WORLD
POETRY

*An Anthology
of Verse from Antiquity
to Our Time*

WORLD POETRY

An Anthology
of Verse from Antiquity
to Our Time

KATHARINE WASHBURN
and
JOHN S. MAJOR
Editors

CLIFTON FADIMAN
General Editor

W · W · NORTON & COMPANY
New York · London
BOOK-OF-THE-MONTH CLUB, INC.

Copyright © 1998 by Katharine Washburn, John S. Major, and Clifton Fadiman

Since this page cannot legibly accommodate all the copyright notices,
pp. 1239-1303 constitute an extension of the copyright page.

The text of this book is composed in Cochin
with the display set in Cochin and Cochin bold
Composition and manufacturing by the Haddon Craftsmen, Inc.
Book design by Antonina Krass.

Library of Congress Cataloging-in-Publication Data
World poetry : an anthology of verse from antiquity to our time /
edited by Katharine Washburn and John S. Major, Clifton Fadiman,
general editor.
p.   cm.
Includes indexes.
ISBN 0-393-04130-1
1. Poetry—Collections.   I. Washburn, Katharine.   II. Major, John S.
III. Fadiman, Clifton, 1904– .
PN6101.W517   1998
808.81—dc21   97-10879
CIP

W. W. Norton & Company, Inc., 500 Fifth Avenue, New York, N.Y. 10110
http://www.wwnorton.com

W. W. Norton & Company Ltd., 10 Coptic Street, London WC1A 1PU

1 2 3 4 5 6 7 8 9 0

For Stanley Burnshaw
and for The Poem Itself

Contents

Part III ᏬᏬ THE POSTCLASSICAL
WORLD (A.D. 250–1200)

Part IV ᏬᏬ THE RISE OF THE
VERNACULAR (950–1450)

Part V ❧ THE RENAISSANCE IN EUROPE; LATE TRADITIONAL VERSE FROM THE AMERICAS, SOUTH ASIA, AND EAST ASIA (1350–1625)

Part VI ❧ THE SEVENTEENTH CENTURY (1600–1700)

Foreword

The year 1928 saw the publication of *An Anthology of World Poetry*, edited by Mark Van Doren. Before this date there had been minor collections of the sort, but Van Doren's one-thousand-plus-page book was the first attempt to reflect, in English translation, the achievements in poetry of every major cultural tradition and some minor ones, including our own Native American. Rather surprisingly, the book was an instant success, both commercially and critically. As editor, scholar, and poet, Van Doren was, of course, beyond cavil. His anthology enjoyed a near sixty-year run before going out of print.

Every anthology mirrors the taste of its time. To begin with, the poetry audience changes its temper and constitution as one generation follows another. In our time, for example, the universalist approach that Van Doren pioneered has become much more pervasive. I do not believe that this is connected with any increase in our sense of world citizenship. On the contrary, nationalism is in the ascendant. Our growing interest in other cultures is largely a consequence of technology, the multiplication of communication of all sorts.

To satisfy our increasing curiosity about other cultures, most of us must depend on translations, and anthologies can only make use of the best that chances to be available. Our time happens, fortunately, to be one of great translation, comparable in this respect to the Elizabethan–Jacobean period. This applies not only to translations of modern work but to the classical canon. In Robert Fitzgerald's version the old Homer is made new.

Finally, it is an odd fact that poetry today pervades our common culture more strikingly than was the case seventy-five years ago. Any new anthology of poetry is in part a consequence of this circumstance.

With this new landscape in mind, I set down in the early 1980s a scheme for an anthology of world poetry that might please a post–Van Doren generation of readers. From that original germ the present effort has evolved.

This book was created under somewhat unusual circumstances, and I am under obligation to the reader to explain them. By the end of 1992 I had worked up a general scheme of the book and, far more important, secured Katharine Washburn and John Major as co-editors. In January 1993 I lost my sight. At this point I intended to dissociate myself from the project but was persuaded to continue as General Editor.

The word *general* is apt. My General Editorship consisted of protracted written and oral discussions with the Editors on the content and direction of the anthology; the auditing of tapes, which allowed me to listen to and approve every proposed poem; and finally, the nomination of certain favorites of my own. In a way, my handicap brought me back to the aural origins of poetry and enabled me to be more sensitive to the actual sound and rhythm of the verse.

The greater part of this work by far, however, is the product of the energy, the taste, and the scholarship of Katharine Washburn and John Major. Whatever substantive virtues it may have are to be credited to them. Their modes of procedure are explained in the Introductions that follow.

My Book-of-the-Month Club colleagues were responsible for recording some of the tapes, and I am most grateful to them. The larger part of the recording was done by my son, Kim, and I thank him. Whatever small contribution I have made would have been impossible without the aid and discriminating judgment of my assistant, Anne Marcus, whom I cannot thank sufficiently.

—Clifton Fadiman

Introduction

I

In his Foreword, Clifton Fadiman has explained this book's genesis, and how Katharine Washburn and I came to be its editors. Here I will deal primarily with the organization and general characteristics of the anthology; I will also remark to some extent on the material in it for which I had direct responsibility. In the second part of the Introduction, Katharine Washburn will write about the larger portion of the book's content for which she had responsibility.

How This Book Is Organized

Conventionally, poems in this book would have been grouped by language, with sections of English verse, French verse, Chinese verse, Japanese verse, Russian verse, and so on, each arranged chronologically. Such a scheme has the virtue of clarity and simplicity, but it almost inevitably privileges the larger and better-known traditions, and leaves less familiar ones (African, Korean, Vietnamese, and the like) ghettoized in a way that makes them all too easy to ignore. Moreover it does not facilitate comparisons of contemporaneous poetry from different parts of the world. An alternative approach would have been to employ chronology alone, presenting the poems in order of, say, poets' birthdates, without regard for the language of the original poem. This, though notionally fair minded, would quite clearly have been unsatisfactory in practice.

Early in the planning phase of this book we all agreed on an organizational scheme that incorporated the best features of both linguistic and chronological categories. Accordingly, this book is divided into eight parts, ranging from the archaic poetry of the Bronze and Iron Ages to the twentieth century. Within each part, poetry is presented in sections defined by broad geographical regions (e.g., southern Europe, East Asia); each section is subdivided by language. Thus in Part II, for example, one finds poetry in the languages of each of the great civilizations of the classical world—Greek, Latin, Prakrit, Tamil, and Chinese. A minor disadvantage

of this plan is that if one wants, for example, to read all of the Chinese po-
etry in the anthology, one has to skip from part to part, reading the Chi-
nese poems in all eight. But this inconvenience is far outweighed by the
fascination of finding intriguing and unexpected possibilities for compar-
ing verse across cultural boundaries. (The book's two indexes — of poets and
translators, and of titles — will facilitate finding individual poems.)

The parts into which the book is divided are approximate; both chronol-
ogy and geography have been bent when it seemed sensible to do so. For
example, the earliest Ottoman love poets chronologically belong in Part V,
but they have been moved to join their successors in Part VI so as not ar-
tificially to break up a continuous tradition of verse. The Mayan Popol Vuh,
of unknown date, may be as early as the Late Classical Maya Period,
around 800–1000; nevertheless I put it in Part IV, reflecting the date when,
so far as we know, it was first recorded in writing. Finally in Part VIII (the
twentieth century), considerations of culture have generally outweighed
those of language; thus, for example, the Japanese poet Nishiwaki Jun-
zaburo and the Filipino poet José Garcia Villa both wrote in English, but
they are included with Japan and the Philippines, respectively, rather than
in the English-language section. Similarly Aimé Césaire and Léopold Sédar
Senghor both write in French, but they are included with the West Indies
and Africa, respectively, rather than with the poets of France

Each of the eight parts is preceded by a brief introduction, which places
the material in context and highlights a few salient points about the con-
tents of that part. There are no headnotes to the poems themselves.

The organization of the book invites readers to undertake a kind of walk
of discovery through world poetry. The number of possible paths is end-
less. Given the many possible ways in which this book might be read, do
broader themes emerge from the poems collected here? To take a much-
contested example, do we find on the basis of this anthology that there is
any such thing as a coherent "Asian literature"? Most readers will agree
that the answer is "Probably not." On the other hand we do find remark-
able continuities both within and among the great cultures of Asia: one can
easily discover within these pages the deep and enduring influence that Chi-
nese poetry had on the verse of Korea and Vietnam and (with somewhat
more complexity and less directly) Japan; or the continuities in Indian
verse in many languages from the Vedic period to modern times. We see,
too, how other strands bind these separate traditions together: the influ-
ence of Islam from North Africa to Indonesia, or of Buddhism from India
to Japan; or how the Persian language links the Middle East with Mughal
India. And beyond that, one sees in these pages how people over vast dis-
tances of time and language and culture all have turned their minds to writ-
ing poetry. This anthology is evidence that all of us can feel at home in the

world's diversity of cultures, and that the poetry of the world can belong to everyone.

Some Notes on the Poetry Itself

It is appropriate here to make clear how the editors divided up responsibility for the book's content. Katharine Washburn covered all of the European languages, plus Persian, Arabic, and Hebrew (the last two having also been, at times, European languages). I was responsible for all non-European languages, plus European-language verse composed by native speakers of Asian, African, and Native American languages. Each of us read all of the material proposed for the book, and had extensive discussions of it, and felt free to make suggestions (and to accept or decline them) about one another's choices, but in the end each of us accepts individual responsibility for the material in our own areas. The remarks that follow, then, reflect my own editorial judgment about non-Western verse, and my own understanding of how this book came together.

My invariable criterion for whether a poem deserved to be included in these pages was this: that it should be able to surprise and delight the common reader. Every page should be a source of pleasure and discovery.

Compiling an anthology amounts to a series of winnowing-down procedures. Generally this involves making explicit, poem-by-poem decisions on the basis of one's knowledge, experience, and taste. The task of deciding what to include entails thousands of decisions about what to leave out. Sometimes choices were bound by agreed-on rules; for example, the decision not to include poetry by anyone born after World War II meant that China's influential young "misty" poets had to be dropped. (The book does include many translations by younger poets.) The final stage of the editorial process, of necessity, consisted of performing several rounds of cuts, successively distressing, painful, and traumatic, to reduce the volume of poetry to fit into the twelve hundred available book pages. One hopes that this process led, in Darwinian fashion, to the survival of the fittest, or in this case of the finest; but there were many fine poems that I would dearly have liked to include, for which there was in the end simply no room.

In the context of what has been included here, I wish to emphasize that this book does not represent an attempt to "cover" world poetry; it is not a "survey of the field." What this means in particular is that are no instances here of a poem included simply to be inclusive. These poems are intended to be read for pleasure, not to score points. In fact I regard this book, both in conception and in realization, as a landmark of multiculturalism; but it is so, one might say, by nature—we are all heirs to many cultures—rather than because it has been cut to fit an ideological pattern.

I have tried to avoid using precious space for things that are readily found elsewhere. Tu Fu, by far the most widely translated of the Chinese poets, is represented here by a smaller selection of poems than his greatness might suggest. Similarly, any good bookstore or library will have several books of translations of Japanese *haiku;* I have included only a very judicious selection of those short gemlike poems here. On the other hand I've made every effort to include material that most readers will previously have been unaware of. Examples include the distinctive verse collected from traditional societies in the South Pacific in the late nineteenth and early twentieth centuries; the sophisticated and witty Inuit verse from the same time period; or the melancholy, beautiful poetry of the Aztecs

The Asian verse here ranges from the famous to, some might say, the very obscure. Some Asian poets — the great T'ang masters Tu Fu, Li Po, and Po Chü-i, or Kalidasa, the defining voice of Sanskrit poetry — are well known in the West, and have been for a long time; their influence can be seen in the work of a number of Western poets represented in this anthology. Others, from the T'ang courtesan-poet Hsüeh T'ao to the brilliant Vietnamese vernacular poet Nguyen Trai, have received much less attention. In the modern era, too, there are artists like the Indonesian poet Rendra, the Nigerian Nobel Prize–winning Wole Soyinka, or the Turkish poet Orhon Veli who are justly famous in their own countries and cultures, but comparatively little known to international audiences. An achievement of this book is that it affords a much broader scope for thinking about world poetry across time than anything ever attempted before. One finds, I believe, that creative genius spans the globe and pervades history, and is not very hard to find.

Something that I think will come as a revelation to many readers is how gloriously the art of translation has flourished in recent decades. This has been true not only with respect to Western-language poetry — where, as Katharine Washburn will remark, many of the best poets of the mid-twentieth century have also been gifted translators — but also in the poetic traditions of Asia, where the contrast between the translations of several generations ago and the best work being done today is astounding. Many Victorian and Edwardian translators from Asian languages, for example, seemed implicitly to assume that because Asian poetry was written by "quaint Oriental gentlemen," it had to be made to sound quaint and exotic in English; nowadays their efforts are acutely embarassing to read.

Naturally, there were exceptions. Early scholars of Chinese literature and philosophy like James Legge and H. A. Giles may have been dull poets, but they were neither inaccurate nor condescending as translators. Arthur Waley and Ezra Pound both were children of the Edwardian era, but they were pioneers of modern translation from Chinese. Waley, in particular, was the first to think through the problem of how to translate the highly compressed and metrical verse of Classical Chinese into satisfactory English verse. His solution, whereby the number of syllables in the Chinese is matched by the number of stressed beats in the English line, has influenced all translators of Chinese verse since.

In Waley's and Pound's time, excellent translations from Asian and African languages were rare; today excellence is the standard to which all competent translators must work. Of course not all old translations are obsolete — obviously some endure brilliantly — nor are all modern ones satisfactory; but it is plain that we are in the midst of a golden age of translation. That is what has made this book both possible and, in a sense, necessary. Compilers of earlier anthologies of world poetry had scant material to go on, once they got past the boundaries of Europe and the English-speaking world — a handful of usually mediocre translations of standard works in Chinese, Japanese, and Sanskrit, and not much else. I, on the other hand, found myself contending with an overabundance of riches.

Still, much more remains to be done. Much of the poetry of the non-Western world remains untranslated or is translated only in unsatisfactory versions. The poetic travel-romances characteristic of eighteenth- and nineteenth-century Thailand, the pithy, humorous Malay *pantuns* (of which there are many collections), and the poetry of Burma are all nearly untouched. Traditional Turkish verse is seriously neglected. Much of the oral poetry of the mountain peoples of mainland and island Southeast Asia, and of Africa as well, has been translated, if at all, as anthropology rather than literature. Some poems that are major works not just within their own cultures but in the context of world literature as a whole still await translators of a skill to do them justice: Balagtas's nineteenth-century Tagalog pastoral fantasy, "Plorante at Laura," and Shota Rustavelli's Georgian masterpiece "The Knight in the Panther Skin," to name only two of the most obvious. There are many splendid translations of Inuit and North American Indian poetry, and of Mayan and Aztec verse, but very little, at least into English, from the Native American languages of South America or of postconquest Central America and Mexico. I hope that this anthology will inspire a new generation of translators to explore these and other neglected traditions.

Conventions and Apparatus

Chinese, Japanese, Korean, and Vietnamese names here are given in their traditional form, i.e., surname first: Yosano Akiko, not Akiko Yosano. I have not tampered with the various Romanization systems for Chinese employed by different translators within their translations, but names of poets are uniformly given in Wade-Giles Romanization, even if the translators had originally given them in *pinyin* or some other system. Similarly, the Romanization of names of poets in other languages (Greek, Russian, etc.)

have been, for the most part, regularized, while leaving names and other foreign-language words within the translated poems spelled according to the translators' preferences. In most cases diacritical marks from words transcribed into our alphabet have been dropped; among the very few exceptions are Japanese long vowels and the Korean short *o*.

As far as has been possible, the typography of the poems in this anthology, including line breaks, centered lines, staggered or broken lines, italicization, boldface, and other typographical features, follows that of the poems as they were originally published or, in the case of previously unpublished translations, the expressed wishes of the translators. In excerpts from longer works, each ellipsis is indicated by a short centered horizontal line in boldface.

—*John S. Major*

II

It is the fate of those who toil at the lower employments of life, to be rather driven by the fear of evil, than attracted by the prospect of good; to be exposed to censure without hope of praise; to be disgraced by miscarriage or punished for neglect, where success would have been without applause or diligence without reward. Among these unhappy mortals is the writer of dictionaries.

—Samuel Johnson, 1775

The map of the world known to poets and their translators has greatly expanded since the publication in 1928 of Mark Van Doren's collection of world poetry; the size available to a similar anthology seventy years later has in the meantime shrunk. The modernist clock was stopped in Professor Van Doren's book, although the program of vigorous exploration of work in other languages was well under way; its contents filled 1376 pages. Even though, this time, two editors, not one, undertook a necessary division of labor and carved up the planet, this new circumference of the globe involved an overwhelming trek; concerns of space (and frequently inflationary permissions fees) proved limiting. I kept Samuel Johnson's quotation on the door of my study and often referred to it while compiling this book, striking out only his final words: where Johnson says "writer of dictionaries," I substituted "anthologist."

My own territory encompassed the poetry of our own language from both the British isles and America, the work of the West from Mesopotamia, Egypt, and the classical world through contemporary Europe in both Western and Eastern European languages, and, because the links are arguably so strong between Europe and the Near East, the poetry of two Semitic tongues—Hebrew and Arabic—and Persian. I stopped gathering poems just at the edge of the Indus River; my co-editor picked up the itinerary into Asia, sub-Saharan Africa, and the Pacific Islands as well as among the native languages of the Americas. We both wish this volume were twice as large; the casualties along the route—poems dropped for want of room— are, just as Dr. Johnson's own apology suggests, painful reminders of a task that involves endless compromise.

The primary emphasis in this book, however, is on contemporary translation, and although the idiom of our own age dominates the language of this collection, I intended no disrespect for the genius of the English translators of the past. (The work of Gavin Douglas, Arthur Golding, Marlowe, Spenser, Dryden, and Pope is given its due in Charles Tomlinson's excellent *Oxford Book of Verse in English Translation.*) Although Marlowe's Ovid, just about all of Dryden and the Sydney *Psalter* were sacrificed, they remain available and as essential as ever, not just for the purposes of translation, but for the language of English poetry.

The room allotted to English-language poetry in this volume will strike many readers as inappropriately narrow. But just as no anthology of world poetry could exclude the poetry of our own language, neither can we hope to accommodate it adequately. I consoled myself with the fact that superb anthologies of English and American poetry already exist (many of them published by Norton), that it was not the chief burden of this book to establish or reinforce the canon of English-language poetry, but simply to allude to its existence: the room allowable for Wordsworth, Milton, Browning, and Donne is not meant to be dismissive of their greatness; the number of pages made available for them does no more than hold down the place for these giants. I hope the surprise of certain inclusions in the book will compensate for the shock of its omissions, and that the absence altogether of Richard Wilbur's Racine, Edwin Morgan's Tasso, Harington's Ariosto, Omar Pound's translation from the Persian of "Gorby and the Rats," and the apparent neglect of a long list of twentieth-century poets from Central Europe and South America will not irritate the reader as much as it haunts this editor.

The selection process became acutely difficult in dealing with late-twentieth-century poets. My preference there (after ruthlessly closing the door to numerous gifted poets born after World War II, many of them still visible in their role as translators) was to select certain English and American poems who fitted best into the landscape of the entire book. The English poems in the final section share a resonance with the past and with the traditions of other languages, other places. I hope that some of the work excluded can be restored in a subsequent edition, and that poets whose birthdate precluded their appearance in a first edition will come into their own in the next.

Part of the understood purpose of the book, and in the joint decision to arrange its contents within a chronological scaffolding, aimed at a museum without walls, where poems could be reproduced without a strict segregation by language and ethnicity, and yet live on the printed page without flattening their distinctiveness. The division (a very imperfect one, with a number of anomalies, but the best my co-editor and I could construct) of the poetry of several millennia into eight discrete units was meant to be suggestive, informing, and a rough chart for readers with no headnotes to guide them. (The headnotes also were hostage to constraints of space.) But something else was intended as well: that the reader of this anthology would enjoy tracking the connections between one tradition, one part of the globe, one poem and another, and would perceive the way in which an image, a theme, a formal innovation, or a technique begins, gathers force, and sails on a strong gust of influence and linkage, sometimes even circumnavigating the globe. Thus the connective tissue binding a poem by the twentieth-century German Bertold Brecht, a Japanese *haiku*, and a *ballade* by François Villon may become more visible. A fragment of Sappho's might recall a love poem in Tamil, and a poem from medieval Wales suggest a richer reading of Dylan Thomas.

This anthology is a collection of poetry in which more than 80 percent of the work exists in translation. Robert Frost's dismissive remark that "poetry is what gets lost is translation" is famous; less celebrated is Octavio Paz's response that "poetry is what gets translated." Well before I came across Paz's retort, experience, instinct, and sheer bravado led me to look *at what poets, across the ages, had chosen to translate*. There were, to be sure, areas of neglect: poems that had yet to find their translators because of the uncanny demands of the original, the relative obscurity of the language together with the lack of a native collaborator to ease the poet along the tightrope. I was lucky to locate living poets who could either resuscitate a poem that existed only in a philologist's warehouse as a learned crib or were willing to stare, propped up by dictionaries and native guides, at a poem that lacked translators altogether. A considerable number of translations were commissioned for this book; many more were simply found by searching for what poets themselves, a few of them polyglots anyway, saw as necessary to translate. Like the distinguished Irish poet Desmond O'Grady who observes of early Celtic literature that "what happens at the corner is as important as what happens at the center," poets have blown off the dust from lost masterpieces and merged the familiar with the unfamiliar, dissolving the barriers of geography into shared experience. Looking through the work of contemporaries turned up many an item, often locked away and unindexed in their *Collected Poems*, sometimes not even identified, strictly speaking, as a translation. I trusted poets, above all, to locate the poems that matter.

The very elastic yardstick here for what is called "translation" needs some explanation. Probably the best taxonomy is that established by John Dryden in his seventeenth-century *Preface to Ovid's Epistles,* where he reduced translation to three "heads." The first, which he called "metaphrase," we would call a humble crib—the turning of a poem word by word and line by line from one language to another. The second head he termed a "paraphrase" or "translation with latitude," allowing the translator to keep the author in view while altering words, but not sense. The third embraced the possibilities of "imitation," a translation in which the poet works from the original text but departs from words and sense as he sees fit, sometimes writing as the author would have done had he lived in the time and place of the reader. Dryden would probably have abided (and admired as I do) the movement of a Satire of Juvenal's from Imperial Rome to London in the late 1960s or happily condoned Christopher Logue's long and dazzling project of translating the *Iliad* with a self-admitted lack of Greek; Logue calls his versions "accounts," invoking the idea of "a kind of middle composition between a translation and a design."

Where some translators here have chosen more conventional methods, cleaving to the meter and staying close to the precise diction of the original, others have taken another, equally demanding route. Their "paraphrases" replicate something they see as intrinsic qualities in one language that can be tightly matched to the properties of another, sacrificing certain aspects of the original poem to allow others a wider play, and imperfectly navigating two worlds to pass through a treacherously narrow gate. Because these distinctions between "metaphrase," "paraphrase," and "imitation," useful though they are, are not well reflected in the informal notation poets themselves often use of "after," or "a version" or an "adaptation" of the original, the latter have been excised altogether from this book. One way or another, using Dryden's categories, these poems are translations and the debate as to how well they steer us through the labyrinth of language and meaning will continue.

A number of poets in this book work on what some critics consider the wilder shores of translation, rearranging the lines of the original to maintain a pattern of rhyme, forfeiting rhyme altogether when its use might distort the original's meaning and intention. Others deliberately use the playful anachronism that uncovers an antique allusion or abandon an alien metrical scheme, which, when employed in English, would appear crabbed and eccentric.

The translations in this book are intended to be read as good English poems, not too battered by the voyage between one foreign language port and another or too deeply compromised by those interlocking compacts with necessity that all gifted translators must make, regret, and stubbornly refashion once more. One of the translator's incidental tasks, and sometimes his main consolation, is to keep the poetry of his own tradition from suffocation and sterility, allowing fresh waves of renewal. The American poet Frank O'Hara wrote in "Salute to the Negro Poets," "From near the sea like Whitman my great predecessor, I call to the spirits of other lands to make fecund my existence." Had this book wanted for an epigraph, O'Hara's line would have served as well as any.

This book bears instead a joint dedication to Stanley Burnshaw, poet, translator, and critic, whose classic *The Poem Itself* makes the most eloquent case against anything other than a collection of poetry in translation that consists simply of a bilingual edition in which the foreign-language poem faces a literal version with a scrupulously annotated interlinear. However arbitrary many of the decisions that went into this book must have seemed to this fine judge of the limits of translation, Stanley Burnshaw's critical presence throughout its assembly was encouraging, enabling, and bracing. He is first and foremost on a long list of those critics, poets, and friends whom John Major and I wish to thank for their generosity and assistance. But since space remains at a premium in a volume where so many poems have fallen away to conserve it, both editors trust that acknowledging their contribution, without listing their names, is sufficient.

—Katharine Washburn

Part I

Poets of
the Bronze
and
Iron Ages
(2200–250 B.C.)

Scholars and archaeologists harvested the poetry of the ancient Near East from many sources: broken tablets recording their cuneiform originals in the library in the ruins of Ninevah, wall carvings in hieroglyphs from Egyptian tombs of the Old Kingdom, and inscriptions on ostraca—shards of earthenware vessels. The intertwining roots of archaic poetry lie in some human equivalent of what geologists call "deep time," their genesis virtually undatable, but still suggestive of the synchrony of the origins of religion with the development of literature.

Hymns and prayers are as central to Mediterranean culture as the rise and fall of the kingdoms of Mesopotamia during the first three millennia. Just as essential to its stock of verse are the exquisite erotic poems of the Egyptian New Kingdom, and the Sumerian *Cycle of Inanna*—the world's first love story. This poetry resembles a wide lake fed by tributaries from the Tigris-Euphrates river basin, Egypt's Nile Valley, and Bronze Age sites in southeastern Europe—like mainland Greece and Minoan Crete—making early use of syllabic scripts.

Cross-currents ripple close to the surface of the ancient world's middle sea. Pharaoh Ankhenaton's monotheistic hymn proclaiming the worship of the sun-disk is a pendant to the thought and wording of the Hebrew verses of Psalm 104. There are close links between the dreamlike Hebrew "Song of Songs" and the invocation in Egyptian love poetry of swallows, herdsmen, flowering quince, and gateways dividing brother and sister, lover and beloved. The governing metaphor for the poetry of the ancient Near East is fertility, reflecting a universal preoccupation with recurring cycles of drought, water, and rebirth.

The *Epic of Gilgamesh*, the tale of a hero's journey to the underworld in search of his lost comrade Enkidu, was available in writing around the same time as the Ionic Greek editions of the *Iliad* and the *Odyssey*, works sharing with *Gilgamesh* the themes of the loss of dear companions in shipwreck and war, the wisdom of women both mortal and divine, and a quest to the land of the dead.

Although Homeric epic was not written down until about 800 B.C. these heroic accounts of battle, exile, and the homecoming of a wanderer who called himself "nobody" resonate with distant memories of Bronze Age

Mycenae and the Trojan War, a clash between invaders from mainland Greece and the inhabitants of a citadel in Asia Minor, around 1150 B.C. The pulse of the Homeric hexameter and the mnemonic device of the formula, yoking nouns and even events to conventional phrases, stitched together the folk tales and legends worked by harpists or "rhapsodes" into mythopoeic narratives of extraordinary unity and literary sophistication.

The Hebrew poetry of the Bible, described as "a blossoming of the desert," emerges from the literary miscellany of a thousand years and written by many hands. Its songs of everyday life accompanying work, dance, and acts of war are sacred texts, depending like Egyptian poetry on a symmetry of units. Their striving for perfection uses semantic parallelism to reinforce a dynamic movement within the line, designing a pattern of repetition jolted by striking variation. The imagery of the religious vision of the Psalms—"devotions upon emergent occasions" as John Donne called them—has attracted translators of genius throughout the history of English poetry.

Given the brilliant tradition of English poets in the wake of the King James Bible, the representation of its accomplishment here is slight. A selection from the Book of Lamentations, a collective dirge bewailing the destruction of Jerusalem after its capture by the Babylonians in 550 B.C. is a recent example of how this verse passed through many workings: a twentieth-century poet here refashioned it from a version in a Quaker Bible published in 1831. In two translations from the fifth-century B.C. Book of Job, a muscular language invoked by the depths of individual suffering parallels the dialogue between deity and man in the theater of classical Greek tragedy.

A haunting exorcism from the Akkadian opens this anthology, calling on the seven great dark planetary demons. Often menacing, inhuman, and incantatory, these archaic voices recite the birth of the gods and their wars with one another. A Pyramid Text from 2300 B.C. Egypt describes the entry of a dead monarch ("The Cannibal King") into the realm of sky and his conquest over lesser gods by eating their hearts, their innards, and thereby their magical powers. In Hesiod's *Theogony*, some fifteen hundred years later, the gods of Greece appear hardly more merciful.

In the civilizations of the ancient Mediterranean and their transition from the use of bronze tools to iron, aristocratic feudal societies gave way to the culture and sensibility of Hesiod's harsh agrarian landscape. Daily ritual, old magic, and hieratic language intersected for millennia in the mysterious well-springs of the poetry of this world. Spontaneity of expression became refined through practice. Like an artisan carefully spinning a final clay pot on the wheel or a farmer taking pleasure in a straight furrow, the poet began to craft the spoken word.

K. W.

The ancient verse of India and China is later than that of archaic western Eurasia, but otherwise shows many of the same characteristics of literature-in-genesis.

Northern India was conquered by Indo-European invaders around 1500 B.C. Many of the indigenous Dravidian-speaking peoples fled to southern India to evade conquest; others stayed and were both dominated and assimilated. Over a period of centuries, the conquerors developed a syncretic religion — ancestral to Hinduism and Buddhism — that featured a pantheon of local and imported deities, a strong component of solar worship, and rituals mediated though the gods Soma and Agni. Representing that tradition here are several hymns, sung or recited in rites of worship, taken from the *Rig Veda*, written around 1200 B.C., and from the somewhat later devotional *Upanishads*.

The Indian section concludes with excerpts from the *Bhagavad-Gita*, India's most important religious text. (The name means "The Song of the Lord"; it is the first of many devotional poems to Lord Krishna.) The *Gita* is a self-contained section of the much larger epic, the *Mahābhārata*, the tale of a deadly rivalry between two related royal clans. The god Krishna aids the noble warrior Arjuna by acting as his charioteer. Arjuna hesitates to join the battle, lamenting the inevitable deaths of his kinsmen/enemies; Krishna instructs him that he must fulfill his *dharma* (the word connotes both "fate" and "duty") as a warrior. A work of remarkable power, the *Gita* is venerated in India and has long been esteemed in the West — Thoreau, for example, had a copy with him at Walden Pond.

The earliest Chinese poetry is found in the *Book of Songs*, a collection of three hundred poems, some of which may have been written down as early as around 800 B.C. on the basis of older oral traditions; the latest may date to 500 B.C. or later. Confucius and his followers valued these poems as sources of moral precepts and social criticism; today scholars see them more straightforwardly as dynastic legends, ritual liturgies, love songs, and literary treatments of popular verse. Complementing the poems from the *Book of Songs* here is an unusual poetic inscription from a sixth-century B.C. bronze bell.

Chinese poetry in a quite different mode is found in the *Elegies of Ch'u*, dating from perhaps the fifth through the third centuries B.C. Many of the poems in the collection are attributed to a high minister of the state of Ch'u (in the Yangtse River Valley) named Ch'ü Yüan, who is supposed to have drowned himself in frustration when his advice was rejected by his king. The poems themselves struck Chinese contemporaries as being shamanistic, lush, sensual, exotic, and unrestrained in contrast to the more austere northern poetry of the *Book of Songs;* that ancient judgment still seems valid. It is interesting to note the close similarity between the *Rig Veda*'s "Creation Hymn" and the creation narrative from the "Heaven Questions" of the *Elegies of Ch'u.*

The section of Chinese verse includes excerpts from Lao-Tzu's *Tao Te Ching.* That founding work of Taoist philosophy is written in verse of great power and beauty—a fact obscured by most English translations but displayed to advantage here.

                                                            J.S.M.

1

Sumer and the Ancient Near East: Poetry in Akkadian, Old Babylonian, and Assyrian; Egypt; Poetry from the Hebrew Bible; Archaic Greek Poetry and the Homeric Tradition

Akkadian

Anonymous (c. 2000 B.C.)

THE SEVEN

They are 7 in number, just 7
In the terrible depths they are 7
Bow down, in the sky they are 7

In the terrible depths, the dark houses
They swell, they grow tall
They are neither female nor male
They are a silence heavy with seastorms
They bear off no women their loins are empty of children
They are strangers to pity, compassion is far from them
They are deaf to men's prayers, entreaties can't reach them
They are horses that grow to great size that feed on mountains
They are the enemies of our friends
They feed on the gods
They tear up the highways they spread out over the roads
They are the faces of evil they are the faces of evil

They are 7 they are 7 they are 7 times 7
In the name of heaven let them be torn from our sight
In the name of the Earth let them be torn from our sight

Jerome Rothenberg

৯৫ Anonymous (c. 2000 B.C.)

From THE CYCLE OF INANNA: THE COURTSHIP
OF INANNA AND DUMAZI

Inanna spoke:
    I bathed for the wild bull,
    I bathed for the shepherd Dumazi,
    I perfumed my sides with ointment,
    I coated my mouth with sweet-smelling amber,
    I painted my eyes with kohl.

    He shaped my loins with his fair hands,
    The shepherd Dumazi filled my lap with cream and milk,
    He stroked my public hair,
    He watered my womb.
    He laid his hands on my holy vulva,
    He smoothed my black boat with cream,
    He quickened my narrow boat with milk,
    He caressed me on the bed.

    Now I will caress my high priest on the bed,
    I will caress the faithful shepherd Dumuzi,
    I will caress his loins, the shepherdship of the land,
    I will decree a sweet fate for him."
. . . .

Ninshubur, the faithful servant of the holy shrine of Uruk,
Led Dumazi to the sweet thighs of Inanna and spoke:
    "My queen, here is the choice of your heart,
    The king, your beloved bridegroom.
    May he spend long days in the sweetness of your holy loins.
    Give him a favorable and glorious reign.
    Grant him the shepherd's staff of judgment.
    Grant him the enduring crown with the radiant and noble diadem.

From where the sun rises to where the sun sets,
From south to north,
From the Upper Sea to the Lower Sea,
From the land of the *huluppu*-tree to the land of the cedar,
Let his shepherd's staff protect all of Sumer and Akkad.

As the farmer, let him make the fields fertile,
As the shepherd, let him make the sheepfolds multiply,
Under his reign let there be vegetation,
Under his reign let there be rich grain.

In the marshland may the fish and birds chatter,
In the canebreak may the young and old reeds grow high,
In the steppe may the *mashgur*-trees grow high,
In the forests may the deer and wild goats multiply,
In the orchards may there be honey and wine,
In the gardens may the lettuce and cress grow high,
In the palace may there be long life.
May there be floodwater in the Tigris and Euphrates,
May the plants grow high on their banks and fills the meadows,
May the Lady of Vegetation pile the grain in heaps and mounds.

O my Queen of Heaven and Earth,
Queen of all the universe,
May he enjoy long days in the sweetness of your holy loins.

Diane Wolkstein and Samuel Noah Kramer

Old Babylonian

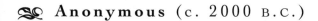 **Anonymous** (c. 2000 B.C.)

From GILGAMESH

Tablet VII

III

In the early hours of the next morning dawning,
Enkidu, sleepless, weeping, cried out to Shamash:

"As for the hunter who saw me in the grasslands,
may the creatures which he hunts, the gazelles and the others,

get away from him free. May the hunter starve
because he saw me at the watering place.

Fill in his hunting pits, unset his traps,
so that he can no longer be a hunter."

With the first light of the early morning dawning,
Enkidu, sleepless, cried out against the harlot:

"As for the harlot who brought me to the city,
this is the curse of Enkidu against her:

May the garbage of the city be what you eat.
May you drink what flows along the alley gutters.

May you importune in the alley shadows.
May you have no home. May you sleep on the city doorsteps.

May there be signs of vomit on your clothes.
May all men curse and revile you and turn away.

Because of you the creatures fled from me,
who dwelt with them and ranged the hills with them."

Then Shamash spoke and said to Enkidu:
"Why do you curse the temple prostitute?

Because of her you eat the food and drink
the palace affords. Because of her you wear

the garments suitable for a prince to wear;
you sit in the place of honor nearest the king;

the great ones of the earth bow down before you.
Gilgamesh is your friend and your companion.

The grief of Gilgamesh for you will be
the cause of woe and wailing in the city.

Gilgamesh the king will build a statue
to celebrate the fame of Enkidu.

When you are gone, then Gilgamesh will wear
the skins of beasts and hairy-bodied wander

grieving in the wilderness for you."
Enkidu heard what Shamash said to him,

and for a time his stormy heart was quiet.
He repented the curse and blessed the harlot, saying:

"This is the blessing of Enkidu on Shamhat:
May no man revile or curse or turn away.

May the old man comb his locks and beard to please you.
May the young unbuckle his belt in joy for you.

May your house be full of gifts, crystal and gold,
carnelian and lapis lazuli,

earrings and filigree ornaments, fine new clothes.
May the priests invite you with honor into the temple."

I V

In the early hours of the next morning dawning,
Enkidu lay in his bed, fear in his belly.

He told a dream to Gilgamesh who was there.
"I had a dream. There was a noise in the sky

and a noise in the earth in answer. On a dark plain
I was alone. But there was one, a man,

with a lion head, and the paws of a lion too,
but the nails were talons, the talons of an eagle.

The face was dark. He took hold of me and seized me.
I fought with him, I hit at him, but he

kept moving about in the dark, too quick for me,
and then with a blow he capsized me like a raft.

I cried out in the dark to Gilgamesh,
'Two people, companions,' but the man overpowered me.

and raged like a wild bull over me in glory,
and Gilgamesh was afraid and did not help me.

Then I was changed into something like a bird,
with a bird's arms, as spindly as a bird's,

and feathered like a bird. He seized an arm
and led me to the dwelling of Irkalla,

the House of Darkness, the House of No Return.
No one comes back who ever enters there.

The garments that they wear are made of feathers.
The food they eat is clay, the drink is dirt.

Stillness and dust are on the door and door bolt.
There is no light of any sort at all.

Dead kings were there, and princes of old kingdoms,
dead high priests and acolytes were there,

dead chanters and anointers, bearers of ointments;
Etana was there and Sumuqan was there,

and on her throne Ereshkigal the Queen
of the Underworld, and kneeling before her was

Belit-Seri the Scribe who holds the tablet
on which the fate of everyone is written.

She turned her head and looked at us and said:
'Who has led here this latest to arrive?' "

Gilgamesh said: "The dream is terrible."
Enkidu said: "We went together through

the dangers of the Forest and we killed
the Bull of Heaven. Do not forget how we,

two people together, prevailed against the terror."
Enkidu lay suffering on the bed of terror

another day and another day and another,
and the long nights between, and day after day

the suffering of Enkidu grew worse.
On the twelfth day he raised up in his bed

and spoke these words to Gilgamesh and said:
"Gilgamesh, who encouraged me in the battle,

saying, 'Two people, companions, they can prevail,'
Gilgamesh is afraid and does not help me!"

After that Gilgamesh heard the death rattle.

Tablet VIII

I

With the first light of the early morning dawning,
in the presence of the old men of the city,

Gilgamesh, weeping, mourned for Enkidu:
"It is Enkidu, the companion, whom I weep for,

weeping for him as if I were a woman.
He was the festal garment of the feast.

On the dangerous errand, in the confusions of noises,
he was the shield that went before in the battle;

he was the weapon at hand to attack and defend.
A demon has come and taken away the companion.

He ranged the hills together with the creatures
whose hearts delight to visit the watering places.

A demon has come and taken him away.
He was the first to find the way through the passes

to go to the Cedar Forest to kill Huwawa.
He sought the wilderness places to find the water

with which to quench our thirst on the way to the Forest.
Together we killed Huwawa; together we fought

the bellowing Bull of Heaven, and killed the Bull,
and together the two of us sat down to rest.

Then a demon came and took away the companion.
You are asleep. What has taken you into your sleep?

Your face is dark. How was your face made dark?"
Enkidu's eyes were unmoving in their sockets.

Gilgamesh touched the heart of the companion.
There was nothing at all. Gilgamesh covered

Enkidu's face with a veil like the veil of a bride.
He hovered like an eagle over the body,

or as a lioness does over her brood.

David Ferry

✀ Anonymous (c. 1500 b.c.)

PRAYER TO THE GODS OF THE NIGHT

The gates of the town are closed. The princes
Have gone to sleep. The chatter of voices

Has quieted down. Doorbolts are fastened.
Not until morning will they be opened.

The gods of the place, and the goddess,
Ishtar, Sin, Adad, and Shamash,

Have gone into the quiet of the sky,
Making no judgments. Only

The voice of a lone wayfarer
Calls out the name of Shamash or Ishtar.

Now house and field are entirely silent.
The night is veiled. A sleepless client

In the still night waits for the morning.
Great Shamash has gone into the sleeping

Heaven; the father of the poor,
The judge, has gone into his chamber.

May the gods of the night come forth—the Hunter,
The Bow, the Wagon, the Yoke, the Viper,

Irra the valiant, the Goat, the Bison,
Girra the shining, the Seven, the Dragon—

May the stars come forth in the high heaven.

Establish the truth in the ritual omen;
In the offered lamb establish the truth.

David Ferry

Assyrian

✇ Anonymous (c. 1000 B.C.)

YOUR THWARTS IN PIECES, YOUR MOORING
ROPE CUT

"Why are you adrift, like a boat, in the midst of the river.

your thwarts in pieces, your mooring rope cut?

Your face covered, you cross the river of the Inner City."

"How could I not be adrift, how could my mooring rope not be cut?

The day I bore the fruit, how happy I was,

happy was I, happy my husband.

The day of my going into labor, my face became darkened,

the day of my giving birth, my eyes became clouded.

With open hands I prayed to Bēlet-ilī:

'You too have borne a child, save my life!'

Hearing this, Bēlet-ilī veiled her face.

'You [. . .], why do you keep praying to me?'

[My husband, who loved me], uttered a cry,

['Why do you take from me] the wife in whom I rejoice?'

[   ] years on end,

[   ] . . . . . .

[   ] Inner City, ... you sounded a wail.

[All] those [many] days I was with my husband,

I lived with him who was my lover.

Death came creeping into my bedroom:

it drove me from my house,

it tore me from my husband,

it set my feet into a land of . . . .

Erica Reiner

Egyptian

✇ Anonymous (c. 2180 B.C.)

From THE CANNIBAL HYMN

The sky is a dark bowl, the stars die and fall.
The celestial bows quiver,
the bones of the earthgods shake and planets come to a halt
when they sight the king in all his power,
the god who feeds on his father and eats his mother.
The king is such a tower of wisdom
even his mother can't discern his name.
His glory is in the sky, his strength lies in the horizon
like that of his father the sungod Atum who conceived him.
Atum conceived the king,
but the dead king has greater dominion.
His vital spirits surround him,
his qualities lie below his feet,
he is cloaked in gods and cobras coil on his forehead.
His guiding snakes decorate his brow
and peer into souls,

ready to spit fire against his enemies.
The king's head is on his torso.
He is the bull of the sky
who charges and vanquishes all.
He lives on the stuff of the gods,
he feeds on their limbs and entrails,
even when they have bloated their bodies with magic
at Nesisi, the island of fire.

He cooks the leftover gods into a bone soup.
Their souls belong to him
and their shadows as well.
In his pyramid among those who live on the earth of Egypt,
the dead king ascends and appears
forever and forever.

Tony Barnstone and Willis Barnstone

✒ Anonymous (c. 1900 B.C.)

DEATH IS BEFORE ME TODAY

Death is before me today
like health to the sick
like leaving the bedroom after sickness.

Death is before me today
like the odor of myrrh
like sitting under a cloth on a day of wind.

Death is before me today
like the odor of lotus
like sitting down on the shore of drunkenness.

Death is before me today
like the end of the rain
like a man's home-coming after the wars abroad.

Death is before me today
like the sky when it clears
like a man's wish to see home after numberless years of captivity.

W. S. Merwin

❧ Anonymous (c. 1500 B.C.)

THE MARSH'S PLANTS BEWILDER

The marsh's plants bewilder.
   My sister's mouth is a lotus,
her breasts mandragoras,
   her arms the limbs of a tree,
her . . .
   her head the love-wood trap,
and I am the gone goose!
   The cord is my . . .
her hair is the lure in the net
   that will ensnare me.

Barbara Hughes Fowler

❧ Anonymous (c. 1567–1085 B.C.)

PLEASANT SONGS OF THE SWEETHEART WHO MEETS YOU IN THE FIELDS: *From* CONVERSATIONS IN COURTSHIP

I

You, mine, my love,
My heart strives to reach the heights of your love.

See, sweet, the bird-trap set with my own hand.

See the birds of Punt,
Perfume a-wing
       Like a shower of myrrh
Descending on Egypt.

Let us watch my handiwork,
The two of us, together in the fields.

II

The shrill of the wild goose
Unable to resist
The temptation of my bait.

While I, in a tangle of love,
Unable to break free,
Must watch the bird carry away my nets.

And when my mother returns, loaded with birds,
And finds me empty-handed,
What shall I say?

That I caught no birds?
That I myself was caught in your net?

III

Even when the birds rise
Wave mass on wave mass in great flight
I see nothing, I am blind
Caught up as I am and carried away
Two hearts obedient in their beating
My life caught up with yours
Your beauty the binding.

IV

Without your love, my heart would beat no more;
Without your love, sweet cake seems only salt;
Without your love, sweet "shedeh" turns to bile.
O listen, darling, my heart's life needs your love;
For when you breathe, mine is the heart that beats.

V

With candour I confess my love;
I love you, yes, and wish to love you closer;
As mistress of your house,
Your arm placed over mine.

Alas your eyes are loose.
I tell my heart: "My lord
Has moved away. During
The night moved away
And left me. I am like a tomb."
And I wonder: Is there no sensation
Left, when you come to me?
Nothing at all?

Alas those eyes which lead you astray,
Forever on the loose.
And yet I confess with candour
That no matter where else they roam
If they roam towards me
I enter into life.

Ezra Pound and Noel Stock

ॐ Akhenaton (c. 1375 b.c.)

HYMN TO THE SUN

A glory,
    eternity in life,
        the Undeposed,

    beauty
    flashing
    powers,

Love,
    the powering,
        the Widening,
        light
        unraveling
        all faces followers of

      All the colors, beams of
      woven thread,
          the Skin

        alight that
        warms itself
        with life.

      The Two Lands,
        shape themselves
            that Love

        flows
        to the
        making,

      Place, man, cattle, creature-kind,
        & tree of every image
           taking place.

        Life-in-shining
        shining
        life,

      The Mother/Father,
        sees the Seeing
           rise upon our

        hearts beat
        dawn lights
        earth entire

As you made. And as you
   pass we settle
       equal to the Dead,

   linen wrapping
   head nostril
   plugged with

Earth that waits
   return in Heaven
       rises overturned

   the
   uplift
   palms upturned to

Light your being is
   the living
       Acts the

   Touch the voicing in
   all Land
   hears Man —

Womansong en-
   throning
       Truth

   gives
   heart the
   Food.

This One, we give, to walk,
   purely to your
       Will, all

   creatures
   dance you
   toward your coming every

Day, you gave your
   Son, forever in your
       Form he

   Acts
   in
   Beauty, saying:

I am
   your Son, my heart
       knows you the

strength
the seat
of powering

Eternal is the Light
  you are the watchful
        Maker,

  solitary
  every
  life

Sees light that breathes
  by light,
        flowers

  Seeding
  Wilderness,
  light stunned by

Light before your
  Face,
          the dancing

  creatures,
  feathers
  up from nests a

Wavering in wing
  goes round
        around

& praises
  living
      Joy

  you
  Are.

John Perlman

Anonymous (1160 B.C.)

THE HARPER'S SONG FOR INHERKHAWY

Sung by his Harpist for the Osiris,
Chief of the Crew in the Place of Truth,
Inherkhawy, who says:

I am this man, this worthy one,
who lives redeemed by abundance of good
tendered by God indeed.

I

All who come into being as flesh
pass on, and have since God walked the earth;
and young blood mounts to their places.

The busy fluttering souls and bright transfigured spirits
who people the world below
and those who shine in the stars with Orion,
They built their mansions, they built their tombs —
and all men rest in the grave.

So set your home well in the sacred land
that your good name last because of it;
Care for your works in the realm under God
that your seat in the West be splendid.

The waters flow north, the wind blows south,
and each man goes to his hour.

II

So, seize the day! hold holiday!
Be unwearied, unceasing, alive,
you and your own true love;
Let not your heart be troubled during your sojourn on earth,
but seize the day as it passes!

Put incense and sweet oil upon you,
garlanded flowers at your breast,
While the lady alive in your heart forever
delights, as she sits beside you.

Grieve not your heart, whatever comes;
let sweet music play before you;
Recall not the evil, loathsome to God,
but have joy, joy, joy, and pleasure!

O upright man, man just and true,
patient and kind, content with your lot,
rejoicing, not speaking evil —

Let your heart be drunk on the gift of Day
  until that day comes when you anchor.

John L. Foster

Anonymous (c. 1100 B.C.)

THE VOICE OF THE SWALLOW, FLITTERING, CALLS TO ME

The voice of the swallow, flittering, calls to me:
  "Land's alight! Whither away?"
No, little bird, you cannot entice me,
  I follow you to the fields no more.

Like you in the dawn mist I rose,
  at sunrise discovered my lover abed
    (his voice is sweeter)
"Wake," I said, "or I fly with the swallow."
And my heart smiled back
  when he, smiling, said:
"You shall not fly,
  nor shall I, bright bird.
    But hand in hand
We shall walk the Nileside pathways,
  under cool of branches, hidden
    (only the swallows watching)
Wide-eyed girl.
  I shall be with you in all glad places."

Can you match the notes of that song, little swallow?
  I am first in his field of girls!
My heart, dear sister, sings in his hand—
  love never harmed a winged creature.

John L. Foster

Anonymous (c. 1100 B.C.)

SEND HIM BACK HARD BY YOUR LADY'S SMALL WINDOW

Send him back hard by your lady's small window
    (she is alone now, there is no other);
Stuff yourself full in her banquet hall!
    Then though bedrock be shaken high,
Though very heaven break down in the storm wind,
    he shall not (lovely lady) be moved.

Lo where she comes to you, bright with her thousand pleasures!
                    Fragrance spreads like a floodtide
Drowning the eyes, and the head whirls.
                    Unable the poor fool before her.
Ah! this is the land of Our Golden Lady! —
                    She gives the girl as your due
That you keep to your service in Her Holy Name
                    able anon, old pecker, to say
You've had the world in your time.

                                        John L. Foster

✖ Anonymous (c. 1100 B.C.)

SONG INSCRIBED ON AN EARTHENWARE VESSEL

Once more you pass her house, deep in thought,
                    darkness is fallen, hiding you:

I would gain entry there,
                    but for me no sort of welcome opens;
Yet the night is lovely for our soft purposes,
                    and doors are meant to give passage!

Doorlatch, my friend, you govern my destiny:
                    heaven for me needs a good turn from you;
(And once safe inside, our longhorn as payment) —
                    oppose no spellbinding power!

Add oxen in praise to the door, as needed,
                    lesser beasts to the lock, slit geese
To doorjamb and lintel, suet for sockets —
                    and let all that moves turn quietly, quietly!

But the choicest cuts of our fine animal —
                    these go instead to the sawyer's apprentice
If he makes us a new door — of rushes,
                    and a tie-latch of brittlest straw.

O then, a man big with love could come anytime,
                    find her house welcoming, open,
Discover the couch decked with closewoven bedclothes,
                    and a lovely young lady restless among them! —

(You walk back and forth in the dark)
                    She whispers:
"The mistress of this choice spot has been lonely.
                    Dear heart, who held you so long?"

                                        John L. Foster

❧ Anonymous (c. 1100 B.C.)

I FOUND MY LOVE BY THE SECRET CANAL

I found my love by the secret canal,
      feet dangling down in the water.
He had made a hushed cell in the thicket, for worship,
      to dedicate this day
To holy elevation of the flesh.

He brings to light what is hidden
      (breast and thigh go bare, go bare),
Now, raised on high toward his altar, exalted,
      Ah! . . .
A tall man is more than his shoulders!

John L. Foster

Hebrew

❧ Anonymous (c. 600 B.C.)

From SONG OF SONGS

2:8–13

The sound of my lover
coming from the hills
quickly like a deer
upon the mountains

Now at my windows,
walking by the walls,
here at the lattices
he calls —

come with me,
my love,
come away

For the long wet months are past,
the rains have fed the earth
and left it bright with blossoms

Birds wing in the low sky,
dove and songbird singing
in the open air above

Earth nourishing tree and vine,
green fig and tender grape,
green and tender fragrance

Come with me,
my love,
come away

　　　　Marcia Falk

5:2–6:3

I was drowsy, but my heart was awake. Listen!
My lover beats at the door.
　　'Sister my love,
open and let me in
　　my dove, my perfection.
my head is soaked with dew
　　hair drenched with the drops of night.'
'I am already undressed,
　　why should I get dressed again,
I've washed my feet
　　and why should I get them dirty?'

He took his hand off the bolted door
　　and my heart sank . . .
I got up to let him in,
my hands sticky with myrrh, fingers
dripping myrrh on the latch
　　and flung the door open —
but he was gone in the darkness.
My heart longed for his voice;
I looked, but did not find him,
called, but he gave no reply.
Soldiers making their rounds in the city
found me, and beat me up,
those Wall-Guards stripped off my coat . . .

I make you swear, daughters of Jerusalem
if you find my lover, tell him
how sick I am with love.

　　　(And what's your lover
　　　　　more than anyone else's,
　　　darling?
　　　　　Why so special
　　　for you to make us promise?)

He has a sparkling appearance —
you'd pick him out of ten thousand.
His face is the purest gold, his hair
a heap of curls, black as a raven.

His eyes float like doves in a pool
suspended, bathing in milk.
His cheeks smell like fragrant spice-beds,
his lips are anemones
        overflowing with myrrh,
his hands gold clasps set in topaz,
an ivory cask his body, lapis-lazuli-veined,
pillars of marble on gold bases—his legs:
the sight of him is like Lebanon,
        grand as the cedars,
his talking, sweetness itself,
        he is altogether delightful.
Daughters of Jerusalem—
        this is my lover and friend.

        (But darling, where can he have got to?
        Tell us which way he went,
        so we can find him with you.)

My lover has gone
        down to his garden
into his spice-beds
        to feed there in the orchards
picking anemones . . .

I am my lover's and he is mine
as he grazes among the anemones.

                                        Peter Jay

❧ Anonymous (c. 550 B.C.)

THE VALLEY OF DRY BONES

From Ezekiel 37:1–11

The hand of the Lord   held me transported
and spirited my spirit   and set me down
in the fell of a valley   filled with bones.

The Lord caused me   to compass the bones
in the open valley.   They were very dry.

And then He addressed me: You, human!
can these bones live?   Lord, I answered,
You alone know.

And then He addressed me: Proffer this prophecy
over these bones: O dry bones!
welcome the Word:

The Lord God gives   this to these:
I will let breath   enter in you
and you will live.
I will make you muscle   and lend you flesh,
settle you with skin,   bring you breath,
and you will live
and know your Lord.

So I proffered the prophecy   commanded of me
and as I uttered it   a clacking clattered
and bone came   bone to bone.
And I saw sinews,   flesh, skin,
come up and cover them.   But yet no breath.

And then He addressed me: Prophet the breath!
You, human!   address the breath!
Say God says: I summon you, breath,
from the four quarters   to breathe in these
that they may live.

So I uttered the summons   commanded of me
and the breath entered   and then they lived.
And then they stood,   an immense army.

And then He addressed me: You, human!
these bones are the host   of all the Chosen.
The cry they utter is:

> Our bones are dry,
> our hope is drained,
> We are cut off.

David Curzon

Anonymous (c. 530 B.C.)

PSALM 137

By the waters of Babylon we sat down and wept:
when we remembered thee, O Sion.

As for our harps, we hanged them up:
upon the trees that are therein.

For they that led us away captive
required of us then a song,
and melody, in our heaviness:
Sing us one of the songs of Sion.

How shall we sing the Lord's song:
in a strange land?

If I forget thee, O Jerusalem:
let my right hand forget her cunning.

If I do not remember thee,
let my tongue cleave to the roof of my mouth:
yea, if I prefer not Jerusalem in my mirth.

Remember the children of Edom, O Lord,
in the day of Jerusalem:
how they said, Down with it, down with it,
even to the ground.

O daughter of Babylon, wasted with misery:
yea, happy shall he be that rewardeth thee,
as thou hast served us.

Blessed shall he be that taketh thy children:
and throweth them against the stones.

Miles Coverdale

✌ Anonymous (c. 400 b.c.)

From JOB

Chapter 3

Then Job spoke and cursed his day and chanted and said:

Be damned, day when I was born
   and the night that said, "A man has been conceived!"
Make that day dark!
No god look after it from above,
   no light flood it.
Foul it, darkness, deathgloom;
   rain-clouds settle on it;
   heat-winds turn it into horror.
That night—black take it!
   May it not count in the days of the year,
may it not come in the count of the months.
That night, that night be barren!
   No joy ever come in it!
Curse it, men who spell the day,
   men skilled to stir Leviathan,
   to stir him up to war again
   and put an end to time.

May its morning stars stay dark,
    may it wait for light in vain,
never look upon the eyelids of the dawn —
because it did not lock the belly's gates
    and curtain off my eyes from suffering.

Why did I not die inside the womb,
    or, having left it, and give up breath at once?
Why did the knees advance to greet me,
    or the breasts, for me to suck?
I would be lying now asleep;
    then I would be at rest
with kings and counselors of the earth
    who build its ruins into palaces,
or with princes, men with gold,
    men who fill their tombs with silver.
Why was I not stillbirth, hidden,
    like infants who never saw the light?
There the wicked cease their trouble,
    there the weary find their rest
where the captives have repose
    and need not heed the taskmaster,
where low and great all abide,
    the slave, now free, beside his lord.

Why is the sufferer given light?
    Why life, to men who gag on bile
who wait for death that never comes,
    though they would rather dig for it than gold;
whose joy exceeds mere happiness,
    thrill to find the grave?
Why, to a man whose way is hidden,
    because a god has blocked his path?
For, my sighs are served to me for bread,
    and my cries are poured for me for water.
One thing alone I feared, and it befell:
    the very thing I dreaded came to me.
No peace had I, no calm, no rest;
but torment came.

                                            R. P. Scheindlin

Chapter 38

> Then the LORD answered Job out of the whirlewind, and sayd,
> Who is this that darkneth counsell by words without knowledge?
> Gird up nowe thy loines like a man; for I will demaund of thee, and
> answere thou me.
> Where wast thou when I layd the foundations of the earth? declare,
> if thou hast understanding.
> Who hath layd the measures thereof, if thou knowest? or who hath
> stretched the line upon it?

Whereupon are the foundations thereof fastened? or who layd the corner stone thereof?

When the morning starres sang together, and all the sonnes of God shouted for joy.

Or who shut up the sea with doores, when it brake foorth as if it had issued out of the wombe?

When I made the cloud the garment thereof, and thicke darkness a swadling band for it,

And brake up for it my decreed place, and set barres and doores,

And said, Hitherto shalt thou come, but no further; and heere shall thy proud waves be stayed.

Hast thou commaunded the morning since thy daies? and caused the day-spring to know his place,

That it might take hold of the endes of the earth, that the wicked might be shaken out of it?

It is turned as clay to the seale, and they stand as a garment.

And from the wicked their light is withholden, and the high arme shalbe broken.

Hast thou entred into the springs of the sea? or hast thou walked in the search of the depth?

Have the gates of death bene opened unto thee? or hast thou seene the doores of the shadow of death?

Hast thou perceived the breadth of the earth? Declare if thou knowest it all.

Where is the way where light dwelleth? and as for darknesse, where is the place thereof?

That thou shouldest take it to the bound thereof, and that thou shouldest know the pathes to the house thereof.

Knowest thou it, because thou wast then borne? or because the number of thy daies is great?

Hast thou entred into the treasures of the snowe? or hast thou seene the treasures of the haile,

Which I have reserved against the time of trouble, against the day of battaile and warre?

By what way is the light parted? which scattereth the East wind upon the earth.

Who hath divided a water-course for the overflowing of waters? or a way for the lightning of thunder,

To cause it to raine on the earth, where no man is: on the wildernesse wherein there is no man?

To satisfie the desolate and waste ground, and to cause the bud of the tender herbe to spring forth.

Hath the raine a father? or who hath begotten the drops of dew?

King James Version

✌ Anonymous (c. 400 B.C.)

From LAMENTATIONS

1

How doth the city sit solitary that was full of people,
and that the steeples and minarets canopied,
and that the stone saints guarded
where the flute was heard in the dawn-light
and the cradle song lowed at dusk,
and the marketplace full of made things,
the first fruits bending the tables
and the pledges and signatures of honor,
honored—how is she become tributary
and her people bounded by gates.
She weepeth sore in the night
and the tears are on her cheeks;
her face is shrouded in fear and
all her beauty is departed.
The guilds and the clans are gone,
gone the pity of the nurses and
teachers. The scavenger dogs
roam the fallow gardens and
run without strength
before their pursuers. How the walls
are stained with a brother's blood
and the night brings sickness to the longing.

2

The scribes have cast the blame
upon a woman, writing *her filthiness
is in her skirts* and the elders have gathered
in judgment under plane trees,
and the virgin is trodden as in a wine-press,
(how the crowd cries out against
the menstruous woman, and the handmaiden,
and the crone, and they are hooded
with the cloud of anger
and pulled into the waiting wagons)
And the mothers of the warriors
are crowned with laurel and the fathers
of the singers are shamed in the square
and the signs are marked upon the doorposts
and the scaffolding built at the edge
of the fairground. Who will teach
the stitches and patterns? And who will
remember the spells of the clover?
And who will know the harmonies of
number, the names and accounts of the stars?

What thing shall I take to witness for thee?
What thing shall I liken unto thee?

3

I have been brought into darkness
surely against me he has turned
he hath set me in dark places
he hath hedged me about
that I cannot get out
he hath made my chain heavy
he hath closed my ways with stone
he was like a bear lying in wait
he hath pulled me to pieces
and made me desolate
that I cannot get out
he hath filled my teeth with dust
and covered me with ashes
I cried out to my rescuers
and they did not hear me,
I turned away, and still
I was hedged about,
the daylight was taken
and the blanket was taken
and the rope and all
my childish things,
I cried out with my throat
and my in-my-heart
and my Lord's Prayer and
my now I lay me down
to sleep, and my health
and my hands, and my
show me myself and my
secrets-and-all-my-sins
forgiven and I counted
the ones I knew and the ones
I dreamed and I measured
the grains of the wood
and the sand, and measured
the shadow cast by the mirror,
but the sun was remote and
cold to me. I turned away,
and still I was hedged about
and anointed in fire
and ashes. I saw
the blue sheen
of the world through
the darkness, and the crust,
and the stain of another,
I touched my hair to my mouth,
and my arms to my legs,

and my mouth to my knee.
I smelled the animal sweetness
and the dampness of leaves
beyond the wall; I heard
the murmurs of my mothers
and my brother, alone in his
whimpering, and I heard the strangers
whisper. But when I cried they did not
hear me, and when I sang
they did not know my song,
and when I spoke, they did
not acknowledge me, and when I left
they did not seek me out
along the cisterns and
streets of the city.
Mercy is new in the morning
they said, and our god
will not stand for such
suffering—oh god of mercy
and golden light.

Susan Stewart

Greek

ஒ Hesiod (c. 700 B.C.)

From THE WORKS AND DAYS

Beware of the month Lenaion, bad days,
    that would take the skin off
an ox; beware of it, and the frosts, which,
    as Boreas,
the north wind, blows over the land, cruelly develop;
he gets his breath and rises on the open water
    by horse-breeding
Thrace, and blows, and the earth
    and the forest groan, as many
oaks with sweeping foliage, many solid fir trees
along the slopes of the mountains his force bends
    against the prospering
earth, and all the innumerable forest
    is loud with him.
The beasts shiver and put their tails
    between their legs, even
those with thick furry coats to cover their hides,
    the cold winds
blow through the furs of even these, for all

their thickness.
The wind goes through the hide of an ox,
    it will not stop him;
it goes through a goatskin, that is fine-haired;
    but not even Boreas'
force can blow through a sheepskin to any degree,
    for the thick fleece
holds him out. It does bend the old man
    like a wheel's timber.
It does not blow through the soft skin
    of a young maiden
who keeps her place inside the house
    by her loving mother
and is not yet initiated in the mysteries of Aphrodite
the golden, who, washing her smooth skin carefully,
    and anointing it
with oil, then goes to bed, closeted
    in an inside chamber
on a winter's day
            that time when old No-Bones the polyp
gnaws his own foot in his fireless house,
    that gloomy habitat,
for the sun does not now point him out any range
    to make for
but is making his turns in the countryside
    and population of dusky
men, and is dull to shed his light
    upon Hellenic peoples.
Then all the sleepers in the forest,
    whether horned or hornless,
teeth miserably chattering, flee away
    through the mountainous
woods, and in the minds of all
    there is one wish only,
the thought of finding shelter, getting behind
    dense coverts
and the hollow of the rock; then like
    the three-footed individual
with the broken back, and head over, and eyes
    on the ground beneath
so doubled, trying to escape the white snow,
    all go wandering.

                    Richmond Lattimore

VISION, *From* THE THEOGONY

children of Zeus
    grant me song

of the gods who are forever
who were born out of Earth and star-lit Sky
          dark Night and Salt Sea

          Speak tell me
how we were born the beginning
          of the ground we walk on
          rivers ponds lakes
sea without end swelling rushing
          stars sending light
          sky cupped overhead
               gods born of them
          the gods givers of good things
dividing wealth among themselves
          honors titles a palace in the mountains
                                             Olympos

Muses living in the houses of Olympos
          who was first?

"Gap was first
          then Earth the great chair with her immense teat

     then Pit hard to see
          deep in the wombs of Earth

     next Love
          loveliest of gods
who unstrings the body
          tames the heart
     breaks the mind
          whether god or man
     within his heart

     the children of Gap were Gloom and Night
          whom Love joined
     their children were bright Air and Day

          Earth's firstborn was star-lit Sky
          a lover to cover her
               equal in every particular

     He made her his chair
          the seat forever for the happy gods

               as soon as his children were born
                    Sky hid them away
          he deprived them of light
shoving them back deep into the wombs of Earth
          he went away and laughed

Earth crowded groaned
she thought of something clever and ugly
she made gray adamant
made a sickle of it
children understand what she wanted done with it
sorrowing in her heart
she encouraged them
"pay him back for what he has done
he was first to hurt"
this is what she said

they were afraid
none of them answered
but great Kronos who thinks around corners was not afraid
he spoke to his wise mother
'I shall do it
I shall finish it
I do not love my father
he was first to hurt'
he spoke huge Earth shook with joy in her heart
she hid him in a place of ambush
She put the sickle with jagged teeth in his hand
she showed him her plan

great Sky came
bringing night
lying heavy on Earth in love and desire
she opened receiving him
their son stretched out his left hand from ambush
in his right he held the great sickle with jagged teeth
he chopped off his father's balls
he threw them to the wind behind him
they flew away a bloody track in the air
which Earth enfolded
in full time she gave birth to the strong Curses
and the great Titans
full-armored bursting with light shaking long spears
and the Meliads nymphs of the ash tree
all over boundless Earth
when his balls cut down by adamant
fell from boundless Earth
into high Sea
battered they swam open currents
from that deathless flesh foam blossomed
inside the pink flower a girl was born and grew
she passed by holy Cythera
she came to Cyprus surrounded by water's flood
she stepped onto land
august lovely goddess
grass sprung up under her tapered feet

Aphrodite born of foam Cytheria the well-garlanded
because she grew inside the bloody foam
because she passed near Cythera
Cyprogene because there she was born
on Cyprus wave washed
Philomedes because she loves Love's bond
she was born inside her father's balls
Love walks with her
Desire follows

Charles Doria

❧ Homer (c. 800–700 B.C.)

From THE ILIAD

From Book XXI

                              Then Achilles,
Leaving the tall enemy with eels at his white fat
And his tender kidneys infested with nibblers,
Pulled his spear out of the mud and waded off,
After the deadman's troop that beat upstream
For their dear lives; then, glimpsing Achilles' scarlet plume
Amongst the clubbed bullrushes, they ran and as they ran
The Greek got seven of them, swerved, eyeing his eighth, and
Ducked at him as Scamander bunched his sinews up,
And up, and further up, and further further still, until
A glistening stack of water, solid, white with sunlight,
Swayed like a giant bone over the circling humans,   '
Shuddered, and changed for speaking's sake into humanity.
And the stack of water was his chest; and the foaming
Head of it, his bearded face; and the roar of it—
Like weir-water—Scamander's voice:

'Indeed, Greek, with Heaven helping out, you work
Miraculous atrocities. Still, if God's Son
Has settled every Trojan head on you,
Why make my precincts the scupper for your dead inheritance?
Do them in the fields, Greek, or—or do them anywhere but here.
Thickened with carcasses my waters stiffen like a putrid syrup,
Downstream, the mouth cakes against standing blood-clots yet,
And yet, you massacre. Come, Greek, quit this loathsome rapture!'

                    Head back, Achilles cried:
'Good, River, good—and you shall have your way . . . presently.
When every living Trojan squats inside his city's wall.
When I have done with Hector, Hector with me, to death.'
                    And he bayed and leapt—

Bronze flame shattering like a divine beast —
Pity the Trojans!

                                 So Scamander
Tried involving the Lord Apollo, thus:
                          'Lord, why the negligence?
Is this the way to keep your Father's word?
Time and again he said: Watch the Trojan flank
Till sundown comes, winds drop, shadows mix and lengthen,
War closes down for night, and nobody is out
Bar dogs and sentries.'

                           Hearing this
The Greek jumped clear into the water, and Scamander
Went for him in hatred: curved back his undertow, and
Hunched like a snarling yellow bull drove the dead up,
And out, tossed by the water's snout on to the fields;
Yet those who lived he hid behind a gentle wave.
Around the Greek Scamander deepened. Wave clambered
Over wave to get at him, beating aside his studded shield so,
Both footholds gone, half toppled over by the bloodstained crud,
Achilles snatched for balance at an elm — ah! — its roots gave —
Wrenched out — splitting the bank, and tree and all
Crashed square across the river, leaves, splintered branches,
And dead birds blocking the fall. Then Achilles wanted out.
And scrambled through the root's lopsided crown, out of the ditch,
Off home.

        But the river Scamander had not done with him.

Forcing its bank, an avid lip of water slid
After him, to smother his Greek breath for Trojan victory.
Aoi! — but that Greek could run! — and put and kept
A spearthrow's lead between him and the quick,
Suck, quick, curve of the oncoming water,
Arms outstretched as if to haul himself along the air,
His shield — like the early moon — thudding against
His nape-neck and his ears, fast, fast
As the black winged hawk's full stoop he went —
And what is faster? — yet, Scamander was nigh on him,
Its hood of seething water poised over his shoulderblades.
Achilles was a quick man, yes, but the gods are quicker than men.
And easily Scamander's wet webbed claw stroked his ankles.

            You must imagine how a gardener prepares
            To let his stored rainwater out, along
            The fitted trench to nourish his best plants.
            Carefully, with a spade, he lifts the stone
            Gagging the throat of his trench, inch by inch,
            And, as the water flows, pebbles, dead grubs,

Old bits of root and dusts are gathered and
Swept along by the speed of it, until
Singing among the plants, the bright water
Overtakes its gardener and his control
Is lost. Likewise Scamander took Achilles.

Each time he stood, looking to see which Part, or whether
Every Part of Heaven's Commonwealth was after him,
The big wave knocked him flat. Up, trying to outleap
The arch of it, Scamander lashed aslant and wrapped his knees
In a wet skirt, scouring the furrows so his toes got no grip.
And Achilles bit his tongue and shrieked: 'Father . . .'
Into the empty sky '. . . will Heaven help me? No?
Not one of you? Later, who cares? But now? Not now. Not this . . .'
Why did my lying mother promise death
Should enter me imaged as Lord Apollo's metal arrowheads?
Or Hector, my best enemy, call Hector for a big hit
Over Helen's creditors, and I'll go brave.
Or else my death is waste.
Trapped like a pig-boy beneath dirty water.

In Heaven, two heard him:
First, the woman Prince, Athena; and with her came
Fishwaisted Poseidon, Lord of the Home Sea.
And dressed as common soldiers they came strolling by,
And held his hand, and comforted him, with:
'Stick, my friend, stick. Swallow the scare for now.
We're with you and, what's more, God knows it, so
Stick. This visitation means one thing—no River
Will put you down. Scamander? . . . He'll subside. And soon.
Now child, do this: Keep after him no matter what.
Keep coming, till—I use your own fine words—
Every living Trojan squats inside his city's wall
And Hector's dead. You'll win. We promise it.'

So the Greek, strong for himself, pushed by, thigh deep,
Towards the higher fields, through water
Bobbing with armoured corpses. Sunlight glittered
Off the intricate visions etched into breastplates
By Trojan silversmiths, and Trojan flesh
Bloomed over the rims of them, leather toggles sunk
To the bone. Picking his knees up, Achilles, now
Punting aside a deadman, now swimming a stroke or two,
Remembered God's best word and struck
Like a mad thing at the river. He beat it
With the palm of his free hand, sliced at it,
At the whorled ligaments of water, yes, sliced at them, Ah! —
There, there—there, and—*there*—such hatred,
Scamander had not thought, the woman Prince,
Scamander had not thought, and now, slice, slice,

Scamander could not hold the Greek! Yet,
Would not quit, bent, like a sharp-crested hyoid bone,
And sucking Achilles to his midst, called out:
'Simois, let's join to finish off this Greek — What's that?
Two against one, you say? Yes. Or Troy is ash,
For our soldiers cannot hold him. Quick, and help, come
Spanned out as a gigantic wave, foot up to peak
A single glinting concave welt, smooth, but fanged
Back in the tumultuous throat of it, with big
Flinty stones, clubbed pumice, trees, and all
Topped by an epaulette of mucid scurf to throttle,
Mash each bone, and shred the flesh and drown away
The impudent who plays at God.
Listen, Simois . . . Nothing can help him now.
Strength, looks — nothing. Why, that heavy armour, how
It will settle quietly, quietly, in ooze,
And his fine white body, aye, slimy and coiled up
I'll suck it down a long stone flue,
And his fellow Greeks will get not one bone back,
And without a barrow to be dug can save their breath
For games.'

                    And the water's diamond head
Shut over Achilles, locked round his waist
Film after film of sopping froth, then
Heaved him sideways up while multitudinous crests
Bubbled around his face, blocked his nostrils with the blood
He shed an hour before.

                    Then Hera, Heaven's queen,
Looked over the cloudy battlements of Paradise
And saw it all and saw the Greek was done and cursed Scamander,
Turned to Hephaestus her son, balanced on a silver crutch
And playing with a bag of flames, who, when his mother
Beckoned with her head, came close and listened:
'Little Cripple, would you fight Scamander for me?
Yes?' — rumpling his hair — 'You must be quick or' —
Giving him a kiss — 'Achilles will be dead. So,
Do it with fire, son; an enormous fire, while' —
Twisting his ear a bit — 'I fetch the white south wind to thrust
Your hot nitre among the Trojan dead, and you must
Weld Scamander wet to bank — now! But . . .
Wait. Little One, don't be talked out of it, eh?
More Gods are threatened than struck, Scamander's promises
Are bought. Now, off with you, and, one last thing —
Sear him, Hephaestus, till you hear me shout!'

                    And the Fire God
From a carroty fuse no bigger than his thumb,
Raised a burning fan as wide as Troy,

And brushed the plain with it until,
Scamander's glinting width was parched
And the smoke stopped sunlight.

          Then the garnet-coloured bricks
Coped with whitestone parapets that were Troy's wall,
Loomed in smoky light, like a dark wicket bounding
The fire's destruction.
Troy's plain was charred and all in cinders
The dead Trojans and their gear. Yet Heaven's Queen
Did not call her son, and the Cripple
Turned on the beaten river.

          Flame ate the elms,
Sad-willow, clover, tamarisk and galingale—the lot.
Rushes and the green, green lotus beds crinkled—wet dust,
The eels and the pike began to broil.
Last of all, Scamander's back writhed like a burning poultice,
Then, reared up, into a face on fire:
'How can I fight you, Cripple? Flames in my throat,
My waters griddled by hot lacquer! Quit—and I'll quit.
As for Troy and Trojans—let 'em burn. Are not we Gods
Above the quarrels of mere humans?'

        You must imagine how the water
        For boiling down the fat of a juicy pig
        After the women pour it in a cauldron,
        Seethes and lifts as the kindling takes
        And the iron sits in a flamy nest.
        Likewise Hephaestus fixed Scamander.

  So the wretched River God called to Heaven:
'Queen, why does your boy pick on me?
What of the other Gods who side with Troy?
I promise to leave off if *he* leaves off. What's more
I swear to turn away when Troy is burnt by Greeks.'

          So she called the Cripple off.
And between the echoing banks
    Scamander
Rushed gently over his accustomed way.

                   Christopher Logue

From THE ODYSSEY

From Book XI

We bore down on the ship at the sea's edge
and launched her on the salt immortal sea,

stepping our mast and spar in the black ship;
embarked the ram and ewe and went aboard
in tears, with bitter and sore dread upon us.
But now a breeze came up for us astern —
a canvas-bellying landbreeze, hale shipmate
sent by the singing nymph with sun-bright hair;
so we made fast the braces, took our thwarts,
and let the wind and steersman work the ship
with full sail spread all day above our coursing,
till the sun dipped, and all the ways grew dark
upon the fathomless unresting sea.
                                                   By night

our ship ran onward toward the Ocean's bourne,
the realm and region of the Men of Winter,
hidden in mist and cloud. Never the flaming
eye of Hêlios lights on those men
at morning, when he climbs the sky of stars,
nor in descending earthward out of heaven;
ruinous night being rove over those wretches.
We made the land, put ram and ewe ashore,
and took our way along the Ocean stream
to find the place foretold for us by Kirkê.
There Perimêdês and Eurýlokhos
pinioned the sacred beasts. With my drawn blade
I spaded up the votive pit, and poured
libations round it to the unnumbered dead:
sweet milk and honey, then sweet wine, and last
clear water; and I scattered barley down.
Then I addressed the blurred and breathless dead,
vowing to slaughter my best heifer for them
before she calved, at home in Ithaka,
and burn the choice bits on the altar fire;
as for Teirêsias, I swore to sacrifice
a black lamb, handsomest of all our flock.
Thus to assuage the nations of the dead
I pledged these rites, then slashed the lamb and ewe,
letting their black blood stream into the wellpit.
Now the souls gathered, stirring out of Erebos,
brides and young men, and men grown old in pain,
and tender girls whose hearts were new to grief;
many were there, too, torn by brazen lanceheads,
battle-slain, bearing still their bloody gear.
From every side they came and sought the pit
with rustling cries; and I grew sick with fear.
But presently I gave command to my officers
to flay those sheep the bronze cut down, and make
burnt offerings of flesh to the gods below
to sovereign Death, to pale Perséphonê.
Meanwhile I crouched with my drawn sword to keep
the surging phantoms from the bloody pit
till I should know the presence of Teirêsias.

One shade came first—Elpênor, of our company,
who lay unburied still on the wide earth
as we had left him—dead in Kirkê's hall,
untouched, unmourned, when other cares compelled us.
Now when I saw him there I wept for pity
and called out to him:

                         'How is this, Elpênor,

how could you journey to the western gloom
swifter afoot than I in the black lugger?'

He sighed, and answered:

                            'Son of great Laërtês,

Odysseus, master mariner and soldier,
bad luck shadowed me, and no kindly power;
ignoble death I drank with so much wine.
I slept on Kirkê's roof, then could not see
the long steep backward ladder, coming down,
and fell that height. My neck bone, buckled under,
snapped, and my spirit found this well of dark.
Now hear the grace I pray for, in the name
of those back in the world, not here—your wife
and father, he who gave you bread in childhood,
and your own child, your only son, Telémakhos,
long ago left at home.

                        When you make sail

and put these lodgings of dim Death behind,
you will moor ship, I know, upon Aiaia Island;
there, O my lord, remember me, I pray,
do not abandon me unwept, unburied,
to tempt the gods' wrath, while you sail for home;
but fire my corpse, and all the gear I had,
and build a cairn for me above the breakers—
an unknown sailor's mark for men to come.
Heap up the mound there, and implant upon it
the oar I pulled in life with my companions.'

He ceased, and I replied:

                           'Unhappy spirit,

I promise you the barrow and the burial.'

                    Robert Fitzgerald

❧ Anonymous (c. 700–600 b.c.)

HOMERIC HYMN TO HERMES: THE STEALING OF APOLLO'S CATTLE

The maid Maia shook her head, here is
No cattle reiver, my lord Apollo, come
And see;

    And there was only
An empty cavern. Wait,
There was in the very plush centre
Tiny as a beam
Of sunlight in a pinhole, a small
Gold cradle that rocked itself.

My son, said the maid, a true
Lovechild to Zeus;
            And indeed there glowed
In the blues and saffrons of the quilts one
Small triumphant head.
              But three days old, said the maid.
And it seemed to the god
The air was filled with the lowing
Of cattle. Maiden, he said, my herds
Are nearby. Where?
            The thief was here,
Here he stood, so recently I can hear
Heifers chew the cud and drop dung —
           Maiden, said Apollo.

My Lord, said the bare truth in her, only Zeus
Comes here.

My cattle were or are in this cavern.

Lord, is Zeus a reiver?

      The god
Was staring at the infant in the cot.
Three days, he said, three days old and

Already a monster.
          Wake up, my newest brother,
And talk to me.
          Take your choice. Speak or
I throw you downstairs into Tartarus.
                I see
I do not discommode you, little thief.

He shook the cradle noting
How the child rode it, all the rough and tumble.

So, child, you too are a power. In that case,
Let us speak as equals.

A great voice filled the cavern.
          My brother is
Too kind. How may we speak as man to man with this
Wet dribble down my chin.

Thunder in Heaven, said Apollo, you could be Heracles.

That thumper, said the babe. No, thank you. Could he
Hide from your all-seeing eye the two cowskins
I pegged outside to dry?

          My cows, the god whispered, the
Sacred ones.

          Who sacrificed when I was born? said the babe.
With Zeus, terrified of his old termagant, hiding
Us here in the wilderness.

          My child, my child, said Maia.

What other sacrifice would have relevance to
A major birth like mine?
          What other
Shake the heavens, give the place a new
Tilt?

     Apollo hung over him in two wide wings.
You laugh, Babe, do you laugh at me?

No, said the little lad, should a child
Three days old, take on the big loud-spoken
Almighties? I haven't finished my
Disquisition with reference to your kine.

     The child sat up. He
Was quite luminous, already stretched
Far beyond the body.
                         I thought, said he,
That heaven too should rejoice when I was born.
So I sacrificed your heifers to the Gods,
To the Twelve.

Apollo said, I see you want me to state
That we Olympians number only
Eleven.

So the twelfth smoke
Arises for a three-day-old, a babe?

Ho, said the child, you shall have your cattle back
At once.

My cattle, Apollo answered, I have already.
Look into your mind, you will not find them there.

The child pondered. That's a trick, a right one
You'll have to teach me.

Some say, said Apollo,
With birch and ferrule. Well, I'm pleased
In one way to have met you, Number Twelve.
Goodbye.

You'll be back, said the babe.

The maiden Maia walked with the god, her face

    Was full of wonder.
        What can I say, my Lord Apollo?

    Behind, in the cave, the earth had begun
    To dance, Apollo turned:
        A child making the music,
                      from
    A shell, a simple shell
        (And that was the first string plucked)

    I thought you'd be back, said the little one.
    All desires pull.
        And you want my shell. Here.

    The music died, Apollo took the shell
    Divining it,
        But could not find his way into a tune.

    You'll have to teach me, said he.

    Some say, said the babe,
    With birch and ferrule. And one must be a god, of course.
    Trees do not dance for common people.

    O Little cattle-robber, would you roast
    Apollo in the sun?
        He laughed, the laughter going forth
    In thunders that rapped the stone heads of hills
    And rained in the valleys.

Teach me, little brother, birch
Your sorry elder, but here's an art I must have.

You have it, said the Babe. Now
Quid pro quo, your royal herds for me.

Hey, said Apollo.

The music stopped.
So, said Apollo, you can stop me
As simply as that.

While the herds are yours, the gift and the shell
Are mine.

Ah, sighed the great God. I'll take the shell.
But tell me, wonder-babe, what will you do
With cattle, they're no toys, they're not exactly
Cradle playthings, what will you do with them?

Eat them, said the little lad. And grow up
To be like Daddy.
This time however I reserve
The twelve best portions for myself, for Hermes,
He said modestly, the youngest and perhaps the fairest
Of the Gods.

Padraic Fallon

ஐ 2

INDIA: THE VEDAS TO THE BHAGAVAD-GITA

Vedic

ஐ *From* The Rig Veda (c. 1500–1200 B.C.)

CREATION HYMN

No thing existed, nor did nothing exist:
there was no air-filled space, no sky beyond.
What held it all? And where? And who secured it?
Was water all there was, deep beyond measure?

There was no death, nor anything immortal —
no sign by which to mark off night and day.
Self-moved where no wind blew, one Being breathed:
other than it no thing had being then.

All was obscure at first, darkness in darkness,
an endless ocean — featureless, unlit:
there, at the heart of nothingness, the One
took on its being, born of an austere heat.

Desire came over it in the beginning —
first seed of all, engendered by the mind.
Wise thinkers who had searched within their hearts
found where what is is bound to what is not,

and stretched their measuring-cord across the void.
Did a "below" exist then, did an "above"?

There were seed-casters, there were primal forces —
power below, strong urgency above.

But who can know for certain, who proclaim it?
Who can explain the birth of this various world?
The gods themselves came into existence later —
who knows the source of this great tangled world?

How it all came about, or was created —
whether or not he fashioned it himself —
he who surveys it from the highest heaven,
he of all beings knows — or perhaps not.

Frederick Morgan

HYMN TO NIGHT

So vast, our Goddess Night, she rises,
star-eyes gazing everywhere;
all her finery of dress displayed.
Space high and low she fills, Eternal Night,
her beauty driving out the dark.
Close on the heels of sister Day
she treads. Let darkness run . . .
As you draw near, we turn for home
like birds that wing to nest.
Life everywhere retreats: man, beast
and bird. Even the soaring hawk
returns to seek out rest.
Night, shield us from the wolf and thief.
Throughout your hours let there be calm.
Pitch dark has brought a shroud for me.
Dawn, drive it, like my debts, away.
Child of Day, to you, as to a calf,
my hymn is offered. Receive it now
as paean to a conqueror.

Edwin Gerow and Peter Dent

DAWN HAS ARISEN, OUR WELFARE IS ASSURED

Arousing the lands where dwell the five peoples,
Dawn has made visible the pathways of Men.
The beautiful dawn clouds convey her radiance.
The light of the Sun has disclosed earth and heaven.

The Dawns advance like clans arrayed for battle,
their bright rays tingeing the sky's distant bounds.
The Sun extends his arms; the rose-colored dawn clouds,
imprisoning the darkness, beam forth their luster.

Goddess Dawn has arisen, endowed with great wealth,
eliciting homage — our welfare is assured!
Noblest of the noble, this Daughter of Heaven
grants to her worshipers varied treasures.

Give to us, Dawn, that copious bounty
with which you have rewarded those who sang your praises!
Loudly they acclaimed you, like the strong bulls that bellowed
as you unbarred the doors of the firm-set mountain.

Prevail on each God to give us his bounty!
Now at your appearing impart to us the charm
of pleasant voices and thoughts for our uplift.
Preserve us evermore, O Gods, with your blessings!

Raimundo Panikkar

MAY THE WIND BLOW SWEETNESS!

May the wind blow sweetness,
the rivers flow sweetness,
the herbs grow sweetness,
for the Man of Truth!

Sweet be the night,
sweet the dawn,
sweet be earth's fragrance,
sweet Father Heaven!

May the tree afford us sweetness,
the sun shine sweetness,
our cows yield sweetness —
milk in plenty!

Raimundo Panikkar

Sandkrit

❧ *From* The Upanishads
(c. 800–500 B.C.)

THE GOLDEN GOD

The Golden God, the Self, the immortal Swan
leaves the small nest of the body, goes where He wants.
He moves through the realm of dreams; makes numberless forms;
delights in sex; eats, drinks, laughs with His friends;
frightens Himself with scenes of heart-chilling terror.
But He is not attached to anything that He sees;
and after He has wandered in the realms of dream and awakeness,
has tasted pleasures and experienced good and evil,
He returns to the blissful state from which He began.
As a fish swims forward to one riverbank then the other,
Self alternates between awakeness and dreaming.
As an eagle, weary from long flight, folds its wings,
gliding down to its nest, Self hurries to the realm
of dreamless sleep, free of desires, fear, pain.
As a man in sexual union with his beloved
is unaware of anything outside or inside,
so a man in union with Self knows nothing, wants nothing,
has found his heart's fulfillment and is free of sorrow.
Father disappears, mother disappears, gods
and scriptures disappear, thief disappears, murderer,
rich man, beggar disappear, world disappears,
good and evil disappear; he has passed beyond sorrow.

Stephen Mitchell

❧ *From* The Bhagavad-Gita
(c. 300 B.C.)

From BOOK ONE

Arjuna, his war flag a rampant monkey,
saw Dhritarashtra's sons assembled
as weapons were ready to clash,
and he lifted his bow.

He told his charioteer:
    "Krishna,

halt my chariot
between the armies,

Far enough for me to see
these men who lust for war,
ready to fight with me
in the strain of battle.

I see men gathered here
eager to fight,
bent on serving the folly
of Dhritarashtra's son."

When Arjuna had spoken,
Krishna halted
their splendid chariot
between the armies.

Facing Bishma and Drona
and all the great kings,
he said, "Arjuna, see
the Kuru men assembled here!"

Arjuna saw them standing there:
fathers, grandfathers, teachers,
uncles, brothers, sons,
grandsons and friends.

He surveyed his elders
and companions in both armies,
all his kinsmen
assembled together.

Dejected, filled with strange pity,
he said this:

"Krishna, I see my kinsmen
gathered here, wanting war.
My limbs sink,
my mouth is parched,
my body trembles,
the hair bristles on my flesh.

The magic bow slips
from my hand, my skin burns,
I cannot stand still,
my mind reels.

I see omens of chaos,
Krishna; I see no good

in killing my kinsmen
in battle.

Krishna, I seek no victory,
or kingship, or pleasures.
What use to us are kingship,
delights, or life itself?

We sought kingship, delights,
and pleasures for the sake of those
assembled to abandon their lives
and fortunes in battle.

They are teachers, fathers, sons,
and grandfathers, uncles, grandsons,
fathers and brothers of wives,
and other men of our family.

I do not want to kill them
even if I am killed, Krishna;
not for kingship of all three worlds,
much less for the earth!

What joy is there for us, Krishna,
in killing Dhritarashtra's sons?
Evil will haunt us if we kill them,
though their bows are drawn to kill.

Honor forbids us to kill
our cousins, Dhritarashtra's sons;
how can we know happiness
if we kill our own kinsmen?"

Saying this in the time of war,
Arjuna slumped into the chariot
and laid down his bow and arrows,
his mind tormented by grief.

From BOOK TWO

[SANJAYA]
　　Arjuna sat dejected,
　　filled with pity,
　　his sad eyes blurred by tears.
　　Krishna gave him counsel.
[LORD KRISHNA]
　　Why this cowardice
　　in time of crisis, Arjuna?

The coward is ignoble, shameful,
foreign to the ways of heaven.

Don't yield to impotence!
It is unnatural in you!
Banish this petty weakness from your heart.
Rise to the fight, Arjuna!
[ARJUNA]
Krishna, how can I fight
against Bhishma and Drona
with arrows
when they deserve my worship?

It is better in this world
to beg for scraps of food
than to eat meals
smeared with the blood
of elders I killed
at the height of their power
while their goals
were still desires.

We don't know which weight
is worse to bear —
our conquering them
or their conquering us.
We will not want to live
if we kill
the sons of Dhritarashtra
assembled before us.

The flaw of pity
blights my very being;
conflicting sacred duties
confound my reason.
I ask you to tell me
decisively — Which is better?
I am your pupil.
Teach me what I seek!

I see nothing
that could drive away
the grief
that withers my senses;
even if I won kingdoms
of unrivaled wealth
on earth
and sovereignty over gods.
[SANJAYA]
Arjuna told this
to Krishna — then saying

"I shall not fight,"
he fell silent.

Mocking him gently,
Krishna gave this counsel
as Arjuna sat dejected,
between the two armies.

[LORD KRISHNA]
You grieve for those beyond grief,
and you speak words of insight;
but learned men do not grieve
for the dead or the living.

Never have I not existed,
nor you, nor these kings;
and never in the future
shall we cease to exist.

Just as the embodied self
enters childhood, youth, and old age,
so does it enter another body;
this does not confound a steadfast man.

Contacts with matter make us feel
heat and cold, pleasure and pain.
Arjuna, you must learn to endure
fleeting things—they come and go!

When these cannot torment a man,
when suffering and joy are equal
for him and he has courage,
he is fit for immortality.

Nothing of nonbeing comes to be,
nor does being cease to exist;
the boundary between these two
is seen by men who see reality.

Indestructible is the presence
that pervades all this;
no one can destroy
this unchanging reality.

Our bodies are known to end,
but the embodied self is enduring,
indestructible, and immeasurable;
therefore, Arjuna, fight the battle!

He who thinks this self a killer
and he who thinks it killed,

both fail to understand
it does not kill, nor is it killed.

It is not born,
it does not die;
having been,
it will never not be;
unborn, enduring,
constant, and primordial,
it is not killed
when the body is killed.

Arjuna, when a man knows the self
to be indestructible, enduring, unborn,
unchanging, how does he kill
or cause anyone to kill?

As a man discards
worn-out clothes
to put on new
and different ones,
so the embodied self
discards
its worn-out bodies
to take on other new ones.

———

If you think of its birth
and death as ever-recurring,
then too, Great Warrior,
you have no cause to grieve.

Death is certain for anyone born,
and birth is certain for the dead;
since the cycle is inevitable,
you have no cause to grieve!

Creatures are unmanifest in origin,
manifest in the midst of life,
and unmanifest again in the end.
Since this is so, why do you lament?

Rarely someone
sees it,
rarely another
speaks it,
rarely anyone
hears it—
even hearing it,
no one really knows it.

The self embodied in the body
of every being is indestructible;
you have no cause to grieve
for all these creatures, Arjuna!

Look to your own duty;
do not tremble before it;
nothing is better for a warrior
than a battle of sacred duty.

If you are killed, you win heaven;
if you triumph, you enjoy the earth;
therefore, Arjuna, stand up
and resolve to fight the battle!

From BOOK ELEVEN

[ARJUNA ASKS]
Tell me—
who are you
in this terrible form?
Homage to you, Best of Gods!
Be gracious! I want to know you
as you are in your begining.
I do not comprehend
the course of your ways.
[LORD KRISHNA]
I am time grown old,
creating world destruction,
set in motion
to annihilate the worlds;
even without you
all these warriors
arrayed in hostile ranks
will cease to exist.

Therefore, arise
and win glory!
Conquer your foes
and fulfill your kingship!
They are already
killed by me.
Be just my instrument,
the archer by my side!

Drona, Bhishma, Jayadratha,
and Karna,
and all the other battle heroes,
are killed by me.

Kill them
without wavering;
fight, and you will conquer
your foes in battle!

[SANJAYA]
Hearing Krishna's words,
Arjuna trembled
under his crown,
and he joined his hands
in reverent homage;
terrified of his fear,
he bowed to Krishna
and stammered in reply.
[ARJUNA]
Krishna, the universe
responds
with joy and rapture
to your glory,
terrified demons
flee in far directions,
and saints throng
to bow in homage.

Why should they not bow
in homage to you, Great Soul,
Original Creator,
more venerable than the creator Brahma?
Boundless Lord of Gods,
Shelter of All That Is,
you are eternity,
being, nonbeing, and beyond.

You are the original god,
the primordial spirit of man,
the deepest treasure
of all that is,
knower and what is to be known,
the supreme abode;
you pervade the universe,
Lord of Boundless Form.

You are the gods of wind,
death, fire, and water;
the moon; the lord of life;
and the great ancestor.
Homage to you,
a thousand times homage!
I bow in homage to you
again and yet again.

I bow in homage
before you and behind you;
I bow everywhere
to your omnipresence!
You have boundless strength
and limitless force;
you fulfill
all that you are.

Barbara Stoler Miller

3

CHINA: THE CHOU DYNASTY AND THE WARRING STATES PERIOD

Chinese

From The Book of Songs (c. 800–500 B.C.)

πολύμτιζ
THE BAMBOOS GROW WELL UNDER GOOD RULE

Dry in the sun by corner of K'i
green bamboo, bole over bole:
Such subtle prince is ours
to grind and file his powers
as jade is ground by wheel;
he careth his people's weal,
stern in attent,
steady as sun's turn bent
on his folk's betterment
                    nor will he fail.

Look ye here on the coves of the K'i:
green bamboo glitteringly!
Of as fine grain our prince appears
as the jasper plugs in his ears
ground bright as the stars in his cap of state;
his acumen in debate
splendid, steadfast in judgement-hall
he cannot fail us
                    nor fall.

In coves of K'i,
bamboo in leaf abundantly.
As metal tried is fine
or as sceptre of jade is clean;
stern in his amplitude,
magnanimous to enforce true laws, or lean
over chariot rail in humour
as he were a tiger
                    with velvet paws.

Ezra Pound

THE GREAT WAR DANCE

I. Lighting Up

Oh Lustrous! the king's army
            when reared
            at times, was dim
            at times, was all aglow!
Thus with his Great Aid,
            we, the favored ones, received it.
Striding high, the king's creation
            initiated the succession
Culminating in this Your Lord's true army.

II. Martial Wu

Oh Brilliant! the Martial King Wu
            fearless, blazing
Truly accomplished, what the Accomplished King Wen
            began for his descendents.
Wu, the successor, received it.
            Conquering the Yin nation, he
            exterminated
            slaughtered
So securing Your merit.

III. Return

Oh Brilliant! the Zhou peoples
Climbing those high mountains
            Narrow ridges
            towering peaks
Gathered at the river.
"All under Vast Heaven"
            is the response of the assembly
            is the Mandate of the Zhou.

IV. Rewards

King Wen's toil came to an end,
We in turn received it,

the spreading bounty.
We then sought to secure
    the Mandate of the Zhou.
Oh, it is bountiful!

V. [Silent Dance]

VI. Staunch

Pacifying the ten thousand nations,
Multiplying the full harvest years,
The Mandate of Heaven is not undone.
Staunch and Martial is King Wu,
    protective of his sons
    in the four regions of the world,
    securing his house.
Oh, shining in Heaven
    Brilliant, he looks over it.

Constance A. Cook

BOSS RAT

Boss Rat, Boss Rat,
Don't eat our millet.
Three years now we've been dealing with you,
Not that we get a bit of appreciation.
It's time for us to be leaving you,
To go to a happy place —
Happy place, happy place,
Where there will be some place for us.

Boss Rat, Boss Rat,
Don't eat our wheat.
Three years now we've been dealing with you,
Not that you ever give us a thing in return.
It's time for us to be leaving you,
To go to a happy land —
Happy land, happy land,
Where we can get some rest.

Boss Rat, Boss Rat,
Don't eat our seedlings.
Three years now we've been dealing with you,
Not that you ever think how hard we work.
It's time for us to be leaving you,
To go to a happy town —
happy town, happy town,
Where we won't always have to groan.

John S. Major

CRANE CALLS

Crane calls in Nine Marshes
    the sound heard in the wild;
Fish deep in the abyss
    or in the shallows.
You play in that garden
where sandlewood was planted:
    All dead leaves below.
Stone of that mountain:
    It could be carved.

Crane calls in Nine Marshes
    the sound heard in Heaven;
Fish in the shallows
    or deep in the abyss.
You play in that garden
where sandlewood was planted:
    All brambles below.
Stone of that mountain:
    It could be worked
into jade.

        Constance A. Cook

SHU IS AWAY

Shu is away in the hunting-fields,
There is no one living in our lane.
Of course there *are* people living in our lane;
But they are not like Shu,
So beautiful, so good.

Shu has gone after game.
No one drinks wine in our lane.
Of course people *do* drink wine in our lane
But they are not like Shu,
So beautiful, so loved.

Shu has gone to the wilds,
No one drives horses in our lane.
Of course people *do* drive horses in our lane.
But they are not like Shu,
So beautiful, so brave.

        Arthur Waley

FOREVER MARTIAL

Majestic and brilliant,
The king gave his command
To Oldsire Nan Ch'ung
And Grandee Huang Fu:
"Muster my six armies,
Make ready my war-weapons.
With reverence and due caution,
I will pacify the southern lands."

The king spoke then to the Lord of Yin,
Saying, "Command my lord Hsiu Fu of Ch'eng:
'Left and right, in columns and ranks,
Let my armies be put on alert.
March to the banks along the Huai River
And see to this Kingdom of Hsu.
Do not linger, do not tarry.
A threefold task: do all in good order.' "

Magnificent, awesome,
The splendor of the Son of Heaven!
Leisurely, calmly, the king's army set out,
Neither bunched up nor straggling.
The Land of Hsu trembled unceasingly:
The tremors that startled the Kingdom of Hsu
Were like thunder, like claps of thunder,
The tremors that startled the Kingdom of Hsu.

Then the king roused his martial might,
So that it too raged like the thunder.
Forward he ordered his tiger-like captains,
Fierce, like true tigers marauding.
His army spread out on the banks of the Huai,
And swiftly made captive both war-chiefs and men.
Securely they held the banks of the Huai,
The troops of the king encamped there.

The king's army innumerable,
As if it were flying, as if it were soaring,
Like the Yangtse, like the Han,
Like the firmness of a mountain,
Like the current of a river,
In columns and ranks,
Beyond measure, indomitable,
Mightily swept through the Kingdom of Hsu.

All that the king did was proper and righteous:
Thus swiftly surrendered the Kingdom of Hsu,
Swiftly, as one, the Kingdom of Hsu.

The Son of Heaven's brilliant achievement:
In every direction the world is at peace.
They come to pay homage, the Kingdom of Hsu,
They will not renege, the Kingdom of Hsu.
The king said, "Now let us go home."

John S. Major

FRUIT PLUMMETS FROM THE PLUM TREE

Fruit plummets from the plum tree
but seven of ten plums remain;
you gentlemen who would court me,
come on a lucky day.

Fruit plummets from the plum tree
but three of ten plums still remain;
you men who want to court me,
come now, today is a lucky day!

Fruit plummets from the plum tree.
You can fill up your baskets.
Gentlemen if you want to court me,
just say the word.

Tony Barnstone and Chou Ping

CYPRESS BOAT

Floating that cypress boat
And floating it goes,
Restless sleepless,
        as with hidden pain.
I do not lack for wine,
        to enjoy to wander.

        My heart is not a mirror.
        You cannot peer in.
        As I have brothers,
        You cannot grab me.
            Go there to tell!
            And meet their anger!

        My heart is not a stone.
        You cannot turn it over.
        My heart is not a mat.
        You cannot roll it up.

Dignity so refined!
Cannot be reckoned!

Pained heart so sad,
   Vexed by pettinesses
   Mixed with ills so many
   Insulted not a little,
Silently I contemplate them
Waking with a slap!

Sun, oh, moon, ah
How lost and small!
Oh heart's pain!
   as unwashed clothes
Silently I contemplate them
   unable to flap my wings and fly.

Constance A. Cook

THE RAT (A CLOSE TRANSLATION AND A PARAPHRASE)

1

Look: rat has skin.
Person, however: no standards.
This person without standards:
Hasn't died? Any reason?

Look: rat has teeth.
Person, however: no restraint.
This person without restraint:
Isn't dead? Why not?

Look: rat has legs.
Person, however: no propriety.
This person without propriety:
Should die! Hurry up!

John S. Major

2

SANS EQUITY AND SANS POISE
   "Dentes habet."
      Catullus

A rat too has a skin (to tan)
A rat has a skin at least

But a man who is a mere beast
might as well die,
his death being end of no decency.

A rat also has teeth
but this fellow, for all his size, is beneath
the rat's level,
why delay his demise?

The rat also has feet
but a man without courtesy need not wait
to clutter hell's gate.

Why should a man of no moral worth
clutter the earth?
This fellow's beneath the rat's modus,
why delay his exodus?

A man without courtesy
might quite as well cease to be.

Ezra Pound

CHUNG TZU

I Beg of you, Chung Tzu,
Do not climb into our homestead,
Do not break the willows we have planted.
Not that I mind about the willows,
But I am afraid of my father and mother.
Chung Tzu I dearly love;
But of what my father and mother say
Indeed I am afraid.

I beg of you, Chung Tzu,
Do not climb over our wall,
Do not break the mulberry-trees we have planted.
Not that I mind about the mulberry-trees,
But I am afraid of my brothers.
Chung Tzu I dearly love;
But of what my brothers say
Indeed I am afraid.

I beg of you, Chung Tzu,
Do not climb into our garden,
Do not break the hard-wood we have planted.
Not that I mind about the hard-wood,
But I am afraid of what people will say.
Chung Tzu I dearly love;

But of all that people will say
Indeed I am afraid.

Arthur Waley

❧ Yun'er (c. 500 B.C.)

YUN'ER'S BELL

The first month, Early auspicious, Dinghai day
I, Yun'er, the younger son of King Kang of Xu,
chose these Auspicious Metals
to cast myself a harmonious bell:
> Endlessly peal and toll!
> Primarily call the Resounding Brilliant One!
> Resounding celebrate the Primal Acheiver!
Drinking wine from a basin,
in harmony the Hundred Nobles meet:
> Skilled in Awesome Deportment.
> Charitable in Luminous Sacrifice.
I feast, please, and entertain
the celebrated guest
and our fathers, brothers, and clan sons:
> Brilliant! Brilliant!
> Glittering! Glittering!
> Extended longevity limitless!
> Sons and grandsons eternally
> Protect and strike this bell!

Constance A. Cook

❧ Attributed to Lao-tzu (c. 300 B.C.)

FIVE CHAPTERS: *From* THE TAO TE CHING

One

The way as "Way" bespoke is no true lasting way;
The name as "Name" no true lasting name.

"Unmanifest" can name creation's quickening;
"Manifest" the mother of millions bred.

Surely is this so:
Through the true unmanifest
Forms potential
Through the true manifest
Forms realized
The mind's eye marks.

These two brought forth,
Be one and the same,
But differ in name.
As one,
a darkling depth
to probe
ever to probe
beyond that portal
whence the millions teem.

Two

Whenever all the world declares fair "fair,"
There is foul.
Whenever all the world declares good "good,"
There is ill.

For,
As "manifest/unmanifest" defines existence,
So
Challenge achievement,
Span dimension,
Level degree,
Sound harmony
Position sequence.

It has always been this way.

And truly that is why
The wise man keeps to the practice of
"not acting for"
And applies the lesson of
"not speaking for."

The ten thousand stir forth
Without his direction,
Live through their lives
Without his possession,
And act of themselves
Unbeholden to him;
His work completed,
He lays no claim.

And this has everything to do
With why his claim holds always true.

Nine

Best be done before the last degree.
Honed too sharp no blade can hold its edge.
Treasure-filled no room remains secure.
Pride in wealth and place yields retribution.

"Tasks fulfilled, doers yield"
Is Heaven's law of motion.

Eleven

When thirty spokes join the wheel-hole,
A void to matter paired,
The carriage functions.
When clay is thrown to form a vase:
A void to matter paired,
The vessel functions.
When door and window vent a room,
A void to matter paired,
The chamber functions.
Surely is this so:
Materials avail,
Having void for function.

Twenty-One

A boundless shaping Power
Attends the moving-mover.
The mover fashions forms
That shine and darkle.
In the darkling shine—a likening;
In the shining dark—forms visible.
In the chambered half-light
A manifest quickening,
Elemental, real:
The pledge of the power.

From ancient times
Down to today
Still these words hold.

For thus we view
the gamut of the million's sources.
Thus can we describe
The gamut of the million's sources.

Moss Roberts

❧ Attributed to Ch'ü Yüan (c. 350–315 B.C.) *From* Ch'u Tz'u (Elegies of Ch'u)

From THE HEAVEN QUESTIONS

1

In the beginning of old,
    all is yet formless, no up or down,

Light is still dim,
    dark is a blur, the only image is a whir.
When bright gets brighter,
    and dark gets darker, the yin couples with the yang,
Then is the round pattern manifold.
    What an achievement that was!
Around turn the cords on the pivot of Heaven.
    Eight Pillars are the buttresses;
Spread out are the nine fields of Heaven
    with their many angles and edges.
The heavens mesh with the twelve Earth Branches,
    the sun and moon bond, and the stars line up.
One leaves from Bright Valley and rests at Shroud Shore
    on its journey from bright to dark,
While the Orb of Night flourishes after death
    and harbors a rabbit in its gut.
Nü Qi got nine sons without a husband.
    Old Qiang is there, and the benevolent nimbus.
Dark as it closes, bright when it opens,
    before the Horn rises the Great Light is hidden.

2

Rebuffed as flood-queller, the people upheld him.
    They said, why worry, employ Gun.
Owl-bearing turtles followed him beak to tail,
    as he fulfilled his task to satisfaction.
But for three long years he was banished to Quill Crag,
    whereupon Old Yu was born from his belly.
Yu inherited the loose ends and completed his father's task.
    While he kept to the plan, his scheme was distinct.
He filled the floodwaters, fathoms deep.
    He raised the nine regions of the square earth.
His winged dragon laid the courses of rivers and seas.
Gun designed it, and Yu completed it.
    Then Kang Hui did rage, and the land leaned southeast.
The nine continents rose, the river valleys deepened,
    and the eastward flow never fills the sea.

3

Long are the lengths, east to west, south to north,
    but the south to north span is the longer.
Kunlun Mountain is a Hanging Garden
    of terraced walls in tiers of nine.
Enter by gates in the Four Directions;
    open the Northwest and a wind escapes.
The Torch Dragon glows where the sun does not reach.
    The Ruo Tree shines before Xihe has risen.
The winter is warm there, and the summer is cold.
    There is a stone forest, and a beast that speaks.
There is a horned dragon bearing on its back a bear.
There is a nine-headed Hydra, and the Shu and Hu.

There is no death there where the long men guard.
There are the nine-jointed Calamus, the blossoms of Xi,
    and snakes that can swallow elephants.
Three Dangers is there, and Black Water that darkens the feet.
    Life there is long, and there is no death.
The Ling fish dwells there and the monster, Qi.
    Yi shot the suns, and how the crow feathers scattered!

Stephen Field

THE YELLOW RIVER'S EARL

With you I will roam to the river's nine channels,
when blasts of wind rise driving waves across stream,
we will ride my coach of waters, its canopy, lotus,
hitched to paired dragons, by basilisks flanked.

I climbed Mount Kun-lun, I gazed all around,
the heart flew aloft, it went sweeping off free.
Soon the sun was to set, I, transfixed, forgot going,
and then to the far shore I looked back with care.

My roofs are of fish scales, halls of the dragon,
turrets of purple cowries, palaces of carmine —
why is the holy one here, down in the water?

We will ride on white turtles, goldfish attend us,
with you I will roam by the river's isles,
where the current is rushing, there we'll go down.

You clasp your hands, journeying eastward;
you go with the Fairest to the southern shores
where the swell of the waves is coming to meet us,
and the schools of fishes, will send off my bride.

Stephen Owen

THE SUMMONS OF THE SOUL

The Lord God said to Wu Yang:
'There is a man on earth below whom I would help:
His soul has left him. Make divination for him.'
Wu Yang replied:
'The Master of Dreams . . .
The Lord God's bidding is hard to follow.'
[The Lord God said:]
'You must divine for him. I fear that if you any longer decline, it will be too
    late.'
Wu Yang thereupon went down and summoned the soul, saying:

'O soul, come back! Why have you left your old abode and fled to the earth's
far corners,
Deserting the place of your delight to meet all those things of evil omen?

'O soul, come back! In the east you cannot abide.
There are giants there a thousand fathoms tall, who seek only for souls to
catch,
And ten suns that come out together, melting metal, dissolving stone.
The folk that live there can bear it, but you, soul, would be consumed.
O soul, come back! In the east you cannot abide.

'O soul, come back! In the south you cannot stay.
There the people have tattooed faces and blackened teeth;
They sacrifice flesh of men and pound their bones for meat paste.
There the venomous cobra abounds, and the great fox that can run a
hundred leagues,
And the great nine-headed serpent, who darts swiftly this way and that,
And swallows men as a sweet relish.
O soul, come back! In the south you may not linger.

'O soul, come back! For the west holds many perils.
The Moving Sands stretch on for a hundred leagues.
You will be swept into the Thunder's Chasm, and dashed in pieces, unable to
help yourself;
And even should you chance to escape from that, beyond is the empty
desert,
And red ants as huge as elephants and wasps as big as gourds.
The five grains do not grow there; dry stalks are the only food;
And the earth there scorches men up; there is nowhere to look for water;
And you will drift there for ever, with nowhere to go in that vastness.
O soul, come back! Lest you bring on yourself perdition.

'O soul, come back! In the north you may not stay.
There the layered ice rises high, and the snowflakes fly for a hundred
leagues and more.
O soul, come back! You cannot long stay there.

'O soul, come back! Climb not to the heaven above,
For tigers and leopards guard the nine gates, with jaws ever
ready to rend up mortal men,
And one man with nine heads that can pull up nine thousand trees,
And the slant-eyed jackal-wolves pad to and fro;
They hang out men for sport and drop them in the abyss,
And only at God's command may they ever rest or sleep.
O soul, come back! Lest you fall into this danger.

'O soul, come back! Go not down to the Land of Darkness,
Where the Earth God lies, nine-coiled, with dreadful horns on his forehead,
And a great humped back and bloody thumbs, pursuing men, swift-footed:
Three eyes he has in his tiger's head, and his body is like a bull's.
O soul, come back! Lest you bring on yourself disaster.

'O soul, come back! and enter the gate of the city.
Skilled priests are there who call you, walking backwards to lead you in.
Qin basket-work, silk cords of Qi, and silken banners of Zheng:
All things are there proper for your recall; and with long-drawn, piercing
    cries they summon the wandering soul.
O soul, come back! Return to your old abode.

'All the quarters of the world are full of harm and evil.
Hear while I describe for you your quiet and reposeful home.
High halls and deep chambers, with railings and tiered balconies;
Stepped terraces, storeyed pavilions, whose tops look on the high mountains;
Lattice doors with scarlet interstices, and carving on the square lintels;
Draughtless rooms for winter; galleries cool in summer;
Streams and gullies wind in and out, purling prettily;
A warm breeze bends the melilotus and sets the tall orchids swaying.
Beyond the hall, in the apartments, the ceilings and floors are vermilion,
The chambers of polished stone, with kingfisher curtains hanging from
    jasper hooks;
Bedspreads of kingfisher seeded with pearls, dazzling in brightness:
Arras of fine silk covers the walls; damask canopies stretch overhead,
Braids and ribbons, brocades and satins, fastened with rings of precious
    stone.
Many a rich and curious thing is to be seen in the furnishings of the
    chamber.
Bright candles of orchid-perfumed fat light up flower-like faces that await
    you;
Twice eight handmaids to serve your bed, each night alternating in duty,
The lovely daughters of noble families, far excelling common maidens.
Women with hair dressed finely in many fashions fill your apartments,
In looks and bearing sweetly compliant, each gently yielding to the other.
But, despite their soft looks, of strong and noble natures, lofty spirits.
Beauty and elegance grace the inner chambers:
Mothlike eyebrows and lustrous eyes that dart out beams of brightness,
Delicate colouring, soft round flesh, flashing, seductive glances.
In your garden pavilion, by the long bed-curtains, they wait your royal
    pleasure:
Of kingfisher feathers its purple curtains and the blue hangings that furnish
    its high hall;
The walls, red; vermilion the woodwork; jet inlay on the roofbeams;
Overhead you behold carved rafters, painted with dragons and serpents;
Seated in the hall, leaning on its balustrade, you look down on a winding
    pool;
Its lotuses have just opened; among them grow water-chestnuts;
And purple-stemmed water-mallows enamel the green wave's surface.
Attendants quaintly costumed in spotted leopard skins wait on the sloping bank;
A light coach is tilted for you to ascend; footmen and riders wait in position.
An orchid carpet covers the ground; the hedge is of flowering hibiscus.
O soul, come back! Why should you go far away?

'All your household have come to do you honour; all kinds of good food are
    ready:

Rice, broom-corn, early wheat, mixed with yellow millet;
Bitter, salt, sour, hot and sweet—there are dishes of all flavours:
Ribs of the fatted ox, tender and succulent;
Sour and bitter blended in the soup of Wu;
Stewed turtle and roast kid, served up with yam sauce;
Geese cooked in sour sauce, casseroled duck, fried flesh of the great crane;
Braised chicken, seethed terrapin, high-seasoned, but not to spoil the taste;
Fried honey-cakes of rice flour and malt-sugar sweetmeats;
Jade-like wine, honey-flavoured, fills the winged cups;
Ice-cooled liquor, strained of impurities, clear wine, cool and refreshing;
Here are laid out patterned ladles, and here is sparkling wine.
O soul, come back! Here you shall have respect and nothing shall harm you.

'Before the dainties have left the tables, girl musicians take up their places.
They set up the bells and fasten the drums and sing the latest songs:
"Crossing the River", "Gathering Caltrops" and "The Sunny Bank".
The lovely girls are drunk with wine, their faces are flushed.
With amorous glances and flirting looks, their eyes like wavelets sparkle;
Dressed in embroideries, clad in finest silks, splendid but not showy;
Their long hair, falling from high chignons, hangs low in lovely tresses.
Two rows of eight, in perfect time, perform a dance of Zheng;
Their *xi-bi* buckles of Jin workmanship glitter like bright suns.
Bells clash in their swaying frames; the catalpa-wood zither's strings are
     swept.
Their sleeves rise like crossed bamboo stems, then slowly shimmer
     downwards.
Pipes and zithers rise in wild harmonies, the sounding drums thunderously
     roll;
And the courts of the palace quake and tremble as they throw themselves
     into the Whirling Chu.
Then they sing songs of Wu and ballads of Cai and play the Da-lü music.
Men and women now sit together, mingling freely without distinction;
Hat-strings and fastenings come untied: the revel turns to wild disorder.
The singing-girls of Zheng and Wei come to take their places among the
     guests;
But the dancers of the Whirling Chu find favour over all the others.
Then with bamboo dice and ivory pieces the game of Liu Bo is begun;
Sides are taken; they advance together; keenly they threaten each other.
Pieces are kinged and the scoring doubled. Shouts of 'five white!' arise.
Day and night are swallowed up in continuous merriment of wine.
Bright candles of orchid-perfumed fat burn in stands of delicate tracery.
The guests compose snatches to express their thoughts as the orchid
     fragrance steals over them;
And those with some object of their affections lovingly tell their verses to
     each other.
In wine they attain the heights of pleasure and give delight to the dear
     departed.
O soul, come back! Return to your old abode.'

David Hawkes

Part II

THE
CLASSICAL
EMPIRES,
EAST AND
WEST
(750 B.C.–A.D. 500)

Every account of the history of Greek literature includes a catalog of its losses. Poetry from the "Lyric Age" of Greece in the seventh century B.C. exists in fragments; pitifully little remains of the experience of the intensity, directness, and simplicity of these individual voices.

In the classical era, choral verse from fifth-century Attic theater is intact only insofar as we have access to the play that contained it. Only seven of a hundred plays of Sophocles have survived to convey their recital of the beauty and terror of old beliefs. His choruses still provide the ancient reassurance (or warning) that however "numberless are the world's wonders" none are "more wonderful than man." To his contemporary Aristophanes, the great scatological playwright who set a satirical contest between two other theatrical masters in *The Frogs*, nothing is more wonderful than mocking mortal pretensions under the Athenian freedom of speech to which Old Comedy gave full rein. (A. E. Housman's irresistible "Fragment of a Greek Tragedy" is, however, neither fragment, tragedy, nor Greek but a parody of certain late Victorian translations of Euripides.)

Monodic Greek poetry, sung in a variety of Aegean dialects by one performer and accompanied by the lyre, was recorded on scrolls of papyrus, gnawed by rats, used on occasion as mattress stuffing, and retrieved erratically. Stray lines unattached to the original poem cropped up in the glosses of grammarians and critics who wished to score a philological point. Although the ancients called Sappho of Lesbos "The Tenth Muse," what we read of her work exists in scraps; the enigmatic archaic smile has left its trace like the expression of a sculptured bust damaged by sea-water and corroded by time. (The translator here of Hipponax's fragments has chained them into a snarling unity.)

Without the labors of the Byzantine compilers of the Greek Anthology, around A.D. 1100, the casualties would be greater still. Hundreds of elegies, epigrams, and exquisite love poems remain in this huge gathering of "a mine of jewels choked with masses of lumber." One of its earliest poets in this collection covering the archaic period, the era of Alexander the Great, the Roman conquest of Greece, and the collapse of the Roman Empire itself, is the savagely satirical Archilochos of Paros. His work has survived from the seventh century B.C., a pioneering age in which Greece expanded into the archipelago and colonized Asia Minor. This soldier of fortune wrote animal fables, indulged his bent for the private vendetta, and took the realm of the defiant individual voice into iambic verse. His blazingly erotic "Fireworks on the Grass" was finally recovered and deciphered in 1975 in a presentation at the Oxford Philological Society under the title "Last Tango on Paros."

The turbulent early history of Greece, its relative stabilization in the sixth and fifth centuries, and the ebullient intellectual adventure of its civilization strongly inform its poetry. Simonides of Keos, Greece's national poet during the time of its greatest peril during the war with Persia, is the author of an epigram celebrating the Spartan dead at the battle of Thermopylae, the central pass forming the main line of defence against the invaders. Pindar's Epinician (Victory) Odes commemorate successes in the sacred games of the fifth century B.C. with verse as stylistically dazzling and formally difficult as the athletic triumphs of the winners.

During the Hellenistic era, the architectonic balance of composition and the "classical" ideal it suggests, gave way to the romantic realism and technical bravura of the third century B.C. In the work of Callimachus, Theocritus, and other learned poets clustered around the Ptolemaic capital of Alexandria, the European tradition began to take a familiar shape, while an old legacy of spleen, invective, and an abrasive misogyny flourished anew.

Religious texts continued to be a conduit between east and west. "The Petelia Tablet," inscribed in gold leaf on a tomb, alludes to the ancient cult of Orphism and its belief that the devotee has escaped from the sorrowful wheel. The "Last Oracle from Delphi" written shortly after the destruction of the temple of Apollo around A.D. 396, was supposedly delivered to an emissary of Julian the Apostate, the pagan and archaizing emperor who tried to restore the oracle. The primitive chant of the Latin "Arval Hymn" takes its name from the priesthood that performed it before the establishment of the Roman Republic.

Indigenous Latin poetry from the time when Rome was a provincial village has almost vanished. What remains in the Latin language are masterworks, owing their greatness not only to Greek models but to a self-conscious and urbane idea of tradition. The Latin poetry of the late Republic and the Empire embraced a useful didacticism and a patriotic vision of Rome frequently at odds with the Stoic ethic of living in harmony with reason. Stoicism was a strong element in the life of Roman writers; Lucretius's first-century B.C. treatise on natural philosophy gave it poetic expression.

The Stoic argument continues to jostle with the introspection and passionate torment of lyric poets like Catullus, whose dark love for the noblewoman he calls "Lesbia" displays a mastery of borrowed Greek meters, if not of the self. The poems are highly wrought, and learned, but take full advantage of the colloquial range of Latin.

In the Augustan Age poetry and history are fused in Virgil's *Aeniad*. The enterprise of writing a Latin epic on the founding of Rome gave an age of relative peace a mythos beginning with an imitation of Homer, yet ending with a synthesis of form and subject whereby what began as derivative evolved into powerful innovation. Ovid, exiled by Augustus in A.D. 8 to a barbarous border town on the Black Sea, not only reconfigured Greek myth in the *Metamorphoses*, but wrote in a Latin so compact, layered, and wily that it remained the sport of poets through the European Renaissance.

In the more rootless poetry of the Silver Age in the second century A.D. satirists roamed at large in the dissolution, corruption and weariness of the Empire. Petronius and Seneca committed suicide; their work gives us a bitter dose of our own modernity. Martial's epigrams still shock with their willful grossness, but the real surprise is the biting wit of the punch line. "I do not like thee, Dr. Fell" is an actual translation of Martial improvised by a seventeenth-century undergraduate under threat of expulsion from Oxford; Dr. Fell was the wrathful dean of Christ College.

The last Latin poem here celebrates the Rite of Spring. Its famous and intricate refrain goes through a new dance step in an elegant series of variations choreographed by the translator. "The Vigil of Venus," probably datable to the reign of Hadrian, looks backward at the spring festival of the pagan goddess and forward to the romantic and sensuous spirit of Medieval Latin lyric.

K. W.

For several centuries before and after the turn of the Common Era, much of the civilized world of Eurasia, East, and West, was under the sway of one or another great empire. In India, the Mauryan Dynasty conquered and held much of the northern subcontinent, though the dynasty did not long outlast its most famous ruler, Asoka the Great. And in China, the Han Dynasty — the first of the great imperial dynasties — expanded and ruled the Chinese empire for four hundred years. In Asia as in Greece and Rome, power, prosperity, and a sense of cultural entitlement encouraged all of the arts, and poetry not least, to flourish.

Indian verse in this period is dominated by secular poetry, generally in short stanzas of rhymed double-lines *(slokas)*. From northern India comes the *Gathasatasapti*, an anthology of poems on love and other topics compiled by King Hala, who ruled a minor kingdom during the first century A.D. The language of these poems is Prakrit, a colloquial counterpart to Sanskrit, which by this time had become largely a literary and liturgical language. In South India Tamil, a Dravidian language, debuts on the stage of world

literature in a great burst of creativity, in short poems—collected in a se-
ries of classical anthologies—that celebrate flirtation and clandestine love
affairs, extol martial valor, and mourn (but also praise) the deaths of young
men in battle.

Chinese poetry in the Han (sometimes—undeservedly—viewed mainly
as a transitional stage between two greater poetic eras) developed from ear-
lier roots. The Ch'u elegy form gave rise to the genre of "rhymeprose"
(such as Chia Yi's "Rhymeprose on an Owl," excerpted here), long, highly
ornamented works in rhymed, grammatically matched lines. The plain
verse of the *Book of Songs* lived on in the poems collected by the Yüeh Fu
(Music Bureau), a government office that was responsible for collecting folk
songs and poetry as a way of gauging public opinion (though the so-called
Yüeh Fu poems that survive are not true folk verse, but literary rework-
ings of folk themes).

J.S.M.

1

Greek Poetry: From the Lyric Age through the Hellenistic Period

Greek

Anonymous (date unknown)

THE PETELIA TABLET

(Inscription on gold foil from a tomb in South Italy, perhaps 4th century B.C.*)*

You will come to a well on the left side of hell's house.
A white cypress stands by it, luminous, pale.
Stay clear of this well at all cost. Don't drink from this well.
You will come to another, where cold water flows
from the marshes of memory. Sentinels stand there.
Say: "I am earth's and the starred sky's child, but the sky's
blood runs in my veins; you can see this yourselves.
Thirst dries me, withers me, give me this instant
the cold water flowing out of memory's marsh."
They will give you water from the sacred wellhead
and you will be known. . . . heroes from then on.
. . . . going to die
. . . . this writing . . . .
. . . . the darkness closing over.

Robert Bringhurst

ஜ Archilochus (c. 650 B.C.)

STRATEGY

Fox knows many,
Hedgehog one
Solid trick.

Guy Davenport

FIREWORKS ON THE GRASS

[   ]
Back away from that, (she said)
and steady on [   ]

Wayward and wildly pounding heart,
there is a girl who lives among us
who watches you with foolish eyes,

a slender, lovely, graceful girl,
just budding into supple line,
and you scare her and make her shy.

O daughter of the highborn Amphimedo,
I replied, of the widely remembered
Amphimedo now in the rich earth dead,

There are, do you know, so many pleasures
for young men to choose from
among the skills of the delicious goddess

it's green to think the holy one's the only.
When the shadows go black and quiet,
Let us, you and I alone, and the gods,

sort these matters out. Fear nothing:
I shall be tame, I shall behave
and reach, if I reach, with a civil hand.

I shall climb the wall and come to the gate.
You'll not say no, Sweetheart, to this?
I shall come no farther than the garden grass.

Nebule I have forgotten, believe me, do.
Any man who wants her may have her.
Aiai! she's past her day, ripening rotten.

The petals of her flower are all brown.
The grace that first she had is gone.
Don't you agree that she looks like a boy?

A woman like that would drive a man crazy.
She should get herself a job as a scarecrow.
I'd as soon hump her as [kiss a goat's butt].

A source of joy I'd be to the neighbors
with such a woman as her for a wife!
How could I ever prefer her to you?

You, O innocent, true heart and bold.
Each of her faces is as sharp as the other.
Which way she's turning you can never guess.

She'd whelp like the proverb's luckless bitch
were I to foster get upon her, throwing
them blind, and all on the wrongest day.

I said no more, but took her hand,
laid her down in a thousand flowers,
and put my soft wool cloak around her.

I slid my arm under her neck
To still the fear in her eyes,
for she was trembling like a fawn,

touched her hot breasts with light fingers,
spraddled her neatly and pressed
against her fine, hard, bared crotch.

I caressed the beauty of all her body
And came in a sudden white spurt
while I was stroking her hair.

Guy Davenport

BE BOLD! THAT'S ONE WAY

Be bold! That's one way
Of getting through life.
So I turn upon her
And point out that,
Faced with the wickedness
Of things, she does not shiver.
I prefer to have, after all,
Only what pleases me.

Are you so deep in misery
That you think me fallen?
You say I'm lazy; I'm not,
Nor any of my kin-people.
I know how to love those
Who love me, how to hate.
My enemies I overwhelm
With abuse. The ant bites!
The oracle said to me:
"Return to the city, reconquer.
It is almost in ruins.
With your spear give it glory.
Reign with absolute power,
The admiration of men.
After this long voyage,
Return to us from Gortyne."
Pasture, fish, nor vulture
Were you, and I, returned,
Seek an honest woman
Ready to be a good wife.
I would hold your hand,
Would be near you, would have run
All the way to your house.
I cannot. The ship went down,
And all my wealth with it.
The salvagers have no hope.
You whom the soldiers beat,
You who are all but dead,
How the gods love you!
And I, alone in the dark,
I was promised the light.

Guy Davenport

MAY HE LOSE HIS WAY ON THE COLD SEA

May he lose his way on the cold sea
And swim to the heathen Salmydessos,
May the ungodly Thracians with their hair
Done up in a fright on the top of their heads
Grab him, that he know what it is to be alone
Without friend or family. May he eat slave's bread
And suffer the plague and freeze naked,
Laced about with the nasty trash of the sea.
May his teeth knock the top on the bottom
As he lies on his face, spitting brine,
At the edge of the cold sea, like a dog.
And all this it would be a privilege to watch,

Giving me great satisfaction as it would,
For he took back the word he gave in honor,
Over the salt and table at a friendly meal.

Guy Davenport

MERCENARY

I don't give a damn if some Thracian ape strut
Proud of that first-rate shield the bushes got.
Leaving it was hell, but in a tricky spot
I kept my hide intact. Good shields can be bought.

Stuart Silverman

ᔆᕱ Semonides

From THE GENEALOGY OF WOMEN

God in His Wisdom from the start
Set Man & Woman poles apart,
And out of Woman's nature drew
A veritable human zoo.

    The slattern SOW 'mid pans & pots
& unwashed clothes & garbage squats,
Her very skin as thick with dirt
As are her stockings, shirt & skirt —
Maid of middens that still battens
On household waste — and fat, fattens.

    Maliciously, the long-nosed VIXEN
Of Good & Bad won't choose betwixt 'em.
Restless, till the heart of rose
Smells like a cabbage — cabbage, rose —
Exudes the stench of human stews
Dressed as the kindliest piece of news.

    Next, the BITCH, whose business is
Everyone else's businesses.
Inquisitive, like the she-fox,
With eye at keyholes, ear at locks,
Nosing for what her neighbor knows,
Yapping the secret to disclose
(Or when there's nothing to disclose).
Threats, blows on the mouth, a kind word,
She stays oblivious as a turd.

Set her where discretion matters,
As host or guest—still she chatters.

————

And last, the humble bumble BEE
That I & Meleagro (he
Who started the Greek Anthology)
And also Rgya Mts'o, sang
(Whose other names were Ts'angs & Dbyangs)—
The BEE in this brute list arrives,
And here we find the best of wives.
What honey would you rather eat
Than that she spins from Love's sweet seat?
What distillation ever comes
More dear than from her honeycombs?
Women, 'tis known, swap tales of Love,
This woman's life of Love is wove:
She has no time for Love's tit-bits
But spews out honey where she sits.
Daily about her wifely chores,
Eager to earn her man's applause.
By night she stills his rightful lust,
By day she mops the household dust.
A happy, useful life, you think,
Spent beside the kitchen-sink?
'Tis true, yet let no man forget,
There comes a time when Love shall set.
And she'll call in her woman's debt.
Love in its fullness like a peach
She'll then accept from each & each.
For this Queen BEE—'tis known to all—
Consumes her lovers in the Fall.

　　Although Man runs to take a wife
She works him mischief all his life.
The even tenour of a day,
The sense that debt is kept at bay,
To all of this he'll kiss goodbye.
And when he thinks he's hit a high,
That God is pleased with him, or Man,
And he has done the best he can,
That's when his wife in ambush waits
Slamming Euphoria's happy gates
With words relentless as the Fates'.
He asks his friends: she makes a scene;
Or, if she would appear serene,
Then's when the poison works the worst,
Then's when she's well & truly curst.
And all the while his wife is *his;*
Others, potential mistresses.
He praises her; the others mocks,
And does not see the paradox.

Of all the woes God's given Man,
Woman, especially Woman's can(—)
Can honestly be said to take
The torta, tart, or bun, or cake.
The sexual drive in Man or Woman
Is all the sexes have in common.
In Man, the sex & love are one,
In her, this union is undone.
From this divorce derives that pain
The whore lays on with whip & cane.
All ills, desires, fruitless prayers,
Discords, empty acts & wars
Are in those eyes, those thighs, that hair
That ride Man's sexual despair.

And who among us now, a boy,
Could carelessly set sail for Troy?
For Helen's gestures, walk, her glance,
More deadly than the haft of lance
That entered once her erstwhile friends,
For us no deathless cause portend—
Merely the *pettiest* of ends.

Is there no other path to tread
Than that of the Achaean dead?

Peter Whigham

∾ Alcman (654–611 B.C.)

DESIRE LOOSENING

Desire loosening
arms, knees, thighs, she
    looks at me
    more meltingly
than sleep or death, such
sweetness carries her—

Astymeloisa, swaying
past me, lifts her garland
    high, a star
    skimming the night air,
or green-gold April sprout, or,
softly, a feather . . .

Rosanna Warren

FRAGMENT 58: NIGHT AND SLEEP

They sleep, the mountain crags and gullies,
headlands and brooks, and the whole race
of footed creatures the black earth pulls from its womb,
mountain beasts and the republic of bees,
and vast fish looming in hollows
of purple sea: they sleep,
too, birds with wide, cloud-tipped wings . . .

Rosanna Warren

❧ Sappho (c. 612 B.C.)

STAR OF EVENING

Hesperus
you bring
home everything
which light of day dispersed:
home the sheep herds
home the goat
home the mother's darling

Paul Roche

ANAKTORIA

Handsome horses O shiver and admire,
Long ships and symmetries of archers,
But black earth's fine sight for me
Is her I love.

Heart's hunger all can understand.
Did not she up and leave the best of men,
Helen that beautifullest of womankind?
[   ]

And forgot her kin and forgot her children
To follow however far into whatever luck
The wild hitherward of her headlong heart
[   ]

[   ]
[   ]
Anaktoria so far away, remember me,
Who had rather

Hear the melody of your walking
And see the torch flare of your smile
Than the long battle line of Lydia's charioteers,
Round shields and helmets.

Guy Davenport

THE ARBOR

He seems to be a god, that man
Facing you, who leans to be close,
Smiles, and, alert and glad, listens
To your mellow voice

And quickens in love at your laughter
That stings my breasts, jolts my heart
If I dare the shock of a glance.
I cannot speak,

My tongue sticks to my dry mouth,
Thin fire spreads beneath my skin,
My eyes cannot see and my aching ears
Roar in their labyrinths.

Chill sweat glides down my back,
I shake, I turn greener than grass.
I am neither living nor dead and cry
From the narrow between.

Guy Davenport

HORSES IN FLOWERS

Come out of Crete
And find me here,
Come to your grove,
Mellow apple trees
And holy altar
Where the sweet smoke
Of libanum is in
Your praise.

Where Leaf melody
In the apples
Is a crystal crash,
And the water is cold.
All roses and shadow,

This place, and sleep
Like dusk sifts down
From trembling leaves.

Here horses stand
In flowers and graze.
The wind is glad
And sweet in its moving.
Here, Kypris [   ]
Pour nectar in the golden cups
And mix it deftly with
Our dancing and mortal wine.

                              Guy Davenport

PERCUSSION, SALT AND HONEY

Percussion, salt and honey,
A quivering in the thighs;
He shakes me all over again,
Eros who cannot be thrown,
Who stalks on all fours
Like a beast.

                              Guy Davenport

LYRIC: THREE VERSIONS

1

The moon has set
and the Pleiades; it is the middle
of the night and the hours go by
and I lie here alone.

                              Jim Powell

2

The moon has set
and the Pleiades. It is
Midnight. Time passes.
I sleep alone.

                              Kenneth Rexroth

3

The Pleiades disappear,
the pale moon goes down.

After midnight, time blurs:
sleepless, I lie alone.

Sam Hamill

PRAYER TO APHRODITE

Eternal Aphrodite, Zeus's daughter, throne
Of inlay, deviser of nets, I entreat you:
Do not let a yoke of grief and anguish weigh
Down my soul, Lady,

But come to me now, as you did before
When, hearing my cries even at that distance
You slammed the door of your father's house —
Golden! and hastened

To harness your chariot. Then pretty sparrows
Drew you forthwith over the dark lands,
Beating their crisp wings. From the outer spheres,
Down through the inner,

Steeply they descended. At last you, Divine Lady,
Beaming your unearthly smile at me,
Asked was I in distress once again — for,
Why had I called you?

And what did my unruly heart demand
Of you now? "And whom do I urge this time
To return your generous friendship? Who,
Sappho, has been stubborn?

For if she avoids you, soon she will come
Knocking; if refuses presents, will shower them
On you; if she loves not, she shall love, and
Learn to be kinder."

I beg you, come. Free me from this oppression.
All that my heart longs to see accomplished,
Goddess, do it. No one could resist if you were
Fighting beside me.

Alfred Corn

✎ Alcaeus (c. 620–658 B.C.)

HER HEART SO STRICKEN

. . . Her heart so stricken, Helen
clutched her breast and wept for Paris
as he, in turn, deceived his host;
and she stole away on his boat,
abandoning her child and her husband's bed . . .

And now how many brothers of Paris
lie planted in black earth
across the plains of Troy?
All for that woman, chariots ground to dust,
noble, olive-skinned men all slaughtered
on her behalf.

Sam Hamill

I LONG FOR THE CALL TO COUNCIL

I long for the call to council
that I will never hear.

Driven from the land that was my father's,
from the land that was his father's before him,

the citizens bicker and battle
as I enter my exile, a wolf in his thicket . . .

wandering the scorched, black world . . .

Sam Hamill

COME TIP A FEW WITH ME

Come tip a few with me,
Melanippus, and you'll see
why you crossed over Acheron
once again searching for the sun.

Come drink. Don't set your sights
too high. Even King Sisyphus —
among all men, the wisest —
thought he might outsmart Death,

only to cross Acheron twice:
the judgment of Fate.
And now he labors endlessly
in Hades.

Come drink, and celebrate
while we are young. Later,
whatever sufferings we undergo,
we will . . . the north wind blows.

Sam Hamill

COME! PUT BY PELOPS' ISLE

Come! Put by Pelops' Isle
Zeus' and Leda's hero sons
Castor and Polydeuces
Come!

Over the earth's breadth and the width
of the Sea come swiftly on strange horses.
You can take away death from these men
great cold threats.

Quick! Up the mast of the well-built ship
bright from afar. Quick! Up the rigging.
In the pain of night bring light
to the dark ship.

Fred Beake

ᗄ Anacreon (570–? B.C.)

COUNT, IF YOU CAN

Count, if you can, every leaf on every tree.
And count each wave that comes ashore
    from every possible sea—
then you might number my plethora of lovers.

Compute if you can the countless loves of Athens,
the infinite passions of Korinth,
and Achaea where the women take your breath away.

Write down the names of all my loves in Lesbos,
remember their names from Ionia, from Karios

and Rhodos,
their names from passionate dark Syria,

and from Krete where Eros runs wild in the streets.
How can I number my many loves in India, in Baktria?
How many did I love in Cadiz?

Sam Hamill

Xenophanes (570–? B.C.)

WAR MEMORIES

In winter, sprawled on soft cushions,
replete and warm, munching on chick-peas
and drinking sweet wine by the fire . . .
that is the time to ask each other:

As if to Odysseus:
   "Who, from where, and why, art thou?"

—Or with a wink:
   "And how many years are on your back, Bold-Heart?"

—Or, quietly:
   "Had you yet reached man's estate, when the Persians came?"

Theodore Blanchard

Ibycus (c. 560 B.C.)

IN SPRING THE QUINCE

In the Spring the quince and the
Pomegranate bloom in the
Sacred Park of the Maidens,
And the vine tendril curls in
The shade of the downy vine leaf.
But for me Love never sleeps.
He scorches me like a blaze
Of lightning and he shakes me
To the roots like a storm out of
Thrace, and he overwhelms my heart
With black frenzy and seasickness.

Kenneth Rexroth

❧ Simonides (556–468 B.C.)

THERMOPYLAE

Go tell the Spartans, thou that passest by,
That here, obedient to their laws, we lie.

William Lisle Bowles

BECAUSE OF THESE MEN'S COURAGE

Because of these men's courage, no smoke rose
Skyward from Tegea's burning. They chose
To leave their children the broad land's township green
With freedom, while in the front line they went down.

Peter Jay

DANAE AND PERSEUS

. . . when in the wrought chest
the wind bowing over
and the sea heaving
struck her with fear, her cheeks not dry,
she put her arm over Perseus and spoke: My child
such trouble I have.
And you sleep, your heart is placid;
you dream in the joyless wood;
in the night nailed in bronze,
in the blue dark you lie still and shine.
The salt water that towers above your head
as the wave goes by you
heed not, nor the wind's voice; you press
your bright face to the red blanket.
If this danger were danger to you
your small ear will attend my words.
But I tell you: Sleep, my baby, and let the sea sleep, let
our trouble sleep; let some change appear

Zeus, father, from you.
This bold word and beyond justice
I speak, I pray you, forgive it me.

Richmond Lattimore

ᜠ Theognis (c. 550 B.C.)

CAPTIVE

I gave you wings. Black stone, blue heave shall take
the shadow of your flight. Where men pass, where
legend is live with music, they will make
your name a song, and you will still be there
when all your bones are gathered underground
to sad and private darkness in the sty
of Hades; you shall live still in the sound
of singing. Even dead you shall not die.
For song is mine and I am yours. Then go.
Continents dip behind your heel, appears
Ocean and spinning water miles below.
You ride on wind and a defeat of years.
I made you this. And now you turn from me
as from a child who will not let you be.

Richmond Lattimore

ᜠ Hipponax (540–? B.C.)

STILL WAITING FOR MY WINTER COAT: A
SEQUENCE OF FRAGMENTS

called on Hermes
strangler of dogs

brother of thieves
a.k.a. Kandaules

(in Scythia):
PLEASE HELP ME OUT

•

ah . . . to wear a mantle
of mountain sheep's wool . . .

•

Hermes lord of Cyllene
great son of Maia

Hipponax begs you:
send me a winter coat

for I am starving

•

unfunny he who drinks his lunch

•

now that was good advice

•

last night while I lay sleeping
someone made off with my clothes

lay in a room on a pallet buck-naked

•

o teeth
you

who used to reside
in my jaw

•

picked tarragon out of a dented bucket
hands shook trembled

like the toothless
when the north wind blows

•

Zeus
Emperor of Olympus

Big Daddy

no scrumptious feast of partridge and hare
no sesame pancakes

no fritters drenched
in honey

no yummy Lebedian figs
from far-off Kamandolos

•

to Hipponax:

> 1 coat
> 1 shirt

> 1 pair of sandals
> 1 pair of winter shoes

> > (and 60 gold bars
> > to hide in the wall)

●

still waiting for my great shaggy coat
to keep me from freezing in winter

and for that pair of winter shoes
to save my poor feet from chilblains

●

Pluto must have gone blind
he's never found his way to my house to tell me

"greetings dear Hipponax
see here I brought you this bag of silver"

●

o great Athena
please grant me a gentle master

one who won't beat me

●

I bow to Hermes
wait for the sun to rise

in his bright shirt

> > > > *Anselm Hollo*

✢ Aeschylus (525–456 B.C.)

CHORUS *From* AGAMEMNON

[*Enter* CHORUS OF OLD MEN. *During following chorus the day begins to dawn.*]
The tenth year it is since Priam's high
Adversary, Menelaus the king

And Agamemnon, the double-throned and sceptre
Yoke of the sons of Atreus
Ruling in fee from God,
From this land gathered an Argive army
On a mission of war a thousand ships,
Their hearts howling in boundless bloodlust
In eagles' fashion who in lonely
Grief for nestlings above their homes hang
Turning in cycles
Beating the air with the oars of their wings,
 Now to no purpose
 Their love and task of attention.

But above there is One,
Maybe Pan, maybe Zeus or Apollo,
Who hears the harsh cries of the birds
Guests in his kingdom,
Wherefore, though late, in requital
He sends the Avenger.
Thus Zeus our master
Guardian of guest and of host
Sent against Paris the sons of Atreus
For a woman of many men
Many the dog-tired wrestlings
Limbs and knees in the dust pressed—
 For both the Greeks and Trojans
 An overture of breaking spears.

Things are where they are, will finish
In the manner fated and neither
Fire beneath nor oil above can soothe
The stubborn anger of the unburnt offering.
As for us, our bodies are bankrupt,
The expedition left us behind
And we wait supporting on sticks
Our strength—the strength of a child;
For the marrow that leaps in a boy's body
Is no better than that of the old
For the War God is not in his body;
While the man who is very old
And his leaf withering away
Goes on the three-foot way
No better than a boy, and wanders
A dream in the middle of the day.

But you, daughter of Tyndareus,
Queen Clytemnestra,
What is the news, what is the truth, what have you learnt,
On the strength of whose word have you thus
Sent orders for sacrifice round?
All the gods, the gods of the town,

Of the worlds of Below and Above,
By the door, in the square,
Have their altars ablaze with your gifts,
From here, from there, all sides, all corners,
Sky-high leap the flame-jets fed
By gentle and undeceiving
Persuasion of sacred unguent,
Oil from the royal stores.
Of these things tell
That which you can, that which you may,
Be healer of this our trouble
Which at times torments with evil
Though at times by propitiations
A shining hope repels
The insatiable thought upon grief
Which is eating away our hearts.

Of the omen which powerfully speeded
That voyage of strong men, by God's grace even I
Can tell, my age can still
Be galvanized to breathe the strength of song,
To tell how the kings of all the youth of Greece
Two-throned but one in mind
Were launched with pike and punitive hand
Against the Trojan shore by angry birds.
Kings of the birds to our kings came,
One with a white rump, the other black,
Appearing near the palace on the spear-arm side
Where all could see them,
Tearing a pregnant hare with the unborn young
Foiled of their courses.

   Cry, cry upon Death; but may the good prevail.
But the diligent prophet of the army seeing the sons
Of Atreus twin in temper knew
That the hare-killing birds were the two
Generals, explained it thus—
In time this expedition sacks the town
Of Troy before whose towers
By Fate's force the public
Wealth will be wasted.
Only let not some spite from the gods benight the
bulky battalions,
The bridle of Troy, nor strike them untimely;
For the goddess feels pity, is angry
With the winged dogs of her father
Who killed the cowering hare with her unborn
young;
Artemis hates the eagles' feast.'
   Cry, cry upon Death; but may the good prevail.

'But though you are so kind, goddess,
To the little cubs of lions
And to all the sucking young of roving beasts
In whom your heart delights,
Fulfil us the signs of these things,
The signs which are good but open to blame.
And I call on Apollo the Healer
That his sister raise not against the Greeks
Unremitting gales to baulk their ships,
Hurrying on another kind of sacrifice, with no feasting,
Barbarous building of hates and disloyalties
Grown on the family. For anger grimly returns
Cunningly haunting the house, avenging the loss
of a child, never forgetting its due.'
So cried the prophet — evil and good together,
Fate that the birds foretold to the king's house,
In tune with this
    Cry, cry upon Death; but may the good prevail.

Louis MacNeice

CHORUS *From* THE SUPPLIANTS

SUPPLIANTS. ZEUS MEN APHIKTOR Shining Father
        Protector of suppliants   shine freely
here on this voyage of women   who set sail
where Nile twists through saltpolished
sand   Hallowed netherland whose sunbruised
boundaries graze desert   leaving it
we flew
        not outlaws hounded publicly
for murder's blood on our hands
            but fugitives
escaping self-built prisons for our own flesh
Agree to marry Egypt's sons   unthinkable!
skin shudders   the unholy thought

    [DANAOS *enters left and climbs to the sanctuary.*]

Our father on earth   heart's guide
and guide for our footsteps   gambling
all for the best among sorrows
            decided
we fly before we were pinioned   over a trembling sea
to light on this earth cupped in the day's hand
and here   it must have been   our lives,
our voyage time out of mind began in

droning of flies round a heifer
warm palm of heaven
blue breathing of Zeus   yes
we swear it!

Land?   shall you welcome
our coming?
With these mightiest swords we implore you   with
branches flowering white unspun wool

O home
O earth and sundazzled water
Highblazing gods and slowgrinding earthpowers
        vital in coffins
O Saviour Zeus
        guarding the flesh houses
of men who honor You   receive as Your suppliants
our fleet of innocence and breathe
a soft air of mercy onshore
                                    But the night-thick
manswarm   self-vaunting, spawned out of Egypt
before one foot pierces the shallows
before sailwings fold   God!
send them seaward   breathe rain, ice and winter
caress them with lightning, thunder, hail
let them face gnashing waves
                                    let them die
before they can man themselves   decency forbid!
in cousin-beds, in bodies seized and
        brutally entered

[*Putting down their branches, the* SUPPLIANTS *sing and dance.*]

O be joyful now sing
        the Zeus-calf born over the sea
        to right an old wrong
        son of our flowerpastured first mother
        child of the heifer filled by Zeus' breath
        caress-child whose name,
            given at birth, proves the virginal
        truth of his fathering:
Epaphos, Caress-born

Sing joy sing homecoming!
        These green shores nourished
        · our earliest mother
while her body learned the first stings of suffering
Remember her pains   count and recount them,
proofs of our good faith
        proofs to astonish the land's children

till they know truth
abides in our unfinished story . . .

Janet Lembke

From THE PERSIANS

The Battle of Salamis

And when the light of the sun had perished
and night came on, the masters of the oar
and men at arms went down into the ships;
then line to line the longships passed the word,
and every one sailed in commanded line.
All that night long the captains of the ships
ordered the sea people at their stations.
The night went by, and still the Greek fleet
gave order for no secret sailing out.
But when the white horses of the daylight
took over the whole earth, clear to be seen,
the first noise was the Greeks shouting for joy,
like singing, like triumph, and then again
echoes rebounded from the island rocks.
The barbarians were afraid our strategy
was lost, there was no Greek panic in
that solemn battle-song they chanted then,
but battle-hunger, courage of spirit;
the trumpet's note set everything ablaze.
Suddenly by command their foaming oars
beat, beat in the deep of the salt water,
and all at once they were clear to be seen.
First the right wing in perfect order leading,
then the whole fleet followed out after them,
and one great voice was shouting in our ears:
"Sons of the Greeks, go forward, and set free
your fathers' country and set free your sons,
your wives, the holy places of your gods,
the monuments of your own ancestors,
now is the one battle for everything."
Our Persian voices answered roaring out,
and there was no time left before the clash.
Ships smashed their bronze beaks into ships,
it was a Greek ship in the first assault
that cut away the whole towering stem
from a Phoenician, and another rammed
timber into another. Still at first
the great flood of the Persian shipping held,
but multitudes of ships crammed up together,
no help could come from one to the other,
they smashed one another with brazen beaks,
and the whole rowing fleet shattered itself.

So then the Greek fleet with a certain skill
ran inwards from a circle around us,
and the bottoms of ships were overturned,
there was no seawater in eyesight,
only wreckage and bodies of dead men,
and beaches and rocks all full of dead.
Whatever ships were left out of our fleet
rowed away in no order in panic.
The Greeks with broken oars and bits of wreck
smashed and shattered the men in the water
like tunny, like gaffed fish. One great scream
filled up all the sea's surface with lament,
until the eye of darkness took it all.

Peter Levi

✒ Pindar (518–446 B.C.)

OLYMPIA XI—FOR AGESIDAMUS OF THE
WESTWIND LOCRIANS: WINNER IN THE BOYS'
BOXING MATCH

Old Time, Old Shifting Trade—Time there is for the luffing sheets,
for the shipmates crying out for a blast to drive them home;
and Time there is for the flash flood, Rain,
Son-at-Arms from the thunderbreast of Sky.
But once let a man catch fire,
          wring some triumph out of the grit of combat:
then my underrun of music,
a founding-stone for annals building against the years,
will mount at the last, an unaging pledge to the works of Greatness;

over the seas of Envy, surge and spring, my votive tablet,
shoring up from your bed of Olympic wreaths perennial!
No, go slow, my heart, slower, lips,
straining to rear this win and make it bear.
God is the Gardener. All our primes,
          flowering out on the coiling force of skill,
yours and mine entwining, stem
from Him alone. Yes Agesidamus, trust to it now
that you're living up to your gift for fists, you sprig of Archestratus,
now, this talisman cast in song—I fling it over your olive wreath
to blaze its bloom of gold and the stock of Locris
where the West Wind waits to fill our sails.
Muse at the cutwater, O my Convoy!
Take this warrant, taut as our cords:
no camp of provincials armed to the teeth to warm
us in as guests, no, nor bludgeon-artists put to rout
by a piece of fine old work; no, in the haven you and I

will raise the craftsmen grasp the heights,
    the spearmen hit the grand finesse forever.
Show me a Trade that sloughs them off—
    the eyes of the vixen glittering Guile,
        or the rival of thunder, the lion's exultation—
all the marks of birth that vault to Triumph on our rushing blood.

Robert Fagles

THE HYPERBOREANS *From* PYTHIAN X

Among them too are the Muses
For everywhere
To flute and string the young girls
Are dancing,
In their hair the gold leaves of the bay:

The dance whirls them away:
Age or disease, no toil,
Battle or ill-day's luck
Can touch them, they
Are holy, they
Will outlast time, exempted
From the anger of the Goddess
And all decay.

Here the hero came
With the head
That shocked a royal house, turning
King and all into stone:
It was long long ago, if
Time means anything;
Long, long ago.

Padraic Fallon

FOR MIDAS, THE MAN FROM AKRAGAS FIRST IN THE FLUTE MATCH 409 B.C., *From* PYTHIAN XII

I ask you
lover of brightness
men's fairest city
Persephone's home & throne
well built, set on a hill
by Akragas' sheep grazed banks
kind, gentle to gods & men alike
take this crown

from Pytho for good Midas
& Midas as well
who beat Hellas at the craft
Pallas discovered
in the insolent Gorgons'
deadly song
unravelled by Athena
maidens worn out
sorrow shed
under snake infested heads
when Perseus slew
their third sister
he brought the Seriphians
their lot, their fate
darkened the ineffable race
of Phorkos, his share for
Polydektes' feast
—his mother's coffer
eternal bondage & bed of need
Medusa's fair cheeks
her head cut off
by Danae's son, born
I know, from a gush of gold
flux of itself.
Saving her lover, the maid
& goddess discovered
a flute
a tool to weave
polytonic musics
& mimic those loud groans
growing from Euryala's quick jaws.
Finding this
she gave what she found
to men to use, called it
many headed music
a sound to rouse feats
a weave of thin bronze & reeds
& call the people
dwelling by the fair site
of the Grace's city
on Kephinos' sacred land
to witness the dance.
Bright success never shines
effortless on men.
A god might end it today.
What fate sets occurs.
Yet time can still cast up
the unexpected, grant
this but not that.

                    Thomas Meyer

✑ Sophocles (496–406 B.C.)

CHORUS *From* OEDIPUS AT KOLONOS

Praise for Kolonos
Come, let us praise this haven of strong horses,
unmatched, brilliant Kolonos, white with sunlight,
where the shy one, the nightingale, at evening
        flutes in the darkness,

the ivy dark, so woven of fruit and vine-leaves
no winter storms nor light of day can enter
this sanctuary of the dancing revels
        of Dionysos.

Here, under heaven's dew, blooms the narcissus,
crown of life's mother and her buried daughter,
of Earth and the Dark below; here, too, the sunburst
        flares of the crocus.

The river's ample springs, cool and unfailing,
rove and caress this green, fair-breasted landscape.
Here have the Muses visited with dances,
        and Aphrodite

has reined her chariot here. And here is something
unheard of in the fabulous land of Asia,
unknown to Doric earth—a thing immortal;
        gift of a goddess,

beyond the control of hands, tough, self-renewing,
an enduring wealth, passing through generations,
here only: the invincible grey-leafed olive.
        Agèd survivor

of all vicissitudes, it knows protection
of the All-Seeing Eye of Zeus, whose sunlight
always regards it, and of Grey-Eyed Athena.
        I have another

tribute of praise for this city, our mother:
the greatest gift of a god, a strength of horses,
strength of young horses, a power of the ocean,
        strength and a power.

O Lord Poseidon, you have doubly blessed us
with healing skills, on these roads first bestowing
the bit that gentles horses, the controlling
        curb and the bridle,

and the carved, feathering oar that skims and dances
like the white nymphs of water, conferring mastery
of ocean roads, among the spume and wind-blown
      prancing of stallions.

———————

What is unwisdom but the lusting after
Longevity: to be old and full of days!
For the vast and unremitting tide of years
Casts up to view more sorrowful things than joyful;
And as for pleasures, once beyond our prime,
They all drift out of reach, they are washed away.
And the same gaunt bailiff calls upon us all,
Summoning into Darkness, to those wards
Where is no music, dance, or marriage hymn
That soothes or gladdens. To the tenements of Death.

Not to be born is, past all yearning, best.
And second best is, having seen the light,
To return at once to deep oblivion.
When youth has gone, and the baseless dreams of youth,
What misery does not then jostle man's elbow,
Join him as a companion, share his bread?
Betrayal, envy, calumny and bloodshed
Move in on him, and finally Old Age —
Infirm, despised Old Age — joins in his ruin,
The crowning taunt of his indignities.

So is it with that man, not just with me.
He seems like a frail jetty facing North
Whose pilings the waves batter from all quarters;
From where the sun comes up, from where it sets,
From freezing boreal regions, from below,
A whole winter of miseries now assails him,
Thrashes his sides and breaks over his head.

Anthony Hecht

CHORUS *From* PHILOCTETES

Not from out of my own life but from the tradition
a story which turns out to be true: of a youth
who dared to approach Zeus' bed.
Kronos' great son
bound him for endless torture
to the endless round of the wheel,
aside from him
what life known or heard of is sadder
than Philoctetes'? innocent man
dragging to his end

he robbed or wronged no man
how can I understand him? I see
the waves of the years of his anguish
break and break on the grey cold stone
he is his own neighbor, he groans
to his neighbor, limping through the heavy
round of day on day on day
no friend to mirror his misery to him, to offer
healing attentiveness, to calm the rage
and quell the pain
with herbs from the good soil.
no choice: between spasms his infant's crawling's
all he can manage on his hunt for his drugs.

alone among the sons of men he's cast out of earth's
gifts. the sowing and the reaping.
enough if now and then his arrow downs
any living thing. poor man
in those ten black years
what did he find to drink
not wine but stagnant water

he's found a good friend now.
the music of his life deepens
through his suffering; he will rediscover a green
continuity
goodbye to the black months.
homing in with our ship
to his Spercheios' banks, his old
countryside, the naiads' woods, he will roam
where the hero of the brazen shield
climbed in fire to the sky over Oeta.

                                    Armand Schwerner

TWO CHORUSES *From* ANTIGONE

Blessed is he whose life has not tasted of evil.
When God has shaken a house, the winds of madness
Lash its breed till the breed is done.
          Even so the deep-sea swell
          Raked by wicked Thracian winds
Scours in its running the subaqueous darkness,
Churns the silt black from sea-bottom;
And the windy cliffs roar as they take its shock.

Here on the Labdacid house long we watched it piling,
Trouble on dead men's trouble: no generation
Frees the next from the stroke of God:

Deliverance does not come.
The final branch of Oedipus
Grew in his house, and a lightness hung above it:
To-day they reap it with Death's red sickle,
The unwise mouth and the tempter who sits in the brain.

The power of God man's arrogance shall not limit:
Sleep who takes all in his net takes not this,
Nor the unflagging months of Heaven—ageless the Master
Holds for ever the shimmering courts of Olympus.
　　　For time approaching, and time hereafter,
　　　And time forgotten, one rule stands:
　　　That greatness never
Shall touch the life of man without destruction.

Hope goes fast and far: to many it carries comfort,
To many it is but the trick of light-witted desire—
Blind we walk, till the unseen flame has trapped our footsteps.
For old anonymous wisdom has left us a saying
　　　"Of a mind that God leads to destruction
　　　The sign is this—that in the end
　　　Its good is evil."
Not long shall that mind evade destruction.

　　　　　　　　　　　　　　　E. R. Dodds

Numberless are the world's wonders, but none
More wonderful than man; the storm-grey sea
Yields to his prows, the huge crests bear him high;
Earth, holy and inexhaustible, is graven
With shining furrows where his plows have gone
Year after year, the timeless labor of stallions.

The lightboned birds and beasts that cling to cover,
The lithe fish lighting their reaches of dim water,
All are taken, tamed in the net of his mind;
The lion on the hill, the wild horse windy-maned,
Resign to him; and his blunt yoke has broken
The sultry shoulders of the mountain bull.

Words also, and thought as rapid as air,
He fashions to his good use; statecraft is his,
And his the skill that deflects the arrows of snow,
The spears of winter rain: from every wind
He has made himself secure—from all but one:
In the late wind of death he cannot stand.

O clear intelligence, force beyond all measure!
O fate of man, working both good and evil!
When the laws are kept, how proudly his city stands!
When the laws are broken, what of his city then?

Never may the anarchic man find rest at my hearth,
Never be it said that my thoughts are his thoughts.

Dudley Fitts and Robert Fitzgerald

Euripides (485–405 B.C.)

CHORUS *From* HIPPOLYTUS

[*The chorus sing of escape*]
O for wings,
swift, a bird,
set of God
among the bird-flocks!
I would dart
from some Adriatic precipice,
across its wave-shallows and crests,
to Eradanus' river-source;
to the place
where his daughters weep,
thrice-hurt for Phæton's sake,
tears of amber and gold which dart
their fire through the purple surface.

I would seek
the song-haunted Hesperides
and the apple-trees
set above the sand drift:
there the god
of the purple marsh
lets no ships pass;
he marks the sky-space
which Atlas keeps —
that holy place
where streams,
fragrant as honey,
pass to the couches spread
in the palace of Zeus:
there the earth-spirit,
source of bliss,
grants the gods happiness.

O ship
white-sailed of Crete,
you brought my mistress
from her quiet palace
through breaker and crash of surf
to love-rite of unhappiness!
Though the boat swept

toward great Athens,
though she was made fast
with ship-cable and ship-rope
at Munychia the sea-port,
though her men stood
on the main-land,
(whether unfriended by all alike
or only by the gods of Crete)
it was evil—the auspice.

On this account
my mistress,
most sick at heart,
is stricken of Kupris
with unchaste thought:
helpless and overwrought,
she would fasten
the rope-noose about the beam
above her bride-couch
and tie it to her white throat:
she would placate the dæmon's wrath,
still the love-fever in her breast,
and keep her spirit inviolate.

H. D.

From ELECTRA

When the long boats came on Troy from Greece
Oars were fans flashed wide under sun
Arching sea girls naked in spume
Girls who leaped while dolphins dived
Drunk with your boat song, while Achilles gazed,
Agamemnon gazed, watched for a river—
Shimmering blade upon Troy's broad shore

And sea girls brought from the Fire God's forge
Armour of blinding gold for Achilles,
Climbed mountain to Pelion's crag—
Where sire had trapped immortal Thetis—
Then heights and glens of the wild hill girls
Echoing shining praise—
Sea born Achilles! Heart of the Greeks!

One night that wanderer from Ilium
Told stories near harbour lights—
I heard of your shield, Achilles!
Those emblems writhed in bronze . . .
Perseus a dragon

Soared over sea, swung the Gorgon's head,
Hermes arrowed alongside . . .
How wonder all Troy trembled . . . ?

And the eye of his shield glared brighter than the sun
Harder then Phaeton's hurtling car
Whose horses flame to the rim of the world
Brighter far than Pleiades, Hyades,
And Hector saw, while spirit died,
Sphinxes poised on the red-gold helm
Victims rigid between their claws,
Lioness reared from Achilles' breast,
Clawed thin air despised by Pegasus . . .

But his sword! Down the sword ran
Black war stallions, cloaked in dust,
Raised far by their radiant stride . . .
Such was a man, whose chief you killed,
Killed with your bed-tricks
Clytemnestra!
So seigneurs of the heaven shall slit you
I'll see when your hot blood shoots
When you'll gasp for the steel
For axe bites deeper than love, at your throat!

Denis Goacher

CHORUS *From* THE TROJAN WOMEN

It is a fearful thing to be flung
from the hand of the living god.
Zeus handed Troy's smoking altars to the Greeks:
the steamy mulch poured on the flame,
the myrrh that climbed the azure roof,
the tall citadel and Ida's high ridges
thick with ivy cut with snow-fed culverts,
mountaintop the sun strikes first and last —
once filled with light, once sacred.

Gone are the offerings and the holy cries
of the dance in the dark night;
gone the night-long festivals,
the golden statues of the gods;
gone the moon-dials that number and trace
the moon's phases in the night's supernal silence.
What did you feel
in the blaze of the besieged city
as the flames licked your chair?
Did the smoke get in your eyes? Make you blind?

Was Troy the sacrifice you had in mind?

O young men, o my mate,
o you, dead, now spirits stumbling
on the wrong shore,
while your bodies lie
above ground, mud-caked and rotting,
for ravens to prey on.
You gods—build me a sea-going vessel
with darting wings
to bring me to the pastures of Argos
where horses graze,
where Cyclopian walls
break the sky.
They are herding the children
like heifers, lowing, down to the gate

MA—MA—

The herdsmen of Achaea are taking me out
of your sight, away from your arms—
leading me down to the midnight boats
whose oars clip the waves
all the way to port
hard by the double-gated island,
Pelops' keep,
where fathers eat their children.

Let that thunder
break the toy ship in the middle sea,
clap the oar with fire,
break Menelaos.
He exiled me, enslaved me,
a wife to constant sorrow.
Break the mirrors, girl's toys,
Helen's first love,
would that they were all shattered.

MENELAUS: May he never return
to Laconia, to the limestone cliffs
of that grubby backwater
where men lie like stones;
to his father's smoky hearth,
to the bronze vault of the goddess.
Who looked on
when he forced great Hellas
to a filthy union
made in the mud of the river-bed?

Mark Rudman and Katharine Washburn

❧ A. E. Housman (1859–1936)

FRAGMENT OF A GREEK TRAGEDY: A PARODY

CHORUS.   O suitably-attired-in-leather-boots
      Head of a traveller, wherefore seeking whom
      Whence by what way how purposed art thou come
      To this well-nightingaled vicinity?
      My object in enquiring is to know,
      But if you happen to be deaf and dumb
      And do not understand a word I say,
      Then wave your hand, to signify as much.

ALCMAEON.   I journeyed hither a Bœotian road.
CHORUS.   Sailing on horseback, or with feet for oars?
ALCMAEON.   Plying with speed my partnership of legs.
CHORUS.   Beneath a shining or a rainy Zeus?
ALCMAEON.   Mud's sister, not himself, adorns my shoes.
CHORUS.   To learn your name would not displease me much.
ALCMAEON.   Not all that men desire do they obtain.
CHORUS.   Might I then hear at what your presence shoots?
ALCMAEON.   A shepherd's questioned mouth informed me that—
CHORUS.   What? for I know not yet what you will say—
ALCMAEON.   Nor will you ever, if you interrupt.
CHORUS.   Proceed, and I will hold my speechless tongue.
ALCMAEON.   —This house was Eriphyla's, no one's else.
CHORUS.   Nor did he shame his throat with hateful lies.
ALCMAEON.   May I then enter, passing through the door?
CHORUS.   Go, chase into the house a lucky foot,
      And, O my son, be, on the one hand, good,
      And do not, on the other hand, be bad;
      For that is very much the safest plan.

ALCMAEON.   I go into the house with heels and speed.
CHORUS.   In speculation   [*Strophe*]
    I would not willingly acquire a name
        For ill-digested thought;
        But after pondering much
    To this conclusion I at last have come:
        Life is uncertain.
        This truth I have written deep
        In my reflective midriff
        On tablets not of wax,
    Nor with a pen did I inscribe it there,
    For many reasons: *Life, I say, is not*
        A stranger to uncertainty.
    Not from the flight of omen-yelling fowls
        This fact did I discover.
    Nor did the Delphic tripod bark it out,
        Nor yet Dodona.
    Its native ingenuity sufficed
        My self-taught diaphragm.

Why should I mention   [*Antistrophe*]
The Inachean daughter, loved of Zeus?
    Her whom of old the gods,
      More provident than kind,
Provided with four hoofs, two horns, one tail,
    A gift not asked for,
    And sent her forth to learn
    The unfamiliar science
    Of how to chew the cud.
She therefore, all about the Argive fields,
Went cropping pale green grass and nettle-tops,
    Nor did they disagree with her.
But yet, howe'er nutritious, such repasts
    I do not hanker after:
Never may Cypris for her seat select
    My dappled liver!
Why should I mention Io! Why indeed?
    I have no notion why.

    But now does my boding heart,   [*Epode*]
    Unhired, unaccompanied, sing
    A strain not meet for the dance.
    Yea even the palace appears
    To my yoke of circular eyes
    (The right, nor omit I the left)
    Like a slaughterhouse, so to speak,
    Garnished with woolly deaths
    And many shipwrecks of cows.
I therefore in a Cissian strain lament;
    And to the rapid,
Loud, linen-tattering thumps upon my chest
    Resounds in concert
The battering of my unlucky head.

ERIPHYLA [*within*]. O, I am smitten with a hatchet's jaw;
    And that in deed and not in word alone.
CHORUS. I thought I heard a sound within the house
    Unlike the voice of one that jumps for joy.
ERIPHYLA. He splits my skull, not in a friendly way,
    One more: he purposes to kill me dead.
CHORUS. I would not be reputed rash, but yet
    I doubt if all be gay within the house.
ERIPHYLA. O! O! another stroke! that makes the third.
    He stabs me to the heart against my wish.
CHORUS. If that be so, thy state of health is poor;
    But thine arithmetic is quite correct.

ᘒ Aristophanes (445–385 B.C.)

PISTHETAIROS' SPEECH *From* THE BIRDS

Whereas now you've been downgraded.
You're the slaves, not lords, of men.
They call you brainless or crazy.
They kill you whenever they can.

The temples are no protection:
the hunters are lying in wait
with traps and nooses and nets
and little limed twigs and bait.

And when you're taken, they sell you
as tiny *hors d'oeuvres* for a lunch.
And you're not even sold alone,
but lumped and bought by the bunch.

And buyers come crowding around
and pinch your breast and your rump,
to see if your fleshes are firm
and your little bodies are plump.

Then, as if this weren't enough,
they refuse to roast you whole,
but dump you down in a dish
and call you a *casserôle.*

They grind up cheese and spices
with some oil and other goo,
and they take this slimy gravy
and they pour it over you!

Yes, they pour it over you!

It's like a disinfectant,
and they pour it piping hot,
as though your meat were putrid,
to sterilize the rot!

Yes, to sterilize the rot!
[*As* PISTHETAIROS *finishes, a long low susurrus of grief runs through the* CHORUS
and the BIRDS *sigh, weep, and beat their breasts with their wings.*]

William Arrowsmith

From THE CLOUDS

The Clouds: The Initiation of Strepsiades

So I hereby bequeath you my body,
 for better, dear girls, or worse.
You can shrink me by slow starvation;
 or shrivel me dry with thirst.
You can freeze me or flay me skinless;
 thrash me as hard as you please.
Do any damn thing you've a mind to—
 my only conditions are these:

that when the ordeal is completed,
 a new Strepsiades rise,
renowned to the world as a WELSHER,
 famed as a TELLER OF LIES,
a CHEATER,
   a BASTARD,
     a PHONEY,
       a BUM,
SHYSTER,
   MOUTHPIECE,
     TINHORN,
       SCUM,
STOOLIE,
   CON-MAN,
     WINDBAG,
       PUNK,
OILY,
  GREASY,
    HYPOCRITE,
      SKUNK,
DUNGHILL,
   SQUEALER,
     SLIPPERY SAM,
FAKER,
  DIDDLER,
    SWINDLER,
      SHAM,
—or just plain Lickspittle.
And then, dear ladies, for all I care,
 Science can have the body,
to experiment, as it sees fit,
 or serve me up as salami.

Yes, you can serve me up as salami!

       William Arrowsmith

Cydias (c. 400 B.C.)

BEWARE

Beware. There are fawns
who, facing the lion,
die of fright just thinking
the lion might be hungry.

Sam Hamill

Plato (c. 427–347 B.C.)

ASTER

You were the morning star among the living:
But now in death your evening lights the dead.

Peter Jay

Anyte (c. 390–350 B.C.)

I, HERMES, HAVE BEEN SET UP

I, Hermes, have been set up
Where three roads cross, by the windy
Orchard above the grey beach.
Here tired men may rest from travel,
By my cold, clean whispering spring.

Kenneth Rexroth

Antiphanes (388–311 B.C.)

A STRANGE RACE OF CRITICS

A strange race of critics,
they perform autopsies on
the poetry of the dead.
Sad bookworms,
they chew through thorns.

No poet's too dull
for them to elucidate, these who defile
the bones of the great.

Callimachus attacked them like a dog.
Out! Into the long darkness,

perpetual beginner, little gnat —
it is a poet you distract.

Sam Hamill

◈ Poseidippus (c. 310 B.C.)

DORICHA

So now the very bones of you are gone
Where they were dust and ashes long ago;
And there was the last ribbon you tied on
To bind your hair, and that is dust also;
And somewhere there is dust that was of old
A soft and scented garment that you wore —
The same that once till dawn did closely fold
You in with fair Charaxus, fair no more.

But Sappho, and the white leaves of her song,
Will make your name a word for all to learn,
And all to love thereafter, even while
It's but a name; and this will be as long
As there are distant ships that will return
Again to your Naucratis and the Nile.

Edwin Arlington Robinson

◈ Heraclitus (c. 300 B.C.)

THE SOIL IS FRESHLY DUG

"The soil is freshly dug, the half-faded wreathes of leaves droop across the
    face of the tombstone.
What do the letters, say, traveller? What can they tell you of the smooth
    bones the slab says it guards?
'Stranger, I am Artemias of Cnidua. I was the wife of Euphro. Labour-pains
    were not withheld
from me. I left one twin to guide my husband's old age, and took the other to
    remind me of him.' "

Edwin Morgan

❧ Leonidas of Tarentum (c. 300 B.C.)

THERIS, THE OLD MAN WHO LIVED BY HIS FISH TRAPS

Theris, the old man who lived by his fish traps
And nets, more at home on the sea than a gull,
The terror of fishes, the net hauler, the prober
Of sea caves, who never sailed on a many oared ship,
Died in spite of Arcturus. No storm shipwrecked
His many decades. He died in his reed hut,
And went out by himself like a lamp at the
End of his years. No wife or child set up this
Tomb, but his fisherman's union.

Kenneth Rexroth

❧ Tymnes (c. 300 B.C.)

THE MALTESE DOG

He came from Malta; and Eumelus says
He had no better dog in all his days,
He called him Bull; he went into the dark,
Along those roads we cannot hear him bark.

Edmund Blunden

❧ Theocritus (c. 300 B.C.)

EPITAPH: JUSTICE

The poet Hipponax lies here.
In justice, this is only fair.
His lines were never dark or deep.
Now he enjoys (like his readers) sleep.

Fred Chappell

IDYL I

THYRSIS.
The whisper of the wind in
        that pine tree,
                goatherd,

is sweet as the murmur of live water;
    likewise
        your flute notes. After Pan
you shall bear away second prize.
    And if he
        take the goat
with the horns,
    the she-goat
        is yours: but if
he choose the she-goat,
    the kid will fall
        to your lot.
And the flesh of the kid
    is dainty
        before they begin milking them.
GOATHERD.
Your song is sweeter,
    shepherd,
        than the music
of the water as it plashes
    from the high face
        of yonder rock!
If the Muses
    choose the young ewe
        you shall receive
a stall-fed lamb
    as your reward,
        but if
they prefer the lamb
    you
        shall have the ewe for
        second prize.
THYRSIS.
Will you not, goatherd,
    in the Nymph's name
        take your place on this
        sloping knoll
among the tamarisks
    and pipe for me
        while I tend my sheep.
GOATHERD.
No, shepherd,
    nothing doing;
        it's not for us
to be heard during the noon hush.
    We dread Pan,
        who for a fact
is stretched out somewhere,
    dog tired from the chase;
        his mood is bitter,

anger ready at his nostrils.
> But, Thyrsis,
>> since you are good at
singing of *The Afflictions of Daphnis,*
> and have most deeply
>> meditated the pastoral mode,
come here,
> let us sit down,
>> under this elm
facing Priapus and the fountain fairies,
> here where the shepherds come
>> to try themselves out
by the oak trees.
> Ah! may you sing
>> as you sang that day
facing Chromis out of Libya,
> I will let you milk, yes,
>> three times over,
a goat that is the mother of twins
> and even when
>> she has sucked her kids
her milk fills
> two pails. I will give besides,
>> new made, a two-eared bowl
of ivy-wood,
> rubbed with beeswax
>> that smacks still
of the knife of the carver.
> Round its upper edges
>> winds the ivy, ivy
flecked with yellow flowers
> and about it
>> is twisted
a tendril joyful with the saffron fruit.
> Within,
>> is limned a girl,
as fair a thing as the gods have made,
> dressed in a sweeping
>> gown.

Her hair
> is confined by a snood.
>> Beside her
two fair-haired youths
> with alternate speech
>> are contending
but her heart is
> untouched.
>> Now,
she glances at one,

smiling,
and now, lightly
she flings the other a thought,
while their eyes,
by reason of love's
long vigils, are heavy
but their labors
all in vain.
In addition
there is fashioned there
an ancient fisherman
and a rock,
a rugged rock,
on which
with might and main
the old man poises a great net
for the cast
as one who puts his whole heart into it.
One would say
that he was fishing
with the full strength of his limbs
so big do his muscles stand out
about the neck.
Gray-haired though he be,
he has the strength
of a young man.
Now, separated
from the sea-broken old man
by a narrow interval
is a vineyard,
heavy
with fire-red clusters,
and on a rude wall
sits a small boy
guarding them.
Round him
two she-foxes are skulking.
One
goes the length of the vine-rows
to eat the grapes
while the other
brings all her cunning to bear,
by what has been set down,
vowing
she will never quit the lad
until
she leaves him bare
and breakfastless.
But the boy
is plaiting a pretty

cage of locust stalks and asphodel,
    fitting in the reeds
        and cares less for his scrip
and the vines
    than he takes delight
        in his plaiting.
All about the cup
    is draped the mild acanthus
        a miracle of varied work,
a thing for you to marvel at.
    I paid
        a Caledonian ferryman
a goat and a great white
    cream-cheese
        for the bowl.
It is still virgin to me,
    its lip has never touched mine.
        To gain my desire,
I would gladly
    give this cup
        if you, my friend,
will sing for me
    that delightful song.
        I hold nothing back.
Begin, my friend,
    for you cannot,
        you may be sure,
take your song,
    which drives all things out of mind,
        with you to the other world.

William Carlos Williams

✑ Callimachus (c. 300–240 B.C.)

EPIGRAM

The demon in the morning,
Unknown. Yesterday, Kharmis
You were in our eyes. Today
We buried you. Yes, Kharmis,
You. Nothing
Your father has ever seen
Has caused him more pain.

Stanley Lombardo and Diane Raynor

NEWS OF YOUR DEATH

News of your death.

Tears, and the memory
of all the times we talked the sun down the sky.

You, Herakleîtos of Halikarnassos,
once my friend, now vacant dust,
    whose poems are nightingales
beyond the clutch of the unseen god.

Stanley Lombardo and Diane Raynor

"PROLOGUE" TO THE AETIA

The malignant gnomes who write reviews in Rhodes
    are muttering about my poetry again—
tone-deaf ignoramuses out of touch with the Muse—
because I have not consummated a continuous epic
    of thousands of lines on heroes and lords
but turn out minor texts as if I were a child
    although my decades of years are substantial.
To which brood of cirrhotic adepts
            I, Callímachus, thus:

A few distichs in the pan outweight *Deméter's Cornucopia,*
    and Mimnermos is sweet for a few subtle lines,
not that fat *Lady* poem. Let "cranes fly south to Egypt"
    when they lust for pygmy blood,
and "the Masságetai arch arrows long distance"
    to lodge in a Mede,
but nightingales are honey-pale
    and small poems are sweet.
So evaporate, Green-Eyed Monsters,
or learn to judge poems by the critic's art
    instead of by the parasang,
and don't snoop around here for a poem that rumbles:
    not I but Zeus owns the thunder.

When I first put a tablet on my knees, the Wolf-God
    Apollo appeared and said:
Fatten your animal for sacrifice, poet,
    but keep your muse slender."
And
    "follow trails unrutted by wagons,
don't drive your chariot down public highways,
    but keep to the back roads though the going is narrow.

We are the poets for those who love
    the cricket's high chirping, not the noise of the jackass."

Long-eared bray for others, for me delicate wings,
    dewsip in old age and bright air for food,
mortality dropping from me like Sicily shifting
    its triangular mass from Enkélados's chest.
No nemesis here:
        the Muses do not desert the gray heads
    of those on whose childhood
            their glance once brightened.

Stanley Lombardo and Diane Raynor

Asclepiades (c. 275–265 B.C.)

HERE LIES ARCHEANASSA

Here lies Archeanassa
the courtesan from Colophon
whose old and wrinkled body
was still Love's proud domain.

You lovers who knew her youth
in its sweet piercing splendor
and plucked those early blooms —
through what a flame you passed!

Frederick Morgan

Aristophanes of Byzantium (257–180 B.C.)

ON THE ADVICE OF PRAXILLA

On the advice of Praxilla,
we are asked to look
under every stone
for a hiding scorpion.

The proverb sounds all right.
But, turning stones,
remember:
poets also bite.

Sam Hamill

❧ Diophanes of Myrina (c. 150 B.C.)

ON LOVE

Love's thrice a robber, however you take it:
He's desperate,
           sleepless,
                    and he strips us naked.

Dudley Fitts

❧ Antipatros (c. 150 B.C.)

NEVER AGAIN, ORPHEUS

Never again, Orpheus
Will you lead the enchanted oaks,
Nor the rocks, nor the beasts
That are their own masters.
Never again will you sing to sleep
The roaring wind, nor the hail,
Nor the drifting snow, nor the boom
Of the sea wave.
You are dead now.
Led by your mother, Calliope,
The Muses shed many tears
Over you for a long time.
What good does it do us to mourn
For our sons when the immortal
Gods are powerless to save
Their own children from death?

Kenneth Rexroth

❧ Meleager (c. 140–70 B.C.)

LOVE'S NIGHT & A LAMP

Love's night & a lamp
judged our vows:
that she would love me ever
& I should never leave her.
Love's night & you, lamp, witnessed the pact.
Today the vow runs:
'Oaths such as these, waterwords.'
Tonight, lamp,

witness her lying
               —in other arms.

Peter Whigham

AT 12 O'CLOCK IN THE AFTERNOON

At 12 o'clock in the afternoon
     in the middle of the street —
     Alexis.

Summer had all but brought the fruit
     to its perilous end:
               & the summer sun & that boy's look

did their work on me.
     Night hid the sun.
               Your face consumes my dreams.

Others feel sleep as feathered rest;
     mine but in flame refigures
          your image lit in me.

Peter Whigham

I WAS THIRSTY

I was thirsty.
It was hot.
I kissed the boy
with girl-soft skin.
My thirst was quenched.
I said: Is that what
upstairs you're up
to Papa Zeus,
is that what strip-
ling Ganymede
at table serves,
under Hera's
watchful eye?

Lip-spilt wine
from soul to soul
as honeyed-sweet
as those vast draughts
Antiochus
pours now for me!

Peter Whigham

WHITE VIOLETS FLOWER

White violets flower
lilies on hill-slopes
narcissus nodding to rain-showers

and the queen of lovers' hopes
the sweet persuasive rose,
Zenophile, more fair than those:

o hills o fields your laughter rings
falsely through the flowered spring
for she outshines your garlanding.

Peter Whigham

Antipater of Sidon (c. 130 B.C.)

PRIAPOS OF THE HARBOR

Now Spring returning beckons the little boats
Once more to dance on the waters: the grey storms
Are gone that scourged the sea. Now swallows build
Their round nests in the rafters, and all the fields
Are bright with laughing green.
                    Come then, my sailors:
Loose your dripping hawsers, from their deep-sunk graves
Haul up your anchors, raise your brave new sails.

It is Priapos warns you, god of this harbor.

Dudley Fitts

THIS IS ANACREON'S GRAVE

This is Anacreon's grave. Here lie
the shreds of his exuberant lust,
but hints of perfume linger by
his gravestone still, as if he must
have chosen for his last retreat
a place perpetually on heat.

Robin Skelton

ꙮ Philodemus (110–40 B.C.)

YOU CRY, WHINE, PEER STRANGELY AT ME

You cry, whine, peer strangely at me.
you're jealous, cling and clutch, kiss too much:
now that's a lover. But when you say, "Here I Am,"
and just lay back, you make me wonder.

George Economou

DEMO AND THERMION BOTH SLAY ME

Demo and Thermion both slay me,
one's a pro, the other still unversed in your ways,
the one I can grope, the other mustn't touch.
I swear, goddess, I don't know which I want more.
I'll say little virgin Demo—I don't want it off the rack,
but long for what's under lock and key.

George Economou

I LOVED—WHO HASN'T?

I loved—who hasn't? I worshipped—hasn't
everyone been in that congregation?
But I was crazy—did a god do it?
The force that through my black hair drives the grey
announces the age of reason—I'm done.
At playtime I played, now I'll act my age.

George Economou

MAKE THE BEDLAMP TIPSY WITH OIL

Make the bedlamp tipsy with oil;
It's the silent confidant of things
We seldom dare to speak of. Then
Let it go out. There are times when
The god Eros wants no living witness.
Close the door tight. Then let the
Bed, the lovers' friend, teach us
The rest of Aphrodite's secrets.

James Laughlin

❧ Scythinus (c. 100 B.C.)

TOO LATE

And now you're ready who while she was here
Hung like a flag in calm. Friend, though you stand
Erect and eager, in your eye a tear,
I will not pity you, nor lend a hand.

J. V. Cunningham

❧ Lucilius (Carus Titus Lucilius, 99–55 B.C.)

LEAN GAIUS, WHO WAS THINNER THAN A STRAW

Lean Gaius, who was thinner than a straw
And who could slip through even a locked door,
Is dead, and we his friends are twice bereft,
In losing him and finding nothing left
To put into the coffin: what they'll do
In Hades with a creature who is too
Shadowy to be a Shade, God knows,
But when we bear him to his last repose,
We'll make it stylish—mourners, black crepe, bier,
The lot, and though he won't himself appear,
His empty coffin's progress will be pious—
THE DEATH OF NOTHING, FUNERAL OF GAIUS!

Peter Porter

❧ Antipater of Thessalonica (c. 11 B.C.)

I'VE NEVER FEARED

I've never feared the setting of the Pleiades
or the hidden reefs beneath the waves
or even the lightning at sea

like I dread friends who drink with me
and remember what we say.

Sam Hamill

ஜௐ Euenos (c. A.D. 50)

TO A SWALLOW

Relish honey. If you please
Regale yourself on Attic bees.
But spare, O airy chatterer,
Spare the chattering grasshopper!

Winging, spare his gilded wings,
Chatterer, his chatterings.
Summer's child, do not molest
Him the summer's humblest guest.

Snatch not for your hungry young
One who like yourself has sung —
For it is neither just nor fit
That poets should each other eat.

John Peale Bishop

ஜௐ Antiphilos (c. A.D. 80)

ON THE DEATH OF THE FERRYMAN, GLAUCUS

Glaucus, pilot of the Nessus Strait, born
    on the coast of Thasos, skilled sea-plowman,
Who moved the tiller unerringly even in his sleep,
    old beyond reckoning, a rag of a sailor's life,
even when death came would not leave his weathered deck.
    They set fire to the husk with him under it
so the old man might sail his own boat to Hades.

W. S. Merwin

ஜௐ Anonymous (c. A.D. 200)

CHRISTIAN EPIGRAM

Egyptian woman,
hidden infant,
and close river —
these are the human
earthly current
in the Pattern-Giver,
see it who can.

John Peck

ᘑ Palladas (c. 360–430)

WHOSE BAGGAGE FROM LAND TO LAND IS DESPAIR

Whose baggage from land to land is despair,
Life's voyagers sail a treacherous sea.
Many founder piteously
With fortune at the helm. We keep
A course this way & that, across the deep,
From here to nowhere. And back again.
Blow foul, blow fair
All come to anchor finally in the tomb.
Passengers armed, we travel from room to room.

Frank Kuenstler

WOMEN ALL CAUSE RUE

women all
cause rue

but can be nice
on occasional

moments two
to be precise

in bed

& dead

Tony Harrison

THE MURDERER & SERAPIS

A murderer spread his pallaisse
beneath a rotten wall
and in his dream came Serapis
and warned him it would fall:

*Jump for your life, wretch and be quick
or in a second you'll be dead.*
He jumped, and tons of crumbling brick
came crashing on his bed.

The murderer gasped with relief,
he thanked the gods above.
It was his innocent belief
they'd saved him out of love.

But once again came Serapis
In the middle of the night,
and once more uttered prophecies
that set the matter right:

*Don't think the gods have let you go
and connive at homicide.
We've spared you that quick crushing, so
we can get you crucified.*

Tony Harrison

HAVING SLEPT WITH A MAN

Having slept with a man
the grammarian's daughter
gave birth to a child, in turn
masculine, feminine & neuter.

Peter Jay

WHERE THE 3 ROADS MEET

where the 3 roads meet
I was surprised to see the great bronze of Hermes

knocked over, flat on the ground:
people used to worship it here . . .

now the invincible guardian
lay flat on the ground

but later that night he appeared by my bed
grinned down at me, said:

"you have to go with the times . . .
that much I learned
when I was a god"

Anselm Hollo

❧ Anonymous (c. A.D. 396)

THE LAST ORACLE FROM DELPHI

Say this to the king: Men wrought this shrine
Now fallen to ruin. A God kept this place.
His laurels are dead. Prophecy's spring
Ran dry. Parched stone, speechless stream.

Katharine Washburn

❧ Paulus Silentiarius (c. A.D. 575)

TANTALOS

Mouth to mouth joined we lie, her naked breasts
Curved to my fingers, my fury grazing deep
On the silver plain of her throat,
                    and then: no more.
She denies me her bed. Half of her body to Love
She has given, half to Prudence:
                    I die between.

Dudley Fitts

✒ 2

LATIN POETRY: FROM ITS ORIGINS
THROUGH THE LATE ROMAN EMPIRE

Latin

✒ Anonymous (c. 700–600 B.C.)

HYMN FOR SEEDTIME AND A SAFE HARVEST
(ARVAL HYMN)

```
now    life in the houses of flesh    help us
now    love in our hearts' hearths    help us
now              fleshfires           help us
```

```
let not war nor sickness    slay hope     at the year's turning
nor abortion nor stillbirth   waste hope   with the months' passing
          nor blood          rust hope    at this moon's waning
```

```
guard fiercely   the pale sprout that roots   in the tender earth
guard fiercely    the soft calf that swims    in the dark before birth
guard fiercely    the red life that screams     into this world
```

```
sower    in turn    sow
semen    in turn    flow
 seed    in turn    grow
```

```
lifeforce    that hardens the swords of men    help us
lifeforce    that ripens and bursts in women   help us
littledeath   that bears the survival of life   help us
      yes    yes    yes    yesyes
```

Janet Lembke

ᴥ Q. Lutatius Catulus (c. 102 B.C.)

WAKING INTUITIVELY

Waking intuitively in the rosegray light of rising sun,
I turned, saw you arise sleepwarm from my heart's side.
And knew (plain Calvinistic conscience, hold your tongue!)
that man, here, breathing, is more beautiful than God.

Janet Lembke

ᴥ Lucretius (Titus Lucretius Carus, 95–54 B.C.)

From DE RERUM NATURA

Darling of Gods and Men, beneath the gliding stars
you fill rich earth and buoyant sea with your presence
for every living thing achieves its life through you,
rises and sees the sun. For you the sky is clear,
the tempests still. Deft earth scatters her gentle flowers,
the level ocean laughs, the softened heavens glow
with generous light for you. In the first days of spring
when the untrammelled allrenewing southwind blows
the birds exult in you and herald your coming.
Then the shy cattle leap and swim the brooks for love.
Everywhere, through all seas mountains and waterfalls,
love caresses all hearts and kindles all creatures
to overmastering lust and ordained renewals.
Therefore, since you alone control the sum of things
and nothing without you comes forth into the light
and nothing beautiful or glorious can be
without you, Alma Venus! trim my poetry
with your grace; and give peace to write and read and think.

Basil Bunting

ᴥ Catullus (Gaius Valerius Catullus, 84–54 B.C.)

BY STRANGERS' COASTS AND WATERS

By strangers' coasts and waters, many days at sea,
    I come here for the rites of your unworlding,
Bringing for you, the dead, these last gifts of the living

And my words—vain sounds for the man of dust.
  Alas, my brother,
You have been taken from me. You have been taken from me,
  By cold chance turned a shadow, and my pain.
Here are the foods of the old ceremony, appointed
  Long ago for the starvelings under the earth:
Take them; your brother's tears have made them wet; and take
  Into eternity my hail and my farewell.

Robert Fitzgerald

CARMEN: 11

Furius and Aurelius, loyal friends
who'll follow Catullus even to the world's ends,
whether he journeys to far India's shore
where the eastern wave beats in with echoing roar,
enters Hyrcania and soft Arab lands,
or visits the Scyth and Parthian archer bands
or plains stained by the sevenfold Nile's rich ooze;
or whether, crossing the high Alps, he views
Caesar's memorials: the Rhine, and Gaul,
and the fierce Britons, remotest tribe of all—
good friends, ready right now to risk with me
all this, and whatever else the gods decree,
go take this one short message to my slut,
short but not sweet. Tell her to live and rut
to her heart's content with the studs she grips so tight
hundreds at once between her legs each night,
not loving a single one in honesty
but draining them dry as bone impartially:
but let her not look to find what once she had,
my love, which by her fault has fallen dead—
as at the meadow's edge a flower lies,
lopped by the heavy plow as it passed by.

Frederick Morgan

IPSITHILLA, MY PET, MY FAVORITE DISH

Ipsithilla, my pet, my favorite dish,
Plump, wanton little rabbit, how I wish
You'd bid me join you for the noonday nap
And let me spend this scorcher in your lap.
How does that sound? Make sure no man nor mouse
Opens your little gate. Don't leave the house.
Just change the sheets, break out your bread and wine,
And one by one, my puss, we'll tear off nine

And melt away in joy. Want to know how?
Then let me come immediately, for now,
Swollen with lunch and dreaming, catching your scent,
I watch my tunic hoisted like a tent.

Robert Mezey

HE SEEMS TO ME ALMOST A GOD

He seems to me almost a god, or even
Eclipses the gods, if that is possible, who,
Sitting turned towards you continuously,
      Watches and catches

Your dulcet laughter—all of which drains my senses,
For always when I turn and face you, Lesbia,
Not a breath remains in my throat, not a sound,
      Nothing is left me.

But my tongue thickens, a white flame travels
Like brandy through my blood, with a mute thunder
My ears pound, and my clouded eyes are quenched by
      Breakers of darkness.

Idleness, Catullus, idleness injures you:
In idleness you take too wild a pleasure,
Idleness that has broken the power of princes
      And prosperous kingdoms.

Robert Mezey

ODI ET AMO

I hate *and* love. Ignorant fish, who even
wants the fly while writhing.

Frank Bidart

UNTO NO BODY

Unto no body my woman saith she had rather a wife be,
    Then to my selfe, though Jove grew a suter of hers.
These be her words, but a woman's words to a love that is eager,
    In wind or water streame do require to be writ.

Sir Philip Sidney

ATTIS

Borne over deep seas in swift ship
To Phrygia, Attis urgent on hungry feet
Fled to black-shagged home of Goddess,
Rabid with need, mind choked on need.
There with flint unloaded his sex,
Then borne on lightness of her new freed body—
Fresh blood blotching earth, feet—
Seized light tambour (Your tambour,
Cybele, Yours, Mother), struck it, rung it,
In tense hand of snow, howled tight-throated
Song to Sisters. *"Up. Go. Scale*
Crags of Cybele, clamber beside me—
Queen's prize herds hunting exile homes,
Flock at my heels who've taken my lead
Through boiling surf on cruel sands,
Gouged Venus from thighs in excess loathing:
Feed Queen's heart with laughter of flight!
Now. To Cybele's piney home
Where cymbals crash, hard tambours answer,
Phryx—flutist—blows grave calamus,
Maenads in ivy fling hot in ring,
Keen as they shake sacred sighs,
Where tramps of the Queen crowd home to dance.
Now, with me, beside me—run to join!"

When Attis—forged woman—summoned sisters,
Quivering tongues hissed *Yes* from dance,
Pocked cymbals crashed, tambours rang glad.
Ida's green sides bore clutching climb
After Attis—quickest, gasping, lost—
Still leader howling through thickening pines,
Unplowed heifer scared, lurching in harness.

There—spent—they dropped at Cybele's door,
Slept hungry blinding sleep that smoothed
Clenched minds, locked limbs.
But—dawn: gold Sun, His scalding eye,
Struck air, packed ground, ferocious sea,
And Attis' sleep. Calmed, sealed eyes
Slit, Attis saw act and losses, saw
Puckering scars, raced in mind
To empty shores, wailed lost home.
"Home—that made me, bore me, that I fled,
Hateful slave, to roam waste Ida—snow-choked,
Ice-ribbed caves of beasts, my own mind beast.
How?—where?—to reclaim you?
For this instant soul is sane, let eyes
See you once. Not again?—home,
Goods, parents, friends, market, ring,

Wrestling-pit? Agony. Groan grinds groan.
What have I not been, what form not filled? —
I woman, cocked boy, boy-child, baby,
Crown of the track, oiled glory of the pit,
Warm doorsills ganged with friendly feet,
Garlands round me to deck my house
At dawn when I stood from my own wide bed:
Now priestess to the gods, slavegirl to Cybele, maenad,
Chained — no hope — to green gelid Ida
With deer grove-haunting, rooting boar,
Each thin breath poisoned by memory.":

The noise of her pink lips — news to gods.
Cybele, bending to lion at Her left, terror of herds,
Said, *"Now. Go. Hunt Attis*
Toward Me. Drive him through woods till, mad, he heels;
Goes down appalled, lashed by your tail
To My ring where pines stagger at your voice."
Wild, She unharnessed yoke, lion crouched,
Roused rage, charged woods toward Attis, tender
By marble sea — slave, girlslave all his life.

Strong Goddess, Goddess Cybele, Goddess Lady of Dindymus —
Spare my house, Queen, from total fury.
Hunt others. Seize others. Others appall.

                                        Reynolds Price

WHAT FOR?

Catullus, what keeps you from killing yourself? No good reason.
That tumor Nonius sits in the chair of a magistrate,
and lying Vatinius swears by his imminent consulship.
Catullus, what keeps you from killing yourself? No good reason.

                                        Charles Martin

LESBIA, LET US LIVE ONLY FOR LOVING

Lesbia, let us live only for loving,
and let us value at a single penny
all the loose flap of senile busybodies!
Suns when they set are capable of rising,
but at the setting of our own brief light
night is one sleep from which we never waken.
Give me a thousand kisses, then a hundred,
another thousand next, another hundred,
a thousand without pause & then a hundred,

until when we have run up our thousands
we will cry bankrupt, hiding our assets
from ourselves & any who would harm us,
knowing the volume of our trade in kisses.

Charles Martin

❧ Virgil (Publius Vergilius Maro, 70–19 B.C.)

From THE AENEID

Opening Invocation

Arms, and the Man I sing, who, forc'd by Fate,
And haughty Juno's unrelenting Hate;
Expell'd and exil'd, left the Trojan Shoar:
Long Labours, both by Sea and Land he bore;
And in the doubtful War, before he won
The Latian Realm, and built the destin'd Town:
His banish'd Gods restor'd to Rites Divine,
And setl'd sure Succession in his Line:
From whence the Race of Alban Fathers come,
And the long Glories of Majestick Rome.
O Muse! the Causes and the Crimes relate,
What Goddess was provok'd, and whence her hate:
For what Offence the Queen of Heav'n began
To persecute so brave, so just a Man!
Involv'd his anxious Life in endless Cares,
Expos'd to Wants, and hurry'd into Wars!
Can Heav'nly Minds such high resentment show;
Or exercise their Spight in Human Woe?

John Dryden

The Sleep of Palinurus

And now the dewy night had nearly come to its halfway
Mark in the heavens: the mariners, sprawled on the hard benches
Beside their oars, were all relaxed in solacing quiet.
Just then did Sleep come feathering down from the stars above,
Lightly displacing the shadowy air, parting the darkness,
In search of you, Palinurus, carrying death in a dream
To your staunch heart. Now, taking the shape of Phorbas, the Sleep-god
Perched up there in the stern-sheets and rapidly spoke these words —
Palinurus, son of Iasus, the seas are bearing the ships on,
Steadily blows the breeze, and you have a chance to rest.
Lay your head down, and take a nap; your eyes are tired with
Watching. I will stand your trick at the helm for a little.
Palinurus could hardly raise his heavy eyes, but he answered —
Are you asking me to forget what lies behind the pacific

Face of the sea and its sleeping waves? to trust this devil?
What? Shall I leave Aeneas to the mercy of tricky winds—
I who, time and again, have been taken in by a clear sky?
While he spoke, Palinurus kept a good grip on the tiller—
By no means would he release it—and a steadfast gaze on the stars.
But look! over his temples the god is shaking a bough
That drips with the dew of Lethe, the drowsy spell of Stygian
Waters. And now, though he struggles, his swimming eyes are closing.
As soon as, taken off guard, he was relaxed in unconsciousness,
The god, leaning down over him, hurled him into the sea
Still gripping the tiller; a part of the taffrail was torn away:
As he fell, he kept calling out to his friends, but they did not hear him.
Up and away skywards the Sleep-god now went winging.
Safe as before, the fleet was scudding upon its course—
Nothing to fear, for Neptune had guaranteed a safe passage.
And now, racing on, they were near the rocky place of the Sirens,
Dangerous once for mariners, white with the bones of many;
From afar the rasp of the ceaseless surf on those rocks could be heard.
Just then Aeneas became aware that his ship was yawing
Badly, her helmsman missing; he brought her back on to course
In the night sea, and deeply sighing, stunned by the loss of his friend, said—
O Palinurus, too easily trusting clear sky and calm sea,
You will lie on a foreign strand, mere jetsam, none to bury you.

                                                    C. Day Lewis

The Pyres

                         Dawn at that hour
Brought on her kindly light for ill mankind,
Arousing men to labor and distress.
By now Aeneas and Tarchon had built up
Their pyres along the curving shore. On them
In the old-time ritual each bore and placed
The bodies of his men. The smoky fires
Caught underneath and hid the face of heaven
In a tall gloom. Round pyres as they blazed
Troops harnessed in bright armor marched three times
In parade formation, and the cavalry
Swept about the sad cremation flame
Three times, while calling out their desolate cries.
Tears fell upon the ground, fell upon armor.
High in air rose the wild yells of men,
The somber song of trumpets. There were some
Who hurled gear taken from the Latin slain
Into the fire, helmets and ornate swords,
And reins and chariot wheels. Others tossed in
Gifts better known—the dead men's shields and weapons
Luck had not attended. On all sides
Death received burnt offerings of oxen,
Throats of swine were bled into the flames

With cattle commandeered from all the fields.
Then over the whole shore they stood to see
Their fellow-soldiers burning, and kept watch
On pyres as they flared: men could not be
Torn from the scene till dew-drenched night came on
And a night sky studded with fiery stars.
The wretched Latins, also, in their quarter,
Built countless pyres, and of their many dead
They buried some, took some inland, or home
Into the city. All the rest they burned,
Heaped up in mammoth carnage, bodies jumbled,
Numberless and nameless. Everywhere
Field strove with field in brightness of thick fires.

Robert Fitzgerald

From GEORGICS I

Who dares deny the burning truth of the sun?
When Caesar was destroyed, the sun was black.
At midday, in a cloudless sky, black!
It warns us of all manner of uprisings—
of wind, of rain, of hail, and of humankind,
for views of the mind change, and the heart conceives
new emotions.

　　　　The earth shook and the sea
shuddered in its bed. It was dark at noon,
and many feared that the darkness would last forever
when Caesar died. The sun had shown it all.
Dogs had howled, and birds had chattered and cried,
and mighty Etna's furnace had boiled up
to answer fire with fire, to turn black rocks
white hot, and melt them runny as rain.
In Germany thunder rolled as if to recall
the clash of an army's weapons—Caesar's own.
The Alps shook as with an army's marching.
There were voices singing out of groves of trees.
Pale ghosts shimmered in the peculiar light.
Cattle spoke. Humans were struck dumb.
Rivers stood still. Plains yawned to chasms.
In the temples, ivory wept and hard bronze
broke into sweat. The Po overflowed its banks
and pretended to farm—herding cattle to death,
and harvesting woods and fields in a labor of rage.
The other omens were awful: wells flowed blood;
wolves howled in the streets of cities; lightning
flashed in the cloudless sky; comets blazed.
Feel it aright, and a man could feel Philippi,

the clang of Roman sword upon Roman sword,
the pools of our blood flowing back together
on the Macedonian plain, and at last the farmer
(always the farmer, first and last the farmer)
driving his curved plow to till the earth
and finding the Roman javelins covered with rust,
or digging with his shovel and striking a helmet.
Wonder at the white bones in the earth,
and feel in your own bones the sun's fire,
the fire of life itself.

        Hail, Caesar!
May the gods allow Caesar, our new Caesar,
to right this overturned time. We have atoned
for old Troy's sins, and with more blood
than Troy ever spilled.

        I feel the dread,
and the sun burns in me, burns like a fever.
The world is full of war, and at home, crime
resembles a war. Men flock to the city
leaving their fields to weeds, their tools to rust.
Plowshares now are beaten into swords.
It's bad in Asia, bad in Europe, bad . . .
No treaties hold, no laws hold, nothing
but Mars, blood red . . . He holds it all,
hurtling through the sky in his chariot.
I feel those wheels rumble. I feel the sway
of speed. The horses are mad and running faster.
They ought to check. They ought to answer the reins.
There ought to be reins.

        But there are none.

           David R. Slavitt

THE FOURTH ECOLOGUE: POLLIO

The ages of the world will not turn back.
The iron rusts and will not shine again
like silver, will not be silver, and the gold . . .
Who believes that? Still there are golden dawns,
springs with their promises.

        We try to believe
as we do with a deadbeat debtor relative,
forgetting the smog of evenings, the brown of August,
the whining stalls that we shall hear again.
And yet we believe, we lend, we lend belief.

At the birth of a baby, then, who can resist
that act of faith? Springs, sunrises lie,
but he has not lied. Not yet. He has not promised
falsely or at all. And if his yowl
demands the whole world, who is to say
he has not the right? Someone must come along
to get us all out of this mess, to make it right,
to save us from what we have been, from what we are.
And so, at the baby's birth, Virgil dreams
of all the rough places smoothed to match the brow
of that tiny creature, all the crooked, flabby
hearts made taut and tight as that new heart
in the delicate chest beneath those flexible ribs.
We will have miracles! Promises will be
kept, even this—that the cradle itself will sprout
ivy, foxglove, acanthus. He dreams of the time
we all yearn for, like men in a desert who yearn
so much for water they see it.

            No plows,
but the earth will offer up crops. No ships on the sea
risking the savage storms, but every land
will produce all things. No tints and dyes for wool,
but sheep will be blue and purple and yellow and green.
The dreams are familiar, but then the need is familiar
and always with us.

            It was all supposed to begin
in Virgil's time, with Pollio, his friend,
as consul, presiding over the new beginning.
And the baby . . .
            But Virgil had to cheat on that.
The trouble is, with these poems, that they take time,
and he had to write it before the baby was born.
And the baby cheated him.

            Marc Antony lost
in the struggle with Octavian, and from his loins
came daughters, daughters of daughters, and then Nero.
Octavian, the other possible father,
also had a child at the right time,
the child that could have been the expected one—
but it was a daughter, Julia, who grew up to be
the notorious whore Tiberius had to banish.
The babies were wrong, but the longing for a baby,
for health, for innocence, for the freshness of starting,
beginning again with nothing yet gone awry,
continued, continues.

            Later, the poet of Naples
gave Virgil into the hands of St. Paul. And Dante

took Virgil with him. The dreams were close enough —
a new beginning.

             But the sheep are not yet blue
nor any of those colors. And ships and planes
scurry and wreck. Plows wound the ground
and a field smells of sweat and diesel fuel . . .

"Oh, if my life could only be longer!" he wrote,
but what would he have seen? What was there new
or better or different? Only his own poem,
itself another promise, another assurance,
beautiful, false, false and still beautiful

as the smile of that little Julia.

             The poem ends:
"Begin, then, child. Recognize your mother,
give her a smile, a sign . . ."

             The sex was wrong,
the baby was wrong, it was all wrong but the hoping,
and we must always hope.

             Let there be no child
who comes into the world without some hope,
some joy in him. And we shall have begun . . .

                                David R. Slavitt

DEATH PLUCKS MY EAR

Death plucks my ear and says,
"Live — I am coming."

                      Oliver Wendell Holmes

Horace (Quintus Horatius Flaccus, 65–8 B.C.)

SOLVITUR ACRIS HIEMS

Winter to Spring: the west wind melts the frozen rancour,
    The windlass drags to sea the thirsty hull;
Byre is no longer welcome to beast or fire to ploughman,
    The field removes the frost-cap from his skull.

Venus of Cythera leads the dances under the hanging
   Moon and the linked line of Nymphs and Graces
Beat the ground with measured feet while the busy Fire-God
   Stokes his red-hot mills in volcanic places.

Now is the time to twine the spruce and shining head with myrtle,
   Now with flowers escaped the earthy fetter,
And sacrifice to the woodland god in shady copses
   A lamb or a kid, whichever he likes better.

Equally heavy is the heel of white-faced Death on the pauper's
   Shack and the towers of kings, and O my dear
The little sum of life forbids the ravelling of lengthy
   Hopes. Night and the fabled dead are near

And the narrow house of nothing, past whose lintel
   You will meet no wine like this, no boy to admire
Like Lycidas, who today makes all young men a furnace
   And whom tomorrow girls will find a fire.

                                        Louis MacNeice

THIS MONUMENT WILL OUTLAST

This monument will outlast metal and I made it
More durable than the king's seat, higher than pyramids.
Gnaw of the wind and rain?
                        Impotent
The flow of the years to break it, however many.

Bits of me, many bits, will dodge all funeral,
O Libitina-Persephone and, after that,
Sprout new praise. As long as
Pontifex and the quiet girl pace the Capitol
I shall be spoken where the wild flood Aufidus
Lashes, and Daunus ruled the parched farmland:

Power from lowliness: "First brought Aeolic song to Italian fashion"—
Wear pride, work's gain! O Muse Melpomene,

By your will bind the laurel.
                        My hair, Delphic laurel.

                                        Ezra Pound

QUIS MULTA GRACILIS

Trailing a wake of heady odors, what slim
Boy in a wreath of roses leads you, Pyrrha,

In some cozy hollow, on; him
    For whom you comb your honey hair

And neatly knot it? O, how often he
Shall weep for constancy and the inconstant
    Gods! Black gales and the cruel sea
        Will amaze this neophyte

Who finds merely being with you golden.
He hopes—careless affection, ever; no thought
    Of shifty breezes. Misery for men
        Who in a body's beauty bask

Content! For me, at the temple wall, I offer
This votive of my foundering to potent
    Neptune; the painted board, and these
        Weeds from shipwreck I have shored.

Stephen Sandy

AN OLD MALEDICTION

What well-heeled knuckle-head, straight from the unisex
Hairstylist and bathed in *Russian Leather,*
Dallies with you these late summer days, Pyrrha,
In your expensive sublet? For whom do you
Slip into something simple by, say, Gucci?
The more fool he who has mapped out for himself
The saline latitudes of incontinent grief.
Dazzled though he be, poor dope, by the golden looks
Your locks fetched up out of a bottle of Clairol,
He will know that the wind changes, the smooth sailing
Is done for, when the breakers wallop broadside,
When he's rudderless, dismasted, thoroughly swamped
In that mindless rip-tide that got the best of me
Once, when I ventured on your deeps, Piranha.

Anthony Hecht

LATE NIGHT ODE

It's over, love. Look at me pushing fifty now,
    Hair like grave-grass growing in both ears,
The piles and boggy prostate, the crooked penis,
    The sour taste of each day's first lie,

And that recurrent dream of years ago pulling
    A swaying bead-chain of moonlight,

Of slipping between the cool sheets of dark
    along a body like my own, but blameless.

What good's my cut-glass conversation now,
    Now I'm so effortlessly vulgar and sad?
You get from life what you can shake from it?
    for me, it's g and t's all day and CNN.

Try the blond boychick lawyer, entry level
    At eighty grand, who pouts about the overtime,
Keeps Evian and a beeper in his locker at the gym,
    And hash in tinfoil under the office fern.

There's your hound from heaven, with buccaneer
    Curls and perfumed war-paint on his nipples.
His answering machine always has room for one more
    Slurred, embarrassed call from you-know-who.

Some nights I've laughed so hard the tears
    won't stop. Look at me now. Why now?
I long ago gave up pretending to believe
    Anyone's memory will give as good as it gets.

So why these stubborn tears? and why do I dream
    Almost every night of holding you again,
Or at least of diving after you, my long-gone,
    Through the bruised unbalanced waves.

J. D. McClatchy

ODE 4.7

Snows dissolving, grass returns to meadow,
    leaves to the wood;
earth changes; past their banks
    diminishing rivers go.

Out from the chorus of nymphs & sisters, naked,
    one of the Graces advances.
No hope for eternity, year & hour admonish,
    taking away the day that sustains us.

Cold softens in west wind, summer overtakes spring,
    goes under in turn
as autumn, apple-bearing, pours down its yield &
    inert winter comes on.

Swift moons repair celestial losses, but we,
    going down to keep faith with Aeneas

& the old, rich kings, Tullus & Ancus,
      are dust & shadow.

Who knows if to this day's tally
      high gods will add another hour?
What's spent in friendship eludes
      survivors' keen hands.

Once you have fallen, once Minos records his
      decision concerning you,
no birth, Torquatus, or eloquence or piety
      can ever restore you,

nor Diane spring from nether darkness
      shame-faced Hippolytus,
Theseus shatter Lethean chains of
      Pirithoous, dear to him.

Michael O'Brien

THE YOUNG MEN COME HERE LESS OFTEN

The young men come less often—isn't it so?—
To rap at midnight on your fastened window;
Much less often. How do you sleep these days?

There was a time your door gave with proficiency
On easy hinges; now it seems apter at being shut.
I do not think you hear many lovers moaning

"Lydia, how can you sleep?
"Lydia, the night is so long!
"Oh, Lydia, I'm dying for you!"

No. The time is coming when *you* will moan
And cry to scornful men from an alley corner
In the dark of the moon when the wind's in a passion

With lust that would drive a mare wild
Raging in your ulcerous old viscera.
You'll be alone and burning then

To think how happy boys take their delight
In the new tender buds, the blush of myrtle,
Consigning dry leaves to the winter sea.

Robert Fitzgerald

TO LEUCONOË

Don't be too eager to ask
      What the gods have in mind for us,
What will become of you,
      What will become of me,
What you can read in the cards,
      Or spell out on the Ouija board,
It's better not to know.
      Either Jupiter says
This coming winter is not
      After all going to be
The last winter you have,
      Or else Jupiter says
This winter that's coming soon,
      Eating away the cliffs
Along the Tyrrhenian Sea,
      Is going to be the final
Winter of all. Be mindful.
      Take good care of your vineyard.
The time we have is short.
      Cut short your hopes for longer.
Now as I say these words,
      Time has already fled
Backwards away—
      Leuconoë—
          Hold on to the day.

David Ferry

❧ Tibullus (Albius Tibullus, 55–19 B.C.)

CROSS THE AEGEAN WITHOUT ME, THEN, MESSALLA

Cross the Aegean without me, then, Messalla—
But think of me, you and your foreign staff. I'm stuck here
In Phaecia, sick, in a foreign land. Death,
Keep your grasping, black hands to yourself
And let me be. I've no mother here
To clutch my charred bones to a sad heart,
Nor sister to spread perfume over my ashes
Or weep with streaming hair beside my grave.
And no Delia, either—who, they say,
Consulted the whole tribe of gods before
Letting me leave the city; three times
She took the sacred lots from the acolyte,
And each time he told her, 'All will be well.'

Promises of return — none of which stopped her
Weeping, terrified, over my journey.
And I, her comforter, after all the farewells
Still found reasons to delay and linger.
Words of ill omen; the flights of birds;
Days of unlucky Saturn. With my foot
Poised on the high road, I claimed my stumbling
Warned of disaster! Let no man leave home
When Love forbids him. Let him look to the gods.

What use to me was your Isis, Delia,
Or the bronze cymbals you clashed so often?
What of your careful rituals — those baths
In clean water, all that chastity?
Help me, goddess, you whose healing powers
Are shown in so many temples. Let my Delia
Watch nightly at your threshold, swathed
In a linen veil; let her sing praises
Twice a day, with her long hair streaming,
So that the whole Egyptian crowd hears her.
And let me worship the gods of hearth and home,
Offering incense as the years go by.

Better to have lived in the old days
When Saturn ruled, before the world was made
So free for travel. Pines had not learnt
To mock the ocean then, or hang sails
For the winds to billow, nor did mariners
Fill their holds with foreign goods. Oxen
Had not been yoked and horses went untamed.
Houses had no doors, and no man set
Stones to mark his boundaries. Even the oaks
Gave honey, and the ewes came to be milked
With bursting udders. Armies did not exist;
Wars were unheard of; no-one forged weapons.
But Jupiter rules now: wounds, killings,
Deaths by water — thousands of ways to go.

Spare my life, Lord. I told you no lies;
I spoke no blasphemies. But if I'm done for,
Let them carve this memorial:
HERE LIES TIBULLUS, SNATCHED BY DEATH'S HAND:
MESSALLA'S FOLLOWER, BY SEA AND LAND.

Because I have served Venus, she herself
Will take my hand to the Elysian fields.
There's singing and dancing there. The birds flit,
Music in all their throats. Cassia grows
With no tilling, and the friendly earth
Spreads its roses over the whole land.
Girls and young men collect in troops

To contest Love's sport, which lasts for ever.
All whom Death took because of their love
Are gathered there, and myrtle binds their brows.

But there's a place of evil, too, buried
In night's chasm. Rivers rage around it.
Tisiphone storms with wild snakes in her hair
As the godless scurry about her. Wild snakes
Hiss from the open mouth of black Cerberus
As he guards the bronze doors. Ixion's there,
Who tried to assault Juno—guilty limbs
Whirling upon a wheel. And there is Tityus
Covering nine acres; vultures tirelessly
Rip his black liver. Tantalus, too,
Waters lapping around him. His thirst rages.
And there Danaus' daughters, who mocked Venus,
Dip their leaking jars in Lethe's stream.
You who would violate my love, or wish me
Long campaigning—this is the place for you.

Be chaste, Delia. Keep your old nurse
Always beside you. Let her guard your honour.
She'll tell rambling tales when the lamps are lit,
Spinning her yarn, while all around you maidens
Droop over their tasks till sleep comes
And the work's forgotten. Let me be there then,
With no warning; let me be like a man
That's dropped from heaven. Then, just as you are,
With long, disordered hair and no sandals,
Run to my arms. I've prayed for this, Delia.
Now let the bright morning star, who rides
On pink horses, quicken that glad day.

Humphrey Clucas

From ADDE MERUM VINOQUE . . .

Fill up my glass again! The anodyne
For this poor lover's pain is sleep—and wine.
And when I've swilled enough to sink a ship,
No busybody better wake me up.
A cruel door stands between my girl and me,
Double-locked with a determined key.

Damn you, door! May rainstorms mildew you,
Or well-aimed lightning burn you through and through.
Aren't you moved by all my misery?
Please, door, open just a crack for me,
But carefully—don't creak. If I just said
Harsh things, may curses light on my own head.

I hope you've not forgotten all my prayers,
And all the times I hung your knob with flowers.

You, Delia, must be bold and cunning too;
Venus helps those who help themselves, you know.
Whether a boy sneaks to a strange room or
Stealthily a girl unlocks the door,
Venus teaches sorties out of bed,
Teaches our footsteps soundlessly to pad,
Or lovers to communicate by sighs
Before the hoodwinked husband's very eyes.
But you must have initiative, and dare
To prowl around at midnight without fear.

Take me—I wander through the streets all night.
Plenty of thieves and muggers are in sight,
But Love protects me from the switchblade knife
Scenario ("Your money or your life!").
In holiness a lover's safety lies;
It's needless to envision plots and spies.
No frosty winter night can do me harm;
Rain falls in torrents, but I'm safe and warm.
True, now I'm suffering; that could turn around
If Delia beckoned me without a sound.

Whoever sees us, please pretend you didn't;
Venus prefers her lovers snugly hidden.
Don't make a racket, do not ask my name
Or blind me with an outthrust torch's flame.
If you were fool enough to see us, then
Pray to the gods that you'll forget again.
The tattletale must learn the parentage
(Tempest and blood) that fuels Venus' rage.

But even if some busybody tells
Your husband all about us, magic spells
Will seal his eyes. A witch has promised me.
I've seen her pull the stars down from the sky.
Her charms can change a running river's flow,
Split open graves and let dead spirits go.
From pyres still smoldering she can wheedle bones,
Commanding ghostly troops with weird groans;
Then, sprinkling milk, she orders them away.
Clouds she disperses from a sullen sky.
In midsummer she can make it snow;
She knows Medea's herbs and where they grow;
The hounds of Hecate she can tame at will.

To cheat him, she's concocted me a spell
To chant three times, and each time spit as well.
From that time on, no matter what he sees,

He'll be unable to believe his eyes.
But keep away from other men! He'll be
Suspicious of every man but me.
This sorceress claimed that she could cure me too;
Her charms and herbs could set me free — of you.
She purified me at the witching hour
By torchlight, and slew victims with her power.
But what I prayed for was a love to share;
Life without you would be bleak and bare.

––––––––

Venus, I've always served you faithfully.
Don't burn your harvest in your rage at me!

Rachel Hadas

Propertius (Sextus Propertius, 50–16 B.C.)

From HOMAGE TO SEXTUS PROPERTIUS

I

Shades of Callimachus, Coan ghosts of Philetas
It is in your grove I would walk,
I who come first from the clear font
Bringing the Grecian orgies into Italy,
                    and the dance into Italy.
Who hath taught you so subtle a measure,
                    in what hall have you heard it;
What foot beat out your time-bar,
          what water has mellowed your whistles?

Out-weariers of Apollo will, as we know, continue
    their Martian generalities,
    We have kept our erasers in order.
A new-fangled chariot follows the flower-hung horses;
A young Muse with young loves clustered about her
                    ascends with me into the æther, . . .
And there is no high-road to the Muses.

Annalists will continue to record Roman reputations,
Celebrities from the Trans-Caucasus will belaud Roman celebrities
And expound the distentions of Empire,
But for something to read in normal circumstances?
For a few pages brought down from the forked hill unsullied?
I ask a wreath which will not crush my head.
              And there is no hurry about it;
I shall have, doubtless, a boom after my funeral,
Seeing that long standing increases all things

regardless of quality.
And who would have known the towers
           pulled down by a deal-wood horse;
Or of Achilles withstaying waters by Simois
Or of Hector spattering wheel-rims,
Or of Polydmantus, by Scamander, or Helenus and Deiphoibos?
Their door-yards would scarcely know them, or Paris.
Small talk O Ilion, and O Troad
                     twice taken by Oetian gods,
If Homer had not stated your case!

And I also among the later nephews of this city
           shall have my dog's day,
With no stone upon my contemptible sepulchre;
My vote coming from the temple of Phoebus in Lycia, at Patara,
And in the mean time my songs will travel,
And the devirginated young ladies will enjoy them
     when they have got over the strangeness,
For Orpheus tamed the wild beasts —
                     and held up the Threician river;
And Citharaon shook up the rocks by Thebes and danced them into a
     bulwark at his pleasure,
And you, O Polyphemus? Did harsh Galatea almost
Turn to your dripping horses, because of a tune, under Aetna?
We must look into the matter.
Bacchus and Apollo in favour of it,
There will be a crowd of young women doing homage to my palaver,
Though my house is not propped up by Taenarian columns from Laconia
     (associated with Neptune and Cerberus),
Though it is not stretched upon gilded beams:
My orchards do not lie level and wide
                     as the forests of Phaecia,
                     the luxurious and Ionian,
Nor are my caverns stuffed stiff with a Marcian vintage,
My cellar does not date from Numa Pompilius,
Nor bristle with wine jars,
Nor is it equipped with a frigidaire patent;
Yet the companions of the Muses
           will keep their collective nose in my books,
And weary with historical data, they will turn to my dance tune.
Happy who are mentioned in my pamphlets,
     the songs shall be a fine tomb-stone over their
     beauty.
     But against this?
Neither expensive pyramids scraping the stars in their route,
Nor houses modelled upon that of Jove in East Elis,
Nor the monumental effigies of Mausolus,
                     are a complete elucidation of death.

Flame burns, rain sinks into the cracks
And they all go to rack ruin beneath the thud of the years.

Stands genius a deathless adornment,
      a name not to be worn out with the years.

Ezra Pound

WHEN THOU MUST HOME TO SHADES OF UNDER GROUND

When thou must home to shades of under ground,
And there ariv'd, a newe admired guest,
The beauteous spirits do ingirt thee round,
White Iope, blith Hellen, and the rest,
To heare the stories of thy finisht love
From that smoothe toong whose musicke hell can move;

Then wilt thou speake of banqueting delights,
Of masks and revels which sweete youth did make,
Of Turnies and great challenges of knights,
And all these triumphes for thy beauties sake:
When thou hast told these honours done to thee,
Then tell, O tell, how thou didst murther me.

Thomas Campion

From THE ODES

A ghost is someone: death has left a hole
For the lead-coloured soul to beat the fire:
    Cynthia leaves her dirty pyre
    And seems to coil herself and roll
      Under my canopy,
Love's stale and public playground, where I lie
And fill the run-down empire of my bed.
I see the street, her potter's field, is red
And lively with the ashes of the dead;

She no longer sparkles off in smoke:
It is the body carted to the gate
    Last Friday, when the sizzling grate
    Left its charred furrows on her smock
      And ate into her hip.
A black nail dangles from a finger tip
And Lethe oozes from her neither lip.
Her thumb-bones rattle on her brittle hands,
As Cynthia stamps and hisses and demands:

Sextus, has sleep already washed away
Your manhood? You forget the window-sill

My sliding wore to slivers? Day
Would break before the Seven Hills
   Saw Cynthia retreat
And climb your shoulders to the knotted sheet.
You shouldered me and galloped on bare feet
To lay me by the crossroads. Have no fear:
Notus, who snatched your promise, has no ear.

But why did no one call in my deaf ear?
Your calling would have gained me one more day.
   Sextus, although you ran away
   You might have called and stopped my bier
   A second by your door.
No tears drenched a black toga for your whore
When broken tilestones bruised her face before
The Capitol. Would it have strained your purse
To scatter ten cheap roses on my hearse?

The State will make Pompilia's Chloris burn:
I knew her secret when I kissed the skull
   Of Pluto in the tainted bowl.
   Let Nomas burn her books and turn
   Her poisons into gold;
The finger-prints upon the potsherd told
Her love. You let a slut, whose body sold
To Thracians, liquefy my golden bust
In the coarse flame that crinkled me to dust.

If Chloris' bed has left you with your head,
Lover, I think you'll answer my arrears:
   My nurse is getting on in years,
   See that she gets a little bread —
   She never clutched your purse;
See that my little humpback hears no curse
From her close-fisted friend. But burn the verse
You bellowed half a life time in my name:
Why should you feed me to the fires of fame?

I will not hound you, much as you have earned
It, Sextus: I shall reign in your four books —
   I swear this by the Hag who looks
   Into my heart where it was burned:
   Propertius, I kept faith;
If not, may serpents suck my ghost to death
And spit it with their forked and killing breath
Into the Styx where Agamemnon's wife
Founders in the green circles of her life.

Beat the sycophant ivy from my urn,
That twists its binding shoots about my bones
   Where apple-sweetened Anio drones

Through orchards that will never burn
  While honest Herakles,
My patron, watches. Anio, you will please
Me if you whisper upon sliding knees:
"Propertius, Cynthia is here:
She shakes her blossoms when my waters clear."

You cannot turn your back upon a dream,
For phantoms have their reasons when they come:
  We wander midnights: then the numb
  Ghost wades from the Lethaean stream:
    Even the foolish dog
Stops its hell-raising mouth and casts its clog;
At cock-crow Charon checks us in his log.
Others can have you, Sextus; I alone
Hold: and I grind your manhood bone on bone.

Robert Lowell

ARIADNE LAY, THESEUS' SHIP SAILING AWAY

Ariadne lay, Theseus' ship sailing away,
languid on lonely shores, the Knossian girl;
and Cepheus' daughter collapsed in first sleep
just free from the hard stone, Andromeda;
no less the Edonian bacchante, worn from dances,
when she fell on grassy Apidanus:
so seemed she, breathing gentle quiet,
Cynthia, supporting her head with slipping hands,
when I came in, dragging my feet with much Bacchus,
and the boys shook the torch late in the night.

Not yet having completely lost sensation,
I lightly try to advance to her, pressing on the couch;
And while a pair commanded me, gripped with lust,
Love on one side, Liber the other, each a hard god,
to lightly try her, her arm thrown up,
and to take kisses, my weapon in hand,
yet I didn't dare disturb my mistress' quiet,
fearing the outbursts of her expert cruelty.

But I remained fixed, my eyes intent,
like Argus with the strange horns of Inachus' daughter.
And now I take the garland from my forehead
and place it on your temples, Cynthia.
Now I delight to redo your fallen hair,
now I give furtive fruits to empty hands.
I lavish all these gifts on ungrateful sleep,
gifts rubbed repeatedly against dangling breasts.

And each time you take breath with a sudden motion,
I stop, believing in an empty sign,
that some vision has brought you unaccustomed fears,
or someone is forcing you unwillingly to be his,
until the moon, running across different windows,
the moon, busy with lingering moonbeams,
opens your composed eyes with its light rays.

So she speaks, fixing her elbow on the soft couch,
"Have another's insults finally brought you
back, expelled from her doors, to our bed?
So where did you consume the long hours of my night,
still languid, my god, with the stars disappearing?

If only you could experience the nights you always
force me to endure, you asshole!
At first I evaded sleep with the purple thread,
and again, exhausted, with song of the Orphic lyre.
Left all alone, I was singing lightly to myself
the frequent long delays when your lover is about.
Then drowsiness pulled me, slipping in its soft wings.
She at last cured my crying."

Vincent Katz

O BEST OF ALL NIGHTS, RETURN AND RETURN AGAIN

(After the Pervigilium Veneris *&* Propertius's *"Nox mihi candida")*

How she let her long hair down over her shoulders, making a love cave
    around her face. Return and return again.
How when the lamplight was lowered she pressed against him, twining her
    fingers in his. Return and return again.
How their legs swam together like dolphins and their toes played like little
    tunnies. Return and return again.
How she sat beside him cross-legged, telling him stories of her childhood.
    Return and return again.
How she closed her eyes when his were open, how they breathed together,
    breathing each other. Return and return again.
How they fell into slumber, their bodies curled together like two spoons.
    Return and return again.
How they went together to Otherwhere, the fairest land they had ever seen.
    Return and return again.
O best of all nights, return and return again.

James Laughlin

✍ Ovid (Publius Ovidius Naso, 43 B.C.–A.D. 19)

From THE METAMORPHOSES

Arethusa Saved

When the god of the river
                    pursues her over Greece
weed-rot on his breath
                    rape on his mind,
at length Arethusa
                    loses her lead,
stops, prays for help
                    from a huntress like herself.

Artemis grants her
                    ground-fog to hide her
and she cowers wetly
                    in condensing cloud
and her own sweat cooling
                    from the cross-country run.
Bubbles itch
                    in her close-bobbed hair;
where her foot touches
                    forms a pool, small
but widening quickly;
                    liquid rolls down her,
excessively, really,
                    covering her body
till the body is obscured:
                    a living sheet of water
has clothed then replaced
                    hair, body, and foot.

The river-god roaming
                    round the cloud's circumference
sniffing at the edge
                    like a dog at a rat-hole
calls out boisterously
                    with country-boy bravado
"Arethusa darling
                    come out and get screwed."
At last the cloud clears
                    —he sees Arethusa
melted to his element,
                    a woman of water.
Roaring with joy
                    he reverts to river
making to plunge upon her

and deluge her with dalliance.
But Artemis opened
many earth-entrances,
cracks underneath her
hair-thin but deep.
Down them the girl slips
soaking out of sight
before his glassy stare
—to be conducted through darkness
to another country,
Sicily, where she springs
(fountain Arethuse)
as virgin stream presiding
over pastoral hymn
with intact hymen,
to be figured on medals
flanked by fish,
hair caught in a net
whom the god never netted.

Thom Gunn

The Death of Orpheus

The Thracian poet's song gets trees, rocks,
& beasts' souls going; suddenly Ciconian women,
their maddened breasts covered with wild animal fleece,
on hilltop spot Orpheus composing strummed
lyre-chords' song:

hair thrown back
in light breeze one cries, "There's our detractor!"
flings thyrsos at the Apollo-poet's melodic mouth:
leaf-covered, it leaves mark but no wound;
another's weapon: stone: shot, but caught
in air itself by harmony of voice & lyre falls
at his feet as if to beg pardon for such craziness!
thoughtless warfare increases unrestrained!
Fury reigns insane! still, all weapons
would be softened by song were it not for
the loud clamor of Phrygian flutes & bent horns,
drums, claps & Bacchic howls blocking lyre
sound: finally, stones redden with the silenced poet's
blood; maenads destroy the famous Orpheus theater:
on birds first, innumerable, still struck
by the singer's voice; snakes & an array of beasts; then
bloody hands turn on Orpheus, gathering like birds
seeing an owl stray in daylight, like dogs
preying on deer dying in morning's amphitheater:
after the poet! throwing leafy green thyrsos
wands not made for this purpose, throwing
dirt clods, branches ripped from trees, stones:

no lack of weapons for madness: oxen nearby
plowing earth & strong farmers, sweating, digging
fields, see this army & flee; leaving tools
scattered there: hoes, rakes, heavy shovels;
the wild-women grab them, horn-threatening oxen
torn apart, & rush back to the poet's death;
his arms out & voice speaking in vain
(first time ever moving no one);
sacrilege, they kill him; & through that mouth,
O Jupiter, that rocks & minds of beasts heard,
his soul breathes out into winds

saddened, birds weep for you, Orpheus, multitudes
of beasts, rocks, forests that often followed your songs;
trees drop leaves & tear their hair for you;
rivers, they say, rose with their tears;
hair down, Naiads & Dryads wear shrouds

his limbs scattered: you, Hebrus River, get
his head & lyre: & wonderful! drifting, mid-stream,
the lyre somehow plays mournfully; the lifeless tongue
murmurs mournfully; river banks respond mournfully;
carried out to sea beyond their native river,
they reach Methymna, on Lesbos shore; here,
a savage snake finds head exposed on sand,
hair dripping wet; but Phoebus comes,
stops the snake, ready to bite: freezes its open
jaws stone: they harden, still gaping

Orpheus-ghost underground recognizes places
seen before: searches Fields of the Blessed & finds
Eurydice; eager embraces; they walk there now
stepping together: or he follows her; or she
follows him with Orpheus looking back at her safely

Bacchus Doesn't Let Evil Go Unpunished:
grieving for his mysteries' missing poet, he ties down
with twisted roots in forest all Thracian women
who saw the crime: toes of those pursuers out, bodies
stuck in solid ground: as bird feels its legs
caught in crafty trapper's snare & shrieks frightened,
tightening the bonds with movement, terrified women try
in vain escaping, soil-stuck; roots hold,
forcing them, struggling; find fingers, feet,
nails are wood advancing up smooth legs;
try striking hand on thigh for lament: slap oak;
breasts, oak; shoulders, oak; they reach out
arms you'd think real branches (& thinking that
you wouldn't be wrong)

Charles Boer

From TRISTIA

3.14

Friend of the arts and artists, scholar, generous patron
   of whose kind notice I used to be proud,
only now do I learn the value of your esteem,
   independent, abiding—the way a friendship
always ought to be but seldom actually is.
   My books are still on your shelves, and you still speak
my ghostly name to the new poets coming along.
   Not just my spirit, but even my corpus
you keep alive and well in the city to which I write
   to thank you and offer the praise that you deserve.
Mine is the fervent gratitude a father would feel
   toward one who had done his abandoned children a kindness,
for those poems of mine to which you still give house room
   are children or rather orphans left behind,
to fend for themselves in whatever way they can on their own
   or with help—for you're their guardian now.
Three of my offspring carry the trait and share the taint
   of my corruption, but keep the rest of the flock
with the kind care you have shown them over the years. Remember
   the thrice five books of the *Metamorphoses,*
snatched, as it were, from the conflagration of my disaster.
   I think with remorse of what I left undone,
how unrevised it has limped into the marketplace.
   And find if you can a place for this new arrival,
the hayseeds still in its hair as it comes shambling in
   from the end of the world. I pray you bear in mind
how and where it came into being and make excuses
   for all its defects. To take up a pen here
is an act of defiance, folly, stubborn pride, habit,
   and the occasion of deep chagrin. There are no books,
nothing to prompt me here or prime the pump to flowing.
   There's no literate talk but only the rattle
of men in armor. Poets don't need enormous throngs
   but a small group to read to, intelligent ears
to appreciate and judge, sometimes to make suggestions
   Not here. And neither is solitude,
that elegant private calm in which one might set to work
   and do one's best. I weep to admit how badly
I grope and fumble. I try for a word and can't think.
   I feel my Latin fading like an inscription
on a stone the wind is wiping back to its first blankness,
   and the wind is full of the grit of Thracian chatter,
Scythian jabber and terrible Getic gobbledygook.
   By a guttering lamp I go over these pitiful pages
looking for any solecisms or Pontine lapses.
   The guards at the gates are supposed to fend off the raids
of the Getic brutes on our outpost. I'm on guard as well,

alert to their subtle incursions, but weary, weary . . .
It's not just a conceit: out here I am Rome.
Think of me kindly, fairly, as you have
for many years, and consider my fate as you read over
    Ovid's lastest work, these halting plaints.

5.14

I have been looking these pages over, my dearest wife,
    and I see what a monument I've erected here
to honor you. What small satisfaction I'm able to take
    from this dejected, depressing work of mine,
comes from the truth of my representation of your virtues.
    As long as people anywhere read Ovid,
you can be sure of the fame your character has deserved.
    If I am a sorry figure, you're still splendid,
a light for time to come, and a model for all women
    to remember and emulate in moments of trial.
Other men can offer their wives expensive gifts,
    but nothing those women wouldn't be glad
to trade for a chance at the immortality you'll have.
    I'm happy for that. To have carved you a place in the annals
of civilization is no small thing and the least I could do
    after what you've done for me, the sole
guardian of my fortunes and vessel of all my hopes.
    My sorry condition is proof of what you've lived with,
showing devotion, courage, forbearance, and even love,
    all the way. My disgrace is the base,
the pedestal for your figurine on the temples' altars.
    Courage without danger to show it off,
or loyalty lacking trials or tests . . . They're easy enough,
    but your demonstrations, which I've been obliged to watch
and admire even though they broke my heart, are amazing.

————

It may turn out that I'm your story's footnote
which is perfectly fine with me. As long as Latin is spoken,
    and as far as the highways of Rome extend, from here
to the furthermost parts of Gaul, your name will be invoked
    along with those of Penelope and Alcestis,
for selflessness and the faithful love that cynics doubt,
    but I can swear exists because I've seen it.
I write to let you know how my adoration grows
    as if you were a demigoddess, but still
my human love remains undiminished from what
    it was on the day we parted. I'd add my thanks,
but that would be wrong. You'd only wrinkle your brow, puzzled,
    entirely unaware of having behaved
in any remarkable way. You haven't acted well,
    or even at all. Your nature expressed itself
in its pure spontaneity as a bird in miraculous grace,
    wheels overhead and astonishes us all.

I stand here on the shore of this bleak coast, observing
  a gull turn on the air, and I think of you.
My eyes brim. My heart brims over. I send my love
  and praise that I hope will last a thousand years.

David R. Slavitt

OVID IN LOVE

1. (Amores I, V)

The day being humid and my head
heavy, I stretched out on a bed.
The open window to the right
reflected woodland-watery light,
a keyed-up silence as of dawn
or dusk, the vibrant and uncertain
hour when a brave girl might undress
and caper naked on the grass.
You entered in a muslin gown,
bare-footed, your fine braids undone,
a fabled goddess with an air
as if in heat yet debonair.
Aroused, I grabbed and roughly tore
until your gown squirmed on the floor.
Oh, you resisted, but like one
who knows resistance is in vain;
and, when you stood revealed, my eyes
feasted on shoulders, breasts and thighs.
I held you hard and down you slid
beside me, as we knew you would.
Oh, come to me again as then you did!

2. (Amores, II, XI)

This strange sea-going craze began
with Jason. Pine from Pelion,
weathered and shaped, was first to brave
the whirlpool and the whistling wave.
I wish the *Argo* had gone down
and seafaring remained unknown;
for now Corinna, scornful of
her safety and my vigilant love,
intends to tempt the winds and go
cruising upon the treacherous blue
waters where no shade-giving ilex,
temple or marble pavement breaks
with its enlightened artistry
the harsh monotony of the sea.

Walk on the beach where you may hear
the whorled conch whisper in your ear;
dance in the foam, but never trust
the water higher than your waist.
I'm serious. Listen to those with real
experience of life under sail;
believe their frightening anecdotes
of rocks and gales and splintered boats.
You won't be able to change your mind
when once your ship is far from land
and the most sanguine seamen cease
their banter as the waves increase.
How pale you'd grow if Triton made
the waters crash around your head—
so much more comfortable ashore
reading, or practising the lyre!
Still, if you're quite determined, God
preserve you from a watery bed:
Nereus' nymphs would be disgraced
if my Corinna should be lost.
Think of me when your shrinking craft
is a poignant pinpoint in the aft-
ernoon, and again when homeward bound
with canvas straining in the wind.
I'll be the first one at the dock
to meet the ship that brings you back.
I'll carry you ashore and burn
thank-offerings for your safe return.
Right there we'll make a bed of sand,
a table of a sand-dune, and
over the wine you'll give a vivid
sketch of the perils you survived—
how, faced with a tempestuous sea,
you hung on tight and thought of me!
Make it up if you like, as I
invent this pleasant fantasy . . .

Derek Mahon

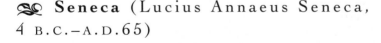 **Seneca** (Lucius Annaeus Seneca,
4 B.C.–A.D. 65)

CHORUS *From* THE TROJANS

After death nothing is, and nothing, death:
The utmost limit of a gasp of breath.
Let the ambitious zealot lay aside
His hopes of heaven, whose faith is but his pride;

Let slavish souls lay by their fear,
　Nor be concerned which way nor where
　After this life they shall be hurled.
Dead, we become the lumber of the world,
And to that mass of matter shall be swept
Where things destroyed with things unborn are kept.
　Devouring time swallows us whole;
Impartial death confounds body and soul.

For Hell and the foul fiend that rules
God's everlasting fiery jails
(Devised by rogues, dreaded by fools),
With his grim, grisly dog that keeps the door,
　Are senseless stories, idle tales,
　　Dreams, whimseys, and no more.

John Wilmot, Earl of Rochester

CHORUS *From* OEDIPUS

CHORUS.　Thebes　　you are finished
　　　　the countryside around is empty　　the farmers all
　　　　dead　　the workers all dead　　their children all
　　　　dead　　the plague owns everything

　　　　what's happened to your armies　　Thebes　　all
　　　　those brave men of yours　　they've gone under the

　　　　plague　　they're finished　　they marched so
　　　　bravely away out　　eastward　　past the last frontiers
　　　　victory after victory　　right away on to the world's
　　　　rim　　leaned their banners against the sun's very
　　　　face　　the conquerors　　where are they?
　　　　everybody ran from them　　the rich nations of the
　　　　rivers　　the marksmen of the hills　　the horsemen
　　　　everybody ran　　towns empty　　scattered　　but
　　　　not any more Thebes　　where are your armies now
　　　　Thebes　　they're finished　　the plague touched
　　　　them and they vanished　　finished　　rubbished into
　　　　earth

　　　　look at the streets　　what are the crowds doing
　　　　black procession　　they're going to the graves and the
　　　　fires　　Thebes is a funeral　　Thebes is choking
　　　　with corpses　　why don't the crowds move　　there
　　　　are too many corpses　　graves can't be dug fast
　　　　enough　　fire can't burn corpses fast enough　　the
　　　　earth's glutted　　death's glutted　　and the piles of
　　　　corpses rot

the plague began with the sheep   it began with the
grass   the grass was suddenly poison   the air was
suddenly stench

a bull at the altar   massive animal   the priest had
hoisted his ax steadied his aim   in that second
before the ax fell   the bull was down   was it
touched by the god   it was touched by the plague

I saw a heifer slaughtered   her body was a sackful
of filthy tar   filthy bubbling tar

everywhere cattle are dead in the fields   dead in
their stalls   on silent farms there are bones in
cloaks   skulls on pillows   every ditch stinks
death   the heat stinks   the silence stinks

a horseman coming breakneck past us   but the
plague caught him up   it caught his horse   mid-
stride   head over heels   full tilt   down
the rider beneath it

everything green has withered   the hills that
were cool with forest   they're dusty ridges
deserts of brittle sticks   the vine's tendril is white
it crumbles when you touch it
where are the gods   the gods hate us   the gods
have run away   the gods have hidden in holes
the gods are dead of the plague   they rot and stink
too

there never were any gods   there's only death

Ted Hughes

✏ Petronius (d. A.D. 65)

DOING, A FILTHY PLEASURE IS, AND SHORT

Doing, a filthy pleasure is, and short;
And done, we straight repent us of the sport:
Let us not then rush blindly on unto it,
Like lustfull beasts, that onely know to doe it:
For lust will languish, and that heat decay
But thus, thus, keeping endlesse Holy-day
Let us together closely lie, and kisse,
There is no labour, nor no shame in this;
This hath pleas'd, doth please, and long will please; never
Can this decay, but is beginning ever.

Ben Jonson

MAN IN THE MIDDLE OF THE STREET

The day's noise was draining away in my mind
    and the light from behind my eyes
when savage Cypris grabbed a handful of my hair
    and yanked me up
    and gave me hell, so:
    "You, my creature, my cocksman, my gash-hound,
    you I catch sleeping alone?
        Get on with it!"
So I leap up and barefoot, bathrobe flapping,
I rush down every alley in town
  and reach the end of none.
Like a man chasing a bus, running one minute,
    the next ashamed to run,
afraid to go home,
      terrified of looking silly
        standing here like this
        in the middle of an empty street
        hearing not one human voice
        not a sound but an occasional backfire
        not so much as a dog.
Am I the only man in the city without a bed of my own?
No pension plan, hard goddess, for your oldest campaigner?

Tim Reynolds

℘ Martial (Marcus Valerius Martialis, A.D. 40–104)

HERE HE IS WHOM YOU READ AND CLAMOR FOR

Here he is whom you read and clamor for,
tasteful reader, the very Martial world-
renowned for pithy books of epigrams
and not even dead yet. So seize your chance:
better to praise him when he can hear
than later, when he'll be literature.

William Matthews

YOU ARE A STOOL PIGEON

You are a stool pigeon and
A slanderer, a pimp and
A cheat, a pederast and

A troublemaker. I can't
Understand, Vacerra, why
You don't have more money.

Kenneth Rexroth

NON TE AMO, SABIDINE

1 On the Occasion of One Dr. Fell's Challenge to Translate an Epigram of Martial's

I do not like thee, Doctor Fell
The reason why I cannot tell.
But this I know and know full well
I do not like thee, Doctor Fell.

Thomas Brown

2 The Truth at Last

I do not love thee, Dr. Fell;
The reason why I'm going to tell
Although you lawyers threaten suit.
For I'm too sick to give a hoot.

Fred Chappell

YOU SOLD A SLAVE JUST YESTERDAY

You sold a slave just yesterday
for twelve hundred sesterces, Cal;
at last the lavish dinner you've
long dreamed about is in the pan.
Tonight! Fresh mullet, four full pounds!

You know I'll not complain, old pal,
about the food. But that's no fish
we'll eat tonight; that was a man.

William Matthews

TED'S STUDIO BURNT DOWN

Ted's studio burnt down, with all his poems.
Have the Muses hung their heads?
You bet, for it was criminal neglect
not also to have sautéed Ted.

William Matthews

YOU LIE AND I CONCUR

You lie and I concur. You "give"
a reading of your wretched verse
and I applaud. You sing and I
too lift my blowsy voice.

You drink, Pontificus, and I
drink up. You fart; I look away.
Produce a cribbage board; I'll find
a chance to lose, to pay.

There's but one thing you do without
me and my lips are sealed. Yet not
a minim of your money's trickled
down to me. So what?

You'll be good to me in your will?
No doubt you'd bounce a check from hell.
So don't hold back on my account;
if die you must, farewell.

William Matthews

SURROUNDED BY EUNUCHS

Surrounded by eunuchs and limp as a tissue,
Almo blames his Pollia for bearing no issue.

William Matthews

OH IF THE GODS WOULD MAKE ME RICH

"Oh if the gods would make me rich," you said —
gods like a joke, and so they did —
"I'd show you all what living's for."
But you dress like a scarecrow and your shoes
are patched. From ten olives you
set six aside; you stretch one scant dinner
until it's two. The tepid pondslime
you call pea soup, the bilge you drink for wine,
the lank, parched whores you call *amours* —
you call this squandering? You anal lout,
act rich or else restore the gods their loot
before they haul you into court.

William Matthews

AGRICULTURE

You've planted seven wealthy husbands
    While the bodies were still warm.
You own, Chloe, what I'd call
    A profit-making farm.

            Fred Chappell

HOW TO DO IT

"Chappell—you who love to jest—
Hear the things that make life blest:
Family money not got by earning;
A fertile farm, a hearthfire burning;
No lawsuits and no formal dress;
A healthy body and a mind at peace;
Friends whom tactful frankness pleases;
Good meals without exotic sauces;
Sober nights that still spark life;
A faithful yet a sexy wife;
Sleep that makes the darkness brief;
Contentment with what you plainly need;
A death not longed for, but without dread."

            Fred Chappell

✌ Juvenal (Decimus Junius Juvenalis, c. A.D. 50–127)

LONDON, GREATER LONDON (AFTER *SATIRE III*)

    Well, it really hurts, to think of him going away.
But he's made the right decision: that's got to be faced,
For what could be worse than—well, yes, the horrors of London
(Culminating in the Festival of Poetry)? . . . His station waggon
Was crammed the day he went. I joined him as far as Richmond,
Through the publishers moved up west, and the Royal Car Parks,
And the spacious villa Estates in the Green Belt.
This is what he said: 'It's unliveable-in:
Gets worse every day; so I'm off, before I'm senile.
Agreed, it's a real break—but what's the good?
How can I cope with London? When a book's bad,
I just can't say it was 'deeply moving' and 'I wonder
if you'd care to inscribe my copy . . . ?' I haven't read Jung.
Don't know any abortionists. Can't play bingo.
It may be the place if you want a coffee-coloured model

Or a Vietnam gymnastics-mistress: but it's not me.
Never mind if they come from Halifax, Oldham, Sydney,
The New Men, New Mannikins, if they don't know about culture
And play the guitar, well, they're so smooth, they're glass;
In those bum-freezer tuxedos, you'd think they were waiters.

And they make for London like waiters. First, they act as
The company soil-pipes; a bit later on, you find
They're all on the Board. Quick Wits, a Bloody Nerve,
All the Answers—and for numbers! It's Cup Final Day.
Smart! Is This Your Choice? He's playing it.
Linguistics, mathematical logic, advertising copy,
Action painting, judo, market forecasts, compering,
Psychiatry, cybernetics—he even knew Sabrina.
The Other-directed Man. Say Fly, he's airborne.
And the knock-out, this one's not from a Comprehensive School
Or College of Advanced Technology: First, Modern Greats, he is,
And 'a poet in his own right.' Can't I dodge their gent's suiting?
Well, we're all entertainers now. Are you laughing? He nearly died.
Pull a long face, he's doubled it (grinning arsewise).
Say it's chilly, he's buttoning his British Warm. Say it's hot,
He's Talking About Jerusalem, he's dripping. We're non-starters.
And as far as Sex goes, Is Nothing Sacred?
Seems the right approach. Respectable married woman,
Teenagers, model husband, nice young man, the lot.
And if that's no good, tries it on with granny on a pension.
All to get the inside news and pull the right strings.

And since we're on the subject, just take a look at
Our educational establishments; that's where you find
The real outsize fiddles. Heads jockeying for places
At the older universities. Lethal testimonials:
'Feel it my duty to add . . .' Public lecturers
Asking for their fee in notes. One day they'll steal
The hairs out of Pegasus's tail: that'll finish it.

There's no place for an ordinary Englishman here.
They want it all, with their well-bred adverse comments
In the Director's ear, drip drop, they don't need to learn how,
They were born dripping. 'Much regret no vacancy occurs
At present,' we read. Just one more off the waiting list.
No good living in a dream-world: it won't get you anywhere,
Out of bed early to go to a Shareholders' Meeting,
Buttoning your pants as you run . . . 'That concludes our business.'
He's having lunch with an American widow or a model.
'Darling why did you stay so long at that horrid committee?'
After all, they can spend the works monthly wage-bill on a girl,
But if some high-class piece takes your fancy, you'd think
Twice before you asked her to flash-of-white-thigh out of her Mark X
For you: what about those little red figures at the bank?

Go up for an interview, take authenticated copies
Of your qualifications, and they'll make 'discreet enquiries'
About your means. That'll tell them, in case you don't know,
Whether you're a security risk. 'How big's his wages-roll?
Is he farming?' (Inland-Revenue-wise). 'How many courses
Does Mrs. Applicant serve at her little dinner parties?'
'Just a few more questions about your financial status . . .'
Which will tell us if you're ethical, you see. The poor man
(Underprivileged I mean) can swear himself blue in the face,
They're taking careful note of his expression of view.
Anything else? Yes. If he's wearing off-the-pegs,
Or his socks dangle, or you glimpse a potato-heel,
Or his collar's not trubenized, or you can see
Where his wife's been stitching at him, it's 'really rather funny.'
Poverty, poverty, what have you worse than this? —
The poor man knows he can find a grin in every smile.

'If you don't mind,' you hear, 'This is a reserved compartment.'
So it is. As you go, you see your places taken by
The sons of ponces, who first saw the light in a clip-joint,
Or a disc-jockey's offspring, a bouncer's, an all-in wrestler's,
A boxing tout's (all been to good schools of course).
Well, I suppose the Prince Consort first thought up First Class Carriages.

Have you ever heard 'a marriage has been arranged'
Into this income-bracket when the young man's not even
Paying at the Standard Rate—let alone, no portfolio
That bulges . . . the way the bride does? Do 'persons of limited means'
Ever get the jackpot legacy? Or made an Alderman?
(I mean in The City, obviously.) It's high time such people started
A New Life somewhere, maybe in Our Great Commonwealth.
The able boy has to fight his home background
The whole way . . . and life in London's worst,
The cost of living's so high. Hospitality, tips,
Even eating out by yourself is really quite something.
In some parts of the country, perhaps, folk don't ride
In a car, till the hearse knocks at the door. Even now
Have gymkhanas and village fêtes, and the children don't call
Westerns *vieille vague*. Men's clothes don't run after the fashion,
And the cops don't drive white Jags. But where we are
It's the Affluent Society to the gusset (Extended Play,
Extended Payments, Creative Fares, and everybody Conforming Upwards).
Monnet talks. The firm is happy to celebrate
Our prospective entry into E.E.C. *(Ha ha.)* All personnel
Cordially invited. Something for the kiddies. Tickets five
Guineas excluding drinks (doubles? but naturally).

You tell me who could get run over in Lundy Island,
Ardnamurchan, Wells-next-the Sea, Durness?
But here it's all underpasses, motor-ways, twelve-mile jams, and

Articulated lorries jack-knifing downhill in the smog,
And a hundred deaths on the Road each Day of National Rejoicing.

 If you could only forget What's On,
And Keeping Abreast, I know just the sort of thing
Would suit you down to the ground: think what a snip
You could pick up in Dorset, the Cotsfolds, unspoilt Suffolk
(Beyond commuter country of course) — and be paying less
Or at least no more than key-money on a mews in Chelsea.
A matured garden (with all main services though),
Then take up roses for pleasure, especially old roses,
And give modest select dinners in flawless taste.
Not gracious — distinguished living. And surely it's something
Even to have one pony for your only daughter to learn on.
. . . There really has been a Decline, a Falling Away —
You could put it so much better than I. Merrie England;
The organic community; a living tradition; wheelwrights.
The old fashioned kind of J.P. — and just the village stocks.
Well, I mustn't dawdle; it's getting towards rush-hour,
I'll be stuck on the by-pass . . . keep in touch . . . I'll look you up
When you're settled at Chipping Camden. Yes, that could tempt me,
It's nippy sometimes on the coast; and I've always been one for hills.'
That's what he said. I thought he put it frightfully well.

John Holloway

THE VANITY OF HUMAN WISHES
From THE TENTH SATIRE

 Let Observation, with extensive view,
Survey mankind, from China to Peru;
Remark each anxious toil, each eager strife,
And watch the busy scenes of crowded life;
Then say how hope and fear, desire and hate
O'erspread with snares the clouded maze of fate,
Where wavering man, betrayed by venturous pride
To tread the dreary paths without a guide,
As treacherous phantoms in the mist delude,
Shuns fancied ills, or chases airy good;
How rarely Reason guides the stubborn choice,
Rules the bold hand, or prompts the suppliant voice;
How nations sink, by darling schemes oppressed,
When Vengeance listens to the fool's request.
Fate wings with every wish the afflictive dart,
Each gift of nature, and each grace of art;
With fatal heat impetuous courage glows,
With fatal sweetness elocution flows,
Impeachment stops the speaker's powerful breath,

And restless fire precipitates on death.
But scarce observed, the knowing and the bold
Fall in the general massacre of gold;
Wide-wasting pest! that rages unconfined,
And crowds with crimes the records of mankind;
For gold his sword the hireling ruffian draws,
For gold the hireling judge distorts the laws;
Wealth heaped on wealth, nor truth nor safety buys,
The dangers gather as the treasures rise.
Let History tell where rival kings command,
And dubious title shakes the madded land,
When statutes glean the refuse of the sword,
How much more safe the vassal than the lord,
Low skulks the hind beneath the rage of power,
And leaves the wealthy traitor in the Tower,
Untouched his cottage, and his slumbers sound,
Though Confiscation's vultures hover round.
The needy traveler, serene and gay,
Walks the wild heath, and sings his toil away.
Does envy seize thee? crush the upbraiding joy,
Increase his riches and his peace destroy;
New fears in dire vicissitude invade,
The rustling brake alarms, and quivering shade,
Nor light nor darkness bring his pain relief,
One shows the plunder, and one hides the thief.
Yet still one general cry the skies assails,
And gain and grandeur load the tainted gales;
Few know the toiling statesman's fear or care,
The insidious rival and the gaping heir.

Samuel Johnson

❧ Hadrian (Publius Aelius Hadrianus, A.D. 76–138)

THE EMPEROR HADRIAN ON HIS SOUL

Soul, little wandering friend,
companion and guest of the body,
to what regions now are you drifting —
naked and pale and constrained
with no hint of the old repartee!

Frederick Morgan

Anonymous (c. a.d. 200)

From THE VIGIL OF VENUS

> "Cras amet qui nunquam amavit quique amavit cras amet."

I

Tomorrow love shall have its way with ingenue and old roué.
Spring has sprung, young, and singing rebirth,
inveigling lovers, as birds overhead mate and the trees
undo themselves and yield like maidens out on the field.

                O Goddess!

Tomorrow love shall have its way with ingenue and old roué.

II

Orange blossoms and myrtle sprays: everywhere are brides' bouquets.
The world turns matchmaker and the woods are alive with whispers
like the giggles of young girls who are minions of Dione, nymph
and mother of Venus, queen of the green season's demesne.

                O Goddess!

Tomorrow love shall have its way with ingenue and old roué.

III

Tomorrow air, water, and fire will all commingle in desire
as Dione, who arose like foam from the deep green sea,
teaches the world to primp, bedeck, sashay,
as wavelets caress with a loving hand the flank of the strand.

                O Goddess!

Tomorrow love shall dictate to the old roué and the ingenue.

X (XII)

Ceres and Bacchus attend the feast. There is much eating and drinking,
and rhapsodists strum their lyres and sing what is in all our hearts,
his vision Apollo's gift that he passes on to us all.
The woods resound with his songs and nightingales' all night long.

                O Goddess!

Tomorrow love shall have its way with ingenue and old roué.

XI

His sister, the goddess Diana, puts by her weapons and thinks
reappraises her fate—for even a virgin may wonder
what she has lost as each sunset bids the world go to bed
and again as each moonrise discovers the intricate postures of lovers . . .

                O Goddess!

Tomorrow love shall ride roughshod over the hearts of mortals and gods.

XII (X)

At the last, for Venus' sake, Diana elects to take a respite
from her pursuit and slaughter of bird and scampering beast.
In this mood, the wood is transformed, and we glimpse a moment of peace,
no bloodshed staining the grass where shepherd lies down with his lass.
                                                                    O Goddess!
Tomorrow love shall have its way with ingenue and old roué.

XIII

On the heights of flowery Hybla, the goddess presides, declaring
freedom, ease, and rapture, but having lived long with constraint,
we do our best as stiff-jointed, and heavy-footed we dance
to the pipe's seductive strain and gambol on Enna's plain.
                                                                    O Goddess!
Tomorrow love shall have its way with ingenue and old roué.

XIV

All the girls of the village, the surrounding farms, and the hillside
pastures attend the summons of Cupid's mother, voluptuous
Venus, whose whispered dictates fill them with apprehension:
they're afraid to fail as indeed they are also afraid to succeed.
                                                                    O Goddess!
Tomorrow love shall have its way with ingenue and old roué.

XV

They blush to hear her sing the praise of the god, her father,
who rains his fertility down from the sky to the lap of the fields,
and they feel in their own laps, a shiver of sudden response,
an opening up of the truth of their powerfully fecund youth.
                                                                    O Goddess!
Tomorrow love shall have its way with ingenue and old roué.

XVI

Her mystery is the power that kindles life from unlikely
opposites that encounter each other: Trojans and Latins
were joined when Aeneas bedded Lavinia; Romulus' sons,
in their lust for those Sabine women, blurred what it meant to be Roman.
                                                                    O Goddess!
Tomorrow love shall have its way with native and with emigré.

XVII (XVIII)

By Venus' command did Mars, her former lover, attend
on Ilia, the Vestal virgin, forced her, and she brought forth
Romulus, Remus, Rome, Caesar. Civilization
and all the good things that it brings come from these passionate springs.
                                                                    O Goddess!
Tomorrow love shall have its way with virgin and with debauché.

XVIII (XVII)

The tide of the huge future begins with these tiny spurts.
The scrotal tingle, the sudden vaginal lubrication
are parts of the general lusts of the world at large. In the fields
the perfume of fresh-turned earth is the tang of their giving birth.
O Goddess!

Tomorrow love shall have its way with ingenue and old roué.

XIX

Venus arouses the woods, the meadows and fields. The hillsides
heave and the hidden valleys open in invitation.
Her son is a country boy whom she nursed at her beautiful bosom
into which he was tucked, clutching, rapt, as he sucked.
O Goddess!

Tomorrow love shall have its way with ingenue and old roué.

XX

Look how the mighty bull, the ram, and the spirited stallion
lie down in their pastures content to feel the good warmth of the earth
as if it were an enormous cow or ewe or mare—
with something of mate and mother, a reliably welcoming other.
O Goddess!

Tomorrow love shall be high priest to every fish and bird and beast.

XXI

High in the sky the trumpeter swans perseverate swan-ness.
And smaller birds in the copse chirrup and coo. . . . Even Procne
and Philomel, the victims of Tereus' terrible lust.
The tunes in which they complain sound much like a lovesong's refrain.
O Goddess!

Tomorrow love shall have its way with ingenue and old roué.

XXII

They sing, but we are mute, dumbstruck with longing and hope
that spring may come to us, too, and our hearts burst into birdsong,
an anthem of celebration, creation, and re-creation.
Hatred is silence and death. Singing requires breath.
O Goddess!

Tomorrow love shall have its way with ingenue and old roué.

David R. Slavitt

❧ 3

India: The Mauryan Dynasty and the Dravidian Kingdoms

Prakrit

❧ Collected by King Hala (First century A.D.)

From THE GATHASAPTASATI

Even He Was Abashed

Even he was abashed
and I laughed
and held him close
when he went for the knot
of my underclothes
and I'd already untied it.

> *Martha Ann Selby*

Those Women

Those women
who can see their lovers
in dreams
are lucky

but without him,
sleep won't come
so who can dream?

> *Martha Ann Selby*

Lone Buck

Lone buck
in the clearing
nearby doe
eyes him with such
longing
that there
in the trees the hunter
seeing his own girl
lets the bow drop

Andrew Schelling

The Newly Wed Girl

The newly wed girl, pregnant already,
asked what she liked about the honeymoon,
cast a glance at her husband,
but not at his face.

David Ray

You Love Her

You love her, while I love you,
and yet she hates you, and says so.
Love ties us in knots,
keeps us in hell.

David Ray

These Women Plunder My Husband

These women plunder my husband
as if he were plums
in the bowl of a blind man.
But I can see them, clear as a cobra.

David Ray

Tamil

From THE CLASSICAL TAMIL ANTHOLOGIES (C. A.D. 50–300)

∞ Ammuvanar

THEY SHOUT OUT THE PRICE OF SALT

They shout out the price of salt harvested from salt flats;
they travel to far distances on dusty roads

as they go in their caravans over long trails
carrying thick staffs.
The life of these salt merchants seems a good one to me.
Her curly hair tossing,
the dress of shoots she wears to ornament her wide, soft loins
swaying with each step,
she cries in every street,
"People of the town! Salt is as cheap as paddy!
Will you buy some?"
"Listen, you with your belly curved and arms supple as bamboo,
you did not tell us the price of the salt of your body,"
I said, standing a little away.
Her anger showing in her large, red-lined eyes blackened with collyrium,
she said, "You, over there, who are you?"
And innocent,
very lovely,
she moved off a little,
smiling,
her few rows of white bangles flashing,
taking my heart with her.

George L. Hart III

◈ Kaccipettu Nannakaiyar

WHAT SHE SAID

My lover capable of terrible lies
at night lay close to me
in a dream
that lied like truth.

I woke up, still deceived,
and caressed the bed
thinking it my lover.

It's terrible. I grow lean
in loneliness,
like a water lily
gnawed by a beetle.

A. K. Ramanujan

◈ Mamalatan

WHAT SHE SAID

Don't they really have
in the land where he has gone

such things
as house sparrows

dense-feathered, the color of fading water lilies,
pecking at grain drying on yards,
playing with the scatter of the fine dust
of the streets' manure
and living with their nestlings
in the angles of the penthouse

and miserable evenings,

and loneliness?

A. K. Ramanujan

❧ Oreruravanar

WHAT HE SAID

Her arms have the beauty
of a gently moving bamboo.
Her eyes are full of peace.
She is faraway,
her place not easy to reach.

My heart is frantic
with haste,
          a plowman with a single ox
          on land all wet
          and ready for seed.

A. K. Ramanujan

❧ Maturaikkataiayattar Makan Vennakan

WHAT SHE SAID TO HER GIRL-FRIEND

Once you said
let's go, let's go
to the gay carnival in the big city;

that day
the good elders spoke of many good omens
for our going.

But he waylaid me,
gave me a slingshot and rattles
for scaring parrots,
and a skirt of young leaves
which he said looked good
on me,

and with his lies
he took the rare innocence
that mother had saved for me.

      And now I am like this.

A. K. Ramanujan

Maturai Eruttalan Centamputan

WHAT SHE SAID

Before I laughed with him
    nightly,

        the slow waves beating
        on his wide shores
        and the palmyra
        bringing forth heron-like flowers
        near the waters,

my eyes were like the lotus
my arms had the grace of the bamboo
my forehead was mistaken for the moon.

    But now

      A. K. Ramanujan

Kannan

WHAT HER GIRL-FRIEND SAID TO HIM

Sir,
    not that we did not hear the noise
    you made trying to open the bolted doors,
    a robust bull elephant
    stirring in the night
    of everyone's sleep;

we did. But as we fluttered inside
like a peacock in the net,
crest broken, tail feathers flying,

our good mother held us close
in her innocence
thinking to quell our fears.

A. K. Ramanujan

Peruñcattan

WHAT HER GIRL-FRIEND SAID

when she sees that her friend's love-sickness is being misunderstood and rites of exorcism are performed to cure her

Cutting the throat of a sacrificial goat,
offering special platters of grain,
and sounding many instruments on the dry islets
in a running river,

none of this will help: they'll put on a show,
but will bring no remedy
for our girl's disease.

And this calling on all the great gods
except the right one, her lover,
as if some demon
possessed her—

it's really painful,

when she is only being faithful
to her secret lover
from the tall hills where
the clouds play games.

A. K. Ramanujan

Kallatanar

WHAT SHE SAID

It would be nice, I think,
if someone didn't mind
the hurry and the long walk,
and went to give him the good word:

the wound that father got
pulling in that big shark
is healed and he's gone back
to the blue-dark of the sea;

and mother's gone to the salt pans
to sell her salt for white rice;

if only someone would reach my man
on his cold wide shore and tell him:
            this is the time to come!

A. K. Ramanujan

✺ Kollan Arici

WHAT HER FRIEND SAID

The great city fell asleep
but we did not sleep.
Clearly we heard, all night,
from the hillock next to our house
the tender branches of the flower-clustered tree
with leaves like peacock feet
let fall
their blue-sapphire flowers.

A. K. Ramanujan

✺ Cempulappeyanirar

WHAT HE SAID

What could my mother be
to yours? What kin is my father
to yours anyway? And how
did you and I meet ever?
            But in love our hearts are as red
earth and pouring rain:
            mingled
beyond parting.

A. K. Ramanujan

✆ Ponmutiyar

ELEGY ON A YOUNG WARRIOR

O heart sorrowing
for this lad
        once scared
of a stick
lifted in mock-anger
when he refused
a drink of milk,
        now
not content with killing
war-elephants
with spotted trunks,
        this son
of the strong man who fell yesterday

seems unaware of the arrow
in his wound,
his head of hair is plumed
like a horse's,
        he's fallen
on his shield,
his beard still soft.

A. K. Ramanujan

✆ Kovurkilar

WE HOPE FOR PATRONS

We hope for patrons,
travel like birds,
and cross wastelands as if they were short,
singing as well as we can with our stumbling tongues.
We find happiness in what we get,
feed our families,
eat without saving,
give without stinting,
and suffer for reputation.
Does this life of a suppliant ever bring harm to others?
Only if you count how we put our enemies to shame in every contest,
walking with our heads held high in joy.
Our lives are no worse than yours
with your fame and the wealth you have gained from ruling the earth.

George L. Hart III

❧ Itaikkunrurkilar

HIS LEGS STRONG AND LITHE

His legs strong and lithe,
his bravery fierce and unyielding,
my lord is like a tiger living in a cramped cave
who stretches, rises up, and sets out for his prey.
But they did not think him hard to fight against.
They rose up bellowing,
"We are best, we are the greatest.
Our enemy is young and there is much plunder."
Those foolish warriors who came with contempt
ran with dim eyes, showing their backs,
but he did not let them be killed then.
He took them to the city of their fathers,
and as their women with fine ornaments died in shame
and the clear *kiṇai* drum sounded,
there he killed them.

George L. Hart III

❧ Ceraman Kottampalattut

GREAT IT MAY BE

Great it may be,
yet my grief has limits,
for it is not strong enough to kill me.
On the weed-strewn salt earth of the burning ground,
on a pile of logs set aflame
she lies,
her bed blazing fire.
My woman is dead, she belongs to the other world,
yet I am still alive.
This life is strange.

George L. Hart III

❧ Kakkaipirtiniyar Naccellaiyar

MANY SAID

Many said,
"That old woman, the one whose veins show
on her weak, dry arms where the flesh is hanging,
whose stomach is flat as a lotus leaf,

has a son who lost his nerve in battle and fled."
At that, she grew enraged and she said,
"If he has run away in the thick of battle,
I will cut off these breasts from which he sucked,"
and, sword in hand, she turned over fallen corpses,
groping her way on the red field.
Then she saw her son lying there in pieces
and she rejoiced more than the day she bore him.

George L. Hart III

✌ Tayankannanar

OVERSPREAD WITH SALTY SOIL

Overspread with salty soil,
overgrown with weeds,
where owls hoot in broad daylight
and demon women live whose mouths gape in the light of the pyres,
the burning ground spewing forth white clouds is fearful.
Their hearts full of desire, lovers weep
and their warm tears put out embers lying among the bones.
The burning ground has seen the back of every man,
for it alone is the end of all men on the earth.
No one has ever seen its back.

George L. Hart III

4

CHINA: THE HAN DYNASTY

Chinese

Chia Yi (201–169 B.C.)
From RHYMEPROSE ON AN OWL

The year was tan-wo, it was the fourth month, summer's first,
The thirty-seventh day of the cycle, at sunset, when an owl flew into my
    house.
On the corner of my seat it perched, completely at ease.
I marveled at the reason for this uncanny visitation
And opened a book to discover the omen. The oracle yielded the maxim:
"When a wild bird enters a house, the master is about to leave."
I should have liked to ask the owl: Where am I to go?
If lucky, let me know; if bad, tell me the worst.
Be it swift or slow, tell me when it is to be.
The owl sighed; it raised its head and flapped its wings
But could not speak—Let me say what it might reply:
All things are a flux, with never any rest,
Whirling, rising, advancing, retreating;
Body and breath do a turn together—change form and slough off,
Infinitely subtle, beyond words to express.
From disaster fortune comes, in fortune lurks disaster,
Grief and joy gather at the same gate, good luck and bad share the same
    abode.

———

Disaster is to fortune as strands of a single rope.
Fate is past understanding—who comprehends its bounds?
Force water and it spurts, force an arrow and it goes far:
All things are propelled in circles, undulating and revolving:
Clouds rise and rain falls, tangled in contingent alternation.

On the Great Potter's wheel creatures are shaped in all their infinite variety.
Heaven cannot be predicted, the Way cannot be foretold,
Late or early, it is predetermined; who knows when his time will be?
Consider then:
Heaven and Earth are a crucible, the Creator is the smith,
Yin and yang are the charcoal, living creatures are the bronze:
Combining, scattering, waning, waxing—where is any pattern?
A thousand changes, myriad transformations with never any end.
If by chance one becomes a man, it is not a state to cling to;
If one be instead another creature, what cause is that for regret?
A merely clever man is partial to self, despising others, vaunting ego;
The man of understanding takes the larger view: nothing exists to take
    exception to.

———

The Perfect Man is above circumstance, Tao is his only friend.
The mass man vacillates, his mind replete with likes and dislikes;
The True Man is tranquil, he takes his stand with Tao.
Divest yourself of knowledge and ignore your body, until, transported, you
    lose self,
Be detached, remote, and soar with Tao. . . .

J. R. Hightower

P'an Chieh-yü (Lady P'an, c. 80 B.C.)

A PRESENT FROM THE EMPEROR'S NEW CONCUBINE

I took a piece of the rare cloth of Ch'i,
White silk glowing and pure as frost on snow,
And made you a fan of harmony and joy,
As flawlessly round as the full moon.
Carry it always, nestled in your sleeve.
Wave it and it will make a cooling breeze.
I hope, that when Autumn comes back
And the North wind drives away the heat,
You will not store it away amongst old gifts
And forget it, long before it is worn out.

Kenneth Rexroth

Liu Chi-hsün (c. 100 B.C.)

LAMENT

My family married me off
to the King of the Wusun,

and I live in an alien land
a million miles from nowhere.
My house is a tent.
My walls are of felt.
Raw flesh is all I eat,
with horse milk to drink.
I always think of home
and my heart stings.
O to be a yellow snow-goose
floating home again!

Tony Barnstone and Chou Ping

Anonymous (c. A.D. 50)

OLD POEM

She went up the hill to pick angelica;
she came down the hill and met her former husband.
She knelt and asked her former husband,
"How do you find the new wife?"
"The new wife I would say is fine,
but she lacks the old wife's excellence.
In face and complexion they're much alike,
but quite unlike in skill of hand.
When the new wife came in the gate,
the old wife left by the side door.
The new wife is good at weaving gauze,
the old wife was good at weaving plain stuff.
Weaving gauze, one does a bolt a day,
weaving plain stuff, five yards or more.
And when I compare the gauze with the plain stuff,
I know the new wife can't equal the old!"

Burton Watson

Pan Chao (A.D. 48–117)

NEEDLE AND THREAD

Tempered, annealed, the hard essence of autumn metals
finely forged, subtle, yet perdurable and straight,

By nature penetrating deep yet advancing by inches
to span all things yet stitch them up together,

Only needle-and-thread's delicate footsteps
are truly broad-ranging yet without beginning!

"Withdrawing elegantly" to mend a loose thread,
and restore to white silk a lamb's-down purity . . .

How can those who count pennies calculate their worth?
They may carve monuments yet lack all understanding.

Rob Swigart

ஜ Anonymous (c. A.D. 100)

TWO POEMS ON THE THEME OF SEPARATION, *From* NINETEEN POEMS IN ANCIENT STYLE

1

Going on always on and on
alive, but parted from you
gone ten thousand miles and more
each to a far edge of the sky

the road is hard and long
with nothing sure about meeting again
Tartar horses lean to the northern wind
Viet birds nest on southern boughs

days advance, the parting grows long
days advance, the sash grows loose
floating clouds hide the bright sun
the wanderer can think of no return
loving you I became old
suddenly the time is late —
enough   I speak no more
try hard to stay well

Charles Hartman

2

Green is the grass on riverbanks,
Dense are the willows in the garden.
Fair is the woman upstairs,
Bright as the moon at her window.
Lovely is her rouge-powdered face,
Slender are her white hands.
At one time she was a singing-girl,
Now she is a wanderer's wife.
He went away and has not returned,
An empty bed, hard to keep alone.

Dell R. Hales

Anonymous (c. A.D. 100)

MULBERRY BY THE PATH

The sun rises at the southeastern corner
And shines upon our Ch'in family's house.
The Ch'in clan has a fair daughter,
She is called Lo-fu.
Lo-fu likes to work with silkworms and mulberry leaves;
She picks mulberry leaves at the wall's south corner.
Green silk strands form the basket cord
A cassia twig forms the basket handle
On her head, a "falling" chignon,
On her ears, "bright moon" pearls;
Of yellow silk her skirt below,
Of purple silk her jacket above.
The passers-by who see Lo-fu
Put down their loads and stroke their beards.
The young fellows who see Lo-fu
Take off their caps and adjust their headcloths.
The tillers forget their ploughs,
The hoers forget their hoes.
When they go home they find fault and are wroth
Just because they've looked at Lo-fu.

The Prefect comes from the South,
His five steeds stop and hesitate.
The Prefect sends his men to ask,
"Who is this pretty woman?"
"The Ch'in clan has a fair daughter,
She is called Lo-fu."
What is Lo-fu's age?
Not quite twenty yet,
A little more than fifteen.
The Prefect asks Lo-fu,
Would she ride with him?
Lo-fu steps forward and replies:
"How stupid is the Prefect!
The Prefect has his own wife,
Lo-fu has her own husband.
"In the East, among more than a thousand horsemen,
My husband holds the top position.
How can you recognize my husband?
A white horse walks behind a black colt.
With green silk strands is tied the horse's tail,
With yellow gold is harnessed the horse's head.
At his hip a sword with 'pulley' hilt,
Worth more than a million.

"At fifteen he was county clerk,
At twenty, provincial court councilor,
At thirty, palace attendant,
At forty, lord governor.
His personal appearance: a pure white complexion,
Fine hair and a slight beard.
Slow is his pace, as becomes a dignitary;
With stately, graceful steps he moves around the office.
The thousands of men assembled there
All say my husband looks superior."

Hans H. Frankel

Anonymous (c. A.D. 100)

THE POMELO

Where pomelo hangs down lovely fruit
Is on the deep hill flank.
I hear you like my sweetness;
In secret, alone, I make myself lovely.
I offer my humble self on a jade dish,
For many years hoping to be eaten.
My fragrance fair does not please you.
Green to yellow — swift the colors change.

Anne Birrell

Sung Tzu-hou (c. A.D. 120)

SONG

On the Eastern Way at the city of Lo-yang
At the edge of the road peach trees and plum-trees grow;
On the two sides, — flower matched by flower;
Across the road, — leaf touching leaf.

A spring wind rises from the north-east;
Flowers and leaves gently nod and sway.
Up the road somebody's daughter comes
Carrying a basket, to gather silkworms' food.
    [*She sees the fruit trees in blossom and, forgetting
    about her silkworms, begins to pluck the branches.*]
With her slender hand she breaks a branch from the tree;
The flowers fall, tossed and scattered in the wind.

    [*The tree says:*]
"Lovely lady, I never did you harm;
Why should you hate me and do me injury?"

[*The lady answers:*]
"At high autumn in the eighth and ninth moons
When the white dew changes to hoar-frost,
At the year's end the wind would have lashed your boughs,
Your sweet fragrance could not have lasted long.
Though in the autumn your leaves patter to the ground,
When spring comes, your gay bloom returns.
But in men's lives when their bright youth is spent
Joy and love never come back again."

Arthur Waley

✆ Ts'ao Ts'ao (Emperor Wen of the Wei Dynasty, 155–220)

VARIANT ON THE SONGS OF THE EAST AND WEST GATES

Wild geese go north of the passes
in no man's country
ten thousand miles and more they lift their wings
and fly or linger by instinct single-file
winters they glean the southern paddies
on a spring day they soar back north

and in the field there is tumbleweed
wind-borne   it scatters and whirls away
long severed from old roots
not in ten thousand years will it join them again

what help is there for a soldier gone to war
how can he ever return from the earth's four borders
the war horse never slips its saddle
the soldier's armor never leaves his back
softly   softly   age comes upon him
when can he go home

a dragon god lurks in the deep spring
a fierce tiger stalks the high ridge
a fox   dying   turns its head to the hill
how can one forget home

David Lattimore

Part III

The
Postclassical
World
(A.D. 250–1200)

In the centuries that followed the decline of the classical empires of Eurasia, the world's literary center of gravity for a time shifted decisively to the East, a fact reflected in the organization of Part III. For while the fall of Rome led to a long-term fragmentation of political power and cultural identity in the West, in India, China, and Japan alike the postclassical centuries saw the rise of new imperial regimes whose splendors outshone those of the past.

South Indian verse of this period is represented in excerpts from the *Kural* of the Tamil poet and sage Tiruvalluvar, regarded still in his native land as a moral teacher of a stature equal to that of Aristotle or Confucius. A shamanistic poem from South India, also in Tamil, reminds us of popular and tribal beliefs and traditions quite foreign to the high culture of India's royal courts. In northern India the rise of the Gupta Empire (c. 320–550) coincided with the high-water mark of classical Sanskrit literature, above all in the plays and poetry of Kalidasa, a master poet of very humble and obscure origns. His work is represented here by excerpts from his gallant, romantic long poem the *Megaduta,* "The Cloud Messenger." In contrast to the extreme formalism of Kalidasa's *sloka* couplets are the more relaxed poems of (or at least attributed to) Bhartrihari, and the sensual love poems of Vidya, King Amaru, and others in the same vein.

In China, the fall of the Han Dynasty in 220 was followed by more than three hundred years of political disunion during which culture nevertheless flourished, fertilized particularly by the growing popularity of the newly imported Buddhist religion. The poet T'ao Ch'ien (also called T'ao Yüan-ming) was in the forefront of a movement to create a new, "modern" style of verse; the anonymous poets who wrote in the name of the courtesan "Midnight" (Tz'u-yeh) added an element of worldly sophistication to China's poetic vocabulary.

The T'ang Dynasty (618–907) saw a great flowering of literary genius, especially during the first half of the eighth century in the work of Wang Wei, Li Po, and Po Chü-i. The mood shifted abruptly with the civil wars of the 750s, which led to the flight of the imperial court to Szechuan Province (see Li Po's "The Road to Shu Is Hard"), during which the imperial guards insisted on executing the emperor's favorite concubine, Yang Kuei-fei (see Po Chü-i's "Song of Everlasting Sorrow"). The incomparable verse of Tu Fu reflects the sober realities of these decades of war and hardship. The T'ang also is distinguished by the verse of women poets like Yü Hsüan-chi and Hsüeh T'ao, and by the emergence of early Korean poetry (in Classical Chinese).

Japan's Nara (610–685) and Heian (695–1185) periods had no imperial antecedents, but marked instead the first emergence of an imperial system in the "country of the eight islands." The first imperial poetry collection, the *Man'yōshū* ("Book of Ten Thousand Leaves"), compiled around 759, contains verse from the previous two centuries or so, including many long poems of irregular form, and some poems in Classical Chinese in pure T'ang style. But long verse was by the late ninth century already a thing of the past, and the *tanka* (or *waka*), in five lines of five, seven, five, seven, and seven syllables, became established as the quintessential Japanese poetic form. The *tanka* was above all occasional verse, which Heian aristocrats learned to compose as easily as they could breathe. Many of the best poets of the era were women (Ono no Komachi, Ki no Tsurayuki, Izumi Shikibu) who found the delicacy of the form a perfect outlet for the passionate but constrained emotions of their exquisite and often brief lives.

J.S.M.

In the gloom the gold gathers the light against it.
— Ezra Pound

In the long stark time after the fall of Rome, the vigor of oral traditions returned, informing words sung by poets, preserved by scribes, and illuminated by a visionary light from the Iron Age. This poetry belonged less to the scorched ruins of Roman cities and villas than to lonely outposts in a dark and dangerous world. The bards who recited the verse of early medieval Europe were usually wanderers or exiles, learned in craft, and keepers of the memories of their folk. Centuries before the coronation of Charlemagne in A.D. 800, they were essential to isolated settlements on the edge of northern forests and coasts.

Before the rise of Islam in the seventh century in northern Africa and the Near East, the bardic poet embodied the tribal spirit of groups of Bedouin nomads traveling the desert in caravan. All of these minstrels inhabited a world in which invasion and dispersal were constant threats, requiring their service as prophets in an era when collective existence was precarious. The poets of fireside and high feast had a common task, inspired by the somber memories and regional myths of the former provinces of Rome. Bardic performance knit together the fragile identity of people for the written word was even scarcer than the legends kept alive under the assimilating drive of Roman civilization. Out of near oblivion, cultural chaos, and narratives surviving through speech alone, the bard composed an intricate music.

Their incantantions link language once more to its most archaic function. They enriched and sustained the developing vernacular tongues of audiences in remote places and managed what was, almost literally, a verbal magic. The epic poetry of the early Middle Ages in Europe was a powerful force in keeping at bay the demons and monsters looming beyond the clearings of scattered townships and villages. Bardic song revived for its hearers dead heroes and a mythical past that, without their retellings, might have slipped as well into the silence of the broken walls, fallen marble, and deserted temples around them.

In many of these traditions, pagan gods and Christian saints coexist as a palimpsest, just as oral poetry maintained a shadowy alliance with the art of the manuscript and its literate practioners. The culture of Ireland passed from the harps of a sacred class of professional poets rooted in the Druid religion to the pens of the Christian hermits and monks who both composed and compiled the literature of the Gaelic language. From their solitary labor comes one of the oldest poetic achievements in the vernacular, and a wealth of lyric poetry that delights with its tender love of the natural world, and a reverence for its Maker. The Celtic epic cycles furnish early models of the poetic imagination in both the adventures of Mad Sweeny after the Battle of Moira in the seventh century A.D., when a saint's curse transformed him into a bird of the air, and the Lament of the Old Woman of Beare, a dramatic archetype of Ireland. Monastic scholarship retrieved as well the heroic tales of Ulster in the *Tain* in which the warrior Cuchulainn, like Achilles, speaks to the body of his foe at a ford in a river.

The Welsh bards, like the Irish, were sacred entertainers at the feast, eulogizing their fallen heroes, exalting great rulers, raiding the underworld of their myths in the *Mabinogion,* and devising a highly elaborate and unique formal metric. The classical convention of a single theme was fractured in their poetic design. The poems show a concentric architecture, shaped uncannily like the stone rings under the forts where they fought with more courage than luck. Bardic glory was a deep element in the history of Wales; Welsh law granted a special reward to the poet who took part in the battle he celebrated. The names of the poets themselves — Taliesin, Aneirin, and Merlin — merge with the necromancers of Arthurian legend who know both past and future.

In Anglo-Saxon England, the bard was a *scop,* a "maker" or "shaper." As in the Celtic traditions, the poet was both historian and holy man, but keeper also of the "word-horde." This narrative and verbal gold included not only the tales of lost battles and dragon-haunted meres from which the heroic-elegiac *Beowulf* springs but also the eloquent testimony to the pain of exile by solitary fate-driven seafarers and wanderers. We have recovered no more than thirty thousand lines of the dazzling debris of Old English poetry. Its varied stock includes the kenning (a poetic convention in which the sea is called the "whale-road") gnomic statements, runes, and riddles posed from a nonhuman point of view. The technical accomplishment of Anglo-Saxon metric still astonishes with its alliteration and almost inimitable strophic base, reminiscent of the slow pull and push of the oar. But the kenning, with its figurative use of language, may be the real bedrock of the conjuring, allusive, and layered game of English language poetry.

The life of Latin poetry continued past the collapse of the empire, receiving a new lease in Christian hymns, and another powerful twelfth-century transfusion from light verse. The manuscript of the *Carmina Burana* houses a famous collection from the Goliardic poets. The generic name for this cluster of learned vagabonds who satirized authority and celebrated drink and subversion comes from both the Latin word for gluttony and the name of the biblical giant Goliath, a lasting symbol of wickedness. These wandering scholars flouted one particular convention with a singular flamboyance: the rules of classical Latin prosody. Robert Frost celebrated their most striking innovation when he wrote how the Goliards "led old Latin verse to rhyme / And to forget the ancient lengths of time, / And so began the modern world for us."

The use of rhyme came with a natural grace to the pre-Islamic poets of Arabia in the verse form of the *qaṣīda*, sung to some traditional tune before a Bedouin audience that clapped its hands in time. In the *qaṣīda*, a three-part ode, the poet typically visits an abandoned campsite to lament the departure of a the girl he loves, remembers his journey on camelback in search of her through a wilderness of sandstorms and desert flowers, and closes with a eulogy on a wealthy neighbor. The poem, each line in the Arabic original ending in the same rhyme, is a string of beads, or *mu'allaqah*, in a necklace "chained by experiences both psychological and lyrical."

Chivalric themes of honor, revenge, and the shifts of fate gradually made their way to Spain, Italy, and the southern Mediterranean, suggesting a striking affinity between the early Arabic ode and the later accomplishment of the European Middle Ages and the Renaissance. The early-sixth-century work of one of the greatest of these Arabic poets, Imr El-Qais, known as "The Errant King," is at home with the poetry of a Europe where, half a millennium later, an anonymous Latin *alba*—a dawn song to wake sleeping lovers—included in this section, contains in its margin a refrain scrawled in the speech of the Provençal troubadours, early evidence of a poetic language about to be born.

K. W.

✎ 1

INDIA: THE GOLDEN AGE OF COURTLY VERSE

Tamil

✎ Tiruvalluvar (c. 500)

From THE KURAL

The Gift of Children

No finer gift could come to man,
Among all the goods he might obtain,
Than to have children who are able
To learn the lessons that are needful.

If one has children
of blameless character,
He will not reap
The fruits of evil deeds
Even in seven rebirths.

Sweeter than ambrosia
are the hands of little children
held up for food.

Sweet is the music of flute and lute
Only to those who know not the melody
Of their little ones' prattle.

Among mankind in all the world
The thing which causes joy
Is, that one's own sons should be
More learned than one's self.

If you ask,
What is a father's reward?
It is that they who note
The learning of the son
Will ask, "What deeds of merit
Has the father done,
To reap from Karma
So fine a fruit?"

Learning

Be thorough in your scholarship,
And let the lessons learned
Govern all your life.

Only the wise have real eyes.
But the foolish man
Has two sores in the sockets
Where his eyes should be.

The scholar is famous because
All like to associate with him.
They languish
When they cannot see him.

As the poor man stands humbly
In the presence of the wealthy,
So the noble will seek knowledge
From men of learning.
They who crave not knowledge
Will remain ignoble.

As the water of a well increases
In proportion to the amount drawn,
So learning increases
With the effort put forth.

Highest of all riches
Is the wealth of learning;
All other wealth will perish.

Kindness and Generosity

Greatest of all forms of wealth
Is the wealth of kindness.
Material goods are riches
To fools only.

They who seek
The virtue of kindness
Must practise it.

It will be found
That kindness should be shown
To all life upon the earth.

They whose minds
Are filled with kindness
Will never enter
A world dark with woes.

No fearful evils
Will e'er overtake
Him who protects
All living beings
And is kind to them.

The wise say that men
Who do cruel deeds
Are those who neglected virtue
And forgot the troubles
Which came to them in consequence.

They who became poor
Because of evil deeds
Can attain prosperity
After fulfilling their destiny.
But unkind folk will perish
And never become great.

Emmons E. White

ᏋᎾ Nakkirar (c. 700)

From THE GUIDE TO LORD MURUKAN

The Shaman and the Red God

The possessed shaman with the spear
wears wreaths of green leaves
        with aromatic nuts between them
and beautiful long pepper,
        wild jasmine and the three-lobed
                white nightshade;

his jungle tribes
        have chests bright with sandal;
the strong-bowed warriors
        in their mountain village
drink with their kin
sweet liquor, honey brew

aged in long bamboos,
they dance rough dances
        hand in hand
                to the beat of small
                        hillside drums;

the women
wear wreaths of buds
        fingered and forced to blossom
                so they smell differently,
wear garlands
        from the pools on the hill
                all woven into chains,

cannabis leaves
        in their dense hair,

white clusters
        from a sacred *katampu* tree
        red-trunked and flowering,
arrayed between large cool leaves
        for the male beetle to suck at,

in leaf-skirts
        shaking
        on their jeweled mounds of venus,
and their gait sways with the innocence
        of peacocks;

the shaman
is the Red One himself,
is in red robes;

young leaf of the red-trunk *aśoka*
flutters in his ears;

He wears a coat of mail,
        a warrior band on his ankle,
                a wreath of scarlet ixora;

has a flute,
        a horn,
        several small instruments
        of music;

for vehicles
        he has a ram,
        a peacock;

a faultless rooster
        on his banner;

the Tall One
   with bracelets on his arms,
   with a bevy of girls, voices
      like lutestrings,

a cloth
cool-looking above the waist-band
tied so it hangs
all the way to the ground;

his hands large
   as drumheads
   hold gently
     several soft-shouldered
      fawnlike women;

he gives them proper places
   and he dances
   on the hills:

and all such things happen
because
of His being
there.

And not only there.

             A. K. Ramanujan

Sanskrit

Kalidasa (c. 450–500)

From THE CLOUD MESSENGER

1

High on the Mount of Rama a yaksha* dwelt, who for
   neglect of duty
  Had lost his great estate, sentenced by his Lord to
   a year of exile;
  Grievous with separation from his dear wife, he stayed
   in hermit groves
  Of gentle shade trees and waters hallowed by the baths
   of Janaka's child.

---

*[yaksha: A nature deity.]

2

On this peak the lovelorn yaksha spent some months
    without his mate;
  The fall of the golden bracelet bared his wasted arm.
    It was the end of Ashadha,
And on that day he saw a cloud embracing the crest,
  Arresting as an elephant stooping to strike a stream-bank
    in play.

3

Before that fountain-head of yearning, Kubera's
    henchman stood
  With an effort restraining his tears, and brooded long.
Descrying a cloud, even a glad man's heart becomes disturbed;
  How much more if she who longs to cling to his neck
    is far away!

4

The rains now at hand, seeking to sustain the life of
    his beloved,
  He thought to induce that cloud to carry her news of
    his welfare;
With fresh kutaja blooms he tendered it the guest-offering
  And with loving heart spoke affectionate words of welcome.

5

Blended of mist, light, water, and wind, what could
    a message mean to a cloud,
  That only the penetrating senses of the living can convey?
Heedless of this, in headlong eagerness, the yaksha shaped
    his prayer;
  For those who are sick with love make humble request of
    sentient and insentient alike.

6

Born in the noblest lineage of clouds, renowned throughout
    the world,
  I know thee for Indra's minister and man, taking what
    shape thou wilt;
Far from my wife by fate's decree, to thee I make entreaty;
  Better vain pleas to the worthy, than to the vulgar, those
    which gain their goal!

7

Thou art a shelter for the burning, the distressed; so, Cloud,
    to my dear one
  Bear a message from me, lonely by Kubera's displeasure.
Go to Alaka, home of the yaksha-lords; its palaces gleam

With moonlight from the head of Shiva, who dwells in an
    outlying park.

12

Embrace and bid farewell to thy dear friend, this lofty mountain,
    Marked on its girdling slopes by Rama's feet adored of men,
Which time and again, in its reunion with thee, displays its love,
    Sending up a burning mist of tears born of long separation.

13

Listen, now, while I describe a path fitting for thy
      journey; thereafter,
    O Cloud, thou shalt hear my message, a worthy draught
      for thine ears.
On this path shalt thou go, resting thy foot on mountains
      whenever weary;
    Whenever spent, drinking the pure waters of fresh streams.

22

Though quickly thou wouldst go for my beloved's sake, my
      friend, I fancy
    Thou mightst delay on this peak and that, fragrant with
      blooming kakubhas,
As peacocks receiving thy visit utter loud cries of welcome
    With love-moistened eyes. Still continue O Cloud, and
      hasten on.

34

Even if thou comest, O Cloud, at another hour to Mahakala,
    Linger there till the sun has passed beyond the range of sight;
By serving as praiseworthy drum at the evening worship
      of Shiva
    Thou shalt attain the perfect reward of thy
      deep-rumbling thunder.

35

There the temple girls, cinctures tinkling with the dance-steps,
      their hands weary
    With the yak-tail fans they gracefully wave, the handle-rings
      studded with bright gems,
Receiving the first drops of thy rain, balm to the marks
      of fingernails,
    Will cast on thee sidelong glances, extending like a row of bees.

37

There, on behalf of women who go to their lovers' dwellings
      by night
    On the king's highway where sight is sealed by darkness a

needle might pierce,
Brighten the ground with lightning smooth as the
        gold-proving touchstone,
   And, since they are timid, let no thunder roar as thy rain
        pelts down.

38

Sojourning that night on some housetop where doves
        are asleep,
   While thy wife, the lightning, is exhausted by
        long-lasting play,
When the sun appears, my friend, resume thy further journey;
   One who makes a friend's need his sworn duty surely does
        not linger.

63

Once seen, thou, who movest unrestrained, wilt not fail to
        know Alaka again;
   Her Ganges-garment falls on that mountain's lap, as on
        a lover's;
At your season she wears on her tall mansions a mass of
        clouds shedding water,
   As a loving woman wears her tresses confined by a
        network of pearls.

64

The palaces there compare with thee in many varied ways:
   Thou hast the lightning, they playful women; thou the
        rainbow, they have paintings;
Thou hast the smooth deep thunder, they tambourines
        beaten at concerts;
   Thou containest waterdrops, they the gemmed pavements;
        thou art lofty, their roofs touch the sky.

71

Our home is there to the north of Kubera's palace,
   Well-marked from afar by its gateway arch as lovely as
        the rainbow,
Near which our "adopted son" has been nurtured by
        my beloved —
   A young coral tree, bending its blossom clusters within
        reach of the hands.

75

And between them is a golden roosting rod with crystal tablet,
   Surrounded at its base with gems the color of unripe
        bamboo shoots,

On which a peacock, friend to you clouds, settles at close of day
  After my love has made it dance, clapping her hands with
    sweetly tinkling bracelets.

78

Slender, nut-brown, with tapering teeth, her lip like a ripe
  red fruit,
  Slight in the waist, her eye like a timid doe, with deep-set
    navel,
Slow-moving from weight of hips, a little stooped with her
  full breasts,
  Thou wilt find there one who shall seem the Creator's
    masterwork among women.

80

Surely the eyes of my beloved are swollen with
  passionate weeping,
  And the hue of her lip now changed by the heat of her sighs;
Resting on her hand and half-hidden by her drooping locks,
  Her face wears the sad look of the moon when thy approach
    eclipses its beauty.

85

Thou wilt find her wasted with care, flung down on one side
  on her lonely mat
  Like the shape of the moon on the eastern horizon with but
    one slim sector left;
The night that passed like a flash with me in the joys she
  yearns for,
  She now finds long in her solitude and spends in burning tears.

90

From this I know that the heart of thy friend's wife is stored
  with love for me,
  That I remember her in this very mood at our first parting.
Truly it is not my self-conceit which makes me extravagant;
  All I have said, my brother, will soon be revealed to thine eyes.

93

If at this time, O Cloud, she should have found the happiness
  of sleep,
  Wait in attendance on her for a single night-watch, abstaining
    from thunder,
Lest, when she has succeeded in finding me, her lover, in a dream,
  Her close embrace, arms entwined like tendrils, should
    suddenly slip from my neck.

94

When she has been refreshed (and the newly opened jasmine
     clusters too),
  Arouse her with a breeze, cooled with thine own drops of water,
And while her gaze is riveted on the window filled by thee,
     containing thy lightning,
  Begin thine address to the noble lady with deep
     thunderous words.

95

Know that I, a cloud, the dear friend of thy husband—no
     widow thou!—
  Am come to deliver his message that is fixed in my heart;
I who with deep yet gentle sounds speed on their way the throngs
  Of weary wanderers who yearn to loosen the wifely braids.

96

At these words she, like Sita lifting her eyes to Hanumant,
  Her heart consoled in its longing, will gaze at thee and pay
     thee her respect,
Whereupon, my friend, she will hearken, all attentive.
     To a woman,
  Tidings brought by a friend from her true love are but
     little less than reunion.

97

To her, both because I bid thee, sir, and for thine
     own satisfaction,
  Speak thus: *Thy consort dwells in the hermit-groves of*
     Rama's Mount;
He lives; but parted, he would know if all is well with thee, my lady.
  This is the prime hope of mortals; calamity comes so readily!

98

With his body thy body he enters; all-haggard body with haggard;
  Fevered with intensely fevered; tear-flowing with tearful;
     incessantly eager
With eager; hotly sighing with yet more abundantly sighing;
  In his thoughts, far distant as he is, and the way barred by
     adverse fate.

99

Who, before thy girl companions, loved to say in thine ear
  Even what might no doubt have been said aloud, for he craved
     to touch thy face,
He, gone beyond the range of hearing and hidden from thine eyes,
  By my mouth sends thee this message, its words fashioned
     of his longing.

104

I would that the night's long watches were compressed as a
    single moment!
I would, too, that the day were at all times mild and balmy!
These prayers of my heart, dancing-eyed girl, so hard to achieve,
    Are rendered hopeless by the fierce-burning anguish of exile
        from thee.

105

See, do I not bear myself up by my self alone, musing on
    many thoughts?
So shouldst thou too, my sweet, yield not wholly to despondence;
Does any one meet with perpetual happiness? Or never-
    ending sorrow?
Downward and upward goes our luck, like the rim of a wheel.

106

When Vishnu has risen from his serpent couch, my curse shall end;
    Close thine eyes and endure the four months that yet remain.
Afterwards in nights of full autumn moonlight, we twain shall enjoy
    Divers heart's desires, imagined while we were parted.

107

And further he said: Once, clinging to my neck on the couch,
    Thou didst fall asleep and awake with a cry, weeping a little;
And when I asked thee over and again, thou saidst, with
    furtive smile,
Wretch, I saw thee in a dream, caressing some woman or other!

108

Know, since I have given this token, that I am in good health,
    And be not mistrustful of me, black-eyed one, from idle report
Which says that affection is apt to wane in separation; for if
    not satisfied,
Passion for the dear one waxes and becomes a mountain
    of love.

109

I hope, fair sir, thou wilt essay this friendly service for me?
    Clearly I need no reply to know thee worthy of my trust.
Without a word thou givest water on request to chataka-birds;
    For the noble make answer to suppliants simply by fulfilling
        their desires.

110

Having granted me this boon, though my mode of prayer
    be unwonted,

Either through friendship or sympathy with me, knowing
   my bereavement,
Then go, O Cloud, wherever thou wilt, as the monsoon augments
   thy majesty;
And mayst thou never, even for a moment, be thus parted
   from the lightning!

Franklin and Eleanor Edgerton

ᕦ Bhartrihari (c. 650)

A MAN MAY TEAR A JEWEL

A man may tear a jewel
From a sea monster's jaws,
Cross a tumultuous sea
Of raging tides,
Or twine garlandwise
A wrathful serpent on his head.
But no man can alter
The thoughts of an obstinate fool.

Barbara Stoler Miller

APATHY IS ASCRIBED TO THE MODEST MAN

Apathy is ascribed to the modest man,
Fraud to the devout,
Hypocrisy to the pure,
Cruelty to the hero,
Hostility to the anchorite,
Fawning to the courteous man,
Arrogance to the majestic,
Garrulity to the eloquent,
Impotence to the faithful.
Does there exist any virtue
Which escapes
The slander of wicked men?

Barbara Stoler Miller

A BALD-HEADED MAN

A bald-headed man, his pate
Pained by the rays of the sun,

Desiring a shady spot,
Went by fate to the foot
Of a wood-apple tree.
Alas, there his head
Was smashed by a large
Falling fruit.
Verily,
Where goes a man deserted by fortune,
There do adversities follow him.

Barbara Stoler Miller

SWEET MAID

Sweet maid, you perform a singular feat
With the archer's bow.
You pierce hearts without arrows,
But with strands of your beauty.

Barbara Stoler Miller

WHILE HIS BODY'S VIGOR IS WHOLE

While his body's vigor is whole
And old age is remote;
While his sensuous powers are unimpaired
And life not yet exhausted;
Only then would a wise man
Strive to perfect his soul.
Why attempt to dig a well
When the house is already burning?

Barbara Stoler Miller

From THE VIDYAKARÀ ANTHOLOGY (C. 600–1100)

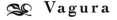 **Vagura**

A LOVE POEM

Bracelets jingle every time
she lifts her arm, and as her dress
falls open, one can see a line
of nailmarks traced upon her breast.
The pestle lifted once again—

happy in her lotus hands —
her necklace beads go swinging free . . .
How beautiful is the threshing girl.

Edwin Gerow and Peter Dent

 ## Vidya

A LOVE POEM

The luck is yours that you can talk about
your lover's playful glance, his words and touch.
For me, I swear that once he puts his hand
upon my girdle, I remember nothing.

Edwin Gerow and Peter Dent

ON MAKESHIFT BEDDING

On makeshift
bedding in the cucumber
garden, the hilltribe
girl clings to
her exhausted lover.
Limbs still chaffing
with pleasure, dissolving
against him she
now and again with
one bare foot
jostles a shell necklace
that hangs from a
vine on the fence —
rattling it
through the night,
scaring the jackals off.

Andrew Schelling

FATE IS A CRUEL AND PROFICIENT POTTER

Fate is a cruel
and proficient potter,
my friend. Forcibly
spinning the wheel

of anxiety, he lifts misfortune
like a cutting tool. Now,
having kneaded my heart
like a lump of clay,
he lays it on his
wheel and gives a spin.
What he intends to produce
I cannot tell.

Andrew Schelling

AND WHAT OF THOSE ARBORS OF VINES

And what of those
arbors of vines
that grow where the river
drops away from Kalinda Mountain?
They conspired in the love
games of herding girls
and watched over the veiled
affairs of Radha.
Now that the days
are gone when I cut their
tendrils, and laid them
down for couches of love,
I wonder if they've
grown brittle and if
their splendid blue flowers
have dried up.

Andrew Schelling

✌ Anonymous

NEXT MORNING

Next morning
when a damnfool parrot—
right before her parents—
starts to mimic
last night's cries of love,
the girl leaps up,
blushing,
claps her hands to
start the children dancing—
jangle of her bracelets

drowning out
the parrot's calls

Andrew Schelling

✿ Anonymous

MY HUSBAND, BEFORE LEAVING

My husband
before leaving on a journey
is still in the house speaking
to the gods and already
separation is climbing like
bad monkeys to the windows.

J. Moussaieff Masson and W. S. Merwin

✿ Anonymous

A LONG TIME BACK

A long time back
when we were first in love
our bodies were always as one
later you became
my dearest
and I became your dearest
alas
and now beloved lord
you are my husband
I am your wife
our hearts must be
as hard as the middle of thunder
now what have I to live for

J. Moussaieff Masson and W. S. Merwin

✿ King Amaru (c. 700)

LYING IN BED

Lying in bed turned away from each other, holding their
    breath, without a word,
though their love was still strong, the weight of
    pride keeping them from making peace,

then a trembling glance out of the side of an eye
   of each met
and the coldness broken with laughter, the two of them
   quickly, closely embraced.

Henry Heifetz

YOU WITH YOUR BEAUTIFUL SWAYING WALK

"You with your beautiful swaying walk, where
 are you going near midnight?"
"To my lover who is worth more than my own
 breath to me."
"But you're so young. How can you be walking
 alone without any fear?"
"Isn't the god of love with his arrows
 always by my side?"

Henry Heifetz

MUCH TOO CLOSE

Much too close to bear his eyes
I turn my own down to my lap.
I do not try to hear
the many soft words in his breath.
I make my hands stop both my ears,
then cup my cheeks that burn
at words he does not even speak.
I try so hard. But now
I feel my dress undoing me,
what do I do?

Peter Dent

❧ Anonymous (c. 750)

COSMOLOGY

The goddess Laksmi
loves to make love to Vishnu
from on top
looking down she sees in his navel
a lotus
and on it Brahma the god
but she can't bear to stop

so she puts her hand
over Vishnu's right eye
which is the sun
and night comes on
and the lotus closes
with Brahma inside

W. S. Merwin and J. Moussieff Masson

҈ 2

CHINA: THREE KINGDOMS PERIOD THROUGH THE T'ANG DYNASTY; KOREA: EARLY POETRY IN THE CHINESE STYLE

Chinese

҈ Juan Chi (210–263)

THE TEN SUNS RISE IN THE EAST

The Ten Suns rise in the East,
their drivers whip them onward, thousands of *li.*
Crossing the sky, they shine down upon China,
suddenly, they sink in the West.

Who says their lustre endures?

That is why the wise man drifts along the river of time.

What is passing cannot remain.
Such are the thorns and thistles of this world.

Thousands of years are just a day.
Life is a dinner-party. Time passes.

Right and wrong, gain and loss —
how can it be worthwhile to vex oneself?

When desire for profit or knowledge come to an end,
so will the sadness of Man.

Graham Hartill and Wu Fusheng

THE MUJIN FLOWERS BLOSSOM ON THE ROLLING GRAVES

The Mujin flowers blossom on the rolling graves,
these hills are lovely, and luminous.
The radiant sun goes down into the trees
as one by one, the flowers fall.
Outside my window a cricket is singing,
transient thing in the thorn.

Mayflies play for their three days,
their wings are as slender and pretty as feathers.
Who are their costumes designed for?
To decorate their little moment.

The life of Man is also brief.
Our hearts know it. We should
    try our best to live.

Graham Hartill and Wu Fusheng

℈ Lu Chi (261–303)

From THE ART OF WRITING

4. The Satisfaction

The pleasure a writer knows is the pleasure all sages enjoy.

Out of non-being, being is born; out of silence, the writer produces a song.

In a single yard of silk, infinite space is found; language is a deluge from one small corner of the heart.

The net of images is cast wider and wider; thoughts search more and more deeply.

The writer spreads the fragrance of new flowers, an abundance of sprouting buds.

Laughing winds lift up the metaphor; clouds rise from a forest of writing brushes.

    Sam Hamill

7. The Music of Words

Like shifting forms in the world
literature takes on many shapes and styles
as the poet crafts ideas
into elegant language.
Let the five tones be used in turn
like five colors in harmony,
and though they vanish and reappear inconstantly

and though it seems a hard path to climb
if you know the basic laws of order and change
your thoughts like a river will flow in channels.
But if your words misfire
it's like grabbing the tail to lead the head:
clear writing turns to mud
like painting yellow on a base of black.

Tony Barnstone and Chou Ping

9. The Riding Crop

Sometimes your writing is a lush web of fine thoughts
that undercut each other and muffle the theme;
when you reach the pole there's nowhere else to go,
more becomes less if you try to improve what's done.
A powerful phrase at the crucial point
will whip the writing like a horse and make it gallop;
though all the other words are in place
they wait for the crop to run a good race.
A whip is always more help than harm;
stop revising when you've got it right.

Tony Barnstone and Chou Ping

Attributed to the Courtesan Tzu Yeh (c. 350–500)

"MIDNIGHT" SONGS

1

It is night again
I let down my silken hair
Over my shoulders
And open my thighs
Over my lover.
"Tell me, is there any part of me
That is not lovable?"

2

I had not fastened my sash over my gown,
When you asked me to look out the window.
If my skirt fluttered open,
Blame the Spring wind.

3

The bare branches tremble
In the sudden breeze.

The twilight deepens.
My lover loves me,
And I am proud of my young beauty.

Kenneth Rexroth and Ling Chung

4

When I started wanting
to know that man,
I hoped our coupled hearts
would be like one.

Silk thoughts threaded
on a broken loom —
who'd have known
the tangled snarls to come?

5

So soon. Today, love, we
part. And our re-
union — when
will that time come?

A bright lamp
shines on an empty place,
in sorrow and longing:
not yet, not yet, not
yet.

Jeanne Larsen

✍ T'ao Ch'ien (T'ao Yüan-ming, 365–427)

POEM ON RETURNING TO DWELL IN THE COUNTRY

In youth I had nothing
    that matched the vulgar tone,
For my nature always
    loved the hills and mountains.
Inadvertently I fell
    into the Dusty Net,
Once having gone
    it was more than thirteen years.
The tame bird
    longs for his old forest —

The fish in the house-pond
    thinks of his ancient pool.
I too will break the soil
    at the edge of the southern moor,
I will guard simplicity
    and return to my fields and garden.
My land and house —
    a little more than ten acres,
In the thatched cottage —
    only eight or nine rooms:
Elms and willows
    shade the back verandah,
Peach and plum trees
    in rows before the hall.
Hazy and dimly seen
    a village in the distance,
Close in the foreground
    the smoke of neighbours' houses.
A dog barks
    amidst the deep lanes,
A cock is crowing
    atop a mulberry tree.
No dust and confusion
    within my doors and courtyard;
In the empty rooms,
    more than sufficient leisure.
Too long I was held
    within the barred cage.
Now I am able
    to return again to Nature.

William Acker

WRITTEN WHILE DRUNK

I built my house near where others dwell,
And yet there is no clamour of carriages and horses.
You ask of me "How can this be so?"
"When the heart is far the place of itself is distant."
I pluck chrysanthemums under the eastern hedge,
And gaze afar towards the southern mountains.
The mountain air is fine at evening of the day
And flying birds return together homewards.
Within these things there is a hint of Truth,
But when I start to tell it, I cannot find the words.

William Acker

UNTITLED

Great men want the four seas. I've only
wanted old age to come unnoticed like

this. My family together in one place,
kids and grandkids looking after each

other still, I linger out mornings over
koto and wine, the winejar never dry.

My clothes a shambles, exhausting every
joy, I sleep late now, and nod off early.

Why live like all those fine men, hearts
stuffed with fire and ice to the end,

their hundred-year return to the grave
nothing but an empty path of ambition?

David Hinton

ॐ Pao Chao (414–466)

THE RUINED CITY

The immense plain
    runs south to the foamy waves of the sea
    and north to the purple passes of the Great Wall.
In it
    canals are cut through the valleys;
    and rivers and roads
    lead to every corner.
In its golden past,
    axles of chariots and carts
    often rubbed against each other
    like men's shoulders.
Shops and houses stood row upon row
And laughter and songs rose up from them.
Glittering and white were the salt fields;
Gloomy and blue were the copper mines.
Wealth and talents
And cavalry and infantry
Reinforced the strict and elaborate
Regulations and laws.
Winding moats and lofty walls
Were dug and built, to ensure
That prosperity would long endure.
People were busy working

On palaces and battlements
And ships and beacon stations
Up and down, far and wide
At all places.
Magnets were installed at mountain passes;
Red lacquer was applied on doors and gates.
The strongholds and fortresses
    would see to it
That for a myriad generations
    the family's rule should last.
But after five centuries or three dynasties
The land was divided like a melon,
Or shared like beans.

Duckweed flourishes in the wells
And brambles block the roads.
Skunks and snakes dwell on sacred altars
While muskdeer and squirrels quarrel on marble steps.
In rain and wind,
Wood elves, mountain ghosts,
Wild rats and foxes
    Yawp and scream from dusk to dawn.
Hungry hawks clash their beaks
As cold owls frighten the chicks in their nests.
Tigers and leopards hide and wait
    for a draught of blood
    and a feast of flesh.
Fallen tree-trunks lie lifelessly across
Those once busy highways.
Aspens have long ceased to rustle
And grass dies yellow
In this harsh frosty air
Which grows into a cruelly cold wind.
A solitary reed shakes and twists,
And grains of sand, like startled birds,
    are looking for a safe place to settle.
Bushes and creepers, confused and tangled,
    seem to know no boundaries.
They pull down walls
And fill up moats.
And beyond a thousand miles
Only brown dust flies.
Deep in my thoughts, I sit down and listen
To this awesome silence.
Behind the painted doors and embroidered curtains
There used to be music and dancing.
Hunting or fishing parties were held
In the emerald forests or beside the marble pools.
The melodies from various states
And works of art and rare fish and horses
Are all now dead and buried.

The young girls from east and south
Smooth as silk, fragrant as orchids
White as jade with their lips red,
Now lie beneath the dreary stones and barren earth.
The greatest displeasure of the largest number
Is the law of nature.
For this ruined city,
I play the lute and sing:
"As the north wind hurries on,
    the battlements freeze.
They tower over the plain
    where there are neither roads nor field-paths.
For a thousand years and a myriad generations,
I shall watch you to the end in silence."

                        C. J. Chen and Michael Bullock

✑ Anonymous (c. 450)

ON THE SLOPE OF HUA MOUNTAIN

O Flowery Mountain slopes,
Now that my lover is dead
How can I live out my lonely life?

O my lover, if you still love me,
Open your sealed coffin for me,
And take me with you.

Why is it, with the world full of men
I am desolated, and long only for you?

I wish I were the ivy,
Climbing high in the pine tree,
And you were the moving clouds,
So we could see each other
As you pass by.

                        Kenneth Rexroth and Ling Chung

✑ Anonymous (c. 500)

MU-LAN

Tsiek tsiek and again *tsiek tsiek*,
Mu-lan weaves, facing the door.
You don't hear the shuttle's sound,
You only hear Daughter's sighs.

They ask Daughter who's in her heart,
They ask Daughter who's on her mind.
"No one is in Daughter's heart,
No one is on Daughter's mind.
Last night I saw the draft posters,
The Khan is calling many troops,
The army list is in twelve scrolls,
On every scroll there's Father's name.
Father has no grown-up son,
Mu-lan has no elder brother.
I want to buy a saddle and horse,
And serve in the army in Father's place."

In the East Market she buys a spirited horse,
In the West Market she buys a saddle,
In the South Market she buys a bridle,
In the North Market she buys a long whip.
At dawn she takes leave of Father and Mother,
In the evening camps on the Yellow River's bank.
She doesn't hear the sound of Father and Mother calling,
She only hears the Yellow River's flowing water cry *tsien tsien.*

At dawn she takes leave of the Yellow River,
In the evening she arrives at Black Mountain.
She doesn't hear the sound of Father and Mother calling,
She only hears Mount Yen's nomad horses cry *tsiu tsiu.*
She goes ten thousand miles on the business of war,
She crosses passes and mountains like flying.
Northern gusts carry the rattle of army pots,
Chilly light shines on iron armor.
Generals die in a hundred battles,
Stout soldiers return after ten years.

On her return she sees the Son of Heaven,
The Son of Heaven sits in the Splendid Hall.
He gives out promotions in twelve ranks
And prizes of a hundred thousand and more.
The Khan asks her what she desires.
"Mu-lan has no use for a minister's post.
I wish to ride a swift mount
To take me back to my home."

When Father and Mother hear Daughter is coming
They go outside the wall to meet her, leaning on each other.
When Elder Sister hears Younger Sister is coming
She fixes her rouge, facing the door.
When Little Brother hears Elder Sister is coming
He whets the knife, quick quick, for pig and sheep.
"I open the door to my east chamber,
I sit on my couch in the west room,
I take off my wartime gown

And put on my old-time clothes."
Facing the window she fixes her cloudlike hair,
Hanging up a mirror she dabs on yellow flower-powder.
She goes out the door and sees her comrades.
Her comrades are all amazed and perplexed.
Traveling together for twelve years
They didn't know Mu-lan was a girl.
"The he-hare's feet go hop and skip,
The she-hare's eyes are muddled and fuddled.
Two hares running side by side close to the ground,
How can they tell if I am he or she?"

Hans H. Frankel

Anonymous (c. 550)

OUR LITTLE SISTER IS WORRIED

Our little sister is worried.
How long should she wait
To get married?
She has often seen the wind
Blow the peach petals from the trees.
She has never seen it
Blow them back on the branches.

Kenneth Rexroth

Han Shan (c. 680–760)

From COLD MOUNTAIN POEMS

There's a Naked Bug at Cold Mountain

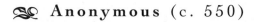

There's a naked bug at Cold Mountain
With a white body and a black head.
His hand holds two book-scrolls,
One the Way and one its Power.
His shack's got no pots or oven,
He goes for a walk with his shirt and pants askew.
But he always carries the sword of wisdom:
He means to cut down senseless craving.

Gary Snyder

Cold Mountain Is a House

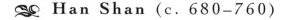

Cold Mountain is a house
Without beams or walls.

The six doors left and right are open
The hall is blue sky.
The rooms all vacant and vague
The east wall beats on the west wall
At the center nothing.
Borrowers don't bother me
In the cold I build a little fire
When I'm hungry I boil up some greens.
I've got no use for the kulak
With his big barn and pasture —
He just sets up a prison for himself.
Once in he can't get out.
Think it over —
You know it might happen to you.

Gary Snyder

I Live in a Little Country Village

I live in a little country village,
Where everyone praises me as someone without compare.

But yesterday I went down to the city,
Where, to the contrary, I was looked up and down by the *dogs!*

Some complained that my trousers were too tight;
Others said that my shirt was a little too long!

If someone could draw off the eyes of the hawk,
Little sparrows could dance with dignity and grace!

Robert Henricks

In Other Days

In other days, I was poor enough to suit,
But now I freeze in utter poverty:
I make a deal — it doesn't quite work out,
I take the road — it ends in misery;
I walk in the mud — my feet slip out from under,
I sit in the shrine — my belly gripes at me —
Since I lost the parti-colored cat,
Around the rice-jar, rats wait hungrily

E. Bruce Brooks

People Ask about Cold Mountain Way

People ask about Cold Mountain Way;
There's no Cold Mountain Road that goes straight through:
By summer, lingering cold is not dispersed,
By fog, the risen sun is screened from view;
So how did one like me get onto it?
In our hearts, I'm not the same as you —

If in your heart you should become like me,
Then you could reach the center of it too

E. Bruce Brooks

℘ **Wang Wei** (699–761)

SONG OF PEACH TREE SPRING

My fishing boat sails the river. I love spring
   in the mountains.
Peach blossoms crowd the river on both banks
   as far as sight.
Sitting in the boat, I look at red trees and forget
   how far I've come.
Drifting to the green river's end, I see no one.

Hidden paths winding into the mountain's mouth.
Suddenly the hills open into a plain
and I see a distant mingling of trees and clouds.
Then coming near I make out houses, bamboo groves
   and flowers
where woodcutters still have names from Han times
and people wear Qin dynasty clothing.
They used to live where I do, at Wuling Spring,
but now they cultivate rice and gardens
   beyond the real world.

Clarity of the moon brings quiet to windows under
   the pines.
Chickens and dogs riot when sun rises out of clouds.
Shocked to see an outsider, the crowd sticks to me,
competing to drag me to their homes and ask
   about their native places.
At daybreak in the alleys they sweep flowers from
   their doorways.
By dusk woodcutters and fishermen return,
   floating in on the waves.

They came here to escape the chaotic world.
Deathless now, they have no hunger to return.
Amid these gorges, what do they know of the world?
In our illusion we see only empty clouds and mountain.
I don't know that paradise is hard to find,
and my heart of dust still longs for home.

Leaving it all, I can't guess how many mountains
   and waters lie behind me,
and am haunted by an obsession to return.
I was sure I could find my way back, the secret paths

again.
How could I know the mountains and ravines would
    change?
I remember only going deep into the hills.
At times the green river touched cloud forests.
With spring, peach blossom water is everywhere,
but I never find that holy source again.

Tony Barnstone, Willis Barnstone, and Xu Haixin

SPRING NIGHT AT BAMBOO PAVILLION, PRESENTING A POEM TO SUBPREFECT QIAN ABOUT HIS STAYING FOR GOOD IN BLUE FIELD MOUNTAINS

Night is quiet. All creatures are resting.
Beyond the forest, occasionally a dog barks.
I remember living here in the mountains,
my only neighbors far west of the ravine.
One morning you came here. I envy you.
Back there we have carriages and official hats.
You prefer picking ferns in this unknown place.

Tony Barnstone, Willis Barnstone, and Xu Haixin

ARRIVING AT BA GORGE IN THE MORNING

Daybreak in late spring, I embark at Ba Gorge,
already missing the emperor's city.
A solitary woman washes in the clear river
as many cocks crow into the morning sun.
Junks form a floating market in this land of waters.
A mountain bridge steps over the treetops.
Climbing high, I see thousands of wells
and two bright rivers far below.
Here people use a strange dialect
but birds repeat the sound of my old home.
The sorrow at leaving my city fades
before the old joy of being in new mountains.

Tony Barnstone, Willis Barnstone, and Xu Haixin

WEEPING FOR YING YAO

How many years can a man possess?
In the end he will be formlessness.

Friend, now you are dead
and thousands of things sadden me.
You didn't see your kind mother into the grave
and your daughter is only ten.
From the vast and bleak countryside
comes the tiny sound of weeping.
Floating clouds turn to dark mist
and flying birds lose their voices.
Travelers are miserable
below the lonely white sun.
I recall when you were alive
you asked me how to learn nonbeing.
If only I'd helped you earlier
you wouldn't have died in ignorance.
All your old friends give elegies
recounting your life.
I know I have failed you,
and weep, returning to my thorn gate.

Tony Barnstone, Willis Barnstone, and Xu Haixin

VISITING HSIANG-CHI MONASTERY

I had not known of Hsiang-chi Monastery
When after several miles I entered a cloudy peak.
Beneath ancient trees, an unused path,
Deep in the mountains—from where?—a bell.
Noise from a spring burbles over sharp rocks,
The sun's light chills the dark pines.
At dusk, by the empty curve of the pond,
Meditation to subdue one's poisonous dragon.

Eva Shan Chou

ᘒᙣ Li Po (701–762)

THE ROAD TO SHU IS HARD

A-eee! Shee-yew! Sheeeeee! So dangerous! So high!
The road to Shu is hard, harder than climbing the sky.
Silkworm Thicket and Fishing Duck
Founded their kingdom in the depths of time,
But then for forty-eight thousand years,
No settlers' smoke reached the Ch'in frontier.
Yet west on T'ai-po Mountain, take a bird road there,
You could cross directly to O-mei's brow.
When earth collapsed and the mountain crashed,
the muscled warriors died.

It was after that when the ladders to heaven
were linked together with timber and stone.
            Up above is
the towering pillar where six dragons turn the sun.
            Down below is
the twisting river colliding waves dash into the turns.
The flight of a yellow crane cannot cross it;
Gibbons and monkeys climb in despair.

Green Mud Ridge—coiling, unwinding—
Nine turns in a hundred steps, round pinnacle and snag.
      Touch the Triad, pass the Well Stars,
            look up to gasp and groan.
      Press a hand to calm your chest,
            sit down for a lingering sigh.

I wonder as you travel west, when will you return?
I fear that a road so cragged and high is impossible to climb.
All I see is a mournful bird that cries in an ancient tree,
            And cocks that fly in pursuit of hens,
                  circling through the forest.
Yet again I hear the cuckoo call in the moonlit night—
      sorrow upon the desolate mountain.
The road to Shu is hard, harder than climbing the sky.
Whenever one shall hear this, it wilts his youth away.

Peak after peak missing the sky by not so much as a foot.
Withered pines hang upside-down clinging to vertical walls.
      Flying chutes and raging current,
            how they snarl and storm!
      Pelted cliffs and spinning stones,
            ten thousand chasms thundrous roar!
      The perils—this is the way they are.
      And woe to that man on a road so far—
Oh why, and for what, would he travel here?
Sword Gallery looms above with soaring crags and spires;
            One man at the pass,
            Ten thousand men are barred.
      And if the guards are not our people,
      They can change into jackals and wolves.

      In the morning avoid fierce tigers,
      In the evening avoid long snakes.
      They sharpen teeth for sucking blood;
            The dead are strewn like hemp.
      Let them talk of pleasure in Brocade City,
            The better thing is hurrying home.
The road to Shu is hard, harder than climbing the sky.
Edging back, I gaze to the west, long and deep my sighs.

                                          Elling O. Eide

INSCRIBED ON THE WALL OF HSÜ HSÜAN-PING'S RETREAT

I go along chanting the wayhouse poem
And come to visit the immortal's dwelling.
His lofty tracks are lost on misty ranges,
The Great Void blocked by clouded forests.
I peer into the courtyard deserted and silent,
  I lean on a column to dawdle in vain.
No doubt turned into a far-flying crane,
He'll be back in a thousand years or so.

Elling O. Eide

THE BALLAD OF LONG BANK

Number One

When my hair was first in bangs,
I used to pick flowers and tease from the door.

Then my love would ride out on a bamboo horse
To circle the wellhead and play with green plums.
We lived together in the village of Long Bank,
Two little children without doubt or mistrust.
  At fourteen, I became your wife,
  A bashful face that never could smile;
I drooped my head, faced the dark wall—
  To your thousand calls, not one reply.
At last fifteen, I unfurrowed my brow,
Vowed to stay with you like ashes with dust.
Could you cling to a piling like the man in a flood,
Would I ever be climbing the Spouse-Vigil Tower?
  I was sixteen when you went away
To Rough River Rock in Threatening Gorge;
In the Fifth Month you must not run afoul,
  And cries of gibbons are sad in the sky.
The tracks by the gate where you slowly departed,
  In each one now the moss grows green.
The moss is deep, I can't sweep it away;
  Autumn is early, we have falling leaves.
In the Eighth Month the butterflies came,
  Flew in pairs through the western garden.
When I think of this, my heart starts breaking,
  I sit and grieve, and my face grows old.

Whenever you finally leave Triple Pa,
Send a letter ahead and let us all know.
I'll go out to meet you, not caring how far—
I'll go right down to Long Wind Shore.

Number Two

I remember when I was a single girl
And knew nothing of smoke and dust in the world,
But now having married a Long Bank man,
I'm at Sandy Point to check on the wind.

In the Fifth Month when the south wind rises,
I think of you coming down from Pa-ling.

In the Eighth Month when the west wind starts,
I worry about you departing from Yang-tzu.

With this coming and going, what is my heartache?
There is little of seeing and too much of parting.
You'll be reaching Hsiang-t'an in how many days?
In my dreams I leap over the wind and the waves.

Last night a wild wind went by;
It blew down trees by the riverside.
Everything water and dark without edges,
Where was a place for a traveller to be?

Visitors from the north have included real nobles,
And the whole of the river was filled with red robes.
Evenings they came along shore for their lodging,
And wouldn't move eastward for several days.
I pity myself at fifteen or so,
I had a pink face with peach blossom skin.
Who would be the wife of a merchant man,
To grieve about water and grieve about wind?

Elling O. Eide

SPRING THOUGHTS

When the grass in Yen is still jade thread,
The mulberries of Ch'in are drooping green boughs.
The days when your mind is filled with returning,
Those are the times when my heart is breaking.
But the spring wind and I have been strangers,
What is it doing in my gauze bedcurtains?

Elling O. Eide

FIGHTING SOUTH OF THE WALL

Number One

Last year fighting at the source of the Sang-kan,
This year fighting on the Onion River road,

They have washed their weapons in the waves
on the seas of T'iao-chih,
They have pastured their horses on grass
in the snows of T'ien-shan.
Across ten thousand miles the long campaigns and battles,
The Three Armies completely exhausted and old.

For the Hsiung-nu murder and killing
are the work of plowing;
From of old they have seen only white-bone
and yellow-sand fields.
Where the House of Ch'in built a wall against the barbarians,
The House of Han still has the signal fires burning.

The signal fires burn without ceasing.
The long campaign has no time for ending.
Fighting in the wilds they die in hand to hand combat;
The loser's horses cry and sorrow toward Heaven.
Crows and kites peck at human intestines
And carry them off to hang them from withered trees.
Soldiers are splattered all over the weeds and the grasses,
And being a general is something useless to be.
Then know that weapons are truly the tools of misfortune,
Only used by The Sage when he has no other way.

Number Two

The battlefield is a swirling blur,
The fighting men like swarms of ants;
The air is heavy and the sun-wheel red,
And the brambles are purple with the dye of blood;
And the crows with their beaks full of human flesh
Have stuffed themselves till they cannot fly.
Yesterday's man on top of the wall
Beneath the wall is a ghost today.
Still the banners are like an array of stars;
And the war drums' sound is not yet done;
And out of my family, husbands and sons,
All are there in the sound of the drums.

Elling O. Eide

INSCRIBED AT SUMMIT TEMPLE

The night we stayed at Summit Temple
I could reach up and touch the stars.
We did not dare to talk aloud
For fear of disturbing the men in Heaven.

Elling O. Eide

DRINKING ALONE IN THE MOONLIGHT

Number One

Beneath the blossoms with a pot of wine,
No friends at hand, so I poured alone;
I raised my cup to invite the moon,
Turned to my shadow, and we became three.
Now the moon had never learned about drinking,
And my shadow had merely followed my form,
But I quickly made friends with the moon and my shadow;
To find pleasure in life, make the most of the spring.

Whenever I sang, the moon swayed with me;
Whenever I danced, my shadow went wild.
Drinking, we shared our enjoyment together;
Drunk, then each went off on his own.
But forever agreed on dispassionate revels,
We promised to meet in the far Milky Way.

Number Two

Now, if Heaven didn't love wine,
There wouldn't be a Wine Star in Heaven.
And if Earth didn't love wine,
Earth shouldn't have the town of Wine Spring.
But since Heaven and Earth love wine,
Loving wine is no crime with Heaven.
The light, I hear, is like a sage;
The heavy, they say, is called the worthy.
If I have drunk with the sage and worthy,
What need have I to search for immortals?
Three cups and I've mastered the Way;
A jarful and I am at one with Nature.
A man can get hold of the spirit of drinking,
But no point explaining to those who abstain.

Elling O. Eide

OLD TAI'S WINE SHOP

When Old Tai goes down below,
He may still make Young Springtime brew;
But there's no Li Po on the Terrace of Night,
So who in hell will he sell it to?

Elling O. Eide

FOR MENG HAO-JAN

I love Master Meng.
Free as a flowing breeze,
He is famous
Throughout the world.

In rosy youth, he cast away
Official cap and carriage.
Now, a white-haired elder, he reclines
Amid pines and cloud.

Drunk beneath the moon,
He often attains sagehood.
Lost among the flowers,
He serves no lord.

How can I aspire
to such a high mountain?
Here below, to his clear fragrance,
I bow.

Greg Whincup

LISTENING TO A MONK FROM SHU PLAYING THE LUTE

The monk from Shu with his green lute-case walked
Westward down Emei Shan, and at the sound
Of the first notes he strummed for me I heard
A thousand valleys' rustling pines resound.
My heart was cleansed, as if in flowing water.
In bells of frost I heard the resonance die.
Dusk came unnoticed over the emerald hills
And autumn clouds layered the darkening sky.

Vikram Seth

IN PRAISE OF A GOLD AND SILVER PAINTED SCENE OF THE BUDDHA MANIFESTATION IN THE PURE LAND OF THE WEST, WITH A PREFACE

I hear that west of the golden sky, in the place where the sun sinks away, separated from China by ten trillion Buddhist lands, there is a World of Ultimate Joy. The Buddha of that country has a height of sixty trillion yojanas, as uncountable as the Ganges' sand. The white hairs between His eyebrows curl and turn to the right like five Sumeru mountains, and the light from His eyes is clear and bright like the waters of the four oceans. He sits erect preaching The Law, abiding forever in tranquility.

The lakes there gleam with golden sand; the banks are lined with jewelled trees. Railings and balconies enclose it all, and netting is stretched on every side. Colored glazes and mother-of-pearl from the giant clam decorate the storied halls. From crystal and carnelian comes the splendor of the glittering stairs. All this the sundry Buddhas have affirmed; these are not mere empty words.

This gold and silver painted scene of the manifestation in the Pure Land of the West was erected for her late husband, His Lordship Wei, Governor of Hu Prefecture, by the lady Ch'in of P'ing-i Commandery. Her Ladyship embodies the purity of ice and jade and exemplifies the teaching of the mother's sage-like goodness. In the love and loyalty of the marriage bond, she hopes for him to be lifted up from the dark paths of purgatory, and for the depth of their children's filial devotion to see him perfected in luminous blessing. Thus has she pledged her precious things and sought out famous artisans.

Applying gold they have created the foundation; painting with silver they have supplied the figures. Through the power of the Eight Dharmas, the waves move on the Blue Lotus pools, and fragrant flowers from the seven jewels shine in relief against the golden ground. Whatever is caressed by the refreshing breeze is as if it were producing the five musical notes, so that a hundred and a thousand kinds of sublime music all seem to be set in play.

Be it one who has already expressed the prayer, or one who has not yet expressed the prayer, be it one who has already been born, or one who has not yet been born, devout contemplation for seven days will give him rebirth into that land. Infinite is the power from the merit of this. We may ponder it, but it is hard to explain. In praise I say,

> Looking toward the west where the sun sinks away,
> Behold afar that Face of Great Compassion.
> Eyes pure as the waters of the four oceans,
> His body shines like a mountain of purple gold.

> By diligent contemplation we can surely be reborn,
> Thus the acclaim of Ultimate Joy.
> Mid pearl netting and trees of precious jewels,
> The flowers of Heaven are scattered in fragrant halls.

> In this painting it is all before our eyes,
> And in prayer we entrust ourselves to that spiritual realm.
> On the ocean of power from the merit of this,
> Let divine intercession be our boat and bridge,
> That eight billion kalpas of human sin

May as frost be swept away by the wind.
Let all think on the Buddha of Eternal Life,
Ever praying for the light of his jade-like hair.

Elling O. Eide

⚬ Meng Hao-jan (689–740)

WRITTEN FOR OLD FRIENDS IN YANG-JOU CITY
WHILE SPENDING THE NIGHT ON THE TUNG-LU
RIVER

I hear the apes howl sadly
In dark mountains.
The blue river
Flows swiftly through the night.

The wind cries
In the leaves on either bank.
The moon shines
On a solitary boat.

These wild hills
Are not my country.
I think of past ramblings
In the city with you.

I will take
These two lines of tears,
And send them to you
Far away
At the western reach of the sea.

Greg Whincup

⚬ Liu Ch'ang-ch'ing (710–785)

ON PARTING WITH THE BUDDHIST PILGRIM
LING-CH'Ê

From the temple, deep in its tender bamboos,
Comes the low sound of an evening bell,
While the hat of a pilgrim carries the sunset
Farther and farther down the green mountain.

Witter Bynner

ꙮ Tu Fu (712–770)

A HAWK IN A PAINTING

From white silk   a whiff of wind and frost
grey goshawk   of art extraordinary
twitching body   alert for wily hares
she glowers askance   like a gloomy Sogdian
swivel and jess   their glitter I'd unleash
and from her lofty perch   call down her power
how she would fall   upon the pack of songsters
sprinkling   blood and feathers across the plain

David Lattimore

BALLAD OF THE ARMY CARTS

Carts clang   and clatter
horses whinny   and neigh
troops   at each man's waist
a bow and arrows
mothers   fathers   wives   and sons
rush to see them off
dust-clouds   so you can't see
Xianyang Bridge
cling to their coat-tails   trample
block the road   weep
sounds of weeping   soar
and crash on cloudbanks
a wayside   passer-by
asks about the soldiers
a soldier   answers
drafts unceasing
some of us   at fifteen
went north to guard the River
now   turned forty
it's west to the army farms
when first we served   town elders
forced on us caps of manhood
home   white-headed
now it's back to man the borders
border forts   drowned
in seas of blood
still unchecked   the Martial Ruler's
urge to burst borders
sir   have you not heard
of Han folk   to the mountains' east
two hundred counties

ten thousand hamlets   a thousand towns
choked in brush   and thorn
though there be   strong wives
to wield plow and hoe
grain overgrows   diked acres
till there's no east or west
though we be   Qin soldiers
steeled to harsh warfare
they drive us   no otherwise
than hens or dogs
reverend sir   though you inquire about us
how can a soldier   dare complain
suppose   this winter
west of the passes   there's no relief of troops
yet county magistrates   press for tax grain
rents   tax grain   where will they come from
know for sure   it's evil to bear a son
all's backward   it's good to bear a daughter
bear girls   at least
you can marry them to neighbors
bear sons   you'll lose them
in steppeland grass
sir   have you not seen
on the shores of Kokonor
white bones   from of old
with none to gather them
new ghosts   are grieving
old ghosts weep
in rain   and darkness
mewing   mewing

David Lattimore

From CROSSING THE BORDER, FIRST SERIES

No. 6 (in a set of nine poems)

Drawing a bow   you must draw a strong one
choosing an arrow   choose a long one
when you shoot a man   first shoot his horse
when you seize bandits   first seize their leader
killing men   in the end should have some limit
to any state   by nature there are bounds
if you can   master an invader
what's the use   of further death and wounds

David Lattimore

MOONLIT NIGHT

In Fuzhou, far away, my wife is watching
The moon alone tonight, and my thoughts fill
With sadness for my children, who can't think
Of me here in Changan; they're too young still.
Her cloud-soft hair is moist with fragrant mist.
In the clear light her white arms sense the chill.
When will we feel the moonlight dry our tears,
Leaning together on our window-sill?

Vikram Seth

DAYTIME DREAM

In the second month, sleeping a lot, all sleepy and dazed,
Are the nights not shorter? —asleep at midday.
With warm air of plum blossoms, eyes grow drunk,
At sun's set by the spring sandbar, dreams lead one away.
The gate and path to my old home lie beneath brambles and thorns,
Ruler and officials in the Central Plains lie by wolves and tigers.
When, when, may one attend to farming, the fighting ended,
And the whole world be without officials seeking money?

Eva Shan Chou

TRAVELING AT NIGHT

Slender grasses,
A breeze on the riverbank,
The tall mast
Of my boat alone in the night.

Stars hang
All across a vast plain.
The moon leaps
In the Great River's flow.

My writing
Has not made a name for me,
And now, due to age and illness,
I must quit my official post.

Floating on the wind,
What do I resemble?
A solitary gull
Between the heavens and the earth.

Greg Whincup

THINKING OF MY LITTLE BOY

Pony Boy   though it's spring we're still apart
oriole songs   in the warmth are at their fullest
separation   seasonal change upsets me
quick and clever   who chatters with you now
a canyon stream   a road in the empty mountains
a rough gate   a village among old trees
I think of you   I grieve and almost sleep
toasting my back   I lean on the sunny rail

David Lattimore

DREAMING OF LI PO

Death at least gives separation repose.
Without death, its grief can only sharpen.
You wander out in malarial southlands,
and I hear nothing of you, exiled

old friend. Knowing I think of you
always now, you visit my dreams, my heart
frightened it is no living spirit
I dream. Endless miles—you come

so far from the Yangtze's sunlit maples
night shrouds the passes when you return.
And snared as you are in their net,
with what bird's wings could you fly?

Filling my room to the roof-beams, the moon
sinks. You nearly linger in its light,
but the waters deepen in long swells,
unfed dragons—take good care old friend.

David Hinton

❧ Han Yü (768–824)

From AUTUMN THOUGHTS

Leaves fall turning turning to the ground,
by the front eaves racing, following the wind;
murmuring voices seem to speak to me
as they whirl and toss in headlong flight.
An empty hall in the yellow dusk of evening:
I sit here silent, unspeaking.

The young boy comes in from outdoors,
trims the lamp, sets it before me,
asks me questions I do not answer,
brings me a supper I do not eat.
He goes and sits down by the west wall,
reading me poetry—three or four poems;
the poet is not a man of today—
already a thousand years divide us—
but something in his words strikes my heart,
fills it again with an acid grief.
I turn and call to the boy:
Put down the book and go to bed now—
a man has times when he must think,
and work to do that never ends.

Burton Watson

Hsüeh T'ao (768–831)

GAZING AT SPRING

Flowers bloom:
no one
to enjoy them with.

Flowers fall:
no one
with whom to grieve.

I wonder when love's
longings
stir us most—

when flowers bloom,
or when flowers fall?

Jeanne Larsen

TRYING ON NEW-MADE CLOTHES: THREE
POEMS

1

In your astral palace, I
am bestowed with scarlet silks

hazy as spirit mists
far beyond the sea.

Cool fur from the frosty moon-hare,
pure thread
of the ice-silk moth:

the Moon Lady smiles
and points
toward the Weaver Woman Star.

2

The Nine Humors split and woven
into nine-colored clouds of dawn,

the Five Magic Beasts reined in
to pull
a five-cloud chariot:

east winds blowing past
the palace of Spring's Lord

stole these designs for
human realms
to dye a hundred flowers.

3

This skirt's in the style
worn in paradise.

It once trailed heavenly
courtiers grasping
magic-mushroom scepters.

Each time they meet at the palace,
come to sing and dance,

they bow from the waist
and chorus, "Step
through the Sky," a star-walker's song.

Jeanne Larsen

DOG PARTED FROM HER MASTER

Yes, she's a good dog,
lived four or five years
within his crimson gates,

fur sweet-smelling,
feet quite clean,
master, affectionate.

Then by chance she
took a nip
and bit a well-loved guest.

Now she no longer sleeps
upon his red silk rugs.

Jeanne Larsen

ஒ Po Chü-i (772–846)

SONG OF EVERLASTING SORROW

The Emperor prized beauty, and longed for a woman to topple a kingdom,
Through a reign of many years he searched without obtaining her.
There was a girl of the Yang family, just about grown,
Who had been reared in the inner chambers—no one knew of her yet,
She had beauty and charms granted by Heaven, difficult to conceal,
And so one day was chosen to be the concubine of her sovereign.
A glance exchanged, a single smile; she showed a hundred charms,
The painted beauties of his Six Palaces seemed to have no allure.
In the cold of early spring she bathed in the Flower-Clear Pool,
The warm spring's water polished her skin translucent white and glossy
    smooth.
A servant helped her up; she was graceful, so helplessly languid—
That was the first time the emperor bestowed his favor on her.
Her clouds of hair, her lovely face, her swaying, gold-shod steps,
Within hibiscus canopies they passed their spring nights in warmth.
The spring nights seemed very short, the sun would rise high;
But from that time His Majesty would not attend the early court.
They took their pleasure at feasts and entertainments without pause,
The spring came, and passed on as night followed night.
There were three thousand other beauties in the women's palace;
For him, all their three thousand charms were combined in one body.
In the golden room, her toilette complete, she seductively attended him all
    night,
In the jade tower, the feasting finished, she harmonized with spring delights.
Her sisters and brothers were all given rank and titles;
To the dismay of many, her glory reflected on her family,
And so throughout the empire the hearts of mothers and fathers
Did not value the birth of a boy, but valued that of a girl.
In the upper stories of Li Palace, piercing the blue sky,
Fairy music wafted on the wind, to be heard everywhere,
Slow-paced songs and languorous dances were played by strings and flutes:
Though he gaze all day, His Majesty could not gaze on her enough.
Then the war-drums from Yü-yang came, shaking the earth,
Abruptly breaking off the songs of the "Rainbow Skirt" and the "Robe of
    Feathers."
The Nine Rings of the Forbidden City threw up smoke and dust,

Thousands mounted, ten thousand in carts moved off to the southwest.
The Imperial banner fluttered, then its movement stopped
West of the city gates more than a hundred *li.*
There the six armies refused to budge, no matter what the cost,
Until he yielded his moth-browed beauty to die before the horses.
Hairpins like flowers flung to the ground, with no one to catch them,
A kingfisher crown, golden birds and hair-tassels of jade.
The Emperor could only cover his face; he was unable to save her.
Looking back, the blood and tears were flowing together.
The yellow dust dispersed, the wind blew cold,
The trail in the clouds twisted around to climb the Chien-ko Pass.

Under O-mei Mountain a few people passed,
Without light, the day-bright colors of flags and pennants faded.
The water of the Shu River is green, Shu Mountain is blue:
The Emperor, day after day, night after night, grieved.
Pacing the palace, he looked at the moon, his wounded heart full of longing,
In the night rain he heard bells, but his feelings cut off their sounds.
Heaven and Earth swung 'round again, and the dragon-cart returned,
When they came to that spot he hesitated, and could not go on.
She was in the earth under the Ma-wei Slope,
He could not see her jade face—the place where she died was empty.
Lord and courtier, when they met, would soak their clothes with tears,
Looking east to the city gates, they trusted their horses to know the way
      back.
When they returned, the pools and parks were as in the olden days,
Hibiscus from Lake T'ai-yi, and Wei-yang Palace willows.
The hibiscus were like her face, the willows like her brows,
So when he looked at them, how could he help but weep?
In the spring wind the peaches and plums blossomed with the days,
In the autumn rains the *wu-t'ung* trees shed their leaves in season.
The West Palace and the Southern Enclosure were full of autumn grasses,
Falling leaves covered the stairs with red, and were not swept away.
The attendants of the Pear Garden, their white hair was new,
The Pepper House eunuchs' young eyebrows began to show their age.
Fireflies flew in the evening halls; he thought quietly of her,
The wick in his lonely lamp burnt out, and yet he would not sleep.
Slowly, slowly, the bells and drums began each long night,
Brighter, brighter the Milky Way, urging the sky to dawn.
The roof-tile mandarin ducks were cold, the frost was bright and thick,
His kingfisher-feather covers were cold, for who was to be with him?
His thoughts were on the distance between life and death, year after year
      without end,
But her spirit would not return, or come to enter his dreams.

A Taoist adept of Ling-chün was a voyager in the heavens
Able because of his devout conviction to contact spirits.
Moved by their sovereign's constant torment of longing,
Some sought out this adept to search diligently for her.
He marshalled the clouds and drove ether before him, quick as lightning,
Up in the sky, down into the earth, he looked for her everywhere.

He rose to the ends of the jade-green sky, he plumbed the Yellow Springs,
In both places, look as he might, he did not see her.
Suddenly he heard of a mountain of immortals in the sea,
The mountain was in the misty realm of emptiness.
Splendid towers and gates rose up from the five-color clouds,
And in the midst of these delights there were many immortals.
Among them was one called "Most Genuine,"
With snowy skin, a flower face, who could be compared with her?
At the gold towers on the west side he knocked on the jade door,
And asked a little jade attendant to inform the one of the paired perfections.
When she heard the Chinese court had sent an envoy from the Emperor,
She was awakened from her dreams in her nine-flowered canopied bed.
Pushing aside her pillow, she dressed and rose like a flying swallow,
Rushed over to open the pearly door and the silver screen.
New-wakened from sleep, her cloud of hair tilted to one side,
Her flower cap was not set straight when she came down to the courtyard.
The wind sighed in her immortal sleeves and raised them up in dancing.
As if this were the dance of the "Rainbow Skirt" and the "Robe of Feathers."
On her jade face from loneliness the tears trickled down,
Like pear blossoms on a branch when the spring brings down the rain.
She restrained her emotions, calmed her eyes and thanked the emperor:
"Since we parted our voices and faces are dim to one another,
Cut off was our happy love in the Court of the Bright Sun,
And the long days and nights in P'eng-lai Palace.
But when I turn my head to gaze down at the mortal world,
I can never see Ch'ang-an, but only fog and dust."
She gave the envoy the old things that were pledges of their love,
A golden hairpin in its case she gave him to take away;
But of the hairpin she kept one branch, of the box she kept one half,
Breaking the hairpin's yellow gold and the hinge of the box.
"Tell him our love should be as whole as this hairpin and its case—
In heaven or in the world of men we will meet again."
About to part, she charged him further to take these words,
In these words was meaning only their two hearts knew:
"On the seventh day of the seventh month, in the Palace of Long Life,
At midnight, with no one else there, we exchanged a secret vow:
That in the heavens we wished to fly, two birds with joined wings,
And on the earth we wished to grow, two trees with branches entwined."
Heaven endures, earth's span is long, but sometime both will end—
This sorrow everlasting will go on forever.

Dore J. Levy

THE RED COCKATOO

Sent as a present from Annam—
A red cockatoo.
Coloured like the peach-tree blossom,
Speaking with the speech of men.

And they did to it what is always done
To the learned and eloquent.
They took a cage with stout bars
And shut it up inside.

Arthur Waley

MADLY SINGING IN THE MOUNTAINS

There is no one among men that has not a special failing:
And my failing consists in writing verses.
I have broken away from the thousand ties of life:
But this infirmity still remains behind.
Each time that I look at a fine landscape:
Each time that I meet a loved friend,
I raise my voice and recite a stanza of poetry
And am glad as though a God had crossed my path.
Ever since the day I was banished to Hsün-yang
Half my time I have lived among the hills.
And often, when I have finished a new poem,
Alone I climb the road to the Eastern Rock.
I lean my body on the banks of white stone:
I pull down with my hands a green cassia branch.
My mad singing startles the valleys and hills:
The apes and birds all come to peep.
Fearing to become a laughing-stock to the world,
I choose a place that is unfrequented by men.

Arthur Waley

THE CHANCELLOR'S GRAVEL-DRIVE

A Government-bull yoked to a Government-cart!
Moored by the bank of Ch'an River, a barge loaded with gravel.
A single load of gravel,
How many pounds it weighs!
Carrying at dawn, carrying at dusk, what is it all for?
They are carrying it towards the Five Gates,
To the West of the Main Road.
Under the shadow of green laurels they are making a gravel-drive.
For yesterday arrove, newly appointed,
The Assistant Chancellor of the Realm,
And was terribly afraid that the wet and mud
Would dirty his horse's hoofs.
The Chancellor's horse's hoofs
Stepped on the gravel and remained perfectly clean;
But the bull employed in dragging the cart

Was almost sweating blood.
The Assistant Chancellor's business
Is to "save men, govern the country
And harmonize Yin and Yang."
Whether the bull's neck is sore
Need not trouble him at all.

Arthur Waley

✎ Liu Tsung-yüan (773–819)

ON COVERING THE BONES OF CHANG CHIN, THE HIRED MAN

The cycle of life is a worrisome thing,
a single breath that gathers and scatters again.
We come by chance into a hubbub of joy and rage
and suddenly we're taking leave again.
To be an underling is no disgrace,
neither is nobility divine;
all at once when breathing stops,
fair and ugly disappear in decay.
You slaved in my stables all your life,
cutting fodder, you never complained you were tired.
When you died we gave you a cheap coffin
and buried you at the foot of the eastern hill.
But then, alas, there came a raging flood
that left you helter-skelter by the roadside.
Dry and brittle, your hundred bones baked in the sun,
scattered about, never to join again.
Luckily an attendant told me of this,
and the vision saddened me to tears,
for even cats and tigers rate a sacrificial offering,
and dogs and horses have their ragged shrouds.
Long I stand here mourning for your soul
yet how could you know of this act?
Basket and spade bear you to the grave
which waterways will keep from further harm.
My mind is now at ease
whether you know it or not.
One should wait for spring to cover up bones,
and propitious is the time now.
Benevolence for all things is not mine to confer;
just call it a personal favor for you.

Jan W. Walls

꩜ Li Ho (791–817)

THE KING OF CH'IN DRINKS WINE

The King of Ch'in rides out on his tiger and roams to the Eight Bounds,
The flash of his sword lights up the sky against the resisting blue:
He is Hsi-ho flogging the sun forward with the sound of ringing glass.
The ashes of the kalpas have flown away, rebellion has never been.
Dragon's heads spout wine and the Wine Star is his guest,
Gold-grooved mandolins twang in the night;
The feet of the rain on Lake Tung-t'ing come blown on a gust from the pan-
   pipes,
Heated by the wine his shout makes the moon run backward!

Under combed layers of silvered cloud the jasper hall brightens,
A messenger from the palace gate reports the first watch.
The jade phoenix of the painted tower has a sweet and fierce voice,
Mermaid silks patterned in crimson have a faint and cool scent.
The yellow swans trip over in the dance. A thousand years in the cup!

Beneath the immortal's tree of candles, where the wax lightly smokes,
The tears flood Blue Zither's drunken eyes.

A. C. Graham

THE GRAVE OF LITTLE SU

> I ride a coach with lacquered sides,
> My love rides a piebald horse.
> Where shall we bind our hearts as one?
> On West Mound, beneath the pines and cypresses.
> Ballad ascribed to the singing girl Little Su, ca. 500

Dew on the secret orchid
Like screaming eyes.
Nowhere, the hearts bound as one.
Evanescent flowers I cannot bear to cut.
Grass like a cushion,
The pine like a parasol;
The wind is a skirt,
The waters are tinkling pendants.
A coach with lacquered sides
Waits for someone in the evening.
The cold green will-o'-the-wisp
Squanders its brightness.
Beneath West Mound
The wind puffs the rain.

A. C. Graham

FLYING LIGHT

Flying light, flying light—
I urge you to drink a cup of wine.
I do not know the height of blue heaven
nor the extent of yellow earth.
I only sense the moon's cold,
sun's burn, sears us.
Eat bear, and you'll grow fat;
eat frog, and you'll waste away.
Where is the Spirit Lady?
And where the Great Unity?
East of the sky is the Jo tree:
underneath, a dragon, torch in mouth.
I will cut off the dragon's feet
and chew the dragon's flesh:
then morning will never return
and evening cannot bend.
Old men will not die
nor young men weep.
Why then swallow yellow gold
or gulp down white jade?
Who is Jen Hung-tzu
riding a white ass through the clouds?
Liu Ch'e, in Mao-ling tomb, is just a heap of bones.
And Ying Cheng rots in his catalpa coffin,
wasting all that abalone.

Arthur Sze

✥ Tu Mu (803–853)

EGRETS

Snowy coats and snowy crests and beaks of blue jade
Flock above the fish in the brook and dart at their own shadows,
In startled flight show up far back against the green hills,
The blossoms of a whole pear-tree shed by the evening wind.

A. C. Graham

✥ Li Shang-yin (812–858)

PHOENIX TAIL ON SCENTED SILK

Phoenix tail on scented silk, flimsy layer on layer:
Blue patterns on a round canopy, stitched deep into the night.
The fan's sliced moon could not hide her shame,

His coach drove out with the sound of thunder, no time to exchange a word.
In the silent room the gold of the wick turned dark:
No message since has ever come, though the pomegranate is red.
The dappled horse stands tethered only on the bank of drooping willows,
Where shall she wait for a kind wind to blow from the South West?

A. C. Graham

BITE BACK PASSION

Bite back passion. Spring now sets.
Watch little by little the night turn round.
Echoes in the house; want to go up, dare not.
A glow behind the screen; wish to go through, cannot.
It would hurt too much, the swallow on a hairpin;
Truly shame me, the phoenix on a mirror.
     On the road back, sunrise over Heng-t'ang.
The blossoming of the morning-star shines farewell on the jewelled saddle.

A. C. Graham

THE CHANCE TO MEET IS DIFFICULT

The chance to meet is difficult,
       but parting is even more difficult.
The east wind is powerless
       as the hundred flowers wither.
A spring silkworm spins silk
       up to the instant of death.
A candle only stops weeping
       when its wick becomes ash.
In the morning mirror, she grieves
       that the hair on her temples whitens.
Chanting poems in the evening,
       she only senses the moonlight's cold.
From here, P'eng Mountain is not too far.
       O Green Bird, seek, seek her out.

Arthur Sze

 **Kuan Hsiu** (832–912)

WRITTEN IN THE MOUNTAINS

A mountain's a palace
for all things crystalline and pure:

there's not a speck of dust
on a single one of all these flowers.

When we start chanting poems like madmen
it sets all the peaks to dancing.
And once we've put the brush to work
even the sky becomes mere ornament.

For you and me the joy's in the doing
and I'm damned if I care about "talent."

But if, my friend, from time to time
you hear sounds like ghostly laughter . . .
It's all the great mad poets, dead,
and just dropping in for a listen.

J. P. Seaton

SONG OF THE PALACE OF CH'EN

Think sad thoughts of other days,
those palace gates, overflowing . . .
Reckless feasting, feckless loves:
no Sages, there.
Jade trees' blossoms singing, there
among a hundred flowers.
Coral jeweled, the very window frames,
sun from the sea, scattered, jewels.
Great ministers to audience; Mi'Lord
still in his cups, and even when he'd sobered
few wise words got past *his* ears.
So. The Palace of Ch'en
is rubble in this farmer's field,
and the peasant's plow turns up the shards
of a courtier's mirror.

J. P. Seaton

BAD GOVERNMENT

Sleet and rain, as if the pot were boiling.
Winds whack like the crack of an axe.
An old man, an old old man,
toward sunset crept into my hut.
He sighed, sighed he, as if to himself,
"These rulers, so cruel: why, tell me
why they must steal till we starve,
and then slice off the skin from our bones?

For a song from some beauty
they'll go back on sworn words;
for a song from some tart,
they'll tear our huts down . . .
for a song, for a sweet song or two,
they'll slaughter ten thousand like me, or
like you. You can cry as you will, let
your hair turn pure white,
let your whole clan go hungry . . .
no good wind will blow
no gentle breeze
begin again.
Lord Locust Plague, and Baron Bandit Bug,
one East, one West, one North, one South,
We're surrounded."

J. P. Seaton

✂ Yü Hsüan-chi (843–868)

LIVING IN THE SUMMER MOUNTAINS

I have moved to this home of Immortals.
Wild shrubs bloom everywhere.
In the front garden, trees
Spread their branches for clothes racks.
I sit on a mat and float wine cups
In the cool spring.
Beyond the window railing
A hidden path leads away
Into the dense bamboo grove.
In a gauze dress
I read among my disordered
Piles of books.
I take a leisurely ride
In the painted boat,
And chant poems to the moon.
I drift at ease, for I know
The soft wind will blow me home.

Kenneth Rexroth and Ling Chung

SPRING THOUGHTS SENT TO TZU-AN

The mountain road is steep, the stone steps are dangerous;
The hard climb hurts me less than thoughts of you.

Ice melts in a far stream: your voice in its sad tune.
Snow on cold peaks like jade reminds me of you.

Don't listen to the singers, springsick with wine.
Don't call your guests to play chess at night.

Like pine or stone our promise stays,
So I can wait for paired wings to join.

I walk alone in the cold end of winter.
Perhaps we'll meet when the moon is round.

What can I give my absent man?
In the pure light, my tears fall: a poem.

Geoffrey Waters

⚔ Anonymous (c. 850)

POEM OF MEDICINE PUNS

His wife then composed a poem with the names of medicines its theme and,
by means of it, asked him a series of questions:
    "I, Belladonna, am the wife of a man named Wahoo,
Who early became a mandrake in Liang.
Before our matrimonyvine could be consomméted, he had to go back,
Leaving me, his wife, to dwell here ruefully alone.
The mustard has not been cut, the flaxseed bed remains unvisited —
Hemlocked in here without any neighbors, I raised my head and sighed
    for my Traveler's Joy:
'Parsley, sage, rosemary, and thyme —
I pray that he'll forget me not!'
Gingerly, I hoped, but I recently heard that the King of Ch'u,
Acting without principle and unleashing a bitterroot heart,
Slaughtered my pawpaw and brother-in-law with a jalap! jalap!
Clovered with shame, weak as a wisp of straw,
And arrowhead-swift, my husband fled with fear as a dog would.
Quick as a periwinkle, he became a fungative,
And hid amongst the stinkbushes;
But hiding became a hell-of-a-bore.
He seemed like a jackal pursued by horehounds;
Laudanum almighty, how he hopsed and hyssopped like a jack-in-the-
    pulpit!
When I think of it, bittersweet tears stain my bleedingheart;
I am arti-choked with antimony.
At nightshade when I sleep, it's hard to endure till the morning's glory;
I recite his name all day until my tongue curls up like a sliver of cypress.
His voice, begging balm, so ingenuous entered my ears;
Drawn by aniseedent causes, I dillied up to the visitor,
And, seeing it was my long orrised honeysuckle whom I mint at the
    gate,
Sloed down my steps to a hibiscus pace.

And then I saw your toothwort smile;
It reminded me of my husband's dog's tooth violets.
Borax you don't remember me but, no madder what caper you're up to,
I'm willing to lay out my scurvy Butter and Eggs."

Tzu-hsü answered in the same cryptic vein:

"Potash! Nitre am I this fellow Wahoo whom you speak of,
Nor am I a fungative from injustice.
Listen while I tell you the currant of my travels.
I was born in Castoria and grew up in Betony Wood;
My father was a Scorpio, my mother a true Lily-of-the-valley.
Gathering up all of my goldenrod and silverweed,
This son of theirs became a Robin-Run-Around.
Rose Hips was my low-class companion,
Nelson Rockyfeldspar my uppercrust chum.
Together with them, I waded Wild Ginger Creek,
And caught cold in its squilling, wintergreen waters;
Saffronly, of the three of us, I found myself alone.
Day after day, my lotus-thread hopes dangled tenuously;
My thoughts were willows waving in the wind.
All alone, I climbed Witch Hazel Mountain;
How hard it was to cross the slippery elms and stone roots!
Cliffs towering above me, I clambered over stoneworts and rockweeds;
Often did I encounter wolfsbanes and tiger thistles.
Sometimes I would be thinking of soft spring beauties,
But suddenly would meet up with a bunch of pigsheads;
My thoughts would linger over midsummer vetches,
Yet I could never see an end to my tormentils.
So I reversed my steps, feeling compelled to spurry back;
Fennelly, I arrived here.
I grow goatsbeard,
Not dog's tooth violets.
Methinks you've scratched a fenugreek but found no tartar,
So furze tell me what you mean and don't make such a rhubarb."

Victor H. Mair

ॐ Ch'en T'ao (c. 860)

TURKESTAN

Thinking only of their vow that they would crush the Tartars—
On the desert, clad in sable and silk, five thousand of them fell. . . .
But arisen from their crumbling bones on the banks of the river at the
border,
Dreams of them enter, like men alive, into rooms where their loves lie
sleeping.

Witter Bynner

Sino-Korean

❧ Anonymous (c. 650)

LAMENT FOR PRINCE CHAGOO

Over the Dragon Rock the moon appears.
How can I bear to watch her beauty rise
Where stars are like ten thousand frozen tears?

Where is Prince Chagoo now? The Silent Hall
Rings to his footsteps while the dim lights ebb
Low in the lamps of death, and shadows fall.

They fold around and draw him to his doom.
The full moon sets behind the willow tree.
Does no faint glimmer pierce that awful gloom?

Dawn breaks above the mountains' jagged rim
The forest stirs with blossom-scented breath.
No perfumed wind can bear new life to him.

The oriole wakes. I wonder why she sings
So gaily all day long beside my door,
When one who loved so well the sound of wings
Hears her no more.

Jenn S. Grigsby

❧ Master Wŏlmyŏng (c. 742–765)

REQUIEM

On the hard road of life and death
That is near our land,
You went, afraid,
Without words.

We know not where we go,
Leaves blown, scattered,
Though fallen from the same tree,
By the first winds of autumn.

Abide, Sister, perfect your ways,
Until we meet in the Pure Land.

Peter H. Lee

❧ Anonymous (c. 750)

THE ORCHID DOOR

Stilled is the lute string after hours of song.
The fountain is a shower of rainbow spray,
Lit by the moon. Upon the littered floor
Guest after guest falls into drunken sleep.
Winecups are drained. The flickering lantern light
Glimmers above a weary dancing girl,
Shines through the amber pins that hold her hair,
Mocks at the peony bud which is her mouth,
The jasmine petals that enfold her eyes.

What are such joys to me? I turn away.
Beyond the Fountain of Ten Thousand Jewels
In fragrant shadow waits an orchid door.

Jean S. Grigsby

❧ Ch'oe Ch'ung (984–1068)

IN THE NIGHT

Light of the silver torch that has no smoke
Recalls me from the seventh world of sleep.
A shadow pine tree grows upon my wall.
On the white paper of my window screen
A shadow hill by shadow brush is drawn.
All life is shadow in my room tonight.
I know not if I wake or if I sleep—
Music breathes through the silence; can it be
Wind in the shadow pine tree, or a song
Drawn from a hidden harp that has no string?

Jean S. Grigsby

ꙮ 3

JAPAN: FROM THE EARLIEST VERSE THROUGH THE HEIAN PERIOD

Japanese

ꙮ Emperor Jomei (593–641)

WRITTEN AFTER CLIMBING KAGUYAMA TO
SURVEY THE LAND

Many are the hills,
the mountains of Yamato,
yet when I ascend heavenly Kaguyama,
the peerless mountain,
when I look down on the land:
where the land stretches,
hearth smoke rises everywhere;
where the water stretches,
water birds fly everywhere.
Ah, a splendid country,
this land Yamato of bounteous harvests!

Helen Craig McCullough

ꙮ Kakinomoto no Hitomaru (c. 680–700)

MOURNING PRINCESS ASUKA

At Asuka, the river of birds in flight,
there are stepping stones crossing the upper reaches,

there is a wood bridge crossing the lower reaches.
The gemmed water weed growing tall,
waving its fronds by the stepping stones,
grows again when it is cut;
the river weed, too,
growing tall, putting forth shoots by the lower bridge,
sprouts again when it withers.
Why, then, should it be that you, O great Princess,
have quite forgotten the palace of the morning,
have quite forsaken the palace
        of the evening of your fair husband —
you who when you stood erect resembled gemweed,
you who when you lay with him bent your limbs to his,
as pliant as river weed?
Your meetings have ceased,
and there is an end to speech exchanged between you
now that you have determined to dwell forever
        at the Kinoe Palace —
you who while you lived in this transitory world,
plucked flowers in spring to decorate your tresses,
and when autumn came decked your head with colored leaves;
you who now and then came to take your pleasure there,
came in company —
walking sleeve beside sleeve spread for sheet at night —
with the husband you gazed on as on a mirror,
gazed and never had enough,
loved more ardently than men admire a full moon.
For my aching heart there is no hope of solice,
while I see the Prince who was wont to visit you like a morning bird,
the grieving widower,
like a tiger thrush,
sorrowing beyond measure
(and surely for this?) —
while I behold him drooping like summer grasses
going yonder, coming here like the evening star,
unsteady as a great ship.
And since it is thus,
I cannot tell what to do.
Yet throughout all time,
through ages longer lasting than heaven and earth,
we will hold ever in mind the sound, at least, the name:
for countless generations,
the River Asuka
stream bearing your honored name,
will be a keepsake preserving the memory of our beloved
Princess.

        Helen Craig McCullough

✢ Yamanoue no Okura (660–733)

A LAMENT FOR THE EVANESCENCE OF LIFE

What we must accept as we journey through the world
is that time will pass like the waters of a stream;
in countless numbers,
in relentless succession,
it will besiege us with assaults we must endure.
They could not detain the period of their bloom,
when, as maidens will,
they who then were maidens encircled their wrists
    with gemmed bracelets from Cathay,
and took their pleasure frolicking hand in hand
    with their youthful friends.
So the months and years went by,
and when did it fall —
that sprinkling of wintry frost on glistening hair
    as black as leopard flower seeds?
And whence did they come —
those wrinkles that settled in,
marring the smoothness of blushing pink faces?
Was it forever,
the kind of life those others led —
those stalwart men,
who, as fine young men will do,
girded at their waists sharp swords, keen-bladed weapons,
took up hunting bows,
clasped them tight in their clenched fists,
placed on red horses saddles fashioned of striped hemp,
climbed onto their steeds,
and rode gaily here and there?
They were not many,
those nights when the fine young men pushed open the doors,
the plank doors of the chamber where the maidens slept,
groped their way close to their loves,
and slept with their arms intertwined with gemlike arms.
Yet already now those who were maidens and youths
    must use walking sticks,
and when they walk over there,
others avoid them,
and when they walk over here,
others show distaste.
Such is life, it seems, for the old.
Precious though life is,
it is beyond our power to stay the passing of time.

Envoi

Would that I might stand a rock through eternity,
unchanged forever —
but life does not allow us to halt the passing of time.

Helen Craig McCullough

LONGING FOR HIS SON, FURUHI

What value to me the seven kinds of treasures
    by which others set store —
the precious things coveted by the run of men?
My son, Furuhi,
the child fair as a white pearl,
born of the union between his mother and me,
used to play with us when the morning star announced
    the dawn of each new day —
to stay close to the bedside where our sheets were spread,
to frolic with us standing and sitting.
And when evening came with the evening star,
he used to take us by the hand and say to us,
"Let's go to bed now,"
and then, in his pretty way,
"Father and Mother,
don't go where I can't see you.
I want to sleep right here in the middle."
And we thought, trusting as people trust a great ship,
"May the time come soon when he becomes an adult;
for good or for ill,
may we behold him a man."
But then suddenly a mighty storm wind blew up,
caught us from the side,
overwhelmed us with its blast.
Helpless, distraught,
not knowing what to do,
I tucked back my sleeves with paper-mulberry cords,
I took in my hand a clear, spotless mirror.
With upturned face,
I beseeched the gods of the sky;
forehead to the ground,
I implored the gods of the earth.
"Whether he be cured or whether he die —
that is for the gods to say."
But though I begged them in frantic supplication,
there resulted not the briefest improvement.
His body wasted,
changing little by little;
he uttered no more the words he had spoken

with each new morning;
and his life came to its end.
I reeled in agony,
stamped my feet, screamed aloud,
cast myself down,
looked up to heaven, beat my breast.
I have lost my son,
the child I loved so dearly.
Is this what life is about?

Envois

He is still so young that he won't know the way to go.
I will give you something—
only carry him on your back,
messenger from the netherworld!

Making offerings,
I utter this petition:
tempt him not afield,
but lead him straight ahead—
show him the way to heaven.

Helen Craig McCullough

Prince Ōtsu (663–686)

ON THE EVE OF HIS EXECUTION

(written in Chinese)

The golden crow lights on the western huts;
Evening drums beat out the shortness of life.
There are no inns on the road to the grave—
Whose is the house I go to tonight?

Burton Watson

Priest Sami Mansei (c. 720)

OUR LIFE IN THIS WORLD

Our life in this world—
to what shall I compare it?
It is like a boat
rowing out at break of day,
leaving not a trace behind.

Steven D. Carter

✑ Lady Kasa (c. 740–770)

LOVE AND FEAR

I love and fear him
steadily as the surf
Roars on the coast at Ise.

Kenneth Rexroth

✑ Princess Uchiko (807–847)

RECALLING A VISIT FROM HIS MAJESTY

(written in Chinese)

Silent was my lonely lodge among the mountain trees
When to this far lake your fairy carriage came.
The lone forest bird tasted the dew of spring;
Cold flowers of the dark valley saw the sun's brightness.
Springs sound close by like the echo of early thunder;
High hills shine clear and green above the evening rain.
Should I once more know the warmth of this fair face,
All my life will I give thanks to the azure skies.

Burton Watson

✑ Ariwara no Narihira (823–880)

From THE ISE MONOGATARI

Regretting the Past

Is that not the moon?
And is not the spring the same
Spring of the old days?
My body is the same body —
Yet everything seems different.

Facing His Own Death

That it is a road
Which some day we all travel
I had heard before,
Yet I never expected
To take it so soon myself.

F. Vos

৯ Ono no Komachi (fl. 850–860)

SIX LOVE POEMS

1

Autumn nights, it seems
are long by repute alone:
scarcely had we met
      when morning's first light appeared,
leaving everything unsaid.

2

Yielding to a love
      that recognizes no bounds,
I will go by night—
for the world will not censure
      one who treads the path of dreams.

3

Though I go to you
      ceaselessly along dream paths,
the sum of those trysts
      is less than a single glimpse
            granted in the waking world.

Helen Craig McCullough

4

Thinking about him
I slept, only to have him
Appear before me—
Had I known it was a dream
I should never have wakened.

Donald Keene

5

Doesn't he realize
that I am not
like the swaying kelp
in the surf,
where the seaweed gatherer
can come as often as he wants.

Kenneth Rexroth and Ikuko Atsumi

6

A diver does not abandon
a seaweed-filled bay. . . .

Will you then turn away
from this floating, sea-foam body
that waits for your gathering hands?

Jane Hirshfield and Mariko Aratani

Ki no Tsurayuki (872–945)

THREE POEMS ON SPRING BLOSSOMS

1

On a spring hillside
    I took lodging for the night;
and as I slept
    the blossoms kept on falling—
even in the midst of my dreams

Steven D. Carter

2

The hue is as rich
    and the perfume as fragrant
        as in days gone by,
but how I long for a glimpse
    of the one who planted the tree.

3

The wind that scatters
    cherry blossoms from their boughs
        is not a cold wind—
and the sky has never known
    snow flurries like these.

Helen Craig McCullough

OUT IN THE MARSH REEDS

Out in the marsh reeds
A bird cries out in sorrow
As though it had recalled
Something better forgotten.

Kenneth Rexroth

❧ Lady Ise (875?–938?)

FOUR POEMS

1

Lightly forsaking
the Spring mist as it rises,
the wild geese are setting off.
Have they learned to live
in a flowerless country?

2

Because we suspected
the pillow would say "I know,"
we slept without it.
Nevertheless my name
is being bandied like dust.

3

A flower of waves
blossoms in the distance
and ripples shoreward
as though a breeze had quickened
the sea and set it blooming.

4

If it is you, there
in the light boat on the pond,
I long to beg you
"Do not go; linger a while
among us here in this place."

Etsuko Terasaki with Irma Brandeis

❧ Anonymous

From THE KOKINSHŪ (905)

Two Poems on Love

1
If this were a world
   in which there were no such thing
     as false promises,
how great would be my delight
   as I listened to your words!

2
Though you made me think
    your love inexhaustible
        as sand on a beach,
the thing that proved limitless
    was your power to forget.

Helen Craig McCullough

⨯ Lady Ukon (c. 950)

Me
you've forgotten
and
I've no remorse.
But
I feel sorry for you
when your lifetime ends,
for
that vow
we vowed
before the gods.

Howard S. Levy

⨯ Lady Murasaki Shikibu (fl. 996–1010)

From THE TALE OF GENJI

Dialogue Poems

GENJI:
The warblers are today as long ago,
But we in the shade of the blossoms are utterly changed.

EMPEROR SUZAKU:
Though kept by mists from the ninefold-garlanded court,
I yet have warblers to tell me spring has come.

PRINCE HOTARU:
The tone of the flute is as it always has been,
Nor do I detect a change in the song of the warbler.

EMPEROR SUZAKU:
The warbler laments as it flies from tree to tree—
For blossoms whose hue is paler than it once was?

Edward Seidensticker

❧ Lady Izumi Shikibu (c. 970–1030)

THREE POEMS ON THE UNCERTAINTY OF LIFE

1

From one darkness
        into another darkness
            I soon must go.
Light the long way before me,
moon on the mountain rim!

2

Being a person
        whom no one will mourn when gone,
I should perhaps
        say for myself while still here —
"Ah, the pity, the pity."

3

So forlorn am I
        that when I see a firefly
            out on the marshes
it looks like my soul rising
        from my body in longing.

Steven D. Carter

IF SOMEONE WOULD COME

If someone would come,
I could show, and have him listen —
evening light shining
        on bush clover in full bloom
            as crickets bring on the night.

Steven D. Carter

IN MY IDLENESS

In my idleness
        I turn to look at the sky —
though it's not as if
        the man I'm waiting for
            will descend from the heavens.

Steven D. Carter

THREE POEMS ON LOVE

1

On nights when hail
falls noisily
on bamboo leaves
I completely hate
to sleep alone.

2

You told me it was
because of me
you gazed at the moon.
I've come to see
if this is true.

3

If you love me,
come. The road
I live on
is not forbidden
by impetuous gods.

Willis Barnstone

AUTUMN, ON RETREAT AT A MOUNTAIN TEMPLE

Although I try
to hold the single thought
of Buddha's teaching in my heart,
I cannot help but hear
the many crickets' voices calling as well.

Jane Hirshfield and Mariko Aratani

ALTHOUGH THE WIND

Although the wind
blows terribly here,
the moonlight also leaks
between the roof planks
of this ruined house.

Jane Hirshfield and Mariko Aratani

TANGLED HAIR

With not a thought
    for my black hair's disarray,
I lay myself down —
soon longing for the one whose hands
    have so often brushed it smooth.

Stephen Carter

❧ A Court Lady (c. 1000–1030)

From THE EIGA MONOGATARI

Dialogue Poems

A SON OF EMPEROR YŌZEI:
Which is worse —
The dusk,
When you wait and wonder,
Or the morning after,
When he says goodbye and leaves?

LADY HON'IN NO JIJŪ:
I comfort myself
With hopeful thoughts
At nightfall,
But I faint with grief
When he takes his leave at dawn.

GOVERNOR TAMEYORI OF SETTSU:
How large it has grown:
The number of those
Who had wished
Merely to remain alive
And who now are dead.

LADY KOŌGIMI:
The living die;
The dead multiply.
How long
Shall we survive
In this transient world?

LORD KORECHIKA:
Though no man's flesh
But melts one day,
How grevious is the loss

Of this sister,
Vanished beneath the snow.

LORD TAKAIE:
With no track
On the plain
Deep in fallen snow,
What will guide us
To your grave?

BISHOP RYŪEN:
I wish only
Never to go home —
Let me die
Here on this plain
Beside my sister.

EMPEROR ICHIJŌ:
My heart
Has journeyed alone
To that plain,
But you, perhaps, are unaware
Of its coming.

William H. and Helen Craig McCullough

◈ Monk Nōin (988–1050?)

SPRING IN A MOUNTAIN VILLAGE

To a mountain village
    at nightfall on a spring day
        I came and saw this:
blossoms scattering on echoes
    from the vespers bell.

Steven D. Carter

◈ Anonymous (c. 1150)

MALEDICTION

May he that bade me trust him, but did not come,
Turn into a demon with three horns on his head,
That all men fly from him!
May he become a bird of the waterfields
Where frost, snow, and hail fall,

That his feet may be frozen to ice!
Oh, may he become a weed afloat on a pond!
May he tremble as he walks with the trembling of the hare,
    with the trembling of the doe!

Arthur Waley

✹ 4

ARABIA: FROM PRE-ISLAMIC VERSE THROUGH THE ELEVENTH CENTURY

Arabic

✹ Imr El-Qais (c. 530)

THE ODE OF IMR EL-QAIS

Rein up
        and we weep here, mourn
a house, a girl—
                where the cornice
of that sand reef curls
between Miqrat and Toodih, Haumal and Dakhool.
North wind, south
                wind interweave; wind
mutilates the traces.
Stag dung is spattered like peppercorns
where the yards and cisterns were.
They loaded up one dawn
by these acacias.
                        It was
like biting a colocynth.

Tending their mounts, my companions
are saying:
        Don't die grieving. Find
        some seemly end.
I cry again. Tears cure.
No solace here.
Not even enough ruin
left to lean on.

You were just this way with the woman before her,
Huwairith's mother. Also with her neighbor
in Masal, Omm el-Rabâb . . .

Perfume stirred around them when they stirred,
like odor of clove on a fresh east breeze,
and tears flowed over my throat as free
as blood, and soaked my scabbard.

You've had your share
of good days with the women.
That day at Dara Juljul
for example, couldn't be equalled.

Or the day I slaughtered my mare
for a gaggle of girls
and passed out presents from the saddle pack.
The girls tossed the fresh-cut camel flesh
high into the air.
                    I cut the suet
into tassles like twilled silk . . .

Or the day I climbed into Onaiza's howdah!
She yelled:
        Go to hell! Do you
        mean to make me walk?
The canopy kept swaying
with the two of us, and Onaiza was saying:
        Imr el-Qais, you'll cripple my camel! Get DOWN!
And then I said to her:

Give him the quirt, and let the reins hang.
Don't hold me off, you sweet little melon.
Why, I've come like this
even to pregnant women.
Even to a nursing mother!
(And diverted her, my dear, from her amulet-laden
little yearling.
Whenever he'd whimper behind her she'd hardly
half turn to him. Her other
half stayed under me.)

And one day, back of a dune,
a girl made excuses, swore her honor, and I said to her:
        Easy, lady. Less of your coquetry.
        Even if it's dead set
        that you're through with me, be decent to me.
        Dazzled you, maybe, this battle
        between me and my love of you?
        Dazed you that whatever order
        you issue, my heart obeys?

Or is it that you think
I have disreputable habits? Then
by all means pile my shirt apart
from yours. These tears have only
one intent: they're meant to strike
with your bright barbed eyes
into the carnage of my heart.

And the prize yolk in the boudoir's shell,
whose tent no man at all
dares even to gaze on —
I've sported with her, totally at leisure.
I've threaded through the garrison that guarded her, eager
every man of them to kill me.
Pleiades lay
            like studs in the sky's folds.
She'd piled all but the last of her clothes,
as for sleep,
            by the curtain when I came.
And she whispered when she saw me:
        I'll be damned. You are
        disarming, I must say.
        And what if . . . I were also to find you
        rather charming?
I led her outside
and she trailed behind her
her finest skirt, dragged the dirt with it,
covered our spoor.
We crossed all the encampment, walked on,
found a soft little hollow in the crusted, wind-whipped sand.
I took her curls in my hand.
She hovered over me . . .

Slender the flanks, tender the ankles,
shapely the belly, taut, white,
not a gram
            of unfirm flesh.
Shoulders burnished like a silver mirror.
Whiteness, where whiteness
first blends into amber,
nourished on the whey of unstirred water.
She turns, there appears
a polished cheek.
She wards me away with the shy eye
of a doe with foal, as in Wajra.
Throat like the throat of a lithe white addax.
Neck not ungainly, no matter how she cocks it.
Not a flaw.
Hair down her back like a black cascade,
                                color of coal.
Luminous curls clustered like dates on the palm,

strands twined upward into
                    ravelled and unravelled braid.
And a waist as supple as my bridle rein.
Thighs like moist, pliant reed.

Motes of musk
brood over her bed in the sun's ray;
she sleeps until noon.

She gives, it is with tenderness.
Caterpillar fingers
like the wooly-worms of Zhabi;
no taint whatever of coarseness;
softly;
probing and gentle
as dental tools of ishil wood.

Goes out at evening, she glows there,
illuminates the gloom like an anchorite's light.
Pubescent boy or gone dreamer would stare
with full-blooded fervour at her
                              standing there
half woman and half girl.

        Men's blindnesses distract them
        from their youthful inclinations.
        My heart is not distracted, knows
        no consolations,
        no diversion from loving you.
        Many have meant to argue against you;
        I've restrained them. I remember,
        my sincerity's won out
        against their censure.

But a night veiled like a breaking wave
broke over me, strewed every variety
of miserable luck in my way.
And I shouted to the night, when its loins stretched over me
and buttock-wash behind me heaved against me:
        Give birth to the dawn!
        What morning, even if you mothered it,
        could look like you?
        You bitch of a night,
        your stars are roped to stones!

I've lugged my kinsmen's waterskin,
laid it over my shoulder-blades
humbly and humped it
down a valley bleak as a wild ass's belly.
Lone jackal wailed
like an exile thinking of his kids.

I answered back:
    Jackal, we've had equal luck.
    Both clean out of money —
    if you ever had any.
    Or if either of us ever
    had anything, it's vanished.
    Whoever farms my acreage
    or yours, goes pretty skinny.

And I've left at first light, birds in their nests,
on a short-haired stallion, sired wild, huge,
attacking, backing, banking, outflanking
all at once — a boulder
            barrelled off the mountain on an avalanche.
Blood's hue simmers in his gray.
The saddle-felt sails
         straight off his back
like a pebble intercepted by a cataract.
He surges to second wind,
thunder under the sea-surge
          of his heartbeat,
like a kettle at full boil.
He flows, while the floating mares
falter and go stringhalt.
The light young jockey blows
         right off his back;
he whips the clothes
        clean off the hard-eyed heavy rider.
He spins like a boy's toy
        hurler-twirler whirled on a string.

Thighs of a gazelle, cannons of an ostrich.
He trots like a wolf, runs like a young fox.
Deep in the heart-girth; the gap between his gaskins
filled to overflow,
and no bone below them askew.
Smooth across the spine as a bride's new griddlestone,
solid as a mill-slab in the ribs.
Blood of big game at his throatlatch — a stain
like tincture of henna combed into an old man's beard.

We sighted a herd, and the cows were like the white-robed
vestals walking circles round the altar-stone.
They turned,
they flew like beads from a breaking necklace,
necklace off a neck
whose father's and mother's
        brothers sit high in the tribe.
We rode down on the fastest;
      the rest

of the herd ran hard together, far in his dust.
And he leaped between lead bull and cow
without breaking a lather.

That day, in sum, there was meat on the fire—
some hung high to cure, some turned
at once to steak and stew.

Sunset breeze, and the eye seemed
almost insufficient to sustain
examination of him, looking him hoof to poll.
He stood saddled and bridled,
close in my gaze, the night through.

 Look NOW at the lightning,
 I show you its glitter,
 flutter of light as of brandished hands
 flashing in the piled cloud.
 The stormlight leaps
 like a penitent's lamps
 when he tips oil to the twisted wicks.

I waited the storm with companions
some distance from Darij, a ways from Othaib,
far off my hope's focus.
Thunderhead swirled
   southward over Qatan,
ran to leeward as far
   as Sitar and Yathbul,
and the water began to come down . . .
Dumped the tamarisks on their whiskers at Kutaifa,
ran the mountain goats out of their lairs
   on the slopes of Qanân,
and left not a palm stump at Taima,
nor any fortification
   or barricade, save those
made out of boulders.

Mount Thabeer, in the thickets of rain,
loomed like a greybeard bundled in his robes.
And at dawn the summit of Mujaimir rose
out of skeins of stormwrack
like a spindle-cap.
And the storm laid out its wares on the desert plain
like a Yemeni unpacking his latest load.

And it seemed, in the early light,
that the valley larks gathered over
nectar laced with nutmeg,
and the carcasses of cougar

drowned down the canyon overnight,
far out in the eye's gaze,
were uprooted onion.

Robert Bringhurst

✇ Antara (b. 550)

THE BLACK KNIGHT

Have the poets left a place
to sew on a patch?
From my camel
I salute the campsite of my longed-for lady
to satisfy my need of her gone absent.
The camp's a ruin now, deserted by departure. To find
her again will prove difficult.
In my heart she occupies
the most highly honoured tabernacle of adoration.
Now she's gone to her family's springtime home,
far from mine.

One dark night they harnessed
their camels for departure;
pack camels champing wild berries,
milch camels black as the wing feathers of ravens.
When her kisses took me through the white mosque of her teeth
it was like musk moved
from her mouth to mine,
or like an unmowed meadow after rain.
Liquid languor.
Like a fly rubbing its legs,
like a one armed man bent to strike flints,
she lazes languidly
morning and evening
while I ride the night on my black stallion,
flesh flanked, broad in girth.

I should never have made it on a barren she-camel,
her tail lashing through the long night's trek
tramping the sand with broad pads ponderously tramping.
At sunset it's like riding a close-footed ostrich
young ostrich flock to,
as Yemeni camels flock to the call
of a voice speaks no Arabic.
They follow the crown of his small head.
He looks like a slave, his ear shorn,
swaggers in swept furs.
And when my camel had drunk she turned and swerved

away from that big beast screams at evening,
a cat padding beside her.
Every time she turns bad-tempered on him
he retaliates with claws and teeth.
Her long journeys have strengthed her stout back
high-hoisted, propped like a pitched tent.
She knelt in the crackling reeds by the pool's edge,
proud-stepper, match for any much-bitten stallion.
And if you should raise your veil to me
what then?
I have been a warring warrior.
Wronged, I wax wild.
Praise me for what you know of me.
Praise my passivity.
I enjoy good wine in cut-glass glasses
when I squander my money,
feast my friends.
And when we sober up I'm no less sought after.
You know my nobility and qualities.
Many's the man I've flattened with one blow
and left him winded on the floor
like a harelip hissing.
I'm never out of the saddle, the frenzy of the fight,
as many may testify.
And I abstain from booty-sharing.
Many's the man others avoided I've taken on
man to man.
And I've left him carrion for famished wolves, wild kites,
all of him
from his lolling head to his limp hand.
No soldier stands sacrosanct to the spear.
How often my sword's sliced
through linked links of coat mail
One, when I strode against him,
bared his back teeth at me
I gutted him on the spot.

Fabulous fawn
hunted by all,
denied to me.
Her turned throat's like young antelope,
like graceful gazelle.

In the thick of battle,
beneath our battle banners,
I wheeled on the mob.
The shout went up:
'Antara!'
The spears stretched straight as well-ropes
sinking into the breast of my black stallion
with his white blaze on his forehead.

In the end,
soaked in his own blood,
he turned his thoroughbred head to me
as though in complaint, sobbing, whispering.
Had he speech he'd have spoken.
Yet he wept.
Then dropped dead in his own dung.
It was a purgation for my soul.
And the horsemen shouted:
'Antara!
Forward! Forward!'

I care for my camels.
I travel by the light of my heart.
I fear death may claim me
before my war's wheel turns
against who've dishonoured me
and threaten me.
Death well may.

Desmond O'Grady

✇ Abu Dhu'ayb Al-Hudhali (d. 649)

LAMENT FOR FIVE SONS LOST IN A PLAGUE

Run down by fate's spite
my body hangs, a mantle on a broom;

with wealth enough to ease all pain
I turn at night from back to belly
side after side after side.

Who put pebbles on my couch when my sons died?

I tried but could not shield
them well enough from fate
whose talon-grip
turns amulet to toy.

Thorns tear out my eyes. I lie,
a flagstone at the feet of Time
all men wear me down
but even those my pain delights
envy that I cannot cringe
at fortune's spite.

Omar S. Pound

℘ Labid (Labid Ibn Rabia, d. 661)

From THE MU'ÁLLAQA

The tent marks in Mínan are worn away,
    where she encamped
and where she alighted,
    Ghawl and Rijám left to the wild,

            And the torrent beds of Rayyán
        naked tracings,
            worn thin, like inscriptions
        carved in flattened stones,

Dung-stained ground
    that tells the years passed
since human presence, months of peace
    gone by, and months of war,

            Replenished by the rain stars
        of spring, and struck
            by thunderclap downpour, or steady,
        fine-dropped, silken rains,

From every kind of cloud
    passing at night,
darkening the morning,
    or rumbling in peals across the evening sky.

            The white pondcress has shot upward,
        and on the wadi slopes,
            gazelles among their newborn,
        and ostriches,

And the wide-of-eyes,
    silent above monthling fawns.
On the open terrain
    yearlings cluster.

            The rills and the runlets
        uncovered marks like the script
            of faded scrolls
        restored with pens of reed,

Or tracings of a tattoo woman:
    beneath the indigo powder,
sifted in spirals,
    the form begins to reappear.

I stopped to question them.
How is one to question
deaf, immutable,
inarticulate stones?

Stripped bare now,
what once held all that tribe —
they left in the early morning
leaving a trench and some thatch,

They stirred longing in you
as they packed up their howdahs,
disappearing in the lairs of cotton,
frames creaking,

Post-beams covered
with twin-rodded curtains
of every kind of cloth brocade
and a black, transparent, inner veil,

Strung out along the route
in groups, like oryx does of Túdih,
or Wájran gazelles, white fawns
below them, soft necks turning,

They faded into the distance
appearing in the shimmering haze
like tamarisks and boulders
on the slopes of Bíshah.

But why recall Nawár?
She's gone.
Her ties and bonds to you
are broken.

The Múrrite lady
has lodged in Fayd,
then joined up with the Hijázi clans.
Who are you to aspire to reach her,

On the eastern slopes
of Twin Mountains or Muhájjar?
Lonebutte has taken her in,
then Marblehead,

Then Tinderlands
if she heads toward Yemen —
I imagine her there — or at Thrall Mountain
or in the valley of Tilkhám.

Cut the bond
with one you cannot reach!
    The best of those who make a bond
are those who can break it.

Give to one who seems to care,
    give again,
but if the love goes lame and stumbles,
    you can break it off

            On a journey-worn mare,
        worn to a remnant,
            with sunken loins
        and a sunken hump.

When flesh shrinks back
    around the joints,
and at the limits of weariness
    ankle thongs fray,

            She is as fleet in the bridle
        as a reddish cloud
            emptied of water
        skimming along on the south wind.

Or a sheen-of-udder,
    mate of a rutted white-belly.
Gnashing and kicking, the driving off of rivals,
    has turned him sallow.

            Bite-scarred, wary,
        he takes her high
            into the hill curves, pregnant,
        recalcitrant, craving.

Above the craglands of Thalabút
    he climbs the vantage points,
wind-swept,
    the way-stones charged with fear,

            Until they scrape back through
        the six dry months of Jumáda,
            month on month of thirst,
        surviving on dew.

They bring their course
    to a binding plan —
strength of intent
    is in the twist of the strands.

Pasterns tear in the briar grass.
Summer winds
flare into dust squalls
and burning winds of Sumúm.

They contend in raising dust.
Its shadow soars
like the smoke of a firebrand,
kindling set ablaze,

Fanned by the north wind,
stoked with brushweed,
the smoke of a blazing,
high-billowing fire.

He pushes on,
keeping her ahead.
She balks.
He drives her forward

Until they break
into the midst of a stream,
split the brimming flow
and clustered reeds,

An enclosing stand of rushes,
some trampled,
some standing,
hedging them in with shade.

———

Or was it a wild one,
wolf-struck?
She lagged behind the herd.
Its lead animal had been her stay.

A flat-nosed one who lost her young,
she does not cease
circling the dune slopes
and lowing,

For a white fawn, rolled in the dust
and dismembered
by contending wolves, ashen,
not about to give up their portion.

They chanced upon her
while she was unaware
and struck. The arrows of fate
do not miss their prey.

   She passes the night
in continuous curtains of rain
   washing around the dune tufts
  in a steady stream,

Flowing along the line of her back,
  runlet on runlet,
on a night the stars
  are veiled in cloud.

   She enters a gnarled tangle
  of roots, casting about
   with her horns, at the base of the dune
  as it drifts and falls away,

Glowing in the face
  of the dark, luminous,
like a seaman's pearl
  come unstrung.

   As night parts from dawn
  she appears in the early light,
   leg shafts slipping
  on the hard, wet sand,

Splashing, confused,
  through the pools of Su'á'id,
back and forth,
  seven pairs of nights and days,

   Until, hope gone,
  her once-full udder dries,
   though suckling and weaning
  are not what withered it down.

She makes out the sound of men,
  muffled, striking fear
from the hidden side,
  human presence, her affliction.

   Dawn finds her turning,
  front and rear,
   placing behind her and ahead
  the source of fear,

Until the archers give up
  and send in their well-trained,
lop-eared, rawhide-collared
  hunting hounds.

They run her down.
She wheels upon them
with a horn, point and shaft,
like a Samharíyya spear,

Driving them off,
sensing death upon her
if she fails, certain,
fated, near,

Kasábi bears down on her.
He is smeared in blood,
and Sukhám, in his place of attack,
is left to die.

———————

On one like that,
when shimmerings dance
in the forenoon
and hills are gowned in mirage,

I bring the issue to a close,
not held back by doubt
or by some critic's rummaging around
for something there to blame.

Or didn't you know, Nawár,
that I
am one who ties a love knot
and cuts it free?

———————

Michael Sells

 5

MEDIEVAL LATIN POETRY, FOURTH THROUGH TWELFTH CENTURIES

Latin

Ausonius (c. 310–395)

THE FIELDS OF SORROW

They wander in deep woods, in mournful light,
Amid long reeds and drowsy-headed poppies,
And lakes where no wave laps, and voiceless streams,
Upon whose banks in the dim light grow old
Flowers that were once bewailed names of kings.

Helen Waddell

I USED TO TELL YOU

I used to tell you, "Frances, we grow old.
The years fly away. Don't be so private
With those parts. A chaste maid is an old maid."
Unnoticed by your disdain, old age crept
Close to us. Those days are gone past recall.
And now you come, penitent and crying
Over your old lack of courage, over
Your present lack of beauty. It's all right.
Closed in your arms, we'll share our smashed delights.
It's give and take now. It's what I wanted,
If not what I want.

Kenneth Rexroth

✥ Sulpicius Lupercus Servasius (c. 400)

RIVERS LEVEL GRANITE MOUNTAINS

Rivers level granite mountains
Rains wash the figures from the sundial,
The plowshare wears thin in the furrow;
And on the fingers of the mighty,
The gold of authority is bright
With the glitter of attrition.

Kenneth Rexroth

✥ Avianus (c. 400–430)

THE CALF AND THE OX

Scampering the pasture, that's how now,
the brown cow, a calf still, sees
in the next field, yoked to a heavy plow,
the dumb ox, and stops to shoot the breeze:
"What's that contraption? What kind of life
is that?" The questions, even the mocking laugh
get no rise from the ox, but a silent stare
at the farmer who carries a glittering butcher knife
and a light halter, coming toward the calf.
Nobody gets to choose which yoke to wear.

David R. Slavitt

✥ Orientius (c. 450)

From POEM ON DIVINE PROVIDENCE

The bulk of these years is already gone out of mind
    because your page is inscribed with no verses.
What conditions have made such silence your product,
    what anguish has squatted on your glum genius?

If the wide sea were to rip broadside into Gaul,
    surging toweringly across its tillage, surely
there is no beast of the field, no grain or fruit or olive
    and no choice place that would not turn rotten;
no plantations and great houses that would not be swept
    by storm crash and fire blast and be left standing blank and sad:

like shouldering a landslide, going through this ten-year slaughter
    strewn by the steel of the Vandals and Visigoths.

And then, too, you trudged among the wagons, eating dust,
    lugging weapons for the Goths, and no small bit of baggage,
beside a white-haired commoner, ruddy with the dust of cities,
    driven the same way a shepherd goads banished sheep.

So you cry over farms laid waste, courtyards deserted,
    and the flame-swept stage scenery of the villas.
How, then, not weep over losses that are truly yours,
    if you could peer into the trampled sanctums
of your heart, their splendors crudded with filth,
    and hobnailed swaggerers in the mind's cramped cell?

John Peck

❧ Anonymous (c. 800)

THE SWAN SEQUENCE

Hear that echo, children,
Swan's cry lost at sea

Bitter he left lake or stream,
Rushes known by his dark farm

"Light goes, my way unfound,
How tell feather from rain?

Cold between close waves,
Who shall find home?

Ocean heads leap nearer,
Shriek poised above death

Neck won't climb, try! climb!
Leave the fish you cannot catch

I scream for the sun I'll never see
I scream for sunset

Then kill me now Orion!
Your arm alone hurls off cloud"

But swan flew quiet, thought the wind,
Could sunrise rescue him?

Yes, one breeze was clever,
Lifting near blinded stars

A land flocks can never leave,
With folded wings, they watch by their last king.

Denis Goacher

⤳ Walafrid Strabo (d. 849)

WITH HIS BOOK, OF GARDENING

for Paul Blackburn

Most learned Father Grimold,
your servant Strabo sends you his book,
a trivial gift and of no account, only for that,
seated in your own garden, where peach and apple
cast their ragged opacities
and your small pupils, laughing, gather up
the shining or furred fruit and bring it you
clutched to the stomach with both hands,
or put it away in bushels,
you might find some utility in it—more,
that you may prune it back,
strengthen, fertilize, transplant
as seems best to you. So may you at last
be brought to such flourishing
as grapples God's trellis toward
the evergreening of unwithering life:
this may Father, Son and Fruitful Spirit grant you.

Tim Reynolds

⤳ Anonymous (c. 1050)

LEVIS EXSURGIT ZEPHIRUS *From* THE CAMBRIDGE SONGS

The wind stirs lightly as the sun's
warmth stirs in the new season's
moment when the earth shows everything
she has, her fragrance on everything.

The spring royally in his excitement
scatters the new season's commandment
everywhere, and the new leaves open,
the buds open, and begin to happen.

The winged and the fourfooted creatures
according to their several natures

find or build their nesting places;
each unknowingly rejoices.

Held apart from the season's pleasure
according to my separate nature
nevertheless I bless and praise
the new beginning of the new days.

seeing it all, hearing it all,
the leaf opening, the first bird call.

David Ferry

Anonymous (c. 1100)

HERIGER AND THE FALSE PROPHET *From* THE CAMBRIDGE SONGS

Heriger the bishop   of Mainz once encountered
a prophet who claimed   that he had been captured
and carried off straightway   right down to Hell.

He furnished details,   this among others:
"Hell is encircled   around and about
By very dense forest."   Such was his story.

Heriger giggled   before he made answer:
"Maybe I'll quarter   in that fat pasture
My swineherd with all my   scrawny little piglets."

The fellow kept lying: "Then was I taken
To the temple of Heaven;   there I saw Jesus
Sitting and eating   a very nice supper.

"And Johann the Baptist   served as the barkeep,
Pouring out goblets   of first-rate vintage
To a bibulous crowd   of saintly carousers."

Then said the bishop: "It was canny of Christ
To choose the Baptizer   to fill up their glasses,
For as we all know   he drank only water.

"But you prove you're a liar   when you tell us that Peter
Works in the kitchen   inspecting the cooking,
For he is the keeper   of the portals of Heaven.

"What honor in Heaven   did the good Lord give you?
At the table celestial   where were you seated?
And what were you offered   that was tasty to eat?"

This prophet responded: "I sat in a corner
With a giblet of tripe,   but only a little
I stole from the cooks,   and I nibbled on that."

Then Heriger ordered him   tied to a pillar
And whipped with those straps   that bind up broomstraw
And preached him a sermon   of harsh-sounding words:

"If ever it happens   that Jesus invites you
Once more to dinner   perhaps you'll remember
Not to behave like   a verminous thief."

Fred Chappell

Peter Abelard (d. 1142)

I AM CONSTANTLY WOUNDED

I am constantly wounded
By the deadly gossip that adds
Insult to injury, that
Punishes me mercilessly
With the news of your latest
Scandal in my ears. Wherever
I go the smirking fame of each
Fresh despicable infamy
Has run on ahead of me.
Can't you learn to be cautious
About your lecheries?
Hide your practices in darkness;
Keep away from raised eyebrows.
If you must murder love, do it
Covertly, with your candied
Prurience and murmured lewdness.

You were never the heroine
Of dirty stories in the days
When love bound us together.
Now those links are broken, desire
Is frozen, and you are free
To indulge every morbid lust,
And filthy jokes about your
Latest amour are the delight
Of every cocktail party.

Your boudoir is a brothel;
Your salon is a saloon;
Even your sensibilities
And your depraved innocence

Are only special premiums,
Rewards of a shameful commerce.
O the heart breaking memory
Of days like flowers, and your
Eyes that shone like Venus the star
In our brief nights, and the soft bird
Flight of your love about me;
And now your eyes are as bitter
As a rattlesnake's dead eyes,
And your disdain as malignant.
Those who give off the smell of coin
You warm in bed; I who have
Love to bring am not even
Allowed to speak to you now.
You receive charlatans and fools;
I have only the swindling
Memory of poisoned honey.

Kenneth Rexroth

Anonymous (c. 1150)

DE RAMIS CADUNT FOLIA (LOVE IN WINTER)

From every limb the leaves are cast,
And greenness dies along the vines;
Since summer's vital heat has passed,
All life declines;
The sun has travelled to the last
Celestial signs.

The winter sets its killing blight
On tender things; most birds have flown;
The nightingale the growing night
Laments alone;
The land seems in the waning light
A monotone.

No ground that is not full of wet,
No field but its green grasses lost;
The golden sun escapes to set
On seas uncrossed;
With snowy days we'll soon be met,
And nights of frost.

Now everything that is must freeze,
And I alone am all afire,
I feel a flame within me seize
My heart entire;

A maiden is the source of these
Pangs of desire.

Her touch is gentle and entwines,
Her virginal, soft kiss excites;
In her bright eye eternal shines
The light of lights;
Nor are there in this world's confines
More holy sights.

To quench a flame within, it's said,
Drink bitter wine excessively;
Yet I must burn and live instead
In misery;
From my own heart the fire's fed
Abundantly.

                    Phillip Holland

∞ Anonymous (c. 1150)

DUM DIANA VITREA *From* THE CARMINA BURANA

When Diana, late at night,
for her crystal lamp reclaims
pink and paler light
kindled from her brother's flames,
western winds soft and fair
fill the air,
clear the sky,
and as by
music falling from above
cast their spell
and compel
hearts once hard to yield to love
as the evening star again
bright and new,
fresh with dew,
charms to sleep mortal men.

O felicity
of sleep careless
that comes to set us free
from all distress,
and through the eyes' entry
making sweet ingress
prepares us for sorcery
of love's progress.

Morpheus, shaper in the mind
brings us for dreams
soft blowing wind,
murmuring of streams
over clean sand running,
mill wheel sound
all night long turning
slowly round and round
softly to mesmerize
day-weary eyes.

After love's blandishing
and soft exchanges,
sleep comes languishing;
new strength outranges
all past sweet experience
and swims in new ecstasies of sense
Lovely to sleep after love's strain,
but lovelier to wake from sleep to love again.

Under green trellises
where Philomela sings the lay
of her sad jealousies,
sweet to sleep the night away,
but sweeter still to play
with a girl in the grass,
and with such beauty pass
all the time away.

Smell of thyme and roses
and all things growing
gently disposes
of all our hearts' undoing,
and the heart in weariness
after love's commerces
softly reposes.

                    Richmond Lattimore

❧ Archpoet (c. 1165)

THE ARCHPOET'S CONFESSION

Boiling over inwardly,
choking on my fury,
sick at heart with bitterness,
only verse can cure me.
Made up of light elements,

air and fire only,
like a fallen leaf I lie
where the winds have blown me.

Let the wise man prudently
seek some kind of stasis,
on a rock foundation build
his enduring basis.
Foolishly I let life slip
like a running river,
underneath the self-same skies
firmly settled never.

Like a ship without a crew
driven on the ocean,
like a straggling bird in air
making errant motion.
Chains will never hold me down,
nor a key confine,
I seek people with a twist
similar to mine.

Gravity of heart and mind
isn't very sunny,
joking is more pleasant and
sweeter far than honey.
Whatsoever Venus bids
is a welcome labor,
Venus loves the young at heart,
loving of their neighbor.

Wide the berth I give myself
in the way of youth,
virtue can't compare with vice,
if you want the truth.
More intent on pleasure than
matters of salvation,
since my soul is surely doomed,
better save my clay skin.

Prelate, you who judge so well,
I must beg your pardon,
sin is deadly and so sweet
I am dead but ardent.
Stricken by the beauty of
girls, past cure, or near it,
those who may escape my touch
I possess in spirit.

It is very hard to hold
nature in subjection;

looking at a virgin with-
out a changed complexion.
We young men are not equipped
such strict rules for keeping,
we are desperate for a cure
for our bodies' leaping.

You say that I love the dice,
nor am inexpert there,
all I know is in the end,
I have lost my shirt there,
Though I'm freezing and exposed,
inside I'm on fire,
verses then and witty songs
come at my desire.

You have heard, in talk of me,
tavern-dwelling brought up,
I can't say I've spared the place,
where I'm often caught up.
There I'll stay until I hear
holy angels chanting
"Rest eternal" to the dead,
and my pardon granting.

I intend to meet my end
in a tavern lying,
at my lips a cup of wine,
drinking as I'm dying.
Choruses of angels will
sing where skies are pinker,
"May the Lord have mercy on
this devoted drinker."

From the cup my lamp is lit,
drink inflames my spirit,
drunk with nectar I fly up
where the gods uprear it.
Tavern wine tastes sweeter than
wine that's mixed with water,
that's the way the churchmen drink,
lest their worships totter.

Certain poets shun the bright
lights of public places,
they're the kind who only write
where their private space is.
Study, sleeplessness, and toil,
hope where it seems hopeless,
that at last they may bring forth
one immortal opus.

Going without food and drink
is some poets' diet,
they avoid the marketplace,
where the people riot.
So that they might make a work
to outlast the ages,
at their desks they perish to
give life to their pages.

Inspiration never comes
like a bolt upon me,
not unless my belly's first
full and wine is drawn me.
Then within my reeling brain
Bacchus drinks me under,
soon Apollo rushes in
speaking words of wonder.

In the bishop's presence I'll
publish my behavior,
following the rule set forth
by our blessed savior.
Let him be the first to cast
stones at me, a poet,
whose mind is not dark with sin,
though he may not show it.

There, I freely have divulged
my own deviations,
just the ones my friends at court
told to try your patience.
Yet among them not a one
stands his own accuser,
though of worldly pleasures he
be a heavy user.

I've alleged against myself
everything about me,
I have spat the poison out
which long ran throughout me.
My old ways no longer please,
I prefer a new life;
though my face remains the same,
Jove beholds my true life.

Spare one who is penitent,
Bishop and Elector—
grant me mercy as my lord
in the private sector.
Though I've lived a life of sin,
from the heart I rue it,

lay upon me penance due,
I will freely do it.

Phillip Holland

Anonymous (c. 950)

ALBA, WITH A REFRAIN FROM THE PROVENÇAL

Two shadows now, north from the translucent
moon, from the unrisen sun west,
watcher cries warning to the unwary:
    Dawn whitens over a dark sea,
    leans across the hills: the light! the light!

Day lies in ambush for the unwakeful
for the sleepers to destroy them
to whom the watcher cries warning still:
    Dawn whitens over a dark sea,
    leans across the hills: the light! the light!

The wind blows chillier from Arcturus.
The stars gutter, dwindling toward the pole.
The Great Bear lumbers east and east.
    Dawn whitens over a dark sea,
    leans across the hills: the light! the light!

Tim Reynolds

6

POETRY IN CELTIC LANGUAGES

Irish Gaelic

Colman mac Lenini (d. 604)

IN PRAISE OF A SWORD GIVEN HIM BY HIS
PRINCE

Blackbirds to a swan,
Feathers to hard iron,
Rock hags to a siren,
    All lords to my lord;
Jackdaws to a hawk,
Cackling to a choir,
Sparks to a bonfire,
    All swords to my sword.

Richard O'Connell

Attributed to Rumann, son of Colman (c. 700)

STORM AT SEA

Tempest on the plain of Lir
Bursts its barriers far and near,
    And upon the rising tide
    Wind and noisy winter ride—
Winter throws a shining spear.

When the wind blows from the east
All the billows seem possessed,
    To the west they storm away
    To the farthest, wildest bay
Where the light turns to its rest.

When the wind is from the north
The fierce and shadowy waves go forth,
    Leaping, snarling at the sky,
    To the southern world they fly
And the confines of the earth.

When the wind is from the west
All the waves that cannot rest
    To the east must thunder on
    Where the bright tree of the sun
Is rooted in the ocean's breast.

When the wind is from the south
The waves turn to a devil's broth,
    Crash in foam on Skiddy's beach,
    For Caladnet's summit reach,
Batter Limerick's grey-green mouth.

Ocean's full! The sea's in flood,
Beautiful is the ships' abode;
    In the Bay of the Two Beasts
    The sandy wind in eddies twists,
The rudder holds a shifting road.

Every bay in Ireland booms
When the flood against it comes —
    Winter throws a spear of fire!
    Round Scotland's shores and by Cantyre
A mountainous surging chaos glooms.

God's Son of hosts that none can tell
The fury of the storm repel!
    Dread Lord of the sacrament,
    Save me from the wind's intent,
Spare me from the blast of Hell.

                     Frank O'Connor

ஜ Anonymous (c. 700)

EPITAPH FOR CU CHUIMNE

Cu Chuimne in his youth
    studied half the truth,

then turned from the second half
    and studied women.

With the fullness of years
    he developed wisdom,
and turned away from women
    to complete his studies.

                        Thomas Kinsella

℘ Anonymous (c. 700)

STANZA

What, my Lord, shall I do with
Work enough to fill a cart?
How build from a thousand boards
A tight little house of art?

                        Lewis Turco

℘ Anonymous (c. 700)

From THE TAIN

Combat of Ferdia and Cúchulainn

'Ferdia of the hosts
and the hard blows, beloved
golden brooch, I mourn
your conquering arm

and our fostering together,
a sight to please a prince;
your gold-rimmed shield,
your slender sword,

the ring of bright silver
on your fine hand,
your skill at chess,
your flushed, sweet cheek,

your curled yellow hair
like a great lovely jewel,
the soft leaf-shaped belt
that you wore at your waist.

You have fallen to the Hound,
I cry for it, little calf.

The shield didn't save you
that you brought to the fray.

Shameful was our struggle,
the uproar and grief!
O fair, fine hero
who shattered armies
and crushed them under foot,
golden brooch, I mourn.'

Thomas Kinsella

✂ Anonymous (c. 700)

THE FORT OF RATHANGAN

The fort over against the oak-wood,
Once it was Bruidge's, it was Cathal's,
It was Aed's, it was Ailill's,
It was Conaing's, it was Cuiline's,
And it was Maelduin's;
The fort remains after each in his turn—
And the kings asleep in the ground.

Kuno Meyer

✂ Anonymous (c. 700)

BRAN AT THE ISLAND OF WOMEN

Bran you're flabbergast
at what for you is mere sea, while I
in my chariot, from a distance, observe
your coracle traverse a floral plain.

You see wave upon
wave leapfrogging over the ocean;
I myself behold in The Plain of Sports
waves of perfect vermilion flowers.

Sea-horses shimmer in summer
as far as your gaze can stretch;
flowers fountain with nectar
in the land of Manannan son of Ler.

The sheen of the sea on which you row,
the spangle of the water

unfurls, green and gold,
into rock solid terrain.

The speckled salmon leaping
from the fleecy sea
are calves and lovely coloured lambs
at ease with one another.

Though you simply see a lone chariot-rider
in the Pleasant Plain of flowers,
it is alive with steeds
of which you have no inkling.

The expanse of the plain and its host
are bedecked with hues of profound beauty,
a stream of silver, steps of gold,
welcome all at every grand feast.

Men and gentle women play
a sweet and comely game
under shading wildwood, contesting fairly,
without sin, without transgression.

Your puny craft navigates over a blossoming,
halcyon wood, bursting with ripe fruit,
blessed with the true scent of the vine;
a wood without decay, without defect.

We are from the beginning of the beginning,
ageless, not being of the clay,
we do not fear fading;
the sin has never reached us.

Greg Delanty

❧ Anonymous (c. 800)

THE OLD WOMAN OF BEARE

The sea crawls from the shore
Leaving there
The despicable weed,
A corpse's hair.
In me,
The desolate withdrawing sea.

The Old Woman of Beare am I
Who once was beautiful.
Now all I know is how to die.
I'll do it well.

Look at my skin
Stretched tight on the bone.
Where kings have pressed their lips,
The pain, the pain.

I don't hate the men
Who swore the truth was in their lies.
One thing alone I hate—
Women's eyes.

The young sun
Gives its youth to everyone,
Touching everything with gold.
In me, the cold.

The cold. Yet still a seed
Burns there.
Women love only money now.
But when
I loved, I loved
Young men.

Young men whose horses galloped
On many an open plain
Beating lightning from the ground.
I loved such men.

And still the sea
Rears and plunges into me,
Shoving, rolling through my head
Images of the drifting dead.

A soldier cries
Pitifully about his plight;
A king fades
Into the shivering night.

Does not every season prove
That the acorn hits the ground?
Have I not known enough of love
To know it's lost as soon as found?

I drank my fill of wine with kings,
Their eyes fixed on my hair.
Now among the stinking hags
I chew the cud of prayer.

Time was the sea
Brought kings as slaves to me.
Now I near the face of God
And the crab crawls through my blood.

I loved the wine
That thrilled me to my fingertips;
Now the mean wind
Stitches salt into my lips.

The coward sea
Slouches away from me.
Fear brings back the tide
That made me stretch at the side
Of him who'd take me briefly for his bride.

The sea grows smaller, smaller now.
Farther, farther it goes
Leaving me here where the foam dries
On the deserted land,
Dry as my shrunken thighs,
As the tongue that presses my lips,
As the veins that break through my hands.

Brendan Kenneally

✣ Anonymous (c. 800)

EPITAPH

"Have you seen Hugh,
The Connacht king in the field?"
"All that we saw
Was his shadow under his shield."

Frank O'Connor

✣ Anonymous (c. 800)

WHENCE ARE YOU, LEARNING'S SON?

"Whence are you, learning's son?"
"From Clonmacnois I come.
"My course of studies done,
    "I'm off to Swords again."
"How are things keeping there?"
"Oh, things are shaping fair—
"Foxes round churchyards bare
    "Gnawing the guts of men."

Frank O'Connor

Anonymous (c. 800)

MONASTIC POEMS: FOUR GLOSSES

1

A wall of woodland overlooks me.
A blackbird sings me a song (no lie!).
Above my book, with its lines laid out;
the birds in their music sing to me.

The cuckoo sings clear in lovely voice
in his grey cloak from a bushy fort.
I swear it now, but God is good!
It is lovely writing out in the wood.

2

How lovely it is today!
The sunlight breaks and flickers
on the margin of my book.

3

A bird is calling from the willow
with lovely beak, a clean call.
Sweet yellow tip; he is black and strong.
It is doing a dance, the blackbird's song.

4

The little bird
let out a whistle
from his beak tip
    bright yellow.
He sends the note
across Loch Laig
    —a blackbird, a branch
    a mass of yellow.

Thomas Kinsella

Anonymous (c. 800)

From SWEENEY ASTRAY

My Dark Night Has Come Round Again

My dark night has come round again.
The world goes on but I return

to haunt myself. I freeze and burn.
I am the bare figure of pain.

Frost crystals and level ice,
the scourging snow, the male-voiced storm
assist at my requiem.
My hearth goes cold, my fire dies.

Are there still some who call me prince?
The King of Kings, the Lord of All
revoked my title, worked my downfall,
unhoused, unwived me for my sins.

Why did He spare my life at Moira?
Why did He grudge me death in battle?
Why ordained the hag of the mill
His hound of heaven and my fury?

The mill-hag's millstone round my neck!
Hell roast her soul! She dragged me down
when I leaped up in agitation.
I fell for that old witch's trick.

Then Lynchseachan was in full cry,
a bloodhound never off my trail.
I fell for his lies too and fell
among captors out of the tree.

They made me face the love I'd lost.
They tied me up and carried me
back to the house. The mockery!
I overheard their victory feast

yet gradually grew self-possessed,
for there were decent people there,
and gaming and constant laughter.
My mind was knitting up at last

but soon unravelled into nightmare.
I was for the high jump once more.
The mill-hag spun her web and swore
her innocence. I leaped for her

and leaped beyond the bounds of sense.
She challenged me a second time.
We kept in step like words in rhyme.
I set the pace and led the dance —

I cleared the skylight and the roof,
I flew away beyond the fortress

but she hung on. Through smooth and rough
I raised the wind and led the chase.

We coursed all over Ireland then.
I was the wind and she was smoke.
I was the prow and she the wake.
I was the earth and she the moon.

But always look before you leap!
Though she was fit for bog and hill,
Dunseverick gave her the spill.
She followed me down off the top

of the fort and spread-eagled
her bitch's body in the air.
I trod the water, watching her
hit the rocks. And I was glad

to see her float in smithereens.
A crew of devils made a corpse
of her and buried it. Cursed
be the ground that housed her bones.

One night I walked across the Fews —
the hills were dark, the starlight dead —
when suddenly five severed heads,
five lantern ghouls, appeared and rose

like bats from hell, surrounding me.
Then a head spoke — another shock!
— This is the Ulster lunatic.
Let us drive him into the sea.

I went like an arrow from a bow.
My feet disdained that upland ground.
Goat-head and dog-head cursed but found
me impossible to follow.

I have deserved all this:
night-vigils, terror,
flittings across water,
women's cried-out eyes.

Seamus Heaney

The Trees of the Forest

Stag on the westward ridge, melodious
One, clamourer with your high nodes
Of point and time. Below, the roe-bucks
Are grazing in a dappled row.

Oak, mighty one, my shelterer,
I lie beneath you, acorn in shell.
Crush of your bark will cure a mastoid,
Swine root among the years of mast.

The water-willow is never hostile.
I pull down sweetness, cross green stile,
Frail blossom of the catkin. Baskets
Are woven, supple as your sap.

The wicked blackthorn, claws sharp as Pangur
Baun's. Each prickle is a pang,
Appetite has been well sustained by
Those berries, juicy, darksome, stainful.

The yew-tree, gloomer in churchyard. Coffins
Go under it, funereal cough.
The yewy yew thickens: a sturdy
One. Winds blow strong. It is unstirred.

Aspen, the trembler, leaves a-racing
Fast as competitions in Thrace.
I hear within it the sound of fray.
That whispering makes me afraid.

Hateful the ash, a nub for chariot.
Let every branch above be charred.
Avoid the ash that brings contention.
Quarrel on chessboard, blows in tent.

Apple tree shaken by many hands,
Wide spreader out of pink bloom, handsome
One. Bark for tanning, wealth in garden.
Sweet crop that every man must guard.

Elder, that women strain, boil twice,
The bark will dry the pus in boil
Out of the flowers will come a greenness.
Dyers make the dark and the pale be seen.

Holly, cold light in woods, silver
As winter moon, icedrip from sill,
The leaves are fierce and disagreeable
Although they glitter like filagree.

Pleasant the whiteness of the May,
I smell and pluck it while I may,
Go by it in the twilight, listen
To music coming from rath and liss.

Pleasant, also, the lofty beech
That comes down to the river beach.
Under the shady shade, I drag
My weariness, sore-footed, bedraggled.

Briar, deceitful friend, you hold me
With tiny fingers, unholy one,
Drawing a drop from small or big vein.
I jump away. Your tricks are vain.

Birch, the smooth, the blessed, sent down
From Heaven, with summer grace and scent,
Delicate one: breezes are leaving
Half of your sweetness with other leaves.

Dear Hazel, bring an end to my story,
Pantry of plenty, my winter store.
Sweet, sweet, is the brown-covered kernel:
Good bite for gallowglass and kern.

Stag of the topmost ridge, melodious
One, clamourer with your high nodes
Of point and tine. Below, the roe-bucks
Are grazing in a dappled row.

Austin Clarke

✇ Anonymous (c. 800)

NORTH-EAST

i

The small bird
let a chirp
from its beak:
    I heard
woodnotes, whin-
gold, sudden:
the Lagan
    blackbird.

ii

Look far: cast
eyes north-east
over tossed
    seascapes.
There's the seal!

And tides fill
and run, all
    whitecaps.

Seamus Heaney

❧ Anonymous (c. 800)

ON THE VIKING RAIDS

Since tonight the wind is high,
The sea's white mane a fury
I need not fear the hordes of Hell
Coursing the Irish Channel.

Frank O'Connor

❧ Anonymous (c. 800)

SEASON SONG *From* THE FINN-CYCLE

Here's a song —
stags give tongue
winter snows
summer goes.

High cold blow
sun is low
brief his day
seas give spray.

Fern clumps redden
shapes are hidden
wildgeese raise
wonted cries.

Cold now girds
wings of birds
icy time —
that's my rime.

Flann O'Brien

⁊⁊ Attributed to Amergin (c. 800)

AMERGIN'S CHARM

[The text restored from mediaeval Irish and Welsh variants.]

I am a stag: *of seven tines,*
I am a flood: *across a plain,*
I am a wind: *on a deep lake,*
I am a tear: *the Sun lets fall,*
I am a hawk: *above the cliff,*
I am a thorn: *beneath the nail,*
I am a wonder: *among flowers,*
I am a wizard: *who but I*
Sets the cool head aflame with smoke?

I am a spear: *that roars for blood,*
I am a salmon: *in a pool,*
I am a lure: *from paradise,*
I am a hill: *where poets walk,*
I am a boar: *renowned and red,*
I am a breaker: *threatening doom,*
I am a tide: *that drags to death,*
I am an infant: *who but I*
Peeps from the unhewn dolmen arch?

I am the womb: *of every holt,*
I am the blaze: *on every hill,*
I am the queen: *of every hive,*
I am the shield: *for every head,*
I am the grave: *of every hope.*

Robert Graves

⁊⁊ Anonymous (c. 850)

THE SCHOLAR AND THE CAT

Each of us pursues his trade,
I and Pangur my comrade,
His whole fancy on the hunt,
And mine for learning ardent.

More than fame I love to be
Among my books and study,
Pangur does not grudge me it,
Content with his own merit.

When—a heavenly time!—we are
In our small room together
Each of us has his own sport
And asks no greater comfort.

While he sets his round sharp eye
On the walls of my study
I turn mine, though lost its edge
On the great wall of knowledge.

Now a mouse drops in his net
After some mighty onset
While into my bag I cram
Some difficult darksome problem.

When a mouse comes to the kill
Pangur exults, a marvel!
I have when some secret's won
My hour of exaltation.

Though we work for days and years
Neither the other hinders;
Each is competent and hence
Enjoys his skill in silence.

Master of the death of mice,
He keeps in daily practice,
I too, making dark things clear,
Am of my trade a master.

Frank O'Connor

℘ Anonymous (c. 850)

TOWARD WINTER (FOUR FRAGMENTS)

1

Sliab Cua, dark and broken, is full of wolf packs.
The wind sweeps down its glens,
wolves howl about its dykes,
the fierce dark deer bellows
across it in the Autumn,
and the crane cries out across its rocks.

2

The night is cold on the Great Bog.
The storm is lashing—no small matter.

The sharp wind is laughing at the groans
echoing through the cowering wood.

3

We are shattered and battered, engulfed,
O King of clear-starred Heaven!
The wind has swallowed us like twigs
swallowed in a red flame out of Heaven.

4

Want and Winter are upon us.
The lake-side is flooded.
Frost has shrivelled the leaves.
The pleasant wave has started muttering.

Thomas Kinsella

Anonymous (c. 1150)

GRANIA'S SONG TO DIARMUID

Stag does not lay his side to sleep;
    He bellows from the mountainside,
And tramples through the woods, and yet
    In no green thicket can he hide.

Not even the birds within their house —
    From bough to bough all night they leap,
And stir the air with startled cries.
    Among the leaves they will not sleep.

The duck that bears her brood tonight
    By many a sheltering bank must creep,
And furrow the wild waters bright;
    Among the reeds she will not sleep.

The curlew cannot sleep at all
    His voice is shrill above the deep
Reverberations of the storm;
    Between the streams he will not sleep.

But you must sleep as in the south
    He who from Conall long ago
With all the arts of speech and song
    Made Morann's daughter rise and go.

Or sleep the sleep that Fionncha found
    In Ulster with his stolen bride,

When Slaney ran from home with him
    And slept no more at Falvey's side.

Or sleep the sleep that Aunya slept
    When with the torchlight round her head
From Garnish and her father's house
    To her beloved's arms she fled.

Or Dedaid's sleep who in the east
    Did not think for one sweet night,
His head upon his lover's breast
    Of the terrors of the flight.

Frank O'Connor

Welsh

৯ে Attributed to Myrddyn (Merlin, c. 550)

YSCOLAN

Your horse is black your cloak is black
your face is black you are black
you are all black—is it you Yscolan?

I am Yscolan the seer
my thoughts fly they are covered with clouds.
Is there no reparation then for offending the Master?

I burned a church I killed the cows that belonged to a school
I threw the Book into the waves
my penance is heavy.

Creator of living things you
greatest of all my protectors forgive me.
He that betrayed you deceived me.

I was fastened for a whole year
at Bangor under the piles of the dam.
Try to think what I suffered from the sea worms.

If I had known what I know now
the liberty of the wind in the moving tree tops
that crime could not be laid to me.

W. S. Merwin

✂ Aneirin (c. 590)

THE GORCHEANU: THREE LAMENTS

I

I sing what I saw:
waste scatter of weaponry
broken battlelines
uproar
slaughter.

Surrounded by splendour—
his household's hospitality—
curved cutlasses hang wide walls,
spiralled wine horns,
the bitter alderwood chalice—
they praised him:
fair skinned,
tough stuff,
matchless.

In his heyday
a war wolf in ford fights.
Spear sharp his snake eyes.
Danger-driven.
Woman-wanted.
Bull of the marriage bed.
I mourn his murder.

The fight's forehead,
full of wave fury,
he death-drove four times
his own tallied followers—
shield
shattered,
his sword swipe a skull splitter.

Proud in his purple,
swigger of strong wine,
he deserved every right
to his titles for terror.
A wonder the wield of his weapons.

Though green grass grows on his gravemound,
though fame fade,
I lament there his death's day;
lament too the men came to Catraeth
who fostered me.

II

I sing
rivet studded shields,
that magic boar, river war, Angle slaughter.

I sing
his fight's fury
barefaced in battle,
bringer of black crows
to bloodstained white corpses.

Headlong his gallop
on knee-tight held horses.
Headlong his hot charge
mad for mad massacre.

I'll praise my prince
till I cease in silence:
border defender,
wise man in war matters.
He gifted his spear to me,
hard hafted, gold gilded.
High his honour
as gift giver.

Focus of any fight
while flung spears fell
on locked battle.

Of the crowd who came down to Catraeth
after our booze-up
myself and three others
got back —
I for a price
in silver, gold and war weapons
because of the power that makes poetry.

III

Northman,
you keep me awake
with your lime-white shield,
your check cloak,
your blood splashed tartan.

Boozing pal,
forever out front in a fracas,
you finally dared
the Deep Divide —
died.

Desmond O'Grady

From THE GODODDIN

Youth
exquisite with man instinct
backbone in battle
many a horsehand high
galloped game thoroughbreds
given head
thick manes streaming
broad shields tiptipping rhythmically
tilting flanks.

Swords blue bladed.

Flash of the golden spurs
gold embroidered the garments.

What anguish between us?
I praise you!

The end?

Battle beds
not marriage.

It's wrong that such friends
should end in the claws of ravens.

II

His coronet bound round his forehead
passion proud
he raised his worked winchorn
high to the watching women
wide of the rim of his shield.

So frenzied his fighting
quarter he granted
only when called for;
stood, stock straight there in the thick of it
until he drew blood.
Who faced him he cut down like corn stalks.

And the tale went untold
on the turf of that ground
outside the tall torn tents
till this single man
of three hundred
returned.

III

Headband loose
this man,
like the circling eagle
closing over the estuary,
his word kept
his after planned
and no turn back.

The enemy
scuttled to short shelter.
No courage controlled them.

No quarter.
No barter.
Nothing.
Yet they lost it.
That's how it went.

IV

Golden this brave's band.
Half the wolf in him
half the temple too.

Jewel clasps on him
and precious things mounted.

Worth of worked horn.
Wolf at the winecup.

In crisis
he helped men work its worth out
for themselves.

Shield: splinters.
Sword: sheared off.

Gone all good council.

He ended in bloodshed.
Blood belongs everywhere.

V

His goldband broad round his forehead
armed to the scalp
this dear friend
dead before daybreak
and all for his battle's boast;
downed at the end in the eyes of two armies.

Five times fifty heads fell to his credit.
Of the fellows who faced him
one hundred knocked in a halfhour.

So many friends,
so many,
given to wolves
not weddings
to scaldcrows not sacraments.

Desmond O'Grady

✎ Anonymous (c. 600)

SONG TO A CHILD

Dinogad's smock is pied, pied—
Made it out of marten hide.
Whit, whit, whistle along,
Eight slaves with you sing the song.

When your dad went to hunt,
Spear on his shoulder, cudgel in hand,
He called his quick dogs, 'Giff, you wretch,
Gaff, catch her, catch her, fetch, fetch!'

From a coracle he'd spear
Fish as a lion strikes a deer.
When your dad went to the crag
He brought down roebuck, boar and stag,
Speckled grouse from the mountain tall,
Fish from Derwent waterfall.

Whatever your dad found with his spear,
Boar or wild cat, fox or deer,
Unless it flew, would never get clear.

Tony Conran

✎ Attributed to Taliesin (c. 700)

EAGLE OF PENGWERN

Eagle of Pengwern, grey-crested, tonight
its shriek is high,
eager for flesh I loved.

Eagle of Pengewern, grey-crested, tonight
    its call is high,
    eager for Cynddylan's flesh.

Eagle of Pengwern, grey-crested, tonight
    its claw is high,
    eager for flesh I love.

Eagle of Pengwern, it called far tonight,
    it kept watch on men's blood;
    Trenn shall be called a luckless town.

Eagle of Pengwern, it calls far tonight,
    it feasts on men's blood;
    Trenn shall be called a shining town.

                                   Gwyn Williams

ஜ Anonymous (c. 850)

THE SPOILS OF ANNWN

I praise a prince, lord of king's country,
Over shores of the world widens his sovereignty.
Impeccable prison had Gweir in Caer Siddi,
As the story relates of Pwyll and Pryderi.
Prior to him, there went to it nobody,
To the heavy grey chain that trussed a true laddie.
Because of the spoils of Annwn he sang bitterly.
It shall last till Doomsday, our own prayer and poetry.
Three shiploads of Prydwen we went on that journey.
Seven alone returned from Caer Siddi.

I make splendid fame, my song they heard it
In the rotating fortress, four-turreted.
It was of the cauldron my first word was uttered.
With breath of nine maidens its fire was lighted.
Head of Annwn owned the cauldron. What nature has it?
Dark round the rim, and pearl-encrusted,
Its destiny is, no coward's food cooks in it.
The flashing sword of Lleawg was thrust in it.
In the hand of Lleminawg they left it
And before Hell's gate a lamp was lighted.
When we went with Arthur, bright and ill-fated,
Seven alone came back from Caer Feddwid.

I make splendid fame, my song is heard more
In the four-turreted fort, isle of the radiant door,

Where jet black and noonday are mingled together.
Bright wine with their retinue they had for liquor.
Three shiploads in Prydwen we put off from shore.
Seven alone returned from Caer Rigor

Tony Conran

⚘ Anonymous (c. 1000)

GEREINT SON OF ERBIN *From* THE BLACK BOOK OF CARMATHEN

Before Gereint, the enemy's punisher,
I saw white stallions with red shins
and after the war-cry a bitter grave.

Before Gereint, the enemy's depriver,
I saw stallions red-shinned from battle
and after the war-cry a bitter pensiveness.

Before Gereint, scourge of the enemy,
I saw stallions girdled in white
and after the war-cry a bitter covering.

At Llongborth I saw vultures
and more than many a bier
and men red before Gereint's unrush.

At Llongborth I saw slaughter,
men in fear and blood on the head
before Gereint, his father's great son.

At Llongborth I saw spurs
and men who would not flinch from spears
and the drinking of wine from shining glass.

At Llongborth I saw armour
and the blood flowing
and after the war-cry a bitter burying.

At Llongborth I saw Arthur,
where brave men struck down with steel,
an emperor, a director of toil.

At Llongborth Gereint was killed,
and brave men from Devon's lowland;
and before they were killed, they killed.

There were fast horses under Gereint's thigh,
long-shanked, wheat-fed;
they were red, in their rush like milky eagles.

There were fast horses under Gereint's thigh,
long-shanked, grain nourished them;
they were red, their rush like black eagles.

There were fast horses under Gereint's thigh,
long-shanked, devourers of grain;
they were red, their rush like red eagles.

There were fast horses under Gereint's thigh,
long-shanked, emptiers of grain;
they were red, their rush like white eagles.

There were fast horses under Gereint's thigh,
long-shanked, with the stride of a stag,
like the roar of burning on a waste mountain.

There were fast horses under Gereint's thigh,
long-shanked, greedy for grain,
blue-gray, their hair tipped with silver.

There were fast horses under Gereint's thigh,
long-shanked, worthy of grain;
they were red, their rush like grey eagles.

There were fast horses under Gereint's thigh,
long-shanked, grain-fed;
they were red, their rush like brown eagles.

When Gereint was born, Heaven's gates were open,
Christ would grant what was asked:
a fair countenance, the glory of Britain.

Gwyn Williams

ঞ্চ Anonymous (c. 1063)

THE SONG OF BLODEUWEDD *From* THE MABINOGION

Not of father nor of mother
Was my blood, was my body.
I was spellbound by Gwydion,
Prime enchanter of the Britons,
When he formed me from nine blossoms,
  Nine buds of various kind:

From primrose of the mountain,
Broom, meadow-sweet and cockle,
   Together intertwined,
From the bean in its shade bearing
A white spectral army
   Of earth, of earthy kind,
From blossoms of the nettle,
Oak, thorn and bashful chestnut—
Nine powers of nine flowers,
    Nine powers in me combined,
      Nine buds of plant and tree.
Long and white are my fingers
      As the ninth wave of the sea.

Robert Graves

ANGLO-SAXON POETRY

Anglo-Saxon

∾ Anonymous (c. 700)

THE RUIN

Well-wrought this wall-stone which fate has broken:
The city bursts, the work of giants crumbles.
Roofs are fallen, towers in ruins,
The gate is gone, frost on the mortar,
The shelters in shards, open to showers,
Eaten by age. Earth has in its grasp
Ruler and workman, removed now, perished,
Held fast in the ground while a hundred generations
Went from the land. This wall remained,
Red-colored, mossy, kingdom on kingdom,
Stood under storms, while all around perished.
Bright were the buildings, many bath-houses,
High-gabled homes, and the sound of soldiers,
Many a mead-hall where men enjoyed themselves
Until mighty fate overturned all.
Many men fell in the days of wrath;
Death took all the valor of earth.
Bulwarks became wrecked foundations,
A fortress in fragments. The builders perished.
Defenders gone under. The courtyard is dreary;
The arch of red stone, the roof with its rafters,
Shed their tiles, and they slip to the earth,
A broken mound. Once many men
Glad and gold-bright, in gleaming array,
Proud and wine-flushed, shone in war-apparel;
Saw the treasure, the silver, the well-set jewels,

Riches, possessions, precious stones,
In the bright fortress of a broad kingdom.
Stone courts stood, the hot stream came
In its broad whelm; a wall enclosed all
Within its bosom. There the baths were,
Hot in the midst. It was a haven.

Michael O'Brien

Anonymous (c. 700)

WULF AND EADWACER: A WOMAN'S LAMENT

It is to my people   as a gift in their lap:
Will they devour him   should he come to their clutches?
    We share no likeness.
Wolf is on island,   I on another.
Fast is that island   thronged in by fen.
Lovers of slaughter   there are on that island.
Will they devour him   should he come in their clutches?
    We share no likeness.
I've suffered wide longing   expecting my Wolf,
When in rain I sat weeping;
When the battle-chafer bent his rough branches about me—
There was bliss in it for me,   and yet it was loathsome.
Wolf, my Wolf,   waiting for thee
Has made me sick;   thy seldom-comings
Make hollow longing,   and not for food.
Hearest thou, Eadwacer?   Our sniveling whelp
Wolf shall snatch off to wood.
That easily is torn   which never was whole
The song of the two of us, together.

Jonathan McKeage

Anonymous (c. 700)

DEOR

An old singer, a young stag, I am Deor,
Dear to the world was once-am, shall be;
Bought never by man-gold, sheep-bleating,
Gain for itself and none beside

Troubles pile up around me   Life is a hunt,
Hounds and pursuit   death to the lonely quarry

    But pain passes, may even this pass too . . .

Wayland in Werma was brought to ruin,
Wracked by the Worm   a woman's vengeance,
The staunch warrior clamorous woes underwent,
Had for his fellows   pain and sorrow,
sharp winter-frost pricked,   found only blain
Once bloody Nith-had   on him laid hands,
Brutally hamstrung him   the better man.

That passed over, so may this . . .

As for myself   let me but say:
I was Bard once   to the famous Heodening folk,
Dear to my Lord,   my name The Deer —
A wild beast, bold stag   precious and proud,
Like gold to kings   once was I called.

That has passed, so even may this . . .

Beadohild in her own heart never was stung
By her brothers' death as she was by her own trouble,
The stain that she had to face once she found
She was pregnant;   never could she remember
Clearly how it happened,   the young girl
Stunned by the blow   before being violated.
Most of us know now of Hilda's rape,
Most of us know her bitter fate.

That passed over, and so may this . . .

Nithhad said after: "Ever awake, ever wracked,
Robbed of all joy since my sons' deaths,
Now I can never sleep . . ."

That passed over, so too may this this . . .

Endless the sorrow of the Jute king, endlessly chained
In sorrowful love that robbed him of sleep's joy.

That passed over, so may this too . . .

Theodoric too, thirty winters he held out, he grieved,
Defending the Maeringas' stronghold;
Many know all too well his cruel story.

It passed, as may this too . . .

We have learned too   of Eormanric,
Wolf-thought like his we have endured;
He who held once in hopeless thrall
all of the Goths in   their wide good Kingdom.
It was a grim King.   Many a warrior cursed,

Waiting ever for worse wishes often enough
That foul rule   would be overthrown.

   That passed too, and so may this . . .

Man sits full of shame, of bliss cheated,
Grieves in his heart and thinks to himself
His part only misery, his share but blame.

Thwarted, let that man think: Throughout the World
The Wise Lord goes ever His way;
To many a man   there falls to his lot
Life-breath, renown and bounty,   but to others
A dish of despair, a goblet of sorrow.

   It passes, it passes, as well may this . . .

I myself, many a winter,   had good luck,
A generous Lord,   till Horrant got
The rights to my lands, (the crafty minstrel),
That my Lord had awarded before, to me to hold.

   That's over and done, so may this be . . .

Horrant now thrives   on his Gudrun Lay
But I was first in England to sing
Clear song to my harp in the Heodenings' house,
Of heroes of old,   their harsh lot,
True words of the great for a great Tribe;
Who now am old, an ailing bard,
But my poem *Deor* that I proudly sang
Still springs like a young hart hid in the woods,
Gladdening itself with its own bounding glee,
Blest in itself as is the Word of Bliss.

   That never will pass, — this will . . .

                                        Peter Russell

℘ Anonymous (c. 700)

CHARM OF THE NINE HEALING HERBS

Mugwort recall
What you showed us all
At Regenmeld
Una you're called
Oldest of herbs
You stand firm

Against the three and the thirty
You stand great
Against all poison and spreading illness
You stand great and firm
Against the wicked demon that wanders
All over this inflicted realm

You Plaintain
Mother of herbs
Wide open to the East
So strong within
Wagons rode over you
Queens on horseback too
Brides swooned over you
Bulls gnawed your root
But you stood strong against them
You fought them all
So fight this spreading illness
These poisons and demons that wander
All over this inflicted realm

On stone in crags
You grow Stime
Fierce you are
You beat back pain
You fight all venoms
So fierce you're called
The grass that defeats the snake

Fly fly Betony
From the smallest to the greatest
From the greatest to the smallest
And back again
Till you cure them both

Recall Camomile
What you showed us all
At Alorford
What came to pass
When a suffering wretch
Held on to his ghost
Because you Camomile
Cured his ills

Wergulu
Wergulu
A seal bore you up
Over the sea's high ridge
You heal all evil brought
By the nine wicked spirits
You stand strong against pain

You beat down poison
Fierce against the three and the thirty
You broke the demon's claw
You hold off the wicked glance
You break the harmful spels
Of every hateful thing

A snake slithered up
It bit a man he died
Then Woden flung nine
Magic brands these
Struck the snake
It burst apart
This freed the nine
Biting poisons
But Apple was given

And broke the harmful spel
And evil dwelt in no man's home

You great great ones
Thyme and Fennel
The High One in his Highness
Made you most blessed
When he hung from the wood
His blood bore your seed
Into the seven worlds
As a gift to help
Both rich and poor

These nine healing herbs
Fight the nine laming demons
And the nine evil poisons
And the nine flying ills
They fight the red poison
And the oozing poison
The white poison and the purple
They fight the yellow poison
And the green poison
The black poison and the blue
And the brown poison
And the crimson

They fight the worm-boil
And water-blister
The thorn-blister and thistle-swell
They fight the ice-blister
And swollen bite

If borne from the East
If borne from the North

If borne from the West
If borne from the South
These nine beat down the flying ills

Christ himself
Stands over all poison
Only I know the power
Of the stream that clears
And the nine slithering ones know it

Now all the fields bloom
Full of healing herbs
When I blow these ills away
The very salt of the sea disappears
And the waters clear forever

David Cloutier

𝕊𝕖 Anonymous (c. 700)

From BEOWULF

Hrothgar Answered

Hrothgar answered   helm of the Shield-Danes:
"Don't ask about happiness!   Horror has returned
to the Danes in Heorot.   Dead is Aeschere
good Yrmenlaf's   guide and blood-brother
my closest adviser   counsel to us all
shoulder-companion when shields were hoisted
defender of my life   when foot-warriors clashed
helmets were swordstruck.   So should a man be
always beside us   as Aeschere was!
He found in Heorot   a hell-spawned murderer
restless hand-killer.   From our high meadhall
that slaughter-stained spirit has   sought her corpse-cave
I know not where.   She now has avenged
the felling of Grendel   that feud you began
with violent grappling that great handgrip
that settled our account   for those cold death-years
the closing of Heorot.   He cringed at your hand
went dying through the night   and now this she-fiend
has avenged her monster-son   vicious man-killer—
too far she has carried   this feud over blood-kin
it seems to us all   aching in our minds
weeping for Aeschere   warrior of my heart
high-minded hall-thane—now his hand is idle
that once granted us   each wish and command.
I have heard evening-tales   hearth-talk of scouts
of hall-messengers   hailing from abroad

that they have sighted   a solitary pair
monstrous moor-walkers   moving through shadows
sorrowful fen-spirits.   They say that one of them
misshapen exile   is most like a woman —
the wanderer with her   woefully deformed
prowled the march-tracks   manlike to their eyes
yet bigger by far   than the best of warriors.
In times long past   tenders of the land
named him Grendel.   No one can say
what creatures spawned them   their kin in this world.
They live secretly   in a shadowy land
dwell by wolf-slopes   wind-tortured bluffs
gloomy fen-hollows   where a forested stream
dives from the bluffs   down past earthlight
flows underground.   Not far from Heorot
measured in miles   the mere lies hidden —
reaching above it   with rime-covered branches
strong-rooted trees   stretch from rock-slopes.
At night may be seen   a strange wonder-sight
fire on the water.   No wiseman lives
who knows the bottom   of that black monster-home.
Though the heath-prancer   by hounds labored
the strong-antlered hart   may seek life-haven
driven from afar   he will die beside it
forfeit his life there   for fear of crossing
plunging his head   in that hell-cursed water.
A surging of waves   swirls to the clouds
when whistling winds   come whirling in anger
to that sorrowful place — the sky hangs gloomy
and the heavens weep.   Our hope for mercy
lies only in your help.   The home of these fiends
dark moor-cavern   monsters' water-den
is not far from Heorot.   Find it if you dare!
I will reward you   with weapons and gold
ancient treasure-gifts   as I earlier did
linked mail-corselets   if you live to return.

Frederick Rebsamen

Such Is the Grief of the Grey-Haired Man

such is the grief of the grey-haired man
who lives to see his young son
ride on the gallows; he grasps at words,
at wretched song, when his son hangs,
a host to ravens, & he cannot help him,
old as he is, or do anything.
every morning he is reminded
of his son's journey; he has no joy
in the hope of other inheritors
within these walls, when his own boy
has proved by deed the power of death.

in his son's house he sees, sick at heart,
the wine-hall empty, the windy rooms
bereft of sound; the riders sleep,
heroes gone under; no harp is heard,
no games in the yard, as there were once.
in his bed, lonely, he must lament
the one he has lost; there is too much room
in castle & country.

Michael O'Brien

✌ Anonymous (c. 750)

THE SEAFARER

May I for my own self song's truth reckon,
Journey's jargon, how I in harsh days
Hardship endured oft.
Bitter breast-cares have I abided,
Known on my keel many a care's hold,
And dire sea-surge, and there I oft spent
Narrow nightwatch nigh the ship's head
While she tossed close to cliffs. Coldly afflicted,
My feet were by frost benumbed.
Chill its chains are; chafing sighs
Hew my heart round and hunger begot
Mere-weary mood. Lest man know not
That he on dry land loveliest liveth,
List how I, care-wretched, on ice-cold sea,
Weathered the winter, wretched outcast
Deprived of my kinsmen;
Hung with hard ice-flakes, where hail-scur flew,
There I heard naught save the harsh sea
And ice-cold wave, at whiles the swan cries,
Did for my games the gannet's clamour,
Sea-fowls' loudness was for me laughter,
The mews' singing all my mead-drink.
Storms, on the stone-cliffs beaten, fell on the stern
In icy feathers; full oft the eagle screamed
With spray on his pinion.
                              Not any protector
May make merry man faring needy.
This he little believes, who aye in winsome life
Abides 'mid burghers some heavy business,
Wealthy and wine-flushed, how I weary oft
Must bide above brine.
Neareth nightshade, snoweth from north,
Frost froze the land, hail fell on earth then,
Corn of the coldest. Nathless there knocketh now

The heart's thought that I on high streams
The salt-wavy tumult traverse alone.
Moaneth alway my mind's lust
That I fare forth, that I afar hence
Seek out a foreign fastness.
For this there's no mood-lofty man over earth's midst,
Not though he be given his good, but will have in his youth greed;
Nor his deed to the daring, nor his king to the faithful
But shall have his sorrow for sea-fare
Whatever his lord will.
He hath not heart for harping, nor in ring-having
Nor winsomeness to wife, nor world's delight
Nor any whit else save the wave's slash,
Yet longing comes upon him to fare forth on the water.
Bosque taketh blossom, cometh beauty of berries,
Fields to fairness, land fares brisker,
All this admonisheth man eager of mood,
The heart turns to travel so that he then thinks
On flood-ways to be far departing.
Cuckoo calleth with gloomy crying,
He singeth summerward, bodeth sorrow,
The bitter heart's blood. Burgher knows not—
He the prosperous man—what some perform
Where wandering them widest draweth.
So that but now my heart burst from my breastlock,
My mood 'mid the mere-flood,
Over the whale's acre, would wander wide.
On earth's shelter cometh oft to me,
Eager and ready, the crying lone-flyer,
Whets for the whale-path the heart irresistibly,
O'er tracks of ocean; seeing that anyhow
My lord deems to me this dead life
On loan and on land, I believe not
That any earth-weal eternal standeth
Save there be somewhat calamitous
That, ere a man's tide go, turn it to twain.
Disease or oldness or sword-hate
Beats out the breath from doom-gripped body.
And for this, every earl whatever, for those speaking after—
Laud of the living, boasteth some last word,
That he will work ere he pass onward,
Frame on the fair earth 'gainst foes his malice,
Daring ado, . . .
So that all men shall honour him after
And his laud beyond them remain 'mid the English,
Aye, for ever, a lasting life's-blast,
Delight 'mid the doughty.
                    Days little durable,
And all arrogance of earthen riches,
There come now no kings nor Cæsars
Nor gold-giving lords like those gone.

Howe'er in mirth most magnified,
Whoe'er lived in life most lordliest,
Drear all this excellence, delights undurable!
Waneth the watch, but the world holdeth.
Tomb hideth trouble. The blade is layed low.
Earthly glory ageth and seareth.
No man at all going the earth's gait,
But age fares against him, his face paleth,
Grey-haired he groaneth, knows gone companions,
Lordly men, are to earth o'ergiven,
Nor may he then the flesh-cover, whose life ceaseth,
Nor eat the sweet nor feel the sorry,
Nor stir hand nor think in mid heart,
And though he strew the grave with gold,
His born brothers, their buried bodies
Be an unlikely treasure hoard.

Ezra Pound

✆ Anonymous (c. 750)

THE WANDERER

Who liveth alone longeth for mercy,
Maker's mercy. Though he must traverse
tracts of sea, sick at heart,
—trouble with oars ice-cold waters,
the ways of exile—Wierd is set fast.

Thus spoke such a 'grasshopper', old griefs in his mind,
cold slaughters, the death of dear kinsmen:

Alone am I driven each day before daybreak
to give my cares utterance.
None are there now among the living
to whom I dare declare me throughly,
tell my heart's thought. Too truly I know
it is in a man no mean virtue
that he keep close his heart's chest,
hold his thought-hoard, think as he may.

No weary mind may stand against Wierd
nor may a wrecked will work new hope;
wherefore, most often, those eager for fame
bind the dark mood fast in their breasts.

So must I also curb my mind,
cut off from country, from kind far distant,
by cares overworn, bind it in fetters;

this since, long ago, the ground's shroud
enwrapped my gold-friend. Wretched I went thence,
winter-wearied, over the waves' bound;
dreary I sought hall of a gold-giver,
where far or near I might find
him who in mead-hall might take heed of me,
furnish comfort to a man friendless,
win me with cheer.
               He knows who makes trial
how harsh and bitter is care for companion
to him who hath few friends to shield him.
Track ever taketh him, never the torqued gold,
not earthly glory, but cold heart's cave.
He minds him of hall-men, of treasure-giving,
how in his youth his gold-friend
gave him to feast. Fallen all this joy.

He knows this who is forced to forgo his lord's,
his friend's counsels, to lack them for long:
oft sorrow and sleep, banded together,
come to bind the lone outcast;
he thinks in his heart then that he his lord
claspeth and kisseth, and on knee layeth
hand and head, as he had at otherwhiles
in days now gone, when he enjoyed the gift-stool.

Awakeneth after this friendless man,
seeth before him fallow waves,
seabirds bathing, broading out feathers,
snow and hail swirl, hoar-frost falling.
Then all the heavier his heart's wounds,
sore for his loved lord. Sorrow freshens.

Remembered kinsmen press through his mind;
he singeth out gladly, scanneth eagerly
men from the same hearth. They swim away.
Sailors' ghosts bring not many
known songs there. Care grows fresh
in him who shall send forth too often
over locked waves his weary spirit.

Therefore I may not think, throughout this world,
why cloud cometh not on my mind
when I think over all the life of earls,
how at a stroke they have given up hall,
mood-proud thanes. So this middle earth
each of all days ageth and falleth.'

Wherefore no man grows wise without he have
his share of winters. A wise man holds out;
he is not too hot-hearted, nor too hasty in speech,

nor too weak a warrior, not wanting in fore-thought,
nor too greedy of goods, nor too glad, nor too mild,
nor ever too eager to boast, ere he knows all.

A man should forbear boastmaking
until his fierce mind fully knows
which way his spleen shall expend itself.

A wise man may grasp how ghastly it shall be
when all this world's wealth standeth waste,
even as now, in many places, over the earth
walls stand, wind-beaten,
hung with hoar-frost; ruined habitations.
The wine-halls crumble; their wielders lie
bereft of bliss, the band all fallen
proud by the wall. War took off some,
carried them on their course hence; one a bird bore
over the high sea; one the hoar wolf
dealt to death; one his drear-cheeked
earl stretched in an earthen trench.
The Maker of men hath so marred this dwelling
that human laughter is not heard about it
and idle stand these old giant-works.

A man who on these walls wisely looked
who sounded deeply this dark life
would think back to the blood spilt here,
weigh it in his wit. His word would be this:
'Where is that horse now? Where are those men? Where is
                                    the hoard-sharer?
Where is the house of the feast? Where is the hall's uproar?

Alas, bright cup! Alas, burnished fighter!
Alas, proud prince! How that time has passed,
dark under night's helm, as though it never had been!

There stands in the stead of staunch thanes
a towering wall wrought with worm-shapes;
the earls are off-taken by the ash-spear's point,
—that thirsty weapon. Their Wierd is glorious.

Storms break on the stone hillside,
the ground bound by driving sleet,
winter's wrath. Then wanness cometh,
night's shade spreadeth, sendeth from north
the rough hail to harry mankind.

In the earth-realm all is crossed;
Wierd's will changeth the world.
Wealth is lent us, friends are lent us,

man is lent, kin is lent;
all this earth's frame shall stand empty.'

So spoke the sage in his heart; he sat apart in thought.
Good is he who keeps faith: nor should care too fast
be out of a man's breast before he first know the cure:
a warrior fights on bravely. Well is it for him who seeks
                                                forgiveness,
the Heavenly Father's solace, in whom all our fastness stands.

Michael Alexander

❧ Anonymous (c. 750)

TWO SEABIRDS *From* THE WANDERER AND THE SEAFARER

When sorrow and sleep both bind him,
the solitary knows: this man must long
lack the kind teachings of a loved lord.
His mind makes him think of his master,
he kisses and clasps his liege-lord,
his head and hands lays on that knee
as once in young days: then he enjoyed
the gift-throne. Again the wretch wakens
to see waves dark like dead leaves before him.
Sleet, frost, and hail all together fall.
The sea fowls bathe, broaden their feathers.

Now in my heart-mood circles my thought;
out of the breastlock, it swings with the flood,
over the whale-domain, over Earth's corners
widely it turns. Then back to me comes
my solitary soarer, greedy and screaming,
urging the whale-path, irresistibly urging
my heart to the lakes of the sea.

John Updike

❧ Anonymous (c. 850)

RIDDLE *From* THE EXETER BOOK

Clothes make no sound when I tread ground
Or dwell in dwellings or disturb the flow.
    And lofty air and gear at times

Above men's towns will lift me:
Brisk breezes bear me far, and then
My frettings loudly rush and ring
Above the people and most clearly sing
    When I forth-fare on air
    And feel and know
        No fold, no flow.

(The Swan)

Geoffrey Grigson

Anonymous (c. 850)

RIDDLE

A meal of words   made by a moth
Seemed to me   when I heard the tale
Curious   and pheomenal:
That such a mite   like a thief in the night
should swallow up   the song of a poet,
The splendid discourse   and its solid setting!
But the strange robber   was none the wiser
For all those words   and all that eating.

(Bookworm)

Edwin Morgan

Anonymous (c. 850)

RIDDLE

The world's wonder, I liven wenches,
A boon to townsfolk, a bane to none,
Though haply I prick her who picks me.
Well-planted, I stand in a bed
With my rogue root. Rarely, mayhap,
Some carline, careless and daring,
Rasps my red tip, wrenches my head,
Lays me to larder. I teach her lore,
This curly-hair who clasps me thus,
And after our meeting moisten her eye.

(Onion)

Lewis Turco

✒ Anonymous (c. 850)

RIDDLE

I saw a strange creature,
a bright ship of the air beautifully adorned,
bearing away plunder between her horns,
fetching it home from a foray.
She was minded to build a bower in her stronghold,
and construct it with cunning if she could do so.
But then a mighty creature appeared over the mountain
whose face is familiar to all dwellers on earth;
he seized on his treasure and sent home the wanderer
much against her will; she went westward
harbouring hostility, hastening forth.
Dust lifted to heaven; dew fell on the earth,
night fled hence; and no man knew
thereafter, where that strange creature went.

(Sun and Moon)

Kevin Crossley-Holland

✒ Attributed to Cynewulf (c. 900)

From THE PHOENIX

When stars are hid in the western wave, dimmed at dawn
& the dusky night steals darkly away
Then strong of wind, & proud of pinion

It looks over the sea, eagerly over the ocean
For the rising sun. When the Bright blesses & burns
in the heavens, & glides eastward over the wide

Water, & climbs over mountains, & salt streams
The grey bird wings from its woodland tree, swift
Aloft, soars to the sky
        Singing and caroling to greet the sun

Frank Kuenstler

THE NATURE OF THE SIREN

Strange things indeed   Are seen in the sea-world:
Men say that mermaids   Are like to maidens
In breast and body   But not so below:

From the navel netherward   Nothing looks human,
For there they are fishes   And furnished with fins.
These prodigies dwell   In a perilous passage
Where swirling waters   Swallow men's vessels;
Cheerily they sing   In their changeable voices
That are high and sweet   And hopeful of harm.
This song makes shipmen   Forget their steering
And sink into drowses,   And deeply they dream:
For their vessels are sunken,   Their voyages over.
But wise men and wary   Will turn from these wiles
And often escape   That evil embrace,
Being warned of the mermaids.   Surely this monster,
Half fish and half woman,   Must harbor some meaning.

Signification

Many of mankind   Resemble the mermaid,
Without they wear lambskin,   Within they are wolves;
Their doctrine is righteous,   Their deeds are the Devil's;
Their actions are not   In accord with their utterance;
These two-natured creatures   Will swear by the cross,
By the sun and the moon,   To steer you astray;
With the sweetest of speeches   They swindle their fellows;
They will steal both your substance   And soul with their falsehood.

Richard Wilbur

Anonymous (c. 991)

From THE BATTLE OF MALDON

"Courage shall grow keener, clearer the will,
the heart fiercer, as our force faileth.
Here our lord lies levelled in the dust,
the man all marred: he shall mourn to the end
who thinks to wend off from this war-play now.
Though I am white with winters I will not away,
for I think to lodge me alongside my dear one,
lay me down by my lord's white hand."

Michael Alexander

Anonymous (c. 1000)

From THE RUNE POEM

We love the daylight,
God's glorious illumination,
hope for rich and wretched.

The oak is on earth for us.
Feed pigs the acorns.
Make a good boat.

The towering ash we love,
its stout trunk steady too
amid a crowd of enemies.

Strapped to the horse
with the rest of the gear,
the bow, ready to go.

The serpent leaves the sea
to feed and dwells encircled
by water, in pure delight.

We hate the clay, the cold flesh,
the pale corpse, the fallen
flowers, the broken promise.

Jim Paul

Part IV

The
Rise of the
Vernacular
(950–1450)

In Old Norse, the language of Norway and Iceland between the ninth and thirteenth centuries, the *skald* was a bard attached to a royal court. Throughout a poetic flight embedded in the prose narrative of *Egil's Saga,* the Viking poet Egil addresses a king who is seriously considering whether or not to cut off the poet's head.

The *Eddas,* and their account of the cosmology and heroic past of pre-Christian Scandinavia, exist in thirty-four lays, reciting the myths of Norse gods and heroes. The Finnish *Kalevala* was written in an alliterative verse so metrically close to early Scandinavian forms that, despite disputes over its dating and even its authenticity, this fusion of old nature myths, folksong, and tribal legends of gods and shamanist poets is generally assigned to the tenth century.

The troubadour, a composer traveling from court to court, is the skald's southern counterpart. Troubadour poetry and its stylization of the medieval idea of courtly love carved out a broad territory. The arc of its influence extended from Provence and the western Iberian peninsula to the Austria and the Rhineland of the German Minnesingers. This verse from the Languedoc invented a fiction of complicated liaisons in keeping with the chivalric code. The thematic triangle involved the poet, the usually married (sometimes chaste) lady of choice, and a husband who was often the poet's patron.

Such vernacular forms from Provence as the aubade and the serenade, and the *cantigas d'amor* of Galician Spain and Portugal made their way to Wales, long after the Norman conquest and the loss of Welsh independence. Away from the reigning culture of cathedral town and manor house, Dafydd ap Gwilym and his poetic fellowship of outlaws and outcasts celebrated a wild "religion of the woods." The technique of *dyfalu* — the use of metaphor to connect the loved one with an image from nature — served as a form of escape and protest, a subversive Celtic annex to Christian society.

Provençal, the language of the Languedoc in southern France and Italy, was so prestigious in the twelfth century that Dante later called it "the mother tongue" of all vernacular poetry. Arnaut Daniel, who made it the instrument of his complex love lyrics, was typical of the troubadour poets; the quarrelsome Bertran de Born, master of the *sirventes* (a form of satire) and the *planh* (a lament for better times, and better patrons) was notorious.

De Born lived as a soldier and died as a monk; he appears among the sowers of discord and strife in Canto Twenty-Eight of Dante's *Inferno*, carrying his own severed head like a lantern. His sovereign and friend, Richard the Lion-Hearted, composed "Forbecause a Prisoner Lies" in captivity, returning from the First Crusade.

The northern French poetry of this era developed separately in a country divided by political, religious and linguistic differences. Charles D'Orléans, refined the *ballade* as well as the *rondeau*, a fixed form constructed on only two rhymes. The formal occasion for the rogue poet François Villon's ballade "I Die of Thirst While at the Fountain Side" was a competition held at the chateau of Blois by D'Orléans himself, requiring each entry to begin with that line, followed by a chain of contradictory refrains.

The much earlier *Song of Roland*, a *chanson de geste* (song of deeds) commemorates a rear-guard action in Charlemagne's expedition in A.D. 778 against the Saracens, and the death of the emperor's greatest paladin. This foundation myth in Old French stands on the threshold of French literature, shaping national consciousness.

The epic form in vernacular languages served a double purpose. It accommodated the heightening of national identity anchored in a historical event, like the ill-fated expedition of the twelfth-century Slavic *Song of Igor's Campaign* or the Spanish epic of another campaign against the Moors in *The Poem of the Cid*. In addition, it assumed the aims of allegory and its symbolic representation of good and evil. The search for divine unity represented in Dante has parallels in the Middle English *Vision of Piers Plowman*. Langland's fourteenth-century Christian allegory is written in a rustic dialect; *Sir Gawain and the Green Knight* is an anonymous romance in the rugged Midlands tongue. Their archaic qualities place them in this section, at a remove from their contemporary Chaucer. Both poems have a medieval focus on the crossing of borders between several worlds: reality and dream, earth, underworld, and paradise, the everyday and the allegorical.

Islamic mysticism in twelfth-century Persia likewise used the allegorical to transform belief into poetry. Farid Ud-Din Attar's *Conference of the Birds* is a Sufi parable anticipating Chaucer's gathering of stories bound by the convention of a pilgrimage. The esoteric doctrine of Sufism, its theology of divine emanations in a world of shadows, claimed its own school of itinerant poets, including Rumi whose ecstatic delineation of mystical stages through music and dancing inspired Goethe and Gandhi.

The equally influential Hafiz (The pen name of Shams-ud-din Muhammed, which means "one who remembers," i.e., knows the Koran by heart) shaped the rhymed quatrains called *rubaiyat* and wrote *ghazals* — short love lyrics. The term *Rubaiyat* has passed into the common language through Edward Fitzgerald's famous pre-Raphaelite rendering in 1859 of the work of the astronomer Omar Khayyam.

Typically, poetry in Persian, an Indo-European language that used the script of the Arab invaders of A.D. 637, had a reciprocal relationship with Arabic culture. But its emblems—nightingales, the wine-flagon, the goblet, and the bearer—are nonetheless distinctive, as is its preoccupation with the ascetic life and wine as a symbol of release from the pessimism of its skeptics and poets.

Many of these traditions emerged from the cauldron of the dazzling syncretic culture of Arab-Andalusia, where the Arabic conquest of Spain and parts of southern Europe ignited an early Eastern Renaissance and a Golden Age for poets in the Semitic languages of Hebrew and Arabic. (The word *troubadour* comes from the Arabic root *tariba.*) These poets were spice merchants, theologians, philosophers, doctors, viziers, and kings: most took their inspiration from the multiracial Muslim host culture and their work reinvigorated antique traditions. Hebrew poets borrowed from Hispano-Arabic conventions, used liturgical modes, and drew on the Bible for themes of diaspora and redemption. One of its greatest poets, Samuel Ben Yosef Ha-Nagid, was the military leader or *nagid* of Spanish Jewry, the prime minister of the Muslim State of Grenada.

In 1928 the Spanish Arabist Emilio Garcia Gomez picked up a copy in Cairo of the 1243 *Codex* of Ibn Sa'id who wanted poems "whose idea is more subtle than the West Wind and whose language is more beautiful than a fair face." The discovery of this book changed the landscape of modern Spanish poetry. The poetic fragments it contained, celebrating "water, green things and a beautiful face" preserve the memory of the place called *al-Andaluz* or "the garden."

K. W.

By the early second millennium of the Common Era, Asian literature came to be enriched by new vernacular verse from hitherto mostly silent regions. The Asian poetry in Part IV begins with excerpts from Paul Kahn's verse reconstruction of the epic *Secret History of the Mongols,* a hagiographic account of the career of Chingis Khan (known now from an early Chinese prose version), and with a passage from a Tibetan harvest drama of early but uncertain date.

With the transition from the T'ang Dynasty to the Sung, Chinese poetry underwent a decisive shift from verse with a regular and highly formal structure of—usually—five or seven words per line, to a more varied lyric form, in which verse was written to the meter of one of several dozen standard melodies. This led to a new outpouring of creative power, particularly in the hands of the great master Su Tung-p'o and the celebrated courtesan-poet Li Ch'ing-chao. In Japan, the end of the Heian Period and a seismic shift in social power from a courtly to a warrior aristocracy finds an echo in the pervasively sad and nostalgic tone of the era's *tanka* poems. In Korea, poetry begins to move away from the model of Classical Chinese verse, especially in the poems of the first Korean vernacular master, Yi Kyubo. And Vietnam, too, having thrown off the yoke of Chinese domination as the T'ang Dynasty came to an end, begins to appear on the literary stage, though still with verse strongly affected by the Chinese model.

In Indian verse of this period one finds a striking movement away from the courtly themes of earlier times and toward Hindu devotional *(bhakti)* poetry, most often in ecstatic praise of the god Krishna; this is seen both in the Kannada verse of (usually) women mystics from South India and in Jayadeva's very influential long poem in Sanskrit, the *Gitagovinda*.

At the end of Part IV we encounter first voices from the New World, in the form of hymns from the Maya creation epic, the *Popol Vuh*. I have placed these hymns here, as having been composed probably around the end of the Classical Maya Period and handed down orally for several centuries before they were recorded in writing by Spanish priests at the beginning of the sixteenth century.

J.S.M.

℘ 1

Northern Europe: Icelandic Saga, Finnish, the Norse Languages, and the German Minnesingers

Iceland

℘ Anonymous (c. 950)

From EGIL'S SAGA

I crossed the deep sea,
My cargo, poetry,
Odin's boundless gift,
On board my sleek ship.
Soon as the ice broke
I'd the ship afloat,
Cabin crammed with praise
For King Eirik's ways.

The prince has shown me
Hospitality.
Praise is my duty,
Praise in poetry.
I have brought my praise
To England, bright praise,
And ask a hearing
To laud this great king.

Prince, consider this:
If I have my wish
Of silence you'll long

Recollect my song.
Few men but have heard
What battles occurred
With you at their head:
Odin saw the dead.

Clang of shield and sword!
Like an angry word
War swirled round Eirik,
Caused him to attack.
Vast rivers of sound!
Sword on sword, rebound-
Ing like wide echoes
Where huge waters flow.

Always there'd appear
A tight fence of spears
Before the bright fields-
Full of the king's shields.
Blood brindled the seal-
Haunted, wave-blue sea.
Loud waves of violence
Broke its long silence.

Arrows cut the air
Like butcher-birds. Where
They struck flesh they killed.
Men fell or were felled.
A clever tactic
That. And King Eirik
Rightly had much fame
Added to his name.

If folk keep silent
I've more to recount.
When the princes met
Wounds ran redder yet.
Sword fractured on sword,
Men died as they fought —
Bravely. They taught us
All that's courageous.

Sword on sword again.
Men advanced on pain
Or death. Sword-points drew
Blood or ran flesh through.
The swords bit so deep
(Wolf-fangs tearing sheep)
In that harsh battle
That many men fell.

Men were spitted on
Spear-points. Dull swords shone
Redly, edges fresh-
Honed to razor flesh.
A clever tactic
That. And King Eirik
Rightly had much fame
Added to his name.

The king's sword dripped blood,
Saucing raven-food.
Arrows made their kill,
Spears helped blood to spill.
The Scots-killer made
Meat for wolves. Death strayed
Here and there. Men fell.
Eagles would feed well.

Eagles flew where those
Corpses lay in rows.
Ravens' jabbing beaks
Gleamed with bloody streaks.
The wolves tore open
New wounds in dead men.
In a thousand rills
Blood ran for birds' bills.

Even the wolves grew
Fat. They couldn't chew
Much more flesh. They crept
Some way off and slept.
By that blood-drenched shore
Eirik threw down more
Corpses than the wolves
Could stomach themselves.

———

The ranks dwindle, they die,
these dear bright friends of mine
who flared in fight and would
fire my drink with delight.
Where now to search for such
silver-free men as those
who beyond land-starred seas
sweetened a poet's words?

John Lucas

ᔔ Anonymous (c. 900–1000)

THE WORDS OF THE ALL-WISE From THE ELDER EDDA

"Bestrew the benches: for my bride and me
    It is time to be turning homeward.
I am eager for this wedding: they are wondering there
    Why I linger so long."

"Of what race are you, White-Nose?
    Were you clasped in the night by a corpse?
I think you must be Thurse-begotten:
    You were never born for a bride."

"All-Wise I am called: under the ground
    I dwell in the dark among stones.
From the Lord-of-chariots I look for good faith:
    It is ill to break an oath."

"I never swore one: I was not at home
    When the gods gave you this pledge.
The bride's father has the best right:
    Permission is for me to give."

"Declare your name, who claim to be
    The father of the fair maid.
Far-wanderer, few know you:
    Whose arm-rings do you wear?"

"The lord Ving-Thor, Longbeard's son,
    Who has travelled wide in the world:
Unless I agree, give my consent,
    You shall never marry the maid."

"You will agree, give your consent
    That I shall marry the maid,
The snow-white woman I desire to have
    Rather than live alone."

"Wise guest, I give you my promise:
    I will not deny you her hand,
If you know what I wish to know concerning
    All the worlds there are.

"Say, Dwarf, for it seems to me
    There is nothing you do not know:
What is earth called, the outstretched land,
    In all the worlds there are?"

"*Earth* by men, *The Fold* by gods,
    Vanes call it *The Ways,*
Giants *Ever-green,* elves *Growing,*
    High gods call it *Clay.*"

"What is heaven called, that all know,
    In all the worlds there are?"

"*Heaven* by men, *The Arch* by gods,
    Wind-Weaver by Vanes,
By giants *High-Earth,* by elves *Fair-Roof,*
    By dwarves *The Dripping Hall.*"

"What is the moon called, that men see,
    In all the worlds there are?"

"*Moon* by men, *The Ball* by gods,
    The Whirling Wheel in Hel,
The Speeder by giants, *The Bright One* by dwarves,
    By elves *Tally-of-Years.*"

"What is sol called, that is seen by men,
    In all the worlds there are?"

"*Sol* by men, *Sun* by gods,
    By dwarves *Dvalin's Doll,*
By giants *Everglow,* by elves *Fair-Wheel,*
    All-Bright by sons of gods."

"What are clouds called, that carry rain,
    In all the worlds there are?"

"*Clouds* by men, *Hope-of-Showers* by gods,
    Wind-Ships by Vanes,
By giants *Drizzle-Hope,* by elves *Weather-Might,*
    In Hel *Helmet-of-Darkness.*"

"What is wind called, that widely fares
    In all the worlds there are?"

"*Wind* by men, *Woe-Father* by gods,
    By holy powers *The Neigher,*
The Shouter by giants, *Travelling-Tumult* by elves,
    Squall-Blast they call it in Hel."

"What is calm called, that cannot stir,
    In all the worlds there are?"
"*Calm* by men, *Stillness* by gods,
    Idle-Wind by Vanes,
Over-Warmth by giants, by elves *Day-Quiet,*
    And *Day-Rest* by dwarves."

"What is sea called, that is crossed by men,
    In all the worlds there are?"

"*Sea* by men, *Still-Main* by gods,
    The Vanes call it *Wave*,
Eel-Home by giants, by elves *Water-Charm*,
    The Dark Deep by dwarves."

"What is fire called, so fierce to men,
    In all the worlds there are?"

"*Fire* by men, *Flame* by gods,
    The Flickering One by Vanes,
The Wolfish by giants, *All-Burner* by elves,
    In Hel *The Corpse-Destroyer.*"

"What is forest called, that flourishes for men,
    In all the worlds there are?"

"*Forest* by men, *Field's-Mane* by gods,
    By heroes *Mountain Sea-Weed*,
Fire-Wood by giants, *Fair-Bough* by elves,
    By Vanes *Wand-of-Charms.*"

"What is night called, that Nör fathered,
    In all the worlds there are?"

"*Night* by men, *The Dark* by gods,
    By holy powers *The Hood*,
Unlight by giants, by elves *Sleep-Pleasure*,
    By dwarves *Spinner-of-Dreams.*"

"What is the seed called, that is sown by men,
    In all the worlds there are?"

"*Brew* by men, *Barley* by gods,
    Vanes call it *The Growth*,
Oats by giants, by elves *Water-Charm*,
    In Hel they call it *The Drooping.*"

"What is ale called, that is quaffed by men,
    In all the worlds there are?"

"*Ale* by men, *Beer* by gods,
    The Vanes call it *Strength*,
Water-Pure by giants, *Mead* in Hel,
    Feast by Suttung's Sons."

"Never have I met such a master of lore
    With such a wealth of wisdom.
I talked to trick you, and tricked you I have:

Dawn has broken, Dwarf,
Stiffen now to stone."

           W. H. Auden and Paul Taylor

Finnish

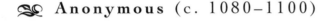 **Anonymous** (c. 1080–1100)

FIRE

From THE KALEVALA

Ilmarinen struck
fire, Väinämöinen
flashed above eight heavens, in
    the ninth sky: a spark
    dropped down through the earth
    through Manala, and
through the smoke-hole caked with soot
    the children's cradle
    it broke maidens' breasts
and burned the mother's bosom.
The mother knew more of it:
she shoved it into the sea
lest the maid go to Mana
lest the fire should burn her up
    lest the flame roast her.

That gloomy Lake Alue
three times on a summer night
foamed as high as the spruces
in the torment of the fire
the flame's overwhelmingness.

    A smooth whitefish swam
    and swallowed the spark:
torment to the swallower
came, hardship to the gulper.
    A grey pike swam up
    swallowed the whitefish
    a light lake-trout swam
    swallowed the grey pike
    a red salmon swam
and swallowed the light lake-trout:
it swam, it darted about
in between the salmon-crags
in the torment of the fire.

It said in these words
it uttered along these lines:
    "Fire once burned much land
one evil summer of fire
one year of flame without help.
A small piece was left unburned
at the turn of Ahti's fence
at the rear of Hirska's bank."
    It was hoed and dug
and Tuoni's maggot was found
and Tuoni's maggot was burned
    in a copper boat
in an iron-bottomed punt.
Its ashes were sown upon
the shore of Lake Alimo:
    flax without like grew
    peerless linen rose
in a single summer night.
It was quickly stripped
now taken to the water
now the linen put in soak.
    The sisters spun it
    the brothers wove cloth
    and fashioned a net.
Sturdy old Väinämöinen
put the young ones on the net.
They drew across the water:
    that fish did not come
for which the net was fashioned.
They drew along the water:
    that fish did not come
for which the net was fashioned.
They drew against the water:
the salmon splashed in the sea.

Sturdy old Väinämöinen
could not bear to put his hand
without mittens of iron:
took his mittens of iron
split open the red salmon —
    the light lake-trout came
from the red salmon's belly
split open the light lake-trout —
    the grey pike came out
he split open the grey pike —
    the smooth whitefish came
split open the smooth whitefish —
    and the spark came out.

    There the fire was lulled
    and the flame was rocked

at a misty headland's tip
    there the fire was lulled
    in a silver sling:
the golden cradle jingled
the copper mantle trembled
    as the fire was lulled.

Keith Bosley

Norwegian

❧ Anonymous (c. 1000)

TWO SPRING CHARMS

(fragments from the Norwegian)

1

Now it is late winter.

Years ago,
I walked through a spring wind
Bending green wheat
In a field near Trondhjem.

2

Black snow,
Like a strange sea creature,
Draws back into itself,
Restoring grass to earth.

James Wright

Swedish

❧ Anonymous (c. 800–900)

THREE SWEDISH SPELLS

Spell against Predatory Animals

I read for wolftooth and bearclaw
that they won't touch my sheep, my cow,
neither large nor small.

I pray them away, past the very last crag
where the swan darkens
and the raven whitens.

A Spell

When meeting a bear, say:

You are bear and I am human.
You were not baptized in the same baptismal as I.
Run in the woods and bite a tree.
Not me.

Spell against Twisting an Ankle

Dave rode across a bridge.
When he came to Tive Wood,
his horse tripped over a root,
twisted a foot.
Odin came by:
"I will cure the twist
of bone, flesh and limb.
Your foot will not ache
and never more break.
+++Amen."

Siv Cedering Fox

✤ Anonymous (c. 800–900)

TWO SWEDISH RIDDLES

Riddle

Father's sickle is hanging
on mother's Sunday skirt.

(The New Moon)

Riddle

An old green witch
stands in a ditch.
Your hand will hurt
if you touch her skirt.

(Nettle)

Siv Cedering Fox

Dutch

 Hadewijch (c. 1250)

LOVE HAS SEVEN NAMES

Love has seven names.
Do you know what they are?
Rope, Light, Fire, Coal
make up its domain.

The others, also good,
more modest but alive:
Dew, Hell, the Living Water.
I name them here (for they
are in the Scriptures),
explaining every sign
for virtue and form.
I tell the truth in signs.
Love appears every day
for one who offers love.
That wisdom is enough.

Love is a ROPE, for it ties
and holds us in its yoke.

It can do all, nothing snaps it.
You who love must know.

The meaning of LIGHT
is known to those who
offer gifts to love,
approved or condemned.

The Scripture tells us
the symbol of COAL:
the one sublime gift
God gives the intimate soul.

Under the name of FIRE, luck,
bad luck, joy or no joy,
consumes. We are seized
by the same heat from both.

When everything is burnt
in its own violence, the DEW,
coming like a breeze, pauses
and brings the good.

LIVING WATER (its sixth name)
flows and ebbs
as my love grows
and disappears from sight.

HELL (I feel its torture)
damns, covering the world.
Nothing escapes. No one has grace
to see a way out.

Take care, you who wish
to deal with names
for love. Behind their sweetness
and wrath, nothing endures.
Nothing but wounds and kisses.

Though love appears far off,
you will move into its depth.

                    Willis Barnstone and Elene Kolb

Middle High German

❧ Walther von der Vogelweide
(c. 1170–1230)

UNDER THE LINDENTREE

Under the lindentree
on the heather
there our bed for two was
and there too
you may find blossoms grasses
picked together
in a clearing of a wood
tandaradei!
            the nightingale sang sweetly.

I came walking
over the field:
my love was already there.
Then I was received
with the words "Noble lady!"
It will always make me happy.
Did he kiss me? He gave me thousands!
tandaradei!
            O look at my red mouth.

He had made
very beautifully
a soft bed out of the flowers.
Anybody who comes by there
knowingly
may smile to himself.
For by the upset roses he may see
tandaradei!
      where my head lay.

If anyone were to know
how he lay with me
(may God forbid it!), I'd feel such shame.
What we did together
may no one ever know
except us two
one small bird excepted
tandaradei!
      and it can keep a secret.

                     Michael Benedikt

der Wilde Alexander (c. 1280)

WHEN WE WERE CHILDREN

I remember how, at that time, in this meadow,
we used to run up and down, playing our games,
tag and games of that sort; and looked for wildflowers,
violets and such. A long time ago.
Now there are only these cows, bothered by flies,
only these cows, wandering about in the meadow.

I remember us sitting down in the field of flowers,
surrounded by flowers, and playing she loves me not,
she loves me; plucking the flower petals.
My memory of childhood is full of those flowers,
bright with the colors of garlands we wore in our dancing
and playing. So time went by among the wildflowers.

Look over there near those trees at the edge of the woods.
Right over there is where we used to find
blueberry bushes, blackberry bushes, wild strawberries.
We had to climb over rocks and old walls to get them.
One day a man called out to us: "Children, go home."
He had been watching from somewhere in the woods.

We used to feast on the berries we found in that place
till our hands and mouths were stained with the colors of all

the berries the blackberries, strawberries, and the blueberries.
It was all fun to us, in the days of our childhood.
One day a man called out, in a doleful voice:
"Go home, children, go home, there are snakes in that place."

One day one of the children went into the grass
that grows high near the woods, among the bushes.
We heard him scream and cry out. He came back weeping.
"Our little horse is lying down and bleeding.
Our pony is lying down. Our pony is dying.
I saw a snake go crawling off in the grass."

Children, go home, before it gets too dark.
If you don't go home before the light has gone,
if you don't get home before the night has come,
listen to me, you will be lost in the dark,
listen to me, your joy will turn into sorrow.
Children, go home, before it gets to be dark.

There were five virgins lingered in a field.
The king went in with his bride and shut the doors.
The palace doors were shut against the virgins.
The virgins wept, left standing in the field.
The servants came and stripped the virgins naked.
The virgins wept, stripped naked, in the field.

David Ferry

Southern Europe: French National Epic; Lyric Poetry in French, Provençal, Spanish, Galicio-Portuguese, and Italian

French

🙰 Attributed to Turoldus (c. 1100)

RONCEVALLES *From* THE SONG OF ROLAND

Evening is coming, the day wears on,
Arms and armour reflect the sun.
Hauberk and helmets, flower-painted shields
Seem to throw flames across the field;
There is glitter from gilded flags and spears.
How sombrely the emperor
Rides! And the French with him, upset
And angry, they cannot forget
Roland, and the danger he is in.
'Seize Ganelon,' orders the king,
'And hand him to the kitchen boys.'
He calls the master cook, and says:
'Besgon, put him under guard.
He has betrayed my house.' There are
A hundred lads there to receive him,
The best and worst of them are pleased.
They pull hairs from his beard and moustache,
Each gives him four blows with his fist.
They beat him with sticks and cudgels, they get
A chain and put it round his neck
Then chain him up just like a bear.

They load him on a donkey, and so
They cosset and look after him
Till they have to give him back to the king.

The mountains are high and full of shadows,
The valleys deep, the streams rapid.
They sound the trumpets as they advance
To give Roland an answer from France.
The emperor rides sombrely,
The French are upset and angry;
Tears start from their eyes, they grieve
And pray to God that he will save
Roland until they reach the place
Where they can save France from disgrace.
What is the point of it? There is none,
The time for praying has already gone.

King Charles rides on in fury,
His white beard outside his byrny.
All the French barons use their spurs,
Not one of them but wishes he were
Already with Roland, their captain
When he is fighting the Saracens.
He is in trouble, cannot survive,
Possibly, till they arrive.
God, those sixty men he has
Are the best that any captain could have!

Roland looks at the mountainside
On which so many Frenchmen have died
And can no longer hold back his tears:
'God have mercy on you peers
And lords, and grant that in Paradise
You may lie among roses and lilies!
I never set eyes on better men.
So long have you served with me and conquered
So many lands for the emperor!
Was it for this he bred you up?
Ah, France, you are the sweetest country,
Now deserted, you may thank me.
French barons, I see you die
And cannot help you in any way.
God help you, he never lies.
Oliver, you are my brother, but I
Have failed you, and I shall die
Of grief, if not in another way.
Let us fight on and finish this day.'

Count Roland is back in the battle,
Laying about him with Durandal.
Faldrun de Pui is cut in two,

Twenty-four others sliced right through:
Never a man so wanted revenge
As Roland for his massacred French!
They run like deer before the dogs,
Those pagans escaping Roland's knocks!
The archbishop says: 'You are doing well;
So a man should do who is able
To bear arms and sit on a horse.
Courage should be a matter of course.
A man without is no good to me:
As well be a monk in a monastery,
Praying all day long for our sins!'
Roland replies: 'Come on, pitch in!'
With that the Franks set to again,
But it didn't go well for the Christians.

When it is known that there will be
No prisoners, men fight desperately.
So with the French, who are like lions.
Marsilie, every inch a baron
Comes riding Gaignon, a fine horse.
He uses his spurs, and with all his force
Charges Bevon, who when at home
Is lord of Dijon and of Beaune.
He smashes his shield, goes through the hauberk
And this one blow completes the work.
Then he kills Yvoire and Ivon,
And with them Gerard of Roussillion.
Count Roland is not far away.
He says to the pagans: 'You will pay
For that, God damn you, they're my men!
Before you touch another of them
You'll find out what my sword is called!'
With that, a blow from Durandal
Which severs Marsilie's right hand.
After that the count Roland
Has off the head of Jurfaleu,
Marsilie's son. The pagans drew
Aside and prayed: 'Help us, Mahomet!
All our gods, help us, and let
Us be avenged on the emperor!
He has sent us a pack of murderers
Who would rather die than leave us in peace.'
They say to each other: 'No more great feats!'
A hundred thousand of them make tracks
For home; no one can call them back.

C. H. Sisson

✺ Anonymous (c. 1100)

LI SONS D'UN CORNET

The note of a trumpet was eating the heart of a thunder-
bolt with vinegar when a dead hobnail caught the course of
a star in a bird-trap. In the air there was a grain of rye, when
the barking of a roasting spit and the stump of a piece of
cloth found a worn-out fart and cut off its ear.

Willard Trask

✺ Jean Bodel (c. 1202)

LES CONGÉS DU LÉPREUX

Plague and sores beyond relief
Have pierced me, skin and bone.
I must set up house with grief,
And travel hence alone.
Death has forced me to content
And with a darkness buys me day;
Poverty has paid my rent,
And counts tomorrow for today.
Pity, with those two red eyes,
And sorrow, looking back on me,
Do these errands I devise
To friends whom I shall never see.

One who taught me how to write,
Gerard of Pontlouvain,
Pity, waft what I indite,
And weep, if it be plain.
What he taught me, now I find
Serviceable to my pain,
So beyond my scabby rind
I touch his friendship yet again.
Now there's nothing sweet or sound
Left about me, but my heart,
Sorrow, as you go your round,
Give him that, and so depart.

Those who catered to my woes
When I was going rotten,
Sorrow, thank, but also those
By whom they were forgotten.
They relieved my body once,

And gave it pleasure in their hour,
And the body I renounce,
But I would not be rude or sour.
Go and tell old Simon Hall,
Now that I peel from head to feet,
With his good men by the wall
I can no longer sit at meat.

Pity, you may say goodbye
To two more I shall miss,
Hugo and Bertyl, and thereby
Look pale, and tell them this:
They may sail for Palestine,
As I had done, and made up three.
With their cross they can carry mine;
The pagans have a truce, for me.
God has quit me of my vow,
I owe no ransom for release.
Say that I go with them now,
Although I die at home in peace.

F. T. Prince

ஒ Eustache Deschamps (1346–1410)

BALLADE 1

The stag was very proud of his swiftness,
Of running ten miles in one breath,
And the wild boar was proud to be fierce,
And the sheep praised her woolly fleece,
And the horse its beauty, and the buck was proud
Of crossing the plain at a bound,
And the one proud of strength was the bull,
The ermine in having a furry skin;
And to them all he said from his shell:
'The snail will get to Easter just as soon.'

What I see first are lions, leopards, bears,
Running the countryside, wolves and tigers
Under pursuit by greyhound and mastiff
And the shouts of men, so hated that if
They're caught each person will attack,
Because of the destruction of the flock;
They're thieves, treacherous and wicked,
And merciless, and for that detested.
Are they strong and fast? Good at a run?
The snail will get to Easter just as soon.

Many see him and the path he's on,
Enclosed in the shell he carries along,
They don't do him harm, they let him be,
And so he goes from week to week,
As many go in their own poor realm
Who live good lives in their simple gown,
And if the world gives them little at all,
They still go on with its good will.
And cow and calf have the meadow's run,
And the snail will get to Easter just as soon.

Prince, among the strong, the rich, the great
There's a lesson they rarely think about;
Their haste can't bring the future on:
The snail will get to Easter just as soon.

David Curzon and Jeffrey Fiskin

BALLADE 2

In Antwerp, Bruges, Ostend and Ghent
I used to order food with flair,
But in every inn to which I went
They always brought me, with my fare,
With every roast and mutton dish,
With boar, with rabbit, pigeon, bustard,
With fresh and with salt-water fish,
Always, never asking, mustard.

I ordered herring, said I'd like
Carp for supper at the bar,
And called for simple boiled pike,
And two large sole, when I ate at Spa.
I ordered green sauce when in Brussels;
The waiter stared and looked disgusted;
The bus boy brought in with my mussels
As always, never asking, mustard.

I couldn't eat or drink without it.
They add it to the water they
Boil the fish in and—don't doubt it—
The drippings from the roast each day
Are tossed into a mustard vat
In which they're mixed, and then entrusted
To those who bring—they're trained at that—
Always, never asking, mustard.

Prince, it's clear a spice like clove
can drop its guard. It won't be busted.

There's just one thing these people serve:
Always, never asking, mustard.

David Curzon and Jeffrey Fiskin

RONDEAU

Fleas, stink, pigs, mold,
The gist of the Bohemian soul,
Bread and salted fish and cold.

Leeks, and cabbage three days old,
Smoked meat, as hard and black as coal;
Fleas, stink, pigs, mold.

Twenty eating from one bowl,
A bitter drink—it's beer, I'm told—
Bad sleep on straw in some filthy hole,
Fleas, stink, pigs, mold,
The gist of the Bohemian soul,
Bread and salted fish and cold.

David Curzon and Jeffrey Fiskin

❧ Charles D'Orléans (1349–1465)

QUANT SOUVENIR ME RAMENTOIT

I was so assailed by the memory
Of that grand beauty I recall
Of her who was my heart's Lady,
The one I could not help but call
My Fountain Ever Bountiful,
Who died alas in recent days,
That I cried out, wiping my eyes,
"All this world means nothing at all!"

Cressid, Isuelt, and Helen, these three,
And many other beauties enthrall
Century on century
With loveliness that cannot pall.
And yet each came in time to fall
Prisoner to Death's emprise;
And so I clearly recognize
That all this world means nothing at all.

Death has desired, it seems to me,
And still desires and ever shall,

To drive his forces powerfully
Against the happy and the pleasurable
By taking all the beautiful
Fine ladies from us, without whose
Presence truly I surmise
All this world means nothing at all.

Love, here's a truth that will appall:
Death wages war without surcease;
If there's no way to make a peace,
Then all this world means nothing at all.

Fred Chappell

LAS! MORT QUI T'A FAIT SI HARDIE

Death, you have made it your pleasure
To take the noble princess
Who was my comfort, my treasure,
And everything to bless
My life. Since my mistress
You take, take once again:
Take me, her servitor.
Better to die than bear
Such torment, sorrow, and pain.

She was beautiful past measure,
In the flower of youth she was.
May God work His displeasure
Upon your faithlessness!
My anguish would be less
If you had taken her when
Old age had burdened her;
But you hastened to show your power
With torment, sorrow, and pain.

I live imprisoned, my leisure
Lonely, companionless . . .
My Lady, goodbye. Now has our
Love departed. This promise
I make to you: largess
Of prayers and, until slain,
My heart, yours evermore,
Forgetting nothing in its sore
Torment, sorrow, and pain.

God, Who art sovereign
Of all, in mercy ordain

That the bright spirit of her
Will only briefly endure
Torment, sorrow, and pain.

Fred Chappell

BALLADE

I was in blossom when I was a child
and as a young man I became the fruit;
but then my mistress Folly shook me wild
and green down from a tree that is the root
of joy. And Reason, who makes all things straight
and acts in ways that no one can envision,
wisely and without malice closed the gate
and laid me ripening on the straw of prison.

There I have lingered in unending rest
deprived of the sweet air of liberty.
I'm happy, and I think it's for the best,
although this idleness is withering me
and I grow old. The spark of foolish lust
is now extinct and dark like my horizon
since they have placed me in this cage of rust
and laid me ripening on the straw of prison.

God give us peace and bring deliverance!
Then I will wade waters of happiness.
Refreshed and lying in the sun of France
I'll clean from me the mildew of duress.
I wait for the sun in stark humility,
for I have hope it will be God's decision
to free me; through his magnaminity
he laid me ripening on the straw of prison.

I am a winter fruit less soft than fruit
of summer. Now I'm in a garrison
to heal my too hard greenness. Destitute,
they laid me ripening on the straw of prison.

Tony Barnstone and Willis Barnstone

LE TEMPS A LAISSIÉ

The weather's cast away its cloak
Of wind and rain and chilling haze;
It clads itself in broideries
Of crystal sunlit rays.

There's not a beast or bird but sings
Or cries out in its own sweet strain:
The weather's cast away its cloak
Of wind and cold and rain.

The whole wide earth is dressed anew:
River, fountain and brook now wear
Drops of silver, jewels of gold—
The weather's cast away its cloak
Of wind and rain and cold.

Stanley Burnshaw

❧ François Villon (1431–1463?)

BALLADE OF THE MEN WHO WERE HANGED

Brother men who come along now, we
Are gone; don't let your feelings petrify
Against us. For if you show some sympathy,
God's grace to you can only magnify.
Five of us up here—or is it six? We fly
By means of ropes the flesh that once was sound
And sleek but now is mere half-eaten rind,
And only we, the bones, left to discuss
Our rotten luck. Don't laugh, but be chagrined—
And pray to God that He show grace to us.

We call you brothers, and we hope you'll see
Our side of things, although our fate came by
Edict of law. You surely must agree
That all men don't possess an equal high
Intelligence. And now that we draw nigh,
Ask of the Virgin's Son that He be kind
And, never stinting mercy, will befriend
And keep us from that Hell so thunderous.
We're dead—and none need pay us any mind,
But pray to God that He show grace to us.

The rain has washed us clean as clean can be;
The sun has blackened us and burnt us dry:
Eyebrows and beards the crows have carried away
And, helped by magpies, dug out every eye.
Nor are we tranquil as the hours go by
But always we drift restless in the wind
That gaily neglects to keep a steady mind.
We've got more holes than a tailor's thimble has.
Don't do our deeds; do just the other kind—
And pray to God that He show grace to us.

Jesu, to Whose domain we're all assigned,
Let Hell not hold us eternally confined,
For that's one place we've got no business.
And brothers, your sneering jokes are quite unkind;
O pray to God that He show grace to us.

Fred Chappell

REMEMBER, IMBECILES AND WITS

Remember, imbeciles and wits,
sots and ascetics, fair and foul,
young girls with little tender tits,
that DEATH is written over all.

Worn hides that scarcely clothe the soul
they are so rotten, old and thin,
or firm and soft and warm and full—
fellmonger Death gets every skin.

All that is piteous, all that's fair,
all that is fat and scant of breath,
Elisha's baldness, Helen's hair,
is Death's collateral:

Three score and ten years after sight
of this pay me your pulse and breath
value received. And who dare cite,
as we forgive our debtors, Death?

Abelard and Eloise,
Henry the Fowler, Charlemagne,
Genée, Lopokova, all these
die, die in pain.

And General Grant and General Lee,
Patti and Florence Nightingale,
like Tyro and Antiope
drift among ghosts in Hell,

know nothing, are nothing, save a fume
driving across a mind
preoccupied with this: our doom
is, to be sifted by the wind,

heaped up, smoothed down like silly sands.
We are less permanent than thought.
The Emperor with the Golden Hands

is still a word, a tint, a tone,
insubstantial-glorious,
when we ourselves are dead and gone
and the green grass growing over us.

Basil Bunting

BALLADE (TWO VERSIONS)

Gone Ladies

Where in the world is Helen gone,
Whose loveliness demolished Troy?
Where is Salome? Where the wan
Licentious Queen of Avalon?
Who sees My Lady Fontenoy?
And where is Joan, so soldier tall?
And She who bore God's only Boy?
Where is the snow we watched last Fall?

Is Thaïs still? Is Nell? And can
    Stem Héloïse aurene.
Whose so-by-love-enchanted man
Sooner would risk castration than
    Abandon her, be seen?
Who does Sheherazade enthral?
And who, within her arms and small,
    Shares Sappho's evergreen?

Through what eventless territory
Are Ladies Day and Joplin swept?
What news of Marilyn who crept
Into an endless reverie?
You saw Lucrece? And Jane? And she,
Salvation's ancient blame-it-all,
Delicious Eve? Then answer me:
Where is the snow we watched last Fall?

Girl, never seek to know from me
    Who was the fairest of them all.
What wouldst thou say if I asked thee:
    Where is the snow we watched last Fall?

Christopher Logue

Ballade of the Ladies of Time Past

O tell me where, in lands or seas,
Flora, that Roman belle, has strayed,
Thais, or Archipiades,
Who put each other in the shade,

Or Echo who by bank and glade
Gave back the crying of the hound,
And whose sheer beauty could not fade.
But where shall last year's snow be found?

Where too is learned Héloïse,
For whom shorn Abélard was made
A tonsured monk upon his knees?
Such tribute his devotion paid.
And where's that queen who, having played
With Buridan, had him bagged and bound
To swim the Seine thus ill-arrayed?
But where shall last year's snow be found?

Queen Blanche the fair, whose voice could please
As does the siren's serenade,
Great Bertha, Beatrice, Alice — these,
And Arembourg whom Maine obeyed,
And Joan whom Burgundy betrayed
And England burned, and Heaven crowned:
Where are they, Mary, Sovereign Maid?
But where shall last year's snow be found?

Not next week, Prince, nor next decade,
Ask me these questions I propound.
I shall but say again, dismayed,
Ah, where shall last year's snow be found?

Richard Wilbur

A BALLADE TO END WITH

Here is poor Villon's final word;
The ink upon his will is dried.
Come see him properly interred
When by the bell you're notified,
And come in scarlet, since he died
Love's martyr, through his gentle heart:
This on one ball he testified
As he made ready to depart.

Nor do I think his claim absurd;
Love hounded him both far and wide,
By such contempt and malice spurred
That, clear to Roussillon, one spied
No thorn in all the countryside
But wore his tattered shirt in part.
So said he (and he never lied)
As he made ready to depart.

And thus and therefore it occurred
That one rag only clothed his hide
When he lay dead; what's more, we heard
How on his bed of death he cried
A pox on Love, who still applied,
Sharper than buckle-tongue, his dart
(A fact which left us saucer-eyed),
As he made ready to depart.

Prince, like a falcon in your pride,
Hear how his pilgrimage did start:
He swigged some dark-red wine, and sighed,
As he made ready to depart.

Richard Wilbur

I DIE OF THIRST WHILE AT THE FOUNTAIN SIDE

I die of thirst while at the fountain side,
Hot as fire, my teeth are chattering,
In my own country, far off I abide,
Near the blaze I burn, still shivering,
Naked as a worm, dressed like my Lord the Mayor,
I laugh in tears and wait, but without hope,
I brighten up again, in sad despair,
I'm joyful, and I don't have any fun,
Powerful, and with no strength to cope,
Well received, dismissed by everyone.

I'm sure of nothing but uncertainties,
I find obscure all that is evident,
Doubtful of nothing but the certainties,
My learning comes by sudden accident,
Winner of everything, a loser overall,
At dawn I say, "God give you a good night,"
When I'm laid out I'm still afraid I'll fall,
I own the bank, without a sou in sight,
Await inheritance, as no-one's son,
Well received, dismissed by everyone.

Careless and carefree, still a working stiff
So I can buy what I don't need to buy,
Those who speak best to me most piss me off,
And those who are most true most often lie,
A friend is anyone who lets me know
That a white swan is just a coal-black crow,
And those who hurt believe they help I see,
Falsehood and truth are all the same to me,
I can recall each thing, and think of none,
Well received, dismissed by everyone.

Merciful Prince, let's hope you like this one,
I've learned a lot, no sense or knowledge won,
I'm someone special, and common in the dock.
What's left to do? Get my junk out of hock.
Well received, dismissed by everyone.

David Curzon and Jeffrey Fiskin

QUATRAIN

France's I am; my lookout's glum.
From Paris (near Pontoise) I come,
And soon my neck, depending from
A rope, will learn the weight of my bum.

Richard Wilbur

Provençal

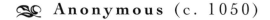

Anonymous (c. 1050)

EN UN VERGIER SOIZ FOLHA D'ALBESPI

Sheltered beneath white hawthorn boughs,
A woman held her loved one close
In her arms, till the watchman cried abroad:
God! It is dawn! How soon it's come!

"How wildly have I wished that the night
Would never end, and that my love
Could stay, and the watchman never cry
God! It is dawn! How soon it's come!

"My love-and-friend, but one more kiss,
Here in our field where the small birds sing;
We shall defy their jealous throats—
God! It is dawn! How soon it's come!

"Still one more close embrace, my love,
Here in our field where the small birds sing,
Till the watchman blow his reedy strain—
God! It is dawn! How soon it's come!

"From the wind beyond where my love has gone,
Thoughtful, contented, I have drunk
A long deep draught of his breath—O God,
God! It is dawn! How soon it's come!"

Envoi

Flowing with grace and charm is she;
Her loveliness draws many eyes,
Whose full heart throbs with a true love:
God! It is dawn! How soon it's come!

Stanley Burnshaw

𝕾 Richard I, Coeur de Lion
(1157–1199)

JA NULS HOMS PRIS NE IRA A RAISON

Forbecause a prisoner lies
With no air or exercise
He has need, to save his health,
Of thoughts that will not give him grief:
I have friends of name and wealth,
But few of them have sent relief.

Ask what they have done for me,
Those who yet go rich and free,
All my barons, tall young men
Of Poitou, England and Touraine;
Once they were my friends, and then
They never knew me false or vain.

Much dishonour they may fear,
Should I lie two winters here.
Men and barons, they all know
Not one could be so poor to me,
I would let him stifle so
For want of money paid in fee.

Some may think my capture sent
As deserved, in punishment;
Others resting from alarms
Live unconcerned in heart or head,
Though the fields are bare of arms
And I do homage to a bed.

Not that I intend excuse
From the chance of war, ill-use,
Close confinement, fear and pain;
But this is over and above.
Of the others none complain,
But worse than all is loss of love.

F. T. Prince

✍ Arnaut Daniel (1180–1210)

EN CEST SONET COIND' A LERI

On this gay and slender tune
I put and polish words and plane
and when I've passed the file they'll be
       precise and firm.
For Love himself pares down and gilds my song
which moves from her whose glances are
the firm light rails that guide all excellence.

I tell you frankly, she I adore and serve
's the loveliest in the world.
Because I'm hers from head to toe
I cleanse myself, and though wind blow in winter
the love flowing within my heart keeps ice
out of the stream the coldest weather.

I burn oil lamps, wax tapers, no pretense I
hear a thousand masses out for my intention,
that God grant me by his intervention
good success with her against
whom all resistance is useless.
And when I think of her auburn hair, her
merry body, svelte and lissom,
I love her better than if they gave me Lusena.

I love her with fire
       seek her with such
excess of desire
       I feel I float.
Loving without stint one loses weight.
Her heart submerges mine in a great flood that nothing
will evaporate.
She takes such usury of love she'll end
       by owning tavern and bartender.

I do not want the Roman Emp.
nor to be elected pope
if I can't
       turn toward her
       where my heart
is kindled to a blaze nothing can quell.
       The meat
browns and catches fire, flames, cracks and splits,
and if she doesn't heal me with a kiss
before New Year's she destroys me, she
damns me to hell. And I

cannot turn from loving her too well.
The pain I put up with's hard, this
solitude wraps me round and is my theme.
                              On this cover
                              I embroider
                              words for rhymes.
My fate is worse than his who plows a field, for
though my field's a little bit of earth, I love,
I love it better than Mondis loved Audierna.

            I am Arnaut
            who gathers the wind
            who hunts with an ox
            to chase a hare
forever, and swims against the current.

Paul Blackburn

Bertran de Born (c. 1180)

PROTESTATION

O let me, Lady, silence calumny
And end these lies envy has laid on me.
In God's name, I pray you! Let them not confuse
Your heart that is all faith and courtesy,
Complaisance, truth and tender loyalty,
However they assail me with abuse.

At first cast may I lose my hawk in air,
See falcons strike it at my wrist and tear
It from me, to pluck it to the bloodied bone,
If ever the love I have of you could bear
I look upon another with desire to share
That bed whereon I get no rest alone.

And now that I may utterly disencumber
My course from shame the protest shall be sombre:
If ever I have failed toward you in thought
When we shall be alone in the high chamber
May my powers fail and my heart not remember
To send blood into my veins for the bout.

If I sit down to tables may my luck
Change so I cannot win by hook or crook;
When I start gaming may the dice conspire
Always to fall upon the lowest stroke;
If ever I sought another and forsook
You whom alone I love, alone desire.

May I share Altafort with other lords
And in the tower may we be four swords
And no love lost among the lot. But rather
May I go always covered round with guards
Crossbowmen, leeches, sergeants and gatewards,
If ever I had heart to love another.

O Lady, leave me for another knight
Nor let me know where to avenge the slight;
May the winds fail me when beyond the sea,
And the King's porters drub me from his sight;
In press of battle may I take first flight,
If they lie not who tell these tales of me.

Lady, I have a goshawk, finely mewed,
Swift to the wild duck, trained and unsubdued
By any bird that flies, heron or swan
Or even the black eagle, and I would
Gladly for your sake see her droop immewed,
Sullen and slow to fly, fat as a capon.

Envious liars, feinting with calumny,
Since through my lady you have troubled me,
You were advised to leave me well alone.

                              John Peale Bishop

SIRVENTES

Spring is a juice, a rejoicing, forcing
leaves out, flowers up.
I like the noise of birds who make
their singing ring in the woods,
and see tents
on the meadows raised,
and pavillions raised,
and a very hellish delight to see
armored horses and armed knights ranging
down the field.

And on the roads I have delight to see
the rabble with their goods in flight
pressed by the skirmishers, and behind
outriders,
            the army crowding in.
And it pleases me in my heart to see
strong castles at siege,
ramparts broke and riven, and
an army on the fosse-brink gudgeoned

in
between palisade and ditch
the stakes close-set.

And I love beyond all pleasure that
lord who horsed, armed and beyond fear is
forehead and spearhead in the attack, and there
emboldens his men with exploits. When
   stour proches and comes to quarters
   may each man pay his quit-rent firmly,
   follow his lord with joy, willingly,
for no man's proved his worth a stiver until
many the blows
he's taken and given.

Maces smashing painted helms,
glaive-strokes descending, bucklers riven,
this to be seen at stour's starting!
And many valorous vassals pierced and piercing
  striking together!
And nickering, wandering lost through the
  battle's thick,
brast-out blood on the broken harness,
  horses of dead men and wounded.

And having once sallied into the stour
no boy with a brassard may think of aught, but
the swapping of heads and hacking off arms —
for here a man is worth more dead
  than shott-free and caught!

I tell you,
I have no such savour of eating soft
food and sleeping and tasting hot wines
as hearing the cries from each side coming
   "AT THEM!"
and see
waiting under the trees
horses whicker and strain,
to hear the shout
   "a RESCUE! to AID!"
and see fall in the fosse and on the green earth
the mighty and mean, and
see in the flanks of the fallen
  the broken
butt-end of lances, their banners flaming!

   Pawn your castles, lords,
   pawn your towns and cities!
   Before you're beat to the draw
    unsheath those swords!

Papiols, rejoice and go
with all haste to Oc-e-No
and tell him that we've got too much
damned PEACE down here!

Paul Blackburn

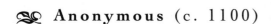 Peire Cardinal (c. 1216–1271)

THE CLERKS PRETEND TO BE SHEPHERDS

The clerks pretend to be shepherds, and under
A show of sanctity are
Ravening cut-throats.
When I see one shimmy
Into a cassock
I think of Alengri the wolf,
Who thought to break into
The sheep-cote but was
Afraid on account of the mastiffs . . .
But then he had an idea.
He pulled a sheepskin over his head
And ate as much as he liked.

Kings, emperors, dukes, counts and knights
Used to rule the world.
Now the priests have the power, got
By robbery, treachery, sermons,
Force and hypocrisy.

Paul Blackburn

Spanish

Anonymous (c. 1100)

GIRL WITH THE DARK HAIR

Girl with the dark hair
If you are asleep, be warned:
Half of our life is a dream
Which runs and slips by us,
As rapid in its flight
As a light sleep wakened,
As brief while we are young
As when age is upon us,

For the sad disclosure
Of our fleet career
When it would wake us comes
Late and avails us nothing.
Your youth and beauty are
No more than a new merchant,
Rich to be left poor
By the lapse of time;
A glory of the world
And a veil for the eyes
And chains for the feet
And fetters for the fingers;
A ground for hazards,
A midden of envy,
A butcher of men,
A famous thief of time.
When death has shuffled
Ugly and fair together
In the narrow sepulcher
The bones do not know each other.
And though the cypress is higher
And the cedar more lovely, neither,
Burned into charcoal, is whiter
Than charcoal from the ash tree.
For in this woeful existence
Delight comes to us in dreams only
And distress and tribulation
When we are widest awake.
Dry autumn will consume
The flower of fresh April,
To unloved ivory
Turning your ebon hair.

W. S. Merwin

❧ Anonymous (c. 1100)

THE GRAY SHE-WOLF

As I was in my hut
Painting my shepherd's crook
The Pleiades were climbing
And the moon waning;
Sheep are poor prophets
Not to keep to the fold.
I saw seven wolves
Come up through a dark gully.
They cast lots as they came
To see who should enter the fold;

It fell to an old she-wolf,
Gray, grizzled and bow-legged,
With fangs lifting her lips
Like the points of knives.
Three times she circled the fold
And could take nothing;
Once more she went round it
And snatched the white lamb,
The Merino's daughter,
Niece of the earless ewe,
Which my masters were saving
For Easter Sunday.
—Come here, my seven pups,
Here, my bitch from Trujilla,
Here, you on the chain,
Run down the gray she-wolf.
If you fetch back the lamb
On milk and bread you will dine;
Fail to fetch her back,
You'll dine on my stick.—
On the heels of the she-wolf
They wore their nails down to crumbs;
Seven leagues they ran her
On the harsh mountains.
Climbing a little ravine,
The she-wolf begins to tire:
—Here, dogs, you can take the lamb,
As sound and well as ever.—
—We do not want the lamb
From your wolving mouth;
Your skin is what we want,
For a coat for the shepherd,
Your tail to make laces
To fasten his breeches,
Your head for a bag
To keep spoons in,
And your guts for lute strings
To make the ladies dance.

W. S. Merwin

෨ Anonymous (c. 1140)

From POEM OF THE CID

1. The Cid Calls His Vassals Together. They'll Go into Exile with Him.

[. . .]
He
turned and looked back to see the towers,

tears running from his eyes:
saw the gate standing ajar,
doors left open without locks,
the porches bare
of either pelts or coverings,
perches empty of falcons, empty of molted hawks. He sighed,
mio Cid, his worries were weighty, and not small.

The Cid spoke well and with great measure:
"Thanks be to thee, my Lord, our
Father, which art in heaven!
It's my enemies have turned
this treachery upon me."

2. Omens on the Road to Burgos.

Then they set spur to horse,
loosed the reins, they opened up then.
Crows flew across to their right
as they were leaving Bivar,
and as they drove down to Burgos,
crows crossed to their left.
The Cid shrugged and shook his head:
"So, we're thrown out of the country, well,
cheer up Fáñez! When we come back to Castille, we'll
come back with all the honors."

3. The Cid Enters Burgos.

The Cid Ruy Díaz came into Burgos,
the pennons of 60 lances with him.
They have to get a look at him,
men and women both.
Townsmen and their wives crowd the windows,
tears in their eyes
and in their mouths
a single sentence:
"God, what a good vassal!
If only he had a worthy lord."

4. No One Will Put the Cid up. Only a Small Girl Addresses Him and That to Tell Him to Go Away. The Cid Finds He Has to Make Camp Outside of Town, on the Sand of the Riverbank.

They would have invited him gladly,
only not one dared,
so great was Alfonso's fury.
The night before, his letter,
sealed with severity and heavy with
warnings,
had gotten to Burgos:

that
to mio Cid Ruy Díaz
no man should give shelter,
or by the king's true word, he'd lose
his goods, his eyes from his head, his soul, and his body.
   Everyone was ashamed, and in sorrow,
    hid from mio Cid,
      and no one chanced a word.
The Campeador rode up to a place
they could stay for the night, and
when he reached the door he found it barred.
For fear of the king they had agreed
   that, unless he broke it down, by
   no means to let him in.
The Cid's men called loudly to those inside,
   they did not answer a word. Mio
    Cid dug in his spurs, raced up to the door,
pulled one foot out of the stirrup and
gave it a helluva kick.
Door was well secured and did not budge.
       Then a little girl of nine years
       leaned above him over the
        balcony:
"Hey Campeador, in a good hour you girded on sword!
   But the king has forbidden it,
   his letter arrived last night
with heavy warnings and stamped with the royal seal.

   We don't dare open to you, or
    put you up,
    for if we did,
      we'd lose our goods and our houses, even
      they eyes out of our faces. Cid,
what would you gain from our misery?
But, with all his holy strength,
may God keep you."
     And she went back into the house.

Then the Cid saw
that he would get no privilege from the king. He
turned from the door and galloped through the town,
dismounted at the church of Santa María,
fell upon his knees
and prayed from the heart.
      The prayer done,
      he rode on,
      rode out of the gates
      and crossed the Arlanzón by the
      bridge near the cathedral.
On the far side of the river,

on the sand of the riverbank,
he had them pitch his tent, and then dismounted.
Mio Cid Ruy Díaz,
who in good hour girded on sword, set
       his tent on the rough sand
           surrounded by good companions,
               when no one would take him in.
So the Cid set down camp
as though he were in the mountains.
       In the great city of Burgos, he
     was forbidden to buy anything
       whatsoever, any provisions,
        and no one dared sell him ration enough
          to feed a single man
          for a single day.

                      Paul Blackburn

Galician-Portuguese

✎ Nuño Fernández Torneol (c. 1225)

THE LADY'S FAREWELL

Awake, my love, who sleep into the dawn!
The birds of all the world cried and are gone.
    I go away in joy.

Awake, my love, who sleep so late at dawn!
It was our love the small birds dwelt upon.
    I go away in joy.

The birds of all the world spoke of our love,
Of my love and of yours cried out above.
    I go away in joy.

The birds of all the world sang loud at day.
It was my love and yours, I heard them say.
    I go away in joy.

It was my love and yours that made their song.
You cut the branches where they clung so long.
    I go away in joy.

It was my love and yours that made their cry—
You cut the branches where they used to fly.
    I go away in joy.

You cut the branches where they used to sing,
And where they came to drink you dried the spring.
    I go away in joy.

You cut the branches where they used to stay,
And dried the waters where they came to play.
    I go away in joy.

              Yvor Winters

ꙮ Pero Meogo (c. 1250)

COSSANTE

Tell me, daughter, my pretty daughter,
Why you waited by the cold water.
    —It was love, alas!

Tell me, daughter, my lovely daughter,
Why you waited by the cold water.
    —It was love, alas!

I waited, mother, by the cold fountain
While the deer came down the mountain.
    —It was love, alas!

I waited by the cold river, mother,
To see the deer, and not for any other.
    —It was love, alas!

You lie, daughter, you lie for your lover,
I never saw deer come down from cover.
    —It was love, alas!

You lie, daughter, for your lover by the fountain,
I never saw deer going up to the mountain.
    —It was love, alas!

              Yvor Winters

CANTIGA DE AMIGO

Through the green grass
the does pass
    lover:
through the green meadow
the bucks go
    lover.

Seeking the does
I washed my tresses
   lover:
seeking the bucks
I washed my locks
   lover.

When I had washed them
with gold I brushed them
   lover:
when I had dried them
with gold I tied them
   lover.

With gold I tied them
till you espied them
   lover:
with gold I bound them
until you found them
   lover.

Keith Bosley

Italian

✤ St. Francis of Assisi (1181–1226)

CANTICLE OF THE CREATURES

Most high, all powerful, good Lord
To You be praise, glory and honor
And all blessing.
To You, Most High, do they belong,
And no one is worthy to say Your name.

Be praised, my Lord, with all Your creatures,
Especially Sir Brother Sun,
Who brings us day; and by whom You give us light,
And he is beautiful and radiant with great splendor.
He is a symbol of You, Most High.

Be praised, my Lord, for Sister Moon and the Stars
In the sky You formed them beautiful and precious and clear.

Be praised, my Lord, for Brother Wind,
And for air, cloud and calm and all weathers
By which You give Your creatures sustenance.

Be praised, My Lord, for Sister Water,
Who is very useful and humble and precious and pure.

Be praised, My Lord, for Brother Fire,
By whom night is lighted,
And he is beautiful and merry and robust and strong.

Be praised, my Lord, for Sister Mother Earth,
Who sustains and governs us,
And brings forth divers fruits and colored flowers and grass.

Be praised, my Lord, for those who pardon for Your love's sake
And put up with weakness and distress.
Blessed are those who will endure in peace,
For by You, Most High, they will be crowned.

Be praised, my Lord, for Sister Bodily Death,
From whom no living man can escape.
Woe to those who die in mortal sin,
Blessed those found doing Your most holy will,
For the Second Death will do them no harm.

Praise and bless my Lord and give thanks
And serve Him with deep humility.

James Schuyler

❧ Jacopone da Todi (c. 1250)

PRAISE OF DISEASES

O Lord, in your courtesy
Send me each infirmity!

Send the quartan fever to me,
Send the constant, tertiary,
Send me fever, double, daily,
And great dropsy's misery.

Send me every kind of toothache,
Headache and the stomach ache,
Make my belly sharply ache,
For my throat a malady.

Trouble in eyes and pain for side,
Imposthume within left side,
Let consumption gnaw me inside,
And all the time insanity.

Let my liver burn with fire,
My spleen grow large, my paunch swell higher,
Lungs go ulcered, and a dire
Cough seize on me, and a palsy.

Let my flesh grow fistular,
And my body carbuncular,
And my cancers such as are
Enough to fill me thoroughly.

Let the gout descend to torment,
Sore eyes bring cause for new lament,
Dysentery keep me bent
And hemorrhoids perpetually.

Let the asthma make me strain,
Let its spasm bring me pain;
Like a dog's make mad my brain,
My mouth with cankers tortured be.

Let the falling sickness maim,
Let me fall in water and flame,
And never find a spot where came
No hurt, but pain me utterly.

Let me go sightless, strike me blind;
Deafness, muteness let me find,
Wretched poverty unkind,
Always ensnared in misery.

Let my fetor stink to heaven
So great that not one person even
Will be who from me is not driven,
Placed in so much agony.

Let this terrible ditch, a site
Regoverci called aright,
Be a place abandoned quite
By every goodly company.

Let ice and hail and tempest rise,
Lightning, thunder, blackest skies,
Let there be no adversities
Which do not hold me at their mercy.

Let the demons out of hell
Be my ministers as well,
Let them try me with evil spell:
This I have earned with my folly.

Until this world of ours is done,
If that long my life shall run,
Till final dissolution
Let harsh death be given me.

Give me when at last I'm dead
To a wolf's belly famishéd;
My bones? Be they in ordure laid,
The wilderness my cemetery.

Let dreadful spirits torment my ghost,
Let them escort me, be my host,
And strong vexations trouble most
With their frightful fantasy.

Let every man who hears my shame,
If he's aghast at my ill-fame,
Cross himself in Jesus' name
Lest he meet ill on his journey.

My Lord, not for revenge or spite
Is all this pain that I indite,
But that You made me in love's delight,
And I have slain You for villainy.

L. R. Lind

❧ Guido Cavalcanti (1255–1300)

LAST SONG: FROM EXILE

Since I do not hope to return ever,
Little ballad, to Tuscany,
Go thou, swift and sleight,
Unto my lady straight
Who, of her courtesy,
Will give thee gentle cheer.

Thou shalt bring news of sighs,
Of deep grief, of much fear:
But guard that none thy journey spies
Who's enemy to gentleness:
Or, sure, for my unhappiness,
Thou'lt be delayed
And so assayed
'Twill be my pain,
Past death, to plain
New grief and many a tear.

Thou feel'st how death, O little song,
Clippeth me close in whom life endeth:
Thou feel'st this heart to beat too strong
So fierce each vital sprite contendeth.
So much consumed is this body now
Its suffering is done, I trow:
Thou, for thy part,
Thou then, prithee,
Take thou this soul with thee
Whenever forth it issueth from my heart.

'Las little ballad! for thy amity
This trembling soul I recommend thee:
Bear it with thee, with all its pity,
To that sweet fair to whom I send thee.
'Las! little ballad! say with a sigh
When thou stand'st her before:
"Here doth your servant lie
Come to make stay with you
Parted from him who
Was Love's servitor."

And thou, bewilderèd and enfeeblèd voice,
Now from this sore heart weeping issue find,
And with this soul and with this little song
Go reasoning of this exhausted mind.
There thou wilt find a lady pleasurable
And of a mind so choice
'Twere thy delight if able
To go her ways before,
My soul: and her adore
For her true worth, for ever.

G. S. Fraser

✑ Dante Alighieri (1265–1321)

THE BANQUET: *DISSERTATION 2, CANZONE 1*

Ye intelligences, turning the third sphere,
Hear out the reasoning within my heart
Stranger than I can openly relate.
The heaven that obeys your moving art
—Such noble natures as you surely are—
I see has brought me to my present state;
So of my suffering any debate
Seems that it rightly should be told to ye:
Wherefore I pray that ye will hear my part.
I would tell the strange history of the heart,

How the sad soul there weeps bitterly
Because a spirit speaks, opposing her,
That comes upon the shining of your star.

My sorrowful heart's life often would be
A thought so sweet that it would rise in flight
Many a time to the feet of our great Sire
To see a Lady glorious in light,
Of whom it spoke so blessedly to me
That my soul spoke, and said: "I would go there."
But, putting her to flight, one does appear
Who lords it with such power over me,
My trembling heart shows outwardly its fear.
And this one made me see a Lady here,
And said: "Who would behold felicity,
Let him look in this Lady's eyes
If he fears not the agony of sighs."

Now comes the adversary, who can slay,
Against my humble thought that would give me
Word of an angel crowned in the skies,
So that my soul cried out, and still must cry,
Saying: "Alas, how is she fled away,
The piteous one who showed my pity's guise."
Then this afflicted heart said of its eyes:
"What hour such a lady looked therein,
Why would they not believe my word of her?"
Always I said: "In such eyes as hers are
One surely stands whose glance can murder men.
It not availed me, that I saw it plain,
Against their gazing whereby I am slain."

"You are not slain, but only as though blind,
Soul in our keeping, with so great lament,"
A spirit of gentle love replied to me.
"Because, upon that Lady all intent,
The life has so been driven from your mind
That you are full of fear, and cowardly.
But she is pity and humility,
Courteous and wise in her magnificence:
Know that she is your Lady from this day!
And having undeceived your eyes you may
See such high miracles her ornaments
That you will say to Love: O my true Lord,
Behold thy handmaid, who will do thy word."

Song, I think they will be few indeed
Who well and rightly understand your sense,
So difficult your speech and intricate.
Wherefore if you should come by any chance
Among such folk so little fit to read

As that you seem not to *communicate*,
I'd have you take heart even at that rate,
My latest and dear one, saying to them:
"Look you at least how beautiful I am."

Howard Nemerov

SONNET: DANTE ALIGHIERI TO GUIDO CAVALCANTI

Guido, I would that Lapo, thou, and I,
Led by some strong enchantment, might ascend
A magic ship, whose charmèd sails should fly
With winds at will where'er our thoughts might wend,
So that no change, nor any evil chance
Should mar our joyous voyage; but it might be,
That even satiety should still enhance
Between our hearts their strict community:
And that the bounteous wizard then would place
Vanna and Bice and my gentle love,
Companions of our wandering, and would grace
With passionate talk, wherever we might rove,
Our time, and each were as content and free
As I believe that thou and I should be.

Percy Bysshe Shelley

SPESSE FIATE VEGNONMI A LA MENTE

Comes often to my memory
the darkness Love has fixed in me
so that I cry, self-pityingly,
"What other man has lived this through?"

For Love attacks me suddenly,
life's energies abandon me,
one spirit only lives and moves
within, because it speaks of you.

Then I, to save myself, must force
my steps: a pallid, empty thing
I come to you to be made whole,

but when I raise my eyes to yours
my heart is seized with shuddering
that from the bloodstream drives my soul.

Frederick Morgan

From THE DIVINE COMEDY

Inferno

CANTO III

THROUGH ME COME INTO THE CITY FULL OF PAIN

THROUGH ME COME INTO ENDLESS SUFFERING

THROUGH ME COME BE AMONG THE LOST

I WAS FASHIONED BY MY HIGH MAKER IMPELLED

BY JUSTICE; I WAS FASHIONED BY DIVINE POWER,

BY UTTER WISDOM, BY ORIGINAL LOVE.

BEFORE ME ONLY ETERNALS WERE CREATED

—ANGELS   HEAVEN   PRIMAL MATTER—

I GO ON FOREVER.

YOU WHO COME IN ABANDON ALL HOPE.

Darkling these words I saw inscribed
atop a doorframe, so I said:

    "Master, the meanings are hard to me."

And like a man familiar with the site, he said:

    "Here all self-doubt must be cast off, and all cowardice
    snuffed out; we've come to the place I told you about
    where you'll see the sad beings bereft of the good
    of the intellect—the knowledge of God."

Then, face aglow, he put his hand on mine
—and I was comforted—and after that he led me in
to things concealed from the quick but not from the dead.
Here through the starless air sighs, cries and loud wails
reverberated; so first I wept. A motley clutch
of tongues, monstrous dialects, agony-words, spikes
of wrath, faint and shrill voices and along with these
the thwack of hands—all created a tumult swirling
in a dun air outside of time, as sand eddies in a whirlwind.
And I, horror girding my head, said:

    "Master, what's this I hear, and who are these beings
    so in thrall to their grief?"

And he to me:

    "This despondency weighs down the miserable souls
    who in life earned neither praise nor blame, who here

keep company with that craven choir of angels
not rebels, not faithful to God, out for themselves only
Justly the heavens chased away such angels
whom Hell's deeps rejected too, to make sure
the infernal shades don't lord it over these cowards."

And I:

"Master, what acute pain afflicts all the spirits here,
who are breaking into lamentation?"

He answered:

"I'll tell you, briefly. These, brought so low
through the blindness of their lives, have no hope
of death, and envy anyone else's fate.
The world casts them out of its concerns.
Pity scorns them; justice loathes them.
Let's stop talking about them. Look and pass by.

I looked — and saw a banner whirling so fast
that I thought it could suffer no
pause; and behind it such a press of beings
that I would not have thought death
could undo so many.
         As I was recognizing some,
I saw and knew the shade of him whose pettiness
of soul had spawned the Great Refusal. Immediately
certain, I understood that these were the malicious cabal
odious to God and to all His enemies. Green
flies and wasps stung these naked contemptible beings
—who'd never *been* alive —
and by their feet disgusting worms were harvesting
the mix of tears and blood that had streaked
their faces. And then peering further, I saw beings
on the bank of a wide river
so that I was moved to say:

"Master, those beings I can just make out
through the hazy light — can you tell me who they are,
and what practice makes them seem so ready
to cross over?"

And he to me:

"You will understand these things when we pause
on the sad banks of the Acheron."

Then, ashamed, eyes cast down because I was afraid
what I said had vexed him, I stopped talking
until we got to the river. Ah an old man in a boat,

his hair turned white by time, was coming towards us,
shouting:

> "This is it, you depraved souls! Give up
> the hopes you'll see the sky again. I've come
> to bring you to the other shore forever dark—
> fire and ice. And you there, you living soul,
> quit the dead."

But when he saw I wasn't leaving, he said:

> "You may *not* go from here. You'll pass
> through another port of entry, in a different way;
> a lighter boat must carry you."

And my leader said to him:

> "Charon, don't torment yourself. This is how it must be,
> so ordered where will and power are one. Stand down."

And at once the scraggly jowls of the denatured
fen's boatman grew quiet; around his eyes fire
wheels were dancing. But as soon as the shades, naked
and worn, heard his menacing words, they grew
pallid and gnashed their teeth, blaspheming against God,
against their parents, against humankind, against the site,
the time, the seed that begot them, their birth.
Then they huddled together by that damned shore
which waits for every man who's not afraid
of God. Demon Charon of the ember eyes
beckons them, gathers them and drubs the laggards
with an oar.
        As in the fall the leaves one after another
are subtracted from the branch, which sees those
spoils grounded, so at the infernal gesture Adam's bad
seed hurtle down from that shore, like falcons recalled.
That's how they go across the dark billows
and before they touch down on the other side, a new
band clusters on this shore.

The courteous master said:

> "My son, all beings who die in the wrath of God
> swarm here from every land, and they can't wait
> to cross the Acheron: divine justice so prods them
> that dread transforms into desire. No good soul
> ever comes by here, so if Charon calls you down
> you can now understand the drift of his words."

When he was done, the dusky surround shook
so strongly that I'm bathed in sweat as I remember

my fear. Through the tear-laden ground earth's
imprisoned winds touched off a scarlet flash
which downed my senses; and I fell like a man
snared by sleep.

Armand Schwerner

CANTO XXI

And so from bridge to bridge we went, talking,
    but not of things I mean to sing to all
    the world; and talking brought us to the top
Where we stopped and took in the next crevasse
    of Malebolge: Oh, those ghostly cries!
    It was preternaturally dark —
You know what it's like in the shipyards of Venice,
    how all winter workers boil the pitch
    to caulk and patch up their leaky ships
When storms keep them off the roughened seas:
    one hammers out a new boat, one plugs
    the cracked seams of an old sea-worn vessel,
One strikes the stern, another bangs on the prow,
    some make oars, others are braiding rope,
    another repairs the main, someone the lug sail;
Well, not with fire, but with immortal heat
    a thick pitch is boiling down there and sticks
    like glue to both banks of the river.
I saw it. But I could not see in it
    anything but huge bubbles the boiling raised.
    The mess kept swelling up, then sinking back.
As if hypnotized, I kept staring down
    until my leader cried out, "Watch it! Watch it!"
    and pulled me back to safety just in time:
That's when I turned, dying to have a look
    at the very thing I should have run from;
    yet at that moment I was seized with fear,
I was running and looking at the same time.
    And there behind us running up along
    the spiny ridge was a black devil.
How wild he looked, how menacing to me
    his every movement, with leathery wings
    spread wide open, and almost flying on his feet.
His shoulder was weighed down by a sinner he'd slung
    across it, and he held the wretch by both his ankles,
    the way a butcher carries a side of beef.
Then from our bridge he called, "Evil Claws,
    I've got a new one for you from Santa Zita.
    Stick him below, I'm going back for more!
That city is well stocked with the likes of him.
    Except for Bonturo, everyone's on the take
    and for a bribe will change a 'no' to 'yes.' "

He flung the wretch down, then ran back along
    the cliff: never was a dog set loose
    in such a hurry to catch a thief.
The sinner he had hurled, heaved up, doubled
    over with pain. But the devils by the bridge
    taunted, "You won't find Old Holy Face here!
Don't think you're swimming in that pure stream,
    the Serchio, and if you don't want to feel
    our hooks, stay down in the steaming pitch."
At once they gripped him with a hundred hooks:
    "Here the dance is done under cover,
    so snatch some on the sly, if you can."
Just like the servant boys of cooks, they hooked
    this meat and shoved him deep into the boiling
    pot: they made certain he wouldn't float.
My good master said, "Crouch down behind
    that jagged rock so it won't seem you're here.
    You'll need that shield to hide from them.
And no matter how they menace me,
    don't be afraid, I've got this under control.
    This isn't the first scuffle I've had."
Once he told me what to do, he left
    and as he walked alone to the sixth bank,
    he made an effort to appear composed.
But the devils, with the frenzy and commotion
    dogs make when they go after some luckless wretch
    who has to beg right there where he stands,
Those devils rushed out from under the bridge
    and turned all their forks against my guide.
    "Not one of you dare touch me," he cried.
"Before you savage me with those forks
    one of you had better listen well —
    then decide whether you want to stick me."
"You go, Knife Tail," all of them were screaming
    so that one moved on up while the rest stayed back
    muttering, "A lot of good it will do him."
But my guide: "Do you really think, Knife Tail,
    when you've seen me come here safe and sound,
    unharmed by any of your wild schemes,
I don't have divine help on my side?
    Let us move on, that's the will of Heaven.
    It's fated I show another this savage place."
At that the devil lost his proud look.
    He let his fork fall to the ground and said:
    "Well, in that case, we'll have to let him go."
Then my guide called me where I sat huddled
    and crouching among the jagged rocks of the bridge:
    "You can feel safe now and come back to me."
At this I stirred and came to him fast as I could.
    But the devils all moved forward too,

so that I doubted they would keep their word.
If you saw the infantry marching out
      under safe conduct from Caprona,
      saw men trembling as they passed their enemies,
You'll know how I huddled up against my guide.
      Not for a moment did I look away
      from the menacing looks those devils gave us;
Though they lowered their hooks, still one jeered:
      "Should I stick him up his behind?" And all
      the others, "Yes, yes! Give it to him!"
But the devil who had been talking
      with my guide spun around and cried,
      "Down, Slob, get down!"
Then to us: "There's no way to go much further
      along the ridge because the sixth arch
      of the bridge is smashed to pieces at the bottom.
So if you still want to go on ahead,
      move up and walk along this rocky ledge:
      there's a cliff nearby where you'll find a path.
At noon yesterday, by my reckoning, exactly
      twelve hundred and sixty-six years had come and gone
      since this road was shattered and left in ruins.
I'm sending some of my men on ahead
      to see if some sinner dare stick up his head
      for air. Go with them—they won't harm you.
Hey you, Buffoon, and you, Ancient Foot,
      you too, Dog Face," he called to the devils,
      "and you, Curly Beard, lead the squad.
Let Windy go and also Dragon Smile,
      then Hog-With-Tusks and also Dog Scratcher.
      Then the Scamp, and you too, Crazy Mad.
Search through the steaming pitch and keep these two
      safe from harm, at least to the next ridge
      that rises over our caves and hideouts."
I said, "Master, must they? Can't we go on
      without their company? Especially
      since you know the way, let's skip the escort.
If you were as shrewd as you usually are,
      you'd see how those devils gnash their teeth.
      With darkened brows they threaten us with harm."
Then my guide said: "Don't be afraid.
      Let them chomp and grind as much as they want
      to cook up a scare in their stew of sinners."
The devils turned to take the left-hand bank.
      But first each stuck out his tongue between his teeth,
      which I took for a signal to their leader.
As reply he made a bugle of his ass.

                                        Susan Mitchell

SESTINA

I have reached, alas, the long shadow
and short day of whitening hills
when color is lost in the grass.
My longing, all the same, keeps green
it is so hooked in the hard stone
that speaks and hears like a woman.

In that same way this new woman
stands as cold as snow in shadow,
less touched than if she had been stone
by the sweet time that warms the hills
and brings them back from white to green,
dressing them in flowers and grass.

Who, when she wreathes her hair with grass,
thinks of any other woman?
The golden waves so mix with green
that Love himself seeks its shadow
that has me fixed between small hills
more strongly than cemented stone.

More potent than a precious stone,
her beauty wounds, and healing grass
cannot help; across plains and hills
I fled this radiant woman.
From her light I found no shadow
of mountain, wall, or living green.

I have seen her pass, dressed in green,
and thought the sight would make a stone
love, as I, even her shadow.
And I have walked with her on grass,
speaking like a lovesick woman,
enclosed within the highest hills.

But streams will flow back to their hills
before this branch, sappy and green,
catches fire (as does a woman)
from me, who would bed down on stone
and gladly for his food crop grass
just to see her gown cast shadow.

The heavy shadow cast by hills
this woman's light can change to green,
as one might hide a stone in grass.

James Schuyler

❧ Francesco Petrarch (1304–1374)

WHOSO LIST TO HUNT

Whoso list to hunt, I know where is an hind,
    But as for me, alas, I may no more
    The vain travail hath wearied me so sore.
I am of them that farthest cometh behind;
Yet may I by no means my wearied mind
    Draw from the Deer: but as she fleeth afore,
    Fainting I follow. I leave off therefore,
Since in a net I seek to hold the wind.
Who list her hunt, I put him out of doubt,
    As well as I may spend his time in vain:
    And, graven with diamonds, in letters plain
There is written her fair neck round about:
    Noli me tangere, for Caesar's I am;
    And wild for to hold, though I seem tame.

Sir Thomas Wyatt

SONNET: WHEN SHE WALKS BY HERE

When she walks by here
The grass bends down, the gentle flowers.
The mark of her foot remains in the damp ground beside water.

You have known her, the slenderness of trees.
Young green branches: making a shadowy wood
The sun breaks with its narrow shafts of gold smoke.

River, that has become her face, takes fire
Looking at me; fire from the sun has washed her.

The stones themselves are burning in my shadow.

Nicholas Kilmer

MY GALLEY

My galley, chargèd with forgetfulness,
Thorough sharp seas in winter nights doth pass
'Tween rock and rock; and eke mine enemy, alas!
That is my Lord, steereth with cruelness;
And every oar a thought in readiness,
As though that death were light in such a case.
An endless wind doth tear the sail apace

Of forcèd sighs, and trusty fearfulness;
A rain of tears, a cloud of dark disdain,
Hath done the wearèd cords great hinderance,

Wreathèd with error and eke with ignorance.
The stars be hid that led me to this pain.
Drownèd is reason that should me comfort,
And I remain despairing of the port.

Sir Thomas Wyatt

THE WOODS ARE WILD AND WERE NOT MADE FOR MAN

The woods are wild and were not made for man.
Now men and weapons fill them with their fear.
I walk there free, the only terror near
being my Sun and the bright rays I scan —

her piercing Love! And I walk singing (but can
such thoughts be wise?) of her who in absence is here,
here in my eyes and heart to make me swear
I saw girls, ladies, where beech and fir trees ran!

I seem to hear her, when I hear the air,
the leaves, the branches, the complaint of birds,
or waters murmuring on through the green grass.

Never so happy, never in silence so rare,
alone in a grim forest, without light, without words —
but still too far out from my Sun I pass!

Edwin Morgan

HE UNDERSTANDS THE GREAT CRUELTY OF DEATH

My flowery and green age was passing away, and I feeling a chill in the fires had been wasting my heart, for I was drawing near the hillside above the grave.

Then my sweet enemy was making a start, little by little, to give over her great wariness, the way she was wringing a sweet thing out of my sharp sorrow. The time was coming when Love and Decency can keep company, and Lovers may sit together and say out all things are in their hearts. But Death had his grudge against me, and he got up in the way, like an armed robber, with a pike in his hand.

John Millington Synge

REMEMBRANCE

They flee from me, that sometime me did seek
    With naked foot, stalking in my chamber.
I have seen them gentle, tame and meek,
      That now are wild, and do not remember
      That sometime they put themselves in danger
          To take bread at my hand; and now they range
          Busily seeking with a continual change.

Thanked be fortune it hath been otherwise
    Twenty times better; but once, in special,
In thin array, after a pleasant guise,
      When her loose gown from her shoulders did fall,
      And she me caught in her arms long and small,
          There with all sweetly did me kiss
          And softly said, 'Dear heart, how like you this?'

It was no dream; I lay broad waking:
    But all is turned, thorough my gentleness,
Into a strange fashion of forsaking;
      And I have leave to go of her goodness,
      And she also to use newfangleness.
          But since that I so kindly am served,
          I would fain know what she hath deserved.

                    Sir Thomas Wyatt

3

THE BEGINNINGS OF SLAVIC POETRY; BYZANTINE GREEK VERSE

Early Russian

Anonymous (c. 1185)

From THE SONG OF IGOR'S CAMPAIGN

Part III

And in the mountains of Kiev, Sviatoslav,
Grand Prince of Kiev and overlord of Igor,
Had a troubling dream vision: *When night stood over the house,*
He said, *they dressed me in a fine black mourning robe,*
And they placed me in a bed cut from yew wood from the steppes.
They ladled blue wine for me, but it was bitter.
From the empty quivers of the heathen nomads
They poured false pearls upon me, stroked my head.
And as I looked at my gold crested roof
I saw no column held it up. Evil sounding ravens
Cried and wildly ranged through all the night of that dream vision.
Outside of Plesensk, at dusk,
The dragon ship was carried out to the blue sea.

And then the nobles said to Sviatoslav,
Grand Prince of Kiev and overlord of Igor:
The black robe is the grief that has shrouded your mind
Since two brave falcons have flown the ancestral throne
To seek, perhaps, the city of Tmutorokan,

Or to dip their golden helmets in the Don.
But Kuman sabers have clipped the falcons' wings.
The captured birds flutter in iron traps.
The blue wine is the sea in which were drowned
Two crimson columns which should support your golden roof.
And the two young moons shrouded themselves in mist.
It was dark that day, more dark than light on the river Kayal.
It was dark on the third day. Now swaggering Kumans
Cry and wildly range through all our land at this dark moment,
Wild as a tribe of panthers: they kill the land
And the scavenging Huns push in on the trails they have beaten.
Disgrace comes crashing down where glory was,
Famine comes down where freedom dwelled.
The Deva that sways back and forth on the tops of the trees
Has swooped down with a screech on our land.
And Gothic maidens are carried out to the blue sea
On barges, wearing Ruthenian golden bracelets,
Singing our evil times and the measure of vengeance
They have taken for their wretched chieftain Sharokan.
And all your soldiers and knights are sorrowful now.

Then Sviatoslav of the Golden Word looked down and said:
O Igor and Vsevolod, do you not know my command?
Why did you fail to come to me for counsel?
The time was not right, but you went ahead
And tore and ripped with your sabers the Kuman land,
Seeking glory for yourselves alone.
But what of that? What glory have you won?
You gained no honor when, without cause, you shed
The blood of the pagan infidel.
Your brave hearts forged of strong steel,
Hearts that were early tempered to strength and warlike rage,
You took to battle. But what your glory has done
To the country now in my old silver age!

Bitter tears were mixed with the word of Sviatoslav:
Our strength is breaking. I cannot see the way
To win it back when even honor stops.
I remember the power of my brother Yaroslav,
How he and his nobles from Chernigov held sway,
And his tribes of Tatrans and Moguts and Shelbirs
And loud Revugs and Topchaks and brave Olbers
Would go to fight for the state of Chernigov.
Without shields, only with knives in their boot tops,
They would charge and conquer armies with yells and whoops.
Even now they thunder in my mind. I hear their cries,
Ringing through ancestral fame the echo stirs,
And now in Kiev the echo falls away and dies . . .

Then Sviatoslav gazed out through his golden door:

But you said: 'We can be heroes too.
We will gain the glory of the future here,
And will also steal whatever glory went before!'
Brothers, is it not a wonder of the times when you
Find older princes becoming young again?
When the swift winged falcon of the grassy plain
Changes his feathers to age, he should climb and soar,
Should knock down mighty birds that come too near
His nest, should not let ravaging little ravens there!
The princes do not help us in our great distress.
Time and the seasons are whirling back in pain
To the first beginning, back to nothingness!...

Harry Strickhausen

Serbo-Croatian

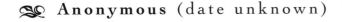 **Anonymous** (date unknown)

THE MESSAGE OF KING SAKIS AND THE LEGEND OF THE TWELVE DREAMS HE HAD IN ONE NIGHT

1

I saw a gold pillar from earth to heaven.

2

I saw a dark towel
hanging from heaven to earth.

3

I saw three boiling kettles:
one of oil, one of butter, and one of water,
and oil boiled over into butter,
and butter into water
but the water boiled all by itself.

4

I saw an old mare with her colt,
and a black eagle pulling grass by its roots
and laying it down before the mare
while the colt neighed.

5

I saw a bitch lying on a dunghill
while the puppies barked from her womb.

6

I saw many monks soaked in pitch
wailing because they can't get out.

7

I saw a beautiful horse
grazing with two heads
one in front, one in the back.

8

I saw precious stones, pearls, and royal wreaths
scattered over the whole kingdom,
but fire came down from heaven
and scorched everything into ashes.

9

I saw the rich giving workers either
gold or silver or rice,
but when they asked for their own reward,
no one was left.

10

I saw evil-faced rocks descending
from the sky
and walking all over the earth.

11

I saw three maidens in a mowed field
bearing wreaths of sunlight on their heads
and sweet-smelling flowers in their hands.

12

I saw men with slits for eyes,
cruel fingernails, and hair that rose up,
and these were the devil's servants.

Charles Simic

Greek

✎ Theodore Prodromos (1098–1150)

TO THE EMPEROR

When I was young, my graying father frowned:
"Let studious zeal, my son, be still your rule.
You see that man? He used to tramp around:
Now a two-breasted horse, a portly mule,
Are his. In student days he went unshod:
Now long, you see, on pointed shoes he's trod.
A student, he went ragged in neglect:
Now he's a horseman, debonairly decked.
Then, the Bath's door he'd never learned to seek:
And now he warmly bathes three times a week.
Fleas, almond-sized, once made his breast their lair:
Now Manuel-pieces, golden, nestle there.
So, follow your old father in these matters:
Devote your diligent life to prosperous Letters."

I studied hard, till I was nearly daft;
And since I'm a mere worker in this craft,
I want some bread, I want a crumb of bread.

Literature I run down, and tears I shed.
"Damn Letters, Christ, and all its devotees,
And damn the chance, the day that spoiled my ease,
When literary studies I began
And hoped to thrive, a literary man."

If an embroiderer I'd been trained instead
To live by decorating robes with thread,
If I'd but plied that trade, so much despised,
I'd open cupboard, finding unsurprised
A wealth of bread and wine there, bought with money,
The salted fry of mackerel, pickled tunny.
Now when I look, on all the shelves are stacks
Of paper crammed away in bursting sacks.
I open my small chest, for crusts I hope,
And still in paper, one more sack, I grope.
I try my wallet, out my purse I spill,
No coins come jingling — only paper still.
I rummage round in every slight recess
Till my defeat I wearly confess:
With fainting heart, I lapse in dull distress,
And, hungry, penned in poverty's harsh fetters,
For broidery I'd exchange my craft of Letters.

Sire, by your Head, what answer can you give?
"Your lad," could I advise a bothered neighbor? —
"Make him a scholar—pleasantly he'll live."
Yet if I added, "Shoes are better labor,"
My wits were addled, everyone would say . . .

Jack Lindsay

MEDIEVAL VERSE FROM THE BRITISH ISLES

Middle English

ை Anonymous (c. 1000–1300)

THE HARROWING *From* DOOMSDAY, THE MYSTERIES

[*All round the still darkened stage the voices of the whole* COMPANY *are heard, here and there, as to their fellows in hell, speaking of the light that has been seen shining through the gloom.*]

VOICES.
This shining that us showers
And divides the darkness drear,
It is the hope that hath been ours
This four thousand and six hundred year.

This flame that on us flares
And dangs the dark in two
Comforts our carking cares.
This doom will God undo.

This lamp that on us lights
To this thought makes me tend:
This never-ending night's
Darkness and doom may end.

[*The voices pass round the entire audience in all parts and then become louder so that they are heard by all, and gradually the individual voices blend into a unison saying:*]

ALL.
Come, Lord, come to hell anon!
Deliver us from darkness drear.
Four thousand six hundred years be gone
Since mankind first came here.

Come, Lord, come to hell anon!
Deliver us from darkness drear.
Four thousand six hundred years be gone
Since mankind first came here.

Come, Lord, come to hell anon.
Deliver us from darkness drear
Four thousand six hundred years be gone
Since mankind first came here.

[*The sounds of this concerted murmured prayer, and outcry, alerts the* DEVILS. *Sirens and alarms as* RIBALD *emerges from a sewer grate.*]

RIBALD.
Since first that hell was made
And I was put therein,
Such sorrow never ere I had
Nor heard I such a din.
Help, Beelzebub, to bind these boys!
Such harrow was never ere heard in hell!

BEELZEBUB.
Why roars thou so, Ribald? Thou roys!
What is betide? Can thou ought tell?

RIBALD.
What? Hears thou not this ugly noise?
These that have lived in limbo long
They make moaning of many joys
And muster great mirth them among.

BEELZEBUB.
Mirth? Nay, nay, that point is past.
More hope of health shall they never have.

RIBALD.
They cry on Christ full fast
And says he shall them save.

BEEZLEBUB.
Ya, if he save them not, we shall.
For they are sparred in special space.
While I am prince and principal
Shall they never pass out of this place.
Say to Satan our sire
And bid him bring also
Lucifer lovely of lyre.

RIBALD.
Already, lord, I go.

[*Three loud knocks at the gates of hell. The voice of* JESUS *is heard on the other side of the gates.*]

JESUS.
Attollite portas principes
Open up ye princes of pains sere
Et elavamini eternales
Your endless gates that ye have here.

RIBALD.
Out, harrow, out! What devil is he
That calls him king over us all?
Hark, Bellzebub!

[*To other* DEVILS]
And hasten ye
For hideously I heard him call.

BEELZEBUB.
Way! Go spar our gates full fast with speed
And set forth watches on the wall,
And if he call or cry
To make us more debate
Lay on him hardily
And garre him gang his gate.

SATAN.
Tell me what boys dare be so bold
For dread to make on us affray?

RIBALD.
It is that Jew that Judas sold
For to be dead the other day.

SATAN.
Ow! This tale in time is told,
This traitor traverses us alway.
He shall be here full hard in hold.
Look that he pass not I thee pray.

BEELZEBUB.
Pass! Nay! He will not wend.
I wean the means to stay
And shapes him for to shend
All hell afore he hie away.

SATAN.
Fie! Fie! Ye fools, thereof he shall fail.
For all his fare I him defy.
I know his tricks from top to tail.
He lives by gauds and guilery.
Thereby he brought forth from our bail

Of late Lazar of Betany.
Therefore I gave to the Jews counsel
That they should garre him die.
But I bid you be not abashed
But boldly make you boun
With tool that ye entrust
And ding the dastard down.

[*They arm themselves with various weapons. Three loud knocks. The voice of* JESUS *is heard again from the other side of the gates of hell.*]

JESUS.
Principes, portas tollite
Undo your gates, ye princes of pride
Et introibit rex glorie
The king of bliss comes in this tide.

SATAN.
Out! Harrow! What harlot is he
That says his kingdom shall be cried?

JESUS.
Ye princes of hell, open your gate
And let my folk forth go.
The prince of peace shall enter thereat
Whether ye will or no.

RIBALD.
What art thou that speaks us so?

JESUS.
A king of bliss that hight Jesus.

RIBALD.
Yea, fast I rede thou go
And meddle thee not with us.

BEELZEBUB.

[*To* DEVILS]
Our gates will last I trust.
They seem so strong to me.

[*Then louder to* JESUS *over the wall*]
But if our bars shall bust
They shall not bust for thee!

JESUS.
This stead shall be no longer stock.
Open up and let my people pass.

[*There is an explosion.*]

RIBALD.
Out! Harrow! Our bail is brok
And busted all our bars of brass.
Tell Lucifer he's loosened t'lock.

BEELZEBUB.
What is limbo lost, alas!
Harrow! Our gates begin to crack.
In sunder, I trow, they go.
All hell is lost, alas, alack!
Alas! I weep with woe.

SATAN.

[*From the back like all good generals*]
I bade ye should be boun,
If he made mischief more,
To ding that dastard down
And set him both sad and sore.

BEELZEBUB.
To set him sore that is soon said!
Come thou thyself and set him sore!
We may not bide his bitter braid.
He will us mar, though we were more.

SATAN.
Fie, faint hearts, wherefore are ye afeared?
Have ye no force to flit him fro?
Look ye in haste to get me geared.
Myself shall to that gadling go.

[SATAN *is armed and equipped, and goes forth to meet* JESUS. SATAN *seems threatening and formidable but* JESUS *defeats him with a simple sign.*]
How, bel ami, abide
With all thy flaunt and fleer
And tell to me this tide
What mischief makes you here.

JESUS.
I come to claim these kin of mine.
Them would I save, I thee now tell.
You had no power them to pine.
But for their good, forced guests of hell
Have they sojourned, not as thine
But in thy ward, as thou wot well.

SATAN.
Ay, but where the devil hast thou been
This four thousand years or more?

JESUS.
Now is the time certain.
My Father ordained before
That they should pass from pain
And dwell in mirth for evermore.

SATAN.
Thy Father knew I well by sight.
He worked as wright his meat to win.

And Mary, methinks, thy mother hight.
They are all thou canst claim as kin.
So who made thee so mickle of might?

JESUS.
Thou wicked fiend, let be thy din!
My Father dwells in heaven on height
With bliss that shall never blin
I am his own son
His forward to fulfil.
Together we are one
Or sunder when we will.

SATAN.
God's son? Then should thou be full glad.
After no chattels need thou crave.
But thou hast lived ay like a lad
And in sorrow like a simple knave.

JESUS.
That was for the heartly love I had
Unto man's soul it for to save,
And for to make thee mazed and mad
And for to goad thee from my grave.
My godhead I covered
In Mary, mother mine,
And ne'er was discovered
By such as thee and thine.

SATAN.
Nay, bel ami, thou must be smit!

JESUS.

[*Calling on his* ANGELS]
Michael, mine angel, make thee boun
And fast yon fiend that he not flit.
And, Devil, I command thee go down
Into thy cell where thou shall sit.

SATAN.
Ow! Ay! Harrow! Help Mahoun!
Now wax I wode out of my wit.

[SATAN *falls into the sewer. Followed by* BEELZEBUB.]
I sink into hell's pit!

Tony Harrison

❧ Anonymous (c. 1300)

THE NAMES OF THE HARE

The man the hare has met
will never be the better of it
except he lay down on the land
what he carries in his hand —
be it staff or be it bow —
and bless him with his elbow
and come out with this litany
with devotion and sincerity
to speak the praises of the hare.
Then the man will better fare.

'The hare, call him scotart,
big-fellow, bouchart,
the O'Hare, the jumper,
the rascal, the racer.

Beat-the-pad, white-face,
funk-the-ditch, shit-ass.

The wimount, the messer,
the skidaddler, the nibbler,
the ill-met, the slabber.

The quick-scut, the dew-flirt,
the grass-bitter, the goibert,
the home-late, the do-the-dirt.

The starer, the wood-cat,
the purblind, the furze cat,
the skulker, the bleary-eyed,
the wall-eyed, the glance-aside
and also the hedge-springer.

The stubble-stag, the long lugs,
the stook-deer, the frisky legs,
the wild one, the skipper,
the hug-the-ground, the lurker,
the race-the-wind, the skiver,
the shag-the-hare, the hedge-squatter,
the dew-hammer, the dew-hopper,
the sit-tight, the grass-bounder,
the jig-foot, the earth-sitter,
the light-foot, the fern-sitter,
the kail-stag, the herb-cropper.

The creep-along, the sitter-still,
the pintail, the ring-the-hill,
the sudden start,
the shake-the-heart,
the belly-white,
the lambs-in-flight.

The gobshite, the gum-sucker,
the scare-the-man, the faith-breaker,
the snuff-the-ground, the baldy skull,
(his chief name is scoundrel.)

The stag sprouting a suede horn,
the creature living in the corn,
the creature bearing all men's scorn,
the creature no one dares to name.'

When you have got all this said
then the hare's strength has been laid.
Then you might go faring forth —
east and west and south and north,
wherever you incline to go —
but only if you're skilful too.
And now, Sir Hare, good-day to you.
God guide you to a how-d'ye-do
with me: come to me dead
in either onion broth or bread.

Seamus Heaney

✆ Anonymous (c. 1327)

SUMMER SUNDAY

On a summer Sunday I saw the sun
    Rising up early on the rim of the east:
Day dawned on the dunes, dark lay the town;
    I caught up my clothes, I would go to the groves in haste;
With the keenest of kennel-dogs, crafty and quick to sing,
    And with huntsmen, worthies, I went to the woods at once.
So rife on the ridge the deer and dogs would run
    That I liked to loll under limbs in the cool of the glades
            And lie down.
        The kennel-dogs quested the kill
        With barking bright as a bell;
        Disheartened the deer in the dell
            And made the ridge resound.

Ridge and rill resounded with the rush of the roes in terror
    And the boisterous barking the brilliant bugle bade.

I stood, stretched up, saw dogs and deer together
    Where they slipped under shrubs or scattered away in the shade.
There lords and ladies with lead-leashes loitered
    With fleet-footed greyhounds that frolicked about and played.
And I came to the ground where grooms began to cry orders,
    And walked by wild water and saw on the other side
        Deep grass.
    I sauntered by the stream, on the strand,
    And there by the flood I found
    A boat lying on the land;
        And so I left the place.

So I left the place, more pleased with my own play,
    And wandered away in the woods to find who I'd find.
I lounged a long while and listened—on a slope I lay—
    Where I heard neither hunter, hound, nor hart, nor hind.
So far I'd walked I'd grown weary of the way;
    Then I left my little game and leaned on a limb
And standing there I saw then, clear as day,
    A woman with a wonderful wheel wound by the wind.
        I waited then.
    Around that wheel were gathered
    Merry men and maids together;
    Most willingly I went there
        To try my fortune.

Fortune, friend and foe, fairest of the fair,
    Was fearful, false, and little of faith, I found.
She spins the wheel to weal and from weal to woe
    In the running ring of the wheelrim running round.
At a look from that lovely lady there,
    I gladly got into the game, cast my goods to the ground!
Ah, could I recount, count up, cunning and clear,
    The virtues of that beauty who in bitterness bound
        Me tight!
    Still, some little I'll stay
    To tell before turning away—
    All my reasons in array
        I'll readily write.

Readily I'll write dark runes to read:
    No lady alive is more lovely in all this land;
I'd go anywhere with that woman and think myself glad,
    So strangely fair her face; at her waist, I found,
The gold of her kirtle like embers gleamed and glowed.
    But in bitter despair that gentle beauty soon bound
Me close, when her laughing heart I had given heed.
    Wildly that wonderful wheel that woman wound,
        With a will.
    A woman of so much might,
    So wicked a wheelwright,

Had never struck my sight,
   Truth to tell.

Truth to tell, sitting on the turf I saw then
   A gentleman looking on, in a gaming mood, gay,
Bright as the blossoms, his brows bent
   To the wheel the woman whirred on its way.
It was clear that with him all was well as the wheel went,
   For he laughed, leaned back, and seemed at his ease as he lay.
A friendly look toward me that lord sent,
   And I could imagine no man more merry than he
      In his mind.
   I gave the knight greeting.
   He said, "You see, my sweeting,
   The crown of that handsome king?
      I claim it by kind!

"By kind to me it will come:
As King I claim the kingdom,
Kingdom by kind.
To me the wheel will wind.
Wind well, worthy dame;
Come fortune, friendly game,
Be game now, set
Myself on that self same seat!"

I saw him seated then at a splendid height,
   Right over against the rim of the running ring;
He cast knee over knee as a great king might,
   Handsomely clothed in a cloak, and crowned as a king.
Then high of heart he grew in his gambling heat;
   Laid one leg on the other leg to his liking;
Unlikely it looked that his lordship would fall in the bet;
   All the world, it seemed, was at his wielding
      By right.
   On my knees I met that king.
   He said, "You see, my sweeting,
   How I reign by the ring,
      Most high in might?

"Most high in might, queen and knight
Come at my call.
Foremost in might,
Fair lords at my foot fall.
Lordly the life I lead,
No lord my like is living,
No duke living need I dread,
For I reign by right as King."

Of kings it seems most sad to speak and set down
   How they sit on that seemly seat awhile, then in wastes are in

sorrow sought.
I beheld a man with hair like the leaves of the horehound,
    All black were his veins, and his brow to bitterness brought;
His diadem with diamonds dripped down
    But his robes hung wild, though beautifully wrought;
Torn away was his treasure—tent, tower, town—
    Needful and needing, naked; and nought
        His name.
        Kindly I kissed that prince.
        He spoke words, wept tears;
        Now he, pulled down from his place,
          A captive had become.

        "Become a captive outcast,
        Once great kings could call
        Me king. From friends I fall,
        Long time from love, now little, lo! at the last.
        Fickle is fortune, now far from me;
        Now weal, now woe,
        Now knight, now king, now captive."
A captive had he become, his life a care;
    Many joys he had lost, and much great mastery.
Then I saw him sorrier still, and hurt still more:
    A bare body in a bed, on a bier they bore him past me,
A duke driven down into death, hidden in the dark.

John Gardner

✵ William Langland (c. 1330–1400)

From PIERS PLOWMAN

Thus I awoke, God knows, when I lived in Cornhill,
With Kit in a cottage, clothed like a loller,
And not very well-liked, believe me,
Among London's lollers and unlettered hermits,
Because I wrote about those men as Reason taught me.
For as I came upon Conscience I met Reason
In a hot harvest when I was in good health
And had strong arms to work with but loved the good life
And to do nothing but to drink and sleep.
Then someone questioned me in my body and soul;
Reason rebuked me, as I roamed about my memories.
    "Can you serve," he said, "or sing in a church,
Or pile hay into stacks or pitch it into carts,
Mow or rake or bend it into sheaves,
Reap or be a head-reaper and rise up early,
Or take a horn and be a hayward and sleep out all night
And guard my grain in the field against pilferers and thieves?

Or make shoes or cloth, or herd sheep and cattle,
Hedge or harrow, or drive hogs and geese,
Or use any skill that serves the community,
So you better thereby those that sustain you?"
  "For sure," I said, "so help me God,
I'm too weak to work with sickle or scythe
And too tall, believe me, to bend down low,
To work like a laborer for any length of time."
  "Then you have land to live off," asked Reason, "or a trust fund
That keeps you in food? For you seem an idler,
A compulsive big-spender or waster of time,
Or do you beg for a living at men's doorways
Or free-load on Fridays and feast-days in churches,
Which is a loller's life that wins little praise
Where righteousness rewards men just as they deserve.
  And then will he render to every man according to his works.
Or perhaps you're physically handicapped
Or got hurt in an accident, whereby you're excused?"
  "When I was young, many years ago,
My father and family supported my schooling,
Till I truly knew what holy merit means
And what's best for the body, according to the book,
And surest for the soul, provided I persevere.
And, in faith, since my friends died I never found
A life that I liked except in these long robes,
And if I should work for a living and have means of support,
That work that I learned best is what I should live by.
  Let every man abide in the same calling in which he was called.
And so I live in London and in the country, too;
The tools of my trade and means of support
Are *pater-noster* and my primer, *placebo* and *dirige,*
And sometimes my psalter and my seven psalms.
So I sing for the souls of such that help me,
And those that feed me I expect to bestow me
A welcome when I come every month or so,
Now with him, now with her; this is how I beg
Without bag or bottle but only with my stomach.
  And moreover it seems to me, Sir Reason,
One should not constrain a clerk to do common labor,
For by the law of Leviticus that our lord ordained,
Crowned clerks, it is naturally understood,
Should neither toil and sweat nor swear in court
Nor fight at the front or grieve a foe.
  See that none render evil for evil.
For all that have been crowned are heaven's heirs
And are Christ's ministers in church and choir.
  The Lord is the portion of my inheritance.
  And elsewhere: Mercy is not constrained.
It becomes clerks to serve Christ
And uncrowned peasants to cart and work.
For no clerk should be crowned who doesn't come

From franklins and free men and married folks.
Serfs and bastards and beggars' children,
They should do the work, and the children of lords
Serve God and good men, as it suits their station,
Some to sing mass, others to sit and write,
To plan and keep track of reasonable spending.
But since serfs' kids have been made bishops
And bastards' boys into archdeacons
And Shoemaker & Son pay silver for knighthood
And lords' sons work for them and mortgage their land
To ride against the enemy in defense of the realm
In behalf of the commons and the king's honor,
And monks and nuns, who should minister to the poor,
Have made their kin knights and bought up knights' lands,
Popes and patrons refused the poor nobility
And picked Simony's sons to keep the sanctuary,
Holy living and love have been long gone,
And will be, till this is worn out or otherwise changed.
    Therefore, Reason, please don't rebuke me,
For I know in my conscience what Christ would have me do.
Prayers of a perfect man and discreetly done penance
Is the dearest labor that pleases our lord.
Non de solo," I said, "for surely *viuit homo,*
Nec in pane et in pabulo, the *pater-noster* witnesses;
Fiat voluntas dei — that furnishes us all things."
    "By Christ," said Conscience, "I don't see how all this applies;
City begging doesn't seem to me to be steadfast perfection
Unless under appointment by priory or minister."
    "That's the truth," I said, "and I must admit
That I have wasted time and time misspent;
But still, I hope, as he that has dealt often
And lost and lost, and at last happened
To buy such a bargain he was set up forever,
And counted his previous losses as not worth a leaf,
Such a winning came his way through words of grace.
    The kingdom of heaven is like unto a treasure hidden in a field.
    The woman that found a silver coin, etc.
So I hope to have from Him that is almighty
A mouthful of his grace, and begin a time
That all times of my time shall turn to profit."
    "I advise you," then said Reason, "to get started
On the life that is commendable and true to your soul" —
"Yeah, and keep it up," said Conscience; and I went to church.

George Economou

Anonymous (c. 1370)

From SIR GAWAIN AND THE GREEN KNIGHT

Then the drawbridge came down, and the thick gates
Drew back, swung open, unbarred. And the knight
Crossed himself and rode across,
He blessed the porter who kneeled before him,
Wished him Godspeed and God's good will
For Gawain; then almost alone, rode off.
Following in his guide's footsteps, leading him
Along the dangerous road to that axe-
Stroke. Trees stood bare, on the slopes
Where they rode, and the rocky cliffs lay frozen.
Clouds blew high, but the sky was ugly;
Mist drizzled, melted on the mountains,
Every hill wore a hat, a cloak
Of fog. Brooks foamed at their banks,
Splashing on the shore, bright, where they flowed.
Their path wound wild, around a wood,
Till the time when the winter sun rises
                  In the sky:
        Snow covered the high
        Hill they rode on, white
        And cold; and the guide
        Drew up, asked Gawain to halt.

I've brought you this far; now you've come close,
Knight, to that place you've been hunting, scurrying
And prying so hard to find. Let
Me speak to you privately, for I know who you are,
And I speak as someone who loves you; if you'll listen
To me, you'll manage this business better.
That place where you're hurrying is dangerous, knight:
The most horrible creature in the world lives
In that wilderness, a grim wildman who loves
To kill, the hugest creature on the earth,
Bigger and stronger than four of Arthur's
Best knights, or Hector, or anyone else.
He waits in that green chapel, grim,
Determined, and no one rides by, no knight
Proud of his sword, but he beats him to death
With one blow. A ruthless man born
Pitiless, who kills priests or peasants,
Monks or abbots, anyone who passes:
Killing is as natural as air to him!
And so I say to you, sitting in your saddle,
If you go there, you're dead; it's the simple truth,
Knight—dead if you'd twenty lives
                  To lose!

He's lived there for years,
He kills as he chooses:
Fight without fear,
Gawain, but you're bound to lose.

"And so, good sir, leave him in peace,
In the name of God pick some different
Path! Ride wherever Christ takes you,
And I'll hurry home, and I promise you, knight,
I swear by God and all His saints,
I'll swear by any oath you ask,
That I'll keep your secret, conceal this story
Forever, keep it from everyone on earth."
"By God," said Gawain, grimly polite,
"I'm grateful, fellow, for all your good wishes;
But however loyally you lied, if I rode
Away, fled for fear, as you tell me,
I'd be a coward no knight could excuse.
Whatever comes, I'm going to that chapel,
And I'll meet that wild man: however it happens
It will happen, for evil or good, as fate
                        Decides;
        However wild
        He may be,
        God can see,
        God can save."

"By Mary!" said the man, "you've said so much
of your bravery that the blame will be yours when you lose
Your life. You want to lose it; proceed,
Your helmet's on your head, your spear's in your hand:
Ride along the rocky side
Of this path; you'll come to a wild valley;
On your left, a little farther down,
You'll see exactly what you want, that green
Chapel, and the green oaf who owns it.
Gawain the noble, go in God's name!
I wouldn't join you for all the gold
In the world, not a foot further through this wood."
And he swung his horse around, dug
His heels in its side, and raced away,
Leaving Gawain with no guide, alone
                      In that wood.
        "Good is good,"
        Said the knight, "I'll not weep
        Or complain: I keep
        My trust in Him, I'll do as He would."

Then he spurred Gringolet down the path,
Across a slope, beside a grove,
Riding a rough road to the valley

Below. Then he looked about. It seemed wild,
No sign of shelter anywhere, nothing
But steep hills on every side,
Gnarled crags with huge rocks,
Crags scratching at the sky! He stopped,
Pulled back on the reins, held Gringolet ready
while he stared this way and that, seeking
The chapel. He saw nothing—except
A queer kind of mound, in a glade
Close by, a rounded knoll near a stream,
Set right on the bank, beside the brook:
And that water bubbled as though it were boiling!
He sent Gringolet forward, stopped
Near the mound, dismounted and tied his horse
To a lime-tree, looping the reins on a branch.
Then he walked closer, walked around
The knoll, trying to think what it was.
He saw holes at the end and the sides,
Saw patches of grass growing everywhere,
And only an old cave inside—
A hole—a crevice in a crag: he couldn't
          Tell.
      "My Lord, my Lord," said that courteous knight,
      "Can this be the chapel?" At midnight,
      Here, the devils of hell
      Could pray their prayers quite well!

By Jesus, it's lonely here; this chapel
Is ugly, gruesome, all overgrown.
But a good place for the green knight,
He could serve the devil properly, here.
By Christ, it's Satan who struck me with this meeting,
I feel it! He's sent me here to destroy me.
What an evil church: may destruction end it!
The most cursed chapel I've ever come to!"
His helmet on his head, spear in his hand,
He climbed across to its rough roof—
Then heard, from a high hill, on a boulder,
Beyond the brook, a violent noise—
What! It clattered on the cliff, as if
To split it, like a grindstone grinding a scythe.
What! It whirred like water at a mill.
What! It rushed and it rang, and it sang
Miserably. "That's meant for me," said Gawain,
"A kind of greeting. By Christ, I'll greet him
          Better.
      God's will be done!—'Alas, alas!'—
      What good is wailing? It never
      Helps; I'll never gasp,
      Though my life be severed."

Then he raised his voice, calling out loud:
"Who lives in this place? who's here as he promised
To be? Gawain is walking right
On your roof. If you want him, come to him quickly,
Now or never, let's have it done with."
"Just wait," said someone up over his head,
"What you're waiting to have, you'll have in a hurry."
But he stayed where he was, working that wheel
With a whirring roar. Then he stopped, and stepped
Down across a crag; came
Through a hole, whirling a fierce weapon,
A long-bladed battle-axe, sharpened for the stroke,
Its massive blade bent to the shaft,
Filed like a knife, on a grindstone four feet
Wide; a leather strap hung at
Its length; and the green man looked as he'd looked
At the start, his skin and his beard and his face,
Except that he skipped like a dancer, setting
His axe-handle on stones and leaping along.
At the brook, to keep dry, he leaned on the handle
And hopped across, and hurried to Gawain,
Grim on a broad battlefield covered
                              With snow.
            And Gawain waited,
            Not bowing low;
            And the green man said: "You came:
            I can trust you now."

                                        Burton Raffel

✑ Anonymous (c. 1400)

THE BLACKSMITHS

Sooty, swart smiths,
                        smattered with smoke,
Drive me to death
                        with the din of their dents.
Such noise at night
                        no man heard, never:
With knavish cries
                        and clattering of knocks!
The crooked cretins
                        call out, "Coal, coal!"
And blow their bellows,
                                that all their brains burst:
"Huff, puff!" says that one;
                                "haff, paff!" that other.

They spit and sprawl
        and spill many spells;
They gnaw and gnash,
          they groan together
And hold their heat
        with their hard hammers.
Of bullhide are their
        broad aprons made;
Their shanks be shackled
        for the fiery flinders;
Heavy hammers they have
        that are hard-handled,
Stark strokes they strike
        on a steely stump:
LUS, BUS! LAS, DAS!
        rants the row —
So doleful a dream,
        the Devil destroy it!
The master lengthens little
        and labors less,
Twines a two
      and touches a trey:
Tick, tack! hick, hack!
        ticket, tacket! tyke, take!
LUS, BUS! LAS, DAS!
        Such lives they lead,
These cobblemares:
        Christ give them grief!
May none of these waterburners
        by night have his rest!

Wesli Court

ꕢ Dame Juliana Berners (b. 1388)

THE PROPERTIES OF A GOOD GREYHOUND

A greyhound should be headed like a Snake,
And necked like a Drake,
Footed like a Cat,
Tailed like a Rat,
Sidèd like a Team,
Chined like a Beam.

The first year he must learn to feed,
The second year to field him lead,
The third year he is fellow-like,
The fourth year there is none sike,

The fifth year he is good enough,
The sixth year he shall hold the plough,
The seventh year he will avail
Great bitches for to assail,
The eighth year lick ladle,

The ninth year cart saddle,
And when he is come to that year
Have him to the tanner,
For the best hound that ever bitch had
At nine year he is full bad.

Seamus Heaney

Welsh

✆ Dafydd Ap Gwilym (c. 1350)

THE RATTLE BAG

As I lay, fullness of praise,
On a summer day under
Trees between field and mountain
Awaiting my soft-voiced girl,
She came, there's no denying,
Where she vowed, a very moon.
Together we sat, fine theme,
The girl and I, debating,
Trading, while I had the right,
Words with the splendid maiden.

And so we were, she was sky,
Learning how to love each other,
Concealing sin, winning mead,
An hour lying together,
And then, cold comfort, it came,
A blare, a bloody nuisance,
A sack's bottom's foul seething
From an imp in shepherd's shape,
Who had, public enemy,
A harsh-horned sag-cheeked rattle
He played, cramped yellow belly,
This bag curse its scabby leg.
So before satisfaction
The sweet girl panicked: poor me!
When she heard, feeble-hearted,
The tones whir, she would not stay.

By Christ, no Christian country,
Cold harsh tune, has heard the like.
Noisy pouch perched on a pole,
Bell of pebbles and gravel,
Saxon rocks making music
Quaking in a bullock's skin.
Crib of three thousand beetles,
Commotion's cauldron, black bag.
Field-keeper, comrade of straw.
Black-skinned, pregnant with splinters,
Noise that's an old buck's loathing,
Devil's bell, stake in its crotch,
Scarred pebble-bearing belly,
May it be sliced into thongs.
May the churl be struck frigid,
Amen, who scared off my girl.

Joseph Clancy

THE WIND

Free-coursing wind from the sky,
Great tumult walking yonder,
Marvelous rough-sounding man,
Mad, without foot, without wing.
Fearful wonder how you're turned
Footless from the sky's mansion,
And with what speed you now run
Over the high escarpment.
No swift horse you need, no bridge
Or boat to cross a river.
You cannot drown, you are warned,
Free you flow, joined to nothing.
Taking nests, winnowing leaves,
None can indict, no rife mob
Or ruler's hand can stay you,
Nor blue blade, nor flood, nor rain.
Sheriff and troop you elude,
Feathered treetops' winnower.
None can strike you (absurd thought),
No fire burn, no guile weaken.
Seen by none, heard by thousands,
Huge bare bed, nest of the rain;
Swift inscriber of the sky,
Leaping nine wildernesses.

God's blessing to the whole world;
A sad roar breaking oak-tops;
Quick far-traveling creature,

Dry-natured trampler of clouds;
Noisily heaping districts
High with snow's barren chaff-heaps.
Tell, north wind from the valley,
Constant hymn, where you're going.
Rough weather storming the sea,
Wild sporter on the seashore;
Fluent author, magician;
Sower, scatterer of leaves;
Loud hilltop laughter, hurler
Of wild masts on white-tipped brine.

You fly the lengths of the world;
Weather on the brow, be high
Tonight, go to Uwch Aeron
Most clear, and with ringing sound.
Don't linger, don't balk, don't fear
Jealousy's slave—complaining,
Accusing Little Hunchback.
I'm banned the place which bred her.

I rue the time that my love
Fell on my golden Morvudd.
By a maid I'm exiled; run
Aloft to her father's house.
Beat the door, for my message
Make it open before dawn.
If chance wills, seek her presence
And moan the sound of my sigh.
Coming from the perfect Signs,
Tell my faithful gentle one
That while I remain on earth
I'll be her true poor lover.
My face is woe without her,
If indeed she's not untrue.
Fly up, you'll see a fair one,
Fly down, elect of the sky,
Go to the yellow-haired girl,
Return safe, you're a good wind.

Daniel Huws

THE MIRROR

That my face was not handsome,
Such potent harm, I'd not dreamt
Until I handled the glass
And plainly saw the grimmest
Of men; the mirror at last
Tells me I'm not good-looking.

My cheek, for this new Enid,
Grows sallow, is far from flushed,

Glass-grey from all my moaning,
A huge yellow-colored bruise.
The long nose could almost be
A razor. Is it not sad?
How dreadful that cheerful eyes
Should become blind auger holes,
And curly hair in fistfuls
Fall uselessly from its root.

There's a curst fate upon me.
I judge that my state must be
That of a rotten quiver,
Or else the mirror's no good.
If I'm to blame, who've endured
Long passion, let death take me.
If it's the freckled mirror
To blame, alas, what a life!

A sad-circled pale round moon,
Magnet-like, full of magic,

Frail-looking gem that beguiles,
Created by magicians;
Swiftest of dreams; cold traitor,
And a brother of the ice.
Most false, unkindest servant,
Hell take the thin wry-mouthed glass!

Nobody gave me my wrinkles
(Supposing I trust the glass)
If not the girl from Gwynedd,
Where they know how to mar looks.

Daniel Huws

DAFYDD AP GWILYM RESENTS THE WINTER

Across North Wales
The snowflakes wander,
A swarm of white bees.
Over the woods
A cold veil lies.
A load of chalk
Bows down the trees.

No undergrowth
Without its wool,

And here below
The big drifts blow,
Blow and billow
Across the heather
Like swollen bellies.
The frozen foam
Falls in fleeces.

Out of my house
I will not stir

No field unsheeted;
No path is left
Through any field;
On every stump
White flour is milled.

Will someone tell me
What angels lift
Planks in the flour-loft
Floor of heaven,
Shaking down dust?
An angel's cloak is
Cold quicksilver.

For any girl,
To have my coat
Look like a miller's,
Or stuck with feathers
Of eider down.

What a great fall
Lies on my country!
A wide wall, stretching
One sea to the other,
Greater and grayer
Than the sea's graveyard.
When will rain come?

Rolfe Humphries

THE PENIS

By God penis, you must be guarded
with eye and hand
because of this lawsuit, straight-headed pole,
most carefully for evermore;
net-quill of the cunt, because of
complaint a bridle must be put on your snout
to keep you in check so that you are not indicted
again, take heed you despair of minstrels.

I consider you the vilest of rolling-pins,
horn of the scrotum, do not rise up or wave about;
gift of the noble ladies of Christendom,
nut-pole of the lap's cavity,
snare-shape, gander
sleeping in its yearling plumage,
neck with a wet head and milk-giving shaft,
tip of a growing shoot, stop your awkward jerking;
crooked blunt one, accursed pole,
the centre pillar of the two halves of a girl,
head of a stiff conger with a hole in it,
blunt barrier like a fresh hazel-pole.
You are longer than a big man's thigh,
a long night's roaming, chisel of a hundred nights;
auger like the shaft of the post,
leather-headed one who is called 'tail.'
You are a sceptre which causes lust,
the bolt of the lid of a girl's bare arse.
There is a pipe in your head,
a whistle for fucking every day.
There is an eye in your pate
which sees every woman as fair;

round pestle, expanding gun
it is a searing fire to a small cunt;
roof-beam of girls' laps,
blunt pod, it dug a family,
snare of skin, nostril with a crop of two testicles.
You are a trouserful of wantonness.
your neck is leather, image of a goose's neckbone;
nature of complete falsity, pod of lewdness,
door-nail which causes a lawsuit and trouble.

Consider that there is a writ and an indictment,
lower your head, stick for planting children.
It is difficult to keep you under control,
cold thrust, woe to you indeed!
Often is your lord rebuked,
obvious is the rottenness through your head.

Dafydd Johnston

✑ Lewis Glyn Cothi (c. 1450)

ON THE DEATH OF HIS SON

One son was a jewel to me:
o Dwynwen, his father bewails his birth!
I have been left pain for love,
to ache for ever without a son.
My plaything is dead and my sides
are sick for Siôn y Glyn.
I moan continually
for a little story-book chieftain.
A sweet apple and a bird
the boy loved, and white pebbles,
a bow made of a thorn twig
and little brittle swords of wood.
He feared a pipe and a scarecrow
and begged his mother for a ball.
He'd sing for anyone,
singing io-o for a nut.
He'd make as though to flatter
and then fall out with me;
then make it up for a chip of wood
or a dice that he desired.
O, that Siôn, sweet innocent,
could live again like Lazarus.
Beuno brought seven heaven-dwellers
back again into this life.
Woe upon woe to my true heart
that Siôn's soul does not make eight.

O Mary, woe for his lying down
and woe to my side for his grave!
Siôn's death stands near me
like two barbs in my breast.
My son, child of my hearth,
my breast, my heart, my song,
my one delight before my death,
my knowing poet, my luxury,
my jewel, and my candle,
my sweet soul, my one betrayal,
my chick learning my song,
my chaplet of Iseult, my kiss,
my nest, (woe that he's gone!)
my lark, my little wizard.
My Siôn, my bow, my arrow,
my suppliant, my boyhood,
Siôn who sends to his father
a sharpness of longing and love.
No more smiles for my lips,
no more laughter from my mouth,
no more sweet entertainment,
no more begging for nuts,
no longer any playing ball
and no more singing aloud.
Farewell, whilst I live below,
my merry darling, my Siôn.

Gwyn Williams

Irish Gaelic

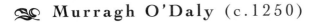

♒ Murragh O'Daly (c.1250)

ON KILLING A TAX COLLECTOR

Why do they stare
And expect me to act penitent?
I but clouted the slave
On a bad deed sent.

Richard O'Connell

ஓ 5

Hebrew and Arabic Verse from Andalusian Spain and the Middle East; the Golden Age of Persian Poetry

Hebrew

ஓ Samuel Ha-Nagid (993–1056)

THE GAZELLE

I'd give everything I own for that gazelle
 who, rising at night to his
   harp and flute,
  saw a cup in my hand
  and said:
"Drink your grape blood against my lips!"
 And the moon was cut like a D,
  on a dark robe, written in gold.

Peter Cole

ONE WHO WORKS AND BUYS HIMSELF BOOKS

One who works
 and buys himself books,
while his heart inside them
 is vain or corrupt

resembles a cripple
 who draws on the wall

a hundred legs,
    then can't get up.

              Peter Cole

FIRST WAR

First war resembles
    a beautiful mouth we
all want to flirt with
    and believe —.

Later it's more
    a repulsive old whore
whose callers are bitter
    and grieve.

              Peter Cole

YOU MOCK ME NOW IN YOUR YOUTH

You mock me now in your youth
    because I've grown old and gray;
I'm old, but I've seen the carpenters
    building their coffins for boys.

              Peter Cole

THE PRISON

The earth is a prison to man all his life.
Therefore I say this truth to the fool:
though you rush about, the sky
surrounds you on all sides. Try to get
out, if you can.

              T. Carmi

✑ Solomon ibn Gabirol (1021–1055)

RIDDLE

Naked without either cover or dress,
    utterly soulless, and hollow —

from its mouth comes wisdom and prudence,
    and in ambush it kills like an arrow.

(The Pen)

Peter Cole

MY HEART THINKS AS THE SUN COMES UP

My heart thinks as the sun comes up
    that what it does is wise:
    as earth borrows its light,
        as pledge it takes the stars.

Peter Cole

✇ Abraham ibn Ezra (1029–1167)

MY STARS

On the day I was born,
The unalterable stars altered.
If I decided to sell lamps,
It wouldn't get dark till the day I died.

Some stars. Whatever I do,
I'm a failure before I begin.
If I suddenly decided to sell shrouds,
People would suddenly stop dying.

Robert Mezey

✇ Moses ibn Ezra (1060–1138)

AND WHERE ARE THE GRAVES

And where are the graves, so many graves
Of all who have died on the earth since the beginning?
Grave tunneling into grave,
Headstone and obelisk crumbled into one dust,
Bodies heaped upon bodies, in motionless orgy—
All sleeping together in deep holes,
Fragments of chalk,
Stained rubies.

Robert Mezey

❧ Yehuda Halevi (1075–1141)

From ON THE SEA

Greetings ladies, kith and kin,
brothers and sisters, from hope's
captive. Purchased by the high seas,
he's placed himself in the hands
of rival winds: the west wind
steers the ship forward, the levant
whips it back. Between him and death —
a step, a plank. He's boxed in
alive in a wooden casket, without earth,
not even a bare four cubits.
He squats to keep his balance,
lies, but cannot stretch his legs,
is sickly, suspicious of strangers,
of pirates and the spookish winds.
Helmsman and crew — mere striplings —
are the Pashas and deputies here.
The wise and learned, unless they can swim,
have neither honor nor grace.
The thought for a moment clouds my face over
but heart and core thrill, for soon,
at the site of ark and altar,
I'll pour out my soul and render to you,
Lord, who bestows favors on the unworthy,
the pick of my songs and praise.

Gabriel Levin

DISTANT DOVE

A distant dove flutters
    above the treeline, un-
able to break loose,
    lurches, swerves, wings
flapping, whirls in
    a flurry round her lover.
She had thought one
    thousand years the limit
of her time, but now
    is ashamed, that she harbored
such fancies. Her long
    absent lover has harrowed
and driven her soul
    to the grave: "Never," she
swears, "will I mention

His name again," but no
sooner said and her
    heart's kindled like tinder.
Why be her adversary?
    Look how she opens wide
her bill to admit
    the spring shower of Your
salvation; believing
    with all her might, never
losing heart—whether
    honored or bowed down to
the dust. Surely our
    God shall come (round Him
rage tongues of fire)
    and not stay silent.

Gabriel Levin

POEM IN PARTS

Pity the heart, my lovely doe,
you've always lived in. Know
the day you stray from me will
be my end. Even now, as my eyes
dare spy your beauty, serpents
guarding your cheeks sting me,
for their venom is drawn from
fire and I am banished by them.

She hooked my heart in
the crescents resting over
her heart, though made of
stone, it engendered two
apples, to the right and
left. Taut as lance heads,
her nipples sting my heart:
though they've not come near
me, their mouths have drunk
my blood—and felt no shame.

Spinning one day like a drunkard from
the wine of her favors, envoys came
bearing me greetings and complaints;
on their return she pleaded: "Messengers

of peace, bear me such words
again and again. My heart is
seduced, my spirit renewed."

One day my hands were
grazing in her garden
caressing her breasts

and she said: "Let
your hands go loose
I'm still unseasoned!

Don't touch, my friend.
I don't care for abuse.

My breasts are full,
soft, and delicate.

Enough, I'll refuse
you, one and all."

Ammiel Alcalay

✖ Anonymous (c. 1250)

YOU AND I

You are Jehovah, and I am a wanderer.
Who should have mercy on a wanderer
if not Jehovah? You create and I decay.
Who should have mercy on the decayed
if not the creator? You are the Judge
and I the guilty. Who should have mercy
on the guilty if not the Judge? You are All
and I am a particle. Who should have mercy
on a particle if not the All?
You are the Living One and I am dead.
Who should have mercy on the dead if not
the Living One? You are the Painter and Potter
and I am clay. Who should have mercy on clay
if not the Painter and Potter? You are the Fire
and I am straw. Who should have mercy on straw
if not the Fire? You are the Listener
and I am the reader. Who should have mercy
on the reader if not the Listener? You
are the Beginning and I am what follows.
Who should have mercy on what follows
if not the Beginning? You are the End and I am
what follows. Who should have mercy on what follows if not the End?

Stanley Moss

⮂ Abraham Abulafia (c. 1250)

THE BATTLE

When Yahweh spoke to me, when I saw His name
spelled out in blood, the pounding in my heart
separated blood from ink and ink from blood,
and Yahweh said to me, "Know your soul's name
is blood and ink is the name of your spirit.
Your father and mother longed with all their hearts
to hear my Name and title given to every generation."
When I heard the clear difference between my spirit
and my soul, I was filled with great joy,
then I knew my soul took the hillside
under its own colors, in the mirror red as blood,
and that my spirit stood its ground in the mirror
that is black as ink, and that there raged
a ferocious war in my heart between blood and ink.
The blood was of the air and the ink of the earth
and the ink defeated the blood, and the Sabbath
overcame all the days of the week.

Stanley Moss

Arabic

⮂ Jafar ibn Uthman al-Mushafi (d. 982)

YELLOW ITS COLOR

Yellow its color
As if it wore
A daffodil slip
A perfume
Penetrating as musk

Perfumed and hard of heart
As that woman I want
Mine its color, lover-color
Passionate, strong

It is pale with a pallor
Loaned from the midst of me
And when she breathes
She breathes its deep odor

It had grown on a branch
Ripe in its odor
And leaves by then had woven
Brocade for its mantle

Hand outstretched
Gently I picked it
In the middle of my room
I placed it with reverence
A censer

Rolled
In ashes, fuzz
Its golden body

Naked in my hand
Under its daffodil slip

It made me think of her
I cannot name
I was breathing so hard
My fingers crushed it

Christopher Middleton and Leticia Garza-Falcón

Ibn Hazm Al-Andalusi (994–1064)

TWICE TIMES THEN IS NOW

You ask how old am I
bleached by the sun
my teeth all gone.
How old am I?

I have no guide
no calendar inside
except a smile
and little kiss
she gave me
by surprise
upon my brow.

And now,
that little while
is all my life
and all reality,
how long or brief
it seems to be.

Omar S. Pound

THE VISIT

You came to me a little while before
The Christians rang their bells. I saw
The halfmoon rising in the sky

Very like an old person's eye-
Brow half-hid by white hair
Or was it the delicate curve of a footsole

Sweetheart, when it was dark, dark everywhere
You put into the sky an aureole,
God's bow on the horizon, I saw it ride
With all the colors of a peacock's pride

Christopher Middleton and Leticia Garza-Falcón

❦ Abu'l Qasim As'ad ibn Billita (c. 1050)

THE ROOSTER

Up he stands
To declare the darkness done for
The bird trimmed with a poppy
Who rolls his lustrous eyes for us

With song he calls to prayer
And he complies with his call
Beating his great plumes
Flexing his shoulder knuckles

The Emperor of Persia
Perhaps wove his crown
Personally Mary the Copt
Hung pendant rings from his ears

He snatched from the peacock
His most attractive cloak
And still not comforted took
His strut from a duck

Christopher Middleton and Leticia Garza-Falcón

✑ Ibn Sharaf (d. 1068)

SATIRE

Chez toi, Mahmout,
What humdinging
Musical soirées —*écoute:*

To singing
Flies mosquitos flute,
And all the dancing girls are fleas.

Christopher Middleton and Leticia Garza-Falcón

✑ Abu I-Salt Umayyah (1067-1134)

THE WHITE STALLION

Pale as the morning star
in the hour of sunrise

he advances proudly,
caparisoned with a saddle of gold.

One who saw him going with me
into battle, envied me and said:

"Who bridled Dawn with the Pleiades?
Who saddled lightning with the half moon?"

Cola Franzen

✑ Muhammad ibn Ghalib al-Rusafi (d. 1177)

BLUE RIVER

The river of diaphanous waters
murmuring between its banks
would have you believe
it is a stream of pearls.

At midday tall trees
cover it with shadows
turning it the color of metal

So now you see it, blue,
wrapped in brocade,
like a warrior in armor
resting in the shade of his banner.

Cola Franzen

❧ Ibn Sara (d. 1123)

EGGPLANT

Spheroid

Fruit,   pleasing

To   taste,   fattened

By   water   gushing   in   all

The   gardens,   glossy   cupped

In   its   petiole,   ah,   heart

Of   a   lamb   in   a

Vulture's

Claws

Christopher Middleton and Letitia Garza-Falcón

❧ Ibn 'Iyad (1083–1149)

GRAINFIELD

Look at the ripe wheat
bending before the wind

like squadrons of horsemen
fleeing in defeat, bleeding
from the wounds of the poppies.

Cola Franzen

ࠗ Abu Bakr ibn Abd al-Malik ibn Quzman (c. 1086–1160)

TO A BEAUTY, WHITE, PURE, AND CONSTANT

Girl, you cut me up inside:
To you my torment I confide.

Longing to blend our sighs
Night after night I've spent
And could not close my eyes:
That you for me are meant
God's writ does recognize—
Leastways my large intent.

Yes you're my lucky star:
On days I see you pass,
Your features luminous,
If you are glad, my soul,
Seeing my flower afar
I'm filled with happiness.

Beauty, your slave is it?
Or captive? Out you go
And over flowers tread.
Your little bed you quit,
A light that fills your room
Spreads through your barrio.

Dawn of your look! My eyes
Answer that early light;
My myrtle tree, my wine—
If nothing suits you quite,
If nothing satisfies,
What misery is mine.

A lover living still,
Fortune exalts him most;
If death became his fate—
One look from you could kill—
Has not the ghost of a
Chance to retaliate.

"Hold up," is what they say,
"Patience, endure, be strong."
This patience, is it, pray,
Circular? Is it long?
Its color green, I ask,
Or yellow as aloe husk?

Hard labor is this love,
Distressing its ordeal.
Now I am skin and bone,
My wardrobe down-at-heel,
Share with me, if you can,
One third of what I feel.

If I am counting right,
Three gifts of God secure
No woman, quite, like you:
A being that is white,
A being that is pure,
A being constant too.

Christopher Middleton and Leticia Garza-Falcón

✥ Abu Amir ibn al-Hammarah (c. 1180)

INSOMNIA

When the bird of sleep
thought to nest
in my eye

it saw the eyelashes
and flew away
for fear of nets.

Cola Franzen

✥ Ali ibn Hariq (d. 1225)

GALLEY OARS

Below deck
There must be serpents

There since Noah's day
Fearing the Deluge

So now sensing
A rise in the water level

Out through the holes
They push their tongues

Christopher Middleton and Leticia Garza-Falcón

Perſian

⁓ Rudaki (c. 920)

ALL THE TEETH EVER I HAD ARE WORN DOWN

Abu'abdulla Ja'far bin Mahmud Rudaki of Samarkand ſays:

All the teeth ever I had are worn down and fallen out.
They were not rotten teeth, they shone like a lamp,
a row of silvery-white pearls set in coral;
they were as the morning star and as drops of rain.
There are none left now, all of them wore out and fell out.
Was it ill-luck, ill-luck, a malign conjunction?
It was no fault of stars, nor yet length of years.
I will tell you what it was: it was God's decree.

The world is always like a round, rolling eye,
round and rolling since it existed: a cure for pain
and then again a pain that supplants the cure.
In a certain time it makes new things old,
in a certain time makes new what was worn threadbare.
Many a broken desert has been gay garden,
many gay gardens grow where there used to be desert.

What can you know, my blackhaired beauty,
what I was like in the old days?
You tickle your lover with your curls
but never knew the time when he had curls.
The days are past when his face was good to look on,
the days are past when his hair was jet black.
Likewise, comeliness of guests and friends was dear,
but one dear guest will never return.
Many a beauty may you have marvelled at
but I was always marvelling at her beauty.
The days are past when she was glad and gay
and overflowing with mirth and I was afraid of losing her.
He paid, your lover, well and in counted coin
in any town where was a girl with round hard breasts,
and plenty of good girls had a fancy for him
and came by night but by day dare not
for dread of the husband and the jail.

Bright wine and the sight of a gracious face,
dear it might cost, but always cheap to me.
My purse was my heart, my heart bursting with words,
and the title-page of my book was Love and Poetry.
Happy was I, not understanding grief,

any more than a meadow.
Silk-soft has poetry made many a heart
stone before and heavy as an anvil.

Eyes turned always towards little nimble curls,
ears turned always towards men wise in words,
neither household, wife, child nor a patron —
at ease of these trials and at rest!
Oh! my dear, you look at Rudaki
but never saw him in the days when he was like that.

Never saw him when he used to go about
singing his songs as though he had a thousand.
The days are past when bold men sought his company,
the days are past when he managed affairs of princes,
the days are past when all wrote down his verses,
the days are past when he was the Poet of Khorassan.

Wherever there was a gentleman of renown
in his house had I silver and a mount.
From whomsoever some had greatness and gifts,
greatness and gifts had I from the house of Saman.
The Prince of Khorassan gave me forty thousand dirhems,
Prince Makan more by a fifth,
and eight thousand in all from his nobles
severally. That was the fine time!
When the Prince heard a fair phrase he gave, and his men,
each man of his nobles, as much as the Prince saw fit.
Times have changed. I have changed. Bring me my stick.
Now the beggar's staff and wallet.

Basil Bunting

SPRING

Spring came,
with colors and scents,
a hundred thousand trimmings
and strange get-up;
perhaps an old man might regain his youth
in such a time,
as the world found strength again
after senescence.

Nature has raised an army:
rain-clouds marshalled by a gentle wind,
storm-lit path,
thunder step,
I have seen a thousand armies
but never one like this.

Look at the cloud weeping
listen to the thunder sighing,
from time to time the sun comes out
between the sullen clouds
like a prisoner
escaping from his guard.

The winter world was sick
but now the scent of jasmine has revived it;
rain falls, smelling of musk,
stripping the earth of its white covering;
the frozen treasure opens into flower
and dry streams flow.

In the distance, the desert tulip gleams
like a bride's finger dyed with henna;
the nightingale is singing in the willow,
the pigeon in the cypress,
strange melodies,
answering,
familiar.

Now is the time to drink and be alive
for now lover and lover
give happiness
one to another.

Geoffrey Squires

PRAYER

The face is turned to Mecca
but what's the use?
the heart goes out to Bokhara
and the stately ladies there.
God will accept the whisperings of love
and ignore the prayer. . . .

Geoffrey Squires

CAME TO ME

Came to me —
        Who?
She.
        When?
In the dawn, afraid.

What of?
Anger.
        Whose?
Her father's.
        Confide!

I kissed her twice.
        Where?
On her moist mouth.
        Mouth?

No.
        What, then?
Cornelian.
         How was it?
Sweet.

      Basil Bunting

Khosravani (c. 960)

There are four kinds of men who'll get no fee from me
Since I've seen not a scrap of profit from their arts—
The doctors with their drugs, the pious with their prayers,
Magicians with their spells, stargazers with their charts.

      Dick Davis

Firdowsi (d. 1020)

WHEN THE SWORD OF SIXTY COMES NIGH HIS HEAD

When the sword of sixty comes nigh his head
give a man no wine, for he is drunk with years.
Age claps a stick in my bridle-hand:
substance spent, health broken,
forgotten the skill to swerve aside from the joust
with the spearhead grazing my eyelashes.

The sentinel perched on the hill top
cannot see the countless army he used to see there:
the black summit's deep in snow
and its lord himself sinning against the army.

He was proud of his two swift couriers:
lo! sixty ruffians have put them in chains.

The singer is weary of his broken voice,
one drone for the bulbul alike and the lion's grousing.

Alas for flowery, musky, sappy thirty
and the sharp Persian sword!
The pheasant strutting about the briar,
pomegranate-blossom and cypress sprig!
Since I raised my glass to fifty-eight
I have toasted only the bier and the burial-ground.

I ask the just Creator
so much refuge from Time
that a tale of mine may remain in the world
from this famous book of the ancients
and they who speak of such matters weighing their words
think of that only when they think of me.

Basil Bunting

ꙮ Abu Sa'id Abul Khayr (967–1048)

FOUR POEMS ON DEATH

1

I'm going to tell You something that is true
And won't take more than two words to explain —
I'll lie beneath the earth still loving You
And with Your kindness I shall rise again.

2

If I've been dead for twenty years or so
And you, believing love gone long ago,
Should stir my dust and say "Whose grave is this?"
"How is my love?" will echo from below.

3

His absence is the knife that cuts your throat?
Let noone glimpse the blood-stains on your coat;
Weep, but in weeping let no listener hear;
Burn, but in burning let no smoke appear.

4

For men and women soon the day draws near
When dreading Judgement they'll grow pale with fear;
Bravely I'll show your beauty then and say
"I must be judged on this, my life is here."

Dick Davis

ஐஓ Omar Khayyam (1048-1131)

From THE RUBAIYAT

A Book of Verses underneath the Bough,
A Jug of Wine, a Loaf of Bread—and Thou
    Beside me singing in the Wilderness—
O, Wilderness were Paradise enow!

Some for the Glories of This World; and some
Sigh for the Prophet's Paradise to come;
    Ah, take the Cash, and let the Credit go,
Nor heed the rumble of a distant Drum!

Look to the blowing Rose about us—'Lo,
Laughing,' she says, 'into the world I blow.
    At once the silken tassel of my Purse
Tear, and its Treasure on the Garden throw.'

And those who husbanded the Golden grain
And those who flung it to the winds like Rain,
    Alike to no such aureate Earth are turned
As, buried once, Men want dug up again.

———

The Worldly Hope men set their Hearts upon
Turns Ashes—or it prospers; and anon,
    Like Snow upon the Desert's dusty Face,
Lighting a little hour or two—is gone.

Think, in this battered Caravanserai
Whose Portals are alternate Night and Day,
    How Sultan after Sultan with his Pomp
Abode his destined Hour, and went his way.

They say the Lion and the Lizard keep
The Courts where Jamshyd gloried and drank deep:
    And Bahram, that great Hunter—the wild Ass
Stamps o'er his Head, but cannot break his Sleep.

I sometimes think that never blows so red
The Rose as where some buried Caesar bled;
    That every Hyacinth the Garden wears
Dropt in her Lap from some once lovely Head.

And this reviving Herb whose tender Green
Fledges the River-Lip on which we lean—
    Ah, lean upon it lightly! for who knows
From what once lovely Lip it springs unseen!

Ah, my Beloved, fill the Cup that clears
TODAY of past Regrets and future Fears:
　　To-morrow!—Why, To-morrow I may be
Myself with Yesterday's Seven thousand Years.

For some we loved, the loveliest and the best
That from his Vintage rolling Time hath prest,
　　Have drunk their Cup a Round or two before,
And one by one crept silently to rest.

And we, that now make merry in the Room
They left, and Summer dresses in new bloom,
　　Ourselves must we beneath the Couch of Earth
Descend—ourselves to make a Couch—for whom?

Ah, make the most of what we yet may spend,
Before we too into the Dust descend;
　　Dust into Dust, and under Dust to lie,
Sans Wine, sans Song, sans Singer, and—sans End!

Edward Fitzgerald

৯৫ Nizami Arudi (c. 1110)

CALLING THE DOCTOR (c. A.D. 1000)

For Basil Bunting

Go find Avicenna
　　　　　or my son will die,
make forty copies of this miniature,
don't paint alembics in his lap
or gardens with mauve rocks behind.
　　　　　Damn court artists
　　　　　their frills and fuss.
Just his features, enough,
that will give you fewer lines
to fight about.
Send one to every court
　　　　　but get them off tonight
with the royal command:
Abu ali ibn sina is sought
　　　　　and must be found.

You've found him.
　　　　　What!
chuckling to himself. How dare he
with my son about to . . .
　　　　　　　　and what?

asking if birds fly through sandstorms
or around,
            chuckling indeed
            I'll chuckle him,
go bring him in.
            Stop it rings
don't sparkle so. Yours is not the light
to hustle him.

Ruler of the world! Your majesty desires?
. . . my son, with the first fuzz of youth
around his chin is
              you understand
about to
            die,
              my son,
                  the king's son,
come and examine him.

Rings, stop jangling like jays.
I wonder which is worse
private or public pain,
a king's child where children reign.

The lad seems worn,
              pulse regular, urine opaque.
That was a fine amber ring
the king wore. No wonder he attracts
such chaff. I'm one straw more.
The boy's so thin, withdrawn,
with saffron down around his chin.

. . . that's odd, before I mention
the disease I know the cure.
            I knew more at ten
than he will ever know, but Muhammad,
Seal of all Prophets,
            tell me more about the soul;
is it within or out, and must I doubt
before I know, or will doubt kill
all knowing?
            The soul needs reason,
and reason, knowing.

Your majesty, send me a man
who knows the town.

You're the city clerk?
Now list
            slowly, please
the quarters of the town;

boy
        your wrist
                don't worry
it's not to bleed you
just to take your pulse again.

Clerk
                you were saying?
the gate to Mazanderan
the Prophet's gate, and Newgate
the oldest one in town,

fine, now list the roads that lead
to Mazanderan: Cobbler's Way,
Bread alley and Indigo lane.

Right! now recite from tax lists
                if you can
each household in Indigo land:
the Jasmine estate, Thanks-be-to-God,
Hassan Firuz, Godspeed, Makepeace
and Worthy the scribe
                                Stop!
That's enough, clerk, take this
for your trouble. Goodbye son,
I'm done and off to tell your father
the cure to kill what's ailing you.

Your majesty, I cannot hide
behind incantations, spells
and magic lore,
                not that I dismiss prayer
                to set a man right,
your son will soon be well
with eyes bright
as alhazen's reflected light:
his sickness: pride.
                He has a secret love
and none he thought loved like him before,
and telling none
                he's burning down;
it's Worthy the scribe's daughter
in Indigo lane by the gate to Mazanderan.
The cure? Arrange a feast, proclaim he's cured,
announce the wedding soon
he'll be up by noon,
                and don't ask how
                I named the bride.

You need no medico for that. I knew
he'd surely lie if asked the name

for which he'd gladly die,
but as your clerk,
          promote him if you wish,
reeled off gates and streets
the pulse would change, and soon
I knew her name. May she be worthy
of your own.

My reward?
Three scribes dumb enough
to copy down exactly what I say
and not what they think I've said,
and a girl from Samarqand
          for my bed.

Omar S. Pound

❧ Anvari (d. 1190)

DRUNKENNESS

I drink but don't get drunk:
I abuse nothing but the goblet:
I worship wine in order to avoid
Worshipping self, like you.

Geoffrey Squires

COMPOSING

I wrote a panegyric on you—and I'm sorry,
     There's no point in these lays of one's own making;
My praise was like a wet dream—when I woke I found
     I'd spent spunk on a worthless undertaking.

Dick Davis

TAKE WHAT HE GIVES YOU

Take what he gives you, even if it's paltry—
     To this lord *paltry*'s quite a bit;
A gift from him's like being circumcised—
     Once in a lifetime, and that's it!

Dick Davis

✺ Attar (Farid Ud-Din Attar, c. 1120–1220)

From THE CONFERENCE OF THE BIRDS

The birds assemble and the hoopoe tells them of the Simorgh

The world's birds gathered for their conference
And said: 'Our constitution makes no sense.
All nations in the world require a king;
How is it we alone have no such thing?
Only a kingdom can be justly run;
We need a king and must inquire for one.'

They argued how to set about their quest.
The hoopoe fluttered forward; on his breast
There shone the symbol of the Spirit's Way
And on his head Truth's crown, a feathered spray.
Discerning, righteous and intelligent,
He spoke: 'My purposes are heaven-sent;
I keep God's secrets, mundane and divine,
In proof of which behold the holy sign
Bismillah etched for ever on my beak.
No one can share the grief with which I seek
Our longed-for Lord, and quickened by my haste
My wits find water in the trackless waste.
I come as Solomon's close friend and claim
The matchless wisdom of that mighty name
(He never asked for those who quit his court,
But when I left him once alone he sought
With anxious vigilance for my return —
Measure my worth by this great king's concern!).
I bore his letters — back again I flew —
Whatever secrets he divined I knew;
A prophet loved me; God has trusted me;
What other bird has won such dignity?
For years I travelled over many lands,
Past oceans, mountains, valleys, desert sands,
And when the Deluge rose I flew around
The world itself and never glimpsed dry ground;
With Solomon I set out to explore
The limits of the earth from shore to shore.
I know our king — but how can I alone
Endure the journey to His distant throne?
Join me, and when at last we end our quest
Our king will greet you as His honoured guest.
How long will you persist in blasphemy?
Escape your self-hood's vicious tyranny —
Whoever can evade the Self transcends

This world and as a lover he ascends.
Set free your soul; impatient of delay,
Step out along our sovereign's royal Way:
We have a king; beyond Kaf's mountain peak
The Simorgh lives, the sovereign whom you seek,
And He is always near to us, though we
Live far from His transcendent majesty.
A hundred thousand veils of dark and light
Withdraw His presence from our mortal sight,
And in both worlds no being shares the throne
That marks the Simorgh's power and His alone —
He reigns in undisturbed omnipotence,
Bathed in the light of His magnificence —
No mind, no intellect can penetrate
The mystery of His unending state:
How many countless hundred thousands pray
For patience and true knowledge of the Way
That leads to Him whom reason cannot claim,
Nor mortal purity describe or name;
There soul and mind bewildered miss the mark
And, faced by Him, like dazzled eyes, are dark —
No sage could understand His perfect grace,
Nor seer discern the beauty of His face.
His creatures strive to find a path to Him,
Deluded by each new, deceitful whim,
But fancy cannot work as she would wish;
You cannot weigh the moon like so much fish!
How many search for Him whose heads are sent
Like polo-balls in some great tournament
From side to giddy side — how many cries,
How many countless groans assail the skies!
Do not imagine that the Way is short;
Vast seas and deserts lie before His court.
Consider carefully before you start;
The journey asks of you a lion's heart.
The road is long, the sea is deep — one flies
First buffeted by joy and then by sighs;
If you desire this quest, give up your soul
And make our sovereign's court your only goal.
First wash your hands of life if you would say:
"I am a pilgrim of our sovereign's Way";
Renounce your soul for love; He you pursue
Will sacrifice His inmost soul for you.

———

The birds, one by one, make excuses, declining the journey.

———

The heron's excuse

The heron whimpered next: 'My misery
Prefers the empty shoreline of the sea.

There no one hears my desolate, thin cry— ⎫
I wait in sorrow there, there mourn and sigh. ⎬
My love is for the ocean, but since— ⎭
A bird—must be excluded from the deep,
I haunt the solitary shore and weep.
My beak is dry—not one drop can I drink—
But if the level of the sea should sink
By one drop, jealous rage would seize my heart.
This love suffices me; how can I start
A journey like the one that you suggest?
I cannot join you in this arduous quest.
The Simorgh's glory could not comfort me;
My love is fixed entirely on the sea.'

The hoopoe answers him

The hoopoe answered him: 'You do not know
The nature of this sea you love: below
Its surface linger sharks; tempests appear,
Then sudden calms—its course is never clear,
But turbid, varying, in constant stress;
Its water's taste is salty bitterness.
How many noble ships has it destroyed,
Their crews sucked under in the whirlpool's void:
The diver plunges and in fear of death
Must struggle to conserve his scanty breath;
The failure is cast up, a broken straw.
Who trusts the sea? Lawlessness is her law;
You will be drowned if you cannot decide
To turn away from her inconstant tide.
She seethes with love herself—that turbulence
Of tumbling waves, that yearning violence,
Are for her Lord, and since she cannot rest,
What peace could you discover in her breast?
She lives for Him—yet you are satisfied
To hear His invitation and to hide.

Afkham Darbandi and Dick Davis

ᕫ Rumi (Jalal ad-din Rumi, 1207–1273)

CARING FOR MY LOVER

Friends, last night I carefully watched my love
sleeping by a spring circled with eglantine.
The houris of paradise stood around him,
        their hands cupped together
between a tulip field and jasmines.

Wind tugged softly in his hair.
His curls smelled of musk and ambergris.
Wind turned mad and tore the hair right off his face
like a flaming oil lamp in a gale.
From the beginning of this dream I told myself
    go slowly, wait
for the break into consciousness. Don't breathe.

Willis Barnstone and Reza Baraheni

FOUR POEMS ON THE NIGHT

1

This night there are no limits to what may be given.
This is not a night but a marriage,
a couple whispering in bed in unison the same words.
Darkness simply lets down a curtain for that.

2

A night full of talking that hurts,
my worst held-back secrets: Everything
has to do with loving and not loving.
This night will pass.
Then we have work to do.

3

Night comes so people can sleep like fish
in black water. Then day.

Some people pick up their tools.
Others become the making itself.

4

Inside water, a waterwheel turns.
A star circulates with the moon.

We live in the night ocean wondering,
What are these lights?

John Moyne and Coleman Barks

HAS ANYONE SEEN THE BOY?

Has anyone seen the boy who used to come here?
Round-faced trouble-maker, quick to find a joke,

slow to be serious, red shirt,
perfect coordination, sly, strong muscled,
with things always in his pocket, reed flute,
work pick, polished and ready for his Talent
    you know that one.
Have you heard stories about him?
Pharoh and the whole Egyptian world
    collapsed for such a Joseph
I'd gladly spend years getting word
    of him, even third or fourth hand.

Coleman Barks and John Moyne

NIGHT AND SLEEP

At the time of night-prayer, as the sun slides down,
the route the senses walk on closes, the route to the invisible opens.

The angel of sleep then gathers and drives along the spirits;
just as the mountain keeper gathers his sheep on a slope.

And what amazing sights he offers to the descending sheep!
Cities with sparkling streets, hyacinth gardens, emerald pastures!

The spirit sees astounding beings, turtles turned to men,
men turned to angels, when sleep erases the banal.

I think one could say the spirit goes back to its old home;
it no longer remembers where it lives, and loses its fatigue.

It carries around in life so many griefs and loads
and trembles under their weight; they are gone; it is all well.

Robert Bly

❧ Sa'di (d. 1292)

LAST NIGHT WITHOUT SIGHT OF YOU

Last night without sight of you my brain was ablaze.
My tears trickled and fell plip on the ground. That I with
sighing might bring my life to a close they would name
you and again and again speak your name till
with night's coming all eyes closed save mine whose every
hair pierced my scalp like a lancet. That was
not wine I drank far from your sight but my heart's
blood gushing into the cup. Wall and door wherever
I turned my eyes scored and decorated with shapes

of you. To dream of Laila Majnun prayed for
sleep. My senses came and went but neither your
face saw I nor would your fantom go from me.
Now like aloes my heart burned, now smoked as a censer.
Where was the morning gone that used on other nights
to breathe till the horizon paled? Sa'di!
Has then the chain of the Pleiades broken
tonight that every night is hung on the sky's neck?

Basil Bunting

THIS I WRITE, MIX INK WITH TEARS

This I write, mix ink with tears,
and have written of grief before, but never so grievously,
to tell Azra Vamiq's pain,
to tell Laila Majnun's plight,
to tell you my own
unfinished story.
Take it. Seek no excuse.
How sweetly you will sing what I so sadly write.

Basil Bunting

FIVE POEMS

1

If you should say to me "Don't mention love"
I'll manage to restrain my tongue by force,
But if you try prohibiting my tears
The Tigris can't be altered in its course.

2

Until you can correct and heal yourself
Be quiet about another man's disgrace —
Don't be the bare-assed bullying constable
Who hits a whore and tells her "Veil your face!"

3

When once the soul is ready to depart, sir,
All surgeons and their science are sure to fail,
Since no dead donkey's going to stand again
However much you pull its ears or tail.

4

He glanced at me one day—but then his mean
Suspicious tutor had to intervene;

He wouldn't let the sunlight fall on me
But like a louring cloud pushed in between.

5

O I repented, wore my pious cloak,
Listened and looked wherever wise men spoke,
But then I saw that cypress-bodied boy
And I forgot their sayings at a stroke.

Dick Davis

✖ Hafiz (1320–1389)

GHAZAL: HALF-WAY THROUGH THE NIGHT

Half-way through the night
            she came by the side of my bed
Wine in hand, blouse torn
            and her hair all over the place
With laughter and tears in her eyes
            mockery in her voice
She laid her head on me
            and plaintively said
Asleep so soon my love?
            you will be love's infidel
If you do not worship wine
            when you are given it;
Forget all that talk of sin
            whining hypocrites
Since the day the world began
            we have had our fill
Whatever was put before us
            we drank and we didn't care
If it was the wine of paradise
            or the dregs of a bad year
O Hafiz many a vow like yours
            has been broken beyond repair
By a girl with a flask of wine
            and disorder in her hair.

Geoffrey Squires

GHAZAL 24: FOR YEARS MY HEART ASKED ME FOR JAMSHID'S CUP

For years my heart asked me for Jamshid's cup.
That which it held it begged from strangers.

It sought the pearl which lies outside the world's shell
from the lost ones who wait by the edge of the sea.

Last night I carried my dilemma to the old Magus
that with his vision he might find the answer.

I found him laughing, drunk, his cup and heart
blazed at one another their dialogue of mirrors.

"Wise man," I said, "when did He give you this world-seeing cup?"
He said, "the day that He built this blue enamel dome.

That friend," he added, "who dignified the gallows,
his sin was this: he spilled the secrets.

In every state God walked with the lost-hearted
who saw nothing and from a distance cried, 'O God!'

All the sleights-of-hand with which Reason tricks us here
were tried before Moses, to no avail.

If the grace of the Holy Spirit commands more help
others will raise the dead as Jesus did."

I asked him, "What do the idols' ringlets seek?"
He said, "Hafiz complains of a tangled heart."

Elizabeth Gray

THREE POEMS ON FRIENDSHIP

1

Desire's destroyed my life; what gifts have I
Been given by the blindly turning sky?
And, such is my luck, everyone I said
"Dear friend" to loathed me by and by.

2

Each "friend" turned out to be an enemy,
Corruption rotted all their "purity";
They say the night is pregnant with new times,
But since no men are here, how can that be?

3

My friend, hold back your heart from enemies.
Drink shining wine with handsome friends like these;

With art's initiates let down your hair —
Stay buttoned up with ignoramuses.

Dick Davis

LIGHT OF MY EYES

Light of my eyes, there *is* something to be said.
Drink and give to drink while the bottle is full.
Old men speaking from experience, as I told you:
'Indeed, you will grow old.
Love has respectable people chained up for the torture.
You'd like to rumple his hair? Give up being good.
Rosary and veil have no such relish as drink.'

Put it in practice. Send for the wine-merchant.
Amongst the drinkers, one lifetime,
one purse cannot cramp you.
A hundred lives for your dear!
(In love's business the devil lacks not ideas,
but listen, listen with your heart to the angel's message.)

Maple leaves wither, gaiety's not everlasting.
Wail, O harp! Cry out, O drum!
May *your* glass never want wine!
Look gently behind you and drink.
When you step over the drunks in your gold-scattering gown
spare a kiss for *Hafiz* in his flannel shirt.

Basil Bunting

꧇ 6

POETRY FROM INNER ASIA

Mongolian

꧇ Anonymous (c. 1250)

From THE SECRET HISTORY OF THE MONGOLS

The Death of Yesugei

As he rode back Yesugei came on a camp of the Tatar,
who were feasting below Mount Chegcher on the Yellow Steppe.
Tired and thirsty, he dismounted to join in the feasting.
But the Tatar recognized who he was, and said to themselves:
"Yesugei of the Kiyan clan is among us here."
They remembered the times he'd defeated them in battle.
Secretly they decided to kill him,
mixing poisons into the drinks he was offered.
On his way back he felt something was wrong
and after riding three days to get back to his tent
he knew he was dying.
Yesugei the Brave spoke from his bed, saying:
"I feel that I'm dying.
Who's here beside me?"
Someone answered him:
"Munglig, the son of Old Man Charakha is here."
Yesugei called the boy over to him and said:
"Munglig, my child, my sons are still very young.
As I rode back from leaving Temujin with his wife's family
I was secretly poisoned by the Tatar.
I can feel that I'm dying now.
Take care of my sons like they were your own little brothers.
Take care of my wife like she was your own elder sister.

Go quickly now, Munglig, my child, and bring Temujin back."
Then Yesugei passed away.
Following Yesugei's last words Munglig went to Dei the Wise and said:
"My Elder Brother Yesugei's heart aches
and he is constantly thinking of his son.
I've come to take Temujin back to him."
Dei the Wise answered him:
"If my friend thinks so much of his son, I'll let him go.
When he's seen his father again, have him quickly come back."
So Father Munglig brought Temujin back to his family.

Temujin Becomes Chingis Khan

Then they moved the whole camp
to the shores of Blue Lake in the Gurelgu Mountains.
Altan, Khuchar, and Sacha Beki conferred with each other there,
and then said to Temujin:
"We want you to be khan.
Temujin, if you'll be our khan
we'll search through the spoils
for the beautiful women and virgins,
for the great palace tents,
for the young virgins and loveliest women,
for the finest geldings and mares.
We'll gather all these and bring them to you.
When we go off to hunt for wild game
we'll go out first to drive them together for you to kill.
We'll drive the wild animals of the steppe together
so that their bellies are touching.
We'll drive the wild game of the mountains together
so that they stand leg to leg.
If we disobey your command during battle
take away our possessions, our children, and wives.
Leave us behind in the dust,
cutting off our heads where we stand and letting them fall to the ground.
If we disobey your counsel in peacetime
take away our tents and our goods, our wives, and our children.
Leave us behind when you move,
abandoned in the desert without a protector."
Having given their word,
having taken this oath,
they proclaimed Temujin khan of the Mongol
and gave him the name Chingis Khan.

The Last Battle and Death of Chingis Khan

Chingis Khan left his camp on Mount Chasutu
and laid siege to the city of Ying-li.
Once he had taken Ying-li
he moved on to Ling-wu
which stood only a few miles from the Tanghut capital.

As Chingis Khan was breaking down the walls of Ling-wu,
Burkhan presented himself with offerings for peace.
He brought out images of the Buddha made from gold.
Then followed bowls and vessels made of silver and gold,
nine and nine,
young boys and young maidens,
nine and nine,
fine geldings and fine camels,
nine and nine,
and every other thing in his realm,
each arranged according to its color and form,
nine and nine.
Chingis Khan ordered Burkhan to present himself outside the closed door of
    his tent.
Burkhan was told to wait there three days,
and on the third day Chingis Khan decided what to do.
He gave Burkhan Khan the new title Shidurghu,
One Who Has Been Made Upright,
and after allowing Burkhan Shidurghu to stand before him,
Chingis Khan said:
"See that he is executed.
Let Tolun Cherbi be the one to see that he is killed."
When Tolun Cherbi sent a report saying:
"I have laid hands on Burkhan and he is dead,"
Chingis Khan made this decree:
"When we were approaching the Tanghut land
to settle the words that Burkhan had sent to me,
when I had been injured while hunting the wild horses of Arbukha,
it was Tolun who advised that I take care of my life and my body,
saying, 'Let it heal,' when he heard of my pain.
Because of these poisonous words from our enemy
Everlasting Heaven has once again increased our strength
and caused our enemy to fall into our hands.
We have taken our vengeance.
Now let Tolun take the great palace tent Burkhan has brought,
along with the bowls and vessels of silver and gold."
Chingis Khan took everything from the Tanghut people.
He gave their ruler Burkhan the name Shidurghu
and then executed him.
He ordered that the men and women of their cities be killed,
their children and grandchildren, saying:
"As long as I can eat food and still say,
'Make everyone who lives in their cities vanish,
kill them all and destroy their homes.
As long as I am still alive
keep up the slaughter."
This is because the Tanghut people made a promise they didn't keep.
Chingis Khan had gone to war with the Tanghut a second time.
He had destroyed them,
and coming back to Mongolia,
in the Year of the Pig,

Chingis Khan ascended to Heaven.
After he had ascended
Yesui Khatun was given most of the Tanghut people who remained.

Paul Kahn (after Francis Woodman Cleaves)

Tibetan

 Anonymous (c. 1350)

From DRIMEH KUNDAN

The Queen wept but thought: It is not appropriate to show such grief;
he must go on this long journey. So she wiped away her tears.
Gedan Zangmo:
>My dearest child, now let me speak not to you but for you.
>To the beings in the boundless ocean of space surrounding us,
>To the conquering Buddhas and Bodhisattvas, the guardians
>Of all directions, please listen to my words:
>This son of mine is leaving; return him with his present virtue
>And in his body. May he be spared acute fatigue as he crosses
>Pass and plain; when he lives in the hill Hashang may it become
>Palatial; when he eats what trees and plants can give
>May he taste a royal nectar; in his thirst may his water become
>Forever milk; when he dresses in leaves and sleeps on moss
>May he walk in the god's five-color cloth and lie on silk.
>When the wild beasts roar may he hear the music of mantra;
>When the rivers roar in their beds of rock, let the sound be
>Om Mani Padme Hung; may the daughters of the gods spare him
>From the narrow valleys' heat; and on frightfulness mountain
>May all the Buddhas be his companions; when his body burns
>With fever, may doctors, like miracles, come with medicine.
>Last,
>Wherever he may live, may he live in delight, may his doings
>And his thoughts spread like the wish-fulfilling leaves.
>>>>>>>>>>Last,

May the two of us soon meet.

Armand Schwerner

7

CHINA: THE SUNG AND YÜAN DYNASTIES

Chinese

Li Yü (937–978)

TO THE TUNE "MEETING HAPPINESS"

Silent and alone, I ascend the west tower.
The moon is like a hook.
In solitude, the *wu tung* trees
imprison the clear autumn in the deep courtyard.
Scissored but not severed,
trimmed, but still massive:
it is the sorrow of parting,
another strange flavor in the heart.

Arthur Sze

Wang Yü-ch'eng (954–1001)

SONG OF THE CROW PECKING AT MY SCARRED
DONKEY

Old crow of Shang Mountain, you are cruel!
Beak longer than a spike, sharper than an arrow.
Go gather bugs or peck at eggs —
Why must you harm this poor scarred beast of mine?
Since I was exiled to Shang-yu last year

There has only been this one lame donkey to move my things.
We climbed the Ch'in Mountains and the Ch'an to get here;
He carried a hundred volumes for me on his back.
The ropes cut his skin to the spine: the scar reached his belly;
Now with half a year's healing he's nearly well again.
But yesterday the crow suddenly swooped down
And pecked through his wound to get the living flesh.
The donkey brayed, my servant cried out and the crow flew away!
Perched on the roof he preened his feathers and scraped his beak.
There was nothing my donkey and my servant could do
Without a crossbow to shoot or nets to spread.
But Shang Mountain has many birds of prey;
I'll ask our neighbor to lend me his autumn hawk:
With claws of iron and hooked talons
He'll snap the crow's neck and feed on his brain!
And this won't serve only to fill his empty gut;
No! It's revenge for my donkey's pain.

Jonathan Chaves

😉 Liu Yung (987–1053)

SONG TO THE TUNE "TING FENG PO"

Because spring brings its miserable green and painful red,
my heart is moved by nothing.
When the sun climbs over the flowers
and orioles fly through the willows,
I remain in bed wrapped in a perfumed blanket.
My face is a mess,
my hair is a mess,
but I'm too shiftless to do a thing about it.
What can I say?
That my cruel lover has left me,
that he's sent not a single letter?

I should have known this would happen.
I wish I had locked up his saddle.
I should have locked him in his study,
brought him pen and paper,
and made him chant his poems.
At least we could have had our days together
instead of being divided.
I would put aside my sewing
and smuggle up against him.
That way, the best years of our lives
would not have gone for nothing.

Sam Hamill

✆ Anonymous (c. 1000)

TO THE TUNE "THE DRUNKEN YOUNG LORD"

Outside my door
              the dog barking
I know what it is
              My lover's here
Off with my stockings
                  down
                    perfumed stairs
My good-for-nothing lover
                  is drunk tonight

I help him into
              my silk-curtained bed
Will he take off the silk gown?
                  O! O! not he
Milord is drunk
              and drunk let him be
Better that
          than sleeping alone

C. H. Kwock and Vincent McHugh

✆ Mei Yao-ch'en (1002–1060)

ON THE DEATH OF A NEWBORN CHILD

The flowers in bud on the trees
Are pure like this dead child.
The East wind will not let them last.
It will blow them into blossom,
And at last into the earth.
It is the same with this beautiful life
Which was so dear to me.
While his mother is weeping tears of blood,
Her breasts are still filling with milk.

Kenneth Rexroth

SORROW

Heaven took my wife. Now it
Has also taken my son.
My eyes are not allowed a
Dry season. It is too much

For my heart. I long for death.
When the rain falls and enters
The earth, when a pearl drops into
The depth of the sea, you can
Dive in the sea and find the
Pearl, you can dig in the earth
And find the water. But no one
Has ever come back from the
Underground Springs. Once gone, life
Is over for good. My chest
Tightens against me. I have
No one to turn to. Nothing,
Not even a shadow in a mirror.

Kenneth Rexroth

A SOLITARY FALCON ABOVE THE BUDDHA HALL OF THE MONASTERY OF UNIVERSAL PURITY

My newly rented home commands a view of the temple hall;
gold and jade-green glitter before my crumbling house.
I gaze at the temple, and watch the flocks of pigeons
bring food and drink to their nested young,
            unaware of the year's drawing to a close.
Bird droppings have dirtied all the carved eaves and painted walls,
and fallen on the heads and shoulders of clay-sculpted Buddhas.
The monastery monks would never dare to shoot the birds with crossbows;
but suddenly there comes a dark falcon, baring his dangerous claws.
Crows caw, magpies screech, mynah birds cry out;
the falcon, excited, flies close in and catches the scent of flesh.
Determination in his heart, outnumbered but unafraid,
in a flash he has crushed the head of a bird and terrified the others.
The dead bird plunges in the void, has not yet reached the ground
when the falcon sweeps down with whirlwind wings and snatches him
            in midair.
Alone on the rooftop, he freely rips and tears,
pecks at the flesh, pulls at the liver, casts away the guts.
The scavengers with no skill of their own, crafty and cowardly,
circle above, waiting to descend, staring with their hungry eyes.
Soon the falcon has eaten his fill and leisurely flies off;
who can distinguish kites from crows in the struggle for the leavings?
All the children point and gesture, the passers-by laugh,
while I thoughtfully intone my poem by the autumnal riverbank.

Jonathan Chaves

✖ Wang An-shih

IN THE STYLE OF HAN SHAN AND SHIH TE

Had I been an ox or horse
I would rejoice to see grass and beans;
If, on the other hand, I were a woman,
the sight of men would please me.
But if I were really me
I would always settle for what I be.
If liking and dislike keep you upset
surely you are being used:
Big man, with all your dignity,
don't mistake what you have for what you are.

Jan W. Walls

✖ Su Tung-p'o (Su Shih, 1036–1101)

ON THE BIRTH OF HIS SON

Families, when a child is born
Want it to be intelligent.
I, through intelligence,
Having wrecked my whole life,
Only hope the baby will prove
Ignorant and stupid.
Then he will crown a tranquil life
By becoming a Cabinet Minister.

Arthur Waley

LYRICS TO THE TUNE "FAIRY GROTTO"

Skin of ice.
Bones of jade.
Always cool and unperspiring.

To the palace by the water
Comes a breeze,
Filling it with hidden fragrance.

Embroidered curtains open.
A ray of moonlight
Peeks in at her.
She is not yet asleep,

But leans against the pillow,
Hairpin awry
And hair tousled.

She rises.
I take her white hand.
In all the doors and courtyards
There is silence.

From time to time
A shooting star
Crosses the Milky Way.

I ask how late it is:
Already midnight.
Golden waves of moonlight fade,
The stars of the Jeweled Cord
Roll low.

On my fingers I count the time
Until the west wind comes again,
Saying nothing of the flowing years
That steal away in darkness.

Greg Whincup

LYRIC TO THE TUNE "THE CHARMS OF NIEN-NU": AT THE RED CLIFF I PONDER OVER ANTIQUITY

The big river goes east
waves washed through a thousand ages of headlong heroes
west of the ancient battlements
men say is Lord Chou's Red Cliff of Three Kingdoms days
jags of rocks peel the clouds
awesome eddies rip the shore
curled into a thousand snowdrifts
rivers   mountains   like paintings
how many champions there once were

far off I think of his lordship that year
newly married to the younger Ch'iao
brave his mien   valor flashing forth
with a feather fan and kerchief
amid talk and laughter
strong enemies scattered as ashes   blown as smoke
godlike I roam the old Kingdoms
till men of spirit must mock
my hair early blossoming white

life in the world as in a dream
a wine libation I pour to the moon in the river

David Lattimore

ROADSIDE FLOWERS, THREE POEMS WITH AN INTRODUCTION

On a trip to the Mountain of the Nine Immortals [in Lin-an] I heard the village boys singing "Roadside Flowers." The old men told me that the consort of the king of Wu-Yüeh each year in spring would always return to her old home in Lin-an. Then the king would write her a letter saying, "Roadside flowers are in bloom—no hurry, but come on home!" The people of Wu took his words and used them to make a song that is tuneful and full of feeling. When I heard it I found it very moving. But the lyrics were too countrified and so I've written new ones.

I

Roadside flowers are blooming, butterflies on the wing;
rivers and hills remain, but not the people of time gone by.
Subjects of a lost ruler, growing older year by year,
as strolling women keep singing, "No hurry, but come on home!"

II

Wild roadside flowers, blooming in boundless numbers;
along the road people vie to see her curtained carriage go by.
If only there were some way to halt spring's heedless passing—
later on, no hurry, she can go on home.

III

Wealth and honor in life were dew on the grass leaf;
now he's gone, they remember him in "Roadside Flowers."
Slow, slow his steps when the ruler left his kingdom,
and still they tell his wife, "No hurry, but come back home."

Burton Watson

READING THE POETRY OF MENG CHIAO

Night: reading Meng Chiao's poems,
characters fine as cow's hair.
By the cold lamp, my eyes blur and swim.
Good passages I rarely find—
lone flowers poking up from the mud—
but more hard words than the *Odes* or *Li sao*—

jumbled rocks clogging the clear stream,
making rapids too swift for poling.
My first impression is of eating little fishes —
what you get's not worth the trouble;
or of boiling tiny mud crabs
and ending up with some empty claws.
For refinement he might compete with monks
but he'll never match his master Han Yü.
Man's life is like morning dew,
a flame eating up the oil night by night.
Why should I strain my ears
listening to the squeaks of this autumn insect?
Better lay aside the book
and drink my cup of jade-white wine.

Burton Watson

ᘏᕬ Li Ch'ing-chao (1084?–1151?)

WRITTEN TO THE TUNE
"THE FISHERMAN'S HONOR"

The sky becomes one with its clouds,
the waves with their mist.
In Heaven's starry river, a thousand sails dance.
As if dreaming, I return to the place
where the Highest lives,
and hear a voice from the heavens:
Where am I going?
I answer, "The road is long,"
and sigh; soon the sun will be setting.
Hard to find words in poems to carry amazement:
on its ninety-thousand-mile wind,
the huge inner bird is soaring.
O wind, do not stop —
My little boat of raspberry wood
has not yet reached the Immortal Islands.

Jane Hirshfield

LYRIC TO THE TUNE "IMMORTAL BY THE RIVER"

The court is deep, deep, deep, how deep
Mists outside the window, fog beyond locked chambers
The tips of the willow, the buds on the plum coming out
Spring at home again in the trees of Mo Ling
I still a stranger within its tranquil walls

Wind, moon, how much there was to sing about
Now, aging, childless
Who could love me, haggard and thin
I've no heart to flirt at lantern festival
Even walking in the snow no longer tempts me

Julie Landau

Attributed to Li Ch'ing-chao

FLIRTATION

After kicking on the swing,
Lasciviously, I get up and rouge my palms.
Thick dew on a frail flower,
Perspiration soaks my thin dress.
A new guest enters.
My stockings come down
And my hairpins fall out.
Embarrassed, I run away,
And lean flirtatiously against the door,
Tasting a green plum.

Kenneth Rexroth and Ling Chung

Kuan Tao-sheng (1262–1319)

MARRIED LOVE

You and I
Have so much love,
That it
Burns like a fire,
In which we bake a lump of clay
Molded into a figure of you
And a figure of me.
Then we take both of them,
And break them into pieces,
And mix the pieces with water,
And mold again a figure of you,
And a figure of me.
I am in your clay.
You are in my clay.
In life we share a single quilt.
In death we will share one coffin.

Kenneth Rexroth and Ling Chung

✣ Yang Wan-li (1124–1206)

SAILING THROUGH THE GORGES

Our boat going upstream barely moves by the inch;
The dark cliffs on both sides deepen into the dusk's gloom
With a clap of thunder the heavens threaten rain;
A wind rushing in from the South Seas beyond the horizon
Angrily blasts the gorges asunder—
A hundred men shout and beat the big drums,
While a single swain flies up the towering mast.
When the sails are rigged, all hold their hands in their sleeves
And sit down to watch their boat—
  a goose feather skimming over the waters.

Kuangchi C. Chang

✣ Sun Pu-erh (b. 1124)

LYRIC

Late Indian summer's
Soft breezes fanning out,
The sun shines
On the hidden cottage
South of the river.
December, and the apricots'
First flowers open.
A person looks,
The blossoms look back:
Plain heart seeing into plain heart.

Jane Hirshfield

✣ Lu Yu (1125–1209)

I HAD OCCASION TO TELL A VISITOR ABOUT AN OLD TRIP I TOOK THROUGH THE GORGES OF THE YANGTZE

Long ago I made that journey, fall rain coming down lightly,
reached the east wall of Chien-p'ing just as gates were closing.
Host at the inn met me with greetings, words rambling on and on,
his young wife grinding and cooking in her cheap white robe.
Old boatmen who work the river, some drunk, some sobered up;
merchants from Shu, peddlers of the gorges, clever at closing a deal;

soon lamps went dark, people getting ready for bed,
though outside we could still hear boats tying up, baggage being unloaded
    from horses.
Mountains steep, rivers treacherous, barbarian tribes close by;
often I saw their mallet-shaped hairdos mingling with city folk.
Now, counting on my fingers, I find it's been forty years! —
sad memories held in my heart, truly from another incarnation.

Burton Watson

NIGHT THOUGHTS

I cannot sleep. The long, long
Night is full of bitterness.
I sit alone in my room,
Beside a smoky lamp.
I rub my heavy eyelids
And idly turn the pages
Of my book. Again and again
I trim my brush and stir the ink.
The hours go by. The moon comes
In the open window, pale
And bright like new money.
At last I fall asleep and
I dream of the days on the
River at Tsa-feng, and the
Friends of my youth in Yen Chao.
Young and happy we ran
Over the beautiful hills.
And now the years have gone by,
And I have never gone back.

Kenneth Rexroth

Kuan Han-ch'ing (c. 1300)

TO THE TUNE "A SPRAY OF FLOWERS" (NOT GIVING IN TO OLD AGE)

I've plucked every bud hanging over the wall,
and picked every roadside branch of the willow.
The flowers I plucked had the softest red petals,
the willows I picked were the tenderest green.
A rogue and a lover, I'll rely
on my picking and plucking dexterity
'til flowers are ruined and willows wrecked.

I've picked and plucked half the years of my life,
a generation entirely spent
    lying with willows, sleeping with flowers.

to "Liang-zhou"
    I'm champion rake of all the world,
    the cosmic chieftain of rogues.
    May those rosy cheeks never change,
        let them stay as they are forever.
    For among the flowers I spend my time,
    I forget my cares in wine;
    I can:
        swirl the tealeaves,
        shoot craps,
        play checkers,
        do a shell game.
    And I know whatever there is to know
        about music in every key—
    nothing sad ever touches me.
    I go with girls with silver harps
        on terraces of silver,
        who play upon their silver harps,
        and smiling, lean on silver screens.
    I go with jade white goddesses
        and take them by their jade white hands,
        then shoulder to jade white shoulder,
        we go upstairs in mansions of jade.
    I go with girls with pins of gold
        who sing their songs of golden threads,
        who raise their golden drinking cups
        and golden flagons brimming full.
    You think I'm too old!
    Forget it!
    I'm the best known lover anywhere,
        I'm center stage,
    I'm smooth,
    sharp, too!
    I'm commander in chief
        of the brocade legions
            and garrisons of flowers.
    And I've played every district and province.

to Ge-wei
    You boys are baby bunnies
        from sandy little rabbitholes
        on grassy hills,
        caught in the hunt
        for the very first time;
    I'm an ol' pheasant cock plumed with gray;
        I've been caged,

I've been snared,
a tried and true stud
    who's run the course.
I've been through ambushes, pot-shots,
    dummy spears,
and I never came out second-best.
So what if they say:
    "A man is finished at middle age" —
you think I'm going to let
    the years just slip away?

Coda
I'm a tough old bronze bean
    that can still go *boing,*
    steamed but not softened,
    stewed but not mush,
    whacked but not flattened,
    baked but not popped.
Who let you boys worm your way in-
    to the brocade noose
    of a thousand coils
    that you can't chop off
    and you can't cut down
    and you can't wriggle out
    and you can't untie?
The moon of Liang's park is what I enjoy,
Kaifeng wine is what I drink,
Luo-yang's flowers are what I like,
Zhang-tai's willows are what I pick.
Me, I can:
    recite poems,
    write ancient script,
    play all stringed instruments —
    woodwinds too;
and I can:
    sing "The Partridge,"
    dance "Dangling Hands,"
    I can hunt
    play soccer,
    play chess,
    shoot craps.
You can
    knock out my teeth,
    scrunch up my mouth,
    lame my legs,
    break both my hands;
but Heaven bestowed on me this gift
    for vice in each assorted kind,
so still I'll never quit.
Not till Yama the King of Hell
    himself gives me the call,

and demons come and nab me,
my three souls sink to Earth below,
my seven spirits float away
    into the murky dark,
then, Heaven, that's the time
I'll walk the lanes of misty flowers
    no more.

Stephen Owen

❧ Lu Chih (c. 1243–1315)

SEVENTY YEARS ARE FEW

I think a man's seventy years are few!
Of his hundred years' allotted span,
Thirty are lost.
Of his seventy years,
Ten are spent as a foolish child,
Ten are spent completely decrepit.
The fifty left divide into days and nights;
Only half have the light of day.
Wind and rain hasten one another,
The hare runs and the crow flies.
Carefully I ponder it all;
What's better than
To be happy and at ease?

Bruce Carpenter

❧ Chao Meng-fu (1254–1322)

AN ADMONITION TO MYSELF

Your teeth are loose, your head is bald,
    you're sixty-three years old;
every aspect of your life
    should make you feel ashamed.
All that's left that interests you
    are the products of your brush:
leave them behind to give the world
    something to talk about.

Jonathan Chaves

✆ Chang Yang-hao (d. c. 1340)

T'UNG PASS

Masses of mountain peaks,
waves as if in a rage —

the road to T'ung Pass
winds among mountains and rivers.

Looking west to the capital,
my heart sinks.

Where the thousand armies
of Ch'in and Han once passed,

I grieve: ten thousand palaces
ground into dust for nothing.

Dynasties rise, people suffer;
dynasties fall, people die.

Sam Hamill

8

JAPAN: THE KAMAKURA AND EARLY MUROMACHI PERIODS

Japanese

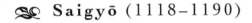 Saigyō (1118–1190)

IN A TREE STANDING

In a tree standing
Beside a desolate field,
The voice of a dove
Calling to its companions—
Lonely, terrible evening.

Donald Keene

I DON'T EVEN KNOW

I don't even know
    whose last remains they hold,
but how fearsome
    on the slopes of Toribe Hill
      are the graves in evening light!

Stephen D. Carter

OUT IN THE HIGH WAVES

Out in the high waves
    in the sea off Ashiya

a boat heads for shore:
oh that I too might make my way
so easily through the world!

Stephen Carter

♋ Kojijū (1121–1201)

ON THE SPIRIT OF THE HEART AS MOON-DISK

Merely to know
The Flawless Moon dwells pure
In the human heart
Is to find the Darkness of the night
Vanished under clearing skies.

Edwin A. Cranston

♋ Fujiwara no Yasusue (c. 1180)

NOTHING WHATSOEVER

Nothing whatsoever
Remains of you in this grass
We once used to tread;
How long ago it was we came —
The garden now is a wilderness.

Donald Keene

♋ Fujiwara no Shunzei (1114–1204)

TWO POEMS

1

Shall I see it again,
This hunting for flowers on the
Beautiful plains of Katano,
When the spring dawn comes
Over the snow of scattered blossoms?

2

The cormorant-boat
Poling down the Ōi River,

Its lanterns aglow:
How many shoals must it cross
Before the dawning of this summer night?

Valerie Durham

Former Chief Priest Jien (1155–1225)

TOO MUCH TO ASK

Too much to ask
but
as I stand
on
this forested hill,
may my
black-dyed
Buddhist robes
cover protect
all who live
in the floating world.

Howard S. Levy

"Shunzei's Daughter" (c. 1171–1241)

BURNING IN SECRET

Burning in secret,
my feelings will consume me.
And how sad to think
that even the smoke of my fire
will end as an aimless cloud.

Stephen D. Carter

Fujiwara no Teika (1162–1241)

THREE POEMS

1

Weary wild geese who came
   through skies once chilled by frost

   now head back north—
and on their departing wings
   fall the soft rains of spring.

2

   After his tryst,
   he too may be looking up
   on his way back home—
while for me a night of waiting
   ends with the dawn moon.

3

   Those long black tresses
     that I roughly pushed aside:
now strand upon strand
     they rise in my mind's eye
       each night as I lie down.

             Stephen Carter

❧ Retired Emperor Go-Toba
(1180–1239)

THERE WERE THOSE I LOVED

There were
those I loved
but
then too
those I hated—
vexing
the things
of this world
as
lone
I ponder.

    Howard S. Levy

❧ Retired Emperor Juntoku
(1197–1242)

ROYAL DWELLINGS

Royal dwellings
but

today
the eaves
are overgrown —
yearning
for the then,
living
in the now.

Howard S. Levy

〜 Jusammi Chikako (c. 1300)

MOON

On this summer night
All the household lies asleep,
And in the doorway,
For once open after dark,
Stands the moon, brilliant, cloudless.

Edwin A. Cranston

KOREA: THE KORYŎ DYNASTY

Korean

ஐ Yo Inlŏ (c. 1050–1100)

MEDITATING ON THE START OF A NEW ERA

My candle burns a flame of jade.
The peachwood comb goes through my hair
This way and that. My head is clean.
The old dead hairs fall to the ground.
I build my topknot fresh and firm.

Would that we so might comb the State
Free of her follies and her greed!
So cast aside old dead ideas
And build new strength to face our foes!

Too soon my candle gutters down.
The flame of jade is lost in grease,
And sleep drowns my desires.

Jean S. Grigsby

ஐ Cho-yong (c. 1050–1100)

SONG

I carouse all night
In moonlit fields
And return home to find,
In my bed, four legs.

Two of these legs,
I have known as they slid
Past my own two legs.
Two of these legs,
I have owned, but now
They are taken.

Michael Stephens and Okhee Yoo

∾ Anonymous (c. 1100–1150)

THINKING OF LADY YANG AT MIDNIGHT

Watching alone by the ancient city wall,
Thinking of one who was too beautiful,
What did I see? What did I hear?

Moonlight, quivering over empty courtyards,
A voice calling out of the midnight shadows.
One name, her name, echoes across the silence.
Light feet, her feet, in shoes of peacock feathers,
Dance through the empty halls. Will they never rest?

Thinking of joys that ended and sorrows which never end
I find my white robe spangled with tears for her.

Jean S. Grigsby

∾ Yi Kyubo (1168–1241)

EVENING ON THE MOUNTAIN:
SONG TO THE MOON IN THE WELL

1

Blue water ripples the well at the corner of the mossy rock.
The new moon is beautifully etched therein.
I scoop out some water but only half a shadow enters my jar.
I fear I'll bring only half the golden mirror home.

2

A mountain monk coveted the moon;
he drew water, a whole jar full;
but when he reached his temple, he discovered
that tilting the jar meant spilling the moon.

Kevin O'Rourke

✺ 10

EARLY VIETNAMESE POETRY

Sino-Vietnamese

✺ Van Hanh (d. 1018)

THE BODY OF MAN

The body of man is like a flicker of lightning
existing only to return to Nothingness.
Like the spring growth that shrivels in autumn.
Waste no thought on the process for it has no purpose,
coming and going like the dew.

Nguyen Ngoc Bich with W. S. Merwin

✺ Khuong Viet (c. 1050)

WOOD AND FIRE

Deep inside wood sleeps primal fire.
Set free, it kindles back to life.
If there's no fire locked up in wood,
where does a tinder's spark come from?

Huynh Sanh Thong

✺ Man Giac (1051–1096)

REBIRTH

Spring goes, and the hundred flowers.
Spring comes, and the hundred flowers.

My eyes watch things passing,
my head fills with years.
But when spring has gone not all the flowers follow.
Last night a plum branch blossomed by my door.

Nguyen Ngoc Bich with W. S. Merwin

Doan Van Kham (c. 1090)

REMEMBERING PRIEST QUANG TRI

Though you fled the Capital for the woods,
Your name came back—fragrance from the hills.
I used to dream of being your disciple;
Then the news: You're gone, your door is shut.
Only sad birdcries in the empty moonlight outside your hut.
Who will compose the epitaph for your grave?
Reverend friends, do not grieve. Look round this temple:
In rivers and mountains, his face still shines.

Nguyen Ngoc Bich

Tran Nhan-tong

SPRING VIEW

The willows trail such glory that the birds are struck dumb.
Evening clouds balance above the eave-shaded hall.
A friend comes, not for conversation,
But to lean on the balustrade and watch the turquoise sky.

Nguyen Ngoc Bich

Nguyen Trai (1380–1442)

A PLOUGH AND A SPADE

A plough and a spade, that's all,
A row of chrysanthemums, and orchids,
A place to plant beans: that's all I need
Friends come, birds sing and flowers wave: welcome!
The moon walks with me when I fetch water for tea.
Old Po Yi stayed pure and stayed happy,
Yen-tzu stayed poor and liked it.
Let the world buzz,
I need no praise, I am deaf to laughter.

Nguyen Ngoc Bich

THE BAMBOO HUT

A bamboo hut and a plum tree bower —
That's where I spend my days, far from the world's talk.
For meals, only some pickled cabbage,
But I've never cared for the life of damask and silk.
There's a pool of water for watching the moon,
And land to plough into flower beds.
Sometimes I feel inspired on snowy nights —
That's when I write my best poems, and sing.

Nguyen Ngoc Bich

❧ Emperor Le Thanh-tong (1142–1497)

STICK AND HAT

They're insignificant when not in use,
But work wonders when properly employed.
In times of peril, sticks strong and true defend the realm;
Whatever the weather, all take shelter beneath their wide-woven hats.
The stick preserves the peace and plenty of the land,
The hat gives shade and refuge to the world.
What marvels they make possible, when used this way:
The hand wields power, as the head directs and leads.

John S. Major (after Huynh Sanh Thong)

THE STONE DOG

With a heavy paw he guards the frontier,
Squatting alone in the middle of the pass,
Paying no heed to the snow or frost,
Never asking for good food or payment.
Staring straight at the visitors' faces,
He is above listening to their gossiping tongues.
With one mind he serves his lord.
A thousand-weight strong, he cannot be swayed.

Nguyen Ngoc Bich

INDIA: SECULAR AND SACRED LYRIC VERSE

Kannaða

⁊ Devara Dasimayya (c. 1000)

THE TATTERED SACK

A man filled grain
in a tattered sack
and walked all night
fearing the toll-gates

but the grain went through the tatters
and all he got was the gunny sack.

It is thus
with the devotion
of the faint-hearted

O Rāmanātha.

A. K. Ramanujan

⁊ Mahadeviyakka (c. 1130–1180)

LIKE AN ELEPHANT

Like an elephant
lost from his herd
suddenly captured,

remembering his mountains,
   his Vindhyas,
     I remember.

A parrot
come into a cage
remembering his mate,
     I remember.

O lord white as jasmine
show me
your ways.
    Call me: Child, come here,
      come this way.

A. K. Ramanujan

A VEIN OF SAPPHIRES

A vein of sapphires
hides in the earth,
a sweetness in fruit;

and in plain-looking rock
lies a golden ore,
and in seeds,
the treasure of oil.

Like these,
the Infinite
rests concealed in the heart.

No one can see the ways
of our jasmine-white Lord.

Jane Hirshfield

I DO NOT CALL IT HIS SIGN

I do not call it his sign,
I do not call it becoming one with his sign.
I do not call it union,
I do not call it harmony with union.
I do not say something has happened,
I do not say nothing has happened.
I will not name it You,
I will not name it I.

Now that the White Jasmine Lord is myself,
What use for words at all?

Jane Hirshfield

Sanskrit

✥ Kshemendra (c. 1150)

From KAVIKANTHABHARANA

A poet should learn with his eyes
the forms of leaves
he should know how to make
people laugh when they are together
he should get to see
what they are really like
he should know about oceans and mountain
in themselves
and the sun and the moon and the stars
his mind should enter into the seasons
he should go
among many people
in many places
and learn their languages

W. S. Merwin and J. Moussaieff Masson

✥ Jayadeva (ca. 1200)

From THE GITAGOVINDA

Song of Krishna: The Fourth Song, Sung with Raga "Ramakari"

Yellow silk and wildflower garlands lie on dark sandaloiled skin.
Jewel earrings dangling in play ornament his smiling cheeks.
    Hari revels here as the crowd of charming girls
    Revels in seducing him to play.

One cowherdess with heavy breasts embraces Hari lovingly
And celebrates him in a melody of love.
    Hari revels here as the crowd of charming girls
    Revels in seducing him to play.

Another simple girl, lured by his wanton quivering look,
Meditates intently on the lotus face of Madhu's killer.

Hari revels here as the crowd of charming girls
Revels in seducing him to play.

A girl with curving hips, bending to whisper in his ear,
Cherishes her kiss on her lover's tingling cheek.
  Hari revels here as the crowd of charming girls
  Revels in seducing him to play.

Eager for the art of his love on the Jumna riverbank, a girl
Pulls his silk cloth toward a thicket of reeds with her hand.
  Hari revels here as the crowd of charming girls
  Revels in seducing him to play.

Hari praises a girl drunk from dancing in the rite of love,
With beating palms and ringing bangles echoing his flute's low tone.
  Hari revels here as the crowd of charming girls
  Revels in seducing him to play.

He hugs one, he kisses another, he caresses another dark beauty.
He stares at one's suggestive smiles, he mimics a willful girl.
  Hari revels here as the crowd of charming girls
  Revels in seducing ihm to play.

The wondrous mystery of Krishna's sexual play in Brindaban forest
Is Jayadeva's song. Let its celebration spread Krishna's favors!
  Hari revels here as the crowd of charming girls
  Revels in seducing him to play.

> When he quickens all things
> To create bliss in the world,
> His soft black sinuous lotus limbs
> Begin the festival of love
> And beautiful cowherd girls wildly
> Wind him in their bodies.
> Friend, in spring young Hari plays
> Like erotic mood incarnate.
>
> Winds from sandalwood mountains
> Blow now toward Himalayan peaks,
> Longing to plunge in the snows
> After weeks of writhing
> In the hot bellies of ground snakes.
> Melodious voices of cuckoos
> Raise their joyful sound
> When they spy the buds
> On tips of smooth mango branches.

Barbara Stoler Miller

Hinði

⚮ Anonymous (c. 1250)

From THE MANTREYA UPANISHAD

"I am I, but also the other.
   I am Brahman, I am the source.
I am the teacher of the whold world.
   I am the whole world.
      I am he!

"I am only I, I am perfect.
   I am pure, I am supreme.
I am spotless and eternal.
   I am I.
      I am always he!

"I am wisdom, I am special.
   I am the moon, I am complete.
I am splendid, I am without grief.
   I am spirit.
      I am the same!

"From honor and dishonor,
   and from qualities I am free.
      I am ŚIVA!
From oneness and duality
   and from opposites I am free.
      I am he!

"From coming into being and ceasing to be
   and from light I am free.
      I shine!
I am the power of the void and the non-void,
   I am both ugly and beautiful.

"I am free from the equal and the unequal.
   I am pure and sempiternal.
   I am the eternal ŚIVA!
I am free from the All and the Non-all.
   I have the nature of goodness.
      I always am!

"I am free from the number one,
   and I do not have the number two.
I am free from the distinction

of being and non-being.
    I am without thoughts.

"I distinguish not between selves,
    For I embody complete bliss.
I am not, I am not another.
    I have no body and the like.

"I have no refuge; I am no refuge.
    I do not have a support.
        From bondage and from freedom I am free.
    I am pure. I am Brahman.
        I am he!

"I am without mind and all such things.
    I am the highest, higher than highest.
I am ever reflective thought.
    Yet I reflect not.
        I am he!

Patrick Olivelle

❧ 12

MAYAN POETRY: THE POPUL VUH

Mayan

❧ Anonymous

From THE POPUL VUH (DATE UNKNOWN)

Two Hymns

1

    Truly now,
double thanks, triple thanks
that we've been formed, we've been given
our mouths, our faces,
we speak, we listen,
we wonder, we move,
our knowledge is good, we've understood
what is far and near,
and we've seen what is great and small
under the sky, on the earth.
Thanks to you we've been formed,
we've come to be made and modeled,
our grandmother, our grandfather,

2

    Wait!
thou Maker, thou Modeler,
look at us, listen to us,
don't let us fall, don't leave us aside,
thou god in the sky, on the earth,
Heart of Sky, Heart of Earth,
give us our sign, our word,

as long as there is day, as long as there is light.
When it comes to the sowing, the dawning,
will it be a greening road, a greening path?
Give us a steady light, a level place,
a good light, a good place,
a good life and beginning.
Give us all of this, thou Hurricane,
Newborn Thunderbolt, Raw Thunderbolt,
Newborn Nanahuac, Raw Nanahuac,
Falcon, Hunahpu,
Sovereign Plumed Serpent,
Bearer, Begetter,
Xpiyacoc, Xmucane,
Grandmother of Day, Grandmother of Light,
when it comes to the sowing, the dawning.

Dennis Tedlock

Part V

THE
RENAISSANCE
IN EUROPE;

LATE TRADITIONAL
VERSE FROM THE
AMERICAS, SOUTH ASIA,
AND EAST ASIA
(1350–1625)

When the twenty-five-year-old Thomas Wyatt, returning to England from a diplomatic mission to the Pope in Italy, escaped capture en route by Spanish troops, his baggage included copies of the fourteenth-century sonnets of Petrarch. The fourteen iambic pentameter lines of the sonnet, divided into an octave and sestet, focused on a single sentiment, migrated through numerous formal variations long after Wyatt recast Petrarch's unattainable Laura as Anne Boleyn and turned the sonnets into English.

Shakespearean, Spenserian, and a later Miltonic type of the sonnet united the break in sense between octave and sestet into a unified whole. In the hands of such poets, the conflict between the desire for a "Laura" and the laurels of fame gave an exquisite and stylized tension to the Petrarchian tradition that dominated European poetry for centuries. Ambassadors and diplomatists in the Renaissance were couriers for new forms of poetry and the revival of classical learning: Renaissance Humanism, the New Learning, and its secularization of social and individual life endowed the Renaissance Man, as accomplished in the world as in his art, as the poet *par excellence* of the age.

Diplomats like Wyatt, who passed in 1537 through Lyons, where Louise Labé and Maurice Scève took part in the school of poetry known as the Pléiade, carved out the trade routes for the poetry of the Renaissance. Labé's sonnets and elegies express the webbed nets of an unhappy love and the intricate games and masques of the Renaissance that disguised them in festival. The force and éclat of the Pléiade (a group of seven young French poets who took their name from a cluster of stars familiar to navigators) dominated French poetry. Many of them served as ambassadors, like Ronsard in Scotland and du Bellay in Rome, and maintained their attachment to the sonnet form and its timeless themes of perishable roses, intimate friendship, and witty conversation. Two versions of a single poem in Ronsard's *Four Sonnets to Helen* are included here. One is Yeats's free adaptation, which turns it into an address to Maude Gonne, a woman he identified in her destructive twentieth-century apparition with Helen of Troy. Humbert Wolfe's translation continues the original thrust of Ronsard's poem.

The poets of the Elizabethan and Jacobean Age of England understood, in their master passion for beauty, wealth, and power, the great mission of translation. Christopher Marlowe, gripped by the Faustian love of learning and the desire to cross the boundaries of language, translated Ovid; Edmund Spenser was in flamboyant competition with the example of Italy and the Continent.

Poets in this era of spies, informers, and fellow courtiers of dubious loyalty often took refuge in translating the past. Some employed not only translation but the subversive forms of the classical world, like Thomas More, the lawyer and lord chancelor under Henry VIII who turned, like many of the civil servants in the history of literature, to the epigram to solve the task of speaking plainly at a dangerous time. (Even Fulke Greville's poem celebrating the supernatural Merlin's unholy laughter at the death of a mortal brother seems to have the elements of a cipher.) But many poems in this section are not easily categorized. W. H. Auden considered John Skelton's inspired doggerel "Upon a Dead Man's Head," written in a springy, supple, and at last colloquial English, the greatest poem of an age, "between two worlds, one dead, the other powerless to be born." And Shakespeare is Shakespeare: an infintesimal portion of his work here stands in for the whole.

The idea of courtly love, grounded in the psychology of the troubadour, now merged with the notion of Platonic love, just as the hunt, instead of providing the feudal table with game, became the sport of noblemen. One of the greatest poems of the Italian revival of classical learning, Angelo Poliziano's "The Tournament," remodels the images of classical texts in enameled vignettes from Hesiod, Homer, and Ovid, while borrowing a Renaissance pictorial vision of the scattering of flowers, gold, birdsong, and leaves over everything in sight. The translator proposes Uccello's *Hunting Scene* as the ideal illustration of this chase.

The map of Renaissance poetry included Portugal, Poland, and just over its horizons, a view of the New World. Street brawls, intrigues, prison, the scaffold, and early death were the material concerns of poets like Sir Walter Raleigh and the one-eyed Luis de Camões, banished courtier and common soldier. Camões was the author of numerous sonnets and *cançoes*, and of a national epic of Portugal that dealt, through classical allusion to Venus and Dionysus, with the exploits of Vasco de Gama's voyage to India. The greatest poet of the Slavic world, a region slow to abandon Latin as a literary language, was Jan Kochanowski. Devastated by the loss of his small daughter, he virtually invented Polish poetry. Friend of Ronsard and civil servant at the court of Szigismund II, he imported the epigram as the Polish *fraska*, participated in the exhilaration of the New Learning through his versions of the Psalms, and wrote the series of Laments for the death of Ursula that broke the literary conventions of 1580.

The boundaries between the poetry of the Renaissance and that of the baroque era are porous. But in the next age, the sonnet began to refract the wrenching divisions and devotional flights of the Counter-Reformation; alchemical experiments and early explorations of the round earth yielded to Newton's "voyage through strange seas of thought" and the settlement of the New World.

K. W.

The Aztec Empire, built on military conquest and human sacrifice, flourished during the fifteenth century before falling to the Spanish. Soon afterward the Franciscan priest Fray Bernardino de Sahagún collected as much literature and lore as he could in Nahuatl, the Aztec language. Many of the short poems collected by Sahagún are attributed to Nezahualcoyotl, ruler of an Aztec principality; their air of resignation reflects a society in which a warrior's highest aim was to achieve a "flowery death" on the battlefield. In this section also are a short excerpt from the Maya prophetic poem of Chilam Balam, and two Inca poems collected shortly after the Spanish Conquest.

The Indian poetry in Part V is drawn from the work of four *bakhti* poets, including Mirabai, one of India's most famous women poets, and Kabir, whose verbal cleverness and undogmatic religious ideas have made him perhaps India's most-translated poet.

Chinese poetry of the Ming period is on the whole undistinguished; among the exceptions, well represented here, are works by women poets like Yang Wen-li and Liang Te-sheng, who were known for their expressive and highly personal verse. Korean poetry flourished in the sixteenth century with the development of *sijo*, three-line poems that put a premium on word play and wit, popular with *kisaeng* female professional entertainers and their wealthy clients. Vietnamese verse during this period continued to proclaim its vernacular independence from China and to draw on earthy folk traditions for verse that is often startlingly bold and funny. Japan, which spent the sixteenth century wracked by civil war, is represented here by works of two Zen monks, along with two shamanic poems from an old collection in Okinawan.

J. S. M.

ENGLISH POETRY: CHAUCER THROUGH SPENSER AND SHAKESPEARE

English

❧ Geoffrey Chaucer (1343–1400)

BALLADE

Hide, Absalom, thy gilte tresses clear;
    Esther, lay thou meekness all a-down;
Hide, Jonathan, all thy friendly mannér;
    Penelope and Marcia Catóun
    Make of your wifehood no comparisón;
        Hide ye your beauties, Isolde and Elaine:
        My lady com'th, that all this may distain.

Thy fairë body let it not appear,
    Lavine; and thou, Lucrece of Romë town,
And Polixene, that broughten love so dear,
    And Cleopatre, with all thy passión,
    Hide ye your truth of love and your renown;
        And thou, Thisbe, that hast for love such pain:
        My lady com'th, that all this may distain.

Hero, Dido, Laodámia, all y-fere,
    And Phyllis, hanging for thy Demophon,
And Cánacé, espièd by thy chere,
    Hypsípylé, betraysèd with Jasón,
    Make of your truthë neither boast ne soun;
        Nor Hypermestre or Ariadne, ye twain:
        My lady com'th, that all this may distain.

From TROILUS AND CRESEYDE

Conclusion

Go, little book, go, my little tragedy
There where God, before your maker dies,
May send him, there to write some comedy!
But never, little book, never envy
Authors, bow to all great poetry,
Kissing the steps where Lucan walked, and where
Vergil walked too, and Statius, Ovid, Homer.

And since our English talks in many tongues,
Spoken and written, everywhere different, I pray
To God that no one, unknowing, scans you wrong,
Reads you aloud in some outlandish way—
But lettered, or read, or sung, it makes no difference,
So long as your sense is clear, oh God I beseech!
—And now, back to my story; I'd started this speech:

Troilus' anger, my story began to tell,
Cost the Greeks more than they had bargained for.
His quick hands sent thousands rolling to hell.
No one could match him, no one on the Trojan side
But Hector, while Hector could breathe and use his eyes.
But oh, he hung, all hangs, on God's sweet will
Whom fierce Achilles caught up with to kill.

And Troilus, after this fierce, this bitter death,
Ascended, a joyful spirit, a passing breath
Of light, high to the eighth and final sphere,
And earth, and water, and air, and fire stayed here;
And there he saw, and stared, and went on staring
At the erratic stars, and with his ears
Listened to the music of the heavenly spheres.

And then he turned, eager, anxious to watch
This tiny bit of ground, this earth, all washed
And held by the sea, and learn'd, at once, how botched
And miserable a world we hold, how couched
In heaven, he'd changed vanity for bliss, the best,
Most perfect bliss; and finally he sought
The field where his body lay, and stared, and thought.

And then he laughed and laughed, seeing the tears
Shed for his death, and the men who mourned his going;
And all we do for blind desire, or fear,
Or hate, or earthly love, is all unknown
In heaven, and heaven is all our hearts need know.
And off he went, to cut my story short,
To live where Mercury sets his house and court.

And that was the end of Troilus, who lived for love!
And that was the end of all his mighty virtue!
And that was the end of royalty, flown above!
And that was the end of desire, the end of worth, too!
And that was the end of earthly fickleness! And how
Troilus met Creseyde, how they loved, you've read
In this book, and how Troilus passed this life, now dead.

Burton Raffel and Selden Rodman

✢ John Skelton (1460–1529)

UPON A DEAD MAN'S HEAD

Skelton Laureat Upon a dead man's head, that was sent to him from an honorable gentlewoman for a token, devised this ghostly meditation in English, convenable in sentence, commendable, lamentable, lacrymable, profitable for the soul.

Your ugly token
My mind hath broken
From worldly lust;
For I have discust
We are but dust,
And die we must.
    It is generall
    To be mortall:
I have well espied
No man may him hide
From Death hollow-eyed,
With sinews widered
And bones shidered,
With his worm-eaten maw,
And his gastly jaw
Gasping aside,
Naked of hide,
Neither flesh nor fell.
    Then by my councell,
Look that ye spell
Well this gospell:
For whereso we dwell
Death doth us quell,
And with us mell.
For all our pampered paunches,
There may be no fraunchise,
Nor worldly bliss,
Redeem us from this:
Our days be dated,
To be checkmated

With draughtès of death,
Stopping our breath,
Our eyen sinking,
Our bodies stinking,
Our gummès grinning,
Our soulès brinning.
To whom, then shall we sue,
For to have rescúe,
But to sweet Jesu,
On us for to rue?
     O goodly child.
Of Mary mild,
Then be our shield!
That we be not exiled
To the dine dale
Of bootless bale,
Nor to the lake
Of fiendès black.
But grant us grace
To see thy face,
And to purcháse
Thine heavenly place,
And thy paláce,
Full of solace,
Above the sky
That is so high;
Eternally
To behold and see
The Trinity!
          Amen.
Myrrez vous y.

William Dunbar (1460–1520)

OF THE CHANGES OF LIFE

I seek about this world unstable
to find one faithful moral fable,
but I cannot for all my wit
so true one maxim find of it
but say, it is deceivable.

For yesterday I did declare
how that the season soft and fair
came in as fresh as peacock feather.
This day it stings me like an adder.
Things conclude me *au contraire.*

Yesterday fair upsprang the flowers,
this day they are all slain with shears;
and fowls in forests that sang clear
now wake up with a dreary cheer.
Full cold are both their beds and bowers.

Next after summer, winter lean,
next after comfort, care keen;
next to dark midnight, mirthful morrow;
next after joy cometh sorrow.
So is this world and ever has been.

Andrew Glaze

Anonymous (c. 1450)

THE BRIDAL MORN

The maidens came
   When I was in my mother's bower;
I had all that I would.
     The bailey beareth the bell away;
     The lily, the rose, the rose I lay.
The silver is white, red is the gold;
The robes they lay in fold.
     The bailey beareth the bell away;
     The lily, the rose, the rose I lay.
And through the glass window shines the sun.
How should I love, and I so young?
     The bailey beareth the bell away;
     The lily, the rose, the rose I lay.

Anonymous (c. 1400–1500)

A LYKE-WAKE DIRGE

This ae nighte, this ae nighte,
   Every nighte and alle;
Fire and sleete, and candle lighte,
   And Christe receive thye saule.

When thou from hence away are past
   Every nighte and alle;
To Whinny-muir thou comest at laste;
   And Christe receive thye saule.

If ever thou gavest hosen and shoon,
    Every nighte and alle;
Sit thee down, and put them on;
    And Christe receive thye saule.

If hosen and shoon thou ne'er gavest nane,
    Every nighte and alle;
The whinnes shall pricke thee to the bare bane
    And Christe receive thye saule.

From Whinny-muir when thou mayst passe,
    Every nighte and alle;
To Brigg o' Dread thou comest at laste;
    And Christ receive thye saule.

From Brigg o' Dread when thou mayst passe,
    Every nighte and alle;
To purgatory fire thou comest at laste,
    And Christe receive thye saule.

If ever thou gavest meate or drinke,
    Every nighte and alle;
The fire shall never make thee shrinke,
    And Christe receive thye saule.

If meate or drinke thou never gavest nane,
    Every nighte and alle;
The fire will burn thee to the bare bane;
    And Christe receive thye saule.

This ae nighte, this ae nighte,
    Every nighte and alle;
Fire and sleete, and candle lighte,
    And Christe receive thye saule.

✸ Anonymous (c. 1500)

WESTERN WIND

Western wind, when will thou blow,
    The small rain down can rain?
Christ, if my love were in my arms
    And I in my bed again!

❧ Anonymous (c. 1500)

THE UNQUIET GRAVE

The wind doth blow today, my love,
    And a few small drops of rain.
I never had but one true-love,
    In cold grave she was lain.

I'll do as much for my true-love
    As any young man may,
I'll sit and mourn all at her grave
    For a twelvemonth and a day.

The twelvemonth and a day being up,
    The dead began to speak:
Oh who sits weeping on my grave,
    And will not let me sleep?

'Tis I, my love, sits on your grave,
    And will not let you sleep,
For I crave one kiss of your clay-cold lips,
    And that is all I seek.

You crave one kiss of my clay-cold lips,
    But my breath smells earthy strong.
If you have one kiss of my clay-cold lips,
    Your time will not be long.

'Tis down in yonder garden green,
    Love, where we used to walk,
The finest flower that ere was seen
    Is withered to a stalk.

The stalk is withered dry, my love,
    So will our hearts decay.
So make yourself content, my love,
    Till God calls you away.

❧ Sir Thomas Wyatt (1503–1542)

MY LUTE, AWAKE

My lute, awake! perform the last
Labor that thou and I shall waste
And end that I have now begun,
For when this song is sung and past,
My lute, be still, for I have done.

As to be heard where ear is none,
As lead to grave in marble stone,
My song may pierce her heart as soon.
Should we then sigh or sing or moan?
No, no, my lute, for I have done.

The rocks do not so cruelly
Repulse the waves continually
As she my suit and affection,
So that I am past remedy,
Whereby my lute and I have done.

Proud of the spoil that thou hast got
Of simple hearts through love's shot,
By whom, unkind, thou hast them won,
Think not he hath his bow forgot,
Although my lute and I have done.

Vengeance shall fall on thy disdain
That makest but game on earnest pain;
Think not alone under the sun
Unquit to cause thy lovers plain
Although my lute and I have done.

Perchance thee lie withered and old
The winter nights that are so cold,
Plaining in vain unto the moon;
Thy wishes then dare not be told.
Care then who list, for I have done.

And then may chance thee to repent
The time that thou hast lost and spent
To cause thy lovers sigh and swoon;
Then shalt thou know beauty but lent,
And wish and want as I have done.

Now cease, my lute; this is the last
Labor that thou and I shall waste
And ended is that we begun.
Now is this song both sung and past;
My lute, be still, for I have done.

⚏ Edmund Spenser (1552–1599)

PROTHALAMION

Calme was the day, and through the trembling ayre,
Sweete breathing *Zephyrus* did softly play
A gentle spirit, that lightly did delay

Hot *Titans* beames, which then did glyster fayre:
When I whom sullein care,
Through discontent of my long fruitlesse stay
In Princes Court, and expectation vayne
Of idle hopes, which still doe fly away,
Like empty shaddowes, did aflict my brayne,
Walkt forth to ease my payne
Along the shoare of siluer streaming *Themmes*,
Whose rutty Bancke, the which his Riuer hemmes,
Was paynted all with variable flowers,
And all the meades adornd with daintie gemmes,
Fit to decke maydens bowres,
And crowne their Paramours,
Against the Brydale day, which is not long:
    Sweete *Themmes* runne softly, till I end my Song.

There, in a Meadow, by the Riuers side,
A Flocke of *Nymphes* I chaunced to espy,
All louely Daughters of the Flood thereby,
With goodly greenish locks all lose vntyde,
As each had bene a Bryde,
And each one had a little wicker basket,
Made of fine twigs entrayled curiously,
In which they gathered flowers to fill their flasket:
And with fine Fingers, cropt full feateously
The tender stalkes on hye.
Of euery sort, which in that Meadow grew,
They gathered some; the Violet pallid blew,
The little Dazie, that at euening closes,
The virgin Lillie, and the Primrose trew,
With store of vermeil Roses,
To decke their Bridegromes posies,
Against the Brydale day, which was not long:
    Sweete *Themmes* runne softly, till I end my Song.

With that, I saw two Swannes of goodly hewe,
Come softly swimming downe along the Lee;
Two fairer Birds I yet did neuer see:
The snow which doth the top of *Pindus* strew,
Did neuer whiter shew,
Nor *Ioue* himselfe when he a Swan would be
For loue of *Leda*, whiter did appeare:
Yet *Leda* was they say as white as he,
Yet not so white as these, nor nothing neare;
So purely white they were,
That euen the gentle streame, the which them bare,
Seem'd foule to them, and bad his billowes spare
To wet their silken feathers, least they might
Soyle their fayre plumes with water not so fayre
And marre their beauties bright,
That shone as heauens light,

Against their Brydale day, which was not long:
    Sweete *Themmes* runne softly, till I end my Song.

Eftsoones the *Nymphes*, which now had Flowers their fill,
Ran all in haste, to see that siluer brood,
As they came floating on the Christal Flood.
Whom when they sawe, they stood amazed still,
Their wondring eyes to fill,
Them seem'd they neuer saw a sight so fayre,
Of Fowles so louely, that they sure did deeme
Them heauenly borne, or to be that same payre
Which through the Skie draw *Venus* siluer Teeme,
For sure they did not seeme
To be begot of any earthly Seede,
But rather Angels or of Angels breede:
Yet were they bred of *Somers-heat* they say,
In sweetest Season, when each Flower and weede
The earth did fresh aray,
So fresh they seem'd as day,
Euen as their Brydale day, which was not long:
    Sweete *Themmes* runne softly, till I end my Song.

Then forth they all out of their baskets drew,
Great store of Flowers, the honour of the field,
That to the sense did fragrant odours yeild,
All which vpon those goodly Birds they threw,
And all the Waues did strew,
That like old *Peneus* Waters they did seeme,
When downe along by pleasant *Tempes* shore
Scattred with Flowres, through *Thessaly* they streeme,
That they appeare through Lillies plenteous store,
Like a Brydes Chamber flore:
Two of those *Nymphes*, meane while, two Garlands bound,
Of freshest Flowres which in that Mead they found,
The which presenting all in trim Array,
Their snowie Foreheads therewithall they crownd,
Whil'st one did sing this Lay,
Prepar'd against that Day,
Against their Brydale day, which was not long:
    Sweete *Themmes* runne softly, till I end my Song.

Ye gentle Birdes, the worlds faire ornament,
And heauens glorie, whom this happie hower
Doth leade vnto your louers blisfull bower,
Ioy may you haue and gentle hearts content
Of your loues couplement:
And let faire *Venus*, that is Queene of loue,
With her heart-quelling Sonne vpon you smile,
Whose smile they say, hath vertue to remoue
All Loues dislike, and friendships faultie guile
For euer to assoile.

Let endlesse Peace your steadfast hearts accord,
And blessed Plentie wait vpon your bord,
And let your bed with pleasures chast abound,
That fruitfull issue may to you afford,
Which may your foes confound,
And make your ioyes redound,
Vpon your Brydale day, which is not long:
    Sweete *Themmes* run softlie, till I end my Song.

So ended she; and all the rest around
To her redoubled that her vndersong,
Which said, their bridale daye should not be long.
And gentle Eccho from the neighbour ground,
Their accents did resound.
So forth those ioyous Birdes did passe along,
Adowne the Lee, that to them murmurde low,
As he would speake, but that he lackt a tong
Yeat did by signes his glad affection show,
Making his streame run slow.
And all the foule which in his flood did dwell
Gan flock about these twaine, that did excell
The rest, so far, as *Cynthia* doth shend
The lesser starres. So they enranged well,
Did on those two attend,
And their best seruice lend,
Against their wedding day, which was not long:
    Sweete *Themmes* run softly, till I end my Song.

At length they all to mery *London* came,
To mery London, my most kyndly Nurse,
That to me gaue this Lifes first natiue sourse:
Though from another place I take my name,
An house of auncient fame.
There when they came, whereas those bricky towres,
The which on *Themmes* brode aged backe doe ryde,
Where now the studious Lawyers haue their bowers,
There whylome wont the Templer Knights to byde,
Till they decayd through pride:
Next whereunto there standes a stately place,
Where oft I gayned giftes and goodly grace
Of that great Lord, which therein wont to dwell,
Whose want too well now feeles my freendles case:
But Ah here fits not well
Olde woes but ioyes to tell
Against the Brydale daye, which is not long:
    Sweete *Themmes* runne softly, till I end my Song.

Yet therein now doth lodge a noble Peer,
Great *Englands* glory and the Worlds wide wonder,
Whose dreadfull name, late through all *Spaine* did thunder,
And *Hercules* two pillors standing neere,

Did make to quake and feare:
Faire branch of Honor, flower of Cheualrie,
That fillest *England* with thy triumphs fame,
Ioy haue thou of thy noble victorie,
And endlesse happinesse of thine owne name
That promiseth the same:
That through thy prowesse and victorious armes,
Thy country may be freed from forraine harmes:
And great *Elisaes* glorious name may ring
Through al the world, fil'd with thy wide Alarmes,
Which some braue muse may sing
To ages following,
Vpon the Brydale day, which is not long:
    Sweete *Themmes* runne softly, till I end my Song.

From those high Towers, this noble Lord issuing,
Like Radiant *Hesper* when his golden hayre
In th'*Ocean* billowes he hath Bathed fayre,
Descended to the Riuers open vewing,
With a great traine ensuing.
Aboue the rest were goodly to bee seene
Two gentle Knights of louely face and feature
Beseeming well the bower of anie Queen,
With gifts of wit and ornaments of nature,
Fit for so goodly stature:
That like the twins of *Ioue* they seem'd in sight,
Which decke the Bauldricke of the Heauens bright.
They two forth pacing to the Riuers side,
Receiued those two faire Brides, their Loues delight,
Which at th'appointed tyde,
Each one did make his Bryde,
Against their Brydale day, which is not long:
    Sweete *Themmes* runne softly, till I end my Song.

∞ Sir Walter Raleigh (1552–1618)

SIR WALTER RALEIGH TO HIS SON

Three things there be that prosper up apace
And flourish, whilst they grow asunder far,
But on a day, they meet all in one place,
And when they meet, they one another mar;
And they be these: the wood, the weed, the wag.
The wood is that which makes the gallow tree;
The weed is that which strings the hangman's bag;
The wag, my pretty knave, betokeneth thee.
Mark well, dear boy, whilst these assemble not,
Green springs the tree, hemp grows, the wag is wild,
But when they meet, it makes the timber rot;

It frets the halter, and it chokes the child.
Then bless thee, and beware, and let us pray
We part not with thee at this meeting day.

✼ Fulke Greville, Lord Brooke (1554–1628)

MERLIN, THEY SAY

Merlin, they say, an English Prophet borne,
When he was young and govern'd by his Mother,
Took great delight to laugh such fooles to scorne
As thought, by Nature we might know a Brother.

His Mother chid him oft, till on a day,
They stood, and saw a Coarse to buriall carried,
The Father teares his beard, doth weepe and pray;
The Mother was the woman he had married.

Merlin laughs out aloud in stead of crying;
His Mother chides him for that childish fashion;
Sayes, Men must mourne the dead, themselves are dying,
Good manners doth make answer unto passion.

The Child (for children see what should be hidden)
Replies unto his Mother by and by,
'Mother, if you did know, and were forbidden,
'Yet you would laugh as heartily, as I.'

✼ Chidiock Tichborne (1558?–1586)

ON THE EVE OF HIS EXECUTION

My prime of youth is but a frost of cares,
    My feast of joy is but a dish of pain,
My crop of corn is but a field of tares,
    And all my good is but vain hope of gain;
        The day is past, and yet I saw no sun,
        And now I live, and now my life is done.

My tale was heard and yet it was not told,
    My fruit is fallen, yet my leaves are green,
My youth is spent and yet I am not old,
    I saw the world and yet I was not seen;
        My thread is cut and yet it is not spun,
        And now I live, and now my life is done.

I sought my death and found it in my womb,
    I looked for life and saw it was a shade,
I trod the earth and knew it was my tomb,
    And now I die, and now I was but made;
        My glass is full, and now my glass is run,
        And now I live, and now my life is done.

Robert Southwell (1561–1595)

THE BURNING BABE

As I in hoary winter's night
    Stood shivering in the snow,
Surprised I was with sudden heat
    Which made my heart to glow;
And lifting up a fearful eye
    To view what fire was near,
A pretty babe all burning bright
    Did in the air appear;
Who scorchèd with excessive heat,
    Such floods of tears did shed,
As though His floods should quench His flames,
    Which with His tears were bred:
'Alas!' quoth He, 'but newly born
    In fiery heats I fry,
Yet none approach to warm their hearts
    Or feel my fire but I!

'My faultless breast the furnace is;
    The fuel, wounding thorns;
Love is the fire, and sighs the smoke;
    The ashes, shames and scorns;
The fuel Justice layeth on.

    And Mercy blows the coals,
The metal in this furnace wrought
    Are men's defilèd souls:
For which, as now on fire I am
    To work them to their good,
So will I melt into a bath,
    To wash them in my blood.'
With this He vanish'd out of sight
    And swiftly shrunk away,
And straight I callèd unto mind
    That it was Christmas Day.

ᦉ Mark Alexander Boyd (1563–1601)

SONNET

Fra bank to bank, fra wood to wood I rin,
　Ourhailit with my feeble fantasie;
Like til a leaf that fallis from a tree,
　Or til a reed ourblowin with the win.

Twa gods guides me: the ane of tham is blin,
　Yea and a bairn brocht up in vanitie;
　The next a wife ingenrit of the sea,
And lichter nor a dauphin with her fin.

Unhappy is the man for evermair
　That tills the sand and sawis in the air;

　But twice unhappier is he, I lairn,
That feidis in his hairt a mad desire,
And follows on a woman throw the fire,
　Led by a blind and teachit by a bairn.

ᦉ Christopher Marlowe (1564–1593)

THE PASSIONATE SHEPHERD TO HIS LOVE

Come live with me and be my love,
And we will all the pleasures prove
That valleys, groves, hills, and fields,
Woods, or steepy mountain yields.

And we will sit upon the rocks,
Seeing the shepherds feed their flocks
By shallow rivers, to whose falls
Melodious birds sing madrigals.

And I will make thee beds of roses
And a thousand fragrant posies;
A cap of flowers and a kirtle
Embroidered all with leaves of myrtle;

A gown made of the finest wool
Which from our pretty lambs we pull;
Fair linèd slippers for the cold,
With buckles of the purest gold;

A belt of straw and ivy buds,
With coral clasps and amber studs.

And if these pleasures may thee move,
Come live with me and be my Love.

The shepherds' swains shall dance and sing
For thy delight each May morning.
If these delights thy mind may move,
Then live with me and be my Love.

﹏ William Shakespeare (1564–1616)

From CYMBELINE

Fear no more the heat of the sun,
   Nor the furious winter's rages;
Thou thy worldly task hast done,
   Home art gone and ta'en thy wages.
Golden lads and girls all must,
As chimney-sweepers come to dust.

Fear no more the frown o' the great,
   Thou art past the tyrant's stroke;
Care no more to clothe and eat;
   To thee the reed is as the oak.
The sceptre, learning, physic, must
All follow this, and come to dust.

Fear no more the lightning-flash,
   Nor the all-dreaded thunder-stone;
Fear not slander, censure rash;
   Thou hast finished joy and moan.
All lovers young, all lovers must
Consign to thee, and come to dust.

No exorciser harm thee!
Nor no witchcraft charm thee!
Ghost unlaid forebear thee!
Nothing ill come near thee!
Quiet consummation have,
And renownèd be thy grave!

SONNET: WHEN I DO COUNT THE CLOCK THAT TELLS THE TIME

When I do count the clock that tells the time,
And see the brave day sunk in hideous night;
When I behold the violet past prime,
And sable curls all silvered o'er with white;

When lofty trees I see barren of leaves,
Which erst from heat did canopy the herd,
And summer's green all girded up in sheaves,
Borne on the bier with white and bristly beard;
    Then of thy beauty do I question make,
That thou among the wastes of time must go,
Since sweets and beauties do themselves forsake,
And die as fast as they see others grow;
        And nothing 'gainst time's scythe can make defence
        Save breed, to brave him when he takes thee hence.

SONNET: WHEN, IN DISGRACE WITH FORTUNE AND MEN'S EYES

When, in disgrace with fortune and men's eyes,
I all alone beweep my outcast state,
And trouble deaf heaven with my bootless cries,
And look upon myself, and curse my fate;
    Wishing me like to one more rich in hope,
Featured like him, like him with friends possessed,
Desiring this man's art, and that man's scope,
With what I most enjoy contented least;
    Yet in these thoughts myself almost despising,
Haply I think on thee, and then my state,
Like to the lark at break of day arising
From sullen earth, sings hymns at heaven's gate;
        For thy sweet love remembered such wealth brings
        That then I scorn to change my state with kings.

SONNET: TH' EXPENSE OF SPIRIT IN A WASTE OF SHAME

Th' expense of spirit in a waste of shame
Is lust in action; and till action, lust
Is perjured, murd'rous, bloody, full of blame,
Savage, extreme, rude, cruel, not to trust;
    Enjoyed no sooner but despisèd straight;
Past reason hunted, and no sooner had,
Past reason hated, as a swallowed bait
On purpose laid to make the taker mad;
    Mad in pursuit, and in possession so;
Had, having, and in quest to have, extreme;
A bliss in proof, and proved, a very woe;
Before, a joy proposed; behind, a dream.
        All this the world well knows; yet none knows well
        To shun the heaven that leads men to this hell.

SONNET XIII

THEY that have power to hurt and will do none,
    That do not do the thing they most do show,
Who, moving others, are themselves as stone,
    Unmovèd, cold, and to temptation slow —
They rightly do inherit heaven's graces,
    And husband nature's riches from expense;
They are the lords and owners of their faces,
    Others, but stewards of their excellence.
The summer's flower is to the summer sweet,
    Though to itself it only live and die;
But if that flower with base infection meet,
    The basest weed outbraves his dignity:
        For sweetest things turn sourest by their deeds;
        Lilies that fester smell far worse than weeds.

SONNET XVI

WHEN in the chronicle of wasted time
    I see descriptions of the fairest wights,
And beauty making beautiful old rhyme,
    In praise of ladies dead and lovely knights,
Then, in the blazon of sweet beauty's best,
    Of hand, of foot, of lip, of eye, of brow,
I see their antique pen would have expressed
    Even such a beauty as you master now.
So all their praises are but prophecies
    Of this our time, all you prefiguring;
And, for they looked but with divining eyes,
    They had not skill enough your worth to sing:
        For we, which now behold these present days,
        Have eyes to wonder, but lack tongues to praise.

From RICHARD THE SECOND

[*Enter* RICHARD *alone.*]

RICHARD. I have been studying how I may compare
    This prison where I live unto the world:
    And for because the world is populous,
    And here is not a creature but myself,
    I cannot do it. Yet I'll hammer it out:
    My brain I'll prove the female to my soul,
    My soul the father, and these two beget
    A generation of stillbreeding thoughts;
    And these same thoughts people this little world,

In humors like the people of this world,
For no thought is contented. The better sort,
As thoughts of things divine are intermixed
With scruples, and do set the word itself
Against the word; as thus: "Come, little ones";
And then again,
"It is as hard to come as for a camel
To thread the postern of a small needle's eye."
Thoughts tending to ambition, they do plot
Unlikely wonders: how these vain weak nails
May tear a passage thorough the flinty ribs
Of this hard world, my ragged prison walls;
And, for they cannot, die in their own pride.
Thoughts tending to content flatter themselves
That they are not the first of fortune's slaves,
Nor shall not be the last, like seely beggars
Who sitting in the stocks refuge their shame,
That many have, and others must, sit there;
And in this thought they find a kind of ease,
Bearing their own misfortunes on the back
Of such as have before endured the like.
Thus play I in one person many people,
And none contented; sometimes am I king,
Then treasons make me wish myself a beggar,
And so I am. Then crushing penury
Persuades me I was better when a king.
Then am I kinged again and, by and by,
Think that I am unkinged by Bolingbroke,
And straight am nothing. But whate'er I be,
Nor I, nor any man that but man is,
With nothing shall be pleased, till he be eased
With being nothing.

[The music plays.]

Music do I hear.
Ha—ha! Keep time! How sour sweet music is
When time is broke, and no proportion kept;
So is it in the music of men's lives:
And here have I the daintiness of ear
To check time broke in a disordered string,
But for the concord of my state and time,
Had not an ear to hear my true time broke.
I wasted time, and now doth Time waste me:
For now hath Time made me his numb'ring clock;
My thoughts are minutes, and with sighs they jar
Their watches on unto mine eyes, the outward watch
Whereto my finger, like a dial's point,
Is pointing still, in cleansing them from tears.
Now, sir, the sound that tells what hour it is
Are clamorous groans which strike upon my heart,

Which is the bell. So sighs, and tears, and groans,
Show minutes, times, and hours; but my time
Runs posting on in Bolingbroke's proud joy,
While I stand fooling here, his Jack-of-the-clock.
This music mads me: let it sound no more.
For though it have holp madmen to their wits,
In me it seems it will make wise men mad.
Yet blessing on his heart that gives it me,
For 'tis a sign of love; and love to Richard
Is a strange brooch in this all-hating world.

From TWELFTH NIGHT

Song

O mistress mine, where are you roaming?
Oh, stay and hear; your true love's coming,
  That can sing both high and low.
Trip no further, pretty sweeting;
Journeys end in lovers meeting,
  Every wise man's son doth know.

What is love? 'Tis not hereafter;
Present mirth hath present laughter;
  What's to come is still unsure.
In delay there lies no plenty,
Then come kiss me, sweet and twenty;
  Youth's a stuff will not endure.

℘ Anonymous (c. 1600)

TEARS

Weep you no more, sad fountains;
  What need you flow so fast?
Look how the snowy mountains
  Heaven's sun doth gently waste.
    But my sun's heavenly eyes
      View not your weeping,
      That now lies sleeping
    Softly, now softly lies
        Sleeping.

Sleep is a reconciling,
  A rest that peace begets.
Doth not the sun rise smiling
  When fair at even he sets?

Rest you then, rest, sad eyes,
   Melt not in weeping,
   While she lies sleeping
Softly, now softly lies
   Sleeping.

Thomas Nashe (1567–1601)

IN TIME OF PESTILENCE

Adieu, farewell earth's bliss,
This world uncertain is;
Fond are life's lustful joys,
Death proves them all but toys,
None from his darts can fly.
I am sick, I must die.
     Lord, have mercy on us!

Rich men, trust not in wealth,
Gold cannot buy you health;
Physic himself must fade,
All things to end are made.
The plague full swift goes by.
I am sick, I must die.
     Lord, have mercy on us!

Beauty is but a flower
Which wrinkles will devour;
Brightness falls from the air,
Queens have died young and fair,
Dust hath closed Helen's eye.
I am sick, I must die.
     Lord, have mercy on us!

Strength stoops unto the grave,
Worms feed on Hector brave,
Swords may not fight with fate,
Earth still holds ope her gate.
Come! come! the bells do cry.
I am sick, I must die.
     Lord, have mercy on us!

Wit with his wantonness
Tasteth death's bitterness;
Hell's executioner
Hath no ears for to hear
What vain art can reply.
I am sick, I must die.
     Lord, have mercy on us!

Haste, therefore, each degree,
To welcome destiny.
Heaven is our heritage,
Earth but a player's stage;
Mount we unto the sky.
I am sick, I must die.
          Lord, have mercy on us!

❦ Thomas Campion (1567–1620)

FIRE, FIRE, FIRE, FIRE

          Fire, fire, fire, fire!
Loe here I burne in such desire
That all the teares that I can straine
Out of mine idle empty braine
Cannot allay my scorching paine.

          Come Trent, and Humber, and fayre Thames,
          Dread Ocean, haste with all thy streames:
          And, if you cannot quench my fire,
          O drowne both mee and my desire.

          Fire, fire, fire, fire!
There is no hell to my desire:
See, all the Rivers backward flye,
And th'Ocean doth his waves deny,
For feare my heate should drinke them dry.

          Come, heav'nly showres, then, pouring downe;
          Come, you that once the world did drowne:
          Some then you spar'd, but now save all,
          That else must burne, and with mee fall.

❦ Sir John Davies (1569–1626)

AFFLICTION

If aught can teach us aught, Affliction's looks,
     Making us look into ourselves so near,
Teach us to know ourselves beyond all books,
     Or all the learned schools that ever were.

This mistress lately plucked me by the ear,
     And many a golden lesson hath me taught;
Hath made my senses quick, and reason clear,
     Reformed my will, and rectified my thought.

So do the winds and thunders cleanse the air;
    So working seas settle and purge the wine;
So lopped and prunèd trees do flourish fair;
    So doth the fire the drossy gold refine.

Neither Minerva nor the learned Muse,
    Nor rules of art, nor precepts of the wise,
Could in my brain those beams of skill infuse,
    As but the glance of this dame's angry eyes.

She within lists my ranging mind hath brought,
    That now beyond myself I list not go;
Myself am centre of my circling thought,
    Only myself I study, learn, and know.

I know my body's of so frail a kind
    As force without, fevers within, can kill;
I know the heavenly nature of my mind,
    But 'tis corrupted both in wit and will;

I know my soul hath power to know all things,
    Yet is she blind and ignorant in all;
I know I am one of nature's little kings,
    Yet to the least and vilest things am thrall.

I know my life's a pain and but a span,
    I know my sense is mocked with everything;
And to conclude, I know myself a man,
    Which is a proud, and yet a wretched thing.

❧ 2

LYRIC VERSE FROM CONTINENTAL EUROPE

French

❧ Maurice Scève (1510–1562)

LES DIZAINS

1

The last day of your sweet companionship
Was a serenity in gloomy winter,
Which made the evening of your absence
An even shadowier thing, to my soul's eye,
Than the Body, which encumbers my life,
And bears the burden of your refusal.
　　For from the moment you left, I've crouched
Like the Hare squatting in his hole,
I've cupped my ear, hearing confusing noise,
Entirely bewildered by the darkness of Egypt.

2

Recollection, key to all my thought,
Ravishes me in its elusive dream,
And, since the memory isn't at all bad,
I let myself be fed by its sweet lie.
　　Then when the ardor gnaws and picks at me,
Throwing itself against the urge to sleep,
Suddenly before my mind can guard
Against the feeling of the hungry flames,
In jerky thought it casts a look at you,
And in the desert a Serpent raises up.

3

White dawn had barely gotten through
Shining forth its rosy head,
When my Mind, canoed
In the confusing bottom of so many wandering things,
Was brought back to me by the hooded ministers
To ready my surrender to the End.
      But you (and you alone) can call
The hour of my death, so you
Will be the incorruptible Perfume
Against the worms of my mortality.

4

When Death will have, after long sufferance,
Ripped my sad spirit from an empty flesh,
I do not want to rest, for centuries, in
A mausoleum or a pyramid.
      But let me huddle, Miss, in the damp tomb
(If I deserve) of your delicious breast.
      For since, before, on earth and under heaven,
You've always waged implacable war on me,
Maybe you'll be, in that prestigious place
After I die, at last, a gentle peace.

5

I'm alone here, she's with her lawful mate;
Me in my pain, she in her cozy bed.
I roll around in these vexating thorns,
And she sleeps nude between his brawny arms.
      That louse, he's got her and he's touching her!
She suffers it, being the Weaker Sex,
And love is raped to serve some phony bond,
A man-made law, maybe, no way divine.
      O Holy Law, you're fair to all but me:
For her wrong-doings I'm the one to pay!

                                        Phillip Lopate

EVERY LONG & WIDE EXPANSE OF SEA

Every long & wide expanse of sea,
Every whirling verge of solid land,
Every mountain ridge both low & high,
Every distant site of day & night,
Every space between, O you who unsettle me,
Will be filled by your inexorability.
      Thus traversing the spans of time,
You will surmount the heights of stars,

Your sacred name, under my lazy spell,
Setting full sail, beyond all heaven & all hell.

Richard Sieburth

❧ Joachim du Bellay (1522–1560)

HEUREUX QUI, COMME ULYSSE, A FAIT UN BEAU VOYAGE

for Claire White

Great joy be to the sailor if he chart
The Odyssey or bear away the Fleece
Yet unto wisdom's laurel and the peace
Of his own kind come lastly to his start.
And when shall I, being migrant, bring my heart
Home to its plots of parsley, its proper earth,
Pot hooks, cow dung, black chimney bricks whose worth
I have not skill to honor in my art.

My home, my father's and grandfather's home.
Not the imperial porphyry of Rome
But slate is my true stone, slate is my blue.
And bluer the Loire is to my reckoning
Than Caesar's Tiber, and more nourishing
Than salt spray is the breathing of Anjou.

Anthony Hecht

ROME

   You, who behold in wonder Rome and all
Her former passion, menacing the gods,
These ancient palaces and baths, the sods
Of seven hills, and temple, arch, and wall,
   Consider in the ruins of her fall,
That which destroying Time has gnawed away —
What workmen built with labor day by day
Only a few worn fragments now recall.

   Then look again and see where, endlessly
Treading upon her own antiquity,
Rome has rebuilt herself with works as just:
   There you may see the demon of the land
Forcing himself again with fatal hand
To raise the city from this ruined dust.

Yvor Winters

TWO POEMS *From* THE REGRETS

1

To walk with sober step, to raise the eyebrow
Soberly, and with sober welcome smile,
Consider well what's to be said, and nod
Implying *Messer Si* or *Messer No.*

To interpose a little *E così,*
Let down your dignity with Son Servitor
And, letting on you'd served with the armed forces
Discuss Florence conquered, and Naples too.

Say Lord to everyone and kiss the hand,
And, acting as the Roman courtiers do,
Hide poverty behind a bright, brave hand:

Which is required behaviour in that Court,
From which on a poor horse, in poor health and poorly dressed,
Unshaved and bankrupt, you return to France.

Dennis Devlin

2

Given all my worries over each day's trivia,
Given the ill-timed troubles that torment me endlessly,
And given all the regrets about which I lament,
You've often been amazed I'm able to sing.

I don't sing, Magny, I weep my boredoms,
Or, more precisely, I sing them while weeping,
And when I sing them, I often enchant them:
And that's why, Magny, I sing day and night.

Like workmen singing when engaged in their work,
Like the ploughman engaged in his ploughing,
Like the pilgrim longing for his home,

Like the traveller while dreaming of his woman,
Like the sailor while pulling at the oar,
Like the prisoner cursing his prison.

David Curzon

LAS, OÙ EST MAINTENANT CE MESPRIS DE FORTUNE

How is it that Fortune now always ignores me?
What has happened to the Me that stood up to all trouble,

That shameless taste for immortality,
That fire whose flame is so rare in the mortal?

Under the rays of fertility the Muses once offered me
Such subtle pleasures in the shadows and dark
In learned dances under the glimmer of the Moon
At their green dancing place beside the brook's bank.

Now Fortune is my true lover I think
And my soul which was once its own self's master
Is slave to Trouble, and regrets cloud it over.

I have no interest in those that come after
And that divine fire is turning to clinker
And the Muses I knew grow further and stranger.

Fred Beake

❧ Pierre de Ronsard (1524–1585)

CORINNA IN VENDOME

Darling, each morning a blooded rose
Lures the sunlight in, and shows
Her soft, moist and secret part.
See now, before you go to bed,
Her skirts replaced, her deeper red —
A colour much like yours, dear heart.

Alas, her petals will blow away,
Her beauties in a single day
Vanish like ashes on the wind.
O savage Time! that what we prize
Should flutter down before our eyes —
Who also, late or soon, descend.

Then scatter, darling, your caresses
While you may, and wear green dresses;
Gather roses, gather me —
Tomorrow, aching for your charms,
Death shall take you in his arms
And shatter your virginity.

Robert Mezey

ROSES

As one sees on the branch in the month of May the rose
In her beautiful youth, in the dawn of her flower,

When the break of day softens her life with the shower,
Make jealous the sky of the damask bloom she shows:
Grace lingers in her leaf and love sleeping glows
Enchanting with fragrance the trees of her bower,
But broken by the rain or the sun's oppressive power,
Languishing she dies, and all her petals throws.
Thus in thy first youth, in thy awakening fair
When thy beauty was honored by lips of Earth and Air,
Atropos has killed thee and dust they form reposes.
O take, take for obsequies my tears, these poor showers,
This vase filled with milk, this basket strewn with flowers,
That in death as in life thy body may be roses.

Vernon Watkins

INVECTIVE AGAINST DENISE, A WITCH

The hatred I reserve for thee
Surpasses the malignity
    Of camel and of bear,
Old witch, unseemly thaumaturge,
Whipped by the Public Hangman's scourge
    The length of the town square.

Luring about you, like a brood,
The vulgar, curious and lewd,
    You shamelessly lay bare
Your haunches to the sight of men,
Your naked shoulder, abdomen
    Emblazoned with blood-smear.

And yet that punishment is slight
Compared to what is yours by right;
    Just Heaven must not bestow
Its mercy on so foul a thing
But rather by its whirlwind bring
    Such proud excesses low.

Still wracked by the brute overthrow
The Titans suffered long ago,
    A brooding Mother Earth,
To spite the Gods, in her old age
Shall, in an ecstasy of rage,
    At last bring you to birth.

You know the worth and power of both
Rare herbals and concocted broth
    Brought from the tropic zone;
You know the very month and hour

To pluck the lust-inducing flower
    That makes a woman groan.

There's not, among the envenomed plants
On mountain or in valley haunts,
    One that your eyes have missed
And has not yielded up its ground
To your bright sickle-blade, and crowned
    Your formidable quest.

When, like a lunatic, all bare,
The moon lets down its mystic hair
    Of cold, enraging light,
You wrap your features in the hide
Of animals, and smoothly glide
    Abroad into the night.

Your least breath ravishes the blood
    Of all dogs in the neighborhood
And sets them on to bark,
Makes rivers flow uphill, reversed,
And baying wolves observe your cursed
    Hegira through the dark.

Chatelaine of deserted spots,
Of mouldered cemetery plots
    Where you are most at home,
Muttering diabolic runes,
You disinter the troubled bones
    From their sequestered tomb.

To grieve a mother more you don
The aspect of her only son
    Who has just met his death,
And you assume the very shape
That makes an aged widow gape
    And robs her of her breath.

You make the spell-bound moon appear
To march through the all-silvered air,
    And cast through midnight's hush
Such tincture on a pallid face
A thousand-cymbaled crashing brass
    Could not restore its flush.

The terror of us all, we fear
Your hateful practice, and we bar
    Your presence from our door,
Afraid you will inflict a pox
Upon our persons, herds and flocks,
    With juice of hellebore.

Often I've watched as you espy
From far away with baleful eye
     Some shepherd on his heights;
Soon after, victim of your arts,
The man is dead, his fleshly parts
     A nest of parasites.

And yet like vile Medea, you
Could sometimes prove life-giving, too;
     You know what secret thing
Gave Aeson back his sapling youth,
Yet by your spells you have in truth
     Deprived me of my spring.

O Gods, if pity dwells on high,
May her requital be to die,
     And may her last repose,
Unblessed by burial, serve as feast
To every gross and shameful beast,
     To jackals and to crows.

                 Anthony Hecht

TWO VERSIONS OF A SONNET *From* SONNETS TO HELEN

1

When you are old and grey and full of sleep,
And nodding by the fire, take down this book,
And slowly read, and dream of the soft look
Your eyes had once, and of their shadows deep;

How many loved your moments of glad grace,
And loved your beauty with love false or true,
But one man loved the pilgrim soul in you,
And loved the sorrows of your changing face;

And bending down beside the glowing bars,
Murmur, a little sadly, how Love fled
And paced upon the mountains overhead
And hid his face amid a crowd of stars.

                 William Butler Yeats

2

When you are old, at evening candle-lit
     beside the fire bending to your wool,
read out my verse and murmur, "Ronsard write

this praise for me when I was beautiful."
And not a maid but, at the sound of it,
   though nodding at the stitch on broidered stool,
will start awake, and bless love's benefit
   whose long fidelities bring Time to school.
I shall be thin and ghost beneath the earth
   by myrtle shade in quiet after pain,
but you, a crone, will crouch beside the hearth
   mourning my love and all your proud disdain.
And since what comes to-morrow who can say?
Live, pluck the roses of the world to-day.

Humbert Wolfe

GÉNÈVRES HÉRISSEZ, ET VOUS, HOUX ESPINEUX

Bush-bristling juniper and you the thorn —
Enjoying holly, one the desert's guest
And one the thicket's; ivy-cover drawn
Across waste caves; sand-spiring spouts and freshets;

   Pigeons that sip at them; you mourning doves
In your unending widowhood; nightingales
Who day-long night-long in appealing jargon
Rehearse the unvaried versicles of your loves;

And you with the red throat, non-indigenous swallow —

   If you should see *la Cara* in this Spring
Abroad for flowers, parting the young grasses,
   Tell her from me I hope for nothing now
From her, no favours. Cut the suffering:
As well be dead as carry on like this.

Donald Davie

᠙ Louise Labé (1525–1566)

I FLEE THE CITY, TEMPLES, AND EACH PLACE

I flee the city, temples, and each place
where you took pleasure in your own lament,
where you used every forceful argument
to make me yield what I could not replace.
Games, masques, tournaments bore me and I sigh

and dream no beauty that is not of you.
And so I try to kill my passion too,
forcing another image to my eye,
hoping to break away from tender thought.
Deep in the woods I found a lonely trail,
and after wandering in a maze I sought
to put you wholly out of mind. I fail.
Only outside my body can I live
or else in exile like a fugitive.

Willis Barnstone

LONG-FELT DESIRES

Long-felt desires, hopes as long as vain —
sad sighs — slow tears accustomed to run sad
into as many rivers as two eyes could add,
pouring like fountains, endless as the rain —
cruelty beyond humanity, a pain
so hard it makes compassionate stars go mad
with pity: these are the first passions I've had.
Do you think love could root in my soul again?
If it arched the great bow back again at me,
licked me again with fire, and stabbed me deep
with the violent worst, as awful as before,
the wounds that cut me everywhere would keep
me shielded, so there would be no place free
for love. It covers me. It can pierce no more.

Annie Finch

✑ Jean Passerat (1534–1602)

SONNET ADDRESSED TO HENRY III ON THE DEATH OF THULÈNE, THE KING'S FOOL

Thulène is dead, my lord. I saw his funeral.
But it is in your power to bring him back again.
Appoint some poet to inherit his domain.
Poets and fools are of the same material.
One scorns advancement. One has nowhere to advance.
In both accounts, the gain is greater than the loss.
Both kinds are quick to anger, difficult to cross.
One speaks on impulse, one leaves everything to chance.
One is light-headed, but the other one is seen
wearing a pretty cap and bells, yellow and green.

One sings his rhymes, the other capers to his chimes.
Yet we are different in one important way.
Fortune has always favored fools, or so they say.
She's seldom favored poets in the best of times.

Richmond Lattimore

Italian

❧ Matteo Maria Boiardo (1441–1494)

IL CANTO DE LI AUGEI DI FRUNDA IN FRUNDA

The song of birds which leaps from leaf to leaf,
The scented breeze that runs from flower to flower,
The shining dew that glitters in each bower,
Rejoice our sight and banish thoughts of grief.
It is because she holds all Nature in fief
Whose will is that the world shall live Love's hour;
Sweet scents and songs—the Spring's own magic power—
Each stream invade, each wind, each emerald sheaf.

Where'er she walks, She by her gaze enstarred
Brings warmth before due season in her arms;
Love's kindled in her look and falls in showers;
At her sweet smile or at her sweet regard
The grass grows green and colours paint the flowers,
The sky is clear, the sea is locked in calms.

Peter Russell

❧ Angelo Politziano (1454–1494)

From THE TOURNAMENT

1

Splendor and pride I celebrate,
Of Tuscan arms and Tuscan men.
Generous and strict, firm their state,
Scholars, knights, and gentlemen,
And her whose power moves us all
From Heaven's third bright parapet,
Lest time and death among them fall,
And fortune turn and men forget.

2

O shining god who breathes desire
Sweet and bitter upon our eyes
And raves until the heart take fire
And burns the hotter for your sighs,
Make gentle all you gaze upon,
Burn out what's base within the mind,
That intellect and love be one,
Direct me, Love, or I am blind.

3

Lighten the weight that holds me so,
Steady my hand, Love, rule my tongue,
Begin and end, that the world know
Yours the honor, when all is sung.
Display the snare, show how you won,
How you the Tuscan baron caught,
Etruscan Leda's youngest son,
And how the cunning net was wrought.

4

Under the laurel tree's great shade,
Florence's peace your wisdom's kept,
Where thrives the best that's thought or made,
High born Lorenzo, too, accept,
That the Laurentian laurel take
This song, whose will from yours receives
Its strength, for splendor, for kindness' sake,
Within the fragrance of its leaves.

5

If fortune quarrel with my song
And noble rivals take my theme,
I was not born to hold my tongue,
But figure bolt and ell and seam
Of all your glory. Boötes
Know, Numidia too, your name.
My duckling words on unfound seas
Become the white swan of your fame.

6

But that great honor lies ahead.
I've yet to grow to reach its height.
Giuliano first I sing instead,
Your brother's triumph new and bright.
Love! Power to these stanzas bring,
Bring martial sounds and hunter's lust—

The great tree's second branch I sing,
And sing of sweat, of blood and dust.

7

Since death divine Achilles took
And Leda's golden daughter died,
Alive they've moved from tongue and book:
Cherishing fame holds time defied.
Silence, Fame, your tall trumpet while
Italian song I sound, or join, then,
Our two lutes in the sweet new style
To sing of Giulio and his men.

8

Lithe in the April of his years,
Princely, bold, careless, free, antique,
Ignorant of love's nectared tears,
The down thin on his boy's flat cheek,
Chaste, swift, by longing unbeguiled,
He rode Sicilian chargers out,
Wild as the high west wind gone wild,
Rode as the storm wind roars about.

9

Like the liquid leopard he sprang,
Or danced a circle reined up tight,
Or fast and keen the long spear sang
Bitter end to the red deer's flight.
Nor knew he what his luck was like,
That next he'd fall with deer and dove,
Let but the golden arrow strike
The muscled hunter stalked by love.

10

They quiver, the apple nymphs, and sigh,
They pant and burn, they faint, they start
When tall Giuliano gallops by,
But cannot thaw his frigid heart.
Indifferent, haughty, unimpressed,
Like woodsman clad but plainly fine,
His high-chinned head, unturning, dressed
In beechen garland or in pine.

11

When burning stars in figured night
Changed the world, then prancer and prince
Homeward rode to the lute's delight,
Secure from nymphs who glance and mince,
Where ancient virtue filled his mind,

And those to whom his heart belonged,
Nine chaste sisters and all their kind,
Diana huntress, virgin thronged.

12

Whenever he saw, blind, alone,
A lover in his anguish bent,
Pity's picture and heart of stone,
For enemy and woman blent
Had with a double blinding light
Stunned dumb his will, and, high and proud,
Took all but glamor from his sight,
Stupid, stumbling, he cried aloud:

13

O silly fool, give all this up,
Call concupiscence by its name,
Part randy goat, part suckling pup,
With flattery to feed the flame.
Take back mind, take back heart. Above
This idle burning mischief climb.
Idiocy calls him Love —
He's but the fire of rutting time.

14

To give to womankind your will,
Worship her face, hark to her tongue,
Be happy with her, sweet or shrill,
Dance to whatever song is sung,
If she's the wind, to be a leaf,
Is to long and fall, to adore
Her and despair, in hope and grief,
Like shifting waves upon a shore.

15

A hidden rock beneath the blue,
The beautiful sweet summer sea,
Or serpent in flowers and true
To its old intent, such is she,
Beautiful woman and her pride
Who takes the foolish with her smile
And under lips and eyes can hide
The hook and halter of her guile.

16

In her face Cupid baits his snare
To catch young eyes, catch manly thought,
Just as the trout all unaware
Is by the trout fly lured and caught.

To all masculine strength of mind,
To all that's noble say farewell
If Love the bastard catch and bind
You in the Lethe of his spell.

17

Finer by far, valorous, free,
To ride and cry with dog and horn
By ancient rock and ancient tree,
Down spoor, to lair, and, winded, torn,
Spear the lost spent heart of the boar,
Away from castle, moat and town,
On flowered hills where high streams roar
And birds and leaves dip green and brown.

18

Delight, delight is in these hills
Where grazing goats and shepherds move.
Green the shadows, some shepherd trills
His whistle, cows low in the grove,
Ram tilts with ram, and orchards bend
Heavy with apples. Like the sea,
Fields of oats, acres without end,
Flow round flock, hill, and laden tree.

19

The shepherd boy unbars the fold,
Drives in his lambs, holds high his crook,
Tells each its name till all are told,
The farmer plies the pruning hook,
Or scythe or ox and plow and trace.
A loose-frocked barefoot girl draws nigh,
Stands watchful at a narrow place
And lets her waddling geese file by.

20

Once the world in its age of gold
Lived in peace on the forest floor,
And neither winds nor hearts were cold,
And mothers gave no sons to war.
No ship set sail upon the sea,
No ox was burdened with a yoke,
Roof and provender was a tree,
Honey and acorns from the oak.

21

No beauty in the warp of lust
Had cruelty yet caught through greed.

Happy were they, true, free, and just.
From untilled fields sprang fecund seed.
Fortuna jealous broke that age,
Broke peace and law, broke godliness,
Broke them with luxurious rage,
With love that is but idleness.

22

So said Giulio in his pride,
Scorning lovers and love's holiness,
Whose haughtiness could not abide
The silly sight of their distress.
And Love's anguished, all on fire, cried
From their pain and their happiness
That scorn was just from the untried
Who had not tasted loveliness.

23

Cupid heard. His godly eyes, sly,
Half closed, and mischief, wakened, curled
His lips. A god, he laughed, am I
Whose torch has set fire to the world.
Great Jove, all hot, I've put with cows,
Man, god, and tree obey my spell,
The sun's in love with laurel boughs,
And Pluto leaves his throne in hell.

24

I can the tiger's rage enchant,
The lion's growl, the dragon's hiss.
Is there a man who says I can't?
O smug and bold, consider this:
You'd fall oh! even if I chanced
To stay my hand. For how devise
A counterforce to stand against
The beauty of a pair of eyes?

25

Wildflower crowned, the west winds blow.
The swallow comes to weave her nest,
Swallow and swallow when the snow
Dies in the warm, the breathing west.
Dawn wakes the wood, spring wakes the year,
Wakes sweet flowers where works the bee,
Wakes a sweetness within the ear,
And wakes the honey-nectared tree. . . .

Guy Davenport

ॐ Michelangelo Buonarotti
(1475–1564)

Very dear though it was I have bought you
a little whatever-it-is for its sweet smell
since by the scent often I find the way
Wherever you are wherever I am
beyond all doubt I will be clear and certain
If you hide yourself from me I pardon you
Taking it always with you where you go
even if I were quite blind I would find you.

W. S. Merwin

"NIGHT" IN THE MEDICI CHAPEL

Sleep's very dear to me, but being stone's
Far more, so long as evil persevere.
It's my good fortune not to see nor hear:
Do not wake me; speak in the softest tones.

William Jay Smith

ON THE PAINTING OF THE SISTINE CHAPEL

To Giovanni da Pistoja

I've grown a goitre by dwelling in this den —
as cats from stagnant streams in Lombardy,
or in what other land they hap to be —
which drives the belly close beneath the chin:

my beard turns up to heaven; my nape falls in,
fixed on my spine: my breast-bone visibly
grows like a harp: a rich embroidery
bedews my face from brush-drops thick and thin.

My loins into my paunch like levers grind:
my buttock like a crupper bears my weight;
my feet unguided wander to and fro;

in front my skin grows loose and long; behind,
by bending it becomes more taut and strait;
crosswise I strain me like a Syrian bow:
    whence false and quaint, I know,
must be the fruit of squinting brain and eye;
for ill can aim the gun that bends awry.

Come then, Giovanni, try
to succour my dead pictures and my fame;
since foul I fare and painting is my shame.

John Addington Symonds

Spanish

❧ St. Teresa of Avila (1515–1582)

POEM

Nothing move thee;
Nothing terrify thee;
Everything passes;
God never changes.
Patience be all to thee.
Who trusts in God, he
Never shall be needy.
God alone suffices.

Yvor Winters

❧ Anonymous (c. 1550)

LAMENT FOR THE DEATH OF GUILLÉN PERAZA

Grieve, ladies, so may God keep you.
Guillén Peraza remained in Palma,
Withered, the flower of his face.

No palm are you, you are broom,
You are cypress of mournful bough,
You are misfortune, dire misfortune.

May molten stone buckle your fields,
May you see no pleasures, only sorrows,
May the sand-pits cover your flowers.

Guillén Peraza, Guillén Peraza,
Where is your shield, where is your spear?
By ill fortune all is ended.

W. S. Merwin

Portuguese

ॐ Luis Vaz de Camões (1524–1580)

DEAR GENTLE SOUL

Dear gentle soul, who went so soon away
Departing from this life in discontent,
Repose in that far sky to which you went
While on this earth I linger in dismay.
In the ethereal seat where you must be,
If you consent to memories of our sphere,
Recall the love which, burning pure and clear,
So often in my eyes you used to see!
If then, in the incurable, long anguish
Of having lost you, as I pine and languish,
You see some merit—do this favour for me:
And to the God who cut your life short, pray
That he as early to your sight restore me
As from my own he swept you far away.

Roy Campbell

ON A SHIPMATE, PERO MONIZ, DYING AT SEA

My years on earth were short, but long for me,
And full of bitter hardship at the best:
My light of day sinks early in the sea:
Five lustres from my birth I took my rest.
Through distant lands and seas I was a ranger
Seeking some cure or remedy for life,
Which he whom Fortune loves not as a wife,
Will seek in vain through strife, and toil, and danger.
Portugal reared me in my green, my darling
Alanguer, but the dank, corrupted air
That festers in the marshes around there
Has made me food for fish here in the snarling,
Fierce seas that dark the Abyssinian shore,
Far from the happy homeland I adore.

Roy Campbell

SONNET: THAT SAD AND JOYFUL DAWN

That sad and joyful dawn,
light full of pity and grief,
while the world wakes in loneliness
I'll praise it and remember it.

The mild light was breaking, shadows
ran from the sun. Light was the eye of the world—
it saw the parting of two souls,
two wills I thought were indivisible.

And light witnessed the tears
that fell from their eyes, ran together, and formed
a river as long and broad as the Amazon—

and heard the bitter, heartsick words
that made the fires of Hell burn cold
and soothed the lost spirits under the world.

David Wevill

SONNET: MY ERRORS MY LOVES MY UNLUCKY STAR

My errors my loves my unlucky star
these three things have been my curse.
My luck and my errors were bad enough
but love was the worst.

I have survived. But the pain
has bitten so deep in the bone
the rage and grief will not let go—
too hurt to want contentment now.

The blunders scattered through my life
are like a broken rosary.
I gave myself to fortune; fortune broke me.

Of love there is hardly a ghost left.
O who what angel of power can assuage
my terrible demon of revenge!

David Wevill

Latin

✑ Sir Thomas More (1477–1535)

TWO EPIGRAMS

The Astrologer

What is it, fool, in the tall stars you'd find
About the earthy morals of your spouse?
Why search so far? Your fears are close at hand.
For while you polled the poles for what she'd do
She did it willingly and on the ground.

J. V. Cunningham

Good Princes and Bad

Good prince? (Guardian Of Flocks.) His bark
Chases bad prince (The Wolf) from fold:
Safe from bad prince in undisturbed sleep.
Watchdog and wolf both partial to sheep.

Katharine Washburn

Polish

✑ Jan Kochanowski (1530–1584)

TO A MATHEMATICIAN

He discovered the age of the sun and he knows
Just why the wrong or the right wind blows.
He has looked at each nook of the ocean's floor
But he doesn't see that his wife is a whore.

Jerzy Peterkiewicz and Burns Singer

IN DEFENCE OF DRUNKARDS

Earth, that drinks rain, refreshes the trees:
Oceans drink rivers: stars quaff up the seas:
So why should they make such a terrible fuss
Over insignificant tipplers like us?

Jerzy Peterkiewicz and Burns Singer

I'D BUY YOU, WISDOM *From* THE LAMENTS

I'd buy you, Wisdom, with all of the world's gold
But is there any truth in what we're told
About your power to purge our human thought
Of want and worry, elevate distraught
Spirits to heaven, up to the highest sphere
Where angels dwell beyond distress and fear?
You see mere trifles in all human things;
Mourning and mirth are two extended wings
On which you bring us equanimity,
Yourself unmoved by Death, calm, changeless, free.
For you, the rich man is the one who owns
No more than what's enough—no precious stones,
Or land, or rents; your piercing eyes behold
Misery lodged beneath the roof of gold.
But if poor people heed your sober voice,
You do not grudge the poor their simple joys.
To think that I have spent my life in one
Long climb towards your threshold! All delusion!
My Wisdom was a castle built on air;
Like all the rest, I'm flung from its top stair.

Stanisław Barańczak and Seamus Heaney

WHERE IS THAT GATE FOR GRIEF *From* THE LAMENTS

Where is that gate for grief which, long ago,
Let Orpheus enter the dark realm below
In search of his lost love? My own dear loss
Is such that I would follow him across
The flood where Charon's ferryboat still moves
Shades whom he puts ashore in cypress groves.
And you, my lovely lute, do not desert
Your singer now: we both have to assert
Our rights before stern Pluto, now with tears,
Now with sad songs, till he at last appears
Softened enough to let my dear girl go
And come to my embrace, and end my woe.
He will not lose her thus; we'll all be his
(If fruit's not ripe, you wait until it is).
Is this god so stone-hearted that he can
Turn a deaf ear to a despairing man?
I never shall return if that is so
But lose my soul to find peace there below.

Stanisław Barańczak and Seamus Heaney

Armenian

✖ Nahabed Kouchag (d. 1592)

I WAS SUFFERING EXILE

I was suffering exile like a rambling
Madman and then of a sudden I met you
When I thought there was no hope
As a parched man comes suddenly on a fresh spring
Plunges his head in and drinks
Until he placates his fever.

Desmond O'Grady

MESOAMERICAN AND ANDEAN POETRY

Toltec

❧ Anonymous (c. 1450?)

THE ARTIST

The artist: disciple, abundant, multiple, restless.
The true artist: capable, practicing, skillful;
maintains dialogue with his heart, meets things with his mind.

The true artist: draws out all from his heart,
works with delight, makes things with calm, with sagacity,
works like a true Toltec, composes his objects, works dexterously, invents;
arranges materials, adorns them, makes them adjust.

The carrion artist: works at random, sneers at the people,
makes things opaque, brushes across the surface of the face of things,
works without care, defrauds people, is a thief.

Denise Levertov with Elvira Abascal

Nahuatl

❧ King Nezahualcoyotl of Texcoco (c. 1402–1472)

WHERE WILL I GO?

Where will I go?
Where will I go?

To the road, to the road
That leads to God.
Are you waiting for us in the Place of the Unfleshed?
Is it within the heavens?
Or is the Place of the Unfleshed only here on earth?

We vanish,
We vanish,
Into his house;
No one abides on earth.
Does someone ask,
"Where are our friends?"
Rejoice!

Thelma D. Sullivan

BE INDOMITABLE, O MY HEART

Be indomitable, O my heart!
Love only the sunflower;
It is the flower of the Giver-of-Life!
What can my heart do?
Have we come, have we sojourned here on earth in vain?

As the flowers wither, I shall go.
Will there be nothing of my glory ever?
Will there be nothing of my fame on earth?
At most songs, at most flowers.
What can my heart do?
Have we come, have we sojourned on earth in vain?

Thelma D. Sullivan

OUR LORD

Our Lord,
Ever-present, Ever-close,
Thinks as he pleases,
Does as he pleases,
He mocks us.
As he wishes, so he wills.
He has us in the middle of his hand
And rolls us about,
Like pebbles we spin and bounce,
He flings us every which way.
We offer him diversion,
He laughs at us.

Thelma D. Sullivan

CAN IT BE TRUE THAT ONE LIVES ON EARTH?

Can it be true that one lives on earth?
Not forever on earth; only a little while here.
Be it jade, it shatters.
Be it gold, it breaks.
Be it a quetzal feather, it tears apart.
Not forever on earth; only a little while here.

Thelma D. Sullivan

FLOWERS OF RED AND BLUE

flowers of red and blue
mix with flowers of fiery red
it is your word your heart
Oh my king
for a little while I can see earth
I cry because death kills
everything I did
everything I sang
for a little while I can see the earth

Stephen Berg (after Angel Maria Garibay K.)

Mayan

ଆ Chilam Balam (c. 1500)

FLIGHT OF THE ITZÁS

They came with a fury
with a rage without reason
with a thirst for blood,
for heads, for jewels.
Came into our lands
to conquer for no quarrel
to seize for the sake of seizing
to claim for an absent king
our lands, our corn, our people.

They came from the east,
those foreign lords,
came to the village of Nacom Balam,
took the town and the people

and the fields and the trees
and even the great black crows.

Then the Itzá went away,
left by the thousands.
Thirteen measures of corn
they had per head,
and nine measures and
three handfuls of grain.
And many of the magicians
from the town went with them
and many of the town's daughters
formed their growing troop.
They did not want to join
the treacherous foreigners,
did not want to bow
to a foreign god,
did not want to pay tribute
to a foreign lord.
They guarded their birds
and their stones,
their jaguars and
their three magic emblems
and fled with spears
deep into the dense forest.

Before the conquerors came
there was no sin,
no sickness, no aches,
no fevers, no pox.
The foreigners stood
the world on its head,
made day become night.
There were no longer
any lucky days
after they came into our lands.
There was no more sound judgement,
no more great vision.
The great teachers never came again
nor any great priests,
just death and blood
and sorrow, sorrow, sorrow!

Christopher Sawyer-Lauçanno

Quechua

Anonymous (c. 1550)

From THE ELEGY FOR THE GREAT INCA
ATAWALLPA

You all by yourself fulfilled
 Their malignant demands,
But your life was snuffed out
 In Cajamarca.

Already the blood has curdled
 In your veins,
And under your eyelids your sight
 Has withered.
Your glance is hiding in the brilliance
 Of some star.

Only your dove suffers and moans
 And drifts here and there.
Lost in sorrow, she weeps, who had her nest
 In your heart.

The heart, with the pain of this catastrophe,
 Shatters.
They have robbed you of your golden litter
 And your palace.
All of your treasures which they have found
 They have divided among them.

Condemned to perpetual suffering,
 And brought to ruin,
Muttering, with thoughts that are elusive
 And far away from this world,
Finding ourselves without refuge or help,
 We are weeping,
And not knowing to whom we can turn our eyes,
 We are lost.

Oh sovereign king,
 Will your heart permit us
To live scattered, far from each other,
 Drifting here and there,
Subject to an alien power,
 Trodden upon?

Discover to us your eyes which can wound
    Like a noble arrow;
Extend to us your hand which grants
    More than we ask,
And when we are comforted with this blessing
    Tell us to depart.

W. S. Merwin

﹏ Anonymous (c. 1550)

TO A TRAITOR

The traitor's skull, we shall drink out of it,
His teeth we shall wear as a necklace,
From his bones we shall make flutes,
Of his skin we shall make a drum,
Then we shall dance.

Willard Trask (after Richard Pietschmann)

❧ 4

India: Devotional Verse

Bengali

❧ Chandidas (c. 1375–1450)

WHY TELL ME WHAT TO DO?

Why tell me what to do?
Dreaming or awake I see only his black skin.
I don't even fix my tangled hair,
just pour it in my lap, and wish it were Krishna.
I call to him, sweet black Krishna,
and cry.
I leave this black hair loosely knotted
so when my dark love comes to mind
I can let it down and brood.
What can I do?
His black skin is always with me.

Tony Barnstone

Hindi

❧ Kabir (c. 1440–1518)

STUDENT, DO THE SIMPLE PURIFICATION

Student, do the simple purification.
You know that the seed is inside the horse-chestnut tree;

and inside the seed there are the blossoms of the tree, and the chestnuts, and
    the shade.
So inside the human body there is the seed, and inside the seed there is the
    human body again.

Fire, air, earth, water, and space—if you don't want the secret one,
you can't have these either.

Thinkers, listen, tell me what you know of that is not inside the soul?
Take a pitcher full of water and set it down on the water—
now it has water inside and water outside.
We mustn't give it a name,
lest silly people start talking again about the body and the soul.
If you want the truth, I'll tell you the truth:
Listen to the secret sound, the real sound, which is inside you.
The one no one talks of speaks the secret sound to himself,
and he is the one who has made it all.

                        Robert Bly

ARE YOU LOOKING FOR ME?

Are you looking for me? I am in the next seat.
My shoulder is against yours.
You will not find me in stupas, not in Indian shrine rooms, nor in
    synagogues, nor in cathedrals:
not in masses, nor kirtans, not in legs winding around your own neck, nor in
    eating nothing but vegetables.
When you really look for me, you will see me instantly—
you will find me in the tiniest house of time.
Kabir says: Student, tell me, what is God?
He is the breath inside the breath.

                        Robert Bly

ETERNITY

The kings shall go, so will their pretty queens,
courtiers and all proud ones shall go.
Pundits chanting the *Vedas* shall go,
and go will those who listen to them.
Masochist yogis and bright intellectuals shall go,
go the moon and sun and water and wind.
Thus says Kabir only those can remain
whose minds are tied to the rocks.

                Arvind Krishna Mehrotra

I CHERISH THAT LOVE

More than anything else
I cherish that love
which gives me
an unfettered life on this earth.
It is like a lotus:
even though the waters
nurture it and make it blossom,
its petals remain
beyond the reach of the lake.
It is like a wife
who enters the fire
at the call of love:
others grieve as she burns,
and yet she refuses
to dishonour love.
It is a dangerous ocean,
this life of ours:
its waters run very deep.

Kabir says:
Listen to me, O man of God:
Very few have seen where it ends.

Pritish Nandy

THE ASCETIC DYES HIS ROBES

The ascetic dyes his robes
instead of dyeing his heart
in the colours of love.
He sits within a temple
and worships a stone deity
instead of the Lord.
He pierces his ears,
grows a beard and matted locks
and looks like a goat.
He escapes into the wilderness
and murders all his desires,
to become an eunuch.
He shaves his head,
dyes his robes,
reads the scriptures
and sermonizes at every opportunity.

Kabir says:
You are entering the gates of death,
shackled.

Pritish Nandy

❧ Mirabai (1498–1565)

ALL I WAS DOING WAS BREATHING

Something has reached out and taken in the beams of my eyes.
There is a longing, it is for his body, for every hair of that dark body.
All I was doing was being, and the Dancing Energy came by my house.
His face looks curiously like the moon, I saw it from the side, smiling.
My family says: "Don't ever see him again!" And implies things in a low
    voice.
But my eyes have their own life; they laugh at rules, and know whose they
    are.
I believe I can bear on my shoulders whatever you want to say of me.
Mira says: Without the energy that lifts mountains, how am I to live?

Robert Bly

THE WILD WOMAN OF THE FORESTS

The wild woman of the forests
Discovered the sweet plums by tasting,
And brought them to her Lord —
She who was neither cultured nor lovely,
She who was filthy in disarrayed clothes,
She of the lowest of castes.
But the Lord, seeing her heart,
Took the ruined plums from her hand.
She saw no difference between low and high,
Wanting only the milk of his presence.
Illiterate, she never studied the Teachings —
A single turn of the chariot's wheel
Brought her to Knowledge.
Now she is bound to the Storm Bodied One
By gold cords of Love, and wanders *his* woods.
Servant Mira says:
Whoever can love like this will be saved.
My Master lifts all that is fallen,
And from the beginning I have been the handmaiden
Herding cows by his side.

Jane Hirshfield

Kashmiri

Lal Ded (14th century)

THE SOUL

The soul, like the moon,
is new, and always new again.

And I have seen the ocean
continuously creating.

Since I scoured my mind
and my body, I too, Lalla,
am new, each moment new.

My teacher told me one thing,
Live in the soul.

When that was so,
I began to go naked,
and dance.

Coleman Barks

ON THE WAY TO GOD

On the way to God the difficulties

feel like being ground by a millstone,
like night coming at noon, like
lightning through the clouds.

But don't worry!
What must come, comes.
Face everything with love,
as your mind dissolves in God.

Coleman Barks

✥ 5

EAST ASIA: MING CHINA; CHOSŎN
KOREA; VIETNAM; MUROMACHI JAPAN

Chinese

✥ Chang Yü (1333–1385)

THE PAVILION FOR LISTENING TO FRAGRANCE

Brilliant, bright—the flowers of the cold season!
Their subtle fragrance arises in the quiet.
Others are hoping to smell them a few times,
but I prefer to use my ears!
The fragrance sends forth jewel-like songs;
singing them out loud, I feel such joy!
And who says there is no fragrance in sound?
Smelling and hearing are really the same thing.
But best of all would be to end all sound,
and also get rid of fragrance and form.
No smelling, and also no hearing at all—
back to the mystery of the Primal One.

Jonathan Chaves

✥ Yang Chi (1334–1383)

FIVE-COLOR

A five-color robe of embroidered silk:
many flowers, and a few sparse branches.

Spring is here, and I'm afraid to put it on:
the butterflies might all land on me!

Jonathan Chaves

Yang Shih-chi (1365–1444)

FOLLOWING THE RHYMES OF SHAO-PAO HUANG'S POEM ON BEING MOVED WHILE VISITING THE FARMERS

There is a drought, the farmers have a hard time finding food:
what terrible suffering in this district!
They comb the fields for pieces of stubble:
they might as well steam sand for rice!
Now the tax collectors are putting on the pressure,
and the autumn harvest seems more distant than ever.
What are we officials doing about it?
Eating meat, growing old in the capital!

Jonathan Chaves

Yang Wen-li (16th century)

NEW YEAR'S EVE

Spring's sun has just turned, the year's about to end,
lanterns and fireworks smoke up the sky; tonight's not so cold.
Aware that tomorrow I will turn another year older,
all night I'll joyfully celebrate the change of seasons.
Seats arranged in the painted hall, gold and jade plates set,
scent of orchid ointment wafts from precious tripods.
By good luck I can even appreciate spring in advance:
plum blossoms fill my sight as I gaze at them, all smiles.

Nancy Hodes and Tung Yuan-fang

THINKING OF MY FAMILY ON AN AUTUMN DAY

Moist the jade dew that borders the flowers,
cool the golden breeze that penetrates the curtain.
Emerald green the autumn waters stretching to the sky,
hazy blue the evening mist that winds around the mountains.

Over and over I ponder the scene, sigh at the season's changes,
think of my family, recall my native place.
Leaning on the balustrade, I stand for a time transfixed,
my heart chasing wild geese that soar towards the south.

Nancy Hodes and Tung Yuan-fang

❧ Wang Chiu-ssu (1468–1551)

TWO POEMS AFTER READING THE POEMS OF MASTER HAN SHAN

1

This crazy man has escaped the world,
with his messy hair and bare feet!
His body sleeps among the clouds of Cold Mountain,
his mind is like the moon in an autumn pond!
He enjoys the company of the monk Feng-kan;
sometimes he visits the Cowrie Palace.
He looks up to heaven, and laughs out loud:
an ocean bird crying in the cool shade!
Flourishing his brush, he inscribes mountainsides:
dragons and snakes writhe in the lofty heights!
Handed down for thousands of years,
his fame will never die out.

2

Floating, floating, the river waters,
naturally forming patterns in the wind.
Beautiful, the jade of Ching Mountain:
carve it, cut it, and it loses its true nature.
Men of talent, striving for fame,
write too much poetry, and damage their souls!
They are like the parrot:
he is able to talk, but he just is not a man!
Where can we find a real recluse
who locks his door to keep out all the dust?

Jonathan Chaves

❧ T'ang Yin (1470–1523)

INSCRIPTION FOR A PORTRAIT

Last night the cherry-apple
    deflowered by the first rain-drops
Its fallen petals slight and frail

their beauty almost articulate.
My mistress rising early
　　leaves her bedroom
In her hand a mirror
　　to admire her painted cheeks.
She asks me 'Which is prettier
　　the petals or my complexion?'
To her question I reply
　　'They win by innocence.'
At hearing this my mistress
　　displays a charming anger
Refusing to believe dead petals
　　surpass a real live person.
She crumbles a handful of blossom
　　to throw in my face —
'Tonight, my dear' she says
　　'sleep with the flowers!'

John Scott and Graham Martin

❧ Huang O (1498–1569)

A FAREWELL TO A SOUTHERN MELODY

The day will come when I will
Share once more the quilts
And pillows I am storing
Away. Once more I will shyly
Let you undress me and gently
Unlock my sealed jewel.
I can never describe the
Ten thousand beautiful sensual
Ways we will make love.

Kenneth Rexroth and Ling Chung

TO THE TUNE "A FLOATING CLOUD CROSSES ENCHANTED MOUNTAIN"

Every morning I get up
Beautiful as the Goddess
Of Love in Enchanted Mountain.
Every night I go to bed
Seductive as Yang Kuei-fei,
The imperial concubine.
My slender waist and thighs
Are exhausted and weak
From a night of cloud dancing.

But my eyes are still lewd,
And my cheeks are flushed.
My old wet nurse combs
My cloud-like hair.
My lover, fragrant as incense,
Adjusts my jade hairpins, and
Draws on my silk stockings
Over my feet and legs
Perfumed with orchids;
And once again we fall over
Overwhelmed with passion.

Kenneth Rexroth and Ling Chung

Mo Shih-lung (c. 1539–1587)

SAYING GOOD-BYE TO A SINGING GIRL WHO HAS DECIDED TO BECOME A NUN

You have called at the gate of the True Vehicle,
             your worldly self is no more.
You have said farewell forever
             to the golden chambers,
                         the wind and the dust.
Lightly you wield the yak-tail whisk;
             your singing fan lies on the floor.
You learn to adjust your meditation cushion,
             and laugh at the dancer's mat.
No more resentment when rouge fades
             like red flowers;
no longer will the feathered hairdo appear in your mirror.
Mist, light, water—quiet Zen mind:
I know a new springtime
             will bloom
                         in the Realm of Emptiness.

Jonathan Chaves

Korean

Yi Inbok (c. 1350)

DRUMBEATS

The courtyard is warmed by the coming of spring.
The moon shines on the high places.

Where people once danced and sang
Drumbeats sound again.

Kevin O'Rourke

❧ Yi Talch'ung (c. 1385)

THE NEGLECTED WIFE

One moon of joy I knew,
And in the waning radiance of that moon
I gave you a folding fan.

Your love was lighter than the fragrant wind
Stirred by these sticks of carven sandalwood.

The moon sank down behind the city wall.
How bitter was the wine we drank at dawn!

Soon came the whisper of a silken skirt.
Soon came the perfume of a jasmine flower.
Swiftly for you there rose another moon.

Your new wife's face is like a jasmine petal
And like a fallen petal it will fade
After the moon goes down.

I think you do not know how cruel you are,
But why was your parting gift to me
Another folding fan?

Jean S. Grigsby

❧ Sung Sammun (1418–1456)

WHITE BANNERS

The long white banners flutter on the breeze.
Drums roll and boom to speed my life away.
Here, there and everywhere are grinning lips
And mocking eyes.
                    I watch the sinking sun.
Where shall I rest when all my pain is ended?
There are no inns within the Yellow Shades—
Where I shall sleep tonight no man can tell.

Jean S. Grigsby

❧ Kim Ku (1488–1534)

I SPY THE THREE-COLORED PEACH BLOSSOM

I spy the three-colored peach blossom
As it floats down the mountain stream.
A free spirit,
I jump in, fully clothed.
I scoop those flowers in my arms
And leap up and down in the water.

Kevin O'Rourke

❧ Anonymous (16th century)

IT IS THE THIRD WATCH

It is the third watch. The girl
   in the bridal bedroom is so gentle,
   so beautiful, I look and look again;
   I can't believe my eyes.
Sixteen years old, peach blossom complexion,
   golden hairpin, white ramie skirt,
   bright eyes agleam in playful glance,
   lips half-parted in a smile.
   My love! My own true love!
Need I say ought
   of the silver in her voice
   and the wonder of her under the quilt.

Kevin O'Rourke

❧ Anonymous (16th century)

LOVE, WHY DON'T YOU COME

Love, why don't you come!
   Why don't you come!
On the way did someone build
   a castle of iron,
   erect a wall within the castle,
   build a house within the wall,
   place a rice-chest within the house,
   put a box within the rice-chest,
   tie you up within the box,
   make the box fast with a pair of
   dragon-turtle locks?

Why don't you come?
With thirty days in the month,
    surely you could save one day for me?

Kevin O'Rourke

Anonymous (16th century)

THE ANGRY BRIDE

Six crock bowls the bride smashed
In a fit of temper on her wedding night.
Are you going to replace them, mother-in-law asked?
The bride replied: Your son has smashed beyond repair
The vessel I brought from home.
Weighed one against the other,
The balance would seem quite fair.

Kevin O'Rourke

Anonymous (16th century)

WIND LAST NIGHT BLEW DOWN

Wind last night blew down
A gardenful of peach blossoms.
A boy with a broom
Is starting to sweep them up.

Fallen flowers are flowers still;
Don't brush them away.

Virginia Olsen Baron and Chung Seuk Park

Anonymous (16th century)

WHEN I THINK ABOUT WHY

When I think about why
You sent that fan to me,
I wonder if you meant
For me to blow out the fire in my heart.

How could I put out a fire with a fan
When teardrops failed?

Virginia Olsen Baron and Chung Seuk Park

✎ Anonymous (16th century)

AGING

Aging is an agony.

Just white hairs, I'd thought;
But now the teeth are falling out
And hearing is a sort
Of fought-off deafness, it seems nothing
That my hair is white.

And she looks at me, she looks at me,
My darling of the night,
As though some bitter cucumber
Were sullying her sight.

Graeme Wilson

✎ Song Sun (1493–1583)

TEN YEARS IT TOOK

Ten years it took
To build my little cottage.
Now the cool wind inhabits half of it
And the rest is filled with moonlight.

There is no place left for the mountain and the stream
So I guess they will have to stay outside.

Virginia Olsen Baron and Chung Seuk Park

✎ Hwang Chini (c. 1506–1544)

I WILL CUT OUT THE MIDDLE WATCH

I will cut out the middle watch
Of this long midwinter night,
And carefully store it away.
When my lover returns I will take it out again,
Unrolling it inch by inch,
To lengthen the night.

John S. Major

✏ Myŏng'ok (16th century)

DREAMS

It is said that a lover seen in dreams
Will prove to be an unfaithful love.
Yet I ache and moan for you, faithless
Lover, and how can I see you except in
Dreams. O love, even though it is only
In dreams that I see you,
Let me see you; let me see you always.

Michael Stephens and Okhee Yoo

✏ Yi Jung (16th century)

THE RIVER DARKENS ON AN AUTUMN NIGHT

The river darkens on an autumn night
And the waves subside as if to sleep.
I drop a line into the water
But the sleepy fish won't bite.

The empty boat and I return
Filled with our catch of moonlight.

Virginia Olsen Baron and Chung Seuk Park

✏ Han Kwak (16th century)

DON'T BRING OUT THE STRAW MAT

Don't bring out the straw mat;
I'll sit on fallen leaves.
Don't bother to light the pine-knot torch;
The moon will rise again tonight.

But I might say yes to wine
And a little dish of mountain herbs.

Virginia Olsen Baron and Chung Seuk Park

❧ Kwŏn Homun (1532–1587)

NIGHTS AFTER RAIN WHEN THE MOON

Nights after rain when the moon
Cuts through the clouds to land on pine branches,
Slanting brilliant light
Across the blue stream,
A flock of seagulls from somewhere
Follows me around.

Kevin O'Rourke

❧ Chŏng Ch'ŏl (1536–1593)

SNOW FALLING IN THE PINE FOREST: TWO POEMS

1

Snow falling in the pine forest,
        every branch a flower.
I'll cut a branch
        and send it to my love.
What matter if it melts
        if he but sees it first?

2

Why does that pine tree stand
        so near the road?
I wish it stood a little back,
        perhaps in the hollow behind.
Everyone equipped with rope and axe
        will want to cut it down.

Kevin O'Rourke

MAGISTRATE

When I was made the magistrate
Of this benighted town
I had not thought to spend my days
In bobbing up and down.

How can so dwarf a township
Produce so vast a crowd

Of visitors concerned to brag
That we have met and bowed?

Greetings, flatteries, farewells:
One bows and bows again.
No wonder magistrates are rarely
Seen as upright men.

Graeme Wilson

Kim Sang'yong (1561–1637)

LOVE IS FALSE

Love is false, that he loves me is a lie.
That he saw me in a dream is a worse lie.
If you are sleepless as I, in which dream
                would you see me?

Chung Chong-wha

Hŏ Nansŏrhŏn (1563–1589)

FOR MY BROTHER HAGOK

The candle light shines low on the dark window,
Fireflies flit across the housetops.
As the night grows colder,
I hear autumn leaves rustle to the ground.
There's been no news for some time from your place of exile.
Because of you,
My mind is never free of worry.

Thinking of a distant temple,
I see a deserted hillside
Filled with the radiance of the moon.

Kichung Kim

Vietnamese

Anonymous (16th century)

THE FARMER'S PRIDE

Some folks transplant rice for wages,
but I have other reasons.

I watch the sky, the earth, the clouds,
observe the rain, the nights, the days,
keep track, stand guard till my legs
are stone, till the stone melts,
till the sky is clear and the sea calm.
Then I feel at peace.

Nguyen Ngoc Bich

✣ Anonymous (16th century)

ANGLING

My rod is made of fine bamboo,
my hook is made of gold.
For bait I use some flashing gems,
then cast my line in the dragon's mouth.
Some people fish in rivers and seas,
but I'm after girls of established families.
If you're already married, let go my bait.
If not, bite, and I'll try to land you.

Nguyen Ngoc Bich

✣ Anonymous (16th century)

GOOD SCHOLARS MAKE BAD HUSBANDS

Girls, don't ever marry students!
Their long backs require great swaths of cloth.
Well-fed, they rest their lazy bones.
In freezing winter weather
while you transplant rice for thirty-six coppers
they read books by the fire,
waiting to eat your earnings.

Nguyen Ngoc Bich

✣ Anonymous (16th century)

TOO LATE FOR A HUSBAND

Where were you in the marriage season?
Now all the available men are gone,
you pitch yourself up and moan to the sky,
"O Heaven, O Earth!
Can't you just toss me a little husband?"

The sky pokes out his head and replies,
"You were too choosy when the merchandise was in.
Go home now, we're all sold out."

Nguyen Ngoc Bich

❧ Nguyen Binh Khiem (1491–1585)

THE HATED RATS

To be born is to want—is it that simple?
Who can be whole, unfed, unfilled, unnourished?
Old saints furrowed the grain-seeded land
to feed parents, fill wives, nourish children.

Yet you came, rat, to tax us. Your gorged body
slinks invisible, sleek, to gnaw away
embattled fields, filled now with hollow stalks,
the storehouse gaping like a child's starved mouth.

The grunting farmer's labor cannot feed
the abyss behind the thin cries of his wife.
To die in want—is it that simple
to those yellow teeth whose hunger maims our flesh?

The strategems of your diseases sidle through us.
Everything, even your own filth, abhors you.
You foresaw the people wasted, emptied, stricken,
but now how our stiffening hands will strangle you,

nor will they loosen until at last they carry
your rank body to the court and marketplace
where beaks will feed and clash, once filled, like cymbals,
proclaiming a peace to nourish our ravaged land.

Nguyen Ngoc Bich

WORRIED

I hate war. I'm worried, of course,
yet content to be here, alone, bound in duty
to my old lord. How can I betray him to face the world?
An immortal must bide his time: I sing a little
to blend my soul with the landscape, I meditate
on Peace and Satisfaction. Modest perhaps, but then
not all of us can choose Fame.

Nguyen Ngoc Bich

Japanese

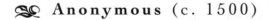 Ikkyū Sōjun (1394–1481)

FOUR POEMS

1

oh green green willow wonderfully red flower
but I know the colors are not there

2

nobody told the flowers to come up nobody
will ask them to leave when spring's gone

3

don't worry please please how many times do I have to say it
there's no way not to be who you are and where

4

ten years of whorehouse joy I'm alone now in the mountains
the pines are like a jail the wind scratches my skin

Stephen Berg

Monk Sōgi (1421–1502)

SPRING

Wait to scatter,
blossoms: for now there's no wind
   I can complain to.

Stephen D. Carter

Okinawan

Anonymous (c. 1500)

From THE OMORO SŌSHI

Before light became time
the sun shone into herself,

long, long before time
the single sun, overflowing,
looked down
and her look was pure desire.
The sun called to her
the first goddess, the deep mother,
and told her to make islands,
told her to make land.
The mother glistened
and made islands,
and grew hot
and made more and more.
But the sun couldn't wait,
she couldn't hold in the want.
"Burning mother," she said, "Stop!
Stop bearing all those islands,
stop making all that land.
Bear me some small, soft people!"

———————

Between Mount Onna and the sea
her father walks
with his hands on his heart,
and her mother from Awa
lies every night
hugging the air.
Up on the mountain
already three months now
in a cave on the peak
their daughter listens
only to goddesses,
bitten by mosquitoes,
bitten by gnats.

                    Christopher Drake

Part VI

THE
SEVENTEENTH
CENTURY
(1600–1700)

The poetic sensibility of the seventeenth century was close to the spirit of the baroque. The word *baroque* was a borrowing from the descriptive language of art history as it applied to the florid architecture of continental Europe where the Roman Catholic religion held its ground against the movement of the Reformation in the north. The actual term *baroque* is supposedly derived from the Portuguese word *barroco,* meaning "a pearl of irregular shape," although some historians insist that it comes from the word *baroco,* used to represent a certain vein of late medieval pedantry. Whatever the source of the word, learning, oddity, and overabundance define the poetic character of the age.

In both poetry and the visual arts, the baroque era was marked by excess, exuberance and a relishing of conceit so vehement that it seems almost perverse. Its yoking of unlikely images, its expressive energy in declaring the sumptuousness of heaven and earth, and its awareness of the loveliness and horror of the physical world informed the metaphysical poetry and theater of Jacobean England, the dynamism of the *siglo de oro* ("century of gold") of Spain, and changed the vocabulary of poets throughout the European Counter-Reformation.

The mystical and voluptuous signature of the poetry in this section was underwritten by an expansion of anatomical, scientific, and technological thought and vocabulary; both the design of the balance spring for watches and the precise definition of the heart as a muscle had considerable impact. This era bid a final farewell to the medieval model of the sun in orbit around the earth. Its early modernity united in a brilliant tension with the doctrinal ferocity and kindling fever of the wars of religion. In the exiled Théophile de Viau's poem included here, there is a reflection of this twilight of the distracted mind, and an image of the world turned upside down. This seventeenth-century French poem became an icon for the surrealists of the 1920s.

Anxiety, incongruous couplings of ideas, and concision were the driving forces of the age that united to produce the wit of the English Metaphysical poets. Samuel Johnson coined their collective name, and like Dryden, disparaged their mazelike models of passion and reasoning. These poets used argument, persuasion, and the sinewy rhetoric of the baroque to imagine a moment of religious or erotic experience. Clergymen, Calvinists, and eccentric and visionary chaplains like Thomas Traherne struck sparks from the comparison of unlikely things to create extravagant conceits and, as with the whirling motion of Bernini's sculptures, added to what was wrought.

The heroes of baroque poetry were as complex as Milton's Lucifer, and the hero of his *Samson Agonistes,* massive embodiments of paradox and double meaning: the blind Samson, once-powerful prisoner of the Philistines in a biblical story from *Judges,* resembles not only Hercules and stubborn humanity in struggle *(agonistes)* but the defiant poet John Milton, in defeat after the Restoration. Milton had a great poet's special custody of the historical imagination of the age of Cromwell and the English Civil War.

The fervor of religious conversion, its imagery of blood and tears, suffused seventeenth-century poetry on the Continent as well. There, its wars of religion, in particular the inferno of the Thirty Years' War, ignited the work of the greatest German poet of the century, Andreas Gryphius. In Gryphius's "Hell" we have something close to Brueghel's "Triumph of Death." By writing German hymns himself and making the singing of the congregation an integral part of the church service, Martin Luther gave the religious lyric a new prestige.

In Catholic Spain, where the *siglo de oro* lasted well beyond one century, dramatists and poets like Lope de Vega combined a Renaissance Spanish ferocity of expression with the panache of the baroque. Luis de Gongora wove Renaissance and popular poetry into an individual and elegant form in the style now known as "Gongorism." The controversy about this poet — grotesque or astonishing — continues, but Gongara emblemizes the Spanish baroque in his lavish use of metaphor and hyperbole, his Latinization of vocabulary, and his steady drawing from classical myth.

Religious ecstacy and a sense of calamity before the will of an unaccountable and fearsome God disturbed the gilt clockwork of the Renaissance world order. The poets born in the next century would inhabit an age of great prose, anticipated here by La Fontaine's allegorical tales of everyday life. This shift in focus was dictated by a rationalizing psychology and a fascination with the structure of society and of the universe.

K. W.

The Ottoman Turks, self-confident, rich, and securely in control of their far-flung empire, indulged poetry writing as a harmless and pleasant occupation; poets responded by creating verse that was romantic and at its best very beautiful, but highly constrained, with a standard vocabulary of images (wine, roses, poplars, and so on) and a conventional attitude of world-weary resignation. The Ottoman Empire controlled much of the

Balkans; the Serbian and Gypsy poetry in this section was written under Ottoman rule.

Indian poetry continues in this section with vernacular devotional verse; Bihari's short lyrics hark back to the secular verse of the old Sanskrit anthologies. Most remarkable here are several Telegu poems to Krishna in which the god is imagined as the patron of a courtesan, who teases, cajoles, and flirts with him—a startlingly direct evocation of the eroticism of religious devotion.

China in this section is represented by the poetry of two famous eccentrics; one recalls (even in his pen name) the T'ang hermit-poet Han Shan, the other ignores the high tradition altogether to derive inspiration from bawdy popular lyrics. Tibet also provides a surprise with the love songs of the sixth Dalai Lama, a romantic and short-lived young man tragically unsuited to his high spiritual office.

The seventeenth century was a glorious age for Japanese literature, seen here in a diversity of styles that seek to escape the strictures of the *tanka* form: the aristocratic intellectual Jōzan and the Zen monk Gensei both wrote in classical Chinese; Bashō perfected the new *haiku* form, and, in the company of poetical friends, created *renga* linked-verse sequences of striking modernity. Chikamatsu, Japan's greatest playwright, is represented by the climactic scene from his most famous play, *The Love Suicides at Sonezaki.* The Asian verse in Part VI concludes with the work of three late Korean masters of the "long *sijo*" style.

J.S.M.

1

England: Metaphysical and Cavalier Poetry

English

John Donne (1572–1631)

From HOLY SONNETS: AT THE ROUND EARTH'S IMAGINED CORNERS BLOW

At the round earth's imagined corners blow
  Your trumpets, angels, and arise, arise
  From death, you numberless infinities
Of souls, and to your scattered bodies go:
All whom the flood did, and fire shall o'erthrow,
  All whom war, dearth, age, agues, tyrannies,
  Despair, law, chance hath slain, and you whose eyes
Shall behold God, and never taste death's woe.
But let them sleep, Lord, and me mourn a space,
  For if above all these my sins abound,
'Tis late to ask abundance of thy grace
  When we are there. Here on this lowly ground
    Teach me how to repent: for that's as good
    As if thou hadst sealed my pardon with thy blood.

ELEGIE 19: TO HIS MISTRIS GOING TO BED

Come, Madam, come, all rest my powers defie,
Until I labour, I in labour lie.
The foe oft-times having the foe in sight,
Is tir'd with standing though he never fight.

Off with that girdle, like heaven's Zone glistering,
But a far fairer world incompassing.
Unpin that spangled breastplate which you wear,
That th' eyes of busy fools may be stopt there.
Unlace yourself, for that harmonious chyme,
Tells me from you that now it is bed time.
Off with that happy busk, which I envie,
That still can be, and still can stand so high.
Your gown going off, such beautious state reveals,
As when from flowry meads th'hills shadow steales.
Off with that wyerie Coronet and shew
The haiery Diademe which on you doth grow:
Now off with those shooes, and then safely tread
In this loves hallow'd temple, this soft bed.
In such white robes, heaven's Angels us'd to be
Receavd by men; Thou Angel bringst with thee
A heaven like Mahomets paradice; and though
Ill spirits walk in white, we easly know,
By this these Angels from an evil sprite,
Those set our hairs, but these our flesh upright.
    Licence my roaving hands, and let them go,
Before, behind, between, above, below.
O my America! my new-found-land,
My kingdome, safeliest when with one man man'd,
My Myne of precious stones, My Emperie,
How blest am I in this discovering thee!
To enter in these bonds, is to be free;
Then where my hand is set, my seal shall be.
    Full nakedness! All joyes are due to thee,
As souls unbodied, bodies uncloth'd must be,
To taste whole joyes. Gems which you women use
Are like Atlanta's balls, cast in mens views,
That when a fools eye lighteth on a Gem,
His earthly soul may covet theirs, not them.
Like pictures, or like books' gay coverings made
For lay-men, are all women thus array'd;
Themselves are mystick books, which only wee
(Whom their imputed grace will dignifie)
Must see reveal'd. Then since that I may know;
As liberally, as to a Midwife, shew
Thy self: cast all, yea, this white lynnen hence,
There is no pennance due to innocence.
    To teach thee, I am naked first; why then
What needst thou have more covering than a man.

GO AND CATCH A FALLING STAR

Go and catch a falling star,
    Get with child a mandrake root,

Tell me where all past years are,
    Or who cleft the Devil's foot,
Teach me to hear mermaids singing,
    Or to keep off envy's stinging,
        And find
        What wind
Serves to advance an honest mind.

I thou be'st borne to strange sights,
    Things invisible to see,
Ride ten thousand days and nights,
    Till age snow white hairs on thee.
Thou, when thou return'st, wilt tell me
    All strange wonders that befell thee,
        And swear
        Nowhere
Lives a woman true, and fair.

If thou find'st one, let me know,
    Such a pilgrimage were sweet;
Yet do not, I would not go,
    Though at next door we might meet;
Though she were true, when you met her,
    And last, till you write your letter,
        Yet she
        Will be
False, ere I come, to two, or three.

THE CANONIZATION

For God's sake hold your tongue, and let me love,
    Or chide my palsy, or my gout,
My five gray hairs, or ruined fortune flout;
With wealth your state, your mind with arts improve;
    Take you a course, get you a place,
    Observe his Honour, or his Grace,
And the King's real, or his stamped face
    Contemplate; what you will, approve,
        So you will let me love.

Alas, alas, who's injured by my love?
    What merchant's ships have my sighs drowned?
Who says my tears have overflowed his ground?
When did my colds a forward spring remove?
    When did the heats which my veins fill
    Add one man to the plaguy Bill?
Soldiers find wars, and lawyers find out still
    Litigious men, which quarrels move,
        Though she and I do love.

Call us what you will, we're made such by love;
    Call her one, me another fly,
We're tapers too, and at our own cost die,
And we in us find the Eagle and the Dove;
    The Phoenix riddle hath more wit
    By us; we two, being one, are it,
So, to one neutral thing both sexes fit.
    We die and rise the same, and prove
        Mysterious by this love.

We can die by it, if not live by love,
    And if unfit for tombs or hearse
Our legend be, it will be fit for verse;
And if no piece of chronicle we prove,
    We'll build in sonnets pretty rooms;
    As well a well-wrought urn becomes
The greatest ashes, as half-acre tombs;
    And by these hymns all shall approve
        Us canonized for love;

And thus invoke us: 'You, whom reverend Love
    Made one another's hermitage;
You, to whom love was peace, that now is rage;
Who did the whole world's soul extract, and drove
    Into the glasses of your eyes,
    So made such mirrors, and such spies,
That they did all to you epitomize,
    Countries, towns, courts: beg from above
        A pattern of your love!'

✆ Ben Jonson (1573–1637)

ON MY FIRST SON

Farewell, thou child of my right hand, and joy;
My sin was too much hope of thee, loved boy:
Seven years thou'wert lent to me, and I thee pay,
Exacted by thy fate, on the just day.
O could I lose all father now! for why
Will man lament the state he should envý
To have so soon 'scaped world's and flesh's rage,
And, if no other misery, yet age?
Rest in soft peace, and asked, say, "Here doth lie
Ben Jonson his best piece of poetry."
For whose sake henceforth all his vows be such
As what he loves may never like too much.

ON SPIES

Spies you are lights in state, but of base stuffe,
Who, when you have burnt your selves down to the snuffe,
Stinke, and are throwne away. End faire enough.

TO DOCTOR EMPIRICK

When men a dangerous disease did 'scape
Of old, they gave a cock to Aesculape;
Let me give two, that doubly am got free
From my disease's danger, and from thee.

✇ Sir Arthur Gorges (?–1625)

HER FACE, HER TONGUE, HER WIT

Her face	Her tongue	Her wit
so fair	so sweet	so sharp
first bent	then drew	then hit
mine eye	mine ear	my heart
Mine eye	Mine ear	My heart
to like	to learn	to love
her face	her tongue	her wit
doth lead	doth teach	doth move
Her face	Her tongue	Her wit
with beams	with sound	with art
doth blind	doth charm	doth knit
mine eye	mine ear	my heart
Mine eye	Mine ear	My heart
with life	with hope	with skill
her face	her tongue	her wit
doth feed	doth feast	doth fill
O face	O tongue	O wit
with frowns	with checks	with smart
wrong not	vex not	wound not
mine eye	mine ear	my heart
This eye	This ear	This heart
shall joy	shall yield	shall swear
her face	her tongue	her wit
to serve	to trust	to fear.

John Webster (c. 1580–1638)

From THE WHITE DEVIL

A Dirge

Call for the robin-redbreast and the wren,
Since o'er shady groves they hover,
And with leaves and flowers do cover
The friendless bodies of unburied men.
Call unto his funeral dole
The ant, the field-mouse, and the mole,
To rear him hillocks that shall keep him warm,
And (when gay tombs are robb'd) sustain no harm;
But keep the wolf far thence, that's foe to men,
For with his nails he'll dig them up again.

Attributed to Orlando Gibbons (1583–1625)

THE SILVER SWANNE, WHO LIVING HAD NO NOTE

The Silver Swanne, who living had no Note,
    When death approacht, unlockt her silent throat.
Leaning her breast against the reedie shore,
    Thus sang her first and last, and sung no more:
Farewell all joyes, O death come close mine eyes,
More Geese than Swannes now live, more fooles than wise.

Robert Herrick (1591–1674)

THE ARGUMENT OF HIS BOOK

I sing of Brooks, of Blossoms, Birds, and Bowers:
Of April, May, of June, and July-Flowers.
I sing of May-poles, Hock-carts, Wassails, Wakes,
Of Bride-grooms, Brides, and of their Bridal-cakes.
I write of Youth, of Love, and have access
By these, to sing of cleanly-wantonness.
I sing of Dews, of Rains, and piece by piece
Of Balm, of Oil, of Spice, of Amber-Greece.
I sing of Time's transhifting; and I write
How Roses first came red, and Lilies white.
I write of Groves, of Twilights, and I sing

The Court of Mab, and of the Fairie-King.
I write of Hell. I sing (and ever shall)
Of Heaven, and hope to have it after all.

UPON JULIA'S CLOTHES

Whenas in silks my Julia goes,
Then, then, methinks, how sweetly flows
That liquefaction of her clothes.

Next, when I cast mine eyes and see
That brave vibration, each way free,
O, how that glittering taketh me!

George Herbert (1593–1633)

JORDAN

Who sayes that fictions onely and false hair
Become a verse? Is there in truth no beautie?
Is all good structure in a winding stair?
May no lines passe, except they do their dutie
    Not to a true, but painted chair?

Is it no verse, except enchanted groves
And sudden arbours shadow course-spunne lines?
Must purling streams refresh a lovers loves?
Must all be vail'd, while he that reads divines,
    Catching the sense at two removes?

Shepherds are honest people; let them sing:
Riddle who list for me, and pull for Prime:
I envie no man's nightingale or spring;
Nor let them punish me with loss of rime
    Who plainly say, *My God, My King.*

EASTER WINGS

            Lord, who createdst man in wealth and store,
              Though foolishly he lost the same,
                Decaying more and more
                    Till he became
                      Most poor:
                      With thee
                    O let me rise

As   larks,   harmoniously,
And sing this day thy victories:
Then shall the fall further the flight in me.

My tender age in sorrow did begin;
And still with sicknesses and shame
Thou didst so punish sin,
That I became
Most thin.
With thee
Let me combine,
And feel this day thy victory;
For, if I imp my wing on thine,
Affliction shall advance the flight in me.

HEAVEN

O who will show me those delights on high?
    Echo.   I.
Thou Echo, thou art mortall, all men know.
    Echo.   No.
Wert thou not born among the trees and leaves?
    Echo.   Leaves.
And are there any leaves, that still abide?
    Echo.   Bide.
What leaves are they? impart the matter wholly.
    Echo.   Holy.
Are holy leaves the Echo then of blisse?
    Echo.   Yes.
Then tell me, what is that supreme delight?
    Echo.   Light.
Light to the mind: what shall the will enjoy?
    Echo.   Joy.
But there are cares and business with the pleasure?
    Echo.   Leisure.
Light, joy, and leisure: but shall they persever?
    Echo.   Ever.

James Shirley (1596–1666)

DEATH THE LEVELLER

The glories of our blood and state
    Are shadows, not substantial things;
There is no armour against Fate;
    Death lays his icy hand on kings:
        Sceptre and Crown

    Must tumble down,
And in the dust be equal made
With the poor crooked scythe and spade.

Some men with swords may reap the field,
    And plant fresh laurels where they kill:
But their strong nerves at last must yield;
    They tame but one another still:
        Early or late
        They stoop to fate,
And must give up their murmuring breath
When they, pale captives, creep to death.

The garlands wither on your brow;
    Then boast no more your mighty deeds!
Upon Death's purple altar now
    See where the victor-victim bleeds.
        Your heads must come
        To the cold tomb:
Only the actions of the just
Smell sweet and blossom in their dust.

Edmund Waller (1607–1687)

SONG

    Go, lovely rose!
Tell her that wastes her time and me
    That now she knows,
When I resemble her to thee,
How sweet and fair she seems to be.

    Tell her that's young,
And shuns to have her graces spied,
    That hadst thou sprung
In deserts, where no men abide,
Thou must have uncommended died.

    Small is the worth
Of beauty from the light retired;
    Bid her come forth,
Suffer herself to be desired,
And not blush so to be admired.

    Then die! that she
The common fate of all things rare
    May read in thee;
How small a part of time they share
That are so wondrous sweet and fair!

✇ John Milton (1608–1674)

From BOOK IV of PARADISE LOST

With thee conversing, I forget all time,
All seasons and thir change, all please alike.
Sweet is the breath of morn, her rising sweet,
With charm of earliest Birds; pleasant the Sun
When first on this delightful Land he spreads
His orient Beams, on herb, tree, fruit, and flow'r,
Glist'ring with dew; fragrant the fertile earth
After soft showers; and sweet the coming on
Of grateful Ev'ning mild, then silent Night
With this her solemn Bird and this fair Moon,
And these the Gems of Heav'n, her starry train:
But neither breath of Morn when she ascends
With charm of earliest Birds, nor rising Sun
On this delightful land, nor herb, fruit, flow'r,
Glist'ring with dew, nor fragrance after showers,
Nor grateful Ev'ning mild, nor silent Night
With this her solemn Bird, nor walk by Moon,
Or glittering Star-Light, without thee is sweet.

From SAMSON AGONISTES

Samson. A little onward lend thy guiding hand
To these dark steps, a little further on;
For yonder bank hath choice of Sun or shade,
There I am wont to sit, when any chance
Relieves me from my task of servile toil,
Daily in the common Prison else enjoin'd me,
Where I a Prisoner chain'd, scarce freely draw
The air imprison'd also, close and damp,
Unwholesome draught: but here I feel amends,
The breath of Heav'n fresh-blowing, pure and sweet,
With day-spring born; here leave me to respire.
This day a solemn Feast the people hold
To *Dagon* their Sea-Idol, and forbid
Laborious works, unwillingly this rest
Thir Superstition yields me; hence with leave
Retiring from the popular noise, I seek
This unfrequented place to find some ease,
Ease to the body some, none to the mind
From restless thoughts, that like a deadly swarm
Of Hornets arm'd, no sooner found alone,
But rush upon me thronging, and present

Times past, what once I was, and what am now.
O wherefore was my birth from Heaven foretold
Twice by an Angel, who at last in sight
Of both my Parents all in flames ascended
From off the Altar, where an Off'ring burn'd,
As in a fiery column charioting
His Godlike presence, and from some great act
Or benefit reveal'd to *Abraham's* race?
Why was my breeding order'd and prescrib'd
As of a person separate to God,
Design'd for great exploits; if I must die
Betray'd, Captiv'd, and both my Eyes put out,
Made of my Enemies the scorn and gaze;
To grind in Brazen Fetters under task
With this Heav'n-gifted strength? O glorious strength
Put to the labour of a Beast, debas't
Lower than bondslave! Promise was that I
Should *Israel* from *Philistian* yoke deliver;
Ask for this great Deliverer now, and find him
Eyeless in *Gaza* at the Mill with slaves,
Himself in bonds under *Philistian* yoke;
Yet stay, let me not rashly call in doubt
Divine Prediction; what if all foretold
Had been fulfill'd but through mine own default,
Whom have I to complain of but myself?
Who this high gift of strength committed to me,
In what part lodg'd, how easily bereft me,
Under the Seal of silence could not keep,
But weakly to a woman must reveal it,
O'ercome with importunity and tears.
O impotence of mind, in body strong!
But what is strength without a double share
Of wisdom? Vast, unwieldy, burdensome
Proudly secure, yet liable to fall
By weakest subtleties, not made to rule,
But to subserve where wisdom bears command.
God, when he gave me strength, to show withal
How slight the gift was, hung it in my Hair.
But peace, I must not quarrel with the will
Of highest dispensation, which herein
Haply had ends above my reach to know:
Suffices that to me strength is my bane,
And proves the source of all my miseries;
So many, and so huge, that each apart
Would ask a life to wail, but chief of all,
O loss of sight, of thee I most complain!
Blind among enemies, O worse than chains,
Dungeon, or beggary, or decrepit age!
Light the prime work of God to me is extinct,
And all her various objects of delight

Annull'd, which might in part my grief have eas'd,
Inferior to the vilest now become
Of man or worm; the vilest here excel me,
They creep, yet see; I dark in light expos'd
To daily fraud, contempt, abuse and wrong,
Within doors, or without, still as a fool,
In power of others, never in my own;
Scarce half I seem to live, dead more than half.
O dark, dark, dark, amid the blaze of noon,
Irrecoverably dark, total Eclipse
Without all hope of day!
O first created Beam, and thou great Word,
Let there be light, and light was over all;
Why am I thus bereav'd thy prime decree?
The Sun to me is dark
And silent as the Moon,
When she deserts the night,
Hid in her vacant interlunar cave.
Since light so necessary is to life,
And almost life itself, if it be true
That light is in the Soul,
She all in every part; why was the sight
To such a tender ball as th' eye confin'd?
So obvious and so easy to be quench't,
And not as feeling through all parts diffus'd,
That she might look at will through every pore?
Then had I not been thus exil'd from light;
As in the land of darkness yet in light,
To live a life half dead, a living death,
And buried; but O yet more miserable!
Myself my Sepulchre, a moving Grave,
Buried, yet not exempt
By privilege of death and burial
From worst of other evils, pains and wrongs,
But made hereby obnoxious more
To all the miseries of life,
Life in captivity
Among inhuman foes.
But who are these? for with joint pace I hear
The tread of many feet steering this way;
Perhaps my enemies who come to stare
At my affliction, and perhaps to insult,
Thir daily practice to afflict me more.

From COMUS

Sabrina

The Spirit. Sabrina fair,
　　　Listen where thou art sitting
　　Under the glassy, cool, translucent wave,
　　　In twisted braids of lilies knitting
　　The loose train of thy amber-dropping hair;
　　　Listen for dear honour's sake,
　　　Goddess of the silver lake,
　　　Listen and save.
　　Listen and appear to us
　　In name of great Oceanus,
　　By the earth-shaking Neptune's mace,
　　And Tethys' grave majestic pace,
　　By hoary Nereus' wrinkled look,
　　And the Carpathian wizard's hook,
　　By scaly Triton's winding shell,
　　And old soothsaying Glaucus' spell,
　　By Leucothea's lovely hands,
　　And her son that rules the strands,
　　By Thetis' tinsel-slippered feet,
　　And the songs of Sirens sweet,
　　By dead Parthenope's dear tomb,
　　And fair Ligea's golden comb,
　　Wherewith she sits on diamond rocks
　　Sleeking her soft alluring locks;
　　By all the nymphs that nightly dance
　　Upon thy streams with wily glance,
　　Rise, rise, and heave thy rosy head
　　From thy coral-paven bed,
　　And bridle in thy headlong wave,
　　Till thou our summons answered have.
　　　　　　　Listen and save!

Sabrina.　　　By the rushy-fringèd bank,
　　Where grows the willow and the osier dank,
　　　My sliding chariot stays,
　　Thick set with agate, and the azurn sheen
　　　Of turkish blue, and emerald green,
　　　　That in the channel strays.
　　Whilst from off the waters fleet
　　Thus I set my printless feet
　　O'er the cowslip's velvet head,
　　　That bends not as I tread.
　　Gentle swain, at thy request
　　　I am here!

❧ Richard Crashaw (1612–1649)

From THE FLAMING HEART: UPON THE BOOK
AND PICTURE OF THE SERAPHICAL SAINT
TERESA

Conclusion

O thou undaunted daughter of desires!
By all thy dow'r of *Lights* and *Fires;*
By all the eagle in thee, all the dove;
By all thy lives and deaths of love;
By thy large draughts of intellectual day,
And by thy thirsts of love more large then they;
By all thy brim-fill'd Bowls of fierce desire
By the last Morning's draught of liquid fire;
By the full kingdom of that final kiss
That seiz'd thy parting Soul, and seal'd thee his;
By all the heav'ns thou hast in him
(Fair sister of the *Seraphim!*)
By all of *Him* we have in *Thee;*
Leave nothing of my *Self* in me.
Let me so read thy life, that I
Unto all life of mine may die.

❧ Anne Bradstreet (c. 1612–1672)

From THE PROLOGUE

I am obnoxious to each carping tongue
Who says my hand a needle better fits.
A poet's pen all scorn I should thus wrong;
For such despite they cast on female wits,
If what I do prove well, it won't advance —
They'll say it's stolen, or else it was by chance.

But sure the antique Greeks were far more mild,
Else of our sex why feignéd they those Nine,
and Poesy made Calliope's own child?
So 'mongst the rest they placed the Arts Divine.
But this weak knot they will full soon untie —
The Greeks did nought but play the fools and lie.

Let Greeks be Greeks, and women what they are.
Men have precedency, and still excel.
It is but vain unjustly to wage war.
Men can do best, and women know it well.

Preëminence in all and each is yours —
Yet grant some small acknowledgment of ours.

And oh, ye high flown quills that soar the skies,
And ever with your prey still catch your praise,
If e'er you deign these lowly lines your eyes,
Give thyme or parsley wreath; I ask no bays.
This mean and unrefinéd ore of mine
Will make your glistering gold but more to shine.

Andrew Marvell (1621–1678)

BERMUDAS

    Where the remote Bermudas ride,
In th' ocean's bosom unespied,
From a small boat that rowed along,
The listening winds received this song:
    "What should we do but sing His praise,
That led us through the watery maze
Unto an isle so long unknown,
And yet far kinder than our own?
Where He the huge sea monsters wracks,
That lift the deep upon their backs;
He lands us on a grassy stage,
Safe from the storms, and prelate's rage.
He gave us this eternal spring
Which here enamels everything,
And sends the fowls to us in care,
On daily visits through the air;
He hangs in shades the orange bright,
Like golden lamps in a green night,
And does in the pomegranates close
Jewels more rich than Ormus shows;
He makes the figs our mouths to meet,
And throws the melons at our feet;
But apples plants of such a price,
No tree could ever bear them twice;
With cedars, chosen by His hand,
From Lebanon, He stores the land;
And makes the hollow seas, that roar,
Proclaim the ambergris on shore;
He cast (of which we rather boast)
The Gospel's pearl upon our coast,
And in these rocks for us did frame
A temple, where to sound His name.
O! let our voice His praise exalt,
Till it arrive at heaven's vault,

Which, thence (perhaps) rebounding, may
Echo beyond the Mexique Bay."
    Thus sung they in the English boat,
An holy and a cheerful note;
And all the way, to guide their chime,
With falling oars they kept the time.

TO HIS COY MISTRESS

Had we but world enough and time,
This coyness, Lady, were no crime.
We would sit down and think which way
To walk, and pass our long love's day.
Thou by the Indian Ganges' side
Shouldst rubies find; I by the tide
Of Humber would complain. I would
Love you ten years before the Flood,
And you should, if you please, refuse
Till the Conversion of the Jews.
My vegetable love should grow
Vaster than empires, and more slow.
An hundred years should go to praise
Thine eyes, and on thy forehead gaze,
Two hundred to adore each breast,
But thirty thousand to the rest.
An age at least to every part,
And the last age should show your heart.
For, Lady, you deserve this state,
Nor would I love at lower rate.
    But at my back I always hear
Time's winged chariot hurrying near,
And yonder all before us lie
Deserts of vast eternity.
Thy beauty shall no more be found,
Nor in thy marble vault shall sound
My echoing song; then worms shall try
That long preserved virginity,
And your quaint honor turn to dust,
And into ashes all my lust.
The grave's a fine and private place,
But none, I think, do there embrace.
    Now therefore, while the youthful hue
Sits on thy skin like morning glew,
And while thy willing soul transpires
At every pore with instant fires,
Now let us sport us while we may;
And now, like amorous birds of prey,
Rather at once our time devour
Than languish in his slow-chapped power.

Let us roll all our strength and all
Our sweetness up into one ball
And tear our pleasures with rough strife
Thorough the iron gates of life.
Thus, though we cannot make our sun
Stand still, yet we will make him run.

ॐ Henry Vaughan (1622–1695)

THEY ARE ALL GONE INTO THE WORLD OF LIGHT!

They are all gone into the world of light!
    And I alone sit lingering here;
Their very memory is fair and bright,
    And my sad thoughts doth clear.

It glows and glitters in my cloudy breast
    Like stars upon some gloomy grove,
Or those faint beams in which this hill is dressed
    After the sun's remove.

I see them walking in an air of glory,
    Whose light doth trample on my days;
My days, which are at best but dull and hoary,
    Mere glimmering and decays.

O holy hope, and high humility,
    High as the heavens above!
These are your walks, and you have showed them me
    To kindle my cold love.

Dear, beauteous death! the jewel of the just,
    Shining nowhere but in the dark;
What mysteries do lie beyond thy dust,
    Could man outlook that mark!

He that hath found some fledged bird's nest may know
    At first sight if the bird be flown;
But what fair well or grove he sings in now,
    That is to him unknown.

And yet, as angels in some brighter dreams
    Call to the soul when man doth sleep,
So some strange thoughts transcend our wonted themes,
    And into glory peep.

If a star were confined into a tomb,
    Her captive flames must needs burn there;

But when the hand that locked her up gives room,
   She'll shine through all the sphere.

O Father of eternal life, and all
   Created glories under Thee!
Resume Thy spirit from this world of thrall
   Into true liberty!

Either disperse these mists, which blot and fill
   My perspective still as they pass;
Or else remove me hence unto that hill
   Where I shall need no glass.

John Dryden (1631–1700)

A SONG FOR ST CECILIA'S DAY, 1687

1

From harmony, from heav'nly harmony
   This universal frame began.
When nature underneath a heap
   Of jarring atoms lay,
   And could not heave her head,
The tuneful voice was heard from high,
   'Arise ye more than dead.'
Then cold, and hot, and moist, and dry,
   In order to their stations leap,
   And music's pow'r obey.
From harmony, from heav'nly harmony
   This universal frame began;
   From harmony to harmony
Through all the compass of the notes it ran,
The diapason closing full in man.

2

What passion cannot music raise and quell!
   When Jubal struck the corded shell,
   His list'ning brethren stood around
   And wond'ring on their faces fell
   To worship that celestial sound.
Less than a god they thought there could not dwell
   Within the hollow of that shell,
   That spoke so sweetly and so well.
What passion cannot music raise and quell!

3

   The trumpet's loud clangour
   Excites us to arms

With shrill notes of anger
  And mortal alarms.
The double double double beat
  Of the thund'ring drum
  Cries hark the foes come!
Charge, charge, 'tis too late to retreat.

4

The soft complaining flute
In dying notes discovers
The woes of hopeless lovers,
Whose dirge is whisper'd by the warbling lute.

5

Sharp violins proclaim
Their jealous pangs and desperation,
Fury, frantic indignation,
Depth of pains and height of passion,
  For the fair, disdainful dame.

6

But oh! what art can teach
  What human voice can reach
The sacred organ's praise?
Notes inspiring holy love,
Notes that wing their heav'nly ways
  To mend the choirs above.

7

Orpheus could lead the savage race,
And trees uprooted left their place,
  Sequacious of the lyre.
But bright Cecilia raised the wonder high'r;
  When to her organ vocal breath was giv'n,
An angel heard and straight appeared
  Mistaking earth for heav'n.

Grand Chorus

As from the pow'r of sacred lays
  The spheres began to move,
And sung the great creator's praise
  To all the blessed above;
So when the last and dreadful hour
This crumbling pageant shall devour,
The trumpet shall be heard on high,
The dead shall live, the living die,
And music shall untune the sky.

◊Q Thomas Traherne (1637–1674)

SHADOWS IN THE WATER

In unexperienced infancy
Many a sweet mistake doth lie,
Mistake though false, intending true,
A seeming somewhat more than view
    That doth instruct the mind
    In things that lie behind,
And many secrets to us show
Which afterwards we come to know.

Thus did I by the water's brink
Another world beneath me think,
And while the lofty spacious skies
Reversèd there abused mine eyes,
    I fancied other feet
    Came mine to touch and meet;
As by some puddle I did play
Another world within it lay.

Beneath the water people drowned,
Yet with another heaven crowned,
In spacious regions seemed to go
Freely moving to and fro;
    In bright and open space
    I saw their very face;
Eyes, hands and feet they had like mine;
Another sun did with them shine.

'Twas strange that people there should walk
And yet I could not hear them talk;
That through a little watery chink
Which one dry ox or horse might drink
    We other worlds should see,
    Yet not admitted be;
And other confines there behold
Of light and darkness, heat and cold.

I called them oft, but called in vain,
No speeches we could entertain;
Yet did I there expect to find
Some other world to please my mind.
    I plainly saw by these
    A new antipodes,
Whom, though they were so plainly seen,
A film kept off that stood between.

By walking men's reversèd feet
I chanced another world to meet;
Though it did not to view exceed
A phantasm, 'tis a world indeed
    Where skies beneath us shine
    And earth by art divine
Another face presents below,
Where people's feet against ours go.

Within the regions of the air,
Compassed about with heavens fair,
Great tracts of land there may be found
Enriched with fields and fertile ground;
    Where many numerous hosts
    In those far distant coasts,
For other great and glorious ends,
Inhabit, my yet unknown friends.

O ye that stand upon the brink,
Whom I so near me, through the chink,
With wonder see; what faces there,
Whose feet, whose bodies, do ye wear?
    I my companions see
    In you, another me.
They seemed others, but are we;
Our second selves those shadows be.

Look how far off those lower skies
Extend themselves! Scarce with mine eyes
I can them reach. O ye my friends
What secret borders on those ends?
    Are lofty heavens hurled
    'Bout your inferior world?
Are ye the representatives
Of other people's distant lives?

Of all the playmates which I knew
That here I do the image view
In other selves; what can it mean?
But that below the purling stream
    Some unknown joys there be
    Laid up in store for me;
To which I shall, when that thin skin
Is broken, be admitted in.

✌ John Wilmot, Earl of Rochester (1647–1680)

SONG

Love a woman? You're an ass!
    'Tis a most insipid passion
To choose out for your happiness
    The silliest part of God's creation.

Let the porter and the groom,
    Things designed for dirty slaves,
Drudge in fair Aurelia's womb
    To get supplies for age and graves.

Farewell, woman! I intend
    Henceforth every night to sit
With my lewd, well-natured friend,
    Drinking to engender wit.

Then give me health, wealth, mirth, and wine,
    And, if busy love entrenches,
There's a sweet, soft page of mine
    Does the trick worth forty wenches.

EPITAPH ON CHARLES II

Here lies our Sovereign Lord the King,
    Whose word no man relies on:
Who never said a foolish thing,
    Nor ever did a wise one.

✌ Attributed to Isobel Gowdie (1662)

THE ALLANSFORD PURSUIT: A RESTORATION

Cunning and art he did not lack
But aye her whistle would fetch him back.

O, I shall go into a hare
With sorrow and sighing and mickle care,
And I shall go in the Devil's name
Aye, till I be fetchèd hame.
        —Hare, take heed of a bitch greyhound
    Will harry thee all these fells around,

For here come I in Our Lady's name
All but for to fetch thee hame.

Cunning and art he did not lack
But aye her whistle would fetch him back.

Yet, I shall go into a trout
With sorrow and sighing and mickle doubt,
And show thee many a crooked game
Ere that I be fetchèd hame,
    —Trout, take heed of an otter lank
    Will harry thee close from bank to bank,
    For here come I in Our Lady's name
    All but for to fetch thee hame.

Cunning and art he did not lack
But aye her whistle would fetch him back.

Yet I shall go into a bee
With mickle horror and dread of thee
And flit to hive in the Devil's name
Ere that I be fetchèd hame.
    —Bee, take heed of a swallow hen
    Will harry thee close, both butt and ben,
    For here come I in Our Lady's Name
    All but for to fetch thee hame.

Cunning and art he did not lack
But aye her whistle would fetch him back.

Yet I shall go into a mouse
And haste me unto the miller's house,
There in his corn to have good game
Ere that I be fetchèd hame.
    —Mouse, take heed of a white tib-cat
    That never was baulked of mouse or rat,
    For I'll crack thy bones in Our Lady's name:
    Thus shalt thou be fetchèd hame.

Cunning and art he did not lack
But aye her whistle would fetch him back.

                    Robert Graves

✆ 2

POETRY IN THE CELTIC LANGUAGES OF SCOTLAND AND IRELAND

Scots Gaelic

✆ Anonymous (date unknown)

OMENS

Early on the morning of Monday,
I heard the bleating of a lamb,

And the kid-like cry of snipe,
While gently sitting bent,

And the grey-blue cuckoo,
And no food on my stomach.

On the fair evening of Tuesday,
I saw on the smooth stone,
The snail slimy, pale,

And the ashy wheatear
On the top of the dyke of holes,

The foal of the old mare
Of sprauchly gait and its back to me.

And I knew from these
That the year would not go well with me.

Alexander Carmichael

Irish Gaelic

❧ Aodhagán O Rathaille (1675–1729)

LAMENT FOR TADHG CRONIN'S CHILDREN

That day the sails of the ship were torn
and a fog obscured the lawns.
In the whitewashed house the music stopped.
A spark jumped up at the gables
and the silk quilts on the bed caught fire.
They cry without tears—
their hearts cry—
for the three dead children.

Christ God neglect them not
nor leave them in the ground!

They were ears of corn!
They were apples!
They were three harpstrings!
And now their limbs lie underground
and the black beetle walks across their faces.
I, too, cry without tears—
my heart cries—
for the three dead children.

Michael Hartnett

❧ Anonymous (18th century)

SO, WE'LL GO NO MORE A-ROVING

So, we'll go no more a-roving
    So late into the night,
Though the heart be still as loving,
    And the moon be still as bright.

For the sword outwears its sheath,
    And the soul wears out the breast,
And the heart must pause to breathe,
    And love itself have rest.

Though the night was made for loving,
    And the day returns too soon,

Yet we'll go no more a-roving
  By the light of the moon.

George Gordon, Lord Byron

๑๑ Attributed to Eileen Dubh O'Connell (1773)

YOUR GRAVE DISFIGURES ME *From* THE DEATH OF ART O'LEARY

My own darling,
Your grave disfigures me

And when your children come home
They will ask where I've left their father
And I will tell them that I left him here
In unconsecrated ground
Because Morris, the accursed
Would not permit you to rest
Amoung your own.

Oh, my darling treasure,
If my cries could reach to great Derrynane
And to Carhen of the yellow apples
Many a light-foot spirited horseman
And many a handsome woman
Would be here without delay
To weep on your grave.

They would cry for vengeance
But you would not be here to lead them.
My love and my own one,
My tears wash over you.
Your corn-ricks are standing
Your tawny cows are milking
And in my heart there is grief for you
Such as the whole of Munster
Could not cure.

Until Art O'Leary comes back to me
My grief will not dissipate
For it is crushed down
Deep in my soul
And closed and fastened
As a lock on a trunk
Where the key has vanished.
Oh, you women weeping out there

Stay on your feet until Art,
Son of Conor, calls for a drink
Before he goes to the Abbey at Kilcrea—
Not to study learning or song
But to bear the weight of clay
And stones.

Patrick Galvin

3

The Baroque in Northern Europe

Frisian

Gysbert Japicx (b. 1603)

LOVELIGHT

Dear Lyltsen, when I'm with thee
(My light, my flame, my sun, my eye),
As dark as may be the deep of night
When stars steer their course through the sky,
No matter how much dark may be,
It's light as daytime sun for me.

But when your flares flare not toward me,
I have no star to steer my turning;
I move then blind as a stick, a stone,
Even though mid-day sun is burning.
What use if the sun in my eyes is bright?
Lylts is all my dark and light.

Roderick Jellema

Swedish

Anonymous (c. 1650)

DEEP IN THE FOREST

Deep in the forest there is a pond,
small, shaded by a pine so tall

its shadow crosses her surface.
The water is cold and dark and clear,
let it preserve those who lie at the bottom
invisible to us in perpetual dark.
It is our heaven, this bottomless
water that will keep us forever still;
though hands might barely touch they'll never
wander up an arm in caress or lift a drink;
we'll lie with the swords and bones
of our fathers on a bed of silt and pine needles.
In our night we'll wait
for those who walk the green and turning earth,
our brothers, even the birds and deer,
who always float down to us
with alarmed and startled eyes.

Jim Harrison

✌ Carl Michael Bellman (1740–1795)

From FREDMANS EPISTLAR, 1790

Fredman's Epistle No. 23

Which is a soliloquy, when Fredman lay by the Creep Inn,
opposite the National Bank, one summer's night in the year
1768

Oh, Mother, Mother, oh what a cipher,
    you in my father's bed!
You, the first spark igniting my poor life;
    I wish I were dead!
    Thanks to your kindling
    here I lie dwindling,
    every step dead tired.
    You lay impassioned;
    cooling, you fashioned
    my hot blood inside.
    Let there be lock and key
    to virginity.
Flauto   _ _ _ to virginity.

Damn the fourposter, damn each wooden slat
    furnished your bridal bed!
Damn your dark eyes and saintly maiden ways that
    turned my father's head!
    God damn the second
    love to you beckoned
    and your soul you sold!
    Damn your sore feet!

                    desiring a seat,
                    into bed you strolled!
                    Or did a table-top
                    serve to start me up?
Flauto   __ __ __ serve to start me up?

          A heart that's true? Not even worth hating;
                    damn mother, father, too!
          Here I lie in the gutter contemplating
                    my decrepit shoes.
                    Mercy, how battered!
                    My coat's all tattered!
                    Shirt as black as soot!
                    Look at this kerchief,
                    this lambskin hairpiece,
                    and my twisted foot!
                    This bad itch just won't stop;
                    come and help me up.
Flauto   __ __ __ come and help me up.

          Feel my two hands so bony and frigid
                    trembling at every noise;
          see how they drop down to my sides, such rigid
                    sterile, hollow straws.
                    Cheeks drawn, eyes weathered,
                    drawn in and gathered,
                    dual infirmity.
                    Heavens! my tongue
                    cannot even sing
                    of all the joys I see;
                    of love's repose and pain,
                    and a glass to drain.
Flauto   __ __ __ and a glass to drain.

          Waken my tongue now! The sweetest liquids
                    splash in the glass, resound.
          I am a heathen, heart and mouth and spirits
                    to the wine-god bound.
                    Poor me, all drunken,
                    down my throat sunken,
                    every treasure chest.
                    Whatever my fate,
                    and even when dead
                    I will slake my thirst.
                    And as I breathe my last
                    I shall raise a glass.
Flauto   __ __ __ I shall raise a glass.

          The pub door opens, shutters unfasten;
                    no one is up or dressed.
          Daybreak compels the morning star to hasten

down to clouds and rest;
sunbeams are streaming,
church towers gleaming,
ah, the air's so warm.
Now where's my jacket?
What's all the racket
down in Bacchus' room?
Pour me a drink, my friend,
or my life will end.

Flauto   __ __ __ or my life will end.

Prosit! your health! I need to gird my loins,
to stand up and raise a tankard.
Ah, now to lubricate these aching joints
and get them well anchored.
Come now, take courage!
Don't get discouraged!
Send that bottle here!
I'm feeling gallant
practically valiant,
nothing more to fear.
Another sip's not bad,
Thank you Mom and Dad.

Flauto   __ __ __ Thank you Mom and Dad.

Thanks for each coupling, here's to each loyal
amorous interlude;
thank you who felled the trees and with your toil
carved my natal bed;
thanks for your passion
and lack of caution,
Father, dear old friend!
If we could meet
we'd chatter and eat,
and drink for days on end.
My brother you should be
just as drunk as me.

Flauto   __ __ __ just as drunk as me.

Rika Lesser

German

ᴥ Andreas Gryphius (1616–1664) ᴥ

HELL

Ah and woe!
Screams! Murder! Wailing! Fear! Cross! Torment! Worms! Indiction!

Pitch! Torture! Hangman! Flame! Stench! Spirits! Cold! Affliction!
    End, then, go,
    High and low!
Sea! Hillocks! Mountains! Rock! Who can endure such friction?
    Engulf it, chasm, gulp down this plaint for dereliction.
    Age-long so!
Terrible demons of caves all in darkness / you that both torture
                    and yourselves are tortured,
    Cannot eternity's eternal fire / ever atone for what your evil
                    has nurtured?
    O cruel dread / live death without remission /
This is the flame of perpetual vengeance / fanned by a fury
                    white-hot and glowing:
Here is the curse of a punishment endless; here is the rage
                    unremittingly growing:
    Perish, mankind! Lest here you know perdition.

(1641. A Baroque sonnet of the Thirty Years' War)

Michael Hamburger

NOT MINE THE YEARS TIME TOOK AWAY

Not mine the years time took away,
not mine the years that might yet be.
Time's wink is mine, and if I tend it, then
the maker of years and eternity is mine.

John Peck

MY COUNTRY WEEPS

We are finished, yet still
            they have not finished with us.
Brazen troops of nations,
            crazed trumpets,
blood-slick sword
            and the big howitzer
have devoured everything that sweat
            and diligence laid away.
Towers flicker, the cathedral
            lies roof through floor,
city hall sits in terror,
            our forces smashed,
girls defiled,
            and wherever we turn
flames, plague, and mortality
            pierce heart and spirit.

Trench and street are the constantly
        refreshed conduits of blood.
For eighteen years now
        our rivers have
brimmed with corpses, slowly
        pushing themselves clear.
Yet still I have said nothing
        of what vexes like death
and dips a lashing beak deeper
        than hunger, pest, and holocaust:
that so much treasure has been
        plundered from our souls.

John Peck

TO THE VIRGIN MARY

No room at the crowded inn for you. And why?
The world itself is too cramped for what's inside you.

Christopher Benfey

EPITAPH FOR MARIANA GRYPHIUS, HIS BROTHER PAUL'S LITTLE DAUGHTER

Born on the run, ambushed by sword and flame,
suckled by smoke, my mother's bitter bargain,
my father's midnight fear, I swam to light
just as the fire's jaws devoured my country.
I took one look at this world and said goodbye.
I knew in a flash all that it had to offer.
If you count my days, I vanished when I was young.
But I was old if you add the things I suffered.

Christopher Benfey

MISERY

What are we *really?* Pain's return address.
A ball for luck, blindfolded, to kick around.
A flick of the switch. A stage darkened by fear.
A candle doused, snow melting on bare ground.
Life slips away like gossip or last night's joke.
Unzip your body like an evening dress
and add your name to the bulging visitors' book
of the dead—you're out of sight and out of mind.

Like dreams we can't remember, or a stream
we're powerless to stop, so will our fame
(such as it is) and honor disappear.
Whatever breathes will vanish into air.
Our graves are large and lonely. What's left to say?
We're smoke that the wind has caught, and blown away.

Christopher Benfey

⁓ Catharina Regina von Greiffenberg (1633–1694)

ON THE INEFFABLE INSPIRATION OF THE HOLY SPIRIT

You unseen lightning flash, you darkly radiant light,
you power that's heart-infused, incomprehensible being!
Something divine within my spirit had its being
That stirs and spurs me: I sense a curious light.

Never by its own power the soul is thus alight.
It was a miracle-wind, a spirit, a creative being,
The eternal power of breath, prime origin of being
That in me kindled for himself this heaven-flaring light.

You mirror-spectrum-glance, you many-colored gleam!
You glitter to and fro, are incomprehensibly clear;
in truth's own sunlight the spirit-dove-flights gleam.

The God-stirred pool has also been troubled clear!
First on the spirit-sun reflecting it casts its gleam,
The moon; then turns about, and earthward, too, is clear.

Michael Hamburger

❧ 4

POETRY IN ROMANCE LANGUAGES

Spanish

❧ St. John of the Cross (1549–1591)

DARK NIGHT

In a dark night, when the light
    burning was the burning of love (*fortuitous*
    night, fated, free, —)
    as I stole from my dark house, dark
    house that was silent, grave, sleeping, —

by the staircase that was secret, hidden,
    safe: disguised by darkness (*fortuitous*
    night, fated, free, —)
    by darkness and by cunning, dark
    house that was silent, grave, sleeping—;

in that sweet night, secret, seen by
    no one and seeing
    nothing, my only light or
    guide
    the burning in my burning heart,

night was the guide
    to the place where he for whom I
    waited, whom I had long ago chosen,
    waits: night
    brighter than noon, in which none can see —;

night was the guide
    sweeter than the sun raw at

dawn, for there the burning bridegroom is
bride
and he who chose at last is chosen.

As he lay sleeping on my sleepless
breast, kept from the beginning for him
alone, lying on the gift I gave
as the restless
fragrant cedars moved the restless winds, —

winds from the circling parapet circling
us as I lay there touching and lifting his hair, —
with his sovereign hand, he
wounded my neck —
and my senses, when they touched that, touched nothing . . .

In a dark night (*there where I*
lost myself, —) as I leaned to rest
in his smooth white breast, everything
ceased
and left me, forgotten in the grave of forgotten lilies.

Frank Bidart

&ep; Luis de Gongora (1561–1627)

THE RUINS OF TIME

This chapel that you gaze at, these stern tombs,
the pride of sculpture . . . Stop here, Passer-by,
diamonds were blunted on this porphyry,
the teeth of files wore smooth as ice. This vault
seals up the earth of those who never felt
the earth's oppression. Whose? If you would know,
stand back and study this inscription. Words
give marble meaning and a voice to bronze.
Piety made this chapel beautiful,
and generous devotion binds these urns
to the heroic dust of Sandoval,
who left his coat of arms, once five blue stars
on a gold field, to climb with surer step
through the blue sky, and scale the golden stars.

Robert Lowell

IV

The whistling arrow flies less eagerly,
and bites the bull's-eye less ferociously;

the Roman chariot grinds less hurriedly
the arena's docile sand, and rounds the goal . . .
How silently, how privately, we run
through life to die! You doubt this? Animal
despoiled of reason, each ascending sun
dives like a cooling meteorite to its fall.
Do Rome and Carthage know what we deny?
Death only throws fixed dice, and yet we raise
the ante, and stake our lives on every toss.
The hours will hardly pardon us their loss,
those brilliant hours that wore away our days,
our days that ate into eternity.

Robert Lowell

A GREAT FAVORIT BEHEADED

The bloody trunck of him who did possesse
    About the rest a haplesse happy state,
    This little Stone doth Seale, but not depresse,
    And scarce can stop the rowling of his fate.

Brasse Tombes which justice hath deny'd t'his fault,
    The common pity to his vertues payes,
    Adorning an Imaginary vault,
    Which from our minds time strives in vaine to raze.

Ten years the world upon him falsly smild,
    Sheathing in fawning lookes the deadly knife
Long aymed at his head; That so beguild
    It more securely might bereave his Life;

Then threw him to a Scaffold from a Throne,
Much Doctrine lyes under this little Stone.

Sir Richard Fanshawe

From THE SPECTRE OF THE ROSE

Learn, flowers, from me, what parts we play
From dawn to dusk. Last noon the boast
And marvel of the fields, today
I am not even my own ghost.

The fresh aurora was my cot,
The night my coffin and my shroud;
I perished with no light, save what
The moon could lend me from a cloud.

And thus, all flowers must die—of whom
Not one of us can cheat the doom.

Learn, flowers, from me, etc.

What most consoles me for my fleetness
Is the carnation fresh with dew,
Since that which gave me one day's sweetness
To her conceded scarcely two:
Ephemerids in briefness vie
My scarlet and her crimson dye.

Learn, flowers, from me, etc.

The jasmine, fairest of the flowers,
Is least in size as in longevity.
She forms a star, yet lives less hours
Than it has rays. Her soul is brevity.
Could ambergris a flower be grown
It would be she, and she alone!

Learn, flowers, from me, etc.

The gillyflower, though plain and coarse,
Enjoys on earth a longer stay,
And sees more suns complete their course
As many as there shine in May.
Yet better far a marvel die
Than live a gillyflower, say I!

Learn, flowers, from me, etc.

To no flower blooming in our sphere did
The daystar grant a longer pardon
Than to the Sunflower, golden-bearded
Methusalem of every garden,
Eyeing him through as many days
As he shoots petals forth like rays.

*Yet learn from me, what parts we play
From dawn to dusk. Last noon the boast
And marvel of the fields, today
I am not even my own ghost.*

Roy Campbell

೨ Lope de Vega Carpio (1562–1635)

JUDITH

Blood from the shoulder drips from couch to floor,
Blood from the savage tyrant who in vain
Beseiged Bethulia's wall, and caused a rain
Of bolts from Heaven to strike him down in war.
The left hand's anguished rigour, like a claw,
Grips back the scarlet curtain, and again
Horror reveals itself: the attitude of pain,
The hideous torso, one blind mass of gore.

Wine's spilt; the heavy mail has disarrayed
The ornaments; the table's overturned;
The guard asleep forget their vicious lord;
And on the rampart the chaste Hebrew maid,
To Israel's people splendidly returned,
Holds up the armoured head as her reward.

Brian Soper

IN SANTIAGO

In Santiago the green
Jealousy seized me,
Night sits in the day,
I dream of vengeance.

Poplars of the thicket,
Where is my love?
If she were with another
Then I would die.

Clear Manzanares.
Oh little river,
Empty of water,
Run full of fire.

W. S. Merwin

From THE KNIGHT OF OLMEDO

1

They slew by night
upon the road
Medina's pride
Olmedo's flower

shadows warned him
not to go
not to go
along that road

weep for your lord
Medina's pride
Olmedo's flower
there in the road

2

Down in the orchard
I met my death
under the briar rose
I lie slain

I was going
to gather flowers
my love waited
among the trees

down in the orchard
I met my death
under the briar rose
I lie slain

8

And you my spent heart's treasure
my yet unspent desire
measurer past all measure
cold paradox of fire

as seeker so forsaken
consentingly denied
your solitude a token
the sentries at your side

fulfilment to my sorrow
indulgence of your prey
the sparrowhawk the sparrow
the nothing that you say

13

Splendidly-shining darkness
proud citadel of meekness
likening us our unlikeness
majesty of our distress

emptiness ever thronging
untenable belonging

how long until this longing
end in unending song

and soul for soul discover
no strangeness to dissever
and lover keep with lover
a moment and for ever

15

I shall go down
to the lovers' well
and wash this wound
that will not heal

beloved soul
what shall you see
nothing at all
yet eye to eye

depths of non-being
perhaps too clear
my desire dying
as I desire

                Geoffrey Hill

LACHRIMAE AMANTIS

What is there in my heart that you should sue
so fiercely for its love? What kind of care
brings you as though a stranger to my door
through the long night and in the icy dew

seeking the heart that will not harbour you,
that keeps itself religiously secure?
At this dark solstice filled with frost and fire
your passion's ancient wounds must bleed anew.

So many nights the angel of my house
has fed such urgent comfort through a dream,
whispered 'your lord is coming, he is close'

that I have drowsed half-faithful for a time
bathed in pure tones of promise and remorse:
'tomorrow I shall wake to welcome him.'

                Geoffrey Hill

❧ Francisco Gomez de Quevedo y Villegas (1580–1645)

HE POINTS OUT THE BREVITY OF LIFE, UNTHINKING AND SUFFERING, SURPRISED BY DEATH

My yesterday was dream, tomorrow earth:
nothing a while ago, and later smoke;
ambitions and pretensions I invoke
blind to the walls that wall me in from birth.
In the brief combat of a futile war
I am the peril of my strategy
and while cut down by my own scimitar
my body doesn't house but buries me.
Gone now is yesterday, tomorrow has
not come; today speeds by, it is, it was,
a motion flinging me toward death. The hour,
even the moment, is a sharpened spade
which for the wages in my painful tower
digs out a monument from my brief day.

Willis Barnstone

ON A CHAPLAIN'S NOSE

Limblike to his own snout, projecting there,
A man was hung. Sufficient it appeared
For all the scribes and pharisees to share,
Protruding like a swordfish from his beard.
It seemed an ill-set dial-hand, a pensile
Alembic, or an elephant, whose hose
Is turned the wrong way up, and less prehensile.
Ovid's was far less noseyfied a nose.

It seems the beak and ram of some huge galley,
Or pyramid of Egypt. The Twelve Tribes
Of noses it exceeds and circumscribes.
For sheer nasality it has no tally.
A nose so fiercely nasal in its bias
Would even spoil the face of Ananias.

Roy Campbell

LOVE CONSTANT BEYOND DEATH

Last of the shadows may close my eyes,
goodbye then white day

and with that my soul untie
its dear wishing

yet will not forsake
memory of this shore where it burned
but still burning swim
that cold water again
careless of the stern law

soul that kept God in prison
veins that to love led such fire
marrow that flamed in glory

not their heeding will leave
with their body
but being ash will feel
dust be dust in love

W. S. Merwin

ON LISI'S GOLDEN HAIR

When you shake loose your hair from all controlling,
Such thirst of beauty quickens my desire
Over its surge in red tornadoes rolling
My heart goes surfing on the waves of fire.
Leander, who for love the tempest dares,
It lets a sea of flames its life consume:
Icarus, from a sun whose rays are hairs,
Ignites its wings and glories in its doom.
Charring its hopes (whose deaths I mourn) it strives
Out of their ash to fan new phoenix-lives
That, dying of delight, new hopes embolden.
Miser, yet poor, the crime and fate it measures
Of Midas, starved and mocked with stacks of treasures,
Or Tantalus, with streams that shone as golden.

Roy Campbell

SONNET

I saw the ramparts of my native land,
One time so strong, now dropping in decay,
Their strength destroyed by this new age's way,
That has worn out and rotted what was grand.

I went into the fields: there I could see
The sun drink up the waters newly thawed,

And on the hills the moaning cattle pawed;
Their miseries robbed the day of light for me.

I went into my house: I saw how spotted,
Decaying things made that old home their prize.
My withered walking-staff had come to bend.
I felt the age had won; my sword was rotted,
And there was nothing on which to set my eyes
That was not a reminder of the end.

John Masefield

THE TOOTHPULLER WHO WANTED TO TURN A MOUTH INTO A GRINDING MACHINE

O you who eat with someone else's teeth,
chewing with molars, mumbling groans to us,
your gluttonous dragon fingers bite beneath
the gums, and pinch and nibble flesh and pus.
You who dissuade us from indulgent forms
of eating dive into a soup like stones
down wells; for a few crumbs, in rampant storms
you plunge in with your grandmother's jawbones.
Because of you, a peeling blames a mouth,
a hazelnut explodes in brave defeat,
its shell still boasting it a fortress bed.
Relieving hurt by pulling out a tooth
is getting rid of pain from head to feet,
and feels the same as pulling off your head.

Willis Barnstone

✌ Pedro Calderon de la Barca (1600–1681)

THOSE WHICH WERE POMP AND DELIGHT

First light of morning, it gives you no warning
Of processions and prizes and matters of state
Noontime's delicious with things meretricious
Despair's chill at midnight will keep you up late.

Heaven yields gleaming to the rainbow's wild seeming
The spectrum of transcience you're haltingly learning
The scarlet is fustian, the gold's been devalued
But while whiteness remains there's no end to your yearning.

The roses awake to a first tryst at daybreak
Time's executioner arrives punctual as dawn
As each bud makes room for cradle and tomb.

So the fortunes of men share the fate of that blossoming
In the space of one moment you are born and you pass:
Centuries, hours, dead men and flowers.

Katharine Washburn

L. L. de Argensola (1559–1613)

DAMON'S LAMENT FOR HIS CLORINDA, YORKSHIRE 1654

November rips gold foil from the oak ridges.
Dour folk huddle in High Hoyland, Penistone.
The tributaries of the Sheaf and Don
bulge their dull spate, cramming the poor bridges.

The North Sea batters our shepherds' cottages
from sixty miles. No sooner has the sun
swung clear above earth's rim than it is gone.
We live like gleaners of its vestiges

knowing we flourish, though each year a child
with the set face of a tomb-weeper is put down
for ever and ever. Why does the air grow cold

in the region of mirrors? And who is this clown
doffing his mask at the masked threshold
to selfless raptures that are all his own?

Geoffrey Hill

Sor Juana Inés de la Cruz (1648–1695)

From THE FIFTH VILLANCICO

In alternating voices, written for the *Feast of the Nativity in Puebla, 1689*

Because my Lord was born to suffer,
let Him stay awake.

Because for me He is awake,
let Him fall asleep.

Let Him stay awake—
there is no pain for one who loves
as painlessness would be.

    Let Him sleep—
    for one who sleeps, in dreaming,
    prepares himself to die.

Silence, now He sleeps!
    Careful, He's awake!
Do not disturb Him, no!
    Yes, He must be waked!
Let Him wake and wake!
    Let Him have his sleep!

Alan S. Trueblood

ON HER PORTRAIT

This that you see, this colorful pretense
That makes a show of its precise virtù
(The colors prove that none of it is true),
Is nothing but painstaking fraudulence;
This ornament in which flattery has done
All that it could to cover up time's smears,
To palliate the horrors of the years
And conquer old age and oblivion,
Is the empty trappings of anxiety,
An airy flower under the wind's weight,
A laughable protection against fate,
A stupid affair, delusive as can be,
A weak solicitude, and, more than this,
It is a corpse, dust, shadow, nothingness.

Robert Mezey

French

✺ Théophile de Viau (c. 1590–1626)

ODE

A raven croaks before me
A shadow darkens my sight
A pair of weasels and a pair
Of foxes cross my path

My horse stumbles
My groom falls badly
I hear the thunder cracking
A spirit appears before me
Charon is calling me to him
I see the center of the earth

This brook runs backward to its source
An ox climbs up a steeple
Blood flows from the rock
An asp mates with a bear
Atop an ancient tower
A snake tears a vulture apart
Fire burns in ice
The sun has gone black
I see the moon is going to fall
That tree has moved from its place.

Phillip Holland

ᴥ Vincent Voiture (1597–1648)

RONDEAU

Lord, I'm done for: now Margot
Insists I write her a rondeau.
Just to think of it gives me pain:
Eight "o" lines and five in "ain"—
A slow boat to China is not so slow.

With five lines down, and eight to go,
I summon Sono Osato,
Adding, with an eye for gain,
            Lord, I'm done.

If from my brain five others flow
My poem will in beauty grow:
Comes eleven, that is plain,
And twelve to follow in its train,
And so thirteen rounds out the show—
            Lord, I'm done!

William Jay Smith

YOU KNOW WHERE YOU DID DESPISE

You know where you did despise
(T'other day) my little eyes,

Little legs, and little thighs,
And some things of little size,
        You know where.

You, 'tis true, have fine black eyes,
Taper legs, and tempting thighs,
Yet what more than all we prize
Is a thing of little size,
        You know where.

Alexander Pope

✌ Jean de la Fontaine (1621–1695)

PHOEBUS AND BOREAS

The sun and the north wind observed a traveler
       Who was cloaked with particular care
Because fall had returned; for when autumn has come,
What we wear must be warm or we dare not leave home.
Both rain and rainbow as the sun shines fitfully,
       Warn one to dress warily
In these months when we don't know for what to prepare,
An uncertain time in the Roman calendar.
Though our traveler was fortified for a gale,
With interlined cloak which the rain could not penetrate,
The wind said, "This man thinks himself impregnable
And his cloak is well sewn, but my force can prevail
       As he'll find in the blast I create,
No button has held. Indeed before I am through,
       I may waft the whole mantle away.
The battle could afford us amusement, I'd say.
Do you fancy a contest?" The sun said, "I do.
       Mere words are unprofitable,
Let us see which can first unfasten the mantle
       Protecting the pedestrian.
Begin: I shall hide; you uncloak him if you can."
Then our blower swelled, swallowed what wind he could,
To form a balloon, and with the wager to win,
       Made demoniacal din.
Puffed, snorted, and sighed till the blast that he brewed
Left ships without a sail and homes without a roof
       Because a mantle proved stormproof.
It was a triumph for the man to have withstood
       The onslaught of wind that had rushed in,
As he somehow stood firm. The wind roared his chagrin —
A defeated boaster since his gusts had been borne.
Controlling clasp and skirt required dexterity,

But the wind found nothing torn
And must stop punctually.

The cloud had made it cool
Till the sun's genial influence caused the traveler to give way,
And perspiring because wearing wool,
He cast off a wrap too warm for the day
Though the sun had not yet shone with maximum force.

Clemency may be our best resource.

Marianne Moore

THE SHRIMP AND HER DAUGHTER

The wise men of yesterday, like the shrimp,
used to walk backwards: in this maritime custom
one turns one's back on safety. It's an artifice
of people who want to dissimulate deeper ends;
they face opposite their true goal, and
their adversaries go the other way. I'll paint
my subject small since my background is so large.
I'll describe a Conqueror—who by himself disabled
hydras of enemies. What his intention is
and what it isn't—that's always a secret. He
conquers. Do eyes see what he hides? Hardly.
Are the fates overturned? His rushing
torrent sweeps everything before him, and a hundred
gods are feeble before this Jupiter. LOUIS
and FATE become the same. But to our fable.
Mother shrimp says one day to her daughter,
'My goodness, how you crawl, child! Won't you
go straight?' 'I'm like you,' says the daughter.
'I'm like the whole family. Should I go straight
when the rest of us are crooked? I'm like
all shrimps.' This shrimp knows nature.
As the twig is bent. Homely habits
rule everything for good and ill.
They form the wise and the noodleheads
(as well as everything in between). And as for
turning my back on my goal—I'll come back
to it. This is always good business,
civilian or military. But let's return
to the subject.

Bruce Boone and Robert Glück

PIG, GOAT, SHEEP

A goat and a sheep, with a fat pig, are
packed into the same cart going to market.
They aren't out for their health, I can
tell you that. They're off to be sold.
Mr. Pig cries all the way as if he had a hundred
butchers at his heels. It's a deafening noise.
The other animals, gentler creatures, decent
sorts, were astonished at his cries: Resist, resist!
They see nothing to fear. Next,
Driver says to Pig—What are you yelling for?
You'll break our eardrums. What's the matter
with you, where are your manners? You should
take a lesson from this well-behaved couple!
Look at Mr. Sheep—has he said a word? He's
got breeding! He's got problems—shoots back
Mr. Pig. If he knew what was happening, he'd
be yelling like I am at the top of my lungs.
And this other polite person—she'd be screaming
like a banshee. Goat supposes she'll be milked,
Sheep thinks he'll be fleeced—if they
only knew! Let's just say I've got my suspicions.
And me? The only thing I've got going
for me is pig meat. I'm a goner. Good-bye
forever, happy piggy days; bye-bye to
my one animal life.
Mr. Pig reasoned subtly and well. Only
what good did it do him?

Bruce Boone and Robert Glück

BOOK 12, #5

A young mouse, poor, no experience
in the field, believed imploring
and giving reasons would convince:

> Let me live
> —a mouse
> of my size
> and upkeep—
> do I burden
> this house?
> Do I starve
> the innkeeper
> and his wife?
> A grain of wheat
> feeds me. A nut

fills me up—
look at
my ribs.
Don't you want
this meal to get fat
for Messrs. Vos Enfants?

Thus the trapped mouse parleyed with the cat.
The other says:

Is this a discourse for the Old and Powerful?
Cat and Old, pardon you? Hardly.
Descend to your death. Go to the nether world.
Die. And for this defeat
harangue the Spinning Sisters. My kittens
will catch plenty of mice to eat.

He pauses, cleans his chops. His fur's plain
brown, set off by a gold button and a bit of
velvet. He shuns rings and wears jewels only
on his shoebuckles, his garters, and his hat,
which is trimmed in Spanish needlepoint
and topped with a white plume. He turns to us
and says:

As for this fable, here's the moral that applies:
Who flatter themselves, believe they can have everything?
Mice.

Bruce Boone and Robert Glück

Isaac De Benserade (c. 1650)

IN BED WE LAUGH, IN BED WE CRY

In bed we laugh, in bed we cry;
And, born in bed, in bed we die.
The near approach a bed may show
Of human bliss to human woe.

Samuel Johnson

✺ 5

CENTRAL EUROPE: POLISH AND FINNISH

Poliأh

✺ Zbigniew Morsztyn (1620–1690)

EMBLEM 51

> The universal sphere is revolved by holy love so
> that it may become more perfectly spherical.
> *Inأcription:* The sphere will be more perfectly a sphere.

Round universe, where only spheres can range
Though sizes differ and the colours change:
The sun, the moon, the stars, the heavy earth
That draped itself in oceans at its birth,
Eternal love allows each to possess
All properties of roundness, nothing less.
And this same love winds up the world, its clock,
And teaches months and years the way to walk:
And all for man, for mortal man, because
He is the image of great nature's laws.
Red heart, red sun, but one vast congruence:
The moon exerts her silver influence
Upon his brain. The same occurs in metals;
In beasts, fish, reptiles; inhabits trees and petals,
Makes Wildness grow and what is sown by hand.
In ants it happens, instructing them to stand
And walk and run. Yet shadows all of these
To what salvation's holy pure decrees
Has promised men by love which will be given
When they live finally through it in Heaven.

Jerzy Peterkiewicz and Burnأ Singer

✆ Waclaw Potocki (1625–1696)

WINTER, BEFORE THE WAR

The frost bit deep. When heavy guns were dragged
Across a marsh no inch of bogland sagged.
The dubious fords raised solid crystal beams.
A glass bridge spanned the deeper parts of streams.
The snow was shameless in its secret keeps
Though clouds had dumped it carelessly in heaps;
But where frost parched it, sparkling silks were spun
And polished lilies to receive the sun.

Someone to whom the war means nothing yet
Glides on a sledge, its runners barely wet,
So light it seems: one horse has leopard spots
And one's hawk-mottled, bird-like as it trots.
A hunter with his hounds treks through the snow.
But, soaking toast in beer by the hearth's glow,
An old man sits. He doesn't want to drive
Off in a sledge. The Spring will soon arrive
And his death with it. Now, since his teeth have gone,
He sucks soaked bread. If any man lives on
Until his youngest grand-daughter gives birth,
This is the last delight he'll find on earth.
In short: the sun reached Capricorn—no more—
And Winter fell from heaven to this hard floor.

Jerzy Peterkiewicz and Burns Singer

Finnish

✆ Anonymous (date unknown)

From THE KANTELETAR

Lullabies, 2:174

Rock the child, rock the small one
        rock the child to sleep!
I will sing the child to sleep
wear him down to the dream-sledge.
        Come, dream, and hide him
        son of dream, take him
        to your golden sleigh
        to the silver sledge!

When he's got into the sledge
    snatched into your sleigh
drive along a road of tin
    level copper ground
    take my tender one
    convey my precious
to a silver mountain ridge
to a golden mountain peak
and into silver backwoods
    to golden birches
where the cuckoos of gold call
    the silver birds sing.

    Rock, rock my dark one
    in a dark cradle —
    a dark one rocking
    in a dark cabin!

Rock the child to Tuonela
the child to the planks' embrace
    under turf to sleep
    underground to lie
for Death's children to sing to
for the grave's maidens to keep!

For Death's cradle is better
and the grave's cot is fairer
cleverer Death's dames, better
the grave's daughters-in-law, large
the cabin in Tuonela
and the grave has wide abodes.

                    Keith Bosley

❧ Anonymous (date unknown)

From TURO, RESCUER OF THE SUN AND MOON

    The one son of God
Turo the tough, crafty man
    promised he would go
    off to seek the moon
    to spy out the sun.
He wound up a ball of dreams
    took a jug of beer
    an ox horn of mead
thrust a whetstone in his breast
a brush in his shirt front, took

a stallion from the stable
    picked out the best foal
he mounted the black stallion
the horse with the flaxen mane
went off in search of the sun
in pursuit of the moonlight.

He set out along the road
    he rides, he reflects
he rode a mile down the road:
a log lies across the road
across and along the road
and he can't get past the log
he could not go over it
neither over nor under
nor could birds fly over it
nor could worms crawl under it.
Turo the tough, crafty man
took some beer out of the jug
some mead out of the ox horn
    splashed the beer on it
    and sprinkled his mead:
    the log split in two
an eternal road appeared
a track ancient as iron
    for the great, the small
    the middling to tread.

He went on a little way
he rode a mile down the road:
a hill lies across the road
across and along the road
and he can't get over it
cannot escape around it;
many men, many horses
are rotting under the hill.
Turo the tough, crafty man
looked some beer out of the jug
some mead out of the ox horn
    spilled the mead on it
    and he splashed his beer:
    the hill fell in two
an eternal road was born
a track ancient as iron
    for the great, the small
    the middling to tread.

He rode on a little way
he did a mile down the road
and he comes upon a sea:

the sea lies across the road
and he can't get over it
cannot escape around it;
many men, many horses
cover the shore with their bones.
Turo the tough, crafty man
took some beer out of his jug
some mead out of the ox horn
    splashed the beer on it
    and sprinkled his mead;
but the sea would not heed that
so he said a word or two:
    the sea broke in two
an eternal road appeared
a track ancient as iron
for the young, the old
for middle-aged to stroll.

He rode on a little way
kept on down the road a bit
and the Demon's cabins loom
and the Demon's roofs glimmer;
there is one shed on a hill
and three maidens in the shed
    are scouring the moon
    and washing the sun.
Turo the tough, crafty man
    saw the moon gleaming
    and the sun shining
and he stepped to the shed door
    takes the ball of dreams
    lobbed the ball of dreams
    at the Demon's maids
and he got the maids to sleep.
    He shouldered the moon
put the sun upon his head
and sets off for his own lands
    for his homelands bound.

He rode on a little way
he did a mile down the road
and hears a rumbling behind
    so he glances back:
they are coming to catch him
    and to seize him fast.
Turo the tough, crafty man
took the whetstone from his breast
and tossed it from his shirt front
    before the pursuers:
    'Let a thick rock grow

a thick, heavy rock
so they can't get over it
   over or round it!'

Turo the tough, crafty man
   rides forward from there
   made a day's journey
and a rumbling follows him
   so he glances back:
the Demon with his dread band
is again coming to catch
   and to seize him fast.
Turo the tough, crafty man
took the brush out of his breast
and tossed it from his shirt front
   before the pursuers:

   'Let a spruce wood grow
with iron boughs on the trees
   so they cannot go
   through it or past it!'
   There a spruce wood grew
with iron boughs on the trees
   and they cannot go
   through it or past it.

Turo the tough, crafty man
   came to his own lands
and brought the sun as he came
and with him conveyed the moon
and he put the sun to shine
the sunlight to make merry
   in a gold-topped spruce
   on the highest boughs
and the moon he raised to gleam
at the top of a tall pine:
   the sun shone brightly
   from the highest boughs
shone upon those with fathers
   the rich, the happy
but not on the fatherless
   the poor, the hapless.

Turo the tough, crafty man
took the sun from where it shone
   from the highest boughs
   to the lowest boughs:
   the sun shone clearly
   from the lowest boughs
shone upon the fatherless

the troubled, those full of care
but not on those with fathers
    not on the lucky.

Turo the tough, crafty man
moved the sun from where it shone
from the lowest boughs to those
in the middle of the tree:
now the sun shone equally
on the rich and on the poor
shone upon those with fathers
    the rich, the cherished
and upon the fatherless
    the poor, the beggars;
and merrily the sun shone
    sweetly the moon gleamed
on the doors of the lucky
on the thresholds of the poor.

Keith Bosley

ᔥ 6

THE OTTOMAN EMPIRE AND THE BALKANS

Turkish

ᔥ Esrefoğlu (d. 1469)

O MY GOD DO NOT PART ME FROM THEE

O my God do not part me from thee
Do not part me from thy sight

To love you is my faith and belief
Do not part my belief from my faith

I've withered, become like the Autumn
Do not part the leaves from the branch

My Master is a rose, I his leaf
Do not part the leaf from the rose

I, a nightingale in my love's garden
Do not part his beak from his song

All the fish breathe in water they say
Do not part the fish from the lake

Esrefoğlu is thy humble slave
Do not part the Sultan from his servant

Taner Baybars

❧ Pir Sultan Abdal (c. 1550)

ILAHI

The rough man entered the lover's garden
It is woods now, my beautiful one, it is woods,
Gathering roses, he has broken their stems
They are dry now, my beautiful one, they are dry

In this square our hide is stretched
Blessed be, we saw our friend off to God
One day, too, black dust must cover us
We will rot, my beautiful one, we will rot

He himself reads and He also writes
God's holy hand has closed her crescent eyebrows
Your peers are wandering in Paradise
They are free, my beautiful one, they are free

Whatever religion you are, I'll worship it too
I will be torn off with you even the Day of Judgement
Bend for once, let me kiss you on your white neck
Just stay there for a moment, my beautiful one, just stay there

I'm Pir Sultan Abdal, I start from the root
I eat the kernel and throw out the evil weed
And weave from a thousand flowers to one hive honey
I am an honest bee, my beautiful one, an honest bee.

Murat Nemet-Nejat

❧ Bâkî (1526–1600)

OH BELOVED, SINCE THE ORIGIN WE HAVE
BEEN

Oh beloved, since the origin we have been
    the slaves of the shah of love
Oh beloved, we are the famed sultan
    of the heart's domain

We are the poppies of this wasteland
    whose hearts are burnt black with grief
Oh beloved, be generous as the cloud,
    don't withhold your water from the thirsty heart

Fate saw we had a jewel inside us and tore
    our hearts apart

Oh beloved, it left our bodies bleeding,
    mined of the precious knowledge of love

Don't let the dust of sadness cloud the waters
    of the fountain of your soul
Oh beloved, for us faces shine bright with pride
    across the Ottoman lands

The poems of Bâkî go around the world
    like the full cup at the gathering of friends
Oh beloved, we are the cup, and we are the cupbearer
    of this turning age

Walter Andrews, Mehmet Kalpakli, and Najaat Black

 Rûhî (1548–1605)

CURSE THE THORNS OF FATE

Curse the thorns of fate, and damn as well its roses
    and its garden
Curse my rivals in love, and damn as well the beloved
    who brings me pain

There is a life made captive by the pleasures
    of wine
Curse the wineseller, and damn as well the wine
    and the drunkard

Since the wasteland of death is home to
    those born to this world
Curse the caravan that crosses this desert, and
    damn as well its guide

What shall we do when fame and glory are bought
    and sold?
Curse the one who sells them to the unworthy
    and damn the one who buys them

In this world, where the opium-eaters are the knowers
    of mysteries
Curse their whirling trances, and damn as well
    their opium and their secrets

When the intelligent fall upon evil ways, and
    the ignorant become powerful
Curse the good luck of this world, and damn
    its bad luck too

Curse the good fortune brought by the turning
    of the heavens, curse misfortune too
Damn both the fixed stars and the planets

Since both this world and Paradise are forbidden
    to the mystics
Remain with Allah—think not of life, nor pray
    for the delights hereafter

Walter Andrews, Mehmet Kalpakli, and Najaat Black

✇ Nâbî (c. 1642–1712)

IN THE GARDEN OF TIME AND DESTINY

In the garden of time and destiny, we have seen both
    the autumn and the spring
We have seen both the time of joy and the time
    of sorrow

Don't be exceedingly proud, for in the tavern
    of good fortune
We have seen one thousand drunks intoxicated
    on pride

We have seen countless stone fortresses
    in the land of worldly fame
And not one could withstand the exploding sigh
    of a broken heart

We have seen a flood of tears from the people
    of grief
With a roar we have seen the deluge engulf
    one thousand homes of luck

We have seen countless swift riders
    of this battlefield
Whose only remaining wealth is the life-taking
    arrow of love's sigh

We have seen many who are proud
    of their high office
Who must one day wait on others, hands folded
      by the door

Oh Nâbî, we have seen many wine drinkers
      at life's party
Who have exchanged a cup full of their desires
      for a beggar's bowl

Walter Andrews, Mehmet Kalpakli, and Najaat Black

❦ Nedîm (d. 1730)

TAKE YOURSELF TO THE ROSE-GARDEN

Take yourself to the rose-garden, it's the season
    of our wandering
Oh swaying cypress, give back the ruined spring
    its reign
Pour down your dark curls, let your cheek be
    dressed in sable
Oh swaying cypress, give back the ruined spring
    its reign

Come rose-mouthed one, your nightingales
    are calling
Come to the garden, that we might forget
    the rose has gone
Come, before the meadow is ravaged
    by winter
Oh swaying cypress, give back the ruined spring
    its reign

Cast your black down onto that red cheek
This year, border your crimson shawl in mink
And if the tulip cups are lacking,
    bring wine cups in their stead
Oh swaying cypress, give back the ruined spring
    its reign

The world is a Paradise, it is the season
    of plentiful fruit
Won't you make the fruit of union ours
    as well?
Secretly bless your lovers, give each of them
    a kiss
Oh swaying cypress, give back the ruined spring
    its reign

Oh my heart-brightening beauty, I heard
    a line of verse
It was lovely, though I don't know what
    it meant
Oh Nedîm, I suppose you spoke the line
    knowingly . . . it is this
Oh swaying cypress, give back the ruined spring
    its reign

Walter Andrews, Mehmet Kalpakli, and Najaat Black

Serbian

➣ **Anonymous** (date unknown)

THE SKY IS STREWN WITH STARS

The sky is strewn with stars
And the wide meadow with sheep.
The sheep have no shepherd
Except for crazy Radoye
And he has fallen asleep.
His sister Janja wakes him:
Get up, crazy Radoye,
Your sheep have wandered off.
Let them, sister, let them.
The witches have feasted on me,
Mother carved my heart out,
Our aunt held the torch for her.

Charles Simic

➣ **Anonymous** (date unknown)

A GIRL THREW AN APPLE TO A CLOUD

A girl threw an apple to a cloud,
And the cloud kept the apple.
The girl prayed to all the clouds:
Brother clouds, give me back my golden apple.
The guests have arrived:
My mother's brothers and my uncles.
Their horses are wild like mountain fairies.
When they tread the dust
The dust doesn't rise.
When they tread on water,
Their hooves don't get wet.

Charles Simic

➣ **Anonymous** (date unknown)

BROTHERLESS SISTERS

Two sisters who had no brother
Made one of silk to share,

Of white silk and of red.
For his waist they used barberry wood,
Black eyes, two precious stones.
For eyebrows sea leeches.
Tiny teeth a string of pearls.
They fed him sugar and honey sweet
And told him: now eat and then speak.

Charles Simic

Romany

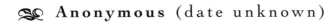 **Anonymous** (date unknown)

THREE GYPSY SONGS

1

see the great vultures,
wheeling above our caravans
may god forgive them, they are
harbingers of the great curse
where is my woman, where is her man
we must hitch up our horses & hit the road

2

moon shines on valley
grass sleeps by river
now why don't you come
sit down with me
& love me a little
as i love you

3

it's *you* puts the green sprig in my hatband
if you should ever leave me
my hat would be a dirty old thing
my heart empty, eyes full of tears
i'd look for green leaves in the woods
but they are the wilting kind
they wouldn't stay green on my hat
where could i find as good a woman
a wife as beautiful
i'd burn my caravan, cut off my hair
& trot off to the darkest part of the woods

to sleep there in my black sorrow
weep & sleep, until the white dog comes
to take me back to you

Anselm Hollo (after Katarina Taikon and Leo Tiainen)

𝕊 7

INDIA: LATE TRADITIONAL SECULAR AND SACRED VERSE

Braj

𝕊 Ruskhan (c. 1550)

IN PRAISE OF KRISHNA

Beautiful his peacock crown,
so stunningly his turban tied;
his forehead graced by dust
raised by herds of cows;
Upon his breast
a forest garland undulates.
    The maiden gazed
upon that fount of nectar,
    and became dumb.
Closing her eyes,
    mirthfully she called out
(while her fellow maiden said:)
"Open your eyes."
"Why open my eyes
    when Krishna's form
    dwells within?"

Allen Shapiro and Stephen Schaffer

❧ Bihari

From THE SATASAI

1

What she said to her companion
Every time I look at him
he seems handsomer.
Like a venturesome swimmer
my glance has dived deep
into the ocean of his loveliness
again and again,
but it could never fathom it.

2

What she said to her confidante
Oh god
how strange are love's ways;
the eyes of lovers
entangle
but what snaps
are family ties!
Love's string joins
tender minds
but it's knotted
in hearts
wicked and jealous!

3

What her companion said
Gazing aloft
you're pointing out to me
how admirably
the pigeons are somersaulting
in their flight.
But by the sparkle in your eyes
the rapture on your face
and the thrills coursing through your body,
I know you're enthralled
not by the pigeons
but by your lover who's flying them!

Krishna P. Bahadur

Marathi

✍ Tukaram (1598–1649)

IN MY VIEW

In my view
God is dead.
Those who have him
Still may.

I speak no more
Of him;
I mouth his name no more.
We mowed each other down.

I praised him.
I damned him.
It was all
A big business.

Now I remain
Quiet.
I am spending
My own life.

Dilip Chitre

Telugu

✍ Ksetrayya (c. 1650)

A COURTESAN TO A YOUNG CUSTOMER

You are handsome, aren't you,
Ādivarāha,
and quite skilled at it, too.

Stop these foolish games.
You think there are no other men
in these parts?
Asking for me on credit,
Ādivarāha?
I told you even then
I won't stand for your lies.

Handsome, aren't you?

Prince of playboys you may be,
but is it fair
to ask me to forget the money?
I earned it, after all,
by spending time with you.
Stop this trickery at once.
Put up the gold you owe me
and then you can talk,
Ādivarāha.

Handsome, aren't you?

Young man:
why are you trying to talk big,
as if you were Muvva Gopāla?
You can make love like nobody else,
but just don't make promises
you can't keep.
Pay up,
it's wrong to break your word.

Handsome, aren't you?

A. K. Ramanujan, Velcheru Narayana Rao, and David Shulman

A COURTESAN TO HER LOVER

Who was that woman sleeping
in the space between you and me?
Muvva Gopāla, you sly one:
I heard her bangles jingle.

As I would kiss you now and then,
I took her lips into mine,
the lips of that woman fragrant as camphor.
You must have kissed her long.

But when I tasted them,
they were insipid
as the chewed-out fiber
of sugarcane.

Who was that woman?

Thinking it was you, I reached out for a hug.
Those big breasts collided with mine.
That seemed a little strange,

but I didn't make a fuss
lest I hurt you, lord,
and I turned aside.

Who was that woman?

You made love to me first,
and then was it her turn?
Does she come here every day?
Muvva Gopāla,
you who fathered the god of desire,
you can't be trusted.
I know your tricks now
and the truth of your heart.

Who was that woman?

A. K. Ramanujan, Velcheru Narayana Rao, and David Shulman

A WIFE TO A FRIEND

Don't tell me what he did in some other country.
What has it got to do with me? For god's sake, stop it.
What are you saying: that he went to her house, fell for her, gave her money
    and begged her?

More likely, she saw his beauty, wanted him,
fell all over him, begged him, melted him with her music.
After all, he's a man. He couldn't contain himself, that's all.

Don't tell me what he did

All decked in jewelry like a wild cassia in bloom,
a temptress on a mission from the Love God,
she must have stood there and said,
"Hey, handsome! It's not good for you to stay alone.
Come over and sleep in my house."

Don't tell me what he did

That Muvva Gopāla, Lord of Madhura, from the day
he made love to me he hasn't known anyone else.
Nor is he up to any tricks, he is a dignified man.
He must have been angry that I wasn't anywhere near.

Don't tell me what he did

A. K. Ramanujan, Velcheru Narayana Rao, and David Shulman

❧ Sarangapani (c. 1720)

THE MADAM TO A YOUNG COURTESAN

Grab whatever cash he has,
that Venugopāla,
and think nothing of the rest.

As they say about lentils,
don't worry
about the chaff.

Does it matter
to which woman he goes,
or how late he stays there?

Just pass the days
saying yes and no,
till the month is over

and grab the cash

What is it to you
if he runs into debt
or if he has an income?

Quietly, tactfully,
lie in wait
like a cat on a wall

and grab the cash

What if he makes love
to her
and only then to you?

What's there
to be jealous about?
When youth passes,
nothing will go your way,

so grab the cash

A. K. Ramanujan, Velcheru Narayana Rao, and David Shulman

8

EAST ASIAN VERSE: EARLY CH'ING DYNASTY CHINA; TIBET; MIDDLE CHOSŎN KOREA; EARLY EDO JAPAN

Chinese

❧ Han-shan Te-ch'ing (1546–1623)

From MOUNTAIN LIVING

1

through a few splinters of
          white cloud motionless
the Buddha wheel bright moon
                    comes flying
to accompany me
          in my mountain stillness
and I smile up at it
     above the dirty suffering world

2

it only took a single flake
          to freeze my mind in the snowy night
a few clangs to smash my dreams
          among the frosted bells
and the stove's night fire fragrance
          too is melted away
yet at my window the moon
          climbs a solitary peak

3

clouds scatter the length of the sky
        rain passes over
the snow melts in the chill valley
           as Spring is born
and though I feel my body's like
        the rushing water
I know my mind's not
           as clear as the ice

James M. Cryer

✍ Feng Meng-lung (1574–1645)

THREE MOUNTAIN SONGS

My Old Man's Small

1

My old man's small, shriveled and shrunk;
When a crummy horse has no bridle, who enjoys the ride?
The river swells, the boat rides high,
Too bad his pole is short.
How will he ever touch bottom?

2

My old man's small and unromantic;
We share the same bedcurtains but not the same pillow.
I joined to your household a fine patch of land;
Too bad you don't know how to plant it.
Every year the harvest of its flowers will be reaped by others.

Smart

Mom is smart,
But her daughter's smart too.
Mom sifted ashes all across the floor,
But I rashly carried my lover into bed and out again,
The two of us sharing a single pair of shoes.

Feeling the Itch

I itched inside and caught my lover's eye,
But once he came to me he wouldn't leave me alone.
From the prow down to the cabin, the deck began to burn;
Luckily my lover put out the fire in my stern.

Richard W. Bodman

❧ Ts'ao Ching-chao (c. 1620)

PALACE POEM

Bejeweled makeup, cloud-coiffure, training golden garments,
small and dainty is the pose she strikes beside the door of jade.
A newcomer still unfamiliar with palace manners,
Head lowered, first she bows to the number one concubine.

Nancy Hodes and Tung Yuan-fang

Tibetan

❧ Tsangyang Gyatso (1683–1706)

From LOVE-POEMS OF THE SIXTH DALAI LAMA

1

I sought my lover at twilight
Snow fell at daybreak.
Residing at the Potala
I am Rigdzin Tsangyang Gyatso
But in the back alleys of Shol-town
I am rake and stud.
Secret or not
No matter.
Footprints have been left in the snow.

2

Wild horses running in the hills
Can be caught with snares or lassos
But not even magic charms can stop
A lover's heart that's turned away.

3

Lover met by chance on the road,
Girl with delicious-smelling body—
Like picking up a small white turquoise
Only to toss it away again.

4

White teeth smiling.
Brightness of skin.
On my seat in the high lama's row

At the quick edge of my glance
I caught her looking at me.

Rick Fields and Brian Cutillo

Japanese Poetry Written in Chinese

✆ Ishikawa Jōzan (1583–1672)

GARDENING CHRYSANTHEMUMS, I THINK OF [T'AO] YÜAN-MING

This gentleman of cultivated virtue
had a hermit's vocation unmatched in his time.
In service or retirement, he avoided success and failure both;
he was intelligent, wise and compassionate.
Caressing a pine tree, he sang the praises of the landscape;
cane in hand, he inspected the fields.
And the fragrance of his love for a hedgeful of chrysanthemums
has lingered in the air for a thousand years!
With lute and books he drove off his old worries;
poetry and wine helped him forget how poor his family was.
When he became drunk, he finished with Heaven and Earth:
how joyful his body, his shadow, his soul!

Jonathan Chaves

EATING ROASTED *MATSUTAKE* MUSHROOMS

You gather them in the shade of pine trees.
You don't boil them, you don't steam them.
Roast them over charcoals glowing red in the brazier:
like the cremation of little naked monks!

Jonathan Chaves

✆ Gensei (1623–1668)

EVENING VIEW FROM GRASS HILL

In love with mountains, I go out my gate,
then lay aside the staff, rest on a pine root.
Autumn rivers border the broad fields,
twilight haze parts me from the distant village.

As dew rises, the edges of the grove whiten;
stars come out and tree tops grow blacker.
I can tell I've been sitting here a long time —
the dark moss already bears my print.

Burton Watson

DISTANT VIEW FROM GRASS HILL

My one puny hut leads right off to the slopes,
but few visitors hike up to the top of Grass Hill.
Cows wandering here and there look almost like flocks of crows;
herons heading home to roost in the village you'd take for darting butterflies.
Clouds break, and beyond the treetops a lone pagoda rises;
where wind parts the reed leaves, the single sail of a homecoming boat.
These scenes have their limits but my mind has none;
still seated on a pine root, I see off the evening sun.

Burton Watson

Japanese

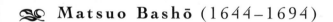 **Matsuo Bashō** (1644–1694)

SIX HAIKU

1

Ancient silent pond
Then a frog jumped right in!
Watersound: kerplunk

John S. Major

2

The temple bell stops —
but the sound keeps coming
out of the flowers.

Robert Bly

3

Such stillness —
The cries of the cicadas
Sink into the rocks.

Donald Keene

4

Skylark
sings all day,
and day not long enough.

Lucien Stryk and Takashi Ikemoto

5

Fish shop—
how cold the lips
of the salted bream.

Lucien Stryk and Takashi Ikemoto

6

Culture's beginnings:
from the heart of the country
rice-planting songs

Sam Hamill

ॐ Nozawa Bonchō (d. 1714), Matsuo Bashō (1644–1694), and Mukai Kyorai (1651–1704)

From THE LINKED-VERSE SEQUENCE THROUGHOUT THE TOWN

Each year it is but a peck of rice
but the land-tax is paid in full
    where five or six logs
still green from cutting lie asoak
    on the boggy ground

Where five or six logs
still green from cutting lie asoak
    on the boggy ground
his fine leather socks grow dirty
as he walks along the muddied path

His leather stockings grow dirty
as he hurries along the muddied path
    the sword attendant
is pulled off at breakneck speed
    by his master's fast horse

The sword attendant
is pulled off at breakneck speed
    by his master's fast horse
making the nearby apprentice spill
the water bucket that he holds

Near where an apprentice spills
the water bucket that he holds
    a house is up for sale
its broken doors and windows covered
    with straw matting

    A house is up for sale
its broken doors and windows covered
    with straw matting
when was it that its chili peppers
took on their ripened color

When was it that the chili peppers
took on their ripened color
    stealthily stealthily
he plaits straw into sandals
    in bright moonlight

    Stealthily stealthily
he plaits straw into sandals
    in bright moonlight
and shaking fleas from the bedcovers
she wakes to early autumn

Shaking fleas from the bedcovers
she wakes to early autumn
    as the half-gallon box
set up as a trap falls in the night
    with a hollow thud

    The half-gallon box
set up as a trap falls in the night
    with a hollow thud
with its lid warped out of line
the storage box cannot be closed

With its lid warped out of line
the storage box cannot be closed
    for a little while
he remains at his hermitage
    and then is off again

    For a little while
I remain at my hermitage

and then am off again
happy in old age that my poems
have won place in a collection

Earl Miner

✑ Chikamatsu Monzaemon (1653–1725)

From THE LOVE SUICIDES AT SONEZAKI

The Journey

NARRATOR: Farewell to the world, and to the night farewell.
    We who walk the road to death, to what should we be likened?
    To the frost by the road that leads to the graveyard,
    Vanishing with each step ahead:
    This dream of a dream is sorrowful.
    Ah, did you count the bell? Of the seven strokes
    That mark the dawn six have sounded.
    The remaining one will be the last echo
    We shall hear in this life. It will echo
    The bliss of annihilation.
    Farewell, and not to the bell alone,
    We look a last time on the grass, the trees, the sky,
    The clouds go by unmindful of us,
    The bright Dipper is reflected in the water,
    The Wife and Husband Stars inside the Milky Way.
TOKUBEI: Let's think the Bridge of Umeda
    The bridges the magpies built and make a vow
    That we will always be Wife and Husband Stars.
NARRATOR: "With all my heart," she says and clings to him:
    So many are the tears that fall between the two,
    The waters of the river must have risen.
    On a teahouse balcony across the way
    A party in the lamplight loudly discuss
    Before they go to bed the latest gossip,
    With many words about the good and bad
    Of this year's crop of lovers' suicides.
TOKUBEI: How strange! but yesterday, even today,
    We spoke as if such things didn't concern us.
    Tomorrow we shall figure in their gossip—
    Well, if they wish to sing about us, let them.
NARRATOR: This is the song that now we hear:
    "Why can't you take me for your wife?
    Although you think you don't want me . . ."
    However we think, however lament,
    Both our fate and the world go against us.
    Never before today was there a day
    Of relaxation, and untroubled night,
    Instead, the tortures of an ill-starred love.

"What did I do to deserve it?
I never can forget you.
You want to shake me off and go?
I'll never let you.
Take me with your hands and kill me
Or I'll never let you go,"
Said the girl in tears.
TOKUBEI: Of all the many songs, that it should be that one,
This very evening, but who is it that sings?
We are those who listen; others like us
Who've gone this way have had the same ordeal.
NARRATOR: They cling to one another, weeping bitterly,
And wish, as many a lover has wished,
The night would last even a little longer.
The heartless summer night is short as ever,
And soon the cockcrows chase away their lives.

Donald Keene

Korean

❧ Yun Sŏndo (1587–1671)

TWO POEMS *From* THE ANGLER'S CALENDAR

1

Is it a cuckoo that cries?
Is it the willow that is blue?
Row away, row away!
Several roofs in a far fishing village
Swim in the mist.
Chigŭkch'ong chigŭkch'ong ŏsawa.
Boy, fetch an old net!
Fishes are climbing against the stream.

2

The sun's fair rays are shining,
The water is calm as oil.
Row away, row away!
Should we cast a net,
Or drop a line on such a day?
Chigŭkch'ong chigŭkch'ong ŏsawa.
The poem of Ch'u Yüan stirs my fancy;
I have forgotten all about fishing.

Peter H. Lee

✌ Kim Sujang (c. 1680–1730)

DECEPTION

Look at that girl in blouse and patterned skirt,
Her face prettily powdered, her hair as yet unpinned.
Yesterday she deceived me,
And now she's off to deceive another.
Fresh cut flowers held firmly in her hand,
Her hips swinging lightly as the sun goes down.

Kevin O'Rourke

MOONLIGHT

Moonlight shines on the lotus pond;
    lotus fragrance pervades my clothes.
There's wine in the golden jug
    and a beauty playing the lute.
    Captivated by the mood
    I sing a sad refrain.
    Pine and bamboo sway to my song;
    cranes dance in the garden.
Thus, happy with relatives,
    glad with friends, I'll live
    the span alloted me by heaven.

Kevin O'Rourke

Part VII

From the Eighteenth Century into the Early Twentieth Century

(1700–1915)

In 1780, the young Johann von Goethe penciled the eight lines of his "Wanderer's Night Song" on the wooden wall of a mountain lodge. Alexander Pushkin, born in the last year of the eighteenth century, wrote another great small poem "On the Hills of Georgia" and, in a brief life ended in a duel, created the literary heritage of Russian poets. Both poets carried the classical styles and almost glacial objectivity of the eighteenth century into the Romantic realism of the nineteenth. Their careers reinforce the vexatious decision here to house two centuries in one section.

The *philosophes* of the Enlightenment, before the tool of reason turned into the ax of the French revolution, influenced poets whose own preferred instrument was the quill pen. André Chenier, awaiting the guillotine, wrote his bitter iambs against his persecutors on smuggled paper. Voltaire, canonized by the Revolution, took the epigraph for his poem on the Lisbon earthquake of 1755 from the sanguine statement of the seventeenth-century philosopher Leibnitz that ours is "the best of all possible worlds." Voltaire's Romantic successor Victor Hugo was a humanitarian active in public life; his experiments with language, rhythms, and the tonalities of words influenced poets for the rest of the nineteenth century.

The eighteenth century was a philosophical age, identifying its own severe proclivities toward stoicism, reason, and detachment with the ancient world. English poets, like John Dryden a generation before, and Alexander Pope looked to the Roman Empire, the Pax Romana in the Age of Augustus for classical models. Giacomo Leopardi's classicism and pessimism united in an aristocratic sensibility congenial to the eighteenth century; his Romantic and patriotic vision of Italy belonged to the next. His meditative final poem on the broom plant, which tenaciously survives on the slopes of Mount Vesuvius, leaves him in a heroic straddle.

Nineteenth-century poets in both England and continental Europe carried on a romantic encounter with history, despite their disenchanted recall of the century of revolution just behind them. (The American Emily Dickinson's mystical seclusion, drawing on Puritan Divines and the poets of both New and Old England, was singular.) Shelley, outraged by a famous cavalry charge on the participants of a reform meeting in Manchester wrote a poetic indictment in 1819 against the administration of Castlereagh. His blend of outraged rebellion against brutal social realities, his unclouded individual equilibrium, and his flight toward mountains and lakes shaped the image of the Romantic poet more, perhaps, than did Keats's less classifiable genius.

Gaelic poets writing during the Protestant Ascendancy in Ireland (located in the previous section of this book to indicate their continuity), like the widowed Eileen O'Leary in her mourning poem on the death of her husband, continued the music of lamentation in the presence of tyranny. The lyric voices of dispossessed poets are audible in the nineteenth century as well. Robert Burns inhabited the genius of the Scots dialect; Goethe collected the folk lyric of the anonymous singers of southeastern Europe and folksong reentered the currents of the century's verse. Guiseppe Belli, the satiric and ribald composer of sonnets in the Romanesco dialect of the ordinary citizens of Rome, wrote under the Napoleonic occupation.

Nineteenth-century nationalism, restless learning, and widespread sympathy with patriotic movements may have inspired the renewed attention to folksong. Yet many Romantic poets were ambivalent toward any claims of nationality, prizing above all the exaltation of the self and a bohemian disdain for authority.

The cradle of the Romantic movement was Germany, where Friedrich Hölderlin, confined in a tower after a bout of madness, merged the classical frieze of pagan gods and goddess into a romantic and febrile landscape of torrents, lakes, and cliffsides. Hölderlin fractured syntax in an individual frenzy to express a oneness with nature and a religious vision uniting Greek pantheism and Christianity. Heinrich Heine's self-division defined the age as well: his melancholy and sense of homelessness as a German Jew living in exile in Paris invade the poems of his last years. He wrote them while paralyzed on his "mattress-grave," his pain slightly relieved by a morphine drip.

The French Symbolist poets began as Romantics but their received reverence for the natural world evolved into revolt against a chilly detailing of reality in the fiction of post-Napoleonic France. Baudelaire saw nature as a temple of "correspondences"; his fellow poets reestablished a richness of discourse and a complex reading of human mystery. Many of the Symbolists were severely alientated from bourgeois society; they prowled the streets and boulevards for an even bleaker view of urban life.

Gérard de Nerval, whose madness took him into suicide in 1855, was the French translator of Goethe's *Faust*. A sonnet included here compiles allusions to Goethe's "Song of Mignon," to the dragon's teeth that sowed the city of Thebes with phantoms of retribution, and recalls both the eruption of Mount Vesuvius in the 1830s and the tomb of Virgil in Naples.

The musical affinities of French Symbolists, along with their ties to Impressionist painters, are familiar. Mallarmé's "Afternoon of a Faun" was set to music by Debussy. while his ellipses, his radical syntax, and his dissonant progression of meaning through metaphor rather than strict narration, altered the language of poetry forever. (Even the chamber music ambiance of Verlaine's delicate lyrics, memorized by generations of French schoolchildren, found a jarring twentieth-century resolution. The opening lines of "Les sanglots longues des violons," broadcast by the Free French during World War II provided the code signaling the uprising of local resistance movements in France after the Normandy invasion.) Symbolist poetry, translated into many languages, probing the psyche of the age to come, had allies and heirs from Russia to the United States. One was the young T. S. Eliot, an undergraduate at Harvard at the end of the century, immersed in Baudelaire and Laforgue and already preoccupied with diagnosing a "dissociation of sensibility," the separation of thought and feeling in poetry. A process under way since the seventeenth century, it reached its climax in the modernist explosion of the twentieth.

K. W.

East of the Euphrates also, the eighteenth and nineteenth centuries were an era of literary change.

The characteristic Persian verse form is the *ghazal,* an intricately rhymed love song lyric; the nineteenth-century master Ghalib wrote *ghazals* both in Persian and in Urdu. Urdu poetry is also represented here in the work of Galib's heir Muhammad Iqbal, the founder of modern Pakistani literature. A very different voice from the subcontinent is that of the Bengali poet Rabindranath Tagore, who consciously saw himself as a bridge between East and West.

Among later Chinese writers Yüan Mei is particularly noteworthy, as China's last great — and highly individualistic — traditional poet. The Japanese verse here features the work of two later *haiku* masters, Buson and Issa, and the hermit-priest Ryokan; the work of Ema Saiko and Tachibana Akemi hints at the beginnings of Japanese modernism. New Asian voices appear in this section: the riddle-like Malay verses called *pantuns,* a poem by the Filipino poet-patriot Rizal, and a Laotian funeral song that preserves, across a period of two thousand years, the ancient south Chinese practice of "summoning the soul" of a newly deceased person (see "The Summons of the Soul" in Part II).

The most exciting development in non-Western literature seen in Part VII, however, is the emergence into world literature of works collected from the oral traditions of the Pacific Islands, the Americas, and Africa. These poems, transcribed by outsiders beginning in the nineteenth century, in some cases reflect oral transmission from much earlier times; other works are contemporary compositions by known poets. What almost always strikes readers encountering this poetry for the first time is not only its beauty but also its remarkable literary sophistication; it makes nonsense of the old belief that these traditional cultures were in any significant way "primitive."

J.S.M.

✺ 1

English-Language Poetry from England, Ireland, and America from the Augustans through the Victorian Age; Late Traditional Verse in Irish Gaelic

English

✺ Alexander Pope (1688–1784)

THE SCALE OF BEING

Far as Creation's ample range extends,
The scale of sensual, mental pow'rs ascends:
Mark how it mounts, to Man's imperial race,
From the green myriads in the peopled grass:
What modes of sight betwixt each wide extreme,
The mole's dim curtain, and the lynx's beam:
Of smell, the headlong lioness between,
And hound sagacious on the tainted green:
Of hearing, from the life that fills the flood,
To that which warbles thro' the vernal wood:
The spider's touch, how exquisitely fine!
Feels at each thread, and lives along the line:
In the nice bee, what sense so subtly true
From pois'nous herbs extracts the healing dew?
How Instinct varies in the grov'ling swine,
Compar'd, half-reas'ning elephant, with thine!
'Twixt that, and Reason, what a nice barrier;
For ever sep'rate, yet for ever near!
Remembrance and Reflection how ally'd;
What thin partitions Sense from Thought divide:
And Middle natures, how they long to join,

Yet never pass th'insuperable line!
Without this just gradation, could they be
Subjected, these to those, or all to thee?
The pow'rs of all subdu'd by thee alone,
Is not thy Reason all these pow'rs in one?

Samuel Johnson (1709–1784)

A SHORT SONG OF CONGRATULATION

Long expected one and twenty,
Lingering year, at length is flown;
Pride and pleasure, pomp and plenty,
Great Sir John, are all your own.

Loosened from the minor's tether,
Free to mortgage or to sell,
Wild as wind, and light as feather,
Bid the sons of thrift farewell.

Call the Betseys, Kates, and Jennys,
All the names that banish care,
Lavish of your grandsire's guineas,
Show the spirit of an heir.

All that prey on vice and folly
Joy to see their quarry fly,
Here the gamester light and jolly,
There the lender grave and sly.

Wealth, my lad, was made to wander,
Let it wander as it will;
Call the jockey, call the pander,
Bid them come, and take their fill.

When the bonny blade carouses,
Pockets full, and spirits high,
What are acres? What are houses?
Only dirt, or wet or dry.

Should the guardian, friend, or mother
Tell the woes of wilful waste,
Scorn their counsel, scorn their pother,
You can hang or drown at last.

❧ Thomas Chatterton (1752–1770)

THE MINSTREL'S SONG

Oh! sing unto my roundelay;
　　Oh! drop the briny tear with me;
Dance no more at holiday;
　　Like a running river be.
　　　　My love is dead,
　　　　Gone to his death-bed,
　　　　All under the willow-tree.

Black his hair as the winter night,
　　White his skin as the summer snow,
Red his face as the morning light;
　　Cold he lies in the grave below.
　　　　My love is dead,
　　　　Gone to his death-bed,
　　　　All under the willow-tree.

Sweet his tongue as the throstle's note,
　　Quick in dance as thought can be,
Deft his tabor, cudgel stout;
　　Oh! he lies by the willow-tree.
　　　　My love is dead,
　　　　Gone to his death-bed,
　　　　All under the willow-tree.

Hark! the raven flaps his wing,
　　In the briarèd dell below;
Hark! the death-owl loud doth sing
　　To the night-mares, as they go.
　　　　My love is dead,
　　　　Gone to his death-bed,
　　　　All under the willow-tree.

See! the white moon shines on high,
　　Whiter is my true love's shroud,
Whiter than the morning sky,
　　Whiter than the evening cloud.
　　　　My love is dead,
　　　　Gone to his death-bed,
　　　　All under the willow-tree.

Here, upon my true love's grave,
　　Shall the barren flowers be laid;
Not one holy saint to save
　　All the coldness of a maid.
　　　　My love is dead,

>Gone to his death-bed,
>All under the willow-tree.

With my hands I'll fix the briars
>Round his holy corse to grow,
Elfin fairy, light your fires,
>Here, my body still shall be.
>>My love is dead,
>>Gone to his death-bed,
>>All under the willow-tree.

Come, with acorn-cup and thorn,
>Drain my own heart's blood away;
Life and all its good I scorn,
>Dance by night, or feast by day.
>>My love is dead,
>>Gone to his death-bed,
>>All under the willow-tree.

Water-witches, crowned with reytes,
>Bear me to your lethal tide.
I die; I come; my true love waits.
>Thus the damsel spake and died.

✌ George Crabbe (1754–1832)

WINTER VIEWS SERENE

The Ocean too has Winter-Views serene,
When all you see through densest Fog is seen;
When you can hear the Fishers near at hand
Distinctly speak, yet see not where they stand;
Or sometimes them and not their Boat discern,
Or half-conceal'd some Figure at the Stern;
The View's all bounded, and from side to side
Your utmost Prospect but a few ells wide;
Boys who, on Shore, to Sea the Pebble cast,
Will hear it strike against the viewless Mast;
While the stern Boatman growls his fierce disdain,
At whom he knows not, whom he threats in vain.
'Tis pleasant then to view the Nets float past,
Net after Net till you have seen the last;
And as you wait till all beyond you slip,
A Boat comes gliding from an anchor'd Ship,
Breaking the silence with the dipping Oar,
And their own Tones, as labouring for the Shore;
Those measur'd Tones which with the Scene agree,
And give a Sadness to Serenity.

SAILING UPON THE RIVER

Among those Joys, 'tis one at Eve to sail
On the broad River with a favourite Gale;
When no rough Waves upon the Bosom ride,
But the Keel cuts, nor rises on the Tide;
Safe from the Stream the nearer Gunwale stands,
Where playful Children trail their idle Hands,
Or strive to catch long grassy Leaves that float
On either side of the impeded Boat:
What time the Moon arising shows the Mud,
A shining Border to the silver Flood;
When, by her dubious Light, the meanest Views,
Chalk, Stones and Stakes obtain the richest Hues;
And when the Cattle, as they gazing stand,
Seem nobler Objects than when view'd from Land:
Then anchor'd Vessels in the way appear,
And Sea-boys greet them as they pass — 'What cheer?'
The sleeping Shell-ducks at the sound arise,
And utter loud their unharmonious Cries;
Fluttering they move their weedy Beds among,
Or instant diving, hide their plumeless Young.

✎ William Blake (1757–1827)

MORNING

To find the Western path
Right thro' the Gates of Wrath
I urge my way;
Sweet Mercy leads me on:
With soft repentant moan
I see the break of day.

The war of swords & spears
Melted by dewy tears
Exhales on high;
The Sun is freed from fears
And with soft grateful tears
Ascends the sky.

THE MENTAL TRAVELLER

I travel'd thro' a Land of Men,
A Land of Men & Women too,

And heard & saw such dreadful things
As cold Earth wanderers never knew.

For there the Babe is born in joy
That was begotten in dire woe;
Just as we Reap in joy the fruit
Which we in bitter tears did sow.

And if the Babe is born a Boy
He's given to a Woman Old,
Who nails him down upon a rock,
Catches his shrieks in cups of gold.

She binds iron thorns around his head,
She pierces both his hands & feet,
She cuts his heart out at his side
To make it feel both cold & heat.

Her fingers number every Nerve,
Just as a Miser counts his gold;
She lives upon his shrieks & cries,
And she grows young as he grows old.

Till he becomes a bleeding youth,
And she becomes a Virgin bright;
Then he rends up his Manacles
And binds her down for his delight.

He plants himself in all her Nerves,
Just as a Husbandman his mould;
And she becomes his dwelling place
And Garden fruitful seventy fold.

An aged Shadow, soon he fades,
Wand'ring round an Earthly Cot,
Full filled all with gems & gold
Which he by industry had got.

And these are the gems of the Human Soul,
The rubies & pearls of a lovesick eye,
The countless gold of the akeing heart,
The martyr's groan & the lover's sigh.

They are his meat, they are his drink;
He feeds the Beggar & the Poor
And the wayfaring Traveller:
For ever open is his door.

His grief is their eternal joy;
They make the roofs & walls to ring;

Till from the fire on the hearth
A little Female Babe does spring.

And she is all of solid fire
And gems & gold, that none his hand
Dares stretch to touch her Baby form,
Or wrap her in his swaddling-band.

But She comes to the Man she loves,
If young or old, or rich or poor;
They soon drive out the aged Host,
A Beggar at another's door.

He wanders weeping far away,
Untill some other take him in;
Oft blind & age-bent, sore distrest,
Untill he can a Maiden win.

And to allay his freezing Age
The Poor Man takes her in his arms;
The Cottage fades before his sight,
The Garden & its lovely Charms.

The Guests are scatter'd thro' the land,
For the Eye altering alters all;
The Senses roll themselves in fear,
And the flat Earth becomes a Ball;

The stars, sun, Moon, all shrink away,
A desart vast without a bound,
And nothing left to eat or drink,
And a dark desart all around.

The honey of her Infant lips,
The bread & wine of her sweet smile,
The wild game of her roving Eye,
Does him to Infancy beguile;

For as he eats & drinks he grows
Younger & younger every day;
And on the desart wild they both
Wander in terror & dismay.

Like the wild Stag she flees away,
Her fear plants many a thicket wild;
While he pursues her night & day,
By various arts of Love beguil'd,

By various arts of Love & Hate,
Till the wide desart planted o'er

With Labyrinths of wayward Love,
Where roam the Lion, Wolf & Boar,

Till he becomes a wayward Babe,
And she a weeping Woman Old.
Then many a Lover wanders here;
The Sun & Stars are nearer roll'd.

The trees bring forth sweet Extacy
To all who in the desert roam;
Till many a City there is Built,
And many a pleasant Shepherd's home.

But when they find the frowning Babe,
Terror strikes thro' the region wide:
They cry "The Babe! the Babe is Born!"
And flee away on Every side.

For who dare touch the frowning form,
His arm is wither'd to its root;
Lions, Boars, Wolves, all howling flee,
And every Tree does shed its fruit.

And none can touch that frowning form,
Except it be a Woman Old;
She nails him down upon the Rock,
And all is done as I have told.

FIVE QUESTIONS, ANSWERS, A PROPHECY AND PARADOXES

The Question Answer'd

What is it men in women do require?
The lineaments of Gratified Desire.
What is it women do in men require?
The lineaments of Gratified Desire.

Lacedemonian Instruction

"Come hither, my boy, tell me what thou seest there."
"A fool tangled in a religious snare."

An Answer to the Parson

"Why of the sheep do you not learn peace?"
"Because I don't want you to shear my fleece."

Merlin's Prophecy

The harvest shall flourish in wintry weather
When two virginities meet together:

The King & the Priest must be tied in a tether
Before two virgins can meet together.

The Look of Love Alarms

The look of love alarms
Because 'tis fill'd with fire;
But the look of soft deceit
Shall win the lover's hire.

JERUSALEM

And did those feet in ancient time
Walk upon England's mountains green?
And was the holy Lamb of God
On England's pleasant pastures seen?

And did the Countenance Divine
Shine forth upon our clouded hills?
And was Jerusalem builded here,
Among these dark Satanic Mills?

Bring me my Bow of burning gold:
Bring me my Arrows of desire:
Bring me my Spear: O clouds unfold!
Bring me my Chariot of fire!

I will not cease from Mental Fight,
Nor shall my Sword sleep in my hand,
Till we have built Jerusalem
In England's green & pleasant Land.

ᴥ Robert Burns (1759–1796)

THE SILVER TASSIE

Go, fetch to me a pint o' wine,
    An' fill it in a silver tassie;
That I may drink, before I go,
    A service to my bonnie lassie.
The boat rocks at the pier o' Leith,
    Fu' loud the wind blaws frae the ferry,
The ship rides by the Berwick-law,
    And I maun leave my bonnie Mary.

The trumpets sound, the banners fly,
    The glittering spears are rankèd ready;

The shouts o' war are heard afar,
    The battle closes thick and bloody;
But it's no the roar o' sea or shore
    Wad mak me langer wish to tarry;
Nor shout o' war that's heard afar,
    It's leaving thee, my bonnie Mary.

JOHN ANDERSON MY JO

John Anderson my jo, John,
When we were first acquent;
Your locks were like the raven,
Your bony brow was bent;
But now tour brow is beld, John,
Your locks are like the snaw;
But blessings on your frosty pow,
John Anderson my jo.

John Anderson my jo, John,
We clamb the hill the gither;
And mony a canty day, John,
We've had wi'ane anither:
Now we maun totter down, John,
And hand in hand we'll go:
And sleep the gither at the foot,
John Anderson my jo.

❧ William Wordsworth (1770–1850)

RESOLUTION AND INDEPENDENCE

1

There was a roaring in the wind all night;
The rain came heavily and fell in floods;
But now the sun is rising calm and bright;
The birds are singing in the distant woods;
Over his own sweet voice the Stock-dove broods;
The Jay makes answer as the Magpie chatters;
And all the air is filled with pleasant noise of waters.

2

All things that love the sun are out of doors;
The sky rejoices in the morning's birth;
The grass is bright with rain-drops;—on the moors
The hare is running races in her mirth;

And with her feet she from the plashy earth
Raises a mist; that, glittering in the sun,
Runs with her all the way, wherever she doth run.

3

I was a Traveler then upon the moor;
I saw the hare that raced about with joy;
I heard the woods and distant waters roar;
Or heard them not, as happy as a boy:
The pleasant season did my heart employ:
My old remembrances went from me wholly;
And all the ways of men, so vain and melancholy.

4

But, as it sometimes chanceth, from the might
Of joy in minds that can no further go,
As high as we have mounted in delight
In our dejection do we sink as low;
To me that morning did it happen so;
And fears and fancies thick upon me came;
Dim sadness—and blind thoughts, I knew not, nor could name.

5

I heard the sky-lark warbling in the sky;
And I bethought me of the playful hare:
Even such a happy Child of earth am I;
Even as these blissful creatures do I fare;
Far from the world I walk, and from all care;
But there may come another day to me—
Solitude, pain of heart, distress, and poverty.

6

My whole life I have lived in pleasant thought,
As if life's business were a summer mood;
As if all needful things would come unsought
To genial faith, still rich in genial good;
But how can He expect that others should
Build for him, sow for him, and at his call
Love him, who for himself will take no heed at all?

7

I thought of Chatterton, the marvelous Boy,
The sleepless Soul that perished in his pride;
Of Him who walked in glory and in joy
Following his plow, along the mountain-side:
By our own spirits are we deified:
We Poets in our youth begin in gladness;
But thereof come in the end despondency and madness.

From THE PRELUDE

    And in the frosty season, when the sun
Was set, and visible for many a mile
The cottage windows through the twilight blazed,
I heeded not the summons:—happy time
It was, indeed, for all of us; to me
It was a time of rapture: clear and loud
The village clock tolled six; I wheeled about,
Proud and exulting, like an untired horse,
That cares not for his home.—All shod with steel,
We hissed along the polished ice, in games
Confederate, imitative of the chase
And woodland pleasures, the resounding horn,
The pack loud bellowing, and the hunted hare.
So through the darkness and the cold we flew,
And not a voice was idle; with the din,
Meanwhile, the precipices rang aloud,
The leafless trees, and every icy crag
Tinkled like iron, while the distant hills
Into the tumult sent an alien sound
Of melancholy, not unnoticed, while the stars,
Eastward, were sparkling clear, and in the west
The orange sky of evening died away.

    Not seldom from the uproar I retired
Into a silent bay, or sportively
Glanced sideway, leaving the tumultuous throng,
To cut across the image of a star
That gleamed upon the ice: and oftentimes
When we had given our bodies to the wind,
And all the shadowy banks, on either side,
Came sweeping through the darkness, spinning still
The rapid line of motion; then at once
Have I, reclining back upon my heels,
Stopped short, yet still the solitary cliffs
Wheeled by me, even as if the earth had rolled
With visible motion her diurnal round;
Behind me did they stretch in solemn train
Feebler and feebler, and I stood and watched
Till all was tranquil as a dreamless sleep.

Surprised by joy—impatient as the wind
    I turned to share the transport—Oh! with whom
    But thee, deep buried in the silent tomb,
That spot which no vicissitude can find?
Love, faithful love, recalled thee to my mind—
    But how could I forget thee? Through what power,
    Even for the least division of an hour,
Have I been so beguiled as to be blind
To my most grievous loss!—That thought's return

Was the worst pang that sorrow ever bore,
Save one, one only, when I stood forlorn,
    Knowing my heart's best treasure was no more;
That neither present time, nor years unborn
    Could to my sight that heavenly face restore.

WITH SHIPS THE SEA WAS SPRINKLED FAR AND NIGH

With Ships the sea was sprinkled far and nigh,
Like stars in heaven, and joyously it showed;
Some lying fast at anchor in the road,
Some veering up and down, one knew not why.
A goodly Vessel did I then espy
Come like a giant from a haven broad;
And lustily along the bay she strode,
Her tackling rich, and of apparel high.
This Ship was naught to me, nor I to her,
Yet I pursued her with a Lover's look;
This Ship to all the rest did I prefer:
When will she turn, and whither? She will brook
No tarrying; where She comes the winds must stir:
On went She, and due north her journey took.

Sir Walter Scott (1771–1832)

LUCY ASHTON'S SONG

Look not thou on beauty's charming;
Sit thou still when kings are arming;
Taste not when the wine-cup glistens;
Speak not when the people listens;
Stop thine ear against the singer;
From the red gold keep thy finger;
Vacant heart and hand and eye,
Easy live and quiet die.

Samuel Taylor Coleridge (1772–1834)

WORK WITHOUT HOPE

All Nature seems at work. Slugs leave their lair—
The bees are stirring—birds are on the wing—

And Winter, slumbering in the open air,
Wears on his smiling face a dream of Spring!
And I, the while, the sole unbusy thing,
Nor honey make, nor pair, nor build, nor sing.

Yet well I ken the banks where amaranths blow,
Have traced the fount whence streams of nectar flow.
Bloom, O ye amaranths! bloom for whom ye may,
For me ye bloom not! Glide, rich streams, away!
With lips unbrightened, wreathless brow, I stroll:
And would you learn the spells that drowse my soul?
Work without Hope draws nectar in a sieve,
And Hope without an object cannot live.

KUBLA KHAN

   In Xanadu did Kubla Khan
     A stately pleasure-dome decree:
   Where Alph, the sacred river, ran
   Through caverns measureless to man
     Down to a sunless sea.
   So twice five miles of fertile ground
     With walls and towers were girdled round:
And there were gardens bright with sinuous rills
Where blossomed many an incense-bearing tree;
And here were forests ancient as the hills,
Enfolding sunny spots of greenery.
But O, that deep romantic chasm which slanted
Down the green hill athwart a cedarn cover!
A savage place! as holy and enchanted
As e'er beneath a waning moon was haunted
By woman wailing for her demon-lover!
And from this chasm, with ceaseless turmoil seething,
As if this earth in fast thick pants were breathing,
A mighty fountain momently was forced;
Amid whose swift half-intermitted burst
Huge fragments vaulted like rebounding hail,
Or chaffy grain beneath the thresher's flail:
And 'mid these dancing rocks at once and ever
It flung up momently the sacred river.
Five miles meandering with a mazy motion
Through wood and dale the sacred river ran,
Then reached the caverns measureless to man,
And sank in tumult to a lifeless ocean:
And 'mid this tumult Kubla heard from far
Ancestral voices prophesying war!

   The shadow of the dome of pleasure
     Floated midway on the waves;

Where was heard the mingled measure
    From the fountain and the caves.
It was a miracle of rare device,
A sunny pleasure-dome with caves of ice!
A damsel with a dulcimer
    In a vision once I saw:
It was an Abyssinian maid,
    And on her dulcimer she played,
Singing of Mount Abora.
Could I revive within me,
    Her symphony and song,
To such a deep delight 'twould win me,
That with music loud and long,
I would build that dome in air,
That sunny dome! those caves of ice!
And all who heard should see them there,
And all should cry, Beware! Beware!
His flashing eyes, his floating hair!
Weave a circle round him thrice,
    And close your eyes with holy dread,
    For he on honey-dew hath fed,
And drunk the milk of Paradise.

❧ Walter Savage Landor (1775–1864)

DIRCE

Stand close around, ye Stygian set,
    With Dirce in one boat conveyed!
Or Charon, seeing, may forget
    That he is old and she a shade.

❧ George Gordon, Lord Byron (1788–1824)

THE DESTRUCTION OF SENNACHERIB

The Assyrian came down like the wolf on the fold,
And his cohorts were gleaming in purple and gold;
And the sheen of their spears was like stars on the sea,
When the blue wave rolls nightly on deep Galilee.

Like the leaves of the forest when summer is green,
That host with their banners at sunset were seen;
Like the leaves of the forest when autumn hath blown,
That host on the morrow lay withered and strown.

For the angel of Death spread his wings on the blast,
And breathed in the face of the foe as he passed;
And the eyes of the sleepers waxed deadly and chill,
and their hearts but once heaved—and for ever stood still!

And there lay the steed with his nostril all wide,
But through it there rolled not the breath of his pride;
And the foam of his gasping lay white on the turf,
And cold as the spray of the rock-beating surf.

And there lay the rider distorted and pale,
With the dew on his brow, and the rust on his mail:
And the tents were all silent—the banners alone—
The lances unlifted—the trumpet unblown.

And the widows of Ashur are loud in their wail,
And the idols are broke in the temple of Baal;
And the might of the Gentile, unsmote by the sword,
Hath melted like snow in the glance of the Lord!

✆ Percy Bysshe Shelley (1792–1822)

From THE MASQUE OF ANARCHY

Written on the Occasion of the Massacre at Manchester

I

As I lay asleep in Italy
There came a voice from over the Sea,
And with great power it forth led me
To walk in the visions of Poesy.

II

I met Murder on the way—
He had a mask like Castlereagh—
Very smooth he looked, yet grim;
Seven blood-hounds followed him:

III

All were fat; and well they might
Be in admirable plight,
For one by one, and two by two,
He tossed them human hearts to chew
Which from his wide cloak he drew.

IV

Next came Fraud, and he had on,
Like Eldon, an ermined gown;

His big tears, for he wept well,
Turned to millstones as they fell.

V

And the little children, who
Round his feet played to and fro,
Thinking every tear a gem,
Had their brains knocked out by them.

VI

Clothed with the Bible, as with light,
And the shadows of the night,
Like Sidmouth, next, Hypocrisy
On a crocodile rode by.

VII

And many more Destructions played
In this ghastly masquerade,
All disguised, even to the eyes,
Like Bishops, lawyers, peers, or spies.

VIII

Last came Anarchy: he rode
On a white horse, splashed with blood,
He was pale even to the lips,
Like Death in the Apocalypse.

IX

And he wore a kingly crown;
And in his grasp a sceptre shone;
On his brow this mark I saw —
'I am God, and King, and Law!'

X

With a pace stately and fast,
Over English land he passed,
Trampling to a mire of blood
The adoring multitude.

XI

And a mighty troop around,
With their trampling shook the ground,
Waving each a bloody sword,
For the service of their Lord.

XII

And with glorious triumph, they
Rode through England proud and gay,

Drunk with intoxication
Of the wine of desolation.

XIII

O'er fields and towns, from sea to sea,
Passed the Pageant swift and free,
Tearing up, and trampling down;
Till they came to London town.

XIV

And each dweller, panic-stricken,
Felt his heart with terror sicken
Hearing the tempestuous cry
Of the triumph of Anarchy.

XV

For with pomp to meet him came,
Clothed in arms like blood and flame,
The hired murderers, who did sing
'Thou art God, and Law, and King.' . . .

XVII

Lawyers and priests, a motley crowd,
To the earth their pale brows bowed;
Like a bad prayer not over loud,
Whispering—'Thou art Law and God.'—

XIX

And Anarchy, the Skeleton,
Bowed and grinned to every one,
As well as if his education
Had cost ten millions to the nation.

✌ John Clare (1793–1864)

I AM

I am—yet what I am, none cares or knows;
    My friends forsake me like a memory lost:
I am the self-consumer of my woes;
    They rise and vanish in oblivion's host,
Like shadows in love's frenzied stifled throes:
And yet I am, and live—like vapours toss't

Into the nothingness of scorn and noise—
    Into the living sea of waking dreams,

Where there is neither sense of life or joys,
    But the vast shipwreck of my life's esteems;
Even the dearest, that I love the best
Are strange—nay, rather, stranger than the rest.

I long for scenes where man hath never trod
    A place where woman never smiled or wept
There to abide with my Creator, God,
    And sleep as I in childhood sweetly slept,
Untroubling, and untroubled where I lie,
The grass below—above the vaulted sky.

WATER-LILIES

The water-lilies on the meadow stream
    Again spread out their leaves of glossy green;
And some, yet young, of a rich copper gleam,
    Scarce open, in the sunny stream are seen.
Throwing a richness upon leisure's eye,
    That thither wanders in a vacant joy;
While on the sloping banks, luxuriantly,
    Tending of horse and cow, the chubby boy,
In self-delighted whims, will often throw
    Pebbles to hit and splash their sunny leaves;
Yet quickly dry again, they shine and glow
    Like some rich vision that his eye deceives,
Spreading above the water, day by day,
In dangerous deeps, yet out of danger's way.

HARES AT PLAY

The birds are gone to bed, the cows are still,
And sheep lie panting on each old mole-hill;
And underneath the willow's grey-green bough,
Like toil a-resting, lies the fallow plough
And timid hares throw daylight fears away
On the lane's road to dust and dance and play,
Then dabble in the grain by naught deterred
To lick the dew-fall from the barley's beard;
Then out they sturt again and round the hill
Like happy thoughts dance, squat, and loiter still,
Till milking maidens in the early morn
Jingle their yokes and sturt them in the corn;
Through well-known beaten paths each nimbling hare
Sturts quick as fear, and seeks its hidden lair.

❧ John Keats (1795–1821)

LA BELLE DAME SANS MERCI

O, what can ail thee, Knight-at-arms
    Alone and palely loitering;
The sedge has wither'd from the lake,
    And no birds sing.

O, what can ail thee, Knight-at-arms
    So haggard and so woe-begone?
The squirrel's granary is full,
    And the harvest's done.

I see a lily on thy brow,
    With anguish moist and fever dew;
And on thy cheeks a fading rose
    Fast withereth too.

I met a lady in the meads
    Full beautiful, a fairy's child:
Her hair was long, her foot was light,
    And her eyes were wild.

I made a garland for her head,
    And bracelets too, and fragrant zone;
She look'd at me as she did love,
And made sweet moan.

I set her on my pacing steed,
    And nothing else saw all day long;
For sidelong would she bend, and sing
    A fairy's song.

She found me roots of relish sweet,
    And honey wild, and manna dew;
And sure in language strange she said,
    'I love thee true.'

She took me to her elfin grot,
    And there she wept and sighed full sore
And there I shut her wild wild eyes
    With kisses four.

And there she lulled me asleep
    and there I dream'd, ah woe betide,
The latest dream I ever dream'd
    On the cold hill side.

I saw pale kings, and princes too,
    Pale warriors, death-pale were they all;
They cry'd—'La belle Dame sans merci
    Hath thee in thrall!'

I saw their starv'd lips in the gloam
    With horrid warning gaped wide,
And I awoke and found me here
    On the cold hill's side.

And this is why I sojourn here
    Alone and palely loitering,
Though the sedge has wither'd from the lake,
    And no birds sing.

TO FANNY BRAWNE

This living hand, now warm and capable
Of earnest grasping, would, if it were cold
And in the icy silence of the tomb,
So haunt thy days and chill thy dreaming nights
That thou would wish thine own heart dry of blood
So in my veins red life might stream again,
And thou be conscience-calmed—see here it is—
I hold it toward you.

ON FIRST LOOKING INTO CHAPMAN'S HOMER

Much have I travell'd in the realms of gold,
    And many goodly states and kingdoms seen;
    Round many western islands have I been
Which bards in fealty to Apollo hold.
Oft of one wide expanse had I been told
    That deep-brow'd Homer ruled as his demesne;
    Yet did I never breathe its pure serene
Till I heard Chapman speak out loud and bold:
Then felt I like some watcher of the skies
    When a new planet swims into his ken;
Or like stout Cortez when with eagle eyes
    He star'd at the Pacific—and all his men
Look'd at each other with a wild surmise—
    Silent, upon a peak in Darien.

SONNET

When I have fears that I may cease to be
    Before my pen has glean'd my teeming brain,
Before high-piled books, in charact'ry,
    Hold like rich garners the full-ripen'd grain;
When I behold, upon the night's starr'd face,
    Huge cloudy symbols of a high romance,
And think that I may never live to trace
    Their shadows, with the magic hand of chance;
And when I feel, fair creature of an hour!
    That I shall never look upon thee more,
Never have relish in the faery power
    Of unreflecting love! —then on the shore
Of the wide world I stand alone, and think
Till Love and Fame to nothingness do sink.

❧ William Barnes (1801–1886)

A WINTER NIGHT

It was a chilly winter's night;
    And frost was glitt'ring on the ground,
And evening stars were twinkling bright;
    And from the gloomy plain around
        Came no sound,
But where, within the wood-girt tow'r,
The churchbell slowly struck the hour;
As if that all of human birth
    Had risen to the final day,
And soaring from the wornout earth
    Were called in hurry and dismay,
        Far away;
And I alone of all mankind
Were left in loneliness behind.

❧ T. L. Beddoes (1803–1849)

SONG ON THE WATER

As mad sexton's bell, tolling
    For earth's loveliest daughter
Night's dumbness breaks rolling
        Ghostlily:
So our boat breaks the water
        Witchingly.

As her look the dream troubles
    Of her tearful-eyed lover,
So our sails in the bubbles
      Ghostlily
Are mirrored, and hover
      Moonily.

Ralph Waldo Emerson (1803–1882)

THE PAST

The debt is paid,
The verdict said,
The Furies laid,
The plague is stayed,
All fortunes made;
Turn the key and bolt the door,
Sweet is death forevermore.
Nor haughty hope, nor swart chagrin,
Nor murdering hate, can enter in.
All is now secure and fast;
Not the gods can shake the Past;
Flies-to the adamantine door
Bolted down forevermore.
None can reenter there, —
No thief so politic,
No Satan with a royal trick
Steal in by window, chink, or hole,
To bind or unbind, add what lacked,
Insert a leaf, or forge a name,
New-face or finish what is packed,
Alter or mend eternal Fact.

Henry Wadsworth Longfellow (1807–1882)

CHAUCER

An old man in a lodge within a park;
    The chamber walls depicted all around
    With portraitures of huntsman, hawk, and hound,
    And the hurt deer. He listeneth to the lark,
Whose song comes with the sunshine through the dark
    Of painted glass in leaden lattice bound;
    He listeneth and he laugheth at the sound,

Then writeth in a book like any clerk.
He is the poet of the dawn, who wrote
    The Canterbury Tales, and his old age
    Made beautiful with song; and as I read
I hear the crowing cock, I hear the note
    Of lark and linnet, and from every page
    Rise odors of ploughed field or flowery mead.

ஊ Alfred, Lord Tennyson (1809–1892)

MAUD

Come into the garden, Maud,
    For the black bat, night, has flown,
Come into the garden, Maud,
    I am here at the gate alone;
And the woodbine spices are wafted abroad,
    And the musk of the rose is blown.

For a breeze of morning moves,
    And the planet of Love is on high,
Beginning to faint in the light that she loves
    On a bed of daffodil sky,
To faint in the light of the sun she loves,
    To faint in his light, and to die.

All night have the roses heard
    The flute, violin, bassoon;
All night has the casement jessamine stirred
    To the dancers dancing in tune;
Till a silence fell with the waking bird,
    And a hush with the setting moon.

I said to the lily, 'There is but one
    With whom she has heart to be gay.
When will the dancers leave her alone?
    She is weary of dance and play.'
Now half to the setting moon are gone,
    And half to the rising day;
Low on the sand and loud on the stone
    The last wheel echoes away.

I said to the rose, 'The brief night goes
    In babble and revel and wine.
O young lord-lover, what sighs are those,
    For one that will never be thine?
But mine, but mine,' so I sware to the rose,
    'For ever and ever, mine.'

And the soul of the rose went into my blood,
    As the music clashed in the hall;
And long by the garden lake I stood,
    For I heard your rivulet fall
From the lake to the meadow and on to the wood,
    Our wood, that is dearer than all;

From the meadow your walks have left so sweet
    That whenever a March-wind sighs
He sets the jewel-print of your feet
    In violets blue as your eyes,
To the woody hollows in which we meet
    And the valleys of Paradise.

The slender acacia would not shake
    One long milk-bloom on the tree;
The white lake-blossom fell into the lake
    As the pimpernel dozed on the lea;
But the rose was awake all night for your sake,
    Knowing your promise to me;
The lilies and roses were all awake,
    They sighed for the dawn and thee.

Queen rose of the rosebud garden of girls,
    Come hither, the dances are done,
In gloss of satin and glimmer of pearls,
    Queen lily and rose in one;
Shine out, little head, sunning over with curls,
    To the flowers, and be their sun.

There has fallen a splendid tear
    From the passion-flower at the gate.
She is coming, my dove, my dear;
    She is coming, my life, my fate;
The red rose cries, 'She is near, she is near;'
    And the white rose weeps, 'She is late;'
The larkspur listens, 'I hear, I hear;'
    And the lily whispers, 'I wait.'

She is coming, my own, my sweet,
    Were it ever so airy a tread,
My heart would hear her and beat,
    Were it earth in an earthy bed;
My dust would hear her and beat,
    Had I lain for a century dead;
Would start and tremble under her feet,
    And blossom in purple and red.

NOW SLEEPS THE CRIMSON PETAL

Now sleeps the crimson petal, now the white;
Nor waves the cypress in the palace walk;
Nor winks the gold fin in the porphyry font:
The fire-fly wakens: waken thou with me.

Now droops the milkwhite peacock like a ghost,
And like a ghost she glimmers on to me.

Now lies the Earth all Danaë to the stars,
And all thy heart lies open unto me.

Now slides the silent meteor on, and leaves
A shining furrow, as thy thoughts in me.

Now folds the lily all her sweetness up,
And slips into the bosom of the lake:
So fold thyself, my dearest, thou, and slip
Into my bosom and be lost in me.

Edward Lear (1812–1888)

THE OWL AND THE PUSSY-CAT

The Owl and the Pussy-cat went to sea
   In a beautiful pea-green boat,
They took some honey, and plenty of money,
   Wrapped up in a five-pound note.
The Owl looked up to the stars above,
   And sang to a small guitar,
"O lovely Pussy! O Pussy, my love,
   What a beautiful Pussy you are,
      You are,
      You are!
What a beautiful Pussy you are!"

Pussy said to the Owl, "You elegant fowl!
   How charmingly sweet you sing!
O let us be married! too long we have tarried:
   But what shall we do for a ring?"
They sailed away, for a year and a day,
   To the land where the Bong-Tree grows,
And there in a wood a Piggy-wig stood,
   With a ring at the end of his nose,
      His nose,
      His nose,
With a ring at the end of his nose.

"Dear Pig, are you willing to sell for one shilling
    Your ring?" Said the Piggy, "I will."
So they took it away, and were married next day
    By the Turkey who lives on the hill.
They dined on mince, and slices of quince,
    Which they ate with a runcible spoon;
And hand in hand, on the edge of the sand,
    They danced by the light of the moon,
        The moon,
        The moon,
They danced by the light of the moon.

Robert Browning (1812–1889)

THROUGH THE METIDJA TO ABD-EL-KADR

I

As I ride, as I ride,
With a full heart for my guide,
So its tide rocks my side,
As I ride, as I ride,
That, as I were double-eyed,
He, in whom our Tribe confide,
Is descried, ways untried,
As I ride, as I ride.

II

As I ride, as I ride,
To our Chief and his Allied,
Who dares chide my heart's pride
As I ride, as I ride?
Or are witnesses denied—
Through the desert waste and wide
Do I glide unespied
As I ride, as I ride?

III

As I ride, as I ride,
When an inner voice has cried,
The sands slide, nor abide,
(As I ride, as I ride)
O'er each visioned homicide
That came vaunting (has he lied?)
To reside—where he died,
As I ride, as I ride.

IV

As I ride, as I ride,
Ne'er has spur my swift horse plied,
Yet his hide, streaked and pied,
As I ride, as I ride,
Shows where sweat has sprung and dried,
—Zebra-footed, ostrich-thighed—
How has vied stride with stride
As I ride, as I ride!

V

As I ride, as I ride,
Could I loose what Fate has tied,
Ere I pried, she should hide
(As I ride, as I ride)
All that's meant me—satisfied
When the Prophet and the Bride
Stop veins I'd have subside
As I ride, as I ride!

Arthur Hugh Clough (1819–1861)

THE LATEST DECALOGUE

THOU shalt have one God only; who
Would be at the expense of two?
No graven images may be
Worshipped, except the currency:
Swear not at all; for, for thy curse
Thine enemy is none the worse:
At church on Sunday to attend
Will serve to keep the world thy friend:
Honour thy parents; that is, all
From whom advancement may befall:
Thou shalt not kill; but need'st not strive
Officiously to keep alive:
Do not adultery commit;
Advantage rarely comes of it:
Thou shalt not steal; an empty feat,
When it's so lucrative to cheat:
Bear not false witness; let the lie
Have time on its own wings to fly:
Thou shalt not covet; but tradition
Approves all forms of competition.
The sum of all is, thou shalt love,
If anybody, God above:
At any rate shall never labour
More than thyself to love thy neighbour.

❧ Matthew Arnold (1822–1888)

DOVER BEACH

The sea is calm tonight.
The tide is full, the moon lies fair
Upon the straits;—on the French coast the light
Gleams and is gone; the cliffs of England stand,
Glimmering and vast, out in the tranquil bay.
Come to the window, sweet is the night-air!
Only, from the long line of spray
Where the sea meets the moon-blanched land,
Listen! you hear the grating roar
Of pebbles which the waves draw back, and fling,
At their return, up the high strand,
Begin, and cease, and then again begin,
With tremulous cadence slow, and bring
The eternal note of sadness in.

Sophocles long ago
Heard it on the Ægæan, and it brought
Into his mind the turbid ebb and flow
Of human misery; we
Find also in the sound a thought,
Hearing it by this distant northern sea.

The Sea of Faith
Was once, too, at the full, and round earth's shore
Lay like the folds of a bright girdle furled.
But now I only hear
Its melancholy, long, withdrawing roar,
Retreating, to the breath
Of the night-wind, down the vast edges drear
And naked shingles of the world.

Ah, love, let us be true
To one another! for the world, which seems
To lie before us like a land of dreams,
So various, so beautiful, so new,
Hath really neither joy, nor love, nor light,
Nor certitude, nor peace, nor help for pain;
And we are here as on a darkling plain
Swept with confused alarms of struggle and flight,
Where ignorant armies clash by night.

❧ Herman Melville (1818–1891)

BILLY IN THE DARBIES

Good of the Chaplain to enter Lone Bay
And down on his marrow-bones here and pray
For the likes just o' me, Billy Budd. — But, look:
Through the port comes the moon-shine astray!
It tips the guard's cutlass and silvers this nook;
But 'twill die in the dawning of Billy's last day.
A jewel-block they'll make of me tomorrow,
Pendant pearl from the yard-arm-end
Like the ear-drop I gave to Bristol Molly —
O, 'tis me, not the sentence they'll suspend.
Ay, Ay, all is up; and I must up too
Early in the morning, aloft from alow.
On an empty stomach, now, never it would do.
They'll give me a nibble — bit o' biscuit ere I go.
Sure, a messmate will reach me the last parting cup;
But, turning heads away from the hoist and the belay,
Heaven knows who will have the running of me up!
No pipe to those halyards. — But aren't it all sham?
A blur's in my eyes; it is dreaming that I am.
A hatchet to my hawser? All adrift to go?
The drum roll to grog, and Billy never know?
But Donald he has promised to stand by the plank;
So I'll shake a friendly hand ere I sink.
But — no! It is dead then I'll be, come to think. —
I remember Taff the Welshman when he sank.
And his cheek it was like the budding pink.
But me they'll lash me in hammock, drop me deep
Fathoms down, fathoms down, how I'll dream fast asleep.
I feel it stealing now. Sentry, are you there?
Just ease these darbies at the wrist,
And roll me over fair,
I am sleepy, and the oozy weeds about me twist.

❧ Walt Whitman (1819–1892)

CROSSING BROOKLYN FERRY

1

Flood-tide below me! I see you face to face!
Clouds of the west — sun there half an hour high — I see you also face to face.
Crowds of men and women attired in the usual costumes, how curious you
   are to me!

On the ferry-boats the hundreds and hundreds that cross, returning home,
  are more curious to me than you suppose,
And you that shall cross from shore to shore years hence are more to me,
  and more in my meditations, than you might suppose.

2

The impalpable sustenance of me from all things at all hours of the day.
The simple, compact, well-join'd scheme, myself disintegrated, every one
  disintegrated yet part of the scheme,
The similitudes of the past and those of the future,
The glories strung like beads on my smallest sights and hearings, on the walk
  in the street and the passage over the river,
The current rushing so swiftly and swimming with me far away,
The others that are to follow me, the ties between me and them,
The certainty of others, the life, love, sight, hearing of others.

Others will enter the gates of the ferry and cross from shore to shore,
Others will watch the run of the flood-tide,
Others will see the shipping of Manhattan north and west, and the heights of
  Brooklyn to the south and east,
Others will see the islands large and small;
Fifty years hence, others will see them as they cross, the sun half an hour
  high,
A hundred years hence, or ever so many hundred years hence, others will
  see them,
Will enjoy the sunset, the pouring-in of the flood-tide, the falling-back to the
  sea of the ebb-tide.

RECONCILIATION

Word over all, beautiful as the sky,
Beautiful that war and all its deeds of carnage must in time be utterly lost,
That the hands of the sisters Death and Night incessantly softly wash again,
  and ever again, this soil'd world;
For my enemy is dead, a man divine as myself is dead.
I look where he lies white-faced and still in the coffin—I draw near,
Bend down and touch lightly with my lips the white face in the coffin.

A NOISELESS PATIENT SPIDER

A noiseless patient spider,
I mark'd where on a little promontory it stood isolated,
Mark'd how to explore the vacant vast surrounding,
It launch'd forth filament, filament, filament, out of itself,
Ever unreeling them, ever tirelessly speeding them.

And you O my soul where you stand,
Surrounded, detached, in measureless oceans of space,
Ceaselessly musing, venturing, throwing, seeking the spheres to connect
    them,
Till the bridge you will need be form'd, till the ductile anchor hold,
Till the gossamer thread you fling catch somewhere, O my soul.

Emily Dickinson (1830–1886)

WILD NIGHTS

Wild nights! Wild nights!
Were I with thee,
Wild nights should be
Our luxury!

Futile the winds
To a heart in port—
Done with the compass,
Done with the chart.

Rowing in Eden!
Ah! the sea!
Might I but moor
Tonight in thee!

AMPLE MAKE THIS BED

Ample make this Bed—
Make this Bed with Awe—
In it wait till Judgment break
Excellent and Fair.

Be its Mattress straight—
Be its Pillow round—
Let no Sunrise' yellow noise
Interrupt this Ground—

SAFE IN THEIR ALABASTER CHAMBERS

Safe in their Alabaster Chambers—
Untouched by Morning—
And untouched by Noon—
Lie the meek members of the Resurrection—
Rafter of Satin—and Roof of Stone!

Grand go the Years—in the Crescent—above them—
Worlds scoop their Arcs—
And Firmaments—row—
Diadems—drop—and Doges—surrender—
Soundless as dots—on a Disc of Snow—

A NARROW FELLOW IN THE GRASS

A narrow Fellow in the Grass
Occasionally rides—
You may have met Him—did you not
His notice sudden is—

The Grass divides as with a Comb—
A spotted shaft is seen—
And then it closes at your feet
And opens further on—

He likes a Boggy Acre
A Floor too cool for Corn—
Yet when a Boy, and Barefoot—
I more than once at Noon
Have passed, I thought, a Whip lash
Upbraiding in the Sun
When stooping to secure it
It wrinkled, and was gone—

Several of Nature's People
I know, and they know me—
I feel for them a transport
Of cordiality—

But never met this Fellow
Attended or alone
Without a tighter breathing
And Zero at the Bone—

✦ Lewis Carroll (Charles Henry Dodgson, 1832–1898)

THE MAD GARDENER'S SONG

He thought he saw an Elephant,
    That practised on a fife:
He looked again, and found it was
    A letter from his wife.

"At length I realize,' he said,
    The bitterness of life!"

He thought he saw a Buffalo
    Upon the chimney-piece;
He looked again, and found it was
    His Sister's Husband's Niece,
'Unless you leave this house,' he said,
    'I'll send for the Police!'

He thought he saw a Rattlesnake
    That questioned him in Greek;
He looked again, and found it was
    The Middle of Next Week.
'The one thing I regret,' he said,
    'Is that it cannot speak!'

He thought he saw a Banker's Clerk
    Descending from the 'bus:
He looked again, and found it was
    A Hippopotamus.
'If this should stay to dine,' he said
    'There won't be much for us!'

He thought he saw a Kangaroo
    That worked a coffee-mill:
He looked again, and found it was
    A vegetable-Pill.
'Were I to swallow this,' he said,
    'I should be very ill!'

He thought he saw a Coach-and-Four
    That stood beside his bed:
He looked again, and found it was
    A Bear without a Head.
'Poor thing,' he said, 'poor silly thing!
    It's waiting to be fed!'

He thought he saw an Albatross
    That fluttered around the lamp:
He looked again, and found it was
    A Penny-Postage Stamp.
You'd best be getting home,' he said,
    'The nights are very damp!'

He thought he saw a Garden-Door
    That opened with a key:
He looked again, and found it was
    A Double Rule of Three:
'And all its mystery,' he said
    'Is clear as day to me!'

He thought he saw an Argument
    That proved he was the Pope:
He looked again, and found it was
    A Bar of Mottled Soap.
"A fact so dread,' he faintly said,
    'Extinguishes all hope!'

William Morris (1834–1896)

POMONA

I am the ancient Apple-Queen,
As once I was so am I now,
For evermore a hope unseen,
Betwixt the blossom and the bough.

Ah, where's the river's hidden Gold?
And where the windy grave of Troy?
Yet come I as I came of old,
From out the heart of Summer's joy.

Thomas Hardy (1840–1928)

AFTERWARDS

When the Present has latched its postern behind my tremulous stay,
    And the May month flaps its glad green leaves like wings,
Delicate-filmed as new-spun silk, will the neighbors say,
    "He was a man who used to notice such things"?

If it be in the dusk when, like an eyelid's soundless blink,
    The dewfall-hawk comes crossing the shades to alight
Upon the wind-warped upland thorn, a gazer may think,
    "To him this must have been a familiar sight."

If I pass during some nocturnal blackness, mothy and warm,
    When the hedgehog travels furtively over the lawn,
One may say, "He strove that such innocent creatures should come to no harm,
    But he could do little for them; and now he is gone."

If, when hearing that I have been stilled at last, they stand at the door,
    Watching the full-starred heavens that winter sees,
Will this thought rise on those who will meet my face no more,
    "He was one who had an eye for such mysteries"?

And will any say when my bell of quittance is heard in the gloom,
    And a crossing breeze cuts a pause in its outrollings,

Till they rise again, as they were a new bell's bloom,
"He hears it not now, but used to notice such things"?

THE DARKLING THRUSH

I leant upon a coppice gate
   When Frost was spectre-gray,
And Winter's dregs made desolate
   The weakening eye of day.
The tangled bine-stems scored the sky
   Like strings of broken lyres,
And all mankind that haunted nigh
   Had sought their household fires.

The land's sharp features seemed to be
   The Century's corpse outleant,
His crypt the cloudy canopy,
   The wind his death-lament.
The ancient pulse of germ and birth
   Was shrunken hard and dry,
And every spirit upon earth
   Seemed fervourless as I.

At once a voice arose among
   The bleak twigs overhead
In a full-hearted evensong
   Of joy illimited;
An agèd thrush, frail, gaunt, and small,
   In blast-beruffled plume,
Had chosen thus to fling his soul
   Upon the growing gloom.

So little cause for carolings
   Of such ecstatic sound
Was written on terrestrial things
   Afar or nigh around,

That I could think there trembled through
   His happy good-night air
Some blessed Hope, whereof he knew
   And I was unaware.

MIDNIGHT ON THE GREAT WESTERN

In the third-class seat sat the journeying boy,
   And the roof-lamp's oily flame
Played down on his listless form and face,

Bewrapt past knowing to what he was going,
   Or whence he came.

In the band of his hat the journeying boy
   Had a ticket stuck; and a string
Around his neck bore the key of his box,
That twinkled gleams of the lamp's sad beams
   Like a living thing.

What past can be yours, O journeying boy
   Towards a world unknown,
Who calmly, as if incurious quite
On all at stake, can undertake
   This plunge alone?

Knows your soul a sphere, O journeying boy
   Our rude realms far above,
Whence with spacious vision you mark and mete
This region of sin that you find you in
   But are not of?

✺ Gerard Manley Hopkins (1844–1889)

NO WORST, THERE IS NONE. PITCHED PAST PITCH OF GRIEF

No worst, there is none. Pitched past pitch of grief,
More pangs will, schooled at forepangs, wilder wring.
Comforter, where, where is your comforting?
Mary, mother of us, where is your relief?
My cries heave, herds-long; huddle in a main, a chief
Woe, world-sorrow; on an age-old anvil wince and sing —
Then lull, then leave off. Fury had shrieked 'No lingering!
Let me be fell: force I must be brief'.

O the mind, mind has mountains; cliffs of fall
Frightful, sheer, no-man-fathomed. Hold them cheap
May who ne'er hung there. Nor does long our small
Durance deal with that steep or deep. Here! creep,
Wretch, under a comfort serves in a whirlwind: all
Life death does end and each day dies with sleep.

FELIX RANDAL

Felix Randal the farrier, O he is dead then? my duty all ended,
Who have watched his mould of man, big-boned and hardy-handsome

Pining, pining, till time when reason rambled in it and some
Fatal four disorders, fleshed there, all contended?

Sickness broke him. Impatient he cursed at first, but mended
Being anointed and all; though a heavenlier heart began some
Months earlier, since I had our sweet reprieve and ransom
Tendered to him. Ah well, God rest him all road ever he offended!

This seeing the sick endears them to us, us too it endears.
My tongue had taught thee comfort, touch had quenched thy tears,
Thy tears that touched my heart, child, Felix, poor Felix Randal;

How far from then forethought of, all thy more boisterous years,
When thou at the random grim forge, powerful amidst peers,
Didst fettle for the great grey drayhorse his bright and battering sandal!

❧ Rudyard Kipling (1865–1936)

THE WAY THROUGH THE WOODS

They shut the road through the woods
    Seventy years ago.
Weather and rain have undone it again,
    And now you would never know
There was once a path through the woods
    Before they planted the trees:
It is underneath the coppice and heath,
    And the thin anemones.
    Only the keeper sees
That, where the ring-dove broods
    And the badgers roll at ease,
There was once a road through the woods.
Yet, if you enter the woods
    Of a summer evening late,
When the night-air cools on the trout-ringed pools
    Where the otter whistles his mate
(They fear not men in the woods
    Because they see so few),
You will hear the beat of a horse's feet
    And the swish of a skirt in the dew,
    Steadily cantering through
The misty solitudes,
    As though they perfectly knew
The old lost road through the woods . . .
But there is no road through the woods.

SEVEN EPITAPHS OF THE WAR

The Coward

I could not look on death, which being known,
Men led me to him, blindfold and alone.

Bombed in London

On land and sea I strove with anxious care
To escape conscription. It was in the air!

Batteries out of Ammunition

If any mourn us in the workshop, say
We died because the shift kept holiday.

A Drifter off Tarentum

He from the wind-bitten North with ship and companions descended,
    Searching for eggs of death spawned by invisible hulls.
Many he found and drew forth. Of a sudden the fishery ended
    In flame and a clamorous breath known to the eye-pecking gulls.

A Dead Statesman

I could not dig; I dared not rob:
Therefore I lied to please the mob.
Now all my lies are proved untrue
And I must face the men I slew.
What tale shall serve me here among
Mine angry and defrauded young?

Convoy Escort

I was a shepherd to fools
    Causelessly bold or afraid.
They would not abide by my rules.
    Yet they escaped. For I stayed.

Common Form

If any question why we died
Tell them, because our fathers lied.

✆ Walter de la Mare (1873–1956)

NAPOLEON

"What is the world, O soldiers?
        It is I:

I, this incessant snow,
    This northern sky;
Soldiers, this solitude
    Through which we go
        Is I.'

✎ Trumbell Stickney (1874–1904)

TWO SONNETS

1

Live blindly and upon the hour. The Lord,
Who was the Future, died full long ago.
Knowledge which is the Past is folly. Go,
Poor child, and be not to thyself abhorred.
Around thine earth sun-wingèd winds do blow
And planets roll; a meteor draws his sword;
The rainbow breaks his seven-coloured chord
And the long strips of river-silver flow;

Awake! Give thyself to the lovely hours.
Drinking their lips; catch thou the dream in flight
About their fragile hairs' aërial gold.
Thou art divine, thou livest,—and as of old
Apollo springing naked to the light,
And all his island shivered into flowers.

2

Be still. The Hanging Gardens were a dream
That over Persian roses flew to kiss
The curlèd lashes of Semiramis.
Troy never was, nor green Skamander stream.
Provence and Troubadour are merest lies.
The glorious hair of Venice was a beam
Made within Titian's eye. The sunsets seem,
The world is very old and nothing is.

Be still. Thou foolish thing, thou canst not wake,
Nor thy tears wedge thy soldered eyes apart,
But patter in the darkness of thy heart.
Thy brain is plagued. Thou art a frighted owl
Blind with the light of life thou'ldst not forsake,
And error loves and nourishes thy soul.

Irish Gaelic

✌ Anonymous (19th Century)

DO YOU REMEMBER THAT NIGHT

Do you remember that night
When you were at the window,
With neither hat nor gloves
Nor coat to shelter you?
I reached out my hand to you,
And you ardently grasped it;
I remained in converse with you
Until the lark began to sing.

Do you remember that night
That you and I were
At the foot of the rowan tree,
And the night drifting snow?
Your head on my breast,
And your pipe sweetly playing?
Little thought I that night
That our love ties would loosen!

Beloved of my inmost heart,
Come some night and soon,
When my people are at rest,
That we may talk together,
My arms shall encircle you
While I relate my sad tale,
That your soft, pleasant converse
Hath deprived me of heaven.

The fire is unraked,
The light unextinguished,
The key under the door,
Do you softly draw it.
My mother is asleep,
But I am wide awake,
My fortune in my hand,
I am ready to go with you.

George Petrie

❧ Anthony Raftery (c. 1784–1835)

I AM RAFTERY

I am Raftery the poet,
Full of hope and love,
With eyes that have no light,
With gentleness that has no misery.

Going west upon my pilgrimage
By the light of my heart,
Feeble and tired
To the end of my road.

Behold me now,
And my face to a wall,
A-playing music
Unto empty pockets.

Douglas Hyde

❧ Patrick Pearse (1879–1916)

NAKED I SAW YOU

Naked I saw you
Beauty's child.
I shut my eyes
Not to yield.

I heard your song
call me near.
I closed my ears
not to hear.

I tasted your mouth,
sweetest of all.
I hardened my heart
not to fall.

I shut my eyes,
my ears I covered;
I hardened my heart,
desire I smothered.

I turned my back
on your embrace,

to the course I've set
I turned my face.

I turned my face
to the course I've set
to what I'll do
though it mean death.

Desmond O'Grady

Welsh

❧ Anonymous (date unknown)

OH SEND TO ME AN APPLE

Oh send to me an apple that hasn't any kernel,
And send to me a capon without a bone or feather,
And send to me a ring that has no twist or circlet,
And send to me a baby that's all grace and good temper.

How could there be an apple that hasn't any kernel?
How could there be a capon without a bone or feather?
How could there be a ring that has no twist or circlet?
How could there be a baby that's all grace and good temper?

The apple in its blossom hadn't any kernel;
And when the hen was sitting there was no bone or feather;
And when the ring was melting it had no twist or circlet;
And when we were in love there was grace and good temper.

Gwyn Williams

❧ Gwallter Mechain (1761–1849)

NIGHTFALL

Silence brought by the dark night: Eryri's
        Mountains veiled by mist:
    The sun in the bed of brine,
    The moon silvering the water.

Tony Conran

≈ Ellis Owen (1789–1868)

EPITAPH: ON THE NEAR-DEATH EXPERIENCE

She lied as much as she could, while she lived;
    Take care you don't revive her,
Or (I do believe) she'd tell
Everyone she'd been to heaven.

                                    Tony Conran

WESTERN AND SOUTHERN EUROPE: THE ROMANTIC ERA TO THE SYMBOLISTS

French

❧ Voltaire (François Marie Arouet de Voltaire, 1694–1778)

A MOUNTAIN MOUNTAINOUS IN PARTURITION

A mountain mountainous in parturition
Broke all the windows of a valley neighbor,
Who tumbled on the run to view her labor,
Thinking a mountain in such huge condition
Might bring forth Hell itself; a town: at least a house.
The mountain was delivered of a mouse.

This story, if I'm sober when I read it,
Strikes me as somewhat tall, if not gigantic:
Yet even for the most approved Romantic
Its literary sense is clear: concede it.
Think of the poet who begins his piece,
"I sing the lords of night and the day's release,"
From which impressive pangs what issue do we find?
A little wind."

        Robert Fitzgerald

From POEM UPON THE LISBON DISASTER; *OR, AN INQUIRY INTO THE ADAGE, "ALL IS FOR THE BEST."*

    Woeful mankind, born to a woeful earth!
Feeble humanity, whole hosts from birth

Eternally, purposelessly distressed!
Those savants erred who claim, "All's for the best."
Approach and view this carnage, broken stone,
Rags, rubble, chips of shattered wood and bone,
Women and children pinioned under beams,
Crushed under stones, piled under severed limbs;
These hundred thousands whom the earth devours,
Cut down to bleed away their final hours.
In answer to the frail, half-uttered cry,
The smoking ashes, will you make reply,
"God, in His bounty, urged by a just cause,
Herein exhibits His eternal laws"?
Seeing these stacks of victims, will you state,
"Vengence is God's; they have deserved their fate"?
What crimes were done, what evils manifest,
By babes who died while feeding at the breast?
Did wiped-out Lisbon's sins so much outweigh
Paris and London's, who keep holiday?
Lisbon is gone, yet Paris drinks champagne.
O tranquil minds who contemplate the pain
And shipwreck of your brothers' battered forms,
And, housed in peace, debate the cause of storms,
When once you feel Fate's catalogue of woe,
Tears and humanity will start and show.
When earth gapes for me while I'm sound and whole
My cries will issue from the very soul.
Hemmed in by Fate's grotesque brutalities,
Wrath of the wicked, death-traps and disease,
Tried by the warring elements, we have borne
Suffering enough to sorrow and to mourn.
You claim it's pride, the first sin of the race,
That human beings, having fallen from grace,
Dream of evading Justice's decree
By means of Man's Perfectibility.
Go ask the Tagus river banks, go pry
Among the smouldering alleyways where lie
The slowly perishing, and inquire today
Whether it's simply pride that makes them pray,
"O heaven save me, heaven pity me."
"All's Good," you claim, "and all's Necessity."
Without this gulf, would the whole universe,
Still stained with Lisbon, be that much the worse?
And has the Great Creative Power no way
To teach us but by violence and decay?

Anthony Hecht

℘ André Chénier (1762–1794)

From HERMES

... When the Euxine goddess with astonished eyes
Beheld the furrowed waves of the Greek ships arise—
The Argonauts of Greece, seeking the Land of Gold—
Orpheus sang to them the mysteries of old
Which as a child he learned from his immortal sire.
High in the helm he sat, and leaned upon his lyre,
And told them of the laws that move creation's days
Through every moment in a hundred different ways;
What power moved the stars, and held them overhead;
Whence came the restless winds that filled the sails they spread,
And what celestial torches filled the darkened west
To guide their ships across blind Amphitrite's breast.
Eager to hear these marvels, eager to obey,
About the demigod the listening princes lay;
His singing held each spellbound, dreaming at his oar,
Listening still, although he sang to them no more.

Paul Schmidt

VIII

We live; we live in squalor. And so? It had to be;
    The squalid eat and sleep, however squalidly.
Even here, in her parks, where death puts us out to graze,
    Where the ax has its random ways,
Love letters are written; lovers and husbands play the fool;
    And the rest: intrigue, gossip, ridicule.
There's singing; there's gambling; and skirts are raised
    And songs composed, and words well phrased;
Bouncing on roofs and panes, someone sent up there
    A balloon inflated by hot air,
Like the speeches of seven hundred elected nits,
    With Barère the best of such wits.
One runs; one jumps; and drinking, laughing, braying goes
    On, among reasoners and politicos;
And from its iron hinges, suddenly, the cry one hears
    Is the door. The purveyor to those tigers appears—
Our lords and judges. Who will be the prey
    The ax calls for today?
Each trembles, listens; and each with glee
    Sees that it's not yet he:
It will be you tomorrow, poor imbecile.

David Curzon and Jeffrey Fiskin

From ELEGIES

III

Happy is he given to sage disciplines,
Nourished by the sacred milk of ancient doctrines,
Just as talents were inherited formerly,
A small and sure income that made for liberty.
He has, in his peaceful and sacred solitude,
Leisure, and sleep, and study, a wood,
Banquets with friends, and at evening, occasionally,
The fresh young kiss of a dark-eyed beauty.
He needn't consider some despot's caprice,
Dissipate himself, and suppress his genius,
Using his pen, and his time, and his honor
In work that's sadly important but obscure.
He needn't get his wayward vessel hurled
Headlong into the floods of the great world;
He needn't suffer twenty speeches by odious
Reasoners when, ever more tedious,
In the long detours of disputation's frivolities,
Twenty separate sides press pompous follies;
The priest and the courtier, the ambitious tyrant,
Nobles and magistrates, the superbly ignorant,
The old usurper, the voracious pirate,
The dignified heirs of our fathers' spirit.
He needn't hear the thunder of a turgid masterpiece
By some arrogant rhymer seated at ease.
He needn't always disguise his belief
Impose eternal silence on his soul,
Betray the truth to acquire relief,
Feign to be foolish to live with fools.

David Curzon and Jeffrey Fiskin

✷ Marceline Desbordes-Valmore
(1786–1859)

MY ROOM

High up here I live
Right against the sky;
Pale and meditative
The moon comes here and I.
Let folks ring below,
What do I care today?
It is no one that I know —
One being gone away.

Unseen by others here
I stitch each silken flower,
Within inward tear on tear
Yet passionless: my tower
Gives me the cloudless sky.
From here I see the blue,
Star on star espy.
I see the tempest too.

Opposite my own
A chair stands through the hours.
His it was, that one;
One instant, it was ours.
There it stands, the chair,
A ribbon signing it,
As in a calm despair —
My case, placed opposite.

Edmund Blunden

A MEMORY

When he grew pale, and his voice trembled,
And suddenly he could no longer speak;
When his eyes, burning beneath the lid,
Gave me a wound I thought he felt alike;
When all his charms, lighted by a fire
       That has never faded,
Were printed in the depth of my desire,
       He did not love. I did.

Louis Simpson

INTERMITTENT DREAM OF A SAD NIGHT

Land of our fathers where at eventide
Across the fields like waves young women glide!

Where fresh pasture and a limpid spring
Make the goat bound and the lake reeds sing!

O native land, my soul is greatly moved
To hear your name that I have always loved;

My soul without an effort turns to song,
And also weeping, for my love is strong!

Love was my life, so I was often sad,
But love was mingled with the grief I had;

That is why I have longed for death in vain,
And though it is suffering, I love again.

My cradle, enchanted hillside where I ranged,
Whose velvet dress I often disarranged,

That is why, toward your distant sky,
Skimming the golden waves of grain I fly.

The cow is lowing on the slope. She has
Fragrant moss to eat, and so much grass,

And follows with a moist, caressing eye,
Calling him to rest, the passerby.

Never did shepherds when sheep wander wide
Find so much water as your streams provide.

An infant when I crawled there, pale and weak,
The air breathed from your woods reddened my cheek.

The sunburned laborers would set me down
Among the new corn that my breath fed on.

Albertine, sister of butterflies, also
Pursued the flowers that grew in the same row.

For liberty is laughing in the field
As in the sky, with neither sword nor shield,

Without fear, sternness or audacity,
Saying, "I am liberty, love me!

The pardon that makes anger disappear,
I give man a voice that is just and clear.

I am the cross exhaling a great breath:
'Father, they are slaying me. I have faith!

The hangman grasps me. I love him! And the more
For he is my brother, father whom I adore!

My blind brother, who throws himself on me,
Whom my love will bring back to your mercy.' "

O absent fatherland! My fertile country
Where the fervent Spaniards came to stay;

True masters of the land, old walnut trees
Shading so well our fathers' resting places;

My father's voice that echoed when he sang:
"Hope" and "Hope" and "Hope" again it rang . . .

The song of men who burned with piety
And yearned to sow the cross beneath our sky,

And many steeples filled with resonant bronze
That still recalls them in its carillons . . .

I am sending you my child, the quick and fair
Who laughs when wind is playing in her hair.

Of all the children you have fed at breast
This one is more enchanting than the rest.

An old man said once, looking in her eyes,
"Her mother must have dreamed her in the skies!"

And often as I lifted her I thought,
My hands beneath her arms, I felt wings sprout!

This fruit of my soul that so gently grew
If I must yield her, it is only to you.

With your milk that comes from a holy fountain
Fill the pure heart of this frail undine.

Mine ran sad and dry, but your milk springs
From virgin soil and happy harvestings.

To veil her forehead that a flame rings round
Open your cornflowers, so gayly crowned:

Do not crush her feet, such little flowers,
And her innocence has all their colors.

One evening women blessed her, standing by
Water, and my heart gave a deep sigh.

In that young heart, bent upon things to be
Your name rang, prophetic memory,

And with all my voice I gave an answer
To the fragrance of your wandering air.

Then let her go where nests sing in the sky,
For children know that they are born to fly.

Already her spirit has a taste for silence
And rises up to where the skylarks dance,

And, isolated, swims beneath the azure,
And comes back down, her throat filled with pure air.

May the gray bird's hymn, so high and pious,
Forever make her soul harmonious!

May your clear streams whose music spoke to me
Moisten her throat with pearls of melody!

Before she goes to her bed of fern and night
Let her go running, curious and light,

To the wood where the moon shines on a tree
In a sheet of tears and trembling quietly,

So she may sleep beneath green images
And they will cover all her infant graces.

The depth of those chaste curtains as they stir
Will keep the air around her heart still pure,

And if she does not have, to play with her,
An Albertine, her faithful follower,

She will face the flowers and dance with them,
But never take the flower from the stem,

Thinking that flowers have their mothers too
And know how to cry as children do.

Not stinging her forehead, your bees down there
Will teach her dreamy head to step with care,

For the insect has a muffled cymbal
That makes the caesura when one muses equal.

So she will go, calm, free, and at peace,
A thread of living water, to happiness,

And the Madonna in the hollow tree
Will see her on the grass with bended knee.

Her sweet weight on my lap, all I would do,
My songs, my kisses, everything spoke of you,

Land of our fathers where at eventide
Across the fields like waves young women glide.

May my daughter climb on your green breast,
Sweet spot in the Universe, and be blessed!

Louis Simpson

ॐ Victor Hugo (1802–1885)

EXPIATION

I

It was snowing. For the first time, conquered
By his conquest, the eagle bowed his head.
Dark days! Slowly the emperor returned,
Leaving behind a Moscow that smoked and burned.
It was snowing. At the end of the white plain
Another stretched, as white and vast again.
The leaders and the flags were swept away . . .
An army yesterday, a herd today.
No longer could one see the wings and center.
It was snowing. Wounded men sought shelter
In the belly of dead horses. Where they camped
One saw buglers frozen, stone mouths clamped
To copper trumpets, silent, white with frost,
Still upright in the saddle at their post.
Ball, grape, and shell were falling with the snow.
The grenadiers, surprised that they shook so,
Marched pensively, ice on the gray moustache.
It was snowing, always snowing! The cold lash
Whistled. These warriors had no bread to eat,
They walked across the ice with naked feet.
No longer living hearts, they seemed to be
A dream lost in a fog, a mystery,
A march of shadows under a black sky.
Vast solitudes, appalling to the eye,
Stretched out, mute and revengeful, everywhere.
The sky was weaving silently, of air,
A shroud for the Grand Army. And each one
Could feel that he was dying, and alone.
"Shall we ever leave this empire of the Czar?
The Czar and the North . . . The North is worse by far."
They jettisoned the guns to burn the wood.
To lie down was to die. Confused, they fled
And were devoured in the fields of snow.
One saw by mounds and ridges that below
Whole regiments were sleeping. Oh the falls
Of Hannibal! The days after Attila!
Fugitives, wounded, caissons, shafts, the mass
Crushed at the bridges as it strove to pass . . .

A hundred woke, ten thousand were left sleeping.
Ney, who had led an army, was escaping,
Fighting to save his watch from three cossacks.
Every night "Qui vive!" Alerts, alarms, attacks!
These phantoms grasped their rifles . . . terrifying
Shadows were rushing towards them, crying
Like vultures. Squadrons of savage men
Struck like a whirlwind and were gone again.
So a whole army would be lost by night.
The emperor was there, he watched, upright
As a tree that must endure the woodsman's blow.
On this giant, a greatness spared till now,
Misfortune the grim woodsman climbed. Each stroke
Of the axe insulted the man, the living oak.
He trembled at the vengeances, each blow
Saw a branch falling to the earth below.
Leaders and soldiers, each in his turn fell.
While love around his tent stood sentinel,
Watching his shadow on the canvas wall,
And those to his bright star remaining loyal
Accused the heavens of lèse-majesté,
Suddenly his inmost soul gave way.
Stunned by disaster, reft of all belief,
The emperor turned to God; the glorious chief
Trembled; he thought that he was expiating
Something perhaps, and contemplating
His legions of the dying and the dead,
"God of the armies," Napoleon said,
"Is this my punishment?" And from the snow
And darkness all around, a voice said, "No."

Louis Simpson

II

Waterloo! Waterloo! Waterloo! dismal plain!
Like an ocean boiling in an overflowing
Vessel of woods, vales, hills, pale
Death combined the dark battalions.
On one side Europe, on the other France.
God at the bloody clash betrayed the heroes,
Victory deserted, fate gave up.
O Waterloo! Alas, I stop and weep!
For those last soldiers of the last war
Were great, they had conquered
The earth, chased twenty kings,
Crossed the Alps and the Rhine,
And their soul sang out in the brazen bugles.

Evening was falling and the struggle
Was fierce and black. He was
On the attack and almost had

The victory; he had Wellington
Pinned against the woods.
His field glass in his hand, sometimes he watched
The heart of the battle, dim point
Trembling with hand-to-hand combat
Like a living thicket, and sometimes
He watched the horizon dark as the sea.
Suddenly with joy he cried out his general's name;
Instead it was the Prussian. Hope switched sides,
The mood of the fighting altered,
The howling combat grew like a flame,
The English artillery crushed our formations.
The plain where our tattered flags fluttered
Was nothing more, in the cries of men dying
With their throats slit, than a flaming
Gulf red as a forge, where regiments
Fell down like walls, where ghastly wounds
Appeared through the enormous plumes
Of tall drum majors fallen like ripened ears of grain.
Dreadful slaughter! fatal moment! the uneasy man
Felt the battle bending under his fingers.
The guard was massed behind a mound,
The guard, last hope and crowning stratagem!
"Now," he shouted, "send in the guard" —

And lancers, grenadiers in gaiters,
Dragoons that Rome would have taken for legionnaires,
Horsemen wearing armor, gunners dragging cannon,
Wearing black busbies or shining helmets,
All of them, those of Friedland and of Rivoli,
Knowing that they were going to die at this celebration,
Hailed their god standing upright in the storm.
Their mouth, in a single shout, cried "Long live the Emperor!"
Then, with measured steps, led by music, without fury,
Calmly smiling at the English grapeshot,
The imperial guard entered the furnace.
Alas! Napoleon looked down and saw,
As soon as they emerged beneath the dark
Cannons spitting jets of sulphur,
One by one in that horrible gulf
The regiments of granite and of steel
Melt like a candle before the fire's blast.
They went on, arms shouldered, heads held high,
Grave and stoical. Not one took one step back.
Sleep, heroic dead! The rest of the army
In shock watched the guard die. Then,
Suddenly lifting up her despairing voice,
Defeat, pale-faced giantess, who
At certain times like a spectre made of smoke
Rises up towering in the midst of armies,
Frightening the proudest battalions,

In an instant turning banners into rags,
Defeat appeared to the shaken soldier, and,
Wringing her hands, cried "Save yourself while you can!"
And every mouth cried—insult! horror!—"Save yourself!"
Across the fields, maddened, desperate, lost,
As if some gale had past over them—
By the heavy battle-wagons covered with dust,
Rolling into ditches, hiding in the rye grass,
Throwing down coats, capes, rifles, and the eagles,
Before the Prussian sabres, these veterans
Shook, screamed, wept, ran—in the blink
Of an eye, like a piece of flaming straw borne
On the wind, this noise which had been the great army
Vanished, and this plain, alas, where now we dream,
Saw them flee before whom the universe had fled.

Forty years have passed, and this corner of the earth,
Waterloo, this solitary, funereal plain,
This ill-fated field where God joined
Together so many nothings,
Still trembles to have seen the flight of giants!

Napoleon saw them flow away like a river;
Men, horses, drums, flags; and in this trial,
Feeling confusedly remorse return,
Lifting his hands to heaven, he said:
My soldiers dead, myself defeated, my
Empire shattered like glass;
Stern God, is this at last my punishment?
Amidst the shrieks, the clamors, and the cannon,
He heard a voice replying to him: No!

                                        Phillip Holland

WORDS IN THE SHADOW

She said, "I am wrong to want something more, it's true.
The hours go by very quietly just so.
You are there. I never take my eyes off you.
In your eyes I see your thoughts as they come and go.

To watch you is a joy I have not yet got through.
No doubt it is still very charming of its kind!
I watch, for I know everything that annoys you,
So that nothing comes knocking when you're not inclined.

I make myself so small in my corner near you.
You are my great lion, I am your little dove.
I listen to your leaves, the peaceful froufrou.
Sometimes I pick up your pen when it falls off.

Without a doubt I have you. Surely I see you.
Thinking is a wine on which the dreamers are drunk,
I know. But sometimes I'd like to be dreamed of too.
When you are like that, in your books, all evening, sunk,

Not lifting your head or saying a word to me,
There is a shadow deep down in my loving heart.
For me to see you whole, it is necessary
To look at me a little, sometimes, on your part."

Louis Simpson

✑ Gérard de Nerval (1808–1855)

EL DESDICHADO

I am the dark one, — the widower, — the unconsoled,
The prince of Aquitaine at his stricken tower:
My sole *star* is dead, — and my constellated lute
Bears the black *sun* of the *Melencolia.*

In the night of the tomb, you who consoled me,
Give me back Mount Posilipo and the Italian sea,
The *flower* which pleased so my desolate heart,
And the trellis where the grape vine unites with the rose.

Am I Amor or Phoebus? . . . Lusignan or Biron?
My forehead is still red from the kiss of the queen;
I have dreamd in the grotto where the mermaid swims . . .

And two times victorious I have crosst the Acheron:
Modulating turn by turn on the lyre of Orpheus
The sighs of the saint and the cries of the fay.

Robert Duncan

TO J — Y COLONNA

Do you know, Daphne, of this old romance
Under the sycomore . . . or white laurel branch,
Under the weeping willow or the olive tree,
This song of love that never ceases to entrance?

Do you recall the Temple with its vast colonnade,
And the bitter lemons that bore the imprint of your teeth,
And the grotto, fatal to all its careless guests,
Where the vanquished dragon's ancient seed now sleeps?

Do you know why the volcano there is now aroused?
Because one day we grazed it with our nimble feet,
And the far horizon lay covered in its cloud!

Ever since a Norman Duke broke your gods of clay,
Beneath the palm that offers Virgil's tomb its shade
The pale hydrangea forever weds the laurel's green.

Richard Sieburth

FANTASY

There is a melody for which I would surrender
All Rossini, all Mozart, all Weber,
An ancient, langorous, funereal tune,
With hidden charms for me alone.

And every time I hear that air,
Suddenly I grow two centuries younger,
I live in the reign of Louis the Thirteenth . . . and see stretched out,
A green slope yellowed by the sunset,

Then a brick castle with stone corners,
Its panes of glass stained by ruddy colors,
Encircled by great parks, and a river
Bathing its feet, flowing between flowers.

Then I see a fair-haired, dark-eyed lady
In old-fashioned costume, at a tall window,
Whom perhaps I have already seen somewhere
In another life . . . and whom I remember!

Geoffrey Wagner

GOLDEN SAYINGS

> All things feel.
> Pythagoras

So you alone are blessed with thought, free-thinking man,
In a world where life bursts forth from everything?
You are free to dispose of forces at your command
But the universe is absent from your well-laid plans.

Honor each creature for the mind in which it takes part:
Each flower is a soul turned towards Nature's face;
Each metal hides some ancient mystery of the heart;
"All things feel!" And all you are is within their art.

Beware, even blind walls may spy on you:
Even dumb matter is imbued with voice . . .
Put not its precious stuff to impious use.

The most obscure of beings may house a hidden god;
And like the new-born eye pouched within its lids,
Pure mind drives its bud through the husk of stones.

Richard Sieburth

Alfred de Musset (1810–1857)

From A NIGHT IN MAY

The Poet

> If all you need, my sister sweet,
> Is but one kiss from friendly lips
> And only one tear from my eyes,
> Gladly I will fulfill your wish;
> And as you lift up to the skies
> Remember how one time we loved.
> For I do not sing of hope,
> Nor of glory, nor of bliss,
> Alas, not even of despair.
> I will choose the silent part
> So as to listen to the heart.

The Muse

Do you believe that I am like the autumn wind
That feeds itself on sorrow even in sepulchres,
And to whom all these tears are simply water drops?
O poet! I'm the one to wake you with a kiss.
The weed that I would tear out of this place—it is
Your idleness; your suffering belongs to God.
Whatever care it is that oppresses your youth:
Do let it widen there, since this fortunate wound
The somber seraphims inflicted on your heart;
For nothing makes us greater than the greatest pain.
But though you suffer it, O poet, do not think
That you must bury it and keep it to yourself.
The sweetest songs are those that sing of saddest thought.
Some memorable ones I know that are pure sobs.
Think of the pelican, who, tired of a long journey,
Returns at nightfall to the reeds he calls his home.
His starving young come running on the shore toward him
When they observe from far his landing on the water.
As they anticipate dividing up the prey
They rush to him with shrieks of joyous expectation.

Nodding their beaks, they shake their hideous, flapping goiters
While slowly he ascends a rock with measured pace
And shelters with his trailing wing his hungry brood.
He stares up at the sky, this mournful fisherman,
Lets blood flow from his side which he has torn for them.
In vain he searched the bottom of the sea for food.
The ocean was depleted and the beach deserted.
He offers them his heart as only nourishment.
In somber silence, lying on the parapet,
Paternal, he divides his entrails with his sons
And with sublime devotion endures his suffering.
He watches as his blood flows from his open breast.
Inebriated with a dreadful tenderness,
At this funereal feast he stumbles, then collapses.
Yet sometimes, sickened by this divine sacrifice,
Tired of dying like this in too long a torment,
He fears his children might not kill him altogether.
Then he raises himself, his wings spread to the wind
And striking at his heart, savagely he calls out
And rends the night with a farewell so desperate
That seabirds on the beach take fright and fly away
And lonely travelers still lingering on shore,
Feeling death in the air, confide their soul to God.
O poet, this is how the truest poets sing.
They leave it to the living to desport themselves;
As for the human banquets they serve up at their feasts,
Most often they resemble that of the pelican.
Whenever they recount their disappointed hopes,
Their tales of love and sadness, loss and forgetfulness,
This is not merely music with which to soothe the heart.
The verses that they sing are dangerous as swords
That trace through the bright air a dazzling arabesque
Which more often than not is tainted with their blood.

The Poet

O my insatiable muse,
Why do you ask so much of me?
A man facing the cutting blast
Will not be writing on the sand.
There was a time, now long since past
When youth, forever on my lips,
Burst into singing like a lark;
But I endured a bitter lot
Which, if I should approximate
To render in my fragile art
Would tear my instrument apart.

Clare Nicolas White

ᘑ Théophile Gautier (1811–1872)

UNKNOWN SHORES

Okay, my starsick beauty! —
blue jeans and tilting breasts,
child of Canaverel —
where would you like to go?

Shall we set course for Mars,
or Venus's green sea,
Aldebaran the golden,
or Tycho Brahe's Nova,
the moons of Sagitta,
or Vega's colonies?

School-minching, bronze Diane,
bane of the launching-pads —
I may not ask again:
wherever you would go

my rocket-head can turn
at will to your command —
to pluck the flowers of snow
that grow on Pluto, or
Capella-wards, to pluck
the roots of asphodel?

I may not ask again:
where would you like to go?

Have you a star, she says,
O any faithful sun
where love does not eclipse?
. . . (The countdown slurs and slips).
—Ah child, if that star shines,
it is in chartless skies,

I do not know of such!
But come, where will you go?

D. M. Thomas

CARMEN

Carmen is thin — a touch of bister
Surrounds her gipsy eye with sin.
Black of her hair is sinister;
The devil tints her tawny skin.

The women say her looks are sick,
Whereof men's wits contract disease;
Prelate of one archibishopric
Conducts the mass before her knees.

For on her nape of amber pale
Her chignon piles a heavy weight,
Which, let fall in her bedroom, will
Wrap her slight body to her feet.

Amid this pallor will explode
A mouth with victory in its laugh.
Red pigment for a scarlet bud
That drinks of hearts their purple life.

A blackamoor made in this wise
Will beat our haughty beauties down,
And the hot glitter of her eyes
Burn up each boring paragon.

In all her gamey flaws there glows
The acrid element she keeps
Of that salt sea from which arose
Nude Venus of the bitter deep.

John Theobald

ART

Yes, artwork is better
When the means used rebel:
  Meter,
Marble, onyx, enamel.

Not for crippling fashion,
Muse, but a straighter walk,
  Put on
High heels, a "learned sock."

In rhythm I despise
The kind like an old shoe,
  The size
Every foot goes into!

Sculptor, do not succumb
To easiness, the clay
  The thumb
Works when the mind's away;

Struggle with Carrara's
Hardness, Paros's rare
      Quarries
Where the pure contours are;

From Syracuse you get
Bronze where a fugitive
      Proud trait
Solidly seems to live;

With skill that's delicate
Unerringly follow
      The agate
Profile of Apollo.

Painter, shun aquarelle.
If you find your color
      Too frail,
See the enameller.

Show sirens with blue scales
Twisting a hundred ways
      The tails
A coat of arms portrays;

In her trefoil nimbus
The Virgin you emboss,
      Jesus,
The globe beneath the cross.

All passes. Art alone
Lasts till eternity.
      The stone
Bust survives the city.

The medal in the ground
Some sweating laborer
      Has found
Reveals an emperor.

The gods themselves have passed,
But poems fill their thrones.
      Words cast
In lines will outwear bronze.

Sculptor, file and chisel
Your dream till it exists,
      Made real
In the block that resists.

          Louis Simpson

⅏ Leconte de Lisle (Charles-Marie-René Lecontede Lisle, 1818–1894)

THE JAGUAR'S DREAM

Lianas in bright bloom hang from mahogany shade,
Motionless where the air is languorous
And buzzing with summer flies. Brushing the moss,
They curl into cradles clutched by the emerald quetzal, swayed
Wildly by monkeys, spun with the yellow spider's silver floss.
Here the bull-killer, slayer of stallions, tired,
Moves among dead tree-stumps moist and soft as sponge,
Implicit violence in his measured tread,
Pelt shimmering with each muscle's plunge,
While from his bay-wide muzzle, drooping with thirst,
A clipped, harsh, rattled breathing shocks
Huge lizards from their sun-trance to a burst
Of chrome-green sparkling over shadowed rocks;
And there where the dark wood blots the sun,
He sprawls across a lichened stone,
Licks satin paws to a lustrous sheen,
Flutters the sleep-heavy lids of gold eyes down
And, as the ghost of his waking force
Twitches his tail and ripples along each side,
He dreams that by some orchard's water course
He leaps and digs his dripping claws
Into a bellowing bull's flesh-swollen hide.

James Lasdun

⅏ Charles Baudelaire (1821–1867)

INTIMATE ASSOCIATIONS

The natural world is a spiritual house, where the pillars, that are alive,
let slip at times some strangely garbled words;
Man walks there through forests of physical things that are also spiritual
    things,
that watch him with affectionate looks.

As the echoes of great bells coming from a long way off
become entangled in a deep and profound association,
a merging as huge as night, or as huge as clear light,
odors and colors and sounds all mean—each other.

Perfumes exist that are cool as the flesh of infants,
fragile as oboes, green as open fields,
and others exist also, corrupt, dense, and triumphant,

having the suggestions of infinite things,
such as musk and amber, myrrh and incense,
that describe the voyages of the body and soul.

Robert Bly

THE SWAN

To Victor Hugo

I

Andromache, I think of you. The Simois,
Little river that once shone with reflections
Of the majesty of your widow's sorrow,
Great with your tears, that now sadly runs,

Brought back to life my fertile memory
As I was crossing the new Carrousel.
Old Paris is no more (the heart of a city
Changes sooner, alas, than the heart of a mortal);

In my mind's eye only, I see barracks,
Rough-hewn capitals and columns, grass,
Blocks turning green in puddles, bric-a-brac
Scattered in windows, shining behind the glass.

There was a display, a menagerie,
And once I saw there, at the time of day
When Labor wakes under a clear, cold sky
And a dust storm rises from the highway,

A swan that somehow had escaped its cage,
Scraping webbed feet on the stony walk,
Over rough ground dragging its white plumage,
Near a dry stream bed opening its beak,

Bathe its wings in the dust. And with a heart
Full of its beautiful native lake, it said,
"Water, when will you rain? Thunder, when will you start?"
I see the unhappy one, so strangely fated,

Toward the sky, like the man in Ovid,
Toward the cruelly blue, ironic sky,
On its convulsive neck stretch its avid head,
As though it were reproaching the Deity!

II

Paris changes! But none of my melancholy
Has budged. New palaces, scaffolds, blocks,

Old suburbs . . . all becomes an allegory.
My memories are heavier than the rocks.

Standing before the Louvre, I feel the weight
Of an image, my big swan, with his insane
Gestures, like exiles, ridiculous but great,
Gnawed by unappeasable desire. And then,

Andromache, you, from your hero's embrace
Torn like cattle, under the hand of Pyyrrhus,
Kneeling by a tomb, praying to empty space;
Widow of Hector, wife of Helenus!

I think of the negress, gaunt, tubercular,
Trudging in the mud, and looking around her
With haggard eyes for the palms of Africa
Behind the huge wall of fog that surrounds her;

Of those who have lost what can never again
Be found. Never! Who water Grief with tears
And like a good she-wolf suckle their pain;
I think of orphans shriveling like flowers.

In the forest where my spirit lives in exile
Memory sounds again . . . *le son du Cor!*
I think of sailors deserted on an isle,
Of captives, the vanquished . . . and many more!

                                          Louis Simpson

THE CLOCK

The Clock, calm, evil god that makes us shiver,
With threatening finger tells us each apart: —
"*Remember!* Soon the vibrant woes will quiver,
Like arrows in a target, in your heart.

To the horizon Pleasure will take flight
As flits a vaporous sylphide to the wings.
Each instant gnaws a crumb of the delight
That for his season every mortal brings.

Three thousand times, each hour, the Second slides,
Whispering 'Remember!' Like an insect shrill
The Present chirrs 'I'm Nevermore. Besides
I've pumped your life-blood with my loathsome bill.'

Remember! Souviens-toi! Esto Memor!
My brazen windpipe speaks in every tongue.

Each minute, foolish mortal, is like ore
From which the precious metal must be wrung.

Remember, Time the gamester (it's the law)
Wins always, without cheating. Daylight wanes.
Night deepens. The abyss with gulfy maw
Thirsts on unsated, while the hourglass drains.

Sooner or later now the hour must be
When Hazard, Virtue (your still-Virgin mate),
Repentance (your last refuge), or all three—
Will tell you 'Die, old Coward, it's too late!' "

Roy Campbell

L'INVITATION AU VOYAGE

My child, my sister,
   dream
 How sweet all things would seem
Were we in that kind land to live together,
 And there love slow and long,
 There love and die among
Those scenes that image you, that sumptuous weather.
 Drowned suns that glimmer there
 Through cloud-disheveled air
Move me with such a mystery as appears
 Within those other skies
 Of your treacherous eyes
When I behold them shining through their tears.

There, there is nothing else but grace and measure,
Richness, quietness, and pleasure.

 Furniture that wears
 The lustre of the years
Softly would glow within our glowing chamber,
 Flowers of rarest bloom
 Proffering their perfume
Mixed with the vague fragrances of amber;
 Gold ceilings would there be,
 Mirrors deep as the sea,
The walls all in an Eastern splendor hung—
 Nothing but should address
 The soul's loneliness,
Speaking her sweet and secret native tongue.

There, there is nothing else but grace and measure,
Richness, quietness, and pleasure.

See, sheltered from the swells
There in the still canals
Those drowsy ships that dream of sailing forth;
It is to satisfy
Your least desire, they ply
Hither through all the waters of the earth.
The sun at close of day
Clothes the fields of hay,
Then the canals, at last the town entire
In hyacinth and gold:
Slowly the land is rolled
Sleepward under a sea of gentle fire.

There, there is nothing else but grace and measure,
Richness, quietness, and pleasure.

Richard Wilbur

A VOYAGE TO CYTHERA

My heart, like a bird ahover joyously,
circled the rigging, soaring light and free;
beneath a cloudless sky the ship rolled on
like an angel drunk with blazing rays of sun.

What is that black, sad island? — We are told
it's Cythera, famed in songs of old,
trite El Dorado of worn-out roués.
Look, after all, it's but a paltry place.

— Isle of sweet mysteries and festive loves,
above your waters antique Venus moves;
like an aroma, her imperious shade
burdens the soul with love and lassitude.

Green-myrtled island, fair with flowers in bloom,
revered by every nation for all time,
where sighing hearts send up their fervent praises
afloat like incense over beds of roses

or like the ringdove's endless cooing call!
— Cythera now was but a meager soil,
a flinty desert moiled with bitter cries.
And yet, half-glimpsed, a strange shape met my eyes.

It was no temple couched in shady groves
where the young priestess, lover of flowers, moves,
her body fevered by obscure desires,
her robe half opened to the fleeting airs;

no—as we passed, skirting the coast so near
our white-spread sails set all the birds astir—
we saw it loom: a three-branched gibbet, high
and black-etched, like a cypress, on the sky.

Perched on their prey, ferocious birds were mangling
with frenzied thrusts a hanged man, ripe and dangling,
each driving like a tool his filthy beak
all through that rot, in every bleeding crack;

the eyes were holes, and from the ruined gut
across the thighs the heavy bowels poured out,
and crammed with hideous pleasures, peck by peck,
his butchers had quite stripped him of his sex.

Beneath his feet, a pack of four-legged brutes
circled and prowled, with upraised avid snouts;
a larger beast was ramping in the midst
like a hangman flanked by his apprentices.

Child of Cythera, born of so fair a sky,
you suffered these defilements silently;
atonement for your impure rituals
and sins that have forbid you burial.

Ridiculous corpse, I know your pains full well.
At sight of your loose-hanging limbs I felt
the bitter-flowing bile of ancient grief
rise up, like a long puke, against my teeth;

poor unforgotten double, in your presence
I felt each beak-thrust of those stabbing ravens,
and the black panthers' jaws—each rip and gash—
that once took such delight to grind my flesh.

The sky was suave, and level was the sea,
but all seemed blood and bitterness to me
from that time on . . . Yes, in this hateful parable
my heart, as in a heavy shroud, found burial.

On your isle, Venus, I saw but one thing standing,
gallows-emblem from which my shape was hanging . . .
God! give me strength and will to contemplate
heart, body—without loathing, without hate.

Frederick Morgan

From AU LECTEUR

To the Reader

Ignorance, error, cupidity, and sin
Possess our souls and exercise our flesh;
Habitually we cultivate remorse
As beggars entertain and nurse their lice.

Our sins are stubborn. Cowards when contrite
We overstuff confession with our pains,
And when we're back again in human mire
Vile tears, we think, will wash away our stains.

Thrice-potent Satan in our cursèd bed
Lulls us to sleep, our spirit overkissed,
Until the precious metal of our will
Is vaporized—that cunning alchemist!

Who but the Devil pulls our waking-strings?
Abominations lure us to their side;
Each day we take another step to hell,
Descending through the stench, unhorrified.

Like an exhausted rake who mouths and chews
The martyrized breast of an old withered whore
We steal, in passing, whatever joys we can,
Squeezing the driest orange all the more.

Packed in our brains incestuous as worms
Our demons celebrate in drunken gangs,
And when we breathe, that hollow rasp is Death
Sliding invisibly down into our lungs.

If the dull canvas of our wretched life
Is unembellished with such pretty ware
As knives or poison, pyromania, rape,
It is because our soul's too weak to dare!

But in this den of jackals, monkeys, curs,
Scorpions, buzzards, snakes—this paradise
Of filthy beasts that screech, howl, grovel, grunt—
In this menagerie of mankind's vice

There's one supremely hideous and impure!
Soft-spoken, not the type to cause a scene,
He'd willingly make rubble of the earth
And swallow up creation in a yawn.

I mean *Ennui!* who in his hookah-dreams
Produces hangmen and real tears together.

How well you know this fastidious monster, reader,
—Hypocrite reader, you—my double! my brother!

Stanley Kunitz

✒ Stéphane Mallarmé (1842–1898)

TOAST

Zero, this spume—a virgin verse
that traces but the cup
just as, far off, a copious troop
of sirens drowns now wrong side up.

We're sailing, oh my various friends,
myself already on the poop,
you as the sumptuous prow that cleaves
the swell of winters and thunder-claps;

a fine intoxication moves
me, fearless of its pitch and roll,
to offer standing here this toast

Star, reef, solitude—to
no matter what may have been worth
the white endeavor of our sail.

Frederick Morgan

VIRGINAL, VIVID, BEAUTIFUL, WILL THIS BE

Virginal, vivid, beautiful, will this be
The day that shatters with a drunken wing
The lake beneath the frost, still mirroring
Flights that were never made, transparency?

A swan of old remembers that it is he,
Superb but helpless, for he would not sing
Of regions where life still was beckoning
When winter spread its sterile, cold ennui.

His whole neck shakes off the white agony
Inflicted by the space he would deny,
But not the earth that grips him horribly.

Phantom, that with pure brilliance lives on,
He lies immobile, dreaming scornfully,
Such dreams as in his exile clothe the Swan.

Louis Simpson

SEA BREEZE

The flesh is sad, alas! And I have read
All the books. To fly! To fly instead!
Birds, I know, are drunk for unknown skies.
Nothing, not old gardens mirrored in eyes,
Holds the heart that still drips with the sea,
O nights! Neither the lamplit mystery
Of a page yet white and undefiled,
Nor the nursing woman and her child.
Steamer, weigh your anchor! I shall go
To some exotic land I do not know.

Despair, whose hopes have often come to grief,
Believes the last wave of a handkerchief!
These masts may be the kind storms do not bend
Toward some greener isle, but foaming send
Onto the rocks, and roll the wreck along.
But, O my sad heart, hear the sailors' song!

Louis Simpson

THE AFTERNOON OF A FAUN

Eclogue

THE FAUN

Those nymphs, I want to capture them.

　　　　　　　　　　　So clear
Their light incarnation, that it floats in air,
Drowsing in leafy slumber.

　　　　　　　　　　Was it a dream
I loved? The shapes of ancient night that seem
Vague end, alas, in branches, and I see
That I, and I alone, was offering me
In triumph the perfect frailty of roses.
Consider . . .

　　　　　　　whether your talk of women is
Inspired, faun, by your fabled senses.
In the cold, blue eyes of the chaster one
Like a tearful fountain, the illusion
Escapes, but then the other, when a breeze
Warms you, is she sighing on your fleece?
But no! In this torpid swooning state
Of morning almost stifled by the heat,
My flute is the only water with its stops,

Sprinkling its harmonies about the copse
Watered with music; and the only breeze
Apart from the two pipes sound quickly empties
Before dispersing in the arid plain,
Is, on the horizon's unwrinkled line,
The serene and artificial exhalation,
Returning to the sky, of inspiration.

O Sicilian marshes that my vanity
Parches, so that suns are filled with envy,
Silent beneath your flowering sparks, RECOUNT
"That I was cutting hollow reeds, the amount
Talent would need, when on the glaucous gold
Of green with fountains on which vines take hold,
An animal whiteness seems to undulate,
And at the slow beginning of the flute
That flight of swans, no, naiads, runs away
Or dives . . ."

           At the fawn's time of day,
All burns, and the art by which the excess
Of hymen wished for by the one who searches
For *la* escaped is unnoticed, I shall wake
At the first transport, in an antique
Flood of light, lily, erect and alone,
And, of all of you, the innocent one.

Aside from the sweet nothings that are murmured,
The kiss, by which treachery is assured,
There is a bite mark on my breast, that was
Virgin till now. I can only suppose,
Due to some august tooth. But no more!
Only the elect know such things, taking for
Their confidant the vast twin reed beneath
The azure, that takes in the troubled breath
And in a solo dreams we were amusing
The beauty all around us, by confusing
It with our song . . . and dreams of a love so high
That it can do without the back and thigh
Of ordinary dreams, the parts I know
And, with both my eyes shut tight, can follow,
A sonorous, vain, montonous line.

Try then, you instrument of flights, malign
Syrinx, again to flower by the lake
Where you are waiting for me! I shall speak
Of goddesses at length, for I am proud
Of the fame I have in paintings with the crowd:
Making off with a girdle in a shadow,
Sucking the light out of some grapes, to show

I have no regrets. Lifting a grapeskin to blow
Into it, and look through it at the sky,
Avid for drink, and so the hours fly.

Nymphs, let us reinflate some MEMORIES.
"My eye makes holes among the reeds and pierces
Each immortal neck that would assuage
Its burning in water with a cry of rage;
And the splendid bath of hair that flashes
And shivers like a jewel vanishes.
I come running up, when on the ground
(Bruised by the taste of evil they have found
In being two) these sleepers are enlaced.
I seize without disjoining them, and haste
To a bed of roses hated by the shade
That spill their perfumes in the sun and fade
Like our frolic, squandering the day."
I love you, anger of virgins, ecstasy
Of the sacred naked burden that would fly
My lips on fire drinking like a flash
Of lightning secret terror of the flesh
From the cold one's feet to the heart of the timid
That innocence gives up together, humid
With wild tears or less unhappy vapors.
"My crime is that, glad to vanquish those terrors,
I separated hair that was entangled
By kisses that the gods themselves had mingled,
For just as I was about to smother
A laugh in the folds of one (keeping the other
By just a finger, so she would take on
The rising fervor of her sister's passion,
The little unblushing one, the innocent),
From my slack arms, by deaths vaguely spent,
The two, ungrateful forever, run away
And leave me sobbing drunk at the end of day."

So what! Others will lead to happiness
My horns as with a noose tied by a tress.
You know, my passion, purple and ripening,
Pomegranates burst, and bees are murmuring;
And that our amorous, responsive blood
Pours out desire in a constant flood.
At the hour when the woods are ash and gold,
The leaves that have lost all their color hold
A festival. It is Venus walking,
Etna, that sets off your lava sparkling
When sad dreams thunder or the flame is low.
I have the queen!

I shall be punished . . .

No,
But the soul drained of words and this dull body
Are succumbing to the silence of midday.
Now I must sleep, forgetting blasphemy,
On the changing sand, and, as pleases me,
Open my mouth to wine's consoling star!

Adieu, you two. I shall see the shade you are.

Louis Simpson

ᘒ Paul Verlaine (1844–1896)

AUTUMN SONG

Violins complain
Of autumn again,
   They sob and moan.
And my heartstrings ache
Like the song they make,
   A monotone.

Suffocating, drowned,
And hollowly, sound
   The midnight chimes.
Then the days return
I knew, and I mourn
   For bygone times.

And I fall and drift
With the winds that lift
   My heavy grief.
Here and there they blow,
And I rise and go
   Like a dead leaf.

Louis Simpson

GREEN

Here you have fruits and flowers and boughs with leaves,
And then my heart, which beats for you alone —
May your white hands not tear it — humble sheaves!
May they seem sweet to you when they are shown!

I come again all covered with the dew
That morning wind has frozen on my brow.

Suffer my weariness, at rest near you,
To dream of quiet that I come to now.

Upon this young breast, let my dull head fall,
Ringing with your last kisses; this, and, best,
Let it grow quiet there from storm and all
In a brief sleep, since you too are at rest.

Yvon Winters

TEARS FALL IN MY HEART

"It rains softly on the town"
Arthur Rimbaud

Tears fall in my heart
Rain falls on the town;
what is this numb hurt
that enters my heart?

Ah, the soft sound of rain
on roofs, on the ground!
To a dulled heart there came,
ah, the song of the rain!

Tears without reason
in the disheartened heart.
What? no trace of treason?
This grief's without reason.

It's far the worst pain
to never know why
without love or disdain
my heart has such pain!

David Curzon

WOMAN AND CAT

They were just playing, lady and cat,
Their sport was a marvelous sight:
White hand, white paw, tit-for-tat,
In the shadow of gathering night.

She tried to conceal (to little avail)
Beneath gloves of the finest black net

A set of deadly agate-hard nails
Honed sharper than razors can whet.

And sweet as sugar, or so it seemed,
The other tucked claws away too;
But let's give the devil, as ever, his due . . .

And suddenly in the boudoir, where
A froth of laughter had filled the air,
Four dazzling points of phosphor gleamed.

John S. Major and Katharine Washburn

THE YOUNG FOOLS

High-heels were struggling with a full-length dress
So that, between the wind and the terrain,
At times a shining stocking would be seen,
And gone too soon. We liked that foolishness.

Also, at times a jealous insect's dart
Bothered our beauties. Suddenly a white
Nape flashed beneath the branches, and this sight
Was a delicate feast for a young fool's heart.

Evening fell, equivocal, dissembling.
The women who hung dreaming on our arms
Spoke in low voices, words that had such charms
That ever since our stunned soul has been trembling.

Louis Simpson

∾ Tristan Corbière (1845–1875)

OLD ROSCOFF

Bolt-hole of brigandage, old keep
Of piracy, the ocean booms
On membranes of your granite sleep
And thunders in your brackish dreams.
Snore the sea and snore the sky,
Snore the fog-horn in your ears;
Sleep with your one watchful eye
On England these three hundred years.

Sleep, old hulk for ever anchored
Where the wild goose and cormorant,

Your elegists, cry to the barred
And salt-laced shutters on the front.
Sleep, old whore of the homing seamen
Heady with wind and wine. No more
Will the hot gold subdue your women
As a spring tide engulfs your shore.

Sleep in the dunes beneath the grey
Gunmetal sky; the flags are gone.
No grape-shot now will ricochet
From spire and belfry. Pungent dawn
Will find your children dream-ensnared
By the great days when giants shook
The timbered piers and cynosured
The streets and market-place; but look—

Your cannon, swept by wintry rain,
Lie prostrate on their beds of mud.
Their mouths will never speak again;
They sleep the long sleep of the dead,
Their only roar the adenoidal
Echoes of equinoctial snores
From the cold muzzles pointing still
At England, trailing a few wild flowers.

Derek Mahon

THE BLINDMAN'S CRIES

(To the tune of the low-Breton air: *Ann hini goz.*)

The eye, murdered, is not yet dead
A wedge still wounds
Nailed coffinless am I
They've planted the nail in my eye
The eye, murdered, is not yet dead
A wedge still wound

Deus misericors
Deus misericors
The hammer beats my head of wood
The hammer which spiked the cross
Deus misericors
Deus misericors

So the birds that eat the dead
Are afraid before my body
My Golotha is unending
Lamma lamma sabactani

You doves of death
Athirst after my body

Like a gunport fire-ruddy
The sore is at the edge
As the lathering gumsocket
Of an old toothless laughing hag
The sore is on the edge
A gunport red

I see circles of gold
The white sun gnaws me
I have two holes pierced by steel
Reddened at the forge of hell
I see a circle of gold
A fire above gnaws me

In the marrow writhes
A tear expressed
In it I see paradise
Miserere de profundis
Within my skull writhes
Sulphur weeping forth

Happy the good deadman
The deadman
        sleeping
                saved
Happy the martyrs the elect
With the Virgin and her Jesus
    O twice happy the deadman
    The deadman
        sleeping
                saved

A knight outside
Rests free of remorse
Blessed in the cemetery
In his granite sleep
    The stone man outside
    Has two eyes free of remorse

O I feel you as before
Yellow sandwastes of Armorica
I feel the rosary at my fingers
And the Christ of bone on timber
    Still for you I hanker
    O defunct sky of Armorica

Pardon for praying loud
If it is fate O Lord

My eyes two ardent chapel founts
The devil's stuck his finger in them
   Pardon for praying so loud
   Against fate O Lord

   I hear the wind from North
   Sounding like a horn
The tally-ho of the departed
Surely I have howled for my turn enough
   I hear the North wind blow
   Hear the deathknelling horn

Martin James

From AFTERWARDS

II

It's getting dark, little thief of starlight!
There're no nights any longer, there're no days.
Sleep . . . till they come for you, child, some morning —
Those who said: *Never!* Those who said: *Always!*

Do you hear their steps? They are not heavy:
Oh, the light feet! — Love has wings . . .
It's getting dark, little thief of starlight!

Don't you hear them asking? . . . You're not listening.
Sleep: it's light, your load of everlastings.
They're not coming at all, your friends the bears,
To throw bricks at your bottle of fireflies.
It's getting dark, little thief of starlight!

Randall Jarrell

Arthur Rimbaud (1854–1891)

From THE DRUNKEN BOAT

Hearing the thunder of the intransitive weirs
I felt my guiding tow-ropes slacken; crazed
Apaches, yelping, nailed my gondoliers
Naked to stakes where fiery feathers blazed.

Not that I cared. Relieved of the dull weight
Of cautious crew and inventoried cargo —
Phlegmatic flax, quotidian grain — I let
The current carry me where I chose to go.

Deaf to the furious whisperings of the sand,
My heart rose to a tidal detonation;
Peninsulas, ripped screaming from the land,
Crashed in a stinging mist of exultation.

Storms smiled on my salt sea-morning sleep.
I danced, light as a cork, nine nights or more,
Upon the intractable, man-trundling deep,
Contemptuous of the blinking lights ashore.

Juice of the oceans, tart as unripe fruit,
Burst on my spruce boards in tongues of brine
That tore the spinning binnacle from its root,
Rinsing the curdled puke and the blue wine.

And then I was submerged in a sea-poem
Infused with milky stars, gulped the profound
Viridian where, disconsolate and calm,
Rapt faces drifted past of the long drowned.

I saw skies split by lightning, granite waves
Shaking the earth, ambrosial dusks and dawns,
Day risen aloft, a multitude of doves —
And, with the naked eye, vouchsafed visions;

Watched horizontal orbs, like spotlights trained
On some barbaric tragedy of old,
Direct their peacock rays along the sun-blind
Waters, and heard their clattering slats unfold.

I dreamed the emerald snow of dazzling chasms,
Kisses ascending to the eyes of the sea,
The circulation of mysterious plasms
And mornings loud with phosphorous harmony.

Trembling, I heard volcanic eructations,
A thrash of behemoths . . . But now, my ears
Weary of this crescendo of sensations,
I thought of Europe and its ancient towers.

Delirious capes! Strewn archipelagoes!
Do you nurse there in your galactic foam
The glistening bodies of obscure flamingoes
Tranced in a prescience of the life to come?

Meuse of the cloud-canals, I would ask of you
Only the pond where, on a quiet evening,
An only child launches a toy canoe
As frail and pitiful as a moth in spring.

Derek Mahon

THIRST

Parents

We are your grandparents,
We are adults,
Covered with the cold sweat
Of the moon, of green fields.
Our dry wines had body!
In the undeceiving sunlight
What does a man need? Drink.

I said: To die among barbarous rivers.

We are your grandparents,
This is our land.
At the foot of the willows there is water:
See the course of the moat
Where the castle is anchored.
Come to our cellars;
Cider, milk.

I said: To go where the cows drink.

We are your grandparents;
Come, take
Liqueurs from our cupboards,
Tea, coffee, so rare;
The kettles are boiling.
See the pictures, the flowers.
We return from the graveyard.

I said: To drain all the vessels!

Michael O'Brien

VOYELLES

A black, E white, I red, U green, O blue, vowels
Some day I'll tell you where your genesis lies;
A—black velvet swarms of flies
Buzzing above the stench of voided bowels,
A gulf of shadow; E—where the iceberg rushes
White mists, tents, kings, shady strips;
I—purple, spilt blood, laughter of sweet lips
In anger—or the penitence of lushes;
U—cycle of time, rhythm of seas,
Peace of the paws of animals and wrinkles
On scholars' brows, strident tinkles;

O—the supreme trumpet note, peace
Of the spheres, of the angels. O equals
X-ray of her eyes; it equals sex.

F. Scott Fitzgerald

O SAISONS, O CHÂTEAUX

O Seasons, O Châteaux,
What angel is there will not fall low?

O Seasons, O Châteaux,

I have made a magic study
Of the good thing that eludes nobody;

Sing it every time you hear
The gallic cock its chanticleer;

Me, I have no will at all,
It's taken me over body and soul,

A spell usurping whatever I be
Blows all abroad, dispersing me,

So that to understand a word
You flee and follow like a bird.

Seasons O, and O Châteaux

Padraic Fallon

THE SLEEPER IN THE VALLEY

This is the green wherein a river chants
Whose waters on the grasses wildly toss
Its silver tatters, where proud sunlight slants
Within a valley thick with beams like moss.

A youthful soldier, mouth agape, head bare,
And nape where fresh blue water cresses drain
Sleeps stretched in grass, beneath the cloud, where
On abundant green the light descends like rain.

His feet on iris roots, smiling perhaps
As would some tiny sickly child, he naps.
O nature, he is cold: make warm his bed.

This quiver of perfume will not break his rest;
In sun he sleeps, his hand on quiet breast.
Upon one side there are two spots of red.

William Jay Smith

A RUNT OF A DREAM

Maybe there is an evening meant
In some mellow aging place
When I shall drink, at peace,
And die then more content:
Seeing that I am patient.

If to pain I could be resigned,
Had coins enough to loose,
Northern wastes should I choose
Or the South-entangled-vine? . . .
—Agh! this drowsing is malign,

It is simply hot air!
And if I start again
Trampling old roads, then
I'll find Nature's green inn bare:
Not even allowed in, there.

Denis Goacher

ᘏ Jules Laforgue (1860–1887)

CLAIR DE LUNE

It comes with the force of a body blow
That the Moon is a place one cannot go.

The world is yours when you advance,
Moon, through magical August silence!

When you toss, majestic mastless wreck
In seas where black cloud-breakers break!

Ah, if my desolate soul could mount
The steps to your pure baptismal fount!

O blinded planet, fatal light
For the migratory Icarian flight!

Great sterile Eye of Suicide,
The disgusted have convened, preside;

Icy skull, make mockery
Of bald, incurable bureaucracy;

O pill of absolute lethargy,
Be dissolved in our cranial cavity!

Diana with overly Doric chlamys,
Take up thy quiver, do thy damage.

With thy one dart inoculate
Wingless Love that sleepeth late!

Planet flooded with powerful spray
May one chaste antifebrile ray

Descend and bathe my sheet tonight
So I may wash my hands of life!

William Jay Smith

COMPLAINT ON THE OBLIVION OF THE DEAD

Ladies and gentlemen
Whose mother is no more,
The old gravedigger
Scratches at your door.

    Six feet down
    Is a dead man's place;
    He hardly ever
    Shows his face.

You blow smoke into your beer,
You wind up your love affair,
Yonder crows chanticleer,
Poor dead beyond the pale!

His finger at his temple,
Look at Grandpa half asleep,
Sister busy with her knitting,
Mother turning up the lamp.

    One who is dead
    Is quite discreet,
      He goes to bed
    Right in the street.

The meal was good, was it?
Now how is everything?
The little stillborn
Get almost no fondling.

On one side of your ledger
Enter the cost of the dance;
On the other, the undertaker's fee
To make your books balance.

Life's a ditty
With a hey-nonny-no.
Eh what, my pretty,
Do you find it so?

Ladies and gentlemen,
Whose sister is no more,
Open up for the gravedigger
Who raps at your door.

Show him no pity,
He will come all the same
To drag you out by the heels
When the moon is full.

Importunate wind,
Howl on.
Where are the dead?
They're gone.

William Jay Smith

SUNDAY PIECE

HAMLET:	Have you a daughter?
POLONIUS:	I have, my lord.
HAMLET:	Let her not walk in the sun; conception is a blessing but not as your daughter might conceive.

Heaven, unmoved, weeps on forever,
Raindrops, shepherdess, dapple the river.

The river takes a Sunday air;
Not a barge is visible anywhere.

Vespers ring out overhead.
The shores are deserted, the lovers fled.

Girls file by in neat little rows,
Some already in winter clothes.

One, unarmed against the cold,
A sad gray figure to behold,

Leaves the others far behind,
And runs—Good Lord, has she lost her mind?—

And hurls herself from the lonely strand,
Unseen by boatman or Newfoundland.

Evening comes; the lights are lit
In the little port. (Ah, the old stage set!)

While rain continues to wet the river,
And Heaven, unmoved, weeps on forever.

William Jay Smith

THE MYSTERY OF THE THREE HORNS

A hunting horn upon the plain
Blares as long as breath holds out
To the quiet country roundabout.
From deep in the forest comes at last,
Loud and clear, an answering blast.
"Tantan!" sings one
To the woodland rills;
And the other: "Tantara!"
To the echoing hills.

The horn on the plain
Feels the veins
Swell in its head;
The other relies
On its lungs instead.

"Oh, where are you hiding,
Pretty horn?
How naughty you are!"

"I'm looking for my sweetheart
Who calls me from afar
To come and watch the Sun go down."

"I love you! Tallyho!
Halloo! Roncevaux!"

"Love is sweet, but don't forget
The lovely Sun is about to set!"

William Jay Smith

German

❧ Johann Wolfgang von Goethe (1749–1832)

THE HOLY LONGING

Tell a wise person, or else keep silent,
because the massman will mock it right away.
I praise what is truly alive,
What longs to be burned to death.

In the calm water of the love-nights,
where you were begotten, where you have begotten,
a strange feeling comes over you
when you see the silent candle burning.

Now you are no longer caught
in the obsession with darkness,
and a desire for higher love-making
sweeps you upward.

Distance does not make you falter,
now arriving in magic, flying,
and, finally, insane for the light,
you are the butterfly and you are gone.

and so long as you haven't experienced
this: to die and so to grow,
you are only a troubled guest
on the dark earth.

Robert Bly

WANDERER'S NIGHT SONG

To every hill crest
Comes rest.
In every tree crest
The forest
Scarcely draws breath.
Each bird-nest is hushed on the heath.
Wait a bit; you
Soon will rest too.

Peter Viereck

MYSTICAL CHORUS *From* FAUST

All that is past of us
Was but reflected;
All that was lost in us
Here is corrected:
All indescribables
Here we descry:
Eternal Womanhood
Leads us on high.

     Louis Macneice

A SONG FROM THE COPTIC

Quarrels have long been in vogue among sages;
 Still, though in many things wranglers and rancorous,
All the philosopher-scribes of all ages
 Join, *una voce,* on one point to anchor us.
Here is the gist of their mystified pages,
Here is the wisdom we purchase with gold —
Children of Light, leave the world to its mulishness,
Things to their natures, and fools to their foolishness;
Berries were bitter in forests of old.

Hoary old Merlin, that great necromancer,
Made me, a student, a similar answer,
When I besought him for light and for lore:
Toiler in vain! leave the world to its mulishness,
Things to their natures, and fools to their foolishness;
Granite was hard in the quarries of yore.

And on the ice-crested heights of Armenia,
And in the valleys of broad Abyssinia,
Still spake the Oracle just as before:
Wouldst thou have peace, leave the world to its mulishness,
Things to their natures and fools to their foolishness;
Beetles were blind in the ages of yore.

     James Clarence Mangan

MIGNON

Know you that land where forest shadows fold
The lemon home in leaves, oranges struck with gold,
Where a young wind slips softly from blue air,
Laurel and myrtle weigh the atmosphere —
O do you know that land?

Yonder! Yonder
Would I with you, O my beloved, wander.

Know you that building? Columned portico,
Chamber and hall of their own substance glow,
And marble figures stand and look at me:
O thou poor child, what have they done to thee?
O do you know that building?
Yonder! Yonder
Would I with you, O my protector, wander.

Know you that mountain, cloud-clustered and grey?
The beast of burden picks his misty way,
The dragon spawns its brood in sweating caves,
Over the tumbled rocks wild water raves —
O do you know that mountain?
Yonder! Yonder
Points our direction; father, let us wander.

Anthony Hecht

ERL-KING

Who spurs on the road when day is done,
Through night, through wind? A father and son.
The father's arm and his cloak enfold
The youngster, to keep him snug from cold.

"My son, why huddle and hide your eyes?"
"The King of the Darkwood, see him rise
—You don't see, father? —all sheeted, crowned?"
"Mist, my son. From the marshy ground."

Dear little fellow, come with me.
We've games to be playing, just you'll see.
I've pretty gardens along the foam,
Gold to wear in my mother's home.

"O father, father! you still can't hear
The King of the Darkwood, coaxing near?"
"Easy, my youngster. Easy there!
In twigs a-wither, a hiss of air."

Fine little fellow, off we go?
I've three tall daughters to curtsy low.
They take hands, dancing the whole night through.
They'll dance you and dandle and rock-a-by you.

"O father, father! you still can't see
His daughters there in the dark, all three?"

"Son, what I see is how they sway,
The wayside willows so old and grey."

*I'm in love with your flesh and its human glow.
And if you're unwilling, I'll see that you go.*
"O father, father! it hurts, his touch
—The King of the Darkwood!—hurts so much!"

The father shudders, the father spurs;
The boy in his arm half moans, half stirs.
Home, under stress and strain, they sped.
There in his arm the boy lay dead.

John Frederick Nims

THREE STANZAS *From* JOURNEY IN WINTER

That man standing there, who is he?
His path lost in the thicket,
Behind him the bushes
Lash back together,
The grass rises again,
The waste devours him.

Oh, who will heal the sufferings
Of the man whose balm turned poison?
Who drank nothing
But hatred of men from love's abundance?
Once despised, now a despiser,
He kills his own life,
The precious secret.
The self-seeker finds nothing.

Oh Father of Love,
If your psaltery holds one tone
That his ear still might echo,
Then quicken his heart!
Open his eyes, shut off by clouds
From the thousand fountains
So near him, dying of thirst
In his own desert.

James Wright

From THE ROMAN ELEGIES

When you tell me that you were unpopular as a child,
and that your mother spoke of you in a rueful

tone of voice, and that all this seemed to go on
for a very long time, the slow time that it took

for you to grow up, I believe you, and I enjoy
thinking about that odd awkward child.

The grapevine flower, you know, is nothing much,
but the ripened fruit gives pleasure to men and gods.

David Ferry

✆ Johann Christian Friedrich Hölderlin (1770–1843)

From TINIAN

Pleasant to wander
In the sacred desert

———

And at the she-wolves' dugs, good spirit,
At the waters, those who wander
Through their native land
                    once wild,

Now tamed, to drink
Like the lost child found;
During spring, when foreign wings
Coming back out of the warm depths of the woods.

                    the day in solitude reposing
And about the sprouting palms
The bees reassemble
With the summer birds

———

David Gascoyne

HALFLIFE

Yellow pears slope down
And wild roses brim
The rim of a lake
You gorgeous swans
So drunk on kissing
Dunk your heads in,
Sobering holy water.

Poor me where do I go for
Flowers in winter, where
On earth is there any
Sunshine with shade.
The walls stay
Speechless and cold, in wind
Creaks the weathervanes crazy.

Vyt Bakaitis

From HYPERION

Schicksalslied

You wander above in brightness
 On airy pathways, blessed beings!
  Glittering winds of heaven
   Gently touch and move you,
    Like a girl's fingers playing
     Over sacred strings.

Free of fate, like a sleeping
 Infant, breathe the heavenly air:
  Forever unspoiled,
   Modest, in the bud,
    The spirit within you
     Blossoming forever,
      And your bliss-filled eyes
       Gazing into the tranquil
        And eternal translucence.

We, though, are destined
 Never to find resting-place;
  We dwindle, we fall,
   We suffering humans,
    Blindly from one
     Hour to the next,
      Like water splashed down
       From rock to rock
        Years without end into the unknown.

M. L. Rosenthal

NO PARDON

Give up on friends.
Make fun of the artist.
Treat deeper meaning as a common trifle.

God will forgive you, but don't you ever
Dare to disturb lovers at their leisure.

Vyt Bakaitis

DESCRIPTIVE POETRY

Get this:
Apollo's god of the press corps.
Awards now go to anyone giving
A faithful account of the facts.

Vyt Bakaitis

PATMOS

The God is near, and
                        difficult to grasp.
But danger fortifies the rescuing power.
In sombre places dwell the eagles; the Alps' sons
Go fearless forth upon the roads of the abyss
Across lightly constructed bridges. And since all round there press
The peaks of time, and those so close
In love, are worn out on the separate heights,
Then give us the innocent waters,
O give us wings, that with the truest thought
We may fly yonder and return to this same place.

I spoke thus. And then rose
A guardian spirit, carried me away
More swiftly and still further than I dreamed,
Far from my house and home.
And as I passed, the light of dawn
Glowed on the shady woods and longed-for streams
Of my own land. I knew the earth no more.
And soon, with mysterious freshness shining
And rapidly growing beneath the footsteps of the sun,
In golden haze there blossomed forth
In a thousand peaks, a thousand glittering spires,

Asia, before my eyes. I blindly sought
For some familiar image.
A stranger to those wide streets where there descends
From Tmolus to the sea the Pactolus adorned with gold
And the Taurus rises with the Messogis,
And the flowering garden like a peaceful fire,
But in the light on high, the silver snow
And sign of immortal life, on the unscaled wall

The age-old ivy grows, and on living pillars
Of cedar and of laurel
Stand the solemn palaces the Gods have built.

And all around the Asiatic gates,
Calling out here and there from the sea's uncertain plain,
There murmur the unshadowed roads.
But the pilot knows the islands.
When I hear
That Patmos was among the nearest isles,
I longed to disembark
And to approach its gloomy caves.

For it is not like Cyprus rich with springs
Or any of the other islands, it is not
In proud display that Patmos stands
But like a poor house full of hospitality,
And when from a wrecked ship, or weeping
For his lost land or for an absent friend
A stranger comes, she listens with good will;

And all her children, and the voices of the hot groves,
And the place where the sand falls, and where the fields are cracked,
And all the sounds
Hear him, and all resounds again
With love for the man's plaint.
Thus it was one day that she took in care
The belov'd of God, the seer
Who in his happy youth had gone
With the All-Highest's Son, inseparable from Him.

David Gascoyne

THE SEASONS

Spring

When Light returns to face the Earth anew,
The wet green valley and the raindrops shiver
With the white blossoms on the crystal river,
A splendid day to cheer the happy few.

Visibility gains from clean distinctions,
From skies atingle with serene extinctions,
Coolly to view the year's delights unfurled
While seeking for perfection in this world.

Summer

Wherever Summer is a country still,
A quality of heat like molten steel

Glows in the tigerlily's dappled crown
Near where an icy rill meanders down.

In unchecked splendor like a royal train
Great spokes of Light wheel over hill and plain,
While, as if Time would temporize with Joy,
At breathless height a swan white cloud soars by.

Autumn

The myths of separation from the Earth,
Of a spirit that departs, then returns,
Return to the same world that gave them birth;
This from self-devouring Time one learns.

Past images Nature did not abandon
When the blaze of Summer abated, and an
Autumnal glow descended, while on high
The spirit of the prophets charged the sky.

As many short-lived things their courses ran,
For a countryman toiling at his plow
The year comes to a happy ending now
In images of a completed span.

Never will Earth's rock-graced rotundity
Vanish like a cloud in the evening. She
Manifests in a steady golden Light
As irreproachable as it is bright.

Winter

When seasons' images pass out of sight and mind
Winter remains, trailing slowly behind.
The field is empty and the prospect milder,
The showers icier, the storm winds wilder.

With the year ending Sabbath fashion, as
An answer to the question that it has
Already vented in the rage of Spring,
Nature burns, a gorgeous unbroken ring.

David Rattray

ALL THE FRUIT IS RIPE

All the fruit is ripe, plunged in fire, cooked,
And they have passed their test on earth, and one law is this:
That everything curls inward, like snakes,
Prophetic, dreaming on

The hills of heaven. And many things
Have to stay on the shoulders like a load
Of failure. However the roads
Are evil. For the handcuffed elements,
Like horses, are going off to the side,
And the old
Laws of the earth. And a longing
For disintegration constantly comes. Many things however
Have to stay on the shoulders. Constancy is essential.
Forwards, however, or backwards we will
Not look. Let us swing
As in a rocking boat on the sea.

Robert Bly

TO THE GERMAN PEOPLE

Do not jeer at the child, when with a whip and spur
    On a horse of wood he thinks himself mighty and great,
        For you Germans, you are also
           Poor at acting, and good at dreaming.

Or am I wrong, like lightning out of clouds, will acts come
    From daydreams? Will books spring to life?
        Lock me up if that happens, my dear ones,
           Make me pay for this blasphemy!

Robert Bly

From HYMNS AND FRAGMENTS

But speech —
God speaks in
Thunderstorms.
I am often possessed of speech
it said anger was enough and of value to Apollo —
Have you love enough, then let your anger only stem from love,
I have often attempted song, but they did not hear you. For
holy Nature wanted it this way. You sang for them in your youth
without singing
you spoke to the deity,
but you have all forgotten that the first-fruits belong
not to mortals, but to the gods,
more common, more daily
must the fruit become, before
it pertain to mortals.

Richard Sieburth

ஆ Novalis (Friedrich von Hardenberg, 1772–1801)

From HYMNS TO THE NIGHT

6

LONGING FOR DEATH

Down into the earth's womb,
Away from Light's kingdoms,
Pain's raging and wild force
Ensigns the happy departure.
We've come in from a narrow boat
Swiftly to heaven's shore.

Blessed be the endless Night to us,
Blessed the endless sleep.
Truly the day has made us hot,
And long care's withered us.
The wish for strange lands is gone away,
And now we want our Father's home.

What should we do in this world now,
With our own love and faith?
The old things have been set aside,
What use could any new ones be
O! There stands alone and in despair
Whoever deeply and truly loves the times gone by.

Those times gone by, where the senses' light
Burned brightly with high flames,
Where the Father's hand and countenance
Were still recognized by humanity,
And with high sense, in simplicity,
Many still matched to His former image.

Endless and full of mystery
Sweet trembling courses through us —
To me it seems an echo sounds
Out of the deep distance of our grief.
Our loved ones too may be longing for us,
And sent to us this yearning breath.

Down now to the sweet bride, on
To Jesus, to the beloved —
Take heart, evening's darkling greys
To the loving, to the grieving.
A dream will break our fetters off,
And sink us forever in our Father's lap.

The past, where still full blooming
And primeval races walked abroad,
And children, for heaven's kingdom's sake,
Yearned for pain and death,
And if also desire and life spoke,
Still many a heart broke from love.

The past, where with youthful ardor
God showed himself to one and all,
And with love's strength committed
His sweet life to an early death,
Did not avoid the fear and pain
Just so He would remain dear to us.

With anxious longing we see them now,
Shrouded in the dark of Night,
And in this temporality
Never will the thirst be quenched.
For we must go away to home
To know and see the holy time.

What holds us back from this trip home,
From our loved ones who have rested so long?
Their graves concluded on our lives' course,
We are sad, we are afraid.
We have no more to search for here —
The heart is full, the world is empty.

Dick Higgins

WHEN GEOMETRIC DIAGRAMS

When geometric diagrams and digits
Are no longer the keys to living things,
When people who go about singing or kissing
Know deeper things than the great scholars,
When society is returned once more
To unimprisoned life, and to the universe,
And when light and darkness mate
Once more and make something entirely transparent,
And people see in poems and fairy tales
The true history of the world,
Then our entire twisted nature will turn
And run when a single secret word is spoken.

Robert Bly

ஐ Joseph von Eichendorff (1788–1857)

ON MY CHILD'S DEATH

Clocks strike in the distance,
Already the night grows late,
How dimly the lamp glistens;
Your bed is all made.

It is the wind goes, only,
Grieving around the house;
Where, inside, we sit lonely
Often listening out.

It is as if, how lightly,
You must be going to knock,
Had missed your way and might be
Tired, now, coming back.

We are poor, poor stupid folk!
It's we, still lost in dread,
Who wander in the dark —
You've long since found your bed.

W. D. Snodgrass

ஐ Heinrich Heine (1797–1856)

SEA-SICKNESS

The grey afternoon clouds
Droop, descending upon the sea
Which rises darkly to meet them,
And between them races the ship.

Sea-sick I sit, still, at the mast
And make meditations about myself,
Very old, ashen-grey meditations,
Which already Father Lot made
When he had enjoyed too much bounty
And found himself so ill afterwards.
Then, now and again, I think of old stories,
How cross-carrying pilgrims of earlier time
Believing, kissed, on the storm-tossed voyage,
The Virgin's image, rich in comfort,
How knights brought low in this sea-emergency
Pressed the dear glove of their cherished lady

Against their lips and were likewise comforted —
I, however, sit and chew disagreeably
An old herring, the salty comforter
In cat-crises and dog's distemper.

Meanwhile the ship contends
With the wild, upheaving tide;
It lands back now like a rearing war-horse
On the stern, so that the rudder cracks,
Now plunges down again headlong,
Into the chasm of moaning water,
Then again, as if carelessly love-weary,
It hovers, thinking to rest
On the black bosom of the giant wave
Which mightily rages on,
And suddenly, a confused sea-cataract,
Crashes into white water-curls
And covers my self with foam.

This rolling and hovering and pitching
Is unendurable!
Vainly my eye peers out, seeking
The German coast. But ah! only water,
And once again water, stirred-up water!

As the traveller in Winter longs at evening
For a hot cup of tea inside him,
So my heart now longs for you,
My German Fatherland.
Though your precious earth may always be covered
With insanity, hussars, bad verses,
And tepidly thin little treatises;
Although your zebras may always
Feed on roses instead of thistles,
Though your aristocratic apes may always
Swagger in grand, idle clothes refinedly,
And think themselves better than all the other
Heavily plodding low-browed cattle;
Though your council of snails may always
Consider itself immortal
Because it crawls on so slowly,
And though it may daily collect its votes
On whether the cheese belongs to the maggots,
And deliberate a long time
On how to perfect Egyptian sheep
So that their wool would grow better
And the shepherd could shear them like others
Without distinction —
Though folly and injustice may always
Cover you whole, O Germany;

Nevertheless I long for you,
For you are at least firm land.

Vernon Watkins

TO THE WORLD WE MUST APPEAR

To the world we must appear
A most peculiar couple:
The lady is weak in the legs,
Her lover can barely hobble.

She is an ailing kitten,
He sick as a dog, and I think
Their heads should both be examined
By some responsible shrink.

"I am a lotus blossom"
Is the notion fixed in her brain,
While her pallid companion
Fancies himself The Moon.

She opens her little cup
Awaiting the lunar bonanza,
But instead of the life-giving touch
All she will get is a stanza.

Francis Golffing

A MEMORY

It's either the Prize or a terminal worry:
O Willy Wisetzki, you left in a hurry.
But the cat, the cat is in clover.

The board proved rotten on which you stood
And they fished you out of the water dead.
But the cat, the cat is in clover.

We followed your body, exquisite child;
They buried you in a flowering field.
But the cat, the cat is in clover.

You escaped early, you have been wise
In getting well ere you caught the disease.
But the cat, the cat is in clover.

Year after year, how often have I
Called you to mind with sadness and envy!
But the cat, the cat is in clover.

Francis Golffing

DEATH IS THE TRANQUIL NIGHT

Death is the tranquil night.
Life is the sultry day.
It darkens; I will sleep now;
The light has made me weary.

Over my bed rises a tree
Wherein sings the young nightingale.
It sings of constant love.
Even in this dream I hear it.

Louise Bogan

DYING IN PARIS

I

DEATH AND MORPHINE

Yes, in the end they are much of a pair,
my twin gladiator beauties—thinner than a hair,
their bronze bell-heads hum with the void; one's more austere,
however, and much whiter; none dares cry down his character.
How confidingly the corrupt twin rocked me in his arms;
his poppy garland, nearing, hushed deaths alarms
at sword-point for a moment.
Soon a pinpoint of infinite regression! And now that incident
is closed. There's no way out,
unless the other turn about
and, pale, distinguished, perfect, drop his torch.
He and I stand alerted for life's Doric, drilled, withdrawing march:
sleep is lovely, death is better still,
not to have been born is of course the miracle.

II

Every idle desire has died in my breast;
even hatred of evil things, even my feeling
for my own and other men's distress.
What lives in me is death.
The curtain falls, the play is done;

my dear German public is goosestepping home, yawning.
They are no fools, these good people:
they are slurping their dinners quite happily,
bear-hugging beer-mugs — singing and laughing.

That fellow in Homer's book was quite right:
he said: the meanest little Philistine living
in Stukkert-am-Neckar is luckier
than I, the golden-haired Achilles, the dead lion.
glorious shadow-king of the underworld.

III

My zenith was luckily happier than my night:
whenever I touched the lyre of inspiration, I smote
the chosen People. Often — all sex and thunder —
I pierced those overblown and summer clouds . . .
But my summer has flowered. My sword is scabbarded
in the marrow of my spinal discs.
Soon I must lose all these half-gods
that made my world so agonizingly half-joyful.

Robert Lowell

REVENGE — ?

Revenge — ? — as if it were a cure
for heartbreak. It is enough re-
venge that no trace of your dazzle
breaks into your interior.

The end: it came to me in dream.
I saw the night corral your heart,
the snake lodged there — your muffled scream —
the hell being you must be.

Mark Rudman

NIGHT THOUGHTS

When I brood on Germany in the night
No hope for sleep. I know I'll lie
Awake with my eyes wide open while
Tears scald my cheeks.

The years are a blur of past and future:
A good twelve of them have passed since I last

Laid eyes on my mother—which may be why
I'm in such a frenzy to see her.

And I am desperate with desire.
I am under the old Mutter's spell.
She circles my mind like a ring of fire.
I hope to god she is alive and well.

She loves me to pieces, the old woman,
And when in her letters her script breaks down,
I know she's shaken to her depths, I know
When the mother in her's shocked by her role.

My mother never leaves my mental space
Free of time past, the twelve long years,
Twelve!—that vanished without a trace
Since our last satisfying hug and kiss.

Don't worry about Germany: it's the picture
Of health. It will outlast us. All and all.
I'll know its borders again by the flare
Of its barbarous oaks and lime-trees' salute.

I wouldn't waste a moment thinking on
Germany were it not for my mother; . . .
Fatherland-is-forever; but the old
Woman, being mortal, may soon grow . . . cold.

Since I left the country death has taken
Many I loved. And now the unbreathing
Impinge too much upon my sympathy.
Numbering the dead does me in.

And yet I feel compelled to count and each
Body added to the tally has a say
In how my mourning grows: hordes of corpses
Crush my chest. What—relief—when they . . . give way.

Praise the lord. And the lighter light of France
That through this window breaks as my wife, well-
Tempered, radiant as dawn, dispels
My German burden with her lovely smile.

Mark Rudman

WORDS, WORDS, WORDS, AND NOTHING DOING

Words, words, words, and nothing doing!
Never flesh, my dear, my poppet! —

Never any dumplings stewing—
Always soul! No roast to top it!

But the horse of passion gallops
Pretty wildly—daily too—
And perhaps the solid wallops
Of the loins aren't good for you.

In that steeple-chase with Cupid,
Gentle child, in fact I fear
You might end up knocked half-stupid:
Love's a savage hunt, my dear.

Yes, I'd say your health demands
Lovers of my kind who linger
On and on with shrivelled glands,
Who can hardly raise a finger.

Therefore by all means unbosom
Till our hearts are hand in glove,
For your health will surely blossom
On such sanitary love.

W. D. Jackson

℘ Eduard Mörike (1804–1875)

REMEMBER IT, MY SOUL

A pine seedling somewhere springs,
Within what woods, who knows?
In who can tell what garden
Some rosebush grows.
Already they are fated—
Remember it, my soul—
Into your grave to strike
Roots and to grow.

Two black colts graze
In open pastures, or
Homeward to the town,
Turn, lively and capering.
How slowly they will pace
Before your corpse,
Perhaps, perhaps before
They have worn loose
Upon their hooves those shoes
That I see glittering.

W. D. Snodgrass

FOREST MURMURS

Stretched out under the oak, in the wood's new leaves,
I lay with my book. To me it is still the sweetest;

All the fairy tales are in it, the Goose Girl and the Juniper Tree
And the Fisherman's Wife—truly, one never gets tired of them.

The curly light flung down to me its green May-shine,
Flung on the shadowy book its mischievous illustrations.

I heard, far away, the strokes of the axe; heard the cuckoo
And the rippling of the brook, a step or two beyond.

I myself felt like a fairy tale; with new-washed senses
I saw, O so clear! the forest, the cuckoo called, O so strange!

All at once the leaves rustle—isn't it Snow-White coming
Or some enchanted stag? Oh no, it's nothing miraculous:

See, my neighbor's child from the village, my good little sweetheart!
She'd nothing to do, and ran to the forest to her father.

Demurely she seats herself at my side, confidentially
We gossip of this and that; and I tell her the story

(Leaving out nothing) of the sorrows of that incomparable
Maiden her mother three times threatened with death.

Because she was so beautiful, the Queen, the vain one, hated her
Fiercely, so that she fled, made her home with dwarfs.

But soon the Queen found her; knocked at the door as a peddler,
Craftily offering the girl her wonderful things to buy;

And forgetting the words of the dwarfs, the innocent child
Let her in—and the dear thing bought, alas! the poisoned comb.

What a wailing there is that night, when the little ones come home!
What work it takes, what skill, before the sleeper awakes!

But now a second time, a third time, in disguise,
The destroyer comes. How easily she persuades the maiden;

Laces in the tender body, strangling it, till she has choked
The breath in the breast; brings, last, the deadly fruit.

Now nothing is any help; how the dwarfs weep!
The poor darling is locked in a crystal coffin, they set it

There on the mountain side in sight of all the stars—
And inside it, unfading forever, the sweet shape sleeps.

So far had I come: all at once, from the thicket behind me,
The song of the nightingale arose in radiant splendor,

Rained through the boughs like honey, sprinkling its fiery
Barbed sounds down over me; I shuddered in terror, in delight—

So one of the goddesses, flying above him unseen,
Betrays herself to a poet with her ambrosial fragrance.

But soon, alas! the singer was silent. I listened a long time
But in vain; and so I brought my story to its end.—

Just then the child pointed and cried: "She's here already,
It's Margaret! See, she's brought Father the milk, in her basket."

Through the branches I could make out her older sister;
Leaving the meadow, she had turned up into the wood.

Bronzed and stalwart, the maid; noon blazed on her cheeks.
We'd have frightened her if we could, but she greeted us first:

"Come along, if you like! Today you don't need any meat
Or soup, it's so warm. My meal is rich and cool."

And I didn't struggle. We followed the sound of the wood-axe.
How willingly I should have led, instead of the child, her sister!

Friend, you honor the Muse who, ages ago, to thousands
Told her stories, but now for a long time has been silent.

Who by the winter fireside, the loom and the work-bench,
Proffered to the folk's creating with her delectable food.

Her kingdom is the impossible: impudent, frivolous, she ladles together
All that's unlikeliest, gleefully gives her prizes to half-wits.

Allowed three wishes, her hero will pick the silliest.
To honor her, now, let me make to you this confession—

How at the side of the girl, the sweet-spoken, the never-silent,
Catching me unawares, the passionate wish overwhelmed me:

If I were a hunter, a shepherd, if I were born a peasant,
If I handled an axe, a shovel—you, Margaret, would be my wife!

Never then would I complain of the heat of the day;
The plainest food, if you served it, would seem a feast.

Each morning, in its magnificence, the sun would meet me—
Each evening, in magnificence, blaze over the ripening fields.

Fresh from the woman's kiss, my blood would grow sweet as balsam;
Boisterous with children, my house would blossom on high.

But on winter nights, when the drifts pile high—by the fireside,
O Muse, maker of the stories of men! I would invoke thee.

Randall Jarrell

THE FORSAKEN GIRL

Ere the cock has crowed,
    The least star dwindled,
I kneel here at the hearth
    Till the fire has kindled.

The warm light is beautiful,
    The flames soar eagerly.
I stare unseeing
    Sunk in my misery.

All at once I remember:
    The whole night through,
Dear one, wicked one,
    I have dreamed of you.

As I remember,
    The tears come one by one.
So the day begins—
    If only it were done!

Randall Jarrell

✑ Theodor Storm (1817–1888)

AT THE DESK

I spent the entire day in official details;
And it almost pulled me down like the others:
I felt that tiny insane voluptuousness,
Getting this done, finally finishing that.

Robert Bly

WOMAN'S RITORNELLE

Blossoming myrtle tree—
I was hoping to gather your sweet fruit;
The blossoms fell; now I can see I was wrong.

Quick, shrivelling winds —
I went out looking for the footprints I left as a child
Along your windbreak, but I could not find them.

Nutmeg herb,
You blossomed once in my great-grandmother's garden;
That was a place a long way from the world, over there.

Dark cypresses —
The world is too interested in gaiety;
It will all be forgotten.

James Wright

ஒ Gottfried Keller (1819–1890)

NOW HAVE I FED AND EATEN UP THE ROSE

Now have I fed and eaten up the rose
which then she laid within my stiffcold hand.
That I should ever feed upon a rose
I never had believed in liveman's land.

Only I wonder was it white or red
The flower that in the dark my food has been.
Give us, and if Thou give, thy daily bread,
Deliver us from evil. Lord. Amen.

James Joyce

VENUS DE MILO

Once our healing nurse, now you're
reduced to being fashionable,
propped in plaster, crockery, tinware
on desktop, stove, and dressing table.

Soup bubbling, small talk's pinging fluff,
yattering brats, domestic riot —
long since accustomed to such stuff,
you show them your surpassing quiet.

How through a shining temple door
one sees you listening into far
expanses, while through the conch of your ear
the sky-blue breakers roar!

John Peck

❧ Friedrich Nietzsche (1844–1900)

UNDISCOURAGED

Wherever you are, dig deeply!
Underneath you'll find water!
Let the dark people go on howling:
"Underneath there is always Hell!"

Robert Bly

AGAINST THE LAWS

Starting now the hours of the clock
will hang on a hair around my neck
starting now the stars will stop
in their courses sun cock-crow shadows
and everything that time proclaimed
is now deaf and dumb and blind
for me all nature is silenced
with the ticking of the law and its measure

W. S. Merwin

NOTES *From* ZARATHUSTRA

They all muddy the water that it may seem deep . . .

They have learned from the sea its vanity too:
is not the sea the peacock of peacocks?

Even before the ugliest of all buffaloes
does it spread out its tail: never
does it tire of its lace-fan of silver
and silk.

I. A. Richards

❧ Christian Morgenstern (1871–1914)

SUMMONS

Korf receives one day from the coppers
one of those B-9 forms, so-called because they aren't:
Who? Where? How? Why? And other such stumpers and stoppers.

Married? Single? Divorced? Separated? Other?
(Supply all relevant and requisite documentation
to support these claims.) *And the Maiden Name of your Mother?*

Visa? Permit de sejour? Papieren? Pass?
Credit rating? Or bluntly and plainly, are you a legitimate person
or are you perhaps nothing? A no-one? A member even of the torturable
    class?

Failure to fill out the form will subject the subject
to penalties only some of which are specified hereinunder—
forfeitures, fines, confinement, etc. Signed, Oberuntergruppenfüher Hecht.

Clearing his throat, with a discreet, "Korf!" he replies, "I insist,
on my right, notwithstanding any covenants and codicils to the contrary,
and as the party of the first part, to deny that I officially exist."

Agape, aghast, a-gasp, the deputy superintendant clutches in what could be
    a coronary.

               David R. Slavitt

ANXIETY FOR THE FUTURE

Korf, whom worry easily attacks,
Can already see the skies
Filled by balloons of every size,
So all day he prepares whole stacks
Of draughts for bylaws and statutes
Of a society for resolute
Maintenance of a zone designed
To keep balloon-egress confined.

Yet even now he can smell doom:
His club already falls behind;
The air, it seems to him, goes blind,
All the landscape turns gloom and tomb.
Therefore he puts down his pen,
Turns on the light (they *all* will, THEN!)
And goes at once to Palmstrom's place;
They sit together, face to face.

After four long hours, finally,
This nightmare is overcome.
First to break the spell is Palmstrom:
"Be a man now, Korf;" says he,
"You've got hold of the wrong era;
As yet, this is a vain chimera

That tricks your intellect away,
Bobbing over your head today."

Korf recovers his own clear sight—
No one is flying in the golden light!
He snuffs his candle, silently;
Then, points to the sun suddenly
And speaks: "If not today, sometime!
One day you will no longer shine,
At least for us—it makes one's teeth
Chatter—the masses underneath! . . ."

Thereafter, von Korf once again
Sits in his room and takes his pen
Drawing up a vast design
For the protection of sunshine.

W. D. Snodgrass

BLUEPRINT FOR DISASTER

A river called the Snake,
unhappy about the lack of any sane ecological policy,
takes itself in hand one fine day
and ups and leaves.

A man called Tony,
watching it mosey along across the prairie,
whips his shooting iron out of his fancy holster
and ups and kills it.

The critter called the Snake,
is ashamed of itself and of what has now happened,
but too late, too late—the entire territory
ups and parches.

The man called Tony,
blowing the smoke from the end of his barrel,
hasn't the foggiest notion of what he has made happen.
Oops, it's dreadful!

The man called Tony,
unrepentant but nevertheless to some degree atoning
(the environment, after all, is all around us)
ups and croaks.

David R. Slavitt

≈ Hugo von Hofmannsthal (1874–1929)

TWILIGHT OF THE OUTWARD LIFE

And children still grow up with longing eyes,
That know of nothing, still grow tall and perish,
And no new traveler treads a better way;

And fruits grow ripe and delicate to cherish
And still shall fall like dead birds from the skies,
And where they fell grow rotten in a day.

And still we feel cool winds on limbs still glowing,
That shudder westward; and we turn to say
Words, and we hear words; and cool winds are blowing

Our wilted hands through autumns of unclutching.
What use is all our tampering and touching?
Why laughter, that must soon turn pale and cry?

Who quarantined our lives in separate homes?
Our souls are trapped in lofts without a skylight;
We argue with a padlock till we die

In games we never meant to play for keeps.
And yet how much we say in saying: "twilight,"
A word from which man's grief and wisdom seeps

Like heavy honey out of swollen combs.

Peter Viereck

TRAVELLER'S SONG

Water pours down in order to swallow us,
Rocks are rolling to smash us,
Shortly on their powerful wings
Birds will come to carry us off.

However beneath us there is a country;
Fruit is always reflected
In its ageless waters.

Marble foreheads and lips of springs
Rise from the flowery acres,
And the easy winds blow.

Robert Bly

ON THE TRANSITORY

My cheeks still feel their breath: how can it be
That these most recent days, these days just past,
Are gone, forever gone, gone totally.

Here is a thing no one can wholly grasp,
Too terrible for tears or for complaint:
That all goes by, that all goes flowing past,

And that this Self of mine, all unconstrained,
Came gliding straight to me from a small child,
Came like a dog uncanny mute and strange,

And: that a hundred years ago, I *was*,
And my ancestors in their death-shrouds are
As close to me as my own hair is close,

As much a part of me as my own hair.

Naomi Replansky

Georg Heym (1887–1912)

SEAFARERS

We saw the brows of countries, worthy of crowns,
and crimson, too, cut down in the day's demise,
and the rustling crests of forests in their thrones
under the hammering wingbeat of solar fires.

A storm arose to deck the flickering trees
with mourning: burning them off like blood descending
in the distance. Thus from a broken heart the embers
of love flare up before its final rending.

We pushed much farther, into the ocean's evening.
Our hands caught fire like a candelabra.
Each vein clear cut, the thick blood eddying
from our fingers, the sunlight eluding our grasp.

Night fell. Somebody sobbed in the dark. We drifted,
hope gone out of our sails and out of our souls.
We kept a silent vigil on the deck
to unravel the shadows, but our light went dead.

One cloud hovered for a moment in the distance
before night went about its shady business.

ung there, staining the sky with indigo
a sweet-voiced dream sounding the depths of the soul.

Christopher Benfey

THE DEMONS OF THE CITIES

The midnight cities cower underfoot;
The demons trample through the urban graves;
Their skipper-beards, a sprout of smoke and soot,
Bristle like chins of Charons needing shaves.

Creeping on fog-shoes where the pavement drowses
And crawling forward slowly room by room,
Their shadows waver over waves of houses
And gobble street-lights in black gulps of gloom.

Their knees are kneeling on the city towers,
Their feet make footstools of the city squares,
And where the rain strews down its bleakest flowers
Their stormy pipe of Pan rears up and blares.

Around their feet each city's dark refrain
Is circling like a rondo of the waters.
An ode to death. Now faint, now shrill again,
The dirge ebbs into darkness till it falters.

The stream they stroll on is a snaky glow,
Its dim back speckled by the yellow glimmer
The lanterns—blanketed in black-out—throw.
The melancholy reptile wallows.

Their weight falls heavy on a bridge's railing
Each time their hands fall heavy into swarms
Of urban flesh, as if some faun were flailing
Across a slimy swamp his outstretched arms.

Now one stands up. He hangs a ghoul's black mask
On the white moon. The leaden heavens spill
Down darkly from a heaven darker still,
Crushing the houses in a jet-black cask.

A snapping sound. A city's backbone splits.
A roof cracks open, reddening its rent
With arson. Demons squat on it like cats
And ululate into the firmament.

A spawning mother bawls where midnight billows;
The steep crescendo of each labor pang

Arches her brawny pelvis from its pillows;
Around her the enormous devils throng.

She's tossed yet anchored. Overhead, her bed's
Whole ceiling shakes with howlings of the tortured.
Red furrow—redder, longer. Now the orchard
Brings forth the fruit. It rips her womb to shreds.

The devils' necks are growing like giraffes'.
The baby has no head. The mother lugs
It with her till she faints; a devil laughs;
Her spine is tickled by cold thumbs of frogs.

Tossing their horns, the demons grow so tall
They gash the very sky for blood to plunder.
Through laps of cities roars their earthquake-thunder
While lightning sizzles where their hoofbeats fall.

Peter Viereck

WITH THE SHIPS OF PASSAGE

With the ships of passage
Scattered we were and tossed
Downward, always downward
Through winters of glittering frost.
Far we wandered and farther;
In the island sea we played;
Tides left us stranded behind,
And the sky was a droning void.

Name me the town
Where I have failed to wait,
Lighting with my searchlight
Heads passing the gate.
Were these your footsteps, you
Whose locks I'd cut?
None in that dying dusk,
None was the face I sought.

Down to the corpses I called,
Searching the sealed-off lair
Where the buried are huddling;
I called.—O you weren't there.
And I crossed a living field;
And the trees of swaying peak
Stood in the shiver of heaven,
And winter had stripped them bleak.

Crows and ravens
I sent out after you;
Into the gray they scattered,
The land receding below.
But down they fell like millstones,
Fell moaning into night's craw,
And held in their beaks of iron
Garlands of weeds and straw.

Sometimes I feel you calling,
The wind thinning your voice;
Your hands—I feel them in trances
Brushing against my brows;
Long ago all of it happened.
And circles to haunt once more.
Muffled in mournful sackcloth,
Strewing ashes on air.

                              Peter Viereck

FINAL VIGIL

How dark the veins of your temples;
Heavy, heavy your hands.
Deaf to my voice, already
In sealed-off lands?

Under the light that flickers
You are so mournful and old,
And your lips are talons
Clenched in a cruel mold.

Silence is coming tomorrow
And possibly underway
The last rustle of garlands,
The first air of decay.

Later the nights will follow
Emptier year by year:
Here where your head lay and gently
Ever your breathing was near.

                              Peter Viereck

Italian

✆ Giuseppe Giocchino Belli
(1791–1863)

GREED

Which of the seven deadly sins is worst?
Pride sneering skyward, avarice shrieking *More*,
Liplicking lust, or anger, one red roar?
No, gluttony, the fifth sin, is the first.
From Adam burst a famine and a thirst
For a wormy apple offered by a whore,
A penny pippin. God has rammed its core
Down all our throats, a canker of the cursed.

That bitch, that bastard. God, I gape aghast as
I contemplate the greed that could have cast us
Into the outer darkness—fed us, rather,
To final fire. But our ingenious master's
As quick to cancel as to cause disasters,
And to this end kindly became a father.

Anthony Burgess

WHAT MIGHT HAVE BEEN

There'd be, if Adam hadn't sold our stock,
Preferring disobedience to riches,
No sin or death for us poor sons of bitches.
Man would range free, powerless to shame or shock,
And introduce all women to his cock,
Without the obstacles of skirt and breeches,
Spreading his seed immeasurably, which is
To say: all round the world, all round the clock.

The beasts would share the happy lot of men,
Despite a natural plenitude of flies.
There'd be no threats of Doomsday coming when
Christ must conduct the dreadful last assize.
Instead, the Lord would look in now and then,
Checking our needs, renewing our supplies.

Anthony Burgess

REVENGE I

Of all the Bible stories that they tell,
This one to come is quite the most fantastic.
A sonnet being so damned inelastic,
I'll require two to tell it really well.
Well, now—the exodists from Egypt's hell
Met the mad Malechites who, dreadful, drastic,
Ferocious, tastelessly enthusiastic,
Fell on the Hebrews, and the Hebrews fell.

God made a memorandum. After all,
The Jews pursued the then correct religion.
After four hundred years he called on Saul.
"The Malechites," he said, "deserve the axe.
Spit the whole nation; roast it like a pigeon.
Don't leave a feather on their fucking backs."

Anthony Burgess

ᕈ Giacomo Leopardi (1798–1837)

SATURDAY NIGHT IN THE VILLAGE

The day
is ready to close;
the girl takes the downward
path homeward from the vineyard,
and jumps from crevice to crevice
like a goat, as she holds a swath
of violets and roses
to decorate her hair and bodice
tomorrow as usual for the Sabbath.

Her grandmother sits,
facing the sun going out,
and spins and starts to reason
with the neighbours, and renew the day,
when she used to dress herself for the holiday
and dance away
the nights—still quick and healthy,
with the boys, companions of her fairer season.

Once again the landscape is brown,
the sky drains to a pale blue,
shadows drop from mountain and thatch,
the young moon whitens.
As I catch
the clatter of small bells,
sounding in the holiday,

I can almost say
my heart takes comfort in the sound.

Children place their pickets
and sentinels,
and splash round and round
the village fountain.
They jump like crickets,
and make a happy sound.
The field-hand,
who lives on nothing,
marches home whistling,
and gorges on the day of idleness at hand.

Then all's at peace;
the lights are out;
I hear the rasp of shavings,
and the rapping hammer
of the carpenter, working all night
by lanternlight—
hurrying and straining himself
to increase his savings
before the whitening day.

This is the most kind
of the seven days; tomorrow, you will wait
and pray for Sunday's boredom and anguish
to be extinguished
in the workdays' grind
you anticipate.

Lively boy,
the only age you are alive
is like this day of joy,
a clear and breathless Saturday
that heralds life's holiday.
Rejoice, my child,
this is the untroubled instant.
Why should I undeceive you?
Let it not grieve you,
if the following day is slow to arrive.

Robert Lowell

ANTISTROPHE

for Michael Peglau

This hill has been standing in my heart a long time,
thick with brush that cuts off much of the horizon.

I sit here, I look out and I think about things —
about long spaces beyond this place, and silence
that is superhuman; about the deep quiet
that happens sometimes in the heart and that almost
replaces the pulse.
                    Whenever there is wind here
I compare its pronunciation of the leaves
to all that silence. And whenever I do that
I think of eternity and the centuries
of the dead as if here living with the present
and the wind's sound. Then my thought drowns, but I find it
sweet, like sweet water, going down in that great sea.

                                        Robert Bringhurst

From THE BROOM; OR, *THE FLOWER OF THE
DESERT*

> *And men loved darkness rather than light.*
> —John, III, 19

Upon the arid shoulder
Of this most terrible mountain,
Vesuvius the destroyer,
Graced by no other tree or flowering plant,
You scatter here your solitary shrubs,
O fragrant-blossoming broom,
Contented with the deserts. So have I seen
Your shoots make beautiful that lonely land
Which girds about the city
Who once had been the mistress of the world,
And to the wayfarer,
Even by her grave and ever-silent aspect,
Gives testimony of an empire lost.
I meet you here once more, O you the lover
Of all sad places and deserted worlds,
The constant comrade of afflicted fortune.
Among these fields, now sown
With barren cinders only, covered up
By lava turned to stone
That rings beneath the passing traveller's feet;
Where the snake nestles, coiled in the hot sun,
Or under the south wind
The rabbit seeks again his hollow den,
Were farmsteads and tilled glebe,
And whitening crops of grain, and here the sound
Of lowing herds of cattle,
Gardens and palaces,
Grateful retreats for leisure

Of mighty lords, and here were famous cities
Which the great mountain, from its fiery mouth
Pouring forth streams of flame, did overwhelm
With those that dwelt in them. Now all around,
One single ruin spreads,
Wherein you take your root, O courteous flower,
As if in pity of the doom of others,
And cast a pleasant fragrance to the skies,
Making the desert glad. Now let him come
And view these slopes, whose wont it is to flatter
Our mortal state; here he may gaze and see
How loving Nature cares
For our poor human race, and learn to value
At a just estimate the strength of Man,
Whom the harsh Nurse, even when he fears it least
With a slight motion does in part destroy,
And may, with one no less
Slight than the last, even now, and with no warning
Wholly annihilate.
Graven upon these cliffs
Is that *magnificent,*
Progressive destiny of Humankind.
Here gaze, and see your image,
O proud and foolish Century,
You who have gone astray
And left the path by reawakening thought
Marked out for you till now, and turning back,
Even of your regress boast,
Proclaiming it advance.
All those fine wits their evil fate has made
You father forth, with flattery receive
Your childish words, although
Deep in their hearts at times
They scorn at you. But I
Would not go to the grave bearing such shame,
Though easily I might
Vie with the rest to imitate their ravings
And make my song acceptable to you;
Rather would I reveal the deep contempt
That lies locked in my breast,
And show it openly, while still I may;
Although I know oblivion
Lies heavy on whom displeases his own age.
But I have learned to laugh
At that bad fate we both will share together.
You dream of liberty, the while you forge
New bonds for thought—through which
Alone Man rose, in part,
From barbarism, whence only civil life
Has grown, and we may guide the common-wealth
To better things. And thus

The truth displeased you, telling
Of that low station and harsh destiny
Nature has given us. So, like a coward
You turned your back upon the light, which showed
This truth to you, and fleeing it, called base
Those who still followed it; and he
Alone was great of soul who, knave or madman,
Could fool himself or others, and would raise
The state of mortal men above the stars:

———

By these deserted banks,
On which the hardened flood
Casts a dark cloak, and still seems moving waves,
Often I sit by night and mark on high
In heaven's purest blue,
The stars burning above this mournful plain,
And where the far-off sea
Becomes their mirror, and the whole world ablaze
With glittering sparks circling the empty sky.
And when I fix my eyes upon those lights,
Which seem to them mere points,
Yet are so vast that all
The earth and sea compared with them are truly
Only a point; to which
Not only Man, but this
Globe, wherein Man is nothing,
Is utterly unknown; and when I see —
Beyond them infinitely more remote —
Those clustering knots of stars
Which look to us like clouds, where are unknown
Not only Man and Earth, but all together;
So infinite in number and in mass,
The golden sun among the rest, our stars,
Or seeming even as themselves appear
To us on earth — a point
Of nebulous light; then to my questing thought
What is it you appear
O son of man? Remembering
Your state below, of which the soil I tread
Bears testimony still, and yet that you
Think lordship and a purpose
Assigned you by the Whole; how many times
You have been pleased to say on this obscure
Grainlet of sand, which bears the name of Earth,
The authors of the universal cause,
Came down, on your account, often conversing
At pleasure with your race, and how this age,
Which seems in knowledge and in civil arts
The most advanced, heaps insult on the wise,
Renewing once again
These long-derided dreams; what feeling then,

Unhappy children of mortality,
What thought of you at last my heart assails?
I cannot say if pity or scorn prevails.

As a small apple falling from the tree,
Which late in autumn-time
Its ripeness and no other force casts down,
Crushes the loved homes of a tribe of ants,
Tunnelled in the soft loam
With infinite toil, their works,
And all their wealth, which, jealously collecting,
That busy race had garnered with long care
And patient forethought through the summer season
Burying and laying waste,
All in a moment; so, falling from on high,
Hurled through the utmost heaven,
A cloud of cinders, pumice-stone, and rocks,
Darkness and ruin, mingled

————

Full eighteen hundred years
Have passed away, since vanished, overwhelmed
By the force of fire, these peopled seats of men:
And the poor husbandman
Tending his vines, whom scarce the scorched, dead soil
Upon these plains affords a livelihood,
Lifts yet suspicious glances
Towards the fatal summit,
Which, now become no milder than before,
Still full of terror stands, still threatening
Disaster for himself, his sons, and their
Impoverished fields. And often
The wretch, upon the roof
Of his poor cottage, lying
Sleepless all night beneath the wandering air,
Time upon time starts up, to mark the flow
Of that dread simmering, which still pours out
From the unexhausted womb
Over the sandy ridge, and shines upon
The shores about Capri,
And Mergellina, and the Bay of Naples.
And if he sees it coming near, or deep
In his domestic well he hears the water
Gurgling and boiling, he awakes his children,
In haste awakes his wife, and snatching up
Whatever they can seize, they go, and fleeing,
See, far behind, their home,
Their little field, which was
The sole protection they possessed from famine,
Prey to the burning flood,
Which hissing, overtakes it, then unappeased,
Spreads ever-during over all they had.

Returns to light of day,
Which old oblivion had quenched for her,
Pompeii, a skeleton,
Out of the grave by greed or piety
Dragged forth into the open;
From her deserted forum
Upright among the ranks
Of broken colonnades, the traveller
May gaze long on the forked peak of the mountain,
And on its smoking crest,
Which threatens still the ruins scattered round,
And in the horror of the secret night,
Among the empty theatres,
Temples defaced, and shattered dwelling-houses,
Where now the bat conceals its progeny,
Like an ill-omened torch
Which darkly flickers through deserted halls,
Still runs the glimmer of the deadly lava,
Which far-off through the shadows
Glows red, and tinges everything around.
Even so, knowing naught of Man, or of the ages
Which he calls ancient, or the long succession
Of various generations,
Nature stays ever fresh, or rather she
Travels so long a course,
That still she seems to stay. While empires fall,
While tongues and peoples pass; nothing she sees;
And Man presumes to boast eternity.

And you, O gentle broom,
Who with your fragrant thickets
Make beautiful this spoiled and wasted land,
You, too, must shortly fall beneath the cruel
Force of the subterranean fire, returning
To this, its wonted place,
Which soon shall stretch its greedy fringe above
Your tender shrubs. You then
Will bend your harmless head, not obstinate
Beneath the rod of fate;
Nor yet till then in vain and cowardly fashion
Bow down to the oppressor yet to come;
Nor upright in mad pride against the stars;
Amid the desert, where
You find your home and birthplace,
Allotted you by fortune, not your will;
But wiser still, and less
Infirm in this than Man, you do not think
Your feeble stock immortal,
Made so by destiny or by ourself.

John Heath-Stubbs

REMEMBERING LEOPARDI'S MOON

A Version

Moon, the year is over.
I scaled this hill a year ago to see you.
My heart was rapid and cold, you
floated over the maples, over there,
the same pasty communion wafer you are now,
you made each leaf visible,
you made the road leaving this fortress glow like an eerie snake.
But I could barely see. I stood there, crying.
In a dream, on one of those nights
when I know I'll die, the whole world
looked crippled, poor, free, everyone stood outside
pointing at you, whispering.
Moon, if I love anyone, it is you.
And then I love a girl fondling me, and games, and my body
when it was straight, gray-veined, milky,
before my father's violence turned it ugly.
It feels good to look back,
to count how many years I've lived,
to resurrect images of childhood. Time —
death, love — quivered with hope then.
I'd climb trees and let myself slip from the top,
trusting the branches to break my fall.
You'd be there, guarding me.
But I feared violent noises and the dark.
At ten, my life was over.
I'd sit in my father's stone library
and read, read with my brother Carlo
in an alcove, drop off to sleep in his lap,
reading. I was healthy until I was ten.
From ten to seventeen I sat in that jail and read —
my father forced me —
until I became those pages: yellow, infinite.
But I won't waste time now trying to see again
what was. Pain's made the world abstract.
Clouds, stars, the night: that's all. Moon,
where are you? Look at me: a hunchback
dressed like a stupid, vicious priest. Pure black.
I pit language against despair each minute of each day
to breathe, to act, not to feel crazy —
the only way I can touch you.

Nothing exists, not even this voice of mine,
these simple words. Illusions are gone:
desire, hope, these two
that made waking possible, dawn after dawn.
They used to make me tremble,
but nothing has value, earth does not care,

life is the narrowness of this poem,
the grind of composition, and what I write—
truculent, useless (though it begs to live) —
is dust even before it reaches your ears.
Sleep. Go back to the chaos of beginnings. Stay there.
No moon above those cool, featureless trees: black
emptiness, which is time, which is—
if we can bear it—all the world is.
The mute path of the stars is crazed, magnificent.
The breeze just now freshens my heavy face.
Nature, sickness, people struggling to love—
what do they mean? Time is the breath of gods,
the air of cities and rich fields,
it gorges each thought, cell, blood and bone,
it is the gods, it is our consciousness,
it means we now
are,
we are,
you, I,
(oh why isn't a hand rubbing my twisted spine?)
are,
each word next to a word stone.

Stephen Berg

Greek

✍ Dionysius Solomos (1798–1857)

THE DESTRUCTION OF PSARA

On the blackened ridge of Psara
Glory walking alone
Recalls the gallant young men:
On her head she wears a crown
Made of what little grass
Remained on that desolate earth.

Edmund Keeley and Philip Sherrard

✍ Anonymous (date unknown)

MOURNING SONGS OF GREECE

1

I beg you, beg you, mother,
don't ever sing your mourning songs

again for me
when the sun begins to set
for that's the hour when
Charon and his Mistress sit for the evening meal.

Ah, I was serving them their wine,
a candle in my hand, —
and when I heard your voice,
my heart beat wildly for you,
the pitcher broke,
the candle tumbled to the ground,
and, oh, a flickering of the light
raced outwards to the dead
and burned the golden treasures
of the brides,
the finery of the grooms.

And Charon, black with rage,
hurled me across the room.
My mouth was filled with blood,
my lips were bitter gall.

2

Close by the shore, the shore,
I sailed until I touched
the reeds,
the reeds that choke the shore.

And I looked down
and saw a sailor's locks
entangled in the seaweeds,
and whirling out from there.

I thought to sail away from there,
but then I stooped and asked, —

Sailor, O sailor,
where have your hands gone now,
where has your body gone,
and where, your golden hair?

The rigging took my hair,
the ropes have carried off
my hands, —
and all my other beauties
are eaten by the fish.

3

My little ship, three-masted,
with your silver sails, your oars,

and with your golden planks,
where will you cast your cables,
where, your ropes?

My cables to the lower world,
my ropes upon dark Hades.
And I shall anchor there, —
before the village graves.

Konstantinos Lardas

❧ 3

Central Europe and Russia

Polish

❧ Ignacy Krasicki (1735–1801)

THE LAMB AND THE WOLVES

The predator's excuse is always good.
Two wolves attacked a lamb in a dark wood.
It said: "I want your legal rights defined."
"You're weak and tender; and it's dark." They dined.

Jerzy Peterkiewicz and Burns Singer

CAGED BIRDS

The young finch asked the old one why he wept:
"There's comfort in this cage where we are kept."
"You who were born here may well think that's so
But I knew freedom once, and weep to know."

Jerszy Peterkiewicz and Burns Singer

THE MASTER AND THE DOG

Because of thieves, a dog barked all night through.
His master, sleepless, beat him black and blue.
On the next night the dog slept; and thieves came.
The silent dog was beaten all the same.

Jerzy Peterkiewicz and Burns Singer

❧ Adam Mickiewicz (1798–1855)

THE YEAR 1812

Year well remembered! Happy who beheld thee!
The commons knew thee as the year of yield,
But as the year of war, the soldiery.

Rumours and skyward prodigies revealed
The poet's dream, the tale on old men's lips,
The spring when kine preferred the barren field.

Short of the acres green with growing tips
They halted lowing, chewed the winter's cud;
The men awaited an apocalypse.

Languid the farmer sought his livelihood
And checked his team and gazed, as if enquiring
What marvels gathered westward while he stood.

He asked the stork, whose white returning wing
Already spread above its native pine
Had raised the early standard of the Spring.

From swallows gathering frozen mud to line
Their tiny homes, or in loud regiments
Ranged over water, he implored a sign.

The thickets hear each night as dusk descends
The woodcock's call. The forests hear the geese
Honk, and go down. The crane's voice never ends.

What storms have whirled them from what shaken seas,
The watchers ask, that they should come so soon?
Or in the feathered world, what mutinies?

For now fresh migrants of a brighter plume
Than finch or plover gleam above the hills,
Impend, descend, and on our meadows loom.

Cavalry! Troop after troop it spills
With strange insignia, strangely armed,
As snow in a spring thaw fills

The valley roads. From the forests long
Bright bayonets issue, as brigades of foot
Debouch like ants, form up, and densely throng;

All heading north as if the bird, the scout,
Had led men here from halcyon lands, impelled
By instincts too imperative to doubt.

War! the war! —a meaning that transpires
To the remotest corner. In the wood
Beyond whose bounds no rustic mind enquires,

Where in the sky the peasant understood
Only the wind's cry, and on earth the brute's
(And all his visitors the neighbourhood),

A sudden glare! A crash! A ball that shoots
Far from the field, makes its impeded way,
Rips through the branches and lays bare the roots.

The bearded bison trembles, and at bay
Heaves to his forelegs, ruffs his mane, and glares
At sudden sparks that glitter on the spray.

The stray bomb spins and hisses; as he stares,
Bursts. And the beast that never knew alarm
Blunders in panic to profounder lairs.

'Whither the battle?'—and the young men arm.
The women pray, 'God is Napoleon's shield,
Napoleon ours', as to the outcome calm.

Spring well remembered! Happy who saw thee then,
Spring of the war, Spring of the mighty yield,
That promised corn but ripened into men.

Donald Davie (after George Rapall Noyes)

THE ACKERMANN STEPPE

I'm swimming in vast stretches of dry ocean.
The car keeps plunging like a boat to cross that far-reaching green.
Through wind-mown waves that turn up streams of embering blossoms,
I glide past islands of redburn sagebrush.
And it gets darker, with no trace of a road or burial marker.
I look up and try to find stars to guide us.
Way up in that bright fog just now, that flicker of morning star
was Dniester's shining peak, the Ackermann Light.
Let's pull up. It really is quiet. Hear those cranes flying by?
No hawk has the eye to spot them now.
I can hear the grasshopper swing slowly on a stalk,
the snake drag its slithering chest along the grass.
Deep into this silence, my ear could pick up
voices from Lithuania. Roll on, there's no one calling.

Vyt Bakaitis

THE STORM

Sails shred, the steering goes, and waves roar doom
in voices from a frightened mob sucked in, then smash up
with the rope torn snapping from all hands.
Sunset fades red, and with it what hope there's left.
With the wind howling glad, and grim swirls
mounting in surges to open up black chasms,
it's death's spirit, wave by wave climbing on board
like some marine charging the battered walls.
Here's one lying half-dead, and one with both his hands wrenched out.
Here's one still hanging on, hugging his friends goodbye,
and they, as they die off, still pray to push death back.
And one calm passenger off by himself now goes
on thinking: lucky for him whose strength's used up,
who still knows how to pray, who still has somebody to die with.

Vyt Bakaitis

Anton Malczewski (1793–1826)

AFTER THE BATTLE

The hill beside the wood had dressed in green
And spread thyme round it in a fragrant screen.
The wind caressed the trees as though it knew
Why the white birches bent like young girls who
Cast tearful shadows when a knight is killed.
That healing haze from which sleep is distilled
Attacked both victors and the prisoners then.
For one thing's sure: shame, glory, pleasure, pain,
Boredom and toil, exhaust us equally.
In front of them, a fire about to die
Threw its last glow across the battlefield.
Far back, above the wood, the sun had wheeled
The likeness of a camp-fire through the trees.
All else was greying. Ravenous colonies
Of carrion birds were shrieking overhead.
Sentries took guard. The camp-fire noises spread.
Men flitted to and fro; and horses crunched
Grass till it tinkled like distant armour.

Jerzy Peterkiewicz and Burns Singer

ঞ Cyprian Norwid (1821–1883)

BUT JUST TO SEE

But just to see a chapel like this room,
No bigger: there to watch Polish symbols loom
In warm expanding series which reveal
Once and for all the Poland that is real.
There the stone-cutter, mason, carpenter,
Poet, and, finally, the knight and martyr
Could re-create with pleasure, work and prayer.
There iron, bronze, red marble, copper could
Unite with native larches, stone with wood,
Because those symbols, burrowed by deep stains,
Run through us all as ores run through rock veins.

Jerzy Peterkiewicz, Burns Singer, and Jon Stallworthy

THOSE WHO LOVE

A woman, parents, brothers, even God
Can still be loved, but those who love them need
Some physical vestige, shadow: I have none.
Cracow is silent now that its hewn stone
Has lost what tongue it had; no banner of
Mazovian linen has been stained to prove
Art obstinate; the peasant's houses tilt;
The native ogives of our churches wilt;
Barns are too long; our patron saints are bored
With being statues; partitioned and ignored,
Form, from the fields to steeples, can't command
One homespun wand or touch one angel's hand.

Jerzy Peterkiewicz, Burns Singer, and Jon Stallworthy

RECIPE FOR A WARSAW NOVEL

Three landlords, stupid ones; cut each in two;
    That'll make six: add stewards, Jews and water
Enough to give full measure: whip the brew
    With one pen, flagellate your puny jotter:
Warm, if there's time, with kisses: that's the cue
    For putting in your blushing gushing daughter
Red as a radish: tighten up: add cash,
A sack of roubles, cold: mix well, and mash.

Jerzy Peterkiewicz, Burns Singer, and Jon Stallworthy

Russian

❧ Prince P. A. Vyazemsky (1792–1878)

THE RUSSIAN GOD

Do you need an explanation
what the Russian God can be?
Here's a rough approximation
as the thing appears to me.

God of snowstorms, God of potholes,
every wretched road you've trod,
coach inns, cockroach haunts, and ratholes —
that's him, that's your Russian God.

God of frostbite, God of famine,
beggars, cripples by the yard,
farms with no crops to examine —
that's him, that's your Russian God.

God of breasts and . . . all sagging,
swollen legs in bast shoes shod,
curds gone curdled, faces dragging —
that's him, that's your Russian God.

God of brandy, pickle vendors,
those who pawn what serfs they've got,
of old women of both genders —
that's him, that's your Russian God.

God of medals and of millions,
God of yard sweepers unshod,
lords in sleighs with two postilions —
that's him that's your Russian God.

Fools win grace, wise men be wary,
there he never spares the rod,
God of everything contrary —
that's him, that's your Russian God.

God of all that gets shipped in here,
unbecoming, senseless, odd,
God of mustard on your dinner —
that's him, that's your Russian God.

God of foreigners, whenever
they set foot on Russian sod,

God of Germans, now and ever—
that's him, that's your Russian God.

Alan Meyers

ॐ Alexander Pushkin (1799–1837)

DEMONS

The moon through total darkness hurrying
Illuminates the snow in flight;
Clouds are whirling, clouds are scurrying,
Dark is the sky, and dark the night.
Across the open plain I'm driven;
The little bell goes *Ding-∂ing-∂ing* . . .
By holy dread my soul is riven,
Such emptiness is gathering.

'Coachman, drive them faster, faster! . . .'
'Can't, sir; they're too tired, you see;
I'm blinded by the blizzard, master;
The roads are drifting heavily;
Can't see the horses—lost the track, sir;
We're done for—we'll be frozen—whey! . . .
Some demon's got us—that's a fact, sir!
A demon's leading us astray.

'Look, there he is! He's teasing, blowing,
Spitting at me . . . Lord! this one's mean—
He's scared the horses—they'll be going
Headlong into some damned ravine;
He's right in front—Lord, isn't he frightening!
Dressed like a milestone (bloody queer);
There he goes, off again, like lightning!
God save us, master—that was near.'

The moon through total darkness hurrying
Illuminates the snow in flight;
Clouds are whirling, clouds are scurrying,
Dark is the sky, and dark the night.
We lurch in circles, strength declining;
Suddenly silent is the bell;
The team has halted . . . 'What's that shining?' . . .
'Tree-stump or wolf, sir—who can tell?'

The storm is howling, the storm is crying,
Drives itself harder, in despair;
The horses snort; away he's flying,
Only his eyes in the grey murk flare;

The horses strain upon their traces;
The little bell goes *Ding-∂ing-∂ing* . . .
I see, amidst the endless spaces,
A host of spirits, gathering.

Numberless and formless devils
In the blizzard's moonlit haze
Twirling in their murky revels,
As leaves swirl in November days . . .
So many! So many! And being carried
Whither? Why do they plaintively sing?
Is there a witch who's getting married?
Some goblin are they burying?

The moon through total darkness hurrying
Illuminates the snow in flight;
Clouds are whirling, clouds are scurrying,
Dark is the sky, and dark the night.
Swarm upon swarm of demons, streaking
On through this limbo without end,
And with their plaintive howls and shrieking
They pounce upon my heart, and rend.

D. M. Thomas

From THE BRONZE HORSEMAN

A Tale of St Petersburg

INTRODUCTION

On a shore washed by desolate waves, *he* stood,
Full of high thoughts, and gazed into the distance.
The broad river rushed before him; a wretched skiff
Sped on it in solitude. Here and there,
Like black specks on the mossy, marshy banks,
Were huts, the shelter of the hapless Finn;
And forest, never visited by rays
Of the mist-shrouded sun, rustled all round.

And he thought: From here we will outface the Swede;
To spite our haughty neighbour I shall found
A city here. By nature we are fated
To cut a window through to Europe,
To stand with a firm foothold on the sea.
Ships of every flag, on waves unknown
To them, will come to visit us, and we
Shall revel in the open sea.

A hundred years have passed, and the young city,
The grace and wonder of the northern lands,

Out of the gloom of forests and the mud
Of marshes splendidly has risen; where once
The Finnish fisherman, the sad stepson
Of nature, standing alone on the low banks,
Cast into unknown waters his worn net,
Now huge harmonious palaces and towers
Crowd on the bustling banks; ships in their throngs
Speed from all ends of the earth to the rich quays;

The Neva is clad in granite; bridges hang
Poised over her waters; her islands are covered
With dark-green gardens, and before the younger
Capital, ancient Moscow has grown pale,
Like a widow in purple before a new empress.
I love you, Peter's creation, I love your stern
Harmonious look, the Neva's majestic flow,
Her granite banks, the iron tracery
Of your railings, the transparent twilight and
The moonless glitter of your pensive nights,
When in my room I write or read without
A lamp, and slumbering masses of deserted
Streets shine clearly, and the Admiralty spire
Is luminous, and, without letting in
The dark of night to golden skies, one dawn
Hastens to relieve another, granting
A mere half-hour to night. I love
The motionless air and frost of your harsh winter,
The sledges coursing along the solid Neva,
Girls' faces brighter than roses, and the sparkle
And noise and sound of voices at the balls,
And, at the hour of the bachelor's feast, the hiss
Of foaming goblets and the pale-blue flame
Of punch. I love the warlike energy
Of Mars' Field, the uniform beauty of the troops
Of infantry and of the horses, tattered
Remnants of those victorious banners in array
Harmoniously swaying, the gleam of those
Bronze helmets, shot through in battle. O martial
Capital, I love the smoke and thunder
Of your fortress, when the empress of the north
Presents a son to the royal house, or when
Russia celebrates another victory
Over the foe, or when the Neva, breaking

Her blue ice, bears it to the seas, exulting,
Scenting spring days.
                    Flaunt your beauty, Peter's
City, and stand unshakeable like Russia,
So that even the conquered elements may make
Their peace with you; let the Finnish waves
Forget their enmity and ancient bondage,

And let them not disturb with empty spite
Peter's eternal sleep!

————————

D. M. Thomas

ODE ON THE HILLS OF GEORGIA

Night over Georgia; mist across the heights.
Before me, the Aragva ripples off.
Only my chained and prancing heart's distress
Remains intense, a pain so filled with you—
Totally you—that all its darkness lights.
How can I help, combustible anew,
But live in love, even a bitter love?—
Being powerless to live in lovelessness.

Peter Viereck

AUTUMN (A FRAGMENT)

> Then, what is not the target for my *drowsy* mind?
> Derzhavin

1

October has come—already now the wood
Casts its last leaves, its branches are all bare;
Autumn has breathed its cold to freeze the road,
Beyond the mill the stream still murmurs there,
But the pond's already ice; my neighbour's load
Of hunting-hounds is shot off with wild blare
To ravage winter crops in distant fields;
They bay until the sleeping forest yields.

2

Now is my time: I hold no brief for spring;
Tiresome thaw with its slush and stench—I'm ill
In spring, blood fevered, mind and heart panting
With longing. Rough-hewn winter meets the bill
Far better; I love its snows; our sledge stealing
Through moonlight, swift, at its own airy will,
While a warm hand stirs from beneath her sable
To press my hand, and make her flush and tremble!

3

What a delight to glide on sharp-shod iron
Across the smooth unruffled river-glass!
Winter festivals all shimmer and fire! . . .

But snow for six months? No, I think I'll pass:
Even for bears in dens it might be fine
At first, but not at last. You can't amass
Pleasure for ever from Juliet in a sledge,
Or vegetate by stove and window-ledge.

4

Summer, you beauty! I would be truly yours
But for the heat and dust, the midges and the flies.
You drain our mental strength, and what tortures
You give us! Like the field, the body cries
For rain; to be where drink and freshness pours;
Only to see old mother winter rise
Once more: pancakes and wine for her farewell,
Ice and ice-cream for her memorial.

5

Late autumn days are no one's favourite,
And yet, you know, I find this season dear.
Its still beauty, its shining placid spirit
Attract me like a Cinderella's tear.
I tell you frankly I can see no merit
In any other season of the year.
Such good, in autumn? Yes, I can discover
Its beckoning essence, and I am no boastful lover.

6

How to persuade you? Were you ever taken
By some unrobust girl wasting away—
Strange, but it's like that. She is stricken,
Death-bent, poor creature, unrepining prey
Of unseen jaws whose grip will never slacken;
She smiles still, with red lips that fade to grey;
Her face has twilight in its blood, not dawn;
Alive today, tomorrow she is gone.

7

Melancholy time, yet magic to the sight!
Leavetaking kinds of beauty please me best:
All nature withering in a sumptuous light,
The groves and forests gold-and-purple-dressed,
The wind-loud tree-crests, the airy delight,
The mists that roll to trouble the sky's rest,
The rare sun-ray and the first test of frost,
The distant menace of winter's grizzled ghost.

8

And with each autumn I bud and bloom once more;
The Russian cold is good and therapeutic;

The everyday routines no longer bore:
Hunger and sleep come sweetly automatic;
Joy dances lightly where my heart's tides pour,
Desire swirls up—I'm young again, an addict
Of life and happiness—that's my organism
(And please forgive this forced prosaicism).

9

My horse is brought; it shakes its mane and takes
Its rider out into the wilderness,
The frostbound glen where every hoofbeat strikes
Flashes, rings loud, while ice cracks in the stress.
But the short day goes grey, and the fire-flakes
Play up in the forgotten grate, now less,
Now more, now smouldering and now flaring:
I read there, or I feed my long thoughts, staring.

10

And I forget the world—and in dear silence
Am dearly lulled by my imagination,
And poetry wakens into consciousness:
My soul is rocked in lyric agitation,
It cries and trembles, and like a dreamer frets
To free itself in full manifestation—
And now a swarm of unseen guests draws near,
Both old friends and imagined shapes are here.

11

And brave thoughts break like waves along my brain,
And rhymes race forward to the rendezvous,
And pen beckons to finger, paper to pen.
One minute, and verse surges freely through.
So a stilled ship drowses on the stilled main,
Till look: a sudden leaping of the crew,
Masts are shinned up and down, sails belly free,
The huge mass moves and slices through the sea.

12

Great to sail off with it! But where to go?
What lands shall we now see: vast Caucasus,
Or some sun-blistered Moldavian meadow,
Or Normandy's snow-gleaming policies,
Or Switzers' pyramid array on show,
Or wild and sad Scottish rock-fortresses . . . ?

Edwin Morgan

REMEMBRANCE

When the loud day for men who sow and reap
Grows still, and on the silence of the town
The unsubstantial veils of night and sleep,
The meed of the day's labour, settle down,
Then for me in the stillness of the night
The wasting, watchful hours drag on their course,
And in the idle darkness comes the bite
Of all the burning serpents of remorse;
Dreams seethe; and fretful infelicities
Are swarming in my over-burdened soul,
And Memory before my wakeful eyes
With noiseless hand unwinds her lengthy scroll.
Then, as with loathing I peruse the years,
I tremble, and I curse my natal day,
Wail bitterly, and bitterly shed tears,
But cannot wash the woeful script away.

Maurice Baring

✹ Vladimir Nabokov (1899–1977)

THE EUGENE ONEGIN STANZA: *From* THE TRANSLATOR'S PREFACE

What is translation? On a platter
A poet's pale and glaring head,
A parrot's screech, a monkey's chatter,
And profanation of the dead.
The parasites you were so hard on
Are pardoned if I have your pardon,
O Pushkin, for my stratagem.
I traveled down your secret stem,
And reached the root, and fed upon it;
Then, in a language newly learned,
I grew another stalk and turned
Your stanza, patterned on a sonnet,
Into my honest roadside prose—
All thorn, but cousin to your rose.

Reflected words can only shiver
Like elongated lights that twist
In the black mirror of a river
Between the city and the mist.
Elusive Pushkin! Persevering,
I still pick up your damsel's earring,
Still travel with your sullen rake:
I find another man's mistake;

I analyze alliterations
That grace your feasts and haunt the great
Fourth stanza of your Canto Eight.
This is my task: a poet's patience
And scholiastic passion blent—
Dove-droppings on your monument.

✠ Fyodor Tyutchev (1803–1873)

SILENTIUM

Be silent, hide yourself:
In the still spirit
Hoard those hauntings
And let their coming
Be like the speechlessness of stars
By night-time waking, rising, homing.

What temerity may sound
Another's depth, survey its ground?
Utter your thoughts
They flow in lies. Dig down
You cloud the spring that feeds the silences.

Learn to live in yourself. There
Thought on thought,
Fretful of glare and stir,
Begets its untold transmutations
And their song
Only in silence may you hear.

Charles Tomlinson

AT VSHCHIZH

After the tumult and the blood
Had died, had dried,
Silence unmade its history:
A group of mounds; on them
A group of oaks. They spread
Their broad unmindful glories
Over the unheard rumour of those dead
And rustle there, rooted on ruin.
All nature's knowledge
Is to stay unknowing—
Ours, to confess confusion:
Dreamt-out by her,

Our years are apparitions in their coming-going.
Her random seed
Spread to their fruitless feat, she then
Regathers them
Into that peace all history must feed.

Charles Tomlinson

THE PAST

(Tsarskoe selo — site of the imperial palace)

Place has its undertone. Not all
Is sun and surface.
There, where across the calm
Gold roofs stream in,
The lake detains the image:
Presence of past,
Breath of the celebrated dead.

Beneath the sun-gold
Lake currents glint . . .
Past power, dreaming this trance of consummation,
Its sleep unbroken by
Voices of swans in passing agitation.

Charles Tomlinson

LAST LOVE

Love at the closing of our days
is apprehensive and very tender.
Glow brighter, brighter, farewell rays
of one last love in its evening splendor.

Blue shade takes half the world away:
through western clouds alone some light is slanted.
O tarry, O tarry, declining day,
enchantment, let me stay enchanted.

The blood runs thinner, yet the heart
remains as ever deep and tender.
O last belated love, thou art
a blend of joy and of hopeless surrender.

Vladimir Nabokov

◎ Mikhail Lermontov (1814–1841)

DREAM

High noon in Daghestan; a lonely valley;
My body heavy on its barren strand;
Lead in my lung, shot as we tried to rally;
Blood trickling from my wound into the sand.

I lay there motionless in that far valley;
Gigantic peaks stood sentinel all round;
The sun's great light fell almost vertically;
Blood flowed out of my wound into the ground.

I dreamt a dream: in rooms illuminated
With candles moved a gracious company,
And many ladies, young and animated,
Were talking very happily of me.

But there was one who did not hear their chatter
And sat beside a window quite alone.
Nothing the others said there seemed to matter;
Her face was still, and she was cold as stone.

For she was dreaming of that distant valley:
A corpse lay rigid on the stony strand;
By boulders sucking waters seemed to dally;
Blood seeped in failing streams into the sand.

W. K. Matthews

◎ Innokenty Annensky (1856–1909)

ONE SECOND

The designs on your blouse are flickering so wildly,
the boiling dust is so white
we don't need smiles or words.
Stay like this,

almost invisible, down,
chalkier than the dusk in autumn
under this streaming willow.
The distance swells with shadow,

one second and the wind jumps past,
spilling the leaves,
one second and my heart wakes up
and feels that it isn't you.

Stay like this, not speaking
or smiling, like a ghost.
Shadows meet, their edges quiver,
the dust listens. It's as soft as your hands.

The clouds drift close to us,
the simmering red sun
softens to nothing through the haze.
Nothing but gloom comes from it.

The horses that pull the funeral cart
are silent, the coffin gleams,
the shield on the box flashes
and wanes as the sky catches in it.

It's late summer
among the willows, on the sand,
in front of the drained yellow flowers
of the shrinking wreath—

I thought the chrysanthemum
that nods like a human head
bent hopelessly
toward the coffin's polished lid

and the two twisted petals
on the tailboard of the hearse
were the gold circles
of the earrings she left behind.

Stephen Berg

THE CAPITOL

It's winter. The city sleeps in its yellow mist.
Yellow snow rots on the pavements and bare ground.
I don't know where you are or where we are,
I just know we're together and can't be torn apart.

Were we invented by our leader's unshakable power?
Did the world forget to attack us until we sank?
We don't have any myths to look back on,
just stones and terrible facts.

things the magician gave us—
lies and a polluted river, the warm color of the faun,
and our own deserts, those numb squares
where citizens were hanged before dawn.

And whatever we had where we lived,
what launched our eagle, what chained
the giant who wore black laurels to the rock there —
all that will be happiness to our children.

He was so courageous, almost like a god!
His own violent horse of the unreal threw him.
Our dictator couldn't trample the snake of greed
so we worship it as the one God.

That's why we huddle together and call it love.
Our only peace is our children, we believe,
as we bend over their toys with them and feel safe
and hear the riderless beast of the state paw the roof.

Stephen Berg

❧ Ivan Bunin (1870–1953)

FLOWERS, AND TALL-STALKED GRASSES

Flowers, and tall-stalked grasses, and a bee,
and azure, blaze of the meridian . . .
The time will come, the Lord will ask his prodigal son:
"In your life on earth, were you happy?"

And I'll forget it all, only remembering those
meadow paths among tall spears of grass,
and clasped against the knees of mercy I
will not respond, choked off by tears of joy.

David Curzon and Vladislav L. Gucrassev

ᘰ 4

PERSIA AND THE INDIAN SUBCONTINENT

Perʃian

ᘰ Mirza Asadullah Khan Ghalib (1797–1869)

NOT ALL, ONLY A FEW, RETURN AS THE ROSE OR THE TULIP

Not all, only a few, return as the rose or the tulip;
What faces there must be still veiled by the dust!

The three stars, three Daughters, stayed veiled and secret by day;
what word did the darkness speak to bring them forth in their nakedness?

Sleep is his, and peace of mind, and the nights belong to him
across whose arms you spread the veils of your hair.

We are the forerunners; breaking the pattern is our way of life.
Whenever the races blurred they entered the stream of reality.

If Ghalib must go on shedding these tears, you who inhabit the world
will see these cities blotted into the wilderness.

Adrienne Rich

I'M NEITHER THE LOOSENING OF SONG NOR THE CLOSE-DRAWN TENT OF MUSIC

I'm neither the loosening of song nor the close-drawn tent of music;
I'm the sound, simply, of my own breaking.

You were meant to sit in the shade of your rippling hair;
I was made to look further, into a blacker tangle.

All my self-possession is self-delusion;
what violent effort, to maintain this nonchalance!

Now that you've come, let me touch you in greeting
as the forehead of the beggar touches the ground.

No wonder you came looking for me, you
who care for the grieving, and I the sound of grief.

Adrienne Rich

FREELY IN HIDDEN FIRE

(written in Urðu)

Freely in hidden fire
my heart burned
Eloquent with silent flames my heart
burned

In my heart
no desire for her
no memory of her—
Fire gutted the house,
whatever was in it
burned

Now I've gone beyond
even Nonbeing:
I sighed—a rush of fire—
the wings of the imagined bird
burned

One
white-hot
slash of the mind
how to convey its power?
One passing thought of madness
and a desert
burned

I have no heart, or I'd show you
a carnival of scars
Too bad, such brilliant fireworks
but the operator
burned

Ghalib I am
and my longing is
cold ash sadness.
My heart saw the "warmth" of the worldly
and burned.

Frances W. Pritchett

GHAZAL

If you've given your heart away
why sing a dirge about it?
If you don't even have a heart in your breast
why should you have a tongue
in your mouth?

She'll act as she always does —
I should behave with style.
Why should I lower myself to ask
why she looks down on me?

Why be faithful? Love — what love?
When I'm bound to bash my head in
any doorstone will do —
You with the heart of stone,
why should I use yours?

When you visit me in my cage,
don't be afraid to tell me
all the news of the garden!
I've already heard that lightning
struck a nest last night.
Why should the nest be mine?

And aren't you wicked enough
to ruin anyone?
With a friend like you
who needs the sky
for an enemy?

If this is testing —
what do you call torment?
Now that you're his
why do you call it
a test
for me?

You ask why it should be
a disgrace

to see him.
Oh, you're right—
you're absolutely right!
Say it again, indeed:
Why should it be?

Frances W. Pritchett

℘ Ghulam-Reza Ruhani (b. 1896)

GAFFER SPEAKS

I remember despotic times
those days were good, everything cheap;
life was slow, uninterfered with,
bread, farthing a loaf,
    and butter, fourpence a pound.
It was quiet and carefree
    no hearts in disarray,
with only a single robber in the land—
        and he a king.

But now, in every hamlet, borough-council,
Chamber of Deputies and Senate House,
thieves are all called:
        Milord and Your Honor!

Those were the days of liberty,
under despotism we were free.

Omar S. Pound

Urðu

℘ Muhammad Iqbal (1877–1938)

MAKE YOUR RADIANT TWINING CURLS

Make your radiant twining curls
more radiant, more twining!
Hunt down mind and thought,
hunt down heart and sight.

Passion may be veiled,
beauty may be veiled.

Reveal yourself,
or else reveal—my self!

You are a fathomless ocean
I am a small stream.
Share your shore with me,
or make me shoreless!

If I am an oyster shell,
in your hands is the radiance of my pearl.
If I am a potsherd—
make me a royal pearl!

If the song of the new spring forms
no part of my lot,
Make this half-scorched breath
a small spring bird.

From the Garden of Paradise, why send
the order for me to set out?
The work of the world is long—
wait for me, for now!

On Judgment Day
when my ledger is opened,
you should feel ashamed—
make me feel ashamed, too!

Frances W. Pritchett

Bengali

✑ Rabindranath Tagore (1858–1941)

THE SONG THAT I CAME TO SING

The song that I came to sing remains unsung to this day.
    I have spent my days in stringing and in unstringing my instrument.
    The time has not come true, the words have not been rightly set; only
there is the agony of wishing in my heart.
    The blossom has not opened; only the wind is sighing by.
    I have not seen his face, nor have I listened to his voice; only I have
heard his gentle footsteps from the road before my house.
    The livelong day has passed in spreading his seat on the floor; but the
lamp has not been lit and I cannot ask him into my house.
    I live in the hope of meeting with him; but this meeting is not yet.

Rabindranath Tagore

YOU DID NOT FIND ME

You did not find me, you did not.
I sat absent minded in a corner,
the lamp had gone out.
You went away seeing no one.
You came to the door
and then forgot,
it would have opened had you knocked.
The boat of my fate ran aground
on this tiny rock.
On a stormy night I sat counting time,
but I failed to hear your chariot's sound.
Shuddering in the thunder's rumbling noise
I pressed my hands tightly round my breast.
In the sky the fiery flame of lightning
wrote a curse, then disappeared.

Pratimer Bowes

5

EAST ASIAN POETRY: REVIVALS AND INNOVATIONS

Chinese

Shih Shu (early 18th century)

ENLIGHTENMENT

the human body is a little universe
its chill tears, so much windblown sleet
beneath our skins, mountains bulge, brooks flow,
within our chests lurk lost cities, hidden tribes.

wisdom quarters itself in our tiny hearts.
liver and gall peer out, scrutinize a thousand miles.
follow the path back to its source, or else be
a house vacant save for swallows in the eaves.

———

as flowing waters disappear into the mist
we lose all track of their passage.
every heart is its own Buddha;
to become a saint, do nothing.

enlightenment: the world is a mote of dust,
you can look right through heaven's round mirror
slip past all form, all shape
and sit side by side with nothing, save Tao.

James H. Sanford

℘ Yüan Chiu-ts'ai (18th century)

A WARM INVITATION

Do not laugh at my tower
Because it is high.
Its height is most useful to me,
For I can see you coming
More than a li away.
Do not come in a cart,
For the noise of a cart
Frightens my birds away.
Do not come riding a horse,
For your horse eats my grass.
Do not come at sunrise,
For I loathe rising at dawn.
Do not come at twilight,
For at sunset
All my flowers are asleep.

Henry H. Hart

℘ Yüan Mei (1716–1798)

MOTTO

When I meet a monk
                    I do bow politely.
When I see a Buddha
                    I don't.
If I bow to a Buddha
                    the Buddha won't know,
But I honor a monk:
                    he's apparently
                    here now.

J. P. Seaton

GROWING OLD (I)

Now that I am old I get up very early
And feel like God creating a new world.
I come and go, meeting no one on the way;
Wherever I look, no kitchen-smoke rises.
I want to wash, but the water has not been heated;
I want to drink, but no tea has been made.
My boys and girls are behind closed doors;

My man-servants and maid-servants are all fast asleep.
At first I am cross and feel inclined to shout;
But all of a sudden remember my young days—
How I too in those early morning hours
Lay snoring, and hated to leave my bed.

Arthur Waley

GROWING OLD (II)

When I was young and had no money to spend
I had a passionate longing for expensive things.
I was always envying people for their fur coats,
For the wonderful things they got to eat and drink.
I dreamt of these things, but none of them came my way,
And in the end I became very depressed.
Nowadays, I have got quite smart clothes,
But am old and ugly, and they do not suit me at all.
All the choicest foods are on my table;
But I only manage to eat a few scraps.
I feel inclined to say to my Creator
'Let me live my days on earth again,
But this time be rich when I am young;
To be poor when one is old does not matter at all.'

Arthur Waley

❧ Liang Te-sheng (1771–1847)

SENT TO MY FOURTH SON, SHAO-WU (TO THE TUNE "SOUTHERN COUNTRYSIDE")

You are far away, blocked by passes and mountains;
my tender heart is churning—going and staying are both hard.
In the splendid hall a night banquet is held,
yet I look on in sorrow,
and the cypress wine, though strong,
          fails to make me smile.

These words I send: please free up your heart;
when the waters rise in spring, boating is good.
For you, tonight, in the remote serenity of your office,
I pine from afar.
Amidst the sound of firecrackers, another year is gone.

Nancy Hodes and Tung Yuan-fang

❧ Wu Tsao (c. 1850)

FOR THE COURTESAN CH'ING LIN

To the tune "The Love of the Immortals"

On your slender body
Your jade and coral girdle ornaments chime
Like those of a celestial companion
Come from the Green Jade City of Heaven.
One smile from you when we meet,
And I become speechless and forget every word.
For too long you have gathered flowers,
And leaned against the bamboos,
Your green sleeves growing cold,
In your deserted valley:
I can visualize you all alone,
A girl harboring her cryptic thoughts.

You glow like a perfumed lamp
In the gathering shadows.
We play wine games
And recite each other's poems.
Then you sing "Remembering South of the River"
With its heart breaking verses. Then
We paint each other's beautiful eyebrows.
I want to possess you completely—
Your jade body
And your promised heart.
It is Spring.
Vast mists cover the Five Lakes.
My dear, let me buy a red painted boat
And carry you away.

Kenneth Rexroth and Ling Chung

❧ Ch'en Yün (1886–1910)

TWILIGHT

The night creeps in,
And every sound of human life
Is hushed.
Even the tinkle of the camel bells
Comes muted through the dusk.
In the faint, dying light
Of the waning moon

The first hibiscus flower
Falls.

Henry H. Hart

✺ Anonymous (c. 1910)

A TOISHAN SONG

if you have a daughter
don't marry her to a scholar
knowing how to close a door
& how to sleep alone.

if you have a daughter,
don't marry her to a farmer
with cowshit on his feet
& dirt all in his hair.

if you have a daughter,
marry her, quickly,
to a U.S.-bound traveler:
once on board the oceanliner
he'll be rich just like Rockefeller.

C. H. Kwock and Gary Gach

Korean

✺ Yi Chŏngbo (c. 1690–1760)

A MEMORY

I'll never forget the boy who slept here last night.
He could be the son of a tilemaker,
The way clay yields to his touch,
Or the scion of a mole,
The way he burrows and thrusts,
Or perhaps the stripling of a seaman,
The way the oar yields to his touch.
His first experience, he avows,
A claim that raises certain doubts.
I've had my share before and I assume I'll have some more,
But the memory of that boy last night
Is a pleasure I shall always store.

Kevin O'Rourke

❧ Kim Pyŏngyŏn (1807–1863)

A SONG FOR MY SHADOW

You follow me as I come and go,
  No one is more polite than you,
You are like me,
  But you are not I.
On the shore under a setting moon
  Your giant shape startles me;
In the courtyard under a midday sun
  Your small pose makes me laugh!
I try to find you on my pillow,
  But you are not there;
When I turn around in front of my lamp,
  We suddenly meet again.
Although I love you in my heart,
  I cannot trust you after all —
When no light is there to shine,
  You leave without a trace!

Richard J. Lynn

Japanese

❧ Ogata Kenzan (1663–1743)

RETROSPECTIVE

All my life through
these eighty-one years
I have done what I wished
in my own way —
the whole world
in a mouthful.

Richard L. Wilson

❧ Yosa Buson (1716–1783)

SIX HAIKU

1

White lotus —
the monk
draws back his blade.

Lucien Stryk and Takashi Ikemoto

2

Such a moon—
the thief
pauses to sing.

Lucien Stryk and Takashi Ikemoto

3

It pierces through me
to stumble in our bedroom
on my dead wife's comb.

Tony Barnstone

4

Avoiding fishnet
and fishing lines,
moon on the water.

Tony Barnstone

5

At the old pond
the frog is aging
among fallen leaves.

Tony Barnstone

6

Plum blossoms scent
rising higher,
the moon's halo.

Tony Barnstone

Ryōkan (1758–1831)

THREE POEMS ON MY BEGGING BOWL

1

Picking violets
by the roadside
I've forgotten and left
my begging bowl—
that begging bowl of mine

2

I've forgotten
my begging bowl

but no one would steal it
no one would steal it —
how sad for my begging bowl

3

In my begging bowl
violets and dandelions
jumbled together —
I offer them to the
Buddhas of the Three Worlds

Burton Watson

DONE WITH A LONG DAY'S BEGGING

Done with a long day's begging,
I head home, close the wicker door,
in the stove burn branches with the leaves still on them,
quietly reading Cold Mountain poems.
West wind blasts the night rain,
gust on gust drenching the thatch.
Now and then I stick out my legs, lie down —
what's there to think about, what's the worry?

Burton Watson

FIRST DAYS OF SPRING

First days of spring — the sky
is bright blue, the sun huge and warm.
Everything's turning green.
Carrying my monk's bowl, I walk to the village
to beg for my daily meal.
The children spot me at the temple gate
and happily crowd around,
dragging at my arms till I stop.
I put my bowl on a white rock,
hang my bag on a branch.
First we braid grasses and play tug-of-war,
then we take turns singing and keeping a kick-ball in the air:
I kick the ball and they sing, they kick and I sing.
Time is forgotten, the hours fly.
People passing by point at me and laugh:
"Why are you acting like such a fool?"
I nod my head and don't answer.
I could say something, but why?

Do you want to know what's in my heart?
From the beginning of time: just this! just this!

Stephen Mitchell

Kobayashi Issa (1763–1827)

FOUR HAIKU

On the Death of the Poet's Daughter Sato

The world of dew
is a world of dew, and yet,
and yet . . .

Conrad Totman

Frog

When he looks at me,
what a sour face he makes,
that frog over there!

Conrad Totman

Insects

Insects, why cry?
We all go
that way.

Robert Bly

Going to Tend Our Family Graves

Going to tend our family graves today,
The old dog trots ahead to show the way.

Harold Stewart

Ema Saikō (c. 1810–1850)

EVENING STROLL

(written in Chinese)

A little drink enjoyed in the east of town;
windy rain of the late autumn
hitting the blinds and banners.
City lights still unlit

and lanterns dark,
we shared an umbrella all the way—
such tenderness!

Conrad Totman (after Nakamura Shin'ichirō)

✆ Tachibana Akemi (1812–1868)

From HAPPINESS IS WHEN

Happiness is when
you find some rice
in the rice bin you thought was empty
and know you're all right
for another month

Happiness is when
you're reading along
aimlessly in a book
and come on someone
exactly like yourself

Happiness is when
you're sick of reading a book
and just then
someone with a familiar voice
knocks at your gate

Happiness is when
you've got some passage
that's supposed to be so difficult
and all by yourself
you figure out the meaning

Happiness is when
sunset finds you in some country temple
or mountain village
and they say "Stay the night!"
and you do

Burton Watson

ᔷ 6

SOUTHEAST ASIA: NEW VERNACULAR TRADITIONS

Vietnamese

ᔷ Anonymous (c. 1700)

THE CHERISHED DAUGHTER

Mother, I am eighteen this year
and still without a husband.
What, Mother, is your plan?
The magpie brought two matchmakers
and you threw them the challenge:
not less than five full *quan,*
five thousand areca nuts,
five fat pigs,
and five suits of clothes.

Mother, I am twenty-three this year
and still without a husband.
What, Mother dear, is your plan?
The magpie brought two matchmakers
and you threw them the challenge:
not less than three full *quan,*
three thousand areca nuts,
three fat pigs,
and three suits of clothes.

Mother, I am thirty-two this year
and still without a husband.
What, Mother darling, is your plan?

The magpie brought two matchmakers
and you threw them the challenge:
not less than one full *quan,*
one thousand areca nuts,
one fat *dog* this time,
and one suit of clothes.

Mother, I am forty-three this year.
Still without a husband.
Mother, look, Mother,
will you please just *give* me away?

Nguyen Ngoc Bich

✖ Nguyen Gia Thieu (1741–1798)

From SORROWS OF AN ABANDONED QUEEN

You were a fool, Old Man of the Moon,
to tie the knot making me an imperial concubine.
Still . . . such unspeakable delights that first night!
To what shall I compare it?
Sunlight gently sporting with the *do-mi* flower?
A peony unfolding to a long-awaited shower?
An apple blossom awakened to love on a spring night?
Or petals on a spring bough softly smiling
as the winter breeze turns away from the plum trees?
Ah, those rainbow dresses rustling in the wind,
those feather-coats dancing, glistening under the moon,
all in harmony with the music and song!
Mattresses stuffed with kingfisher-down, exhaling perfume of musk,
jewels at my waist flashing with moonlight!
Only a few drops of rain: The peony swayed
in the Pavilion of Perfume.
Then the pure lute notes in the Green Hall,
the wailing flutes in the Red Floor Room,
each melody more intoxicating than the last,
more searing, more shattering to the mind!
Magnificent eyebrows beside a dragon figure:
What a beautiful couple we were!
The flower thanked Heaven for his grace;
willingly she accepted the name of Beauty.

Day in, day out, I was close to my shining Prince,
waited on him in the morning, served him in the afternoon.
The Moon-viewing Pavilion: nothing but tender embraces.
The Royal Palace: nothing but laughter, caresses in the snow.
My cheeks needed no potions to entrance:
Kings would give kingdoms, generals their castles.

Musicians would play "Night Stroll" in the Imperial Garden
or "Palace Flower" on the Spring Approach Terrace
while I slept in my glory,
the imperial colors blazing under the moon.
And oh, within the screens, his awesome majesty shone
and every moment was bliss.
Gold coins by the thousands
would not buy a spring dream by his side.

Now I wander in cinnamon walls
through the night's five watches, gradually despairing.
In night rain at the Moon-waiting Pavilion I pace,
toss through the dark hours on the Cool Wind Terrace.
Copper-cold are the inner rooms,
smashed the phoenix mirror,
shredded the bonds of love.
I wander in a dull dream,
my mind is lost.

Tonight the wind is cold, rain thuds
on the banana leaves as the hours crawl.
A firefly flickers on the wall.
The screens are dew-soaked, the lights dim.
The clock goes full circle but my eyes never close;
the weight of solitude falls, crushes my heart.
What words will ever describe this?
In one night a million memories invade my brain.
Soon the sun will leave my window.
When will it end, this perfume-and-powder life?
What if he comes again?
Will I still be beautiful?

Nguyen Ngoc Bich

Ho Xuan Huong (fl. c. 1800)

ON SHARING A HUSBAND

Screw the fate that makes you share a man.
One cuddles under cotton blankets; the other's cold.
Every now and then, well, maybe or maybe not,
once or twice a month, oh, it's like nothing.
You try to stick to it like a fly on rice
but the rice is rotten. You work like a servant,
but without pay. If I had known how it would go
I surely would have lived alone.

John Balaban

✌ Tran Te Xuong (1868–1909)

THE NEW YEAR'S SEASON AND ITS POETASTERS

You don't find so many of them on regular days, in normal months.
How come they swarm from their crevices at New Year's?
It must be that their bellies are stuffed with steamed rice and meat,
so now they excrete these wordy things.

Nguyen Ngoc Bich

WOMEN

Tea is one, wine another, women the third:
My three follies that leave me no peace.
I shall have to give up whichever I can.
I should be able to give up tea, I think. And wine.

Nguyen Ngoc Bich with W. S. Merwin

✌ Nguyen Khuyen (1835–1909)

TO THE SINGING GIRL NAMED LUU

Long ago when you wanted to marry me,
I snubbed you by calling you too naïve and young.
Now that you're ripe for marrying,
it's I who want to marry you. You say I'm too old?
I've grown old, yes, but not like other men:
I'm ten times better at making love.

Nguyen Ngoc Bich

THE MAN WHO FEIGNS DEAFNESS

There's a man I know who feigns deafness.
He throws such wild looks that you think him dumb as well.
Who is to know he is deaf only during working hours?
That kind of deafness I would love to learn.
    In a crowd his face is wooden
    but at night he has a monkey's ear.
He roams in the rear garden, the front yard, smoking a pipe, chewing a betel
    cud, drinking five or seven excellent cups of tea, and quoting verses
    from the Kieu,

he is all ears one moment and deaf the next.
Who wouldn't like to be that kind of deaf?
But it's not easy to be deaf that way:
Ask him how, and he will just say "Eh?"

Nguyen Ngoc Bich

✇ Nguyen Van Lac (c. 1875)

SHRIMPS

They are no lords, no marquesses or dukes.
Yet they all brandish swords and sport long beards.
They splash in water, popping their red eyes,
quite unaware their heads are full of shit.

Huynh Sanh Thong

Lao

✇ Anonymous (date unknown)

THE CALL OF THE SOUL

Come swiftly, soul
By forgotten footpath
And unswept track
Out of trackless
Wild or salt waste
Return to us

Do not delay on the road
Nor hesitate overlong
In the cobra's nest
Or the tiger's thicket

Do not let riverflood
Dissuade you nor
Any other voice
Persuade you but

Come swiftly back
To these well-wrought
Timbers hooked eaves

Open eyes and mouth
Of your own house

Ronald Perry

Malay

❧ Anonymous (c. 1900)

TWO PANTUNS

1

They wear
    bangles on their arms
I wear
    bracelets on my ankles.
They say
    Mustn't do that!
I do
    as I damn well please.

2

A thousand doves
    fly past
one lands
    in my yard.
I want to die
    on her fingertips
and be buried
    in the palms of her hands.

R. J. Wilkinson and R. O. Winstedt

Filipino-Spanish

❧ José Rizal (1861–1896)

WATER AND FIRE

Water are we, you say, and yourselves fire;
so let us be what we are
and co-exist without ire,
and may no conflagration ever find us at war.

But, rather, fused together by cunning science
within the cauldrons of the ardent breast,
without rage, without defiance,
do we form steam, fifth element indeed:
progress, life, enlightenment, and speed!

Nick Joaquín

℘ 7

THE PACIFIC ISLANDS

Maori

℘ Anonymous (date unknown)

COSMOGONY

From the conception the increase,
From the increase the swelling,
From the swelling the thought,
From the thought the remembrance,
From the remembrance the consciousness, the desire.

The word became fruitful;
It dwelt with the feeble glimmering;
It brought forth night;
The great night, the long night,
The lowest night, the loftiest night,
The thick night, to be felt,
The night to be touched, the night unseen,
The night following on,
The night ending in death.

From the nothing the begetting,
From the nothing the increase,
From the nothing the abundance,
The power of increasing, the living breath;
It dwelt with the empty space,
It produced the atmosphere which is above us.

The atmosphere which floats above the earth,
The great firmament above us, the spread out space dwelt with the early dawn,

Then the moon sprung forth;
The atmosphere above dwelt with the glowing sky,
Forthwith was produced the sun,
They were thrown up above as the chief eyes of Heaven:
Then the Heavens became light,
The early dawn, the early day, the mid-day. The blaze of day from the sky.

Richard Taylor

Melanesia

✆ Anonymous (date unknown)

I CAME FROM UNDER THE EARTH

I came from under the earth;
I part the bamboo leaves before me,
    I look to the heights,
I face two red clouds;
        They make me weep,
        If they were nearer
That would be the color of my song.

Jean Guiart

Caroline Islands

✆ Anonymous (20th century)

GIRL'S SONG

I am happy in my love,
I want to find my beloved.
He is happy too;
I from Elato, he from Ifaluk.

By night he comes to me
Where I lie on the mat,
Pulls aside the wall mats,
Takes off two of them and comes in —
Bold lover, heedless of who may be there.
I call out, "Who is that?"
He is like my sweetheart —
Then I know that it is he.

I know the strong, firm body
Tattooed black like a man-of-war bird,
A bird from far Ifaluk.

He came to Elato to find me.
"That is the woman I want for my love."
"Do you love me?"—"If you love me I do."
He pulls me to the tattooing on his collarbone
And the tattooing of his arm.
He lays my head on the tattooing of his chest.
I say, "No! I will not stay here!"
(I lie, for I love him well.)
I say, "How much will you give me?
It is money I want; lots of it."
(I am lying; I love him dearly.)
Then he loves me fiercely;
Our bodies melt into one.

At night we go out from the house,
Walk around on the sand,
And find a beautiful place
In the woods on a bed of coconut leaves.
There we lie down together,
Where the fragrant lamul-tree grows.
He takes off his loincloth,
He pulls me to him,
He hugs me tight,
He puts me on his thighs
(Strong young thighs they are).
He says to me,
"I want to sleep in your house every night."
I say, "I am afraid. You are too fierce."
He is a fine man in face and body.
At last I say, "I am not afraid. We two will sleep together."
He sits up. "I am telling you the truth.
I was lying when I said I was afraid."

He is like the black ura-fish,
His thighs are as fresh as sea water.
He looks only at me.
All the women come and dance, but he likes me best.
They all paint their cheeks with turmeric
And put on fine new skirts;
He cannot rest until he finds me.

In the evening he bathes and anoints himself for me,
Puts on a new loincloth and a wreath,
And comes by night to find me.
We meet in another place now!
He comes into the house. When he sees me:

"I love you."—"I have not forgotten,
Black fish of Ifaluk!"
Like the swift perang-fish he comes.
His home is far away,
But he covers the distance in a flash.
"Never mind what the people say,
The people of Elato are not gossiping.
They think it is right for us to marry.
Like two trees growing straight together,
Though you come from a distant island,
Tattooed like the black Ifaluk fish."
He has come, and I belong to him;
We love each other well,
Each feels the other as part of himself.

Edwin Grant Burrows

Gilbert Islands

℘ Anonymous (20th century)

SATIRE

That man came shouting, "I am a chief."
Certainly he looks lazy enough for the title;
He also has the appetite of a king's son,
And a very royal waddle.
But he shouts, "I am a chief":
Therefore I know he is not one.

Sir Arthur Grimble

Fijian

℘ Anonymous (19th century)

THE SHADES OF THE NEWLY BURIED COMPLAIN
TO THE GODS

O Gods, it is terrible to be buried this way,
Buried on our backs, staring up at the sky,
Seeing the clouds scudding across the sky,
Feeling bruised by the feet that trample above us.

Shattered: our ribs, the rafters of our house;
Rotted: the eyes with which we looked at each other;
Caved in: the noses with which we kissed each other;
Decayed: the breasts with which we fondly embraced;
Withered: the thighs that we wrapped round each other;
Vanished: the lips with which we shared laughter;
Fallen out: the teeth with which we bit;
Gone: the hand that wielded the mock-spear;
Rolled away: the heavy hawkstone balls;
Scattered: the razor-breaking pubic hair.

Listen to the lament of the mosquito:
So may they die, so may they pass onward,
But I miss the ears they have taken away!
Listen to the lament of the fly:
So may they die, so may they pass onward,
But I miss the eyes from which I drank tears!
Listen to the lament of the black ant:
So may they die, so may they pass onward,
But I miss the penises they have carried away!

John S. Major (after Basil H. Thompson)

Hawaiian

✖ Anonymous (19th century)

THE WOMAN WHO MARRIED A CATERPILLAR

Kumuhea the night-caterpillar loves the woman
with his daylight man-body takes her for wife, handsome
man huge caterpillar, at night
gorges on sweet-potato leaves
Kumuhea huge night-caterpillar
bloated back home mornings
soft Kumuhea flabby Kumuhea, through
him shiftless the wife starves
Where does he go nights, her father says, Where
does he go nights, says the hemp string
his wife fastens to track him where he goes nights;
after him through brush on his crawl
the long string snarls, the night—
caterpillar is strong with anger, tears
into leaves all around
        the people cry Kane help us
        night-caterpillar kills our food, do him in
        in his hill-cave home, he
        kills our food

merciful Kane slices him to bits
we now call cut-worm cut-worm cut-worm

Armand Schwerner

✌ Anonymous (19th century)

FOREST TREES OF THE SEA

No, it is not too soon.

I have seen in my heart
that sea of forest trees
of tall-masted ships returning
to Honolulu's harbor of Māmala,
making every sea-murmur a word—
Māmala's murmur of unresting love.

Love's home is Diamond Head.
Love's shelter is where Pearl Harbor hills reach out to sea.
Love's gaze is keen and long.

Perhaps I should write a letter.
Perhaps I should show my love by asking his:
Come back, dear love, bring ease to me,
comfort of mind.

For you I sing my song
of forest trees on the unresting sea.

Mary Kawena Pukui and Alfons L. Korn

✌ Queen Lili'u-o-ka-lani (1838–1917)

THE LAWN SPRINKLER

O whirly-water
gentle rain shower on the move
what do you think you're up to
circling, twirling so quietly?

CHORUS
You there! You there!
(bass)   Yea, yea—coming up!
(hips swinging)   As you revolve,
                  when—oh, when
(bass)   will you—will you—
                  will you ever hold still?

Amazing
the way you take over: irresistible.
Come, slow down a little —
so I can drink!

Mary Kawena Pukui and Alfons L. Korn

ॐ Anonymous (19th century)

BEHOLD

Above, above
all birds in air

below, below
all earth's flowers

inland, inland
all forest trees

seaward, seaward
all ocean fish

sing out and say
again the refrain

Behold this lovely world

Mary Kawena Pukui and Alfons L. Korn

8

NATIVE AMERICAN POETRY

Cora

∾ Anonymous (19th century)

THE EAGLE ABOVE US

In the sky the eagle, there is his place, there far above us.
Now he appears there.
He holds his world fast in his talons.
The world has put on a gray dress, a beautiful, living, watery dress of clouds.
There he is, far above us in the middle of the sky.
There he waits for the words of Tetewan.
Shining, he looks down on his world.
He looks far into the west.
Shining, he looks upon the water of life.
His countenance is full of terrible disaster.
His eye is glorious.
His feet are already dark-red.

There he is, far above us in the middle of the sky.
There he remembers those who live here on earth.
He spreads his wings over them.
Under his spread wings the gods rain, under them the dew falls.
Beautiful dew of life appears here on earth.

Here he speaks above us.
Here below men hear it, beautiful are the words that are heard here below.
They are heard below, where Mother Tetewan dwells far in the underworld.
There the Mother hears him.
She too speaks: Tetewan's words are heard here above.
Here they meet the words of the eagle, here they both come together.
We hear them already mingled together.

The eagle's words fade away over the far water of life.
There the Mother's words blew away.
There they die away in the middle of the sky.
There very far off they die away.

Willard Trask (after Konrad Theodor Preuss)

Navajo

ﻬ Anonymous (20th century)

SHOOTINGWAY CEREMONY PRAYER

Dark young pine, at the center of the earth originating,
I have made your sacrifice.
Whiteshell, turquoise, abalone beautiful,
Jet beautiful, fool's gold beautiful, blue pollen beautiful,
    reed pollen, pollen beautiful, your sacrifice I have made.
This day your child I have become, I say.

Watch over me.
Hold your hand before me in protection.
Stand guard for me, speak in defense of me.
As I speak for you, speak for me.
As you speak for me, so will I speak for you.
    May it be beautiful before me,
    May it be beautiful behind me,
    May it be beautiful below me,
    May it be beautiful above me,
    May it be beautiful all around me.

    I am restored in beauty.
    I am restored in beauty.
    I am restored in beauty.
    I am restored in beauty.

Gladys A. Reichard

Tewa

ﻬ Anonymous (19th century)

SONG OF THE SKY LOOM

O our Mother the Earth, O our Father the Sky,
Your children are we, and with tired backs

We bring you the gifts you love.
Then weave for us a garment of brightness;
May the warp be the white light of morning,
May the weft be the red light of evening,
May the fringes be the falling rain,
May the border be the standing rainbow.
Thus weave for us a garment of brightness,
That we may walk fittingly where birds sing,
That we may walk fittingly where grass is green,
Our our Mother the Earth, O our Father the Sky.

Herbert J. Spinden

Alsea

✣ Anonymous (19th century)

MOON ECLIPSE EXORCISM

come out come out come out
the moon has been killed

        who kills the moon? crow
        who often kills the moon? eagle
        who usually kills the moon? chicken hawk
        who also kills the moon? owl
        in their numbers they assemble
        for moonkilling
come out, throw sticks at your houses
come out, turn your buckets over
spill out all the water don't let it turn
bloody yellow
from the wounding and death
of the moon

o what will become of the world, the moon
never dies without cause
only when a rich man is about to be killed
is the moon murdered

look all around the world, dance, throw your sticks, help out,
look at the moon,
        dark as it is now, even if it disappears
it will come back, think of nothing
I'm going back into the house
        and the others went back

Armand Schwerner (after Leo J. Frachtenberg)

Osage

✑ Anonymous (c. 1900)

PLANTING INITIATION SONG

I have made a footprint, a sacred one.
I have made a footprint, through it the blades push upward.
I have made a footprint, through it the blades radiate.
I have made a footprint, over it the blades float in the wind.
I have made a footprint, over it I bend the stalk to pluck the ears.
I have made a footprint, over it the blossoms lie gray.
I have made a footprint, smoke arises from my house.
I have made a footprint, there is cheer in my house.
I have made a footprint, I live in the light of day.

Francis La Flesche

Chippewa

✑ Anonymous (19th century)

SOMETIMES I GO ABOUT PITYING MYSELF

Sometimes I go about pitying myself
and all the time
I am being carried on great winds across the sky.

Robert Bly (after Frances Densmore)

Nootka

✑ Anonymous (c. 1900)

SONG TO BRING FAIR WEATHER

You, whose day it is, make it beautiful.
Get out your rainbow colors,
So it will be beautiful.

Frances Densmore

Kwakiutl

Anonymous (19th century)

PRAYER TO THE SOCKEYE SALMON

Welcome, o Supernatural One, o Swimmer,
who returns every year in this world
that we may live rightly, that we may be well.
I offer you, Swimmer, my heart's deep gratitude.

I ask that you will come again,
that next year we will meet in this life,
that you will see that nothing evil should befall me.
O Supernatural One, o Swimmer,
now I will do to you what you came here for me to do.

Jane Hirshfield

Inuit

Anonymous (19th century)

MOTHER'S SONG

it's quiet in the house so quiet
outside the snowstorm wails
the dogs curl up noses under their tails
my little son sleeps on his back
his mouth open
his belly rises and falls
breathing
is it strange if I cry for joy

Stephen Berg

Anonymous (19th century)

SPIRIT SONG

spirit in the sky
come down here
right away
bite the world to death

I rise
up to the spirits
magician friends help me
reach the spirits

child child child
spirit
that can bite evil
come to us

and spirit at the bottom of the
earth I'm calling you I
live near you on top
bite our enemies

join your brother from the sky
each bite an eye out
of evil's face
so it can't see us

Stephen Berg

ᔕᑲ Tuglik (19th century)

TUGLIK'S SONG

put on all the bracelets beads rings
we own for this
we're only girls
huddled together
in hard times without food
bellies shrunken
dishes empty
but suddenly
we feel lovely
our skin boats float through the air
the ropes fly too
the earth's
loose in the air
look way out there
see it
the men drag beautiful seals home
there's plenty again
remember
the smell of the boiling pots
slabs of blubber slapped down by the side bench
feast days keep us together
hug them kiss them
they bring us so much

Stephen Berg

ঙ্গ Paulinaq (c. 1900)

DEATH SONG FOR AIJUK, DREAMED BY PAULINAQ

I am filled with joy
When the day peacefully dawns
Up over the heavens,
    ayi, yai ya.

I am filled with joy
When the sun slowly rises
Up over the heavens,
    ayi, yai ya.

But else I choke with fear
At greedy maggot throngs;
They eat their way in
At the hollow of my collarbone
And in my eyes,
    ayi, yai ya.

Here I lie, recollecting
How stifled with fear I was
When they buried me
In a snow hut out on the lake.
    ayi, yai ya.

A block of snow was pushed to,
Incomprehensible it was
How my soul should make its way
And fly to the game land up there,
    ayi, yai ya.

That door-block worried me,
And ever greater grew my fear
When the fresh-water ice split in the cold,
And the frost-crack thunderously grew
Up over the heavens,
    ayi, yai ya.

Glorious was life
In winter.
But did winter bring me joy?
No! Ever was I so anxious
For sole-skins and skins for kamiks,
Would there be enough for us all?
Yes, I was ever anxious,
    ayi, ya ya.

Glorious was life
In summer.
But did summer bring me joy?
No! Ever was I so anxious
For skins and rugs for the platform,
Yes, I was ever anxious,
    ayi, yai ya.

Glorious was life
When standing at one's fishing hole
On the ice.
But did standing at the fishing hole bring me joy?
No! Ever was I so anxious
For my tiny little fish-hook
If it should not get a bite,
    ayi, yai ya.

Glorious was life
When dancing in the dance-house,
But did dancing in the dance-house bring me joy?
No! Ever was I so anxious,
That I could not recall
The song I was to sing.
Yes, I was ever anxious,
    ayi, yai ya.

Glorious was life . . .
Now I am filled with joy
For every time a dawn
Makes white the sky of night,
For every time the sun goes up
Over the heavens.
    Ayi, yai, ya.

              W. E. Calvert

∾ Uvavnuk (19th century)

SHAMAN SONG

The great sea
frees me, moves me,
as a strong river carries a weed.
Earth and her strong winds
move me, take me away,
and my soul is swept up in joy.

              Jane Hirshfield

Takomaq (late 19th century)

IMPROVISED SONG OF JOY

The lands around my dwelling
Are more beautiful
From the day
When it is given me to see
Faces I have never seen before.
All is more beautiful,
All is more beautiful,
And life is thankfulness.
These guests of mine
Make my house grand.

Knud Rasmussen

Anonymous (19th century)

I THINK OVER AGAIN MY SMALL ADVENTURES

I think over again my small adventures,
My fears,
Those small ones that seemed so big,
For all the vital things
I had to get and to reach;
And yet there is only one great thing,
The only thing,
To live to see the great day that dawns
And the light that fills the world.

Unknown

❧ 9

AFRICA: POETRY

San

❧ Anonymous (19th–early 20th century)

THE DAY WE DIE

The day we die
the wind comes down
to take away
our footprints.

The wind makes dust
to cover up
the marks we left
while walking.

For otherwise
the thing would seem
as if we were
still living.

Therefore the wind
is he who comes
to blow away
our footprints.

Arthur Markowitz

Pygmy

✤ Anonymous (19th century)

SONG OF A MARRIAGEABLE GIRL

Will a man come for me?
The good spirit of the forest knows.
He could tell little Medje;
But he will not tell.
There are things it is not right to know:
If there will be dew on the grass tomorrow,
If the fish will come to the trap and be caught,
If a spell put on the gazelle
Will let my father kill it.

Willard Trask (after O. de Labrouhe)

Yoruba

✤ Anonymous (c. 1900)

THE LAZY MAN

When the cock crows,
the lazy man smacks his lips and says:
So it is daylight again, is it?
And before he turns over heavily,
before he even stretches himself,
before he even yawns—
the farmer has reached the farm,
the water carriers arrived at the river,
the spinners are spinning their cotton,
the weaver works on his cloth,
and the fire blazes in the blacksmith's hut.

The lazy one knows where the soup is sweet
he goes from house to house.
If there is no sacrifice today,
his breastbone will stick out!
But when he sees the free yam,
he starts to unbutton his shirt,
he moves close to the celebrant.
Yet his troubles are not few.

When his wives reach puberty,
rich men will help him to marry them.

Bakare Gbadamosi and Ulli Beier

℘ Anonymous (19th century)

OSHUN, THE RIVER GODDESS

Brass and parrots' feathers
on a velvet skin.
White cowrie shells
on black buttocks.
Her eyes sparkle in the forest,
like the sun on the river.
She is the wisdom of the forest
she is the wisdom of the river.
Where the doctor failed
she cures with fresh water.
Where medicine is impotent
she cures with cool water.
She cures the child
and does not charge the father.
She feeds the barren woman with honey
and her dry body swells up
like a juicy palm fruit.
Oh, how sweet
is the touch of child's hand!

Ulli Beier

Bini

℘ Anonymous (19th century)

PRAISE SONG FOR THE OBA OF BENIN

He who knows not the Oba
let me show him.
He has mounted the throne,
he has piled a throne upon a throne.
Plentiful as grains of sand upon the earth
are those in front of him.
Plentiful as grains of sand upon the earth
are those behind him.
There are two thousand people
to fan him.

He who owns you
is among you here.
He who owns you
has piled a throne upon a throne.
He has lived to do it this year;
even so he will live to do it again.

John Bradbury

Bagirmi

❧ Anonymous (c. 1900)

LOVE SONG

I painted my eyes with black antimony
I girded myself with amulets.

I will satisfy my desire,
you my slender boy.
I walk behind the wall.
I have covered my bosom.
I shall knead colored clay
I shall paint the house of my friend,
O my slender boy.
I shall take my piece of silver
I will buy silk.
I will gird myself with amulets
I will satisfy my desire
the horn of antimony in my hand,
O my slender boy!

Ulli Beier (after H. Gaden)

Akan

❧ Anonymous (19th century)

LULLABY

Someone would like to have you for her child
but you are mine.
Someone would like to rear you on a costly mat
but you are mine.
Someone would like to place you on a camel blanket

but you are mine.
I have you to rear on a torn old mat.
Someone would like to have you for her child
but you are mine.

Kwabena Nketia

Ewe

✆ Anonymous (19th century)

THE DEAD MAN ASKS FOR A SONG

Sing me a song of the dead,
That I may take it with me.
A song of the underworld sing me,
That I may take it with me
And travel to the underworld.

The underworld says,
Says the underworld:
It is beautiful in the grave.
Beautiful is the underworld
But there is no wine to drink there.
So I will take it with me
And travel to the underworld
And travel to the underworld.

Sing me a song of the dead,
That I may take it with me.
A song of the underworld sing me,
That I may take it with me
And travel to the underworld.

Willard Trask (after Jakob Spieth)

Galla

✆ Anonymous (19th century)

LOVE SONG

If I might be an ox,
An ox, a beautiful ox,

Beautiful but stubborn;
The merchant would buy me,
Would buy and slaughter me,
Would spread my skin,
Would bring me to the market.
The coarse woman would bargain for me;
The beautiful girl would buy me.
She would crush perfumes for me;
I would spend the night rolled up around her;
I would spend the afternoon rolled up around her.
Her husband would say: "It is a dead skin!"
But I would have my love!

Enrico Cerulli

Berber

✺ Mririda N'ait Attik (date unknown)

PRAISE TO THE TATTOO MISTRESS

Afakem! *Afakem*! Lalla Taouchamt!
By my neck, you are unequalled
for your needles large and small!
You know so well how to use the soot and ivy,
the blue of your tattoo never fades.
Your designs have no rival in the land.
It is well known how the women and girls of our village
fight for your skills—
no man would marry before he knew
that his bride was pricked by your needle.
Prick and pat, our beloved Lalla Taouchamt!
You have nothing to fear little Afannia,
Lalla Mbarka is not an apprentice!
If your skin is as touchy as the pupil of your eye,
her hand can be lighter than a thistle seed.
If you cry out when the tattoos are placed upon your calves
your husband will mock you!
Don't jump around like a little goat,
you will anger Lalla Mbarka, my dear,
and she will ask for the hedgehog's quills.
Afakem! Lalla Mbarka, what a beautiful tattoo!
May God give you his blessings.
May you remain forever in his grace!

Daniel Halpern and Paula Paley

Part VIII

THE
TWENTIETH
CENTURY
(1915–)

Throughout the non-Western world in the first half of the twentieth century, anti-imperial and anticolonial movements appeared and gathered strength; hand in hand with these movements came the creation of new national literatures. The experience of China is typical: Galvanized both by the anti-imperialist, social activist May Fourth Movement (named for anti-Japanese demonstrations on May 4, 1919) and by the powerful influence of such newly translated writers as Ibsen and Dickens, Chinese poets deliberately discarded traditional forms and themes and set out to create a new literature that would be politically and socially conscious and "modern" without being "Western." The new Chinese literature flourished briefly before falling victim to home-grown political repression; but similar movements took hold and grew in Turkey, India, Indonesia, and many other countries; Japan, in particular, produced modern poetry of great sophistication and inventiveness.

In Africa, poetry became no longer just the orally transmitted work of anonymous authors, but literature created self-consciously by individuals who see themselves as poets in the Western sense. Similarly Aimé Césaire, with Léopold Sédar Senghor a pioneer of the *Négritude* movement, helped to create a distinctive West Indian poetry that now flourishes both in French and in English.

Above all, the poetry in Part VIII makes clear that a great achievement of the twentieth century has been the creation of a genuine world literature, multivocal and proud of the distinctiveness of its many voices, but nevertheless part of one great chorus.

J.S.M.

Guillaume Apollinaire scratched his small notorious poem, "O God What a Lovely War" as a caption to a drawing on a soap tin of two gunners facing a shellburst overhead in a battle during World War I. This poet, friend of Picasso and Braque, was a victim of both the general carnage of the Great War and the pandemic influenza of 1918. The Expressionist Georg Trakl was another casualty of the European catastrophe: Trakl, a cocaine addict and suicide in a military hospital, drew from the great symbolist warehouse of association and hallucinatory meaning which twentieth-century modernism ransacked for a new poetics just before the war. Stefan George's prophetic "The Antichrist," written long before the poet died in exile from the Third Reich, gained an historical lease on memory when the leader of a plot to assassinate Hitler in 1944 recited it to friends the night before his failed attempt. A late poem of Robert Desnos, addressed to his wife, was recited to a fellow inmate at the Terezin concentration camp; it is now inscribed on the walls of a memorial in Paris to the two hundred thousand French Jews deported during the Shoah.

The ebullience of twentieth-century modernism had a dark undertow, realized in the vast tally of poets like these, either destroyed in two world wars or silenced or exiled by the homicidal political regimes of our age. Its energies included a ferocious eclecticism, a passionnate revival of the past, and with that, a committment to translation by English and American poets so powerful as to make our own century second only in its appetites and accomplishment as the Elizabethan Age. (T. S. Eliot's "The Waste Land" refers to past traditions as "these fragments I have shored against my ruin.") Eliot's colleague, Ezra Pound, who opened anew the book of poetry from classical Latin through Provençal and the work of early Chinese poets, remains the patron of those who ferry poetry from one language to another.

Thanks in great part to the example of Pound's adventurous reading, and his conviction that the task of translation was a major responsibility for living poets, this book is able to include poetry from quarters of Europe that have long gone without English-language readers. The unique idiom of American poetry, without Pound's authority, might have been trapped in a sullen provincalism: he connected the American vernacular with a European past.

In twentieth-century Europe, poetry flourished where ordinary citizens and poets themselves frequently did not: in Russia, Marina Tsvetayeva, onetime lover of Osip Mandelstam, inherited the incantations of Russian antiquity, returned to Russia during the Great Terror of 1937, and after the loss of both husband and child, hanged herself. Mandelstam's poems survived in part because his wife committed them to memory before his death in the Gulag; Boris Pasternak disguised his own poems as the work of his doomed hero in his novel, *Dr. Zhivago*. Eugenio Montale likewise turned to the autobiographical in a series of motets in which an impossible love, and the pressure of circumstance in Fascist Italy, forced the poetic imagination inward.

A recovery of lost languages, a revival of literary traditions in long eclipse, is part of twentieth-century poetic ingenuity and art. Poetry in the caustic Yiddish language (much of it written in America) enjoyed a Golden Age in the first part of the century. Verse in two ancient tongues, Hebrew and

Gaelic, has once more come into its own. Memory became an obsessive and incandescent concern for poets in an age where historical recollection is often corrupted into *Agitprop* or turned mute in the observance of collective tragedy. The German poet Johannes Bobrowski, who wrote as a Christian poet in a postwar Marxist state, found an ancient homeland in language: the sorcerous and archaic speech of the ancient Pruzzians in a long-vanished Eastern Europe. One of his translators has called his naming of an imaginary country, "Samartia," "a language of lost content, creating what never was and what cannot be." Many poets from Eastern Europe carry on Bobrowski's forlorn intention and his despairing poetic of forgotten territories and the crystalline word.

Poets in cultures under the stress of the contemporary tirelessly unpack the past, like the Irish Austin Clarke who wrote in the mode of the Jacobite song, referring to lyrics written during a period of national eclipse in which the very word *heifer* was an encoded word for Ireland. Clarke thought the symbol harkened back to cattle myths originating in the *Rig Veda*. In the poetry of Vasko Popa, the reader can find a short history of the Serbian people and legends using mythological, alchemical, and Christian symbolism: his Saint Sava, patron saint of the Serbian people, shepherds and protects the wolves who represents the Serbs themselves. The Mexican Octavio Paz, whose *Sunstone* is excerpted here, structured it on the complex Aztec calendar and its measurement of the cycles of the planet Venus. The poem is a single cyclic sentence in which the first six lines are repeated as the last.

The eclectic drive of modernist poetry, like the exotic wanderings of the twentieth-century painters closely associated with many poets, was strong in Spain and in the poetry of Latin America. Lorca's lament for the death of a Spanish bullfighter is not only a premonition of his own violent death but a tribute to multiple traditions: Gongora's manneristic metaphors, the *romanceros* and Arabic *qasidas* of medieval Spain, and the demonic irrationality of the flamenco dancer. Lorca, whom Robert Bly calls "the poet of desire" was shot by Falangist soldiers in the opening days of the Spanish Civil War. Pablo Neruda, a continent away in Chile, was shattered by Lorca's death and probed Macchu Picchu as a place between "the inner roots of the poet and the past of Latin American man."

The modernist experiment, the great variety of poets who undertook its challenge, using intricate strategies from Expressionism and Surrealism onward resulted in much work that is often perceived as "difficult." If its difficulty requires defense, perhaps it is most helpful to remember Coleridge's advice that "poetry gives most pleasure only when . . . not perfectly understood," and I. A. Richards's afterthought that "faint stars are seen best when you do not stare at them too directly."

The final section of this book unfolds the ways in which world poetry, from the earliest millennia to the present, has come full circle. Rafael Alberti, in exile, recreates a museum of the mind of ravaged Europe; Osip Mandelstam echoes Ovid's departure from his loved ones; Gunnar Ekelöf travels to the netherworld of dreams and visions where there is no barrier between past and present: such poets cross borders without dissolving the unique achievement and vividness of cultural differences. Thus they intensify, make necessary, and provide what we identify as "the poem itself."

K. W.

❦ 1

POETRY IN THE LANGUAGES OF CONTINENTAL EUROPE

German

❦ Stefan George (1868–1933)
THE ANTICHRIST

"He comes from the mountain, he stands in the grove!
Our own eyes have seen it: the wine that he wove
From water, the corpses he wakens."

O could you but hear it, at midnight my laugh:
My hour is striking; come step in my trap;
Now into my net stream the fishes.

The masses mass madder, both numbskull and sage;
They root up the arbors, they trample the grain;
Make way for the new Resurrected.

I'll do for you everything heaven can do.
A hair-breadth is lacking—you gape too confused
To sense that your senses are stricken.

I make it all facile, the rare and the earned;
Here's something like gold (I create it from dirt)
And something like scent, sap, and spices—

And what the great prophet himself never dared:
The art without sowing to reap out of air
The power still lying fallow.

The Lord of the Flies is expanding his Reich;
All treasures, all blessings are swelling his might . . .
Down, down with the handful who doubt him!

Cheer louder, you dupes of the ambush of hell;
What's left of life's essence, you squander its spells
And only on doomsday feel paupered.

Then you'll hang out your tongues, but the trough has been
            drained;
You'll panic like cattle whose farm is ablaze . . .
And dreadful the blast of the trumpet.

                                        Peter Viereck

DO NOT PONDER TOO MUCH

Do not ponder too much
Meanings that cannot be found—
The symbol-scenes that no man understands:

The wild swan that you shot, that you kept alive
In the yard, for a while, with shattered wing—
He reminded you, you said, of a faraway creature:
Your kindred self that you had destroyed in him.
He languished with neither thanks for your care nor rancor,
But when his dying came,
His fading eye rebuked you for driving him now
Out of a known into a new cycle of things.

                                        Stanley Burnshaw

❧ Rainer Maria Rilke (1875–1926)

ORPHEUS, EURYDICE, HERMES

This was the eerie mine of souls.
Like silent silver-ore
they veined its darkness. Between roots
the blood that flows off into humans welled up,
looking dense as porphyry in the dark.
Otherwise, there was no red.

There were cliffs
and unreal forests. Bridges spanning emptiness
and that huge gray blind pool
hanging above its distant floor

like a stormy sky over a landscape.
And between still gentle fields
a pale strip of road unwound.

They came along this road.

In front the slender man in the blue cloak,
mute, impatient, looking straight ahead.
Without chewing, his footsteps ate the road
in big bites; and both his hands hung
heavy and clenched by the pour of his garment
and forgot all about the light lyre,
become like a part of his left hand,
rose tendrils strung in the limbs of an olive.
His mind like two minds.
While his gaze ran ahead, like a dog,
turned, and always came back from the distance
to wait at the next bend —
his hearing stayed close, like a scent.
At times it seemed to reach all the way back
to the movements of the two others
who ought to be following the whole way up.
And sometimes it seemed there was nothing behind him
but the echo of his own steps, the small wind
made by his cloak. And yet
he told himself: they were coming, once;
said it out loud, heard it die away . . .
They *were* coming. Only they were two
who moved with terrible stillness. Had he been allowed
to turn around just once (wouldn't that look back
mean the disintegration of this whole work,
still to be accomplished) of course he would have seen them,
two dim figures walking silently behind:

the god of journeys and secret tidings,
shining eyes inside the traveler's hood,
the slender wand held out in front of him,
and wings beating in his ankles;
and his left hand held out to: her.

This woman who was loved so much, that from one lyre
more mourning came than from women in mourning;
that a whole world was made from mourning, where
everything was present once again: forest and valley
and road and village, field, river, and animal;
and that around this mourning-world, just as
around the other earth, a sun
and a silent star-filled sky wheeled,
a mourning-sky with displaced constellations —:
this woman who was loved so much . . .

But she walked alone, holding the god's hand,
her footsteps hindered by her long graveclothes,
faltering, gentle, and without impatience.
She was inside herself, like a great hope,
and never thought of the man who walked ahead
or the road that climbed back toward life.
She was inside herself. And her being dead
filled her like tremendous depth.
As a fruit is filled with its sweetness and darkness
she was filled with her big death, still so new
that it hadn't been fathomed.

She found herself in a resurrected
virginity; her sex closed
like a young flower at nightfall.
And her hands were so weaned from marriage
that she suffered from the light
god's endlessly still guiding touch
as from too great an intimacy.

She was no longer the blond woman
who sometimes echoed in the poet's songs,
no longer the fragrance, the island of their wide bed,
and no longer the man's to possess.

She was already loosened like long hair
and surrendered like the rain
and issued like massive provisions.
She was already root.

And when all at once the god stopped
her, and with pain in his voice
spoke the words: he has turned around—,
she couldn't grasp this and quietly said: who?

But far off, in front of the bright door
stood someone whose face
had grown unrecognizable. He just stood and watched,
how on this strip of road through the field
the god of secret tidings, with a heartbroken expression,
silently turned to follow the form
already starting back along the same road,
footsteps hindered by long graveclothes,
faltering, gentle, and without impatience.

Franz Wright

AUTUMN DAY

Lord: it is time. The summer was immense.
Stretch out your shadow on the sundial's face,
and on the meadows let the winds go loose.

Command the last fruits to be full in time;
grant them even two more southerly days,
press them toward fulfillment soon and chase
the last sweetness into the heavy wine.

Whoever has no house now, will build none.
Who is alone now, will stay long alone,
will lie awake, read, get long letters written,
and through the streets that follow up and down
will wander restless, when the leaves are driven.

John Felsteiner

ARCHAIC TORSO OF APOLLO

We never knew his head and all the light
that ripened in his fabled eyes. But
his torso still glows like a candelabra,
in which his gazing, turned down low,

holds fast and shines. Otherwise the surge
of the breast could not blind you, nor a smile
run through the slight twist of the loins
toward that center where procreation thrived.

Otherwise this stone would stand deformed and curt
under the shoulders' invisible plunge
and not glisten just like wild beasts' fur;

and not burst forth from all its contours
like a star: for there is no place
that does not see you. You must change your life.

Edward Snow

THE PANTHER

Im Jardin des Plantes, Paris

Always passing bars has dulled
His sight so, it will hold no more.
For him, there are a thousand bars;
Behind the thousand bars, no world.

The soft walk of his strong, lithe strides
Turns in the smallest of all orbits
Like the dance of force around an axis
Where a great will stands stupefied.

Only sometimes, the curtain of his eye
Lifts, noiselessly—an image enters,
That runs through his tense, arrested members
Into the heart, to die.

W. D. Snodgrass

BEFORE SUMMER RAIN

All at once something
from the green world's gone;
something . . . the park comes right up
to the window—without a sound.

A plover whistles in the wood,
grave and urgent, like Jerome,
desert saint poised to translate
out of whiteness, skulls and bones,

whose effort the rain will echo.
The chateau walls, as if oppressed
by the brooding paintings in their frames,
recede; reluctant to hear our words betray us.

And the worn tapestries are strewn
with the off light of childhood
afternoons you feared would never end.

Mark Rudman

SPRING HAS RETURNED

Spring has returned. The earth is
like a child who knows poems.
Many, many . . . She gets the prize
for the hardship of extensive learning.

Her teacher was strict.
We liked the white in the old man's beard.
Now, as to what the blue is, the green,
we can ask her: She knows, she knows.

Earth, off from work, lucky one, play now
with us children. We want to catch you,
jubilant earth. The most joyous succeeds.

Ah, what the old man taught her—the manifold
and what is written in roots and in long,
difficult stems: She sings it. She sings.

Charles Haseloff

🙊 Gottfried Benn (1886–1956)

THIS IS BAD

Someone hands you an English thriller,
highly recommended.
You don't read English.

You've worked up a thirst
for something you can't afford.

You have deep insights,
brand new, and they sound
like an academic glossing Hölderlin.

You hear the waves at night
ramping against the shore
and you think: that's what waves do.

Worse: you're asked out
when at home you get better coffee,
silence, and you don't expect to be amused.

Awful: not to die in summer
under a bright sky
when the rich dirt
falls easily from the shovel.

Harvey Shapiro

BEFORE A CORNFIELD

Thus he addressed the cornfield:
The truth and beauty of cornflowers
look good to female painters.
I'll take the dark poppies.
They make me think of bloody crusts,

menstruation,
stress, gasps, hunger, death.
In short, the way a man goes to it.

Harvey Shapiro

QUATERNARY

I

The worlds are drunk and drinking
to create new room,
and the last Quaternaries are sinking
the Ptolemaic dream.
Decline, holocausts, failures
in toxic spheres, cold,
still a few Stygian souls
solitary, high and old.

II

Come—let them rise and sink
the cycles are breaking out,
violin, age-old Sphinx,
and from Babylon a gate,
Jazz from the Rio del Grande,
Swing and a prayer,
by sinking fires, from the border,
where in ash all things disappear.

I slit the gorge of the mutton
and filled the fosse with blood,
the shadows came, met one
another here—I listened hard—
each one drank and recounted
tales of swords and decaying,
the steer- and swan-mounted
women cried in their train.

Quaternary cycles—scenes,
but they leave you unaware,
is the last thing now the tears
or is it desire—
or refracting a few colors
if both are a rainbow,
mirrored or deceived—
you know, you don't know.

Colossal brains are bending
over their then and when,
they watch the thread unwinding

that the ancient spider spins,
with snuffling in every distance
on everything that fails,
breeding their own resistance
the world observing itself.

One of God's dreams
looked for a while at itself,
playfully, and in derision
the old Spinnerman looks too,
then he gathers asphodels
and wanders along the Styx—
leave suffering for the last ones
leave them stories to tell
All Souls' Evening—
"Fini du tout."

Teresa Iverson

Georg Trakl (1887–1914)

TO THE CHILD ELIS

Elis, when the blackbird calls in the black forest,
This is your oblivion.
Your lips drink the cool of the blue rockspring.

Let go, when your brow softly bleeds
Ancient legends
And dark readings of birdflight.

But you pass with soft footsteps into the night
Which is hanging full of purple grapes,
And you move your arms more beautifully in the blue.

A thornbush sings
Where your moonlit eyes are.
Oh how long, Elis, have you been dead!

Your body is a hyacinth,
Into which a monk dips his waxen fingers.
A black cavern is our silence,

From which at times a gentle beast steps
And slowly lowers its heavy eyelids.
Upon your temples drops black dew,

The final gold of fallen stars.

Robert Firmage

ELIS

1

Perfect is the silence of this golden day.
"Beneath ancient oaktrees
You appear, Elis, at rest with wide eyes.

Their blue mirrors the slumber of lovers.
On your mouth
Their rosy sighs were stilled.

At evening the fisherman hauled in his heavy nets.
A good shepherd
Leads his flock along the forest's edge.
Oh how righteous, Elis, are your days!

Softly the blue silence
Of the olive tree sinks near the naked walls,
The dark song of an old man dies away.

A golden skiff,
Your heart rocks, Elis, on the lonely sky.

2

A gentle glockenspiel sings in Elis' breast
At evening,
When his head sinks into the black pillow.

A blue prey
Bleeds softly in the thornbrush.

A brown tree stands in isolation there;
Its blue fruits have fallen from it.

Signs and stars
Sink softly in the evening pond.

Beyond the hill it has turned winter.

At night
Blue doves drink up the icy sweat
That flows from Elis' crystal brow.

Along black walls
Forever drones the lonely wind of God.

Robert Firmage

DECLINE

to Karl Borromaeus Heinrich

Above the white pond
The wild birds have flown away.
An icy wind blows from our stars at evening.

Above our graves
The shattered brow of night is bowed.
We rock beneath the oaktrees in a silver skiff.

The white walls of the city ring forever.
Beneath thorn arches,
O my brother, we blind hands climb toward midnight.

Robert Firmage

DE PROFUNDIS

It is a stubble field, where a black rain is falling.
It is a brown tree, that stands alone.
It is a hissing wind, that encircles empty houses.
How melancholy the evening is.

Beyond the village,
The soft orphan garners the sparse ears of corn.
Her eyes graze, round and golden, in the twilight
And her womb awaits the heavenly bridegroom.

On the way home
The shepherd found the sweet body
Decayed in a bush of thorns.

I am a shadow far from darkening villages.
I drank the silence of God
Out of the stream in the trees.

Cold metal walks on my forehead.
Spiders search for my heart.
It is a light that goes out in my mouth.

At night, I found myself in a pasture,
Covered with rubbish and the dust of stars.

In a hazel thicket
Angels of crystal rang out once more.

James Wright

✍ Bertolt Brecht (1898–1956)

CONTEMPLATING HELL

Contemplating Hell, as I once heard it,
My brother Shelley found it to be a place
Much like the city of London. I,
Who do not live in London, but in Los Angeles,
Find, contemplating Hell, that it
Must be even more like Los Angeles.

Also in Hell,
I do not doubt it, there exist these opulent gardens
With flowers as large as trees, wilting, of course,
Very quickly, if they are not watered with very expensive water. And
    fruitmarkets
With great heaps of fruit, which nonetheless

Possess neither scent nor taste. And endless trains of autos,
Lighter than their own shadows, swifter than
Foolish thoughts, shimmering vehicles, in which
Rosy people, coming from nowhere, go nowhere.
And houses, designed for happiness, standing empty,
Even when inhabited.

Even the houses in Hell are not all ugly.
But concern about being thrown into the street
Consumes the inhabitants of the villas no less
Than the inhabitants of the barracks.

Robert Firmage

ON READING A RECENT GREEK POET

After the wailing had already begun
along the walls, their ruin certain,
the Trojans fidgeted with bits of wood
in the three-ply doors, itsy-bitsy
pieces of wood, fussing with them.
And began to get their nerve back and feel hopeful.

John Peck

OF POOR B. B.

I, Bertolt Brecht, came out of the black forests.
My mother moved me into the cities while I lay

Inside her body. And the chill of the forests
Will be inside me till my dying day.

In the asphalt city I'm at home. From the very start
Provided with every unction and sacrament:
With newspapers. And tobacco. And brandy.
To the end mistrustful, lazy and content.

I'm polite and friendly to people. I put on
A stiff hat because that's what they do.
I say: they're animals with a quite peculiar smell
And I say: Does it matter? I am too.

Sometimes in the morning on my empty rocking chairs
I'll sit a woman or two, and with an untroubled eye
Look at them steadily and say to them:
Here you have someone on whom you can't rely.

Towards evening it's men that I gather around me
And then we address one another as 'gentlemen'.
They're resting their feet on my table tops
And say: Things will get better for us. And I don't ask: When?

In the gray light before morning the pine-trees piss
And their vermin, the birds, raise their twitter and cheep.
At that hour I drain my glass in town, then throw
The cigar butt away and worriedly go to sleep.

We have sat, an easy generation
In houses thought to be indestructible
(Thus we built those tall boxes on the island of Manhattan
And those thin antennae that amuse the Atlantic swell.)

Of those cities will remain: what passed through them, the wind!
The house makes glad the consumer: he clears it out.
We know that we're only tenants, provisional ones,
And after us there will come: nothing worth talking about.

In the earthquakes to come, I very much hope,
I shall keep my Virginia alight, embittered or no,
I, Bertolt Brecht, carried off to the asphalt cities
From the black forests inside my mother long ago.

Michael Hamburger

CONCERNING THE INFANTICIDE, MARIE FARRAR

Marie Farrar, born in April,
No marks, a minor, rachitic, both parents dead,

Allegedly, up to now without police record,
Committed infanticide, it is said,
As follows: in her second month, she says,
With the aid of a barmaid she did her best
To get rid of her child with two douches,
Allegedly painful but without success.
But you, I beg you, check your wrath and scorn
For man needs help from every creature born.

She then paid out, she says, what was agreed
And continued to lace herself up tight.
She also drank liquor with pepper mixed in it
Which purged her but did not cure her plight.
Her body distressed her as she washed the dishes,
It was swollen now quite visibly.
She herself says, for she was still a child,
She prayed to Mary most earnestly.
But you, I beg you, check your wrath and scorn
For man needs help from every creature born.

Her prayers, it seemed, helped her not at all.
She longed for help. Her trouble made her falter
And faint at early mass. Often drops of sweat
Broke out in anguish as she knelt at the altar.
Yet until her time had come upon her
She still kept secret her condition.
For no one believed such a thing had happened,
That she, so unenticing, had yielded to temptation.
But you, I beg you, check your wrath and scorn
For man needs help from every creature born.

And on that day, she says, when it was dawn,
As she washed the stairs it seemed a nail
Was driven into her belly. She was wrung with pain.
But still she secretly endured her travail.
All day long while hanging out the laundry
She racked her brains till she got it through her head
She had to bear the child and her heart was heavy.
It was very late when she went up to bed.
But you, I beg you, check your wrath and scorn
For man needs help from every creature born.

She was sent for again as soon as she lay down:
Snow had fallen and she had to go downstairs.
It went on till eleven. It was a long day.
Only at night did she have time to bear.
And so, she says, she gave birth to a son.
The son she bore was just like all the others.
She was unlike the others but for this
There is no reason to despise this mother.

You, too, I beg you, check your wrath and scorn
For man needs help from every creature born.

Accordingly I will go on with the story
Of what happened to the son that came to be.
(She says she will hide nothing that befell)
So let it be a judgment upon both you and me.
She says she had scarcely gone to bed when she
Was overcome with sickness and she was alone,
Not knowing what would happen, yet she still
Contrived to stifle all her moans.
And you, I beg you, check your wrath and scorn
For man needs help from every creature born.

With her last strength, she says, because
Her room had now grown icy cold, she then
Dragged herself to the latrine and there
Gave birth as best she could (not knowing when)
But toward morning. She says she was already
Quite distracted and could barely hold
The child for snow came into the latrine
And her fingers were half numb with cold.
You too, I beg you, check your wrath and scorn
For man needs help from every creature born.

Between the latrine and her room, she says,
Not earlier, the child began to cry until
It drove her mad so that she says
She did not cease to beat it with her fists
Blindly for some time till it was still.
And then she took the body to her bed
And kept it with her there all through the night:
When morning came she hid it in the shed.
But you, I beg you, check your wrath and scorn
For man needs help from every creature born.

Marie Farrar, born in April,
An unmarried mother, convicted, died in
The Meissen penitentiary,
She brings home to you all men's sin.
You who bear pleasantly between clean sheets
And give the name "blessed" to your womb's weight
Must not damn the weakness of the outcast,
For her sin was black but her pain was great.
Therefore, I beg you, check your wrath and scorn
For man needs help from every creature born.

                                        H. R. Hays

THE MASK OF EVIL

On my wall hangs a Japanese carving,
The mask of an evil demon, decorated with gold lacquer.
Sympathetically I observe
The swollen veins of the forehead, indicating
What a strain it is to be evil.

H. R. Hays

❧ Friedrich Georg Jünger (b. 1898)

ULTIMA RATIO

Like vapour, the titanic scheme
is dissipated,
everything grows rusty now
that they created.

They hoped to make their craze
the lasting Plan,
now it falls apart everywhere,
sheet steel and span.

Raw chaos lies heaped up
on wide display.
Be patient. Even the fag-ends
will crumble away.

Everything they made contained
what brought their fall
and the great burden they were
crushes them all.

Les Murray

❧ Johannes Bobrowski (1917–1965)

WOODLAND GOD

Jagged mouth,
thicket, the eyes
overgrown with reeds, the convulsive
head of the hunchback—

through the ferns
he steps, flays the birch-tree,
scatters

alder branches;
over the crows' nests
he drags the wind.

But restless, the men
follow after him; he kills
suddenly, in the middle of prosperity.
Listen! In the fog he reels,
drunk with berry-pulp. Swallow,
my small animal of pain
sets out from its cry.

Rich Ives

DEAD LANGUAGE

He with the beating wings
outside who brushes the door,
that is your brother, you hear him.
Laurio he says, water,
a bow, colourless, deep.

He came down with the river,
drifting around mussel
and snail, spread like a fan
on the sand and was green.

Warne he says and *wittan*,
the crow has no tree,
I have the power to kiss you,
I dwell in your ear.

Tell him you do not
want to listen —
he comes, an otter, he comes
swarming like hornets, he cries,
a cricket, he grows with the marsh
under your house, he whispers
in the well, *smordis* you hear,
your black alder will wither,
and die at the fence tomorrow.

Ruth Mead and Matthew Mead

NOVGOROD: COMING OF THE SAINTS

Now
as day breaks, light

sets out over the shores, the lake
lifts into cumulus,
around its wings birds
darken and shine,

where the wood image
floated, green graining
and the dark face
of Nicholas, a wave's
green fingers pressed it
under the river,

and came Anthony
the Stranger, a stone
wafting him over the waveless
flood, bore the man
who stepped easily
ashore: he
had seen the city,

towers and roofs,
over mountains those walls
lifting and plunging in volleys
of dark and bright fliers,
and one turret inscribed
steeply against sky.

So be it. Across my way
a cross has fallen,
sayeth Anthony, a stone —
So, fool, you also, fool,
go, fools and holy babes
over the quivering bridge.

They pass on crutches, rags
flapping their spindly arms, ancient
windbirds out of the winters.

Down the road you come shouting!
Lift this stone for me.

                    John Peck

IN THE TORRENT

Downstream the raft plunged
in the pale gray of the foreign
shore, glittering,
receding, in the gray

of slanting surfaces, mirror
light flashing.

Borne down, the Baptist's
severed head, hair
matted, uprooted
where a hand's blue-tinged
loose nails scratched.

As I loved you, your heart
was unruly, the roast spitted on the beating
fire, the mouth, that poured open,
open, the torrent
came down and rose
with the herons, leaves
fell and filled its bed.

We bent down over the stunned
fish, wearing scales
trod the cricket's song,
over the sand, out of shoreline
arbors, we came
here to sleep, no one
walked around the bed, no one
put out the mirror, no one
will wake us
in time.

Mark Rudman

ஐ Paul Celan (Paul Ancel, 1920–1970)

DEATH FUGUE

Black milk of daybreak we drink it at sundown
we drink it at noon in the morning we drink it at night
we drink and we drink it
we dig a grave in the breezes there one lies unconfined
A man lives in the house he plays with the serpents he writes
he writes when dusk falls to Germany your golden hair
                                      Margarete
he writes it and steps out of doors and the stars are flashing
                                  he whistles his pack out
he whistles his Jews out in earth has them dig for a grave
he commands us strike up for the dance

Black milk of daybreak we drink you at night
we drink in the morning at noon we drink you at sundown
we drink and we drink you

A man lives in the house he plays with the serpents he writes
he writes when dusk falls to Germany your golden hair
                                        Margarete
your ashen hair Shulamith we dig a grave in the breezes
                                there one lies unconfined.

He calls out jab deeper into the earth you lot you others sing
                                now and play
he grabs at the iron in his belt he waves it his eyes are blue
jab deeper you lot with your spades you others play on for
                                        the dance

Black milk of daybreak we drink you at night
we drink you at noon in the morning we drink you at
                                        sundown
we drink you and we drink you
a man lives in the house your golden hair Margarete
your ashen hair Shulamith he plays with the serpents

He calls out more sweetly play death death is a master from
                                        Germany
he calls out more darkly now stroke your strings then as
                                smoke you will rise into air
then a grave you will have in the clouds there one lies
                                        unconfined

Black milk of daybreak we drink you at night
we drink you at noon death is a master from Germany
we drink you at sundown and in the morning we drink and
                                we drink you
death is a master from Germany his eyes are blue
he strikes you with leaden bullets his aim is true
a man lives in the house your golden hair Margarete
he sets his pack on to us he grants us a grave in the air
he plays with the serpents and daydreams death is a master
                                        from Germany
your golden hair Margarete
your ashen hair Shulamith

                        Michael Hamburger

SHOT FORTH

SHOT FORTH
in the emerald race,

hatching of grubs, hatching of stars, with every
keel

I search for you,
Fathomless.

Katharine Washburn and Margaret Guillemin

PSALM

No One kneads us anew from earth and clay,
no one addresses our dust.
No One.

Laudeamus te, No One.
For your sake would we
bloom forth
unto
You.

Nothing
were we, and are we and
will be, all abloom:
this Nothing's-, this
nomansrose.

With
stylus heaven-bright,
with stamen heaven-wasted,
with corona dyed in crimson
by words of darker purple, words we sang
over, o over
the thorn.

Katharine Washburn and Margaret Guillemin

MATIÈRE DE BRETAGNE

Gorselight, yellow, the slopes
fester to heaven, the thorn
courts the wound, bells are tolling
down there, it is evening, the Void
rolls its oceans to vespers
the bloodsail is heading for you.

Dry, landlocked
the streambed behind you, silt
chokes its hour, the milky
creeks whisper in mud, stonedriller,
clumped below, gapes into arch-blue, a shrub

transitory, beautiful,
greets your memory.

(Hands, did you
know me? I took
the forked path you showed me, my mouth
spewed its gravel, I went on, my time,
a wandering snowdrift, cast its shadow—did you know me?)

Hands, the wound
thorncourted, bells toll,
hands, the Void, its oceans
hands, in gorselight, the
bloodsail
is heading for you.

You
you teach
you teach your hands
you teach your hands you teach
you teach your hands
                    to sleep.

Katharine Washburn and Margaret Guillemin

✎ Erich Fried (1921–1988)

THE MEASURES TAKEN

The lazy are slaughtered
the world grows industrious

The ugly are slaughtered
the world grows beautiful

The foolish are slaughtered
the world grows wise

The sick are slaughtered
the world grows healthy

The sad are slaughtered
the world grows merry

The old are slaughtered
the world grows young

The enemies are slaughtered
the world grows friendly

The wicked are slaughtered
the world grows good

Michael Hamburger

❧ Ingeborg Bachmann (1926–1973)

FOG LAND

In winter my loved one retires
to live with the beasts of the forest.
That I must be back before morning
the vixen knows well, and she laughs.
Now the low clouds quiver! And down
on my upturned collar there falls
a landslide of brittle ice.

In winter my loved one retires,
a tree among trees, and invites
the crows in their desolation
into her beautiful boughs. She knows
that as soon as night falls the wind
lifts her stiff, hoar-frost-embroidered
evening gown, sends me home.

In winter my loved one retires,
a fish among fishes, and dumb.
Slave to the waters she ripples
with her fins' gentle motion within,
I stand on the bank and look down
till ice floes drive me away,
her dipping and turning hidden.

And stricken again by the blood-cry
of the bird that tautens his pinions
over my head, I fall down
on the open field: she is plucking
the hens, and she throws me a whitened
collar bone. This round my neck,
off I go through the bitter down.

My loved one, I know, is unfaithful,
and sometimes she stalks and she hovers
on high-heeled shoes to the city
and deeply in bars with her straw
will kiss the lips of the glasses,
and finds words for each and for all.
But this language is alien to me.

It is fog land I have seen,
It is fog heart I have eaten.

Michael Hamburger

ARIA I

Wherever we turn in the storm of roses,
thorns illuminate the night. And the thunder
of a thousand leaves, once so quiet on the bushes,
is right at our heels.

Wherever the roses' fire is put out,
rain washes us into the river. Oh distant night!
Yet a leaf that touched us now floats on the waves,
following us to the sea.

Mark Anderson

∿ Hans Magnus Enzenberger (b. 1929)

THE DIVORCE

At first it was an imperceptible tremor of the skin—
"Whatever you say"—where the flesh is darkest.
"What's wrong?"—Nothing. Opaque dreams
of embraces, but on the morning after
the other looks different, strangely bony.
Razor-sharp misunderstandings. "That time in Rome—"
I never said that.—Pause. Rapidly beating heart,
a kind of hate, strange.—"That's not the point."
Repetitions. Brilliantly clear the certainty:
everything is wrong from now on. Odourless, in focus
like a passport photo, this unknown person
with the tea glass at the table, eyes staring.
It is no use no use no use:
litany in the brain, a touch of nausea.
End of reproaches. Slowly the room
fills up to the ceiling with guilt.
The plaintive voice is a stranger's, but the shoes
that drop with a crash to the floor, the shoes are not.
The next time, in an empty restaurant,
slow motion, breadcrumbs, they talk about money,
laughing. The dessert tastes of metal.
Two untouchables. Strident rationality.
"Things could be much worse." But at night
the vindictiveness, the noiseless struggle, anonymous
like two bony barristers, two big crabs

in the water. Then the exhaustion. Slowly
the scabs peel off. Another tobacconist,
a new address. Pariahs, awfully relieved.
Shadows getting paler. Here are the papers.
Here are the keys. Here is the scar.

Herbert Graf

Yiddish

✺ Abraham Reisen (1876–1953)

HOUSEHOLD OF EIGHT

Household of eight.
Beds are two.
When it gets late,
What do they do?

Three with father,
Three with mother:
Limbs
Over each other.

When it's night
And they go to bed,
Mother begins
To wish she were dead.

A resting place
All her own.
Narrow—
But you sleep alone.

Nathan Halper

✺ Moyshe Leyb-Halpern (1886–1933)

IN CENTRAL PARK

Whose fault is it that your tree can't be seen,
Garden of snow, my garden of snow?
Whose fault is it that your tree can't be seen
When the woman strolling through you displays
A bosom that rises and falls in the ways
That a boat on the ocean will toss and careen

Over troubled waves, with twin pirates, yo-ho,
Who cry out that they are twin pirates, yo-ho!
Garden of snow, my garden of snow.

Whose fault is it that there's no stag hereabouts,
Garden of snow, my garden of snow?
Whose fault is it that there's no stag hereabouts
When a priest, who should be as devout as a child
Runs after his hat in the wind so wild—
Hey and ho and hello, he shouts,
And the hat, wildly springing to and fro,
Doesn't hear, wildly springing to and fro,
Garden of snow, my garden of snow?

Whose fault is it that I'm foreign to you,
Garden of snow, my garden of snow?
Whose fault is it that I'm foreign to you
When my funny shawl and my cap appear
Like nothing that anyone else wears here,
When I still have a beard that the wind picks through
Like a woman through straw, for the egg below
For her sick child, a chicken's egg below—
Garden of snow, my garden of snow.

John Hollander

LONG FOR HOME

Long for home and hate your homeland.
What can you be
But a tiny twig
Snapped from a withered tree?
An ashen speck
In a burning tower?
Little soul, raging on your day of woe,
When a man here goes astray
What can he aspire to
But insanity,
To rend himself and be alone?
Weep, then, for your passing years.
Like rain upon the ocean
Fall your tears.

Meyer Schapiro

Dutch

Martinus Nijhoff (1898–1945)

THE NEW STARS

The long-ago, still guiltless generations
gave animals and heroes constellations.
Now that we've committed Golgotha, other
radiations reach us through the night from afar.

Our splendid points of light are torturer's tools,
we see rod, scourge and nails shining like jewels,
the crown of thorns goes trembling up to heaven,
while dice and long-shafted spear nightly are thrown.

Hidden high amidst this immense luster
the crucified one's arms open, secretly.

Who is performing his passion now under
sublunary twilight and Pilate's eye?

Peter, the Handmaiden, Barabas without irons.

No cock crows. No dog barks. It stays out, our sun.

Raphael Rudnik

THE LIGHT

The light, God's white light breaks and must bedizen:
Colors are the deeds done by light as it breaks.
Life itself breaks, bright crowds of things happen,
my soul must break into words as it speaks.

Only to those who dare to die, life is given:
O see! blood run down the nails as it leaks!
My windows are open, the doors all open—
Here is my heart, my body, how it breaks!

The ground lies soft with spring. A hazy green
Weaves itself through the trees. People are seen
Walking alongside calm ponds in the grass.

Upon that pole, a body strong bonds fasten,
soul torn between love and words until broken:
These are the deeds of the man I once was.

Raphael Rudnik

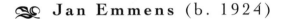 Jan Emmens (b. 1924)

THE LION OF JUDAH

Now that I know so much, I know better
that I feel much less, only
sometimes I've a hankering to be
the Lion of Judah, Cuirassier
of eighteen-thirty, frog in the Achterhoek,
a queer mug altogether, Sinbad's Roc,
townclerk of Amalfi in eleven-eighty.

I see of course that this is out of the question,
and rake with care at my garden, astounding myself
over a pebble, three ants and a sparrow
who feels uneasy in all that silence.

Adrienne Rich

Fritzi Harmsen van Beek (b. 1927)

INTRODUCTION TO A PRAYER

One day when the sun shone on the water and Golden-
march found the cuckoo's young in her bed

more lovable than dandelions, stronger than chick-
like mimosa feathers (or probably the opposite)

and called him Dog's Frog for, naked, red and with
the grim face of dependency on love was he. And:

—Little father, little father, may I keep him?—No child,
you must return him to the King of Life and Death.

And Death, so she took a long knife and butchered the old
neck in the late hour, to let the blood drain off

with the sunset. So she did. And her young in a basin by
the window to let it grow like a cabbage. Hey, dollikin,

then the tables grew crooked, the mirrors blurred and
money still scarcer. And when his small voice

wept: Eat heartily, she sat with wolves and magicians
deep in the gardens, or worse, high on the roof trans
parent with wellbeing but too torn and too badly informed
to see the spoon in their beaks, as amorous

as a waiter and much more obsequious. Bad service was
often the complaint, but ah well, pom pom pom. So she got

a beating on her behind with a bunch of plastic flowers
bought with money from his piggybank and he asked for a reckoning!

Well, she said: Think of me as of that cat, whose penance
you wrote out for her because she couldn't write herself:

"Mothers may not eat mice, enchanted rabbits,
princes or dragons. Dieu des Enfants, may they fast

and pray, amen." Repeat a thousand times.

Clare Nicolas White

Finno-Swedish

❧ Edith Södergran (1892–1923)

MY CHILDHOOD TREES

My childhood trees stand tall in the grass
and shake their heads: what has become of you?
Rows of pillars stand like reproaches: you're unworthy
                              to walk beneath us!
You're a child and should know everything,
so why are you fettered by your illness?
You have become a human, alien and hateful.
As a child, you talked with us for hours,
your eyes were wise.
Now we would like to tell you the secret of your life:
the key to all secrets lies in the grass by the
                              raspberry patch.
We want to shake you up, you sleeper,
we want to wake you, dead one, from your sleep.

Stina Katchadourian

ARRIVAL IN HADES

See, here is eternity's shore,
here the stream murmurs by,
and death plays in the bushes
his same monotonous melody.

Death, why were you silent?
We have come a long way
and are hungry to hear,
we have never had a nurse
who could sing like you.

David McDuff

THE NET

I have the net into which all fishes go.
Blissfully the fisherwoman's quiet breast heaves
when she draws the silver load to herself.
I lift up the riches of the earth on my shoulders.
I bear you, I bear you to a fairy-tale pond.
Upon the shore stands a fisherman with golden fishing rods.
There are gods somewhere behind the densest forests,
we wandering human children want to go nowhere but there.
Up to seek the burning sun of the future beyond the forest.

David McDuff

Swedish

✑ Harry Martinsen (1904–1978)

PEONIES

Summer grew, broadened out;
thickened into positive clumps.
Dark-red farm peonies bulged in the rain.
When they opened their firm-knotted rag balls, she came by,
the lusty queen.
She looked for heavy bouquets,
luxuriant repasts for the senses.
The greenery was wet. Life-wet was the summer-saga:
She had prepared only for life, not for autumn.
Deep in her flesh defiantly she knew

that in time Death would wave to her
with his banner of hay.

William Jay Smith and Leif Sjöberg

Gunnar Ekelöf (1907–1968)

From GUIDE TO THE UNDERWORLD

1

Alone in the quiet Night
the only time I call my own!
Alone in the dark, tied to pain
I see how the Day distracted from the Truth
The Day's Truth: a rain of pinpoints
against skin, hearing and other senses
Alone in the Night fighting against the Truth —
Its pinpoint, its sharp point of light
comes closer in the dark. And that this is
fair play! — The Day gave me
a rain of pinpoints. Can life be pained
out of you? Then let me have Night
whose sting, a single one, a decisive one
is aimed at the light of your eye, the jewel of your soul
is aimed at your heart's being or not being —
You see the point coming close and you beat it aside
It comes close again, you parry
And the darkness receives your lunges
hides them in its dark breast, where perhaps another he
beats wounded — your mirror image
in a mirror-world.

2

*TO THE DIODAR OF SORIA
LIEUTENANT OF THE SACRED SULTAN OF BABYLON*

Ever since I sailed from Calinda in Erminia,
from the Taurus Mountains I described to you, past Cyprus,
a vision, O Diodario, has followed me:
I stood at the rail of the heeling ship
and observed both coasts. Calms
but the ship's rigging took life from an unknown swell
Between the higher coast and the lower was an optical illusion
The sun's reflection from Taurus lengthened the day
The low coast's white cities and small white houses
shone as if the Moon were more brilliant at Paphos
The sea spread out clear and transparent
as if it were one single glance, contemplating

We lay in dead calm. If the wind had blown
the sea's glances would have been beyond reckoning
like the glances of the inhabitants of the cities and houses —
But these houses and cities lay in the past
a distance impossible to sound!
To moor and go ashore, no one could do that!
You will find proof that what we see
is unreal in Time when you see the moonlight
silver the sea's horizon: It is the sun
being mirrored there. But when our eye
in its turn receives the waves' reflections
then our eye has far to go to the horizon
And who can measure an external distance
against the inner distance of the eye?

3

The weather on Death's sea is unpredictable, especially in winter
After a stormy voyage, when the water-casks had been smashed to bits
and lay like rattling ballast in the bilge, and we thirsted
and though the skipper had both seen and invoked Alexander's sister
we ran aground and had to wade to the left bank
of the river that is said to separate Memory from Oblivion:
The left bank, that is memory's, has no water
but on the right, that is oblivion's, there is water

A shadow caught hold of me, she said:
I am *your* shadow, I go where you go!
I shall follow you wherever you go!
I broke free and walked away
halved and indignant:
—As if I were your creature or your image?
Who dares to bargain with the old Jew?
A woman's heart? I go, circumcised
my way, and you must go, unpurchased
the other way!
She laughed:
—Go with your godhead! Look down below!
You, who are favored by god, look deeper!
I said:
—Who here is favored by god?
She replied:
—Look downward, you, endowed with an imageless god!
I looked down. Yes, alone with you, deep under
your womb, in the universe under your feet
that I should have anointed with oil and wild honey
I saw Satan burning in his cloak
made from the fire that has always tormented mortals
with that unendurable glare of riches
with their own obduracy against him. With the eyes of the Shadow
I saw him and the cloak around him like the light

of a distant, majestically burning star
—Even I saw him so, far beyond
the provincial solar arc, far beyond godliness.

4

CAVE OF THE NYMPHS

There is a cave on this coast
accessible only when the sea is calm
a cave with sharp stones that press into your back
a cave with women's names scrawled on the walls
Young fishermen have led their prey here
Strangers, shipwrecked, have been brought here
On the wall the names of women brought here before have made lust grow
Truly, a sacrificial cave

And these young men, who have feigned indifference, rowed them past
and pointed: "There's a cave!" and these girls
who let themselves be rowed and went ashore
believed themselves alone with their secret
or almost alone—
Oh, they are in good company:
For all time a sacrificial cave
Long ago other names were here
Long ago a storming sea crashed down
ancient altars of undressed stone
But for the seer emerges, transparent, in rigid sculpture
the image of the naked woman, the ravished woman
impersonal as the horizon's cleft out there in the cave's mouth
under the seducer with the impersonal face
eyes that speak nothing but the haughtiness of taming
the anonymity of the taker, of the taken
of the taking
The anonymity of the rite and the anonymity of the god—
For every woman, no matter how well tried,
loses her virginity here once again
before the impersonal one who says nothing,
impersonal as the horizon you see through the opening of the cave
over his back
When it is over
and he is gone.

5

"Give me poison to die or dreams to live"—Just now
more than dreams to live I want poison to die
Captain without crew, for they all
have eaten of the lotus, turned to swine I refuse to command—
Alone, exhausted steersman, I too was driven ashore
on a beach strange to me, with these corpses as cargo
Give me water! I have had nothing but brine
Give me water from some stream or spring

Give me the magic water that will wash away the blood
Give me back the island where I was sunk in dreams
There I walked under freedom's yoke, in golden reins
He who has once been stranded in its sucking cleft
doesn't struggle with the rudder, hasn't hands to sail
What he must do is teach them to caress —
Like the prince who once dipped his head in a spring
for one moment felt the vertiginous welling of time
back in Time, 1001 years back, I see you mirror
yourself in your glance that is mine. So have I been stranded
with the Nymph who gives poison to die or dreams to live
With no chart, with no stars, with and against currents
I have once been stranded on the island of the red-blonde nymph.

6

The black shore
you near it, drowning —
bold one of Thásos, who keep swimming
The black shore nears you
drowning one

Now the Swell carries you farther
than the stroke — bold one of Thásos
The swell carries you forward. Perhaps you are
already drowned, but you keep floating
The swell carries you forward, inexorable

You swim no longer, you are drowned
bold one of Thásos. Wind and waves carry
your head closer to the Black Shore
where it shall be dashed against the sharp rock
You drowned one of Thásos.

They say the Moon has set, and
the Pleiades as well, boding
winter. Midnight goes
by. But I lie alone —

I also saw them once
but only six. They say the Seventh
who was involved with a mortal
does not like to be seen

or it is said they dance
in a ring, and the seventh
moves farthest away in the ring
hidden by the others.

The Boulder is rolled upon me
heavy as the Memory I push.

Once I could see, but was mortal.
That is why I lie alone.

It has been said of the Blind Man:
He shall love the invisible.
That is what befits his fate.
That is why he lies alone.

                    Rika Lesser

AYÍASMA*

A one-eyed prison-warder
In charge of the hidden
Sacred well
Gives us water
To pour over our hands
The same water that purified
Mad emperors tormented
By power and suspicion
O filthy lust after power!

I was with Romanós
Beheld the slaughter and the treachery
O filthy lust after power!
Water to cleanse our hands —
Surely even this
The simplest of actions
Can cleanse our hands from all they desired to seize
Our simple hands:
From lust after power from lust after lust —

You say: I am innocent
Because all is possible —

This possible evil
Was sufficient according to our measure.

                    W. H. Auden and Leif Sjöberg

[*Ayíasma (Hagíasma): purifying well. 'The water cult is still alive in Greece and the Near East. A glass of cold water is the holy welcoming drink among the people.']

✎ Tomas Tranströmer (b. 1931)

ALONE

I

One evening in February I came near to dying here.
The car skidded sideways on the ice, out
on the wrong side of the road. The approaching cars—
their lights—closed in.

My name, my girls, my job
broke free and were left silently behind
further and further away. I was anonymous
like a boy in a playground surrounded by enemies.

The approaching traffic had huge lights.
They shone on me while I pulled at the wheel
in a transparent terror that floated like egg white.
The seconds grew—there was space in them—
they grew big as hospital buildings.

You could almost pause
and breathe out for a while
before being crushed.

Then something caught: a helping grain of sand
or a wonderful gust of wind. The car broke free
and scuttled smartly right over the road.
A post shot up and cracked—a sharp clang—it
flew away in the darkness.

Then—stillness. I sat back in my seat-belt
and saw someone coming through the whirling snow
to see what had become of me.

II

I have been walking for a long time
on the frozen Östergötland fields.
I have not seen a single person.

In other parts of the world
there are people who are born, live and die
in a perpetual crowd.

To be always visible—to live
in a swarm of eyes—
a special expression must develop.
Face coated with clay.

The murmuring rises and falls
while they divide up among themselves
the sky, the shadows, the sand grains.

I must be alone
ten minutes in the morning
and ten minutes in the evening.
— Without a programme.

Everyone is queuing at everyone's door.

Many.

One.

Robin Fulton

TO FRIENDS BEHIND A FRONTIER

I

I wrote so meagrely to you. But what I couldn't write
swelled and swelled like an old-fashioned airship
and drifted away at last through the night sky.

II

The letter is now at the censor's. He lights his lamp.
In the glare my words fly up like monkeys on a grille,
rattle it, stop, and bare their teeth.

III

Read between the lines. We'll meet in 200 years
when the microphones in the hotel walls are forgotten
and can at last sleep, become trilobites.

Robin Fulton

BLACK POSTCARDS

I

The calendar full, future unknown.
The cable hums the folksong from no country.
Falling snow on the lead-still sea. Shadows
                wrestle on the dock.

II

In the middle of life it happens that death comes
and takes your measurements. This visit
is forgotten and life goes on. But the suit is
                    sewn in the silence.

Joanna Bankier

HOMEWARDS

A telephone call ran out in the night and glittered over the countryside
    and in the suburbs.
Afterwards I slept uneasily in the hotel bed.
I was like the needle in a compass carried through the forest by an orienteer
    with a thumping heart.

Robin Fulton

ELEGY

I open the first door.
It is a large sunlit room.
A heavy car passes outside
and makes the china quiver.

I open door number two.
Friends! You drank some darkness
and became visible.

Door number three. A narrow hotel room.
View on an alley.
One lamppost shines on the asphalt.
Experience, its beautiful slag.

Robert Bly

❧ Lars Gustafsson (b. 1936)

BALLAD OF THE DOGS

When Ibn Batutta, Arabian traveller,
physician, clear-eyed observer of the world,
born in Maghreb in the fourteenth century, came
to the city of Bulgar, he learnt about the Darkness.
This 'Darkness' was a country, forty days' travel
further to the north. At the end of Ramadan,

when he broke his fast at sunset, he had barely time
to intone the night prayer before day
broke again. The birches glimmered whitely.
Ibn Batutta, Arabian traveller, journeyed
no further north than Bulgar. But the tales he heard
of the Darkness, and of the visits there, engrossed him.
This journey is made only by rich merchants,
who take hundreds of sledges with them, loaded
with food, drink and firewood, for the ground there
is covered with ice and no-one can keep his balance.
Except the dogs: their claws take firm hold
of the eternal ice. No trees, no stones,
no huts can serve the traveller as landmarks.
Only those long-lived dogs are guides into
the Country of the Darkness, those old dogs
who have made the journey many times before.
They can cost a thousand dinars, or even more,
since for their knowledge there is no substitute.
At meals they are always served before the men:
otherwise the leading dog grows angry
and escapes, leaving its master to his fate.
In the great Darkness. After they have travelled
for forty days the merchants make a halt,
place their wares on the ground and return to their camp.
Returning on the following day they find
heaps of sable, ermine, miniver,
set down a little apart from their own pile.
If the merchant is content with this exchange
he takes the skins. If not, he leaves them there.
Then the inhabitants of the Darkness raise
their bid with more furs, or else take back
everything they laid out before, rejecting
the foreigners' goods. Such is the way they trade.
Ibn Batutta returned to Maghreb, and there
at a great age he died. But these dogs,
mute but sagacious, lacking the power of speech
and yet with a blind certainty that guides them
across wind-polished ice into the Darkness,
will never leave us in peace.
We speak, and what we say knows more than we do.
We think, and what we thought runs on before us,
as if that thought knew something we didn't know.
Messages travel through history, a code
masquerading as ideas
but meant for someone other than ourselves.
The history of ideas is not a knowledge of the mind.
And the dogs go on, with sure and swishing steps,
deeper into the Darkness.

Phillip Martin

Norwegian

❧ Rolf Jacobsen (b. 1907)

MEADOWSWEET

Meadowsweet, those dizzying flowers
that arrive midway through summer,
like a secret order swirling their censers
along dips and gullies all over the green fields.

They serve as retinue for the royal clouds
Cumulus and Nimbus, who have descended to the Earth—
so they will not be led through the ditches naked,
but in long processions
with lights swirling like clouds.

Roger Greenwald

GASLIGHT

Now the potato plants are flowering. They've lit up their streets,
rows of whispering lights down endless avenues
in great cities whose cellars are dense with food.
Remote, the moon is growing whiter in its vault,
and the hills shine back faintly
with this sea of lights, these millions of flickering gaslamps
on unending boulevards, far off
where no clocks toll and no trains run
—in those green cities, cellars dark with food.

Roger Greenwald

CRUST ON FRESH SNOW

My soul is hard as stone. I slept with the wind.
He's an unfaithful lover. Now he's with someone else.
He hummed words, prattled in my ear
and stroked my hair. I gave him all my whiteness.
I let him chisel dreams in my soul—of clouds,
fierce seas, and soft flowery hills.
Now I see, cold, it was them he loved.
Where is he now? Tonight my heart froze.

Olav Grinde

✺ Olaf H. Hauge (b. 1908)

ACROSS THE SWAMP

It is the roots from all the trees that have died
out here, that's how you can walk
safely over the soft places.
Roots like these keep their firmness, it's possible
they've lain here centuries.
And there is still some dark remains
of them under the moss.
They are still in the world and hold
you up so you can make it over.
And when you push out into the mountain lake, high
up, you feel how the memory
of that cold person
who drowned himself here once
helps hold up your frail boat.
He, really crazy, trusted his life
to water and eternity.

Robert Bly

Danish

✺ Piet Hein (b. 1905)

NOBLE FUNERALS ARRANGED

The Nobel prize
needs a candidate.
Of course, by the hopeful crowd
you're stunned,
but none is sufficiently
well-known and great,
or sufficiently
Moribund.
Remember, it's not
a scholarship late—
it is
a funeral benefit fund.

Martin Allwood

ꙮ Tove Ditlevsen (1918–1976)

THE ETERNAL THREE

There are two men in the world, who
Are crossing my path, I see,
And one is the man I love,
The other's in love with me.

And one exists in the nightly dreams
Of my sombre soul evermore,
The other stands at the door of my heart
But I will not open the door.

And one once gave me a vernal breath
Of happiness squandered—alack!
The other gave me his whole long life
And got never an hour back.

And one lives hot in the song of my blood
Where love is pure, unbound—
The other is one with the humdrum day
where all our dreams are drowned.

Between these two every woman stands,
In love, belovèd, and white—
And once every hundred years it happens
That both in one unite.

Martin Allwood with John Hollander and Inga Allwood

Finnish

ꙮ Paavo Haavikko (b. 1931)

From THE WINTER PALACE

Bastard Son is born with a tooth in his mouth and hair on his
                                        / head,
he sits at the end of the living-room bench, not in a cradle, not
                                        / on anyone's
        knee,
his hair is ruddy like a snowy spruce forest, and under the
                                        / ruddy glow
Bastard Son walks through the forest, no hat on his head,

he goes out into the world, he is a giant, an inch tall,
he goes out into the world.

Ten years have passed, and the Princess is sleeping, the Giant
/ growing
while sleeping he just grows,
again ten years, and the giant's a giant, full-grown
he walks through the forest.

He sees a dream about three men who carried the world,
they carried the world on their shoulders,
he is amazed, and he is amazed, he laughs, and as he laughs
he falls down, and as he falls down he falls down the way
/ oaks fall down
when they do,
they fall down full length and lie on the ground and sleep,

they sleep, they dream, they fall, the bearers of the world.
In the dream: a golden vessel, in the dream: an open sky.
    The vessels were gold.
The King's men tied our feet to the tops of young trees, bent
/ the trees down.

The colour green bursts in a rage in the trees, we hate
/ immortality.
    It is torn apart.
The green greens in us, we slam into the door-jamb of the air,
    the air weeps for us.

We were the King's bowmen, we are the leaves on the tree,
/ the leaves
    touch air,
we are not weighty like the King's coffers, we go,
    trees,
into the ruddy glow.

                        Anselm Hollo

THREE SHORT POEMS

1

You can't take with you
        even the little bit that's been stolen from you
In Hell, small change
        is perfectly useless

2

The soul against the state.
        The willow against the jail.

No, it grows by the wall,
 a life sentence, with its roots,
outside the walls,
 a living shadow.
The soul against the state.
 The willow against the jail.

3

The woman raises her garment, rain, wind, darkness rise,
when she is full, comes the child,
children, and children bring poverty,
we have visitors: darkness, wind, poverty.

       Anselm Hollo

FIFTEEN EPIGRAMS IN PRAISE OF THE TYRANT

1.

Twice, three times
 may Fate strike. Thereafter
it's the numb beating the numb.

2.

Take heart, Ovid. No sentence
 is longer than life.

3.

Look, life has been constructed this way to make sure
 you won't ever again yearn for this world.

4.

Hades is an even worse place.
 There aren't even any women there.

5.

Don't smile. So you won't become a Buddha
 with that lower-jaw smile. Don't laugh,
so you won't be shown, every moment,
 a reason for doing so.

6.

When you go to the tyrant. Keep your head on a platter.
 Carry the platter in the crook of your arm.
The sharp edge won't hurt.

7.

Before you ask for justice. Make sure
    that you won't get it, just by accident.

8.

The tyrant inspires small poems.
    He doesn't understand what's so special about him.

9.

Plant trees. Exactly against this tree
    may Fascism decisively strike its head.

10.

Precisely the way you divide your small change between two
                                     / pockets
    the tyrant pours your wages in the form of molten gold
into your ears.

11.

When the tyrant is young. Everyone waits
    for him to come to his senses.
Old. For him to die.

12.

It has been proposed that the stars should be removed from sight.
    No one has been against that. The proposal has already
                                   / been accepted.

13.

I always bow down deep before a small tree and a great tyrant.
Great awareness is greater than a small one.
    Be aware.

14.

How decisively
    one's brief moments of clear insight
are ameliorated
             by a good, plausible ideology.

15.

Don't say this to an old idol that's lost its nose.
    It hates everything in existence.

Anselm Hollo

THE BOWMEN

Statecraft and Foresight have gone to their mountain council,
my lord planted his great banner, we have no business there,
alone, I am nothing, it stands to reason,
come and read, I return to Worms and take nail and hammer,

the hand touches the sky, the foot bears down on the ground,
henceforth may nothing separate the hand from the sky, the
/ foot from the
ground,

in the mountains, always winds water and fire, brown dirt,
out of the elements emerge war, bloodshed, and riot,
plague, bad sudden death,
Statecraft and Foresight appear, so do the black men,

honour craves violence,
Foresight sees best when flames glow in the glasses,

but we are here not so much to search in wisdom
as in our hearts,
all of us here not so much to demonstrate foresight
as our readiness.

Anselm Hollo

Estonian

❧ Jaan Kaplinski (b. 1941)

WE STARTED HOME

We started home, my son and I.
Twilight already. The young moon
stood in the western sky and beside it
a single star. I showed them to my son
and explained how the moon should be greeted
and that this star is the moon's servant.
As we neared home, he said
that the moon is far, as far
as that place where we went.
I told him the moon is much, much farther
and reckoned: if one were to walk
ten kilometers each day, it would take
almost a hundred years to reach the moon.
But this was not what he wanted to hear.

The road was already almost dry.
The river was spread on the marsh; ducks and other waterfowl
crowed the beginning of night. The snow's crust
crackled underfoot—it must
have been freezing again. All the houses' windows
were dark. Only in our kitchen,
a light shone. Beside our chimney, the shining moon,
and beside the moon, a single star.

Sam Hamill and Rina Tamm

Lithuanian

❧ Tomas Venclova (b. 1937)

CANTO ELEVEN

> "How, Elpenor, did you get over to the land of shades
> so fast?"
>
> *Odyssey* XI.57

I'm not sure it happened. Through the branches
We suddenly saw one vast deserted harbor,
A concrete pier showing pale and calm
In shade above the muddy water,
Split pile-stakes poking out from the surf.
A wind, starting up from level stretches,
Had steered the sand false, in whorls far darker
Than snapped ship's rigging. It had
The wild air skewered onto masts, all
Wound up in ropes, then heaved down hard
On the whole cove, each thistle and dune.
Heat fluttered the horizon
Like a flag in shreds. There was a boy
Poling a raft knocked together out of disintegrating boards
Across a low stream. The way things looked,
He should have been glad for company.
We saw no one, other than him, on shore.
Something told us this place was just one more
Of many that bring Ithaca to mind.

We were right in the day's fire-core.
The war long past, the journey since
Had crammed our brains full, just like the wave
That snuffs a careless swimmer's breath.
The crunching underfoot was shell, bone,
Pitted rock. Afterwards we lay

Out in the grass, with every trace of nature gone,
Though nature had, far longer back, lost track of us.

A vaulting sunrise. Hissing salt
An unseen moon urged on
Replays the cycle, a tide the soggy corks float on.
Out on iron-clad timbers
Mollusks flash in the sun.

All that darkness a patient gravity
Zeroes in with each surge! One way foam echoes
Is half in memory's cave, half exposed here
Between the dredger's backbone and the pier.

Something gently rasping crept past us.
Shouldering his oar, one voyager
Was walking inland, where no one ever saw
An oar before. Out by the base of a dune
A sand-mole beamed its beady glare
On a trident rusting in sand.

There is no wave. It's some force greater
Than the sum of drops, every split second
The water slips further back from itself, a hairline
Island, death's equator, the grass palmed under
In turning back, in changing over. No history or myth
Had ever made us an offer like this.

Once we changed course, space changed.
First by some trick of perspective,
As if we had each sand-grain shining in our path
Under a magnifying glass, or saw whole
Outcrops of rock through the wrong end of a scope.
Like sounds in some undefined recital hall,
the contours things had fell off. For once
We all agreed it was the heat, so we were not
The least surprised when we happened on our friend
Down by the warehouse wall, the very first of those
You get to see only after your death.

He was the first one.

Vyt Bakaitis

Latvian

❧ Imants Ziedonis (b. 1933)

AT MARUŽA'S

In a shack of trimmed fir struts and a mud floor
trampled solid, a large clay tureen was buried
to the lip in the middle of the floor.
Not many came by here, but down the road a piece —
houses and clearings, and well-worked fields.

Ruža blended her herbal brew here.

Once upon a time, a grim German monk with cross and bible
stumbled into this calm wooded corner
and saw serpents suckling a cow.
The monk blessed himself, cut a hefty branch,
and slew the biggest snake.

So it goes. But no one knew why
Ruža was so suddenly aware.
Horrified, she leapt through the shack door
and began loud wailing:
"O Milk-Mother, my Milk-Mother!"
Coiled and beautiful, with golden ears,
milk leaking from the huge serpent,
seeping into the mouldering, stumpy earth.

And suddenly there was also wailing
in all the houses: "O murdered, O my Milk-Mother!"

As with church bells in later years,
women called through the woods
and in the clustered houses of almost every clan
there was always a woman protecting serpents.
And the lamenting assembled at Ruža's
and cast green grass over the serpent
and wept in the green weeds.

So it was done, Maruža told me.
Ruža didn't own a cow,
but she knew some milk spells —
and when she clapped her knife-handle against
a crock, serpents and toads lugged
themselves from caves, out from under
the thresholds of huts,
and spewed white milk suckled from cows

into the tureen in the middle of the floor.
Ruža always had enough milk.

But the monk reported to holy Rome:

> . . . The first Litvaks I met worshipped (tended) snakes, and every head of a household kept a snake in a corner which he fed and, while she slept in the hay, brought her sacrifice.

And the monks learned much more: how to launch
toads into the air from a slab of see-saw wood,
a toad at one end, a big stone dropped,
catapulting the little creature, who plummets
and splatters, soaking the earth with milk.
And wrote to Rome:

> . . . This non-German people is still in thrall to false gods; they pray to the sun, moon, stars, fire, water, the river, believing garter snakes and evil toads are gods; which, as I myself have to some extent seen, were fat and swollen. After they've been thrown or battered, they burst their bodies leaking bountiful milk.

And during the war, German officers fed at our table, swilling our milk, and stuffed like pigs, undid their belt buckles and passed foul wind; we all felt ashamed, since for children this was forbidden, but apparently among them it's quite common. Probably knights also farted at table, maybe monks as well.

And wrote to Rome:

> The garter snakes were so tame and lethargic that . . . even their children played with them . . . They slept in the children's cradles and supped with children from the same bowl.

Some incomprehensible code of cleanliness sent them into a rage. First they murdered the serpents and sawed down sacrificial linden trees, then they began to burn witches. Even the secret stayed secret. And they wrote to Rome:

> . . . It is clearly known, toads and snakes suckle cows, but what baffling allows them to beguile on demand suckled milk into saucers, and hand it down regained, retained . . .

Barry Callaghan

Russian

ஒ Alexander Blok (1880–1921)

From THE TWELVE

X

making tracks
marching on

   who there

     come on out

but it's the wind
it's the red flag
the red flag marches on

moving on
making tracks

   who there

but it's the dog

aw come on the voice says
get lost you mangy mutt
back where you belong

but he won't get lost
because this is where

moving on
the dog trots on
the dog has joined the 12

got to keep movin got to keep movin
blues fallin down like hail

& the days & the nights
keep on worrying me

for a hellhound on my trail yes
hellhound
on my trail

XI

hey

stop

password

halt   who there

a flag

a sign

no   dumb darkness
no there's someone there

by those houses
can't you see

what the hell play it safe
cut that out   here goes

ack-ack-ack

from the houses back

ack-ack-ack

the blizzard has a good laugh *ack*

ack-ack-ack

ack-ack-ack

sleep hugs the city
the Neva & its silent towers

empty streets & no law
no more juice either
but we'll make it till dawn

see that money-bags at the corner
nose in his collar
something   at his heels   it's a dog

see the bourgeois & the hungry doggy
that's them all right
the bourgeois & his world

the old world
a mangy stray

but who made all that snow
funnels pillars tunnels of snow
wind   wind
no one can stand against

God he says what a night

shut your trap Petya
the voices say
don't you start gospeling now

XII

moving on
trudging on
hungry dog stays on the spoor
and in front   the bloodied flag

& in front of the flag
invisible in the snow
walks one more man

& he walks in stillness
& melts the snowflakes
like a lamp

& he has a wreath on his head
white as roses can be

in front of the blood-drenched flag
walks Jesus Christ

Anselm Hollo

Anna Akhmatova (1889–1966)

THE MUSE

When in the night I await her coming,
My life seems stopped. I ask myself: What
Are tributes, freedom, or youth compared
To this treasured friend holding a flute?
Look, she's coming! She throws off her veil
And watches me, steady and long. I say:
"Was it you who dictated to Dante the pages
Of Hell?" And she answers: "I am the one."

Stanley Burnshaw

From REQUIEM

1935–1940

No foreign sky protected me,
no stranger's wing shielded my face.
I stand as witness to the common lot,
survivor of that time, that place.

1961

Instead of a Preface

In the terrible years of the Yezhov terror I spent seventeen months waiting in line outside the prison in Leningrad. One day somebody in the crowd identified me. Standing behind me was a woman, with lips blue from the cold, who had, of course, never heard me called by name before. Now she started out of the torpor common to us all and asked me in a whisper (everyone whispered there):
"Can you describe this?"
And I said: "I can."
Then something like a smile passed fleetingly over what had once been her face.

Leningrad
1 April 1957

Dedication

Such grief might make the mountains stoop,
reverse the waters where they flow,
but cannot burst these ponderous bolts
that block us from the prison cells
crowded with mortal woe . . .
For some the wind can freshly blow,
for some the sunlight fade at ease,
but we, made partners in our dread,
hear but the grating of the keys,
and heavy-booted soldiers' tread.
As if for early Mass, we rose
and each day walked the wilderness,
trudging through silent street and square,
to congregate, less live than dead.
The sun declined, the Neva blurred,
and hope sang always from afar.
Whose sentence is decreed? . . . That moan,
that sudden spurt of woman's tears,
shows one distinguished from the rest,
as if they'd knocked her to the ground
and wrenched the heart out of her breast,
then let her go, reeling, alone.
Where are they now, my nameless friends
from those two years I spent in hell?

What specters mock them now, amid
the fury of Siberian snows,
or in the blighted circle of the moon?
To them I cry, Hail and Farewell!

March 1940

Prologue

That was a time when only the dead
could smile, delivered from their wars,
and the sign, the soul, of Leningrad
dangled outside its prison house;
and the regiments of the condemned,
herded in the railroad yards,
shrank from the engine's whistle song
whose burden went, "Away, pariahs!"
The stars of death stood over us.
And Russia, guiltless, beloved, writhed
under the crunch of bloodstained boots,
under the wheels of Black Marias.

I

At dawn they came and took you away.
You were my dead: I walked behind,
In the dark room children cried,
the holy candle gasped for air.
Your lips were chill from the icon's kiss,
sweat bloomed on your brow—those deathly flowers!
Like the wives of Peter's troopers in Red Square
I'll stand and howl under the Kremlin towers.

1935

2

Quietly flows the quiet Don;
into my house slips the yellow moon.
It leaps the sill, with its cap askew,
and balks at a shadow, that yellow moon.

This woman is sick to her marrowbone,
this woman is utterly alone,

with husband dead, with son away
in jail. Pray for me. Pray.

3

No, not mine: it's somebody else's wound.
I could never have borne it. So take the thing
that happened, hide it, stick it in the ground.
Whisk the lamps away
                    . . . Night

4

They should have shown you—mocker,
delight of your friends, hearts' thief,
naughtiest girl of Pushkin's town—
this picture of your fated years,
as under the glowering wall you stand,
shabby, three hundredth in line,
clutching a parcel in your hand,
and the New Year's ice scorched by your tears.
See there the prison poplar bending!
No sound. No sound. Yet how many
innocent lives are ending . . .

5

For seventeen months I have cried aloud,
calling you back to your lair.
I hurled myself at the hangman's foot,
You are my son, changed into nightmare.
Confusion occupies the world,
and I am powerless to tell
somebody brute from something human,
or on what day the word spells "Kill!"
Nothing is left but dusty flowers,
the tinkling thurible, and tracks
that lead to nowhere. Night of stone,
whose bright enormous star
stares me straight in the eyes,
promising death, ah soon!

6

The weeks fly out of mind,
I doubt that it occurred:
how into your prison, child,
the white night blazing, stared;
and still, as I draw breath,
they fix their buzzard eyes
on what the high cross shows,
this body of your death.

7

The Sentence

The word dripped like a stone
on my still living breast,
Confess: I was prepared,
am somehow ready for the test.

So much to do today:
kill memory, kill pain,

turn heart into a stone,
and yet prepare to live again.

Not quite. Hot summer's feast
brings rumors of carouse.
How long have I foreseen
this brilliant day, this empty house?

To Death

You will come in any case—so why not now?
How long I wait and wait. The bad times fall.
I have put out the light and opened the door
for you, because you are simple and magical.
Assume, then, any form that suits your wish,
take aim, and blast at me with poisoned shot,
or strangle me like an efficient mugger,
or else infect me—typhus be my lot—
or spring out of the fairy tale you wrote,
the one we're sick of hearing, day and night,
where the blue hatband marches up the stairs,
led by the janitor, pale with fright.
It's all the same to me. The Yenisei swirls,
the North Star shines, as it will shine forever;
and the blue luster of my loved one's eyes
is clouded over by the final horror.

The House on the Fontanka
19 August 1939

9

Already madness lifts its wing
to cover half my soul.
That taste of opiate wine!
Lure of the dark valley!

Now everything is clear.
I admit my defeat. The tongue
of my ravings in my ear
is the tongue of a stranger.

No use to fall down on my knees
and beg for mercy's sake.
Nothing I counted mine, out of my life,
is mine to take:

not my son's terrible eyes,
not the elaborate stone flower
of grief, not the day of the storm,
not the trial of the visiting hour,

not the dear coolness of his hands,
not the lime trees' agitated shade,
not the thin cricket sound
of consolation's parting word.

4 May 1940

Stanley Kunitz and Max Hayward

1915

I'm sick. I hear the cranes
call over the icy fields.
their wings pale gold underneath
in the crumbling, muggy light,

their wings a dense, low cloud
the color of the brushwood
stacked years ago against my house.
Brown? Gray? I say to the cranes

the gold on their wings is the river's.
They can't hear me, of course, but I speak.
They swerve. Their wings rumble.
They shadow rock dynamiters blasted back

all along one hillside to put a road in.
That first time we touched naked I kissed you there.
Pockets and cracks of snow melt in the rocks.
Ten feet away winter-pugged sparrows

land in a birch that's as tall as I am,
stay for a minute, scoot off when I touch my hair.
I feel the river inside me, thawing, along. Its heaviness.
In this fever your sweet, moist, pubic tangle.

Stephen Berg

THE GUEST

Everything's just as it was: fine hard snow
beats against the dining room windows,
and I myself have not changed:
even so, a man came to call.

I asked him: "What do you want?"
He said, "To be with you in hell."
I laughed: "It seems you see
plenty of trouble ahead for us both."

But lifting his dry hand
he lightly touched the flowers.
"Tell me how they kiss you,
tell me how you kiss."

And his half-closed eyes
remained on my ring.
Not even the smallest muscle moved
in his serenely angry face.

Oh, I know it fills him with joy—
this hard and passionate certainty
that there is nothing he needs,
and nothing I can keep from him.

Jane Kenyon

Boris Pasternak (1890–1960)

From DR. ZHIVAGO

Winter Night

A snowstorm made the earth tremble
through its whole frame.
A candle-flame upon a table,
only a candle-flame.

Like midges swarming in the summer,
winging to a spark,
the flakes flew in a thick shimmer
to the window from the dark.

The blizzard blew. Its rime and stubble
clung to the pane.
A candle-flame upon a table,
only a candle-flame.

High up on the bright-lit ceiling
shadows were tossed:
hands cross-clasped, feet cross-leaning,
fate in a cross.

And two small shoes fell with a clatter
to the floor, useless,
and wax drops from the night-light spattered
weeping upon a dress.

And all things faded, misted, feeble,
a grey-white dream.

A candle-flame upon a table,
only a candle-flame.

The candle felt a hidden shaking
blow hot temptation:
wings raised, like an angel's, taking
a cross-like station.

All February, storm rocked the gable
and found there the same
candle-flame upon a table,
only a candle-flame.

                    Edwin Morgan

THE CHRISTMAS STAR

It was winter. The wind
Blew from the plain.
And the infant was cold
In the cave in the slope of a hill.

The breath of an ox
Warmed him. The livestock
Stood in the cave.
A warm mist drifted over the manger.

Having shaken hay-dust
And grains of millet off their sheepskins,
Shepherds stared sleepily
From a cliff into the midnight distance.

Far off were a snow-covered field,
A graveyard, gravestones, fences,
A cart's shafts in a snowdrift,
And, above the graveyard, a star-filled sky.

And nearby, unseen until then,
More humble than an oil-lamp
In a a hut's window, a star
Glimmered over the road to Bethlehem.

It blazed like a haystack, apart
From heaven and God.
Like a reflection from arson,
Like a farmstead or a threshing floor in flames.

It towered like a burning rick
Of hay or straw

In the midst of a universe
Alarmed by this new star.

A growing glow, red above the star,
Was portending something,
And three astrologers hastened
To the call of that unprecedented night.

Behind them trod gift-laden camels;
Harnessed donkeys, each smaller than the one
In front, were going down the hill in little steps.

And all that was to come later
Sprang up far off like a strange vision.
All thoughts of the ages, all dreams, all worlds,
All the future of galleries and museums,
All pranks of fairies, all works of magicians,
All fir trees on earth, all dreams of children.

All the tremor of lighted candles, festoons,
All the splendor of colored tinsel . . .
. . . Even more cruel and furious, the wind blew from the field . . .
. . . All the apples, all the gold glass globes.

Part of the pond was hidden by alder trees,
But, through rooks' nests and treetops,
Part of it was seen quite well from here.

The shepherds could make out clearly
The donkeys and camels plodding along the mill-pond.
—Let's go with everyone and worship the miracle,
They said, closing their coats around them.

Shuffling about in the snow made them warm.
Tracks of bare feet, like sheets of mica,
Let over the bright meadow and behind the hovel.
Sheep dogs growled in the star's light
At the tracks, as at the flame of a candle's stub.

The winter night resembled a fairy tale,
And someone from the snow-covered mountain range
Was constantly mingling, unseen, with the rest.
The dogs wandered, looked back with caution,
And sensed danger, and pressed close to the herdsboy.

Along the same road, through the same land,
Several angels walked with the throng,
Their incorporeality made them invisible,
But each of their steps left a footprint.

A horde of men stood around the rock.
Day was breaking. The trunks of the cedars showed.
—Who are you? Mary asked them.
—We're a shepherd tribe and envoys from heaven;
We came to sing praises to both of you.
—You cannot all go in. Wait outside.

In the haze before dawn, gray as ashes,
The drovers and shepherds stamped about.
Those who came on foot bickered with riders.
By a log hollowed out for a trough
Camels brayed, donkeys kicked.

Day was breaking. The dawn
Swept the last stars, bits of ashes, from the sky.
Of the vast rabble, Mary allowed
Only the Magi to enter the cleft in the rock.

He slept, all luminous, in the oak manger,
Like a moonbeam in the hollow of a tree.
Instead of a sheepskin, he was warmed
By the lips of a donkey and the nostrils of an ox.

They stood in the shadow, as in the dusk of a barn;
They whispered, groping for words.
Suddenly, in the dark, one touched another
To move him a bit to the left of the manger,
And the other turned: from the threshold, like a guest,
The Christmas star was looking at the Maiden.

Nina Kossman

HAMLET

The din quiets. I step onto the boards.
Leaning against the jamb of the door
I try to discern in the distant echo
What will happen in my days.

Through axes of a thousand binoculars
The murk of the night is aimed at me.
If you will, Abba, Father,
Remove this cup from me.

I love your inexorable intent
And I agree to play my part.
But a different drama is on now,
This once, I ask you to spare me.

But the order of acts has been arranged
And the end cannot be forestalled.
I'm alone. All else, sunk to the Pharisee.
To live one's life is no stroll in the park.

Nina Kossman

From ILLNESS

8

At dusk you appear, a school-girl still,
a school-girl. Winter. The sunset a woodsman hacking
in the forest of hours. I lie back to wait for dusk.
At once we're hallooing; back and forth we call.

But the night! A torture chamber, bustling hell.
Come—if anything could bring you!—see for yourself.
Night's your flitting away, your engagement, wedding,
last proceedings of a hangman's court against me.

Do you remember that life, the flakes like doves
in flock thrusting their breasts against the howling
and, the tempest swirling them, fiendishly
dashed to the pavements?

You ran across the street, winds billowing under us,
a flying carpet—sleds, cries, crystals headlong!
For life, inspired by the blizzard, gushed
like blood into a crimson cloud.

Do you remember that moment, the hawkers,
the tents, the jostling crowd, the coins, a puppy's
moist nose? Those bells, encumbered by snow,
do you remember their grumbling before the holidays?

Alas, love, I must summon it all.
What can replace you? Pills? Patent-medicines?
Frightened by my bottomless insomnia, sweat-soaked,
I look sideways from my pillow as with a horse's eye.

At dusk you appear, still taking exams.
It's recess: robins flutter, headaches, textbooks.
But at night how they clamor for thirst, how glaring
their eyes, the aspirins, the medicine bottles.

Theodore Weiss

✒ Osip Mandelstam (1891–1938)

O LORD, HELP ME TO LIVE THROUGH THIS NIGHT

O Lord, help me to live through this night—
I'm in terror for my life, your slave:
to live in Petersburg is to sleep in a grave.

Clarence Brown and W. S. Merwin

LIGHTHEARTEDLY TAKE FROM THE PALMS OF MY HANDS

Lightheartedly take from the palms of my hands
A little sun, a little honey,
As Persephone's bees commanded us.

Not to be untied, the unmoored boat;
Not to be heard, fur-shod shadows;
Not to be silenced, life's thick terrors.

Now we have only kisses,
Bristly and crisp like bees,
Which die as they fly from the hive.

They rustle in transparent thickets of night,
Their homeland thick forest of Taigetos,
Their food—honeysuckle, mint, and time.

Lightheartedly take then my uncouth present:
This simple necklace, of dead, dried bees
Who once turned honey into sun.

James Greene

THE ODE ON SLATE

And star speaks unto star
M. LERMONTOV

A mighty junction of star with star,
The flinty path in an older song
In language of flint and air combined:
Flint meets water and ring joins horseshoe;
On the soft shale of the clouds
A milky slate-gray sketch is drawn:

Not the discipleship of worlds
But the delirious dreams of mooning sheep.

Amid thick night we standing sleep
Beneath a cozy sheepskin cap.
To its source the stream burbles back
Like a warbler, chain or speech.
Here terror writes, here writes displacement
In a milky lead-pencil hand,
And here is shaped a rough-draft version
Of running water's own disciples.

The steeply sloping goats' home cities
Are a mighty layering of flints:
But in any case the mountain ridges
Are churches and settlements of sheep.
The overhanging cliff face preaches
While time tempers and water teaches
And the translucent glades of air
With all things have long been filled.

Like a dead hornet from beside a hive
The many-hued day is swept off in scorn,
And night, the she-kite, carries off
The burning chalk and feeds the slate.
From the iconoclastic board

Wipe away the day's impressions
And shake those transparent apparitions
Like a fledgling from the hands.

The fruit swelled up. The grapes grew ripe.
The day was stormy as days can be.
A friendly game of knucklebones. At noon,
The coats of vicious sheepdogs;
Like garbage from the icy heights,
The seamy side of fresh green imagery,
Hungry water flows and turns
And plays about like a tiny beast.

And like a spider crawls to me,
Where each join is spattered by the moon;
On a shuddering steep-pitched slope
I hear the juddering screech of slate:
Is it your voices, oh my memory,
Playing teacher as they tear the night
And hunting with slate pencils through the woods,
Scavenging from the beaks of birds?

It's only from the voice we'll know
That there was scratching and conflict there;

So we draw the hard pencil in the one direction
Indicated by the voice.
I tear the night, the burning chalk,
For the sake of an instantaneous record.
I change for noise the song of arrows
And for order the clatter of bustards' wings.

Who am I? Not a real stone mason,
No shipwright I; I don't roof buildings,
I'm a double-dealer with a double soul,
The friend of night, the day's assailant.
Blesséd be he who first dubbed flint
The disciple of running water.
Blesséd be he who thongs first tied
To the feet of hills and on firm ground.

And now I study the rough-hewn ledger
Of the scratches made in the slate-pencil summer:
The language of flint and air combined
With a stratum of darkness and a stratum of light.
And I want to place my fingers
In the flinty path from the older song
As in a lesion, binding, joining
Flint to water, ring to horseshoe.

Bernard Meares

TRISTIA

I have learnt by heart the lesson of goodbyes
In bareheaded laments in the night.
Oxen chew, waiting lengthens,
The last hour of the watch in the city.
And I bow to ceremonial cock-crowing nights
When lifting their lading of grief for the journey
Eyes red with crying search the horizon
And singing of Muses blends with the weeping of women.

Who can know from the word 'goodbye'
What kind of separation lies before us,
Or what the cock's clamour promises
When a light burns in the acropolis
And in his stall the lazy ox chews:
Why the cock,
The herald of new life,
Beats on the city walls with his wings?

And I like the way of weaving:
The shuttle comes and goes, the spindle hums,

And—flying to meet us like swan's down—
Look, barefooted Delia comes!
Oh how meagre the basis of life,
How threadbare the language of elysium!
Everything existed of old, everything recurs anew,
The flash of recognition is all that we welcome.

So be it: a translucent manikin
On a clean clay plate—
A squirrel's stretched-out skin:
Bent over the wax, a girl examines it.
Not for us to guess at Grecian Erebus:

For women wax, what bronze is for men.
On us our fate falls only in battles;
Their death they die in divination.

James Greene

THE STALIN EPIGRAM

Our lives no longer feel ground under them.
At ten paces you can't hear our words.

But whenever there's a snatch of talk
it turns to the Kremlin mountaineer,

the ten thick worms his fingers,
his words like measures of weight,

the huge laughing cockroaches on his top lip,
the glitter of his boot-rims.

Ringed with a scum of chicken-necked bosses
he toys with the tributes of half-men.

One whistles, another meouws, a third snivels.
He pokes out his finger and he alone goes boom.

He forges decrees in a line like horseshoes,
One for the groin, one the forehead, temple, eye.

He rolls the executions on his tongue like berries.
He wishes he could hug them like big friends from home.

Clarence Brown and W. S. Merwin

MOUNDS OF HUMAN HEADS

Mounds of human heads recede in mist.
Unseen in their midst, I grow small. But in books
we were raised on and games children play
I will rise from the dead to say—: the sun.

Mark Rudman

WHEN PSYCHE, WHO IS LIFE, DESCENDS AMONG THE SHADES

When Psyche, who is life, descends among the shades,
Following Persephone into half-transparent forest,
The blind swallow hurls itself at her feet
With Stygian affection and green twig

Phantoms in a throng speed towards their new companion,
They meet the fugitive with lamentations,
In front of her they wring thin hands,
Perplexed with diffident expectations.

One holds out a mirror, another a phial of perfumes—
The soul likes trinkets, after all is feminine.
And dry complainings, like fine rain,
Sprinkle the leafless forest with transparent voices.

And not knowing what to do in this friendly hubbub,
The soul senses weight and size no longer.
She breathes on the mirror and is slow to hand over
The lozenge of copper to the master of the ferry.

James Greene

Marina Tsvetayeva (1892–1941)

From POEM OF THE END

Like a thick horse's mane,
Rain in eyes. And hills.
We've passed the suburbs again,
We've left the city walls.

Stepmothers aren't mothers
With generous stock,
Not for us—there's nowhere
For us, here we must croak.

We're brother and sister.
A field. And a fence.
Life is a suburb.
Out of town, build your house.

Ladies and gentlemen,
It's a hopeless affair.
The suburbs are legion,
The cities are—where?

The rain beats and rages.
We stand, breaking. Adieu.
After three months, three ages,
Our first time as two.

Wasn't it Job, God,
You asked for a loan?
The venture's miscarried:
We're out of town.

Out of town! Understand? Out! You must move
Beyond! You've crossed on your own!
Life is the place where no one may live:
It's the Jewish zone . . .

So isn't it a hundredfold more worthy
To become an eternal Jew?
Since for everyone who's not wholly a shit
Life is equal to

A pogrom of Jews! Life's for converts,
The Judases of faith.
Go to hell, the penal islands, anywhere,
But not to life,

That spares only the traitor, sends only the lamb
To the executioner's knife.
On this document I stamp,
On my ticket for life.

I crush it. In vengeance for David's shield.
Into the mangled bodies' mess.
It's intoxicating that a Jew refused life,
That he didn't say yes?

Expect no mercy. The ghetto enfolds
The chosen few.
In this most Christian of all worlds
The poet's a Jew.

                    David McDuff

BEWARE

But for two, even mornings'
Joy is too small.
As you draw inside
Turn your face to the wall

(For the Spirit's a pilgrim,
Walks alone its way),
Let your hearing drop
To the primal clay.

Adam, listen hard
Over the sources,
Hear what rivers' veins
Are telling their shores.

You are the way and the end,
The path and the house.
By two no new lands
Can be opened out.

To the brows' lofty camp
You are bridge and breach.
(God is a despot,
Jealous of each).

Adam, listen hard
Over the source,
Hear what rivers' veins
Are telling their shores:

'Beware of your servant:
When the proud trump plays
Don't appear in our Father's house
Fettered, a slave.

Beware of your wife:
Casting off mortal things,
When the naked trump sounds
Don't appear wearing rings.'

Adam, listen hard
Over the source,
Hear what rivers' veins
Are telling their shores:

'Beware. Don't build towers
On closeness and kin.
(Far more firm than *her*
In our hearts is *Him*.)

Don't be tempted by eagles.
King David still cries
To this day for his son
Who fell into the skies.'

Adam, listen hard
Above the source,
Hear what rivers' veins
Are telling their shores:

'Beware of graves,
More ravenous than whores.
The dead rot, they are gone,
Beware sepulchres.

From yesterday's truths
Remain filth and stench.
Give up to the winds
Your earthly ash.'

Adam, listen hard
Over the source,
Hear what rivers' veins
Are telling their shores:

'Beware.'

David McDuff

AN ATTEMPT AT JEALOUSY

How is your life with the other one,
Simpler, isn't it? One stroke of the oar
Then a long coastline, and soon
Even the memory of me

Will be a floating island
(In the sky, not on the waters):
Spirits, spirits, you will be
Sisters, and never lovers.

How is your life with an ordinary
Woman? without godhead?
Now that your sovereign has
Been deposed (and you have stepped down),

How is your life? Are you fussing?
Flinching? How do you get up?
The tax of deathless vulgarity,
Can you cope with it, poor man?

"Scenes and hysterics—I've had
Enough! I'll rent my own house."
How is your life with the other one
Now, you that I chose for my own?

More to your taste, more delicious
Is it, your food? Don't moan if you sicken.
How is your life with an *image*,
You, who walked on Sinai?

How is your life with a stranger
From this world? Can you (be frank)
Love her? Or do you feel shame
Like Zeus's reins on your forehead?

How is your life? Are you
Healthy? How do you sing?
How do you deal with the pain
Of an undying conscience, poor man?

How is your life with a piece of market
Stuff, at a steep price?
After Carrara marble,
How is your life with the dust of

Plaster now? (God was hewn from
Stone, but he is smashed to bits.)
How do you live with one of a
Thousand women, after Lilith?

Sated with newness, are you?
Now you are grown cold to magic,
How is your life with an
Earthly woman, without a sixth

Sense? Tell me: are you happy?
Not? In a shallow pit? How is
Your life, my love? Is it as
Hard as mine with another man?

Elaine Feinstein

❧ Nikolai Zabolotsky (1903–1968)

THE SIGNS OF THE ZODIAC ARE FADING

The signs of the Zodiac are fading
Above the wide expanse of fields.
And the animal, the Dog, sleeps,

And the bird, the Sparrow, slumbers.
Mermaids soar, broad in the beam,
Soar straight up into the heavens,
With their arms as stout as boughs
And their breasts as round as turnips.
A witch, seated on a triangle,
Turns into a puff of smoke,
And a corpse with female goblins
Nimbly dances the cakewalk.
In a group then, after this
Pale magicians chase a Fly,
While the moon's unmoving face
Gazes down upon the hillside.

The signs of the Zodiac are fading
Above the houses of the village.
And the animal, the Dog, sleeps
And the fish, the Plaice, is slumbering.
The watchman's clapper goes clack clack,
The animal, the Spider, sleeps.
The Cow sleeps, the Fly is sleeping,
Above the earth the moon is hanging.
Above the earth is a great vessel
Full of water, upside down.
The goblin of the woods has plucked
A small log from his shaggy beard.
Daintily the siren dangles
Her leg from behind a cloud.

The ogre has bitten off
The gentleman's unmentionable.
All is lost in the confusion
Of this dance, in all directions
Hamadryads fly and Britons,
Fleas and witches and dead men.

Candidate of ages past,
Captain of the years to come,
Oh my reason! All these monsters
Spring from your delirium,
Spring from your imagination,
Spasms of the sleeping mind,
Suffering that has gone uneased—
All that has no real existence.

Lofty is the earth's dwelling place.
It is late and time to sleep!
Reason, my poor warrior,
You should slumber until dawn.
Why hesitate? Why be anxious?
The day is over, you and I—

Half-animal and half-divine —
Fall asleep upon the threshold
Of a life that's new and young.

The watchman's clapper goes clack clack.
The animal, the Spider, sleeps,
The Cow sleeps, the Fly is sleeping,
Above the earth the moon is hanging.
Above the earth is a great vessel
Full of water, upside down.
The potato plant is sleeping.
You had better sleep as well.

Daniel Weissbort

ஐ Andrei Vozensensky (b. 1933)

WAR BALLAD

The piano has crawled into the quarry. Hauled
In last night for firewood, sprawled
With frozen barrels, crates and sticks,
The piano is waiting for the axe.

Legless, a black box, still polished;
It lies on its belly like a lizard,
Droning, heaving, hardly fashioned
For the quarry's primordial art.

Blood red: his frozen fingers cleft,
Two on the right hand, five on the left,
He goes down on his knees to reach the keyboard,
To strike the lizard's cord.

Seven fingers pick out rhymes and rhythm,
The frozen skin steaming, peeling off them,
As from a boiled potato. Their schemes,
Their beauty, ivory and anthracite,
Flicker and flash like the great Northern lights.

Everything played before is a great lie;
The reflections of flaming chandeliers,
—Deceit, the white columns, the grand tiers
In warm concert-halls—wild lies.

But the steel of the piano howls in me,
I lie in the quarry and I am deft
As the lizard. I accept the gift.

I'll be a song for Russia, I'll be
an étude, warmth and bread for everybody.

Stanley Moss

Joseph Brodsky (1940–1996)

From NEW STANZAS TO AUGUSTA

TO M. B.

I

September came on Tuesday.
It poured all night.
The birds had all flown south.
I was so much alone, so brave,
I did not even watch them go.
The empty sky is broken now.
Rain-curtains close the last clear spot.
I need no south.

George L. Kline

Ukrainian

Bogdan Boychuk (b. 1927)

A FAIRY TALE

Once upon
she was the only child,
called Princess.

> *you came to me*
> *in spring,*
> *your bare feet*
> *warmed*
> *violet buds*
> *to bloom.*

When Princess' father and mother
went on a journey,
never to return,
she befriended her walls
and talked to them.

The walls listened
for they loved her soft voice.

> *wind in the clearing*
> *tried to suck*
> *your youthful*
> *breasts,*
> *to blow away*
> *your beauty.*

The neighbors envied
the Princess' solitude:
they sent a witch to take
her walls away, to breathe
a bad spell on her eyes, lips, ears,
and Princess became blind,
lost her voice, became deaf.

> *inflamed mouths,*
> *spattered with red,*
> *hurled curses*
> *on our love.*

Young Princess lay at the crossroad
in the shadow of a tree.
The years passed by, trampling her
into the ground.

> *I embraced you*
> *and we took*
> *what ripened for us*
> *under the moon,*
> *so kiss me*
> *once more.*

Then came the Prince.
With his glance he nailed
the witch to a pole,
recovered Princess' home
and came to the crossroads.
With a breath he opened
Princess' eyes and ears,
returned her speech.
Her white arms
like two roads
stretched toward him.

> *kiss me, for soon*
> *the wind will blow*
> *your beauty away*

and cold will flow out
of your heart.

They lived on opposite sides
of the road
to the end of their time.

Sometimes happy.

David Ignatow

Polish

∾ Aleksander Wat (1900–1967)

From PERSIAN PARABLES

By a great, swift water
on a stony bank
a human skull was lying
and shouting: Allah la ilah.

And in that cry such horror
and such supplication
so great was its despair
that I asked the helmsman:

For what can it still cry out? Of what is it still afraid?
What divine judgement could strike it yet again?

Suddenly there came a wave
took hold of the skull
and tossing it about
smashed it against the bank.

Nothing is ultimate
—the helmsman's voice was hollow—
and there is no bottom to evil.

Czeslaw Milosz

∾ Czeslaw Milosz (b. 1911)

ENCOUNTER

We were riding through frozen fields in a wagon at dawn.
A red wing rose in the darkness.

And suddenly a hare ran across the road.
One of us pointed to it with his hand.

That was long ago. Today neither of them is alive,
Not the hare, nor the man who made the gesture.

O my love, where are they, where are they going
The flash of a hand, streak of movement, rustle of pebbles.
I ask not out of sorrow, but in wonder.

Czeslaw Milosz and Lillian Vallu

DEDICATION

You whom I could not save
Listen to me.
Try to understand this simple speech as I would be ashamed of another.
I swear, there is in me no wizardry of words.
I speak to you with silence like a cloud or a tree.

What strengthened me, for you was lethal.
You mixed up farewell to an epoch with the beginning of a new one,
Inspiration of hatred with lyrical beauty,
Blind force with accomplished shape.

Here is the valley of shallow Polish rivers. And an immense bridge
Going into white fog. Here is a broken city,
And the wind throws the screams of gulls on your grave
When I am talking with you.

What is poetry which does not save
Nations or people?
A connivance with official lies,
A song of drunkards whose throats will be cut in a moment,
Readings for sophomore girls.
That I wanted good poetry without knowing it,
That I discovered, late, its salutary aim,
In this and only this I find salvation.

They used to pour millet on graves or poppy seeds
To feed the dead who would come disguised as birds.
I put this book here for you, who once lived
So that you should visit us no more.

Czeslaw Milosz

PREPARATION

Still one more year of preparation.
Tomorrow at the latest I'll start working on a great book

In which my century will appear as it really was.
The sun will rise over the righteous and the wicked.
Springs and autumns will unerringly return,
In a wet thicket a thrush will build his nest lined with clay
And foxes will learn their foxy natures.

And that will be the subject, with addenda. Thus: armies
Running across frozen plains, shouting a curse
In a many-voiced chorus; the cannon of a tank
Growing immense at the corner of a street; the ride at dusk
Into a camp with watchtowers and barbed wire.

No, it won't happen tomorrow. In five or ten years.
I still think too much about the mothers
And ask what is man born of woman.
He curls himself up and protects his head
While he is kicked by heavy boots; on fire and running,
He burns with bright flame; a bulldozer sweeps him into a clay pit.
Her child. Embracing a teddy bear. Conceived in ecstasy.

I haven't learned yet to speak as I should, calmly.

Czeslaw Milosz

READING THE JAPANESE POET ISSA: (1762–1826)

*A good world —
dew drops fall
by ones, by twos*

A few strokes of ink and there it is.
Great stillness of white fog,
waking up in the mountains,
geese calling,
a well hoist creaking,
and the droplets forming on the eaves.

Or perhaps that other house.
The invisible ocean,
fog until noon
dripping in a heavy rain from the boughs of the redwoods,
sirens droning below on the bay.

Poetry can do that much and no more.
For we cannot really know the man who speaks,
what his bones and sinews are like,
the porosity of his skin,
how he feels inside.
And whether this is the village of Szlembark
above which we used to find salamanders,

garishly colored like the dresses of Teresa Roszkowska,
or another continent and different names.
Kotarbiński, Zawada, Erin, Melanie.
No people in this poem. As if it subsisted
by the very disappearance of places and people.

> *A cuckoo calls*
> *for me, for the mountain,*
> *for me, for the mountain*

Sitting under his lean-to on a rocky ledge
listening to a waterfall hum in the gorge,
he had before him the folds of a wooded mountain
and the setting sun which touched it
and he thought: how is it that the voice of the cuckoo
always turns either here or there?
This could as well not be in the order of things.

> *In this world*
> *we walk on the roof of Hell*
> *gazing at flowers*

To know and not to speak.
In that way one forgets.
What is pronounced strengthens itself.
What is not pronounced tends to nonexistence.
The tongue is sold out to the sense of touch.
Our human kind persists by warmth and softness:
my little rabbit, my little bear, my kitten.

Anything but a shiver in the freezing dawn
and fear of oncoming day
and the overseer's whip.
Anything but winter streets
and nobody on the whole earth
and the penalty of consciousness.
Anything but.

Czeslaw Milosz and Robert Haas

A SONG ON THE END OF THE WORLD

On the day the world ends
A bee circles a clover,
A fisherman mends a glimmering net.
Happy porpoises jump in the sea,
By the rainspout young sparrows are playing
And the snake is gold-skinned as it should always be.

On the day the world ends
Women walk through the fields under their umbrellas,
A drunkard grows sleepy at the edge of a lawn,
Vegetable peddlers shout in the street
And a yellow-sailed boat comes nearer the island,
The voice of a violin lasts in the air
And leads into a starry night.

And those who expected lightning and thunder
Are disappointed.
And those who expected signs and archangels' trumps
Do not believe it is happening now.
As long as the sun and the moon are above,
As long as the bumblebee visits a rose,
As long as rosy infants are born
No one believes it is happening now.

Only a white-haired old man, who would be a prophet
Yet is not a prophet, for he's much too busy,
Repeats while he binds his tomatoes:
There will be no other end of the world,
There will be no other end of the world.

Warsaw, 1944

Tony Milosz

✌ Zbigniew Herbert (b. 1924)

ELEGY OF FORTINBRAS

for C. M.

Now that we're alone we can talk prince man to man
though you lie on the stairs and see no more than a dead ant
nothing but black sun with broken rays
I could never think of your hands without smiling
and now that they lie on the stone like fallen nests
they are as defenceless as before The end is exactly this
The hands lie apart The sword lies apart The head apart
and the knight's feet in soft slippers

You will have a soldier's funeral without having been a soldier
the only ritual I am acquainted with a little
There will be no candles no singing only cannon-fuses and bursts
crepe dragged on the pavement helmets boots artillery
horses drums drums I know nothing exquisite
those will be my manoeuvres before I start to rule
one has to take the city by the neck and shake it a bit

Anyhow you had to perish Hamlet you were not for life
you believed in crystal notions not in human clay
always twitching as if asleep you hunted chimeras
wolfishly you crunched the air only to vomit
you knew no human thing you did not know even how to breathe

Now you have peace Hamlet you accomplished what you had to
and you have peace The rest is not silence but belongs to me
you chose the easier part an elegant thrust
but what is heroic death compared with eternal watching
with a cold apple in one's hand on a narrow chair
with a view of the ant-hill and the clock's dial

Adieu prince I have tasks a sewer project
and a decree on prostitutes and beggars
I must also elaborate a better system of prisons
since as you justly said Denmark is a prison
I go to my affairs This night is born
a star named Hamlet We shall never meet
what I shall leave will not be worth a tragedy

It is not for us to greet each other or bid farewell we live on archipelagos
and that water these words what can they do what can they do prince

Czeslaw Milosz

THE ENVOY OF MR. COGITO

Go where those others went to the dark boundary
for the golden fleece of nothingness your last prize

go upright among those who are on their knees
among those with their backs turned and those toppled in the dust

you were saved not in order to live
you have little time you must give testimony

be courageous when the mind deceives you be courageous
in the final account only this is important

and let your helpless Anger be like the sea
whenever you hear the voice of the insulted and beaten

let your sister Scorn not leave you
for the informers executioners cowards — they will win
they will go to your funeral and with relief will throw a lump of earth

the woodborer will write your smoothed-over biography

and do not forgive truly it is not in your power
to forgive in the name of those betrayed at dawn

beware however of unnecessary pride
keep looking at your clown's face in the mirror
repeat: I was called—weren't there better ones than I

beware of dryness of heart love the morning spring
the bird with an unknown name the winter oak

light on a wall the splendor of the sky
they don't need your warm breath
they are there to say: no one will console you

be vigilant—when the light on the mountains gives the sign—arise and go
as long as blood turns in the breast your dark star

repeat old incantations of humanity fables and legends
because this is how you will attain the good you will not attain
repeat great words repeat them stubbornly
like those crossing the desert who perished in the sand

and they will reward you with what they have at hand
with the whip of laughter with murder on a garbage heap
go because only in this way will you be admitted to the company of cold
     skulls
to the company of your ancestors: Gilgamesh Hector Roland
the defenders of the kingdom without limit and the city of ashes

Be faithful Go

Bogdana and John Carpenter

WHAT MR COGITO THINKS ABOUT HELL

The lowest circle of hell. Contrary to prevailing opinion it is inhabited neither
by despots nor matricides, nor even by those who go after the bodies of oth-
ers. It is the refuge of artists, full of mirrors, musical instruments, and pictures.
At first glance this is the most luxurious infernal department, without tar, fire,
or physical tortures.

Throughout the year competitions, festivals, and concerts are held here.
There is no climax in the season. The climax is permanent and almost absolute.
Every few months new trends come into being and nothing, it appears, is ca-
pable of stopping the triumphant march of the avant-garde.

Beelzebub loves art. He boasts that already his choruses, his poets, and
his painters are nearly superior to those of heaven. He who has better art has
better government—that's clear. Soon they will be able to measure their
strength against one another at the Festival of the Two Worlds. And then we
will see what remains of Dante, Fra Angelico, and Bach.

　　　Beelzebub supports the arts. He provides his artists with calm, good board, and absolute isolation from hellish life.

Bogдana anд John Carpenter

APOLLO AND MARSYAS

The real duel of Apollo
with Marsyas
(absolute pitch
versus immense range)
takes place in the evening
when as we already know
the judges

have awarded victory to the god

bound tight to a tree
meticulously stripped of his skin
Marsyas
howls
before the howl reaches his tall ears
he reposes in the shadow of that howl

shaken by a shudder of disgust
Apollo is cleaning his instrument

only seemingly
is the voice of Marsyas
monotonous
and composed of single vowel
Aaa

in reality
Marsyas relates
the inexhaustible wealth
of his body

bald mountains of liver
white ravines of aliment
rustling forests of lung
sweet hillocks of muscle
joints bile blood and shudders
the wintry wind of bone
over the salt of memory
shaken by a shudder of disgust
Apollo is cleaning his instrument

now to the chorus
is joined the backbone of Marsyas

in principle the same A
only deeper with the addition of rust

this is already beyond the endurance
of the god with nerves of artificial fibre

along a gravel path
hedged with box

the victor departs
wondering
whether out of Marsyas' howling
there will not some day arise
a new kind
of art—let us say—concrete

suddenly
at his feet
falls a petrified nightingale

he looks back
and sees
that the hair of the tree to which Marsyas was fastened
is white
completely

Czeslaw Milosz and Peter Dale Scott

Wislawa Szymborska (b. 1923)

THE TWO APES OF BRUEGHEL

Here's my dream of a final exam:
two apes, in chains, sitting at a window.
Outside the sky is flying
and the sea bathes.

I am taking the test on human history.
I stammer and blunder.

One ape, staring at me, listens with irony,
the other seems to doze—
but when I am silent after a question,
she prompts me
with a soft clanking of the chain.

Sharon Olds

A TERRORIST IS WATCHING

The bomb will go off in the bar at one-twenty.
Now it's only one-sixteen.
Some will still manage to go in.
Some to go out.

The terrorist has already crossed the street.
At this distance he's safe,
and has a view like in the movies:

A woman in a yellow jacket—she goes in.
A man in sunglasses—he goes out.
Boys in jeans—they are talking.
One-seventeen and four seconds.
The smaller one is lucky and rides off on a bike,
but the taller one goes in.

One-seventeen and forty seconds.
A young woman, a green ribbon in her hair, is walking,
But a bus suddenly blocks the view.
The young woman is nowhere to be seen.
Was she stupid enough to go in?
We'll see when they carry them out.

One-nineteen.
Nobody goes in.
Instead, one man, fat and bald, goes out.
But he seems to be looking for something in his pockets
and at one-twenty, less ten seconds,
he goes back for his silly gloves.

It's one-twenty.
How the time crawls.
Maybe, it's now.
No, not yet.
Yes, now.
The bomb goes off.

Austin Flint

Czech

❧ Vladimir Holan (1905–1980)

DURING AN ILLNESS

A melting icicle, a leaking tap,
counting drops of medicine.

Tibet sees by water. We by tears.

Jarmila and Ian Milner

❧ Miroslav Holub (b. 1923)

IN THE MICROSCOPE

Here too are dreaming landscapes,
lunar, derelict.
Here too are the masses,
tillers of the soil.
And cells, fighters
who lay down their lives
for a song.

Here too are cemetaries,
fame and snow.
And I hear murmuring,
the revolt of immense estates.

Ian Milner

POLONIUS

Behind every arras
he does his duty
unswervingly.
Walls are his ears,
keyholes his eyes.

He slinks up the stairs,
oozes from the ceiling,
floats through the door
ready to give evidence,
prove what is proven,

stab with a needle
or pin on an order.

His poems always rhyme,
his brush is dipped in honey,
his music flutes
from marzipan and cane.

You buy him
by weight, boneless,
a pound of wax flesh,
a pound of mousy philosophy,
a pound of jellied
flunkey.

And when he's sold out
and the left-overs wrapped
in a tasselled obituary,
a paranoid funeral notice,
and when the spore-creating mould
of memory
covers him over,
when he falls
arse-first to the stars,

the whole continent will be lighter,
earth's axis straighten up
and in night's thunderous arena
a bird will chirp in gratitude.

Ian Milner

ŽITO THE MAGICIAN

To amuse His Royal Majesty he will change water into wine.
Frogs into footmen. Beetles into bailiffs. And make a Minister

out of a rat. He bows, and daisies grow from his finger-tips.
And a talking bird sits on his shoulder.

There.

Think up something else, demands His Royal Majesty.
Think up a black star. So he thinks up a black star.
Think up dry water. So he thinks up dry water.
Think up a river bound with straw-bands. So he does.

There.

Then along comes a student and asks: Think up sine alpha
greater than one.

And Žito grows pale and sad: Terribly sorry. Sine is
between plus one and minus one. Nothing you can do about that.
And he leaves the great royal empire, quietly weaves his way
through the throng of courtiers, to his home

in a nutshell.

George Theiner

Serbian

🙝 Vasko Popa (1922–1991)

THE BATTLE ON THE BLACKBIRD'S FIELD

Singing we ride over the field
To encounter the armoured dragons

Our most lovely wolf-shepherd
His flowering staff in his hand
Flies through the air on his white steed

The crazed thirsty weapons
Savage each other alone in the field

From the mortally wounded iron
A river of our blood streams out
Flows upward and streams into the sun

The field stands up erect beneath us

We overtake the heavenly rider
And our betrothed stars
And together we fly through the blue

From below there follows
The blackbird's farewell song

Anne Pennington

ST. SAVA'S JOURNEY

He journeys over the dark land

With his staff he cuts
The dark beyond him into four

He flings thick gloves
Changed into immense cats
At the grey army of mice

Amid the storm he releases his chains
And lashes the ancient oaken land
To the fixed stars

He washes his wolves' paws
That no trace of the dark land
Should remain on them

He journeys without a path
And the path is born behind him

Anne Pennington

SONG OF THE TOWER OF SKULLS

To Svetozar Brkitch

For the great-eyed sunflower you gave us
Blind stone your unface
And what now monster

You made us one with yourself
With the emptiness in your empty poison-tooth
With your dock-tailed eternity
Is that all your secret

Why now flee into our eye-sockets
Why hiss with darkness and sting with horror
Is that all you can do

That's not our teeth chattering it's the wind
Idle at the sun's fair
We grin at you grin up at heaven
What can you do to us

Our skulls are flowering with laughter
Look at us look your fill at yourself
We mock you monster

Anne Pennington

Branko Miljkovic (1934–1961)

SLEEPERS

Awake I steal what they dream.

MINERS

They descended into hell after injustice
on which it is possible to warm oneself.

AGON

While the river banks are quarreling,
The waters flow quietly.

SEA WITHOUT POETS

You wait for a right moment
To attune yourself to words
But there is no such poet
Nor a word fully free
O bitter and blind sea
In love with shipwreck.

Charles Simic

Slovenian

Veno Taufer (dates unknown)

From THE PRAYERS AND GAMES
OF THE WATER PEOPLE

mother loves me loves me not
mother hates me hates me not
water watches watches not
deep eye
glaring eye
fish eye

on soft belly
rising
coming
gaping
or singing
no voice no voice
but all around us
breathing
breathing us in
catching us overtaking us
it breathes
blazing cold
smoky winds
the tongue's vapor
all fall down with names so high
all rise up with names so deep
open up with mouths so wide
your eyes stare
your teeth shine
we'll drink down to your name
but we'll not drink it up
nor use it in vain

full mouth full eye
staring skull
the ear's vortex
circled by hair
the body is drawn off
under the soul's cloud

run slow dull times run
drip happiness drip away
bite stone gnaw bone
back give it back

a drop for you
and a drop for me
like counting potatoes
this drop is wet
that one dried up

a shadow herds wind herds clouds
breeds day
the sun rises the sun falls
dry like a tree
the sun stares through a hole
gray like a mouse
the water runs off
beneath a mousy shadow
a fat shadow which drinks it all
it will ride upon the thunder

the cloud bursts the sun stares
from its belly of water
that fatter shadow drinks it all up
that ever drier shadow
when will I see the sun
when I see the sea
when the stone looks out of my head
when the stone floats
when the fish drowns
and there's no shore in sight

Milne Holton

Slavo-Macedonian

❧ Slavko Janevski (dates unknown)

SAILOR'S SONG

I left along the distant roads, my apple tree, and now you bloom alone,
my heart is my helmsman, blind yet seeking blue bays,
if I hear the wind in the evening, I forebode your ruin . . .
Has someone's hunger pulled you out by the roots
as I roamed alone?

When the blackbird whistles shrilly three times at dawn,
do not wait for the sun. Listen, I am still digging roads,
on a mast I carry a black flag from tavern to tavern
and hide the pain under my skull.
Oh does the blue lightning bring you a blue downfall,
and do the rains lash you?

I have no more strength to come calm and tall
and to lean my forehead against the sleepy water,
from the blows to rest my hands on the rye until dawn,
and then to go nowhere . . .
My apple tree, the autumn is already here, there is no shore to sail to.
And so I dream of a secluded, small, and deserted harbor.

Vasa D. Mihailovich

SILENCE

When poppies tear themselves away
from their roots
and start Indian file

toward their sunset,
don't go after them.
There are no more weddings.
At each step stands a single autumn,
foolish, white, and stark naked.

When poppies leave only waste behind,
shut up the rain within yourself.
Let it toll in the gutter of your veins
under the familiar ceiling,
and keep quiet.

When the wind alights on your window
with three high-pitched squeaks
and the sob of a young crane,
again keep quiet.

For poppies silence is golden.

Charles Simic

Hungarian

✒ Attila Józef (1905–1937)

ENCOURAGING

In China swings the mandarin.
Today cocaine has killed again.
The straw is rustling: go to sleep.
Today cocaine has killed again.

Through windows of department stores
the poor see where the dollar goes.
The straw is rustling: go to sleep.
The poor see where the dollar goes.

Buy yourself sausage, buy yourself bread,
guard your life well, hold up your head.
The straw is rustling: go to sleep.
Guard your life well, hold up your head.

And one day you'll find even this:
a woman who will cook and kiss.
The straw is rustling: go to sleep.
A woman who will cook and kiss.

John Bátki

DEAD LANDSCAPE

The water smokes, the bulrushes
sag and wilt into the wilderness.
The sky cowers deep in its quilt.
Thick silence cracks in the snow-filled
    field.

Gross and greasy the silent sundown;
flat the plain, featureless and round.
Only a single barge, heard
slapping self-absorbed on the furred
    lake.

Newborn time rattles in the cold
branches of the icy wood.
Chittering frost finds some moss here,
ties up its skeletal horse here
    to rest.

Then the vines. And among them plums.
Damp straw on the stocks and stumps.
And a procession of thin stakes,
good for old peasants' walking-sticks
    in the end.

A croft—this countryside revolves
all round it. Winter with its claws
keeps cracking plaster till it falls
in pieces from the homestead walls:
    cat's-play.

The pigsty door gapes wide open.
It sags and creaks, the wind's playpen.
What if a sucking-pig trots in
and a field of corn should sport and spin
    on the cob!

The room small, the peasants small.
Dried leaves in the smoker's bowl.
For these ones, no prayer will work.
They sit there, deep in the dark,
    thinking.

The vines are freezing for the landlord.
His is the crackling of the wood.
His is the pond and under its ice
it is for him the good fish hides
    in the mud.

Edwin Morgan

❧ Sándor Weöres (1913–1989)

MONKEYLAND

Oh for far-off monkeyland,
ripe monkeybread on baobabs,
and the wind strums out monkeytunes
from monkeywindow monkeybars.

Monkeyheroes rise and fight
in monkeyfield and monkeysquare,
and monkeysanatoriums
have monkeypatients crying there.

Monkeygirl monkeytaught
masters monkeyalphabet,
evil monkey pounds his thrawn
feet in monkeyprison yet.

Monkeymill is nearly made,
miles of monkeymayonnaise,
winningly unwinnable
winning monkeymind wins praise.

Monkeyking on monkeypole
harangues the crowd in monkeytongue,
monkeyheaven comes to some,
monkeyhell for those undone.

Macaque, gorilla, chimpanzee,
baboon, orangutan, each beast
reads his monkeynewssheet at
the end of each twilight repast.

With monkeysupper memories
the monkeyouthouse rumbles, hums,
monkeyswaddies start to march,
right turn, left turn, shoulder arms —

monkeymilitary fright
reflected in each monkeyface,
with monkeygun in monkeyfist
the monkeys' world the world we face.

Edwin Morgan

SONG: BOUNDLESS SPACE

When I was no one yet,
light, clear light,
in the winding brooks
I often slept.

As I almost became someone,
a great force rolled me,
stone, rough stone,
ice-veined, down the slope.

And, finally, I have brightened
to live, flame, naked flame,
in rounded, boundless space,
showing our real country.

William Jay Smith

✒ Ferenc Juhász (b. 1926)

BIRTH OF THE FOAL

As May was opening the rosebuds,
elder and lilac beginning to bloom,
it was time for the mare to foal.
She'd rest herself, or hobble lazily

after the boy who sang as he led her
to pasture, wading through the meadowflowers.
They wandered back at dusk, bone-tired,
the moon perched on a blue shoulder of sky.

Then the mare lay down,
sweating and trembling, on her straw in the stable.
The drowsy, heavy-bellied cows
surrounded her, waiting, watching, snuffing.

Later, when even the hay slept
and the shaft of the Plough pointed south,
the foal was born. Hours the mare
spent licking the foal with its glue-blind eyes.

And the foal slept at her side,
a heap of feathers ripped from a bed.
Straw never spread as soft as this.
Milk or snow never slept like a foal.

Dawn bounced up in a bright red hat,
waved at the world and skipped away.

Up staggered the foal,
its hooves were jelly-knots of foam.

Then day sniffed with its blue nose
through the open stable window, and found them—
the foal nuzzling its mother,
velvet fumbling for her milk.

Then all the trees were talking at once,
chickens scrabbled in the yard,
like golden flowers
envy withered the last stars.

David Wevill

THE RAINBOW-COLORED WHALE

Now your grave is sinking,
like your back
when the scalpel
cut away your ribs.

They say, the wreath
we laid at your head was withered,
the plank's gone rotten
that propped your dead heart.

Your grave is sinking deeper,
a black mouth lying in wait.
Every day I bring fresh earth
in a big willow basket.

But the earth I bring in the evening
is gone by morning
by nightfall has sunk without trace.

As if you were eating
and eating your way through the earth,
forever upward,
with those toothless gums.

The salt-spray eating the coral
becomes the coral—
the worm devoured you,
now you devour the worm.

You eat through it all
like a huge grub,

insatiable mouth without stomach,
munching into daylight.

Tons of stones and clay—
nothing can stop those jaws!
What can you want in our world
with your dead will?

Skull, Nothing,
what is it you want?
Learn the final lesson.
You are alone now.

Rainbow-colored whale,
swimming the waters under the earth,
obey the laws of the earth,
the vows of death and burial.

Earth swallowed you whole,
and you swallowed the whole world.
No hope, no body left—
it's time you understood.

Rainbow-colored whale, thrashing and
churning the clogged waters under the earth,
you are a predator now,
not worthy of what you were.

When you were alive your skin
was a breathing marsh of colors,
your sweat gushed in little
squirts, like hypodermics.

But you haven't noticed
how naked you've grown,
how the black earth
has melted you.

Those cold eyes that knew
the stone-green world of boulder and pine
have burst by now,
soft, like seaweed pods.

You didn't even know
they'd betrayed you—
sold every ounce of you
for Judas-gold!

The traces left in the air
by your wandering desires—

gone forever,
under the hoarfrost.

And whatever sediment remained
of your heart
has been turned to stone,
melted away with the waters.

Little by little
time has eaten
the tartar from your teeth,
the grief from your eyes.

And it's time you learned
not to see hope in such signs.
When a man dies,
he loses his will to live.

My grief for you was like thorns,
but the thorns have withered.
The green tree of your absence
is slowly beginning to flower.

The tusks of the black boar,
the tusks of the black boar that
slashed you open —
the sting has gone out of the wound.

But why were you never
as hungry as this —
so hungry I feel you
unwinding out of the grave?

No man has the right
to live it all over again!
I haven't the strength
to bury you twice!

Look, your sea's dried up —
don't thrash about
in the earth's black surf
as if it were water.

You'd swallow the sun
like a goldfish?
Strain the sumac tree
through your teeth, like parsley?

Bone-flower,
burrowing toward the light,

don't ever blossom. Don't gnaw
into our moonlight with your rat's teeth.

Larva,
don't eat your way into my heart.
I live with your absence.
You don't exist.

Life here is peaceful
without you.
Flower then, flower into
the death wish of the lily.

David Wevill

❧ János Pilinszky (1921–1981)

HARBACH 1944

To Gábor Thurzó

At all times I see them.
The moon brilliant. A black shaft looms up.
Beneath it, harnessed men
haul a huge cart.

Dragging that giant wagon
which grows bigger as the night grows
their bodies are divided among
the dust, their hunger and their trembling.

They are carrying the road, they are carrying the land,
the bleak potato fields,
and all they know is the weight of everything,
the burden of the skylines

and the falling bodies of their companions
which almost grow into their own
as they lurch, living layers,
treading each other's footsteps.

The villages stay clear of them,
the gateways withdraw.
The distance, that has come to meet them,
reels away back.

Staggering, they wade knee deep
in the low, darkly-muffled clatter
of their wooden clogs
as through invisible leaf litter.

Already their bodies belong to silence.
And they thrust their faces towards the height
as if they strained for a scent
of the far-off celestial troughs

because, prepared for their coming
like an opened stock-yard,
its gates flung savagely back,
death gapes to its hinges.

Janos Csokits and Ted Hughes

Romanian

✐ Tudor Arghezi (Ion Theodorescu, 1880–1967)

FLOWERS OF MILDEW

I wrote them with my nail on the plaster
On a wall of empty cracks,
In the dark, in my solitude,
Unaided by bull lion vulture
Of Luke Mark and John,
Verses for all seasons,
Verses of the pit
Of thirst for water
And of hunger for ashes,
Verses of today.
When my angel nail was blunted
I let it grow again,
But it didn't,
Or else I knew nothing of it.

Dark. Rain beat down far off, outside.
My hand hurt me, like a claw
That can't be clenched.
I forced myself to write with my left-hand nails.

Michael Impey and Brian Swann

THE LAST HOUR

In the sky
Iron and bronze hour strikes.
In a star

Velvet hour struck.
Hour of felt strikes
In citadel tower.
In hour of wool
Old time is heard
And paper hour
Tears. Near princely epitaph
Hour of dust strikes.

Last night, sister,
The hour never struck.

Michael Impey and Brian Swann

Spanish

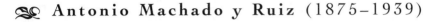

✣ Antonio Machado y Ruiz (1875–1939)

SUMMER NIGHT

It is a beautiful summer night.
The tall houses leave
their balcony shutters open
to the wide plaza of the old village.
In the large deserted square,
stone benches, burning bush and acacias
trace their black shadows
symmetrically on the white sand.
In its zenith, the moon; in the tower,
the clock's illuminated globe.
I walk through this ancient village,
alone, like a ghost.

Willis Barnstone

PEOPLE POSSESS FOUR THINGS

People possess four things
that are no good at sea:
anchor, rudder, oars
and the fear of going down.

Robert Bly

PRIMAVERA

Now spring has come
No one knows how.

Samuel Menashe

PORTRAIT

My childhood is memories of a patio in Seville,
and a garden where sunlit lemons are growing yellow;
my youth twenty years on the earth of Castile;
what I lived a few things you'll forgive me for omitting.

A great seducer I was not, nor the lover of Juliet;
—the oafish way I dress is enough to say that—
but the arrow Cupid planned for me I got,
and I loved whenever women found a home in me.

A flow of leftist blood moves through my body,
but my poems rise from a calm and deep spring.
There is a man of rule who behaves as he should, but more
than him, I am, in the good sense of the word, good.

I adore beauty, and following contemporary thought
have cut some old roses from the garden of Ronsard;
but the new lotions and feathers are not for me;
I am not one of the blue jays who sing so well.

I dislike hollow tenors who warble of love,
and the chorus of crickets singing to the moon.
I fall silent so as to separate voices from echoes,
and I listen among the voices to one voice and only one.

Am I classic or Romantic? Who knows. I want to leave
my poetry as a fighter leaves his sword, known
for the masculine hand that closed around it,
not for the coded mark of the proud forger.

I talk always to the man who walks along with me;
—men who talk to themselves hope to talk to God someday—
My soliloquies amount to discussions with this friend,
who taught me the secret of loving human beings.

In the end, I owe you nothing; you owe me what I've written.
I turn to my work; with what I've earned I pay
for my clothes and hat, the house in which I live,
the food that feeds my body, the bed on which I sleep.

And when the day arrives for the last leaving of all,
and the ship that never returns to port is ready to go,
you'll find me on board, light, with few belongings,
almost naked like the children of the sea.

Robert Bly

FOUR POEMS

1

A frail sound of a tunic trailing
across the infertile earth,
and the sonorous weeping
of the old bells.

The dying embers
of the horizon smoke.
White ancestral ghosts
go lighting the stars.

—Open the balcony-window. The hour
of illusion draws near. . . .
The afternoon has gone to sleep
and the bells dream.

2

Figures in the fields against the sky!
Two slow oxen plow
on a hillside early in autumn,
and between the black heads bent down
under the weight of the yoke,
hangs and sways a basket of reeds,
a child's cradle;
and behind the yoke stride
a man who leans towards the earth
and a woman who, into the open furrows,
throws the seed.
Under a cloud of carmine and flame,
in the liquid green gold of the setting,
their shadows grow monstrous.

3

Naked is the earth
and the soul howls to the wan horizon
like a hungry she-wolf.

What do you seek,
poet, in the sunset?

Bitter going, for the path
weighs one down, the frozen wind,
and the coming night and the bitterness
of distance. . . . On the white path
the trunks of frustrate trees show black,
on the distant mountains
there is gold and blood. The sun dies. . . .
                    What do you seek,
poet, in the sunset?

4

We think to create festivals
of love out of our love,
to burn new incense
on untrodden mountains;
and to keep the secret
of our pale faces,
and why in the bacchanals of life
we carry empty glasses,
while with tinkling echoes and laughing
foams the gold must of the grape. . . .
A hidden bird among the branches
of the solitary park
whistles mockery. . . . We feel
the shadow of a dream in our wine-glass,
and something that is earth in our flesh
feels the dampness of the garden like a caress.

John Dos Passos

✺ Juan Ramón Jiménez (1881–1958)

TO THE BRIDGE OF LOVE

To the bridge of love,
old stone between tall cliffs
      —eternal meeting place, red evening—,
I come with my heart.
      —My beloved is only water,
that always passes away, and does not deceive,
that always passes away, and does not change,
that always passes away, and does not end.

James Wright

THE DAWN BRINGS WITH IT

The dawn brings with it
that sadness of arriving, by train,

at a station that is not one's own.
    How disagreeable, those rumblings
of a new day that one knows cannot last long—
    —Oh my life!—
Overhead, as the day breaks, a child is crying.

                                        James Wright

❧ Jorge Guillén (1893–1984)

I WANT TO SLEEP

I shall be still stronger,
Still clearer, purer, so let
The sweet invasion of oblivion come on.
I want to sleep.

If I could forget myself, if I were only
A tranquil tree,
Branches to spread out the silence,
Trunk of mercy.

The great darkness, grown motherly,
Deepens little by little,
Brooding over this body that the soul—
After a pause—surrenders.

It may even embark from the endless world,
From its accidents,
And, scattering into stars at the last,
The soul will be daybreak

Abandoning myself to my accomplice,
My boat,
I shall reach on my ripples and mists
Into the dawn.

I do not want to dream of useless phantoms,
I do not want a cave.
Let the huge moonless spaces
Hold me apart, and defend me.

Let me enjoy so much harmony
Thanks to the ignorance
Of this being, that is so secure
It pretends to be nothing.

Night with its darkness, solitude with its peace,
Everything favors

My delight in the emptiness
That soon will come.

Emptiness, O paradise
Rumored about so long:
Sleeping, sleeping, growing alone
Very slowly.

Darken me, erase me,
Blessed sleep,
As I lie under a heaven that mounts
Its guard over me.

Earth, with your darker burdens,
Drag me back down,
Sink my being into my being:
Sleep, sleep.

James Wright

Federico García Lorca (1898–1936)

THE SLEEPWALKING BALLAD

Green, how I love you, green.
Green wind, green branches.
Ship up on the sea,
horse in the mountain ranches.
With shadows at her waist
she dreams at her balcony window
green flesh, green hair
and eyes of cold silver.
Green, how I love you, green.
Huge stars of frost
come out with the fish-shadow
to open the dawn's pass.
The figtree strokes the wind
with its sandpaper talons,
the thieving cat of a mountain
bristles its sour aloes.
But who will come? And from where?
She lingers on the balcony,
green flesh, green hair
dreaming of the bitter sea.

"Friend, I want to swap
my saddle for your mirror
my horse for your house
my knife for your bed-cover.

Friend, I have come bleeding
from the passes of Cabra."
"If I could, young man,
I would close the bargain.
But I am no longer myself
nor is my house my own."
"Friend, I wish to die
decently at home
with white linen bed-clothes.
Do you not see this wound
I have from breast to throat?"
"On your white shirt you have
three hundred dark roses.

Your blood smells pungent
as through your sash it oozes."
But I am no longer myself
nor is my house my own."
"At least let me climb up
to the high balcony alone,
let me climb, let me up
to the green balconies
where the water sounds
on the moon's many balconies."

And now the two friends climb
up to the green stairs,
leaving a trail of blood,
leaving a trail of tears.
Small lanterns of tin
on the roofs quaked:
a thousand drums of crystal
wounded the daybreak.
Green, how I love you, green.
Green wind, green branches
The two friends climb
and the strong wind launches
a strange taste in the mouth.
mint, gall and basil.
"Friend, where is she? Tell me
where is your bitter girl?
How often she waited for you!
How often she would wait
on this green balcony,
cool face, black hair."

Over the face of the well
the gipsy girl shivered,
green flesh, green hair
and eyes of cold silver.
An icicle of the moon

over the water held her:
the night became as secret
as a little square.

Green, how I love you, green.
Green wind, Green branches.
Ship up on the sea,
Horse in the mountain ranches.

Michael Hartnett

SONG OF THE RIDER

In the black moon
of the highwaymen
spurs are jingling.

Black horse,
where are you carrying
your dead rider?

The hard spurs
of the motionless bandit
who lost his reins.

Cold horse,
what a flowery scent
of the knife!

In the black moon
the sides of the Sierra Morena
are bleeding.

Black horse,
where are you carrying
your dead rider?

Cold horse,
what a flowery scent
of the knife!

In the black moon
a shriek —and the long
horn of the bonfire.

Black horse,
where are you carrying
your dead rider?

Edwin Honig

From LAMENT FOR IGNACIO SANCHEZ MEJIAS

1. *The Goring and the death*

At five in the afternoon.
It was exactly five in the afternoon.
A boy brought the white sheet
at five in the afternoon.
A basketful of lime in readiness
at five in the afternoon.
Beyond that, death and death alone
at five in the afternoon.

The wind carried off wisps of cotton
at five in the afternoon.
And oxide dispersed glass and nickel
at five in the afternoon.
Dove locked in struggle with leopard
at five in the afternoon.
A thigh with a horn of desolation
at five in the afternoon.
The bass strings began to throb
at five in the afternoon.
The bells of arsenic, the smoke
at five in the afternoon.
At street corners silence clustering
at five in the afternoon.
Only the bull with upbeat heart
at five in the afternoon.
When snow-cold sweat began to form
at five in the afternoon.
when iodine had overspread the ring
at five in the afternoon,
death laid eggs in the wound
at five in the afternoon.
At five in the afternoon.
At exactly five in the afternoon.

A coffin on wheels is the bed
at five in the afternoon.
Bones and flutes resound in his ear
at five in the afternoon.
The bull was bellowing in his face
at five in the afternoon.
Death pangs turned the room iridescent
at five in the afternoon.
In the distance gangrene on the way
at five in the afternoon.
Lily-trumpet in the verdant groin
at five in the afternoon.
The wounds burned with the heat of suns

at five in the afternoon,
and the throng burst through the windows
at five in the afternoon.
At five in the afternoon.
Horrifying five in the afternoon!
The stroke of five on every clock.
The dark of five in the afternoon.

————

4. Absence of the Soul

The bull does not know you, nor the fig tree,
nor horses, nor the ants on your floors.
The child does not know you, nor the evening,
because your death is forever.

The saddleback of rock does not know you,
nor the black satin where you tore apart.
Your silent recollection does not know you
because your death is forever.

Autumn will return bringing snails,
misted-over grapes, and clustered mountains,
but none will wish to gaze in your eyes
because your death is forever.

Because your death is forever,
like everyone's who ever died on Earth,
like all dead bodies discarded
on rubbish heaps with mongrels' corpses.

No one knows you. No one. But I sing you —
sing your profile and your grace, for later on.
The signal ripeness of your mastery.
The way you sought death out, savored its taste.
The sadness just beneath your gay valor.

Not soon, if ever, will Andalusia see
so towering a man, so venturesome.
I sing his elegance with words that moan
and remember a sad breeze in the olive groves.

Alan S. Trueblood

THE UNFAITHFUL WIFE

And I took her to the river
believing she was single
but she had a husband. . . .

It was the night of Santiago
and, as if in duty bound
as the crickets flared up
the streetlamps died down.
At the last street corners
I touched her sleeping breasts
and they opened to me swiftly
like spikes of hyacinth.
The starch of her petticoats
sounded in my ears
like long pieces of silk
cut by sharp shears.
The treetops grew enormous
without their light of silver
and a horizon of dogs
barked very far from the river.

Past brambles, reeds and thorntrees
I took her by the hand.
Under her clustered locks of hair
I made a hollow in the sand.
Neither flower nor shell
had a skin so fine,
nor with such brilliance
did moon-mirrors shine.

Like frightened fish
they slipped from me, her thighs:
one full of cold,
the other full of fire.
On the best highway
that night I was riding
saddling a mare of mother-of-pearl
without stirrups or bridle.

Smeared with sand and kisses
I took her from the river
and the air above us battled
the swords of the lily.

Then I behaved as I am,
a true gipsy after all:
I gave her a sewing-basket
of satin the colour of straw.

Michael Hartnett

CASIDA OF THE DARK DOVES

Through the laurel branches
I saw two dark doves.
The sun was one,
the other was the moon.
Dear neighbors, I said,
where is my tomb?
In my tail, said the sun.
In my throat, said the moon.
And I who was walking around
with the earth at my waist,
saw two snow eagles
and a girl undressed.
One was the other
and the girl neither one.
Dear eagles, I said,
where is my tomb?
In my tail, said the sun.
In my throat, said the moon.
Through the laurel branches
I saw two doves undressed.
One was the other
and both neither one.

Edwin Honig

❧ **Rafael Alberti** (b. 1902)

BOSCH

The devil—
blubber-lipped,
asshole-hipped,
anus-eyed,
tail-wide,
& caprihorny,
Beelzebuggering,
cummingbirding,
sniffing,
whiff-emitting,
strumpeting,
fart-trumpeting
through a funnel.
Loving & dancing,
drinking & prancing,
singing & laughing,
smelling & touching,
eating, fucking,

sleeping & sleeping,
weeping & weeping.

Mandrake, mandrake,
The devil has a crooked stake.

Cock-a-doodle-do!
I ride and I crow,
go mounted on a doe
& on a porcupine,
on a camel, on a lion,
on a burro, on a bear,
on a horse, on a hare,
and on a bugler.

Cork, cork,
The devil has a small pitchfork.

Love in a garden,
nude . . . ah, summer!
Garden of Delights.
On one foot the appletree
& on all fours the flower
(And your lovers,
asses bare to the wind,
to perching birds, small bouquets.)

Prickster, dickster,
The devil is a trickster.

The devil jackrabbit
jackoffrabbit
packoffrabbit
fackoffrabbit,
with his satyry,
  summery,
  cuntery
  company,
jabs,
grabs,
dabs,
nabs,
stabs
with an enema.

Bellies, nostrils,
lizards' tails,
dolphins flying,
ears impaled,
eyes gape-mouthed,
lost brooms,
boats in dread,
vomitings & wounds,
the dead.

He preaches, he preaches,
The devil puts on leeches.

Ladders sliding,
potlids flowing,
cauldrons blowing.
In the lethal
chamberpots,
the most infernal
rags, shoe-toes—
sad, ultimate
scarecrows.

He scythes, he scythes,
Devil cobweb harvests lives.

Nightshade
nightmare,
dark,
polluted,
untransmuted
fruits,
tears,
fear,
& gnashing
teeth
without
cease.

Uneasy painter:
your palette ascends to the skies,
but on a horn your paintbrush flies

to Hell.

Carolyn Tipton

GIOTTO

O Lord, praise be
    to Brother Paintbrush. In Thy divine
    face of dew he has moistened himself, & dipped
    into Thy blood has come to shine.

O Lord, praise be
    to Brother Wall, open to me,
    to fresh lime, able to beat
    cold, water, air, heat—
    Sister Lime, with her pure white
    everlasting dream of life.

O Lord, praise be
    to the pencil, to the pen who drafts Brother Design.
    Praise be to the outline
    manifesting itself out of mist;
    praise be to Sister Light who clarifies it.

O Lord, praise be
    to the human form,
    ardent analogue of her vaster
    Sister Architecture.

O Lord, praise be
    to Brother Color, to his rainbow:
    to green, to white, to red & yellow,
    to black & gold & rose,
    to fraternal violet, and
    to the one whose bright language paints Thy praise
    when, looking up, I raise
    my hand to gather in the humble birds,
    and see/hear the lauding words
    of blue, of good Brother Indigo.

O Lord, praise be
    to solemn & deliberate movement,
    to the rigid landscape & hieratic sea. Praise be
    to the angel: a sail who has no need of Brother Wind,
    to a symmetry not tiresome to behold,
    to the rectilinear psalm of the robe.

O Lord, praised be
    what Thou has done for me.
    In this dark age Thou hast made me sweet & gentle,
    and clothed me in a garment like no other:
    the bright habit of Painting's eldest brother.

Carolyn Tipton

Spanish/Mexico

Alfonso Reyes (1889–1959)

TO-AND-FRO OF SAINT THERESA

She weaves away at the bower,
sword shuttling in the loom,
branchy, hitherandthithering
Saint Theresa's moon.

The eyes in sparkling flight
caught among the lashes
free and captive give
battle and sue for peace.

A wizened darky trembles
entangled in his guitar,
a runaway bridegroom in
a slip of a wench's arms.

Wench in an hour won,
free though consenting, and alien.
How all flows, how all
departs whence all abides!

From the flowers' cups
drops of essence shed:
all in the instant that ends
in another is begun.

Below the sea escapes
in the same light it hales
and escaping never
escapes from the hands of earth

On his lively mare the rider
of the air passes and passes
not: he bides in the shadow,
rowelling jingling spurs.

It is life journeyed through
as to a far remove!
A coming and going, a being
in flight and ever near!

A being beside me, and she
dead these years!
A deluding of all as by
Zeno with his arrow!

Time twines into the voice;
languor takes the song.
With agile feet the angels
suffer to come on earth.

Flying quiet moon,
heron self-ensnared,
in scrolls of leaves she moves
and moves not, wheels and wheels not.

                              Samuel Beckett

✑ Octavio Paz (b. 1914)

From SUNSTONE

a crystal willow, a poplar of water,
a tall fountain the wind arches over,
a tree deep-rooted yet dancing still,
a course of a river that turns, moves on,
doubles back, and comes full circle,
forever arriving:
     the calm course
of the stars or an unhurried spring,
water with eyes closed welling over
with oracles all night long,
a single presence in a surge of waves,
wave after wave till it covers all,
a reign of green that knows no decline,
like the flash of wings unfolding in the sky,

a path through the wilderness of days to come,
and the gloomy splendor of misery like a bird
whose song can turn a forest to stone,
and the imminent joys on branches that vanish,
the hours of light pecked away by the birds,
and the omens that slip past the hand,

a sudden presence like a burst of song,
like the wind singing in a burning building,
a glance that holds the world and all
its seas and mountains dangling in the air,
body of light filtered through an agate,
thighs of light, belly of light, the bays,
the solar rock, cloud-colored body,
color of a brisk and leaping day,
the hour sparkles and has a body,
the world is visible through your body,
transparent through your transparency,

I travel my way through galleries of sound,
I flow among echoing presences,
I cross transparencies as though I were blind,
a reflection erases me, I'm born in another,
oh forest of pillars that are enchanted,
through arches of light I travel into
the corridors of a diaphanous fall,

I travel your body, like the world,
your belly is a plaza full of sun,
your breasts two churches where blood
performs its own, parallel rites,

my glances cover you like ivy,
you are a city the sea assaults,
a stretch of ramparts split by the light
in two halves the color of peaches,
a domain of salt, rocks and birds,
under the rule of oblivious noon,

dressed in the color of my desires,
you go your way naked as my thoughts,
I travel your eyes, like the sea,
tigers drink their dreams in those eyes,
the hummingbird burns in those flames,
I travel your forehead, like the moon,
like the cloud that passes through your thoughts,
I travel your belly, like your dreams,

your skirt of corn ripples and sings,
your skirt of crystal, your skirt of water,
your lips, your hair, your glances rain
all through the night, and all day long
you open my chest with your fingers of water,
you close my eyes with your mouth of water,
you rain on my bones, a tree of liquid
sending roots of water into my chest,

I travel your length, like a river,
I travel your body, like a forest,
like a mountain path that ends at a cliff
I travel along the edge of your thoughts,
and my shadow falls from your white forehead,
my shadow shatters, and I gather the pieces
and go on with no body, groping my way,
the endless corridors of memory, the doors
that open into an empty room
where all the summers have come to rot,
jewels of thirst burn at its depths,
the face that vanishes upon recall,
the hand that crumbles at my touch,
the hair spun by a mob of spiders
over the smiles of years ago,

setting out from my forehead, I search,
I search without finding, search through a moment,
a face of storm and lightning-flashes
racing through the trees of night,
a face of rain in a darkened garden,
relentless water that flows by my side,

I search without finding, I write alone,
there's no one here, and the day falls,
the year falls, I fall with the moment,

I fall to the depths, invisible path
over mirrors repeating my shattered image,
I walk through the days, the trampled moments,
I walk through all the thoughts of my shadow,
I walk through my shadow in search of a moment,

I search for an instant alive as a bird,
for the sun of five in the afternoon
tempered by walls of porous stone:
the hour ripened its cluster of grapes,
and bursting, girls spilled out from the fruit,
scattering in the cobblestone patios of the school,
one was tall as autumn and walked

a face I can see to see my face,
to see life until its death, a face
of the sea, bread, rocks and a fountain,
source where all our faces dissolve
in the nameless face, the faceless being,
the unspeakable presence of presences . . .

—————

I want to go on, to go further, and cannot:
as each moment was dropping into another
I dreamt the dreams of dreamless stones,
and there at the end of the years like stones
I heard my blood, singing in its prison,
and the sea sang with a murmur of light,
one by one the walls gave way,
all of the doors were broken down,
and the sun came bursting through my forehead,
it tore apart my closed lids,
cut loose my being from its wrappers,
and pulled me out of myself to wake me
from this animal sleep and its centuries of stone,
and the sun's magic of mirrors revived
a crystal willow, a poplar of water,
a tall fountain the wind arches over,
a tree deep-rooted yet dancing still,
a course of a river that turns, moves on,
doubles back, and comes full circle,
forever arriving:

Eliot Weinberger

THE KEY OF WATER

After Rishikesh
the Ganges is still green.
The glass horizon
breaks among the peaks.

We walk upon crystals.
Above and below
great gulfs of calm.
In the blue spaces
white rocks, black clouds.
You said:

> *Le pays est plein de sources.*

That night I washed my hands in your breasts.

Elizabeth Bishop

Spanish/Chile

✑ Gabriela Mistral (1889–1957)

NIGHT

Sleep, my child; because of you
The western skies their light efface;
There is no glitter save the dew,
Nor any whiteness, save my face.

My little son, because you dream,
The road lies hushed, in peace unfurled,
Nothing murmurs save the stream;
I am alone in a sleeping world.

A slow mist drowns the silent land,
A blue sigh fades in darkening skies;
Like a gentle, soothing hand
Upon the earth a quiet lies.

Not my child alone I've sung,
Cradling him, to easy sleep;
The earth too, as my cradle swung,
Drifted into slumber deep.

Alice Jane McVan

✑ Pablo Neruda (Ricardo Neftari Reyes, 1904–1973)

IF EACH DAY FALLS

If each day falls
inside each night,

there exists a well
where clarity is imprisoned.

We need to sit on the rim
of the well of darkness
and fish for fallen light
with patience.

                    William O'Daly

DRUNK AS DRUNK ON TURPENTINE

Drunk as drunk on turpentine
From your open kisses,
Your wet body wedged
Between my wet body and the strake
Of our boat that is made out of flowers,
Feasted, we guide it—our fingers
Like tallows adorned with yellow metal—
Over the sky's hot rim,
The day's last breath in our sails.

Pinned by the sun between solstice
And equinox, drowzy and tangled together
We drifted for months and woke
With the bitter taste of land on our lips,
Eyelids all sticky, and we longed for lime
And the sound of a rope
Lowering a bucket down its well. Then,
We came by night to the Fortunate Isles,
And lay like fish
Under the net of our kisses.

                    Christopher Logue

A DIFFERENT SHIP

A different ship will sail by on the sea
at its particular hour, it appears,
Not iron with orange
flags flying:
no one knows the port of departure
or the hour:
but all is in readiness.
The finest salon in the fleet, with everything
planned for the passenger's convenience.
Even the spray is spread fine

as the pile of a carpet
with stars in the threads,
and beyond lies the blue
and the green, the ultramarine movement.
Everything waits.
The reefs open out
scrubbed clean and eternal:
they rise from the sand
like a cordon of castles,
a cordon of towers.
All things
are amenable,
all silence, welcome:
even the watchers forget their habitual distractions
and wait for some presence that must not be missed:
they are wearing their sabbatical best,
they have polished their boots,
and slicked down their hair.
They grow old as they wait
and the ship never passes.

Ben Belitt

FINAL

Matilde, sleeping
that feverish sleep, a day or a year,
here or there,
nailed down
to my backbone, or breaking it,
bleeding real blood,
waking, at times,
or comatose, lost:
clinical beds, foreign windows,
the white uniform of the caretakers,
that sloth in my feet.

Later, those journeys
and my ocean again:
your head on my pillow,

your hands flying
in light, in my light,
my terrain.

How lovely it was to live
while you lived!

The world is bluer, the night
more terrestrial, while I sleep,
grown enormous, in the brief clasp of your hands.

Ben Belitt

❧ Nicanor Parra (b. 1914)

JOURNEY THROUGH HELL

On a saddle without a horse
I made a journey through hell.

In the first circle I saw
A few figures reclining
On bags of wheat.

In the second circle
Some men riding bicycles
Didn't know where to stop
Because of the flames.

In the third circle I saw
Only one human figure
It appeared to be a hermaphrodite.

A thin and twisted figure
Feeding crows.

I went on trotting and galloping
Through a space of hours
Until in a forest I came upon a cabin
Where a witch lived.

A dog tried to bite me.

In circle four
An old man with a long beard
Bald as a watermelon
Building a little boat
In a bottle.

He gave me a kind look.

In circle five
I saw some students
Playing Indian hockey
With a ball of rags.

It was savagely cold.
I had to pass the night
Keeping vigil in a graveyard
Sheltered behind a tomb
To keep from freezing.

The next day I went on
Into some hills
I saw for the first time
The skeletons of trees
Burned by the tourists.

Two circles were left.

In one I saw myself
Sitting at a black table
Eating the flesh of a bird:
My only companion
Was a kerosene stove.

In the seventh circle
I saw absolutely nothing
All I heard were strange sounds
I heard a horrible laughter
And a deep breathing
That tore open my soul.

                              Miller Williams

Spanish/Peru

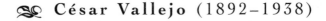 **César Vallejo** (1892–1938)

XXXIV

Finished the stranger, with whom, late
at night, you returned to words for words.
Now there won't be anyone who waits for me,
readies my place, good itself ill.

Finished the heated afternoon;
your great bay and your clamor; the chat
with your exhausted mother
who offered us a tea full of evening.

Finally finished everything: the vacations,
your obedience of hearts, your way
of demanding that I not go out.

And finished the diminutive, on behalf of
my majority in the endless ache
and our having been born like this for no cause.

Rebecca Seiferle

BLACK STONE ON A WHITE STONE

I'll die in Paris on a rainy day,
a day which I can already remember.
I'll die in Paris—and I won't skip town—
maybe on Thursday, like today, in autumn.

It must be Thursday, since today Thursday, as
I set these lines down, I've put my shoulder bones
on wrong, and never like today have I turned,
with all my road, to see myself alone.

César Vallejo is dead. Everyone beat him
although he didn't do a thing to them;
they beat him hard with a big stick and hard

also with a gross rope; witnesses are
the Thursdays and the crooked shoulder bones,
the lonely solitude, the rain, the roads.

Willis Barnstone

IN THAT CORNER WHERE WE SLEPT TOGETHER

In that corner where we slept together
so many nights, now I sit down
to take a walk. The bedstead of the dead lovers
was taken away, or something must have happened.

You came early for other matters
and now you're gone. It's the corner
where beside you I read one night
between your tender nipples
a story by Daudet. It is our lovers'
corner. Don't mistake it.

I've begun to remember the lost days
of summers, your coming and going,
small and fed up and pale in the rooms.

On this rainy night,
already far from them both, suddenly I jump up . . .

They are two doors coming open, shutting,
two doors that come and go with the wind
shadow   to   shadow.

Tony Barnstone and Willis Barnstone

THE BLACK CUP

The night is a cup of evil. A watchman's stinging
whistle pierces through it like a vibrating pin.
Listen, you little slut, how come, if you're already gone,
the wave is still black and still burning me up.

The Earth spreads coffin edges in its shadow.
Listen, you little tramp, don't come back.

My flesh swims, swims
in the cup of shadow that keeps on hurting me;
my flesh swims in it
as in the swampy heart of a woman.

Star coal . . . I've felt
the dry frictions of clay
fall across my diaphanous lotus.
Ah, woman! For you
this flesh of instinct exists. Ah, woman!

So, oh black chalice, even now with you gone
I choke on dust;
and more desires to drink paw inside my flesh.

Tony Barnstone and Willis Barnstone

Spanish/Argentina

✎ Jorge Luis Borges (1899–1986)

EWIGKEIT

Turn on my tongue, O Spanish verse; confirm
Once more what Spanish verse has always said
Since Seneca's black Latin; speak your dread
Sentence that all is fodder for the worm.
Come, celebrate once more pale ash, pale dust,
The pomps of death and the triumphant crown
Of that bombastic queen who tramples down

The petty banners of our pride and lust.
Enough of that. What things have blessed my clay
Let me not cravenly deny. The one
Word of no meaning is Oblivion.
And havened in eternity, I know
My many precious losses burn and stay:
That forge, that night, that risen moon aglow.

Richard Wilbur

BARUCH SPINOZA

A haze of gold, the Occident lights up
The window. Now, the assiduous manuscript
Is waiting, weighed down with the infinite.
Someone is building God in a dark cup.
A man engenders God. He is a Jew
With saddened eyes and lemon-colored skin;
Time carries him the way a leaf, dropped in
A river, is borne off by waters to
Its end. No matter. The magician moved
Carves out his God with fine geometry;
From his disease, from nothing, he's begun
To construct God, using the word. No one
Is granted such prodigious love as he:
The love that has no hope of being loved.

Willis Barnstone

POSSESSION OF YESTERDAY

I know the things I've lost are so many that I could not begin to count them
and that those losses
now, are all I have.
I know that I've lost the yellow and the black and I think
Of those unreachable colors
as those that are not blind can not.
My father is dead, and always stands beside me.
When I try to scan Swinburne's verses, I am told, I speak with my father's
      voice.
Only those who have died are ours, only what we have lost is ours.
Ilium vanished, yet Ilium lives in Homer's verses.
Israel was Israel when it became an ancient nostalgia.
Every poem, in time, becomes an elegy.
The women who have left us are ours, free as we now are from misgivings,
from anguish, from the disquiet and dread of hope.
There are no paradises other than lost paradises.

Nicomedes Suarez Arauz

THE LABYRINTH

Zeus, Zeus himself could not undo these nets
of stone encircling me. My mind forgets
the persons I have been along the way,
the wanted way of monotonous walls,
which is my fate. The galleries seem straight
but curve furtively, forming secret circles
at the terminus of years; and the parapets
have been worn smooth by the passage of days.
Here, in the tepid alabaster dust,
are tracks that frighten me. The hollow air
of evening sometimes brings a bellowing,
or the echo, desolate, of bellowing.
I know that hidden in the shadows there
lurks another, whose task is to exhaust
the loneliness that braids and weaves this hell,
to crave my blood, and to fatten on my death.
We seek each other. Oh, if only this
were the last day of our antithesis!

John Updike

OEDIPUS AND THE RIDDLE

At dawn four-footed, at midday erect,
And wandering on three legs in the deserted
Spaces of an afternoon, thus the eternal
Sphinx had envisioned her changing brother
Man, and with afternoon there came a person
Deciphering, appalled at the monstrous other
Presence in the mirror, the reflection
Of his decay and of his destiny.
We are Oedipus; in some eternal way
We are the long and threefold beast as well—
All that we will be, all that we have been.
It would annihilate us all to see
The huge shape of our being; mercifully
God offers us issue and oblivion.

John Hollander

THE DAGGER

To Margarita Bunge

A dagger rests in a drawer.
It was forged in Toledo at the end of the last

century. Luis Melian Lafinur gave it to
    my father, who brought it from Uruguay.
    Evaristo Carriego once held it in his hand.
Whoever lays eyes on it has to pick up the
    dagger and toy with it, as if he had always
    been on the lookout for it. The hand is
    quick to grip the waiting hilt, and the
    powerful obeying blade slides in and out
    of the sheath with a click.
This is not what the dagger wants.
It is more than a structure of metal; men
    conceived it and shaped it with a single end
    in mind. It is, in some eternal way, the
    dagger that last night knifed a man in
    Tacuarembo and the daggers that rained on
    Caesar. It wants to kill, it wants to shed
    sudden blood.
In a drawer of my writing table, among draft
    pages and old letters, the dagger dreams
    over and over again its simple tiger's dream. On
    wielding it the hand comes alive because
    the metal comes alive, sensing itself, each
    time handled, in touch with the killer for
    whom it was forged.
At times I am sorry for it. Such power and
    single-mindedness, so impassive or innocent
    its pride, and the years slip by, unheeding.

Norman Thomas Di Giovanni

Catalan

ଛ J. V. Foix (Josep Vicenc Foix, 1893–1988)

SONNET

Alone, in mourning, wearing an archaic black gown,
I stray often into dark solitudes,
Uncharted plains where high slate-mounds surround
Me, and everywhere I'm blocked by ocean-deep whirlpools.

And I ask: Where's this? for what antique grounds,
What dead skies or pastures long mute
Are you headed, maniac? toward what never-to-be-found
Miraculous star do you beat onward heavy-footed?

Alone I'm immortal. Palpable in that landscape
Of a thousand years back, strangeness isn't strange to me:
I know myself at home; parched deserts can't derange me

Or the coldest snowcapped peaks. I've got my lands back safe
Just where I used to wander: in the live-trap God arranged for me.
Or the one the Devil made Him; in exchange for me.

M. L. Rosenthal

Portuguese

 **Fernando Pessoa** (1888–1935)

SEGUE O TEU DESTINO

Follow your nose,
Water your plants,
Love your roses.
All else is the shade
Of alien wildwood.

Always the actual
Either more, or less
Than what we wish.
We only are
Selfsame to ourself.

Sweetest to live alone.
Grand and golden
Plainly to live.
Lay pain upon altars
Ex voto to the gods.

View life at a distance
With never a question.
There's nothing it can
Tell you. The answer
Is beyond the gods.

But unperturbed
Emulate Olympus
In your heart.
The gods are gods because
They do not heed.

David Wright

AUTOPSYCHOGRAPHY

The poet is a fake.
His faking seems so real
That he will fake the ache
Which you should really feel.

And those who read his cries
Feel in the paper tears
Not two aches which are his
But one which is not theirs.

And so round in its ring
Entertaining the mind
Goes this train on a string —
The heart that trails behind.

Keith Bosley

✺ Fernando Pessoa as Ricardo Reis

I THE ROSES LOVE IN THE GARDENS OF ADONIS

I the roses love in the gardens of Adonis,
Lydia, I love those fast fleeting roses
    That on the day they are born
    On that same day they die.
Light for them is everlasting: born
After the sun comes up, they die
      Before Apollo rounds
      His visible track.
So let us make our life *a single day*,
And willingly ignore the night to come,
    The night already past,
    The little while we last.

Edwin Honig

NO ONE IN THE WIDE WILDERNESS OF THE WOOD

No one in the wide wilderness of the wood
Of a world not for our unraveling
    Ever comes face to face with God.
We hear in the wind only what the wind bears.

Our loves, our gods, all we think upon,
      Like us, passes on, passes on.

Katharine Washburn

✍ Fernando Pessoa as Alberto Caeiro

RATHER THE BIRD FLYING BY AND LEAVING NO TRACE

Rather the bird flying by and leaving no trace
Than the passing beast leaving tracks in the earth.
The bird going by is forgotten, and should be.
The beast, no longer there (and so perfectly useless),
Shows it was there (also perfectly useless).
Remembering betrays Nature
Because yesterday's Nature is not Nature.
What's past is nothing; remembering is seeing nothing.

Fly, bird, fly away; teach me to disappear!

Edwin Honig

Portuguese/Brazil

✍ Carlos Drummond de Andrade (b. 1902)

DON'T KILL YOURSELF

Carlos, calm down, love
is what you are seeing:
a kiss today, tomorrow no kiss,
the day after tomorrow is Sunday
and nobody knows what will happen
on Monday.

It's useless to resist
or to commit suicide.
Don't kill yourself. Don't kill yourself.
Save all of yourself for the wedding
though nobody knows when or if
it will ever come.

Carlos, earthy Carlos, love
spent the night with you

and your deepest self
is raising a terrible racket,
prayers,
victrolas,
saints in procession,
ads for the best soap,
a racket for which nobody knows
the why or wherefor.

Meanwhile, you walk
upright, unhappy.
You are the palm tree, you are the shout
that nobody heard in the theater
and all the lights went out.
Love in darkness, no, in daylight
is always sad, Carlos, my boy,
don't tell anyone,
nobody knows or will know.

Mark Strand

Vinicius de Moraes (b. 1913)

SONG

Never take her away,
The daughter whom you gave me,
The gentle, moist, untroubled
Small daughter whom you gave me;
O let her heavenly babbling
Beset me and enslave me.
Don't take her; let her stay,
Beset my heart, and win me
That I may put away
The firstborn child within me,
That cold, petrific dry
Daughter whom death once gave,
Whose life is a long cry
For milk she may not have,
And who, in the night-time, calls me
In the saddest voice that can be
Father, Father, and tells me
Of the love she feels for me.
Don't let her go away,
Her whom you gave—my daughter—
Lest I should come to favor
That wilder one, that other
Who does not leave me ever.

Richard Wilbur

Italian

❧ Umberto Saba (1883–1957)

ULYSSES

O sad Ulysses in decline, seer
of terrible omens, does
no sweetness in your soul foment
Desire
for a
pale dreamer of shipwrecks,
who loves you?

Stephen Sartarelli

THE GOAT

I had a conversation with a goat.
She was tied up, alone, in a field.
Full up with grass, wet
with rain, she was bleating.

That monotonous bleat was brother
to my own pain. And I replied in kind, at first
in jest, and then because pain is eternal
and speaks with one voice, unchanging.
This was the voice I heard
wailing in a lonely goat.

In a goat with a Semitic face
I heard the cry of every woe on earth,
every life on earth.

Stephen Sartarelli

❧ Giuseppe Ungaretti (1888–1970)

WHERE THE LIGHT

Like the undulant lark
In glad wind above young fields
My arms know you are light, come

Let us forget all about down there
And about evil and heaven

And my blood quickly towards war,
And of footsteps in the shadow of memory
In the red colours of new mornings.

Where the leaf moves light no longer,
Dreams and angers having crossed the river
Where evening is spread
I shall carry you
To the hill of gold.

That unchangeable, ageless gold
In its lost nimbus
Shall be our winding-sheet.

Dennis Devlin

WAKE

All night long
sitting alongside
my dead friend
(he with white teeth
gnashed in a grin
at the pale moon
he with stiff hands
reaching for
the darkest zone
of my own silence)
    I have been writing
    love letters.

I have never
felt so much
    alive.

George Garrett

Eugenio Montale (1896–1981)

MOTETTI

I

You know this: I must lose you again and cannot.
Every action, every cry strikes me
like a well-aimed shot, even the salt spray
that spills over the harbor walls
and makes spring
dark against the gates of Genoa.

Country of ironwork and ship masts
like a forest in the dust of evening.
A long drone comes from the open spaces
scraping like a nail on a windowpane. I look
for the sign I have lost, the only pledge
I had from you.
Now hell is certain.

II

Many years, and one of them a little harder
on a foreign lake burning in the sunsets.
Then you came down from the mountains to bring me back
Saint George and the Dragon.

If only I could print them on the banner
rising and falling in the brutal wind
of my heart—and descend for you
into a chasm of fidelity, forever.

III

Frost on the windowpanes; the sick
always with each other yet always
alone; and at the tables long
soliloquies about the cards.

This was your exile. Now I think
of mine again, of the morning when I heard
the bomb they called the "ballerina"
go off between the rocks.

And it lasted a long time—like oriental fireworks
on the evening of a festival.

A hard wing brushed past you, touching your hands,
but to no purpose: this was not your card.

IV

Far away, still I was with you
when your father
went into darkness and left you his goodbye.
What did I learn
in that moment? That until then
the ravages of the past
had spared me
only for this:

I had not met you yet
and had to. I know this
from the pain of today, and would

even if the hours bent
back on themselves and brought
me once again to Cumerlotti
or Anghébeni, among the exploding
shells, the screams,
the panic of the squadrons.

V

The long goodbyes, the whistles in the dark,
the waving, coughing, lowering of windows:
it's time. Maybe
the automatons are right. Staring from the passageways,
they seem buried.

————————

—Can you hear it too? The harsh
litany of the express, the terrifying,
steady rhythm of a dance?

VI

I had almost lost
hope of ever seeing you again;

and I asked myself if this thing
cutting me off
from every trace of you, this screen
of images,
was the approach of death, or truly
some dazzling
vision of you
out of the past,
bleached, distorted,
fading:

(under the arches at Modena
I saw an old man in a uniform
dragging two jackals on a leash).

VII

The black and white
flight of swallows rising
and falling in a line
from the telegraph
pole to the sea
does not ease the pain
you feel by the water
nor bring you back
to somewhere
you have left.

The elder tree
already sheds its thick
perfume above the upturned
earth, and the tempest
washes itself away.
If this clear light
signifies a truce,
the sweet threat of you
consumes it.

VIII

Here is the sign; it trembles
over a wall that is turning
itself to gold:
the fretwork of a palm leaf
burnt by the blinding
dazzle of sunrise.

The sound of steps coming down
so lightly from the greenhouse
is not muffled
by the snow, is still
your life, your blood
in my veins.

IX

If the green lizard darts
out of the stubble under
the great whip —

the sail flapping with wind
sinks into the nothingness
beyond the rocks —

the cannon at noon sounds
fainter than your heart,
and if the clock
strikes without a sound —

what then? Then it means nothing

that a flash of lightning
can change you into something
rich and strange. You chose another shape.

Dana Gioia

THE LEMON TREES

Listen: the laureled poets
stroll only among shrubs
with learned names: ligustrum, acanthus, box.
What I like are streets that end in grassy
ditches where boys snatch
a few famished eels from drying puddles:
paths that struggle along the banks,
then dip among the tufted canes,
into the orchards, among the lemon trees.

Better, if the gay palaver of the birds
is stilled, swallowed by the blue:
more clearly now, you hear the whisper
of genial branches in that air barely astir,
the sense of that smell
inseparable from earth,
that rains its restless sweetness in the heart.
Here, by some miracle, the war
of conflicted passions is stilled,
here even we the poor share the riches of the world—
the smell of the lemon trees.

See, in these silences when things
let themselves go and seem almost
to reveal their final secret,
we sometimes expect
to discover a flaw in Nature,
the world's dead point, the link that doesn't hold,
the thread that, disentangled, might at last lead us
to the center of a truth.
The eye rummages,
the mind pokes about, unifies, disjoins
in the fragrance that grows
as the day closes, languishing.
These are the silences where we see
in each departing human shade
some disturbed Divinity.

But the illusion dies, time returns us
to noisy cities where the sky is only
patches of blue, high up, between the cornices.
Rain wearies the ground; over the buildings
winter's tedium thickens.
Light grows niggardly, the soul bitter.
And, one day, through a gate ajar,
among the trees in a courtyard,
we see the yellows of the lemon trees;
and the heart's ice thaws,
and songs pelt

into the breast
and trumpets of gold pour forth
epiphanies of Light!

William Arrowsmith

THE EEL

The eel, the siren
of cold seas,
who leaves the Baltic for our seas,
our estuaries, rivers, rising
deep beneath the downstream flood,
from branch to branch, from twig to smaller twig,
ever more inward,
bent on the heart of rock,
infiltrating
muddy passages, until one day
light glancing off the chestnuts strikes
her slithering in stagnant pools,
in the ravines cascading down
from the Appennine escarpments to Romagna;
eel, torch, whiplash
arrow of Love on earth,
whom only our gullies
or dried-up Pyrenaean brooks draw back
to Edens of generation;
green spirit that finds life
where only drought and desolation sting;
spark that says that everything
begins when everything
seems charcoal, buried stump;
brief rainbow, iris,
twin to the one your lashes frame
that you set shining virginal among
the sons of men, sunk in your mire —
can you fail to see her as a sister?

Jonathan Galassi

HAUL YOUR PAPER BOATS

Haul your paper boats
to the parched shore, and then to sleep,
little commodore: may you never hear
swarms of evil spirits putting in.

The owl flits in the walled orchard,
a pall of smoke lies heavy on the roof.

The moment that spoils months of labor is here:
now the secret crack, now the ravaging gust.

The crack widens, unheard perhaps.
The builder hears his sentence passed.
Now only the sheltered boat is safe.
Beach your fleet, secure it in the brush.

William Arrowsmith

ECOLOGUE

Losing myself in the swaying gray
of my olives garrulous
with quarreling birds
and freshets singing —
how good it used to be!
How the heel sank
in the cracked earth
among tiny blades of thin-leaved
silver! Random
thoughts came springing to mind
in that air too still.

Now the watered blue is gone.
The family pine leaps out;
breaking the grisaille;
overhead a patch of sky
burns, a spiderweb
is torn by a passing step: all around
a lost hour sheds its chains.
Nearby, the roar of a train
begins, then swells. A shot
cracks in the glassy air.
A flock of birds, a cloudburst,
crashes past, O Instant, an armful
of your bitter bark, ashes
blow by, vanish: the distance explodes,
a furious baying.

Soon the idyll can be reborn.
The phase that depends on the sky
is recomposed; streamers
struggle free . . . ;
                    the thicket of beans
is erased, folded in haze.
Swift wings no longer serve,
boldness of purpose is no help;
only the grave cicadas endure
in these Saturnalias of heat.

For an instant in the thick scrub
a woman's apparition flickers,
then vanishes. No Maenad, she.

Later on the moon lifts her horns.
This was when we came back home
from our useless wanderings.
On the face of the world
no trace could be found
of the wild orgy that lasted
all afternoon. Troubled,
we'd walk down among the thistles.
Where I live that's the time
when the hares begin to whistle.

William Arrowsmith

⁂ Salvatore Quasimodo (1901–1968)

AND SUDDENLY IT IS EVENING

Everyone stands alone at the heart of this earth
Stunned by a ray of sunlight
and suddenly it is evening.

J. Ruth Gendler

STREET IN AGRIGENTO

There lasts a wind which I remember, burning
In the names of sidelong horses
Galloping over the great plains, a wind
Which stains and chafes the sandstone, and the heart
Of the mournful sculptured pillars, overthrown
On the grass.

Dennis Devlin

MILAN, AUGUST 1943

In vain, search in the dust
Poor hand, the city's dead.
It is dead; and we have heard the last
Tremor from the fleet; and the nightingale
Has fallen from the aerial high on the Convent-roof
Where it sang before sunset.

Do not dig wells in the courtyards:
The living are no longer thirsty.
And the dead—do not touch them, so swollen, so red;
Leave them on the earth of their own homes:
The city is dead, is dead.

Peter Russell

DEAD OF WINTER

Your clear hands call my name.
They dance in the dark light of the fire
With the odor of oakwood and roses
And death. Dead of winter.

What became of the starving birds?
They fell into a waste of snow.
So it is with words.
They flash like sudden angels, go
Away like ghosts. So with the trees
And us, too, made of morning breeze.

George Garrett

FROM THE WILLOW BRANCHES

And how were we able to sing
with the foreign foot on our heart,
among the dead abandoned in the piazzas
on the grass hard with ice, to the lament
of the boys' lamb, to the black howl
of the mother who went to meet her son
crucified on the telegraph pole?
Our lyres too were hung, by vow,
from the willow branches;
they swayed lightly in the sad wind.

Michael Egan

 **Cesare Pavese** (1908–1950)

THE GOAT GOD

To the boy who comes in summer the country
is a land of green mysteries. Certain kinds of plants
are bad for the she-goat: her paunch begins to swell

and she has to run it off. When a man's had his fun with a girl—
girls are hairy down there—her paunch swells with a baby.
The boys snigger and brag when they're herding the nannies,
but once the sun goes down, they start looking nervous and scared.
The boys can tell if a snake's been around, they know
by the wriggling trail he leaves behind him in the dust.
But nobody knows when a snake is sliding through the grass.
The nannies know. There are nannies who like to lie
in the grass, on top of the snake, they like being suckled.
Girls like it too, they like being touched.

When the moon rises, the nannies get skittish,
and the boys have to round them up and prod them home. Otherwise,
the wild goat goes berserk. Rearing up in the meadow, ramping,
he gores the nannies and disappears. Sometimes girls in heat
come down to the woods, at night, alone;
they lie in the grass and bleat, and the wild billy comes running.
But once the moon is high, he goes berserk, he gores them.
And that's why the bitches bay in the moonlight,
because they've caught the scent of the wild goat leaping
on the hill, they've sniffed the smell of blood.
And the animals in the stalls start quivering.
All but the hounds, the big ones, they're gnawing at their ropes,
and one, a male, breaks loose and tears off after the goat,
and the goat spatters the dogs with blood—hotter, redder
than any fire—until they're all crazy drunk, wild
with blood, dancing and ramping and howling at the moon.

At dawn the dog comes home, savaged and snarling,
and the bitch is his reward. The peasants kick her to him.
If the boys come home at dark, with one of the nannies missing,
or a girl goes roaming at night, they're punished, beaten.
They make their women pregnant, the peasants, and go on working
just the same. Day or night they wander where they like.
They aren't afraid of hoeing by moonlight, or making a bonfire
of weeds and brush in the dark. And that's why the ground
is so beautifully green, and the plowed fields at dawn
are the color of sunburned faces. They harvest the grapes,
they eat and sing. They husk the corn, they dance and drink.
The girls are all giggling, then one girl suddenly remembers
the wild goat. Up there, on the hilltop, in the woods
and rocky ravines, the peasants saw him butting his head
against the trees, looking for the nannies. He's gone wild,
and the reason why is this: If you don't make an animal work,
if you keep him only for stud, he likes to hurt, he kills.

William Arrowsmith

French

❧ Francis Jammes (1868–1938)

A PRAYER TO GO TO PARADISE WITH THE DONKEYS

to Máire and Jack

When I must come to you, O my God, I pray
It be some dusty-roaded holiday,
And even as in my travels here below,
I beg to choose by what road I shall go
To Paradise, where the clear stars shine by day.
I'll take my walking-stick and go my way,
And to my friends the donkeys I shall say,
'I am Francis Jammes, and I'm going to Paradise,
For there is no hell in the land of the loving God.'
And I'll say to them: 'Come, sweet friends of the blue skies,
Poor creatures who with a flap of the ears or a nod
Of the head shake off the buffets, the bees, the flies . . .'

Let me come with these donkeys, Lord, into your land,
These beasts who bow their heads so gently, and stand
With their small feet joined together in a fashion
Utterly gentle, asking your compassion.
I shall arrive, followed by their thousands of ears,
Followed by those with baskets at their flanks,
By those who lug the carts of mountebanks
Or loads of feather-dusters and kitchen-wares,
By those with humps of battered water-cans,
By bottle-shaped she-asses who halt and stumble,
By those tricked out in little pantaloons
To cover their wet, blue galls where flies assemble
In whirling swarms, making a drunken hum.
Dear God, let it be with these donkeys that I come,
And let it be that angels lead us in peace
To leafy streams where cherries tremble in air,
Sleek as the laughing flesh of girls; and there
In that haven of souls let it be that, leaning above
Your divine waters, I shall resemble these donkeys,
Whose humble and sweet poverty will appear
Clear in the clearness of your eternal love.

Richard Wilbur

❧ Paul Valéry (1871–1945)

HELEN

It is I, O Azure, come from the caves below
To hear the waves clamber the loudening shores,
And see those barks again in the dawn's glow
Borne out of darkness, swept by golden oars.

My solitary hands call back the lords
Whose salty beards beguiled my finger-tips;
I wept. They sang the prowess of their swords
And what great bays fled sternward of their ships.

I hear the martial trumpets and the deep-
Sea conches cry a cadence to the sweeps;
The oarsmen's chantey holds the storm in sway;

And high on the hero prows the Gods I see,
Their antique smiles insulted by the spray,
Reaching their carved, indulgent arms to me.

Richard Wilbur

THE GRAVES BY THE SEA

This tranquil vault, assuming files of doves,
Is quivering between the pines and tombs.
The perfect noon composes there with fires
The sea, the sea, the always rebegun!
After abstracting thought, what recompense
In this long gazing on the calm of gods!

Sacred travail of purest lights consumes
The many diamonds in this sightless foam,
And massive peace bethinks itself alive.
When one sun trusts itself above the void,
The pure effectings of a deathless cause,
Times scintillates, and wisdom is the dream.

The constant hoard, Athena's simple shrine,
Calmness of strength, and visible reserve,
The prideful depths, Eye holding in yourself
So rich a sleep beneath your veils of fire,
Oh my own silence! Building in the soul,
The vault a thousand tiles, heavy with gold!

Temple of time, my essence found in breath,
I climb and use myself to this pure point,

Engulfed inside my vision of the sea.
And for that sovereign gift I owe the gods,
The calm explosion of this light now seeds
A regal scorn in staring down on heights.

Just as fruit melts in our possessing it,
Changing its absence to deliciousness
Inside a mouth in which its form will die,
So here I scent the fumes from my own pyre,
And to the soul consumed the sky intones
The rumors of these seething, changing shores.

That clearest sky observes me too in change.
After astringent pride, after so strange
An idleness, yet filled with pending power,
I now give up myself to burnished space;
Over houses of the dead my future shade
Subdues me to its own gaunt pace on graves.

The soul at solstice naked to its fires,
I am sustaining you, refulgent justice
Of light itself, your shafts so pitiless!
I cede you pure back to your primal place:
Regard yourself! . . . But to reflect the light
Requires that other part of dismal shade.

For my sole self, inside myself alone,
Close to a heart, the poem's humid source,
Between a nothingness and pure event,
I wait the echo from my breadth within,
That cistern bitter, grave, and resonant,
Soul's vibrant mold, forever possible!

Do you know, false prisoner of leaves,
Gulf devourer of these slender rails,
On my closed eyes, a secrecy that stuns,
What body drags me to its languid end,
What brow attracts it to a soil of bones?
A spark remembers there my absent ones.

Sacred and closed in bodiless pure fire,
A chthonic fragment sacrificed to light,
This fatal place is pleasing, held by suns,
Composed of gold, of stone, and sombre trees,
Where so much marble trembles over shades —
A faithful ocean sleeping on my tombs!

Shining bitch-hound, keep out idolaters!
When by myself, my peace a shepherd's smile,
I keep and graze the flock, mysterious
White sheep, of all my quiet tombs for hours,

Keep away from here the cautious doves,
The useless dreams, the busy, prying angels!

Once here, the future is an idleness.
Sharp insects cut across the brittleness;
Everything is burnt, destroyed or shrunk
Into I know not what severe an essence. . . .
Life must be vast, so drunk it is on absence,
And bitterness is sweet, the mind is pure.

The hidden dead fit firmly in this earth,
Which holds them warm to drain their mystery.
The Noon on heights immobile, absolute
There knows itself, agrees with self alone . . .
Complete pure head, and flawless diadem,
I am the secret, living change in you.

You only have my soul to hold your fears.
My guilt, uncertainties, my blind constraints,
These flaw the water of your perfect stone. . . .
But in their darkness under marble slabs
A people vague among the roots of trees
Have slowly come to seize your primal side.

They have dissolved into thick nothingness.
Red clay drinks our own kind colorless —
Arteries of flowers absorb the given blood.
Where are the dead's unique, quick idioms,
Their arts of being selves, their only souls?
Worms work through where tears were formed.

The sharp cries of girls aroused and felt,
The eyes, the teeth, the eyelids fluid wet,
The maddening breast which teases with desire,
The blood which blazes in the yielding lips,
The final gifts, the fingers guarding them,
All goes to earth, falls back into the game.

And you, proud soul, do you expect some dream
Not stained by all these colors that deceive,
Which sea and gold make here to eyes of flesh?
Will you then sing when you are only air?
My presence now is porous — all must die:
Your sacred restlessness must cease and lie.

Gaunt immortality, gilt-lettered black,
Consolatrix fixed hideously with laurel,
Who transforms death into a mother's breast —
That pious ruse and myth too beautiful —
Who does not know, who yet cannot refuse
The stretched eternal grin, the empty skull.

Father in the depths, unhoused heads,
Lying beneath the weight of spaded soil,
Who are the earth and who confute our steps,
The true gnawing, the irrefutable worm
Is not for you asleep beneath these slabs—
He lives off life—it's me he never quits!

Love, perhaps, or even hatred of the self?
His secret tooth forms such a part of me
That any name seems right—no matter what!
He sees, feels, dreams, desires and wills!
It is my flesh he likes; even in sleep
I lie transfixed by his unclosing eyes. . . .

Zeno! Cruel Zeno, the Eleatic one!
You cut me with that arrow feathered taut,
Which quivering will fly but never move,
The sound begetting, arrow killing me!
Ah sun, a tortoise shadow for the soul,
Achilles motionless in breathless strides!

But no! . . . Arise! Into successive time!
My body, break apart this pensive mold;
My chest, inhale the naissance of the wind!
A coolness, rising off the breathing sea,
Gives back my soul . . . Ah salty potency!
Run into waves to re-emerge alive!

Yes! Giant sea endowed with ecstasies,
Hide of Bacchic panther, chlamys slit
By thousands of those icons of the sun,
Hydra absolute, drunk in your blue flesh,
Biting endlessly your glittering tail
In noise as deep as silence is its like,

The wind is rising! . . . We must try to live!
Immense air riffles through my taken book;
A reckless wave bursts pulverized on rock.
Let brilliant pages scatter in the flaws!
And crash, waves, crush this tranquil vault
Where crying taut sails plunged, predators!

John Finlay

❧ O. V. de Milosz (1877–1939)

KING DON LUIS

King don Luis wanted to see again
The palace called Sweet Years.

Cloak of grief and a black horse.

Bell in the blank of evening:
Never so ominous as this —

Harsh as the wind's hurry
Through abandoned houses.

Indeed, it is a sound
Travelling farther than time.

Doors swinging into reveries
Over men dead, and women.

Treacherous advent, entering
From what dreams, what shores.

Over my mind it sleeps
In false glimmers of poison.

And the tall beggar, most certainly,
Is that sound's body.

On the road into exile.
Sinister, self-encountering!

I see two eyes nearly headless,
Two eyes on two legs of thread.

Farther than the forgotten,
Deeper than the drowned.

The black horse pricks its ears.

The king's blood would cry out
The smell of silence is so old.

John Peck

ᔓ Guillaume Apollinaire (William Apollineris de Kostrowitski, 1880–1918)

MIRABEAU BRIDGE

Under the Mirabeau Bridge there flows the Seine
    Must I recall
  Our loves recall how then
After each sorrow joy came back again

Let night come on bells end the day
The days go by me still I stay

Hands joined and face to face let's stay just so
    While underneath
The bridge of our arms shall go
Weary of endless looks the river's flow

    Let night come on bells end the day
    The days go by me still I stay

All love goes by as water to the sea
    All love goes by
How slow life seems to me
How violent the hope of love can be

    Let night come on bells end the day
    The days go by me still I stay

The days the weeks pass by beyond our ken
    Neither time past
Nor love comes back again
Under the Mirabeau Bridge there flows the Seine

    Let night come on bells end the day
    The days go by me still I stay

Richard Wilbur

ZONE

In the end you are weary of this ancient world

This morning the bridges are bleating Eiffel Tower oh

Weary of living in Roman antiquity and Greek

Here even the motor-cars look antique
Religion alone has stayed young religion
Has stayed simple like the hangars at Port Aviation

You alone in Europe Christianity are not ancient
The most modern European is you Pope Pius X
And you whom the windows watch shame restrains
From entering a church this morning and confessing your
You read the handbills the catalogues the singing posters
So much for poetry this morning and the prose is in the papers
Special editions full of crimes
Celebrities and other attractions for 25 centimes

This morning I saw a pretty street whose name is gone
Clean and shining clarion of the sun
Where from Monday morning to Saturday evening four times a day
Directors workers and beautiful shorthand typists go their way
And thrice in the morning the siren makes its moan
And a bell bays savagely coming up to noon
The inscriptions on walls and signs
The notices and plates squawk parrot-wise
I love the grace of this industrial street
In Paris between the Avenue des Ternes and the Rue Aumont-Thiéville

There it is the young street and you still but a small child
Your mother always dresses you in blue and white
You are very pious and with René Dalize your oldest crony
Nothing delights you more than church ceremony
It is nine at night the lowered gas burns blue you steal away
From the dormitory and all night in the college chapel pray
Whilst everlastingly the flaming glory of Christ
Wheels in adorable depths of amethyst
It is the fair lily that we all revere
It is the torch burning in the wind its auburn hair
It is the rosepale son of the mother of grief
It is the tree with the world's prayers ever in leaf
It is of honour and eternity the double beam
It is the six-branched star it is God
Who Friday dies and Sunday rises from the dead
It is Christ who better than airmen wings his flight
Holding the record of the world for height

Pupil Christ of the eye
Twentieth pupil of the centuries it is no novice
And changed into a bird this century soars like Jesus
The devils in the deeps look up and say they see a
Nimitation of Simon Magus in Judea
Craft by name by nature craft they cry
About the pretty flyer the angels fly
Enoch Elijah Apollonius of Tyana hover
With Icarus round the first airworthy ever
For those whom the Eucharist transports they now and then make way
Host-elevating priests ascending endlessly
The aeroplane alights at last with outstretched pinions
Then the sky is filled with swallows in their millions
The rooks come flocking the owls the hawks
Flamingoes from Africa and ibises and storks
The roc bird famed in song and story soars
With Adam's skull the first head in its claws
The eagle stoops screaming from heaven's verge
From America comes the little humming-bird
From China the long and supple
One-winged peehees that fly in couples

Behold the dove spirit without alloy
That ocellate peacock and lyre-bird convoy
The phoenix flame-devoured flame-revived
All with its ardent ash an instant hides
Leaving the perilous straits the sirens three
Divinely singing join the company
And eagle phoenix peehees fraternize
One and all with the machine that flies

Now you walk in Paris alone among the crowd
Herds of bellowing buses hemming you about
Anguish of love parching you within
As though you were never to be loved again
If you lived in olden times you would get you to a cloister
You are ashamed when you catch yourself at a paternoster
You are your own mocker and like hellfire your laughter crackles
Golden on your life's hearth fall the sparks of your laughter
It is a picture in a dark museum hung
And you sometimes go and contemplate it long

To-day you walk in Paris the women are blood-red
It was and would I could forget it was at beauty's ebb

From the midst of fervent flames Our Lady beheld me at Chartres
The blood of your Sacred Heart flooded me in Montmartre
I am sick with hearing the words of bliss
The love I endure is like a syphilis
And the image that possesses you and never leaves your side
In anguish and insomnia keeps you alive
Now you are on the Riviera among
The lemon-trees that flower all year long
With your friends you go for a sail on the sea
One is from Nice one from Menton and two from La Turbie
The polypuses in the depths fill us with horror
And in the seaweed fishes swim emblems of the Saviour

You are in an inn-garden near Prague

You feel perfectly happy a rose is on the table
And you observe instead of writing your story in prose
The chafer asleep in the heart of the rose

Appalled you see your image in the agates of Saint Vitus
That day you were fit to die with sadness
You look like Lazarus frantic in the daylight
The hands of the clock in the Jewish quarter go to left from right
And you too live slowly backwards
Climbing up to the Hradchin or listening as night falls
To Czech songs being sung in taverns

Here you are in Marseilles among the water-melons

Here you are in Coblentz at the Giant's Hostelry

Here you are in Rome under a Japanese medlar-tree

Here you are in Amsterdam with an ill-favoured maiden
You find her beautiful she is engaged to a student in Leyden
There they let their rooms in Latin cubicula locanda
I remember I spent three days there and as many in Gouda

You are in Paris with the examining magistrate
They clap you in gaol like a common reprobate

Grievous and joyous voyages you made
Before you knew what falsehood was and age
At twenty you suffered from love and at thirty again
My life was folly and my days in vain
You dare not look at your hands tears haunt my eyes
For you for her I love and all the old miseries

Weeping you watch the wretched emigrants
They believe in God they pray the women suckle their infants
They fill with their smell the station of Saint-Lazare

Like the wise men from the east they have faith in their star
They hope to prosper in the Argentine
And to come home having made their fortune
A family transports a red eiderdown as you your heart

An eiderdown as unreal as our dreams
Some go no further doss in the stews
Of the Rue des Rosiers or the Rue des Écouffes
Often in the streets I have seen them in the gloaming
Taking the air and like chessmen seldom moving
They are mostly Jews the wives wear wigs and in
The depths of shadowy dens bloodless sit on and on
You stand at the bar of a crapulous café
Drinking coffee at two sous a time in the midst of the unhappy

It is night you are in a restaurant it is superior
These women are decent enough they have their troubles however
All even the ugliest one have made their lovers suffer

She is a Jersey police-constable's daughter

Her hands I had not seen are chapped and hard

The seams of her belly go to my heart

To a poor harlot horribly laughing I humble my mouth

You are alone morning is at hand
In the streets the milkmen rattle their cans

Like a dark beauty night withdraws
Watchful Leah or Ferdine the false

And you drink this alcohol burning like your life
Your life that you drink like spirit of wine

You walk towards Auteuil you want to walk home and sleep
Among your fetishes from Guinea and the South Seas
Christs of another creed another guise
The lowly Christs of dim expectancies
Adieu Adieu
Sun corseless head

Samuel Beckett

MEADOW SAFFRON

The meadow is venomous but pleasant in autumn.
The cows at pasture
Slowly poison themselves.
The saffron, color of roundness and lilacs,
Flowers. Your eyes are like those flowers,
Blue-shadowed like their circles and this autumn,
And my life, for your eyes' sake, slowly poisons itself.

The little children come crashing from school,
Wearing their jackets and playing harmonicas.
They gather the saffron, which resembles their mothers,
Daughters of daughters, and is the shade of your eyelids,

Which flutter as flowers flutter in the mad wind.

The guardian of the herd sings very sweetly,
While, swaying and moaning, slowly the cattle abandon
Forever the sweet grass flowering cruelly in autumn.

Robert Mezey

THE CAVALIER'S FAREWELL

Oh God! what a lovely war
With its songs its long leisure hours
I have polished and polished this ring
The wind with your sign is mingling

Farewell! the trumpet call is sounding
He disappeared down the winding road
And died far off while she
Laughed at fate's surprises.

Anne Hyde Greet

THE TRAVELLER

Open the door where I knock weeping

Life is variable as well as Euripos

You were watching a group of clouds fall
With the orphan liner towards future fevers
And all these regrets all repentances
      Remember

Blurred fishes arching underwater flowers
One night it was the ocean
And rivers let themselves go there

I remember I can still remember

One night I went into a depressing bar
Next to Luxembourg
At the back of the place a Christ was taking off
Someone had a weasel
Someone had a porcupine
People were playing cards
And you had forgotten me

Do you remember the long orphanage of train stations
We criss-crossed cities that revolved all day
And nightly vomited the sun of days

O sailors o moody women and you my companions
      Do you all remember

Two sailors who were never separated
Two sailors who never spoke to each other
The younger in dying fell on his shoulder

      O you dear companions
The electric ringing of stations harvesters' songs
Butcher's sledge a regiment of streets without number
Bridge cavalry nights whitened in alcohol
The cities I've seen were living like fools

Do you remember the suburbs and the querulous herd of landscapes

Cypresses projected their shadows on the moon
That night at the close of summer I heard
A bird languorous constantly annoyed
And the perpetual sound of a large somber river

But at the same time that dying all the watching
All the watching of all the eyes
Rolled towards the estuary
The banks were deserted grassy silent
And the mountain on the other shore came across clearly

Then without sound without anything living seen
Living shadows passed across the mountain
In profile or turning their blurred faces suddenly
And holding the shadow of their lances forward

The shadows against the perpendicular mountain
Expanded or at certain times contracted brusquely
And these bearded shadows wept in a human fashion
Gliding step by step across the clear mountain

Do you see anyone you know in these old photographs
Remember that day the bee fell in the fire
It was at the end of summer remember

Two sailors who were never separated
The oldest wore an iron chain around his neck
The youngest kept his blond hair braided

Open the door where I knock weeping
Life is variable as well as Euripos

Rachel Blau

✑ Jules Supervielle (1884–1960)

RAIN AND THE TYRANTS

I stand and watch the rain
Falling in pools which make
Our grave old planet shine;
The clear rain falling, just the same
As that which fell in Homer's time
And that which dropped in Villon's day
Falling on mother and on child
As on the passive backs of sheep;

Rain saying all it has to say
Again and yet again, and yet
Without the power to make less hard
The wooden heads of tyrants or
To soften their stone hearts,
And powerless to make them feel
Amazement as they ought;
A drizzling rain which falls
Across all Europe's map,
Wrapping all men alive
In the same moist envelope;
Despite the soldiers loading arms,
Despite the newspapers' alarms,
Despite all this, all that,
A shower of drizzling rain
Making the flags hang wet.

David Gascoyne

✺ Pierre Reverdy (1889–1960)

ENDLESS JOURNEYS

All those seen from behind who were moving away singing
Who had been seen passing along the river
Where even the reeds repeated their prayers
Which the birds took up louder and farther on
They are the first to arrive and will not go away
They counted each step of the road
Which vanished as they went along
       They walked on the hard rock
At the edge of the fields they stopped
At the edge of the water they slaked their thirst
   Their feet raised a cloud of dust
And it was a coat embroidered by the sunlight
All who were going away
walking in that desert
And for whom the sky had now opened
Were still looking for the tip of land at the world's end
The wind that pushed them continued on its rounds
   And the door closed again
A black door
    Night

John Ashbery

❧ Yvan Goll (1891–1950)

THE SALT LAKE

(written in German)

Like some winter animal the moon licks the salt of your hand,
Yet still your hair foams violet as a lilactree
From which a small shrewd wood-owl calls.

The city we sought stands built for us, the dream city
Where the streets are all black and all white.
You walk in the glittering snow of expectancy
My road is bound by the rails of dark reason.

The houses are drawn in chalk against the sky
And their doors are cast of lead;
Only there under the gables do yellow candles
Grow like the nails for countless coffins.

For all too soon we arrive at the salt lake.
There the kingfishers with their long bills lie in ambush;
All night barehanded I struggle against them
Until at last I make our bed from their warm down.

George Hitchcock

THE FERRY OF LEAD

In our time men die before they are dead
Sitting on their suitcase filled with empty boxes
They watch the dance of the eternal wave
As they wait for the ferry

The past withers from their memory
The song starves on their lips
The song of the ancient goatherd
Loved by the young honeysuckle

The goat with Juno's eyes will go on haunting the hill
And the black wine in the suburbs of Corinth
Will fire the poet's loves again
When all of us are dead on the ferry of lead

Galway Kinnell

✲ Paul Éluard (Eugène Grindel, 1895–1952)

THE DEAF AND BLIND

Do we reach the sea with clocks
In our pockets, with the noise of the sea
In the sea, or are we the carriers
Of a purer and more silent water?

The water rubbing against our hands sharpens knives.
The warriors have found their weapons in the waves
And the sound of their blows is like
The rocks that smash the boats at night.

It is the storm and the thunder. Why not the silence
Of the flood, for we have dreamt within us
Space for the greatest silence and we breathe
Like the wind over terrible seas, like the wind

That creeps slowly over every horizon.

Paul Auster

LADY LOVE

She is standing on my lids
And her hair is in my hair
She has the colour of my eye
She has the body of my hand
In my shade she is engulfed
As a stone against the sky

She will never close her eyes
And she does not let me sleep
And her dreams in the bright day
Make the suns evaporate
And me laugh cry and laugh
Speak when I have nothing to say

Samuel Beckett

❧ André Breton (1896–1966)

THE MARQUIS DE SADE

The Marquis de Sade has gone back inside the erupting volcano
Which he'd come from
With his beautiful hands still fringed
His girlish eyes
And that every-man-for-himself intellect which was
His alone
But from his phosphorescent study with its lamps of viscera
He hasn't stopped flinging the mysterious commands
That crack open the darkness of morality
It's through that crack I see
The great creaking shadows the old mined-out husk
Dissolve
So that I can love you
The way the first man loved the first woman
In total freedom
The freedom
For which fire itself became man
For which the Marquis de Sade defied the centuries with his great abstract
    trees
Of tragic acrobats
Clinging to the Virgin gossamer of desire

Bill Zavatsky and Jack Rogow

IN THE EYES OF THE GODS

To Louis Aragon

"A little before midnight down by the docks.
If a disheveled woman follows you don't pay any
                                attention.
It's the azure. You don't have to be afraid of the azure.
There'll be a large blond vase in a tree.
The bell tower of the town with blended colors
Will be your reference point. Take your time,
Remember. The brown geyser hurling fern shoots into the
                                                sky
Salutes you."
The letter sealed with a fish's three corners
Was now passing by in the light of the suburbs
Like an animal tamer's sign.
                        All the same,
The beautiful woman, the victim, the one known
In the neighborhood as the little reseda pyramid
Unstitched just for herself a cloud like

A sachet of pity.
               Later the white armor
Which used to take care of household and other chores
Taking it easy now more than ever,
The child with the seashell, the one supposed to be . . .
But shh.
          A brazier was already baring
Its breast to a delightful cloak-
And-dagger story.
                  On the bridge, at the same time,
Like so the cat-headed dew rocked back and forth.
Night,—and their illusions would be lost.
Here are the white Fathers coming back from vespers
With the immense key hanging above them.
Here are the gray heralds; finally here's her letter
Or her lip: my heart is a cuckoo for God.

But by the time she speaks, nothing's left except a wall
Flapping inside a tomb like an unbleached sail.
Eternity searches for a wristwatch
A little before midnight down by the docks.

                          Bill Zavatsky and Jack Rogow

ഇ Louis Aragon (1897–1982)

RICHARD II FORTY

My country now is like a barge
Left by the haulers to the reef
And I am like that king in charge
Of more misfortune than belief
Still am I king of all my grief

For living now is just a dodge
For tears the wind's no handkerchief
In all I love my hate must lodge
What I have lost gives them relief
Still am I king of all my grief

The heart knows how to beat no more
The blood just stirs so cold and brief
Let two and two not add to four
When Grundy says fly like a thief
Still am I king of all my grief

Whether the sun should live or die
The colours wither from the leaf
Sweet Paris of my youth goodbye

And Quai-aux-Fleurs in spray and sheaf
Still am I king of all my grief

Desert the woods the fountains flee
You birds so quarrelsome be brief
Your songs are sent to Coventry
The bird-catcher reigns as chief
Still am I king of all my grief

There is a time to suffer pain
When Joan brought Vaucouleurs relief
Oh cut France into shreds again
The light was pallid on the leaf
Still am I king of all my grief*

Peter Dale

*Written after the fall of France in World War II.

Francis Ponge (b. 1899)

THE PLEASURES OF THE DOOR

Kings do not touch doors.

They do not know that happiness: to push before them with kindness or rudeness one of these great familiar panels, to turn around towards it to put it back in place—to hold it in one's arms.

. . . The happiness of grabbing by the porcelain knot of its belly one of these huge single obstacles; this quick grappling by which, for a moment, progress is hindered, as the eye opens and the entire body fits into its new environment.

With a friendly hand he holds it a while longer before pushing it back decidedly thus shutting himself in—of which, he, by the click of the powerful and well-oiled spring, is pleasantly assured.

Raymond Federman

RHETORIC

I assume that we are talking about saving a few young men from suicide and a few others from becoming cops or firemen. I have in mind those who commit suicide out of disgust, because they find that *others* own too large a share of them.

To them one should say: at least let the minority within you have the right to *speak*. Be poets. They will answer: but it is especially there, it is always there that I feel others within me; when I try to express myself, I am unable to do so. Words are ready-made and express themselves: they do not express me. Once again I find myself suffocating.

At that moment, teaching the art of *resisting words* becomes useful, the art of saying only what one wants to say, the art of doing them violence, of forcing them to submit. In short, it is a matter of public safety to found a rhetoric, or rather, to teach everyone the art of founding his own rhetoric.

This saves those few, those rare individuals who must be saved: those who are aware, and who are troubled and disgusted by the others within them.

Those individuals who make the mind progress, and who are, strictly speaking, capable of changing the reality of things.

Serge Gavronsky

❧ Robert Desnos (1900–1945)

NO, LOVE IS NOT DEAD

No, love is not dead in this heart and these eyes and this mouth that proclaimed the beginning of its own requiem.
Listen, I've had enough of the picturesque, of colors and charm.
I love love, its tenderness and its cruelty.
The one I love has only a single name, a single form.
Everything goes. Mouths cling to this mouth.
The one I love has only one name, one form.
And some day if you remember it
O you, form and name of my love,
One day on the sea between America and Europe,
When the last ray of sun flashes on the undulating surface of the waves, or else one stormy night beneath a tree in the country, or in a speeding car,
One spring morning Boulevard Malesherbes,
One rainy day,
At dawn before putting yourself to bed,
Tell yourself, I summon your familiar ghost, that I was the only one to love you more and what a pity it is you didn't know it.
Tell yourself you shouldn't be sorry for anything: before me Ronsard and Baudelaire sang the sorrows of old women and dead women who despised the purest love.
You, when you die,
You will still be beautiful and desirable.
I'll already be dead, completely enclosed in your immortal body, in your astonishing image present forever among the perpetual wonders of life and eternity, but if I outlive you
Your voice and how it sounds, your gaze and how it shines,
The smell of you and of your hair and many other things will still go on living in me,
In me, and I'm no Ronsard or Baudelaire,
Just me Robert Desnos who, for having known and loved you,
Is as good as they are.
Just me Robert Desnos who, for loving you

Doesn't want to be remembered for anything else on this despicable
earth.

Bill Zavatsky

I'VE DREAMED OF YOU SO MUCH

I've dreamed of you so much you're losing your reality.
Is there still time to reach that living body and kiss
onto that mouth the birth of the voice so dear to me?
I've dreamed of you so much that my arms, accustomed
to being crossed on my breast while hugging your shadow,
would perhaps not bend to the shape of your body.
And, faced with the real appearance of what has haunted
and ruled me for days and years, I would probably
become a shadow.
O sentimental balances.
I've dreamed of you so much it's no longer right
for me to awaken. I sleep standing up, my body exposed
to all signs of life and love, and you
the only one who matters to me now, I'd be less able
to touch your face and your lips than the face and the lips
of the first woman who came along.
I've dreamed of you so much, walked so much, spoken
and lain with your phantom that perhaps nothing more is left me
than to be a phantom among phantoms and a hundred times more
    shadow
than the shadow that walks and will joyfully walk
on the sundial of your life.

William Kulik

✎ René Char (b. 1907)

ON THE BELL FRIEZE OF A ROMAN CHURCH

Home for receiving those from whom God has withdrawn,
Back stiff, stone-blue.

Despair desiring shadows
Sought without end
In its love and vertebrae.

Truth's secret tears,
The offer of some refuge.

Mark Rudman

❧ Yves Bonnefoy (b. 1923)

WHAT HOUSE WOULD YOU BUILD FOR ME

What house would you build for me,
What black writing when the fire comes?
. . .
I drew back from your signs a long time,
You hurled me from all densities.
. . .
But now endless night watches over me,
On dark horses I escape from you.

Galway Kinnell and Richard Pevear

REMEMBER THE ISLAND WHERE THEY BUILD THE FIRE

Remember the island where they build the fire
Out of every olive tree thriving on the slopes;
In order that night should arch higher and at dawn
The only wind be that of sterility.
So many charred roads will make up a kingdom
Where the pride we once knew can reign again,
For nothing can swell an eternal force
But an eternal flame and the ruin of everything.
For myself I will go back to that earth of ashes,
I will lay down my heart on its ravaged body.
Am I not your life in its deepest alarms,
Whose only monument is the Phoenix's pyre?

Galway Kinnell and Richard Pevear

French Poetry in Canada

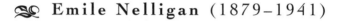

❧ Emile Nelligan (1879–1941)

WATTEAU, A DREAM

As shepherds in the red dusk went to hurry
Their big black goats with golden-wheezing flutes
And pressed on homewards from beyond the buttes
Along a hedgerow bristling with holly,

Schoolboy gypsies fresh from our study halls
With chalk dust in our hair, virginity,
Ink blotches, and unstained serenity,
We hunted nuts and laughed at waterfalls;

And, in the valley where a sheepdog ran
Yapping before the tranquil sons of Pan
Whose piping floated plaintive down the brae,

Although our coats were thin and rations sparse
Still radiant in our palaces of hay
We breakfasted on dawn and supped on stars.

David Rattray

❧ Anne Hébert (b. 1916)

THE TOMB OF KINGS

My heart's on my fist
Like a blind falcon.

This taciturn bird gripping my fingers
Lamp swollen with wine and blood,
I go down
Toward the tomb of kings
Amazed
Barely born.

What Ariadne's thread leads me
Through the muffled labyrinths?
Echoes of footsteps swallow themselves.

(In what dream
Was this child's ankle bound
Like a spellbound slave?)

The author of the dream
Pulls the thread
And naked steps start coming
One by one
Like the first drops of rain
At the bottom of wells.

The smell already stirs in swollen storms,
Oozes under the doorsills
Into the round and secret rooms
Where the walled-in beds are raised.

The dead's torpid desire tugs at me.
Astonished I watch
The blue encrusted stones
Shining among black bones.

A few patiently wrought tragedies
On the breasts of reclining kings
Are offered to me
Like jewels
Without regret or tears.

In one straight line:
The smoke of incense, dried rice-cakes,
And my trembling flesh:
Humble and ritual offering.

A gold mask on my absent face,
Violet flowers for my eyes,
The shadow of love, precise little lines of my make-up.
And this bird that I have
Breathes
And complains strangely.

A long shiver
Like the wind catching from tree to tree
Stirs seven great ebony Pharaohs
In their solemn decorated cases.

Only the depth of death persists,
Simulating the final agony
Seeking its appeasement
And its eternity
In a thin clash of bracelets,
Vain circles of foreign games
Around the sacrificed flesh.

Avid for the fraternal source of evil in me,
They lay me down and drink me:
Seven times I feel the grip of bones,
The dry hand hunting my heart to break it.

Livid and satiated with foul dreams,
My limbs freed
And the dead thrown out of me, assassinated,
What reflection of dawn wanders in here?
Why does this bird shiver
And turn toward dawn
Its punctured eyes?

A. Poulin

Walloon

❧ Willy Bal (b. 1916)

FIRE!

> There was the cottage blazing,
> The parson was ringing the bell,
> Local copper in a flap,
> The mayor swearing blue-murder.

But folks were out after berries and nutting,
Building castles in spain or chasing the girls,
Cheek by jowl in the shop of day-dreams.
The sharpest were gleaning, afraid of losing a grain.
> Step by step they got on with their business
> And it all mounted up by and by.
Mickle and muckle, hand over hand, they laid in,
Sharp fellows; and by way of relaxing
Between two good strokes, they passed on a joke.

> And the world thundered
> Like a skittle-alley floor.
> The world split at the seams
> Like an old bit of rag.

That was surely the neighbour's went up!
When the lot's burned, the fire will go out.
If you want to live quietly, turn a deaf ear.

Yann Lovelock

Scots Gaelic

❧ Iain Crichton Smith (b. 1928)

YOU ARE AT THE BOTTOM OF MY MIND

Without my knowing it you are the bottom of my mind
like a visitor to the bottom of the sea
with his helmet and his two large eyes
and I do not rightly know your appearance or your manner
after five years of showers
of time pouring between me and you:

nameless mountains of water pouring
between me hauling you on board
and your appearance and manner in my weak hands.
You went astray
among the mysterious plants of the sea-bed
in the green half light without love,

and you will never rise to the surface
though my hands are hauling ceaselessly
and I do not know your way at all,
you in the half-light of your sleep
haunting the bed of the sea without ceasing
and I hauling and hauling on the surface.

Iain Crichton Smith

THE OLD WOMAN

Tonight she is sitting by a window
and the street a Bible under her gaze.
The curtains have received many washings.
There is a glitter from the flowered floor.

The world was once without shape
men and women like a red fever
moving about flesh and mind,
nostrils tasting love and rage.

Moon and sun in the sky,
hand like a salmon leaping to hand,
the fish of the world in a net,
pain that would not let the heart rest.

And everything was put in order,
table in its place, chair in its place,
this room is the mirror of her thoughts,
armoury from which no growing music will come.

For the music that will harmonise it
is youth itself that will never return.
Her eye is sweeping the streets.
Time is crouching in the window.

Iain Crichton Smith

☙ Sorley MacLean (1911–1996)

HALLAIG

"Time, the deer, is in the wood of Hallaig"

The window is nailed and boarded
through which I saw the West
and my love is at the Burn of Hallaig,
·a birch tree, and she has always been

between Inver and Milk Hollow,
here and there about Baile-chuirn:
she is a birch, a hazel,
a straight, slender young rowan.

In Screapadal of my people
where Norman and Big Hector were,
their daughters and their sons are a wood
going up beside the stream.

Proud tonight the pine cocks
crowing on the top of Cnoc an Ra,
straight their backs in the moonlight —
they are not the wood I love.

I will wait for the birch wood
until it comes up by the cairn,
until the whole ridge from Beinn na Lice
will be under its shade.

If it does not, I will go down to Hallaig,
to the Sabbath of the dead,
where the people are frequenting,
every single generation gone.

They are still in Hallaig,
MacLeans and MacLeods,
all who were there in the time of Mac Gille Chaluim
the dead have been seen alive.

The men lying on the green
at the end of every house that was,
the girls a wood of birches,
straight their backs, bent their heads.

Between the Leac and Fearns
the road is under mild moss
and the girls in silent bands
go to Clachan as in the beginning,

and return from Clachan
from Suisnish and the land of the living;
each one young and light-stepping,
without the heartbreak of the tale.

From the Burn of Fearns to the raised beach
that is clear in the mystery of the hills,
there is only the congregation of the girls
keeping up the endless walk,

coming back to Hallaig in the evening,
in the dumb living twilight,
filling the steep slopes,
their laughter a mist in my ears,

and their beauty a film on my heart
before the dimness comes on the kyles,
and when the sun goes down behind Dun Cana
a vehement bullet will come from the gun of Love;

and will strike the deer that goes dizzily,
sniffing at the grass-grown ruined homes;
his eye will freeze in the wood,
his blood will not be traced while I live.

Sorley MacLean

Welsh

✜ Roland Jones (1909–1962)

FOAM

The Sea-god, when he walked the beach, shared out
　　　The hems of his silk surplice
To break as a thread of silver
On the cold bed of the rocks.

Tony Conran

✜ David Emrys James (1891–1952)

HORIZON

Look, a mirage, like a round rim, a strange
　　　Wizard's masterpiece about us:

An old line that's not there,
A boundary that never ends.

Tony Conran

Greek

✑ Constantine Cavafy (1863–1933)

DAYS OF 1908

That year he found himself without a job.
Accordingly he lived by playing cards
and backgammon, and by the occasional loan.

A position had been offered in a small
stationer's, at three pounds a month. But he
turned it down unhesitatingly.
It wouldn't do. That was no wage at all
for a sufficiently literate young man of twenty-five.

Two or three shillings a day, won hit or miss—
what could cards and backgammon earn the boy
at *his* kind of working-class café,
however quick his play, however slow his picked
opponents? Worst of all, though, were the loans—
rarely a whole crown, usually half;
sometimes he had to settle for a shilling.

But sometimes for a week or more, set free
from the ghastliness of staying up all night,
he'd cool off with a swim, by morning light.

His clothes by then were in a dreadful state.
He had the one same suit to wear, the one
of much discolored cinnamon.

Ah days of summer, days of nineteen-eight,
excluded from your vision, tastefully,
was that cinnamon-discolored suit.

Your vision preserved him in the very act of
casting it off, throwing it all behind him,
the unfit clothes, the mended underclothing.
Naked he stood, impeccably fair, a marvel—
his hair uncombed, uplifted, his limbs tanned lightly
from those mornings naked at the baths, and at the seaside.

James Merrill

WAITING FOR THE BARBARIANS

What are we waiting for: packed in the forum?

    The barbarians are due here today.

Why isn't anything going on in the senate?
Why have the senators given up legislating?

    Because the barbarians are coming today.
    What's the point of senators and their laws now?
    When the barbarians get here, they'll do the
        legislating.

Why did our emperor set out so early
to sit on his throne at the city's main gate,
in state, wearing the crown?

    Because the barbarians are coming today
    and the emperor's waiting to receive their leader.
    He's even got a citation to give him,
    loaded with titles and imposing names.

Why have our two consuls and praetors shown up today
wearing their embroidered, their scarlet togas?
Why have they put on bracelets with so many amethysts,
rings sparkling with all those emeralds?
Why are they carrying elegant canes
so beautifully worked in silver and gold?

    Because the barbarians are coming today
    and things like that dazzle barbarians.

And why don't our distinguished orators push forward as usual
to make their speeches, say what they have to say?

    Because the barbarians are coming today
    and they're bored by rhetoric and public speaking.

Why this sudden bewilderment, this confusion?
(How serious everyone looks.)
Why are the streets and squares rapidly emptying,
everyone going home so lost in thought?

    Because it's night and the barbarians haven't come.
    And some people just in from the border say
    there are no barbarians any longer.

Now what's going to happen to us without them?
The barbarians were a kind of solution.

Edmund Keeley and Philip Sherrard

ITHAKA

When you set out for Ithaka
pray that your road's a long one,
full of adventure, full of discovery.
Laistrygonians, Cyclops,
angry Poseidon — don't be scared by them:
you won't find things like that on your way
as long as your thoughts are exalted,
as long as a rare excitement
stirs your spirit and your body.
Laistrygonians, Cyclops,
wild Poseidon — you won't encounter them
unless you bring them along inside you,
unless your soul raises them up in front of you.

Pray that your road's a long one.
May there be many a summer morning when —
full of gratitude, full of joy —
you come into harbors seen for the first time;
may you stop at Phoenician trading centers
and buy fine things,
mother of pearl and coral, amber and ebony,
sensual perfumes of every kind,
as many sensual perfumes as you can;
may you visit numerous Egyptian cities
to fill yourself with learning from the wise.

Keep Ithaka always in mind.
Arriving there is what you're destined for.
But don't hurry the journey at all.
Better if it goes on for years
so you're old by the time you reach the island,
wealthy with all you've gained on the way,
not expecting Ithaka to make you rich.

Ithaka gave you the marvellous journey.
Without her you wouldn't have set out.
She hasn't anything else to give.

And if you find her poor, Ithaka won't have fooled you.
Wise as you'll have become, and so experienced,
you'll have understood by then what an Ithaka means.

Edmund Keeley and Philip Sherrard

THE CITY

You said, 'I will go to another land, I will go to another sea.
Another city will be found, a better one than this.

Every effort of mine is a condemnation of fate;
and my heart is—like a corpse—buried.
How long will my mind remain in this wasteland.
Wherever I turn my eyes, wherever I may look
I see black ruins of my life here,
where I spent so many years destroying and wasting.'

You will find no new lands, you will find no other seas.
The city will follow you. You will roam the same
streets. And you will age in the same neighbourhoods;
and you will grow gray in these same houses.
Always you will arrive in this city. Do not hope for any other—
There is no ship for you, there is no road.
As you have destroyed your life here
in this little corner, you have ruined it in the entire world.

Rae Dalven

℘ Yannos Ritsos (1909–1990)

THE END OF DODONA II

With the gods overthrown like that, nobody knew which way to turn.
The sick stayed in bed with their eyes closed.
Their woolen socks rotted away in their shoes, along with two flowers in a
    glass.
The cunning ones adjusted quickly. They put on their best clothes again,
circulated in the marketplace, discussed things, did business. They
    undertook
the defense against the invader. They changed the names of streets
and temples: improvised substitutions. Zeus and Dione
gave way to Jesus and the Virgin. Theodosius
added the finishing touches—what altars and sanctuaries, and that huge tree
overwhelmed by votive offerings.
                          And still
a number of people (including the best) haven't yet come to their senses.
    They're waiting once again
for better gods and people. They fume, protest,
dream, hope. We, the few (who, to some degree anyway, use their heads),
we've given up such luxuries, given up thinking itself.
We plow our small plot of land, look at the clouds once in a while,
calm now, almost secure. One day we found, thrown into a ditch,
that statuette that used to strike metal tools with its wand
and give out prophetic sounds. For a moment that moved us. We said
we'd set it aside for safekeeping somewhere. But what's the point?
Are we supposed to cling to relics these days?
And what if they dug it up on us? We left it there. Covered it with two
    handfuls of dirt.

The dog was in a hurry. It smelled the trees. Large raindrops were already
   falling.

Edmund Keeley

✆ Yannis Papaionnou (1913–1972)

NIGHTS WITHOUT HOPE (REBETIKO SONG)

Late nights without hope
I walk the streets alone.
Before your shuttered window
I spend sad hours.

How I long to meet you
to find old joys again,
again to give you kisses
so black despair will leave.

But who knows where you wander
there in some foreign land.
I wonder if you think of me
or suffer for someone else.

Gail Holst-Warhaft

✆ Odysseus Elytis (b. 1911)

THIS WIND THAT LOITERS

This wind that loiters among the quinces
This bug that sucks the vines
This stone that the scorpion wears next to his skin
And these stacks on the threshing floor
That play the giant to small barefoot children.

The images of the Resurrection
On walls that the pine-trees scratched with their fingers
This whitewash that carries the noonday on its back
And the cicadas, the cicadas in the ears of the trees.

Great summer of chalk
Great summer of cork
The red sails slanting in gusts of wind
On the sea-floor white creatures, sponges
Accordions of the rocks

Perch from the fingers even of bad fishermen
Proud reefs on the fishing lines of the sun.

No one will tell our fate, and that is that.
We ourselves will tell the sun's fate, and that is that.

Edmund Keeley and Philip Sherrard

THE MAD POMEGRANATE TREE

Inquisitive matinal high spirits à perdre haleine

In these all-white courtyards where the south wind blows
Whistling through vaulted arcades, tell me, is it the mad pomegranate tree
That leaps in the light, scattering its fruitful laughter
With windy wilfulness and whispering, tell me, is it the mad pomegranate
    tree
That quivers with foliage newly born at dawn
Raising high its colours in a shiver of triumph?

On plains where the naked girls awake,
When they harvest clover with their light brown arms
Roaming round the borders of their dreams—tell me, is it the mad
    pomegranate tree,
Unsuspecting, that puts the lights in their verdant baskets
That floods their names with the singing of birds—tell me
Is it the mad pomegranate tree that combats the cloudy skies of the world?

On the day that it adorns itself in jealousy with seven kinds of feathers,
Girding the eternal sun with a thousand blinding prisms
Tell me, is it the mad pomegranate tree
That seizes on the run a horse's mane of a hundred lashes,
Never sad and never grumbling—tell me, is it the mad pomegranate tree
That cries out the new hope now dawning?

Tell me, is that the mad pomegranate tree waving in the distance,
Fluttering a handkerchief of leaves of cool flame,
A sea near birth with a thousand ships and more,
With waves that a thousand times and more set out and go
To unscented shores—tell me, is it the mad pomegranate tree
That creaks the rigging aloft in the lucid air?

High as can be, with the blue bunch of grapes that flares and celebrates
Arrogant, full of danger—tell me, is it the mad pomegranate tree
That shatters with light the demon's tempests in the middle of the world
That spreads far as can be the saffron ruffle of day
Richly embroidered with scattered songs—tell me, is it the mad pomegranate
    tree
That unfastens with haste the silk apparel of day?

In petticoats of April first and cicadas of the feast of mid-August
Tell me, that which plays, that which rages, that which can entice
Shaking out of threats their evil black darkness
Spilling in the sun's embrace intoxicating birds
Tell me, that which opens its wings on the breast of things
On the breast of our deepest dreams, is that the mad pomegranate tree?

Edmund Keeley and Philip Sherrard

George Seferis (George Seferiadis, 1900–1971)

From MYTHICAL STORY

Bottle in the Sea

Three rocks, a few burnt pines, an abandoned chapel
and farther above
the same landscape repeated starts again;
three rocks in the shape of a gate-way, rusted,
a few burnt pines, black and yellow,
and a square hut buried in whitewash;
and farther above, the same landscape
recurs level after level
to the horizon, to the darkening sky.

Here we moored the ship to splice the broken oars
to drink water and to sleep.
The sea which embittered us is deep and unexplored
and unfolds a boundless calm.
Here among the pebbles we found a coin
and threw dice for it.
The youngest won it and disappeared.

We set out again with our broken oars.

Edmund Keeley and Philip Sherrard

STRATIS THE SAILOR BY THE DEAD SEA

> *Sometimes you see, in chapels built upon the legendary spots,*
> *the relevant passage from the Gospel, in English, and*
> *underneath the words:* THIS IS THE PLACE GENTLEMEN.
> *Letter of S.S. from Jerusalem, 22nd July, 1942*

Jerusalem, ungoverned city,
Jerusalem, city of the refugee.

Sometimes you see at noon
On asphalt of the road go slipping
A flock of black leaves scattered—
They go by, the birds of passage under the sun,
But you do not raise your head.

Jerusalem, ungoverned city.

Unknown tongues from Babel
With no relation to the grammar
To the Life of the Saints or to the Psalter
Which once they taught you to spell out in autumn
When they tied up the fishing boats to the quays;
Unknown tongues stuck fast
Like old cigarette-butts upon broken lips.

Jerusalem, city of the refugee.

But their eyes all speak the same word,
Not, God forgive us, the Word that became Man,
Not travelling to see new places, but
The dark train of escape, where babies
Feed upon the filth and the sins of parents
And the middle-aged feel growing wider
The gap between the body
That drags behind them like a wounded camel
And the soul with its courage inexhaustible, as they say.
There are also the ships that carry them
Upright, like embalmed bishops, in the holds,
So that one evening they may come to anchorage
On the sea bottom, among the weeds there, gently.

Jerusalem, ungoverned city.

Down to the river Jordan
Came three holy monks,
And tied up to the bank there
A small red sailing ship.
Three from the Holy Mountain,
Sailing for three months,
Came to the bank of Jordan
And tied on to a branch
Their votive offering,
A gift of the refugee.
Three months without food,
Three months without drink,
Three months without sleep,
And they came from the Holy Mountain,
They came from Thessaloniki,
The three slave monks.
All of us are like the Dead Sea

Many fathoms below the level of the Aegean.
Come with me. I shall show you what the place is like.

Down in the Dead Sea
There are no fishes
There are no sea weeds
No sea urchins
There is no life.
There are no creatures
Feeding stomachs
Able to hunger
Feeding nerves
Able to feel pain.

THIS IS THE PLACE GENTLEMEN . . .
Down in the Dead Sea
Cruel contempt
Is not the business
Of any person,
Nobody cares.
The heart and the mind
Grow stiff in the salt,
The bitter salt;
They take their places
Among the minerals.

THIS IS THE PLACE GENTLEMEN . . .
Down in the Dead Sea
Friend and enemy,
Children, wife,
Uncles and cousins,
Go and find them.
They stay in Gomorrah
Down at the bottom
Perfectly happy
In not expecting
Any signal.

GENTLEMEN,
          We will now continue our tour
Many fathoms below the level of the Aegean.

                                        Rex Warner

Hebrew

❧ Avraham Ben Yitzhak (1883–1950)

BLESSED ARE THEY THAT SOW

Blessed are they that sow and shall not reap
For they wander far.

Blessed are they that freely give all that they have,
The glory of their youth has made the sunlight richer
And they threw away their medals at the crossroads.

Blessed are they whose pride brims over their banks
And becomes white and humble
When the rainbow raises its arch in the clouds.

Blessed are they that know their hearts cry out in
          the wilderness,
Silence flowers on their lips.

Blessed, blessed are they, they shall be gathered
          to the heart of the world,
Warm in the coat of forgetfulness,
Eternal silence their offering
And their reward.

        Robert Mezey

❧ Yehuda Amichai (b. 1924)

MY MOTHER ONCE TOLD ME

My mother once told me
Not to sleep with flowers in the room.
Ever since, I don't sleep
With flowers, I sleep
Alone, without them.

There were lots of flowers,
But I never had enough time.
And beloved people push off
From my life,
Like boats from the shore.

My mother told me
Not to sleep with flowers:

Don't sleep. The mother of my childhood
Won't sleep.

The wooden banister I clutched
When they dragged me off to school
Was burned down long ago.
But my clutching hands remained
Clutching.

> *Benjamin Harshaw and Barbara Harshaw*

MY SON

Because of love and because of making love
And because the pain of the unborn
Is greater than the pain of the born,
I said to the woman: "Let us make a man
In our own image." And we did. But he grows
Different from us,
Day by day.

Furtively he eavesdrops on his parents' talk,
He doesn't understand but he grows on those words,
As a plant grows without understanding
Oxygen, nitrogen, and other elements.

Later on he stands before the opened
Holy Arks of legend
And before the lighted display windows
Of history, the Maccabean wars, David and Goliath,
The suicides of Masada, the ghetto uprising,
Hannah and her seven sons,
He stands with gaping eyes
And, deep down, he grows a vow like a big flower.
To live, to live, not to die like them.

When he writes, he starts the letters from the bottom.
When he draws two fighting knights
He starts with the swords, then come the hands,
And then the head. And outside the page
And beyond the table—hope and peace.

Once he did something bad in school
And was punished: I saw him,
Alone in an empty classroom,
Eating with the gestures of a tamed beast.
I told him, fight me
But he fights the school,
Law and order.

I told him, pour out your wrath on me
But he caresses me and I caress him.

The first real
Big school outing
Is the outing from which
They never return.

Benjamin Harshaw and Barbara Harshaw

BIBLICAL MEDITATIONS

1

When Jacob rolled the stone off the well,
Other options were closed,
My history opened.
But my voice remained inside, in the hollow echo.

2

Prophet: he himself is rough, he has to
Smooth the world, like sandpaper.

3

I think of the miracle
Of splitting the Red Sea, of the children
Of Israel and Pharaoh's army:
The latter drowned in the sea,
And the former in thousands of years of history.
What's better?

4

Prophet: God removed the bandage
From his mouth, too soon.

Benjamin Harshaw and Barbara Harshaw

✑ Dan Pagis (1930–1986)

SNAKE

The sand is swift, overflowing,
burrowing inside itself, searching
for remnants, tombstones, ancestors'
bones.
I never understood this hunger

for the past. I
am a series of instants,
shed my skin with ease,
forget,
outsmart myself.
In all this desert only I can guess
who was who.

Stephen Mitchell

WRITTEN IN PENCIL IN THE SEALED RAILWAY CAR

here in this carload
i am eve
with abel my son
if you see my other son
cain son of man
tell him i

Stephen Mitchell

DRAFT OF A REPARATIONS AGREEMENT

All right, gentlemen who cry blue murder as always,
nagging miracle-makers,
quiet!
Everything will be returned to its place,
paragraph after paragraph.
The scream back into the throat.
The gold teeth back to the gums.
The terror.
The smoke back to the tin chimney and further on and inside
back to the hollow of the bones,
and already you will be covered with skin and sinews and you will live,
look, you will have your lives back,
sit in the living room, read the evening paper.
Here you are. Nothing is too late.
As to the yellow star: immediately
it will be torn from your chest
and will emigrate
to the sky.

Stephen Mitchell

TWELVE FACES OF THE EMERALD

1

I am exceedingly green: chillgreen.
What have I to do
with all the greenishness of chance?
I am the green-source,
the green-self,
one and incomparable.

2

The most suspicious flash
in the cat's eye
at the most acute moment
aspires
to be
me.

3

What have I to do with you, or the living grass?
Among you I am a stranger —
brilliant, cold, playing with my eternities.

4

The emperor Nero, artist in stage-lighting,
raises me to his red eye:
only my green can pacify his blood.
Through me he observes the end of the burning world.

5

Slander! I am not
envious of the diamond: fickle duke,
reckless, lacking in self-control:
daggers! fireworks!
I, on the contrary, am moderate,
know how to bide my time,
to pour, green and accurate,
the poison.

6

As if I shared a secret. Shade of blue,
hint of red in a polished facet,
hesitating violet —
they're gone, they're gone.
I, the green-source,
abolish the colours of the rainbow.

7

You think that you will find your image
in mine.
No. I shall not leave a trace of you;
you never were in me.
Mirror facing mirror facing mirror, enchanted,
I am reflected in I.

8

With one flick of the hand
I smash your days into twelve
green nights.

9

I am all eye.
I shall never sleep.

10

And so I put on a face,
twelve facets apparently transparent.

11

Fragments of light:
they indeed are my soul: I shall not fear.
I shall not die.
I have no need to compromise.

12

You will never find the secret of my power.
I am I: crystallized carbon
with a very small quantity
of chromium oxide.

                    Stephen Mitchell

꩜ T. Carmi (b. 1925)

SHORT SONG

Nothing is deeper
than your sleep,
nothing quicker
than my hand,
nothing more complete
than our night.

All the winds
say dews;
the body, love.

Nothing is shorter
than my song;
it guards your sleep
from my hand.

Grace Schulman

Armenian

✍ Moushegh Ishkhan (b. 1913)

THE ARMENIAN LANGUAGE IS THE HOME OF THE ARMENIAN

The Armenian language is the home
and haven where the wanderer can own
roof and wall and nourishment.
He can enter to find love and pride,
locking the hyena and the storm outside.
For centuries its architects have toiled
to give its ceilings height.
How many peasants working
day and night have kept
its cupboards full, lamps lit, ovens hot.
Always rejuvenated, always old, it lasts
century to century on the path
where every Armenian can find it when he's lost
in the wilderness of his future, or his past.

Diana der Hovanessian

POETRY IN NON-EUROPEAN LANGUAGES; POETRY IN ENGLISH AND FRENCH FROM NON-EUROPEAN CULTURES

Turkish

≈ Nazim Hikmet (1902–1963)

RUBAI

I hope I do not sound boasting,
but I've gone like a bullet
        through the ten years
            of my slavery.
And if we discount these liver pains,
my heart hasn't changed, nor my head.

Send me books with happy endings.
The aeroplane with broken wings
        should touch down safely;
the doctor leave the operating theater
                    with smiles;
        the blind boy see the light again;
and just before a partisan is shot
            by a firing squad,
he should be rescued and set free;
a letter I've been waiting for
                    for ten years
reaches me
        one morning
            amid the clamour of birds;
the poet's books should sell
                    by the million;

lovers meet
    wed and celebrate in joy;
no one should be deprived
    of bread, rose, the sun
        and liberty.
Oh, send me books with happy endings,
because I believe
    that our great adventure
        just as it has done out there
          will end happily
            here
              one day.

                  Taner Baybars

ABOUT MOUNT ULUDAĞ

For seven years now Uludağ and I have been staring each other in the eye.
It hasn't moved an inch,
    and neither have I,
yet we know each other well.
Like all living things, it knows how to laugh and how to get mad.

Sometimes,
    in winter, especially at night,
        when the wind blows from the south,
with its snowy forests, plateaus, and frozen lakes
        it turns over in its sleep,
and the Old Man who lives way up there at the very top—
    his long beard flying,
        skirts billowing—
rides howling on the wind down into the valley . . .

Then sometimes,
    especially in May, at sunup,
    it rises like a brand-new world—
        huge, blue, vast,
        free and happy.
Then there are days
    when it looks like its picture on the pop bottles.
And then I understand that in its hotel I can't see
    lady skiers sipping cognac
    are flirting with the gentlemen skiers.

And the day comes
when one of its beetle-browed mountain folk, having
butchered his neighbor at the altar of sacred property,
        comes to us as a guest in his yellow homespun trousers
          to do fifteen years in cellblock 71.

             Randy Blasing and Mutlu Konuk

❧ Fazil Hüsnü Dağlarca (b. 1914)

THE SULTAN OF THE ANIMALS IS THE NIGHT

The sultan of the animals is the night
Jet-black, gleaming, furry night.
Like a female animal it gives me courage
As I think of my love.

Evoking magnificent legends
Blood in dreams,
Savage memories come charging
From starknaked mountains.

All of us animals, beasts and birds,
Crowd the marsh at this moment of tryst.
The white of my teeth glimmers
With relish and eagerness of love.

Ahmet Ö. Evin

❧ Oktay Rifat (b. 1914)

THE FLUTE

When he likened the cemetery to a herd of sheep
Or the day he felt like it, he wrote on a piece of paper:
"Death is to join the herd." And yet there was
Neither cemetery nor flute nor shepherd in this assertion.
The sound of the flute came from afar, light and playful.
The whistle had plunged into silence when it returned
To the grave saying "Here are the shepherds!" Sheep stirred.
All this, he never wrote down, but buried—better that way—
In a single line: "Death is to join the herd."
Now the flute played for him alone, but it can suddenly stop.

Talat Sait Halman

❧ Orhan Veli Kanik (1914–1950)

EROL GÜNEY'S CAT

Poem on the attitude adopted
by Erol Güney's cat toward
social problems in the spring:

A male cat and a slice of liver
Is all she wants out of life.
How marvelous!

> Poem concerning the pregnancy
> of Erol Güney's cat:

That's just what you get, see,
For slipping out into the street on a spring day.
Now you have to lie there
Thinking and worrying
Your head off.

> *Talat Sait Halman*

I AM LISTENING TO ISTANBUL

I am listening to Istanbul with my eyes closed
First a breeze is blowing
And leaves swaying
Slowly on the trees;
Far, far away the bells of the
Water carriers ringing,
I am listening to Istanbul with my eyes closed.

I am listening to Istanbul with my eyes closed
A bird is passing by,
Birds are passing by, screaming, screaming,
Fish nets being withdrawn in fishing weirs,
A woman's toe dabbling in water,
I am listening to Istanbul with my eyes closed.

I am listening,
The cool Grand Bazaar,
Mahmutpasha twittering
Full of pigeons,
Its vast courtyard,
Sounds of hammering from the docks,
In the summer breeze far, far away the odor of sweat,
I am listening.

I am listening to Istanbul with my eyes closed
The drunkenness of old times
In the wooden seaside villa with its deserted boat house
The roaring southwestern wind is trapped.
My thoughts are trapped
Listening to Istanbul with my eyes closed.

I am listening to Istanbul with my eyes closed
A coquette is passing by on the sidewalk,

Curses, sings, sings, passes;
Something is falling from your hand
To the ground,
It must be a rose.
I am listening to Istanbul with my eyes closed.

I am listening to Istanbul with my eyes closed
A bird is flying round your skirt;
I know if your forehead is hot or cold
Or your lips are wet or dry;
Or if a white moon is rising above the pistachio tree
My heart's fluttering tells me . . .
I am listening to Istanbul with my eyes closed.

Murat Nemet-Nejat

Ece Ayhan (b. 1931)

EPITAFIO

They came drowned in the afternoon to the blue house on the wharf of brown broadcloth cafes. Her fate was in Spanish.

They are bending their heads again, for their sister, as in the morning. She promised. She will comb their hair and part it in the middle. The deadtangle.

And it is calling them, screaming, screaming, from an alley of card players, a children's game with thousands. The jack is up.

They see it and how they laugh with their enduring chuckles. But they can't join the game. What can one do? Their bundles are being wrapped. They are in a hurry. Rotten . . .

Will she appear again before them the fat woman who wants the hooks and eyes of her winter coat to be clasped, and their sister, also, on the mossy rocky road to Africa?

Murat Nemet-Nejat

Feyyaz Kayacan (b. 1919)

DIVISION OF LABOR

I have problems
I know them well
They know me well
We get on nicely together
I let them worry me rent-free

Sometimes when I am reading a book
I lift my head to give them
The look of sustained recognition.
Sometimes when I'm eating my heart out
They lift their heads
To look at me and relax.

Feyyaz Fergar

ஜ Ali Püsküllüoğlu (b. 1935)

AN OLD PIRATE IN THESE WATERS

I am too old to burn ships, even if I am a pirate don't mind me
The loneliness of big waters goes by my door
My beard grows long, my hair disheveled, I am a big man but
How can I bear it, three worms,
Hungry, crawl, eat in my hand,
Rub their freckled faces and wet noses and mouths.

This wife of Potiphar is my demon, I brought her from the Caribbean Seas;
She grew on those solitary islands;
There were worms in my hand, dolphins and sparrows,
Here is my universe: one wife of Potiphar, rain, a sailboat.

More beautiful than the freckled woman's picture and dying,
Tied to life more than me, the puppies were orphaned in the evening;
I took the freckled bitches to my bed;
I called one Potiphar's wife, the other sailboat, the third rain;
They lick my hand on and off, on and off they warm me,
And they rub their freckled faces, their wet noses, their mouths.

Murat Nemet-Nejat

ஜ Özdemir İnce (b. 1938)

WIND, ANT, HISTORY

The wind had hanged itself on the plane tree
"death is God's command," they said, "but why did he destroy himself?
he was young, brave, had a bright future,
like magic, all things good and beautiful were his."

It was autumn,
rain kept coming down in torrents,
an ant drenched way down to its marrows
was looking for the safety of a hole
among the fibers of the oily rope.

"Let me pass on a secret to you," said the ant to the rain:
"this wind didn't commit suicide, they hanged him."

Talat Sait Halman

Urdu

✺ Faiz Ahmad Faiz (1911–1984)

ANY LOVER TO ANY BELOVED

Today, if the breath of breeze
wants to scatter petals in the garden of memory,
why shouldn't it?
                    If a forgotten pain
in some corner of the past
wants to burst into flame again, let it happen.
Though you act like a stranger now—
come—be close to me for a few minutes.
Though after this meeting
            we will know even better what we have lost,
and the gauze of words left unspoken
hangs between one line and another,
neither of us will mention our promises.
Nothing will be said of loyalty or faithlessness.

If my eyelashes want to tell you something
about wiping out the lines
left by the dust of time on your face,
you can listen or not, just as you like.
And what your eyes fail to hide from me—
            if you care to, of course you may say it,
            or not, as the case may be.

Naomi Lazard

BEFORE YOU CAME

Before you came things were just what they were:
the road precisely a road, the horizon fixed,
the limit of what could be seen;
a glass of wine no more than a glass of wine.

Then the world took on the tints of my heart;
magnolia-petaled happiness of seeing you,
slate the color that fell
when I was fed up with everything.

With your advent roses burst into flame;
you were the author of dried-up leaves,
the dust, poison, blood.
You colored the night black.

As for the sky, the road, the cup of wine:
one was my tear-drenched shirt,
the other an aching nerve;
the third a mirror that never reflected the same thing.

This was all before you left me.

Now you have come back. Stay.
This time things will fall into place again;
the road can be the road,
the sky, sky;
the glass of wine, as it should be, the glass of wine.

Naomi Lazard

ஜ Akhtar-ul-Iman (b. 1915)

COMPROMISE

Whenever I kissed her,
the smell of cigarettes filled my nostrils.
I've always thought of smoking as a vice,
but now I'm used to it,
it's a part of me.
She too has got used to my stained teeth.
Whenever we meet, we become strangers to words,
only our breathing, sweat, and loneliness
fill the room.
Maybe our souls are dead,
our senses have run dry,
or this story's repeated over and over again:
life's always going through the pangs of birth,
new messiahs come and go to the cross,
a dusty man in the back rows
pushes his way to the front,
climbs the pulpit, and says,
'The crucified man was ours!
His blood is our heritage!'
Then he swallows all the ideals,
all that had caused calumny,
and spits them out as commentaries
and interpretations,
the last resort of helpless people,

maybe all people.
I look for the ideal man in vain.
People dream and ride the high winds,
then reach a stage when they weep bitterly
and break like branches.
They find loved ones,
who're the focus of their desires and lives,
then come to hate them
even while loving them still.
I hate her, she despises me.
But when we meet
in the loneliness, the darkness,
we become one whole, like a lump of kneaded clay,
hatred leaves, silence stays,
the silence that covered the earth
after it was created,
and we go on breaking
like branches.
We don't talk about the dreams we once dreamt,
we don't talk about the joys,
we simply go on breaking.
I'm fond of drinking,
she's addicted to smoking,
wrapped in a sheet of silence we cling to each other,
we go on breaking
like tender branches.

C. M. Naim and Vinay Dharwadker (after Gopi Chand Narang and David Paul
Douglas, and Adil Jussawalla and Akhtar-ul-Iman)

✇ Ahmed Nadeem Qasmi (b. 1916)

THOUGHT

In the deep silence of nights
when the moon is drowsy
and flower-laden branches
rock a lullaby—

dissolved in the lake's mirror
when stars still their motion
each tree becomes an etching
and each flower a mystery—

And from dust to sky
when time curves visibly
between my thought and Allah
lie years of trenched silence—

over my sizzling body
someone sprinkles dew
from His invisible height
it seems, calling out my name.

Raja Changez Sultan

Marathi

✌ **Sadanand Rege** (1923–1982)

OLD LEAVES FROM THE CHINESE EARTH

(I bought a Chinese book at a second-hand book shop.
I got a man who spoke Japanese to explain it to me.
All that I could make out of it is what follows.)

I am Chiang Liang.
Once I was crossing the bridge,
And an old man was sitting there.
As soon as he saw me,
He took off one of his shoes
And threw it deliberately into the river,
And said to me:
My good fellow,
My shoe has fallen into the river,
Please fish it out for me.
I was furious.
But I curbed my temper
And jumped into the water.
As soon as I had come up with the shoe,
He threw the other into the river.
'Oh, there goes the other one too.'
I dived into the water again
And came back with the second shoe,
When he threw the first one back into the river.
I was furious. He said:
Meet me here again after thirteen years.

After thirteen years
There was no one on the bridge.
Only the sun blazed down on it,
The size of a tiger's jaw.
I waited a long time for the old man.
Then I came down and looked into the water:
There was my own face behind the sun,
There was nobody on the bridge except the sun.
But someone spoke out of my bones:

One shoe is life, the other is death.
I recognized the voice.

                    Dilip Chitre

✸ Hira Bansode (b. 1939)

WOMAN

She, the river,
said to him, the sea:
        All my life
        I've been dissolving myself
        and flowing towards you
        for your sake
        in the end it was I
        who turned into the sea
        a woman's gift
        is as large as the sky
                but you went on
                worshipping yourself
                you never thought
                of becoming a river
                and merging
                with me

                    Vinay Dharwadker

Hindi

✸ G. M. Muktibodh (1917–1964)

THE VOID

The void inside us
has jaws,
those jaws have carnivorous teeth;
those teeth will chew you up,
those teeth will chew up everyone else.
The dearth inside
is our nature,
habitually angry,
in the dark hollow inside the jaws
there is a pond of blood.
This void is utterly black,
is barbaric, is naked,

disowned, debased,
completely self-absorbed.
I scatter it,
give it away,
with fiery words and deeds.
Those who cross my path
find this void
in the wounds
I inflict on them.
They let it grow,
spread it around,
scatter it and give it away
to others,
raising the children of emptiness.
The void is very durable,
it is fertile.
Everywhere it breeds
saws, daggers, sickles,
breeds carnivorous teeth.
That is why,
wherever you look,
there is dancing, jubilation,
death is now giving birth
to brand new children.
Everywhere
there are oversights
with the teeth of saws,
there are heavily armed mistakes:
the world looks at them
and walks on,
rubbing its hands.

                              Vinay Dharwadker

ᘒ Dhoomil (1935–1975)

THE CITY, EVENING, AND AN OLD MAN: ME

I've taken the last drag
and stubbed out my cigarette in the ashtray,
and now I'm a respectable man
with all the trappings of civility.

When I'm on vacation
I don't hate anyone.
I don't have any protest march to join.
I've drunk all the liquor
in the bottle marked

FOR DEFENCE SERVICES ONLY
and thrown it away in the bathroom.
That's the sum total of my life.
(Like every good citizen
I draw the curtains across my windows
the moment I hear the air-raid siren.
These days it isn't the light outside
but the light inside that's dangerous.)

I haven't done a thing to deserve
a statue whose unveiling
would make the wise men of this city
waste a whole busy day.
I've been sitting in a corner of my dinner plate
and leading a very ordinary life.

What I inherited were citizenship
in the neighbourhood of a jail
and gentlemanliness
in front of a slaughter-house.
I've tied them both to my own convenience
and taken them two steps forward.
The municipal government has taught me
to stay on the left side of the road.
(To succeed in life you don't need
to read Dale Carnegie's book
but to understand traffic signs.)

Other than petty lies
I don't know the weight of a gun.
On the face of the traffic policeman
doing his drill in the square
I've always seen the map of democracy.

And now I don't have a single worry,
I don't have to do a thing.
I've reached the stage in life
when files begin to close.
I'm sitting in my own chair on the verandah
without any qualms.
The sun's setting on the toe of my shoe.
A bugle's blowing in the distance.
This is the time when the soldiers come back,
and the possessed city
is now slowly turning its madness
into windowpanes and lights.

Vinay Dharwadker

❧ Agyeya (Sachchidananda Vatsyayan, 1911–1986)

HIROSHIMA

On this day, the sun
Appeared — no, not slowly over the horizon —
But right in the city square.
A blast of dazzle poured over,
Not from the middle sky,
But from the earth torn raggedly open.

Human shadows, dazed and lost, pitched
In every direction: this blaze,
Not risen from the east,
Smashed in the city's heart —
An immense wheel
Of Death's swart suncar, spinning down and apart
In every direction.

Instant of a sun's rise and set.
Vision-annihilating flare one compressed noon.

And then?
It was not human shadows that lengthened, paled, and died;
It was men suddenly become as mist, then gone.
The shadows stay:
Burned on rocks, stones of these vacant streets.

A sun conjured by men converted men to air, to nothing;
White shadows singed on the black rock give back
Man's witness to himself.

Agyeya and Leonard Nathan

Bengali

❧ Samar Sen (b. 1916)

LOVE

Like a poisonous snake in my blood
unwinds this desire for you.

Sometimes I see a strange yellow moon in the sky
restless spring trembles among the leaves

and in the dark a red gravel path
stretches like an idle dream.

All day and all night
my desire for you
unwinds like a poisonous snake.

Pritish Nandy

SOLITARY

Embarrassed presently,
      stumbling through the future:
I sometimes wonder
if you and I should escape together
from this unpleasantly truthful earth
      to where
the blue skies descend on the waters
            lovingly
and in some lonely wolf-infested village
      build our small home —
there will be milk, eggs and corn
      all produced in the home
and at night
we will listen to the song of mosquitoes
      from the bamboo fields
            nearby
and in the afternoon
      the bride will come
            with sad bovine eyes
      to the moss-green lakes
to fetch water,
      absentminded, lonely,
knitting an ancient sorrow in the wind.

Pritish Nandy

✆ Tushar Roy (b. 1938)

NOWADAYS

A leper opens the hydrant, drinks water.
Or perhaps the hydrant was leaking.
The night descends on the city in a gang.
A car goes past coughing like an imbecile,

polluting the air.
Someone, despite infinite care, stumbles headlong

into a drain. Three rickshaws, rushing past
the last gaslight, disappear by some prestidigitator's trick.

And I, from Fear Lane, after miles
of meandering, stand here by a wall
in Bentinck Street. Near the Market.
The wind blows dry like monkeynuts.

The warmth of reeling lamps caresses my cheeks.
The smell of kerosene, timber, lac,
jute, the pungent odor of hides mingle
with murmur of dynamos, form polarities

like a bow-string, hold the dead and the living
together, sharpen contraries.

Ron D. K. Banerjee

Tamil

R. Meenakshi (b. 1944)

IF HOT FLOWERS COME TO THE STREET

Red cassia flowers
are a forest fire,
or so they say.
It's an April event
called a summer fire.
Anarchy in green.
An explosion of buds.
Fire in the snow.

On the head of Lord Shiva
of the snow mountains
there are red matted locks,
        gleaming cassia flowers,
        and the Ganga.

In his red hand,
        fire,
        a small drum,
        a deer.

And a snake at his throat.
That snake

won't strike the deer.
The fire in his hand
won't burn the Ganga.

But in our street
even flies
will swarm to hot flowers.

Martha Ann Selby

Indian Poets Writing in English

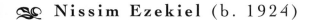

❧ Nissim Ezekiel (b. 1924)

From HYMNS IN DARKNESS

I met a man once
who had wasted half his life,

partly in exile from himself,
partly in a prison of his own making.

An energetic man, an active man.
I liked his spirit
and saw no hope for him.

Yet, he had the common touch;
he could, for instance, work with his hands.

To others, all attentive.
To his own needs, indifferent.

A tireless social human being,
destined always
to know defeat
like a twin-brother.

I saw him cheerful
in the universal darkness
as I stood grimly
in my little light.

❧ A. K. Ramanujan (1929–1993)

LOVE POEM FOR A WIFE, 2

After a night of rage
that lasted days,
quarrels in a forest,
waterfalls, exchanges, marriage,
exploration of bays
and places
we had never known
we would ever know,
my wife's always
changing syriac face,
chosen of all faces,
a pouting difficult child's
changing in the chameleon
emerald
wilderness of Kerala,
small cousin to tall

mythic men, rubber plant
and peppervine,
frocks with print patterns
copied locally
from the dotted
butterfly,
grandmother wearing white
day and night in a village

full of the colour schemes
of kraits and gartersnakes;
adolescent in Aden among stabbing
Arabs, betrayed and whipped
yet happy among ships
in harbour,
and the evacuees,
the borrowed earth

under the borrowed trees;
taught dry and wet,
hot and cold
by the monsoon then,
by the siroccos now
on copper
dustcones, the crater
townships in the volcanoes

of Aden:
          I dreamed one day

that face my own yet hers,
with my own nowhere
to be found; lost; cut
loose like my dragnet
past.
I woke up and groped,
turned on the realism

of the ceiling light,
found half a mirror
in the mountain cabin
fallen behind the dresser
to look at my face now
and the face
of her sleep, still asleep
and very syriac on the bed

behind: happy for once
at such loss of face,
whole in the ambivalence
of being halfwoman half-
man contained in a common
body,
androgynous as a god
balancing stillness in the middle

of a duel to make it dance:
soon to be myself, a man
unhappy in the morning
to be himself again,
the past still there,
a drying
net on the mountain,

in the morning, in the waking
my wife's face still fast
asleep, blessed as by
butterfly, snake, shiprope,
and grandmother's other
children,
by my only love's only
insatiable envy.

❧ Dilip Chitre (b. 1938)

MY FATHER TRAVELS

My father travels on the late evening train
Standing among silent commuters in the yellow light.

Suburbs slide past his unseeing eyes.
His shirt and pants are soggy, and his black raincoat
Is stained with mud, his bag stuffed with books
Is falling apart. His eyes dimmed by age
Fade homeward through the humid monsoon night.
Now I can see him getting off the train
Like a word dropped from a long sentence.
He hurries across the length of the grey platform,
Crosses the railway line and enters the lane.
His chappals are sticky with mud, but he hurries on.

Home again, I see him drinking weak tea,
Eating a stale chapati, reading a book.
He goes into the toilet to contemplate
Man's estrangement from a man-made world.
Coming out, he trembles at the sink,
The cold water running over his brown hands.
A few droplets cling to the greying hair on his wrists.
His sullen children have often refused to share
Jokes and secrets with him. He will now go to sleep
Listening to the static on the radio, dreaming
Of his ancestors and grandchildren, thinking
Of nomads entering a subcontinent through a narrow pass.

Chinese

⋙ Lü Hsün (1881–1936)

HESITATION

Lonely, desolate, the new literary scene;
Peaceful, tranquil, the old battlefields.
'Tween earth and sky remains a single warrior
Shouldering a lance, wandering aimlessly, alone.

William R. Schultz

CALL TO ARMS

Take up the pen: fall into the net of law;
Resist the times: offend popular sentiments.
Accumulated abuse can dissolve the bones,
And so, one gives voice to the empty page.

William R. Schultz

Hu Shih (1891–1962)

DREAM AND POETRY

It's all ordinary experience,
All ordinary images.
By chance they emerge in a dream,
Turning out infinite new patterns.

It's all ordinary feelings,
All ordinary words.
By chance they encounter a poet,
Turning out infinite new verses.

Once intoxicated, one learns the strength of wine,
Once smitten, one learns the power of love:
You cannot write my poems
Just as I cannot dream your dreams.

September 10, 1921

Kai-yu Hsu

Kuo Mo-jo (1892–1978)

EARTHQUAKE

The earth revives,
All beings tremble,
But this is only for a second,
Then all is hushed.

There is silence after the heave,
A silence like annihilation,
Sunshine smiles to the children,
To the dazed and terrified children.

I remember this once happened in my youth,
Mother told me 'twas an enormous turtle opening and shutting
its eyes.
Under the earth is there truly a giant turtle?
I saw it with the eye of a youthful mind.

Now the enormous turtle is dead
And yet I see it soaring through the air.
I know that the quake was caused by a volcano
But how does this knowledge benefit my soul?

Harold Acton and Ch'en Shih-hsiang

❧ Mao Tse-Tung (1893–1976)

LYRICS

1

To the tune "Spring in the Gardens of the
Princess of the Ch'in River": Snow

Glitter of a northern kingdom
a thousand icebound miles
ten thousand miles awhirl with snow
gaze at the Great Wall   on either side
a single unending blur
up and down the Yellow River
the mighty surge stock-still
yet mountains   dancing   are silver snakes
high plains a-gallop are beeswax elephants
struggling to outmatch God in heaven
on a clear day
like white chiffon beneath red
seductive past measure

rivers and mountains as lovely as these
have moved unnumbered champions to vie in homage
yet sadly Ch'in Shih-huang and Han Wu-ti
lacked a touch of polish
T'ang T'ai-tsung and Sung T'ai-tsu
scarcely were equal to the *Songs* and *Sorrows*
and the glory of his time
Chingis Khan
only knew how to draw the bow and shoot great hawks
and all have vanished long ago
to count our "headlong heroes"
come   look at this morning

David Lattimore

2

To the tune "Spring in the Gardens of the
Princess of the Ch'in River": Ch'angsha

I stand alone in the cold autumn
the River Hsiang goes north
by the shore of Orange Island
red all around the myriad mountains
rows of woods drenched utterly in color
the brimming river jade-green   clear
a hundred barges fight for the current

eagles swoop down the long void
fish whirl through shallows
ten thousand species this frosty day vie for freedom
restless in this infinitude
I ask the huge hazy earth
who rules all that floats or drowns

once I wandered here   hand in hand with many comrades
I remember those exalted   crowded   months and years
my lucky harmony with fellow students
wind-tossed flowers just in bloom
with the fervor of scholars
robust and cavalier
we pointed to these hills and streams
our writings sluiced the muddy   spread the pure
lords of ten thousand doors that year were cowdung
don't you remember
pounding the waves even to midstream
we splashed those winging vessels to a halt

David Lattimore

RETURN TO SHAOSHAN

I regret the passing, the dying, of the vague dream:
my native orchards, thirty-two years ago.
Yet red banners roused the serfs, who seized three-pronged lances
when the warlords raised whips in their black hands.
We were brave and sacrifice was easy
and we asked the sun, the moon, to alter the sky.
Now I see a thousand waves of beans and rice and am happy.
In the evening haze heroes are coming home.

Willis Barnstone
with Ko Ching-po

♉ Wen I-to (1898–1946)

DEAD WATER

Here is a ditch of hopelessly dead water.
A cool breeze would not raise the slightest ripple on it.
You might throw in some scraps of copper and rusty tins,
or dump in as well the remains of your meal.

Perhaps the green on copper will turn into emeralds,
or the rust on tin will sprout a few peach blossoms.

Let grease weave a layer of fine silk-gauze, and
mould steam out a few red-glowing clouds.

Let the dead water ferment into a ditch of green wine,
floating with pearls of white foam;
but the laughter of small pearls turning into large pearls
is broken by spotted mosquitoes stealing the wine.

Thus a ditch of hopelessly dead water
can yet claim a bit of something bright.
And if the frogs can't endure the utter solitude,
let the dead water burst into song.

Here is a ditch of hopelessly dead water.
Here beauty can never reside.
You might as well let ugliness come and cultivate it,
and see what kind of world comes out.

Arthur Sze

❧ Chu Hsiang (1904–1933)

THE PAWNSHOP

Beauty runs a pawnshop,
Accepting only the hearts of men.
When the time comes for them to redeem their belongings,
She has already closed the door.

Kai-yu Hsu

❧ Feng Chih (b. 1905)

SONNET

We often pass a night warm and intimate
In an unfamiliar room whose shape
In the daytime we have no way to know,
Let alone its past, its future. The plain

Endlessly stretches before our window.
We vaguely remember the road we came by
In the dusk: such is our knowledge.
Tomorrow, we will leave and return no more.

Close our eyes then! Let these warm, intimate nights
And unfamiliar places weave in our heart:
Our life is like the plain outside the window.

Upon the misty plain we recognize
A tree, a flash of lake-light; within the boundlessness
Is hidden the forgotten past, the seen-unseen future.

Wai-Lim Yip

❧ Li Kuang-t'ien (1906–1968)

A DEAD TURK

Was he English, or French?
Some said he was a Turk.
Anyway, he was a foreigner
Ending his journey
In this village.
Here
No one hears any chanting from a church,
Or any prayer;
Only several calls of a rooster at noon,
Those several sad reports,
Announced the departure of this man.
Was it cholera, or scarlet fever?
Who knows?
Some said his was homesickness.
But people here don't understand
What homesickness is.
They proceed from homes to the fields,
And from fields
To their homes,
Walking back and forth
For ten generations, a hundred generations,
While the roadside weeds turn yellow and green again.

Migrant birds come and go.
They are familiar with all these
And they know
Whose dog it is that barks like a wail,
Or the old man of which family
Has lost several teeth . . .
They never paid attention
To why there are people leaving their hometown
To travel here and there
Like tumbleweeds in autumn wind
Like homeless souls,
Like this Turk.
Now, the Turk
Is lying down on an earthen *kang* in a small inn,
His face covered
By perpetual peace.

In peace perhaps
He is listening to people talk —
They don't know how
To dispose of this strange person:
"Throw him into a mountain creek?"
Someone asked.
Another wanted to drop him in the river,
Letting him follow the water away
And leave nothing behind, not even a trace.
Yet a third one said, "He too is a man,
He too has a soul,
Only when the dead are in peace
Can the living live on undisturbed."

They are, then, to bury the Turk in earth,
In a pauper's graveyard where
There are graves of orphans and widows,
That have been reduced to handfuls of dirt,
Where the bleached bones of beggars and night prowlers
Are gleaming under the weeds dark green,
Where those having sold all they had
And having been drunkards and gamblers over half of their lives
Also go to stay.
To this home for all homeless souls
They now are sending that Turk.
He,
A lonely traveler
From the shores of the Black Sea,
Had once dreamed of strange lands
And their beautiful sights.
He also had heard fairy tales of the Orient,
About someone summoning the wind and the rain,
About an old fox explaining sutras and parables at midnight.
There were also in the Orient women with bound feet,
Their shoes resembling tiny bridges,
And people said of them, each step a water lily.
There were the blue sky and yellow sea of the Heavenly Kingdom,
Limitless huge plains,
And golden dust . . .
But did he ever dream
Of occupying a plot of the Oriental earth,
Together with these lost Oriental souls,
Lying down,
And of letting the warm East wind blow
And cold rains drench
The mound of weedy dirt that covers pleasant dreams?
Perhaps
Perhaps he still thinks of Istanbul,
Of the Turkish prairie,
And of the cattle and sheep over there.

Now only the hard-working farmers here
Will walk from their homes to the fields
And again from the fields
Back to their homes.
Smoking their long pipes
And cloaked in the morning sun and the afterglow,
They'll pass by
Time and time again.
Perhaps by chance they'll mention:
On a certain day in a certain month of a certain year,
There was such and such a human being. . . .

Kai-yu Hsu

❧ Ai Ch'ing (1910–1996)

THE CHILEAN CIGARETTE PACK

A Chilean cigarette pack
bears the portrait of the Statue
of Liberty. Holding her torch on high,
still, she stands in shadow.

As an ad or trademark,
she is allowed her place on the packet.
You can buy the thing for a few cents
and it will go up in smoke . . .

be thrown to the roadside;
walked and spat upon.
In symbol or in fact,
liberty is but a pack of cigarettes.

Huangling Nieh

❧ Tsang K'o-chia (b. c. 1910)

THE STREET ANGEL

A pair of feet, born so nimble,
Whirl around like the wind.
A soft scent wafts from the hem of her clothes;
Love blossoms all over the patterns of the carpet.
(She never said that she was tired.)

She knows how to use clever words
To coax the awkward pleasure of a patron.
She knows, too, how to use her wordless glances

To coat other people's hearts with honey.
(She never revealed her own heart.)

Red-colored and green-colored wine
Pin a spring blossom on her cheeks.
The scent of flesh intoxicates more than the wine's scent,
While her youth burns brighter than fire.
(Youth flees so fast she has no time to reflect.)

Her throat is gifted for singing,
Note after note draw an echo from your heart.
Joy, sorrow, she knows how to sing them all,
You need only name your choice.
(She never sings her own song.)

Alone she bears a night of solitude,
The lamp shines on four walls of quiet grief.
Memory lights up the way from the beginning,
She heaves a deep sigh and closes her eyes.
(This moment she has only herself in the world.)

Kai-yu Hsu

☙ Ho Ch'i-fang (1912-1977)

GET DRUNK

To Those Who Sing Ever So Gently

Get drunk, get drunk,
Those truly drunk are lucky
For paradise belongs to them.

If alcohol, books,
And lips that drip honey . . .
If none of these can cover up man's suffering,
If you proceed from being dead drunk to half sober
To fully awake finally,
Wouldn't you keep your hat cocked and
Your eyes half closed,
To act slightly intoxicated throughout your life?

The flies shivering in the cold wind
Flutter their wings before the paper window pane,
Dreaming of dead bodies,
Of watermelon rinds in high summer,
And of a dreamless void.

In the epilogue of my ridicule
I hear my own shame:

"You too are only buzzing and buzzing
Like a fly."

If I were a fly,
I'd await the sound of a fly swatter
Smashing on my head.

Kai-yu Hsu

✖ Ch'en Meng-chia (1911–1966)

AN OLD WHITE RUSSIAN

Glorious days he had, and a chivalrous spirit.
Now he is old:
How much has he suffered from the wind and the cold?
He coughs, he pants, but still keeps silence
Like a great desert in Siberia.
The hurricane rolled his tent away and rolled
Withal his folk, his cattle, and his stars,
And whirled him to the strange land by the sea.

As a peak rising sheer
In autumn, tranquil and austere,
He still has dignity.
A lump in his breast
Will now and then induce a cough or sigh,
And lightly quiver down
Small dewy drops upon his yellow beard.
He does not speak, he only nods his head.

Keeping eternal silence, pipe in mouth,
Across the page his eyes run to and fro;
Something troubles his mind,
He raises his eyes and lo:
In a casual glance they find
The portrait of Nicholas, divine and bold.
Maybe the cold
Makes him cough out again; he calls: "Natasha!"

Harold Acton and Ch'en Shih-hsiang

✖ Jen Jui (d. 1949)

MIDNIGHT

Midnight. The flowing water of Hu T'o River
Sounds more distinctly.

Suddenly a strong wind blows.
The wind's sound and the water's sound
Together become an enormous roar.
I cannot sleep in peace.
The voices of nature speak
To the troubled hearts of men.
I lie quietly, stilling my heart.
I refuse to remember
The tragic death of the father of my sons.
I refuse to remember
The husband and wife
Embracing, leaning against each other,
Or the sons and daughters around their knees.
I will not imagine
My youngest son's fate on the battlefield.
With all my heart I long for the dawn.
The cruelty of Fascism
The violence and corruption of the enemy
Have turned white the hair of mothers
And wrinkled their foreheads.
At last the dawn comes.
But with it come again
Savage battles, young men falling,
Others taking their places
In heroic sacrifice.
How many of my friends
Are already mothers of martyrs?
Perhaps I am one of them.

Kenneth Rexroth and Ling Chung

❦ Yen Chen (c. 1950s)

ON THE WILLOW BANK

The river bank is white like silver.
The morning moon, shaped like
a gold sickle, is standing on the snow.
The willows on both shores
are cast against thousands of clouds.
The travelling bells ring quick —
like beans jumping in the frying pan.

Bells ring quick, bells ring near;
the wheels speed on ahead.
The Red Banners sway in the wind
like peach blossoms in the groves.
The commune's cart is returning;
the snow whirls up to the sky.

O full-laden carts, what do you carry?
Seeds, tools, or fertilizers?
Passers-by cannot see well
and stop on the road, asking.

The easing driver
brushes his hands and shrugs,
in a low voice —
"What we carry is spring."

Smiles the one who asks.
Smiles the one who answers.
Their smiles beam like the flashing wheels.
Wheels have trodden a thousand miles
and ahead will keep on flying.

Arthur Sze

Korean

✺ Han Yongwun (1879–1944)

THE ARTIST

I'm no artist but in bed
I can paint with my fingertip
your breast your mouth and cheeks,
and surely that crooked smile
that floats around
your eyebrows as you sleep.

When the neighbors are gone
and even the crickets quiet
I am still too shy to sing
the songs you taught me
to the sleeping cat.

I am not a poet but I can describe
your glance, your voice,
the way you walk in the garden
before coming to bed,
even each separate pebble
on the path that runs
the twenty steps from here to there.

Bruce Taylor

✑ Yi Jang'hi (Jang-hi Lee, 1902–1928)

THE SPRING IS A CAT

On a cat's fur soft as pollen,
The mild Spring's fragrance lingers.

In a cat's eyes round as golden bells,
The mad Spring's flame glows.

On a cat's gently closed lips,
The soft Spring's drowsiness lies.

On a cat's sharp whiskers,
The green Spring's life dances.

Chang-soo Koh

✑ Kim Sowŏl (1903–1934)

YEARS FROM NOW

Should you come to me
Years from now,
I shall say: "I have forgotten."

Should you scold me,
I shall say: "After much longing I have forgotten."

Should you persist in scolding me,
I shall say: "For lack of trust I have forgotten."

Not yesterday, not today,
But years from now,
I shall say: "I have forgotten."

Kevin O'Rourke

✑ Kim Kwangsŏp (1905–1977)

HAVING DIED

The general becomes a sword
The sovereign becomes a mausoleum
The rich become a fence
The poor become stones and sand.

I would become a cloud,
in the arms of a favoring wind
travel a thousand miles,
rain on the grasses burning
on a tomb.

David R. McCann

Byok Namkung (20th century)

GRASS

Grass, summer grass,
Dew drenched grass of Yoyogi fields,
Gently, as if kissing a lover's lips,
I tread you with my bare feet.
Are you not truly the lips of the earth?

Should this, however, distress you,
I suggest that when I die
I turn to earth and go beneath your roots
To make you spring up high.

Should this still distress you,
Then I suggest that you and I,
Animate as we are, each
Walking the perimeters of immortality

Shall meet again
On that eternal road.
Then you can become me and I you
And you can tread gently on me
As I now tread on you.

Kevin O'Rourke

No Ch'ŏnmyŏng (1912–1957)

A NAMELESS WOMAN

I wish to be a nameless woman
way out on a small hillside.
With gourd-vines on the roof of my cottage,
pumpkins and cucumbers in a hemp-garden,
the moon invited into my yard
over a fence made of roses,
and my arms full of stars;
the owl-hooting dark will not make me lonely.

In a village where the train never stops,
eating millet-cake soaked in a brass basin,
talking with a close friend until late at night
about the secrets of the fox-haunted mountains,
while a shaggy dog barks at the moon,
I shall be happier than a queen.

Ko Won

ᘏ Sŏ Chŏngju (b. 1915)

SELF-PORTRAIT

Father was a serf, seldom came home at night.
At home my grandmother, old as
The shriveled root of leek,
And a blossoming date tree.
Big with child, Mother wanted just one apricot.

I was a mother's son with dirty fingernails
Under a lamp by the mud wall.
With bushy hair and staring eyes,
I am said to resemble Grandpa on Mother's side,
Who in 1894 went to sea and never returned.

For twenty-three years the wind has reared two-thirds of me,
And the world has become a more embarassing place.
Some have read a convict in my eyes,
Others an idiot in my mouth.
Yet I will repent nothing.

At each dawn, brightly assailing,
The dews of poetry settled on my brow,
Mixed with drops of blood.
And I have come this far panting
Like a sick dog with his tongue hanging out
In the sun and in the shade.

Peter H. Lee

OWL

What the devil is his gripe
that he comes moaning in the night,
clearly cradling some complaint
against my father and mother,
against me and my wife to be?
My poems first, then my face,

a single hair out of place . . .
Indeed he's known to spy by day,
far away in the shadow of gloom,
reciting his weird incantations.
Though blood-red waves from the other
world drench his wings, he turns
unblinking eyes to the sky. Owl . . . owl . . .
long ago you built your round nest
and dwelt in the dark night of my mind.

Kevin O'Rourke

ELEPHANTS OF THAILAND

The elephants of Thailand perform their bows extremely well.
To their mothers and fathers, of course;
and also to their offspring they bow
very well indeed.
          Familiar living creatures,
of course; and to living creatures
not so familiar, they perform their deep bows.
To anything that can be seen
as well as what might very well
never be seen they perform
their deep formal bows without fail.
They enjoy in the gap
between time and distance
their relatively uneventful independence.

David R. McCann

WANDERER'S BOUQUET

Once one year, and I don't know when,
so lonely I could not stand it,
I became a wanderer and spent the year
roaming the mountain district,
and as I did I broke and gathered
a handful of flowers, a bouquet.
That bouquet of flowers I
gave to some child by the roadside.

That child by the roadside
by now must have grown,
and perhaps being lonely he too
has plucked a handful of flowers
to give to some other child.

And after some tens of years have passed,
crossing over yet one more bridge,
might that present of the bouquet
pass on to a child I haven't seen?

And so on a certain day
one thousand, or one thousand five hundred
years from now, below a mountain
where the sky is clearing after rain,
on a vast plain as the sun begins to fall,
where the hand of a new wanderer extends the bouquet,
is the child coming to receive it?

David R. McCann

❧ Pak Mokwŏl (1919–1978)

PRAYER IN FOUR VERSES

1

The Lord has shown me
His hands held out together,
His empty hands.
There falls only my sorrow
Upon his palms like snow.
Now, Lord, your hands are full
Like snow-laden boughs of an evergreen.

2

I have nothing, Lord.
Fill me with the lonely emptiness
From which everything is drained,
Until I am like an empty vase
Left at random on a table.

3

Something I feel
Of sorrow and of ecstasy
Fretting to an irritation.
A moonlit edge of hill,
Ever swept by the wind,
Which I call life.
The whole universe
Glowing white with moonbeams.

4

A thin thirst is spread in me
Like the violet twilight over a December field.

Crossing over the chilled waters of half-mockery and half-regret,
I proceed towards you, Lord.
Drench my cheeks with hot tears
And drown me in your mercy.

Kim Chong-gil

✆ Ko Changsu (Chang-soo Koh, b. 1934)

OCEAN LINER

Slowly the ocean-liner
moves in dreamy motion
as if an island were shifting ground,
weary of its fixed gravity.

Like a baby whale coming for milk,
the pilot boat comes near,
snuggles the ship for a while
and then reluctantly moves away,
leaving the island on the sea.

A little hurt despite its elegance,
the ocean liner struggles over the boundary
between affection and disowning
and gradually travels into memory.

Chang-soo Koh

Japanese

✆ Yosano Akiko (1878–1942)

From TANGLED HAIR

A thousand lines
Of black black hair
All tangled, tangled—
And tangled too
My thoughts of love!

After he came up from the bath,
I gave him

My purple robe
To protect him from the wind —
How beautiful he looked!

    Kissing his fingers,
    I thought them too slender
    For the hilt of the sword
    Raised against
    The devils of this world!

To punish
Men for their endless sins,
God gave me
This fair skin,
This long black hair!

               Sanford Goldstein and Seishi Shinoda

From THE CHANNEL BOAT

What shall I wear to sleep in alone?
An under-kimono of silk crepe
dyed the hushed red of dawn.
It touches the skin
like heavy mist falls on flowers.
Each time I wear it I'm glad
I was born a woman.

In the candle's glowing flame
its smallest motion
has a beauty that makes me catch my breath
even in this bedroom without you.
It's strange but
as I slip under the quilts
in the cold February bed
my heart returns to the days
when I was a girl and first loved you.

My husband traveler
are you sleeping now in France?
If a bird of paradise comes into your dreams
it is me.

    Janine Beichman

❧ Saitō Mokichi (1882–1953)

From MOTHER DIES

From far off I have brought medicines, she watches me because I am her son

I go near her, she watches me and says, she says something because I am her son

On the vermillion-lacquered spear on the wall-beam I see dust; close to mother, in the morning, I see it

I have offered prayers to the sunlight coming out of the mountains. The flowers of columbines continue to bloom

Lying by mother, who's close to death, night hushed, frogs in distant paddies are heard in heaven

Mulberry fragrance drifts blue at daybreak, it is unbearable, I call to my mother

Going near the eyes of mother who's close to death, I said, Columbines are blooming

It's spring, light flows, and I'm sad. Perhaps by now, gnats are born in the grassfields

As I rub the forehead of mother who's close to death, my tears keep flowing—as I come to myself

Away from mother's eyes, for some time, I watch—how sad the silkworms asleep

My mother, my mother who is going to die, mother with sagging breasts, who gave birth to me

With two red-throated swallows perched on the crossbeam, mother with sagging breasts comes to death

People who are alive gathered and saw my mother's life go to death, go to death

I come alone, stand in the silkworm room, and my loneliness becomes extreme

Hiroaki Sato and Burton Watson

❧ Takamura Kōtarō (1883–1956)

WHALE SPOUTING

When May entered the Black Current off Kinkazan Island
the sea suddenly blossomed,
shimmered like a dome of blue cellophane.
The waves, brilliantly flowing, were wincing under the midday sun
coursing ever closer to the land.
The sperm whale, after spouting once, dived deep again,
pillowed the giant weight of his head on the waters.
Enraptured by this warm current, salt-rich and silky,
he now lets his mind flow free, losing himself in boundless dreams
That I am not a dolphin, not a grampus,
but my very self, a sperm whale,
makes me the happiest creature in the world, the whale thinks.
Ah, it's no use fighting against the present.
The whale knows nothing beyond the moment.
He is always reveling on the crest of existence.
He doesn't bother about hypotheses, he doesn't get into metaphysics.
The whale, intoxicated with dreams on the brink of slumber,
has intimations of unknown territory approaching,
is half frightened, half relieved.
Once more he reared up, and into the May sky
spouted his bellyful of the Current, almost a rainbow.
The lookout siren is hooting at Ayukawa Port on the Oshika Peninsula,
but this colossal optimist is blissfully unaware of it.

James Kirkup and Akiko Takemoto

❧ Kitahara Hakashū (1885–1942)

SECRET SONG OF THE HERETICS

I believe in the heretical teachings of a degenerate age, the witchcraft of the
    Christian God,
The captains of the black ships, the marvelous land of the Red Hairs,
The scarlet glass, the sharp-scented carnation,
The calico, arrack, and *vinho tinto* of the Southern Barbarians;
The blue-eyed Dominicans chanting the liturgy who tell me even in dreams
Of the God of the forbidden faith, or of the blood-stained Cross,
The cunning device that makes a mustard seed big as an apple,
The strange collapsible spyglass that looks even at Paradise.
They build their houses of stone, the white blood of marble
Overflows in crystal bowls; when night falls, they say, it bursts into flame.
That beautiful electrical dream is mixed with the incense of velvet
Reflecting the bird and beasts of the world of the moon.

I have heard their cosmetics are squeezed from the flowers of poisonous
    plants,
And the images of Mary are painted with oil from rotted stones;
The blue letters ranged sideways in Latin or Portuguese
Are filled with a beautiful sad music of heaven.

Oh, vouchsafe unto us, sainted padres of delusion,
Though our hundred years be shortened to an instant, though we die on the
    bloody cross,
It will not matter; we beg for the Secret, that strange dream of crimson
Jesus, we pray this day, bodies and souls caught in the incense of longing.

                                                  Donald Keene

❧ Nishiwaki Junzaburō (1894–1982)

JANUARY IN KYOTO

(written in English)

Janus, old man,
Your name is damp and grey and too prolonged
A ring to rattle in my verse;
You double-faced, diluted churl of churls,
You corn-dull, poppy-wilted, beaver-brown,
You snow-eater, a parasite on roots and berries,
Iconoclast of gins and perries,
You're really one of the pariah dogs
Yelping, thrash-worth, at the belated gods.
I know the deities would rather inflate
And flow in pipes than in metric odes, but now
You suddenly brought us shy myth,
When we, disguised as Zeus and Hermes, went
Looking for orchids that will hang oblong and dim
At cuckoo-crow at the hell lady's door,
In the Hiei foot-hills by pebbly-purring streams.

We went into a peasant's cottage to see
How one cleans and adorns one's range
With a sprig of rue and a tangle of hips
To honour the bluff god of the kitchen fire.
The old baucis-and-philemon tree rustled its top:
"Reverend sirs, you are early. Well now."
My friend, a Ben Jonson scholar at the university,
And a complete parr angler, could speak
The Yase doric: "Look what we've got,
Such lovely slender buds; may we leave
These things with you by this mercury bush,

As we're going to see Emau Convent up there?"
Again we went out into loam land, dreaming
Of Angels and pottery crystal-beaming:
This time as tinkers we wandered . . .
Post-orchid journey it will be named.
A redolent trek, there was a smell
Of yellow plum blossom in the turnip fields.
"Who is it walking with you, strangers?"
"It is a woman."
She is in holy visibility:
That was an old woman with the help of a stick
On her way from Shu-gaku-in to Iwakura
To draw out money, the account book on her head,
Nicely done up in a peony-patterned cloth
Probably to ransom her helen out of peonage.
She had a leer like a boar
And had a stutter like Darley;
But it might be thunder if she chose to parley.
Excited by our indignation on the boar ravages,
With fury and frothing she made a Delphic utterance:
"It only took them a night to devour
A middlesex acre (as Macaulay says) of your yams;
Last year they shot a huge one, but nobody
Could bear him anyway, so there you are . . ."
So saying she glowered at us and passed by.
Now I come to the second nonnes tale:
We greeted the ancress in a most elegant way;
Unrobed, aproned, head tonsured as azure as
The kingfisher's wings, sweeping up fallen leaves
Among the landscape stones green with moss,
Herself indistinguishable from the blue.
"Good morning, Madame Eglantine, may I
See your garden? Wonderful!
And do you happen to know my relation
Who is a prioress living near Kitano-Tenjin?"
"I wouldn't know, sir. But how odd, when I've been
Of the same tribe nearly all my life.
Bo tree, that. Very, very rare."
"Perhaps you could let me have a twig in the spring;
I'd like to graft it on a stock . . . mulberry it is."
Enlightenment . . . an entwining of rose and bay.
"By all means. Secretum secretorum!"
When we returned full circle to the roots
Of our orchids, we maundered to sanctify
Fertility . . . magic jabber . . . over cups of tea.
The wife decanted golden mead to immortalize
Our chats and our pseudo-godliness, but we tried
Hard to hide our mortality . . .

A MAN WHO READS HOMER

Dawn and dusk
Quiet like the sides of a gold coin
Came every day through
A tamarind tree to his throat.
Those days he lodged upstairs
At a dyer's, reading Homer.
Those days he had a coral pipe
Painted with a heart's-ease.
All the Gallics laughed, "Yours
Is like a pipe resembling a girl's letter
Or a Byzantine love story—oui!"
Yet the phosphorescent smoke encircles a cockscomb
And also a goddess' thigh.

Masaya Saito

✆ Mitsuharu Kaneko (1895–1975)

MOUNT FUJI

Like the inside of a picnic box
Japan is tiny and self-contained

From corner to corner, with scrupulous care,
We are all counted, one by one,

so that we get called up to fight in the forces
in a most disgraceful way.

Census register book, be burned to ashes
so that no one may remember my son.

My son,
come here and hide away between my hands,
come and hide underneath my hat for a little while.

Your father and mother, in the inn at the mountain foot,
discussed the matter all night long.

Rain was falling all night long,
drenching the naked trees,
with the sounds of breaking twigs.

My son, drenched to the skin,
dragging a heavy rifle, gasping for breath,
I see you tramping along in a daze.
Where are you, my son?

Not knowing where you are,
your father and mother go wandering to look for you
in a night-long dream that lasts until
daybreak brings to an end the long, disturbed night.

We wake to see the rain is over, but
not our nightmare. And in a vacant sky,
dull as damnation, like some
shabby old bathrobe faded in the wash,
—Mount Fuji.

James Kirkup and Akiko Takemoto

✺ Saitō Fumi (b. 1909)

THREE TANKA

1

The palm of the hand
is not aware of dying as
without compulsion
it becomes cold and hardened
and only slightly shrunken.

2

With wings that will not ever
be folded a butterfly
will be made to soar
indefinitely in the white
hours of continuation.

3

As a landscape in the far distance
is how human life appears
and in autumn wind
upon the extended fields
a black locomotive goes.

Edith Macombe Shiffert and Yūki Sawa

✺ Ishigaki Rin (b. 1920)

HANDS

My outspread hands,
the hands in front of me.

These are alive,
alive and moving.

These hands some day will be old.
These hands some day will stop moving.

They will be folded by the hands of others who will mourn over me,
will be placed on my cold chest,
and stay for a while
in the world where my soul will no longer exist.
Ah, when the outside world is filled with light
and a soft breeze blows just like today,
what will the dry skin of these hands see and feel
for the eyes
that are closed?

Hands,
where will you dispose of
all the memories
of the many things you have held?
Tell me.
        (When I look away,
        I see a procession of many creatures
        moving away one after another
        waving their hands like flower petals.
        Where are they going?)

Unmistakably, these are the expressions of my hands,
vivid and sad,
of the living hands of my mortal self.

When I put my hands together, they feel strangely warm,
giving me a singular sense,
certain but imperceptible,
that they are mine
and that some day they will be gone.

                    Naoshi Koriyama and Edward Lueders

ॐ Tamura Ryūichi (b. 1923)

INVISIBLE TREE

I saw little tracks in the snow.
Looking at them,
I saw for the first time
the world that is governed by small animals,
little birds and beasts in the woods.
Take a squirrel, for instance.

Its tracks come down an old elm,
cross the trail,
and disappear into the fir woods.
There is no momentary hesitation, no anxiety, no clever question mark.
Or take a fox, for instance.
His tracks go endlessly in a straight line
down the valley road north of the village.
The hunger I know has never drawn
a straight line like his.
My heart has never had
such a resilient, blind, affirmative rhythm as in these tracks.
Or take a bird, for instance.
Its tracks are clearer than its voice,
the print of its claws sharper than its life.
Its wings are printed on the slope of snow.
The fears I've known have never drawn
such a simple pattern.
My heart has never had
such a sensual, heretical, affirmative rhythm as in these wingprints.

Suddenly the huge setting sun hangs on the summit of Mt. Asama.
Something makes forests,
pushes open the mouth of the valley,
rips apart the cold air.
I return to the hut.
I make a fire in the stove.
I am
an invisible tree,
an invisible bird,
an invisible small animal.
I think only
of the invisible rhythms.

Naoshi Koriyama and Edward Lueders

ᘒ Ibaragi Noriko (b. 1926)

WHAT A LITTLE GIRL HAD ON HER MIND

What a little girl had on her mind was:
Why do the shoulders of other men's wives
give off so strong a smell like magnolia;
or like gardenias?
What is it,
that faint veil of mist,
over the shoulders of other men's wives?
She wanted to have one,
that wonderful thing

even the prettiest virgin cannot have.

The little girl grew up.
She became a wife and then a mother.
One day she suddenly realized;
the tenderness
that gathers over the shoulders of wives,
is only fatigue
from loving others day after day.

Kenneth Rexroth and Ikuko Atsumi

WHEN I WAS PRETTIEST IN MY LIFE

When I was prettiest in my life,
the cities crumbled down,
and the blue sky appeared
in the most unexpected places.

When I was prettiest in my life,
a lot of people around me were killed,
in factories, in the sea, and on nameless islands.
I lost the chance to dress up like a girl should.

When I was prettiest in my life,
no men offered me thoughtful gifts.
They only knew how to salute in the military fashion.
They all went off to the front, leaving their beautiful eyes behind.

When I was prettiest in my life,
my head was empty,
my heart was obstinate,
and only my limbs had the bright color of chestnuts.

When I was prettiest in my life,
my country lost in a war.
"How can it be true?" I asked,
striding, with my sleeves rolled up, through the prideless town.

When I was prettiest in my life,
jazz music streamed from the radio.
Feeling dizzy, as if I'd broken a resolve to quit smoking,
I devoured the sweet music of a foreign land.

When I was prettiest in my life,
I was most unhappy,
I was most absurd,
I was helplessly lonely.

Therefore I decided to live a long time, if I could,
like old Rouault of France,
who painted magnificent pictures in his old age.

Naoshi Koriyama and Edward Lueders

Lao

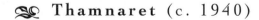 **Thamnaret** (c. 1940)

NIGHTSONG

These are my countries, my forests
And fields full of fires
In the peacock's gold eye
A world and an occasion—love
In my crazy house on stilts
And my latitude of gold inhabited
By a race of dancers
Whose slightest posturing
Is itself both end and beginning
As, from the end of innocence
They contrive an eloquence
Ambiguous as leaves
Wind rising, in the fire—
Trees the firefly's sermon:
This night, the End of Desire
Your love will be like a stone

Your love will be like a stone
In your mouth, you will be
Blind, you will not see the sun
Nor know the moon's urgency
Trembling on the verge of
Light; but dark will be your own
Heart's house, timbered with shadows
Whose walls lengthen and sway
Like dancers, open and close
Like those enormous, dreaming trees
That celebrate their death
In constant seasons of leaves
Until, in an excess of
Love at last you will be undone
In your house (like your heart)
At the heart of a stone

This is my world and weather
Countries of my ruined house

Locked in their fastnesses
Their colors fading on my sleeve
All this landscape gone to seed:
Cities of stone, cities
Of sandalwood returned
Each year to their own dust
Under the immemorial, fading fall
Of constant suns, of constant snows
That drink the wildest weather up
Under the drinking trees
Alas! I am not what I was
Am more foreign now for being loved
But O, if I could only wear
The singing countries of my heart
Once more upon my sleeve

Ronald Perry

Vietnamese

✺ Tu Mo (1900–1976)

THE MANDARINS GOT THEIR RAISE

You'd think all these mandarins, big shots,
small shots, with their fat checks, would be rolling
in gravy, but no! They're hard up, too, it seems,
like any petty official.

Grimacing, grumbling, they draft a petition
to claim that they're hungry and hurting
for cash. They tighten their belts, but still
can barely afford to feed the wife and kids.

Then where will they get the money
for car repairs, for champagnes and wines
to feast the grandees who happen
to visit their homes?

And where will their wives get money
for rubies, diamonds, trinkets of gold,
damasks, silks, and costly gowns
to grace their charming bodies?

And money for buying houses and land?
And security for old age?
And legacies for their children
to guard against future want?

Such a pity the mandarins suffer so!
The State, of course, must raise their pay.
Poor mandarins, they just want to be happy,
they want to live like kings.

The mandarins got their raise, so did the people:
raised taxes, levies, tolls.
Who cares if the loincloth is more shredded?
Who measures the common misery?

Magnificent salaries, lavish raises,
but no sympathy for the masses. All right:
You've got your raise. Now just stop squeezing
the vise around us. That's all we beg.

Nguyen Ngoc Bich

✑ The Lu (1907–1989)

GREEN NOSTALGIA

Soliloquy of a Tiger in a Zoo

I chew a bitter cud, lying
in an iron cage as days and months drag by.
Dwarfish gawkers, their tiny eyes eager
with ignorant presumption, mock my jungle pride.
A blow of destiny swept me behind
these bars of shame,
a curiosity, a toy, equated
with a bunch of crazy bears
and a pair of stupid leopards.

Now I live only in the memory
of those days when I walked freely
in my own territory.
Ah, I see clearly the stretches
of hills and forest, shady patches, twisted trunks;
I hear the blast of winds, torrents shaking the hillside,
and my own terrible immortal voice
rolling through the spaces as I glide
among silent shadows, prickling leaves, fiery grasses,
my skin undulating in rhythmic waves.
When my eyes sparked green and gold in the cave,
nothing moved.
I knew I was king of animals
in an empire with no name
and no beginning.

Golden nights by the brook, where are they,
when I was drunk with the smell of quarry

and the taste of melting moonbeams?
Stormy days when the woods' four corners shook,
as my calm gaze swept over the changing realm,
where are they? And the dawns, the sunbathed branches,
celebrations of birds as I slept, the blood-drenched
evenings when I watched the torrid sun sink
till the vast and secret dark was mine alone —
where are they?

Now only the permanent grudge, the lump of hate
for tended gardens, stunted flowers,
vulgar, phony, never changing,
lawns trimmed to fashion, straight-line paths
with trees at equal intervals, a clogged trickle
to pass for a brook, oozing through mounds of dirt.
The tangled mysteries of jungle foliage
are mocked by a foolish clump of leaves.

Solemn landscape!
Land I'll never see again,
where our holy race ruled
and I roamed in liberty:
Do you know how in these vacant days
my mind flows back in giant forest dreams
to repossess your frontiers,
o my terrible wilderness!

Nguyen Ngoc Bich

✎ Do Tan (b.c. 1940)

TWENTY YEARS

The girl grew up to become a woman
the boy grew up to become a man
man met woman in the forbidden wood
their child was the gift of spring.

The spring child joined the revolution
the revolution was a ravening cannibal
man's portion was exile, prison, bullets,
with sun, roses, and a blood-reeking flag.

The woman weeps for the girl that was
the man weeps for the boy that was
their child sleeps the eternal sleep in the earth
the spring hangs its head and sighs.

Nguyen Ngoc Bich

❧ Du Tu Le (b.c. 1940)

WHAT I LEAVE TO MY SON

No point in leaving you a long list
of those who have died:
Even if I limit it to my friends and your uncles
it won't do. Who could remember them all?
My son, isn't it true?
The obituaries leave me indifferent
as the weather. Sometimes they seem to matter
even less: How can that be, my son?

I'll leave you, yes,
a treasure I'm always seeking, never finding.
Can you guess? Something wondrous,
something my father wanted for me
although (poor man!) it's been nothing
but a mirage in the desert
of my life.
My soul will join his now, praying
that your generation may find it —
simply peace —
simply a life better than ours
where you and your friends won't be forced
to drag grief-laden feet down the road
to mutual murder.

Nguyen Ngoc Bich

❧ Ha Thi Thao (b.c. 1940)

OUR SON'S PROFESSION

you ask what our son's profession should be
I say teach him to paint
so he can sketch maps of Vietnam
where the hate we're creating will be blotted out
teach him to cut the barbed wire
that pierces the festering waist of our land
teach him medicine
so he can heal the clotted wounds of the past
last teach him the land's language
of acid fields and saline waters
then you can burn all the rest of the books
I'll spread my thin arms to hide the fire
as for the ashes just sweep them aside
with the years of bleeding and weeping

let our son remake this land
let him complete the circle
whose diameter now is the river of shame
you and I will stand north and south
and watch over our young boy as he sleeps

Nguyen Ngoc Bich

๑ Le Ngoc Hiep (1944–1970)

I AM SAD

When I got back to base
I sensed something had happened.
They said you went to hospital
and my heart was torn and sad.
I always think of you, Bui Huu Phai.
Your life runs out like a red silk banner.
Your many friends are waiting
anxious for news about you.
Dear brother, my feelings well up
and I wish so much to see you.
Stronger than vast oceans or blue mountains,
because mountains fall and seas dry up,
my feelings for you endure.
My feelings for you, unshakable.
You and I must keep safe
and march on home in victory soon.
I came to Ha-Tay on the first ship
nurturing this dream, not losing heart.
Perhaps we mustn't dream about life.
Life is now too hard, dear brother.
So many dreams float in air.
The more I think, the sadder I get.
How can one find his way to the future?
I think of you and weep these long nights.
I think of us chatting in an immense dusk,
listening to poems sung in the evening
the two of us drinking tea together.
Wouldn't that be a happy moment?
These images seem so real in this poem,
but right now they're hard to believe
as I hold this pen and write you.

John Balaban with T. L. Nguyen

Filipino Poets Writting in English

✌ José Garcia Villa (b. 1906)

NOW I PRIZE YELLOW STRAWBERRIES

Now I prize yellow strawberries —
With their dignities of silk and
Their archbishpal opulence —
Rivalling God the peacock only.

Assuming neither space nor time,
A purely intellectual fruit,
Yet of matchless elegance. This
Is my intellectual religion.

For I would not have bishops lean
Nor peacocks irreligious, but
Temper them to that great gold pitch
Of the first-ascending bridegroom.

So, to the tune of yellow strawberries,
Announce to philosophy my arrival —
O a little irreverent perhaps
But religiously, peerlessly musical.

INVITING A TIGER FOR THE WEEKEND

Inviting a tiger for a weekend.
The gesture is not heroics but discipline.
The memoirs will be splendid.

Proceed to dazzlement, Augustine.
Banish little birds, graduate to tiger.
Proceed to dazzlement, Augustine.

Any tiger of whatever colour
The same as jewels any stone
Flames always essential morn.

The guest is luminous, peer of Blake.
The host is gallant, eye of Death.
If you will do this you will break

The little religions for my sake.
Invite a tiger for a weekend,
Proceed to dazzlement, Augustine.

I WAS SPEAKING OF ORANGES TO A LADY

I was speaking of oranges to a lady
of great goodness when O the lovely

giraffes came. Soon it was all their
splendor about us and my throat

ached with the voice of great larks.
O the giraffes were so beautiful as

if they meant to stagger us by such
overwhelming vision: Let us give

each a rose said my beautiful lady
of great goodness and we sent the

larks away to find roses. It was
while the larks were away that

the whitest giraffe among them
and the goldest one among them

O these two loveliest ones sought
and found us: bent before us two

kneeling with their divine heads
bowed. And it was then we knew

why all this loveliness was sent
us: the white prince and the golden

princess kneeling: to adore us
brightly: we the Perfect Lovers.

Indonesian

✌ Rendra (W. S. Rendra, b. 1935)

THE MOON'S BED, THE BRIDE'S BED

The moon's bed, the bride's bed:
An azure blue sky
Held up by ancient hands;
A cricket flutters about,
Shrilling a love song to the net.

The moon's bed, the bride's bed:
A Chinese junk with a thousand sails
Crossing the sea of sleep;
Stars fall one by one,
Yawning with sweet visions.

The moon's bed, the bride's bed:
A kingdom of ghosts and spirits,
Drunk with the flavour of incense;
Dreams scatter, one by one,
Cracked by brittle truth.

Burton Raffel

THE WORLD'S FIRST FACE

In the pale moonlight
He carries his bride
Up that hill,
Both of them naked,
Bringing nothing but themselves.

So in all beginnings
The world is bare,
Empty, free of lies,
Dark with silence —

A silence that sinks
Into the depths of time.
Then comes light,
Existence,
Man and animals.
So in all beginnings
Everything is bare,
Empty, open.

They're both young,
Both have come a long way.
Passing through dawns bright with illusion,
Skies filled with hope,
Rivers lined with comfort,
They have come to the afternoon's warmth,
Both of them dripping with sweat —

And standing on a barren coral reef.
So evening comes,
Bringing dreams
And a bed
Lined with gleaming coral necklaces.

They raise their heads:
Millions of stars in the sky.
This is their inheritance,
Stars and more stars,
More than could ever blink and go out.

In the pale moonlight
He carries his bride
Up that hill,
Both of them naked:
The world's first face.

Burton Raffel

TALL WEEDS

You're the woman I love best and forget fastest, my love,
Because in this evil silence weeds grew over my miserable heart,
Tall weeds, with long torturing roots.

They're dark weeds, soft, painful.
She's dark and swaying
And she blossoms in sin.
My heart's still yours
But weeds grow in my breast.

Burton Raffel

BABY AT THE BOTTOM OF THE RIVER

There is a song, there is a moaning in the song
there is a song not torn from a mouth
not even the cold and blue mouth.
The cold bodiless wind.
The rustle of the grass.
A song torn from a hole, a wound
in the small white heart of a soul.

There is a baby, there is a life wasted at the bottom of the river
there is bitterness
which stabs the sun through the crystal water
there is a life outside its power and knowledge.
Why was it not killed as blood in the womb
why was it not rejected when it knocked at the door of the womb?
Invited in as a wanted guest
stored away as the ripe fruit of the body
when it had the right to face the sun's arrows
alas, they put it to rest at the bottom of the river!

The river water is very cold
it washes the whole day long
the eyes gaze and never focus
the body grows whiter and gravel enters its flesh.
There is a song, there is a moaning in the song.

Harry Aveling

♀ Toeti Heraty (b. 1935)

CYCLUS

not for a moment shall I allow
confusion of thought and bitterness
              invade
the uncrossable forest
now that you have gone

gone—decently—allowing me time
              to pack
before I hurl myself into the flames, a
faithful widow and pure maiden
              I expected more
than an honest handshake
              and a faint smile
past hopes, present sorrows
form barriers, breathe deeply
              in the race with time
count the months and days, waste
time, we arrived too soon

lost from my life, free
from conditional embrace, on an island
run aground in the final shift of hope
              balanced tight
in bitter reckoning
at the border, wave and
listen silently for a sound
              a sign, a proof
that you are ready for the role
reluctantly tethered to age
              among men
because you caressed with words, warmed
              with desire, fructified
the heart with honeyed pleasure and the rainbow
softly the fingers sought, pierced
didn't you want to know it all?

              you wanted it all
being strange, perhaps love and

death are the same, a sleep
          bringing dreams to the bed
wed, intimately and cruelly
still strange, still recent
          gone

Harry Aveling

Ajip Rosidi (b. 1938)

ONLY IN POETRY

In the train
I read poetry: Rendra and Mayakovsky
Yet the words I hear are yours
Above the rhythm of the wheels.
I look outside:
Rice-fields and mountains
And a poem rises
From every bead of sweat
On the brow of the farmer
Throughout his long and lonely day.

I know you know
That life drifts between heaven and earth
Adam was expelled from Paradise
Then searched for Eve.

The poet's fate
Is to knock on door after door
And never find: Restlessly
Refusing
To surrender to his situation.

In the valley I see your calm face.
From the valley your hand stretches forth.

In the train
I read poetry: submission to emotion
Which through the iron fingers of Time
Determines the path of Fate: stretching out
Into the realm of dreams which I shape to no avail.

I know.
You know.
In poetry
Everything is clear and definite.

Harry Aveling

❧ Sapardi Djoko Damono (b. 1940)

MASK

for Danarto

1

He enjoyed making masks.
and would peel off his faces,
one after another and hang them on the wall.
"I like playing with them," the director said.

At night, as the play was being staged,
he sought his face among the wheezing,
shouting and complaining masks
but it wasn't there. It seemed he had more faces

to peel away, one after another.

2

"Where is my mask?" he asked to no one
in particular. In the changing room: a broken mirror,
rouge and powder in disarray;
but no mask. "Where

is my mask?" he asked. Low-watt bulbs,
cobwebs on the ceiling,
and a tranquilizer in his palm. But the mask
was not there. Perhaps the director had meant: The Tyrant

must create a mask from his own face.

3

But a mask may not become human;
a mask must follow the king's orders,
obey the commander's rules, knowing all too well
the eyes of the audience and the beating

of their hearts. Oh, dear God,
to never be listed in the play bill or receive a wage
just to be hung from the wall when the play is over.
Even when only the two of them remain behind the empty stage
the director pays no heed.

The mask has no right to become human.

John H. McGlynn

✌ Sutardji Calzoum Bachri (b. 1942)

SOLDIERS

let the young people
    climb in your
        cannons

don't disturb them
    let them rub
        together
            in your cannons

go away
    lie down and rest
        sleep
            whistle
    and if you want
    pick grass
    to help you whistle
            in the valleys
                sky
                fields
                at home

just do
    whatever you want

but please
    don't disturb them
        let them ram the barrels
        with their bodies
            light their torches
            and explode

Harry Aveling

Aborigine Poets Writing in English

✌ Manila Koordada (mid-20th century)

YOU CAN'T ESCAPE YOUR LIFE RECORD

In this dream I walked
and then sat down in an area.
Suddenly, they ambushed me

with jabiri, spears.
They came from everywhere
until I was surrounded
by all those people with spears.
I couldn't escape.

There's a history kept on you.
All your life's actions can look at you like spears.
You can't escape your life record.
The spear-holders are all spirit men,
they make you face your life record after you die.

✋ Anonymous (20th century)

Recorded by Billy Marshall-Stoneking

From PASSAGE

See there, that tree is a digging stick
left by the giant woman who was looking
for honey ants;
That rock, a dingo's nose;
There, on that mountain, is the footprint
left by Tjangara on his way to Ulamburra;
Here, the rockhole of Warnampi—very dangerous—
and the cave where the nyi-nyi women escaped
the anger of marapulpa—the spider.
Wati Kutjarra—the two brothers—travelled this way.
There, you can see, one was tired
from too much lovemaking—the mark of his penis
dragging on the ground;
Here, the bodies of the honey ant men
where they crawled from the sand—
no, they are not dead—they keep coming
from the ground, moving toward the water at Warumpi—
it has been like this for many years:
the Dreaming does not end; it is not like the whiteman's way.
What happened once happens again and again.
This is the Law,
This is the power of the Song.
Through the singing we keep everything alive;
through the songs . . . the spirits keep us alive.

Zapotec

✒ Pancho Nácar (1909–1963)

THE FOREIGNER WHO DIED IN JUCHITÁN

He died, in our land where he came to stay.
His death hurt no one.
Only an old mat wrapped him
and covered his face on the way to the grave.

Friendless, he had not even one offering,
dead now and bound for the grave.
He was borne on the shoulders of our people.
His own had already forgotten him.

An old neighbor from the cemetery
who guided the life of his only son,
cut wild flowers from along the road
and placed them on the quiet face.

The boy cut the limb of a tree
which filled the path with shadows,
and made a cross with a log
to mark the fresh grave.

When people visit the dead,
men of pure soul
will leave him flowers of *cordoncillo,*
though he died alone in Juchitán.

Brian Swann

Cree

✒ Jacob Nibenegenesabe (c. 1880–1974)

From THE WISHING BONE CYCLE

1

I try to make wishes right
but sometimes it doesn't work.
Once, I wished a tree upside down

and its branches
were where the roots should have been!
The squirrels had to ask the moles
"How do we get down there
to get home?"
One time it happened that way.
Then there was the time, I remember now,
I wished a man upside down
and his feet were where his hands
should have been!
In the morning his shoes
had to ask the birds
"How do we fly up there
to get home?"
One time it happened that way.

2

There was an old woman I wished up.
She was the wife
of an old pond.
You could watch her swim in her husband
if you were
in the hiding bushes.
She spoke to him by the way she swam
gently.
One time in their lives there was no rain
and the sun began making the pond smaller.
Soon the sun took the whole pond!
For many nights the old woman slept
near the hole where her husband once lived.
Then, one night, a storm came
but in the morning there still was no water
in her husband's old house.
So she set out on a journey to find her husband
and followed the puddles on the ground
which were the storm's footprints.
She followed them for many miles.
Finally she came upon her husband
sitting in a hole. But he was in the wrong hole!
So the old woman brought her husband home
little by little in her hands.
You could have seen him come home
if you were
in the hiding bushes.

Howard Norman

West Indian Poets Writing in French

✑ Aimé Césaire (b. 1913)

BLANK TO FILL IN ON THE VISA OF POLLEN

If there were nothing in the desert but
a single drop of water dreaming far below,
in the desert if there were nothing but
a windborne spore dreaming far above
it would suffice
rusting of weapons, splitting of stones, anarchy of darkness
desert, desert, I endure your challenge
blank to fill in on the visa of pollen.

Gregson Davis

LAY OF THE ROVER

     All that ever was dismembered
In me has been dismembered
all that ever was mutilated
in me has been mutilated
in the center of the platter, bereft of breath
the sliced fruit of the moon eternally roving
toward the contour it must find, its other half

and yet what is left you from the past

     barely perhaps some horse sense
a pricking of the ears or a trembling in night rain
     and when they are singing of Christmas once again
     to muse upon the stars
     that are astray

here comes the shortest day of the year
everything everywhere has declined on cue
words faces dreams
even the air has become poisoned
when a hand reaches toward me
I barely make the connection
my mind is fixed on the tear-drenched season
the day had a flavor of childhood
of deep layers, of mucus
toward the sun wrongly oriented
rail upon rail an empty station

where grasping at nothing the same arm
forever complaining in vain became hoarse

Fragmented sky, flayed curve
back of flogged slaves
pain exchequer of the Trades
closed cabbala, forgotten codes
I confront my silent past

Isle of gore of sargasso
isle: grip of shark-sucker
isle: after-laugh of whales
isle: thin expression, risen bubble
isle: great heart outpoured
height most distant most hidden
tipsy tired exhausted fisherwoman
tipsy attractive hand of the fowler
isle out of joint, isle disjointed
every isle beckons
every isle is a widow
Benin Benin O aggrey bead
Ife that was Uphaz
a mouth of the Zambesi
toward an Ophir free of Albuquerque
shall we forever extend our arms?

once upon a time O Dismembered One
the Goddess piece by fragment
put back together her dissevered lover
and the fourteen fragments
took their seat triumphant in the rays of evening

I have invented a secret cult
my sun is the one that is eternally awaited
the most beautiful of suns is the nighttime sun

Body of woman isle restored
body of woman amply freighted
body of woman foam-begotten
body of woman isle rediscovered
never so transported
it fails to transport to heaven
o night turned ranunculus
a polypary's secret
body of woman tread of the palm-tree
by grace of the sun coiffed with a nest
wherein the phoenix dies and is reborn
we are souls of high degree
bodies of the night, living avatars
faithful trees, gushing wine
myself the flebilant sybil.

Congealed waters of my several childhoods
where oars could scarcely penetrate
millions of birds of my childhoods
where oh where was that perfumed isle
lit up with giant suns
the season the clime so delicious
the year paved with precious stones?

While quartered in the zones' crises
dark amalgam in full cry
I saw a male bird go down
the stone embedded in his forehead
I observe the low point of the year

Polluted body artfully moulting
space: wind of faith betrayed
space: false pride of a planet

slow rural diamond-monger prince
would I fall prey to nigromancy?
Now stronger than Antilia or even Brazil
mile stone in the distance
sword of a flame that torments me
I fell the trees of Eden

Gregson Davis

SINCE AKKAD, SINCE ELAM, SINCE SUMER

Intruder, uprooter
Puff of wind suffered, puff onrushing
Master of three roads, you have before you a man
who has walked much.
Since Elam. Since Akkad. Since Sumer.
Master of three roads, you have before you a man
who has borne much.
Since Elam. Since Akkad. Since Sumer.
I have borne the body of the commandant. I have borne the railroad of the
    commandant. I have borne the locomotive of
the commandant, the cotton of the commandant. I have borne on my woolly
    head (which does so well without a pad) God, the machine, the route —
    the God of the commandant.
Master of three roads I have borne under the sun, I have borne in the mist I
    have borne over smoldering shards managing ants
I have borne the parasol I have borne the explosive I have borne the iron
    collar.
Since Akkad. Since Elam. Since Sumer.
Master of three roads, Master of three waterways, may it please that for
    once — the first time since Akkad since Elam since Sumer — with my
    snout ostensibly more tanned than the callous of my feet but in fact

milder than the crow's fastidious beak and as if draped in the bitter folds
formed by my grey surrogate skin (uniform I am forced to wear each
winter)
I advance across the dead leaves with my small witchdoctor steps

toward the place where lurks in triumph the inexhaustible mandate of men
tossed to the snarled and sneering hurricane.
Since Elam since Akkad since Sumer.

Gregson Davis

West Indian Poets Writing in English

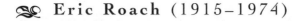

❧ Eric Roach (1915–1974)

AT GUARACARA PARK

the bronze god running,
beauty hurtling through the web of air,
motion fusing time and space
exploding our applauses . . .

speed was survival there in the green heat
where the lithe hero dashed
from the leopard's leap,
fled to cover from the feral fang
or ran the antelope across the plains.

and speed and stamina were the warrior's pride
where impis of assegais and swords and shields
tore tigerish through the brush and raided
and bounced back upon the kraals
panting from wounds and weariness,
brandishing the trophies of their cradling war.
the slave ships could not break our bones
nor strip our tendons, nor the long slaving
years narrow our arteries nor disease
our lungs nor shrivel up our hearts,
but left love thundering to this running man.

not fame's wreath crowns him
but Ogun's aura now; that blaze of flame
that savaged history back beyond our memories
our dreams and searchings.
the blood of the fierce gods we lost,
the pantheon of the kraals made him immortal
or he would have been a scarecrow in the canes.

❧ Martin Carter (b. 1927)

BITTER WOOD

Here be dragons, and bitter
cups made of wood; and the hooves
of horses where they should not
sound. Yet on the roofs of houses
walk the carpenters, as once did
cartographers on the spoil
of splendid maps. Here is where
I am, in a great geometry, between
a raft of ants and the green sight
of the freedom of a tree, made
of that same bitter wood.

❧ Andrew Salkey (b. 1928)

DRY RIVER BED

he came back
by plane,
train,
bus
and cart

his expectations
were plain:
family,
eyecorner familiarity,
back-home self,
or so he thought

1

during the last stretch,
on foot,
over the hard dirt road,
a beggar smiled at him,
and held out his left hand,
like a reaping hook

he gave him
nearly all his small change

2

further along the way,
a tatter of children

offered him pebbly mangoes,
at a price

he handed over
the rest of his change,
without taking the mangoes

3

on the narrative veranda,
where all the village tales
had perched
and taken off again,
his mother stood,
as light as the money
he'd just given away

in his embrace,
her body, wrapped wire,
felt smaller
than he remembered,
her face drawn tight
and frightened

4

everything was diminished,
whittled by long urban knives:
the road outside,
the front garden,
the lean-to house,
the back yard,
the lives

5

all his family
and neighbours
were knocking softly
at death's door,
waiting patiently,

spit fringing their cracked lips,
wizened frowns
sliding
into their collapsed cheeks

6

the villagers clawed at him
and what little he'd brought back,

they picked him clean
as a eucalyptus

7

he quickly saw
that home was a dry river bed;
he knew he'd have to run away, again,

or stay and be clawed to death
by the eagle
hovering over the village;
nothing had changed

8

he walked alone,
for a while;
not even his footprints
sank behind him,
in the dust;

no niche,
no bounce-back,
no mirror, anywhere,
in which to see himself,
merely the sunlight
mocking everybody, everywhere,
and the circling eagle

Edward Kamau Braithwaite (b. 1930)

NAIMA

for John Coltrane

Propped against the crowded bar
he pours into the curved and silver horn
his old unhappy longing for a home

the dancers twist and turn
he leans and wishes he could burn
his memories to ashes like some old notorious emperor

of rome. but no stars blazed across the sky when he was born
no wise men found his hovel. this crowded bar
where dancers twist and turn

holds all the fame and recognition he will ever earn
on earth or heaven. he leans against the bar
and pours his old unhappy longing in the saxophone

❧ Derek Walcott (b. 1930)

THE POLISH RIDER

The grey horse, Death, in profile bears the young Titus
To dark woods by the dying coal of day;
The father, with worn vision portrays the son
Like Durer's knight astride a Rozinanate;
The horse disturbs more than the youth delights us.
The warrior turns his sure gaze for a second,
Assurance looks its father in the eye,
The inherited, bony hack heads accurately
Towards the symbolic forests that have beckoned
Such knights, squired by the scyther, where to lie.
But skill dispassionately praises the rider,
Despair details the grey, cadaverous steed,
The immortal image holds its murderer
In a clear gaze for the next age to read.

Senegal

❧ Birago Diop (1906–1989)

VANITY

If we tell, gently, gently
All that we shall one day have to tell,
Who then will hear our voices without laughter,
Sad complaining voices of beggars
Who indeed will hear them without laughter?

If we cry roughly of our torments
Ever increasing from the start of things,
What eyes will watch our large mouths
Shaped by the laughter of big children
What eyes will watch our large mouths?

What heart will listen to our clamouring?
What ear to our pitiful anger
Which grows in us like a tumour
In the black depth of our plaintive throats?

When our Dead come with their Dead
When they have spoken to us with their clumsy voices:
Just as our ears were deaf

To their cries, to their wild appeals
Just as our ears were deaf
They have left on the earth their cries,
In the air, on the water, where they have traced their signs
For us, blind deaf and unworthy Sons
Who see nothing of what they have made
In the air, on the water, where they have traced their signs.

And since we did not understand our dead
Since we have never listened to their cries
If we weep, gently, gently
If we cry roughly of our torments
What heart will listen to our clamouring,
What ear to our sobbing hearts?

Gerald Moore and Ulli Beier

℘ Léopold Sédar Senghor (b. 1906)

NOCTURNE (I ACCOMPANIED YOU)

(for khalam)

I accompanied you as far as the village of granaries,
To the gates of Night, and I was speechless
Before the golden riddle of your smile. A brief twilight
Fell over your face, like a divine joke.
From the top of a hill shaded from light, I saw your bright pagne
Fade and your crest like a sun drop behind the rice-field shade
When anguish assailed me, ancestral fears more treacherous
Than panthers—the mind cannot expel them farther than the day's
Horizons. Will this night last forever? Departure without good-bye?
I shall cry in the shadows, in the motherly hollow of the Earth,
I shall sleep in my silent tears
Until the milky dawn of your mouth touches my brow.

Melvin Dixon

NOCTURNE (SHE FLIES SHE FLIES)

(for two horns and a balafong)

She flies she flies through the white flat lands, and patiently I take my aim
Giddy with desire. She takes her chances to the bush
Passion of thorns and thickets. Then I will bring her to bay in the chain of
    hours
Snuffing the soft panting of her flanks, mottled with shadow
And under the foolish Great Noon, I will twist her arms of glass.

The antelope's jubilant death rattle will intoxicate me, new palm wine
And I will drink long long the wild blood that rises to her heart
The milk blood that flows to her mouth, odours of damp earth.

Am I not the son of Dyogoye? Dyogoye the famished Lion.

John Reed and Olive Wake

TO NEW YORK

(for jazz orchestra and trumpet solo)

New York! At first I was bewildered by your beauty,
Those huge, long-legged, golden girls.
So shy, at first, before your blue metallic eyes and icy smile,
So shy. And full of despair at the end of skyscraper streets
Raising my owl eyes at the eclipse of the sun.
Your light is sulphurous against the pale towers
Whose heads strike lightning into the sky,
Skyscrapers defying storms with their steel shoulders
And weathered skin of stone.
But two weeks on the naked sidewalks of Manhattan —
At the end of the third week the fever
Overtakes you with a jaguar's leap
Two weeks without well water or pasture all birds of the air
Fall suddenly dead under the high, sooty terraces.
No laugh from a growing child, his hand in my cool hand.
No mother's breast, but nylon legs. Legs and breasts
Without smell or sweat. No tender word, and no lips,
Only artificial hearts paid for in cold cash
And not one book offering wisdom.
The painter's palette yields only coral crystals.
Sleepless nights, O nights of Manhattan!
Stirring with delusions while car horns blare the empty hours
And murky streams carry away hygenic loving
Like rivers overflowing with the corpses of babies.

II

Now is the time for signs and reckoning, New York!
Now is the time of manna and hyssop.
You have only to listen to God's trombones, to your heart
Beating to the rhythm of blood, your blood.
I saw Harlem teeming with sounds and ritual colors
And outrageous smells —
At teatime in the home of the drugstore-deliveryman
I saw the festival of Night begin at the retreat of day.
And I proclaim Night more truthful than the day.
It is the pure hour when God brings forth

Life immemorial in the streets,
All the amphibious elements shining like suns.
Harlem, Harlem! Now I've seen Harlem, Harlem!
A green breeze of corn rising from the pavements
Plowed by the Dan dancers' bare feet,
Hips rippling like silk and spearhead breasts,
Ballets of water lilies and fabulous masks
And mangoes of love rolling from the low houses
To the feet of police horses.
And along sidewalks I saw streams of white rum
And streams of black milk in the blue haze of cigars.
And at night I saw cotton flowers snow down
From the sky and the angels' wings and sorcerers' plumes.
Listen, New York! O listen to your bass male voice,
Your vibrant oboe voice, the muted anguish of your tears
Falling in great clots of blood,
Listen to the distant beating of your nocturnal heart,
The tom-tom's rhythm and blood, tom-tom blood and tom-tom.

III

New York! I say New York, let black blood flow into your blood.
Let it wash the rust from your steel joints, like an oil of life
Let it give your bridges the curve of hips and supple vines.
Now the ancient age returns, unity is restored,
The reconciliation of Lion and Bull and Tree
Idea links to action, the ear to the heart, sign to meaning.
See your rivers stirring with musk alligators
And sea cows with mirage eyes. No need to invent the Sirens.
Just open your eyes to the April rainbow
And your ears, especially your ears, to God
Who in one burst of saxophone laughter
Created heaven and earth in six days,
And on the seventh slept a deep Negro sleep.

Melvin Dixon

David Diop (1927–1960)

THE VULTURES

In those days
When civilization kicked us in the face
When holy water slapped our cringing brows
The vultures built in the shadow of their talons
The bloodstained monument of tutelage
In those days
There was painful laughter on the metallic hell of the roads
And the monotonous rhythm of the paternoster

Drowned the howling on the plantations
O the bitter memories of extorted kisses
Of promises broken at the point of a gun
Of foreigners who did not seem human
Who knew all the books but did not know love
But we whose hands fertilize the womb of the earth
In spite of your songs of pride
In spite of the desolate villages of torn Africa
Hope was preserved in us as in a fortress
And from the mines of Swaziland to the factories of Europe
Spring will be reborn under our bright steps.

Gerald Moore and Ulli Beier

Egypt

✥ Andrée Chedid (b. 1921)

WHO REMAINS STANDING?
First,
erase your name,
unravel your years,
destroy your surroundings,
uproot what you seem,
and who remains standing?
Then,
rewrite your name,
restore your age,
rebuild your house,
pursue your path,
and then,
endlessly,
start over, all over again.

Samuel Haze and Mirène Ghossein

✥ Joyce Mansour (b. 1928)

SEATED ON HER BED

Seated on her bed legs spread open
A bowl before her
Looking for food but seeing nothing
A woman with eyelids eaten by flies
Moaned
The flies came in through the window

Left by the door
Went into her bowl
Red eyes black flies
Eaten by a woman
Who saw nothing

Willis Barnstone

Algeria

ᘒ Malika O'Lahsen (b. 1930)

IT TOOK ONE HUNDRED YEARS

They are cutting up into pieces
My body and my sun
They are cutting them up into pieces
You
    You will be white
You
    You will be black
Hunger
    Laziness
        Unwillingness

It took
    One hundred years
To make me a savage
It took
    One hundred years
Even more

They are cutting everything up into pieces
Departments
Districts
They are clipping out pictures
With border barbed wire
They are cutting up my body
To make it into History

Eric Sellin

Angola

❧ Augustinho Neto (1922–1979)

KINAXIXI

I was glad to sit down
on a bench in Kinaxixi
at six o'clock of a hot evening
and just sit there . . .

Someone would come
maybe
to sit beside me

And I would see the black faces
of the people going uptown
in no hurry
expressing absence in the
jumbled Kimbundu they conversed in.

I would see the tired footsteps
of the servants whose fathers also were servants
looking for love here, glory there, wanting
something more than drunkenness in every
alcohol.

Neither happiness nor hate.

After the sun had set
lights would be turned on and I
would wander off
thinking that our life after all is simple
too simple
for anyone who is tired and still has to walk.

W. S. Merwin

Zimbabwe

✤ Dennis Brutus (b. 1924)

NIGHTSONG: CITY

Sleep well, my love, sleep well:
the harbour lights glaze over restless docks,
police cars cockroach through the tunnel streets

from the shanties creaking iron-sheets
violence like a bug-infested rag is tossed
and fear is immanent as sound in the wind-swung bell;

the long day's anger pants from sand and rocks;
but for this breathing night at least,
my land, my love, sleep well.

Kenya

✤ Marjorie Oludhe Macgoye (b. 1928)

A FREEDOM SONG

Atieno washes dishes,
Atieno plucks the chicken,
Atieno gets up early,
Beds her sacks down in the kitchen,
Atieno eight years old,
Atieno yo.

Since she is my sister's child
Atieno needs no pay,
While she works my wife can sit
Sewing every sunny day:
With her earnings I support
Atieno yo.

Atieno's sly and jealous,
Bad example to the kids
Since she minds them, like a schoolgirl
Wants their dresses, shoes and beads,
Atieno ten years old,
Atieno yo.

Now my wife has gone to study
Atieno is less free.
Don't I keep her, school my own ones,
Pay the party, union fee,
All for progress: aren't you grateful
Atieno yo?

Visitors need much attention,
All the more when I work night.
That girl spends too long at market,
Who will teach her what is right?
Atieno is rising fourteen,
Atieno yo.

Atieno's had a baby
So we know that she is bad.
Fifty fifty it may live
And repeat the life she had
Ending in post-partum bleeding,
Atieno yo.

Atieno's soon replaced.
Meat and sugar more than all
She ate in such a narrow life
Were lavished on her funeral.
Atieno's gone to glory,
Atieno yo.

Ghana

✿ Kwesi Brew (b. 1928)

A PLEA FOR MERCY

We have come to your shrine to worship—
We the sons of the land.
The naked cowherd has brought
The cows safely home,
And stands silent with his bamboo flute
Wiping the rain from his brow;
As the birds brood in their nests
Awaiting the dawn with unsung melodies;
The shadows crowd on the shores
Pressing their lips against the bosom of the sea;
The peasants home from their labours
Sit by their log fires
Telling tales of long ago.
Why should we the sons of the land

Plead unheeded before your shrine,
When our hearts are full of song
And our lips tremble with sadness?
The little firefly vies with the star,
The log fire with the sun
The water in the calabash
With the mighty Volta.
But we have come in tattered penury
Begging at the door of a Master.

South Africa

✑ Ingrid Jonker (1933–1965)

THE CHILD WHO WAS SHOT DEAD BY SOLDIERS AT NYANGA

The child is not dead
the child lifts his fists against his mother
who shouts Afrika! shouts the breath
of freedom and the veld
in the locations of the cordoned heart

The child lifts his fists against his father
in the march of the generations
who shout Afrika! shout the breath
of righteousness and blood
in the streets of his embattled pride

The child is not dead
not at Langa nor at Nyanga
not at Orlando nor at Sharpeville
nor at the police station at Phillippi
where he lies with a bullet through his brain

The child is the dark shadow of the soldiers
on guard with rifles, saracens and batons
the child is present at all assemblies and law-givings
the child peers through the windows of houses and into the hearts
                                        of mothers

this child who just wanted to play in the sun at Nyanga is
                                        everywhere
the child grown to a man treks through all Africa
the child grown into a giant journeys through the whole world

Without a pass

≫ J. G. Mocoancoeng (20th century)

DROUGHT

When the sun is hot, it is burning
The land is not ugly, it is terrifying.
People are sweating but they are not wet
The earth is parched,
O drought

Animals are not grazing, but pulling stalks
They are not lean, they are dying
O! The earth has no water
The land is dry, so dry.

The young man is exhausted
He holds his waist and says,
"We are dying."
He is looking at the herd of cattle.
He shakes his head and says,
"We see you."

In the churches prayers are rising
Lord, Rain!
Lord we are going!
On the land vultures are feeding
The fire has come.

The wind is dry, it petrifies
It's not wind, but clouds of sand
in the air
The land is so dry.

But far in the east
there is a dark cloud
It is true God has heard us
Look, it moves!

Mongane Wally Serote and Philip Bryant

Nigeria

Wole Soyinka (b. 1934)

NIGHT

Your hand is heavy, Night, upon my brow,
I bear no heart mercuric like the clouds, to dare
Exacerbation from your subtle plough.

Woman as a clam, on the sea's crescent
I saw your jealous eye quench the sea's
Fluorescence, dance on the pulse incessant

Of the waves. And I stood, drained
Submitting like the sands, blood and brine
Coursing to the roots. Night, you rained

Serrated shadows through dank leaves
Till, bathed in warm suffusion of your dappled cells
Sensations pained me, faceless, silent as night thieves.

Hide me now, when night children haunt the earth
I must hear none! These misted calls will yet
Undo me; naked, unbidden, at Night's muted birth.

Congo

Jean-Baptiste Tati-Loutard (b. 1938)

EARLY

I got up early and faced the east
Which I thought was made of bright red brick
Like an old temple for the worship of Fire
In the eastern axis
In the minaret I saw a body worked over by ruin
Ready to collapse in a fateful fall
Like a bird about to break with space
Which had borne it up to the clouds
The muezzin called out as though the new age
Would appear at the end of his cry.

Eric Sellin

❧ 3

Modern Poetry in English

English

❧ A. E. Housman (1859–1936)

HER STRONG ENCHANTMENTS FAILING

Her strong enchantments failing,
    Her towers of fear in wreck,
Her limbecks dried of poisons
    And the knife at her neck,

The Queen of air and darkness
    Begins to shrill and cry,
'O young man, O my slayer,
    To-morrow you shall die.'

O Queen of air and darkness,
    I think 'tis truth you say,
And I shall die to-morrow;
    But you will die today.

❧ William Butler Yeats (1865–1939)

SAILING TO BYZANTIUM

I

That is no country for old men. The young
In one another's arms, birds in the trees
—Those dying generations—at their song,

The salmon-falls, the mackerel-crowded seas,
Fish, flesh, or fowl, commend all summer long
Whatever is begotten, born, and dies.
Caught in that sensual music all neglect
Monuments of unageing intellect.

II

An aged man is but a paltry thing,
A tattered coat upon a stick, unless
Soul clap its hands and sing, and louder sing
For every tatter in its mortal dress,
Nor is there singing school but studying
Monuments of its own magnificence;
And therefore I have sailed the seas and come
To the holy city of Byzantium.

III

O sages standing in God's holy fire
As in the gold mosaic of a wall,
Come from the holy fire, perne in a gyre,
And be the singing-masters of my soul.
Consume my heart away; sick with desire
And fastened to a dying animal
It knows not what it is; and gather me
Into the artifice of eternity.

IV

Once out of nature I shall never take
My bodily form from any natural thing,
But such a form as Grecian goldsmiths make
Of hammered gold and gold enamelling
To keep a drowsy Emperor awake;
Or set upon a golden bough to sing
To lords and ladies of Byzantium
Of what is past, or passing, or to come.

TO A FRIEND WHOSE WORK HAS COME TO
NOTHING

Now all the truth is out,
Be secret and take defeat
From any brazen throat,
For how can you compete,
Being honour bred, with one
Who, were it proved he lies,
Were neither shamed in his own
Nor in his neighbours' eyes?

Bred to a harder thing
Than Triumph, turn away
And like a laughing string
Whereon mad fingers play
Amid a place of stone,
Be secret and exult,
Because of all things known
That is most difficult.

SOLOMON AND THE WITCH

And thus declared that Arab lady:
'Last night, where under the wild moon
On grassy mattress I had laid me,
Within my arms great Solomon,
I suddenly cried out in a strange tongue
Not his, not mine.'
                    Who understood
Whatever has been said, sighed, sung,
Howled, miau-d, barked, brayed, belled, yelled, cried, crowed,
Thereon replied: 'A cockerel
Crew from a blossoming apple bough
Three hundred years before the Fall,
And never crew again till now,
And would not now but that he thought,
Chance being at one with Choice at last,
All that the brigand apple brought
And this foul world were dead at last.
He that crowed out eternity
Thought to have crowed it in again.
For though love has a spider's eye
To find out some appropriate pain —
Aye, though all passion's in the glance —
For every nerve, and tests a lover
With cruelties of Choice and Chance;
And when at last that murder's over
Maybe the bride-bed brings despair,
For each an imagined image brings
And finds a real image there;
Yet the world ends when these two things,
Though several, are a single light,
When oil and wick are burned in one;
Therefore a blessed moon last night
Gave Sheba to her Solomon.'
'Yet the world stays.'
                    'If that be so,
Your cockerel found us in the wrong
Although he thought it worth a crow.

Maybe an image is too strong
Or maybe is not strong enough.'

'The night has fallen; not a sound
In the forbidden sacred grove
Unless a petal hit the ground,
Nor any human sight within it
But the crushed grass where we have;
And the moon is wilder every minute.
O! Solomon! let us try again.'

THE SECOND COMING

Turning and turning in the widening gyre
The falcon cannot hear the falconer;
Things fall apart; the centre cannot hold;
Mere anarchy is loosed upon the world,
The blood-dimmed tide is loosed, and everywhere
The ceremony of innocence is drowned;
The best lack all conviction, while the worst
Are full of passionate intensity.

Surely some revelation is at hand;
Surely the Second Coming is at hand.
The Second Coming! Hardly are those words out
When a vast image out of *Spiritus Mundi*
Troubles my sight: somewhere in sands of the desert.
A shape with lion body and the head of a man
A gaze blank and pitiless as the sun,
Is moving its slow thighs, while all about it
Reel shadows of the indignant desert birds.
The darkness drops again; but now I know
That twenty centuries of stony sleep
Were vexed to nightmare by a rocking cradle,
And what rough beast, its hour come round at last,
Slouches towards Bethlehem to be born?

AT GALWAY RACES

There where the course is,
Delight makes all of the one mind,
The riders upon the galloping horses,
The crowd that closes in behind:
We, too, had good attendance once,
Hearers and hearteners of the work;
Aye, horsemen for companions,

Before the merchant and the clerk
Breathed on the world with timid breath.
Sing on: somewhere at some new moon,
We'll learn that sleeping is not death,
Hearing the whole earth change its tune,
Its flesh being wild, and it again
Crying aloud as the racecourse is,
And we find hearteners among men
That ride upon horses.

✇ Edward Arlington Robinson
(1869–1935)

EROS TURANNOS

She fears him, and will always ask
    What fated her to choose him;
She meets in his engaging mask
    All reasons to refuse him;
But what she meets and what she fears
Are less than are the downward years,
Drawn slowly to the foamless weirs
    Of age, were she to lose him.

Between a blurred sagacity
    That once had power to sound him,
And Love, that will not let him be
    The Judas that she found him,
Her pride assuages her almost,
As if it were alone the cost.—
He sees that he will not be lost,
    And waits and looks around him.

A sense of ocean and old trees
    Envelops and allures him;
Tradition, touching all he sees,
    Beguiles and reassures him;
And all her doubts of what he says
Are dimmed with what she knows of days—
Till even prejudice delays
    And fades, and she secures him.

The falling leaf inaugurates
The reign of her confusion;
The pounding wave reverberates
The dirge of her illusion;
And home, where passion lived and died,

Becomes a place where she can hide,
While all the town and harbor side
Vibrate with her seclusion.

We tell you, tapping on our brows,
    The story as it should be, —
As if the story of a house
    Were told, or ever could be;
We'll have no kindly veil between
Her visions and those we have seen, —
As if we guessed what hers have been,
    Or what they are or would be.

Meanwhile we do no harm; for they
    That with a god have striven,
Not hearing much of what we say,
    Take what the god has given;
Though like waves breaking it may be,
Or like a changed familiar tree,
Or like a stairway to the sea
    Where down the blind are driven.

℘ Robert Frost (1874–1963)

THE DRAFT HORSE

With a lantern that wouldn't burn
In too frail a buggy we drove
Behind too heavy a horse
Through a pitch-dark limitless grove.

And a man came out of the trees
And took our horse by the head
And reaching back to his ribs
Deliberately stabbed him dead.

The ponderous beast went down
With a crack of a broken shaft.
And the night drew through the trees
In one long invidious draft.

The most unquestioning pair
That ever accepted fate
And the least disposed to ascribe
Any more than we had to hate,

We assumed that the man himself
Or someone he had to obey

Wanted us to get down
And walk the rest of the way.

PROVIDE, PROVIDE

The witch that came (the withered hag)
To wash the steps with pail and rag
Was once the beauty Abishag,

The picture pride of Hollywood.
Too many fall from great and good
For you to doubt the likelihood.

Die early and avoid the fate.
Or if predestined to die late,
Make up your mind to die in state.

Make the whole stock exchange your own!
If need be occupy a throne,
Where nobody can call *you* crone.

Some have relied on what they knew,
Others on being simply true.
What worked for them might work for you.

No memory of having starred
Atones for later disregard
Or keeps the end from being hard.

Better to go down dignified
With boughten friendship at your side
Than none at all. Provide, provide!

NEITHER OUT FAR NOR IN DEEP

The people along the sand
All turn and look one way.
They turn their back on the land.
They look at the sea all day.

As long as it takes to pass
A ship keeps raising its hull;
The wetter ground like glass
Reflects a standing gull.

The land may vary more;
But wherever the truth may be —

The water comes ashore,
And the people look at the sea.

They cannot look out far.
They cannot look in deep.
But when was that ever a bar
To any watch they keep?

❧ Edward Thomas (1878–1917)

LIGHTS OUT

I have come to the borders of sleep,
The unfathomable deep
Forest where all must lose
Their way, however straight,
Or winding, soon or late;
They cannot choose.

Many a road and track
That, since the dawn's first crack,
Up to the forest brink,
Deceived the travellers,
Suddenly now blurs,
And in they sink.

Here love ends,
Despair, ambition ends;
All pleasure and all trouble,
Although most sweet or bitter,
Here ends in sleep that is sweeter
Than tasks most noble.

There is not any book
Or face of dearest look
That I would not turn from now
To go into the unknown
I must enter and leave, alone,
I know not how.

The tall forest towers;
Its cloudy foliage lowers
Ahead, shelf above shelf;
Its silence I hear and obey
That I may lose my way
And myself.

✌ Wallace Stevens (1879–1955)

TEA AT THE PALAZ OF HOON

Not less because in purple I descended
The western day through what you called
The loneliest air, not less was I myself.

What was the ointment sprinkled on my beard?
What were the hymns that buzzed beside my ears?
What was the sea whose tide swept through me there?

Out of my mind the golden ointment rained,
And my ears made the blowing hymns they heard.
I was myself the compass of that sea:

I was the world in which I walked, and what I saw
Or heard or felt came not but from myself;
And there I found myself more truly and more strange.

OF MERE BEING

The palm at the end of the mind,
Beyond the last thought, rises
In the bronze distance,

A gold-feathered bird
Sings in the palm, without human meaning,
Without human feeling, a foreign song.

You know then that it is not the reason
That makes us happy or unhappy.
The bird sings. Its feathers shine.

The palm stands on the edge of space.
The wind moves slowly in the branches.
The bird's fire-fangled feathers dangle down.

STARS AT TALLAPOOSA

The lines are straight and swift between the stars.
The night is not the cradle that they cry,
The criers, undulating the deep-oceaned phrase.
The lines are much too dark and much too sharp.

The mind herein attains simplicity.
There is no moon, on single, silvered leaf.
The body is no body to be seen
But is an eye that studies its black lid.

Let these be your delight, secretive hunter,
Wading the sea-lines, moist and ever-mingling,
Mounting the earth-lines, long and lax, lethargic.
These lines are swift and fall without diverging.

The melon-flower nor dew nor web of either
Is like to these. But in yourself is like:
A sheaf of brilliant arrows flying straight,
Flying and falling straightway for their pleasure,

Their pleasure that is all bright-edged and cold;
Or, if not arrows, then the nimblest motions,
Making recoveries of young nakedness
And the lost vehemence the midnights hold.

William Carlos Williams (1883–1963)

RALEIGH WAS RIGHT

We cannot go to the country
for the country will bring us no peace
What can the small violets tell us
that grow on furry stem in
the long grass among lance-shaped leaves?

Though you praise us
and call to mind the poets
who sung of our loveliness
it was long ago!
long ago! when country people
would plow and sow with
flowering minds and pockets at ease —
if ever this were true.

Not now. Love itself a flower
with roots in a parched ground.
Empty pockets make empty heads.
Cure it if you can but
do not believe that we can live
today in the country
for the country will bring us no peace.

A SORT OF A SONG

Let the snake wait under
his weed
and the writing
be of words, slow and quick, sharp
to strike, quiet to wait,
sleepless.
—through metaphor to reconcile
the people and the stones.
Compose. (No ideas
but in things) Invent!
Saxifrage is my flower that splits
the rocks.

DANSE RUSSE

If I when my wife is sleeping
and the baby and Kathleen
are sleeping
and the sun is a flame-white disc
in silken mists
above shining trees,—
if I in my north room
dance naked, grotesquely
before my mirror
waving my shirt round my head
and singing softly to myself:
"I am lonely, lonely.
I was born to be lonely,
I am best so!"
If I admire my arms, my face,
my shoulders, flanks, buttocks
against the yellow drawn shades,—

Who shall say I am not
the happy genius of my household?

D. H. Lawrence (1885–1930)

MIDDLE OF THE WORLD

This sea will never die, neither will it ever grow old
nor cease to be blue, nor in the dawn
cease to lift up its hills

and let the slim black ship of Dionysos come sailing in
with grape-vines up the mast, and dolphins leaping.

What do I care if the smoking ships
of the P. & O. and the Orient Line and all the other stinkers
cross like clock-work the Minoan distance!
They only cross, the distance never changes.

And now that the moon who gives men glistening bodies
is in her exaltation, and can look down on the sun
I see descending from the ships at dawn
slim naked men from Cnossos, smiling the archaic smile
of those that will without fail come back again,
and kindling little fires upon the shores
and crouching, and speaking the music of lost languages.

And the Minoan Gods, and the Gods of Tiryns
are heard softly laughing and chatting, as ever;
and Dionysos, young, and a stranger
leans listening on the gate, in all respect.

✤ Ezra Pound (1885–1972)

From THE PISAN CANTOS

From LXXX

Tudor indeed is gone and every rose,
Blood-red, blanch-white that in the sunset glows
Cries: 'Blood, Blood, Blood!' against the gothic stone
Of England, as the Howard or Boleyn knows.

Nor seeks the carmine petal to infer;
Nor is the white bud Time's inquisitor
Probing to know if its new-gnarled root
Twists from York's head or belly of Lancaster;

Or if a rational soul should stir, perchance,
Within the stem or summer shoot to advance
Contrition's utmost throw, seeking in thee
But oblivion, not thy forgiveness, FRANCE.

———

From LXXXI

What thou lovest well remains,
                  the rest is dross
What thou lov'st well shall not be reft from thee
What thou lov'st well is thy true heritage

Whose world, or mine or theirs
                    or is it of none?

First came the seen, then thus the palpable
        Elysium, though it were in the halls of hell,
What thou lovest well is thy true heritage

The ant's a centaur in his dragon world.
Pull down thy vanity, it is not man
Made courage, or made order, or made grace,
        Pull down thy vanity, I say pull down.
Learn of the green world what can be thy place
In scaled invention or true artistry,
Pull down thy vanity,
                            Paquin pull down!
The green casque has outdone your elegance.

'Master Thyself, then others shall thee beare'
        Pull down thy vanity
Thou art a beaten dog beneath the hail,
A swollen magpie in a fitful sun,
Half black half white
Nor knowst'ou wing from tail
Pull down thy vanity
        How mean thy hates
Fostered in falsity,
        Pull down thy vanity,
Rathe to destroy, niggard in charity,
Pull down thy vanity,
        I say pull down.

But to have done instead of not doing
        this is not vanity
To have, with decency, knocked
That a Blunt should open
        To have gathered from the air a live tradition
or from a fine old eye the unconquered flame
This is not vanity.
        Here error is all in the not done,
all in the diffidence that faltered.

❧ H. D. (Hilda Doolittle) (1886–1961)

From HELEN IN EGYPT

This is the spread of wings,
whether the Straits claimed them
or the Cyclades,

whether they floundered on the Pontic seas
or ran aground before the Hellespont,
whether they shouted Victory at the gate,

whether the bowmen shot them from the Walls,
whether they crowded surging through the breach,
or died of fever on the smitten plain,

whether they rallied and came home again,
in the worn hulks, half-rotted from the salt
or sun-warped on the beach,

whether they scattered or in companies,
or three or two sought the old ways of home
whether they wandered as Odysseus did,

encountering new adventure, they are one;
no, I was not instructed, but I "read" the script,
I read the writing when he seized my throat,

this was his anger,
they were mine, not his,
the unnumbered host;

mine, all the ships,
mine, all the thousand petals of the rose,
mine, all the lily-petals,

mine, the great spread of wings,
the thousand sails,
the thousand feathered darts

that sped them home,
mine, the one dart in the Achilles-heel,
the thousand-and-one, mine.

❧ Marianne Moore (1887–1972)

SILENCE

My father used to say,
'Superior people never make long visits,
have to be shown Longfellow's grave
or the glass flowers at Harvard.
Self-reliant like the cat—
that takes its prey to privacy,
the mouse's limp tail hanging like a shoelace from its mouth—
they sometimes enjoy solitude,

and can be robbed of speech
by speech which has delighted them.
The deepest feeling always shows itself in silence;
not in silence, but restraint'.
Nor was he insincere in saying, 'Make my house your inn'.
Inns are not residences.

❧ Edwin Muir (1887–1959)

THE CHILD DYING

Unfriendly friendly universe,
I pack your stars into my purse,
And bid you, bid you so farewell.
That I can leave you, quite go out,
Go out, go out beyond all doubt,
My father says, is the miracle.

You are so great, and I so small:
I am nothing, you are all:
Being nothing, I can take this way.
Oh I need neither rise nor fall,
For when I do not move at all
I shall be out of all your day.

It's said some memory will remain
In the other place, grass in the rain,
Light on the land, sun on the sea,
A flitting grace, a phantom face,
But the world is out. There is no place
Where it and its ghost can ever be.

Father, father, I dread this air
Blown from the far side of despair,
The cold cold corner. What house, what hold,
What hand is there? I look and see
Nothing-filled eternity,
And the great round world grows weak and old.

Hold my hand, oh hold it fast—
I am changing!—until at last
My hand in yours no more will change,
Though yours change on. You here, I there,
So hand in hand, twin-leafed despair—
I did not know death was so strange.

❧ T. S. Eliot (1888–1965)

THE LOVE SONG OF J. ALFRED PRUFROCK

> *S'io credesse che mia risposta fosse*
> *A persona che mai tornasse al mondo,*
> *Questa fiamma staria senza più scosse.*
> *Ma per ciò che giammai di questo fondo*
> *Non tornò vivo alcun, s'i'odo il vero,*
> *Senza tema d'infamia ti rispondo.*

Let us go then, you and I,
When the evening is spread out against the sky
Like a patient etherised upon a table;
Let us go, through certain half-deserted streets,
The muttering retreats
Of restless nights in one-night cheap hotels
And sawdust restaurants with oyster-shells:
Streets that follow like a tedious argument
Of insidious intent
To lead you to an overwhelming question . . .
Oh, do not ask, "What is it?"
Let us go and make our visit.

 In the room the women come and go
Talking of Michelangelo.

The yellow fog that rubs its back upon the window-panes
The yellow smoke that rubs its muzzle on the window-panes
Licked its tongue into the corners of the evening,
Lingered upon the pools that stand in drains,
Let fall upon its back the soot that falls from chimneys,
Slipped by the terrace, made a sudden leap,
And seeing that it was a soft October night,
Curled once about the house, and fell asleep.

 And indeed there will be time
For the yellow smoke that slides along the street,
Rubbing its back upon the window-panes;
There will be time, there will be time
To prepare a face to meet the faces that you meet;
There will be time to murder and create,

And time for all the works and days of hands
That lift and drop a question on your plate;
Time for you and time for me,
And time yet for a hundred indecisions,
And for a hundred visions and revisions,
Before the taking of a toast and tea.

In the room the women come and go
Talking of Michelangelo.

And indeed there will be time
To wonder, "Do I dare?" and, "Do I dare?"
Time to turn back and descend the stair,
With a bald spot in the middle of my hair —
[They will say: "How his hair is growing thin!"]
My morning coat, my collar mounting firmly to the chin,
My necktie rich and modest, but asserted by a simple pin —
[They will say: "But how his arms and legs are thin!"]
Do I dare
Disturb the universe?
In a minute there is time
For decisions and revisions which a minute will reverse.

For I have known them all already, known them all: —
Have known the evenings, mornings, afternoons,
I have measured out my life with coffee spoons;
I know the voices dying with a dying fall
Beneath the music from a farther room.
So how should I presume?

And I have known the eyes already, known them all: —
The eyes that fix you in a formulated phrase,
And when I am formulated, sprawling on a pin,
When I am pinned and wriggling on the wall,
Then how should I begin
To spit out all the butt-ends of my days and ways?
And how should I presume?

And I have known the arms already, known them all —
Arms that are braceleted and white and bare
[But in the lamplight, downed with light brown hair!]
What perfume from a dress
That makes me so digress?
Arms that lie along a table, or wrap about a shawl.
And should I then presume?
And how should I begin?

Shall I say, I have gone at dusk through narrow streets
And watched the smoke that rises from the pipes
Of lonely men in shirt-sleeves, leaning out of windows?

I should have been a pair of ragged claws
Scuttling across the floors of silent seas.

And the afternoon, the evening, sleeps so peacefully!
Smoothed by long fingers,
Asleep . . . tired . . . or it malingers,

Stretched on the floor, here beside you and me.
Should I, after tea and cakes and ices,
Have the strength to force the moment to its crisis?
But though I have wept and fasted, wept and prayed,
Though I have seen my head [grown slightly bald] brought in upon a platter,
I am no prophet—and here's no great matter;
I have seen the moment of my greatness flicker,
And I have seen the eternal Footman hold my coat, and snicker,
And in short, I was afraid.

And would it have been worth it, after all,
After the cups, the marmalade, the tea,
Among the porcelain, among some talk of you and me,
Would it have been worth while,
To have bitten off the matter with a smile,
To have squeezed the universe into a ball
To roll it toward some overwhelming question,
To say: "I am Lazarus, come from the dead,
Come back to tell you all, I shall tell you all"—
If one, settling a pillow by her head,
        Should say: "That is not what I meant at all.
        That is not it, at all."

And would it have been worth it, after all,
Would it have been worth while,
After the sunsets and the dooryards and the sprinkled streets,
After the novels, after the teacups, after the skirts that trail along the floor—
And this, and so much more?—
It is impossible to say just what I mean!
But as if a magic lantern threw the nerves in patterns on a screen:
Would it have been worth while
If one, settling a pillow or throwing off a shawl,
And turning toward the window, should say:
        "That is not it at all,
        That is not what I meant, at all."

No! I am not Prince Hamlet, nor was meant to be;
Am an attendant lord, one that will do
To swell a progress, start a scene or two,
Advise the prince; no doubt, an easy tool,
Deferential, glad to be of use,
Politic, cautious, and meticulous;
Full of high sentence, but a bit obtuse;
At times, indeed, almost ridiculous—
Almost, at times, the Fool.

        I grow old . . . I grow old . . .
I shall wear the bottoms of my trousers rolled.

Shall I part my hair behind? Do I dare to eat a peach?
I shall wear white flannel trousers, and walk upon the beach.
I have heard the mermaids singing, each to each.

I do not think that they will sing to me.

I have seen them riding seaward on the waves
Combing the white hair of the waves blown back
When the wind blows the water white and black.

We have lingered in the chambers of the sea
By sea-girls wreathed with seaweed red and brown
Till human voices wake us, and we drown.

John Crowe Ransom (1888–1974)

CAPTAIN CARPENTER

Captain Carpenter rose up in his prime
Put on his pistols and went riding out
But had got wellnigh nowhere at that time
Till he fell in with ladies in a rout.

It was a pretty lady and all her train
That played with him so sweetly but before
An hour she'd taken a sword with all her main
And twined him of his nose for evermore.

Captain Carpenter mounted up one day
And rode straightway into a stranger rogue
That looked unchristian but be that as may
The Captain did not wait upon prologue.

But drew upon him out of his great heart
The other swung against him with a club
And cracked his two legs at the shinny part
And let him roll and stick like any tub.

Captain Carpenter rode many a time
From male and female took he sundry harms
He met the wife of Satan crying "I'm
The she-wolf bids you shall bear no more arms."

Their strokes and counters whistled in the wind
I wish he had delivered half his blows
But where she should have made off like a hind
The bitch bit off his arms at the elbows.

And Captain Carpenter parted with his ears
To a black devil that used him in this wise

O Jesus ere his threescore and ten years
Another had plucked out his sweet blue eyes.

Captain Carpenter got up on his roan
And sallied from the gate in hell's despite
I heard him asking in the grimmest tone
If any enemy yet there was to fight?

"To any adversary it is fame
If he risk to be wounded by my tongue
Or burnt in two beneath my red heart's flame
Such are the perils he is cast among.

"But if he can he has a pretty choice
From an anatomy with little to lose
Whether he cut my tongue and take my voice
Or whether it be my round red heart he choose."

It was the neatest knave that ever was seen
Stepping in perfume from his lady's bower
Who at this word put in his merry mien
And fell on Captain Carpenter like a tower.

I would not knock old fellows in the dust
But there lay Captain Carpenter on his back
His weapons were the old heart in his bust
And a blade shook between rotten teeth alack.

The rogue in scarlet and grey soon knew his mind
He wished to get his trophy and depart
With gentle apology and touch refined
He pierced him and produced the Captain's heart.

God's mercy rest on Captain Carpenter now
I thought him Sirs an honest gentleman
Citizen husband soldier and scholar enow
Let jangling kites eat of him if they can.

But God's deep curses follow after those
That shore him of his goodly nose and ears
His legs and strong arms at the two elbows
And eyes that had not watered seventy years.

The curse of hell upon the sleek upstart
That got the Captain finally on his back
And took the red red vitals of his heart
And made the kites to whet their beaks clack clack.

✒ Hugh MacDiarmid (Christopher Murray Grieve, 1892–1978)

O WHA'S THE BRIDE?

O wha's the bride that cairries the bunch
O' thistles blinterin' white?
Her cuckold bridegroom little dreids
What he sall ken this nicht.

For closer than gudeman can come
And closer to'r than hersel',
Wha didna need her maidenheid
Has wrocht his purpose fell.

O wha's been here afore me, lass,
And hoo did he get in?
—A man that deed or was I born
This evil thing has din.

And left, as it were on a corpse,
Your maidenheid to me?
—Nae lass, gudeman, sin' Time began
'S hed ony mair to gi'e.

But I can gi'e ye kindness, lad,
And a pair o' willin' hands,
And you sall ha'e my breists like stars,
My limbs like willow wands.

And on my lips ye'll heed nae mair,
And in my hair forget,
The seed o' a' the men that in
My virgin womb ha'e met. . . .

PERFECT

ON THE WESTERN SEABOARD OF SOUTH UIST

Los muertos abren los ojos a los que viven

I found a pigeon's skull on the machair,
All the bones pure white and dry, and chalky,
But perfect,
Without a crack or a flaw anywhere.

At the back, rising out of the beak,
Were domes like bubbles of thin bone,

Almost transparent, where the brain had been
That fixed the tilt of the wings.

E. E. Cummings (1894–1962)

MY FATHER MOVED THROUGH DOOMS OF LOVE

my father moved through dooms of love
through sames of am through haves of give,
singing each morning out of each night
my father moved through depths of height

this motionless forgetful where
turned at his glance to shining here;
that if (so timid air is firm)
under his eyes would stir and squirm

newly as from unburied which
floats the first who, his april touch
drove sleeping selves to swarm their fates
woke dreamers to their ghostly roots

and should some why completely weep
my father's fingers brought her sleep:
vainly no smallest voice might cry
for he could feel the mountains grow.

Lifting the valleys of the sea
my father moved through griefs of joy;
praising a forehead called the moon
singing desire into begin

joy was his song and joy so pure
a heart of star by him could steer
and pure so now and now so yes
the wrists of twilight would rejoice

keen as midsummer's keen beyond
conceiving mind of sun will stand,
so strictly (over utmost him
so hugely) stood my father's dream

his flesh was flesh his blood was blood:
no hungry man but wished him food;
no cripple wouldn't creep one mile
uphill to only see him smile.

Scorning the pomp of must and shall
my father moved through dooms of feel

his anger was as right as rain
his pity was as green as grain

septembering arms of year extend
yes humbly wealth to foe and friend
than he to foolish and to wise wise
offered immeasurable is

proudly and (by octobering flame
beckoned) as earth will downward climb,
so naked for immortal work
his shoulders marched against the dark

his sorrow was as true as bread:
no liar looked him in the head;
if every friend became his foe
he'd laugh and build a world with snow.

My father moved through theys of we,
singing each new leaf out of each tree
(and every child was sure that spring
danced when she heard my father sing)

then let men kill which cannot share,
let blood and flesh be mud and mire,
scheming imagine, passion willed,
freedom a drug that's bought and sold

giving to steal and cruel kind,
a heart to fear, to doubt a mind,
to differ a disease of same,
conform the pinnacle of am

though dull were all we taste as bright,
bitter all utterly things sweet,
maggoty minus and dumb death
all we inherit, all bequeath

and nothing quite so least as truth
—i say though hate were why men breathe—
because my father lived his soul
love is the whole and more than all

❧ Charles Reznikoff (1894–1970)

FOUR SONGS OF THE CITY

1

Showing a torn sleeve, with stiff and shaking fingers the old man
pulls off a bit of the baked apple, shiny with sugar,
eating with reverence food, the great comforter.

2

In steel clouds
to the sound of thunder
like the ancient gods:
our sky, cement;
our earth, cement;
our trees, steel;
instead of sunshine,
a light that has no twilight,
neither morning nor evening,
only noon.

Coming up the subway stairs, I thought the moon
only another street-light—
a little crooked.

3

If there is a scheme,
perhaps this too is in the scheme,
as when a subway car turns on a switch,
the wheels screeching against the rails,
and the lights go out—
but are on again in a moment.

4

What are you doing in our street among the automobiles, horse?
How are your cousins, the centaur and the unicorn?

❧ David Jones (1895–1974)

From THE ANATHEMATA

Ship's master:
      before him, in the waist and before it
           the darling men.
Cheerily, cheerily
         with land to leeward

known-land, known-shore, home-shore
home-light.
                    Cheerly, cheerly men
'gin to work the ropes.
And she bears up for it
                    riding her turning shadow.
The incurning *aphlaston* lanterns high above him
behind him
          the plank-built walls converge
to apse his leaning nave.
To his left elbow
                    the helmsman
is quite immobile now
                         by whose stanced feet
coiled on the drying hemp-coil
                    with one eye open
the still ship's cat
                    tillers, just perceptibly
her tip of tail.
He inclines himself out-board
                    and to her-ward.
The old padrone
                    the ancient staggerer
                    the vine-juice skipper.
What little's left
                    in the heel of his calix
asperging the free-board
                    to mingle the dead of the wake.
Pious, eld, bright-eyed
                    marinus.
Diocesan of us.
                    In the deeps of the drink
his precious dregs
                    laid up to the gods.
Libation darks her sea.
He would berth us
                    to schedule.

❧ Robert Graves (1895–1985)

THE COOL WEB

Children are dumb to say how hot the day is,
How hot the scent is of the summer rose,
How dreadful the black wastes of evening sky,
How dreadful the tall soldiers drumming by.

But we have speech, to chill the angry day,
And speech, to dull the rose's cruel scent.

We spell away the overhanging night,
We spell away the soldiers and the fright.

There's a cool web of language winds us in,
Retreat from too much joy or too much fear:
We grow sea-green at last and coldly die
In brininess and volubility.

But if we let our tongues lose self-possession,
Throwing off language and its watery clasp
Before our death, instead of when death comes,
Facing the wide glare of the children's day,
Facing the rose, the dark sky and the drums,
We shall go mad no doubt and die that way.

COUNTING THE BEATS

You, love, and I,
(He whispers) you and I,
And if no more than only you and I
What care you or I?

Counting the beats,
Counting the slow heart beats,
The bleeding to death of time in slow heart beats,
Wakeful they lie.

Cloudless day,
Night, and a cloudless day;
Yet the huge storm will burst upon their heads one day
From a bitter sky.

Where shall we be,
(She whispers) where shall we be,
When death strikes home, O where then shall we be
Who were you and I?

Not there but here,
(He whispers) only here,
As we are, here, together, now and here,
Always you and I.

Counting the beats,
Counting the slow heart beats,
The bleeding to death of time in slow heart beats,
Wakeful they lie.

❧ Edmund Blunden (1896–1974)

THE MIDNIGHT SKATERS

The hop-poles stand in cones,
The icy pond lurks under,
The pole-tops steeple to the thrones
Of stars, sound gulfs of wonder;
But not the tallest there, 'tis said,
Could fathom to this pond's black bed.

Then is not death at watch
Within these secret waters?
What wants he but to catch
Earth's heedless sons and daughters?
With but a crystal parapet
Between, he has his engines set.

Then on, blood shouts, on, on,
Twirl, wheel whip above him,
Dance on this ball-floor thin and wan,
Use him as though you love him;
Court him, elude him, reel and pass,
And let him hate you through the glass.

❧ Austin Clarke (1896–1974)

THE LOST HEIFER

When the black herds of the rain were grazing
In the gap of the pure cold wind
And the watery hazes of the hazel
Brought her into my mind,
I thought of the last honey by the water
That no hive can find.

Brightness was drenching through the branches
When she wandered again,
Turning the silver out of dark grasses
Where the skylark had lain,
And her voice coming softly over the meadow
Was the mist becoming rain.

✒ Louise Bogan (1897–1970)

WOMEN

Women have no wilderness in them,
They are provident instead,
Content in the tight hot cell of their hearts
To eat dusty bread.

They do not see cattle cropping red winter grass,
They do not hear
Snow water going down under culverts
Shallow and clear.

They wait, when they should turn to journeys,
They stiffen, when they should bend.
They use against themselves that benevolence
To which no man is friend.

They cannot think of so many crops to a field
Or of clean wood cleft by an axe.
Their love is an eager meaninglessness
Too tense, or too lax.

They hear in every whisper that speaks to them
A shout and a cry.
As like as not, when they take life over their door-sills
They should let it go by.

✒ Hart Crane (1899–1932)

VOYAGES

I

Above the fresh ruffles of the surf
Bright striped urchins flay each other with sand.
They have contrived a conquest for shell-shucks,
And their fingers crumble fragments of baked weed
Gaily digging and scattering.

And in answer to their treble interjections
The sun beats lightning on the waves,
The waves fold thunder on the sand;
And could they hear me I would tell them:

O brilliant kids, frisk with your dog,
Fondle your shells and sticks, bleached
By time and the elements; but there is a line

You must not cross nor ever trust beyond it
Spry cordage of your bodies to caresses
Too lichen-faithful from too wide a breast.
The bottom of the sea is cruel.

II

And yet this great wink of eternity,
Of rimless floods, unfettered leewardings,
Samite sheeted and processioned where
Her undinal vast belly moonward bends,
Laughing the wrapt inflections of our love;

Take this Sea, whose diapason knells
On scrolls of silver snowy sentences,
The sceptred terror of whose sessions rends
As her demeanors motion well or ill,
All but the pieties of lovers' hands.

And onward, as bells off San Salvador
Salute the crocus lustres of the stars,
In these poinsettia meadows of her tides, —
Adagios of islands, O my Prodigal,
Complete the dark confessions her veins spell.

Mark how her turning shoulders wind the hours,
And hasten while her penniless rich palms
Pass superscription of bent foam and wave, —
Hasten, while they are true, —sleep, death, desire,
Close round one instant in one floating flower.

Bind us in time, O Seasons clear, and awe.
O minstrel galleons of Carib fire,
Bequeath us to no earthly shore until
Is answered in the vortex of our grave
The seal's wide spindrift gaze toward paradise.

≈ Allen Tate (1899–1979)

THE MEDITERRANEAN

Quem das finem, rex magne, dolorum?

Where we went in the boat was a long bay
A slingshot wide, walled in by towering stone —
Peaked margin of antiquity's delay,
And we went there out of time's monotone:

Where we went in the black hull no light moved
But a gull white-winged along the feckless wave,

The breeze, unseen but fierce as a body loved,
That boat drove onward like a willing slave:

Where we went in the small ship the seaweed
Parted and gave to us the murmuring shore,
And we made feast and in our secret need
Devoured the very plates Aeneas bore:

Where derelict you see through the low twilight
The green coast that you, thunder-tossed, would win,
Drop sail, and hastening to drink all night
Eat dish and bowl to take that sweet land in!

Where we feasted and caroused on the sandless
Pebbles, affecting our day of piracy,
What prophecy of eaten plates could landless
Wanderers fulfil by the ancient sea?

We for that time might taste the famous age
Eternal here yet hidden from our eyes
When lust of power undid its stuffless rage;
They, in a wineskin, bore earth's paradise.

Let us lie down once more by the breathing side
Of Ocean, where our live forefathers sleep
As if the Known Sea still were a month wide—
Atlantis howls but is no longer steep!

What country shall we conquer, what fair land
Unman our conquest and locate our blood?
We've cracked the hemispheres with careless hand!
Now, from the Gates of Hercules we flood

Westward, westward till the barbarous brine
Whelms us to the tired land where tasseling corn,
Fat beans, grapes sweeter than muscadine
Rot on the vine: in that land were we born.

✌ Basil Bunting (1900–1985)

From BRIGGFLATTS

Riding silk, adrift on noon,
a spider gleams like a berry
less black than cannibal slug
but no less pat under elders
where shadows themselves are a web.
So is summer held to its contract
and the year solvent; but men
driven by storm fret,

reminded of sweltering Crete
and Pasiphae's pungent sweat,
who heard the god-bull's feet
scattering sand,
breathed byre stink, yet stood
with expectant hand
to guide his seed to its soil;
nor did flesh flinch
distended by the brute
nor loaded spirit sink
till it had gloried in unlike creation.

———————

Furthest, fairest things, stars, free of our humbug,
each his own, the longer known the more alone,
wrapt in emphatic fire roaring out to a black flue.
Each spark trills on a tone beyond chronological compass,
yet in a sextant's bubble present and firm
places a surveyor's stone or steadies a tiller.
Then is Now. The star you steer by is gone,
its tremulous thread spun in the hurricane
spider floss on my cheek; light from the zenith
spun when the slowworm lay in her lap
fifty years ago.

The sheets are gathered and bound,
the volume indexed and shelved,
dust on its marbled leaves.
Lofty, an empty combe,
silent but for bees.
Finger tips touched and were still
fifty years ago.
Sirius is too young to remember.

Sirius glows in the wind. Sparks on ripples
mark his line, lures for spent fish.

Fifty years a letter unanswered;
a visit postponed for fifty years.

She has been with me fifty years.

Starlight quivers. I had day enough.
For love uninterrupted night.

From SECOND BOOK OF ODES

A thrush in the syringia sings.

'Hunger ruffles my wings, fear
lust, familiar things.

Death thrusts hard. My sons
by hawk's beak, by stones,
trusting weak wings
by cat and weasel, die.

Thunder smothers the sky.
From a shaken bush I
list familiar things,
fear, hunger, lust.'

O gay thrush!

Yvor Winters (1900–1968)

TO MY INFANT DAUGHTER (II)

Alas, that I should be
So old, and you so small!
You will think naught of me
When your dire hours befall.

Take few men to your heart!
Unstable, fierce, unkind,
The ways that men impart.
True love is slow to find.

True art is slow to grow.
Like a belated friend,
It comes to let one know
Of what has had an end.

Laura Riding (1901–1991)

SUMMARY FOR ALASTOR

Because my song was bold
And you knew but my song,
You thought it must belong
To one brave to behold.

But finding me a shy
And cool and quiet Eve,
You scarcely would believe
The fevered singer was I.

And you caressed the child
That blushed beneath your eyes,

Hoping you might surprise
The hidden heart and wild.

And being only human,
A proud, impetuous fool
Whose guise alone was cool,
I let you see the woman.

Yet, though I was beguiled
Through being all too human,
I'm glad you had the woman
And not the trustful child.

For though the woman's weeping
And still must weep awhile,
The dreaming child can smile
And keep on safely sleeping.

✆ Kenneth Fearing (1902–1961)

LOVE, 20C THE FIRST QUARTER MILE

All right, I may have lied to you, and about you, and made a few
   pronouncements a bit too sweeping, perhaps, and possibly forgotten to
   tag the bases here or there,
And damned your extravagance, and maligned your tastes, and libeled your
   relatives, and slandered a few of your friends,
O.K.,
Nevertheless, come back.

Come home. I will agree to forget the statements that you issued so
   copiously to the neighbors and the press,
And you will forget that figment of your imagination, the blonde from
   Detroit;
I will agree that your lady friend who lives above us is not crazy, bats, nutty
   as they come, but on the contrary rather bright,
And you will concede that poor old Steinberg is neither a drunk, nor a
   swindler, but simply a guy, on the eccentric side, trying to get along
(Are you listening, you bitch, and have you got this straight?)

Because I forgive you, yes, for everything,
I forgive you for being beautiful and generous and wise,
I forgive you, to put it simply, for being alive, and pardon you, in short, for
   being you.

Because tonight you are in my hair and eyes,
And every street light that our taxi passes shows me you again, still you. And
   because tonight all other nights are black, all other hours are cold and
   far away, and now, this minute, the stars are very near and bright.

Come back. We will have a celebration to end all celebrations.
We will invite the undertaker who lives beneath us, and a couple of the boys
    from the office, and some other friends,
And Steinberg, who is off the wagon, by the way, and that insane woman
    who lives upstairs, and a few reporters, if anything should break.

✍ Langston Hughes (1902–1967)

MOTHER TO SON

Well, son, I'll tell you:
Life for me ain't been no crystal stair.
It's had tacks in it,
And splinters,
And boards torn up,
And places with no carpet on the floor—
Bare.
But all the time
I'se been a-climbin' on,
And reachin' landin's,
And turnin' corners,
And sometimes goin' in the dark
Where there ain't been no light.
So boy, don't you turn back.
Don't you set down on the steps
'Cause you finds it's kinder hard.
Don't you fall now—
For I'se still goin', honey,
I'se still climbin',
And life for me ain't been no crystal stair.

✍ Stevie Smith (1902–1971)

TO THE TUNE OF "THE COVENTRY CAROL"

The nearly right
And yet not quite
In love is wholly evil
And every heart
That loves in part
Is mortgaged to the devil.

I loved or thought
I loved in sort
Was this to love akin
To take the best

And leave the rest
And let the devil in?

O lovers true
And others too
Whose best is only better
Take my advice
Shun compromise
Forget him and forget her.

❧ Patrick Kavanagh (b. 1905)

SHANCODUFF

My black hills have never seen the sun rising,
Eternally they look north towards Armagh.
Lot's wife would not be salt if she had been
Incurious as my black hills that are happy
When dawn whitens Glassdrummond chapel.

My hills hoard the bright shillings of March
While the sun searches in every pocket.
They are my Alps and I have climbed the Matterhorn
With a sheaf of hay for three perishing calves
In the field under the Big Forth of Rocksavage.

The sleety winds fondle the rusty beards of Shancoduff
While the cattle-drovers sheltering in the Featherna Bush
Look up and say: 'Who owns them hungry hills
That the water-hen and snipe must have forsaken?
A poet? The by heavens he must be poor'
I hear and is my heart not badly shaken?

❧ Stanley Burnshaw (b. 1906)

HOUSE IN ST. PETERSBURG

If my mother had never been the protected child
Of a dreamy scholar in a protected house,
        I would not be writing these lines—

If the sign hung in the window of that house
Had told a different lie from the lie it told,
        I would not be writing these lines—

If the bribed police who winked at the sign had lived—
If the old one had not choked in a swilling night,
        I would not be writing these lines—

If the young recruit had been briefed with the well-bribed word
By his well-bribed captain before he walked by the house,

Or if he had never tripped on a cobble of ice
And ripped his shirt as he sprawled on a gashing stone,
    I would not be writing these lines —

If he had not then remembered the house with the sign
Because of the word it had always said to the street,

Or if when he asked the service of needle and thread
Father or child could have brought him needle and thread,
    I would not be writing these lines —

If the suddenly tongueless man of a stricken house
Had dared to speak with his eyes and a bag of gold,

Or if the gold had said to the young recruit
What it always said when the hunted spoke to the law,
    I would not be writing these lines —

If the young recruit had not shouted guilt in the street
So that passersby turned round to assault the house,

If he had not screamed the name as he climbed the steps
To the barracks and flung his find in his captain's face,

Or if when the captain scanned the innocent's eyes
He had found a gleam that confessed it was not too late,
    I would not be writing these lines —

If the innocent had not shouted again and again
And again — if the captain could have closed up his ears,

Or if his major, cursing his luck and loss,
Had never signed the papers to pillage and seize,
    I would not be writing these lines —

If the child and father, clinging with dread in the snows
Of night, had failed before they reached the frontier,

Or if their boat, lost in a wild North Sea,
Had not been sighted and saved on a Scottish shore,
    I would not be writing these lines —

Or, when they voyaged again, if their battered ship
Had not groped through its trial to the promised port,

Or if when they saw the sun of a friending earth
They had not danced in the recklessness of its air,
      I would not be writing these lines —

If the father after the years of dancing and grief
Had sought his sleep on an alien hill of Home,
      I would not be writing these lines—

Or if my mother, walking in tears from his grave,
Had not returned, one April, to join his sleep,
      I would not be writing these lines—

And if she herself, before, in a long ago,
Had never told this tale to a young one's eyes,
      I would not be singing her song.

W. H. Auden (1907–1973)

THE THREE COMPANIONS

'O where are you going?' said reader to rider,
'That valley is fatal when furnaces burn,
Yonder's the midden whose odours will madden,
That gap is the grave where the tall return.'

'O do you imagine,' said fearer to farer,
'That dusk will delay on your path to the pass,
Your diligent looking discover the lacking
Your footsteps feel from granite to grass?'

'O what was that bird,' said horror to hearer,
'Did you see that shape in the twisted trees?
Behind you swiftly the figure comes softly,
The spot on your skin is a shocking disease?'

'Out of this house'—said rider to reader,
'Yours never will'—said farer to fearer,
'They're looking for you'—said hearer to horror,
As he left them there, as he left them there.

THE WANDERER

Doom is dark and deeper than any sea-dingle.
Upon what man it fall
In spring, day-wishing flowers appearing,
Avalanche sliding, white snow from rock-face,
That he should leave his house,
No cloud-soft hand can hold him, restraint by women;
But ever that man goes
Through place-keepers, through forest trees,

A stranger to strangers over undried sea,
Houses for fishes, suffocating water,
Or lonely on fell as chat,
By pot-holed becks
A bird stone-haunting, an unquiet bird.

There head falls forward, fatigued at evening,
And dreams of home,
Waving from window, spread of welcome,
Kissing of wife under single sheet;
But waking sees
Bird-flocks nameless to him, through doorway voices
Of new men making another love.

Save him from hostile capture,
From sudden tiger's leap at corner;
Protect his house,
His anxious house where days are counted
From thunderbolt protect,
From gradual ruin spreading like a stain;
Converting number from vague to certain,
Bring joy, bring day of his returning,
Lucky with day approaching, with leaning dawn.

Louis MacNeice (1907–1963)

THALASSA

Run out the boat, my broken comrades;
Let the old seaweed crack, the surge
Burgeon oblivious of the last
Embarkation of feckless men,
Let every adverse force converge —
Here we must needs embark again.

Run up the sail, my heartsick comrades;
Let each horizon tilt and lurch —
You know the worst: your wills are fickle,
Your values blurred, your hearts impure
And your past like a ruined church —
But let your poison be your cure.

Put out to sea, ignoble comrades,
Whose record shall be noble yet;
Butting through scarps of moving marble
The narwhal dares us to be free;
By a high star our course is set,
Our end is life. Put out to sea.

THE SUNLIGHT ON THE GARDEN

The sunlight on the garden
Hardens and grows cold,
We cannot cage the minute
Within its nets of gold.
When all is told
We cannot beg for pardon.

Our freedom as freelances
Advances towards its end;
The earth compels, upon it
Sonnets and birds descend;
And soon, my friend,
We shall have no time for dances.

The sky was good for flying
Defying the church bells
And every evil iron
Siren and what it tells;
The earth compels,
We are dying, Egypt, dying

And not expecting pardon,
Hardened in heart anew,
But glad to have sat under
Thunder and rain with you,
And grateful too
For sunlight on the garden.

❧ A. D. Hope (b. 1907)

MEDITATION ON A BONE

> A piece of bone, found at Trondhjem in 1901, with the
> following runic inscription (about A.D. 1050) cut on it:
> *I loved her as a maiden; I will not trouble Erlend's detestable
> wife; better she should be a widow.*

Words scored upon a bone,
Scratched in despair or rage —
Nine hundred years have gone;
Now, in another age,
They burn with passion on
A scholar's tranquil page.

The scholar takes his pen
And turns the bone about,
And writes those words again.

Once more they seethe and shout,
And through a human brain
Undying hate rings out.

"I loved her when a maid;
I loathe and love the wife
That warms another's bed:
Let him beware his life!"
The scholar's hand is stayed;
His pen becomes a knife

To grave in living bone
The fierce archaic cry.
He sits and reads his own
Dull sum of misery.
A thousand years have flown
Before that ink is dry.

And, in a foreign tongue,
A man, who is not he,
Reads and his heart is wrung
This ancient grief to see,
And thinks: When I am dung,
What bone shall speak for me?

George Oppen (1908–1984)

PSALM

> *Veritas sequitur . . .*

In the small beauty of the forest
The wild deer bedding down —
That they are there!

                Their eyes
Effortless, the soft lips
Nuzzle and the alien small teeth
Tear at the grass

                The roots of it
Dangle from their mouths
Scattering earth in the strange woods.
They who are there.

                Their paths
Nibbled thru the fields, the leaves that shade them
Hang in the distances
Of sun

               The small nouns
Crying faith
In this in which the wild deer
Startle, and stare out.

✑ Theodore Roethke (1908–1963)

THE WAKING

I wake to sleep, and take my waking slow.
I feel my fate in what I cannot fear.
I learn by going where I have to go.

We think by feeling. What is there to know?
I hear my being dance from ear to ear.
I wake to sleep, and take my waking slow.

Of those so close beside me, which are you?
God bless the Ground! I shall walk softly there,
And learn by going where I have to go.

Light takes the Tree; but who can tell us how?
The lowly worm climbs up a winding stair;
I wake to sleep, and take my waking slow.

Great Nature has another thing to do
To you and me; so take the lively air,
And, lovely, learn by going where to go.

This shaking keeps me steady. I should know.
What falls away is always. And is near.
I wake to sleep, and take my waking slow.
I learn by going where I have to go.

✑ Elizabeth Bishop (1911–1979)

CASABIANCA

Love's the boy stood on the burning deck
trying to recite "The boy stood on
the burning deck." Love's the son
    stood stammering elocution
      while the poor ship in flames went down.

Love's the obstinate boy, the ship,
even the swimming sailors, who
would like a schoolroom platform, too,

or an excuse to stay
on deck. And love's the burning boy.

❧ J. V. Cunningham (1911–1985)

FOUR EPIGRAMS

1

Homer was poor. His scholars live at ease,
Making as many Homers as you please,
And every Homer furnishes a book.
Though guests be parasitic on the cook,
The moral is: *It is the guest who dines.*
I'll write a book to prove I wrote these lines.

2

Time heals not: it extends a sorrow's scope
As goldsmiths gold, which we may wear like hope.

3

Within this mindless vault
Lie *Tristan* and *Isolt*
Tranced in each other's beauties.
They had no other duties.

Epitaph for someone or other

Naked I came, naked I leave the scene,
And naked was my pastime in between.

INTERVIEW WITH DOCTOR DRINK

I have a fifth of therapy
In the house, and transference there.
Doctor, there's not much wrong with me,
Only a sick rattlesnake somewhere

In the house, if it be there at all,
But the lithe mouth is coiled. The shapes
Of door and window move. I call.
What is it that pulls down the drapes,

Disheveled and exposed? Your rye
Twists in my throat: intimacy
Is like hard liquor. Who but I
Coil there and squat, and pay your fee?

✇ Irving Layton (b. 1912)

AN AUBADE

It is early morning.
The cocks have stopped crowing.
The villagers are waking from dreams
of religious exaltation and buggery.
In their heads while shaving
or stirring their coffee
they carefully lock up their schemes
for profit and cuckoldry.
At the approach of this band of light
men arise to cheat or murder.
O wondrous Light! O wondrous Sun!
It has brought back their colours
to cowsheds and gardenias
to chickens and village dogs
who begin to squawk and bark
at their strange appearance.
From faraway mournful fields
the asses are braying,
'We want wimmin. We want wimmin.'
On the road the pellets of goatshit
look like stunted olives.
In other lands it is dark, dark.
North Ireland, Vietnam.
There light explodes like a bomb
or comes upon the night
like an assassin.
I sit on my bed and light a cigarette.
My girl is still sleeping.
When she awakes how will I
who read Husserl and Camus
tell her of my simple need of her
and that she must never leave me?

THE BLACK HUNTSMEN

Before ever I knew men were hunting me
I knew delight as water in a glass in a pool;
The childish heart then
Was ears nose eyes twiceten fingers,
And the torpid slum street, in summer,
A cut vein of the sun
That shed goldmotes by the million
Against a boy's bare toe foot ankle knee.

Then when the old year fell out of the window
To break into snowflakes on the cold stones of City Hall
I discovered Tennyson in a secondhand bookstore;
He put his bugle for me to his bearded mouth,
And down his Aquitaine nose a diminutive King Arthur
Rode out of our grocery shop bowing to left and to right,
Bearing my mother's *sheitel* with him;
And for a whole week after that
I called my cat Launcelot.

Now I look out for the evil retinue
Making their sortie out of a forest of gold—
Afterwards their dames shall weave my *tzitzith*
Into a tapestry,
Though for myself I had preferred
A death by water or sky.

❧ Robert Hayden (1913–1980)

MIDDLE PASSAGE

Jesús, Estrella, Esperanza, Mercy:

> Sails flashing to the wind like weapons,
> sharks following the moans the fever and the dying;
> horror the corposant and compass rose.

Middle Passage:
>   voyage through death
>   to life upon these shores.

> "10 April 1800—
> Blacks rebellious. Crew uneasy. Our linguist says
> their moaning is a prayer for death,
> ours and their own. Some try to starve themselves.
> Lost three this morning leaped with crazy laughter
> to the waiting sharks, sang as they went under."

Desire, Adventure, Tartar, Ann:

> Standing to America, bringing home
> black gold, black ivory; black seed.
>> *Deep in the festering hold thy father lies,*
>> *of his bones New England pews are made,*
>> *those are altar lights that were his eyes.*

Jesus Saviour Pilot Me
Over Life's Tempestuous Sea

We pray that Thou wilt grant, O Lord,
safe passage to our vessels bringing
heathen souls unto Thy chastening.

Jesus Saviour

    "8 bells. I cannot sleep, for I am sick
with fear, but writing eases fear a little
since still my eyes can see these words take shape
upon the page & so I write, as one
would turn to exorcism. 4 days scudding,
but now the sea is calm again. Misfortune
follows in our wake like sharks (our grinning
tutelary gods). Which one of us
has killed an albatross? A plague among
our blacks—Ophthalmia: blindness—& we
have jettisoned the blind to no avail.
It spreads, the terrifying sickness spreads.
Its claws have scratched sight from the Capt.'s eyes
& there is blindness in the fo'c'sle
& we must sail 3 weeks before we come
to port."

      What port awaits us, Davy Jones'
or home? I've heard of slavers drifting, drifting,
playthings of wind and storm and chance, their crews
gone blind, the jungle hatred
crawling up on deck.

Thou Who Walked On Galilee

    "Deponent further sayeth *The Bella J*
left the Guinea Coast
with cargo of five hundred blacks and odd
for the barracoons of Florida:

    "That there was hardly room 'tween-decks for half
the sweltering cattle stowed spoon-fashion there;
that some went mad of thirst and tore their flesh
and sucked the blood;

    "That Crew and Captain lusted with the comeliest
of the savage girls kept naked in the cabins;
that there was one they called The Guinea Rose
and they cast lots and fought to lie with her:

    "That when the Bo's'n piped all hands, the flames
spreading from starboard already were beyond
control, the negroes howling and their chains
entangled with the flames:

"That the burning blacks could not be reached,
that the Crew abandoned ship,
leaving their shrieking negresses behind,
that the Captain perished drunken with the wenches:

"Further Deponent sayeth not."

Pilot Oh Pilot Me

✺ Randall Jarrell (1914–1965)

VARIATIONS

I

"I lived with Mr. Punch, they said my name was Judy,
I beat him with my rolling-pin, he hit me with his cane.
I ran off with a soldier, he followed in a carriage,
And he drew a big revolver and he shot me through the brain.
But that was his duty, he only did his duty—"

Said Judy, said the Judy, said poor Judy to the string.

"O hear her, just hear her!" the string said softly.
And the string and Judy, they said no more.
Yes, string or Judy, it said no more.
But they hanged Mr. Punch with a six-inch rope,
And "Clap," said the manager; "the play is over."

II

"I lay like a swan upon the down of Heaven.
When the clouds came the rain grew
Into the rice of my palaces, the great wits
Were the zithers of my garden, I stood among sedge
And held to the peoples the gold staff of God."

Said Grace, said Good, O said the son of God.

The wives and wise, the summer's willows
Nodded and were fed by the wind; when the snow fell
And the wind's steps were pink in the pure winter,
Who spared his charcoal for the son of God,
The vain wind failing at the pass to Hell?

III

"I lived in a room full of bears and porridge,
My mother was dead and my nurse was horrid.
I sat all day on a white china chamber

And I lay all night in my trundle bed.
And she wasn't, she wasn't, O not a bit dead!"

The boy said, the girl said—and Nurse she said:

"I'll stew your ears all day, little hare,
Just as God ate your mother, for you are bad,
Are bad, are bad—" and the nurse is the night
To wake to, to die in: and the day I live,
The world and its life are her dream.

IV

"I was born in a hut, my wit is heavy.
My sister died, they killed my father.
There is no time I was not hungry.
They used me, I am dying.
I stand here among graves."

The white, the yellow, the black man said.

And the world said: Child, you will not be missed.
You are cheaper than a wrench, your back is a road;
Your death is a table in a book.
You had our wit, our heart was sealed to you:
Man is the judgment of the world.

❧ Dylan Thomas (1914–1953)

IN MY CRAFT OR SULLEN ART

In my craft or sullen art
Exercised in the still night
When only the moon rages
And the lovers lie abed
With all their griefs in their arms,
I labour by singing light
Not for ambition or bread
Or the strut and trade of charms
On the ivory stages
But for the common wages
Of their most secret heart.

Not for the proud man apart
From the raging moon I write
On these spindrift pages
Nor for the towering dead
With their nightingales and psalms
But for the lovers, their arms
Round the griefs of the ages,

Who pay no praise or wages
Nor heed my craft or art.

John Berryman (1914–1972)

HENRY'S UNDERSTANDING

He was reading late, at Richard's, down in Maine,
aged 32? Richard & Helen long in bed,
my good wife long in bed.
All I had to do was strip & get into my bed,
putting the marker in the book, & sleep,
& wake to a hot breakfast.

Off the coast was an island, P'tit Manaan,
the bluff from Richard's lawn was almost sheer.
A chill at four o'clock.
It only takes a few minutes to make a man.
A concentration upon now & here.
Suddenly, unlike Bach,

& horribly, unlike Bach, it occurred to me
that *one* night, instead of warm pajamas,
I'd take off all my clothes
& cross the damp cold lawn & down the bluff
into the terrible water & walk forever
under it out toward the island.

David Ignatow (b. 1914)

RESCUE THE DEAD

Finally, to forgo love is to kiss a leaf,
is to let rain fall nakedly upon your head,
is to respect fire,
is to study man's eyes and his gestures
as he talks,
is to set bread upon the table
and a knife discreetly by,
is to pass through crowds
like a crowd of oneself.
Not to love is to live.

To love is to be led away
into a forest where the secret grave

is dug, singing, praising darkness
under the trees.

To live is to sign your name,
is to ignore the dead,
is to carry a wallet
and shake hands.

To love is to be a fish.
My boat wallows in the sea.
You who are free,
rescue the dead.

❧ Synsey Goodsir Smith (1915–1975)

THE KENLESS STRAND

My sails by tempest riven
The sea a race
Whaur suld be lown and lither
Aa's dispeace.

Dispeace o hairt that visions
Reefs it downa ride,
Dispeace o mind in rapids
Nane can guide:

And aye a face afore me
And anither face,
Ane luve's ancient tragedy
And ane its peace.

Here, on luve's fludetide I run
There, the unkent strand
Abune, the seamaws' tireless grief
Ayont, nae hyne, nae end.

[*kenless strand*, boundless shore; *riven*, torn; *lown*, calm; *lither*, idleness; *downa*, dare not; *aye*, always; *ane*, one; *fludetide*, floodtide; *unkent*, unknown; *abune*, above; *seamaws*, seagulls; *ayont*, beyond; *hyne*, haven.]

❧ Peter Viereck (b. 1916)

"VALE" FROM CARTHAGE

(for my brother, G.S.V. Jr., 1918–44, killed fighting the Nazis)

I, now at Carthage. He, shot dead at Rome.
Shipmates last May. "And what if one of us,"
I asked last May, in fun, in gentleness,

"Wears doom, like dungarees, and doesn't know?"
He laughed, *"Not see Times Square again?"* The foam,
Feathering across that deck a year ago.
Swept those five words—like seeds—beyond the seas
    Into his future. There they grew like trees,
      And as he passed them there next spring, they laid
      Upon his road of fire their sudden shade.
Though he had always scraped his mess-kit pure
And scrubbed redeemingly his barracks floor,
Though all his buttons glowed their ritual-hymn
Like cloudless moons to intercede for him,
No furlough fluttered from the sky. He will
Not see Times Square—he will not see—he will
Not see Times
            change; at Carthage (while my friend,
Living those words at Rome, screamed in the end)
I saw an ancient Roman's tomb and read
"Vale" in stone. Here two wars mix their dead:
    Roman, my shipmate's dream walks hand in hand
    With yours tonight ("New York again" and "Rome"),
    Like widowed sisters bearing water home
    On tired heads through hot Tunisian sand
    In good cool urns, and says, "I understand."
Roman, you'll see your Forum Square no more.
What's left but this to say of any war?

W. S. Graham (b. 1917)

TO MY FATHER

Yes as alike as entirely
You my father I see
That high Greenock tenement
And the whole shipyarded front.

As alike as a memory early
Of 'The Bonny Earl o' Moray'
Fiddled in our high kitchen
Over the sleeping town

These words this one night
Feed us and will not
Leave us without our natures
Inheriting new fires.

The March whinfires let fall
From the high Greenock hill
A word fetched so bright
Out of the forehead that

A fraction's wink and I
And my death charge round softly.
My birth and I so softly
Charge round the outward journey.

Entirely within the fires
And winter-harried natures
Of your each year, the still
Foundered man is the oracle

Tented within his early
Friendships. And he'll reply
To us locked in our song.
This night this word falling

Across kindling skies

NIGHT'S FALL UNLOCKS THE DIRGE OF THE SEA

Night's fall unlocks the dirge of the sea
To pour up from the shore and befriending
Gestures of water waving, to find me
Dressed warm in a coat of land in a house
Held off the drowned by my blood's race
Over the crops of my step to meet some praise.

The surge by day by night turns lament
And by this night falls round the surrounding
Seaside and countryside and I can't
Sleep one word away on my own for that
Grief sea with a purse of pearls and debt
Wading the land away with salt in his throat.

By this loud night traded into evidence
Of a dark church of voices at hand
I lie, work of the gruff sea's innocence
And lie, work of the deaths I find
On the robbed land breathing air and
The friendly thief sea wealthy with the drowned.

❧ Robert Lowell (1917–1977)

THE DEAD IN EUROPE

After the planes unloaded, we fell down
Buried together, unmarried men and women;

Not crown of thorns, not iron, not Lombard crown,
Not grilled and spindle spires pointing to heaven
Could save us. Raise us, Mother, we fell down
Here hugger-mugger in the jellied fire:
Our sacred earth in our day was our curse.

Our Mother, shall we rise on Mary's day
In Maryland, wherever corpses married
Under the rubble, bundled together? Pray
For us whom the blockbusters marred and buried;
When Satan scatters us on Rising-day,
O Mother, snatch our bodies from the fire:
Our sacred earth in our day was our curse.

Mother, my bones are trembling and I hear
The earth's reverberations and the trumpet
Bleating into my shambles. Shall I bear,
(O Mary!) unmarried man and powder-puppet,
Witness to the Devil? Mary, hear,
O Mary, marry earth, sea, air and fire;
Our sacred earth in our day is our curse.

❧ Robert Duncan (1919–1988)

From MY MOTHER WOULD BE A FALCONRESS

My mother would be a falconress,
And I her gay falcon treading her wrist,
would fly to bring back
from the blue of the sky to her, bleeding, a prize,
where I dream in my little hood with many bells
jangling when I'd turn my head.

My mother would be a falconress,
and she sends me as far as her will goes.
She lets me ride to the end of her curb
where I fall back in anguish.

I dread that she will cast me away,
for I fall, I mis-take, I fail in her mission.

She would bring down the little birds.
And I would bring down the little birds.
When will she let me bring down the little birds,
pierced from their flight with their necks broken,
their heads like flowers limp from the stem?

I tread my mother's wrist and would draw blood.
Behind the little hood my eyes are hooded.

I have gone back into my hooded silence,
talking to myself and dropping off to sleep.

For she has muffled my dreams in the hood she has made me,
sewn round with bells, jangling when I move.
She rides with her little falcon upon her wrist.
She uses a barb that brings me to cower.
She sends me abroad to try my wings
and I come back to her. I would bring down
the little birds to her
I may not tear into, I must bring back perfectly.
I tear at her wrist with my beak to draw blood,
and her eye holds me, anguisht, terrifying.
She draws a limit to my flight.
Never beyond my sight, she says.

She trains me to fetch and to limit myself in fetching.
She rewards me with meat for my dinner.
But I must never eat what she sends me to bring her.

Yet it would have been beautiful, if she would have carried me,
always, in a little hood with the bells ringing,
at her wrist, and her riding
to the great falcon hunt, and me
flying up to the curb of my heart from her heart
to bring down the skylark from the blue to her feet,
straining, and then released for the flight. . . .

✖ Keith Douglas (1920–1944)

VERGISSMEINNICHT

Three weeks gone and the combatants gone
returning over the nightmare ground
we found the place again, and found
the soldier sprawling in the sun.

The frowning barrel of his gun
overshadowing. As we came on
that day, he hit my tank with one
like the entry of a demon.

Look. Here in the gunpit spoil
the dishonoured picture of his girl
who has put: *Steffi. Vergißmeinnicht*
in a copybook gothic script.

We see him almost with content,
abased, and seeming to have paid

and mocked at by his own equipment
that's hard and good when he's decayed.

But she would weep to see today
how on his skin the swart flies move;
the dust upon the paper eye
and the burst stomach like a cave.

For here the lover and killer are mingled
who had one body and one heart.
And death who had the soldier singled
has done the lover mortal hurt.

Tunisia [May–June] 1943

❧ Hayden Carruth (b. 1921)

OF DISTRESS BEING HUMILIATED BY THE CLASSICAL CHINESE POETS

Masters, the mock orange is blooming in Syracuse without scent, having
    been bred by patient horticulturists
To make this greater display at the expense of fragrance.
But I miss the jasmine of my back-country home.
Your language has no tenses, which is why your poems can never be
    translated whole into English;
Your minds are the minds of men who feel and imagine without time.
The serenity of the present, the repose of my eyes in the cool whiteness of
    sterile flowers.
Even now the headsman with his great curved blade and rank odor is
    stalking the byways for some of you.
When everything happens at once, no conflicts can occur.
Reality is an impasse. Tell me again
How the white heron rises from among the reeds and flies forever across the
    nacreous river at twilight
Toward the distant islands.

❧ Richard Wilbur (b. 1921)

BALLADE FOR THE DUKE OF ORLÉANS

> *who offered a prize at Blois, circa 1457, for the best ballade*
> *employing the line "Je meurs de soif auprès de la fontaine."*

Flailed from the heart of water in a bow,
He took the falling fly; my line went taut;
Foam was in uproar where he drove below;

In spangling air I fought him and was fought.
Then, wearied to the shallows, he was caught,
Gasped in the net, lay still and stony-eyed.
It was no fading iris I had sought.
I die of thirst, here at the fountain-side.

Down in the harbor's flow and counter-flow
I left my ships with hopes and heroes fraught.
Ten times more golden than the sun could show,
Calypso gave the darkness I besought.
Oh, but her fleecy touch was dearly bought:
All spent, I wakened by my only bride,
Beside whom every vision is but nought,
And die of thirst, here at the fountain-side.

Where does that Plenty dwell, I'd like to know,
Which fathered poor Desire, as Plato taught?
Out on the real and endless waters go
Conquistador and stubborn Argonaut.
Where Buddha bathed, the golden bowl he brought
Gilded the stream, but stalled its living tide.
The sunlight withers as the verse is wrought.
I die of thirst, here at the fountain-side.

Envoi

Duke, keep your coin. All men are born distraught,
And will not for the world be satisfied.
Whether we live in fact, or but in thought,
We die of thirst, here at the fountain-side.

✑ Philip Larkin (1922–1985)

DAYS

What are days for?
Days are where we live.
They come, they wake us
Time and time over.

They are to be happy in:
Where can we live but days?

Ah, solving that question
Brings the priest and the doctor
In their long coats
Running over the fields.

GOING

There is an evening coming in
Across the fields, one never seen before,
That lights no lamps.

Silken it seems at a distance, yet
When it is drawn up over the knees and breast
It brings no comfort.

Where has the tree gone, that locked
Earth to the sky? What is under my hands,
That I cannot feel?

What loads my hands down?

Louis Simpson (b. 1923)

CARENTAN O CARENTAN

Trees in the old days used to stand
And shape a shady lane
Where lovers wandered hand in hand
Who came from Carentan.

This was the shining green canal
Where we came two by two
Walking at combat-interval.
Such trees we never knew.

The day was early June, the ground
Was soft and bright with dew.
Far away the guns did sound,
But here the sky was blue.

The sky was blue, but there a smoke
Hung still above the sea
Where the ships together spoke
To towns we could not see.

Could you have seen us through a glass
You would have said a walk
Of farmers out to turn the grass,
Each with his own hay-fork.

The watchers in their leopard suits
Waited till it was time,

And aimed between the belt and boot
And let the barrel climb.

I must lie down at once, there is
A hammer at my knee.
And call it death or cowardice,
Don't count again on me.

Everything's all right, Mother,
Everyone gets the same
At one time or another.
It's all in the game.

I never strolled, nor ever shall,
Down such a leafy lane.
I never drank in a canal,
Nor ever shall again.

There is a whistling in the leaves
And it is not the wind,
The twigs are falling from the knives
That cut men to the ground.

Tell me, Master-Sergeant,
The way to turn and shoot.
But the Sergeant's silent
That taught me how to do it.

O Captain, show us quickly
Our place upon the map.
But the Captain's sickly
And taking a long nap.

Lieutenant, what's my duty,
My place in the platoon?
He too's a sleeping beauty,
Charmed by that strange tune.

Carentan O Carentan
Before we met with you
We never yet had lost a man
Or known what death could do.

James Dickey (1923–1997)

THE HEAVEN OF ANIMALS

Here they are. The soft eyes open.
If they have lived in a wood

It is a wood.
If they have lived on plains
It is grass rolling
Under their feet forever.

Having no souls, they have come,
Anyway, beyond their knowing.
Their instincts wholly bloom
And they rise.
The soft eyes open.

To match them, the landscape flowers,
Outdoing, desperately
Outdoing what is required:
The richest wood,
The deepest field.

For some of these,
It could not be the place
It is, without blood.
These hunt, as they have done,
But with claws and teeth grown perfect.

More deadly than they can believe.
They stalk more silently,
And crouch on the limbs of trees,
And their descent
Upon the bright backs of their prey

May take years
In a sovereign floating of joy.
And those that are hunted
Know this as their life,
Their reward: to walk

Under such trees in full knowledge
Of what is in glory above them,
And to feel no fear,
But acceptance, compliance.
Fulfilling themselves without pain

At the cycle's center,
They tremble, they walk
Under the tree,
They fall, they are torn,
They rise, they walk again.

ᗯ Harvey Shapiro (b. 1924)

NATIONAL COLD STORAGE COMPANY

The National Cold Storage Company contains
More things than you can dream of.
Hard by the Brooklyn Bridge it stands
In a litter of freight cars,
Tugs to one side; the other, the traffic
Of the Long Island Expressway.
I myself have dropped into it in seven years
Midnight tossings, plans for escape, the shakes.
Add this to the national total—
Grant's tomb, the Civil War, Arlington,
The young President dead.
Above the warehouse and beneath the stars
The poets creep on the harp of the Bridge.
But see,
They fall into the National Cold Storage Company
One by one. The wind off the river is too cold,
Or the times too rough, or the Bridge
Is not a harp at all. Or maybe
A monstrous birth inside the warehouse
Must be fed by everything—ships, poems,
Stars, all the years of our lives.

November 22, 1963

ᗯ Frank O'Hara (1926–1966)

A STEP AWAY FROM THEM

It's my lunch hour, so I go
for a walk among the hum-colored
cabs. First, down the sidewalk
where laborers feed their dirty
glistening torsos sandwiches
and Coca-Cola, with yellow helmets
on. They protect them from falling
bricks, I guess. Then onto the
avenue where skirts are flipping
above heels and blow up over
grates. The sun is hot, but the
cabs stir up the air. I look
at bargains in wristwatches. There
are cats playing in sawdust.
               On
to Times Square, where the sign
blows smoke over my head, and higher

the waterfall pours lightly. A
Negro stands in a doorway with a
toothpick, languorously agitating.
A blonde chorus girl clicks: he
smiles and rubs his chin. Everything
suddenly honks: it is 12:40 of
a Thursday.
           Neon in daylight is a
great pleasure, as Edwin Denby would
write, as are light bulbs in daylight.
I stop for a cheeseburger at JULIET's
CORNER. Giulietta Masina, wife of
Federico Fellini, *è bell' attrice.*
And chocolate malted. A lady in
foxes on such a day puts her poodle
in a cab.
           There are several Puerto
Ricans on the avenue today, which
makes it beautiful and warm. First
Bunny died, then John Latouche,
then Jackson Pollock. But is the
earth as full as life was full, of them?
And one has eaten and one walks,
past the magazines with nudes
and the posters for BULLFIGHT and
the Manhattan Storage Warehouse,
which they'll soon tear down. I
used to think they had the Armory
Show there.
           A glass of papaya juice
and back to work. My heart is in my
pocket, it is Poems by Pierre Reverdy.

Robert Bly (b. 1926)

AFTERNOON SLEEP

I

I was descending from the mountains of sleep.
Asleep I had gazed east over a sunny field,
And sat on the running board of an old Model A.
I awoke happy, for I had dreamt of my wife,
And the loneliness hiding in grass and weeds
That lies near a man over thirty, and suddenly enters.

II

When Joe Sjolie grew tired, he sold his farm,
Even his bachelor rocker, and did not come back.

He left his dog behind in the cob shed.
The dog refused to take food from strangers.

III

I drove out to that farm when I awoke;
Alone on a hill, sheltered by trees.
The matted grass lay around the house.
When I climbed the porch, the door was open.
Inside were old abandoned books,
And instructions to Norwegian immigrants.

ꔮ John Hollander (b. 1929)

ADAM'S TASK

> *And Adam gave names to all cattle, and to the fowl of the air,*
> *and to every beast of the field . . .*
>
> Genesis 2:20

Thou, paw-paw-paw; thou, glurd; thou, spotted
    Glurd; thou, whitestap, lurching through
The high-grown brush; thou, pliant-footed,
    Implex; thou, awagabu.

Every burrower, each flier
    Came for the name he had to give:
Gay, first work, ever to be prior,
    Not yet sunk to primitive.

Thou, verdle; thou, McFleery's pomma;
    Thou; thou; thou—three types of grawl;
Thou, flisket; thou, kabasch; thou, comma-
    Eared mashawk; thou, all; thou, all.

Were, in a fire of becoming,
    Laboring to be burned away,
Then work, half-measuring, half-humming,
    Would be as serious as play.

Thou, pambler; thou, rivarn; thou, greater
    Wherret, and thou, lesser one;
Thou, sproal; thou, zant; thou, lily-eater.
    Naming's over. Day is done.

ஒ Adrienne Rich (b. 1929)

GHAZAL

7/24/68:ii

The friend I can trust is the one who will let me have my death.
The rest are actors who want me to stay and further the plot.

At the drive-in movie, above the PanaVision,
beyond the projector beams, you project yourself, great Star.

The eye that used to watch us is dead, but open.
Sometimes I still have a sense of being followed.

How long will we be waiting for the police?
How long must I wonder which of my friends would hide me?

Driving at night I feel the Milky Way
streaming above me like the graph of a cry.

ஒ Ted Hughes (b. 1930)

WODWO

What am I? Nosing here, turning leaves over
Following a faint stain on the air to the river's edge
I enter water. What am I to split
The glassy grain of water looking upward I see the bed
Of the river above me upside down very clear
What am I doing here in mid-air? Why do I find
this frog so interesting as I inspect its most secret
interior and make it my own? Do these weeds
know me and name me to each other have they
seen me before, do I fit in their world? I seem
separate from the ground and not rooted but dropped
out of nothing casually I've no threads
fastening me to anything I can go anywhere
I seem to have been given the freedom
of this place what am I then? And picking
bits of bark off this rotten stump gives me
no pleasure and it's no use so why do I do it
me and doing that have coincided very queerly
But what shall I be called am I the first
have I an owner what shape am I what
shape am I am I huge if I go
to the end on this way past these trees and past these trees
till I get tired that's touching one wall of me

for the moment if I sit still how everything
stops to watch me I suppose I am the exact centre
but there's all this what is it roots
roots roots roots and here's the water
again very queer but I'll go on looking

ஐ Geoffrey Hill (b. 1932)

From THE MERCIAN HYMNS

I

King of the perennial holly-groves, the riven sandstone: overlord of the M5:
   architect of the historic rampart and ditch, the citadel at Tamworth, the
   summer hermitage in Holy Cross: guardian of the Welsh Bridge and the
   Iron Bridge: contractor to the desirable new estates: saltmaster:
   moneychanger: commissioner for oaths: martyrologist: the friend of
   Charlemagne.

'I liked that,' said Offa, 'sing it again.'

II

A pet-name, a common name. Best-selling brand, curt graffito. A laugh; a
   cough. A syndicate. A specious gift. Scoffed-at horned phonograph.

The starting-cry of a race. A name to conjure with.

V

So much for the elves' wergild, the true governance of England, the gaunt
   warrior-gospel armoured in engraved stone. I wormed my way
   heavenward for ages amid barbaric ivy, scrollwork of fern.

Exile or pilgrim set me once more upon that ground: my rich and desolate
   childhood. Dreamy, smug-faced, sick on outings—I who was taken to
   be a king of some kind, a prodigy, a maimed one.

VI

The princes of Mercia were badger and raven. Thrall to their freedom, I dug
   and hoarded. Orchards fruited above clefts. I drank from honeycombs
   of chill sandstone.

'A boy at odds in the house, lonely among brothers.' But I, who had none,
   fostered a strangeness; gave myself to unattainable toys.

Candles of gnarled resin, apple-branches, the tacky mistletoe. 'Look' they
   said and again 'look.' But I ran slowly; the landscape flowed away, back
   to its source.

In the schoolyard, in the cloakrooms, the children boasted their scars of
dried snot; wrists and knees garnished with impetigo.

XXIX

'Not strangeness, but strange likeness. Obstinate, outclassed forefathers, I
too concede, I am your staggeringly-gifted child.'

So, murmurous, he withdrew from them. Gran lit the gas, his dice whirred in
the ludo-cup, he entered into the last dream of Offa the King.

Sylvia Plath (1932–1963)

THE COLOSSUS

I shall never get you put together entirely,
Pieced, glued, and properly jointed.
Mule-bray, pig-grunt and bawdy cackles
Proceed from your great lips.
It's worse than a barnyard.

Perhaps you consider yourself an oracle,
Mouthpiece of the dead, or of some god or other.
Thirty years now I have labored
To dredge the silt from your throat.
I am none the wiser.

Scaling little ladders with gluepots and pails of lysol
I crawl like an ant in mourning
Over the weedy acres of your brow
To mend the immense skull plates and clear
The bald, white tumuli of your eyes.

A blue sky out of the Oresteia
Arches above us. O father, all by yourself
You are pithy and historical as the Roman Forum.
I open my lunch on a hill of black cypress.
Your fluted bones and acanthine hair are littered

In their old anarchy to the horizon-line.
It would take more than a lightning-stroke
To create such a ruin.
Nights, I squat in the cornucopia
Of your left ear, out of the wind,

Counting the red stars and those of plum-color.
The sun rises under the pillar of your tongue.
My hours are married to shadow.

No longer do I listen for the scrape of a keel
On the blank stones of the landing.

✑ Anonymous

LITTLE FRIEND

> A woman visiting her son remembers what she has
> read on the front page of her newspaper the week
> before, a conversation between a bomber, in flames
> over Germany, and one of the fighters protecting it:
> Randall Jarrell

"Then I heard the bomber call me in:
'Little Friend, Little Friend,
I got two engines on fire.
Can you see me, Little Friend?'
I said, 'I'm crossing right over you.
Let's go home.' "

✑ David Rattray (1936–1993)

THEY DON'T HAVE TO HAVE THAT LOOK

They don't have to have that
Look the ancient Greeks imagined
Nor do they always strike a colorful voodoo
Pose but they're real and exist
As indisputably as anything you can
Touch or see or feel and you
Will have a posse of them on your ass
One day. They're already with you
Wherever you are, sleeping now
Sleeping in the marrow of your bones
Soon they'll rise up in full cry
You'll wonder if you're hearing things
At last you'll know they're there and
Real as every filthy thing you did
They'll fill your dreams
Make your hair go dead and stand
Between you and the comfort you will need as
Never before as they rot your gums and
Tear the teeth out of your head
And when you end up on that hospice bed
They'll pour out of the teevee screen and
Bubble in the I.V. tubes and hum and sing and
Screech at you out of every stainless steel

Utensil in the intensive care unit until they
Cluster on the ceiling overhead to drop on
You in the extremity of your terror
And you will be screaming loud.

❧ Les Murray (b. 1938)

THE GODS

There is no Reynard fox. Just foxes.
I'm the fox who scents this pole.
As a kit on gravel, I brow arched Play? to a human.
It grabbed to kill, and gave me a soul.

We're trotting down one hen-stalk gully.
Soul can sit up inside, and be.
I halt, to keep us alive. Soul basks in
scents of shadow, sound of honey.

Call me the lover in the dew
of one in his merriment of blur.
Fragile as the first points of a scent
on the mind's skin settle his weights of fur.

A light not of the sky attends
his progress down the unleaped dim —
There's a young false-hoofed dog human coming
and the circling gunshot scent of him

eddies like sickness. I freeze, since their
ears point them, quicker than a wagtail's beak.
I must be Not for a while, *repressing*
all but the low drum of the meek.

Dreams like a whistle crack the spring;
a scentless shape I have not been
threads the tall legs of deities
like Hand, and Colour, and Machine.

❧ Alexander Scott (1920–1989)

From SCOTCHED

Scotch God	*Scotch Love*
Kent His	Barely
Faither.	A bargain.

Scotch Religion
Damn
Aa.

Scotch Free-love
Canna be
Worth much.

Scotch Optimism
Through a gless,
Darkly.

Scotch Lovebirds
Cheap
Cheep.

Scotch Pessimism
Nae
Gless.

Scotch Passion
Forgot
Mysel.

Scotch Drink
Nip
Trip.

Scotch Education
I tellt ye
I tellt ye.

Seamus Heaney (b. 1939)

THE TOLLUND MAN

I

Some day I will go to Aarhus
To see his peat-brown head,
The mild pods of his eye-lids,
His pointed skin cap.

In the flat country nearby
Where they dug him out,
His last gruel of winter seeds
Caked in his stomach,

Naked except for
The cap, noose and girdle,
I will stand a long time.
Bridegroom to the goddess,

She tightened her torc on him
And opened her fen,
Those dark juices working
Him to a saint's kept body,

Trove of the turfcutters'
Honeycombed workings.
Now his stained face
Reposes at Aarhus.

II

I could risk blasphemy,
Consecrate the cauldron bog

Our holy ground and pray
Him to make germinate

The scattered, ambushed
Flesh of labourers,
Stockinged corpses
Laid out in the farmyards,

Tell-tale skin and teeth
Flecking the sleepers
Of four young brothers, trailed
For miles along the lines.

III

Something of his sad freedom
As he rode the tumbril
Should come to me, driving,
Saying the names

Tollund, Grauballe, Nebelgard,
Watching the pointing hands
Of country people,
Not knowing their tongue.

Out there in Jutland
In the old man-killing parishes
I will feel lost,
Unhappy and at home.

Derek Mahon (b. 1941)

AN UNBORN CHILD

(for Michael and Edna Longley)

I have already come to the verge of
Departure. A month or so and
I shall be vacating this familiar room.
Its fabric fits me almost like a glove
While leaving latitude for a free hand.
I begin to put on the manners of the world,
Sensing the splitting light above
My head, where in the silence I lie curled.

Certain mysteries are relayed to me
Through the dark network of my mother's body
While she sits sewing the white shrouds
Of my apotheosis. I know the twisted
Kitten that lies there sunning itself

Under the bare bulb, the clouds
Of goldfish mooning around upon the shelf.
In me these data are already vested;

I know them in my bones—bones which embrace
Nothing, for I am completely egocentric.
The pandemonium of encumbrances
Which will absorb me, mind and senses,
Intricacies of the maze and the rat-race,
I imagine only. Though they linger and,
Like fingers, stretch until the knuckles crack,
They cannot dwarf the dimensions of my hand.

I must compose myself at the nerve centre
Of this metropolis, and not fidget—
Although sometimes at night, when the city
Has gone to sleep, I keep in touch with it,
Listening to the warm red water
Running in the sewers of my mother's body;
Or the moths, soft as eyelids, or the rain
Wiping its wet wings on the window-pane.

And sometimes too, in the small hours of the morning
When the dead filament has ceased to ring,
After the goldfish are dissolved in darkness
And the kitten has gathered itself up into a ball
Between the groceries and the sewing,
I slip the trappings of my harness
To range these hollows in discreet rehearsal
And, battering at the concavity of my caul,

Produce in my mouth the words, 'I want to live!'—
This my first protest, and shall be my last.
As I am innocent, everything I do
Or say is couched in the affirmative.
I want to see, hear, touch and taste
These things with which I am to be encumbered.
Perhaps I needn't worry; give
Or take a day or two, my days are numbered.

DEJECTION

Bone-idle, I lie listening to the rain,
Not tragic now nor yet to frenzy bold.
Must I stand out in thunder-storms again
Who have twice come in from the cold?

✑ David Curzon (b. 1941)

From MIDRASHIM: PROVERBS 6:6

Go to the ant, you sluggard,

and watch it lug an object
forward single file
with no short breaks for
coffee, gossip, a croissant,

and no stopping to apostrophize
blossom, by-passed because
pollen is not its job,
no pause for trampled companions:

consider her ways —and be content.

✑ Armand Schwerner (b. 1932)

From TABLET XXVI

he is not quite dead.

In this stony ground of the great artificer
In the holes, between hillocks.....................hot............
Urus compose themselves in his breath which is the hot wind
Of the desert of his words but also in his bitter [noun]-trap he is
Inhospitable to lost cows and goats, brutal to the lost. Where
Is the room in him for the tame, the life of milk and riverrun fields,
Overcome as he totters over the cave of his stomach, his dank words heavy
on his [peritoneum], he cradles his belly,
Great carpenter of the insides.
The sweet language waters grow
From his stomach,...............his +++++++++, his ....
From his testicles, and in his heart the semen grows
Into the fetus-form of his [verbs.] That will kill him in a great fire
Separated from a house. That will sicken him in a vast house
Cut away from the life of flame and scorching. He goes. May he die.
He leaves. May he die. We will continue ++++++++++++++++++++
In the bleached world. He dies.
We will store what even his greed can't curb. Still riddles pierce us.
He is who? A she. Giving out. Leaping in. Cut away and thinning out. Deep
Song. Great shaken word-stuff +++++++++++++++ missing
        +++++++++++..........
Leaving a change.
The barley of his words

Swells in the wrong ground of his liver, the child of his verbs puffs up
For this bearing, he is shaken .... ++++++++++++++++

he is someone else, perhaps an animal.

He races inside his messages of fleet means. He is the calling voice
Of the names inside the wheat and the barley. He can't say them
Forever. He tells them +++++++++++++++++++++++++++++++++++++++
Through the inside of his eyes, he sees
The inside of his eyes and finds the animal names of plants.
He looks and tells. He lives inside the scorching sun, he also leans
+++++++++++ upwards +++++++++++ downwards ++++++..................
In his long trial toward heat
...................................the name of the water falling, the voice
In the water slithering and trekking underneath the soil calling
To receive the good names, to say the good names and to receive
And to receive.................like the king of the hurricane who draws
Lightning and +++++++++++++++++++++++++ the sound, the proper
Voice for the saying, the murmuring, the uttering, the chant
Of wheat and barley changed by murmur into animal liveliness,
By uttering, by striking his stomach and opening the....................................

he will surely never die.

The world is made of his voice.

(Scholar/Translator's Key:............:untranslatable
+++++:missing
[ ]: supplied by the S/T)

Acknowledgments

(Acknowledgment credits follow the order of the text.)

Part I: POETS OF THE BRONZE AND IRON AGES

Anonymous, "The Seven," translated by Jerome Rothenberg, from Jerome Rothenberg, ed., *Technicians of the Sacred: A Range of Poetries from Africa, America, Asia, and Oceania* (New York: Doubleday, 1968). Reprinted with the permission of the translator.

"Inanna Spoke," translated by Diane Wolkstein and Samuel Noah Kramer from *Inanna: Queen of Heaven and Earth* (New York: Harper & Row, Publishers, 1983). Copyright © 1983 by Diane Wolkstein and Samuel Noah Kramer. Reprinted with the permission of Diane Wolkstein and Mildred Kramer.

Anonymous, ["In the early hours of the next morning dawning,"] from *Gilgamesh: A New Rendering in English,* translated by David Ferry. Copyright © 1993 by David Ferry. Reprinted with the permission of Farrar, Straus & Giroux, Inc.

Anonymous, "Prayer to the Gods of the Night" ["The gates of town are closed. The princes"], translated by David Ferry, from Tsvi Abusch, John Huehnergard, and Piotr Steinkeller, eds., *Lingering Over Words: Studies in Ancient Near East Literature in Honor of William L. Moran* (Atlanta: Scholars Press, 1990), Harvard Semitic Studies #37. Reprinted in *Dwelling Places* (Chicago: Phoenix Press/The University of Chicago Press, 1993). Copyright © 1990 by Harvard University. Reprinted with the permission of the author and Harvard Semitic Studies.

Anonymous, "Your Thwarts in Pieces, Your Mooring Rope Cut" ["Why are you adrift, like a boat, in the midst of the river,"], translated by Erica Reiner, from *Your Thwarts in Pieces, Your Mooring Rope Cut: Poetry from Babylonia and Ancient Assyria.* Copyright © 1985 by Michigan Slavic Publications. Reprinted with the permission of Michigan Slavic Publications, Department of Slavic Languages and Literatures, University of Michigan.

Anonymous, *from* "The Cannibal Hymn" ["The sky is a dark bowl, the stars die and fall."], translated by Tony Barnstone and Willis Barnstone. Original translation. Reprinted with the permission of the translators.

Anonymous, ["Death is before me today"], translated by W. S. Merwin, from *Selected Translations 1968–1978* (New York: Atheneum Publishers, 1979). Copyright © 1979 by W. S. Merwin. Reprinted with the permission of Georges Borchardt, Inc. for the author.

Anonymous, ["The marsh's plants bewilder."], translated by Barbara Hughes Fowler, from *Love Lyrics of Ancient Egypt.* Copyright © 1994 by The University of North Carolina Press. Reprinted with the permission of the publisher.

Anonymous, "Pleasant Songs of the Sweetheart Who Meets You in the Fields," translated by Ezra Pound and Noel Stock, from *Poems of Ancient Egypt.* Copyright © 1960, 1962 by Ezra

Pound and Noel Stock. Reprinted with the permission of New Directions Publishing Corporation.

Pharaoh Akhenaton, "Hymn to the Sun," translated by John Perlman, from Don Wellman, ed., *Translations; Experiments in Reading, Fascicles a and b* (1983). Reprinted with the permission of the translator.

Anonymous, ["All who come into being as flesh"] (Harper's Song), translated by John L. Foster, from *Echoes of Egyptian Voices: An Anthology of Ancient Egyptian Poetry.* Copyright © 1992 by John Lawrence Foster. Reprinted with the permission of the translator and University of Oklahoma Press.

Anonymous, ["The voice of the swallow, flittering, calls to me:"], translated by John L. Foster, from *Love Songs of the New Kingdom.* Copyright © 1969, 1970, 1971, 1972, 1973, 1974 by John L. Foster. Reprinted with the permission of the author and the University of Texas Press.

Anonymous, "Send him back hard by your lady's small window," translated by John L. Foster, from *Love Songs of the New Kingdom.* Copyright © 1969, 1970, 1971, 1972, 1973, 1974 by John L. Foster. Reprinted with the permission of the author and the University of Texas Press.

Anonymous, "Once More You Pass Her House, Deep in Thought," translated by John L. Foster, from *Love Songs of the New Kingdom.* Copyright © 1969, 1970, 1971, 1972, 1973, 1974 by John L. Foster. Reprinted with the permission of the author and the University of Texas Press.

Anonymous, "I found my love by the secret canal," translated by John L. Foster, from *Love Songs of the New Kingdom.* Copyright © 1969, 1970, 1971, 1972, 1973, 1974 by John L. Foster. Reprinted with the permission of the author and the University of Texas Press.

Anonymous, *from* "The Song of Songs" ["The sound of my lover"], translated by Marcia Falk, from *The Song of Songs: A New Translation.* Copyright © 1973, 1977, 1982, 1990 by Marcia Lee Falk. Reprinted with the permission of HarperCollins Publishers, Inc.

Anonymous, "The Valley of Dry Bones" ["The hand of the Lord held me transported"], translated by David Curzon. Original translation. Reprinted with the permission of the translator.

Anonymous, "Job, Chapter 3" ["Then Job spoke and cursed his day and chanted and said:"], translated by Raymond P. Scheindlin. Original translation. Reprinted with the permission of the translator.

Anonymous, *from* "The Book of Lamentations" ["How doth the city sit solitary that was full of people"], translated by Susan Stewart, from *The Denver Quarterly* 29 (Spring 1994). Reprinted with the permission of the translator.

Hesiod, "Works and Days" ["Beware the Month of Lenaion, bad days"] from *Hesiod*, translated by Richmond Lattimore. Copyright © 1959 by The University of Michigan Press. Reprinted with the permission of the publishers. "Children of Zeus (Theogeny)", translated by Charles Doria, in Charles Doria and Harris Lenowitz, *Origins: Creation Myths from the Ancient Mediterranean.* Copyright © 1976 by Charles Doria and Harris Lenowitz. Reprinted with the permission of Doubleday, a division of Bantam Doubleday Dell Publishing Group, Inc.

Homer, from *The Iliad*, Book XXI ["Then Achilles/Leaving the tall enemy with eels at his white fat' "], translated by Christopher Logue, from *Songs* (London: Hutchinson, 1959). Reprinted with the permission of the translator. From *The Odyssey*, Book XI ["We bore down on the ship at the sea's edge"], translated by Robert Fitzgerald. Copyright © 1961, 1963 by Robert Fitzgerald, renewed 1989, 1991 by Benedict R. C. Fitzgerald on behalf of the Fitzgerald children. Reprinted with the permission of Random House, Inc.

Anonymous, "The Stealing of Apollo's Cattle" ["The Maid Maia shook her head, here is"], (Homeric hymn to Hermes), translated by Padraic Fallon, from Padraic Fallon, *Poems and Versions*, edited by Brian Fallon. Copyright © 1983 by the Padraic Fallon Estate. Reprinted with the permission of Carcanet Press, Ltd.

Anonymous, "Creation Hymn" from "The Rig Veda" (X, 129), translated by Frederick Morgan, from *Refractions* (Omaha: Abattoir Editions, 1981). Copyright © 1981 by Frederick Morgan. Reprinted with the permission of the translator.

Anonymous, "Hymn to Night," translated by Edwin Gerow and Peter Dent, from Keith Bosely, ed., *Poetry of Asia: Five Millenniums of Verse from Thirty-Three Languages*. Reprinted with the permission of Weatherhill, Inc.

Anonymous, "Dawn has Arisen, Our Welfare is Assured" and "May the Winds Blow Sweetness!," translated by Raimundo Panikkar, from *The Vedic Experience: Mantramañjarî* (Berkeley: University of California Press, 1977). Reprinted with the permission of the translator.

Anonymous, "The Golden God," from "The Upanishads," translated by Stephen Mitchell, from *The Enlightened Heart: An Anthology of Sacred Poetry*. Copyright © 1989 by Stephen Mitchell. Reprinted with the permission of HarperCollins Publishers, Inc. HarperCollins Publishers, Inc.

Anonymous, *from* "The Bhagavad Gita" ["Arjuna, his war flag a rampant monkey"], ["Arjuna sat dejected,"], and ["Tell me—"], translated by Barbara Stoler Miller, from *The Bhagavad-Gita*. Copyright © 1986 by Barbara Stoler Miller. Reprinted with the permission of Bantam Books, a division of the Bantam Doubleday Dell Publishing Group, Inc.

Confucius, "The bamboos grow well under good rule" ["Dry in the sun by the corner of K'i"], translated by Ezra Pound, from *Shih-Ching: The Classical Anthology Defined by Confucius*. Copyright 1954 by the President and Fellows of Harvard College and renewed © 1982 by Mary de Rachrwitz and Omar Pound. Reprinted with the permission of Harvard University Press.

Anonymous, "The Great War Dance," translated by Constance A. Cook. Original translation. Reprinted with the permission of the translator.

Anonymous, "Boss Rat," translated by John S. Major. Original translation. Reprinted with the permission of the translator.

Anonymous, "Crane Calls," translated by Constance A. Cook. Original translation. Reprinted with the permission of the translator.

Anonymous, "Shu is Away," translated by Arthur Waley, from *The Book of Songs*. Copyright 1937 by George Allen & Unwin, Ltd. Reprinted with the permission of George Allen & Unwin, Ltd., a division of HarperCollins Publishers, Ltd.

Anonymous, "Forever Martial," translated by John S. Major. Original translation. Reprinted with the permission of the translator.

Anonymous, "Fruit Plummets from the Plum Tree," translated by Tony Barnstone and Chou Ping. Original translation. Reprinted with the permission of Tony Barnstone.

Anonymous, "Cypress Boat," translated by Constance A. Cook. Original translation. Reprinted with the permission of the translator.

Anonymous, "The Rat (A Close Translation and a Paraphrase)" translated by John S. Major. Original translation. Reprinted with the permission of the translator.

Ezra Pound, "Sans Equity and Sans Posse" ["A rat too has a skin (to tan)"] from *Shih-Ching: The Classical Anthology Defined by Confucius*. Copyright 1954 by the President and Fellows of Harvard College. Reprinted with the permission of Harvard University Press.

Anonymous, "Chung Tzu," translated by Arthur Waley, from *The Book of Songs.* Copyright 1937 by George Allen & Unwin, Ltd. Reprinted with the permission of George Allen & Unwin, Ltd., a division of HarperCollins Publishers, Ltd.

Yun'er, "Yun'er's Bell," translated by Constance A. Cook. Original translation. Reprinted with the permission of the translator.

Lao-tzu (attributed), "Five Chapters from the Tao Te Ching," translated by Moss Roberts. Original translation. Reprinted with the permission of the translator.

Ch'ü Yüan (attributed), "The Heaven Questions" translated by Stephen Field. Original translation. Reprinted with the permission of the translator. "The Yellow River's Earl," translated by Stephen Owen, from *An Anthology of Chinese Literature: Beginnings to 1911.* Copyright © 1996 by Stephen Owen and The Council for Cultural Planning and Development of the Executive Yuan of the Republic of China. Reprinted with the permission of the translator and W. W. Norton & Company, Inc. "The Summons of the Soul," translated by David Hawkes, from *Ch'ü Yhan: The Songs of the South,* translated, annotated, and introduced by David Hawkes. Copyright © 1985 by David Hawkes. Reprinted with the permission of Penguin Books, Ltd.

Part II: THE CLASSICAL EMPIRES, EAST AND WEST

Anonymous, "The Petelia Tablet," translated by Robert Bringhurst, from *The Beauty of the Weapon: Selected Poems 1972–1982.* Originally in *Arion.* Copyright 1982 by Robert Bringhurst. Reprinted with the permission of Copper Canyon Press, P. O. Box 271, Port Townsend, WA 96368 and McClelland & Stewart, Ltd.

Archilochus, "Strategy" and "Fireworks on the Glass," translated by Guy Davenport, from *Thasos and Ohio: Poems and Translations, 1950–1980* San Francisco: North Point Press, 1980) Reprinted with the permission of the translator. "Be Bold! That's One Way!" and ["May he lose his way on the cold sea"], translated by Guy Davenport, from *Carmina Archilochi: The Fragments of Archilochus.* Copyright © 1964, 1980 by the Regents of the University of California. Reprinted with the permission of the University of California Press. "Mercenary" ["I don't give a damn if some Thracian ape strut"], translated by Stuart Silverman, from Peter Jay, ed., *The Greek Anthology and Other Ancient Greek Epigrams* (New York: Oxford University Press, 1973). Reprinted with the permission of the translator.

Semonides, "The Genealogy of Women" (excerpt) ["God in His Wisdom from the start"], translated by Peter Whigham, from *Things in Common: Properly Selected Poems 1942–1982.* Reprinted with the permission of Black Swan Books, Ltd.

Alcman, ["Desire loosening"] and "Fragment 58: Night and Sleep" ["They sleep, the mountains crags and gullies,"], translated by Rosanna Warren, excerpted from "A Garland from Alcman" from *Stained Glass.* Copyright © 1993 by Rosanna Warren. Reprinted with the permission of W. W. Norton & Company, Inc.

Sappho, "Star of Evening," translated by Paul Roche, from *The Love Songs of Sappho.* Copyright © 1961, 1991 by Paul Roche. Reprinted with the permission of Dutton Signet, a division of Penguin Books USA Inc. "Anaktoria," "The Arbor," "Horses in Flowers" ["Come out of Crete"], and "Percussion, Salt and Honey," translated by Guy Davenport, from *Thasos and Ohio: Poems and Translations, 1950–1980* (San Francisco: North Point Press, 1980). Reprinted with the permission of the translator. "Lyric" ["The moon has set,"], translated by Jim Powell, from *Sappho: A Garland.* Copyright © 1993 by Jim Powell. Reprinted with the permission of Farrar, Straus & Giroux, Inc. "Lyric" ["The moon has set"], translated by Kenneth Rexroth, from *Poems from the Greek Anthology.* Copyright © 1962 by University of Michigan Press. Reprinted with the permission of the publishers. Sappho, "Lyric" ["The Pleiades disappear,"], translated by Sam Hamill, from *The Infinite Moment.* Copyright © 1991, 1992 by

Sam Hamill. Reprinted with the permission of New Directions Publishing Corporation. "Prayer to Aphrodite," translated by Alfred Corn, from *The West Door.* Originally in *The Paris Review* 88. Copyright © 1982 by Alfred Corn. Reprinted with the permission of Viking Penguin, a division of Penguin Books USA Inc.

Alcaeus, [". . . Her heart so stricken, Helen"], ["I long for the call to council"], ["Come tip a few with me,"], translated by Sam Hamill, from *The Infinite Moment.* Copyright © 1991, 1992 by Sam Hamill. Reprinted with the permission of New Directions Publishing Corporation. ["Come! Put by Pelop's Isle"], translated by Fred Beake, from *Acumen Magazine* 19 (April 1994). Reprinted with the permission of the translator.

Anacreon, "Count, If You Can," translated by Sam Hamill, from *The Infinite Moment.* Copyright © 1991, 1992 by Sam Hamill. Reprinted with the permission of New Directions Publishing Corporation.

Xenophanes, "War Memories," translated by Theodore Blanchard. Original translation. Reprinted with the permission of the translator.

Ibycus, "In Spring the Quince," translated by Kenneth Rexroth, from *Poems from the Greek Anthology.* Copyright © 1962 by University of Michigan Press. Reprinted with the permission of the publishers.

Simonides, ["Because of these men's courage, no smoke rose"], translated by Peter Jay, from Peter Jay, ed., *The Greek Anthology and Other Ancient Greek Epigrams* (New York: Oxford University Press, 1973). Reprinted with the permission of the translator. "Danae and Perseus," translated by Richmond Lattimore, from *The Hudson Review* IV, no. 4 (Winter 1952). Copyright 1952 by The Hudson Review, Inc. Reprinted with the permission of *The Hudson Review.*

Theognis, "Captive" ["I gave you wings. Black stone, blue heave shall take"], translated by Richmond Lattimore, from *Poems from Three Decades.* Reprinted with the permission of The University of Chicago Press.

Hipponax, "Still Waiting for My Winter Coat: A Sequence of Fragments," translated by Anselm Hollo, from *Sulfur* no. 33. Reprinted with the permission of the translator.

Aeschylus, "Chorus from 'Agamemnon' " ["The tenth year it is since Priam's high"], translated by Louis MacNeice, from *Agamemnon by Aeschylus.* Copyright 1937 by Louis MacNeice. Reprinted with the permission of Harcourt Brace and Company and Faber and Faber, Ltd. "Chorus from 'The Suppliants' " ["ZEUS MEN APHIKTOR Shining Father"], translated by Janet Lembke, from *The Suppliants.* Reprinted with the permission of Oxford University Press. "The Battle of Salamis" from "The Persians," translated by Peter Levi. Reprinted with the permission of John Johnson, Author's Agent, Ltd.

Pindar, "Olympia XI—For Agesidamus of the Westwind Locrians: Winner in the Boys' Boxing Match," translated by Robert Fagles, from *Arion.* Copyright © by Robert Fagles. Reprinted with the permission of Georges Borchardt, Inc. for the translator. "The Hyperboreans," translated by Padraic Fallon, from Padraic Fallon, *Poems and Versions,* edited by Brian Fallon. Copyright © 1983 by the Padraic Fallon Estate. Reprinted with the permission of Carcanet Press, Ltd. "For Midas, The Man From Akraga's First in the Flute Match 409 B.C., An Ode" ["I ask you"] (12th Pythian Ode), translated by Thomas Meyer, from *Staves Calends Legends* (Highlands, North Carolina: The Jargon Society, 1979). Reprinted with the permission of the translator.

Sophocles, "Praise for Kolonos," translated by Anthony Hecht, from *Collected Earlier Poems.* Copyright © 1977, 1990 by Anthony E. Hecht. Reprinted with the permission of Alfred A. Knopf, Inc. "Philoctetes" (excerpt), translated by Armand Schwerner, from *The Work, The Joy, and the Triumph of the Will* (Minneapolis: New Rivers Press, 1977). Reprinted with the permission of the translator. "Antigone" (excerpt), translated by E. R. Dodds, from *The Greeks and the Irrational.* Copyright © 1951, 1963 by The Regents of the University of California.

Reprinted with the permission of the University of California Press. "Choral Ode" from "Antigone," translated by Dudley Fitts and Robert Fitzgerald, from *The Oedipus Cycle: An English Version.* Copyright 1939 by Harcourt Brace, renewed © 1977 by Cornelia Fitts and Robert Fitzgerald. Reprinted with the permission of Harcourt Brace and Company.

Euripides, "Electra" (excerpt) ["When the long boats came on Troy From Greece"], translated by Denis Goacher, from *Tranversions* (Pemsnett: Gr/Ew Books, 1973). Reprinted with the permission of the translator. "The Trojan Women" (excerpt), translated by Katharine Washburn and Mark Rudman, from *The Denver Quarterly.* Reprinted with the permission of the translators.

Aristophanes, "The Birds" (excerpt) and "The Clouds" (excerpt), translated by William Arrowsmith, from *Three Comedies.* Copyright © 1961 by University of Michigan Press. Reprinted with the permission of the publishers.

Plato, "Aster," translated by Peter Jay, from Peter Jay, ed., *The Greek Anthology and Other Ancient Greek Epigrams* (New York: Oxford University Press, 1973). Copyright © 1973 by Peter Jay. Reprinted with the permission of the translator.

Anyte, ["I, Hermes, have been set up"], translated by Kenneth Rexroth, from *Poems from the Greek Anthology.* Copyright © 1962 by The University of Michigan Press. Reprinted with the permission of the publishers.

Antiphanes, ["A strange race of critics,"], translated by Sam Hamill, from *The Infinite Moment.* Copyright © 1991, 1992 by Sam Hamill. Reprinted with the permission of New Directions Publishing Corporation.

Heracleitus, ["The soil is freshly dug, the half-faded wreathes of leaves"], translated by Edwin Morgan, from *The Second Life.* Copyright © 1967 by Edwin Morgan. Reprinted with the permission of the translator.

Leonides of Tarentum, ["Theris, the old man who lived by his fish traps"], translated by Kenneth Rexroth, from *Poems from the Greek Anthology.* Copyright © 1962 by University of Michigan Press. Reprinted with the permission of the publishers.

Tymmes, "The Maltese Dog," translated by Edmund Blunden, from *Edmund Blunden: Selected Poems,* edited by Robin Marsack. Copyright © 1982 by Mrs. Claire Blunden. Reprinted with the permission of Carcanet Press, Ltd.

Theocritus, "Epitaph: Justice," translated by Fred Chappell, from *C* (Baton Rouge: Louisiana State University Press, 1993). Reprinted with the permission of the translator. "Idyl I" ["The whisper of the wind in"], translated by William Carlos Williams, from *The Collected Poems of William Carlos Williams, Volume II, 1939–1962,* edited by Christopher MacGowan. Copyright © 1962 by William Carlos Williams. Reprinted with the permission of New Directions Publishing Corporation.

Callimachus, "Epigram" ["The demon in the morning"], ["News of your death."], and "Prologue to the 'Aitia'," translated by Stanley Lombardo and Diane Raynor, from *Callimachus: Hymns, Epigrams, Select Fragments.* Copyright © 1988 by The Johns Hopkins University Press. Reprinted with the permission of the publishers.

Asclepiades, ["Here lies Archeanassa"], translated by Frederick Morgan, from *Poems: New and Selected,* with revisions by the translator. Copyright © 1987, 1995 by Frederick Morgan. Reprinted with the permission of the translator and the University of Illinois.

Aristophanes of Byzantium, ["On the advice of Praxilla"], translated by Sam Hamill, from *The Infinite Moment.* Copyright © 1991, 1992 by Sam Hamill. Reprinted with the permission of New Directions Publishing Corporation.

Diophanes, "On Love," translated by Dudley Fitts, from *Poems from the Greek Anthology.* Copyright © 1956 by Dudley Fitts. Reprinted with the permission of New Directions Publishing Corporation.

Antipatros, ["Never again, Orpheus"], translated by Kenneth Rexroth, from *Poems from the Greek Anthology.* Copyright © 1962 by University of Michigan Press. Reprinted with the permission of the publishers.

Meleager, ["Love's night & a lamp"], ["At 12 o'clock in the afternoon"], ["I was thirsty"], and ["White violets flower"], translated by Peter Whigham, from *The Poems of Meleager.* Copyright © 1975 by Peter Whigham and Peter Jay. Reprinted with the permission of University of California Press.

Antipater of Sidon, "Priapos of the Harbor," translated by Dudley Fitts, from *Poems from the Greek Anthology.* Copyright © 1956 by Dudley Fitts. Reprinted with the permission of New Directions Publishing Corporation. ["This is Anacreon's grave. Here lie"], translated by Robin Skelton, from *200 Poems from the Greek Anthology* (Seattle: University of Washington Press, 1972). Originally published in *Arion.* Reprinted with the permission of the translator.

Philodemos, ["You cry, whine, peer strangely at me."], translated by George Economou, from *Harvard Advocate* (1982), "Translation Issue." Reprinted with the permission of the translator. ["Demo and Thermion both slay me,"] and ["I loved—who hasn't? I worshiped—hasn't], translated by George Economou, from *harmonies & fits* (Norman, Okla.: Point Riders Press, 1987). Copyright © 1983, 1987 by George Economou. Reprinted with the permission of the translator. ["Make the bedlamp tipsy with oil;"] translated by James Laughlin, from *Sulphur,* no. 33. Reprinted with the permission of the translator.

Scythinos, "Too Late," translated by J. V. Cunningham, from *Collected Poems and Epigrams* (Athens, Ohio: The Swallow Press, 1971). Reprinted with the permission of Jessie Cunningham.

Lucilius, ["Lean Gaius, who was thinner than a straw"], translated by Peter Porter, from *The Greek Anthology* (London: Allen Lane, 1973). Reprinted with the permission of the translator.

Antipater of Thessalonica, ["I've never feared the setting of the Pleiades"], translated by Sam Hamill, from *The Infinite Moment.* Copyright © 1991, 1992 by Sam Hamill. Reprinted with the permission of New Directions Publishing Corporation.

Euenos, "To a Swallow," translated by John Peale Bishop, from *Selected Poems.* Copyright 1941 by John Peale Bishop, renewed © 1969 by Margaret G. H. Bronson. Reprinted with the permission of Scribners, a division of Simon & Schuster, Inc.

Antiphilos, "On the Death of the Ferryman, Glaucus," translated by W. S. Merwin, from *Selected Translations 1968–1978* (New York: Atheneum Publishers, 1979). Copyright © 1979 by W. S. Merwin. Reprinted with the permission of Georges Borchardt, Inc. for the author.

Anonymous, "Christian Epigram, Palatine Anthology," translated by John Peck, from *Poems and Translations of Hï-Lö* (Bronx: The Sheep Meadow Press, 1993). Reprinted with the permission of the translator.

Palladas, ["Whose baggage from land to land is despair"], translated by Frank Kuenstler, from Peter Jay, ed., *The Greek Anthology and Other Ancient Greek Epigrams* (New York: Oxford University Press, 1973). Reprinted with the permission of the translator. "Women All Cause Rue" and "A Murderer & Serapis," translated by Tony Harrison, from *Palladas Poems: A Selection* (London: Anvil Press Poetry, 1975). Copyright © 1975 by Tony Harrison. Reprinted with the permission of Gordon Dickerson for the author. ["Having slept with a man"], translated by Peter Jay, from Peter Jay, ed., *The Greek Anthology and Other Ancient Greek Epigrams* (New York: Oxford University Press, 1973). Reprinted with the permission of the translator. ["where the 3 roads meet"], translated by Anselm Hollo, from *Corvus: Poems by Anselm Hollo* (Minneapolis: Coffee House Press, 1995). Reprinted with the permission of the translator.

Anonymous, "The Last Oracle From Delphi," translated by Katharine Washburn. Original translation. Reprinted with the permission of the translator.

Leuconoë" [Odes I.11: "Don't be too eager to ask"], translated by David Ferry, from *The Boston Review* (December 1993/January 1994). Reprinted with the permission of the translator.

Tibullus, ["Cross the Aegean without me, then, Messalla—"], translated by Humphrey Clucas, from *Agenda* 16, nos. 3–4. Reprinted with the permission of *Agenda*. "Adde Merum Vinoque" (excerpt) ["Fill up my glass again! The anodyne"], translated by Rachel Hadas, from *Other Worlds Than This*. Copyright © 1994 by Rachel Hadas. Reprinted with the permission of Rutgers University Press.

Propertius, "The Odes" ["A ghost is someone: death has left a hole"], translated by Robert Lowell, from *Lord Weary's Castle*. Copyright 1946 and renewed © 1974 by Robert Lowell. Reprinted with the permission of Harcourt Brace & Company. ["Ariadne lay, Theseus' ship sailing away"], translated by Vincent Katz, from *Charm: Sextus Propertius*. Copyright © 1995 by Sun & Moon Press. Reprinted with the permission of the publishers. "O Best of All Nights, Return and Return Again," translated by James Laughlin, from *The Owl of Minerva*. Copyright © 1987 by James Laughlin. Reprinted with the permission of Copper Canyon Press, P. O. Box 271, Port Townsend, WA 98368.

Ovid, "Arethusa Saved" from "The Metamorphoses," translated by Thom Gunn, from *After Ovid* (New York: Farrar, Straus & Giroux, 1995). Reprinted with the permission of the translator. "The Death of Orpheus" ["the Thracian poet's song gets trees, rocks,"], translated by Charles Boer, from *Ovid's Metamorphoses*. Copyright © 1989 by Charles Boer. Reprinted with the permission of Spring Publications. "Tristia" (excerpts), translated by David R. Slavitt, from *Ovid's Poetry of Exile*. Copyright © 1990 by The Johns Hopkins University Press. Reprinted with the permission of the publishers. "Ovid in Love" [*Amores* I, V: "The day being humid and my head" and II, XI: "This strange sea-going craze began"], translated by Derek Mahon, from *Selected Poems* (London: Penguin Books, 1991). Copyright © 1990 by Derek Mahon. Reprinted with the permission of the translator.

Seneca, "Oedipus" (excerpt) ["Thebes   you are finished"]" translated by Ted Hughes, from *Seneca's Oedipus*. Copyright © 1972 by Doubleday, a division of Bantam Doubleday Dell Publishing Group, Inc. Reprinted with the permission of Doubleday, a division of Bantam Doubleday Dell Publishing Group, Inc. and Olwyn Hughes Literary Agency.

Petronius, "Man in the Middle of the Street," translated by Tim Reynolds, from *Arion* 3, no. 4 (Winter 1964). Reprinted with the permission of the translator.

Martial, ["Here he is whom you read and clamored for,"], translated by William Matthews, from *Selected Poems and Translation 1969–1991*. Copyright © 1992 by William Matthews. Reprinted with the permission of Houghton Mifflin Company. All rights reserved. ["You are a stool pigeon and"], translated by Kenneth Rexroth, from *Poems from the Greek Anthology*. Copyright © 1962 by The University of Michigan Press. Reprinted with the permission of the publishers. "Non te amo, Sabidine" ["I do not like thee, Dr. Fell"], translated by Fred Chappell, from *C* (Baton Rouge: Louisiana State University Press, 1993). Reprinted with the permission of the translator. ["You sold a slave just yesterday"], ["Ted's studio burnt down, with all his poems"], and ["You lie and I concur. You 'give' "], translated by William Matthews, from *Selected Poems and Translations, 1969–1991*. Copyright © 1992 by William Maxwell. Reprinted with the permission of Houghton Mifflin Company. All rights reserved. ["Surrounded by eunuchs and limp as a tissue,"] and [" 'Oh if the gods would make me rich,' you said—"], translated by William Matthews, from *The Mortal City: 100 Epigrams by Martial* (New York: Houghton Mifflin Company, 1991). Copyright © 1991 by William Matthews. Reprinted with the permission of the translator. "Agriculture" and "How to Do It," translated by Fred Chappell, from *C* (Baton Rouge: Louisiana State University Press, 1993). Reprinted with the permission of the translator.

Juvenal, "London, Greater London" (After Juvenal, *Satire III*), by John Holloway, from *New Poems* (New York: Charles Scribner's Sons, 1970). Originally published in *Arion*. Reprinted with the permission of the translator.

Hadrian, "The Emperor Hadrian On His Soul," translated by Frederick Morgan, from *Poems New and Selected*. Copyright © 1987 by Frederick Morgan. Reprinted with the permission of the translator and the University of Illinois Press.

Anonymous, *The Vigil of Venus* (excerpt) ["Tomorrow Love Shall have its way with ingenue and old roué], translated by David R. Slavitt. Original translation. Reprinted with the permission of the translator.

Anonymous, ["Even he was abashed"] and ["Those women"] , from the *Gathasaptasati* of King Hala, translated by Martha Ann Selby, from *Sulfur* (Fall 1993). Reprinted with the permission of the translator.

Anonymous, ["Lone buck"], from the *Gathasaptasati* of King Hala, translated by Andrew Schelling, from *Dropping the Bow: Poems from Ancient India*. Copyright © 1991 by Andrew Schelling. Reprinted with the permission of Broken Moon Press.

Anonymous, ["The newly wed girl, pregnant already,"], ["You love her while I love you"], and ["These women plunder my husband"], from the *Gathasaptasati* of King Hala, translated by David Ray, from *Translation Magazine* 12 (1984). Reprinted with the permission of *Translation Magazine*.

Ammuvanar, "They Shout Out the Price of Salt," translated by George L. Hart III, from *Poets of the Tamil Anthologies: Ancient Poems of Love and War*. Copyright © 1979 by Princeton University Press. Reprinted with the permission of the publisher.

Kaccipettu Nannakaiyar, "What She Said," translated by A. K. Ramanujan, from *The Interior Landscape: Love Poems from a Classical Tamil Anthology* (Bloomington: Indiana University Press, 1967). Copyright © 1967 by A. K. Ramanujan. Reprinted with the permission of Molly A. Daniels-Ramanujan.

Mamalatan, "What She Said," translated by A. K. Ramanujan, from *The Interior Landscape: Love Poems from a Classical Tamil Anthology* (Bloomington: Indiana University Press, 1967). Copyright © 1967 by A. K. Ramanujan. Reprinted with the permission of Molly A. Daniels-Ramanujan.

Oreruravanar, "What He Said," translated by A. K. Ramanujan, from *The Interior Landscape: Love Poems from a Classical Tamil Anthology* (Bloomington: Indiana University Press, 1967). Copyright © 1967 by A. K. Ramanujan. Reprinted with the permission of Molly A. Daniels-Ramanujan.

Maturaikkataiayattar Makan Vennakan, "What She Said to Her Girl-Friend," translated by A. K. Ramanujan, from *The Interior Landscape: Love Poems from a Classical Tamil Anthology* (Bloomington: Indiana University Press, 1967). Copyright © 1967 by A. K. Ramanujan. Reprinted with the permission of Molly A. Daniels-Ramanujan.

Maturai Eruttalan Centamputan, "What She Said," translated by A. K. Ramanujan, from *The Interior Landscape: Love Poems from a Classical Tamil Anthology* (Bloomington: Indiana University Press, 1967). Copyright © 1967 by A. K. Ramanujan. Reprinted with the permission of Molly A. Daniels-Ramanujan.

Kannan, "What Her Girl-Friend Said to Him," translated by A. K. Ramanujan, from *The Interior Landscape: Love Poems from a Classical Tamil Anthology* (Bloomington: Indiana University Press, 1967). Copyright © 1967 by A. K. Ramanujan. Reprinted with the permission of Molly A. Daniels-Ramanujan.

Peruñcattan, "What Her Girl-Friend Said," translated by A. K. Ramanujan, from *The Interior Landscape: Love Poems from a Classical Tamil Anthology* (Bloomington: Indiana University Press, 1967). Copyright © 1967 by A. K. Ramanujan. Reprinted with the permission of Molly A. Daniels-Ramanujan.

Kallataanar, "What She Said," translated by A. K. Ramanujan, from *The Interior Landscape: Love Poems from a Classical Tamil Anthology* (Bloomington: Indiana University Press, 1967).

Copyright © 1967 by A. K. Ramanujan. Reprinted with the permission of Molly A. Daniels-Ramanujan.

Kollan Arici, "What Her Friend Said," translated by A. K. Ramanujan, from *Poetry of Asia: Five Millenniums of Verse from Thirty-Three Languages,* edited by Keith Bosley (New York: Weatherhill, 1979). Reprinted with the permission of Molly A. Daniels-Ramanujan.

Cempulappeyanirar, "What He Said," translated by A. K. Ramanujan, from *Poetry of Asia: Five Millenniums of Verse from Thirty-Three Languages,* edited by Keith Bosley (New York: Weatherhill, 1979). Reprinted with the permission of Molly A. Daniels-Ramanujan.

Ponmutiyar, "Elegy on a Young Warrior," translated by A. K. Ramanujan, from *Poetry of Asia: Five Millenniums of Verse from Thirty-Three Languages,* edited by Keith Bosley (New York: Weatherhill, 1979). Reprinted with the permission of Molly A. Daniels-Ramanujan.

Kovurkilar, "We Hope for Patrons," translated by George L. Hart III, from *Poets of the Tamil Anthologies: Ancient Poems of Love and War.* Copyright © 1979 by Princeton University Press. Reprinted with the permission of the publisher.

Itaikkunrurkilar, "His Legs Strong and Lithe," translated by George L. Hart III, from *Poets of the Tamil Anthologies: Ancient Poems of Love and War.* Copyright © 1979 by Princeton University Press. Reprinted with the permission of the publisher.

Ceraman Kottampuluttut, "Great It May Be," translated by George L. Hart III, from *Poets of the Tamil Anthologies: Ancient Poems of Love and War.* Copyright © 1979 by Princeton University Press. Reprinted with the permission of the publisher.

Kakkaipirttiniyar Naccellaiyar, "Many Said, 'That Old Woman' . . . ," translated by George L. Hart III, from *Poets of the Tamil Anthologies: Ancient Poems of Love and War.* Copyright © 1979 by Princeton University Press. Reprinted with the permission of the publisher.

Tayankannanar, "Overspread With Salty Soil," translated by George L. Hart III, from *Poets of the Tamil Anthologies: Ancient Poems of Love and War.* Copyright © 1979 by Princeton University Press. Reprinted with the permission of the publisher.

Chia Yi, "Rhymeprose on an Owl" (excerpt), translated by John Robert Hightower, from Cyril Birch, ed., *An Anthology of Chinese Literature: From Early Times to the Fourteenth Century.* Copyright © 1965 by Grove Press, Inc. Reprinted with the permission of Grove/Atlantic, Inc.

P'an Chieh-yü, "A Present from the Emperor's New Concubine," translated by Kenneth Rexroth, from *One Hundred More Poems from the Chinese: Love and the Turning Year.* Copyright © 1970 by Kenneth Rexroth. Reprinted with the permission of New Directions Publishing Corporation.

Liu Chi-hsün, "Lament," translated by Tony Barnstone and Chou Ping. Original translation. Reprinted with the permission of Tony Barnstone.

Anonymous, "Old Poem," translated by Burton Watson, from *The Columbia Book of Chinese Poetry: From Early Times to the Thirteenth Century.* Copyright © 1984 by Columbia University Press. Reprinted with the permission of the publishers.

Pan Chao, "Needle and Thread," translated by Rob Swigart. Reprinted with the permission of the translator.

Anonymous, "Nineteen Poems in Ancient Style" (excerpt) ["Going on always on and on"], translated by Charles Hartman, from *Sunflower Splendor: Three Thousand Years of Chinese Poetry,* edited by Wu-chi Liu and Irving Yucheng Lo (Bloomington: Indiana University Press, 1975). Reprinted with the permission of the translator.

Anonymous, "Nineteen Poems in Ancient Style" (excerpt) ["Green is the grass on riverbanks,"], translated by Dell R. Hales, from *Sunflower Splendor: Three Thousand Years of Chinese Poetry,* edited by Wu-chi Liu and Irving Yucheng Lo (Bloomington: Indiana University Press, 1975). Reprinted with the permission of the translator.

Anonymous, "Mulberry by the Path," translated by Hans H. Frankel, from Cyril Birch, ed., *Studies in Chinese Literary Genres.* Copyright © 1974 by The Regents of the University of California. Reprinted with the permission of University of California Press.

Anonymous, "The Pomelo," translated by Anne Birrell, from *Popular Songs and Ballads of Han China.* Copyright © 1993. Reprinted with the permission of University of Hawai'i Press.

Sung Tzu-hou, "Song," translated by Arthur Waley, from *A Hundred and Seventy Chinese Poems.* Copyright 1919 by Alfred A. Knopf, Inc., renewed 1947 by Arthur Waley. Reprinted with the permission of Constable Publishers, Ltd.

Ts'ao Ts'ao, "Variant on the Songs of the East and West Gates," translated by David Lattimore, from *The Harmony of the World* (Providence: Copper Beech Press, 1980). Reprinted with the permission of the translator.

Part III: THE POSTCLASSICAL WORLD

Tiruvalluvar, ["The Gift of Children"] "Learning," and "Kindness and Generosity" from "The Kural," translated by Emmons E. White, from *The Wisdom of India.* Copyright © 1968. Reprinted with the permission of Peter Pauper Press.

Nakkirar, "The Shammon and The Red God" from "The Guide to Lord Murukan," translated by A. K. Ramanujan, from *Hymns for the Drowning* (Princeton: Princeton University Press, 1981). Copyright © 1981 by A. K. Ramanujan. Reprinted with the permission of Molly A. Daniels-Ramanujan.

Kalidasa, "The Cloud Messenger" (excerpts), translated by Franklin and Eleanor Edgerton, from *The Cloud Messenger.* Copyright © 1964 by The University of Michigan. Reprinted with the permission of The University of Michigan Press.

Bhartrihari (ascribed), ["A man may tear a jewel"], ["Apathy is ascribed to the modest man"], ["A bald-headed man, his pate"], ["Sweet maid, you perform a singular feat"], and ["While his body's vigor is whole"], translated by Barbara Stoler Miller, from *Bhartrihari: Poems.* Copyright © 1967 by Columbia University Press. Reprinted with the permission of the publishers.

Vagura, "A Love Poem" from the Vidyakara Anthology, translated by Edwin Gerow and Peter Dent, from Keith Bosley, ed., *Poetry of Asia: Five Millenniums of Verse from Thirty-Three Languages.* Reprinted with the permission of Weatherhill, Inc.

Vidya, "On Makeshift Bedding" from the Vidyakara Anthology, translated by Edwin Gerow and Peter Dent, from Keith Bosley, ed., *Poetry of Asia: Five Millenniums of Verse from Thirty-Three Languages.* Reprinted with the permission of Weatherhill, Inc. "On Makeshift Bedding," "Fate is a Cruel and Proficient Potter" and "And What of Those Arbors of Vines" from the Vidyakara Anthology, translated by Andrew Schelling, from *Dropping the Bow: Poems from Ancient India.* Copyright © 1991 by Andrew Schelling. Reprinted with the permission of Broken Moon Press.

Anonymous, "Next Morning" from the Vidyakara Anthology, translated by Andrew Schelling, from *Dropping the Bow: Poems from Ancient India.* Copyright © 1991 by Andrew Schelling. Reprinted with the permission of Broken Moon Press.

Anonymous, "My Husband, Before Leaving," translated by W. S. Merwin and J. Moussaieff Masson, from *Sanskrit Love Poems.* Copyright © 1977 by Columbia University Press. Reprinted with the permission of the publishers.

Anonymous, "A Long Time Back," translated by W. S. Merwin and J. Moussaieff Masson, from *Sanskrit Love Poems.* Copyright © 1977 by Columbia University Press. Reprinted with the permission of the publishers.

King Amaru, "Lying In Bed" and "You With Your Beautiful Swaying Walk," translated by Henry Heifetz, from *Translation Magazine* VII. Reprinted with the permission of *Translation*

Magazine. "Much Too Close," translated by Peter Dent, from *Agenda* (Spring–Summer 1973). Reprinted with the permission of *Agenda.*

Anonymous, "Cosmology," translated by W. S. Merwin and J. Moussaieff Masson, from *Sanskrit Love Poems.* Copyright © 1977 by Columbia University Press. Reprinted with the permission of the publishers.

Juan Chi, "The Ten Suns Rose in the East" and ["The Mujin Flowers Blossom on the Rolling Graves"], translated by Graham Harthill and Wu Fusheng, from *Songs of My Heart: The Chinese Lyric Poetry of Ruan Chi.* Copyright © 1988 by Graham Harthill and Wu Fusheng. Reprinted with the permission of The Wellsweep Press.

Lu Chi, "The Satisfaction," translated by Sam Hamill, from *The Art of Writing.* Originally published in *American Poetry Review* (May–June 1986). Copyright © 1986, 1991 by Sam Hamill. Reprinted with the permission of Milkweed Editions. "The Music of Words" and "The Riding Crop" from "The Art of Writing," translated by Tony Barnstone and Chou Ping. Original translation. Reprinted with the permission of Tony Barnstone.

Tzu Yeh (attributed), " 'Midnight' Songs" ["It is night again"], ["I had not fastened my sash over my gown,"], and ["The bare branches tremble"], translated by Kenneth Rexroth and Ling Chung, from *Women Poets of China.* Copyright © 1972 by Kenneth Rexroth and Ling Chung. Reprinted with the permission of New Directions Publishing Corporation.

T'ao Ch'ien, "Poem on Returning to Dwell in the Country" and "Written While Drunk," translated by William Acker, from Cyril Birch, ed., *An Anthology of Chinese Literature: From Early Times to the Fourteenth Century.* Copyright © 1965 by Grove Press, Inc. Reprinted with the permission of Grove/Atlantic, Inc. ["Great men want the four seas. I've only"], translated by David Hinton, from *Selected Poems of T'ao Ch'ien.* Copyright © 1993 by David Hinton. Reprinted with the permission of Copper Canyon Press, P. O. Box 271, Port Townsend, WA 98368.

Pao Chao, "The Ruined City," translated by C. J. Chen and Michael Bullock, from Cyril Birch, ed., *An Anthology of Chinese Literature: From Early Times to the Fourteenth Century.* Copyright © 1965 by Grove Press, Inc. Reprinted with the permission of Grove/Atlantic, Inc.

Anonymous, "On the Slope of Hua Mountain," translated by Kenneth Rexroth and Ling Chung, from *Women Poets of China.* Copyright © 1972 by Kenneth Rexroth and Ling Chung. Reprinted with the permission of New Directions Publishing Corporation.

Anonymous, "Mu-lan," translated by Hans H. Frankel, from *The Flowering Plum and the Palace Lady: Interpretations of Chinese Poetry.* Copyright © 1976 by Yale University. Reprinted with the permission of Yale University Press.

Anonymous, "Our Little Sister is Worried," translated by Kenneth Rexroth, from *One Hundred More Poems from the Chinese: Love and the Turning Year.* Copyright © 1970 by Kenneth Rexroth. Reprinted with the permission of New Directions Publishing Corporation.

Han Shan, "There's a Naked Bug at Cold Mountain" and "Cold Mountain Is a House" from "Cold Mountain Poems" translated by Gary Snyder, from Cyril Birch, ed., *An Anthology of Chinese Literature: From Early Times to the Fourteenth Century.* Copyright © 1965 by Grove Press, Inc. Reprinted with the permission of Grove/Atlantic, Inc. "I Live in a Little Country Village" from "Cold Mountain Poems," translated by Robert Hendricks, from *The Poetry of Han Shan: A Complete, Annotated Translation of Cold Mountain.* Copyright © 1990 by State University of New York. Reprinted with the permission of SUNY Press. "In Other Days" and "People Ask About Cold Mountain Way," translated by E. Bruce Brooks, from *Other Mountains: Two Thousand Years of Chinese Poetry in Context* (Amherst: privately printed, 1993). Reprinted with the permission of the translator.

Wang Wei, "Song of Peach Tree Spring," "Spring Night at Bamboo Pavilion, Presenting a Poem to Subprefect Qian about His Staying for Good in Blue Field Mountains," "Arriving at Ba Gorge in the Morning," and "Weeping for Ying Yao," translated by Tony Barnstone, Willis Barnstone, and Xu Haixiu, from *Laughing Lost in the Mountains: Poems by Wang Wei*

(Hanover, New Hampshire: University Press of New England, 1991). Reprinted with the permission of the translators. "Visiting Hsiang-chi Monastery," translated by Eva Shan Chou. Original translation. Reprinted with the permission of the translator.

Li Po, "The Road to Shu is Hard," "Inscribed on the Wall of Hsaü Hsüan-ping's Retreat," "The Ballad of Long Bank," "Spring Thoughts," "Fighting South of the Wall," "Inscribed at Summit Temple," "Drinking Alone in the Moonlight," and "Old Tai's Wine Shop," translated by Elling P. Eide, from *Poems of Li Po* (London: Anvil Press Poetry, 1983). Copyright © 1983 by Elling P. Eide. Reprinted with the permission of the translator. "For Meng Hao-jan," translated by Greg Whincup, from *The Heart of Chinese Poetry*. Copyright © 1967 by Greg Whincup. Reprinted with the permission of Doubleday, a division of Bantam Doubleday Dell Publishing Group, Inc. "Listening to a Monk from Shu Playing the Lute," translated by Vikram Seth, from *Three Chinese Poets*. Copyright © 1992 by Vikram Seth. Reprinted with the permission of HarperCollins Publishers, Inc. "In Praise of a Gold and Silver Painted Scene of the Buddha Manifestation in the Pure Land of the West, With a Preface," translated by Elling P. Eide, from *Poems of Li Po* (London: Anvil Poetry Press, 1983). Copyright © 1983 by Elling P. Eide. Reprinted with the permission of the translator.

Meng Hao-jan, "Written for Old Friends in Yang-jou City While Spending the Night on the Tung-lu River," translated by Greg Whincup, from *The Heart of Chinese Poetry*. Copyright © 1967 by Greg Whincup. Reprinted with the permission of Doubleday, a division of Bantam Doubleday Dell Publishing Group, Inc.

Liu Ch'ang-ch'ing, "On Parting with the Buddhist Pilgrim Ling-ch'ê," translated by Witter Bynner, from James Kraft, ed., *The Works of Witter Bynner: The Chinese Translations*. Copyright 1929 by Witter Bynner. Reprinted with the permission of Farrar, Straus & Giroux, Inc.

Tu Fu, "A Hawk in a Painting," "Ballad of the Army Carts," and "Crossing the Border" (Part 6), translated by David Lattimore. Original translations. Reprinted with the permission of the translator. "Moonlit Night," translated by Vikram Seth, from *Three Chinese Poets*. Copyright © 1992 by Vikram Seth. Reprinted with the permission of HarperCollins Publishers, Inc. "Daytime Dream," translated by Eva Shan Chou. Original translation. Reprinted with the permission of the translator. "Traveling at Night," translated by Greg Whincup, from *The Heart of Chinese Poetry*. Copyright © 1967 by Greg Whincup. Reprinted with the permission of Doubleday, a division of Bantam Doubleday Dell Publishing Group, Inc. "Thinking of My Little Boy," translated by David Lattimore, from *The Harmony of the World* (Providence: Copper Beech Press, 1980). Reprinted with the permission of the translator. "Dreaming of Li Po," translated by David Hinton, from *The Selected Poems of Tu Fu*. Copyright © 1989 by David Hinton. Reprinted with the permission of New Directions Publishing Corporation.

Han Yü, "Autumn Thoughts," translated by Burton Watson, from *The Columbia Book of Chinese Poetry: From Early Times to the Thirteenth Century*. Copyright © 1984 by Columbia University Press. Reprinted with the permission of the publishers.

Hsüeh T'ao, "Gazing at Spring," "Trying on New-Made Clothes," and "Dog Parted from Her Master," translated by Jeanne Larsen, from *Brocade River Poems: Selected Works of the Tang Dynasty Courtesan Xue Tao*. Copyright © 1987 by Princeton University Press. Reprinted with the permission of the publishers.

Po Chü-yi, "Song of Everlasting Sorrow," translated by Dore J. Levy, from *Chinese Narrative Poetry: The Late Han through T'an Dynasties*. Copyright © 1988 by Duke University Press. Reprinted with the permission of the publishers. Po Chü-yi, "The Red Cockatoo," "Madly Singing in the Mountains," and "The Chancellor's Gravel-Drive," translated by Arthur Waley, from *A Hundred and Seventy Chinese Poems*. Copyright 1919 by Alfred A. Knopf, Inc., renewed 1947 by Arthur Waley. Reprinted with the permission of Constable Publishers, Ltd.

Liu Tsung-yüan, "On Covering the Bones of Chang Chin, the Hired Man," translated by Jan W. Wells, from Wu-chi Liu and Irving Yucheng Lo, eds., *Sunflower Splendor: Three Thousand Years of Chinese Poetry* (Bloomington: Indiana University Press, 1975). Reprinted with the permission of the translator.

Li Ho, "The King of Ch'in Drinks Wine," translated by A. C. Graham, from *Poems of the Late T'ang*. Copyright © 1965, 1977 by A. C. Graham. Reprinted with the permission of Penguin Books, Ltd. "The Grave of Little Su," translated by A. C. Graham, from Cyril Birch, ed., *An Anthology of Chinese Literature: From Early Times to the Fourteenth Century*. Copyright © 1965 by Grove Press, Inc. Reprinted with the permission of Grove/Atlantic, Inc. "Flying Light," translated by Arthur Sze. Original translation. Reprinted with the permission of the translator.

Tu Mu, "Egrets," translated by A. C. Graham, from *Poems of the Late T'ang*. Copyright © 1965, 1977 by A. C. Graham. Reprinted with the permission of Penguin Books, Ltd.

Li Shang-yin, ["Phoenix tail on scented silk, flimsy layer on layer:"] and ["Bite back passion. Spring now sets."], translated by A. C. Graham, from *Poems of the Late T'ang*. Copyright © 1965, 1977 by A. C. Graham. Reprinted with the permission of Penguin Books, Ltd. ["The chance to meet is difficult"], translated by Arthur Sze. Original translation. Reprinted with the permission of the translator.

Kuan Hsiu, "Written in the Mountains," "Song of the Palace of Ch'en," and "Bad Government," translated by J. P. Seaton, from *Sulfur* (Fall 1993). Copyright © 1993 by J. P. Seaton. Reprinted with the permission of the translator.

Yü Hsuan-chi, "Living in the Summer Mountains," translated by Kenneth Rexroth and Ling Chung, from *Women Poets of China*. Copyright © 1972 by Kenneth Rexroth and Ling Chung. Reprinted with the permission of New Directions Publishing Corporation. "Spring Thoughts Sent to Tzu-an," translated by Geoffrey Waters, from Willis and Aliki Barnstone, eds., *Book of Women Poets from Antiquity to Now* (New York: Schocken Books, 1980). Reprinted with the permission of the translator.

Anonymous, "Poem of Medicine Puns," translated by Victor H. Mair, from Victor H. Mair, ed., *The Columbia Book of Traditional Chinese Literature*. Copyright © 1994 by Columbia University Press. Reprinted with the permission of the publishers.

Ch'en T'ao, "Turkestan," translated by Witter Bynner, from James Kraft, ed., *The Works of Witter Bynner: The Chinese Translations*. Copyright 1929 by Witter Bynner. Reprinted with the permission of Farrar, Straus & Giroux, Inc.

Master Wŏlmyŏng, "Requiem," translated by Peter H. Lee, from Keith Bosley, ed., *Poetry of Asia: Five Millenniums of Verse from Thirty-Three Languages*. Reprinted with the permission of Weatherhill, Inc.

Emperor Jomei, "Written After Climbing Kaguyama to Survey the Land," translated by Helen Craig McCullough, from Steven D. Carter, ed., *Traditional Japanese Poetry*. Copyright © 1991 by the Board of Regents of the Leland Stanford Junior College. Reprinted with the permission of Stanford University Press.

Kakinomoto no Hitomaru, "Mourning Princess Asuka," translated by Helen Craig McCullough, from *Brocade by Night: "Kokin Wakashu" and the Court Style in Japanese Classical Poetry*. Copyright © 1985 by the Board of Regents of the Leland Stanford Junior College. Reprinted with the permission of Stanford University Press.

Yomanoue no Okura, "A Lament for the Evanescence of Life," translated by Helen Craig McCullough, from *Brocade by Night: "Kokin Wakashu" and the Court Style in Japanese Classical Poetry*. Copyright © 1985 by the Board of Regents of the Leland Stanford Junior College. Reprinted with the permission of Stanford University Press. "Longing for His Son, Furuhi," translated by Helen Craig McCullough, from Steven D. Carter, ed., *Traditional Japanese Poetry*. Copyright © 1991 by the Board of Regents of the Leland Stanford Junior College. Reprinted with the permission of Stanford University Press.

Prince Ōtsu, "Approaching Death," translated by Burton Watson. Reprinted by permission.

Priest Sami Mansei, ["Our life in this world—"], translated by Steven D. Carter, from Steven D. Carter, ed., *Traditional Japanese Poetry*. Copyright © 1991 by the Board of Regents of the Leland Stanford Junior College. Reprinted with the permission of Stanford University Press.

Lady Kasa, "Love and Fear," translated by Kenneth Rexroth, from Donald Keene, ed., *Anthology of Japanese Literature: From The Earliest Times to the Christian Era*. Copyright © 1955 by Grove Press, Inc. Reprinted with the permission of Grove/Atlantic, Inc.

Princess Uchiko, "Recalling a Visit to His Majesty," translated by Burton Watson, from *The Country of Eight Islands*. Copyright © 1986 by Columbia University Press. Reprinted with the permission of the publishers.

Ariwara no Narihira, "Two Poems from the *Ise Monogatari*" ["Regretting the past"] and ["Facing his own death"], translated by F. Vos, from Donald Keene, ed., *Anthology of Japanese Literature: From The Earliest Times to the Christian Era*. Copyright © 1955 by Grove Press, Inc. Reprinted with the permission of Grove/Atlantic, Inc.

Ono no Komachi, "Six Love Poems" ["Autumn nights, it seems"], ["Yielding to a love"], and ["Though I go to you"], translated by Helen Craig McCullough, from *Brocade by Night: "Kokin Wakashu" and the Court Style in Japanese Classical Poetry*. Copyright © 1985 by the Board of Regents of the Leland Stanford Junior College. Reprinted with the permission of Stanford University Press. ["Thinking about him"], translated by Donald Keene, from Donald Keene, ed., *Anthology of Japanese Literature: From The Earliest Times to the Christian Era*. Copyright © 1955 by Grove Press, Inc. Reprinted with the permission of Grove/Atlantic, Inc. ["Doesn't he realize"], translated by Kenneth Rexroth and Ikuko Atsumi, from *Women Poets of Japan*. Copyright © 1977 by Kenneth Rexroth and Ikuko Atsumi. Reprinted with the permission of New Directions Publishing Corporation. ["A diver does not abandon"], translated by Jane Hirshfield and Mariko Aratami, from *The Ink Dark Moon: Love Poems by Ono no Komachi and Izumi Shikibu, Women of the Ancient Japanese Court* (New York: Vintage Books, 1990). Copyright © 1988, 1990 by Jane Hirshfield and Mariko Aratami. Reprinted with the permission of Jane Hirshfield.

Ki no Tsurayuki, "Three Poems on Spring Blossoms": ["On a spring hillside"], translated by Steven D. Carter, from Steven D. Carter, ed., *Traditional Japanese Poetry*. Copyright © 1991 by the Board of Regents of the Leland Stanford Junior College. Reprinted with the permission of Stanford University Press. ["The hue is as rich"], translated by Helen Craig McCullough, from *Kokin Wakashu: The First Imperial Anthology of Japanese Poetry*. Copyright © 1985 by the Board of Regents of the Leland Stanford Junior College. Reprinted with the permission of Stanford University Press. ["The wind that scatters"], translated by Helen Craig McCullough, from Steven D. Carter, ed., *Traditional Japanese Poetry*. Copyright © 1991 by the Board of Regents of the Leland Stanford Junior College. Reprinted with the permission of Stanford University Press. ["Out in the marsh reeds"], translated by Kenneth Rexroth, from *One Hundred Poems from the Japanese*. Copyright © 1955 by Kenneth Rexroth. Reprinted with the permission of New Directions Publishing Corporation.

Lady Ise, "Four Poems" ["Lightly forsaking"], ["Because we suspected"], ["A flower of waves"], and ["If it is you, there"], translated by Etsuko Terasaki with Irma Brandeis, from Willis and Aliki Barnstone, eds., *Book of Women Poets from Antiquity to Now* (New York: Schocken Books, 1980). Reprinted with the permission of Etsuko Terasaki.

Anonymous, "Two Poems on Love from the *Kokinshū*" ["If this were a world"] and ["Though you made me think"], translated by Helen Craig McCullough, from *Brocade by Night: "Kokin Wakashu" and the Court Style in Japanese Classical Poetry*. Copyright © 1985 by the Board of Regents of the Leland Stanford Junior College. Reprinted with the permission of Stanford University Press.

Lady Ukon, ["Me/you've forgotten"], translated by Howard S. Levy, from *Japan's Best Loved Poetry Classic: Hyakunin Isshu* (South Pasadena, Calif.: Landstaff, 1976). Reprinted by permission.

Lady Murasaki Shikibu, "Dialogue Poems": ["The warblers are today as long ago"], translated by Edward Seidensticker *The Tale of the Genji.* Copyright © 1976 by Edward G. Seidensticker. Reprinted with the permission of Alfred A. Knopf, Inc.

Lady Izumi Shikibu, "Three Poems on the Uncertainty of Life": ["From one darkness"], ["Being a person"], and ["So forlorn am I"]; ["If someone would come,"] and ["In my idleness"], translated by Steven D. Carter, from *Traditional Japanese Poetry: An Anthology.* Copyright © 1991 by the Board of Regents of the Leland Stanford Junior College. Reprinted with the permission of Stanford University Press. "Three Poems On Love": ["On nights when hail"], ["You told me it was"], and ["If you love me,"] translated by Willis Barnstone, from Willis and Aliki Barnstone, editors, *A Book of Women Poets from Antiquity to Now.* Copyright © 1980 by Schocken Books, Inc. Reprinted with the permission of Schocken Books, published by Pantheon Books, a division of Random House, Inc. "Autumn, On Retreat at a Mountain Temple" and "Although the Wind," translated by Jane Hirshfield and Mariko Aratani, from *The Ink Dark Moon: Love Poems by Ono no Komachi and Izumi Shikibu, Women of the Ancient Japanese Court* (New York: Vintage Books, 1990). Reprinted with the permission of Jane Hirshfield. "Tangled Hair," translated by Steven D. Carter, from *Traditional Japanese Poetry: An Anthology.* Copyright © 1991 by the Board of Regents of the Leland Stanford Junior College. Reprinted with the permission of Stanford University Press.

Anonymous (A Court Lady), "Dialogue Poems" from *The Eiga Monogatari,* translated by Helen Craig McCullough and William H. McCullough, from *A Tale of Flowering Fortunes: Annals of Japanese Aristocratic Life in the Heien Period.* Copyright © 1980 by the Board of Regents of the Leland Stanford Junior College. Reprinted with the permission of Stanford University Press.

Monk Nōin, "Spring in a Mountain Village," translated by Steven D. Carter, from *Traditional Japanese Poetry: An Anthology.* Copyright © 1991 by the Board of Regents of the Leland Stanford Junior College. Reprinted with the permission of Stanford University Press.

Anonymous, "Malediction," translated by Arthur Waley, from Donald Keene, ed., *Anthology of Japanese Literature: From The Earliest Times to the Christian Era.* Copyright © 1955 by Grove Press, Inc. Reprinted with the permission of Grove/Atlantic, Inc.

Imr El-Qais, "The Ode of Imr El-Qais," translated by Robert Bringhurst, from *Cadastre* (Spencer, Indiana: Kanchenjunga Press, 1973). Reprinted with the permission of the translator.

Antara, "The Black Knight," translated by Desmond O'Grady, from *Trawling Tradition: Translations 1954–1994* (University of Salzberg Press, 1994). Reprinted with the permission of the translator.

Abu Dhu'ayb Al-Hudhali, "Lament for Five Sons Lost in a Plague," translated by Omar S. Pound, from *Arabic and Persian Poems in English.* Copyright © 1986 by Omar Pound. Reprinted with the permission of Three Continents Press.

Labid Ibn Rabia, "The Mu'állaqa (excerpt) ["The tent marks in Mánan are worn away,"], translated by Michael Sells, from *Desert Tracings: Six Classic Arabic Odes* (Middletown, Conn.: Wesleyan University Press, 1989). Copyright © 1989 by Michael A. Sells. Reprinted with the permission of University Press of New England.

Ausonius, "The Field of Sorrow," translated by Helen Waddell, from *Medieval Latin Lyrics* (New York: W. W. Norton & Company, 1977, originally Constable and Barnes and Noble, 1948). Reprinted with the permission of Mary M. Martin and Constable Publishers. ["I used to tell you, 'Frances, we grow old."], translated by Kenneth Rexroth, from *Poems from the Greek Anthology.* Copyright © 1962 by The University of Michigan Press. Reprinted with the permission of the publishers.

Sulpicius Lupercus Servasius, ["Rivers level granite mountains"], translated by Kenneth Rexroth, from *Poems from the Greek Anthology.* Copyright © 1962 by The University of Michigan Press. Reprinted with the permission of the publishers.

Avianus, "The Calf and the Ox," translated by David Slavitt, from *The Fables of Avianus*. Copyright © 1993 by The Johns Hopkins University Press. Reprinted with the permission of the publishers.

Orientius, "Poem on Divine Province" (excerpt) ["The bulk of these years is already gone out of mind"], translated by John Peck, from *Poems and Translations of Hi-lö* (Bronx: The Sheep Meadow Press, 1993). Reprinted with the permission of the translator.

Anonymous, ["Hear that echo, children,"], translated by Denis Goacher, from *Tranversions* (Pemsnett: Gr/Ew Books, 1973). Reprinted with the permission of the translator.

Walifrid Strabo, ["Most learned Father Grimold,"], translated by Tim Reynolds, from *Arion* III, no. 4 (Winter 1964). Reprinted with the permission of the translator.

Anonymous, "Levis Exsurgit Zephirus" from "The Cambridge Songs," translated by David Ferry, from *Dwelling Places* (Chicago: Phoenix Press/University of Chicago Press, 1993). Copyright © 1993 by David Ferry. Reprinted with the permission of the translator.

Anonymous, "Heriger and the False Prophet" from "The Cambridge Songs," translated by Fred Chappell. Original translation. Reprinted with the permission of the translator.

Abelard, ["I am constantly wounded"], translated by Kenneth Rexroth, from *Poems from the Greek Anthology*. Copyright © 1962 by The University of Michigan Press. Reprinted with the permission of the publishers.

Anonymous, "De ramis cadunt folia," translated by Phillip Holland. Original translation. Reprinted with the permission of the translator.

Anonymous, "Dum Diana Vitrea" from "The Carmina Burana," translated by Richmond Lattimore, from *Poems from Three Decades*. Copyright © 1972 by Richmond Lattimore. Reprinted with the permission of The University of Chicago Press.

Anonymous, "The Archpoet's Confession," translated by Phillip Holland. Original translation. Reprinted with the permission of the translator.

Anonymous, "Alba, With a Refrain from the Provençal," translated by Tim Reynolds, from *Arion* III, no. 4 (Winter 1964). Reprinted with the permission of the translator.

Colman mac Lenini, "In Praise of a Sword Given Him By His Prince," translated by Richard O'Connell, from *Translation Magazine*. Reprinted with the permission of *Translation Magazine*.

Rumann, son of Colmann (attributed), "Storm At Sea," translated by Frank O'Connor, from *Kings, Lords, and Commons: An Anthology from the Irish* (New York: Alfred A. Knopf, 1959). Copyright © 1959 by Frank O'Connor. Reprinted with the permission of Writers House, Inc.

Anonymous, "Epitaph for Cu Chuimne," translated by Thomas Kinsella, from *The New Oxford Book of Irish Verse* (New York: Oxford University Press, 1986). Reprinted with the permission of the translator.

Anonymous, "Stanza" ["What, my Lord, shall I do with"], translated by Lewis Turco, from *Ancient Music* (New York: Oxford University Press, forthcoming). Copyright © 1997 by Lewis Putnam Turco. Reprinted with the permission of the translator. All rights reserved by Matham Press Enterprises.

Anonymous, "The Cattle-Raid of Cooley," translated by Thomas Kinsella, from *The Tain* (Oxford: Oxford University Press, 1970). Reprinted with the permission of the translator.

Anonymous, "Bran at the Island of Women," translated by Greg Delanty. Original translation. Reprinted with the permission of the translator.

Anonymous, "The Old Women of Beare," translated by Brendan Kenneally, from *Love of Ireland: Poems from the Irish*. Reprinted with the permission of Mercier Press, Cork.

Anonymous, "Epitaph" [" 'Have you seen Hugh,' "], translated by Frank O'Connor, from *Kings, Lords, and Commons: An Anthology from the Irish* (New York: Alfred A. Knopf, 1959). Copyright © 1959 by Frank O'Connor. Reprinted with the permission of Writers House, Inc.

Anonymous, [" 'Whence are you, learning's son?"], translated by Frank O'Connor, from *Kings, Lords, and Commons: An Anthology from the Irish* (New York: Alfred A. Knopf, 1959). Copyright © 1959 by Frank O'Connor. Reprinted with the permission of Writer's House, Inc.

Anonymous, "Monastic Poems: Four Glosses," translated by Thomas Kinsella, from *The New Oxford Book of Irish Verse* (New York: Oxford University Press, 1986). Reprinted with the permission of the translator.

Anonymous, "My Dark Night Has Come Round Again," translated by Seamus Heaney, from *Sweeney Astray: A Version from the Irish*. Copyright © 1983 by Seamus Heaney. Reprinted with the permission of Farrar, Straus & Giroux, Inc. and Faber and Faber, Ltd.

Anonymous, "The Trees of the Forest" from "Sweeney Astray," translated by Austin Clarke, from *Selected Poems*. Copyright © 1991 by Dardis Clarke. Reprinted with the permission of The Lilliput Press, Ltd., Dublin.

Anonymous, "North-East," translated by Seamus Heaney, from *The Harvard Advocate* (1982). Reprinted with the permission of the translator.

Anonymous, "On the Viking Raids," translated by Frank O'Connor, from *Kings, Lords, and Commons: An Anthology from the Irish* (New York: Alfred A. Knopf, 1959). Copyright © 1959 by Frank O'Connor. Reprinted with the permission of Writers House, Inc.

Anonymous, "Season Song" from "The Finn-Cycle," translated by Flann O'Brian, from *At Swim-Two-Birds*. Reprinted with the permission of Walker and Company.

Amergin (attributed), "Amergin's Charm," translated by Robert Graves, from *Poems of Robert Graves* (New York: Doubleday/Anchor, 1958). Copyright © 1958 by Robert Graves. Reprinted with the permission of Carcanet Press, Ltd.

Anonymous, "The Scholar and the Cat," translated by Frank O'Connor, from *Kings, Lords, and Commons: An Anthology from the Irish* (New York: Alfred A. Knopf, 1959). Copyright © 1959 by Frank O'Connor. Reprinted with the permission of Writer's House, Inc.

Anonymous, "Toward Winter," translated by Thomas Kinsella, from *The New Oxford Book of Irish Verse* (New York: Oxford University Press, 1986). Reprinted with the permission of the translator.

Anonymous, "Grania's Song to Diarmuid," translated by Frank O'Connor, from *Kings, Lords, and Commons: An Anthology from the Irish* (New York: Alfred A. Knopf, 1959). Copyright © 1959 by Frank O'Connor. Reprinted with the permission of Writers House, Inc.

Myrddin (attributed), "Yscolan," translated by W. S. Merwin, from *Selected Translations 1968–1978* (New York: Atheneum Publishers, 1979). Copyright © 1979 by W. S. Merwin. Reprinted with the permission of Georges Borchardt, Inc. for the author.

Aneirin, "The Gorcheanu: Three Laments," translated by Desmond O'Grady. Original translation. Reprinted with the permission of the translator. "The Gododdin" (excerpt) ["Youth"], translated by Desmond O'Grady, from *The Gododdin* (Dublin: The Dolman Press, 1977). Reprinted with the permission of the translator.

Anonymous, "Song to a Child," translated by Tony Conran, from *Welsh Verse: Translations by Tony Conran, Third Edition*. Copyright © 1967, 1986, 1991 by Tony Conran. Reprinted with the permission of Poetry Wales Press, Ltd.

Taliesin (attributed), "Eagle of Pengwern," translated by Gwyn Williams, from *The Burning Tree* (London: Faber and Faber, 1956). Copyright © 1956 by Gwyn Williams. Reprinted with the permission of Daisy Williams.

Anonymous, "Gereint Son of Erbin" from "The Black Book of Carmathen," translated by Gwyn Williams, from *The Burning Tree* (London: Faber and Faber, 1956). Copyright © 1956 by Gwyn Williams. Reprinted with the permission of Daisy Williams.

Robert Graves, "The Song of Blodeuwedd" from *Collected Poems*. Copyright © 1975 by Robert Graves. Reprinted with the permission of Oxford University Press, Inc. and Carcanet Press, Ltd.

Anonymous, "The Ruin," translated by Michael O'Brien, from *The Ruin* (New York: Cairn Editions, 1986). Reprinted with the permission of the translator.

Anonymous, "Wulf and Eadwacer," translated by Jonathan McKeage, from *Harvard Advocate* (Summer 1982). Reprinted with the permission of the translator.

Anonymous, "Deor," translated by Peter Russell. Original translation. Reprinted with the permission of the translator.

Anonymous, "The Charm of the Nine Healing Herbs," translated by David Cloutier, from *Translations: Experiments in Reading* (New York: ARS Press, 1983). Reprinted with the permission of the translator.

Anonymous, "Beowulf" (excerpt) ["Hrothgar Answered"], translated by Frederick Rebsamen, from *Beowulf: A Verse Translation*. Copyright © 1991 by Frederick Rebsamen. Reprinted with the permission of HarperCollins Publishers, Inc. ["such is the grief of the grey-haired man"], translated by Michael O'Brien, from *Blue Springs* (Sun Press, 1976). Reprinted with the permission of the translator.

Anonymous, "The Wanderer," translated by Michael Alexander from *The Earliest English Poems*. Copyright © 1977 by Michael Alexander. Reprinted with the permission of the translator and Penguin Books, Ltd.

Anonymous, "Two Sea-birds," translated by John Updike, from *The Harvard Advocate* (Summer 1982). Reprinted with the permission of the translator.

Anonymous, "The Swan," translated by Geoffrey Grigson, from *A Skull in Salop and Other Poems* (London: Macmillan, 1967). Copyright © 1967 by Geoffrey Grigson. Reprinted with the permission of David Higham Associates, Ltd.

Anonymous, "Riddle" ["A meal of words   Made by a moth"], translated by Edwin Morgan, from *Nine* III. Copyright by Edwin Morgan. Reprinted with the permission of the translator.

Anonymous, "Riddle" ["The world's wonder, I liven wenches"], translated by Lewis Turco, from *Ancient Music* (New York: Oxford University Press, forthcoming). Copyright © 1978 by Lewis Putnam Turco. Reprinted with the permission of the translator. All rights reserved by Mathom Press Enterprises.

Anonymous, ["I saw a strange creature"], translated by Kevin Crossley-Holland, from *Exeter Book Riddles, Revised Edition*. Copyright © 1993 by Kevin Crossley-Holland. Reprinted with the permission of Penguin Books, Ltd.

Cynewulf (attributed), "The Phoenix" (excerpt) ["When stars are hid in the western wave, dimmed at dawn"], translated by Frank Kuenstler. Original translation. Reprinted with the permission of the translator. "The Nature of the Siren," translated by Richard Wilbur, from *The Whale and Other Uncollected Translations* (Rochester: BOA Editions 1982). Reprinted with the permission of the translator.

Anonymous, "The Battle of Maldon" (excerpt) ["Courage shall grow keener, clearer the will"] translated by Michael Alexander from *The Earliest English Poems*. Copyright © 1977 by Michael Alexander. Reprinted with the permission of the translator and Penguin Books, Ltd.

Part IV: THE RISE OF THE VERNACULAR

Anonymous, ["I crossed the deep sea,"], translated by John Lucas, from Christine Fell, ed., *Egil's Saga* (London: Everyman's Library/J. M. Dent & Sons, 1975). Reprinted with the permission of the translator.

Edda Saemundar, "The Words of the All-Wise," translated by W. H. Auden and Paul Taylor, from *The Elder Edda*. Reprinted with the permission of Faber and Faber, Ltd.

Anonymous, "Fire" from "The Kalevala," translated by Keith Bosley, from Matti Kuusi, Keith Bosley, and Michael Branch, eds., *Finnish Folk Poetry* (Helsinki: Finnish Lit. Society, 1977). Reprinted with the permission of the translator.

Anonymous, "Two Spring Charms," translated by James Wright, from *The Bough Will Not Break* (Middletown, Conn.: Wesleyan University Press, 1963). Copyright © 1963 by James Wright. Reprinted with the permission of University Press of New England.

Anonymous, "Three Swedish Spells": "Spell Against Predatory Animals," "A Spell" ["When meeting a bear"], and "Spell Against Twisting an Ankle," translated by Siv Cedering Fox, from *Antaeus* 16 (Winter 1975), Special Translation Issue. Copyright © 1975. Reprinted by permission.

Anonymous, "Two Swedish Riddles": "Riddle" ["Father's sickle is hanging"], and "Riddle" ["An old green witch"], translated by Siv Cedering Fox, from *Antaeus* 16 (Winter 1975), Special Translation Issue. Copyright © 1975. Reprinted by permission.

Hadewijch, ["Love has seven names"], translated by Willis Barnstone and Elene Kolb, from Willis and Aliki Barnstone, editors, *A Book of Women Poets from Antiquity to Now*. Copyright © 1980 by Schocken Books, Inc. Reprinted with the permission of Schocken Books, published by Pantheon Books, a division of Random House, Inc.

Walther von der Vogelweide, "Under the Lindentree," translated by Michael Benedikt, from Angel Flores, ed., *Medieval Age* (New York: Dell, 1963). Reprinted with the permission of the Estate of Angel Flores.

der Wilde Alexander, "When We Were Children," translated by David Ferry from *Dwelling Places* (Chicago: Phoenix Press/University of Chicago, 1993). Reprinted with the permission of the translator.

Turoldus (attributed), "Roncelalles" (excerpt) ["Evening is coming, the day wears on,"], translated by C. H. Sisson, from *The Song of Roland*. Copyright © 1983 by C. H. Sisson. Reprinted with the permission of Carcanet Press, Ltd.

Anonymous, "Li Sons d'un cornet," translated by Willard Trask, from *Medieval Lyrics of Europe* (New York: NAL/The World Publishing Co., 1969). Copyright © 1969 by Willard R. Trask. Reprinted by permission.

Jean Bodel, "Les Congés du Lépreux," translated by F. T. Prince, from *Collected Poems*. Copyright © 1979 by F. T. Prince. Reprinted with the permission of The Sheep Meadow Press.

Eustache Deschamps, "Ballade 1," "Ballade 2," and "Rondeau," translated by David Curzon and Jeffrey Fiskin. Reprinted with the permission of the translators.

Charles d'Orléans, "Quant Souvenir me ramentoit" and "Las! Mort qui t'a fir si hardie," translated by Fred Chappell. Original translations. Reprinted with the permission of the translator. "Ballade" ["I was in blossom when I was a child"], translated by Tony and Willis Barnstone. Original translation. Reprinted with the permission of the translators. "Le temps a laisié," translated by Stanley Burnshaw, from *Caged in an Animal's Mind* (New York: Holt, Rinehart and Winston, 1964). Reprinted with the permission of the translator.

François Villon, "Ballade of the Men Who Were Hanged," translated by Fred Chappell. Original translation. Reprinted with the permission of the translator. "Remember, imbeciles and wits," translated by Basil Bunting, from *The Complete Poems of Basil Bunting.* Reprinted with the permission of Oxford University Press, Ltd. "Gone Ladies," translated by Christopher Logue, from *Selected Poems of Christopher Logue* (London: Faber and Faber, 1996). Reprinted with the permission of the translator. "Ballade of the Ladies of Time Past," translated by Richard Wilbur, from *New and Collected Poems.* Copyright © 1988 by Richard Wilbur. Reprinted with the permission of Harcourt Brace and Company. "A Ballade to End With," translated by Richard Wilbur, from *Walking to Sleep: New Poems and Translations.* Copyright © 1969 by Richard Wilbur. Reprinted with the permission of Harcourt Brace and Company. "I die of thirst while at the fountain side," translated by David Curzon and Jeffrey Fiskin. Original translations. Reprinted with the permission of the translators. "Quatrain" ["France's I am, my lookout's glum."], translated by Richard Wilbur, from *The Whale and Other Uncollected Translations* (Rochester: BOA Editions, 1982). Reprinted with the permission of the translator.

Anonymous, "En un Vergier Soiz Folha d'Albespi," ["Sheltered beneath white hawthorn boughs"], translated by Stanley Burnshaw, from *Caged in an Animal's Mind* (New York: Holt, Rinehart and Winston, 1963). Reprinted with the permission of the translator.

Richard I, Coeur de Lion, "Ja Nuls Homs Pris ne Ira a Raison," translated by F. T. Prince, from *Collected Poems.* Copyright © 1979 by F. T. Prince. Reprinted with the permission of The Sheep Meadow Press.

Arnaut Daniel, "En cest sonet coind' a leri" ["On this gay and slender tune"], translated by Paul Blackburn, from George Economou, ed., *Proensa: An Anthology of Troubadour Poetry.* Copyright © 1968 by Joan Blackburn. Reprinted with the permission of the University of California Press.

Bertran de Born, "Protestation," translated by John Peale Bishop, from *Collected Poems of John Peale Bishop.* Copyright 1948 by Charles Scribner's Sons. Reprinted with the permission of Scribners, a division of Simon & Schuster, Inc. "Sirventes," translated by Paul Blackburn, from George Economou, ed., *Proensa: An Anthology of Troubadour Poetry* (Berkeley: University of California Press, 1986). Copyright © 1978 by Joan Blackburn. Reprinted with the permission of the University of California Press.

Peire Cardinal, "The Clerks Pretend To Be Shepherds," translated by Paul Blackburn, from Angel Flores, ed., *Medieval Age* (New York: Dell, 1963). Reprinted with the permission of the Estate of Angel Flores.

Anonymous, "Girl with the Dark Hair" and "The Gray She-Wolf," translated by W. S. Merwin, from *From the Spanish Morning* (New York: Atheneum Publishers, 1985). Copyright © 1961 by W. S. Merwin. Reprinted with the permission of Georges Borchardt, Inc. for the author.

Anonymous, "Poem of the Cid" (excerpt), translated by Paul Blackburn, from *Sulfur,* #33. Reprinted with the permission of Estate of Paul Blackburn.

Nuño Fernández Torneol, "The Lady's Farewell," translated by Yvor Winters, from *Collected Poems.* Copyright © 1960 by Yvor Winters. Reprinted with the permission of The Ohio University Press/Swallow Press, Athens.

Pero Meogo, "Cossante," translated by Yvor Winters, from *Collected Poems.* Copyright © 1960 by Yvor Winters. Reprinted with the permission of The Ohio University Press/Swallow Press, Athens. "Cantiga D'Amigo," translated by Keith Bosley, from *Agenda* 21, no. 4 and 22, no. 1. Copyright © by Keith Bosley. Reprinted with the permission of the translator.

St. Francis of Assisi, "Canticle of Creatures," translated by James Schuyler, as found in Anne Waldman, ed., *Out of this World* (New York: Crown Publishers, 1989). Reprinted with the permission of the Estate of James Schuyler.

Jacopone da Todi, "Praise of Diseases," translated by L. R. Lind, from *Lyric Poetry of the Italian Renaissance* (New Haven, Conn.: Yale University Press, 1954). Reprinted with the permission of the translator.

Guido Cavalcanti, "Last Song: From Exile," translated by G. S. Fraser, from *The Traveller Has Regrets*. Reprinted with the permission of The Harvill Press, Ltd.

Dante Alighieri, "The Banquet: Dissertation 2, Canzone 1," translated by Howard Nemerov, from *The Collected Poems of Howard Nemerov* (Chicago: The University of Chicago Press, 1977). Reprinted with the permission of Mrs. Howard Nemerov. ["Comes often to my memory"], translated by Frederick Morgan, from *Poems New and Selected*. Copyright © 1987 by Frederick Morgan. Reprinted with the permission of the translator and the University of Illinois Press. "Inferno" (Canto XXI), translated by Susan Mitchell, from Daniel Halpern, ed., *Dante's Inferno: Translations by 20 Contemporary Poets* (Hopewell, New Jersey: The Ecco Press, 1993). Reprinted with the permission of the translator. "The Inferno" (Canto III), translated by Armand Schwerner. Original translation. Reprinted with the permission of the translator. ["I have reached, alas, the long shadow"], translated by James Schuyler, from *Selected Poems of James Schuyler*. Copyright © 1988 by James Schuyler. Reprinted with the permission of Farrar, Straus & Giroux, Inc.

Francesco Petrarch, "Sonnet 162 from *Rime*" ["When she walks by here"], translated by Nicholas Kilmer, from *Songs and Sonnets From Laura's Lifetime* (San Francisco: North Point Press, 1982). Reprinted with the permission of the translator. ["The woods are wild and were not made for man,"], translated by Edwin Morgan, from Peter France and Duncan Glen, eds., *European Poetry in Scotland: An Anthology of Translations*. Copyright © 1989. Reprinted with the permission of Edinburgh University Press.

Anonymous, "The Song of Igo's Campaign" (excerpt), translated by Harry Strickhausen, from Angel Flores, ed., *Medieval Age* (New York: Dell, 1963). Reprinted with the permission of the Estate of Angel Flores.

Anonymous, "The Message of King Sakis and the Legend of the Twelve Dreams He Had in One Night," translated by Charles Simic, from *The Horse Has Six Legs*. Copyright © 1992 by Charles Simic. Reprinted with the permission of Graywolf Press, St. Paul. Minnesota.

Theodore Prodromos, "To the Emperor," translated by Jack Lindsay, from Angel Flores, ed., *Medieval Age* (New York: Dell, 1963). Reprinted with the permission of the Estate of Angel Flores.

Anonymous, "The Harrowing," translated by Tony Harrison, from *The Mysteries* (London: Faber and Faber, 1985). Copyright © 1985 by Tony Harrison. Reprinted with the permission of Gordon Dickerson for the author.

Anonymous, "The Names of the Hare," as found in Seamus Heaney and Ted Hughes, eds., *The Rattle Bag* (London: Faber and Faber, 1982). Reprinted with the permission of Seamus Heaney.

Anonymous, "Summer Sunday," translated by John Gardner, from *The Alliterative Morte Arthure*. Copyright © 1971 by Southern Illinois University. Reprinted with the permission of Southern Illinois University Press.

William Langland, "Piers Plowman" (excerpt) ["Thus I awoke, God knows, when I lived in Cornhill,"], translated by George Economou, from *Piers Plowman: A Translation of C-Text* (Philadelphia: University of Pennsylvania Press, 1996). Reprinted with the permission of the translator.

Anonymous, ["Then the drawbridge came down, and the thick gates"], translated by Burton Raffel, from *Sir Gawain and the Green Knight*. Copyright © 1970 by Burton Raffel. Reprinted with the permission of New American Library, a division of Penguin Books USA Inc.

Anonymous, "The Blacksmiths," translated by Wesli Court (Lewis Putnam Turco), from *Curses and Laments* (Stevens Point, Wisc.: Song, 1980). Copyright © 1978 by Lewis Putnam

Turco. Reprinted with the permission of translator. All rights reserved by Mathom Press Enterprises.

Dafydd Ap Gwilym, "The Rattle Bag," translated by Joseph Clancy, from *The Earliest Welsh Poetry* (London: Macmillan Press, 1965). Reprinted with the permission of the translator. "The Wind" and "The Mirror," translated by Daniel Huws, from *Arion*, VI, no. 1 (Spring, 1967). Reprinted with the permission of the translator. "Dafydd ap Gwilym Resents the Water," freely arranged from the prose translation by Nigel Heseltine by Rolfe Humphries, from *The New Yorker Book of Poetry* (New York: William Morrow, 1974). Reprinted with the permission of Helen S. Humphries. "The Penis," translated by Dafydd Johnston, from *Medieval Welsh Erotic Poetry* (Caerdydd: Tafol Press, 1991). Reprinted with the permission of the publishers.

Lewis Glyn Cothi, "On the Death of His Son," translated by Gwyn Williams, from *The Burning Tree* (London: Faber and Faber, 1956). Copyright © 1956 by Gwyn Williams. Reprinted with the permission of Daisy Williams.

Murragh O'Daly, "On Killing a Tax Collector," translated by Richard O'Connell, from *Translation Magazine*. Reprinted with the permission of *Translation Magazine*.

Samuel ben Yosef Ha-Nagid, "The Gazelle," "One Who Works and Buys Himself Books," "First War," and "You Mock Me Now in Your Youth," translated by Peter Cole, from *Selected Poems of Samuel Ha-Nagid*. Copyright © 1996 by Princeton University Press. Reprinted with the permission of the publishers. "The Prison," translated by T. Carmi, from T. Carmi, ed., *The Penguin Book of Hebrew Verse* (London: Penguin Books, 1981). Copyright © 1981 by T. Carmi. Reprinted with the permission of Jilah Peled-Charney.

Solomon ibn Gabirol, "A Riddle" and "My Heart Thinks as the Sun Comes Up," translated by Peter Cole. Original translation. Reprinted with the permission of the translator.

Abraham ibn Ezra, "My Stars," translated by Robert Mezey, from *Selected Translations 1960–1980* (Kalamazoo: Westigan Review Press, 1981). Reprinted with the permission of the translator.

Moses ibn Ezra, ["And where are the graves, so many graves"], translated by Robert Mezey, from *A Book of Dying* (Santa Cruz: Kayak Books, 1970). Reprinted with the permission of the translator.

Yehuda Halevi, "On The Sea" (excerpt) ["Greetings ladies, kith and kin"] and "Distant Dove," translated by Gabriel Levin from *The Jerusalem Post Magazine* (November 21, 1986). Revised 1996 for this anthology. Reprinted with the permission of the translator. "Poem in Parts," translated by Ammiel Alcalay, from *Sulfur* #33. Reprinted with the permission of the translator.

Anonymous, "You and I," translated by Stanley Moss, from *The Intelligence of Clouds* (New York: Harcourt Brace, 1989). Reprinted with the permission of the translator.

Abraham Abulafia, "The Battle," translated by Stanley Moss, from *The Intelligence of Clouds* (New York: Harcourt Brace, 1989). Reprinted with the permission of the translator.

Ja'far ibn 'Uthman al-Mushafi, "Yellow Its Color," translated by Christopher Middleton and Leticia Garza-Falcon, from *Andalusian Poems*. Copyright © 1993 by Christopher Middleton and Leticia Garza-Falcon. Reprinted with the permission of David R. Godine, Publisher, Inc.

Ibn Hazm al-Andalusi, "Twice Times Then Is Now," translated by Omar Pound, from *Arabic and Persian Poems in English*. Copyright © 1986 by Omar Pound. Reprinted with the permission of Three Continents Press. "The Visit," translated by Christopher Middleton and Leticia Garza-Falcon, from *Andalusian Poems*. Copyright © 1993 by Christopher Middleton and Leticia Garza-Falcon. Reprinted with the permission of David R. Godine, Publisher, Inc.

Abu'l Qasim As'd ibn Billita, "The Rooster," translated by Christopher Middleton and Leticia Garza-Falcon, from *Andalusian Poems*. Copyright © 1993 by Christopher Middleton and Leticia Garza-Falcon. Reprinted with the permission of David R. Godine, Publisher, Inc.

Ibn Sharaf, "Satire" ["Chez toi, Makmout,"], translated by Christopher Middleton and Leticia Garza-Falcon, from *Andalusian Poems*. Copyright © 1993 by Christopher Middleton and Leticia Garza-Falcon. Reprinted with the permission of David R. Godine, Publisher, Inc.

Abu Amir ibn al-Hammarah, "The White Stallion," translated by Cola Franzen, from *Poems of Arab Andalusia*. Copyright © 1989. Reprinted with the permission of City Lights Books.

Muhammad ibn Ghalib al-Rusafi, "Blue River," translated by Cola Franzen, from *Poems of Arab Andalusia*. Copyright © 1989. Reprinted with the permission of City Lights Books.

Ibn Sara, "Eggplant," translated by Christopher Middleton and Leticia Garza-Falcon, from *Andalusian Poems*. Copyright © 1993 by Christopher Middleton and Leticia Garza-Falcon. Reprinted with the permission of David R. Godine, Publisher, Inc.

Ibn'Iyad, "Grainfield," translated by Cola Franzen, from *Poems of Arab Andalusia*. Copyright © 1989. Reprinted with the permission of City Lights Books.

Abu Bakr ibn Abd al-Malik ibn Quzman, "To a Beauty, White, Pure, and Constant," translated by Christopher Middleton and Leticia Garza-Falcon, from *Andalusian Poems*. Copyright © 1993 by Christopher Middleton and Leticia Garza-Falcon. Reprinted with the permission of David R. Godine, Publisher, Inc.

Abu I-Salt Umayyah, "Insomnia," translated by Cola Franzen, from *Poems of Arab Andalusia*. Copyright © 1989. Reprinted with the permission of City Lights Books.

Ali ibn Hariq, "Galley Oars," translated by Christopher Middleton and Leticia Garza-Falcon, from *Andalusian Poems*. Copyright © 1993 by Christopher Middleton and Leticia Garza-Falcon. Reprinted with the permission of David R. Godine, Publisher, Inc.

Rudaki, "All the teeth ever I had are worn down and fallen out," translated by Basil Bunting, from *The Complete Poems of Basil Bunting*. Reprinted with the permission of Oxford University Press, Ltd. "Spring" and "Prayer," translated by Geoffrey Squires, from *Delos* 2 (1968). Reprinted with the permission of the translator. ["Came to me—"], translated by Basil Bunting, from *The Complete Poems of Basil Bunting*. Reprinted with the permission of Oxford University Press, Ltd.

Khosravani, ["There are four kinds of men who'll get no fee from me"], translated by Dick Davis, from *Borrowed Ware: Medieval Persian Epigrams*. Copyright © 1996 by Dick Davis. Reprinted with the permission of Anvil Press Poetry, Ltd.

Firdowsi, ["When the sword of sixty comes nigh his head"], translated by Basil Bunting, from *The Complete Poems of Basil Bunting*. Reprinted with the permission of Oxford University Press, Ltd.

Abu Sa'id Abul Kayhr, "Four Quatrains" ("I'm going to tell you something that is true," "If I've been dead for twenty years or so," "His absence is the knife that cuts your throat?," and "For men and women soon the day draws near"), translated by Dick Davis, from *Borrowed Ware: Medieval Persian Epigrams*. Copyright © 1996 by Dick Davis. Reprinted with the permission of Anvil Press Poetry, Ltd.

Nizami Arudi, "Calling the Doctor," translated by Omar Pound, from *Arabic and Persian Poems in English*. Copyright © 1986 by Omar Pound. Reprinted with the permission of Three Continents Press.

Anvari, "Drunkenness," translated by Geoffrey Squires, from *Delos* 2 (1968). Reprinted with the permission of the translator. "Composing" and ["Take what he gives you, even if it's paltry"], translated by Dick Davis, from *Borrowed Ware: Medieval Persian Epigrams*. Copyright © 1996 by Dick Davis. Reprinted with the permission of Anvil Press Poetry, Ltd.

Farid Ud-Din Attar, "The Conference of the Birds" (excerpt) ["The world's birds gathered for their conference"], translated by Afkham and Dick Davis, from *The Conference of the Birds*. Copyright © 1984 by Afkham and Dick Davis. Reprinted with the permission of Penguin Books, Ltd.

Jalal ad-din Rumi, "Caring for my Lover," translated by Willis Barnstone, Reza Baraheni and Tony Barnstone. Reprinted with the permission of Willis Barnstone. ["This night there are no limits"] and ["Night comes so people can sleep like fish"], translated by John Moyne and Coleman Barks, from *Unseen Rain.* Copyright © 1986. Reprinted with the permission of Threshold Books, 139 Main Street, Brattleboro, VT 05301. ["A night full of talking that hurts"] and ["Inside water, a waterwheel turns."], translated by John Moyne and Coleman Barks, from *The Essential Rumi* (San Francisco: HarperSanFrancisco, 1995). Reprinted with the permission of Coleman Barks. "Has Anyone Seen the Boy?," translated by John Moyne and Coleman Barks, from *These Branching Moments.* Copyright © 1988 by Coleman Barks. Reprinted with the permission of Copper Beach Press. "Night and Sleep," translated by Robert Bly, from *Night and Sleep* (Cambridge: Yellow Moon Press, 1981). Copyright © 1981 by Robert Bly. Reprinted with the permission of the translator.

Sa'di, "Last night without sight of you my brain was ablaze" and "This I write, mix ink with tears," translated by Basil Bunting, from *The Complete Poems of Basil Bunting.* Reprinted with the permission of Oxford University Press, Ltd. "Five Poems": ["If you should say to me 'Don't mention love',"] ["Until you can correct and heal yourself"], ["When once the soul is ready to depart, sir,"], ["He glanced at me one day—but then his mean,"], and ["O I repented, wore my pious cloak,"], translated by Dick Davis, from *Borrowed Ware: Medieval Persian Epigrams.* Copyright © 1996 by Dick Davis. Reprinted with the permission of Anvil Press Poetry, Ltd.

Hafiz, "Ghazzal" ["Half-way through the night"], translated by Geoffrey Squires, from *Delos* 2 (1968). Reprinted with the permission of the translator. "Ghazal 24" ["For years my heart asked me for Jamshid's cup"], translated by Elizabeth Gray, from *The Green Sea of Heaven: Fifty Ghazals from the Diwan of Hafiz* (Ashland, Oregon: White Cloud Press, 1995). Originally published in *Ploughshares* II, no. 4. Copyright © 1995 by Elizabeth Gray. Reprinted by permission. "Three Poems on Friendship": ["Desire's destroyed my life, what gifts have I"], ["Each 'friend' turned out to be an enemy"], and ["My friend, hold back your heart from enemies"], translated by Dick Davis, from *Borrowed Ware: Medieval Persian Epigrams.* Copyright © 1996 by Dick Davis. Reprinted with the permission of Anvil Press Poetry, Ltd. "Light of my eyes," translated by Basil Bunting, from *The Complete Poems of Basil Bunting.* Reprinted with the permission of Oxford University Press, Ltd.

Anonymous, "The Death of Yesugei," "Temujin Becomes Chingis Khan," and "The Last Battle and Death of Chingis Khan," translated by Paul Kahn, from *The Secret History of the Mongols: The Origin of Chingis Khan,* adapted by Paul Kahn from the translation of Francis Woodman Cleaves (San Francisco: North Point Press, 1984). Reprinted with the permission of the translator.

Anonymous, from the Harvest Festival Drama *Drimeh Kundan,* "The Queen wept but thought: . . ." translated by Armand Schwerner, from Ronald Gross and George Quasha, eds., *Open Poetry: Four Anthologies of Expanded Poems* (New York: Simon & Schuster, 1971). Reprinted with the permission of the translator.

Li Yu, "To The Tune of 'Meeting Happiness'," translated by Arthur Sze. Original translation. Reprinted with the permission of the translator.

Wang Yü-ch'eng, "Song Of The Crow Peeking At My Scarred Donkey," translated by Jonathan Chaves, from Wu-chi Liu and Irving Yucheng Lo, eds., *Sunflower Splendor: Three Thousand Years of Chinese Poetry* (Bloomington: Indiana University Press, 1975). Reprinted with the permission of the translator.

Liu Yung, "Song To The Tune 'Ting Feng Po,'" translated by Sam Hamill, from *Midnight Flute: Chinese Poems of Love and Longing.* Originally in *American Poetry Review* 12, no. 6 (November–December 1983). Copyright © 1994 by Sam Hamill. Reprinted with the permission of Shambhala Publications.

Anonymous, "To The Tune 'The Drunken Young Lord'," translated by C. H. Kwock and Vincent McHugh, from Cyril Birch, ed., *An Anthology of Chinese Literature* (New York: Grove

Press, 1965). Copyright © 1965 by Grove Press, Inc. Reprinted with the permission of Grove/Atlantic, Inc.

Mei Yao-ch'en, "On The Death Of A Newborn Child" and "Sorrow," translated by Kenneth Rexroth, from *One Hundred Poems from the Chinese*. Copyright © 1959 by Kenneth Rexroth. Reprinted with the permission of New Directions Publishing Corporation. "A Solitary Falcon Above The Buddha Hall of Universal Purity," translated by Jonathan Chaves, from Wu-chi Liu and Irving Yucheng Lo, eds., *Sunflower Splendor: Three Thousand Years of Chinese Poetry* (Bloomington: Indiana University Press, 1975). Reprinted with the permission of the translator.

Wang An-shih, "In The Style Of Han Shan And Shih Te," translated by Jan W. Walls, from Wu-chi Liu and Irving Yucheng Lo, eds., *Sunflower Splendor: Three Thousand Years of Chinese Poetry* (Bloomington: Indiana University Press, 1975). Reprinted with the permission of the translator.

Su Tung-p'o, "On The Birth Of His Son," translated by Arthur Waley, from *A Hundred and Seventy Chinese Poems*. Copyright 1919 by Alfred A. Knopf, Inc., renewed 1947 by Arthur Waley. Reprinted with the permission of Constable Publishers, Ltd. "Lyrics to the Tune 'Fairy Grotto,' " translated by Greg Whincup, from *The Heart of Chinese Poetry*. Copyright © 1967 by Greg Whincup. Reprinted with the permission of Doubleday, a division of Bantam Doubleday Dell Publishing Group, Inc. "Lyric to the Tune 'The Charms Of Nien-nu': At The Red Cliff I Ponder Over Antiquity," translated by David Lattimore, from *The Harmony of the World* (Providence: Copper Beech Press, 1980). Reprinted with the permission of the translator. "Roadside Flowers, Three Poems With An Introduction," and "Reading The Poetry of Meng Chiao," translated by Burton Watson, from *Selected Poems of Su Tung-p'o*. Copyright © 1994 by Burton Watson. Reprinted with the permission of Copper Canyon Press, P. O Box 271, Port Townsend, WA 98368.

Li Ch'ing-chao, "Written To The Tune 'The Fisherman's Honor'," translated by Jane Hirshfield, from Jane Hirshfield, ed., *Women in Praise of the Sacred: Forty-Three Centuries of Spiritual Poetry by Women* (New York: HarperCollins Publishers, 1994). Reprinted with the permission of the translator. "Lyric To The Tune 'Immortal By The River'," translated by Julie Landau, from *Translation Magazine* XVII (1986). Reprinted with the permission of the translator.

Anonymous (attributed to Li Ch'ing-chao), "Flirtation," from *Women Poets of China*. Copyright © 1972 by Kenneth Rexroth and Ling Chung. Reprinted with the permission of New Directions Publishing Corporation.

Kuan Iao-sheng, "Married Love," translated by Kenneth Rexroth and Ling Chung, from *Women Poets of China*. Copyright © 1972 by Kenneth Rexroth and Ling Chung. Reprinted with the permission of New Directions Publishing Corporation.

Yang Wang-li, "Sailing Through The Gorges," translated by Kuangchi C. Chang, from *The Hudson Review* VIII, no. 1 (Spring 1955). Copyright © 1955 by The Hudson Review, Inc. Reprinted with the permission of *The Hudson Review*.

Sun Pu-erh, "Lyric," translated by Jane Hirshfield, from Jane Hirshfield, ed., *Women in Praise of the Sacred: Forty-Three Centuries of Spiritual Poetry by Women* (New York: HarperCollins Publishers, 1994). Reprinted with the permission of the translator.

Lu Yu, "I Had Occasion To Tell A Visitor About An Old Trip I Took Through The Gorges Of The Yangtze," translated by Burton Watson, from *Translation Magazine* IV (1980). Reprinted with the permission of *Translation Magazine*. "Night Thoughts," translated by Kenneth Rexroth, from *One Hundred Poems from the Chinese*. Copyright © 1959 by Kenneth Rexroth. Reprinted with the permission of New Directions Publishing Corporation.

Kuan Han-ching, "To the Tune 'A Spray of Flowers' (Not Giving In to Old Age)," translated by Stephen Owen, from *An Anthology of Chinese Literature: Beginnings to 1911*. Copyright © 1996 by Stephen Owen and The Council for Cultural Planning and Development of the

Executive Yuan of the Republic of China. Reprinted with the permission of the translator and W. W. Norton & Company, Inc.

Lu Chih, "Seventy Years Are Few," translated by Bruce Carpenter, from *Translation Magazine* IV (1977). Reprinted with the permission of the translator.

Chao Meng-fu, "An Admonition To Myself," translated by Jonathan Chaves, from *Columbia Book of Later Chinese Poetry*. Copyright © 1986 by Columbia University Press. Reprinted with the permission of the publishers.

Chang Yang-hao, "T'ung Pass," translated by Sam Hamill, from *Midnight Flute: Chinese Poems of Love and Longing*. Copyright © 1994 by Sam Hamill. Reprinted with the permission of Shambhala Publications.

Monk Saigyō, ["In a tree standing"], translated by Donald Keene, from Donald Keene, ed., *Anthology of Japanese Literature: From The Earliest Times to the Christian Era*. Copyright © 1955 by Grove Press, Inc. Reprinted with the permission of Grove/Atlantic, Inc. "I don't even know," translated by Stephen D. Carter, from *Traditional Japanese Poetry: An Anthology*. Copyright © 1991 by the Board of Regents of the Leland Stanford Junior College. Reprinted with the permission of Stanford University Press.

Fujiwara no Yasusue, ["Nothing whatsoever"], translated by Donald Keene, from Donald Keene, ed., *Anthology of Japanese Literature: From The Earliest Times to the Christian Era*. Copyright © 1955 by Grove Press, Inc. Reprinted with the permission of Grove/Atlantic, Inc. ["Shall I see it again"] and ["The cormorant-boat"] translated by Valerie Durham, from *The Harvard Advocate* CXV, no. 4 (1982). Reprinted by permission.

Former Chief Priest Jien, ["Too much to ask"], translated by Howard S. Levy, from *Japan's Best Loved Poetry Classic: Hyakunin Isshu* (South Pasadena: Langstaff, 1976). Reprinted by permission.

"Shunzei's Daughter," "Burning in secret," translated by Stephen D. Carter, from *Traditional Japanese Poetry: An Anthology*. Copyright © 1991 by the Board of Regents of the Leland Stanford Junior College. Reprinted with the permission of Stanford University Press.

Fujiwara no Teika, "Three Poems": ["Weary wild geese who came"], ["After his tryst,"], and ["Those long black tresses"], translated by Stephen D. Carter, from *Traditional Japanese Poetry: An Anthology*. Copyright © 1991 by the Board of Regents of the Leland Stanford Junior College. Reprinted with the permission of Stanford University Press.

Retired Emperor Go-Toba, ["There were"], translated by Howard S. Levy, from *Japan's Best Loved Poetry Classic: Hyakunin Isshu* (South Pasadena: Langstaff, 1976). Reprinted with the permission of the translator.

Retired Emperor Jun Toku, ["Royal dwellings"], translated by Howard S. Levy, from *Japan's Best Loved Poetry Classic: Hyakunin Isshu* (South Pasadena: Langstaff, 1976). Reprinted by permission.

Jusammi Chikako, "Moon," translated by Edwin A. Cranston, from Jane Hirshfield, ed., *Women in Praise of the Sacred: Forty-Three Centuries of Spiritual Poetry by Women* (New York: HarperCollins Publishers, 1994). Reprinted with the permission of the translator.

Cho-yong, "Song" ["I carouse all night"], translated by Michael Stephens and Okhee Yoo, from *Translations* by Michael Stephens (Red Hanrahan Books, 1984). Reprinted with the permission of Michael Stephens.

Yi Kyu Bo, "Evening on the Mountain: Song on The Moon In The Well" (1 & 2), translated by Kevin O'Rourke, from *Tilting the Jar, Spilling the Moon*. Reprinted with the permission of The Dedalus Press, Dublin.

Van Hanh, "The Body of a Man," translated by Nguyen Ngoc Bich with W. S. Merwin, from Nguyen Ngoc Bich, ed., *A Thousand Years of Vietnamese Poetry* (New York: Alfred A. Knopf,

1975). Copyright © 1962, 1967, 1968, 1969, 1970, 1971, 1972, 1974 by The Asia Society. Reprinted with the permission of The Asia Society.

Khuong Viet, "Wood and Fire," translated by Huynh Sanh Thong, from *The Heritage of Viet-namese Poetry* (New Haven, Conn.: Yale University Press, 1979). Reprinted with the permission of the translator.

Man Giac, "Rebirth," translated by Nguyen Ngoc Bich with W. S. Merwin, from Nguyen Ngoc Bich, ed., *A Thousand Years of Vietnamese Poetry* (New York: Alfred A. Knopf, 1975). Copyright © 1962, 1967, 1968, 1969, 1970, 1971, 1972, 1974 by The Asia Society. Reprinted with the permission of The Asia Society.

Doan Van Kham, "Remembering Priest Quang Tri," translated by Nguyen Ngoc Bich, from *A Thousand Years of Vietnamese Poetry* (New York: Alfred A. Knopf, 1975). Copyright © 1962, 1967, 1968, 1969, 1970, 1971, 1972, 1974 by The Asia Society. Reprinted with the permission of The Asia Society.

Tran Nhan-tong, "Spring View," translated by Nguyen Ngoc Bich, from *A Thousand Years of Vietnamese Poetry* (New York: Alfred A. Knopf, 1975). Copyright © 1962, 1967, 1968, 1969, 1970, 1971, 1972, 1974 by The Asia Society. Reprinted with the permission of The Asia Society.

Nguyen Trai, "A Plough and a Spade," translated by Nguyen Ngoc Bich, from *Translation Magazine* II (1974). Reprinted with the permission of *Translation Magazine*. "The Bamboo Hut," translated by Nguyen Ngoc Bich, from *A Thousand Years of Vietnamese Poetry* (New York: Alfred A. Knopf, 1975). Copyright © 1962, 1967, 1968, 1969, 1970, 1971, 1972, 1974 by The Asia Society. Reprinted with the permission of The Asia Society.

Emperor Le Thanh-tong, "Stick and Hat," translated by John Major (after the translation of Huynh Sanh Thong). Original translation. Reprinted with the permission of the trans-lator. "The Stone Dog," translated by Nguyen Ngoc Bich, from *A Thousand Years of Viet-namese Poetry* (New York: Alfred A. Knopf, 1975). Copyright © 1962, 1967, 1968, 1969, 1970, 1971, 1972, 1974 by The Asia Society. Reprinted with the permission of The Asia Society.

Devara Dasimayya, "The Tattered Sack," translated by A. K. Ramanujan, from *Speaking of Siva.* Copyright © 1973 by A. K. Ramanujan. Reprinted with the permission of Penguin Books, Ltd.

Mahadeviyakka, "Like an elephant," translated by A. K. Ramanujan, from *Speaking of Siva.* Copyright © 1973 by A. K. Ramanujan. Reprinted with the permission of Penguin Books, Ltd. "A Vein Of Sapphires" and "I Do Not Call It His Sign" translated by Jane Hirshfield, from Jane Hirshfield, ed., *Women in Praise of the Sacred: Forty-Three Centuries of Spiritual Poetry by Women* (New York: HarperCollins Publishers, 1994). Reprinted with the permission of the translator.

Kshemendra, "Kavikanthabharana" (excerpt) ["A poet should learn with his eyes"], trans-lated by W. S. Merwin and J. Moussaief Masson, from Vinay Dharwadker and A. K. Ra-manujan, ed., *The Oxford Anthology of Modern Indian Poetry* (New York: Oxford University Press, 1994). Copyright © 1994 by W. S. Merwin. Reprinted with the permission of Georges Borchardt, Inc. for the author.

Jayaveda, "The Fourth Song, sung with Raga 'Ramakari'," translated by Barbara Stoller Miller, from *Gitagovinda.* Copyright © 1977 by Columbia University Press. Reprinted with the permission of the publishers.

Anonymous, "The Maitreya Upanishad" (excerpt) ["I am I, but also the other"], translated by Patrick Olivelle, from *Samnyasa Upanishads: Hindu Scriptures on Asceticism and Renunciation.* Copyright © 1992 by Oxford University Press, Inc. Reprinted with the permission of the publisher.

Anonymous, Two hymns from the *Popul Vuh:* "Truly now,/Double thanks, triple thanks" and "Wait!/Thou maker, thou Modeler," translated by Dennis Tedlock, from *Popol Vuh: The Definitive Edition of the Mayan Book of the Dawn of Life and the Glories of Gods and Kings.* Copyright © 1985 by Dennis Tedlock. Reprinted with the permission of Simon & Schuster, Inc.

Part V: The Renaissance in Europe; Late Traditional Verse from the Americas, South Asia, and East Asia

Geoffrey Chaucer, "Conclusion," translated by Burton Raffel and Selden Rodman, from Seldon Rodman, ed., *100 British Poets* (New York: New American Library, 1974). Reprinted with the permission of the translators.

William Dunbar, "Of the Changes in Life," translated by Andrew Glaze, from Seldon Rodman, ed., *100 British Poets* (New York: New American Library, 1974). Reprinted with the permission of the translator.

Maurice Scève, "Les Dizains" (excerpt) ["The last day of your sweet companionship"], translated by Phillip Lopate. Original translation. Reprinted with the permission of the translator. "259" ["Every long and wide expanse of sea"], translated by Richard Sieburth. Original translation. Reprinted with the permission of the translator.

Joachim du Bellay, "Heureux Qui, Comme Ulysse, a Fair un Beau Voyage . . . ," translated by Anthony Hecht, from *Collected Earlier Poems.* Copyright © 1990 by Anthony E. Hecht. Reprinted with the permission of Alfred A. Knopf, Inc. "Rome," translated by Yvor Winters, from *Collected Poems.* Copyright © 1960 by Yvor Winters. Reprinted with the permission of The Ohio University Press/Swallow Press, Athens. "The Regrets" (excerpt) ["To walk with sober step, to raise the eyebrow"], translated by Dennis Devlin, from *Translations Into English.* Reprinted with the permission of The Dedalus Press, Dublin. "The Regrets" (excerpt) ["Given all my worries over each day's trivia,"], translated by David Curzon and Jeffrey Fiskin. Original translations. Reprinted with the permission of the translators. ["How is it that Fortune always ignores me?"], translated by Fred Beake, from *Towards the West and Other Poems* (University of Salzburg Press, 1995). Reprinted with the permission of the translator.

Pierre de Ronsard, "Corinna in Verdome," translated by Robert Mezey, from *The Lovemaker: Poems by Robert Mezey* (Iowa City: The Cummington Press, 1961). Reprinted with the permission of the translator. "Roses," translated by Vernon Watkins, from *Mirror of French Poetry.* Copyright © by Vernon Watkins. Reprinted with the permission of Faber and Faber, Ltd. "Invective Against Denise, a Witch," translated by Anthony Hecht, from *The Transparent Man.* Copyright © 1990 by Anthony E. Hecht. Reprinted with the permission of Alfred A. Knopf, Inc. ["When you are old, at evening, candle-lit"], translated by Humbert Wolfe, from *Sonnets Pour Helene.* Copyright 1934 by The Macmillan Company. Reprinted with the permission of Simon & Schuster, Inc. ["Bush-bristling juniper and you the thorn—"], translated by Donald Davie, from *Collected Poems of Donald Davie.* Copyright © 1990 by Donald Davie. Reprinted with the permission of The University of Chicago Press.

Louise Labé, "I Flee the City, Temples, and Each Place," translated by Willis Barnstone, from *The Secret Reader* (Hanover, New Hampshire: University Press of New England, 1996). Reprinted with the permission of the translator. "Sonnet" ["Long-felt desires, hopes as long as vain—"], translated by Annie Finch. Original translation. Reprinted with the permission of the translator.

Jean Passerat, "Sonnet Addressed to Henry III on the Death of Thulene, the King's Fool," translated by Richmond Lattimore, from *Continuing Conclusions: New Poems and Translations.* Copyright © 1983 by Richmond Lattimore. Reprinted with the permission of Louisiana State University Press.

Matteo Maria Boiardo, ["The song of birds which leaps from leaf to leaf"], translated by Peter Russell. Original translation. Reprinted with the permission of the translator.

Angelo Ambrogio de Benedetto Politziano, "The Tournament" (excerpt) ["Splendor and pride I celebrate,"], translated by Guy Davenport, from *Delos* 2 (1970). Reprinted with the permission of the translator.

Michelangelo Buonarroti, ["Very dear though it was I have brought you"], translated by W. S. Merwin, from *Selected Translations 1968–1978* (New York: Atheneum Publishers, 1979). Copyright © 1979 by W. S. Merwin. Reprinted with the permission of Georges Borchardt, Inc. for the author. " 'Night' in the Medici Chapel," translated by William Jay Smith, from *Collected Translations*. Copyright © 1985 by William Jay Smith. Reprinted with the permission of New Rivers Press.

St. Teresa of Avila, ["Nothing move thee;"], translated by Yvor Winters, from *Collected Poems*. Copyright © 1960 by Yvor Winters. Reprinted with the permission of The Ohio University Press/Swallow Press, Athens.

Anonymous, "Lament for the Death of Guillén Peraza," translated by W. S. Merwin, from *Selected Translations 1948–68* (New York: Atheneum Publishers, 1968). Copyright © 1968 by W. S. Merwin. Reprinted with the permission of Georges Borchardt, Inc. for the author.

Luis Vaz de Camões, "Dear Gentle Soul," translated by Roy Campbell, from *The Collected Poems of Roy Campbell, Volume III* (Chicago: Henry Regnery, 1960). Reprinted with the permission of Francisco Campbell Custodio and AD Donker Publishers. "Sonnet 10" and "Sonnet 140," translated by David Wevill, from *Delos* 4 (1970). Reprinted with the permission of the translator.

Sir Thomas More, "The Astrologer," translated by J. V. Cunningham, from *The Collected Poems and Epigrams of J. V. Cunningham* (Chicago: The Swallow Press, 1971). Reprinted with the permission of Jessie Cunningham. "Concerning Good Princes and Bad: Taxonomy," translated by Katharine Washburn. Original translation. Reprinted with the permission of the translator.

Jan Kochanowski, "To a Mathematician" and "In Defence of Drunkards," translated by Jerzy Peterkiewicz, Burns Singer, and Jon Stallworthy, from *Five Centuries of Polish Poetry 1450–1970*. Reprinted with the permission of Oxford University Press, Ltd. "I'd Buy You, Wisdom" and "Where Is That Gate for Grief," translated by Stanislaw Baranczak and Seamus Heaney, *The Laments of Jan Kochanowski*. Copyright © by Stanislaw Baranczak and Seamus Heaney. Reprinted with the permission of Farrar, Straus & Giroux, Inc.

Nahabed Kouchag, "I Was Suffering Exile," translated by Desmond O'Grady, from *Off-License* (Dublin: The Dolman Press, 1968). Reprinted with the permission of the translator.

Anonymous, From the *Toltec Codica de la Real Academia:* "The Artist," translated by Denise Levertov with Elvira Abascal, from *With Eyes at the Back of Our Heads*. Copyright © 1958, 1959 by Denise Levertov Goodman. Reprinted with the permission of New Directions Publishing Corporation.

King Nezahualcoyotl of Texcoco (attributed), "Where Will I Go?," "Be Indomitable, O My Heart!," "Our Lord," "Can it Be True That One Lives on Earth?," translated by Thelma D. Sullivan, from T. J. Knab, ed., *A Scattering of Jades: Stories, Poems, and Prayers of the Aztecs*. Copyright © 1994 by T. J. Knab. Reprinted with the permission of Simon & Schuster, Inc.

Anonymous, "Flowers Of Red And Blue," translated by Stephen Berg, from *The Steel Cricket: Versions 1958–1997* (Port Townsend, Wash.: Copper Canyon Press, 1993). Reprinted with the permission of the translator.

Chilam Balam, "Flight Of The Itzás," translated by Christopher Sawyer-Lauçanno, from *The Destruction of the Jaguar: Poems from the Books of Chilam Balam*. Copyright © 1987. Reprinted with the permission of City Lights Books.

Anonymous, "The Elegy For the Great Inca Atawallpa" (excerpt) ["You all by yourself fulfilled"], translated by W. S. Merwin, from *Selected Translations 1968–1978* (New York: Atheneum Publishers, 1979). Copyright © 1979 by W. S. Merwin. Reprinted with the permission of Georges Borchardt, Inc. for the author.

Anonymous, "To a Traitor," translated by Willard Trask (adapted from the prose translation of R. Pietschmann), from Willard Trask, ed., *The Unwritten Song.* Copyright © 1967 by Willard Trask. Reprinted with the permission of Simon & Schuster, Inc.

Chandidas, "Why Tell Me What To Do?," translated by Tony Barnstone. Original translation. Reprinted with the permission of the translator.

Kabir, "Student, do the simple purification" and "Are You Looking for Me?," translated by Robert Bly, from *The Kabir Book.* Copyright © 1971, 1977 by Robert Bly. Reprinted with the permission of Beacon Press and Macmillan Press Ltd. "Eternity," translated by Arvind Krishna Mehrotra, from *Delos* 6 (1971). Reprinted with the permission of the translator. "I Cherish That Love," and "The Ascetic Dyes His Robes," translated by Pritish Nandy, from *Love: The First Syllable* (New Delhi: Tarang Paperbacks/Vikas Publishing House, 1983). Copyright © 1983. Reprinted with the permission of Vikas Publishing House Pvt Ltd, New Delhi.

Mirabai, "All I Was Doing Was Breathing," translated by Robert Bly, from *Mirabai Versions* (Squid Ink Press, 1993). Copyright © 1993 by Robert Bly. Reprinted with the permission of the translator. "The Wild Woman Of The Forests," translated by Jane Hirshfield from Jane Hirshfield, ed., *Women in Praise of the Sacred: Forty-Three Centuries of Spiritual Poetry by Women* (New York: HarperCollins Publishers, 1994). Reprinted with the permission of the translator.

Lal Ded, "The Soul" and "On The Way To God," translated by Coleman Barks, from *Lalla: Naked Songs* (Athens, Georgia: Maypop Books, 1992). Reprinted with the permission of Coleman Barks.

Chang Yü, "The Pavilion for Listening to Fragrance," translated by Jonathan Chaves, from *Columbia Book of Later Chinese Poetry.* Copyright © 1986 by Columbia University Press. Reprinted with the permission of the publishers.

Yang Chi, "Five-Color," translated by Jonathan Chaves, from *Columbia Book of Later Chinese Poetry.* Copyright © 1986 by Columbia University Press. Reprinted with the permission of the publishers.

Yang Shih-ch'i, "Following the Rhymes of Shao-pao Huang's Poem on Being Moved While Visiting the Farmers," translated by Jonathan Chaves, from *Columbia Book of Later Chinese Poetry.* Copyright © 1986 by Columbia University Press. Reprinted with the permission of the publishers.

Yang Wen-li, "New Year's Eve" and "Thinking of My Family on an Autumn Day," translated by Nancy Hodes and Tung Yuan-fang. Original translation. Reprinted with the permission of the translators.

Wang Chiu-su, "After Reading The Poems of Master Han Shan," translated by Jonathan Chaves, from *Translation Magazine* XVII (1986). Reprinted with the permission of *Translation Magazine.*

T'ang Yin, "Inscription For A Portrait," translated by John Scott and Graham Martin, from *Love and Protest.* Reprinted with the permission of HarperCollins Publishers, Inc and Andre Deutsch Ltd.

Huang O, "A Farewell to a Southern Melody" and "To the Tune 'A Floating Cloud Crosses Enchanted Mountain'," translated by Kenneth Rexroth and Ling Chung, from *Women Poets of China.* Copyright © 1972 by Kenneth Rexroth and Ling Chung. Reprinted with the permission of New Directions Publishing Corporation.

Mo Shih-lung, "Saying Good-bye to a Singing Girl Who Has Decided to Become a Nun," translated by Jonathan Chaves, from *Columbia Book of Later Chinese Poetry*. Copyright © 1986 by Columbia University Press. Reprinted with the permission of the publishers.

Yi In-bok, "Drumbeats," translated by Kevin O'Rourke, from *The Cutting Edge*. Reprinted with the permission of Yonsei University Press.

Kim Ku, ["I spy the three-colored peach blossom"], translated by Kevin O'Rourke, from *Translation Magazine* XII (1984). Reprinted with the permission of *Translation Magazine*.

Anonymous, ["It is the third watch. The girl"], translated by Kevin O'Rourke, from *Tilting the Jar, Spilling the Moon*. Reprinted with the permission of The Dedalus Press, Dublin.

Anonymous, ["Love, why don't you come!"], translated by Kevin O'Rourke, from *Tilting the Jar, Spilling the Moon*. Reprinted with the permission of The Dedalus Press, Dublin.

Anonymous, "The Angry Bride," translated by Kevin O'Rourke, from *The Cutting Edge*. Reprinted with the permission of Yonsei University Press.

Anonymous, "Wind Last Night Blew Down," translated by Virginia Olsen Baron and Chung Seuk Park, from *Sunset in a Spider Web: Sijo Poetry of Ancient Korea*. Copyright © 1974 by Virginia Olsen Baron. Reprinted with the permission of Henry Holt and Company, Inc.

Anonymous, "When I Think About Why," translated by Virginia Olsen Baron and Chung Seuk Park, from *Sunset in a Spider Web: Sijo Poetry of Ancient Korea*. Copyright © 1974 by Virginia Olsen Baron. Reprinted with the permission of Henry Holt and Company, Inc.

Anonymous, "Aging," translated by Graeme Wilson, from *Translation Magazine* XIII (1984). Reprinted with the permission of *Translation Magazine*.

Song Soon, "Ten Years It Took," translated by Virginia Olsen Baron and Chung Seuk Park, from *Sunset in a Spider Web: Sijo Poetry of Ancient Korea*. Copyright © 1974 by Virginia Olsen Baron. Reprinted with the permission of Henry Holt and Company, Inc.

Hwang Chin-i, "I Will Cut Out the Middle Watch," translated by John S. Major. Original translation. Reprinted with the permission of the translator.

Myong-ok, "Dreams," translated by Michael Stephens and Okhee Yoo, from *Translations* (Red Hanrahan Books, 1984). Reprinted with the permission of the translator.

Yi Jung, "The River Darkens on an Autumn Night," translated by Virginia Olsen Baron and Chung Seuk Park, from *Sunset in a Spider Web: Sijo Poetry of Ancient Korea*. Copyright © 1974 by Virginia Olsen Baron. Reprinted with the permission of Henry Holt and Company, Inc.

Han Kwak, "Don't Bring Out the Straw Mat," translated by Virginia Olsen Baron and Chung Seuk Park, from *Sunset in a Spider Web: Sijo Poetry of Ancient Korea*. Copyright © 1974 by Virginia Olsen Baron. Reprinted with the permission of Henry Holt and Company, Inc.

Kwŏn Ho-mun, ["Nights after rain when the moon"], translated by Kevin O'Rourke, from *Translation Magazine* XII (1984). Reprinted with the permission of *Translation Magazine*.

Chŏng Ch'ŏl, "Snow Falling in the Pine Forest: Two Poems," translated by Kevin O'Rourke, from *Tilting the Jar, Spilling the Moon*. Reprinted with the permission of The Dedalus Press, Dublin. "Magistrate," translated by Graeme Wilson, from *Translation Magazine* XIII (1984). Reprinted with the permission of *Translation Magazine*.

Kim Sang-Yong, "Sijo" ["Love is false, that he loves me is a lie."], translated by Chung Chong-wha, from *Love In Mid-Winter Night* (KPI Ltd., 1985). Reprinted by permission.

Anonymous, "The Farmer's Pride," "Angling," "Good Scholars Make Bad Husbands," and "Too Late for a Husband," translated by Nguyen Ngoc Bich, from *A Thousand Years of Vietnamese Poetry* (New York: Alfred A. Knopf, 1975). Copyright © 1962, 1967, 1968, 1969, 1970, 1971, 1972, 1974 by The Asia Society. Reprinted with the permission of The Asia Society.

Nguyen Binh Khiem, "The Hated Rats," translated by Nguyen Ngoc Bich, from *A Thousand Years of Vietnamese Poetry* (New York: Alfred A. Knopf, 1975). Copyright © 1962, 1967, 1968, 1969, 1970, 1971, 1972, 1974 by The Asia Society. Reprinted with the permission of The Asia Society. "Worried," translated by Nguyen Ngoc Bich, from *Translation Magazine* II (1974). Reprinted with the permission of *Translation Magazine.*

Ikkyū Sōjun, "Four Poems," translated by Stephen Berg. Original translations. Reprinted with the permission of the translator.

Monk Sōgi, "Spring," translated by Stephen D. Carter, from *Traditional Japanese Poetry: An Anthology.* Copyright © 1991 by the Board of Regents of the Leland Stanford Junior College. Reprinted with the permission of Stanford University Press.

Anonymous, "The Omoro Sōshi," (excerpts), ["Before light became time"] and ["Between Mount Onna and the sea"], translated by Christopher Drake, from *The Harvard Advocate* CXV, no. 4 (Summer 1982). Reprinted with the permission of the translator.

Part VI: The Seventeenth Century

Anonymous, "Omens," translated by Alexander Carmichael, from *Carmina Gadelica, Volume 1* (Noroton, Conn.: Vineyard Books, 1972). Reprinted by permission.

Aodhagán O Rathaille, "Lament for Tadhg Cronin's Children," translated by Michael Hartnett, from *A Farewell to English* (Co Meath, Ireland: The Gallery Press, 1978). Reprinted with the permission of The Gallery Press.

Eileen Dubh O'Connell (attributed), "Your Grave Disfigures Me," translated by Patrick Galvin, from *The Death of Art O'Leary* (Cork: Killeen Fine Editions, 1994). Reprinted with the permission of the publishers.

Gysbert Japicx, "Lovelight," translated by Roderick Jellema, from *Delos* 1. Also collected in Roderick Jellema, ed., *The Sound That Remains: A Historical Collection of Frisian Poetry* (Grand Rapids: William B. Eerdmans Publishing Company, 1990). Reprinted with the permission of the translator.

Anonymous, "Deep in the Forest," translated by James Harrison, from *Locations* (New York: W. W. Norton & Company, 1969). Copyright © 1969 by James Harrison. Reprinted with the permission of the translator.

Carl Michael Bellman, "Fredman's Epistle No. 23" ["O mother, mother, oh what a cipher"], translated by Rika Lesser. Original translation. Copyright © 1997 by Rika Lesser. Reprinted with the permission of the translator.

Andreas Gryphius, "Hell," translated by Michael Hamburger, from *Collected Poems 1941–1994.* Copyright © 1995 by Michael Hamburger. Reprinted with the permission of Anvil Press Poetry, Ltd. "Not Mine the Years Time Took Away," translated by John Peck. Original translation. Reprinted with the permission of the translator. "My Country Weeps," from John Peck, from *Poems and Translations of Hĩ-Lö* (Bronx: The Sheep Meadow Press, 1993). Reprinted with the permission of the translator. "To The Virgin Mary," "Epitaph For Mariana Gryphius, His Brother Paul's Little Daughter," and "Misery," translated by Christopher Benfey. Original translations.

Catharina Regina von Greiffenberg, "On the Ineffable Inspiration of the Holy Spirit," translated by Michael Hamburger, from *Collected Poems 1941–1994.* Copyright © 1995 by Michael Hamburger. Reprinted with the permission of Anvil Press Poetry, Ltd.

St. John of the Cross, "Dark Night," translated by Frank Bidart, from *Into The Western Night: Collected Poems 1965–1990.* Copyright © 1990 by Frank Bidart. Reprinted with the permission of Farrar, Straus & Giroux, Inc.

Luis de Gongora, "The Ruins of Time" and "IV" ["The whistling arrow flies less eagerly,"], translated by Robert Lowell, from *Near the Ocean.* "The Ruins of Time" first appeared in *Po-*

etry. Copyright © 1967 by Robert Lowell. Reprinted with the permission of Farrar, Straus & Giroux, Inc. "The Spectre of the Rose" (excerpt) ["Learn, flowers, from me, what parts we play"], translated by Roy Campbell, from *Collected Poems of Roy Campbell, Volume 2: Translations* (Chicago: Henry Regnery, 1960). Reprinted with the permission of Francisco Campbell Custodio and AD Donker Publishers.

Lope de Vega Carpio, "Judith," translated by Brian Soper, from *Nine* III, no. 1 (Autumn 1951). Reprinted with the permission of the translator. "In Santiago," translated by W. S. Merwin, from *Selected Translations 1948–1968* (New York: Atheneum Publishers, 1968). Copyright © 1968 by W. S. Merwin. Reprinted with the permission of Georges Borchardt, Inc. for the author. "The Pentecost Castle" (excerpt) ["They slew by night"], translated by Geoffrey Hill, from *Tenebrae.* Copyright © 1978 by Geoffrey Hill. Reprinted with the permission of Houghton Mifflin Company. All rights reserved. "Lachrimae Amantis," translated by Geoffrey Hill, from *Collected Poems.* Copyright © 1985 by Geoffrey Hill. Reprinted with the permission of Oxford University Press, Inc. and Penguin Books, Ltd.

Francisco Gomez de Quevedo y Villegas, "He Points Out the Brevity of Life, Unthinking and Suffering, Surprised by Death," translated by Willis Barnstone, from *The Secret Reader* (Hanover, New Hampshire: University Press of New England, 1996). Reprinted with the permission of the translator. "On a Chaplain's Nose," translated by Roy Campbell, from *Collected Poems of Roy Campbell, Volume 2: Translations* (Chicago: Henry Regnery, 1960). Reprinted with the permission of Francisco Campbell Custodio and AD Donker Publishers. "Love Constant Beyond Death," translated by W. S. Merwin, from *Selected Translations 1968–1978* (New York: Atheneum Publishers, 1978). Originally appeared in *TriQuarterly.* Copyright © 1978 by W. S. Merwin. Reprinted with the permission of Georges Borchardt, Inc. for the author. "On Lisi's Golden Hair," translated by Roy Campbell, from *Collected Poems of Roy Campbell, Volume 2: Translations* (Chicago: Henry Regnery, 1960). Reprinted with the permission of Francisco Campbell Custodio and AD Donker Publishers. "The Toothpuller Who Wanted to Turn a Mouth into a Grinding Machine," translated by Willis Barnstone, from *Six Masters of the Spanish Sonnet* (Carbondale: Southern Illinois University Press, 1983). Reprinted with the permission of the translator.

Pedro Calderon de le Barca, "Those Which Were Pomp and Delight," translated by Katharine Washburn. Original translation. Reprinted with the permission of the translator.

L. L. de Argensola, "Damon's Lament for His Clorinda, Yorkshire 1654," translated by Geoffrey Hill, from *Collected Poems.* Copyright © 1985 by Geoffrey Hill. Reprinted with the permission of Oxford University Press, Inc. and Penguin Books, Ltd.

Sor Juana Inés de la Cruz, "The Fifth Villancico" (excerpt) ["Because my Lord was born to suffer,"], translated by Alan S. Trueblood, from *A Sor Juana Anthology.* Copyright 1928 by the President and Fellows of Harvard College. Reprinted with the permission of Harvard University Press. "On Her Portrait," translated by Robert Mezey. Original translation. Reprinted with the permission of the translator.

Vincent Voiture, "Rondeau," translated by William Jay Smith, from *Collected Translations.* Copyright © 1985 by William Jay Smith. Reprinted with the permission of New Rivers Press.

Jean de la Fontaine, "Phoebus and Boreas," translated by Marianne Moore, from *The Fables of La Fontaine.* Copyright 1945 by Marianne Moore. Reprinted with the permission of Penguin Books Ltd. "The Shrimp and Her Daughter," "Pig, Goat, Sheep," and "Book 12 #5," translated by Bruce Boone and Robert Glück, from *La Fontaine* (San Francisco: Black Star Series). Reprinted with the permission of the translators.

Zbigniew Morsztyn, "Emblem 51," translated by Jerzy Peterkiewicz, Burns Singer, and Jon Stallworthy, from *Five Centuries of Polish Poetry.* Reprinted with the permission of Oxford University Press, Ltd.

Waclaw Potocki, "Winter, Before the War," translated by Jerzy Peterkiewicz, Burns Singer, and Jon Stallworthy, from *Five Centuries of Polish Poetry.* Reprinted with the permission of Oxford University Press, Ltd.

Anonymous, "The Kanteletar" (excerpts), "Lullabies," translated by Keith Bosley from *World's Classics Paperbacks* (New York: Oxford University Press, 1992). Reprinted with the permission of the translator.

Anonymous, "Tuno, Rescuer of the Sun and Moon" (excerpt) ["The one son of God"], translated by Keith Bosley from *World's Classics Paperbacks* (New York: Oxford University Press, 1992). Reprinted with the permission of the translator.

Esrefoğlu, "O My God Do Not Part Me From Thee," translated by Taner Baybars, from Keith Bosley, ed., *Poetry of Asia: Five Millenniums of Verse from Thirty-Three Languages*. Reprinted with the permission of Weatherhill, Inc.

Pir Sultan Abdal, "Ilahi," translated by Murat Nemet-Nejat, from *Talisman Magazine*. Reprinted with the permission of the translator.

Bâkî, ["Oh beloved, since the origin we have been slaves"], translated by Walter G. Andrews, Mehmet Kalpakli, and Najaat Black. Reprinted by permission.

Rûhî, ["Curse the thorns of fate, and damn as well its roses"], translated by Walter G. Andrews, Mehmet Kalpakli, and Najaat Black. Reprinted by permission.

Nâbî, ["In the garden of time and destiny, we have seen"], translated by Walter G. Andrews, Mehmet Kalpakli, and Najaat Black. Reprinted by permission.

Nedîm, ["Take yourself to the rose-garden, it's the season"], translated by Walter G. Andrews, Mehmet Kalpakli, and Najaat Black. Reprinted by permission.

Anonymous, ["The sky is strewn with stars"], ["A girl threw an apple to a cloud,"] and "Brotherless sisters," translated by Charles Simic, from *The Horse Has Six Legs*. Copyright © 1992 by Charles Simic. Reprinted with the permission of Graywolf Press, St. Paul. Minnesota.

Anonymous, "Three Gypsy Poems," translated by Anselm Hollo (after translations by Katarina Taikon and Leo Tiainen), from *Antaeus* 16 (Winter 1975). Reprinted with the permission of the translator.

Ruskhan, "In Praise of Krishna" ["Beautiful his peacock crown"], translated by Allen Shapiro and Stephen Shaffer, from *Translation Magazine* VII (1980). Reprinted with the permission of *Translation Magazine*.

Bihari, "Three Poems from the Satasai" ["What she said to her companion," "What she said to her confidante," and "What her companion said"], translated by Krishna P. Bahadur, from *The Satasai* (New Delhi: Penguin Classics/UNESCO, 1990). Reprinted with the permission of Penguin Books India Pvt. Ltd.

Tukaram, "In My View," translated by Dilip Chitre, from *Translation Magazine* V (1978). Reprinted with the permission of *Translation Magazine*.

Ksetrayya, "A Courtesan to a Young Customer," "A Courtesan to Her Lover," and "A Wife to a Friend," translated by A. K. Ramanujan, Velcheru Narayana Rao, and David Shulman, from *When God is a Customer*. Copyright © 1994 by The Regents of the University of California. Reprinted with the permission of the University of California Press.

Sarangapani, "The Madam to a Young Courtesan," translated by A. K. Ramanujan, Velcheru Narayana Rao, and David Shulman, from *When God is a Customer*. Copyright © 1994 by The Regents of the University of California. Reprinted with the permission of the University of California Press.

Han-shan Te-ch'ing, "Mountain Living," translated by James M. Cryer, from J. P. Seaton and Dennis Maloney, eds., *A Drifting Boat: An Anthology of Chinese Zen Poetry*. Copyright © 1994 by White Pine Press. Reprinted with the permission of the publishers, 10 Village Square, Fredonia, NY 14063.

Feng Meng-lung, "Three 'Mountain Songs'," translated by Richard W. Bodman, from *Columbia Book of Traditional Chinese Literature*. Copyright © 1994 by Columbia University Press. Reprinted with the permission of the publishers.

Ts'ao Ching-chao, "Palace Poem," translated by Nancy Hodes and Tung Yuan-fang. Original translation. Reprinted with the permission of the translators.

Tsangyang Gyatso, "Love-poems of the Sixth Dalai Lama," translated by Rick Fields and Brian Cutillo, from *The Turquoise Bee: The Lovesongs of the Sixth Dalai Lama*. Copyright © 1994 by Rick Fields, Brian Cutillo, and Mayumi Oda. Reprinted with the permission of Harper-Collins Publishers, Inc.

Ishikawa Jōzan, "Gardening Chrysanthemums, I Think of [T'ao] Yüan-ming" and "Eating Roasted Matsutake Mushrooms," translated by Jonathan Chaves, from Jonathan Chaves, J. Thomas Rimer, Stephen Aldiss and Hiroyuki Suzuki, eds., *Shisendo: Hall of Poetry Immortals* (New York: Weatherhill, 1991). Reprinted with the permission of Weatherhill, Inc.

Gensei, "Evening View from Grass Hill" and "Distant View from Grass Hill," translated by Burton Watson, from *Grass Hill: Poems and Prose by the Japanese Monk Gensei*. Copyright © 1983 by Columbia University Press. Reprinted with the permission of the publishers.

Matsuo Bashō, "Six Haiku": ["Ancient silent pond"], translated by John S. Major. Original translation. Reprinted with the permission of the translator. ["The temple bell stops—"], translated by Robert Bly, from *The Sea and the Honeycomb: A Book of Tiny Poems* (Boston: A Seventies Press Book/Beacon Press, 1971). Copyright © 1971 by Robert Bly. Reprinted with the permission of the translator. ["Such stillness—"], translated by Donald Keene, from Donald Keene, ed., *Anthology of Japanese Literature: From The Earliest Times to the Christian Era*. Copyright © 1955 by Grove Press, Inc. Reprinted with the permission of Grove/Atlantic, Inc. ["Skylark"] and ["Fish shop—"], translated by Lucien Stryk and Takashi Ikemoto, from *Zen Poetry: Let the Spring Breeze Enter*. Originally in *American Poetry Review* 3 (May–June 1976). Copyright © 1995 by Lucien Stryk and Takashi Ikemoto. Reprinted with the permission of Grove/Atlantic, Inc. ["Culture's Beginnings"], translated by Sam Hamill, from *Narrow Road to the Interior*. Copyright © 1991 by Sam Hamill. Reprinted with the permission of Shambhala Publications.

Nozawa Bonchō, Matsuo Bashō, and Mukai Kyorai, "Throughout the Town," translated by Earl Miner, from *Japanese Linked Verse: An Account with Translations of Renga and Haikai Sequences* (Princeton: Princeton University Press, 1979). Reprinted by permission.

Chikamatsu Monzaemon, "The Journey" (from "The Love Suicides at Sonezaki"), translated by Donald Keene, from Donald Keene, ed., *Anthology of Japanese Literature: From The Earliest Times to the Christian Era*. Copyright © 1955 by Grove Press, Inc. Reprinted with the permission of Grove/Atlantic, Inc.

Yun Sŏndo, "Two Poems" from "The Angler's Calendar," translated by Peter H. Lee. reprinted by permission.

Kim Su-jang, "Deception," translated by Kevin O'Rourke, from *The Cutting Edge*. Reprinted with the permission of Yonsei University Press. "Moonlight," translated by Kevin O'Rourke, from *Titling the Jar, Spilling the Moon*. Reprinted with the permission of The Dedalus Press, Dublin.

Part VII: FROM THE EIGHTEENTH CENTURY INTO THE
EARLY TWENTIETH CENTURY

Emily Dickinson, "Wild Nights! Wild Nights!," "Ample make this bed—" "Safe in their Alabaster Chambers—" (version of 1861), and "A narrow Fellow in the grass" from *The Complete Poems of Emily Dickinson*, edited by Thomas H. Johnson. Copyright 1929, 1935 by Martha Dickinson Bianchi, renewed © 1957, 1963 by Mary L. Hampson. Copyright 1951, © 1955, 1979, 1983 by the President and Fellows of Harvard College. Reprinted with the permission of The Belknap Press of Harvard University Press.

Walter de la Mare, "Napoleon" from *The Complete Poems of Walter de la Mare* (New York: Alfred A. Knopf, 1970). Reprinted with the permission of The Literary Trustees of Walter de la Mare and The Society of Authors as their representative.

Padraic (Patrick) Pearse, "Naked I Saw You," translated by Desmond O'Grady, from *Trawling Tradition: Translations 1954–1994* (University of Salzberg Press, 1994). Reprinted with the permission of the translator.

Voltaire, ["A mountain mountainous in parturition"], translated by Robert Fitzgerald, from *The Harvard Advocate*, Special Translation Issue (Summer 1982). Copyright © 1982 by Robert Fitzgerald. Reprinted by permission. "Poem Upon The Lisbon Disaster," translated by Anthony Hecht from *Collected Earlier Poems*. Copyright © 1977, 1990 by Anthony E. Hecht. Reprinted with the permission of Alfred A. Knopf, Inc.

André Chénier, "Hermes" (excerpt) ["When the Euxine goddess with astonished eyes"], translated by Paul Schmidt from *Delos* (1971). Reprinted with the permission of the translator. ["We live, we live in squalor. And so? It had to be;"] and ["Happy is he given to sage disciplines,"], translated by David Curzon and Jeffrey Fiskin. Original translations. Reprinted with the permission of the translators.

Marceline Desbordes-Valmore, "My Room," translated by Edmund Blunden, from *Edmund Blunden: Selected Poems*, edited by Robin Marsack. Copyright © 1982 by Mrs. Claire Blunden. Reprinted with the permission of Carcanet Press, Ltd. "A Memory" and "Intermittent Dream of a Sad Night," translated by Louis Simpson. Original translations. Reprinted with the permission of the translator.

Victor Hugo, "Expiation," translated by Louis Simpson. Original translation. Reprinted with the permission of the translator. "Expiation, Part II: The Atonement," translated by Phillip Holland. Original translation. Reprinted with the permission of the translator. "Words in the Shadow," translated by Louis Simpson. Original translation. Reprinted with the permission of the translator.

Gérard de Nerval, "El Desdichado," translated by Robert Duncan, from *Bending the Bow*. Copyright © 1968 by Robert Duncan. Reprinted with the permission of New Directions Publishing Corporation. "To J—y Colonna," translated by Richard Sieburth. Original translation. Reprinted with the permission of the translator. "Fantasy," translated by Geoffrey Wagner, from Gérard de Nerval, *Selected Writings*. Copyright © 1957 by The University of Michigan Press. Reprinted with the permission of the publishers. "Golden Sayings," translated by Richard Sieburth. Original translation. Reprinted with the permission of the translator.

Alfred de Musset, "The Poet" ["If all you need, my sister sweet,"], "The Muse" ["Do you believe that I am like the autumn wind"], and "The Poet" ["O my insatiable muse,"], translated by Claire Nicolas White, from *A Night in May* (Francestown, New Hampshire: Typographeum, 1989). Reprinted with the permission of the translator.

Théophile Gautier, "Unknown Shores," translated by D. M. Thomas, from *Penguin Modern Poets: D. M. Black, Peter Redgrave, D. M. Thomas* (London: Penguin Books, 1968). Copyright © 1968 by D. M. Thomas. Reprinted with the permission of John Johnson, Authors' Agent, Ltd. "Carmen," translated by John Theobald, from *The Lost Wine: Seven Centuries of French into English Lyrical Poetry* (La Jolla: Green Tiger Press, 1980). Reprinted by permission. "Art," translated by Louis Simpson. Original translation. Reprinted with the permission of the translator.

After Leconte de Lisle, "The Jaguar's Dream," translated by James Lasdun, from *A Jump Start*. Copyright © 1987 by James Lasdun. Reprinted with the permission of James Lasdun and W. W. Norton & Company, Inc.

Charles Baudelaire, "Intimate Associations," translated by Robert Bly from *News of the Universe: Poems of Twofold Consciousness* (San Francisco: Sierra Club Books, 1990). Copyright © 1990 by Robert Bly. Reprinted with the permission of the translator. "The Swan," translated by Louis Simpson. Original translation. Reprinted with the permission of the translator. "The Clock," translated by Roy Campbell from *Nine* III, 3. Reprinted with the permission of Francisco Campbell Custodio and AD Donker Publishers. "L'Invitation Au Voyage," translated by Richard Wilbur, from *Things of This World*. Copyright © 1988 by Richard Wilbur. Reprinted with the permission of Harcourt Brace and Company. "A Voyage to Cythera," translated by Frederick Morgan, from *Poems New and Selected*. Copyright © 1987 by Frederick Morgan. Reprinted with the permission of the translator and the University of Illinois Press. "To the Reader" from "Au Lecteur," translated by Stanley Kunitz, from *Poems 1928–1978* (Boston: Atlantic Monthly Press, 1978). Copyright © 1958 by Stanley Kunitz. Reprinted with the permission of Darhansoff & Verrill Literary Agency.

Stéphane Mallarmé, "Toast," translated by Frederick Morgan, from *Poems New and Selected*. Copyright © 1987 by Frederick Morgan. Reprinted with the permission of the translator and the University of Illinois Press. "Vivid, Virginal, Beautiful, Will This Be," translated by Louis Simpson. Original translation. Reprinted with the permission of the translator. "Sea Breeze" and "The Afternoon of a Faun," translated by Louis Simpson. Original translations. Reprinted with the permission of the translator.

Paul Verlaine, "Autumn Song," translated by Louis Simpson. Original translation. Reprinted with the permission of the translator. "Green," translated by Yvor Winters, from *Collected Poems*. Copyright © 1960 by Yvor Winters. Reprinted with the permission of Ohio University Press. "Tears Fall in My Heart," translated by David Curzon. Original translation. Reprinted with the permission of the translator. "Woman and Cat," translated by Katharine Washburn and John S. Major. Original translation. Reprinted with the permission of the translators. "The Young Fools," translated by Louis Simpson. Original translation. Reprinted with the permission of the translator.

Tristan Corbière, "Old Roscoff," translated by Derek Mahon, from *Selected Poems* (London: Penguin Books, 1991). Copyright © 1990 by Derek Mahon. Reprinted with the permission of the translator. "The Blindman's Cries," translated by Martin James, from *Quarterly Review of Literature* II, no. 1 (Fall 1944). Copyright 1944 by Martin James. Reprinted with the permission of the Peekner Literary Agency, Inc. "Afterwards" (excerpt): Rondel # II ["It's getting dark, little thief of starlight!"], translated by Randall Jarrell, from *The Complete Poems*. Copyright © 1969 by Mary Jarrell. Reprinted with the permission of Farrar, Straus & Giroux, Inc.

Arthur Rimbaud, "The Drunken Boat" (excerpt) ["Hearing the Thunder"], translated by Derek Mahon, from *Selected Poems* (London: Penguin Books, 1991). Copyright © 1990 by Derek Mahon. Reprinted with the permission of the translator. "Thirst," translated by Michael O'Brien. Original translation. Reprinted with the permission of the translator. "Voyelles," translated by F. Scott Fitzgerald, from Sheilah Graham, *College of One* (London: Weidenfeld & Nicolson and New York: Viking Penguin, 1967). Copyright © 1981 by Scottie Fitzgerald Lanahan. Reprinted with the permission of Harold Ober and Associates, Inc. "O Seasons, O Châteaux," translated by Padraic Fallon, from *Poems and Versions*, edited by Brian Fallon. Copyright © 1983 by the Padraic Fallon Estate. Reprinted with the permission of Carcanet Press, Ltd. "The Sleeper in the Valley," translated by William Jay Smith, from *Collected Translations*. Copyright © 1985 by William Jay Smith. Reprinted with the permission of New Rivers Press. "A Runt of a Dream," translated by Denis Goacher, from *Transversions* (Premsnett: Gr/Ew Books, 1973). Reprinted with the permission of the translator.

Jules Laforgue, "Claire de Lune," "Complaint on the Oblivion of the Dead," "Sunday Piece," and "The Mystery of the Three Horns," translated by William Jay Smith, from *Collected Translations*. Copyright © 1985 by William Jay Smith. Reprinted with the permission of New Rivers Press.

Johann Wolfgang von Goethe, "The Holy Longing," translated by Robert Bly, from *News of the Universe: Poems of Twofold Consciousness* (San Francisco: Sierra Club Books, 1990). Copyright © 1990 by Robert Bly. Reprinted with the permission of the translator. "Wanderer's Night Song," translated by Peter Viereck. Original translation. Reprinted with the permission of the translator. "Mystical Chorus of *Faust*" (excerpt) ["All that is past of us"], translated by Louis MacNeice, from *Goethe's Faust* (London: Faber and Faber, 1951). Copyright 1951 by Louis MacNeice. Reprinted by permission. "Mignon," translated by Anthony Hecht, from *Hika.* Copyright © by Anthony E. Hecht. Reprinted with the permission of the translator. "Erl-King," translated by John Frederick Nims, from *Poems in Translation: Sappho to Valéry.* Copyright © 1990 by University of Arkansas Press. Reprinted with the permission of the publishers. "Three Stanzas From Journey in Winter," translated by James Wright, from *The Bough Will Not Break* (Middletown, Conn.: Wesleyan University Press, 1963). Copyright © 1963 by James Wright. Reprinted with the permission of University Press of New England. "Roman Elegy VIII," translated by David Ferry, from *Dwelling Places* (Chicago: University of Chicago Press, 1993). Copyright © 1993 by David Ferry. Reprinted with the permission of the translator.

Johann Christian Friederich Hölderlin, "Tinian" (excerpt) ["Pleasant to wander"], translated by David Gascoyne from *Collected Verse Translations* (Oxford: Oxford University Press, 1970). Reprinted with the permission of the translator. "Halflife," translated by Vyt Bakaitis. Original translation. Reprinted with the permission of the translator. "Schicksalslied" from "Hyperion" ["You wander above in brightness"], translated by M. L. Rosenthal. Previously uncollected translation. Reprinted with the permission of Dr. Sally M. Gall, Literary Executor, Estate of M. L. Rosenthal. "No Pardon" and "Descriptive Poetry," translated by Vyt Bakaitis. Original translations. Reprinted with the permission of the translator. ["The God is near, and"], translated by David Gascoyne, from *Hölderlin's Madness* (London: J. M. Dent & Sons, 1936). Reprinted with the permission of the translator. "All the Fruit Is Ripe" and "To the German People," translated by Robert Bly, from *The Sea and the Honeycomb: A Book of Tiny Poems* (Boston: A Seventies Press Book/Beacon Press, 1971). Copyright © 1971 by Robert Bly. Reprinted with the permission of the translator. "Hymns and Fragments" (excerpt) ["But speech —"], translated by Richard Sieburth, from *Hymns and Fragments.* Copyright © 1994 by Princeton University Press. Reprinted with the permission of the publishers.

Novalis, " 'Longing for Death'," translated by Dick Higgins, from *Hymns to the Night.* Copyright © 1978, 1984, 1988 by Richard C. Higgins. Reprinted with the permission of McPherson & Company. "When Geometric Patterns," translated by George Arman (Robert Bly), from *News of the Universe: Poems of Twofold Consciousness* (San Francisco: Sierra Club Books, 1990). Originally in *The Sixties,* #8 (Spring 1966). Copyright © 1966 by Robert Bly. Reprinted with the permission of the translator.

Joseph von Eichendorff, "On My Child's Death," translated by W. D. Snodgrass, from *After Experience: Poems and Translations* (New York: Harper & Row, 1967). Reprinted with the permission of the translator.

Heinrich Heine, "Sea-Sickness," translated by Vernon Watkins, from *Collected Poems.* Copyright © 1955 by Vernon Watkins. Reprinted with the permission of Faber and Faber, Ltd. ["To the world we must appear"] and "A Memory," translated by Francis Golffing, from *Likenesses* (Francestown, New Hampshire: Typographeum Press, 1979). Reprinted with the permission of the translator. "From Heine" ["Death is the tranquil night"], translated by Louise Bogan, from *Collected Poems.* Copyright 1954 by Louise Bogan. Reprinted with the permission of The Noonday Press, a division of Farrar, Straus & Giroux, Inc. "Dying in Paris," translated by Robert Lowell, from *Imitations.* Copyright © 1958 by Robert Lowell. Reprinted with the permission of The Noonday Press, a division of Farrar, Straus & Giroux, Inc. ["Revenge — ? — as if it were a cure"] and "Night Thoughts," translated by Mark Rudman. Original translations. Reprinted with the permission of the translator. "Words, Words, Words, and Nothing Doing!," translated by W. D. Jackson, from *Modern Poetry in Translation* (Summer 1994). Reprinted by permission.

Eduard Mörike, "Remember It, My Soul," translated by W. D. Snodgrass, from *After Experience: Poems and Translations* (New York: Harper & Row, 1967). Reprinted with the permission of the translator. "Forest Murmurs" and "The Forsaken Girl," translated by Randall

Jarrell, from *The Complete Poems*. Copyright © 1969 by Mrs. Randall Jarrell. Reprinted with the permission of Farrar, Straus & Giroux, Inc.

Theodor Storm, "At the Desk," translated by Robert Bly, from *The Sea and the Honeycomb: A Book of Tiny Poems* (Boston: A Seventies Press Book/Beacon Press, 1971). Copyright © 1971 by Robert Bly. Reprinted with the permission of the translator. "Women's Ritornelle," translated by James Wright, from *The Sixties*, no. 8 (Spring 1966), edited by Robert Bly. Copyright © 1966 by James Wright. Reprinted with the permission of Anne Wright.

Gottfried Keller, "Venus de Milo," translated by John Peck, from *Poems and Translations of Hi-Lö* (Bronx: The Sheep Meadow Press, 1993). Reprinted with the permission of the translator.

Friedrich Nietzsche, "Against the Laws," translated by W. S. Merwin, from *Selected Translations 1948–1968* (New York: Atheneum Publishers, 1968). Copyright © 1968 by W. S. Merwin. Reprinted with the permission of Georges Borchardt, Inc. for the author. "Notes" from "Zarathustra," translated by I. A. Richards, from *Good-bye Earth and Other Poems*. Copyright © 1958 by I. A. Richards. Reprinted with the permission of Harcourt Brace and Company.

Christian Morgenstern, "Summons" and "Blueprint for Disaster" translated by David Slavitt. Original translations. Reprinted with the permission of the translator. "Anxiety for the Future," translated by W. D. Snodgrass and Lore Segal, from *Gallows Song* (Ann Arbor: The University of Michigan Press, 1967). Originally published in *Mademoiselle* (1951). Reprinted with the permission of W. D. Snodgrass.

Hugo von Hofmannsthal, "Twilight of the Outward Life," translated by Peter Viereck, from *Strike Through The Mask* (New York: Charles Scribner's Sons, 1950). Reprinted with the permission of the translator. "Traveller's Song," translated by Charles Reynolds (Robert Bly), from *The Sixties* # 8 (Spring 1966). Copyright © 1966 by Robert Bly. Reprinted with the permission of the translator. "On The Transitory," translated by Naomi Replansky. Original translation. Reprinted with the permission of the translator.

Georg Heym, "Seafarers," translated by Christopher Benfey. Original translation. Reprinted with the permission of the translator. "With The Ships Of Passage," translated by Peter Viereck, from *Tide and Continuities: Last and First Poems*. Copyright © 1995 by Peter Viereck. Reprinted with the permission of University of Arkansas Press. "Final Vigil," translated by Peter Viereck, from *Tide and Continuities: Last and First Poems*. Copyright © 1995 by Peter Viereck. Reprinted with the permission of University of Arkansas Press.

Guiseppe Giocchino Belli, "Greed," "What Might Have Been," and "Revenge I," translated by Anthony Burgess, from *ABBA ABBA*. Originally in *Translation Magazine*. Copyright © 1977 by Anthony Burgess. Reprinted with the permission of Little, Brown and Company.

Giacomo Leopardi, "Saturday Night In The Village," translated by Robert Lowell, from *Imitations*. Copyright © 1961 by Robert Lowell. Reprinted with the permission of Noonday Press, a division of Farrar, Straus & Giroux, Inc. "Antistrophe," translated by Robert Bringhurst, from *Cadastre* (Bloomington: Kanchanjunga Press, 1973). Reprinted with the permission of the translator. "The Broom" (excerpt) ["Upon the arid shoulder"], translated by John Heath-Stubbs, from *Poems of Giacomo Leopardi* (New York: New Directions Publishing Corporation, 1948). Reprinted with the permission of the translator. "Remembering Leopardi's Moon: A Version," translated by Stephen Berg, from *The Steel Cricket: Versions 1958–1997* (Townsend, Wash.: Copper Canyon Press, 1997). Reprinted with the permission of the translator.

Dionysius Solomos, "The Destruction of Psara," translated by Edmund Keeley and Phillip Sherrard, from *Six Poets of Modern Greece* (New York: Alfred A. Knopf, 1961). Reprinted with the permission of Edmund Keeley.

Anonymous, "Mourning Songs Of Greece," translated by Konstantinos Lardas, from *Translation Magazine* II, (1974). Reprinted with the permission of *Translation Magazine*.

Ignacy Krasicki, "The Lamb and The Wolves," "Caged Birds," and "The Master and The Dog," translated by Jerzy Peterkiewicz, Burns Singer and Jon Stallworthy, from *Five Centuries of Polish Poetry*. Reprinted with the permission of Oxford University Press, Ltd.

Adam Mickiewicz, "The Year 1812," translated by Donald Davie from *Collected Poems of Donald Davie*. Copyright © 1990 by Donald Davie. Reprinted with the permission of The University of Chicago Press. "The Ackermann Steppe" and "The Storm," translated by Vyt Bakaitis, from *Mothers of Mud* 1, no. 3 (1981). Reprinted with the permission of the translator.

Antoni Malczewski, "After the Battle" from Jerzy Peterkiewicz, Burns Singer, and Jon Stallworthy, *Five Centuries of Polish Poetry*. Reprinted with the permission of Oxford University Press, Ltd.

Cyprian Norwid, "But Just To See," "Those Who Love," and "Recipe For A Warsaw Novel" from Jerzy Peterkiewicz, Burns Singer, and Jon Stallworthy, *Five Centuries of Polish Poetry*. Reprinted with the permission of Oxford University Press, Ltd.

Prince P. A. Vyazemsky, "The Russian God," translated by Alan Meyers, from *An Age Ago: A Selection of Nineteenth-Century Russian Poetry*. Copyright © 1988 by Alan Meyers. Reprinted with the permission of Farrar, Straus & Giroux, Inc.

Alexander Pushkin, "Demons" and "A Tale of St. Petersburg" from "The Bronze Horseman," translated by D. M. Thomas, from *The Bronze Horseman and Other Poems* (London: Martin Secker & Warburg 1982). Copyright © 1982 by D. M. Thomas. Reprinted with the permission of John Johnson, Authors' Agent, Ltd. "Ode On the Hills of Georgia," translated by Peter Viereck, from *Tide and Continuities: Last and First Poems* (Fayetteville: University of Arkansas Press, 1995). Copyright © 1995 by Peter Viereck. Reprinted with the permission of the translator. "Autumn (A Fragment)," translated by Edwin Morgan, from *Sweeping Out the Dark*. Copyright © 1994 by Edwin Morgan. Reprinted with the permission of Carcanet Press, Ltd.

Vladimir Nabokov, "The Eugene Onegin Stanza" from "The Translator's Preface" from *Eugene Onegin: A Novel in Verse*. Copyright © 1964 by Princeton University Press, renewed 1992 by Dmitri Nabokov. Reprinted with the permission of the publishers.

Fyodor Tyutchev, "Silentium," "At Vshchizh," and "The Past," translated by Charles Tomlinson, from *Selected Poems 1951–1974*. Copyright © 1978 by Charles Tomlinson. Reprinted with the permission of Oxford University Press, Ltd. "Last Love," translated by Vladimir Nabokov, from *Three Russian Poets*. Copyright 1944 by Vladimir Nabokov. Reprinted with the permission of New Directions Publishing Corporation.

Mikhail Lermontov, "Dream," translated by W. K. Matthews, from *Translation* (Phoenix Press, 1947). Reprinted by permission.

Innokenty Annensky, "One Second" and "The Capitol," translated by Stephen Berg, from *The Steel Cricket: Versions 1958–1997* (Port Townsend, Wash.: Copper Canyon Press, 1993). Reprinted with the permission of the translator.

Ivan Bunin, "Flowers, and tall-stalked grasses, and a bee," translated by David Curzon and Vladimir Guerassev. Original translation. Reprinted with the permission of David Curzon.

Mirza Asadullah Khan Ghalib, ["Not all, only a few, return as the rose or the tulip;"] and ["I'm neither the loosening of song nor the close-drawn tent of music;"], translated by Adrienne Rich, from *Delos* I (1968). Reprinted with the permission of the author. ["Freely in hidden fire"], translated by Frances W. Pritchett, from *Delos* III (1991). Reprinted with the permission of the translator.

Muhammad Iqbal, "Ghazel," translated by Frances W. Pritchett. Original translation. Reprinted with the permission of the translator.

Ghulam-Reza Ruhani, "Gaffer Speaks," translated by Omar Pound, from *Arabic and Persian Poems in English*. Copyright © 1986 by Omar Pound. Reprinted with the permission of Three Continents Press.

Rabindranath Tagore, "The Song That I Came To Sing," translated by Rabindranath Tagore, from Sisir Kumur Ghose, ed., *Forty Poems of Rabindranath Tagore* (New Delhi: Arnold-Heinemann, 1984). Reprinted by permission. "You Did Not Find Me," translated by Pratima Bowes, from *Some Songs and Poems* (London: East/West Publications, 1981). Reprinted by permission.

Shih Shu, "Enlightenment," translated by James H. Sanford, from J. P. Seaton and Dennis Maloney, eds., *A Drifting Boat: An Anthology of Chinese Zen Poetry.* Copyright © 1994 by White Pine Press. Reprinted with the permission of the publishers, 10 Village Square, Fredonia, NY 14063.

Yüan Chiu-ts'ai, "A Warm Invitation," translated by Henry H. Hart, from *The Charcoal Burner and Other Poems.* Copyright © 1974 by University of Oklahoma Press. Reprinted with the permission of the publishers.

Yüan Mei, "Motto," translated by James H. Sanford, from J. P. Seaton and Dennis Maloney, eds., *A Drifting Boat: An Anthology of Chinese Zen Poetry.* Copyright © 1994 by White Pine Press. Reprinted with the permission of the publishers, 10 Village Square, Fredonia, NY 14063. "Growing Old (I&II)," translated by Arthur Waley, from *Yuan Mei: Eighteenth-Century Chinese Poet.* Copyright © 1956 by Arthur Waley. Reprinted with the permission of Stanford University Press and Unwin Hyman.

Liang Te-sheng, "Sent to My Fourth Son, Shao-wu (To the Tune of 'Southern Countryside')," translated by Nancy Hodes and Tung Yuan-fang. Original translation. Reprinted with the permission of the translators.

Wu Tsao, "For the Courtesan Ch'ing Lin," translated by Kenneth Rexroth and Ling Chung, from *Women Poets of China.* Copyright © 1972 by Kenneth Rexroth and Ling Chung. Reprinted with the permission of New Directions Publishing Corporation.

Ch'en Yün, "Twilight," translated by Henry H. Hart, from *A Garden of Peonies.* Copyright 1938 by the Board of Regents of the Leland Stanford Junior College, renewed © 1966 by Henry H. Hart. Reprinted with the permission of Stanford University Press.

Anonymous, "A Toishan Song," translated by C. H. Kwock and Gary Gach, from Jerome Rothenberg, ed., *Technicians of the Sacred: A Range of Poetries from Africa, America, Asia, and Oceania* (New York: Doubleday, 1968). Reprinted with the permission of Jerome Rothenberg.

Kim Pyŏng-yŏn, "A Song for My Shadow," translated by Richard J. Lynn, from Peter H. Lee, ed., *Anthology of Korean Literature.* Copyright © 1981 by The University Press of Hawai'i. Reprinted with the permission of the publishers.

Ogata Kenzan, "Retrospective," translated by Richard L. Wilson, from Masahiko Kawahara, ed., *The Ceramic Art of Ogata Kenzan.* Reprinted with the permission of Kodansha Publications, Ltd.

Yosa Buson, ["White Lotus—"] and ["Such a moon—"], translated by Lucien Stryk and Takashi Ikemoto from *American Poetry Review* 3 (May–June 1976). Copyright © 1976. Reprinted by permission. ["It pierces through me"], ["Avoiding fishnet"], ["At the old pond"], and ["Plum blossoms scent"], translated by Tony Barnstone. Original translations. Reprinted with the permission of the translator.

Ryōkan, "The Begging Bowl" ("Picking violets," "I've forgotten," and "In my begging bowl"), and "Done with a long day's begging," translated by Burton Watson, from *Ryōkan: Zen Monk-Poet of Japan.* Copyright © 1977 by Columbia University Press. Reprinted with the permission of the publishers. "First Days of Spring," translated by Stephen Mitchell, from Stephen Mitchell, ed., *The Enlightened Heart: An Anthology of Sacred Poetry.* Copyright © 1989 by Stephen Mitchell. Reprinted with the permission of HarperCollins Publishers, Inc.

Kobayashi Issa, "On The Death of the Poet's Daughter Sato" and "Frog," translated by Conrad Totman, from *Early Modern Japan.* Copyright © 1993 by The Regents of the University of California Press. Reprinted with the permission of the University of California Press. "Insects," translated by Robert Bly, from *The Sea & the Honeycomb* (Boston: Beacon Press, 1971). Copyright © 1971 by Robert Bly. Reprinted with the permission of the translator. "Going to Attend Our Family Graves," translated by Harold Stewart, from *A Net of Fireflies*. Reprinted with the permission of Charles E. Tuttle.

Ema Saikō, "Evening Stroll," translated by Conrad Totman after the translation of Nakamura Shin'ichirō, from *Early Modern Japan*. Copyright © 1993 by The Regents of the University of California. Reprinted with the permission of the University of California Press.

Tachibana Akemi, "Happiness is When" (excerpt), translated by Burton Watson, from *The Country of Eight Islands*. Copyright © 1986 by Columbia University Press. Reprinted with the permission of the publishers.

Anonymous, "The Cherished Daughter," translated by Nguyen Ngoc Bich, from *Translation Magazine* II (1974). Reprinted with the permission of *Translation Magazine*.

Nguyen Gia Thieu, "Sorrows Of An Abandoned Queen" (excerpt) ["You were a fool, . . ."], translated by Nguyen Ngoc Nich, from *A Thousand Years of Vietnamese Poetry* (New York: Alfred A. Knopf, 1975). Copyright © 1962, 1967, 1968, 1969, 1970, 1971, 1972, 1974 by The Asia Society. Reprinted with the permission of The Asia Society.

Ho Xuan Huong, "On Sharing a Husband," translated by John Balaban. Original translation. Reprinted with the permission of the translator.

Tran Te Xuong, "The New Year's Season and Its Poetasters" and "Women," translated by Nguyen Ngoc Bich, from *A Thousand Years of Vietnamese Poetry* (New York: Alfred A. Knopf, 1975). Copyright © 1962, 1967, 1968, 1969, 1970, 1971, 1972, 1974 by The Asia Society. Reprinted with the permission of The Asia Society.

Nguyen Khuyen, "To the Singing Girl Named Luu," translated by Nguyen Ngoc Bich, from *A Thousand Years of Vietnamese Poetry* (New York: Alfred A. Knopf, 1975). Copyright © 1962, 1967, 1968, 1969, 1970, 1971, 1972, 1974 by The Asia Society. Reprinted with the permission of The Asia Society. "The Man Who Feigns Deafness," translated by Nguyen Ngoc Bich, from *Translation Magazine* II (1974). Reprinted with the permission of *Translation Magazine*.

Nguyen Van Lac, "Shrimps," translated by Huynh Sanh Thong. Reprinted by permission.

Anonymous, "The Call of the Soul," translated by Ronald Perry, from *The Hudson Review* XXI, no. 4 (Winter 1968–1969). Copyright © 1969 by Ronald Perry. Reprinted with the permission of *The Hudson Review*.

Anonymous "Two Pantuns," translated by R. J. Wilkinson and R. O. Winstedt, from *Pantum Melayu* (Singapore: Malaya Publishing House, 1961). Reprinted by permission. Malaya Publishing House.

José Rizal, "Water are we, you say, and yourselves fire," translated by Nick Joaquín, from *The Complete Poems and Plays of José Rizal* (Manila: Far Eastern University, 1976). Copyright © 1976. Reprinted by permission.

Anonymous, ["I came from under the earth"], translated by Jean Guiart, from André Malraux and George Sallas, eds., *The Arts of the South Pacific* (New York: Golden Press, 1963). Reprinted by permission.

Anonymous, "Girl's Song," translated by Edwin Grant Burrows, from *Flower In My Ear: Arts and Ethos of Ifaluk Atoll*. Copyright © 1963. Reprinted with the permission of University of Washington Press.

Anonymous, "Satire," translated by Sir Arthur Grimble, from *Return to the Islands: Life and Legend in the Gilberts*. Copyright © 1957. Reprinted with the permission of William Morrow and Company.

Anonymous, "The Shades of the Newly Buried Complain to the Gods," translated by John S. Major (from the translation of Basil H. Thompson). Original selection. Reprinted with the permission of John S. Major.

Anonymous, "The Woman Who Married a Caterpillar," translated by Armand Schwerner, from Walter Lowenfels, ed., *The Belly of the Shark* (New York: Vintage, 1973). Reprinted with the permission of the translator.

Anonymous, "Forest Trees of the Sea," translated by Mary Kawena Pukui and Alfons L. Korn, from *The Echo of Our Song: Chant and Poems of the Hawaiians.* Copyright © 1973. Reprinted with the permission of University of Hawai'i Press.

Queen Lili'u-o-ka-lani, "The Lawn Sprinkler," translated by Mary Kawena Pukui and Alfons L. Korn, from *The Echo of Our Song: Chant and Poems of the Hawaiians.* Copyright © 1973. Reprinted with the permission of University of Hawai'i Press.

Anonymous, "Behold," translated by Mary Kawena Pukui and Alfons L. Korn, from *The Echo of Our Song: Chant and Poems of the Hawaiians.* Copyright © 1973. Reprinted with the permission of University of Hawai'i Press.

Anonymous, "The Eagle Above Us," translated by Willard Trask (from the German translation by Konrad Theodor Preuss) from *The Unwritten Song.* Copyright © 1967 by Willard Trask. Reprinted with the permission of Simon & Schuster, Inc.

Anonymous, "Moon Eclipse Exorcism," translated by Armand Schwerner, from Jerome Rothenberg and Alfred Van der Marck eds., *Shaking the Pumpkin: Traditional Poetry of the Indian North Americas* (1986). Reprinted with the permission of the translator.

Anonymous (after Frances Densmore), "Sometimes I go about pitying myself," translated by Robert Bly, from *The Sea and the Honeycomb: A Book of Tiny Poems* (Boston: A Seventies Press Book/Beacon Press, 1971). Copyright © 1971 by Robert Bly. Reprinted with the permission of the translator.

Anonymous, "Prayer to the Sockeye Salmon," translated by Jane Hirshfield, from Jane Hirshfield, ed., *Women in Praise of the Sacred: Forty-Three Centuries of Spiritual Poetry by Women* (New York: HarperCollins Publishers, 1994). Reprinted with the permission of the translator.

Anonymous, "Mother's Song" and "Spirit Song," translated by Stephen Berg, from *The Steel Cricket: Versions 1958–1997* (Port Townsend, Wash.: Copper Canyon Press, 1993). Reprinted with the permission of the translator.

Tuglik, "Tuglik's Song," translated by Stephen Berg, from *The Steel Cricket: Versions 1958–1997* (Port Townsend, Wash.: Copper Canyon Press, 1993). Reprinted with the permission of the translator.

Uvavnuk, "Shaman Song," translated by Jane Hirshfield, from Jane Hirshfield, ed., *Women in Praise of the Sacred: Forty-Three Centuries of Spiritual Poetry by Women* (New York: HarperCollins Publishers, 1994). Reprinted with the permission of the translator.

Takomaq, "The lands around my dwelling," translated by Knud Rasmussen, from *The Intellectual Culture of the Iglulik Eskimos* (Copenhagen: Gyldendalske Boghandel, 1929). Reprinted with the permission of the heirs of Knud Rasmussen, c/o Sand and Sorensen Law Firm, Copenhagen.

Anonymous, (Kalahari Bushmen), "The Day We Die," translated by Arthur Markowitz, from *Translation Magazine* II (1974). Reprinted with the permission of *Translation Magazine.*

Anonymous, "Song of a Marriageable Girl" (after the French of O. de Labrouhe), translated by Willard Trask, from *The Unwritten Song.* Copyright © 1967 by Willard Trask. Reprinted with the permission of Simon & Schuster, Inc.

Anonymous, "The Lazy Man," translated by Bakare Gbadamosi and Ulli Beier, from *African Poetry: An Anthology of Traditional African Poems* (Cambridge: Cambridge University Press, 1966). Reprinted with the permission of Ulli Beier.

Anonymous, "Oshun, The River Goddess," translated by Ulli Beier, from *Delos* II (1968). Reprinted with the permission of the translator.

Anonymous, "Praise Song for The Oba of Benin," translated by John Bradbury, from Ulli Beier, ed., *African Poetry: An Anthology of Traditional African Poems* (Cambridge: Cambridge University Press, 1966). Reprinted by permission.

Anonymous, "Love Song" (from the French of H. Gaden), translated by Ulli Beier, from *African Poetry: An Anthology of Traditional African Poems* (Cambridge: Cambridge University Press, 1966). Reprinted with the permission of the translator.

Anonymous, "Lullaby," translated by Kwabena Nketia, from Ulli Beier, ed., *African Poetry: An Anthology of Traditional African Poems* (Cambridge: Cambridge University Press, 1966). Reprinted by permission.

Anonymous, "The Dead Man Asks For a Song" (after the German of Jakob Spieth), translated by Willard Trask, from *The Unwritten Song*. Copyright © 1967 by Willard Trask. Reprinted with the permission of Simon & Schuster, Inc.

Mririda N'ait Attik, "Praise to the Tattoo Mistress," translated by Daniel Halpern and Paula Paley, from *Translation Magazine* II (1974). Reprinted in *Songs of Mririda: Courtesan of the High Atlas* (Greensboro, North Carolina: Unicorn Press, 1974). Reprinted with the permission of Daniel Halpern.

Part VIII: THE TWENTIETH CENTURY

Stefan George, "The Antichrist," translated by Peter Viereck, from *Parnassus* (September 1987). Reprinted with the permission of the translator. ["Do not ponder too much"], translated by Stanley Burnshaw, from *Caged in an Animal's Mind*, Holt Rinehart & Winston, 1963). Reprinted with the permission of the translator.

Rainer Maria Rilke, "Orpheus, Eurydice, Hermes," translated by Franz Wright, from *The Unknown Rilke: Expanded Edition*. Copyright © 1983 by Oberlin College. Reprinted with the permission of Oberlin College Press. "Autumn Day," translated by John Felstiner, from *Paul Celan: Poet, Survivor, Jew* (New Haven, Conn.: Yale University Press, 1995). Reprinted with the permission of the translator. "Archaic Torso of Apollo" translated by Edward Snow, from *New Poems* (San Francisco: North Point Press, 1987). Reprinted with the permission of the translator. "The Panther," translated by W. D. Snodgrass, from *After Experience* (New York: Harper & Row, 1960). Reprinted with the permission of the translator. "Before Summer Rain," translated by Mark Rudman. Reprinted with the permission of the translator. Sonnet 21 from *Sonnets to Orpheus* ["Spring has returned. The earth is"], translated by Charles Haseloff, from *Sonnets to Orpheus* (1979). Reprinted with the permission of the translator.

Gottfried Benn, "This is Bad" and "Before a Cornfield," translated by Harvey Shapiro. Original translations. Reprinted with the permission of the translator. "Quaternary," translated by Teresa Iverson, from *The Partisan Review* (Summer 1993). Reprinted with the permission of the translator.

Georg Trakl, "To the Child Elis," "Elis," and "Decline," translated by Robert Firmage, from *Song of the West* (San Francisco: North Point Press, 1988). Reprinted with the permission of the translator. "De Profundis," translated by James Wright, from *Above the River: The Complete Poems* (Middletown, Conn.: Wesleyan University Press, 1990). Copyright © 1990. Reprinted with the permission of University Press of New England.

Bertolt Brecht, "Contemplating Hell," translated by Robert Firmage from *Romances of Departure* (1981). Reprinted with the permission of the translator. "On Reading a Recent Greek Poet," translated by John Peck. Previously unpublished. Reprinted with the permission of the translator. "Of Poor B. B.," translated by Michael Hamburger, from *Collected Poems 1941–1994*. Copyright © 1995 by Michael Hamburger. Reprinted with the permission of Anvil Press Poetry, Ltd. "Concerning the Infanticide, Marie Farrar" and "The Mask of Evil," translated by H. R. Hays, from *Selected Poems*. Copyright 1947 by Bertolt Brecht and H. R. Hays. Reprinted with the permission of Grove/Atlantic, Inc.

Friedrich Georg Jünger, "Ultima Ratio," translated by Les Murray, from *Translations from the Natural World*. Copyright © 1994 by Les Murray. Reprinted with the permission of Farrar, Straus & Giroux, Inc.

Johannes Bobrowski, "Woodland God" translated by Richard Ives, from *Evidence of Fire: An Anthology of Twentieth Century German Poetry* (Seattle: Owl Creek Press, 1988). Reprinted with the permission of the translator. "Dead Language," translated by Ruth and Matthew Mead, from *Shadow Lands: Selected Poems of Johannes Bobrowski*. Copyright © 1961 by Deutsch Verlags-Anstalt. English translation copyright © 1966, 1975, 1984 by Matthew Mead. Reprinted with the permission of Anvil Press Poetry, Ltd. "Novgorod: Coming of the Saints," translated by John Peck, from *Poems and Translations of Hï-Lö* (Bronx: The Sheep Meadow Press, 1993). Reprinted with the permission of the translator. "In The Torrent," translated by Mark Rudman, from *Pequod* (1994). Reprinted with the permission of the translator.

Paul Celan, "Death Fugue," translated by Michael Hamburger, from *Collected Poems 1941–1994*. Copyright © 1995 by Michael Hamburger. Reprinted with the permission of Anvil Press Poetry, Ltd. "Farmstead of Time" (excerpt) ["Shot forth",] "Psalm," and "Matière de Bretagne" translated by Katharine Washburn and Margaret Guillemin, from *Paul Celan: Last Poems* (San Francisco: North Point Press, 1986). Reprinted with the permission of the translators.

Erich Fried, "The Measures Taken" translated by Michael Hamburger, from *Collected Poems 1941–1994*. Copyright © 1995 by Michael Hamburger. Reprinted with the permission of Anvil Press Poetry, Ltd.

Ingeborg Bachmann, "Fog Land," translated by Michael Hamburger, from *Collected Poems 1941–1994*. Copyright © 1995 by Michael Hamburger. Reprinted with the permission of Anvil Press Poetry, Ltd. "Aria I," translated by Mark Anderson, from *In the Storm of Roses: Selected Poems of Ingeborg Bachmann* (Princeton: Princeton University Press, 1986). Reprinted by permission.

Hans Magnus Enzensberger, "The Divorce," translated by Herbert Graf, from *Sulfur* III, no. 3 (1984). Reprinted by permission.

Abraham Reisen, "Household of Eight," translated by Nathan Halper, from Irving Howe and Eliezer Greenberg, eds., *A Treasury of Yiddish Poetry* (New York: Holt, Rinehart & Winston, 1969). Reprinted by permission.

Moyshe Leyb-Halpern, "In Central Park," translated by John Hollander, from Ruth Wise, Irving Howe, Chone Schmeruk, eds., *The Penguin Book of Yiddish Verse* (New York: Penguin Books, 1987). Reprinted with the permission of the translator. "Long for Home," translated by Meyer Shapiro, from Irving Howe and Eliezer Greenberg, eds., *A Treasury of Yiddish Poetry*. Copyright © 1969 by Irving Howe and Eliezer Greenberg. Reprinted with the permission of Henry Holt and Company, Inc.

Martinus Nijhoff, "The New Stars" and "The Light," translated by Raphael Rudnik. Original translations. Reprinted with the permission of the translator.

Jan Emmens, "The Lion of Judah," translated by Adrienne Rich, from Jean Garrigue, *Translations by American Poets* (Athens: Ohio University Press, 1970). Copyright © 1970 by Adrienne Rich. Reprinted with the permission of the translator.

Fritzi Harmsen van Beek, "Introduction to a Prayer," translated by Clare Nicolas White, from James S. Holmes and William Jay Smith, eds., *Dutch Interiors: Postwar Poetry of the Netherlands and Flanders* (New York: Columbia University Press, 1984). Reprinted with the permission of the translator.

Edith Södergran, "My Childhood Trees," translated by Stina Katchadourian, from *Love and Solitude: Selected Poems of Edith Södergran, Third Edition*. Copyright © 1981, 1985, 1992, 1996 by Stina Katchadourian. Reprinted with the permission of Fjord Press. "Arrival in Hades" and "The Net," translated by David McDuff, from *Complete Poems of Edith Södergran, Second Edition* (Newcastle-Upon-Tyne: Bloodaxe Books, 1992). Reprinted with the permission of the translator.

Harry Martinsen, "Peonies," translated by William Jay Smith and Leif Sjöberg, from *The Forest of Childhood: Poems from Sweden.* Copyright © 1985 by William Jay Smith. Reprinted with the permission of New Rivers Press.

Gunnar Ekelöf, "Guide to the Underworld" (excerpts), translated by Rika Lesser, from *Guide to the Underworld.* Copyright © 1980 by the University of Massachusetts Press. Reprinted with the permission of the publishers. "ayfasma," translated by W. H. Auden and Leif Sjöberg, from *Selected Poems,* Copyright © 1972 by W. H. Auden and Leif Sjöberg. Reprinted with the permission of Pantheon Books, a division of Random House, Inc.

Tomas Tranströmer, "Alone" and "To Friends Behind a Frontier," translated by Robin Fulton, from *Collected Poems.* Copyright © 1981 by Robin Fulton. Reprinted with the permission of Bloodaxe Books Ltd. "Black Postcards," translated by Joanna Bankier, from Robert Haas, ed., *Tomas Tranströmer, Selected Poems 1954–1986* (Hopewell, New Jersey: The Ecco Press, 1987). Originally in *The Threepenny Review* (1986). Reprinted with the permission of the translator. "Homewards," translated by Robin Fulton, from *Collected Poems.* Copyright © 1981 by Robin Fulton. Reprinted with the permission of Bloodaxe Books Ltd. "Elegy," translated by Robert Bly. Reprinted with the permission of the translator.

Lars Gustafsson, "Ballad of the Dogs," translated by Phillip Martin, from *Quarterly Review of Literature, Poetry Series* IV, vol. XXIII (1982), edited by Theodore Weiss. Reprinted with the permission of *Quarterly Review of Literature.*

Rolf Jacobson, "Meadowstreet," translated by Roger Greenwald, from *Metamorphosis: The Journal of the Five College Seminar on Literary Translation* I, no. 2 (April 1993). Reprinted with the permission of the translator. "Gaslight," translated by Roger Greenwald, from *Metamorphosis: The Journal of the Five College Seminar on Literary Translation* I, no. 2 (April 1993). Revised 1996 by the translator. Reprinted with the permission of the translator. "Crust on Fresh Snow," translated by Olav Grinde, from *Modern Poetry in Translation: 1983.* Reprinted by permission.

Olaf H. Hauge, "Across the Swamp," translated by Robert Bly, from *Trusting Your Life to Water and Eternity: 20 Poems of Olaf H. Hauge.* Copyright © 1987 by Robert Bly. Reprinted with the permission of Milkweed Editions.

Piet Hein, "Noble Funerals Arranged," translated by Martin Allwood, from Martin Allwood, ed., *Modern Scandinavian Poetry: The Panorama of Poetry 1900–1975* (New York: New Directions Publishing Corporation, 1982). Copyright © 1982 by Martin Allwood. Reprinted by permission.

Tove Ditlevsen, "The Eternal Three," translated by Martin Allwood, Inga Allwood, and John Hollander, from Martin Allwood, ed., *Modern Scandinavian Poetry: The Panorama of Poetry 1900–1975* (New York: New Directions Publishing Corporation, 1982). Copyright © 1982 by Martin Allwood. Reprinted by permission.

Paavo Haavikko, ["Bastard Son is born with a tooth in his mouth and hair on his"], "Three Short Poems," "Fifteen Epigrams in Praise of the Tyrant," and "The Bowmen," translated by Anselm Hollo, from *Paavo Haavikko: Selected Poems* (Manchester: Carcanet Press, 1991). Reprinted with the permission of the translator.

Jaan Kaplinski, ["We started home, my son and I,"], translated by Sam Hamill and Rina Tamm, from *The Wandering Border.* Copyright © 1987. Reprinted with the permission of Copper Canyon Press, P. O. Box 271, Port Townsend, WA 96368.

Tomas Venclova, "Canto 11," translated by Vyt Bakaitis. Original translation. Reprinted with the permission of the translator.

Imants Ziedonis, "At Maruža's," translated by Barry Callaghan, from Flowers of Ice. First published by Exile Editions, Ltd. (Canada), 1987. Copyright © 1987 by Imants Ziedonis. English translation copyright © 1990. Reprinted with the permission of The Sheep Meadow Press.

Alexander Blok, "The Twelve" (excerpt) ["making tracks"], translated by Anselm Hollo, from *The Twelve and Other Poems* (Gnomon Press, 1971). Reprinted with the permission of the translator.

Anna Akhmatova, "The Muse," translated by Stanley Burnshaw, from *Caged in an Animal's Mind* (New York: Holt, Rinehart and Winston, 1963). Reprinted with the permission of the author. "Requiem" (requiem), translated by Stanley Kunitz with Max Hayward, from *Poems of Akhmatova* (Boston: Little, Brown and Company/Atlantic Monthly Press, 1967). Copyright © 1967 by Stanley Kunitz with Max Hayward. Reprinted with the permission of the Darhansoff & Verrill Literary Agency. "1915," translated by Stephen Berg, from *The Steel Cricket: Versions 1958–1997* (Port Townsend, Wash.: Copper Canyon Press, 1993). Reprinted with the permission of the translator. "The Guest," translated by Jane Kenyon with Vera Samdomirsky Dunham, from *Anna Akhmatova: Twenty Poems* (St. Paul: Nineties Press, 1985). Reprinted by permission.

Boris Pasternak, "Winter Night," translated by Edwin Morgan. Reprinted with the permission of the translator. "The Christmas Star" and "Hamlet," translated by Nina Kossman, as found in David Curzon, ed., *The Gospels in Our Images* (New York: Harcourt Brace, 1995). Reprinted with the permission of the translator. "Illness" (excerpt), ["At dusk you appear, a school-girl still"], translated by Theodore Weiss, from Jean Garrigue, *Translations by American Poets* (Athens: Ohio University Press, 1970). Reprinted with the permission of the translator.

Osip Mandelstam, ["O Lord, help me to live through this night—"], translated by Clarence Brown and W. S. Merwin, from *Osip Mandelstam: Selected Poems* (New York: Atheneum Publishers, 1974). Copyright © 1973 by Clarence Brown and W. S. Merwin. Reprinted with the permission of Simon & Schuster, Inc. and Oxford University Press, Ltd. ["Lightheartedly take from the palms of my hands"], translated by James Greene, from *Osip Mandelstam*. Copyright © 1977 by James Greene. Reprinted with the permission of Elek Books, Ltd. "The Ode on Slate," translated by Bernard Meares, from *Osip Mandelstam: Fifty Poems*. Copyright © 1977 by Bernard Meares. Reprinted with the permission of Persea Books. "Tristia," translated by James Greene, from *Osip Mandelstam*. Copyright © 1977 by James Greene. Reprinted with the permission of Elek Books, Ltd. "The Stalin Epigram," translated by Clarence Brown and W. S. Merwin, from *Osip Mandelstam: Selected Poems* (New York: Atheneum Publishers, 1974). Copyright © 1973 by Clarence Brown and W. S. Merwin. Reprinted with the permission of Simon & Schuster, Inc. and Oxford University Press, Ltd. ["Mounds of Human Heads," translated by Mark Rudman. Original translation. Reprinted with the permission of the translator. ["When Psyche, who is life, descends among the shades,"], translated by James Greene, from *Osip Mandelstam*. Copyright © 1977 by James Greene. Reprinted with the permission of Elek Books, Ltd.

Marina Tsvetayeva, "Poem of the End" (excerpt) ["Like a thick horse's mane"] and "Beware," translated by David McDuff. Reprinted with the permission of the translator. "An Attempt at Jealousy," translated by Elaine Feinstein, from *Selected Poems of Tsvetayeva*. Copyright © 1971 by Oxford University Press, Inc. Reprinted with the permission of the publishers. "The Signs of the Zodiac are fading," translated by Daniel Weissbort, from Albert C. Todd and Max Hayward, eds., *Twentieth-Century Russian Poetry* (New York: Anchor Books, 1994). Reprinted with the permission of the translator.

Andrei Vozensensky, "War Ballad," translated by Stanley Moss. Original translation. Reprinted with the permission of the translator.

Joseph Brodsky, "New Stanzas to Augusta," translated by George L. Kline, from *Joseph Brodsky: Selected Poems*. Copyright © 1973 by Joseph Brodsky. Reprinted with the permission of Farrar, Straus & Giroux, Inc.

Bohdan Boychuk, "A Fairy Tale," translated by David Ignatow, from David Ignatow and Mark Rudman, *Memories of Love: The Selected Poems of Bohdan Boychuk*. Copyright © 1989 by Bohdan Boychuk. Copyright © 1989 by David Ignatow and Mark Rudman. Reprinted with the permission of The Sheep Meadow Press.

Aleksander Wat, "Persian Parables" (excerpt) ["By a great, swift river"], translated by Czeslaw Milosz, *Postwar Polish Poetry, Third Edition.* Copyright © 1983 by The Regents of the University of California. Reprinted with the permission of University of California Press.

Czeslaw Milosz, "Encounter," translated by Czeslaw Milosz and Lillian Valle, from *The Collected Poems 1931–1987.* Copyright © 1988 by Czeslaw Milosz Royalties, Inc. Reprinted with the permission of The Ecco Press. "Dedication," translated by Czeslaw Milosz, from *The Collected Poems 1931–1987.* Copyright © 1988 by Czeslaw Milosz Royalties, Inc. Reprinted with the permission of The Ecco Press. "Preparation" and "Reading the Japanese Poet Issa: (1762–1826)," translated by Czeslaw Milosz and Robert Haas, from *The Collected Poems 1931–1987.* Copyright © 1988 by Czeslaw Milosz Royalties, Inc. Reprinted with the permission of The Ecco Press. "A Song on the End of the World," translated by Anthony Milosz, from *The Collected Poems 1931–1987.* Copyright © 1988 by Czeslaw Milosz Royalties, Inc. Reprinted with the permission of The Ecco Press.

Zbigniew Herbert, "Elegy of Fortinbras," translated by Czeslaw Milosz and Peter Dale Scott, from *Selected Poems.* Originally published as part of the Penguin Modern European Poets, 1968. Copyright © 1968 by Zbigniew Herbert. Reprinted with the permission of The Ecco Press. "The Envoy of Mr. Cogito" and "What Mr. Cogito Thinks About Hell," translated by Bogdana and John Carpenter, from *Selected Poems of Zbigniew Herbert.* Reprinted with the permission of Oxford University Press, Ltd. "Apollo and Marsyas," translated by Czeslaw Milosz and Peter Dale Scott, from *Selected Poems.* Originally published as part of the Penguin Modern European Poets, 1968. Copyright © 1968 by Zbigniew Herbert. Reprinted with the permission of The Ecco Press.

Wislawa Szymborska, "The Two Apes of Brueghel," translated by Sharon Olds, from *Quarterly Review of Literature Poetry Series* IV, vol. XXXIII. Reprinted with the permission of *Quarterly Review of Literature.* "A Terrorist is Watching," translated by Austin Flint, from *Quarterly Review of Literature Poetry Series* IV, vol. XXXIII. Reprinted with the permission of *Quarterly Review of Literature.*

Vladimir Holan, "During an Illness," translated by Jarmila and Ian Milner, from *Selected Poems.* Copyright © 1971 by Jarmila and Ian Milner. Reprinted with the permission of Penguin Books, Ltd.

Miroslav Holub, "In the Microscope," translated by Ian Milner. Reprinted by permission. "Polonius," translated by Jarmila and Ian Milner, Ewald Oser and George Theiner, from *Before & After.* Reprinted with the permission of Bloodaxe Books, Ltd. "Žito the Magician," translated by George Theiner, from Before & After. Reprinted with the permission of Bloodaxe Books Ltd.

Vasko Popa, "The Battle on the Blackbird's Field," "St. Sava's Journey," and "Song of the Tower of Skulls," translated by Anne Pennington, from *Earth Erect.* Copyright © 1973 by Anne Pennington. Reprinted with the permission of Anvil Press Poetry, Ltd.

Branko Miljkovic, "Sleepers," "Miners," "Agon," and "Sea Without Poets," translated by Charles Simic, from *The Horse Has Six Legs.* Copyright © 1992 by Charles Simic. Reprinted with the permission of Graywolf Press, Saint Paul, Minnesota.

Veno Taufer, "The Prayers and Games of the Water People," (excerpt) ["mother loves me loves me not"], translated by Milne Holton, from *Delos* Second Series, I, no. 1 (1988). Reprinted with the permission of the translator.

Slavko Janevski, "Sailor's Song," translated by Vasa D. Mihailovich, from Milne Holton and Graham W. Reid, eds., *Reading the Ashes: An Anthology of the Poetry of Modern Macedonia.* Copyright © 1977. Reprinted with the permission of University of Pittsburgh Press.

Attila József, "Encouraging," translated by John Batki, as found in Anne Waldman, ed., *Out of this World* (New York: Crown Publishers, 1991). Reprinted with the permission of the translator. "Dead Landscape," translated by Edwin Morgan, from *Sweeping Out the Dark.* Copyright © 1994 by Edwin Morgan. Reprinted with the permission of Carcanet Press, Ltd.

Sándor Weöres, "Monkeyland," translated by Edwin Morgan, from *Selected Poems of Sándor Weöres*. Copyright © 1970 by Edwin Morgan. Reprinted by permission. "Song: Boundless Space," translated by William Jay Smith, from Miklos Vajda, ed., *Eternal Moment: Selected Poems of Sándor Weöres*. Copyright © 1988 by William Jay Smith. Reprinted with the permission of Anvil Press Poetry, Ltd.

Ferenc Juhász, "Birth of the Foal" and "The Rainbow-Colored Whale," translated by David Wevill, from *Delos* 4 (1970). Reprinted with the permission of the translator.

Janos Pilinszky, "Harbach 1944," translated by Janos Csokits and Ted Hughes, from *The Desert of Love: Selected Poems*. Copyright © 1989 by Janos Csokits and Ted Hughes. Reprinted with the permission of Anvil Press Poetry, Ltd.

Tudor Arghezi, "Flowers of Mildew" and "The Last Hour," translated by Michael Impey and Brian Swann, from *Selected Poems of Tudor Arghezi*. Copyright © 1976 by Princeton University Press. Reprinted with the permission of the publishers.

Antonio y Ruiz Machado, "Summer Night," translated by Willis Barnstone, from *The Secret Reader* (Hanover, Vermont: University Press of New England, 1996). Copyright © 1996 by Willis Barnstone. Reprinted with the permission of the translator. "People Possess Four Things," translated by Robert Bly, from *The Sea and the Honeycomb* (Boston: Beacon Press, 1971). Copyright © 1971 by Robert Bly. Reprinted with the permission of the translator. "Primavera," translated by Samuel Menashe. Original translation. Reprinted with the permission of the translator. "Portrait," translated by Robert Bly, from *Time Alone: Selected Poems of Antonio Machado* (Middletown, Conn.: Wesleyan University Press, 1983). Copyright © 1983 by Robert Bly. Reprinted with the permission of the translator. "Four Poems," translated by John Dos Passos, from *Rocinante to the Road Again* (1922). Reprinted with the permission of Estate of John Dos Passos, Elizabeth H. Dos Passos, Co-Executor.

Juan Ramón Jimenéz, ["To the bridge of love,"] and ["The dawn brings with it"], translated by James Wright, from *Collected Poems* (Middletown, Conn.: Wesleyan University Press, 1971). Copyright © 1971 by James Wright. Reprinted with the permission of University Press of New England.

Jorge Guillén, "I Want to Sleep," translated by James Wright, from *Collected Poems* (Middletown, Conn.: Wesleyan University Press, 1971). Copyright © 1971 by James Wright. Reprinted with the permission of University Press of New England.

Federico Garcia Lorca, "The Sleepwalking Ballad," translated by Michael Hartnett, from *Collected Poems, Volume 2*. Reprinted with the permission of Carcanet Press, Ltd. "Song of the Rider," translated by Edwin Honig, from *Four Puppet Plays/Play Without A Title/The Divan Poems and Other Plays/Prose Poems and Dramatic Pieces by Federico Garcia Lorca*. Copyright © 1990 by Edwin Honig. Reprinted with the permission of The Sheep Meadow Press. "Lament for Ignacio Sanchez Mejias" (excerpt) ["1. The Goring and the Death" and 4: Absense of the Soul"], translated by Alan S. Trueblood, from *Selected Verse* (New York: Farrar Straus & Giroux, 1995). Reprinted by permission. Federico Garcia Lorca, "The Unfaithful Wife," translated by Michael Hartnett, from *Collected Poems, Volume 2*. Reprinted with the permission of Carcanet Press, Ltd. "Casida of the Dark Doves," translated by Edwin Honig, from *Four Puppet Plays/Play Without A Title/The Divan Poems and Other Plays/Prose Poems and Dramatic Pieces by Federico Garcia Lorca*. Copyright © 1990 by Edwin Honig. Reprinted with the permission of The Sheep Meadow Press.

Rafael Alberti, "Bosch" and "Giotto," translated by Carolyn Tipton, from *To Painting* (Chicago: Northwestern University Press, forthcoming). Copyright © by Carolyn Tipton. Reprinted with the permission of the translator.

Alfonso Reyes, "To-and-Fro of Saint Theresa," translated by Samuel Beckett, from Octavio Paz, ed., *An Anthology of Mexican Poetry*. Reprinted with the permission of Indiana University Press.

Octavio Paz, "Sunstone" (excerpt), translated by Eliot Weinberger, from *The Collected Poems of Octavio Paz 1957–1987*. Copyright © 1987, 1991 by Eliot Weinberger. Reprinted with the permission of New Directions Publishing Corporation. "The Key of Water," translated by Elizabeth Bishop, from *The Complete Poems 1927–1979*. Copyright © 1983 by Alice Helen Methfessel. Reprinted with the permission of Farrar Straus Giroux, Inc.

Pablo Neruda, ["If each day falls"], translated by William O'Daly, from *Sea and the Bells*. Copyright © 1988 by William O'Daly. Reprinted with the permission of Copper Canyon Press, P. O. Box 271, Port Townsend, WA 98368-0271. ["Drunk as drunk on turpentine"], translated by Christopher Logue, from *Selected Poems of Christopher Logue*. Copyright © 1996 by Christopher Logue. Reprinted with the permission of the translator and Faber and Faber, Ltd. "A Different Ship" and "Final," translated by Ben Belitt, from *Late and Posthumous Poems 1968–1974*. Copyright © 1988 by Ben Belitt. Reprinted with the permission of Grove/Atlantic, Inc.

Nicanor Parra, "Journey Through Hell," translated by Miller Williams, from *Antipoems: New and Selected*. Copyright © 1985 by Miller Williams. Reprinted with the permission of New Directions Publishing Corporation.

César Vallejo, ["Finished the stranger, with whom, late"] (XXXIV), translated by Rebecca Seiferle, from *Trilce*. Copyright © 1992. Reprinted with the permission of The Sheep Meadow Press. "Black Stone on a White Stone," translated by Willis Barnstone. Original translation. Reprinted with the permission of the translator. "In That Corner Where We Slept Together" and "The Black Cup," translated by Tony and Willis Barnstone. Original translations. Reprinted with the permission of the translators.

Jorge Luis Borges, "Ewigkeit," translated by Richard Wilbur, from *New and Collected Poems*. Copyright © 1988 by Richard Wilbur. Reprinted with the permission of Harcourt Brace and Company. "Baruch Spinoza," translated by Willis Barnstone, from *The Secret Reader* (Hanover, Vermont: University Press of New England, 1996). Copyright © 1996 by Willis Barnstone. Reprinted with the permission of the translator. "Possession of Yesterday," translated by Nicomedes Suarez Arauz, from *Los Conjurados* for *24 Conversations with Borges*. Copyright © 1988, 1989 by Emece Editores, S.A., Buenos Aires and Maria Kodama, Executrix, the Estate of Jorge Luis Borges, by arrangement with Emece Editores and the Estate of Jorge Luis Borges. All rights reserved. "The Labyrinth," translated by John Updike, from Norman Thomas Di Giovanni, ed., *In Praise of Darkness* (New York: E. P. Dutton, 1974). Reprinted with the permission of the translator. "Oedipus and the Riddle," translated by John Hollander, from Norman Thomas di Giovanni, ed., *Selected Poems 1923–1967* (New York: Delacorte Press 1972). Reprinted with the pemission of the translator. "The Dagger," translated by Norman Thomas Di Giovanni, from *Selected Poems 1923–1967*. Reprinted by permission.

J. V. Foix, "Sonnet" ["Alone, in mourning, wearing an archaic black gown,"], translated by M. L. Rosenthal, from *As For Love: Poems and Translations*. Copyright © 1987 by M. L. Rosenthal. Reprinted with the permission of Oxford University Press, Inc.

Fernando Pessoa, "Segue o teu destino," translated by David Wright, from *Modern Poetry in Translation*, New Series, #5 (Summer 1994). Reprinted with the permission of the translator. "Autopsychography," translated by Keith Bosley, from *Agenda* 21, no. 4 and 22, no. 1. Reprinted with the permission of the translator. (As Ricardo Reis): "I the roses love in the gardens of Adonis," translated by Edwin Honig from *Selected Poems by Fernando Pessoa* (Swallow Press, 1971). Reprinted with the permission of the translator. ["No one in the wide wilderness of the wood"], translated by Katharine Washburn. Original translation. Reprinted with the permission of the translator. (As Alberto Caeiro): ["Rather the bird flying by and leaving no trace"], translated by Edwin Honig from *Selected Poems by Fernando Pessoa* (Swallow Press, 1971). Reprinted with the permission of the translator.

Carlos Drummond de Andrade, "Don't Kill Yourself," translated by Mark Strand, from Charles Simic and Mark Strand, eds., *Another Republic* (New York: The Ecco Press, 1976). Copyright © 1976 by Mark Strand. Reprinted with the permission of the translator.

Vinicius de Moraes, "Song," translated by Richard Wilbur, from *New and Collected Poems*. Copyright © 1985 by Richard Wilbur. Reprinted with the permission of Harcourt Brace and Company.

Umberto Saba, "Ulysses" and "The Goat," translated by Stephen Sartarelli. Original translations. Reprinted with the permission of the translator.

Giuseppe Ungaretti, "Where the Light," translated by Dennis Devlin, from *Translations Into English*. Copyright © 1992 by The Dedalus Press. Reprinted with the permission of The Dedalus Press, Dublin. "Wake," translated by George Garrett, from *Luck's Shining Child* (Palaemon Press, 1981). Reprinted with the permission of the translator.

Eugenio Montale, "Motetti," translated by Dana Gioia, from *Mottetti: Poems of Love*. Copyright © 1990 by Dana Gioia. Reprinted with the permission of Graywolf Press, Saint Paul, Minnesota. "The Lemon Trees," translated by William Arrowsmith, from *Cuttlefish Bones*. Copyright 1948 by Arnoldo Mondadori Editore, Milan. English translation copyright © 1992 the Estate of William Arrowsmith. Reprinted with the permission of W. W. Norton & Company, Inc. "The Eel," translated by Jonathan Galassi, from Eugenio Montale, *Collected Poems 1916–1956* (New York: Farrar, Straus & Giroux, 1997). Reprinted with the permission of the translator. "Haul Your Paper Boats" and "Ecologue," translated by William Arrowsmith, from *Cuttlefish Bones*. Copyright 1948 by Arnoldo Mondadori Editore, Milan. English translation copyright © 1992 the Estate of William Arrowsmith. Reprinted with the permission of W. W. Norton & Company, Inc.

Salvatore Quasimodo, "And Suddenly It Is Evening," translated by J. Ruth Gendler, from *Changing Light* (New York: HarperCollins Publishers, 1991). Reprinted with the permission of the translator. "Street in Agrigento," translated by Dennis Devlin, from *Translations Into English*. Copyright © 1992 by The Dedalus Press. Reprinted with the permission of The Dedalus Press, Dublin. "Milan, August 1943," translated by Peter Russell. Reprinted with the permission of the translator. "Dead of Winter," translated by George Garrett, from *Luck's Shining Child* (Palaemon Press, 1981). Reprinted with the permission of the translator. "From the Willow Branches," translated by Michael Egan, from *Antaeus* 2, no. 16 (Winter 1975). Reprinted with the permission of the translator.

Cesar Pavese, "The Goat God," translated by William Arrowsmith, from *Hard Labor* (New York: Grossman Publishers, 1976). Copyright © 1976 by William Arrowsmith. Reprinted with the permission of Marianne Meyer.

Francis Jammes, "A Prayer to Go to Paradise with the Donkeys," translated by Richard Wilbur, from *New and Collected Poems*. Copyright © 1988 by Richard Wilbur. Reprinted with the permission of Harcourt Brace and Company.

Paul Valéry, "Helen," translated by Richard Wilbur, from *New and Collected Poems*. Copyright © 1988 by Richard Wilbur. Reprinted with the permission of Harcourt Brace and Company. "The Graves By the Sea," translated by John Finlay, from *Mind and Blood: The Collected Poems of John Finlay*. Reprinted with the permission of John Daniel & Company.

O. V. de Milosz, "King Don Luis wanted to see again," translated by John Peck from *Poems and Translations of Hï-Lö* (Bronx: The Sheep Meadow Press, 1993). Reprinted with the permission of the translator.

Guillaume Apollinaire, "Mirabeau Bridge," translated by Richard Wilbur, from *New and Collected Poems*. Copyright © 1988 by Richard Wilbur. Reprinted with the permission of Harcourt Brace and Company. "Zone," translated by Samuel Beckett, from *Collected Poems in English and French*. Copyright © 1977 by Samuel Beckett. Reprinted with the permission of Grove/Atlantic, Inc. "Meadow Saffron," translated by Robert Mezey, from *The Lovemaker* (Iowa City: The Cummington Press, 1961). Copyright © 1961 by Robert Mezey. Reprinted with the permission of the translator. "The Cavalier's Farewell," translated by Anne Hyde Greet, from *Calligrammes, poemes de la paix et de la guerre (Poems of Peace and War) (1913–1916)*. Copyright © 1980 by The Regents of the University of California. Reprinted with the permission of University of California Press. "The Traveller," translated by Rachel Blau-du Plessis, from *Eventorium Muse* (Spring 1967). Copyright © 1967 by Rachel Blau-du Plessis. Reprinted with the permission of the translator.

Jules Supervielle, "Rain and the Tyrants," translated by David Gascoyne, from *Selected Verse Translations* (New York: Oxford University Press, 1970). Reprinted with the permission of the translator.

Pierre Reverdy, "Endless Journeys," translated by John Ashbery, from Paul Auster, ed., *The Random House Book of Twentieth Century French Poetry* (New York: Random House, 1982). Copyright © by John Ashbery. Reprinted with the permission of Georges Borchardt, Inc. for the author.

Yvan Goll, "The Salt Lake," translated by George Hitchcock, from *Yvan Goll: Poems* (Kayak Books, 1968). Reprinted with the permission of the translator. "The Ferry of Lead," translated by Galway Kinnell, from *Yvan Goll: Poems* (Kayak Books, 1968). Reprinted with the permission of the translator.

Paul Éluard, "The Deaf and the Blind," translated by Paul Auster, from Paul Auster, ed., *The Random House Book of Twentieth Century French Poetry* (New York: Random House, 1982). Copyright © 1982 by Paul Auster. Reprinted with the permission of the Carol Mann Agency. "Lady Love," translated by Samuel Beckett, from *Collected Poems in English and French*. Copyright © 1977 by Samuel Beckett. Reprinted with the permission of Grove/Atlantic, Inc.

André Breton, "The Marquis de Sade," and "In the Eyes of the Gods," translated by Bill Zavatsky and Zack Rogow, from *Earthlight*. Copyright © 1993 by Sun & Moon Press. Reprinted with the permission of the publishers.

Louis Aragon, "Richard II Forty," translated by Peter Dale, from *Narrow Straits: Poems from the French* (Hippopotamus Press, 1985). Copyright © 1985 by Peter Dale. Reprinted with the permission of the translator.

Francis Ponge, "The Pleasures of the Door," translated by Raymond Federman, from Paul Auster, ed., *The Random House Book of Twentieth Century French Poetry* (New York: Random House, 1982). Reprinted with the permission of the translator. "Rhetoric," translated by Serge Gavronsky, from *The Power of Language: Texts and Translations*. Copyright © 1979 by the Regents of the University of California. Reprinted with the permission of the University of California Press.

Robert Desnos, "No, Love is Not Dead," translated by Bill Zavatsky, from Paul Auster, ed., *The Random House Book of Twentieth Century French Poetry* (New York: Random House, 1982). Reprinted with the permission of the translator. "I've Dreamed of You So Much," translated by Carolyn Forché and William Kulik, from Carolyn Forché and William Kulik, eds., *William Kulik: The Selected Poems of Robert Desnos* (New York: The Ecco Press, 1991). Copyright © 1991 by William Kulik. Reprinted with the permission of William Kulik.

René Char, "On the Bell Frieze of a Roman Church," translated by Mark Rudman. Reprinted with the permission of the translator.

Yves Bonnefoy, ["What house would you build for me."] and ["Remember the island where they build the fire"], translated by Galway Kinnell and Richard Pevear, from *Yves Bonnefoy: Early Poems 1947–1959*. Reprinted with the permission of The Ohio University Press/Swallow Press, Athens.

Anne Hébert, "The Tomb of Kings," translated by A. Poulin from *Selected Poems*. Originally in *Quarterly Review of Literature Poetry Series* 21, nos. 3–4. Copyright © 1987 by A. Poulin. Reprinted with the permission of BOA Editions, Ltd., 260 East Avenue, Rochester, NY 14604.

Willy Bal, "Fire!," translated by Yann Lovelock, from *The Colour of the Weather*. Copyright © 1979 by Yann Lovelock. Reprinted with the permission of The Menard Press.

Iain Crighton Smith, "You Are at the Bottom of My Mind" and "The Old Woman" from *Modern Scottish Gaelic Poems: A Bilingual Anthology*. Reprinted with the permission of the author.

Sorley MacLean, "Hallaig" from *Spring Tide and Neap Tide: Selected Poems 1932–72* (Edinburgh: Cannongate Publishing, 1981). Reprinted with the permission of Cannongate Books Limited, Edinburgh.

Roland Jones, "Foam," translated by Tony Conran, from *Welsh Verse.* Copyright © 1967, 1986, 1992 by Tony Conran. Reprinted with the permission of Poetry Wales Press.

David Emrys James, "Horizon," translated by Tony Conran, from *Welsh Verse.* Copyright © 1967, 1986, 1992 by Tony Conran. Reprinted with the permission of Poetry Wales Press.

Constantin Cavafy, "Days of 1908," translated by James Merrill, from *Grand Street* 6, no. 250. Reprinted with the permission of the Estate of James Merrill. "Waiting For the Barbarians" and "Ithaka," translated by Edmund Keeley and Phillip Sherrard, from *C. P. Cavafy: Selected Poems, Revised Edition,* edited by George Savidis. English translation copyright © 1975 by Edmund Keeley and Phillip Sherrard, revised edition copyright © 1992 by Princeton University Press. Reprinted with the permission of the publisher. "The City," translated by Rae Dalvin, from *The Complete Poems of Cavafy.* Copyright 1948 by Rae Dalvin. Reprinted with the permission of Harcourt Brace and Company.

Yannos Ritsos, "The End of Dodona II," translated by Edmund Keeley, from *Repetitions, Testimonies, Parentheses.* Copyright © 1991 by Princeton University Press. Reprinted with the permission of the publishers.

Yannis Papaionnou, "Nights Without Hope (Rebetiko Song)," translated by Gail Holst-Warhaft, from *Road to Rebetika: Music of a Greek Sub-Culture: Songs of Love, Sorrow, and Hashish, Third Edition* (Athens: Denise Harvey & Co., 1975, 1989). Reprinted by permission.

Odysseus Elytis, "This Wind that Loiters" and "The Mad Pomegranate Tree," translated by Edmund Keeley and Philip Sherrard, from *Six Poets of Modern Greece* (New York: Alfred A. Knopf, 1961). Reprinted with the permission of Edmund Keeley.

George Seferis, "Bottle in the Sea" from "Mythical Story," translated by Edmund Keeley and Phillip Sherrard, from *Six Poets of Modern Greece* (New York: Alfred A. Knopf, 1961). Reprinted with the permission of Edmund Keeley. "Stratis the Sailor by the Dead Sea," translated by Rex Warner, from *George Seferis Poems* (Boston: Atlantic Monthly Press/Little Brown, 1960). Copyright © 1960 by Rex Warner. Reprinted by permission.

Avraham Ben Yitzhak, "Blessed Are They That Sow," translated by Robert Mezey, from *A Book of Dying* (Santa Cruz: Kayak Books, 1970). Copyright © 1970 by Robert Mezey. Reprinted with the permission of the translator.

Yehuda Amichai, "My Mother Once Told Me," "My Son," and "Biblical Meditations," translated by Benjamin and Barbara Harshaw, from *Yehuda Amichai: A Life of Poetry.* Copyright © 1994 by Benjamin and Barbara Harshaw. Reprinted with the permission of HarperCollins Publishers, Inc.

Dan Pagis, "Snake," "Written in Pencil in the Railway Car," "Draft of a Reparations Agreement," and "Twelve Faces of the Emerald," translated by Stephen Mitchell, from *The Selected Poetry of Dan Pagis.* Copyright © 1996 by The Regents of the University of California. Reprinted with the permission of the translator and the University of California Press.

T. Carmi, "Short Song," translated by Grace Schulman, from *At the Stone of Losses* (Philadelphia: Jewish Publication Society of America, 1983). Reprinted with the permission of the translator.

Moushegh Ishkan, "The Armenian Language is the Home of the Armenian," translated by Diana der Hovanessian. Reprinted with the permission of the translator.

Nazim Hikmet, "Rubai," translated by Taner Baybars, from *Delos.* Reprinted with the permission of the translator. "About Mount Uludag," translated by Randy Blasing and Mutlu Konuk, from *Poems of Nazim Hikmet.* Originally published in *American Poetry Review* III, no. 2

(March/April 1974). Copyright © 1994 by Randy Blasing and Mutlu Konuk. Reprinted with the permission of Persea Books.

Fazil Hüsnü Dağlarcer, "The Sultan of the Animals is the Night," translated by Ahmet Ö. Evin, from Translation Magazine XIX. Reprinted with the permission of Translation Magazine.

Oktay Rifat, "The Flute," translated by Talat Sait Halman, from *Translation Magazine* XIX. Reprinted with the permission of *Translation Magazine*.

Orhan Veli Kanik, "Erol Güney's Cat," translated by Talat Sait Halman, from *I Am Listening to Istanbul: Selected Poems of Orhan Veli Kanik* (New York: Corinth Books, 1971). Reprinted by permission. "I Am Listening to Istanbul," translated by Murat Nemet-Nejat, from *I, Orhan Veli* (Hanging Loose Press, 1989). Reprinted with the permission of the translator.

Ece Ayhan, "Epitafio," translated by Murat Nemet-Nejat. Reprinted with the permission of the translator.

Feyyaz Kayacan, "Division of Labor," translated by Feyyaz Fergar, from *Translation Magazine* XXI. Reprinted with the permission of *Translation Magazine*.

Ali Püsküllüoğlu, "An Old Pirate in These Waters," translated by Murat Nemet-Nejat. from Translation Magazine XIX. Reprinted with the permission of the translator.

Özdemir İnce, "Wind, Ant, History," translated by Talat Sait Halman, from *Translation Magazine* XIX. Reprinted with the permission of *Translation Magazine*.

Faiz Ahmad Faiz, "Any Lover To Any Beloved" and "Before You Came," translated by Naomi Lazard, from *Translation Magazine* XI (1983). Reprinted with the permission of *Translation Magazine*.

Akhtar-ul-Iman, "Compromise," translated by Vinay Dharwadker, from Vinay Dharwadker and A. K. Ramanujan, eds., *The Oxford Anthology of Modern Indian Poetry* (New Delhi: Oxford University Press, 1994). Reprinted with the permission of the translator.

Ahmed Nadeem Qasmi, "Thought," translated by Raja Changez Sultan, from *Translation Magazine* III (1976). Reprinted with the permission of *Translation Magazine*.

Sadanand Rege, "Old Leaves from the Chinese Earth," translated by Dilip Chitre, from Dilip Chitre, ed., *An Anthology of Marathi Poetry* (Bombay: Normala Sadanand Publishers, 1967). Reprinted by permission.

Hira Bansode, "Woman," translated by Vinay Dharwadker, from Vinay Dharwadker and A. K. Ramanujan, eds., *The Oxford Anthology of Modern Indian Poetry* (New Delhi: University Press, 1994). Reprinted with the permission of the translator.

G. M. Muktibodh, "The Void," translated by Vinay Dharwadker, from Vinay Dharwadker and A. K. Ramanujan, eds., *The Oxford Anthology of Modern Indian Poetry* (New Delhi: University Press, 1994). Reprinted with the permission of the translator.

Dhoomil, "The City, Evening, and an Old Man: Me," translated by Vinay Dharwadker, from Vinay Dharwadker and A. K. Ramanujan, eds., *The Oxford Anthology of Modern Indian Poetry* (New Delhi: University Press, 1994). Originally in *TriQuarterly*. Reprinted with the permission of the translator.

Agyeya, "Hiroshima," translated by Agyeya and Leonard Nathan, *Signs and Silence* (Delhi: Simant, 1976). Reprinted by permission.

Samar Sen, "Love" and "Solitary," translated by Pritish Nandy, from *The Complete Poems of Samar Sen* (Calcutta: Writer's Workshop Books, 1970). Reprinted by permission.

Tushar Roy, "Nowadays," translated by Ron D. K. Banerjee, from *The Harvard Advocate* CXV, no. 4 (1982). Reprinted with the permission of the translator.

R. Meenakshi, "If Hot Flowers Come to the Street," translated by Martha Ann Selby from Vinay Dharwadker and A. K. Ramanujan, eds., *The Oxford Anthology of Modern Indian Poetry*

(New Delhi: Oxford University Press, 1994). Reprinted with the permission of the translator.

Nissim Ezekiel, ["I met a man once"] from *Hymns in Darkness*. Reprinted with the permission of Oxford University Press, New Delhi.

A. K. Ramanujan, "Love Poem for a Wife, 2," from *The Collected Poems of A. K. Ramanujan* (New Delhi: Oxford University Press, 1995). Reprinted with the permission of Molly A. Daniels-Ramanujan.

Dilip Chitre, "My Father Travels," from Keki N. Daruwalla, ed., *Indian English Poetry 1960–1980*. Reprinted with the permission of Vikas Publishing House Pvt Ltd., New Delhi.

Lü Hsün, "Hesitation" and "A Call to Arms," translated by William R. Shultz, from Wu-chi Liu and Irving Yucheng Lo, eds., *Sunflower Splendor: Three Thousand Years of Chinese Poetry* (Bloomington: Indiana University Press, 1975). Reprinted with the permission of the translator.

Hu Shih, "Dream and Poetry," translated by Kai-yu Hsu, from *Twentieth-Century Chinese Poetry*. Copyright © 1963, 1964 by Kai-yu Hsu. Reprinted with the permission of Doubleday, a division of Bantam Doubleday Dell Publishing Group, Inc.

Kuo Mo-jo, "Earthquake," translated by Harold Acton and Ch'en Shih-Hsiang, from *Modern Chinese Poetry*. Reprinted with the permission of Gerald Duckworth, Ltd.

Mao Tse-tung, "Lyrics" ["Glitter of a northern kingdom"] and ["I stand alone in the cold autumn"], translated by David Lattimore, from *The Harmony of the World*. Reprinted with the permission of the translator. "Return to Shaoshan," translated by Willis Barnstone with Ko Ching-po, from *The Poems of Mao Tse-tung* (New York: Harper & Row, 1972). Reprinted with the permission of Willis Barnstone.

Wen I-to, "Dead Water," translated by Arthur Sze. Original translation. Reprinted with the permission of the translator.

Chu Hsiang, "The Pawnshop," translated by Kai-yu Hsu, from *Twentieth-Century Chinese Poetry*. Copyright © 1963, 1964 by Kai-yu Hsu. Reprinted with the permission of Doubleday, a division of Bantam Doubleday Dell Publishing Group, Inc.

Feng Chih, "Sonnet" ["We often pass a night warm and intimate"], translated by Wai-Lim Yip, from *Lyrics from the Shelters: Modern Chinese Poetry 1930–1950* (New York: Garland Publishers, 1992). Reprinted by permission.

Li Kuang-t'ien, "A Dead Turk," translated by Kai-yu Hsu, from *Twentieth-Century Chinese Poetry*. Copyright © 1963, 1964 by Kai-yu Hsu. Reprinted with the permission of Doubleday, a division of Bantam Doubleday Dell Publishing Group, Inc.

Ai Ch'ing, "The Chilean Cigarette Pack," translated by Huangling Nieh, from *Literature of the Hundred Flowers, II: Poetry and Fiction*. Copyright © 1981 by Columbia University Press. Reprinted with the permission of the publishers.

Tsang K'o-chia, "The Street Angel," translated by Kai-yu Hsu, from *Twentieth-Century Chinese Poetry*. Copyright © 1963, 1964 by Kai-yu Hsu. Reprinted with the permission of Doubleday, a division of Bantam Doubleday Dell Publishing Group, Inc.

Ho Ch'i-fang, "Get Drunk," translated by Kai-yu Hsu, from *Twentieth-Century Chinese Poetry*. Copyright © 1963, 1964 by Kai-yu Hsu. Reprinted with the permission of Doubleday, a division of Bantam Doubleday Dell Publishing Group, Inc.

Ch'en Meng-chia, "An Old White Russian," translated by Harold Acton and Ch'en Shih-Hsiang, from *Modern Chinese Poetry*. Reprinted with the permission of Gerald Duckworth, Ltd.

Jen Jui, "Midnight," translated by Kenneth Rexroth and Ling Chung, from *Women Poets of China*. Copyright © 1972 by Kenneth Rexroth and Ling Chung. Reprinted with the permission of New Directions Publishing Corporation.

Yen Chen, "On the Willow Bank," translated by Arthur Sze. Original translation. Reprinted with the permission of the translator.

Hang Yong-woon, "The Artist," translated by Bruce Taylor, from *Translation* XI (1983). Reprinted with the permission of the translator.

Jang-hi Lee, "The Spring is a Cat," translated by Chang So Ko, from *Best Loved Poems of Korea* (Seoul: Hollym Corporation, 1984). Reprinted with the permission of the translator.

Kim So-wol, "Years from Now," translated by Kevin O'Rourke, from *The Cutting Edge*. Reprinted with the permission of Yonsei University Press.

Kim Kwang-sŏp, "Having Died," translated by David R. McCann, from *Translation Magazine* XIII (1984). Reprinted with the permission of *Translation Magazine*.

Nam-Kung Byok, "Grass," translated by Kevin O'Rourke, from *The Cutting Edge*. Reprinted with the permission of Yonsei University Press.

No Ch'ŏn-myŏng, "A Nameless Woman," translated by Ko Won, from *Translation Magazine* XIII (1984). Reprinted with the permission of the translator.

Sŏ Chŏngju, "Self-Portrait," translated by Peter H. Lee, from *Anthology of Korean Poetry: From the Earliest Era to the Present* (New York: John Day Publishers, 1964). Reprinted with the permission of the translator. "Owl," translated by Kevin O'Rourke, from *Titling the Jar, Spilling the Moon*. Copyright © 1993 by Kevin O'Rourke. Reprinted with the permission of The Dedalus Press, Dublin. "Elephants of Thailand" and "Wanderer's Bouquet," translated by David R. McCann, from *Selected Poems of Sŏ Chŏngju*. Copyright © 1988 by Columbia University Press. Reprinted with the permission of the publishers.

Pak Mog-wŏl, "Prayer in Four Verses," translated by Kim Chong-gil, *Translation Magazine* XIII (1984). Reprinted with the permission of *Translation Magazine*.

Koh Chang-soo, "Ocean Liner" from *Anthology of Contemporary Korean Poetry* (Seoul: International Publishing House, 1987). Reprinted with the permission of the author.

Yosano Akiko, "Tangled Hair" (excerpt) ["A thousand lines"], translated by Sanford Goldstein and Seishi Shinoda, from *Tangled Hair*. Reprinted with the permission of Charles E. Tuttle Publishing Co., Inc., Tokyo, Japan. "The Channel Boat" (excerpt) ["What shall I wear to sleep in alone?"], translated by Janine Beichman, from *Journal of Association of Teachers of Japanese* 25, no. 1 (April 1991). Reprinted by permission.

Saitō Mokichi, "Mother Dies" (excerpt) ["From far off I have brought medicines, she watches me because I am her son"], translated by Hiroaki Sato and Burton Watson, from *From the Country of Eight Islands*. Copyright © 1986 by Columbia University Press. Reprinted with the permission of the publishers.

Takamura Kōtarō, "Whale Spouting," translated by James Kirkup and Akiko Takemoto, from *Translation Magazine* XVII (1986). Reprinted with the permission of *Translation Magazine*.

Kitahara Hakashū, "Secret Song of the Heretics," translated by Donald Keene, from *Modern Japanese Literature*. Copyright © 1956 by Grove Press, Inc. Reprinted with the permission of Grove/Atlantic, Inc.

Nishiwaki Junzaburō, "January in Kyoto." Reprinted with the permission of Chikuma Shobo Publishing Co. Ltd. "A Man Who Reads Homer," translated by Masaya Saito, from *Translation Magazine* XXIV. Reprinted with the permission of *Translation Magazine*.

Kaneko Mitsuharu, "Mount Fuji," translated by James Kirkup and Akiko Takemoto, from *Translation Magazine* XVII (1986). Reprinted with the permission of *Translation Magazine*.

Saitō Fumi, "Three Tanka," translated by Edith Macombe Shiffert and Yuki Sawa, from *Anthology of Modern Japanese Poetry*. Reprinted with the permission of Charles E. Tuttle Publishing Co., Inc., Tokyo, Japan.

Ishigaki Rin, "Hands," translated by Naoshi Koriyama and Edward Leuders, from *Like Underground Water.* Copyright © 1995. Reprinted with the permission of Copper Canyon Press, P. O. Box 271, Port Townsend, WA 98368.

Tamura Ryūichi, "Invisible Tree," translated by Naoshi Koriyama and Edward Leuders, from *Like Underground Water.* Copyright © 1995. Reprinted with the permission of Copper Canyon Press, P. O. Box 271, Port Townsend, WA 98368.

Noriko Ibaragi, "What a Little Girl Had on Her Mind," translated by Kenneth Rexroth and Ikuko Atsumi, from *Women Poets of Japan.* Copyright © 1977 by Kenneth Rexroth and Ikuko Atsumi. Reprinted with the permission of New Directions Publishing Corporation. "When I Was Prettiest in My Life," translated by Naoshi Koriyama and Edward Leuders, from *Like Underground Water.* Copyright © 1995. Reprinted with the permission of Copper Canyon Press, P. O. Box 271, Port Townsend, WA 98368.

Thamnaret, "Nightsong" translated by Ronald Perry, from *The Hudson Review* XIII, no. 1 (Spring 1960). Copyright © 1960 by Ronald Perry. Reprinted with the permission of *The Hudson Review.*

Tu Mo, "The Mandarins Got Their Raise," translated by Nguyen Ngoc Nich, from *A Thousand Years of Vietnamese Poetry* (New York: Alfred A. Knopf, 1975). Copyright © 1962, 1967, 1968, 1969, 1970, 1971, 1972, 1974 by The Asia Society. Reprinted with the permission of The Asia Society.

The Lu, "Green Nostalgia: Soliloquy of a Tiger in a Zoo," translated by Nguyen Ngoc Bich, from *A Thousand Years of Vietnamese Poetry* (New York: Alfred A. Knopf, 1975). Copyright © 1962, 1967, 1968, 1969, 1970, 1971, 1972, 1974 by The Asia Society. Reprinted with the permission of The Asia Society.

Do Tan, "Twenty Years," translated by Nguyen Ngoc Bich, from *A Thousand Years of Vietnamese Poetry* (New York: Alfred A. Knopf, 1975). Copyright © 1962, 1967, 1968, 1969, 1970, 1971, 1972, 1974 by The Asia Society. Reprinted with the permission of The Asia Society.

Du Te Le, "What I Leave to My Son," translated by Nguyen Ngoc Bich, from *A Thousand Years of Vietnamese Poetry* (New York: Alfred A. Knopf, 1975). Copyright © 1962, 1967, 1968, 1969, 1970, 1971, 1972, 1974 by The Asia Society. Reprinted with the permission of The Asia Society.

Ha Thi Thao, "Our Son's Profession," translated by Nguyen Ngoc Bich, from *A Thousand Years of Vietnamese Poetry* (New York: Alfred A. Knopf, 1975). Copyright © 1962, 1967, 1968, 1969, 1970, 1971, 1972, 1974 by The Asia Society. Reprinted with the permission of The Asia Society.

Le Ngoc Hiep, "I Am Sad" translated by John Balaban, from *Asian Art and Culture* II, no. 1, (Winter 1994). Reprinted with the permission of the translator.

José Garcia Villa, "Now I Prize Yellow Strawberries," "Inviting a Tiger for a Weekend," and "I was Speaking of Oranges to a Lady," from *Have Come, Am Here.* Copyright 1942 by José Garcia Villa. Reprinted with the permission of Viking Penguin, a division of Penguin Books USA Inc.

(W. S.) Rendra, "The Moon's Bed, The Bride's Bed," "The World's First Face," and "Tall Weeds," translated by Burton Raffel, from *Rendra: Ballads and Blues* (Kuala Lampur: Oxford University Press, 1974). Reprinted with the permission of Penerbit Fajar Bakti Sdn. Bhd. "Baby at the Bottom of the River," translated by Harry Aveling, from *Rendra: Ballads and Blues* (Oxford University Press, 1974). Reprinted by permission.

Toeti Heraty, "Cyclus," translated by Harry Aveling, from Harry Aveling, ed., *Contemporary Indonesian Poetry* (St. Lucia: University of Queensland Press, 1975). Reprinted by permission.

Ajip Rosidi, "Only In Poetry," translated by Harry Aveling, from Harry Aveling, ed., *Contemporary Indonesian Poetry* (St. Lucia: University of Queensland Press, 1975). Reprinted by permission.

Sapardi Djoko Damono, "Mask," translated by John H. McGlynn, from *Suddenly the Night: The Poetry of Sapardi Djoko Damono* (Jakarta: The Lontar Foundation, 1988). Reprinted by permission.

Sutardji Calzoum Bachri, "Soldiers," translated by Harry Aveling, from *Arjuna in Meditation: Three Young Indonesian Poets* (Calcutta: Writer's Workshop/Saffronbird Books, 1976). Reprinted by permission.

Manila Koordada, "You Can't Escape Your Life Record" from *Yorro Yorro: Aboriginal Creation and the Renewal of Nature [Regeneration of the World]: Rock Paintings and Stories from [The Art and Stories of] the Australian Kimberly* (Rochester, Vermont: Inner Traditions, 1993). Reprinted by permission.

Billy Marshall-Stoneking, "The Dreaming," from "Passage" ["See there, that tree is a digging-stick"], from *Singing the Snake: Poems from the Western Desert* (Pymble: Angus & Robertson, 1990). Reprinted with the permission of ETT Imprint, Australia.

Pancho Nácar, "The Foreigner Who Died in Juchitán," translated by Brian Swann, from *Translation Magazine* III (1976). Reprinted with the permission of the translator.

Aimé Césaire, "Blank to Full In on the Visa of Pollen," "Lay of the Rover," and "Since Akkad, since Elam, since Sumer," translated by Gregson Davis. Reprinted by permission.

Eric Roach, "At Guaracara Park" from *Student Arts Group* 1, no. 3 (1970) [San Fernando, Trinidad]. Reprinted by permission.

Martin Carter, "Bitter Wood" from *Selected Poems* (London: Demerara Publishers, 1990). Reprinted by permission.

Andrew Salkey, "Dry River Bed" from *Away*. Copyright © 1980 by Andrew Salkey. Reprinted by permission.

Edward Kamau Braithwaite, "Naima" from *Jah Music* (Savacou Publications, 1986). Reprinted by permission.

Derek Walcott, "The Polish Rider" from *Selected Poems*. Copyright © 1964 by Derek Walcott. Reprinted with the permission of Farrar, Straus & Giroux, Inc.

Birago Diop, "Vanity," translated by Gerald Moore and Ulli Beier, from Gerald Moore and Ulli Beier, eds., *The Penguin Book of Modern African Poetry, Third Edition* (London: Penguin Books, 1984), page 240. Originally in *Leurres et lueurs* (Présence Africaine, 1960). Reprinted by permission.

Léopold Sédar Sénghor, "Nocturne (I Accompanied You)," translated by Melvin Dixon, from *Sénghor: The Collected Poetry*. Copyright © 1991 by the Rector and Visitors of The University of Virginia. Reprinted with the permission of the University Press of Virginia. "Nocturne (She Flies She Flies)," translated by John Reed and Clive Wake, from *Nocturnes* (New York: The Third Press, 1971). Reprinted by permission. "To New York," translated by Melvin Dixon, from *Sénghor: The Collected Poetry*. Copyright © 1991 by the Rector and Visitors of the University of Virginia. Reprinted with the permission of the University Press of Virginia.

David Diop, "The Vultures," translated by Gerald Moore and Ulli Beier, from Gerald Moore and Ulli Beier, eds., *The Penguin Book of Modern African Poetry, Third Edition* (London: Penguin Books, 1984), page 246. Originally in *Coupes de pilon Leurres et lueurs* (Présence Africaine, 1956). Reprinted by permission.

Andrée Chedid, "Who Remains Standing?," translated by Samuel Haze and Mirène Ghossein from *The Heinemann Book of African Women's Poetry* (London: Heinemann, 1995). Reprinted by permission.

Joyce Mansour, "Seated on Her Bed," translated by Willis Barnstone, from *The Heinemann Book of African Women's Poetry* (London: Heinemann, 1995). Reprinted with the permission of the translator.

Malika O'Lahsen, "It Took One Hundred Years," translated by Eric Sellin, "It Took One Hundred Years" from Stella and Frank Chipasula, eds., *The Heinemann Book of African Women's Poetry* (London: Heinemann, 1995). Reprinted by permission.

Augustino Neto, "Kinaxixi," translated by W. S. Merwin, from *Black Orpheus* 15 (1964). English translation copyright © 1964 by W. S. Merwin. Reprinted with the permission of Georges Borchardt, Inc. for the author.

Dennis Brutus, "Nightsong: City" from *Sirens, Knuckles, Boots* (Ibadan: Mbari Publications, 1963). Reprinted with the permission of the author.

Marjorie Oludhe Macgoye, "A Freedom Song" from *Song of Nyarloka and Other Poems*. Copyright © 1977 by Marjorie Oludhe Macgoye. Reprinted with the permission of Oxford University Press, Ltd.

Kwesi Brew, "A Plea for Mercy" from *Okyeame* 1 (1961). Reprinted by permission.

Ingrid Jonker, "The Child Who Was Shot Dead by Soldiers at Nyanga" from Stella and Frank Chipasula, eds., *The Heinemann Book of African Women's Poetry* (London: Heinemann, 1995). Reprinted by permission.

J. G. Mocoancoeng, "Drought," translated by Mongane Wally Serote and Philip Bryant, from *Translation Magazine* III (1976). Reprinted with the permission of the publishers.

Wole Soyinka, "Night" from Gerald Moore and Ulli Beier, eds., *The Penguin Book of Modern African Poetry, Third Edition* (London: Penguin Books, 1984). Reprinted with the permission of the author.

Jean-Baptiste Tati-Loutard, "Early," translated by Eric Sellin, from *Translation Magazine* XV (1985). Reprinted with the permission of *Translation Magazine*.

Robert Frost, "The Draft Horse," "Provide, Provide," and "Neither Out Far Nor In Deep" from *The Poetry of Robert Frost*, edited by Edward Connery Lathem. Copyright 1936 by Robert Frost. Copyright © 1969 by Henry Holt and Co., Inc. Reprinted with the permission of Henry Holt and Company, Inc.

Wallace Stevens, "Tea at the Palace of Hoon" from *Collected Poems of Wallace Stevens*. Copyright 1923 and renewed 1951 by Wallace Stevens. "Of Mere Being" from *Opus Posthumous*. Copyright 1957 by Elsie Stevens and Holly Stevens. "Stars at Tallapoosa" from *Collected Poems of Wallace Stevens*. Copyright 1923 and renewed 1951 by Wallace Stevens. All reprinted with the permission of Alfred. A. Knopf, Inc.

William Carlos Williams, "Raleigh Was Right" and "A Sort of Song" from *The Collected Poems of William Carlos Williams, Volume II: 1939–1962*. Copyright 1944, 1953 by New Directions Publishing Corporation. "Danse Russe" from *The Collected Poems of William Carlos Williams, Volume I: 1909–1939*. Copyright 1938, 1944. 1945 by New Directions Publishing Corporation. All reprinted with the permission of the publishers.

D. H. Lawrence, "Middle of the World" from *Complete Poems of D. H. Lawrence*. Copyright © 1964, 1971 by Angelo Ravagli and C. M. Weekley, Executors of the Estate of Frieda Lawrence Ravagli. Reprinted with the permission of Viking Penguin, a division of Penguin Books USA Inc.

Ezra Pound, Canto LXXX (excerpt) ["Tudor indeed is gone and every rose" to "But oblivion, not thy forgiveness, FRANCE"] and Canto LXXXI (excerpt) ["What thou lovest well remains" to "all in the diffidence that faltered"] from *The Pisan Cantos* (1948). Reprinted in *The Cantos of Ezra Pound*. Copyright 1948 by Ezra Pound. Reprinted with the permission of New Directions Publishing Corporation.

H. D. (Hilda Doolittle), "Helen in Egypt" (excerpt) ["This is the spread of wings"] from *Collected Poems 1912–1944*. Copyright © 1962 by The Estate of Hilda Doolittle. Reprinted with the permission of New Directions Publishing Corporation.

Marianne Moore, "Silence" from *Complete Poems*. Copyright 1935 by Marianne Moore, renewed © 1963 by Marianne Moore and T. S. Eliot. Reprinted with the permission of Simon & Schuster, Inc.

Edwin Muir, "The Child Dying" from *Collected Poems*. Copyright © 1960 by Willa Muir. Reprinted with the permission of Faber and Faber, Ltd.

T. S. Eliot, "The Love Song of J. Alfred Prufrock" from *T. S. Eliot: The Complete Poems and Plays 1909–1950* (New York: Harcourt Brace, 1952). Originally published in *Poetry* (1915). Copyright 1915 by T. S. Eliot. Reprinted with the permission of Faber and Faber, Ltd.

John Crowe Ransom, "Captain Carpenter" from *Chills and Fever* (New York: Alfred A. Knopf, 1924). Reprinted with the permission of Helen Forman.

Hugh MacDiarmid, "O Wah's The Bride?" from *Complete Poems*, edited by Michael Grieve and William Russell Aitken. Copyright © 1993 by Michael Grieve. Reprinted with the permission of Carcanet Press, Ltd. "Perfect" from *Selected Poetry*. Copyright © 1993 by Michael Grieve. Reprinted with the permission of New Directions Publishing Corporation.

E. E. Cummings, "my father moved through dooms of love" from *Complete Poems 1904–1962*, edited by George J. Firmage. Copyright 1923, 1925, 1926, 1931, 1935, 1938, 1939, 1940, 1944, 1945, 1946, 1947, 1948, 1949, 1950, 1951, 1952, 1953, 1954, © 1955, 1956, 1957, 1958, 1959, 1960, 1961, 1962, 1963, 1966, 1967, 1968, 1972, 1973, 1973, 1975, 1976, 1977, 1978, 1979, 1980, 1981, 1982, 1983, 1984, 1985, 1986, 1987, 1988, 1989, 1990, 1991 by the Trustees for the E. E. Cummings Trust. Copyright © 1973, 1976, 1978, 1979, 1981, 1983, 1985, 1991 by George James Firmage. Reprinted with the permission of Liveright Publishing Corporation.

Charles Reznikoff, "Four Songs of the City" from *Poems 1918–1975: The Complete Poems of Charles Reznikoff*. Copyright © 1977 by Marie Fyrkin Reznikoff. Reprinted with the permission of Black Sparrow Press.

David Jones, ["Ship's master:"], from *The Anathemata*. Copyright 1952 by David Jones. Reprinted with the permission of Faber and Faber, Ltd.

Robert Graves, "The Cool Web" and "Counting the Beats" from *Collected Poems*. Copyright © 1975 by Robert Graves. Reprinted with the permission of Oxford University Press, Inc. and Carcanet Press, Ltd.

Edmund Blunden, "The Midnight Skaters" from *Edmund Blunden: Selected Poems*, edited by Robin Marsack. Copyright © 1982 by Mrs. Claire Blunden. Reprinted with the permission of Carcanet Press, Ltd.

Austin Clarke, "The Lost Heifer" from *Selected Poems*. Copyright © 1991 by Dardis Clarke. Reprinted with the permission of The Lilliput Press, Ltd., Dublin.

Louise Bogan, "Women" from *The Blue Estuaries: Poems 1923–1968*. Copyright © 1968 by Louise Bogan. Reprinted with the permission of Farrar, Straus & Giroux, Inc.

Hart Crane, "Voyages I and II" from *Complete Poems of Hart Crane*, edited by Marc Simon. Copyright 1933, © 1958, 1966 by Liveright Publishing Corporation. Copyright © 1986 by Marc Simon. Reprinted with the permission of Liveright Publishing Corporation.

Allen Tate, "The Mediterranean" from *The Collected Poems 1919–1976*. Copyright © 1976 by Allen Tate. Reprinted with the permission of Farrar, Straus & Giroux, Inc.

Basil Bunting, ["Riding silk, adrift on noon,"] from *Briggflatts: An Autobiography* (London: Fulcrum Press, 1966) and ["A thrush in the syringa sings,"] from *Second Book of Odes*, both reprinted in *The Complete Poems of Basil Bunting*. Both reprinted with the permission of Oxford University Press, Ltd.

Yvor Winters, "To My Infant Daughter (II)" from *The Giant Weapon*. Copyright 1943 by Yvor Winters. Reprinted with the permission of New Directions Publishing Corporation.

Laura (Riding) Jackson, "Summary for Alastor" from Elizabeth Friedman, Alan J. Clark, and Robert Nye, eds., *First Awakenings: The Early Poems of Laura Riding*. Originally published in *The Fugitive* IV (March 21, 1925). Copyright © 1992 by The Board of Literary Management of the late Laura (Riding) Jackson. Reprinted with the permission of Persea Books, Inc. In conformity with the late author's wish, her Board of Literary Management asks us to record that, in 1941, Laura (Riding) Jackson renounced, on grounds of linguistic principle, the writing of poetry: she had come to hold that "poetry obstructs general attainment to something better in our linguistic way-of-life that we have."

Kenneth Fearing, "Love, 20c the First Quarter Mile" from *New and Selected Poems*. Reprinted with the permission of Indiana University Press.

Langston Hughes, "Mother to Son" from *The Collected Poems of Langston Hughes*, edited by Arnold Rampersad and David Roessel. Copyright © 1994 by the Estate of Langston Hughes. Reprinted with the permission of Alfred A. Knopf, Inc.

Stevie Smith, "To The Tune of 'The Coventry Carol' " from *Collected Poems*. Copyright © 1972 by Stevie Smith. Reprinted with the permission of New Directions Publishing Corporation.

Patrick Kavanagh, "Shancoduff" from *Collected Poems* (New York: W. W. Norton & Company, 1964). Copyright © 1964 by Patrick Kavanagh. Reprinted with the permission of Devin-Adair Publishers, Inc., Old Greenwich, Connecticut 06830.

Stanley Burnshaw, "House in St. Petersburg, from *Caged in an Animal's Mind* (New York Holt, Rinehart and Winston, 1963). Copyright © 1963 by Stanley Burnshaw. Reprinted with the permission of the author.

W. H. Auden, "The Three Companions" and "The Wanderer" from *Collected Poems*. Copyright © 1991 by the Estate of W. H. Auden. Reprinted with the permission of Random House, Inc.

Louis MacNeice, "Thalassa" and "The Sunlight on the Garden" from *Selected Poems of Louis MacNeice*. Reprinted with the permission of Wake Forest University Press and Faber and Faber, Ltd.

A. D. Hope, "Meditation On a Bone" from *Collected Poems 1930–1970*. Reprinted with the permission of HarperCollins Publishers Australia.

George Oppen, "Psalm" from *Collected Poems*. Copyright © 1975 by George Oppen. Reprinted with the permission of New Directions Publishing Corporation.

Theodore Roethke, "The Waking" from *The Collected Poems of Theodore Roethke*. Copyright 1954 by Theodore Roethke, renewed © 1982 by Beatrice Roethke, Administratrix of the Estate of Theodore Roethke. Reprinted with the permission of Doubleday, a division of Bantam Doubleday Dell Publishing Group, Inc.

Elizabeth Bishop, "Casabianca" from *The Complete Poems 1927–1979*. Copyright © 1979, 1983 by Alice Helen Methfessel. Reprinted with the permission of Farrar, Straus & Giroux, Inc.

J. V. Cunningham, "Four Epigrams" and "Interview With Doctor Drink" from *The Exclusions of a Rhyme* (Allan Swallow, 1960). Copyright © 1960 by J. V. Cunningham. Reprinted with the permission of Jessie Cunningham.

Irving Layton, "An Aubade" from *The Love Poems of Irving Layton*. Copyright © 1980 by Irving Layton. "The Black Huntsmen" from *A Wild Peculiar Joy*. Copyright © 1982 by Irving Layton. Both reprinted with the permission of McClelland & Stewart, Ltd.

Robert Hayden, "Middle Passage" from Frederick Glaysher, ed., *The Collected Poems of Robert Hayden*. Copyright © 1966 by Robert Hayden. Reprinted with the permission of Liveright Publishing Corporation.

Randall Jarrell, "Variations" from *Collected Poems*. Reprinted with the permission of Farrar, Straus & Giroux, Inc.

Dylan Thomas, "In My Craft or Sullen Art" from *The Poems of Dylan Thomas*. Copyright 1939, 1946 by New Directions Publishing Corporation. Reprinted with the permission of New Directions Publishing Corporation and David Higham Associates, London, as agents for the Trustees of the Copyrights of Dylan Thomas.

John Berryman, "Henry's Understanding" from *Collected Poems 1937–1971*. Copyright © 1972 by John Berryman. Reprinted with the permission of Farrar Straus & Giroux, Inc.

David Ignatow, "Rescue the Dead" from *Rescue the Dead* (Middletown, Conn.: Wesleyan University Press, 1968). Copyright © 1968. Reprinted with the permission of University Press of New England.

Peter Viereck, " 'Vale' from Carthage" from *Tide and Continuities: Last and First Poems* (Fayetteville: University of Arkansas Press, 1995). Copyright © 1995 by Peter Viereck. Reprinted with the permission of the author.

W. S. Graham, "To My Father" from *The White Threshold*. Copyright 1949 by W. S. Graham. Reprinted with the permission of Faber and Faber, Ltd.

Robert Lowell, "The Dead in Europe" from *Lord Weary's Castle*. Copyright 1944 by Robert Lowell. Reprinted with the permission of Harcourt Brace and Company.

Robert Duncan, "My Mother Would Be a Falconress" from *Bending the Bow*. Copyright © 1968 by Robert Duncan. Reprinted with the permission of New Directions Publishing Corporation.

Keith Douglas, "Vergissmeinnicht" from *Complete Poems*, edited by Desmond Graham. Copyright © 1978 by Marie J. Douglas. Reprinted with the permission of Oxford University Press, Ltd.

Hayden Carruth, "Of Distress Being Humiliated by the Classical Chinese Poets" from *Collected Shorter Poems 1946–1991*. Copyright © 1989 by Hayden Carruth. Reprinted with the permission of Copper Canyon Press, P. O. Box 271, Port Townsend, WA 98368-0271.

Richard Wilbur, "Ballade for the Duke of Orléans" from *Advice to a Prophet and Other Poems*. Copyright © 1961 and renewed 1989 by Richard Wilbur. Reprinted with the permission of Harcourt Brace and Company.

Philip Larkin, "Days" from *Collected Poems*, edited by Anthony Thwaite. Copyright © 1988, 1989 by the Estate of Philip Larkin. Reprinted with the permission of Farrar, Straus & Giroux, Inc. and Faber and Faber, Ltd. "Going," from *The Less Deceived*. Copyright © 1955 by Philip Larkin. Both reprinted with the permission of The Marvell Press.

Louis Simpson, "Carentan O Carentan" from *Collected Poems* (Paragon House, 1988). Copyright © 1988 by Louis Simpson. Reprinted with the permission of the author.

James Dickey, "The Heaven of Animals" from *Poems 1957–1967* (Middletown, Conn.: Wesleyan University Press, 1967). Copyright © 1967 by James Dickey. Reprinted with the permission of University Press of New England.

Harvey Shapiro, "National Cold Storage Company" from *National Cold Storage Company* (Middletown, Conn.: Wesleyan University Press, 1988). Copyright © 1988 by Harvey Shapiro. Reprinted with the permission of the author.

Frank O'Hara, "A Step Away From Them" from *Lunch Poems*. Copyright © 1964 by Frank O'Hara. Reprinted with the permission of City Lights Books.

Robert Bly, "Afternoon Sleep" from *Silence in the Snowy Fields* (Middleton, Conn.: Wesleyan University Press, 1962). Copyright © 1962 by Robert Bly. Reprinted with the permission of the author.

Index of Poets
and Translators

Page numbers in roman refer to poets; page numbers in *italics* refer to translators. Poems attributed to "Anonymous" are indexed by translator only.

Index of Titles